Butler

Directory of Victoria

Correct and complete map of the colony

Butler

Directory of Victoria
Correct and complete map of the colony

ISBN/EAN: 9783741166525

Manufactured in Europe, USA, Canada, Australia, Japa

Cover: Foto ©ninafisch / pixelio.de

Manufactured and distributed by brebook publishing software (www.brebook.com)

Butler

Directory of Victoria

BUTLER & BROOKE'S

NATIONAL

DIRECTORY OF VICTORIA,

FOR

1 8 6 6 — 6 7;

INCLUDING A

CORRECT AND COMPLETE MAP OF THE COLONY,

AND

THE VICTORIAN YEARLY ADVERTISER.

𝕸𝖊𝖑𝖇𝖔𝖚𝖗𝖓𝖊:

PUBLISHED BY BUTLER & BROOKE, 60 LITTLE COLLINS STREET EAST.
SOLD BY GEO. ROBERTSON AND W. B. STEPHENS.
1866.

W. M. WILLIAMS, PRINTER, POST-OFFICE PLACE, MELBOURNE.

PREFACE.

In presenting the "National Directory of Victoria" to the notice of the public, the publishers have to express regret that the issue of the work has been slightly delayed beyond the advertised date; but they trust this will be overlooked, as the delay has been owing chiefly to their desire to add to the completeness of the work and enhance its value as a Directory.

The names and addresses, in each town and township, have been separately arranged, in alphabetical order; but the scattered population has been classed under the various districts, thus—"The Lodden District Commercial Directory," &c. This plan, they trust, will meet with the approval of the public.

To Wilson and Mackinnon's "Bradshaw's Guide to Victoria" they are indebted for a portion of the up-country information, which they have made as complete as practicable under the circumstances.

In conclusion, the publishers beg to return their sincere thanks, first, for the universal support which their attempt to supply a long-felt desideratum has received; and, secondly, to those gentlemen who have rendered valuable assistance in the compilation of the work, amongst whom they would specially recognise Mr. R. Grundy, of Ballarat, to whose exertions they owe a great portion of valuable information respecting that important district.

BUTLER & BROOKE,
Publishers.

CONTENTS.

	PAGE
Preface	
Calendar for 1866	
Calendar for 1867	
Melbourne and Suburban Directory	1
Geelong Directory	188
Ashby Directory	204
Newtown and Chilwell Directory	212
The Western District Directory	219
Sandhurst Directory	235
Sandhurst District Directory	251
Castlemaine Directory	256
Echuca Directory	283
Ballarat and Ballarat East Directory	287
Buninyong Directory	312
Browns Directory	314
Scarsdale Directory	315
Creswick Directory	318
Smythesdale Directory	322
Clunes Directory	324
Kyneton Directory	329
Malmsbury Directory	331
Taradale Directory	335
Lauriston Directory	338
Beechworth Directory	339
Kilmore Directory	343
Wangaratta Directory	348
Albury Directory	348
Ovens District Directory	350
Gipps Land Directory	350

	PAGE
Wood's Point Directory	372
Loddon, Wimmera, and Rodney Districts Commercial Directory	384
Bourke, Evelyn, and Mornington Districts Commercial Directory	391
Talbot, Ripon, Grenville, and Dalhousie Districts Commercial Directory	395
Deniliquin District Commercial Directory	404
Names, &c., too late	406
Squatting Directory	A1
GENERAL INFORMATION—	
Colony of Victoria	i.
Government of Victoria	ii.
Parliament of Victoria	iii.
Gold Office—Treasury	viii.
Corporation of the City of Melbourne	ix.
Churches	ix.
Coaches	xi.
The Travellers' Road Guide	xii
Country Districts	xv.
Steamers from Melbourne	xxxvii.
Postal	xxxvii.
Money Orders	xl.
Consuls and Consular Agents	xli.
Electric Telegraph	xlii.

Calendar for 1866.

JANUARY.		FEBRUARY.		MARCH.	
Sun.	7 14 21 28	Sun.	4 11 18 25	Sun.	4 11 18 25
Mon.	1 8 15 22 29	Mon.	5 12 19 26	Mon.	5 12 19 26
Tues.	2 9 16 23 30	Tues.	6 13 20 27	Tues.	6 13 20 27
Wed.	3 10 17 24 31	Wed.	7 14 21 28	Wed.	7 14 21 28
Thur.	4 11 18 25	Thur.	1 8 15 22	Thur.	1 8 15 22 29
Fri.	5 12 19 26	Fri.	2 9 16 23	Fri.	2 9 16 23 30
Sat.	6 13 20 27	Sat.	3 10 17 24	Sat.	3 10 17 24 31

APRIL.		MAY.		JUNE.	
Sun.	1 8 15 22 29	Sun.	6 13 20 27	Sun.	3 10 17 24
Mon.	2 9 16 23 30	Mon.	7 14 21 28	Mon.	4 11 18 25
Tues.	3 10 17 24	Tues.	1 8 15 22 29	Tues.	5 12 19 26
Wed.	4 11 18 25	Wed.	2 9 16 23 30	Wed.	6 13 20 27
Thur.	5 12 19 26	Thur.	3 10 17 24 31	Thur.	7 14 21 28
Fri.	6 13 20 27	Fri.	4 11 18 25	Fri.	1 8 15 22 29
Sat.	7 14 21 28	Sat.	5 12 19 26	Sat.	2 9 16 23 30

JULY.		AUGUST.		SEPTEMBER.	
Sun.	1 8 15 22 29	Sun.	5 12 19 26	Sun.	2 9 16 23 30
Mon.	2 9 16 23 30	Mon.	6 13 20 27	Mon.	3 10 17 24
Tues.	3 10 17 24 31	Tues.	7 14 21 28	Tues.	4 11 18 25
Wed.	4 11 18 25	Wed.	1 8 15 22 29	Wed.	5 12 19 26
Thur.	5 12 19 26	Thur.	2 9 16 23 30	Thur.	6 13 20 27
Fri.	6 13 20 27	Fri.	3 10 17 24 31	Fri.	7 14 21 28
Sat.	7 14 21 28	Sat.	4 11 18 25	Sat.	1 8 15 22 29

OCTOBER.		NOVEMBER.		DECEMBER.	
Sun.	7 14 21 28	Sun.	4 11 18 25	Sun.	2 9 16 23 30
Mon.	1 8 15 22 29	Mon.	5 12 19 26	Mon.	3 10 17 24 31
Tues.	2 9 16 23 30	Tues.	6 13 20 27	Tues.	4 11 18 25
Wed.	3 10 17 24 31	Wed.	7 14 21 28	Wed.	5 12 19 26
Thur.	4 11 18 25	Thur.	1 8 15 22 29	Thur.	6 13 20 27
Fri.	5 12 19 26	Fri.	2 9 16 23 30	Fri.	7 14 21 28
Sat.	6 13 20 27	Sat.	3 10 17 24	Sat.	1 8 15 22 29

Calendar for 1867.

JANUARY.		FEBRUARY.		MARCH.	
Sun.	... ... 6 13 20 27	Sun.	... ... 3 10 17 24	Sun.	... ... 3 10 17 24 31
Mon.	... ... 7 14 21 28	Mon.	... ... 4 11 18 25	Mon.	... ... 4 11 18 25
Tues.	... 1 8 15 22 29	Tues.	... ... 5 12 19 26	Tues.	... ... 5 12 19 26
Wed.	... 2 9 16 23 30	Wed.	... ... 6 13 20 27	Wed.	... ... 6 13 20 27
Thur.	... 3 10 17 24 31	Thur.	... ... 7 14 21 28	Thur.	... ... 7 14 21 28
Fri.	... 4 11 18 25	Fri.	... 1 8 15 22	Fri.	... 1 8 15 22 29
Sat.	... 5 12 19 26	Sat.	... 2 9 16 23	Sat.	... 2 9 16 23 30

APRIL.		MAY.		JUNE.	
Sun.	... ... 7 14 21 28	Sun.	... ... 5 12 19 26	Sun.	... ... 2 9 16 23 30
Mon.	... 1 8 15 22 29	Mon.	... ... 6 13 20 27	Mon.	... ... 3 10 17 24
Tues.	... 2 9 16 23 30	Tues.	... ... 7 14 21 28	Tues.	... ... 4 11 18 25
Wed.	... 3 10 17 24	Wed.	... 1 8 15 22 29	Wed.	... ... 5 12 19 26
Thur.	... 4 11 18 25	Thur.	... 2 9 16 23 30	Thur.	... ... 6 13 20 27
Fri.	... 5 12 19 26	Fri.	... 3 10 17 24 31	Fri.	... ... 7 14 21 28
Sat.	... 6 13 20 27	Sat.	... 4 11 18 25	Sat.	... 1 8 15 22 29

JULY.		AUGUST.		SEPTEMBER.	
Sun.	... ... 7 14 21 28	Sun.	... ... 4 11 18 25	Sun.	... 1 8 15 22 29
Mon.	... 1 8 15 22 29	Mon.	... ... 5 12 19 26	Mon.	... 2 9 16 23 30
Tues.	... 2 9 16 23 30	Tues.	... ... 6 13 20 27	Tues.	... ... 3 10 17 24
Wed.	... 3 10 17 24 31	Wed.	... ... 7 14 21 28	Wed.	... ... 4 11 18 25
Thur.	... 4 11 18 25	Thur.	... 1 8 15 22 29	Thur.	... ... 5 12 19 26
Fri.	... 5 12 19 26	Fri.	... 2 9 16 23 30	Fri.	... ... 6 13 20 27
Sat.	... 6 13 20 27	Sat.	... 3 10 17 24 31	Sat.	... ... 7 14 21 28

OCTOBER.		NOVEMBER.		DECEMBER.	
Sun.	... ... 6 13 20 27	Sun.	... ... 3 10 17 24	Sun.	... 1 8 15 22 29
Mon.	... ... 7 14 21 28	Mon.	... ... 4 11 18 25	Mon.	... 2 9 16 23 30
Tues.	... 1 8 15 22 29	Tues.	... ... 5 12 19 26	Tues.	... 3 10 17 24 31
Wed.	... 2 9 16 23 30	Wed.	... ... 6 13 20 27	Wed.	... 4 11 18 25
Thur.	... 3 10 17 24 31	Thur.	... ... 7 14 21 28	Thur.	... ... 5 12 19 26
Fri.	... 4 11 18 25	Fri.	... 1 8 15 22 29	Fri.	... ... 6 13 20 27
Sat.	... 5 12 19 26	Sat.	... 2 9 16 23 30	Sat.	... ... 7 14 21 28

MELBOURNE AND SUBURBAN DIRECTORY.

1866-67.

THE FOLLOWING ARE THE ABBREVIATIONS USED:—

Brighton, Btn.
Brunswick, Bk.
Carlton, Carl.
Collingwood, Col.
East Collingwood, E. C.
East Melbourne, E. M.
Emerald Hill, Em. H.
Essendon, Ess.
Fitzroy, F.
Flemington, Flem.
Footscray, Foy.
Hawthorn, Haw.
Heidelberg, Heid.
Hotham, Hot.

North Melbourne, N. M.
Northcote, Nth.
Pentridge, Pent.
Prahran, Pra.
Preston, Pres.
Richmond, Rd.
Sandridge, San.
South Yarra, S. Y.
St. Kilda, St. K.
Toorak, Tk.
West Melbourne, W. M.
Williamstown, Wms.
Windsor, Wr.

A.

Aaron, M., 73 Argyle st, F
Aarons, Abraham, china and glass warehouse, 24 Derby st, E C
Aarons, Israel, cigar maker, 133 Little Lonsdale st east
Aarons, J , Fitzroy st, F
Aarons, Joseph, auctioneer and trade assignee, 6 Collins st east
Abadee, Moses, pawnbroker, Bay st, San
Abadee, S., Raglan st, San
Abbey, D., carpenter, Mt. Alexander road, Ess
Abboo, Massung, Chinese Club, 51 Park street, Em H
Abbott and Co. (Abbott, Robert Main), printers, 10 Post office place
Abbott, William, Nott st, San
a'Beckett, E. F., registrar, secretary, and librarian Melbourne University
a'Beckett, M., solicitor, 19 Temple court, Collins street west

a'Beckett, Thomas, barrister, 73 Little Collins street west, and Alma road, St K
a'Beckett, T. T., M.L.C., Surrogates' office, 91 Little Collins st west
a'Beckett, W. A. C., Cochran st, Btn
Aberdeen Line of Ships, 59 Little Collins st west
Abraham, David, boot and shoe dealer, 197 Elizabeth st
Abraham, L., 50 King William st, F
Abraham, Maurice, working optician, 99 Queen st
Abrahams, Joseph, Fellmongers' Arms, 182 Victoria st, Rd
Abrahams, J., broker, 46 York st, Em H
Abrahams, Louis, Stanley st, W M
Absalom, G., 45 Market st, Em H
Abson, M., 3 Market st, Em H
Accidental Injury Insurance Co., 26 Collins st east
Acclimatisation Society's office, 30 Swanston st; depôt, Royal park
Ackerill, —, Lereson st, Hot

B

Achilles Mining Association, 86 Elizabeth st
Ackerman, Mrs., Flint st, E M
Acres, R., crinoline manufacturer, 245 Victoria parade, E C, and 20 Bridge road, Rd
Acroyd, Wm., painter and gilder, Bay st, San
Acton, Thomas, cabinetmaker, 194 Johnson st, E C
Acut, John, Fitzroy st, St K
Adam, Mrs., grocer, 94 York st, Em H
Adam, John, Beach st, San
Adam, Rev. G., Wilson st, Bru
Adames and Co. (Clarke, Joseph Lewis), silk and ribbon warehousemen, 51 Elizabeth st
Adams, A., plumber, Cremorne st, Rd
Adams, A. C., Hanmer st, Wmn
Adams, Geo., saddler and harness maker, 3 Franklyn st east
Adams, J., Lygon st, Carl
Adams, James, 10 James st, F
Adams, John, Victoria terrace, Cardigan st, Carl
Adams, John, saddler, 94 Elizabeth st
Adams, J., 75 Kerr st, F
Adams, J., dealer, Yarra st, E C
Adams, J. S., store and P. O., Alphington
Adams, Reuben T., Barkly Arms, Ann st, Wmn
Adams, Thomas, Paddington hotel, 156 Little Collins st east
Adams, T. W., Faraday st, Carl
Adamson, John, Cardigan st, Carl
Adamson, J., Pelham st, Carl
Adamson, James, Cliff st, Pra
Adamson, T., crown prosecutor, Ivanhoe
Adamson, T. —, carver, Byron st, Hot
Adamson, T., 239 Moray st, Em H
Adamson, William, Hoddle st, Rd
Adamson, William, Cochrane st, Dtn
Adamson, Wm., seedsman, 71 Collins st west
Adcock, —, pastrycook, High st, St K
Adcock, A. F., notary public and conveyancer, 26 Queen st
Adcock, Geo. C., bookseller, 66 Bridge road, Rd
Adderly, Edwin, Darling st, Pra
Adderly, Mrs., confectioner, 160½ Bourke st east
Addis, James Clement, forwarding agent, 18 Queen st
Addison, Mark S., 28 Church st, Em H
Addy, Charles, Chapel st, Pra
Adet, Edward, Victoria st, F C
Aerated Bread Co., 203 Bourke st west
A'Fon, —, Chinese merchant, 61½ Little Bourke st east
Agamemnon, Break o' Day, Catherine Reef and Comet M. Co.'s (Bendigo), 37 Market st
Agamemnon G. M. Co., 31 Queen st

Age Newspaper Office, 67 Elizabeth st
Age of Progress Q. M. Co., Eldon Chambers, Collins st west
Agg, Alfred H., Com. of Audit, 178 Collins st. east
Agnew, A., Barry st, Carl
Agnew, G. F., commission merchant, 41 Flinders lane east
Agnew, Richard S., Wreckyn st, Hot
Agra and Masterman's Bank, 85 Queen st
Ahern, Daniel, Lygon st, Carl
Ahern, Tim., grocer, 23 Lonsdale st east
Ah Moy, Clarendon st, E M
Ainslie, James, Jolimont square, E M
Ainslie, Mrs., ladies' school, 40 Powlett st, E M
Ainsworth, A. B., High st, Pra
Ainsworth, J., tailor, 67 Cobden st, Em H
Ainsworth, John, 79 Victoria st, east
Airey, R., cabinetmaker, 101 William st
Aitken, Alex. E., insurance agent, Bay st, San
Aitken, James, 3 Gore st, F
Aitken, J., stationer, Church st, Btn
Aitken, J., china dealer, 30 Rosslyn st, W M
Aitken, Robert, 28 Villiers st, Hot
Aitken, Robt. and Wm., millers and corn merchants, 66 Elizabeth st extension
Aitken, R. W., Berkeley st, Carl
Aitken, Thomas, brewer and malster, 216 Victoria parade
Aitken, Wm. (of R. and W. Aitken), Yea
Aitkens, D., Caledonia hotel, Cole st, Wmn
Aitkins, —, Wreckyn st, Hot
Aitkins, James, Swan st, Rd
Aitkins, R., Hoddle st, Rd
Ajax, Alma United Leads, and Aurora M. Co.'s, 64 Elizabeth st
Akerly, W. J., 185 King st
Akerman, Mrs., 13 Gertrude st, F
Akhurst, W. M., journalist, 18½ Young st, F
Albert, Wm., pastrycook and fruiterer, 21 Elizabeth st
Albon, Thomas, brickmaker, Morland and Parker sts, Fcy
Albury, Thomas, baker, New st, Btn
Alcock, E., Bailey st, Hot
Alcock, Henry Upton, timber merchant and billiard table manufacturer, 132 Russell st, 95 Little Bourke st east
Alcock, J., 94 Madeline st, Carl
Alcock, S., Cardigan st, Carl
Alcorn, Eliz., storekeeper, Lincoln square Carl
Alder, Charles, Station place, San
Alder, J., Weston st, Bk
Alder, James, 23 Coventry st, Em H
Alderson, Chris., 45 Cardigan st, Carl
Aldinga and Economical G. M. Co.'s, Drummond's point, 55 Elizabeth st

Aldwinckle, J., draper, 33 Bourke st east
Alexander, A., bootmaker, 197 King st
Alexander, A., Gertrude st, F
Alexander and Devonshire, furriers, 114 Swanston st
Alexander, Charles, butcher, 149 Brunswick st, 64 Gertrude st, F
Alexander, Geo., pawnbroker, 102 Bridge road, Rd
Alexander, J., Baker, Bay st, Btn
Alexander, J. F., House st, San
Alexander, J., James st, F
Alexander, Jon, 23 Marion st, F
Alexander, John, Gertrude st, F
Alexander, Moses A., Rosslyn st, W M
Alexander, Mrs., Dalgety st, St K
Alexander, M., Fitzroy st, F
Alexander, Walter, Williams road, Tk
Alexander, Wm., general store, Flemington road, Hot
Alford, Charles, carrier, Flem Bnk
Alford, J., store, Cochrane st, Btn
Alford, S., bootmaker, Pent
Alhambra, Bourke st east
Alison, John, bonded warehouse keeper, 111 Flinders lane west
Allamby, Wm., fruiterer, 32 Queensberry st, Carl
Allan, —, 60 Kerr st, F
Allan, —, Moor st, F
Allan, —, 57 Thomson st, Wmn
Allan, A., fishmonger, 100 Bourke st east
Allan, George G., merchant, 11 Market st and Alma road, St K
Allan, Geo. L., Park st, Btn
Allan, James, 63 Queensberry st, Carl
Allan, J., 115 Little Bourke st, west
Allan, J., boarding-house, Yarra st, Held
Allan, Rt., pawnbroker, 105 Stephen st
Allan, R., York st, Em II
Allan, Wm., Abbotsford st, Hot
Allan, W. H., Charles st, Pra
Allanson, W., grocer, 15 Coventry st west, Em II
Allard, A. M., butcher, 124 Russell st
Allars, Charles, broker, High st, St K
Allbut, W., Capel st, W M
Allee, John, St. Kilda road, Btn
Allen, —, 13 James st, Wmn
Allen, —, Marion st, Fitzroy
Allen, A., Chapel st, Pra
Allen, A., Albert st, Pra
Allen, Adam, Perry st, E C
Allen, A. P., plumber, 166 Brunswick st, F
Allen, Charles, painter, Bignell's lane, Bourke st east
Allen, C. E., watchmaker, 83 Swanston st
Allen, Dennis, Salutation hotel, Latrobe st, east
Allen, George, Rouse st, San
Allen, Henry, pawnbroker, Little Bourke st east
Allen, J., Railway place, San

Allen, J. G., Park st, Btn
Allen, J., Charles st, Bk
Allen, J. B., corn store, Hoddle st, E C
Allen, John Harwood, George st, E M
Allen, J. W., accountant, Domain road, S Y
Allen, J., marble mason, 49 Smith st, F
Allen, John, grocer, Bay st, San
Allen, J., Melbourne Gin Palace, Bourke st east
Allen, L., pawnbroker, 194 Stephen st
Allen, Mary, Barry st, Carl
Allen, Mrs., grocer, Madeline st, Carl
Allen, Mrs., grocer, Blackwood st, Hot
Allen, Mrs., Peel st, E C
Allen, Mrs., Grey st, St K
Allen, Mrs., Victoria st, Carl
Allen, Mrs., Dalgety st, St K
Allen, Robert, wholesale fruiterer, 25 William st
Allen, Thomas, Union st, Punt road, Pra
Allen, Thomas, Highett st, Hd
Allen, William, 132 Gertrude st, F
Allen, W., 47 Drummond st, Carl
Allen, W., 22 Lonsdale st east
Allen, William, Lady Franklyn hotel, 19 Wellington st, E C
Allen, Wm. H., chemist, 36 Wellington st, E C
Allen, William H., patentee of Allen's ointment, 51 Temple court
Allendale, William, Pelham st, Carl
Alkerdice, J., grocer, 76 Dorcas st, Em H
Allester, Wm. J., Myrtle Hotel, 31 Coventry st, Em H
Alliance British and Foreign Life Assurance Company, 121 Little Collins st west
Alliance Building and Investment Society, Bank place, Collins st west
Allingham, J. S., solicitor, 72 Queen st
Allison, —, dairy, Swan st, Rd.
Allison, Henry, undertaker, 40 Victoria st, W M
Allison, Wm., store, 138 Latrobe st east
Allman, Miss, seminary, Highett st, Rd
Alloo, —, Bank st west, Em II
Allport, Curzon, solicitor, 21 Queen st
Allport, George L., 35 Bell st, F
Allright, G. M., Lygon st, Carl
Allum, Frederick, 214 Cardigan st, Carl
Allwell, Miss, school, 9 Palmer st, F
Alma and Amelia Quartz Mining Company, 31 Collins st west
Alma Lease Gold Mining Company, 122 Collins st west
Alma United Leads Gold Mining Company, 64 Elizabeth st
Almond, J., 43 Bank st east, Em II
Alner, W., Hoddle st, E C
Alpha Mines, 86 Elizabeth st
Alsop, Geo., carpenter and builder, Kew
Alsop, J., Alma st east, St K
Alston, Thomas, Waterloo st, St K

Alston and Brown, silk mercers and drapers, 47 Collins st west
Alston, David, pawnbroker, 27 Bourke st west
Alston, Thomas, painter, 96 High st, St. K.
Altham, J., Punt road, Rd
Altmann, E., Punt road, Rd
Altmann, and Lindsay, contractors, 110 Lonsdale st east
Alves, John, fishing tackle maker, 81½ Elizabeth st
Amark, Frederick, 136 Russell st
Ambler, Catherine, pawnbroker and earthenware stores, 137 and 139 Lonsdale st east
Ambler, J., Domain st, S Y
Ambler, W. L., letter-press printer, Bourke st east
Ambridge, J., Chetwynd st, Hot
Amedee, E., tailor, 145 Little Bourke st east
Amery, Edwin, George st, E M
Ames, Andrew, Lothian st, Hot
Amess, Samuel, builder and contractor, 1 and 7 William st north
Amies, Thomas, European hotel, 145 Swanston st
Amos, Chas. H., carpenter, Robe st, St K
Amos, James, Dryburgh st, Hot
Amos, Robt., ironworks, Dudley st, W M
Amos, Mrs., Inkerman st, St K
Amslock, Henry, mining agent & broker, 70 Temple court, Collins st west
Amsterdam Underwriters, 49 Collins st west
Anders, J. J., shoemaker, 164 Wellington st, E C
Anderson, —, turner, 217 George st, F
Anderson, Adam, 10 Mackenzie st
Anderson, Alfred, Greville st, Pra
Anderson, Andrew, Bond st, S Y
Anderson, Andrew, Barkly st, Bk
Anderson, Arthur, Wellington parade, E M
Anderson, A. Wm., Lothian st, Carl
Anderson, Charles, Marlou st, F
Anderson, Charles, Fawkner st, St K
Anderson, Chas., baker, Fitzroy st, St K
Anderson, Colonel, Punt road, S Y
Anderson, David, Lothian st, Hot
Anderson, Edward, greengrocer, 87 Lonsdale st east
Anderson, E., clothier, 85 Gertrude st, F
Anderson, F., Brighton st, Hd
Anderson, Hon. R. S., Cotham road, Kew
Anderson, James, 49 Cardigan st, Carl
Anderson, James, Capel st, Hot
Anderson, James, Napier st, Em H
Anderson, James, tailor, 122 Bridge road, Rd
Anderson, J. E., 99 Raglan st, Em H
Anderson, James M., Railway place, San
Anderson, Jas., watchmaker, Bay st, San
Anderson, James, Hoddle st, E C
Anderson, James, Nicholson st, Carl
Anderson, John, grocer, 22 Palmer st, F
Anderson, J., St. Kilda st, Bln
Anderson, J., Morris street, Wmn
Anderson, John, Peel st, Hot.
Anderson, John, boarding house, 118 King st
Anderson, John, Royal George hotel, Hoddle st, E C
Anderson, J., James st, Wmn
Anderson, John J., Park st, Em H
Anderson, J. F., 103 Victoria parade, F
Anderson, John Jas., port gauger, 27 Market st
Anderson, Lawrance, plumber, 224 Elizabeth st, and 140 Cambridge st, E C
Anderson, L., plumber, Little Latrobe st east
Anderson, Magnus, tentmaker, 266 Elizabeth st
Anderson, Miss, 27 Nicholson st, F
Anderson, Mrs., Carlton st, Carl
Anderson, Mrs., Graham st, San
Anderson, Mrs. C. W., store, Beach st, San
Anderson, R., contractor, 108 Arden st, Hot
Anderson, Robert, 210 Napier st, F
Anderson, R. H., Nicholson st, F
Anderson, Robert, machinist and gasfitter, 137 Little Collins st east
Anderson and Marshall, merchants, 63 Little Collins st west
Anderson and Sandilands, solicitors, &c., 91 Little Collins st west
Anderson and Stewart, shipsmiths, Nelson place, Wmn
Anderson and Wright, timber yard and sawmills, 72 Flinders lane east
Anderson, Thos. Y., and Co., ladies' outfitters, 13, 15, and 59 Bourke st east
Anderson, T. Y., Turret lodge, Wr
Anderson, T. Y., 36 Rathdowne st, Carl
Anderson, Thomas, Kew
Anderson, Thomas, Abbotsford st, Hot
Anderson, Thomas, Dryburgh st, Hot
Anderson, W., Barkly st, Bk
Anderson, Walter, chemist, Chapel st, Pra
Anderson, Wm., King William st, F
Anderson, Wm., Carlton st, Carl
Anderson, Wm., Westgarth st, F
Anderson, Wm., Railway place, San
Anderson, Wm., 14 Victoria parade, E M
Anderson, Wm., dealer, 83 Wellington st, E C
Anderson, W. A. D., Punt road, S Y
Anderson, W. S., merchant and importer, 120 Collins st west
Anderson, W. S., and Co., merchants and importers, 120 Collins st west
Andrade, Abraham, grocer, Cambridge st, E C
Andre, J. J., 55 Little Oxford st, E C
Andrew, Edwin, Argyle st, St K
Andrew, Henry, Albert st, E M
Andrew, J., Queensberry st, Hot

Andrew, John, and Co., drapers, 11 and 19½ Lonsdale st west
Andrew, Matthew, Murphy st, S Y
Andrew, P., 94 Durves st, Em H
Andrew, Robert, 98 Dover road, Wmn
Andrews, C., 38 King William st, F
Andrews, G., Clarendon st, Em H
Andrews, G., Berkeley st, Carl
Andrews, Henry, coal merchant, 63 Russell street
Andrews, James, inspector of nuisances, 96 Cardigan st, Carl
Andrews, J., wheelwright, Main st, Heid
Andrews, John, 85 Gore st, F
Andrews, Joseph, 32 Cremorne st, Rd
Andrews, Robert, 8A Palmer st, F
Andrews, Robert, greengrocer, 82 Clarendon st, Em H
Andrews, Robert E., 48 Ann st, Wmn
Andrews, Thomas, Rowena parade, Rd
Andrews, Thomas, 10 Rathdowne st, Carl
Andrews, W., 67 George st, F
Andrews, W., 25 Victoria st, E C
Andrews, W., Webb st, F
Andrews, W. J., Vere st, E C
Anear, Henry, 96 Drummond st, Carl
Angel, Mrs., 58 Cambridge st, E C
Angel, Stephen, 25 Stanley st, W M
Anglor, S., chemist, Northcote
Anglers' Society, 30 Swanston st
Anglo-Swiss G. M. Co., 31 Collins st west
Angus, Henry, bootmaker, 29 Little Lonsdale st west
Angus, Robt., contractor, 68 Napier st, F
Angus, S., Davis st, S Y
Ankers, C., coal and wood yard, High st, St K
Anketell, Wm., returning officer, Pent
Annandale, Mrs., 21 Napier st, Em H
Ansear, B., 33 Pont road, S Y
Ansear, Rev. S., Parker st, Wmn
Annis, A., Lothian st, Hot
Ansett, Henry, 126 Flinders lane east
Anstead, J., Caledonian hotel, Coventry st west, Em H
Anthony, F., C.E., municipal surveyor, 32 Collins st east, and Bk
Anthony, Thomas, and Co., timber merchants, a'Beckett st west
Anthony, Thomas, Church st, Rd
Antisell, R., 11 Church st, Rd
Antonio, B., dining rooms, 63 Bourke st east
Aplin, C. D., geologist, agent, and surveyor, 68 Temple court, Collins st west
Aplin, F., painter, 224 George st, F
Aplin, F., 38 Stanley st, E C
Apollo Music Hall, 172 Bourke st east
Apperly, Henry, sculptor, 20 Barkly st, Carl
Appert, Pierre, l'unt road, Pra
Appleby, J., fruiterer, Sydney road, Bk
Appleton and Littlewood, drapers, 45 and 47 Collins st east

Appleton, Laurence Fredk., Barnett st, St K
Appleton, Richard W., 6 Osborne st, Pra
Appleton, John, tinsmith, Flem
Appold, Mrs., embroideress, Albert st, Pra
Apps, William George, undertaker, 165 Fitzroy st, F
Apted, William, 240 Napier st, F
Arbray, S., 103 Kerr st, F
Arch, Arthur, hatter, 297 Victoria parade, E C
Archibald, Wm., 49 King William st, F
Archer, David, Railway place, San
Archer, W. H. (Registrar-General), Haw
Archer, Mrs., Sackville st, E C
Ardern, J., Commercial road, Pra
Ariel, Thomas H., Stoke st, San
Argo and Britannia Gold Mining Co.'s, 31 Queen st
Argus Newspaper office, 76 Collins st east
Armbrecht, H., working jeweller, 79 Russell st
Armitage, Benjamin, 93 Bouverie st, Carl
Arms, Mrs., Rathdowne st, Carl
Armsted, George, Banksia st, Heid
Armstrong, D., Scott's hotel und Eas
Armstrong, Emery, grocer, 65 Cecil st, Wmn
Armstrong, James, and Co., grocers and bakers, High st, Pra
Armstrong, John, Britannia hotel, corner of Lonsdale and Swanston sts
Armstrong, John, cabinetmaker, 86 Napier st, F
Armstrong, John, 173 Swanston st
Armstrong, J., Heath st, San
Armstrong, Mrs., 123 Kerr st, F
Armstrong, Mrs., 10 Fitzroy st, St K
Armstrong and Merriman, carriage repository, 214 Elizabeth st
Armstrong, R. A., Hotherwood st, Rd
Armstrong, Thomas, grocer, Elizabeth st north
Armstrong, Thos., 32 Rathdowne st, Carl
Armstrong, Thomas, grocer, 79 Leveson st, Hot
Armstrong, W., Station place, San
Armstrong, W., grocer, Sackville st, E C
Armstrong, William, 153 Queensberry st, Hot
Armstrong, Z., botcher, Elizabeth st north
Armytage, C. H., Gardiner's Creek road, Pra
Arnell, —, 159 Elizabeth st
Arnold, Albert G., chemist, 134 High st, St K
Arnold, Andrew, 24 Clarendon st, Em H
Arnold, Ann, *Herald* agency and fancy repository, Clarendon st, Em H
Arnold Brothers, blacking and vinegar works, 10 Franklin st west
Arnold, Charles H., manufacturer of fancy goods, 42 Post Office place, and 125 Swanston st

Arnold, G., surgeon, High st, St K
Arnold, Henry, bootmaker, 104 Drummond st, Carl
Arnold, H., carrier, Elizabeth st north
Arnold, James F., corn merchant, Rathdowne st, Carl
Arnold, Joseph, 89 Chetwynd st, Hot
Arnold, Mrs., Easy st, E C
Arnold, Mrs., Albert st, Fcy
Arnold, R., South road, Bro
Arnold, W., Denby st, Bro
Arnold, W., Bay st, San
Arnoldi, X., engraver, 87 Russell st
Arnot, Andrew, 141 Lonsdale st east
Aroott, Wm., stationer, 54 High st, St K
Arrowshire, George, Punt road, Rd
Arrow, D., 119 Westgarth st, F
Arter, F., Yarra st, E C
Arthur, Mrs., Greville st, Pra
Arthur, Samuel, 20 Johnston st, F
Arthur, Thomas, 40 Johnston st, E C
Arthur, William, 57 Johnston st, E C
Arthurs, George, 21 Gifford st, Wmn
Ashby, R., 132 Gore st, F
Asher, J., Rathdowne st, Carl
Ashforth, Wm., 327 Lygon st, Carl
Ashley and Smith, watchmakers and jewellers, 95 Flinders lane east
Ashley, Edmd., importer of coachmakers' materials, Therry st, St K
Ashley, Mrs., Carlton st, Carl
Ashmore, Mrs., Hoddle st, E C
Ashmore, William, 90 Madeline st, Carl
Ashmore and Goer, wine and spirit merchants, 20 King st
Ashton, E., Gardiner's creek road, Pra
Ashton, Fletcher, 164 Albert st, F M
Ashton, George (H.M.C.), 68 Pascoe st, Wmn
Ashton, J. M., butcher, Chapel st, Pra
Ashton, Michael, organist, Sackville st, E C
Ashworth, E., Davis st, Pra
Ashworth, John, 77 Harmer st, Wmn
Ashworth, Simeon, 178 Madeline st, Carl
Asiatic Banking Corporation, 21 Collins st west
Askmore, Charles, butcher, 157 Brunswick st, F
Asmussen, A., Railway hotel, Elizabeth st
Aspinall, Butler C., barrister, 29 Temple court, Collins st west
Aspinwall, William, Darling st, S Y
Astley, Thomas, Rowena parade, Rd
Astley, William, Rowena parade, Rd
Atchison, J., Barkly st, Bk
Atchison, J. D., 67 Napier st, F
Atchison and Lumsden, timber merchants, &c., 19 Flinders st west
Athenæum and Free Library, Kew
Athens, Mrs., midwife, Latrobe parade
Atkin, C. A., chemist, 45 Errol st, Hot
Atkin, Wm., chemist, 96 Spencer st north
Atkins, George, Fitzroy st, F

Atkins, John, 22 Bank st west, Em H
Atkins, John, barrister, 22 Temple court, Collins st west
Atkins, Josiah, hay and corn store, Bridge road, Rd, and Chapel st, Pra
Atkins, Thomas, 60 Ann st, Wmn
Atkins, William, bootmaker, 146 Collins st west
Atkins, W. H., Northcote
Atkinson, —, Raglan st, San
Atkinson and Co., corn store, &c., High st, St K
Atkinson, F. C., medical practitioner, 187 Stephen st
Atkinson, G. W., Clyde st, St K
Atkinson, Henry, butcher, 120 Little Lonsdale st east
Atkinson, James, Berkely st, Carl
Atkinson, John, tailor, 26 Little Collins st west
Atkinson, John, 244 Moray st, Em H
Atkinson, John, Brighton st, Rd
Atkinson, Mrs., 4 Dover villas, Victoria parade, E C
Atkinson, R., butcher, Church st, Bro
Atkinson, R., butcher, Villiers st, Hot
Atkinson, Robert, butcher, 62 Clarendon st, Em H
Atkinson, T. G., Barkly st, Carl
Atkinson, Thomas G., 91 Moor st, F
Atkinson, G. F., saddler, 146 Brunswick st, F
Atkinson, Wm., Berkely st, Carl
Atkinson, Susan, Caroline st, Pra
Atkyns, E. A., solicitor, 18 and 19 Eldon Chambers, Collins st west and Haw
Attenborough, Wm., Domain road
Attenborough, Thos., stables, Blossom alley, Post Office place
Attenborough, Winfield, solicitor, 26 and 28 Collins st west
Attfield, Edward, boot and shoe dealer, High st, Pra
Attfield, E., Haw
Attrill, Mrs., 14 Napier st, F
Audit Department Offices, 176 Collins st east
Audley, G., carpenter, 316 Bridge road, Rd
Augur, Fred., greengrocer, High st, Pra
Auld, John, grocer, 88 Little Oxford st, E C
Auld, John, 9 Pelham st, Carl
Aulton, Hy., 79 Raglan st, Em H
Aumaliksy, Raimond, marine store, 197 Bourke st west
Aust, Mrs., laundress, Perry st, E C
Austin, —, brushmaker, 234 Moray st, Em H
Austin, —, tanner, Flemington Bank
Austin and Ellis, architects and surveyors, 60 Elizabeth st
Austin, George Gordon, Cross Keys hotel, Lonsdale st east
Austin, G., 153 Moray st, Em H

Austin, G., 63 Young st., F
Austin, Henry, Lothian st, Flot
Austin, Jas. Edward, King William st., F
Austin, J. H., Peel st., Pra
Austin, J. T., coach trimmer, 120 Napier st, Em H
Austin, J., 20 Dorcas st west, Em H
Austin, Mrs., 28 Nelson place, Wmn
Austin, Mrs. Fanny, grocer, Barkly st, Carl
Austin, Richard, schoolmaster, Union st, Punt road, Pra
Austin, S. A., store, 210 Little Collins st east
Austin, Thomas, Kew
Austin, Wm., Bay st, Btn
Austin, William, tailor, Morland st, Fey
Australasian Financial Agency Company, 17 Eldon Chambers, Collins st west
Australasian Fire and Life Insurance Company, 75 Collins st west
Australasian Sub-marine Limited Working Company, 61 Collins st east
Australasian Newspaper Office, 76 Collins st east
Australian Alliance Assurance Company, 53 Elizabeth st and 2 Collins st west
Australian Evangelist Office, 76 Collins st east
Australian Express Company, 90 Bourke st east
Australian Gold and Silver Mining Co., 3 Little Collins st west
Australian Lloyds, Hall of Commerce, 48 Collins st west
Australian Medical Journal Office, 76 Collins st east
Australian Mortgage, Land, and Finance Company, 22 and 24 Queen st
Australian Monthly Magazine Company (Limited), 23 Post Office place
Australian Mutual Provident Society's Office, 107 Collins st west
Australian Newspaper Office, Church st, Rd
Australian Pastoral Investment Co., 70 Queen st
Australian Stage Company, 35 Bourke st east
Australian Steam Navigation Company, 10 Elizabeth st
Australian Trust and Agency Company, corner Bond st and Flinders lane west
Australian Trust Company, 50 William st
Australian United Loan and Discount Association, 61 and 63 Flinders lane east
Australian Wine Company, 73 Bourke st west
Austrian Lloyds Steam Navigation Co., 22 Collins st west
Antard, C., and Co., 65 Flinders st west
Antard, C., 44 Gore st, F
Aveling, G., Millswyn st, Pra
Avery, Edward, 137 Cecil st, Em II

Avery, Joseph, builder, 26 Smith st, E C
Avins, Henry, Painter, 121 Moor st, F
Avis, Thomas, and Co., cabinetmakers, &c., 50 Errol st, Hot
Ayers, J., saddler, Chapel st, Pra
Ayers, John, Weston st, Bk
Aylwin, J. H., 154 Bourke st east
Aylwin, Herbert, 113 Moray st, Em II
Aylwin, Percy, draper, New st, Btn
Azzopaid, (A), ironmonger, 14 Post Office Place
Azzopaid, Antonio, ironmonger, Angelo lane, 7 Bourke st east

B.

Bachelor, William, Lennox st, Rd
Bachholtz, F., 37 Little Lonsdale st west
Backus, T. L., Chapel st, Pra
Bacon, Thomas, wine and spirit merchant, 165 Bourke st east
Badcock, J., manager Bank of New South Wales, Collins st west
Baddington, W., bootmaker, Gardiner's creek road, Tk
Badger, A. G., Wellington parade, E M
Badham, T. W., solicitor, 68 Little Collins st west and Flem
Badley, Wm., 152 Madeline st, Carl
Baeyertz, E., Barkly st, St K
Baeyertz, Charles, manager branch National Bank of Australasia, Rd
Bagge, Herman C., Victoria parade, E M
Baggott, Frederick, bottle dealer, 27 Franklin st west, and Oxford st, Hot
Baggs, Thomas, Wellington st, St K
Bages, W., 17 Nelson road, Em H
Bagley, J. C., Victoria st, W M
Bagley, Rev. J., Lennox st, Rd
Bagnall, John, 130 Elgin st, Carl
Bagot, Robert C., surveyor, 50 William st and Flem
Bagsley, D., 113 Oxford st, E C
Bailey, Chas., bootmaker, 40 Oxford st, E C
Bailey, Edward, Tivoli place, S Y
Bailey, Thomas, 33 Queen st
Bailey, Edward, Goodwood st, Rd
Bailey, Enoch, 136 Johnston st, F
Bailey, F., milliner, Victoria st, Hot
Bailey, Job, 30 Perry st, E C
Bailey, M., 49 Nelson place, Wmn
Bailey, Thomas, market gardener, Pres
Bailey, William, Cecil st, Wmn
Bailey, William, 28 Elgin st, Carl
Bailey, William, Domain road, S Y
Bailey, Wm., corn factor, 9 Flinders st, west
Bailhache, Philip, 147 Bonverie st, Carl
Baillie, J., grocer, High st, St K
Baillie, J. M., 112 Westgarth st, F
Baillie, W. G., St K
Baillie and Butters, stock and share brokers, 49 Collins st west

Baillie, John, 78 Lonsdale st east
Baillie and Robertson, carpenters and joiners, 30 Post Office place
Baillie, Thomas, Carlisle st, E St K
Bailliere, F. F., publisher, 104 Collins st east
Bain, John, Franklin st, W M
Bain, Mrs. 201 Smith st, F
Bain and Royal, coopers, rear 94 Little Bourke st west
Bain, John, greengrocer, 79 Moray st, Em H
Bainbridge, Wm., shoemaker, 118 Queen st
Baines, Edward, wholesale ironmonger, 11 Little Collins st east
Baines, James, baker, 42 Gertrude st, 129 Brunswick st, F, and Hoddle st, E C
Baird, J., builder, Hanmer st, Wmn
Baird, J., 124 Johnston st, F
Baker, —, cab proprietor, Gardiner's ck rd
Baker and Bettison, ship joiners, Beach st, San
Baker, C., Haw
Baker, Captain, 62 Raglan st east, Em H
Baker, Charles, Leicester st, F
Baker, Charles, Hoddle st, E C
Baker, E. H., chemist, Clarendon st, Em H
Baker, Edward, confectioner, 166 King st
Baker, George, Miller st, W M
Baker, G., carrier, Carpenter st, Bin
Baker, George, lime and cement merchant, 8 Cardigan st, Carl
Baker, J., Wilson st, Btn
Baker, John, Wood st, Moor st, F
Baker, John J., fishmonger, 40 Swanston st, and Geelong
Baker, John G., saddler, Church st, Rd
Baker, John R., commission and insurance agent, &c, Eldon Chambers, Collins st west
Baker, J. W., Coventry st, Em H
Baker, Mrs., draper, New st, Btn
Baker, T., Hope st, Bk.
Baker, Thomas, Union st, Pra
Baker, William, Young Queen hotel, Pent
Baker, William, carpenter, 133 Little Collins st west
Balch, Mrs., Fitzroy st, St K
Balchin, Jas., grocer, 216 Bourke st west
Bald, George Thompson, accountant, 69 Collins st west
Bald Hill Gold Mining Company, 66 Little Collins st west
Balderson, R., Chapel st, Pra
Balderson, R., tailor and outfitter, 9 Collins st east
Baldwin, John, general dealer, 166 Madeline st, Carl
Baldwin, J, Hay st, San
Baldwin, John, 54 Bouverie st, Carl
Baldwin, Richard, Church st, Rd
Baldwin, Mrs., Grosvenor st, Pra

Baldwin, Reuben, cab proprietor, 127 Flinders lane east
Baldwin, W., painter and glazier, Little Latrobe st east
Bale, G., clothier and hairdresser, 139 Flinders st west
Balfour, James, Jolimont terrace, E M
Balharry, Jas., shipbroker, Strand, Wmn
Ball, Ambrose, Smith st, E C
Ball, Charles, Pres
Ball, J. W., bookseller, 40 Brunswick st, F
Ball, George, 2 Greeves st, F
Ballantyne, Rev. James, Rathdowne st, Carl
Ballarat Star office, 36 Collins st east
Ballard, Benjamin, 4 James st, F
Ballard, Thomas, Wellington st, Rd
Ballard, Henry, Illawarra st, Wmn
Balleny, Robert, baker, 77 Bank st west, Em H
Ballingall, James, 27 Condell st, F
Ballingall, William, Domain road, S Y
Ballinger, James, 113 Bouverie st, Carl
Ballinger, Joseph, 85 Gore st, F
Ballock, Archibald, Perry st, E C
Balmer, Benjamin, 23 Cobden st, Em H
Balmer, Mrs., 28 Cobden st, Em H
Balston, J., Bank st east, Em H
Bamber, John, 2 Lincoln square, Carl
Bamber, Thomas, 8 Greeves st, F
Bamber, —, 82 Kerr st, F
Bamfield, Henry, dairyman, Hoddle st, E C
Bamford, James, surgeon dentist, 109 Swanston st
Bance, Edmund, baker, Chapel st, Pra
Bance, H. P., Caroline st, S Y
Bancroft, E., merchant, 85 Flinders st west
Bancroft, George, Alma st, St K
Bancroft, Richard, Westbury st, St K
Bancroft, R. K., Halfway House, Albert st, E M
Band, R , Perry st, E C
Bane, Thomas, Duke of Kent hotel, 16 Latrobe st west
Bankes, F., 10 Gloucester terrace, Fitzroy st, St K
Bank of Australasia, 27 Collins st west
Bank of New South Wales, 51 Collins st west
Bank of Victoria, 34 & 36 Collins st east
Bank Place, 77 Collins st west
Banks Brothers, Bell and Co., warehousemen, Flinders court, Flinders lane west
Banks, Frederick, 10 Gloucester terrace, St K
Banks, John, Graham st, Young st, F
Banks, Mrs., milliner, 63 Clarendon st, Em H
Banks, Thomas, 133 Little Lonsdale st west
Banks, William, Btn
Banner, R. G., Victoria hotel, Bay st, San
Banner, Richard, Dow st, San
Bannerman, A. F., 121 Faraday st, Carl

Bannon, E., Swan st, Rd
Bannon, F., Capel st, Hot
Bannon, Sylvester, Argyle square, Carl
Baragwanath, James, carpenter, 208 Victoria st, Rd
Baragwanath, Michael, engineer and machinist, 87 Little Bourke st east
Baragwanath, Peter, 113 Bank st west, Em H
Barber, B., Gore st, F
Barber, James, 61 Argyle st, F
Barber, G. F. A., 14 Ann st, W mn
Barber, Mrs., Dorcas st east, Em H
Barber, Thomas, 41 Market st, Em H
Barber, Wm., wharf carrier, corner of Flinders and Elizabeth sts
Barbler, E. A., 98 Moray place, Em H
Barbour, R., timber merchant, 120 Latrobe st west
Barclay, Henry, 87 Fitzroy st, F
Barclay, Henry, mining agent, 36 Collins st west
Barclay, C. S., Brunswick hotel, Brunswick st, F
Bard, T., 43 Kerr st, F
Bardin, Rev. C. P. M., Albion st east, Bk
Bardsley, Wm., Henry st, Pra
Bardwell, Everett, solicitor, 68½ Queen st
Bardwell, Thomas Hill, merchant and squatter, 73 Flinders lane west
Bardwell, W., tailor, 59 Flinders st east
Barfoot, J. R., Studley st, E C
Barfoot, Mrs. Sarah, midwife, 86 Dorcas st, Em H
Barfoot, U., 73 York st east, Em H
Barker, —, 117 Wellington st, E C
Barker, Edward, surgeon, 53 Latrobe st east
Barker, F., Graham st, San
Barker, J., bootmaker, Mill st, Btn
Barker, J., Gipps st, E M
Barker, J. W., Gardiner's Creek road, S Y
Barker, John, Powlett st, E M
Barker, Mrs., Commercial road, Pra
Barker, Mrs., midwife, 188 Napier st, F
Barker, Wm., 35 Stanley st, W M
Barker, Wm., merchant, 118 Little Collins st west
Barkley, Joseph, 53 Victoria st, Carl
Barkley, Mrs. Mary, 116 Johnston st, F
Barlow, Allan, 283 King st
Barlow, J., Victoria st west, Ilk
Barlow, John, Fitzroy st, St K
Barlow, Rev. John, Nicholson st, Carl
Barlow, Rev. Robert B., St. Mark's Parsonage, Carlton st, Carl
Barlow, Wm., Bell Inn, Perry st, E C
Barlow, W., Station place, San
Barmby Brothers, butchers, Bridge road, Rd
Barmingham, H., Union st, Bk
Barnard, Asher, Princess terrace, F
Barnard, Daniel and Reuben, tobacconists and hairdressers, 44 Bourke st east

Barnard, Francis, chemist, Kew
Barnard, Mrs., Ferguson st, Wmn
Barnard, Wm., baker and grocer, Cambridge st, E C
Barnes, R., 38 M'Arthur place, Carl
Barnes, E., Dover Castle hotel, Palmerston st, Carl
Barnes, F., Jackson st, St K
Barnes, James, Barkly st, Carl
Barnes, Joseph, chemist, Queensberry st, Hot
Barnes, J., Swan st, Rd
Barnes, Samuel, High st, Pra
Barnes, Wm., brickyard, Brunswick road
Barnes, W., Hodgson st, Bk
Barnes, Wm., tailor, 138 Bridge road, Rd
Barnes, Wm., draper, Nelson place north, W mn
Barnes, W. E., Cardigan st, Carl
Barnett, A., cabinetmaker, 155 Lonsdale st west
Barnett, A. R., stockbroker, 35 Little Collins st west
Barnett, B., grocer, 120 and 114 Russell st
Barnett, Asher, confectioner, Russell st
Barnett, Isaac, pawnbroker, 117A Swanston st
Barnett, J., Canning st, Carl
Barnett, John, general dealer, 207 Swanston st
Barnett, Joseph, Yarra st, Pra
Barnett, J., tobacconist, Smith st, F C
Barnett, Joseph, 143 Little Lonsdale st
Barnett, Lewis, dealer, 100 Little Lonsdale st east
Barnett, Lewis, 103 Bourke st west
Barnett, Mrs., Smith st, F
Barnett, Mrs., Ferguson st, Wmn
Barnett, S., Napier st, F
Barnett, Wm., farmer, Hawden st, Heid
Barnfield, Thomas, Barnfield's hotel, Barkly st, Carl
Barnfield, Robert, General Havelock hotel, Victoria parade, E C
Barnicoat, Wm. John, Leveson st, Hot
Barou, Wm., Chapel st, Pra
Barnsdale, S. P., M.D., surgeon, 54 Errol st, Hot
Barr, W., Dover place, Wmn
Barr, Wm., 151 Little Lonsdale st west
Barras, Matthew, Williams road, Pra
Barrett, Charles, hairdresser, 110 Smith st, E C
Barrett, G., Reilly st, F
Barrett, James, M.D., surgeon, 16 Bank st west, Em H
Barrett, T., Brunswick road, Bk
Barrett, Thomas, Pent
Barrett, Thomas, Ferguson st, Wmn
Barrett, Wm., Church st, Rd
Barrie, John, Cardigan st, Carl
Barrow, J. L., Haw
Barrow, Louis, 185 Flinders st east
Barrows, S. C., Wellington parade, E M

Barry, —, Dow st, San
Barry, David, carrier, Flemington Bank
Barry, David, Queensberry st, Hot
Barry, Dr., Mona place, Punt road, S Y
Barry, Edward, Spencer st north
Barry, James, Spanish hotel, 113 Elizabeth st
Barry, J. W., sharebroker, 55 Temple court, Collins st west, and Flem
Barry, John M., architect, C.E., 83 Swanston st
Barry, John, Stanley st, W M
Barry, Richard, bootmaker, 139 Elizabeth st
Barry, Sir Redmond, judge, Rathdowne st, Carl
Barry, Thomas, 10 Bank st east, Em H
Barry, —, Stanley st, E C
Barstow, Joseph, Easy st, Smith st, E C
Barstow, J. F., 66 Lygon st, Carl
Barter, H. M., station master, Spencer st
Barthold, G. J., clothing factory, 127 Spring st
Bartholomew, A., 301 Lygon st, Carl
Bartholomew, Arthur, draughtsman, 55 Rathdowne st, Carl
Bartholomew, David, Greenhythe, Fey
Bartholomew, G., 291 Victoria parade, E C
Bartlam, Henry, Victoria st, St K
Bartlett, A., Wellington st, E C
Bartlett, F. J., plasterer, Church st, Rd
Bartlett, George, perambulator maker, Queensberry st, Carl
Bartlett, Jno., hairdresser, 237 Elizabeth st
Bartlett, John, bootmaker, Gardiners' Creek road, Prn
Bartlett, J., Happy Home hotel, Nott st, San
Bartlett, Thomas J., Cremorne st, Rd
Bartlett, William, Octavia st, St K
Bartlett, Mrs. Easy st, Smith st, E C
Bartlett, Sydney, Electra st, Wmn
Barton, G., 166 Madeline st, Carl
Barton, Robert, baker, 34 Chetwynd st, Hot
Barton, Wm., Barton's hotel, 40 William st and 93 Little Collins st east
Barton, H., Fergusson st, Wmn
Barton, Wm., 73 Rathdowne st, Carl
Barton, W. H., 124 Moray st, Em H
Barton, —, schoolmaster, Ivanhoe
Bartram, Mrs., dressmaker, Wreckyn st, Hot
Bartren, J., 121 Westgarth st, F
Barwick, W. P., Drummond st, Carl
Barwise, John, 36 Villiers st, Hot
Barward, Mrs., Fawkner st, St K
Barwood, James, coal yard, Leveey st, Rd
Barwood, James E., candlemaker, Lenney st, Brighton st, Rd
Bason, George, Grange road, Tk
Basch, J., Queen st
Baskerville, Thomas, 193 Latrobe st west
Bassett, A., Stoke st, San

Basnett, James, Mount Gambier hotel, Palmer st, F
Bastett, Wm., 65 Argyle st, F
Bassett, Wm., 41 Fitzroy st, F
Bastard, S., Stanley st, E C
Bastard, Thomas, bootmaker, High st, St K
Bastings, F., grocer, Northcote
Bastings, Wm., bootmaker, Northcote
Baston, W., George st, F
Bastow, Henry H., architect and surveyor, Oxford Chambers, Collins st west
Batcheldor, Fred., stationer, High st, Prn
Bate, T., Lennox st, Hd
Batelier, Henri, cutler and tinsmith, Queensberry st
Bateman, A., butcher, Flem
Bateman, Wm., Pelham st, Carl
Bateman, Wm., Belfast
Bates, —, bootmaker, Wells st, Bin
Bates, C., Napier st, F
Bates, Charles, Latrobe st west
Bates, Ezekiel, 123 Rathdowne st, Carl
Bates, Henry, boatbuilder, 70 Cole st, Wmn
Bates, Henry, 25 Market st, Em H
Bates, Mrs. Madeline st, Carl
Bates, Thomas T., ironmonger, 46 High st, St K, and 171 and 173 Elizabeth st
Bates, Wm., Margaret st, Prn
Bates, Wm., and Co., provision merchants, 165 Swanston st
Bates, Charles, and Lecroisette, Thomas, cocoa and chocolate manufacturers, Latrobe st west
Bath, Edwin, Fergusson st, Wmn
Batho, Charles, Brunswick st, Bk
Baths and Washhouses, Swanston st north
Batten, Edward H., broker, 18 Queen st
Batten, F. W., Bay st, Bin
Batten, Jos., 90 Dudley st, W M
Batten, John, 11 King William st, F
Batten, Mrs. W. R., milliner and dressmaker, 110 Brunswick st, F
Battersby, Alexander, Wellington st, St K
Battersby, James, 76 Rathdowne st, Carl
Battersby, John, Fergusson st, Wmn
Battinson, John, cabinetmaker, Therry st
Battinson, John, Barkly st, Carl
Battlecombe, J., grocer, Hanover and Webb sts, F
Battle, John, Marion st, F
Batty, —, Kent st, Leicester st, F
Batty, Wm., Grey st, E M
Bavin, T. J., Dalgety st, St K
Baxter, —, Ballic st, Hot
Baxter, Charles, Church st, Rd
Baxter, James, Clyde st, St K
Baxter, Mrs., 115 Wellington st, E C
Baxter, —, 35 Errol st, Hot
Baxter, W., High st, St K
Bayldon and Graham, merchants and tallow-chandlers, 53 Flinders st west
Bayldon, Richard G., Nicholson st, F

Bay AND SUBURBS. Bel 11

Bayles, W., M.L.A. (of Bayles, Wm., and Co.), Dandenong road, St K
Bayles, Wm. and Co., merchants, 97 Collins st west
Bayley, George, 3 Villiers st, Hot
Bayley, J., Williams' road, Prn
Bayley, James, Windsor terrace, Wellington st, Prn
Bayley, J. H., earthenware dealer, Gardiner's Creek road, S Y
Bayley, T., 66 Johnston st, F
Bayley, Rev. Thomas A., George st, F
Bayley, Wm., 72 Wellington st, E C
Bayne, Wm., Abbotsford st, Hot
Baynes, George, solicitor, 85 Little Collins st west
Baynham and Barslow, timber yard, corner of Smith and Derby sts, E C
Bayston, F., 61 Kerr st, F
Bazaglo, ——, poundkeeper, Pent
Beacham, John C., ivory turner, &c., 123 Little Collins st east
Beal, Mrs. Thomas, soap manufacturer, Commercial road, Prn
Beale, M., and Son, fancy repository, 124 Bridge road, Rd
Beale, W. N., carpenter, Blessington st, St K
Beamen, Richard, Derby st, E C
Beaney, James George, surgeon, 154 Collins st east
Bear, Hon. J. P., 25 Victoria parade, F.
Bear, J., Ivanhoe
Bear, T. H., Heidelberg road
Bear's Horse Market, 70 Bourke st west
Bearcroft, F. W., accountant, 1 Bank place, Collins st west
Beard, A., Carlisle st west, St K
Beard, J., Hoddle st, E C
Beasant, Stephen, 49 Bank st west, Em H
Beasley, Nathaniel, fruiterer, Errol st, Hot
Beath, David, Cotham road, Kew
Beacon, Angus, butcher, Provost st, Hot
Beacon, Archd., Provost st, Hot
Beaton, Jas., cooper, 16 Post Office place
Beattie, Robert, commission agent, 27 Dorcas st, Em H
Beatty, John, Wellington st, St K
Beatty, R., Albert st, Prn
Beauchamp and Rocke, auctioneers, 38 and 40 Collins st east
Beauchamp, Horatio, Alma road, St K
Beauchamp, Mrs., 103 Gertrude st, F
Beaugards, John, tailor, Palmerston st, Carl
Beaumont, E., Barkly st, Carl
Beaumont, G., Davis st, Prn
Beaumont, Joshua, Spencer st north
Beaumont, Samuel, wireworker, 226 Bourke st east
Beaumont, Mrs., Roose st, San
Beavan, P., Spencer st north
Beaver, ——, inspector, Cecil st, Wmn
Becker, F., Punt road, Rd

Becher, Rev. Michael Henry, St. James's Deanery, William st
Becker, Thomas, Railway place, San
Beckett, D., Margaret terrace, Bk
Beckett, J., St. James's schools, William st
Beckford, Mrs., 139 Gore st, F
Beckinson, H., sweep, 57 Pelham st, Carl
Beckwith Brothers, merchants, 1 Market st, 65 and 67 Flinders st
Beckx, G. C., Belgian consul, Avoca st, S Y
Beckx, Gustave, and Co., merchants, 89 Queen st
Beddy, Henry, Victoria parade, E M
Bedford, Charles, coal and wood yard, Royal lane, Bourke st east
Bedggood, Daniel, boot importer, 15 Collins st west
Bee, John, builder, 45 Napier st, Em H
Beeby, Mrs., 128 Gertrude st, F
Beech, George, boot and shoe manufactory, Domain st, S Y
Beehive, Bell's Reef, Eaglehawk and Grand Junction Mining Association (Maldon), 37 Market street
Beeling, Henry, Arden st, Hot
Beer, Charles, plumber and gasfitter, Sydney road, Bk
Beer, Ernest, boot and shoe maker, 35 Little Collins st east
Beer, Mrs., school, Moray st, Em H
Beer, Rev. Joseph, Park hill terrace, Hoddle st, E M
Beer, Robert, 53 Lygon st, Carl
Beers, Charles N., bookseller and stationer, 71 Swanston st
Beeston, George, storekeeper, Haw
Beeston, Henry, outfitter, 135 Elizabeth st
Beeston, Mrs., 82 Napier st, Em H
Beggs, John, Stork hotel, Elizabeth st
Behan, J. W., 49 Lygon st, Carl
Behin, Michael, greengrocer, 21 Coventry st, Em H
Behney, John, bootmaker, Beach st, San
Bohn and Frederick, general dealers, 30 Post Office place
Behrens, Ditmar, tobacconist, 164 Bourke st east
Beith, J., Barkly st, Bk
Beith, J., cooper, Railway place, San
Belcher, E., laundress, 15 Little Lonsdale st east
Belcher, Mrs., 3 Albert st, E M
Belcher, Thos., butcher, 148 Brunswick st
Belcher, Wm., carpenter, Northcote
Belfast Steam Packet Office, 31 Market st
Belfield, J., contractor, Macarthur place, Carl
Belfield, Wm., painter, 11 James st, Wmn
Belinfante, Solomon, merchant, Jolimont, E M
Bell, Alexander, High st, St K
Bell, Alexander, Chetwyod st, Hot
Bell, Ann, grocer, 110 Napier st, F

Bell, Benjamin, grocer, 110 Napier st, F
Bell, R. J., Caroline st, S Y
Bell, Bruce, and Co., wholesale grocers and wine merchants, 19 Queen st
Bell and Butt, undertakers, Lennox st, Rd
Bell, David, Cremorne st, Rd
Bell, Edward, Lennox st, Rd
Bell, F., Punt road, S Y
Bell, E., Kew
Bell, F., Pent
Bell, Fred. G., Chetwynd st, Hot
Bell, George S., Charles st, Fcy
Bell, George, William st, S Y
Bell, H., 49 Charles st, F
Bell, Hy., 44 Dudley st, W M
Bell, Henry, Arthur st, Commercial road, Pra
Bell, Henry, 113 Bouverie street, Carl
Bell, James, Swan st, ltd
Bell, James, cabinetmaker, Gipps st, E M
Bell, James, 12 Faraday st, Carl
Bell, J., bootmaker, High st, St K
Bell, John, grocer, Rathdowne st, Carl
Bell, Joshua, Webb st, F
Bell, Mrs., 29 Dorcas st, Em H
Bell, W. M. and Co., merchants, 121 Little Collins st west, bonded stores, Church st, Bourke st west
Bell, W. M., Tivoli, S Y
Bell, W. M., Bolton, Btn
Bell and Westwood, cabinetmakers, 11 Chetwynd st, Hot
Bell, William, Hoddle st, Rd
Bell, W., George st, E. M.
Bell's Life office, 9 Bourke st east
Bellamy, Humphrey, 18 Palmer st, F
Bellatt, A. B., hay and corn store, Haw
Bellin, John, auctioneer and land agent, 66 Gertrude st, F
Bellingham, Samuel, Flem Rd
Bellis, George, 33 Bank st, Em H
Bellman, James, 4 Albert st, E M
Bellman, John, and Co., brewers, 24 Bouverie st, Carl
Belton, G., carpenter, Arthur-seat road, Btn
Bencraft, Charles C., Haw
Bencraft, George, oatmeal and flour miller, 73 Flinders lane west
Bencraft and Smith, solicitors, 45 Temple court, Collins st west
Bencraft, George, High st, St K
Bendigo Waterworks Co., 64 Elizabeth st
Benevolent Asylum, Victoria and Curzon sts. Hot
Benford, John, Richmond terrace, Rd
Benger, Mrs, 104 Napier st, Em H
Bengrey, George, grocer, High st, Pra
Benjamin, Benjamin, George st, E M
Benjamin, David, furniture dealer, 120 Clarendon st, Em H
Benjamin, D., 39 Market st, Em H
Benjamin, David, furniture dealer, 191 Swanston st

Benjamin, David, commission agent, 52 Little Collins st west, and 156 Collins st east
Benjamin, Elias, Victoria Parade
Benjamin, H. and L., tentmakers, 93 and 201 Elizabeth st
Benjamin, Henry, Errol st, Hot
Benjamin, Isaiah, Bridport st west, Em H
Benjamin, Lawrence, clothier and outfitter, 126 Elizabeth st
Benjamin, Lewis, general dealer, 56 Bridge rd, Rd
Benjamin, M., 62 Little Collins st west
Benjamin, M., 158 Collins st east
Benjamin, Mrs., E., 302 Victoria parade, E M
Benjamin, Mrs., stay and corset maker, and servants' registry, 217 Bourke st east
Benjamin, S., merchant, 9 Queen st, and 17 Napier st, F
Benjamin, Samuel, clothier and outfitter 1 Bourke st west
Benjamin, S., money broker, 87 Bourke st west
Benjamin, Solomon, importer, 9 Queen st, and 17 Napier st, F
Benjamin, S., importer, 19 Lonsdale st west
Benjamin, U., painter, &c., 46 Madeline st Carl
Benn, John, Balmarino, S Y
Benn, R., builder, Stephen st
Bennet, T. K., 29 Russell st
Bennet, Thomas Knight, butcher, 115 and 117 Bourke st east, 154 Little Collins st east
Bennett, C., 89 Smith st, F
Bennett, E., 52 Hanover st, F
Bennett, E., Smith st, F
Bennett, Eli, Miller st, Bk
Bennett, E., 51 Wellington st, E C
Bennett, E., Canning st, Carl
Bennett, George, Alphington
Bennett, H., Hoddle st, E C
Bennett, H., produce store, Sydney road, Bk
Bennett, J., boarding-house, 110 Queen st
Bennett, Joseph, Gifford st, Wmn
Bennett, J. H., 231 Smith st, F
Bennett, J., Cecil st north, Wmn
Bennett, John, Bedford st, Hot
Bennett, John B., corner Fitzroy and Acland sts, St K
Bennett, John, Kew
Bennett, Mrs., 57 Kerr st, F
Bennett, Mrs., 71 Smith st, F
Bennett, Mrs., 52 Montague st, Em H
Bennett, M., Station place, San
Bennett, Nathaniel, Terminus hotel, Fitzroy st, St K
Bennett, Peter, fruiterer, corner Little Lonsdale and Swanston sts
Bennett, Robert, Fitzroy st, St K

Bennett and Taylor, solicitors, 107 Collins st west
Bennett, Wm., furniture dealer, 162 Swan st, Rd
Bennett, Wm., Morphy st, S Y
Bennett, Wm. B., 154 Bourke st east
Bennetts, C., builder, 273 Brunswick st, F
Bennetts, W. and A., general merchants, 154 to 158 Brunswick st, F
Bennie, Alexander, George st, E M
Bennie, J., 17 Smith st, F
Benson Brothers, wholesale druggists, 124 Russell st
Benson, Charles, Assembly hotel, 105 Bourke st east
Benson, G., bootmaker, 4 Gertrude st, F
Benson, John, butcher, 115 Flinders st west, and 127 Collins st west
Benson, Mrs., Richmond terrace, Rd
Benson, Philip, Abbotsford st, Hot
Benson, R. G., estate agent, &c., 18 Collins st east
Benson, R., car proprietor, Flem
Benson, Wm., Carlisle st east, St K
Bent, Wm., 13 Grattan st, Carl
Bent, Wm., dealer, King st north
Bent, Wm., secretary, Hobart Town and Launceston and Tasmanian Insurance Companies, 62 Collins st west
Bentley, G. V., 13 Caroline st, S Y
Bentley, Henry, 15 Three chain road, Em H
Bentley, Rev. J., Edward st, Bk
Bentley, James, 32 Bouverie st, Carl
Bentley, Seth, upholsterer and undertaker, Beach st, San
Bentley, Wm., grocer, 222 Elizabeth st, 122 Clarendon st
Bentwitch, Morris, tobacconist, 11 Collins st west
Benyon, James, Ballarat arms hotel, 39 Coventry st west, Em H
Beresford, D., Bay st, Rin
Beresford, D. F., store, Bay st, San
Berg, C. K., musician, Station place, San
Berghoff, Charles, Carlisle st east, St K
Beryhoff and Touzel, importers of Havannah cigars, 18 Collins st west
Bergin, P., 23 Pelham st, Carl
Bergin, P., 186 Madeline st, Carl
Bergin, Thomas, Victoria st, St K
Bergin, Thomas H., 3 Flinders st west
Bergin, Thomas S., grocer and wine and spirit merchant, 123 Flinders st west
Berin, J., 83 Moray st, Em H
Beringer, John, watchmaker, 11 Gertrude st, F
Bernie, James, Morris st, Wmn
Berry, A., Lennox st, Hd
Berry, Graham, Trinian st, Pra
Berry, Henry, 2 Somerset cottages, Nicholson st, Carl
Berry, Henry, 73½ Rathdown st
Berry, J., Bristol st, Fcy

Berry, Joseph, ironmonger, &c., 62 Wellington st, E C
Berry, Wm., tailor, 9 M'Arthur st, Carl
Berthean, Charles E., insurance broker, 49 Collins st west
Bertenshaw, Thomas, photographer, 79 Gertrude st, F
Bertram, Rev. Dixon, Walters st, Fcy
Besant, Alfred, grocer, Hoddle st, E C
Beskinson, H., sweep, 57 Pelham st, Carl
Bessieres, —, 96 Bourke st east
Besson, C., restaurant, 202 Lonsdale st east
Best, Alban Thomas, chemist, 163 Brunswick st, F
Best, Captain J., Osborne st, Wmn
Best, James, Hawke st, W M
Best, John, 46 Bouverie st, Carl
Best, Miss, dressmaker, 39 Russell st
Best, Robert, 135 Rose st, F
Bestwick, Wm., 8 Hanover st, F
Bet-bet Reef Mining Company, 37 Market st
Bethune, Andrew, 103 Lygon st, Carl
Bethune, R., tailor, 189 Lygon st, Carl
Betts, Thomas, Westbury st, St K
Bevan, George, Commercial road, Pra
Bevan, James, and Co., livery stables and coach proprietors, 19 Lonsdale st west, and 35 Bourke st east
Beyers, Edward, Westbury st, St K
Beynon, Captain, Little Nelson st, Wmn
Biagi, G., Italian Consul, 36 William st
Bibby, James, contractor, 178 Drummond st, Carl
Bible Christian Chapel, Gore st, F
Bible, Mrs., Ackland st, St K
Bible and Tract Society's office, 17 Swanston st
Bice, F., 74 Leicester st, F.
Bichner, O. F., 59 King William st, F
Bickerton, J. K., accountant and mining manager, 9 Elizabeth st
Bickerton, Richard Frederick, Neptune st, St K
Bickford, Rev. James, Princess st, St K
Biddle, W. C., Mitchell st, St K
Biddulph, F. H., Wilson st, Pra
Bidgood, Mrs., 274 Smith st, E C
Biers, Henry, 46 Russell st
Biggin, Wm., baker, Rowena parade, Rd
Biggins, —, 19 Victoria st, E C
Biggs, A. E., Haw
Bignell, Henry, manager Graziers' Company, and butcher, 163 Bourke st east
Bignell, W., baker, New st, Bin
Bigwood, Frederick, auctioneer, 79 Collins st west
Bill, Joseph, boarding-house, 297 Elizabeth st
Bickford, Jos. C., Howard st, Hot
Billin, John, 3 Smith st, F
Billing, James, Carlisle st east, St K
Billing, Nathaniel, architect, 91 Queen st

Billing, Richard A., barrister, 12 Temple court
Billyeld, Henry, rivet maker, 48 Wellington st, E C
Bilton, A., 72 Young st, F
Bilton, Charles, Kew
Bince, John, Highett st, Rd
Bindon, H. H., Station place, San
Bindon, Samuel H., M.L.A., barrister, 19 Temple court, Collins st west
Binet, E., Wellington st, Fcy
Binet, Michael, leather seller, 112 Swanston st
Biney, O., Rosslyn st, W M
Binge, Frederic, surgeon dentist, 95 Swanston st
Binge, George, chemist and druggist, 286 Brunswick st, F
Binge, Joseph M., chemist and dentist, 88 Brunswick st, F
Binney, E. N., 78 Collins st west
Binney, R. H., 1 Milton st, St K
Binney, W., Gardiner's creek road, Tk
Binnly, Wm., Gardiner's creek road, Tk
Binstead, George, 132 Rose st, F
Biram, R., grocer, 106 Queen st
Birch, Fredk., Cardigan st, Carl
Birch, F., fruiterer, 43 Victoria parade
Birch, John, Hoddle st, E C
Birch, G., Williams road, Pra
Birch, George, Graham st, San
Birch, John, bootmaker, 89 Wellington st, E C
Birchall, W. H., Rowena parade, Rd
Bird, —, Villiers st, Hot
Bird, A., dealer, 183 Stephen st
Bird, E., Thomson st, E C
Bird Island Guano Company, 80 Queen st, and Eastern Market, Bourke st east
Bird, J., Victoria st, W M
Bird, J., Pent
Bird, James, tailor, 36 Stephen st
Bird, Samuel D., physician, 66 Elizabeth st
Bird, Mrs., 130 Westgarth st, F
Bird and Son, news agents, &c., 4 Bourke st west, and 98 Queen st north
Bird, T. J., 43 Kerr st, F
Birkett, M., Barkly st, Ilk
Birkmire, J., Tivoli place, Pont road, S Y
Birks, Thomas, Rennie st, Fcy
Birmingham, M., Royal brickfields, Bk
Birmingham, T., Park hotel, Vere st, E C
Birmingham, W., Royal brickfields, Bk
Birrell, James, 74 Dudley st, W M
Birnie, —, 46 Coventry st west, Em H
Bishop, —, Dalgety st, St K
Bishop, Alexander, Victorian hotel, corner of Lonsdale and Stephen sts
Bishop, Francis, 6 Alfred place, Collins st east
Bishop, George, Simpson street, E M
Bishop, J., Grattan st, Carl
Bishop, John, grocer, Hoddle st, E C

Bishop, J., dealer, 23 Victoria st, E C
Bishop, James, 299 Fitzroy st, F
Bishop, Mrs., 87 Cecil st, Em H
Bishop, T., 45 Rosslyn st, W M
Bishop, Wm., 1 Cole st, Wmn
Bissell, Samuel, 44 Charles st, F
Bissell, J., 116 Madeline st, Carl
Blaber, Robert, 205 Albert st, E M
Black, —, 36 Bank st west, Em H
Black, A., Chetwynd st, W M
Black, A., Stoke st, San
Black, Charles, 42 George st, F
Black, David, grocer, 171 Little Bourke st east
Black, D., blacksmith, Moray st, Em H
Black, D., store, St Andrew st, Btn
Black, D., produce merchant, Eastern Market and Romeo lane
Black, Donald, 12 Leicester st, Carl
Black, George, stock and share broker, 10 Collins st west, and 84 Drummond st, Carl
Black, George, Church st, Btn
Black, Henry, grocer, 175 Bourke st west
Black, J., 106 Moray st, Em H
Black, James, Cremorne st, Rd
Black, J., 5 Carlton st, Carl
Black, J. and R., bakers, 45 Madeline st, Carl
Black, J., M.D., surgeon, 97 Bourke st west
Black, Miss, dressmaker, Graham st, San
Black, Mrs., 119 Spencer st
Black, Mrs., Lothian st, Hot
Black, Neil, M.L.C., Melbourne Club
Black, Robert, 55 Young st, F
Black, Robert, contractor, 118 Bank st west, Em H
Black, Thomas, M.D., surgeon, Robe st, St K
Black, Wm., bootmaker, 68 Victoria st, Rd
Black, Wm., 152 Victoria parade, E M
Black, Wm. H., bootmaker, 149 King st
Blackall, Wm., 67 Bouverie st, Carl
Blackaly, Daniel, shoemaker, Eastern Market, Bourke st, east
Blackburn, Francis, tobacconist, 53 Bourke st west
Blackburn, James, Avoca st, S Y
Blackburn, James, turner, Hoddle st, E C
Blackburn, James, architect, C.E., and mining agent, 55 Elizabeth st
Blackburn, John, Bendigo stables, Leicester st, Carl
Blackburn, John, Roden st, W M
Blackburn, J. B., Little Nelson st, Wmn
Blackburn, Mrs., Rachael, 3 George st, F
Blackett, Cuthbert Robert, chemist and druggist, Gertrude st, F
Blackett, Mrs. M., Princes st, F
Blackett, Thomas M., chemist, 76 Stevedore st and Nelson place, Wmn
Blackham, George, Lygon st, Carl

Blackham, H., 109 Gertrude st, F
Blackie, J., chemist and registrar, Preston
Blacklock, James. Tivoli place, S Y
Blacklock, J., cabinetmaker, 18 Little Bourke st west
Blacklock, John, tailor, Hosie lane, off Flinders lane east
Blackman, C., gardener, New st, Bun
Blackman, H. S., Elgin st, Carl
Blackman, James, Thomson st, E C
Blackmore, F. N., Halifax st, Btn
Blackmore, Mark, waterproof clothing manufacturer, 133 Flinders st west
Blackmore, Mrs., Graham st, San
Blackshaw, Joseph, bookseller and news agent, 34 Cardigan st, Carl
Blacksmiths' Society, meet at Trades Hall, Lygon st, Carl
Blackson, Joseph, tailor, &c., 186 Bourke st east
Blackwall Line of Packets, White, W. P., and Co., 10 Elizabeth st
Blackwell, H., William st, Prn
Blackwell, John, grocer, Bridge road, Rd
Blackwell, William, 33 Lygon st, Carl
Blackwell, R. T., William st, S Y
Blackwood, James, Orrong road, Tk
Blackwood, J. H., M.L.A., 76 Adderley st, W M
Blade, Jeremiah, butcher, corner of Brunswick and Farie sts, F
Blagden, George, Gipps st, E M
Blair, Alexander, Saltwater River, Fcy
Blair, D., 160 Moor st, F
Blair, Ellen, confectioner, 116 Gertrude st, F
Blair, George, 100 Argyle st, F
Blair, James, 48 Napier st, F
Blair, J., Saltwater River, Fcy
Blair, James W., chemist, 30 Bourke st east
Blair, John, surgeon, 101 Collins st east
Blair, Mrs., Nicholson st, F
Blair, Wm., 79 Raglan st, Em H
Blair, Wm. N., ironmonger, 79 Raglan st, Em H
Blake, Henry, Thompson st, W mn
Blake, T. S., Pelham st, Carl
Blake, Wm., Lothian st, Hot
Blake, Wm., Canning st, Carl
Blake, Wm., florist and sealsman, Greville st, Prn
Blake, Wm., Queensberry st, Hot
Blake, Wm., 31 Bourke st west
Blakemore, E. V., corner of Caroline st and Domain road, S Y
Blakemore, John, butcher, 49 Stevedore st, Wmn
Blakeway, John Edwin, scale maker, 285 Elizabeth st
Blam, Robert, Victoria parade, F M
Blanchard, C., 44 Napier st, F
Blanchard, Charles, saddler, 39 William st
Blanchard, J., 48 King William st, F

Blanchard, John, Valiant st, E C
Blanchard, Wm., U. S. consul, 91 Little Collins st west
Blanchfield, —, grocer, Wellington st, E C
Blandfield, W., 53 Napier st, F
Blannin, Wm., 49 Palmer st, F
Blanshard, David, butcher, Gardiner's Creek road, Prn
Blanshard, Mrs., registry office, Gardiner's Creek road, Prn
Blanshard, Robert, 33 Lygon st, Carl
Blanton, Thomas, Rathdowne st, Carl
Blay, Mrs., St. David's st, F
Blazey, Wm., pianoforte maker, 10 Bridge road, Rd, and 81 Collins st east
Bleach, Mrs., 174 Bridge road, Rd
Bleasdale, Wm., Drummond st, Carl
Blowett, G., 120 Brunswick st, F
Blewitt, Gabriel, 63 Oxford st, E C
Bligh, Francis, J., Btn road
Bligh and Harbottle, merchants, &c., 43 Flinders lane west
Bliss, Alfred, auctioneer, &c., 34 Collins st west, and Lennox st, Rd
Blizard, Mrs., Lennox st, Rd
Blom, O., teacher, off Gisborne st, E M
Blomberg, Mrs., 104 Cecil st, Em H
Blomfield, Benjamin G., coffee roaster, 14 Post Office place
Blomfield, Henry, clothing manufacturer, 85 Fitzroy st, F
Bloomfield, James, Abbotsford st, Hot
Bloomington, Israel, boot importer, Elizabeth st
Bloor, Mrs., accoucheuse, 59 Spring st
Bloor, Samuel, Exchange hotel, William st
Bloxham, Edward John, squatter, 2 Jolimont square, E M
Blue, Thomas S., baker, 12 Market st, Em H
Blum, Thomas, 68 Hotham st, E M
Blumfield, —, Flemington road, Hot
Blundell and Ford, stationers, printers, and publishers, 44 Collins st west, 51 and 53 Flinders lane west
Blundell and Hurry, solicitors and notaries public, 69 Collins st west
Blundell, James J., Beach road, Btn
Blundell, Martin P., Punt road, S Y
Blundell, Richard, Balaclava road, Caulfield
Blyth, D., Albert st, Rk
Blyth, Edgar C., Palmerston st, Carl
Blyth, J., Dalgety st, St K
Blyth, J., 41 Three-chain road, Em H
Blythe, James, 226 George st, F
Boadle, Mrs., 39 Pelham st, Carl
Board of Education, Model schools, Spring st
Board of Examiners for Civil Service, Government house
Board of Science, Building Museum, Queen st

Board of Agriculture, offices off Queen st
Board, James, merchant, 75 Flinders lane east and Kew
Boardman, Thomas, 102 Elgin st, Carl
Bobardt, Otto, mechanical engineer, &c., 121 King st
Bocquet, Alfred, 74 Little Collins st west
Boddington, Alfred, Buckly st, Fcy
Boddington, Robert, millwright, 4 Queensberry st, Carl
Bodley, Sidney, Capel st, Hot
Bodkin, Miss, milliner, 253 Elizabeth st
Body, —, Young st, F
Body, Alexander, 136 Johnston st, E C
Rody, Edward, Haw
Roedacker, W., Llardet st, San
Bogg, John W., Tk
Bogg, J., 17 Nelson road, Em H
Boggiano, Louis, 82 Swanston st, and Little Collins st east
Bogie, A., florist, Punt road, Pra
Bogie, James, Fergusson st, Wmn
Bogle, Andrew (manager of the Royal Bank of India), Breckinhill Lodge, Elsternwick
Bogle, John S., baker, 139 Bouverie st, Carl
Bohling, C., Flemington road, Hot
Bohn, J. C., shoemaker, 110 Little Lonsdale st east
Boilermakers' Society, meet at Trades' hall, Lygon st, Carl
Boland, Edward, Abbotsford st, W M
Boland, Jeremiah, Champion hotel, Brunswick and Gertrude sts, F
Boland, John, Loughmore Castle hotel, Leveson and Arden sts, Hot
Boland, John, Hen and Chickens hotel, 82 Flinders lane east
Boland, J. M., Crown and Anchor hotel, Napier st, F
Boland, Patrick, Cross st, Hot
Bold, Elizabeth, milliner, 34 Queensberry st, Hot
Bold, J., glasscutter, Queensberry st, Hot
Boler, Miss, 20 Adderly st, W M
Boles, W., 21 St. David's st, F
Bolger, James C., Australasian hotel, 232 Elizabeth st
Bolger, Mrs., 137 Little Collins st east
Bolman, Mrs., 150 Brunswick st, F
Bolton, J., Osborne st, Wmn
Bolton, Mrs., High st, Hot
Bolton, Mrs., general storekeeper, 2 Beach st, San
Bolton, Richard, 6 Berkeley st, Carl
Bond, Alicia, provision dealer, 139 Lonsdale st east
Bond, Howard, 92 Westgarth st, F
Bond, John and Alexander, bootmakers, Chapel st, Pra
Bond, Mrs., 32 Grattan st, Carl
Bond, Mrs., Rowena parade, Rd
Bond, Stephen, Crockford st, San

Bond, Thomas, Union terrace, Canning st, Carl
Bond, Wm., bootmaker, 53 Barkly st, E M
Bone, G., 19 Drummond st, Carl
Bone, J. H., bazaar, Queensberry st, Hot
Bone, Mrs., 17 Dover place, Wmn
Boneila, James, 74 Spencer street north
Bones, John, painter and paperhanger, 204 Bridge road, Rd
Bones, John, Lisathdowne st, Carl
Boness, John, cabinetmaker, 16 a'Beckett st, east
Boon, William, George st, E M
Bonnar, George, 71 Dorcas st, Em H
Bonneau, H. C., Kew
Bolten, H. James, 16 Adderley st, W M
Bonwick, —, academy, Acland st, St K
Bonwick, Walter, Haw
Boubler, R., greengrocer, Nott st, San
Booker, George, 104 Fitzroy st, F
Booker, J., Lennox st, Rd
Booker, J., sexton, Crescent, Btn
Booth, A., Fitzroy st, F
Booth, F. S., Alma st east, St K
Booth, James, 10 Jeffcott st, W M
Booth, J., bootmaker, Brunswick st, F
Booth, James, grocer, 92 Clarendon st, Em H
Booth, John, smith, Wellington st, E C
Booth, H., butcher, Errol st, Hot
Booth, Isaac, Flem
Boothby, George, Curzon st, Hot
Borman, J., bootmaker, Errol st, Hot
Boraman, Samuel, jun., bootmaker, 47 Errol st, Hot
Bore, —, 62 Montagne st, Em H
Borland, J., wheelwright, Banksia st, Fleid
Borlase, Jas. Skipp, solicitor, 69 Queen st
Borley, William, gardener, Pres
Boroondara Building Society, 18 Collins st east
Boroondara Cemetery Office, Haw
Borrowman, John, Victoria st, Hot
Borrowman, Mrs. G., 6 Bridport st, Em H
Bortowman, William, Rotherwood st, Rd
Borthwick, Alexander, oil and colorman, 38 Market st, Em H
Borthwick, Mrs., 12 Dorcas st, Em H
Boseley, E., nightman, 24 High st, St K
Bosely, W., plumber, 119 Russell st
Bosisto, Joseph, chemist, 181 Bridge road, Rd
Boston, R., greengrocer, 110 Drummond st, Carl
Boston, Thomas, gardener, Brown st, Heid
Boswarva, H. M., Cremorne st, Rd
Boswarva, N. F., Cremorne st, Rd
Boswell, Alex., tailor, 110 Swan st, Rd
Boswell, George, Canning st, Carl
Boswell, Thomas, blacksmith, Banksia st, Heid
Bosworth, Frederick, plumber and painter, 140 Bridge road, Rd
Botanic Gardens, S Y

Botterill, J., Caroline st, S Y
Bottle, William, saddler, 253 Elizabeth st
Bottomley, Joseph, money broker, 39 Albert st, E M
Bottomley, S., Young st, F
Bottow, J., tailor, Madeline st, Carl
Boulger, D. W., St. Helier's st, E C
Boulter, Miss, dressmaker, 12 Palmer st, F
Boulter, Samuel F., bacon curer, Pres
Boulter, Wm., tailor, High st, Pra
Boulter, Wm., Gipps st, E C.
Bourke, John, 300 Lygon st, Carl
Bourke, John, Carpentaria hotel, Queen st
Boorke, T., 142 Kerr st, F
Bourn, James, corn dealer, Therry st
Bourn, James F., 14 Nicholson st, F
Bourne, John, Studley park
Bovey, W., 95 Young st, F
Bow, F., boarding-house, Franklin st
Bow, Henry, 151 Little Nelson st, Wmn
Bow, Wm., 41 Thomson st, Wmn
Bowater, Benj., grocer, Bedford st, Hot
Bowater, John, Vincent's hotel, Smith st, E C
Bowden, —, Marion st, F
Bowden, H., Rosel, South Elsternwick
Bowden, John, fruiterer, Domain st, S Y
Bowen, W., 114 Bank st west, Em H
Bowen, Wm., chemist, 43 Collins st west
Bower, Charles G., grocer and wine merchant, High st, St K
Bower, James A., general store, 44 Derby st, E C
Bower, Mrs., Peel st, Pra
Bowers, J., 26 Villiers st, Hot
Bowes, Denis, Roscrea hotel, Northcote
Bowes, Mrs., grocer, 71 Rathdowne st, Carl
Bowbey, Thomas, Union st, Pra
Bowie, Robert, M.D., Northcote
Bowker, H., dairy, Otter st, E C
Bowland, P., Cross st, Hot
Bowler, George, shoemaker, Banksia st, Brid
Bowler, James, Williams road, Pra
Bowler, Mrs., Powlett st, E M
Bowley, W. B., Yarra st, Fcy
Bowman, Amos, 123 Napier st, F
Bowman and Co. (Bowman, Joseph; Edmonds, James), bakers, 171 Little Lonsdale st east
Bowman, Mrs., 222 Victoria parade, E M
Bowman, Robert, Gardiner's Creek road
Bowman, Wm., 26 Queensberry st, Carl
Bowring, Charles, bootmaker, Chapel st, Pra
Bowring, James, shoemaker, Hoddle st, E C
Bowring, Joseph, baker, 46 Wellington st, E C
Bowzer, Mrs., Chapel st, St K
Box, H., and Co., importers of saddlers' and coachmakers' ironmongery, 71½ Little Collins st west

Box, E., carpenter, 336 George st, F
Box, H., Haw
Box, John, Albert st, E M
Box, Samuel, 226 George st, F
Boxall, Henry, 11 Pelham st, Carl
Boyall, James, Berkely st, Carl
Boyce, James, Smith st, E C
Boyce, H., bootmaker, Madeline st, Carl
Boyd and Currie, shipping agents, Lloyds' room, Collins st west
Boyd, J., butcher, 32 and 34 Coventry st, Em H
Boyd, James, Chapel st, Pra
Boyd, John, Graham st, San
Boyd, John, 34 William st
Boyd, J. F., High st, St K
Boyd, Mrs., teacher, 21 Smith st, F
Boyd, Mrs., 75 Queensberry st, Hot
Boyd, Rev. J. S., Ess
Boyd, Thomas, Gardiner's Creek road, Pra
Boyd, T. E. (of Boyd and Currie), S Y
Boyle, A., livery stables, Fawkner st, St K
Boyes, Bros., saw makers, 151 Russell st
Boylan, Patrick, Empire hotel, Errol st, Hot
Boyle, C., and Sons, blacksmiths, 264 Elizabeth st
Boyle, Miss, fruiterer, 316 Elizabeth st
Boyle, Samuel, porter bottler, 94 Little Bourke st west
Boyle, Thomas, Fent
Boyle, Thomas, 160 William st
Boyle, Thomas, Baillie st, Hot
Boyne, C., Pelham st, Carl
Boyne, George, paperhanger and painter, 61 Barkly st, Carl
Brache, J., engineer, Northcote
Bracher, John, grocer, 2 Bouverie st, Carl
Bracher and Parsons, coffee roasters and spice merchants, 66 Elizabeth st
Bracher, Wm., Dudley st, W M
Bracken, James, grocer, 220 Moray st, Em H
Bradbury, Thomas, 66 Stanley st, W M
Bradbury, Wm., Victoria st, W M
Brade, Mrs., milliner, High st, St K
Braddon, Wm., Station place, San
Braden, T., grocer, 59 Condell st, F
Bradford, Charles, Victoria st west, Hot
Bradford, Edwin, saddler, 41 Little Bourke st west
Bradford, Joseph, drysalter, 10 Franklin st west
Bradley, Allen, market gardener, Simpson's road, lid
Bradley, C. F., sec. National Building Society, 1 Bank place, Collins st west, and Kew
Bradley, Elgar, Carlisle st east, St K
Bradley, Edward, cabinetmaker, Royal lane, Bourke st east
Bradley, Henry, Flemington road

D

Bradley, M., 243 Victoria parade, E C
Bradley, Thomas, Arden st, Hot
Bradshaw, George, general dealer, 128 Russell st
Bradshaw, George M., and Co., hosiers and outfitters, 59 and 61 Collins st east
Bradshaw's Guide to Victoria, office, 78 Collins st east
Bradshaw, T., 36 Dorcas st west, Em II
Bradshaw, Mrs, Cardigan st, Carl
Bradshaw, S. J., Brighton st, Rd
Bradwell, W., Levison st, Hot
Brady, —, George st, F
Brady, J., and Co., sharebrokers, &c., 90 Collins st west
Brady, James, 68 Little Collins st east
Brady, John, 68 Little Collins st east
Brady, Joseph, civil engineer, Bay st, Bru
Brady, Michael, 105 Argyle st, F
Brady, Mrs., Wellington st, E C
Brady, Obadiah, grocer, 242 Napier st, F
Brady, Patrick, Hotham st east, F M
Brady, Thomas, cab proprietor, 79 Wellington st, E C
Brady, W. J., 61 Little Park st, Em II
Brady, Wm., 68 Little Collins st east
Bragge, J., grocer, 151 Lygon st, Carl
Bragge, J. D., surgeon, and registrar of births and deaths, Haw
Bragge, James, 178 Drummond st, Carl
Bragge, F., Heidelberg road
Braham, David, solicitor, 64 Little Collins st west
Braid, A., 89 Chetwynd st, Hot
Braim, John, 132 Moore st, F
Brain, J., farrier, High st, Pra
Brain, Joseph, Adderly st, W M
Brain, Mrs., Henry st, Windsor
Brain, T., letter carrier, Osborne st, Pra
Braman, J., Cole st, Wmn
Bramble, John, Tennyson st, St K
Bramston, C., oyster saloon, 135 Bourke st east
Bramwell, T., bootmaker, 128 Lonsdale st east
Brand, W., 141 Moor st, F
Brandenburger, Miss, teacher of music, 12 McKenzie st
Brandon, James, Waltham st, Rd
Brandon, G., George st, F
Brandt, W., 69 Charles st, F
Branford, A. G., Electra st, Wmn
Branscombe, Wm., 264 Elizabeth st
Branston, W. H., 146 Latrobe st west
Branthwaite, T., grocer, 16 Ann st, Wmn
Brasch, Platshek, and Co., warehousemen, 74 Little Collins st east
Brasch, Woolf, pawnbroker, 240 Swanston st
Braslan, James, Provost st, Hot
Brasnell, Mrs. Wm., private boardinghouse, 40 Coventry st, Em II
Brass, Thomas, dairyman, 228 Little Collins st east

Bray, C. E., 13 Napier st, Em II
Bray, J., draper, Howard st, Hot
Bray, Jacob Saul, 223 Napier st, F
Bray, James, Victoria st, Nicholson st, F
Bray, Thomas, china, &c., dealer, 160 Little Collins st east
Bray, W., Railway place, San
Bray, Wm., 23 Pelham st, Carl
Bray, Wm., 110 Coventry st, Em II
Brazendale, James, High st, Pra
Brazier, Mrs , Villiers st, Hot
Brealy, W., High st, St K
Brear, Henry T., grocer and provision merchant, 40 Elizabeth st exension
Brearly, James, Royal Exchange hotel, 34 Gertrude st, F
Brearly, Josh., saddler, 272 Elizabeth st
Bredius, C. P., Grey st, St K
Breed, H., High st, St K
Breen, J., Sackville st, Smith st, E C
Breen, M., Railway place, San
Breeze, Mrs., Easy st, Smith st, E C
Breeze, J., Union st, Bk
Brehaney, J., brewery, Little Nelson st, Wmn
Brehany, John, Cole street, Wmn
Brennan, James, Hoddle st, Rd
Bremner, David, Abbotsford st, Hot
Brenan, James, 13 Barkly st, Carl
Brenchley, James, grocer, Church st, Rd
Brendel, John, tailor, 78 Victoria st, Rd
Benjamife, J., 4 Carlton terrace, King William st, F
Brennan, H., Mistletoe hotel, M'Kenzie st
Brennan, Martin, Murchison st, Nicholson st, Carl
Brennan, Patrick, bootmaker, Ferguson st, Wmn
Brennan, T., clerk, Spencer st
Brennan, Thos., photographer, 203 King st
Brenner, —, Byron st, Hot
Brenner, Cornelius, Courtney st, Hot
Brett, J., 83 Kerr st, F
Brew, G., Shamrock hotel, Ann st, Wmn
Brewer, John, carpenter, Brown st, Heid
Brewer, John, 105 Little Bourke st west
Brewer, Wm., livery stable keeper, 117 Little Collins st west
Brewster, Geo. F., commission agent, &c., Graham st, San
Brewster, J., 11 Leveson st, Hot
Bricklayers' Society, meet at Trades hall, Lygon st, Carl
Brickley, M., Albion hotel, Bridge road, Rd
Bricknell, George, 212 Gore st, F
Bride, H. N., surveyor, Haw
Bridge, John, Spencer st
Bridge, John, station st, Fcy
Bridger, John, Commercial road, Pra
Bridges, F., Punt road, Rd
Bridges, J., Sydney road, Bk
Bridges, Mrs., school, Park st, Bru
Bridgeman, Thomas, dyer, High st, Pra

Brierly, John P., ironmonger, Elizabeth st extension
Briggs, Benjamin, Pres
Briggs, D. O., Princes st, F
Briggs, John, 112 Gertrude st, F
Briggs, Mrs., nurse, 209 Napier st, F
Briggs, Mrs. J., 140 Fitzroy st, F
Briggs, Walter, Punt road, Pra
Briggs, Wm., hairdresser, 169 Stephen st
Bright Brothers and Co., merchants, Flinders lane west and Bond st
Bright, C., 43 Three chain road, Em H
Bright, C. E. Torwak
Bright, H., 134 Flinders lane east
Bright, James, saddler, 162 Brunswick st, F
Bright, Mrs., 31 Cecil st, Em H
Brightwell, J., undertaker, 66 Smith st, E C
Brims, Alexander, 27 Bridport st, Em H
Briockman, Otto, jeweller and goldsmith, 85 Little Bourke st west
Brinkley, Mrs., 10 Hanover st, F
Britnanny, Mrs., Inkerman st, St K
Brimon, J. W., carpenter and builder, Rouse st, San
Brisbane and Co., iron and steel merchants, &c., 245 Elizabeth st, and 11 Collins st east
Brisson, H., 93a Nicholson st, F
Britannia Life Assurance Co. Agency, corner of Queen and Collins sts, west
British and Foreign Marine Insurance Co., 50 Collins st west
British Nation Life Assurance Association, 25 Market st
Brin, Henry, 43 Provost st, Hot
Britz, Pat., Provost st, Hot
Brittain, Eliza, hay and corn dealer, 63 Brunswick st, F
Britten, F. J., grocer, corner of Gardiner's creek road, and Caroline st, Pra
Britten and Son, grocers, ironmongers, and drapers, corner Swan and Church sts, Rd
Britton, A. C., Courtney st, Hot
Broaich, James, farrier, 4 Nicholas lane, Bourke st west
Broadbent, Anthony, 145 Albert st, E M
Broadbent Brothers, general carriers, 50 Elizabeth st
Broadbent, J., Miller st, Bk
Broadbent, John, Fawkner st, St K
Broadbent, Joseph, 8 Grey st, E M
Broadbent, Thos., 59 Greville st, Pra
Broadbent and Kitchingman, grocers and wine merchants, corner of Bourke and Swanston sts
Broadbridge, Samuel, boot and shoe dealer, 83 Victoria st, E C
Broadhead, George, Greeves st, F
Broadhurst, William, grocer, 93 Wellington st, E C
Broadley, Mrs. Ruth, 270 Smith st, E C

Broadley, T. B., Perry st, F C
Broadway, Thos., Inkerman st east, St K
Brock, Alexander, Pres
Brock, J. A., Wellington st, St K
Brock, James, actuary of Melbourne Savings' Bank, Haw
Brock, Mrs., Dalgety st, St K
Brock, Robert, engraver, 83 Cecil st, Em H
Brock, T., Edward st, Bk
Brockie, Joan, labour mart, 84 Collins st east
Brockman, Wm., Bridge road, Rd
Broderick, Edmund, Market hotel, 17 Market st, Em H
Brodie, David, collar maker, 8 Elizabeth st extension
Brodie, Edward, Henry st, Pra
Brodie, E. W., Henry st, Pra
Brodie, G. S., 3 Fitzroy terrace, Clarendon st, E M
Brodie, John C., 8 Hanmer st, Wmn
Brodie, Mrs., Douglas parade, Wmn
Brodie, Phillip, 35 Stephen st
Brodie, Robert, 107 Little Bourke st west
Brodribb, Crisp and Lewis, solicitors, &c., 51 Little Collins st west
Brodribb, K. E., 51 Little Collins st west
Brodribb, W. A., Park st, Bro
Brolin, A., 93 Young st, F
Brolin, Alex., cabinetmaker, 54 Gertrude st, F
Bromby, John, Drummond st, Carl
Bromley, Thos. P., 348 Wellington st, E C
Bronard, W., Bay st, Bro
Bronckhorst and Smale, solicitors, &c., 105 Collins st west
Bronckhorst, H. A., notary public, Rd
Bronken, Emil, locksmith, 29 Little Lonsdale st east
Brook, Benjamin, 88 Gore st, F
Brook, Henry Wm., baker, 210½ Bourke st east
Brook, J., Jeffcott st, W M
Brook, John, 229 King st
Brooke, J., cabinetmaker, 66 Moray st, Em H
Brooke, J. H., Heidelberg road
Brooke, W. H., bonded store proprietor, 61 William st
Brooke, W. H., Clyde st, St K
Brookes, H., 147 Argyle st, F
Brookes, John Peter, sign writer, 3 Little Collins st west, and Barkly st, Fcy
Brookman, A., confectioner, &c., 210½ Bourke st east
Brookman, D., Blackwood st, Hot
Brookman, J., Courtney st, Hot
Brooks and Halkenstein, tanners, Morland st, Fcy
Brooks and Higgins, builders and timber merchants, 41 Gore st, F
Brooks, Edward, 40 George st, F
Brooks, F., Ocean Child hotel, 52 Bridge road, Rd

Brooks, Henry, importer of plate-glass and builders' materials, 39 Elizabeth st, and Clarendon st, E M
Brooks, Henry H., baker and confectioner, 136 Little Bourke st east
Brooks, Jeannette, 33 Little Lonsdale st west
Brooks, John, watchmaker, 49 Errol st, Hot
Brooks, John, Kensington
Brooks, John, furniture dealer, 41 Swanston st
Brooks, Jonathan, coffee roaster, 90 Little Oxford st, E C
Brooks, Leicester, Barton cottage, Kensington
Brooks, W., 25 Church st, Em H
Brooks, Wm., Prince Alfred hotel, Church st, Rd
Brophy, Mrs., Pres
Brosnan, C., 83 Bouverie st, Carl
Brotchie, David, boot and shoe warehouse, Cecil st, Wmn
Brotchie, Richard, general dealer, 128 Brunswick st, F
Brotherton, Benj., grocer, 30 Argyle st, F
Brotherton, Henry, 70 Bank st west, Em H
Brougham, P., Crescent, Bin
Broughton, E. S., Bridge road, Rd
Broughton, J. H., boot closer, 76 Bridge road, Rd
Broughton, Mrs., 38 Napier st, F
Brown, —, mercer, &c., 41 and 43 Bourke st east
Brown, —, dentist, Hoddle st, E C
Brown, A., Smith st, E C
Brown, A., tailor, 45 Franklin st, W M
Brown, A., bootmaker, Courtenay st, Hot
Brown, Adam, blacksmith, Pres
Brown, Alfred, tailor, 50 Bouverie st, Carl
Brown, Andrew, Rising Sun hotel, Post Office place
Brown, Archibald, grocer, Peel st, E C
Brown, Captain, 26 James st, Wmn
Brown, Catherine, Exchange hotel, corner of Swanston and Little Collins st east
Brown, Charles, boarding-house keeper, 167 Bourke st west
Brown, Charles, builder, Ramsden st, E C
Brown, Charles, Milton st, W M
Brown, Charles F. E., stock and commission agent, 33 Bourke st west
Brown, Colin, ship broker, &c., 100 Collins st west
Brown, D., 295 Victoria parade, E C
Brown, Duncan, undertaker, &c., 39 York st, Em H
Brown, E., 26 Gore st, F
Brown, E. E., Carpenter st, Bin
Brown, Francis, Ballaarat road, Fey
Brown, G., livery stables, corner of Gardiner's Creek road and Ralston st, S Y
Brown, G., 51 Rathdowne st, Carl
Brown, G. A., Pres

Brown, G. C., draper, William st, Bin
Brown, G. W., 252 Little Collins st east
Brown, Gavin G., and Co., stock and share brokers, Hall of Commerce, 48 Collins st west
Brown, George, accountant, 10 Bourke st west
Brown, George, 128 Johnston st, E C
Brown, George, 51 Rathdowne st, Carl
Brown, George, Railway place, San
Brown, George, Mercer st, Geelong
Brown, George S., Upper Haw
Brown, Gilbert, Punt road, S Y
Brown, Gilbert W., Haw
Brown, H., Douglas parade, Wmn
Brown, H., Weston st, Bk
Brown, H. W., 25 Gore st, F
Brown, Hannah, Victoria st, Hot
Brown, Henry, builder, Ramsden st, E C
Brown, Henry, Peel st, Hot
Brown, J., draper, New st, Bin
Brown, J., gasfitter, 150 Little Lonsdale st west
Brown, J., bootmaker, 64 Arden st, Hot
Brown, J., Weston st, Bk
Brown, J., Nott st, San
Brown, J., 23 Webb st, F
Brown, J., South road, Bin
Brown, J., Williams road, Pra
Brown, J., Rowena parade, Rd
Brown, J. D., 225 Clarendon st, Em H
Brown, J. E., 101 Raglan st east, Em H
Brown, J. G., Greeves st, F
Brown, J. S., 139 Johnston st, E C
Brown, J. W., and Co., masons, Madeline st, Carl
Brown, James, Wellington st, Rd
Brown, James, Elgin st, Carl
Brown, James, dealer, 20 Alfred place, Collins st east
Brown, James, 172½ Lonsdale st west
Brown, John, 127 Leicester st, F
Brown, John, cattle dealer, Firm Bank
Brown, John, Railway place, San
Brown, John, 61 York st west, Em H
Brown, John, 49 Rathdowne st, Carl
Brown, John, 18 Hotham st, E M
Brown, John, 7 Pelham st, Carl
Brown, John, Geelong road, Fey
Brown, John, Dorcas st east, Em H
Brown, John P., Three chain road, Em H
Brown, John H., accountant, &c., Hall of Commerce, 48 Collins st west
Brown, Mrs., greengrocer, Smith st, E C
Brown, Mrs., Graham st, San
Brown, Mrs., labour office, 8 Bourke st west
Brown, Mrs., Punt road, S Y
Brown, Mrs., milliner, Chapel st, Pra
Brown, Mrs., Esplanade, St K
Brown, Mrs., Ralston st, Pra
Brown, Mrs., Neptune st, St K
Brown, Mrs., Gardiner's creek road, Pra
Brown, Peter, Marion st, F

Brown, Osborne, and Co., forwarding agents, 7 Western Market, Collins st west
Brown and Patterson, sailmakers, King st
Brown and Slight, engravers, &c., 56 Raglan st, Em H
Brown, R., Flem
Brown, Rev. P., Haw
Brown, Rev. E., Nth
Brown, Rev. J., Brown st, Heid
Brown, Robert, Victoria st west, Hot
Brown, Robert, 70 Stanley st, W M
Brown, S., 55 Raglan st, Em H
Brown, Samuel, miller, Flem Bank
Brown, Sarah, greengrocer, 186½ Smith st, E C
Brown, T., plumber, Bay st, Bto
Brown, T. S., and Co., bakers, High st, St K
Brown, W., jun., fellmonger, beef curer, &c., 110 Flinders lane west, Yarra bank
Brown, W. W., Peel st, W M
Brown, Walter, bag manufacturer and machine sewer, 63 Little Collins st west
Brown, William, Wellington st, St K
Brown, William, Saracen's Head hotel, 12 Bourke st west
Brown, William, dairyman, 184 Little Collins st east
Brown, William White, Robe st, St K
Brown, Wm., Stewart st, Bk
Brown, Wm., Wreckyn st, Hot
Brown, Wm., boatbuilder, Pant road, Rd
Brown, Wm., 71 Smith st, F
Brown, Wm., greengrocer, Brunswick st, F
Brown, Wm., importer of hardware, 17 Little Collins st east, and Stewart st, Bk
Brown, Wm., engineer, Wellington st, E C
Browne and Reid, tea and coffee merchants, 46 Elizabeth st
Browne, E. E., Carpenter st, Btn
Browne, H., 8 Kerr st, F
Browne, John, corn dealer, 167 Little Lonsdale st east
Brownbill, James, baker, 176 Smith st, E C
Brownbill, Joseph, Sackville st, Smith st, E C
Browning, J. C., 38 Dorcas st, Em H
Browning, John, jeweller and pawnbroker, 167 and 169 Elizabeth st
Brownless, Anthony C., physician, 117 Collins st east
Brownless, C., Stoke st, San
Browless, Mrs., school, Railway place, San
Browse, —, butcher, 112 Smith st, E C
Broyer, C., medical botanist, 120 Madeline st, Carl
Bruce, Andrew, and Co., booksellers, 93 Bourke st east
Bruce and M'Donough, tailors, 98 King st
Bruce Bros., booksellers, 68 Elizabeth st
Bruce, Henry A., 1 George st, E M

Bruce, James, fruiterer, Howard st, Hot
Bruce, John, Hoddle st, E C
Bruce, John, Jolimont terrace, E M
Bruce, Joseph, grocer, High st, Pra
Bruce, Mansfield, Studley park
Bruce, Mrs. O. V. A., Ess
Bruce, Mrs. Sarah, Ess
Bruce, Mrs., 154 Moor street, F
Bruce, Robert, butcher, Chapel st, Pra
Bruce, Samuel, 208 Cardigan st, Carl
Bruford, Mrs., Queensberry st, Hot
Brumner, James, Cole st, Wm
Brunckhman, R., shoemaker, Main st, Heid
Brunet, Gustave, tabacconist, coal, and wood merchant, 95 and 86 Swanston st
Brunston and Gillespie, produce merchants, 57 Flinders st west
Brunston, John, Yarra st, Pra
Brunt, J., dealer, Bedford st, Hot
Brunton, —, 49 Victoria st, Carl
Brunton, David, 6 Marchison st, Nicholson st, Carl
Brunton, H. H., Station place, San
Brunton, Henry, City Coffee-house, 16 Bourke st east
Brunton, Thomas, baker, 380 Spencer st
Brunton, Thomas, produce merchant, 139 Lonsdale st
Brunton, W. J., Bridport st, Em H
Brush and MacDonnell, jewellers, &c., 89 Collins st west
Brush, Samuel, Acland st, St K
Brusher, T., oyster dealer, 121 Swanston st, and 36 Little Collins st east
Bruenan, Timothy, builder, 132 Latrobe st west
Bryan, Ann, Essex hotel, Cardigan st, Carl
Bryan, P., Elgin st, Carl
Bryant, Charles, Alma st, F
Bryant, Frederick, Hoddle st, E C
Bryant, J., Rathdowne st, Carl
Bryant, J. M., Cricketers' hotel, Swanston st
Bryant, Jabez, and Co., hosiers, &c., 161 Swanston st
Bryant, John M., 10 Royal terrace, Nicholson st, F
Bryant, W., 14 Rosslyn st, W M
Bryden, T., hat manufacturer, 76 Fitzroy st, F
Brydie and Ferguson, grocers, 51 Leveson st, Hot
Bryer, James, 43 Victoria parade, F
Brymer, Robert, bootmaker, Leveson st, Hot
Buchan, John, land agent and money broker, 75 Little Collins st east
Buchan, Thomas, 93 Dudley st, W M
Buchanan, Charles, engraver and lithographer, 62 Collins st east
Buchanan, Cunningham, 105 Coventry st, Em H

22   Buc   MELBOURNE   Bur

Buchanan, J., Sydney road, Bk
Buchanan, John, tinsmith, Bay st, San
Buchanan, Mrs., saddler, &c., 230 Elizabeth st
Buchanan, Mrs., 122 Napier st, F
Buchanan, Wm., Railway tavern, Greville st, Pra
Bocirde, V. H., Hanmer st, Wmn
Buck, Adolph T., egg and butter dealer, 46 Stephen st
Buckham, G., tinsmith, Wellington st, E C
Buckham, James, tinsmith, 219 Smith st, E C
Buckham, John, tent and pavilion maker, 287 Elizabeth st
Buckett, Stephen, 55 Moray st, Em H
Buckhurst, Wm. P., auctioneer, 116 Clarendon st, Em H
Buckingham, H., Cardigan st, Carl
Buckland, S. V., Geelong
Buckland, Thomas, 188 Lygon st, Carl
Buckley, —, Johnston st, E C
Buckley and Nunn, drapers, 27 Bourke st east
Buckley, C., Gardiner's creek road, Tk
Buckley, J. A., 67 Gore st, F
Buckley, J. W., Illawara st, Wmn
Buckley, John, Orrong road, Tk
Buckley, John, Arthur seat, Commercial road, Pra
Buckley, Mars, Hayington, Tk
Buckley, Robert, Avoca st, S Y
Buckley, Wm., 74 George st, F
Bodd, R. H., inspector-general of schools, offices, Spring st, and Cochrane st, Bru
Buddee, J., Bay st, Bts
Buddee, Julius, professor of music, 55 Stephen st
Budemeyer, F., candlemaker, Flem Bank
Budge, David, Wellington st, St K
Budge, Henry, and Co., estate and commission agents, 38 Collins st east, and Nicholson st, F
Budge, John, Simpson st, E M
Budge, John, 78 Victoria st, W M
Bugden, Wm., turncock, Victoria parade, E M
Bugg, Robert, 21 Marion st, F
Buich, Christie, and Lyell, warehousemen, 21 Flinders lane west
Buick, J., Sandhurst
Building Museum, Queen st north
Bull, —, 64 St David st, F
Bull, F. W., C.E. and surveyor, Park st, Bts
Bull, George, 160 Young st, F
Bull, J., Cecil st, Wmn
Bull, Thomas, furniture dealer, 104 Smith st, E C
Bull, W., 120 Douglas parade, Wmn
Bull, Wm., gardener, Pres
Bullen, Frederick, Haw
Bullen, F. and G., outfitters, 131 and 133 Russell st

Bullen, Henry, watchmaker, 14 Lonsdale st west, and Bendigo st, Pra
Buller, Mrs., 15 Pelham st, Carl
Bulley, C., Gipps st, E M
Bulley and John, leather merchants, 21 Post Office place
Bulley, Wm., baker, Chapel st, Pra
Bulling, Joseph, plasterer, Albert st, Pra
Bulling, Wm., 16 Perry st, E C
Bullock, Cornelius, Harrison's road, Fcy
Bullock, John, Hanmer st, Wmn
Bullock, W. C., 84, David st, F
Bullman, J., St. David st, F
Bollon, J., 111 Leicester st, F
Bulman, Mrs., 150 Kerr st, F
Bultitude, Ann, Black Prince hotel, Baillie st, Hot
Buncle, John, watchmaker and jeweller, McKillop st, Bourke st west
Buncle, John, engineer and millwright, Wreckyn st, Hot
Bonnett, Thomas, 32 Cobden st, Em H
Bungaalice Extended Tin Mining Company, 31 Queen st
Bunny, B. F., barrister, 21 Temple Court, Collins st west
Bunny, Henry J., 162 Cardigan st, Carl
Bunting, Geo., store, Cole st south, Wmn
Borchall, Arthur, accountant, 147 Bourke st east and Haw
Burchett, J., Barkly st, Bk
Burden, Stephen, 33 Moor st, F
Burfield, James, 144 Fitzroy st, F
Burge, Henry, Acland st, St K
Borge, Mrs., dressmaker, 21 Lonsdale st east
Burgess, A., Swan st, Rd
Burgess, C., cab proprietor, 315 Smith st, F
Burgess, D., picture framer, 74 Gore st, F
Burgess, George, painter, &c., Howard st, Hot
Burgess, H., Lygon st, Carl
Burgess, Mrs., dressmaker, 126 Young st, F
Burgess, O., Nth
Burgess, Sewell, Victoria st, Hot
Burgess, Thomas, Pont road, Wr
Burgess, Wm., Lygon st, Carl
Burgess, Wm., grocer, 103 Elgin st, Carl
Burgon, P., 18 Fitzroy st, F
Burgoyne, G. F., Haddle st, Rd
Burgoyne, Mrs., 155 Moor st, F
Burke, A., Victoria st west, Hot
Burke, E., Hanover st, P
Burke, E., furniture broker, corner Lonsdale and Russell sts
Burke, E., 37 Moor st, F
Burke, Edmund, 28 Douglas parade, Wmn
Burke and Ollard, solicitors, 99½ Collins st west
Burke, J., 54 Ann st, Wmn
Burke, J. L. and C., coal and produce merchants, 103 Flinders st west

Burke, Richard, 122 Napier st, F
Burke, P. H., chemist, Bridge road, Rd
Burke, Mrs., Fitzroy st, St K
Burke, Thomas, 114 Coventry st, Em H
Burke, Thomas, Wellington st, Rd
Burke, Thomas, Colgin's hotel, 3 a'Beckett st, Carl
Burklit, Mrs., Octavia st, St K
Burman, Henry, store, Howard st, Hot
Burman, W., painter, 41 Madeline st, Carl
Burmeister, Leopold, chronometer and watchmaker, 27 Little Bourke st east
Burn, E. W., grocer and baker, Easy st, Smith st, E C
Burn, J., Berkeley st, Carl
Burn, Wm., builder, Wellington st, Rd
Burnatine, Wm., Raglan st west, Em H
Burns, John, Pelham st, Carl
Burnes, Adam, Brighton road, St K
Burnes, James, dairyman, Millswyn st, S Y
Burney, T., Bendigo st, Hot
Burnley, James, 149 Church st, Rd
Burns, Andrew, 9 Johnston st, E C
Burns, Forest, grocer, Chapel st, Pra
Burns, George H., grocer, 1 Little Bourke st west
Burns, George, carpenter, New st, Btn
Burns, J., Pelham st, Carl
Burns, J., Palmerston st, Carl
Burns, James, Union st, Wr
Burns, James, grocer, 55 Stanley st, W M
Burns, John, tanner, Flem Bank
Burns, Mrs., 55 Rose st, F
Burns, Mrs., Marion st, F
Burns, Mrs., Lothian st, Hot
Burns, Nelson, Station place, San
Burns, P., 132 Leicester st, F
Burns, Richard, Higbett st, Rd
Burns, Wm., Lennox st, Rd
Burns, W., butcher, Douglas parade, Wmn
Burns, Wm., 202 Johnston st, E C
Burnside, Henry, 163 Wellington st, E C
Burrage, Thomas Allan, importer of fancy goods, 63 Swanston st, 3½ Collins st west
Burrell, George, secretary Pilot Board, Thomson st, and Dover road, Wmn
Burrell, James, grocer, 77 Spencer st
Burrell, James G., 175 Fitzroy st, F
Burridge, Jos., Cole st, Wmn
Burrington, Mrs., Hobe st, St K
Burrowes, W., Gifford st, Wmn
Burrows, George, Twyford st, Wmn
Burrows, H. B., Richmond terrace, Rd
Burrows, Henry, Drummond st, Carl
Burrows, James, Dryburgh st, Hot
Burston, Lake, bookmaker, 93 Swanston st, and 6 Carson's cottages, Collins st east
Bart, G., 27 Coventry st, Em H
Bart, J., Stephen st
Bart, J. Ward E., produce merchant, 60 Stephen st,

Burt, J. W., Elgin st, Carl
Burt, Mrs., 67 York st west, Em H
Burtenshaw, F. G., carpenter, 401 Lygon st, Carl
Burton, Captain O. S., Bridge road, Rd
Burton, F. A., 30 Smith st, E C
Burton, George, Albert st west, Bk
Burton, John, farmer, Pres
Burton, Joseph H., coach builder, 61 Latrobe st east
Burton, Thomas, boot and shoe dealer, 182 and 176 Bridge road, Rd
Burton, Thomas, Arden st, Hot
Burton, Wm., Belvidere hotel, Victoria parade, F
Burton, Wm., contractor, Station st, Fcy
Burton, Wm. T., Western Port hotel, Queen st
Burtt, John G., M.L.A., Cecil st, Em H
Burtt, John Wesley, hay and corn store, 66 Stephen st
Burward, J., 111 George st, F
Bury, Fredk. John, curator of the estates of deceased persons, 59 Temple court, Collins st west
Bury, J. C., Chambers st, Pra
Bury, Mrs., dressmaker, Chapel st, Pra
Busbridge, S., butcher, Commercial road, Pra
Buse, S., Dover road, Wmn
Bushell, N. E., Royal Oak hotel, 73 Swanston st
Bushman, C. L., 4 Alma terrace, Moray st, Em H
Butchart, —, New st, Btn
Butchart, George, Caulfield
Butcher, James, Grey st, east, E M
Butcher, M., Station place, San
Butcher, T., 62 Cambridge st, E C
Buteux, David, fruiterer, 34 Swanston st
Butler and Moss, hay salesmen and farmers' agents, Eastern Market
Butler, Edward, pawnbroker, 79 Drummond st, Carl
Butler, G. S., M.D., Buckland st, Heid
Butler, George, Alma st, F
Butler, J., blacksmith, Perry st, E C
Butler, James, Capel st, W M
Butler, John, 20 Regent st, F
Butler, Joseph, secretary Equitable Loan and Investment Co., 105 Elizabeth st
Butler, M., grocer, Baille st, Hot
Butler, Michael, builder, 149 Little Lonsdale st west
Butler, Mrs., Peel st, Hot
Butler, Mrs., Spring st, F
Butler, R., Lincoln cottages, Bouverie st, Carl
Butler, T., Mill st, Btn
Butler, Wm., grocer, 82 Bridge road, Rd
Butler's Reef Gold Mining Company, 54 Queen st
Butlin, George, 28 Cardigan st Carl

Butt, Charles, Lennox st, Rd
Butt, David, 15 Rose st, F
Butt, George, Howard st, Hot
Butterfield, Joseph, 151 Lygon st, Carl
Butterfield, Thomas, Hope st, Bk
Butters, James S., Boundary road, Tk
Butterworth, J. H., Clarke st, E C
Butterworth, Samuel, 9 Owen st, Nicholson st, Carl
Buttner and Hallenstein, merchants, 1 Flinders st west
Buttolph, W. G., baker, 48 Bridge road, Rd
Button, Edward, 140 George st, F
Butts, Cornelius, Castlemaine st, Fry
Buvelot, Louis, photographer, 92 Bourke st east
Buzzard, Thomas Meredith, bookseller, stationer, and librarian, 181 Bourke st east, and 4 Collins st east
Byrne, A., Hawthorne hotel, Haw
Byrne, Andrew, 80 Stanley st, W M
Byrne, D., mason, 48 Latrobe st east
Byrne, H., 191 Victoria parade, E C
Byrne, J. P., cabinetmaker, 56 Cambridge st, E C
Byrne, James, Stanley st, W M
Byrne, James, 49 Latrobe st west
Byrne, James, Argus hotel, Collins st east
Byrne, M., dairy, 23 King st
Byrne, M. G., barrister, 30 Temple court, Collins st west
Byrne, Michael, Railway family hotel, 102 King st
Byrne, Robert, auctioneer, &c., corner of Nott and Spring sts, San., and 40 Collins st east
Byrne, Thomas, kerosene oil merchant, 54 Swanston st
Byrne, Thomas, Blackwood st, Hot
Byrnes, Rev. William, St. Mary's parsonage, Howard st, Hot

C.

Caddford, James, 102 George st, E M
Caddy, J., 76 Johnston st, F
Caile, Frederick, Avoca st, S Y
Caile, James, miller, Bridge road, Rd
Cadman, William, Domain road, S Y
Caffin, James, 208 Madeline st, Carl
Caffin, W., draper, Sydney road, Bk
Cahill, H., 223 Swan st, Rd
Cahill, James, Harp of Erin hotel, 22 Cecil st, Wmn
Cahill, Joseph, William st, Pra
Cairncross, Mrs., 15 Cecil st, Wmn
Cairns, J., Punt road, S Y
Cairns, John, Walsh street, S Y
Cairns, Rev. Adam, D.D., Gipps st west, Dudley st, W M
Caldecott, C. J., Charles st, F
Calder, Allen, Wilson st, Pra
Calder, John, artist and photographer, Dryburgh st, Hot

Calder, Henry, Domain st, S Y
Caldhoun, J., 14 Faraday st, Carl
Caldwell, Rev. James, 61 Gore st, F
Cale, Richard O., sawmaker, 209 Smith st, F
Caledonian and Mountaineer Mining Coa., Eldon Chambers, Collins st west
Calfen, William, Peel st, Pra
Calhoun, A., grocer, Stoke st, San
Call, F., Strand, Wmn
Callaghan, J., carpenter, 3 Nicholas lane
Callaghan, J., bootmaker, 94 Queensberry st, Carl
Callaghan, J. and R., clothiers and boot importers, 159 Swanston st
Callaghan, James, Wellington parade, E M
Callaghan, M., 22 Rosslyn st, W M
Callaghan, Mrs., greengrocer, Drummond st, Carl
Callaghan, R., 28 Gore st, F
Callaghan, Thomas, 140 Moray st, Em H
Callaghan, William, Fitzroy st, F
Callahan, J., Hoddle st, Rd
Callard, P., blacksmith, 79 Coventry st. and 92 Moray st, Em H
Callender, A., 35 Cardigan st, Carl
Callender and Co., merchants and wholesale stationers, 41 and 43 King st
Callender, J., Alma st east, St K
Callenen, —, 142 Moor st, F
Callow, M. J., Star and Garter hotel, Robe st, St K
Callum, D. M., Carlisle st, St K
Calvert, E. M., dressmaker, 208½ Little Collins st east
Calvert, Michael, 21 Wellington st, E C
Calvert, Samuel, engraver, 7 George st, F
Calvert, Thomas, fruiterer and poulterer, 2 and 3 Eastern Market
Cambie, David, 125 Argyle st, F
Cambourne, F., Clifton hotel, Derby st, E C
Cameron, Alexander, Pent
Cameron, D., baker, 85 Victoria st, Carl
Cameron, D., Park st, S Y
Cameron, J. F., saddler, 3 Bourke st west
Cameron, John, draper, Gardiner's creek road, S Y
Cameron, John, Caroline st, S Y
Cameron, John, 12 Grattan st, Carl
Cameron, John, 403 Lygon st, Carl
Cameron, John, draper, Gardiner's Creek road, Prn
Cameron, John, 104 Park st, Em H
Cameron, John, Balmoral Castle hotel, Commercial road, Pra
Cameron, Miss, 128 Lygon st, Carl
Cameron, Mrs., 73 Dorcas st west, Em H
Cameron, Mrs., Newport Arms hotel, 15 Latrobe st west
Cameron, Mrs., Foresters' Arms, Drummond st, Carl
Cameron, V. L., 53 Little Collins st east, and 11 Brougham st road

Cameron, Wm., Railway place, San
Cameron, Wm., Stoke st, San
Cameron, Wm., merchant, 61 William st
Campbell, A. P., stock and share broker, 99½ Collins st west
Campbell, Alexander, Queensberry st, Carl
Campbell, Alex., harbour master, 119 Spencer st
Campbell, Alfred, French polisher, 140 Little Collins st, and Gipps st, Rd
Campbell, C., Cliff st, S Y
Campbell, Catherine, bookseller, 81 Gertrude st, F
Campbell, Charles, Cliff st, Pra
Campbell, D., Grey st, St K
Campbell, D., and Co., stock salesmen and commission agents, 47 Bourke st west
Campbell, D. S., Vauclue, Rd
Campbell and Graham, hairdressers, 95 Swanston st
Campbell and Judd, wine and spirit merchants, Bank place, 77 Collins st west
Campbell, George W., Punt road, Pra
Campbell, Hon. Wm., M.L.C., Melbourne Club
Campbell, Isabella, store, 89 Leveson st, Hot
Campbell, J., 49 Market st, Em H
Campbell, J., 100 Nicholson st, F
Campbell, J., Capel st, Hot
Campbell, J. W., watchmaker, 41 Cardigan st, Carl
Campbell, James, 61 Cremorne st, Rd
Campbell, James, Davis st, S Y
Campbell, James, 2 Hagian st, Em H
Campbell, John, 7 Railway place, Wmn
Campbell, John, 5 Swan st, Rd
Campbell, John, Palmerston st, Carl
Campbell, John, 73 Hanmer st, Wmn
Campbell, John, 20 Hanmer st, Wmn
Campbell, Mrs., 121 Lonsdale st east
Campbell, Mrs., 15 Cecil st, Wmn
Campbell, Mrs., 9 Victoria parade, F
Campbell, Norman, Osborne st, Pra
Campbell, O. R., 213 Albert st, E M
Campbell, Patrick, baker, Fitzroy st, St K
Campbell, R. S., Porter st, Pra
Campbell, Robert, teacher, Inkerman st east, St K
Campbell, Robert, 105 Clarendon st, E M
Campbell, Ronald, M.L.A., Parliament house
Campbell, T., hairdresser, 5 King st
Campbell, W., Punt road, Rd
Campbell, W. H., mining agent, 52 Collins st east
Campbell, Wm., Wellington parade, E M
Campbell, Wm., Gardiner's creek road, S Y
Campbell, Wm. H., M.D., surgeon, 196 Collins st east
Campl, John and A., looking-glass manufacturers, 122 Russell st
Campion, Henry, 581 Church st, Rd

Campion, Wm., 122 Madeline st, Carl
Candler, Curtis, coroner and mining company's manager, 38 Temple court, Collins st west
Candid, —, whip maker, 39 Victoria st, Carl
Candy, G., 380 Smith st, E C
Candy, Wm., herbalist, 68 George st, F
Cane, Matthias, Stoke st, San
Cane, S., Grosvenor st, E C
Cane, Samuel, Drummond st, Carl
Cann, George, Prince Alfred hotel, Pres
Cann, Wm., Chapel st, Pra
Cannam, Charles C., marble mason, Punt road, Pra
Canney, Thos., Leveson st, Hot
Cannon, M., 46 King William st, F
Cannon, Wm., Great Britain hotel, Stoke st, San
Conobbio, D., carpenter, 230 Lonsdale st east
Canter, W. J., grocer, 25 Peel st, Hot
Canterbury, John, coal and wood merchant, 70 Flinders lane east
Canterbury, Mrs., 124 Flinders lane
Canterford, Wm., bootmaker, 14 Bank st, Em H
Cantlon, —, Esplanade, St K
Cantlow, R., hairdresser, 79 Smith st, F
Canton, F. E., dentist, &c., 126 Bridge road, Rd
Canton Marine Insurance Company, 11 Little Collins st west
Cantor, Jacob A., 78 Leicester st, Carl
Cantwell, D., Barkly st, Carl
Cantwell, M., Royal hotel, Nelson place, Wmn
Cape, Matthew W., Ralston st, Pra
Capon, George, butcher, Russe st, San
Caporu, Thomas, Railway place, San
Capp, P., 193 Victoria parade, E C
Capron, Thomas, Kew
Carbis, C., blacksmith, Buckley st, Foy
Card, Wm., coach painter, 8 Bridge road, Rd
Cardiff, John, 55 Rathdown st, Carl
Cardwell, E., 17 Palmer st, Foy
Cardwell, Wm. H., Haw
Care, T., grocer, Harmsworth st, E C
Carew, Thomas, saddler, 299 Elizabeth st
Carey, G. J., Brigadier-General, C.B., Commander of H. M. Forces—office, Military Barracks
Carey, Mrs., 85 Chetwynd st, Hot
Carey, P., gardener, Hawden st, Hoid
Carey, W., gardener, Mill st, Bm
Carey, Wm., High st, Pra
Carey, Wm., butcher, Flem Bank
Carfrae, James, 2 Faraday st, Carl
Carfrae, John, 27 Victoria parade, F
Carlile, J. S., ironmonger, 40 and 42 Gertrude st, F
Carlisle, W. J., veterinary surgeon, 18 Little Latrobe st

Carlisle, J., 82 Dryburgh st, Hot
Carlos. W. H., accoutrement maker, 162 Bourke st west
Carlow, S. J., 4 George st, E M
Carlstein, A., Golden Fleece hotel, corner Russell and Little Bourke sts
Carlton and Hagin, agents, Wharf, and 23 Spencer st
Carlton Schools, Faraday st, Carl
Carlton, Wm., tailor, Hoddle st, E C
Carmichael, J., grocer, Easy st, E C
Carmichael, M., 40 Franklin st, W M
Carnahy, George, tailor, 58 Elizabeth st
Carnaby, J. H., Bouverie st, Carl
Carnaby, Wm., bootmaker, 80 Queen st
Carns, P., carpenter, 83 Raglan st, Em H
Carne, W. J., 169 Smith st, F
Carnell, Mrs. M., 62 Hanover st, F
Carnie, Alexander, farmer, Ess
Caro, Jacob, ironmonger, 96 Elizabeth st
Caroline, Jos., coach painter, 32 Latrobe st east
Carp, W. H., colonial wine and luncheon rooms, 36 Collins st west
Carpenter, Charles, general store, 15 Beach st, San
Carpenter, Charles, hairdresser, Beach st, San
Carpenter, Edwin, Cardigan st, Carl
Carpenter, Thomas, M.L.A., Parliament House
Carpenters and Joiners' Society; meet at Trades Hall, Lygon st, Carl
Carr, George, 85 Napier st, F
Carr, Harriet, Wellington st, E C
Carr, Hugh Bernard, and Son, upholsterers and blind makers, 128 Spring st
Carr, J. R., storekeeper, Btn
Carr, J., Rose st, Rd
Carr, John, hairdresser, 175 King st
Carr, Robert, Douglas parade, Wmn
Carr, W., Ball st, St K
Carr, Wm., greengrocer, 248 King st
Carrick, R. W., 37 Dorcas st west, Em H
Carrick, W. C., Sir Henry Barkly hotel, Silver bank, Rd
Carrighan, A., Dow st, San
Carrington, —, Church st, Btn
Carol, John, greengrocer, Flem Bank
Carrol, H., saddler, Nth
Carroll, Charlotte, ladies' school, Canning st, Carl
Carroll, Dennis, Howard st, Hot
Carroll, J., grocer, 134 Johnston st, E C
Carroll, J., dining rooms, 35 Lonsdale st west
Carroll, J., livery stable keeper, Leveson st, Hot
Carroll, James, Odd Fellows' hotel, Little Lonsdale st east
Carroll, John, Queensberry st, Carl
Carroll, Mrs, Bedford st, Hot
Carroll, Peter, 44 Stanley st, W M
Carroll, Peter, 115 Oxford st, E C

Carroll, Peter, Boab inn, Elizabeth st
Carroll, Robert J., saddler, 32 Elizabeth st, north extension
Carroll, Thomas, 128 Church st, Rd
Carruthers and James, drapers and outfitters, 80 Elizabeth st
Carruthers, John, Haw
Carruthers, Wm., 80 Elizabeth st
Carson, James, carpenter, Railway place, San
Carson, John, importer of boots and shoes, 39 Collins st east
Carstairs, A., 11 Russell st
Carter, Albinus J., 29 Courtney st, Hot
Carter, Charles, painter and paperhanger, 75 Queen st
Carter, Ernest, dentist, 30 Russell st
Carter, Gro., tailor, 167 Spring st
Carter, George and Samuel, butchers, 20 Gertrude st, F
Carter, Godfrey D., wine, spirit, and provision merchant, 49 Flinders lane west, and Malvern
Carter, Henry, New st, Btn
Carter, John, hairdresser, 133 Little Collins st east
Carter, John, Grey st, St K
Carter, John, 268 Johnston st, E C
Carter, John, Raglan st, San
Carter, Joseph, builder, 91 Palmer st, F
Carter, Mrs., 108 Johnston st, F
Carter, Mrs., 60 Gore st, F
Carter, Rev. W., Pent
Carter, Richd., 177 Little Lonsdale st east
Carter, Richd., 87 Levison st, Hot
Carter, Samuel, Rouse st, San
Carter, S. J., bricklayer, 104 Napier st, Em H
Carter, W., greengrocer, 61 Peel st, E C
Carter, Wm., designer, printer, &c., 88 Ferrars st, Em H
Carter, Wm., Chapel st, St K
Carter, Wm., High st, Pra
Carter, Wm., Gardiner's creek road, Tk
Cartledge, H., grocer, 23 Johnston st, F
Cartledge, J., 145 Rose st, F
Cartwright, F., 71 Coventry st, Em H
Cartwright, F. C., Cecil st, Em H
Cary, Robt. D., 92 Argyle st, F
Casey, J. J., M.L.A., Gertrude st, F
Casey, John, Curzon st, Hot
Casey, John, grocer, Hoddle st, E C
Casey, Mrs., fruiterer, 109 High st, St K
Cash, W. D., 113 Argyle st, F
Cashion, Jas., Little Collins st west
Cashmore, Michael, butcher, 147 Russell st
Casselden, John, news agent, 179 Little Lonsdale st
Cassell, James, 56 Young st, F
Cassell, John, Hoddle st, Rd
Cassell, Mrs., Williams road, Pra
Cassidy, James, 209 George st, F
Casson, John, Lincolnshire arms hotel, Em

Cannon, John, fancy goods dealer, 231 Elizabeth st
Castle, E., 5 Woodland terrace, George st, F
Castle, J., 17 Market st, Em H
Castle, John, sawmaker, 13 Latrobe st west
Castlemaine Paving Company, 62 Little Collins st west
Castleman, Fredk., 25 Rathdowne st, Carl
Catchpole, W., draper, 84 Brunswick st, F
Cater, James, Park st, S Y
Cater, Mrs., 87 Gore st, F
Catherod, F., Canning st, Carl
Catholic Apostolic Church, M'Kenzie st., top of Russell st
Catholic Education Committee office (St Francis) Lonsdale st east,
Cattach, James, British Crown hotel, Smith st, E C
Cattenach, A., saddler, Chapel st, Pra
Catterall, E., 27 Smith st, F
Cattanan, C., bootmaker, Edward st, Bk
Cattlin, Edward, carrier, Bay st, San
Cattnach, Thos., builder, 44 Queensberry st, Hot
Caudle, George, draper and outfitter, 130 Smith st, E C
Caughey, Alex., Upper Haw
Caughey, Robert, Haw
Caulfield, Mrs., Provost st, Hot
Caulton, John, Hoddle st, Rd
Cavan, Wm., Capel st, Hot
Cavanagh, J., 14 Little Lonsdale st east
Cavanagh, Joseph, 120 Argyle st, F
Cavanagh, T., Albert st west, Bk
Cavanagh, W., Union st, Bk
Cavalier, S., 139 Bouverie st, Carl
Cavell, George T., Park st, E C
Cavenagh, George, Lennox st, Rd
Cay, Edward, High st, Pra
Cayzer, F., bootmaker, 42 Johnston st, F
Cayzer, Francis D., bootmaker, 185 Smith st, F
Cayzer, Henry, carpenter, 80 Elgin st, Carl
Cayzer, John, shoemaker, Johnston st, F
Cecil, Wm., grocer, Leicester st, Carl
Cederberg, J. P., engraver, 82 Queen st
Central Bank of Western India, 48 Collins st west
Central Board of Health office, 178 Collins st east
Chadwick, John, Peel st, Pra
Chadwick, Matthew, 30 Faraday st, Carl
Chadwick, Wm., Farmers' hotel, Ess
Chalk and Price, warehousemen, 8 Collins st east
Chalk, John, Wallis st, Th
Chalker, J., Railway place, San
Chalker, Wm., builder, 5 Spring st
Challis, James, Pier hotel, Nelson place, Wm
Chalmond, Mrs., Webb st, F

Chalmers, James, Gardiner's creek road, S Y
Chamber of Commerce, 48 Collins st west
Chamberlain, B., Williams road, Pra
Chamberlain, Robert, produce merchant, 281 Brunswick st, F
Chamberlain, R., 98 Kerr st, F
Chamberlain, Wm. E., Wellington st, St K
Chambers and Clutten, monumental masons, &c., corner Lonsdale and Stephen sts
Chambers, E., railway truck works, Nicholson st, Fcy
Chambers, Enoch, engineer and ironfounder, 40 and 42 Little Collins st east; Charles st, Fra; and Patent Slip, Wmn
Chambers, George, Mackenzie st
Chambers, James, Gardiner's creek road, S Y
Chambers, Mrs., 75 Lygon st, Carl
Chambers, Mrs., Arden st, Hot
Chambers, T. W., Inkerman st east, St K
Chambers, Thomas, greengrocer, 69 Barkly st, Carl
Chambers, Thomas, 2 Albert terrace, Moray st, Em H
Chambers, W., 195 Cardigan st, Carl
Chambers, William, Union st, S Y
Chambers, William, Chapel st, Pra
Chambers, William, 10 Berkeley st, Carl
Champ, W. T. N., inspector-general of penal establishments, Pent
Champion, Benjamin, Queen's Arms hotel, 27 Swanston st
Champion, Mrs., 42 Bouverie st, Carl
Champion, Mrs., 112 York st east, Em H
Chance Prospecting Gold Mining Company, Gipps Land, 31 Collins st west
Chancellor and Sons, grocers, 66 Errol st, Hot
Chandler, Joseph, Ivanhoe, Heid
Chandler, Joseph, 81 Smith st, F
Chandler, Nun (manager Central Bank of India), 7 Royal terrace, F
Chandler, Stephen, market gardener, Pres
Chandler, Thomas, 115 Stephen st
Chandler, Wm., agent, 227 Swanston st
Chaney, J., 55 Twyford st, South Wmn
Chapel, R., 5 Bendigo st, Hot
Chaplin, Edward, accountant, &c., 64 Elizabeth st
Chaplin, J. T., Goodwood st, Rd
Chaplin, Thomas, grocer, 34 Bridge road, Rd
Chapman, A., storekeeper, Flem
Chapman, G., grocer, Chapel st, Pra
Chapman, George, music warehouse, 117 Swanston st
Chapman, H., storekeeper, Nicholson st, Carl
Chapman, Josiah, coachbuilder, 144 High st, St K
Chapman, L., greengrocer, 146 Brunswick st, F

Chapman, H., grocer, Canning st, Carl
Chapman, Mrs., 3 Granite terrace, Gertrude st, F
Chapman, S., professor of music, 175 Victoria parade, E C
Chapman, Thomas, Flem
Chapman, Thomas, Curzon st, Hot
Chapman, Thomas, butcher, 39 Leveson st, Hot
Chapman, T. O., 130a Rose st, F
Chapman, T. S., 76 Moray place, Em H
Chapman, W., 25 York st east, Em H
Chapman, W. G., saddler, Pent
Chapman, Wm., hay and corn dealer, 247 Victoria parade, E C
Chard, John, Sarsfield Inn, 76 Little Bourke st
Chard, John, storekeeper, Flem
Chard, Wm., builder, 14 Franklyn st west
Charge, Thomas, painter and paperhanger, 17 Cambridge st, E C
Charles, B., Madeline st, Carl
Charles, C., fruiterer, 47 Albert st, E M
Charles, H., 94 Dryburgh st, Hot
Charles, J., Carlisle st east, St K
Charles, Robert, forwarding agent, 3 Latrobe st east
Charles, Thomas, bootmaker, 91 Victoria st, Carl
Charles, Thomas, Berkeley st, Carl
Charleston Amalgamated and Good Spec Mining Company, 64 Elizabeth st
Charlton, Francis, Greville st, Pra
Charlton, James F., coachpainter, 53 Rathdowne st, Carl
Charlton, John, Ivanhoe, Heid
Charlwood and Son, printers, booksellers, &c., 7 Bourke st east; printing office, Angelo lane
Charlwood, C. J., 165 Victoria parade, F
Charlwood, E., 26 Napier st, F
Charsley, Edward, Malvern Hill
Charter, J., 24 Cobden st, Em H
Chase, C., hairdresser, Bay st, San
Chase, Rev. S. L., St. Paul's parsonage, Flinders st east
Chaston, Wm., 42 McArthur place, Carl
Chathand, H. J., tailor, 33 Wellington st, E C
Chatterton, Mrs., 1 Alma terrace, Moray st, Em H
Chavasse, J. L., gardener, Denby st, Btn
Chaavus, Charles, 25 Roden st, W M
Cheese, G., 17 York st west, Em H
Cheese, James, butcher, 17 Curzon st, Hot
Cheeseman, Thomas, Highett st, Rd
Cheetham, Daniel, 79 Stanley st, W M
Cheetham, R., Commercial road, Pra
Cheetham, Wm., Commercial road, Pra
Cherrington, Wm., dealer, 89 Flinders st west
Cherry, Thomas, off 61 Little Collins st east

Cherry, Thomas, 124 Queen st
Cherry, T., Webb st, F
Cheshire, Edwin, 7 Ferguson st, Wmn
Cheshire, Joseph, fishmonger, 130 Bourke st east, and off Little Collins st east
Cheshire, Mrs., general store, Wreckyn st, Hot
Chesney, J., 139 Cecil st, Em H
Chester, Edward C., Whitelaw st, Fcy
Chessell, Charles, 56 York st, Em H
Chevalier, Nicholas, artist, 53 Spring st
Chew, Thomas, 66 Hank st east, Em H
Chew, Thomas, Hay st, Btn
Chewton Flagging and Slate Mining Company, 42 Elizabeth st
Chidley, J. J., fruiterer, Gardiner's creek road, S Y
Child, Jas., store, 184 and 186 Little Bourke st
Child, Jos., Napier st, F
Child, Wm., 150 Little Bourke st west
Chinese Club-house, 75 Little Bourke st east
Chinese Court-house, 71 Little Bourke st east
Chinese Joss-house, Cobden st, Em H
Chinnick, H. J, 128 Johnston st, E C
Chisholm, David, Argyle st, Pra
Chisholm, John Moffatt, 26 Collins st west
Chisholm, James, 171 Lygon st, Carl
Chisholm, Wm. K., Niagara hotel, 28 Lonsdale st west
Chislett, John, Kew
Chittock, E., tailor, 66 Lygon st, Carl
Chitty, Wm., Church st, Hd
Chivers, John C., 5 Bridport st, Em H
Chomley, A. W., secretary Crown Law department, 192 Collins st east
Chomley, Mrs., High st, Pra
Christian, Henry, rope maker, Kew
Christian, Robert, 101 High st, St K
Christian, Wm., boarding-house, 96 King street
Christian Review, 51 Flinders lane west
Christie, James, brickmaker, Commercial road, Pra
Christie, L. S., Ballaarat
Christie, Mrs., boarding-house, 115 Queen street
Christieson, Henry, Peel st, Pra
Christmas,—, Jeweller, 72 Brunswick st, F
Christmas, John, mason, Stephen st
Christopher, James, 6 James st, F
Christopher, John, Brunswick st, F
Christopherson, John, 4 Grey st, E M
Christy, —, Grange road, Tk
Christy, Alexander, Howard st, Hot
Christy, George, Howard st, Hot
Christian Banner office, 123 Argyle st, F
Christy, Robert, 125 Moray st, Em H
Chrystal, Wm., 138 Victoria st, W M
Chronicle, Williamstown, office of, 22 Ann st, Wmn
Chummings, Wm., 30 Brunswick st, F

Chung Hankee, storekeeper, 83 Little Bourke st east
Church of England Grammar School, St. Kilda road
Church of England Life Assurance office, 8 Elizabeth st
Church of England Sunday School Institute Book Depôt, 91 Little Collins st west
Church, J. C., market gardener, Pres
Church, Richard, Hotham st, E M
Churcher, Wm., 158 Johnston st, E C
Churches, James, baker, 57 Peel st, E C
Churchman, James, Standard hotel, 160 Little Collins st east
Churches, R., timber merchant, High st, St K
Churchyard, John, Drummond st, Carl
Churchyard and Cane, wine coopers, 110 Flinders lane east
Chute, —, 2 Westbourne terrace, Grey st, St K
City Loan Company, 60 Elizabeth st
City of Melbourne Gas and Coke Company, 9 Collins st west
City Police Court, Swanston st
City and Suburban Building Society, 18 Collins st east
Clancy, Charles, general dealer, 206 Little Collins st east
Civil Service Gold Mining Company, 69 Collins st west
Clancy, Mrs., 55 Roden st, W M
Clancy, M., bootmaker, Victoria st, Carl
Clapham, Edwin, Nicholson st, Carl
Clapham, S., 90 York st west, Em U
Clapham, Thomas J., 56 Argyle st, F
Clapp, Oliver B., merchant, 65 Little Collins st east
Clapperton, George, draper, 29 Madeline st, Carl
Clapperton, Wm., 74 Bouverie st, Carl
Clapperton, Wm., 26 Queensberry st, Carl
Clare, Mrs., Clyde st, St K
Clare, John, 38 Coventry st west, Em H
Claridge, Charles J., customs agent, Custom-house and Carl
Claridge, T., Carlton st, Carl
Clark, Alexander, Kew
Clark, A., 8 Nicholson st, F
Clark, A., Peel st, Pra
Clark, Alexander J., carpenter, 23 Palmer st, F
Clark, Bernard, Chetwynd st, Hot
Clark, B. R., Dow st, San
Clark, Candid, 74 Cardigan st, Carl
Clark, C., storekeeper, Bay st, Btn
Clark, C. G., shipping reporter, 5 Stoke st, San
Clark, D., Punt road, Pra
Clark, D. G., Rd
Clark, David, Nelson st, Pra
Clark, Edward, house and land agent, 3 Graham st, San

Clark, Frederick S., 24 John st, Wmn
Clark, George, house and land agent, 7 Drummond st, Carl
Clark, George, 137 Elizabeth st
Clark, George, draper and outfitter, 63 and 67 Bourke st east, F
Clark, Henry, chair caner, off Little Bourke st east
Clark, H., 11 Baillie st, Hot
Clark, J., Davis st, Pra
Clark, J., outfitter, 97 Kerr st, F
Clark, J. R., and Co., chemical manufacturers, Yarra bank and 23 Flinders lane west
Clark, James, 25 Little Lonsdale st west
Clark, John, saddler and harness maker, 137 Elizabeth st
Clark, John T., butcher, Commercial road, Pra
Clark, John, Dryburgh st, Hot
Clark, John J., Electra st, Wmn
Clark, John, Arthur's Seat road, Bin
Clark, John, Ruden st, Wmn
Clark, John, tinsmith, 8 Gertrude st, F
Clark, John, 80 Dorcas st, Em H
Clark, John, shipwright, River side south
Clark, John, Arthur st, Pra
Clark, M., 313 Victoria parade, E C
Clark, Mrs. J. B., china warehouse, 130 Clarendon st, Em H
Clark, Mrs. M. A., Junction hotel, Pelham st, Carl
Clark, R., Nicholson st, Carl
Clark, Robert, Elizabeth st
Clark and Sons, tanners, curriers, and leather sellers, 137 Elizabeth st
Clark, Thomas, Hoddle st, Rd
Clark, Thomas, 65 Little Nelson st, Wmn
Clark, T. F., Nelson road, Em H
Clark, Wm., cabinetmaker, 166 Elizabeth st, and Barry st, Carl
Clark, W. A., mathematical instrument maker, 33 Little Collins st west, and Drummond st, Carl
Clark, Wm., Pascoe st, Wmn
Clark, Wm., photographer, 142 Bridge road, Rd
Clark, Wm., Therry st
Clarke, Alex., 132 Drummond st, Carl
Clarke, B., bootmaker, 170 Smith st, E C
Clarke, C., post office, Church st, Btn
Clarke, Charles E., 42 Lonsdale st west
Clarke, C. E., 86 Elizabeth st
Clarke, D., 1 Church st, Em H
Clarke, D., 78 York st, Em H
Clarke, George, architect, 70 Leicester st, Carl
Clarke, Hy., parliamentary agent, Bourke st east
Clarke, Henry J., Wellington st, St K
Clarke, H. S. John, surgeon, 132 Victoria st, Rd
Clarke, J., saddler, Sydney road, Bk
Clarke, J., surgeon, 26 Park st west, Em H

Clarke, J. L., Sydney road, Bk
Clarke, J. L., Sydney road, Bk
Clarke, James, Victoria st, W M
Clarke, John, Nott st, San
Clarke, John, St Kilda road, Btn
Clarke, John, 97 Kerr st, F
Clarke, John, wine merchant and corn factor, 139 Smith st, F
Clarke, Joseph, warehouseman, 11a Flinders lane west, and Erin st, Rd
Clarke, Mary Ann, Junction hotel, corner of Pelham and Elizabeth st extension
Clarke, Miss, 49 Bouverie st, Carl
Clarke, Mrs., Kew
Clarke, W., 33 Bouverie st, Carl
Clarke, Mrs., Cremorne st, Rd
Clarke, Mrs., upholstress, 59 Flinders lane east
Clarke, Mrs., Domain road, S Y
Clarke, Mrs., 47 Lygon st, Carl
Clarke, Rev. W., 5 Lyons st, Wmn
Clarke, Rev. M., 45 St David st, F
Clarke, Richard T., printer, 84 and 88 Moor st, F
Clarke, Robson, Carlisle st west, St K
Clarke, S., Fortune of War hotel, 203 Napier st, F
Clarke, S., bootmaker, 36 Stephen st
Clarke, T., 126 Moray st, Em H
Clarke, T., 96 Dudley st, W M
Clarke, T., Thomson st, Wmn
Clarke, T. P., 51 Nelson road, Em H
Clarke, Thomas, grocer and fruiterer, 29 Douglas parade, Wmn
Clarke, Thos., Southey st, St K
Clarke, Thos., grocer, 42 York st, Em H
Clarke, W., Sackville st, E C
Clarke, W., Little Nelson st, Wmn
Clarke, W., 50 Kerr st, F
Clarke, W., 52 Kerr st, F
Clarke, W., gardener, South road, Btn
Clarke, W. J., stockholder, 60 Collins st west
Clarke, W. T., Dow st, San
Clarke, W. G., Kerr st, F
Clarke, Wm., Williams road, Pra
Clarke, Wm., junr., 64 Elizabeth st, and St K
Clarke, Wm., confectioner, 68 Gertrude st, F
Clarke, Wm., Barry st, Carl
Clarke, Wm., Carlton st, Carl
Clarke, Wm., 52 Kerr st, F
Clarke, Wm., Canning st, Carl
Clarke, Wm., 52 Little Latrobe st
Clarke, Wm., Capel st, W M
Clarke, Wm., junr., Darkly st, St K
Clarke, Wm., 33 Cremorne st, Rd
Clarke, Wm. John Turner, M.L.C., 60 Collins st west and Ess
Clarke, Wm., and Sons, bankers, bullion and share brokers, 85 Elizabeth st
Clarkson, Wm., North Star hotel, corner Provost and Abbotsford sts, Hot

Clare, J., 40 Jeffcott st, W M
Clary, John, cattle dealer, Flem Bank
Clarson, Shallard, and Co., printers and label manufacturers, 74 Little Collins st east
Clarson, W., Wellington parade, E M
Clasby, Martin, Telegraph hotel, 66 Little Bourke st west
Classon, Nickels, C., 76 Coventry st east, Em H
Clavey, Wm. R., surgeon, 31 Dorcas st, Em H
Clay, Charles, Hoddle st, E C
Clay, Frederick L., solicitor, Victoria st, E C
Clay, John H., cabinetmaker, 65 Condell st, F
Clay, Mrs., Graham st, San
Clay, T., veterinary forge, Rouse st, San
Clay, Wm., hairdresser, &c., 44 Queen st
Clayton, Charles, Victoria hotel, Peel st, Hot
Clayton, George, Lothian st, Hot
Clayton, James, grocer, 40 King William st, F
Clayton, John H., solicitor, 64 Little Collins st east
Clayton, Mrs., Brighton st, Rd
Clayton, R., 69 George st, F
Cleal, Jacob, Parisian cafe, 108 Bourke st east
Cleary, Edmond, shoemaker, 158 King st
Cleary, E. J., Australian hotel, Rathdowne st, Carl
Cleary, John, storekeeper, Flem
Cleary, Patrick, shoemaker, 126 Little Bourke st west
Cleeland, John, Albion hotel, 37 Bourke street east
Clegg, P., stonemason, Chapel st, Pra
Clegg, Robert H., 47 Victoria st, Hot
Cleghorne, Arthur, tannery, White Horse st, Fcy
Cleland, R., general dealer, 91 Stephen st
Clelland, Mrs., 42 Darkly st, Carl
Clement, Thomas, Berkeley st, Carl
Clements, G., 83 Westgarth st, F
Clements, H., 150 Little Lonsdale st west
Clements, Tobias, Cricketers' hotel, pastry cook, 58 Swanston st
Clendinnen, Joseph James, jeweller, 7 Bourke st east
Clerley, R., 34 Bouverie st, Carl
Cleve, Salt, merchant, acting consul Hamburg, Bremen, and Hanover, 38 Flinders lane west
Cleveland, Wm., merchant, 9 Flinders st west
Cleveland, Wm., 3 Dalgety st, St K
Cleverdon, W., 91 Park st, Em H
Clews, F., cabinetmaker, 69 Johnston st, E C
Cliff, E., Prince of Wales hotel, Chapel st, Pra

Clifford, —, Argyle st east, St K
Clifford, James, Church st, Rd
Clifford, Wm., 30 Fitzroy st, F
Clifton, George, furniture dealer, Chapel st, Pra
Climance, George, Wellington parade, E M
Clinch, James, 9 Stanley st, W M
Clinn, J. N., engineer, Pres
Clinton, James, Fletcher's hotel, Haw
Clinton, Mrs., school, Brighton st, Rd
Clipperton, John, solicitor, 81 Little Collins st east
Clissold, George, grazier, Ascot vale, Flem
Close, J. S., 39 Smith st, F
Close, Wm., storekeeper, Railway place, San
Clothier, Robert, Essex st, Fcy
Clothier, Wm., Essex st, Fcy
Clough, F., Victoria st, E C
Clough, J. H. and Co., wool brokers, 111 and 113 Collins st west
Clough, J. H., Chapel st, S Y
Clough, Richard, blacksmith, 11 Little Nelson st, W on
Clough's Circular and Pastoral Advertiser office, 99 Bourke st west
Clowes, Wm., Jollmont
Clowles, Thomas, Rowena parade, Rd
Clubb, Thomas Joseph, and Mrs., surgical bandage makers, 136 Collins st east
Clune, Patrick, Union st, S Y
Clutten, George, Inkerman st, St K
Clutterbuck, Henry, Kew
Clydesdale, David, greengrocer, 58 Lygon st, Carl
Coad, Henry, 26 Grattan st, Carl
Coates, —, grocer, 107 Queen st
Coates, J., painter, New street, Bin
Coates, Miss, draper, Chapel st, Pra
Coates, Mrs., 238 King st
Coates, Mrs., Gardiner's creek road, S Y
Coates, Walter, Victoria st, Bin
Coates, Wm., painter and glazier, 70 Queen st
Cobb and Co.'s coach office, 35 Bourke st east
Cobb, Charles, 55 St. David's st, F
Cobb, Mrs., 70 Lonsdale st west
Cobb, Wm., 33 Curzon st, Hot
Cobham, Alexander, Osborne st, South W nn
Caton, J., 41 Cecil st, Em H
Cobourn, G., Moor st, F
Cochran, Hugh, grocer, 70 Swan st, Rd
Cochran, W., Ralston st, Pra
Cochrane and O'Brien, importers of fancy drapery, 52 Flinders lane west
Cochrane, Edward, Station place, San
Cochrane, J., Cochrane st, Bin
Cochrane and Hadford, tinsmiths, 19 Post Office place
Cochrane, Wm., Caroline st, S Y
Cock, Thomas, farmer, Braybrook road, Ess

Cock, Thomas, Provost st, Hot
Cocking, Samuel, Kew
Cockbill, Henry, nightman, &c., Barkly st, St K
Cockbill, John, nightman, 23 Little Bourke st west
Cockbill, Wm., nightman, 42 Little Bourke st west
Cockburn, C., Cardigan st, Carl
Cockburn, John, pastrycook, 39 Bourke st east, and 56 and 58 Swanston st
Cockburn, J., Spencer st, near Roden st
Cockburn, John, confectioner, &c., 19 Collins st west, and 136 Collins st east
Cockburn, Oasley, Rotherwood st, Hd
Cockerill, John F., Abbotsford st, Hot
Cockes, Thomas, carpenter, 99 Flinders st east
Cocklan, J., bootmaker, Berkeley st, Carl
Cockles, James, Pelham st, Carl
Coffey, Thomas, Courtney st, Hot
Coffey, Wm., Stockade hotel, Nicholson st, Carl
Cogan, E. W., Greville st, Pra
Coe, James, gardener, Pres
Cogally, Martin, Curzon st, Hot
Coggins, Thomas, sharebroker and mining agent, 3 Collins st west
Coghill, George, 51 Three chain road, Em H
Coglan, Mrs., 128 Madeline st, Carl
Cogswell, L. H., Stewart street, Bk
Cogvin, John, Oxford arms hotel, Oxford st, E C
Cohen, A. Abraham, china and glass dealer, 120 and 131 Swanston st
Cohen, Andrew, gingerbeer manufacturer, Little Collins st
Cohen, A. J., Commercial road, Pra
Cohen Brothers, furniture importers, Queen's Arcade, Lonsdale st
Cohen, David, outfitter and passage broker, 73 Flinders st west
Cohen, David, 120 Little Lonsdale st west
Cohen, E., and Co., merchants, 36 Little Collins st west
Cohen, E., 18 Napier st, F
Cohen, Edward, M.L.A., Clarendon st, E M
Cohen, E. L., 2 George st, F
Cohen, George, hairdresser, Beech st, San
Cohen, Jos., 9 Royal terrace, Nicholson st, F
Cohen, Lewis, Victoria st, W M
Cohen, Louis, Druid's hotel, 172 Russell st
Cohen, Louis, pawnbroker, 176 Russell st
Cohen, L., 153 Spring st
Cohen, L., dealer, Market lane, Bourke st east
Cohen, Mendel, dealer, 162 Russell st
Cohen, Mrs. E., clothier, 73 Elizabeth st, and Smith st, E C
Cohen, Mrs., 47 Franklin st west
Cohen, Mrs., Marion st, F

Cohen, Mrs., furniture mart, 118 Smith st, E C
Cohen, P., 115 Victoria parade, F
Cohen, P., & Co., cigar divan, 103 Bourke st east
Cohen, Samuel H., Wellington st, St K
Cohen, S. H., and Co., auctioneers, 30 Collins st west
Cohen, Simeon, King William st, F
Cohen, Victor, watchmaker, 216 Smith st, E C
Cohen, Wm., cab proprietor, South Andley st, E C
Cohn, Henry, Rifle Brigade hotel, Elgin st, Carl
Cohn, E., erated waters maker, off 24 Little Collins st east
Coker, Thomas, Esplanade, St K
Coker, Thomas, and Co., stock, share, and money brokers, 69 Collins st west
Colclough, R. and J., grocers and provision merchants, &c., 167 Clarendon st, Em H
Colclough, Richard, produce merchant, 107 Clarendon st, Em H
Coldon, Miss, dressmaker, Princes st, F
Cole Brothers, painters and paperhangers, 12 Napier st, F
Cole, E. W., bookseller, 14 Eastern market
Cole, G., cabinetmaker, 88 Oxford st, E C
Cole, Hon. Geo. W., M.L.C., merchant, &c., Cole's Wharf, Flinders st west
Cole, James H., Capel st, W M
Cole, Jas., bootmaker, 36 Rathdowne st, Carl
Cole, John, locksmith, whitesmith, &c., 21 Little Collins st east
Cole, John H., draper, 231 Lygon st
Cole, John, 26 M'Arthur place Carl
Cole, John, 132 Moor st, F
Cole, John, Pent
Cole, Josias, 97 Wellington st, E C
Cole, Miss, Cliff st, Pra
Cole, Robert, 85 Jeffcott st, W M
Cole, T., 108 Moor st, F
Cole, T. C., Haw
Cole, Thomas, draper, Stanley st, E C
Cole, Thos., Carson's lane, Little Collins st east
Coleman, B., 40 Little Lonsdale st east
Coleman, Edward, 52 Young st, F
Coleman, J., 22 Barkly st, Carl
Coleman, Mrs., Cecil st, Em H
Coleman, Mrs., 121 Gertrude st, F
Coleman, Mrs., 106 York st, Em H
Coles, George, baker, 154 Bridge road, Rd
Coles, J., Albert st, Pra
Coles, Robert, Builders arms hotel, Cardigan st, Carl
Coles, Samuel, baker, Haw
Coles, S., accountant, Ray st, Bm
Coles, Thomas, grocer, 96 Elgin st, Carl
Colgin, John, 3 a'Beckett st east

Colgin, M., Villiers st, Hot
Coliban Gold Mining Company, 54 Queen street
Collard, Geo. M., butcher, Clyde st, St K
Colley, Wm., Rotherwood st, Rd
Colley, Wm., South Audley st, E C
Collis, Jonas, York st, Hm
Collie, Joseph, secretary Victorian Fire and Marine Insurance Company, 82 Collins st east
Collie, Wm., painter, Ralston st, Pra
Collie, Wm., 45 Howard st, Hot
Collier, Mrs., Wellington st, St K
Collier, Thomas, wood and coal dealer, 323 Brunswick st, F
Collingwood Assembly Hall, 56 Gertrude st, F
Collingwood, Fitzroy, and District Gas and Coke Company, 26 Swanston st
Collingwood Gold Mining Company's Office, 55 Elizabeth st
Collingwood Observer office, 23 Smith st, F
Collins and Co., flock and bone-dust manufacturers, Yarra bank
Collins, Callaghan, off 132 Collins st east
Collins, Christopher, painter, 173 Little Lonsdale st east
Collins, Denis, 13 Bouverie st, Carl
Collins, James, confectioner, 9 High st, St K
Collins, John, John st, Wmn
Collins, John, harnessmaker, 3 Elizabeth st extension
Collins, John K., All England Eleven hotel, Railway place, San
Collins, J., man cook, Gardiner's creek road, S Y
Collins, John, 227 Swan st, Rd
Collins, John, 208 Johnston st, E C
Collins, John, 70 Barkly st, Carl
Collins, J., 80 York st, Em H
Collins, John, Abbotsford st, Hot
Collins, M., Hoddle st, Rd
Collins, Mrs., 149 George st, F
Collins, Mrs., Cremorne st, Rd
Collins, Robert, butcher, 96 Elgin st, Carl
Collins, T., Reilly st, F
Collins, Thomas, Elgin st, Carl
Collins, Walter, Railway place, San
Collins, W., 46 Coventry st, Em H
Collins, W., coachsmith, 124 Gore st, F
Collis, Alfred, 64 Lygon st, Carl
Collis, F., 108 Westgarth st, F
Collis, T., Byron st, Hot
Collis, Wm., lithographer, 12 Smith st, F
Collison, C. C., Hoddle st, Rd
Collison, John, tanner, Flem bank
Colliver, —, Sackville st, E C
Collocott, James, 182 George st, F
Collonder, Francis, ironmonger, 111 High st, St K
Colls, Benjamin, 10 Queensberry st, Hot
Colman, —, 10 Dover place, Wmn
Colman, B., 60 Coventry st east, Em H

Colman, Isaac, 143 Flinders lane east
Colman, J., 129 Moor st, F
Colman, R., storekeeper, Pent
Colman, Mrs., 55 Kerr st, F
Colonial Bank of Australasia, corner of Elizabeth st and Little Collins st east
Colonial Life Assurance Company (of Edinburgh), 96 Collins st west
Colquhoun, Gideon A., 28 Moor st, F
Colson, Wm., hay and corn dealer, Chapel st, Pra
Colter, Edwin, 224 Johnston st, E C
Colville, Henry, grocer, 181 Smith st, F
Colville, R., Trinnian st, Pra
Colvin, James, Beehive hotel, Haw
Colvin, James, Fitzroy Arms, 139 King st and Little Bourke st west
Comen, Ellen, dressmaker, 3 Bouverie st, Carl
Comban, S., 17 Stevedore st, Wmn
Comerford, Wm., 132 Argyle st, F
Comisky, W., boarding-house, 118 Little Lonsdale st west
Commendlog, Mrs., dressmaker, 351 Elizabeth st
Commissariat Office, corner of King and Little Collins st west
Commissioners of Audit, 178 Collins st east
Comport, M., 46 Swan st, Rd
Comport, Wm., Berkeley st, Carl
Compton, —, Inkerman st, St K
Compton, C. Henry, professor of music, Chapel st, St K
Compton, W. H., Punt road, Rd
Comrie and Co., importers, 144 Little Collins st east
Comyns, Charles L., Haw
Comyns, J. R., Macarthur place, Carl
Conacher, D., cabinetmaker, Ralston st, Pra
Cooden, Edward, Lygon st, Carl
Condon, Thomas, Condon's hotel, 60 William st
Condron, Thomas, Cavan hotel, 328 Brunswick st, F
Coney, Richard, 178 Napier st, F
Congdon, J., Madeline st, Carl
Congregational College, corner of Elgin and Madeline sts, Carl
Conlay, P., Hyde st, Fzy
Conlen, Peter, draper, Chapel st, Pra
Conley, James, head master National Schools, Bell st, F
Conlon, P. T., architect, 30 Queen st
Connell and Clark, timber merchants, 13 William st
Connell, D., Cole st, Wmn
Connell, David, Ivanhoe, Heid
Connell and Hogarth, importers, 15 and 17 Swanston st
Connell, John, 2 Grattan st, Carl
Connell, John, 101 Bouverie st, Carl
Connell, John, Kew

Connell, John, 55 Dorcas st west, Em H
Connell, John, ironmonger, 89 Elizabeth st
Connell, Peter, 53 Smith st, F
Connell, Thomas, Haw
Connell, W., 263 Victoria parade, E C
Connelley, Charles, Flemington hotel, Flem
Connelley, Mrs., St Kilda st, Bta
Connelley, 11 Macarthur place, Carl
Connolly, W., Nth
Conner, James, bootmaker, Mount Alexander road, Ess
Conner, Mrs., 172 Victoria st, Rd
Conner, Wm., Princes st, Flem
Connibere, C., draper, High st, St K
Connobee, George, Station place, San
Connolly, James, boarding-house keeper, 169 Bourke st west
Connor, Daniel, 42 Little Nelson st, Wmn
Connor, J. H., M.L.A., Parliament house
Connor, John, Curzon st, Hot
Connor, John, chemist, Elizabeth st, extension
Connor, John, Little Nelson st, Wmn
Connor, Jos., 36 George st, F
Connor, T. G., Punt road, S Y
Conolly, Philip, 142 Little Bourke st west
Conrad, Edward M., stevedore, Stevedore st, Wmn
Conran, Mrs., Governor Hotham hotel, Haw
Conroy, James, grocer, 40 Nelson place east, Wmn
Conroy, Mrs., 105 Faraday st, Carl
Conroy, Michael, Station place, San
Conroy, Mrs., Thompson st, Wmn
Conroy, Wm. C., Conroy's Royal hotel, Victoria st, Carl
Considine, J. W., chemist, 49 Peel st, E C
Constable, Wm., general dealer, 143 King st
Constable, Marmaduke, mining agent, 9 Elizabeth st
Constantine, Mrs., straw bonnet maker, 67 Smith st, F
Convent of the Good Shepherd, Clarke st, E C
Convent of the Sisters of Mercy, Nicholson st, F
Conway, F., boot warehouse, Chapel st, Pra
Conway, —, Nott st, San
Conway, Francis, 131 Johnston st, F
Conway, John, 21 Cross st, Hot
Conway, Patrick, 7A Wellington st, St K
Conway, Patrick, grocer, 259 King st
Cook, A., ferryman, River Bank
Cook and Fox, account book manufacturers, 58 Queen st
Cook and Richards, cabinetmakers, Franklin st, W M
Cook, B. J., Fernyhurst, Ess
Cook, Frederic, manager, Melbourne Banking Co., Queen st

Cook and Co., printers, Leveson st, Hot
Cook, F. T., working jeweller, 151 Spring street
Cook, George, Mount Erica hotel, High st, Prn
Cook, George, 93 Victoria st, Hot
Cook, Henry, 94 Smith st, F
Cook, J., Andrew st, Wind
Cook, J., Punt road, S Y
Cook, James, Latrobe st west
Cook, John, 176 Napier st, F
Cook, Richard, tinsmith, Blackwood st, Hot
Cook, Robert, Abbotsford st, Hot
Cook, Thomas, 45 Rathdowne st, Carl
Cook, Thomas, Nicholson st, Carl
Cook, Thomas A., blacksmith, Buckley st, Em
Cook, Thomas, 138 Cardigan st, Carl
Cook, W. and D., Sydney road, Bk
Cook, Wm., accountant, &c., 32 Queen st
Cook, William, builder, Commercial road, Prn
Cook, Wm., store, 60 Gore st, F
Cook, Wm. C., pawnbroker, Bay st, San
Cook, Wm., 176 Lygon st, Carl
Cooke, Abel, 59A St. David st, F
Cooke, B., Alabama hotel, Victoria st, Rd
Cooke, B. and H., timber merchants, Spencer st, opposite railway
Cooke, C. F. D., sign writer, 106 Russell st
Cooke, Charles, 192 Little Bourke st east
Cooke, H., merchant, 5 Bond st, and Yarra Falls
Cooke, John H., accountant, 20 and 21 Eldon chambers, Collins st west
Cooke, M., 1 Trafalgar place, Hot
Cooke, Mrs., 27 Barkly st, Carl
Cooke, Mrs., 50 Bank st west, Em H
Cooke, R., contractor, 70 Johnston st, E C
Cooke, Richard S., Hoddle st, E M
Cooke, T., Peel st, E C
Cooke, Thomas, tailor, Bay st, Bin
Cooke, W., 81 Bank st west, Em H
Cooke, W. H., grocer, Williams road, Prn
Cookson and Brown, tailors and outfitters, 43 Bourke st east
Cookson, John, 41 Dorcas st, Em H
Cooley, George, Collingwood hotel, Webb st, F
Cooling, Richard Henry, tailor and outfitter, 45 and 47 Bourke st east
Coombes, James, 182 Drummond st, Carl
Coombes, Joseph B., Berkeley st, Carl
Coombes, Lidwell, and Ellis (Trade Protection Society), 36 Collins st west
Coombes, Richard, bootmaker, 259 Elizabeth st
Coombes, Wm., 10 Henry st, F
Cooney, C., Wembury st, St K
Cooney, Patrick, bootmaker, 23 Little Lonsdale st east
Cooney, Wm., bootmaker, 37 Little Lonsdale st west

Coop, James, lead pipe manufacturer and engineer, 28 Little Collins st west
Coop, James, Illawarra st, Wmn
Coop, R., 88 Stanley st, Wmn
Cooper and Spencer, farriers, 9 Little Collins st east
Cooper, Alexander, 10 Marion st, F
Cooper, C., surgeon, 64 Queensberry st, Carl
Cooper, Edmund H., chemist, 158A King st
Cooper, Edward W., solicitor, 41 Swanston st
Cooper, George, Lennox st, Rd
Cooper, Harriet, Sir C. Darling hotel, 164 Swanston st
Cooper, H., clothier, 213 Bourke st east
Cooper, J. T., Burnett st, St K
Cooper, John, 3 Regent terrace, Faraday st, Carl
Cooper, John, Park st, S Y
Cooper, John, Charles st, F
Cooper, John T., Gurner st, St K
Cooper, Miss, milliner, 61 Gertrude st, F
Cooper, Mrs., hat and bonnet manufacturer, Chapel st, Prn
Cooper, Mrs., Bedford hotel, corner of Lonsdale and Swanston sts
Cooper, Peter, bootmaker, 89 Smith st, F
Cooper, Richard, Walsh st, S Y
Cooper, Richd., consul for Portugal, 2d Queen st
Cooper, Richard Austin, Hammams hotel, 140 Bourke st east
Cooper, R. W. G., wine broker, 26 Queen st, and Walsh st, S Y
Cooper, T., 100 Montague st, Em H
Cooper, Thomas, commission agent, 26 Queen st
Cooper, Thomas, coachbuilder, Ess
Cooper, Wm., 4 Cumberland place, Little Lonsdale st east
Coose, J., Railway place, San
Coote, F. J., Kensington
Cope, —, 86 Cambridge st, E C
Cope, Alfred, Patterson st, E C
Cope Brothers and Nephew, merchants, 101 Little Collins st east
Cope, Edward, M.L.A., Patterson st, E C
Cope, Joseph, Kew
Cope, Thomas, Church st, Rd
Cope, Thomas, Patterson st, E C
Cope, T., storekeeper, 139 Flinders st west
Copeland, James, Upper Haw
Coppick, John, 50 Jeffcott st, W M
Copley and Sons, basket makers, &c., Franklin st west
Copley, W., Stockade hotel, Nicholson st, F
Coppel, Elias, watchmaker and jeweller, 18 Bourke st east, and Franklin st west
Copperthwaite, Wm., 102 Moray st, Em H
Coppin, Fdk., 159 Cardigan st, Carl
Coppin, George, Rd
Coppin, Michael, Arden st, Hot

Coppins, T., dairyman, 14 York st west, Em H
Copplestone, John, Bridport st, Em H
Copplestone, Wm., 125 Queensberry st, Hot
Corben, J., builder, Barry st, Carl
Corben, R., 197 Faraday st, Carl
Corben, Stephen, Cardigan st, Carl
Corben, T., Pelham st, Carl
Corbett, J., tailor, 112 Latrobe st east
Corbett, Matthew, Lothian st, Hot
Corbett, Rev. J. F., Westbury st, St K
Corbett, R. G., 30 Little Collins st west
Corboy, Michael, bootmaker, 34 Little Collins st east
Corcoran, James, West End hotel, corner of Spencer and Latrobe st
Corcoran, J., bootmaker, 50 Latrobe st east
Corcoran, Wm. P., hairdresser, 46 and 236 Swanston st
Cord, W., 14 Railway place, Wmn
Core, W., butcher, Wilson st, Btn
Corr, Thomas, 86 Leveson st, Hot
Corfield, J. P., bootmaker, Grey st, St K
Corfield, James, dealer, Curzon st, Hot
Cork, Wm., 67 Stanley st, Wmn
Corkhill, Robert, Pent
Corlett, Frederick, Barry st, Carl
Corlett, Thomas A., Gardiner's creek road, Pra
Corley, T., Wellington st, St K
Cormack, H., 81 Leicester st, Carl
Cormick, Wm., tailor, 87 Faraday st, Carl
Corneille, Wm., government contractor, 59 Bourke st west
Cornell, Edward, draper and outfitter, 63 and 64 Madeline st, Carl
Cornell, F., photographer, Madeline st, Carl
Cornell, H. and A., drapers and boot dealers, Chapel st, Prahran
Cornell, T. W., Lincoln cottages, Bouverie st, Carl
Cornfoot, David, plumber and tinsmith, Peel st, E C
Cornick, E., 80 Moor st, F
Cornish Brothers, law stationers, 79 Little Collins st west
Cornish and Bruce, railway contract, 91 Little Collins st west
Cornish, Ebenezer, 34 Carlton st, Carl
Cornish, Jane, Victoria st, Carl
Cornwall Fire and Marine Insurance Agency, 26 Queen st
Cornwall, F. L., Chambers st, Pra
Cornwell, H., butcher, 147 Lonsdale st east
Cornwell, Alfred, pottery, off Sydney road
Coronel, H., 103 Latrobe st east
Corp, John, bootmaker, Bay st, Btn
Corry, Joseph, Haw
Corteen, Daniel, timber yard, Howard st, W M

Cosgrave, John J., 62 Stanley st, W M
Cosgrave, John, city treasurer, Kensington, Flem
Cosgrave, J., storekeeper, New st, Btn
Cosham, T. H., store, 25 Bank st west, Em H
Costano, Thomas, storekeeper, Flem bank
Cossu, C., Vice Italian Consul, 36 William street
Costella, W., Station place, San
Costello, C., Galway hotel, 129 Flinders lane east
Costello, Henry, 28 Cobden st, Em H
Costello, Wm., Graham st, San
Coster, F., Robe st, St K
Coster, Thomas, builder, 191 Smith st, F
Cott, Edward, 2 Wellington st, E C
Cottell, James, Chapel st, Pra
Cotter, Edmund, tollkeeper, Richmond bridge
Cotter, Miss B., Punt road, Rd
Cottingham, Mary, draper, Latrobe st
Cottren, J., grocer, Commercial and Williams roads, Pra
Couch, Samuel, blacksmith, 35 Derby st, E C
Courke, William, Grey st, St K
Coughland, D., 140 George st, F
Coughlin, John, dairyman, Flem
Coulson, A., 124 Leicester st, F
Coulson Bros., chairmakers, 36 a'Beckett st east
Coulson, Edward, builder, William st north
Coulson, T., 128 Leicester st, F
Coulson, Wm., carrier, 152 Swan st, Rd
Coulsoo, W., grocer, Victoria st, Hot
Coulter, W., Gardiner's creek road, Pra
Coulthard, —, carpenter, Smith st, E C
Coulthard, —, 253 Lygon st, Carl
Coulton, T., Sackville st, E C
Councill, W., 47 Nelson road, Em H
Counsel, Loughlin, civil engineer, 22 Arden st, Hot
Counsel, Richard, 85 Montague st, Em H
County Court, Swanston st north
Counter, John, Hoddle st, E C
Coupar, James, tailor and outfitter, 3 Victoria st, Carl
Coupland, S., draper, 129 Brunswick st, F
Courier, A., 12 Barry st, Carl
Court, T. P., Bay st, Btn
Courteen, Daniel, 17 Howard st, Hot
Courtis, John, auctioneer and commission agent, 22 Nelson place, Wmn
Courtney, Edward, official assignee, 53 Temple court, Collins st west
Cousens, Charles, 20 Market st, Em H
Cousens, Mrs., Punt road, Pra
Cousins, C., 96 Moray place, Em H
Cousins, E., carpenter, Millewyn st, S Y
Cousins, H., professor of music, 113 Bouverie st, Carl
Cousland, A., 142 Moray st, Em H
Coutie, J., bootmaker, 155 Elizabeth st

Cootle, David, Blackwood st, Hot
Coventry, Thomas, market gardener, Cape st, Hcld
Coventry, Thomas, bootmaker, Gardiner's creek road, Pra
Cover, Thomas, Elphinstone st, Fcy
Coverlid, Henry, hairdresser, 124 Little Bourke st east
Coverlid, John, gingerbeer manufacturer, Church st, Rd
Cowan, A. K., Kenmure Arms hotel, Flinders st west
Cowan, James, Station place, San
Cowan, John, grocer, 56 Queensberry st, Carl
Cowan, John, storekeeper, 76 Elgin st, Carl
Cowan, Matthew, bootmaker, Little Bridge, Em
Coward, Joseph, Whitehall st, Fcy
Cowderoy, Benjamin, valuer, &c., 46 Collins st west
Cowdie, A., 11 Victoria st west, Hot
Cowell, James, 136 Flinders lane east
Cowell, Joshua, 125 Nicholson st, F
Cowell, Joshua, M.L.A., Abbotsford
Cowell and Milne, bootmakers, 67 Collins st west
Cowen, Ann, registry office, 100 Collins st east
Cowen, —, 119 Fitzroy st, F
Cowen, T., 110 York st east, Em H
Cowen, Wm., watchmaker, Cubitt st, Rd
Cowie, Mrs., grocer, 24 Faraday st, Carl
Cowie, Robert John, Caulfield
Cowie, Wm., 9 True street, Carl
Cowieson, J., 13 York st west, Em H
Cowley, George E. (actuary Australasian Insurance Company), Coldblow, Malvern Hill
Cowley, Captain, Electra st, Wmn
Cowley, Miss, milliner, Argyle st west, St K
Cowlishaw, F., ironmonger, Chapel st, Pra
Cowlishaw, T., ironmonger, 91 Bridge road, Rd
Cowper, Charles, 27 York st, Em H
Cowper, W., lighterage agent, 37 William street
Cox, C., builder, Nth
Cox, Charles, painter, 38 Bourke st west
Cox, Edward, Roden st, W M
Cox, F., Goodwood st, Rd
Cox, George, tripe dresser, Greville st, Pra
Cox, George R., architect, 41 Swanston st
Cox, H., 38 Coventry st, Em H
Cox, James, Fitzroy
Cox, John, 11 Nelson place east, Wmn
Cox, J., painter and glazier, 116 High st, St K
Cox, John, 92 Stanley st, W M
Cox, John, dairyman, 164 Ferrars st, Em H
Cox, Mrs., 163 Queensberry st, Hot
Cox, Wm. Samuel, pork butcher, 106 Bourke st east

Cox, R., Cecil st, Em H
Coxhead, G., dealer, 107 Argyle st, F
Coxhead, H., draper, 157 Victoria st, E C
Cozon, Mrs., Bridge road, Rd
Cozon, W. J., Britannia hotel, 162 Clarendon st, Em H
Coyle, D., fruiterer, 155 Little Bourke st east
Cosens, John, Carlton Inn, Leicester st, Carl
Crabb, James, bootmaker, 251 Swanston st
Craggs, Mrs., Gardiner's creek road, S Y
Craib, George, draper, 67 Bourke st east
Craig, A. C., 34 George st, F
Craig, George, Baillie st, Hot
Craig, Henry, grocer, 101 Bourke st east
Craig, J., Curzon st, Hot
Craig, James, outfitter, Bay st, San
Craig, Jas., butcher, 66 Queensberry st, Carl
Craig, John, 19 Bell st, F
Craig, Matthew, Regent st, F
Craig, Robert, Greville st, Pra
Craig, Robert, 171 Lygon st, Carl
Craine, T., timber merchant and coach builder, 3 Latrobe st west
Crambe, Wm., M.D., surgeon, 113 Victoria st, E C
Cramer, Albert, manufacturing jeweller, 18 Little Bourke st west
Cramp, John, butcher, 119 Brunswick st, F
Cramplin, Geo. J., butcher, Kew
Crane, E., painter, &c., 58 Nelson place, Wmn
Crang, C. H., engineer, Richmond terrace, Rd
Cranston, George, High st, Pra
Cranston, J., Provost st, Hot
Cranston, Samuel, draper, Russell st
Cranwell, Mark, Kew
Crasks, Francis N., plasterer, Henry st, Pra
Craven, George, plumber and gasfitter, 96 Victoria st, Rd
Craven, John, town clerk, Grosvenor st, Pra
Craven, Moses, Cardigan st, Carl
Craven, Mrs., 116 Raglan st east, Em H
Craven, Richard B., Bay st, San
Craven, S., Weston st, Bk
Craven, S., 219 Victoria parade, E C
Crawford, D., carpenter, 127 Elgin st, Carl
Crawford, E., High st, Pra
Crawford, G. H., Gardiner's creek road, Pra
Crawford, J., Arden st, Hot
Crawford, James, High st, Hot
Crawford, W., builder, 42 Rathdowne st, Carl
Crawley, Charles, market gardener, Pres
Crawley, John, draper, Chapel st, Pra
Crawshaw, Jos., 145 Cardigan st, Carl
Crawshaw, Wm., Reilly st, F

Creak, Mrs., milliner, 67 Wellington st, E C
Creber, Wm. James W., solicitor, &c., 60 Queen st
Cree, Robert B., livery stable keeper, Stephen st, and Grey st, St K
Creed, Frederick, grocer, 47 Stanley st, E C
Creek, Mrs, 110 Stevedore st, Wmn
Creek, John, school, Ferguson st, Wmn
Creek, Samuel, Cole st, Wmn
Creeke, Robert, bootmaker, 2 Nelson place, North Wmn
Creeke, R., 34 Nelson place, Wmn
Creerand, James, dining rooms, 97 Flinders st west
Creeth, Wm. J., Carlisle st, St K
Crerib, W. J., Peel st, Pra
Cregin, P., registry office, 134 Smith st, E C
Crespin, T. T., Bridge road, Rd
Cress, Mrs., Arden st, Hot
Cresswell and Son, solicitors, 55 Little Collins st east
Cresswell, Charles, Beach, Btn
Cresswell, Hy., Octavia st, North St K
Cresswell, Hurdman, Charles
Cresswell, C., Henry st, Pra
Creswick, Henry, and Co., pastoral agency, 54 Queen st
Creswick, Henry, M.L.A., Parliament House
Crew, Samuel, 80 Napier st, F
Crews, J. B., M.L.A., Chapel st, Pra
Crews, J. B., and Co., auctioneers, Chapel st, Pra
Crewther, J., Barkly st, Bk
Cribb, Miss, draper, 166 Elizabeth st
Chrichsen, Charles, Bond st, E C
Crichton, Wm., grocer, 39 Madeline st, Carl
Crick, T., butcher, Twyford st, Wmn
Cricketers' Gold Mining Company, 64 Elizabeth st
Crickmer, S., Ship Inn, 66 Flinders lane west
Crighton, James, 7 Spencer terrace, Little Bourke st west
Crisp and Co., brewers, Cambridge st, E C
Crisp, C., Pelham st, Carl
Crisp, Edward, Derby st, E C
Crisp, George, watchmaker and jeweller, 46 Queen st
Crisp, T., Wellington st, Btn
Crispin, Henry, contractor, 151 Ross st, F
Croad, J., Wellington st. St K
Croaker, D., 117 Leveson st, Hot
Crocker, Robert, Punt road, Pra
Crockford, Edward J., Chequers Inn, Bay st, Nan
Croft, John, bootmaker, 62 Johnston st, E C
Croft, Mrs., 209 Moray st, Em H
Croft, Robert T., cheesemonger, 135A Bourke st east

Croft, Wm., Madeline st, Carl
Croke, James, Thompson st, South Wmn
Croker, H. D., surgeon, hydropathic establishment, 30 Regent st, F
Croker, J., Hotham Arms hotel, Strand, Wmn
Croker, James, grocer, 94 Little Collins st west
Cromay, James, Richmond terrace, Rd
Crombie, Edward E., Park st, S Y
Crompton and Child, butchers, 141 King st
Crompton, Robert, Richmond terrace, Rd
Crompton, Thomas, 150 Little Bourke st west
Cron, Robert, Henry st, Pra
Cron, Robert, Rowena parade, Rd
Cronan, Bartholomew, steam bonnet shape manufacturer, 39 Victoria parade, F
Cronan, P., baker, Chapel st, Pra
Crone, Jerome, watchmaker, 136 Smith st, E C
Croner, T., Villiers st, Hot
Cronin, —, Patterson st, E C
Cronin, D., 94 George st, F
Cronin, J., Peel st, Pra
Crook, B., Albert st west, Bk
Crook, Mrs., Webb st, F
Crook, T., saddler, Acling st, Btn
Crook, T. G., painter, Cliff st, Pra
Crouke and Hewlett, surgeons, 43 Drummond st, Carl
Crooke, Edward, 5 Grey st, E M
Crooke, Edward, 5 Barkly terrace, Grey st, St K
Crooke, L., Punt road, S Y
Crooke, Robert, national teacher, 27 Bank st, Em H
Crooke, Wm., surgeon, corner of Gertrude and Brunswick sts, F
Crooked River Quartz Mining Company, Temple court, Collins st west
Croom, John, 106 Lygon st, Carl
Cropley, Henry, Dryborgh st, Hot
Cropper, Wm. H., stock and share broker, 49 Collins st west
Crosby, B., Church st, Rd
Crosby, J., 190 Victoria parade, E M
Crosby, Mrs., Esplanade, St K
Crosby, Mrs., Murphy st, S Y
Crosby, Wm., and Co., merchants, 35 Market st
Crosby, Wm., 120 Wellington parade, F M
Cross, Alfred, bedding factory, 3 and 13 Lonsdale st east
Cross and Co., hay and corn dealers, Errol st, Hot
Cross, Charles, Manadon House hotel, 23 Stanley st, W M
Cross, Edwin, Peel st, Pra
Cross, John, coffee roaster, 276 Elizabeth st, and Austin st, Fcy
Cross, Joseph, 16 Barkly st, Carl
Cross, Mrs., 140 Cardigan st, Carl
Cross, Wm., 24 Young st, F

Crossland, Jeremiah, greengrocer, 144 Moray st, Em H
Crossley, Mrs., Punt road, Rd
Crothers, Charles, 148 Wellington st, E C
Crouch and Wilson, architects, &c., 69 Elizabeth st
Crouch, Mrs., 117 Gertrude st, F
Crouch, T. J., Argyle st, St K
Croucher, Mrs., Russell st
Crouchen, James R., 103 Victoria st east
Crow, John, plumber, Flem
Crowe, John, 158 Madeline st, Carl
Crowe, Stephen, 146 Elgin st, Carl
Crowell, E. L., 19 Lonsdale st west
Crowfoot, Frederick, 76 Kerr st, F
Crowl, John, bootmaker, Stanley st, E C
Crowl, J., draper, 146 Clarendon st, Em H
Crowl, Michael, 36 Elgin st, Carl
Crowl, Vincent, Sir Charles Darling hotel, corner Morris and Little Nelson sts, Wmn
Crowley, J., 58 George st, F
Crown Lands offices, Latrobe st west
Crown Solicitors and Law offices, 192 Collins st east
Crowson, Samuel, 141 Johnston st, E C
Crowson, Thomas, Charles st, F
Crowther, John Edward, agent, Fitzroy st, St K
Crowther, Thos., Richmond terrace, Rd
Cruickshank, Wm., shoemaker, 42 High st, St K
Cruickshank, Wm., and Co., outfitters, Beach st, and Bay st, San
Croley, A., importer and manufacturer, 41 Flinders lane east
Crump, John, Condell st, F
Crump, Wm., importer of boots and shoes, 133 Little Collins st east
Crutch, Wm., coachbuilder, 5, 7, and 11 Latrobe st, west
Crutchfield, Henry, engraver, 93 Little Collins st east
Cuddy, John, Charles st, Pra
Culhane, John, Hotham arms hotel, Leveson st, Hot
Cullen, James, Argyle st west, St K
Cullen, P., painter, 81 Errol st, Hot
Cullen, Park, 5 Victoria st, Hot
Cullen, Richard, 20 Hoden st, W M
Culliford, S., 40 Chetwynd st, Hot
Culligan, John, Curzon st, Hot
Cullingford, Hector, Victoria st, Hot
Cully, C. J., Cremorne st, Richmond
Cully, Mrs., Osborne st south, Wmn
Cully, Mrs., Pelham st, Carl
Cultra, Wm., seedsman, 293 Elizabeth st
Cumberland, Wm., Bridge road, Rd
Cumming, J., farrier, a'Beckett st east
Cuming, A., commission agent, 18 Collins st east, and Park st, S Y
Cumming, Alexander, 49 Drummond st, Carl
Cumming, Duncan, 39 Victoria parade, F

Cumming, James, 123 Elgin st, Carl
Cumming, James, surgeon dentist, 67 Swanston st
Cumming, John, Waterman's arms, 8 Little Collins st west
Cumming, Wm., Acland st, St K
Cummings, Hugh, Berkeley st, Carl
Cummins, —, Barkly st, Carl
Cummins, James, 92 Argyle st, F
Cummins, Mrs., 180 Napier st, F
Cummins, Richard, machine maker and sewer, &c., 110 Collins st east
Cunningham and Macredie, wool brokers, and stock and station agents, wool stores, Collins st west
Cuningham, F., Chambers' terrace, Gardiner's creek road, Pra
Cuningham, H., Jolimont
Coolif, Elias, grocer, 219 Bourke st east
Cunnett, Ann, Dover road, Wmn
Cunningham, —, Abbotsford st, W M
Cunningham, —, Adderly st, W M
Cunningham, A., St Kilda road, Bin
Cunningham, P., builder, St Regent st, F
Cunningham, Alexander (manager of National Bank), Haw
Cunningham, C., Albert st, Pra
Cunningham, Frank, Gardiner's creek road, Pra
Cunningham, George, M.L.A., Parliament house
Cunningham, Gray, 146 Queen st
Cunningham, J., 54 Victoria st, W M
Cunningham, James, 226 Johnston st, E C
Cunningham, P., builder, 35 Regent st, F
Cunningham, Robert F., carpenter, 10 Elizabeth st north
Cunningham, R., ironmonger, Chapel st, Pra
Cunningham, S., High st, Pra
Cunningham, Mrs., Wellington st, E C
Cunnington, John, solicitor, &c., for taking affidavits, 45 Swanston st
Cupit, Charles, baker and confectioner, 56 Queen st
Curator of Intestate Estates Office, Temple court, Collins st west
Currier and Adel, importers, 21 Market st
Curle, Wm., 16 Curzon st, Hot
Curley, J., Arthur's Seat road, Bin
Carr, E. M., Gardiner's creek road, Pra
Carr, R., Napier st, F
Carms, Mrs., 136 Johnston st, F
Curran, Mrs, 34 Stanley st, W M
Currie, Anthony, 93 Lygon st, Carl
Currie, Archibald, Albert st
Currie, J., china store, 76 Wellington st, E C
Currie, John, grocer and wine and spirit merchant, corner of Swanston st and Post Office place
Currie, Michael, grocer, 249 Smith st, F
Currie, William, land agent, 29 York st, Em H
Currill, Donald, 20 Barry st, Carl

Curry, J., Thompson st south, Wmn
Curry, Joseph, 65 George st, F
Curry, Patrick, Council hotel, Kew
Curson, A. J., 39 Cremorne st, Rd
Curtain, John, Leicester hotel, Leicester st, Carl
Curtain, Michael, 170 Victoria parade, E M
Curtayne, John, manager Union Bank, Southey st, St K
Curten, John, 2 Queensberry st, Carl
Curtis, —, Balllie st., Hot
Curtis, Charles, Kew
Curtis, Charles, 195 Lygon st, Carl
Curtis, Chas , 39 Three chain road, Em H
Curtis, C., Wells st. Btn
Curtis, Chas., fruiterer, Smith st, E C
Curtis, J. H., 28 Drummond st, Carl
Curtis, Matthew, St. Andrew's st, Btn
Curtis, Matthew, broker, 70 Flinders lane west, and Dorcas st, Em H
Curtis, Miss M , Powlett st, E M
Curtis, Mrs., Johnston st, F
Curtis, Miss, 16 Victoria parade, E M
Curtis, M., 9 Faraday st, Carl
Curtis, Peter, 160 Johnston st, E C
Curtis, S., coachbuilder, 123 Gertrude st, F
Curtis, Samuel, 9 Alma st, St K
Curtis, Thomas, grocer, 95 and 170 High st, St K
Cortis, Thomas W., 50 Villiers st, Hot
Curtise, H. C., surgeon, Railway place, San
Cusack, Roger, 27 Lygon st, Carl
Cushing, Joshua H., Grey st, St K
Custom House and Offices, Flinders st west, and Nelson place east, Wmn
Customs and Immigration Office, 27 Thompson st, Wmn
Cuthbert, A., Hanmer st, Wmn
Cuthbert, David, Henry st, F
Cuthbert, George, 54 Franklin st west
Cuthbert, John, 17 Richmond terrace, Rd
Cuthbert, William Wallace, stock and share broker, Hall of Commerce
Cuthbertson, R., Rowens parade, Rd
Cutler, Charles, 64 Oxford st, E C
Cutler, Chas., watchmaker, Lennox st, Rd
Cutler, Christopher, Bricklayers' Arms hotel, Church st, Rd
Cutler, E., Union st, Rd
Cutler, George C., chemist, 38 Grattan st, Carl
Cutler, Wm., 66 Oxford st, E C
Cutolo, Signor, musical artist, Gardiner's creek road, S Y
Cutten, Charles E., solicitor, Greville st, Pra
Cuttle, Hannah, Curzon st, Hot
Cutts, W., carrier, New st, Btn
Cuts, W. H., M.D., 5 Collins st east, and 119 William st
Cutts, George, miller, Flem bank
Cutts, Henry, miller, Flem bank

D.

Dabbs, Charles, city inspector, Wilson st, Pra
Da Costa, H. F., 29 Gore st, F
Daer, Andrew, plumber, &c., Howard st, Hot
Daffron, J., 80 Drummond st, Carl
Dagg, Frederick, Moreland st, Fcy
Dagno, P., dairyman, 13 John st, Wmn
Daily, George P., 174 Napier st, F
Daily Law List, 56 Little Collins st west
Daintree, Richard, Wellington st, Btn
Daish, William, secretary to Second and Third Union Building Societies, &c., 82 Collins st east
Dakers, John, 191 Lonsdale st west
Dakers, John, 197 Lonsdale st west
Dakin, Thomas, builder, 40 and 111 Queen st
Dalcon, George, 6 Wellington st, E C
Dale, Mrs., Webb st, F
Dale, Mrs.. store, Strand, Wmn
Dale, Robert, typefounder, 31 Victoria st, Carl
Daley, John, undertaker, 193 Spring st
Daley, Wm., 23 Rathdowne st, Carl
Dalgarno, J., store, Douglas parade, Wmn
Dalgety and Co., merchants, 86 and 88 Bourke st west, and 59 Little Collins st west
Dalgrity, James, carpenter, Gipps st, E M
Dalglish, Andrew, Hoddle st, Rd
Dalglish and Adamson, grocers, 62 Cardigan st, Carl, and 113 Brunswick st, F
Dalglish, Wm., 70 Cardigan st, Carl
Dall, Wm., builder, Alfred place, Collins st east
Dell, Wm. C., Victoria parade, E M
Dallachy, —, grocer, 138 Wellington st, E C
Dallas, John, Punt road, S Y
Dallaway, James S., basket maker, 20 Post Office place, and Fcy
Dally, J. G., draper, 120 Smith st, E C
Dally, John, woodyard, Bouverie st, Carl
Dally, Thomas, 10 Argyle st, F
D'Aloustel, Charles A., Carson's cottages, Collins st east
Dalrymple, —, 188 Church st, Rd
Dalrymple and Hudson, ship and commission agents, 23 Market st
Dalrymple, P. J., King st
Dalrymple, Thomas, wood and coal yard, Crockford st, San
Dalton, J., butcher, 49 Bank st west, Em H
Dalton, John, grocer, 343 Elizabeth st, and 2 Latrobe st
Dalton, Richard, store, Thompson st, South Wm
Dalton, W. H., 69 Bourke st west, and 15 Park st, Em H
Daly, —, Nicholson st, Carl

Daly, John, Barry st, Carl
Daly, John, Hill farm, Bk
Daly, Mrs., 93 Gore st, F
Dalzell, Wm. James, Haw
Dalzell, Robert, Drummond st, Carl
Dalziell, Wm., Birmingham hotel, 1 Johnston st west, F
Dame, Van Frederick, Marion st, F
Dammen, George, and Co., tobacconists, 62 Collins st east
Dampsey, M., Canning st, Carl
Damyon, James, customs agent and Russian consul, Market st
Dando, Henry, Graham st, San
Dane, Captain J., M.L.A., Esplanade, 8 K
Dance, Abraham, boot and shoemaker, 12 Ann st, Wmn
Dangerfield James, Dryburgh st, Hot
Danheir, P., store, Leicester st, Carl
Daniel, Charles, 83 Nelson road, Em U
Daniel, Rev. G., Bm
Daniel, W., Douglas parade, Wmn
Daniel, Wm., Neptune st, St K
Daniell, W., carpenter, Church st, Rd
Dardancill, D., merchant, 32 King st, and William st, Bm
Daniels, George F., 50 Little Latrobe st
Daniels, Henry, Curzon st, Hot
Daniels, Mrs., 26 Fitzroy st, E C
Daniels, Thomas, grocer, 135 Little Lonsdale st east
Danker, H., blacksmith, Graham st, San
Danks, John, and Co., importers and candle mould manufacturers, 42 Bourke st west
Danks, John, Park st, Em H
Danks, Samuel, Park st, Em H
Dannehey, John, cab proprietor, Alfred place, Collins st west
Dannelli, S., macaroni manufacturer, Sydney road, Bk
Danworth, P., 4 Trafalgar place, Hot
Darby, J. C., brazier, 65 Brunswick st, F
Darby, P., furniture dealer, 78 Brunswick st, F
Darby, Richard, tinsmith, Sackville st, E C
Darby, W., Cecil st east, Wmn
Darbyshire, G. C., C.E., 66 Temple court, Collins st west, and Wyndham, Werribee
Darbyshire, J., King and Jeffcott sts
Darbyshire, Jas., gardener, Cochrane st, Bm
D'Aranjo, Mdm., 5 Albert st, E M
Darcy, James, Rouse st, San
D'Arcy, —, Otter st, E C
D'Arcy, Thomas, shoemaker, 119 Leveson st, Hot
Dare, C., fruiterer, Gardiner's creek road, Pra
Dare, John George, money broker and insurance agent, 114 Elizabeth st
Darey, J., 215 Swan st, Rd
Dark, Stephen, bootmaker, 5 Victoria st, Carl

Dargan, Richard, 127 Johnston st, E C
Darling Quartz Mining Company, 56 Elizabeth st
Darling, Rev. H., 37 Three Chain road, Em H
Darling, T., Higbett st, Rd
Darlow, H., Nth
Darlow, Wm., Palmerston st, Carl
Darvern, F., boarding-house, 50 Latrobe st east
Darvall, Tom, Davis st, Pra
Daubeny, Wm., 21 Cecil st, Wmn
Daugleish, Alexander, Nott st, San
Daunt, Edward R., commission agent, 85 Queen st
Davenport, J., Rosslyn st, W M
Davenport, J., 108 Moray st, Em H
Davey, John, 89 Leveson st, Hot
Davey, James, bootmaker, 9 Bouverie st, Carl
Davey, Joseph, baker, Flemington road, Hot
Davey, Joseph, Queensberry st, Hot
David, A., 207 Clarendon st, Em H
David, Thomas, 15 Steredore st, Wmn
Davidson, A., tobacconist, 123 King st
Davidson, A., baker, 58 Victoria st, Rd
Davidson, Archd., grocer, 113 Collins st east
Davidson, Churchill, Argyle st, St K
Davidson, Edwin, bootmaker, 167 Fitzroy st, F
Davidson, Elizabeth, Sir John Franklyn hotel, Wellington st, E C
Davidson, H., builder, 56 Wellington st, E C
Davidson, J., 1 Victoria terrace, Cardigan st, Carl
Davidson, John, 121 Steredore st, Wmn
Davidson, James, storekeeper, corner Heath and Raglan sts, San
Davidson, J. M., 187 Clarendon st, Em H
Davidson, John S., outfitter, 44 Elizabeth st
Davidson, K., Hanover st, Wmn
Davidson, Mrs., 32 Franklin st, W M
Davidson, Mrs., 45 Thompson st, Wmn
Davidson, Thomas, 15 Russell st
Davidson, Wm., butcher, 138 Smith st, E C
Davies and Son, coopers, 270 Elizabeth st
Davies, B. G., M.L.A., Gertrude st, F
Davies, Charles, solicitor, 37 Gertrude st, F
Davies, Christopher, and Davies, drapers, 107 Brunswick st, F
Davies, Cornelius, grocer, 31 Victoria st, Carl
Davies, D., 42 Queensberry st, Carl
Davies, D. W., chemist, Johnston st, E C
Davies, Francis W., Harmsworth st, E C
Davies, George, cooper, 270 Elizabeth st
Davies, George, 1 Jeffcott st, W M
Davies, H., cabinetmaker, 35 Johnston st, E C
Davies, H., 70 Park st, Em H

Davies, John, 23 Park st west, Em H
Davies, John, 146 Lonsdale st west
Davies, John, Nelson road, Em H
Davies, John, 95 Chapel st, Pra
Davies, John, Halfway House hotel, York st west, Em H
Davies, John, clothier and outfitter, 1 Collins st west
Davies, M., dressmaker, Franklin st
Davies, Maurice Coleman, ship broker, &c., 37 Market st
Davies, Miss H., school, 11 Spring st
Davies, Mrs., 97 Cecil st, Em H
Davies, Mrs., 27 Church st, Em H
Davies, Mrs., Chapel st, Pra
Davies, Mrs., Chambers st, Pra
Davies, R. H., churn maker, 284 King st
Davies, Rev. John, Kew
Davies, Robt. B., solicitor, 78 Elizabeth st
Davies, Stephen, painter, 105 Little Bourke st west
Davies, Wm., 35 Cremorne st, Rd
Davies, Wm., 167 Lonsdale st west
Davies, Wm., photographer, 5 Collins st west, 7, 91, and 94 Bourke st east
Davies, Wm., clothier and outfitter, 81 and 85 Swanston st
Davies, Wm., Royal Mail hotel, 39 Wellington st, Pra
Davis, Aaron, 76 Cobden st, Em H
Davis, Aaron H., Australian Arms hotel, 170 Little Bourke st east
Davis, Aquila John, photographer, 83 Swanston st
Davis, Alexander, baker, Church st, Rd
Davis and Garrett, wine and spirit merchants, 19 Elizabeth st
Davis, Charles, 65 Cremorne st, Rd
Davis, Charles, Canning st, Carl
Davis, D. E., agent, 42 Elizabeth st
Davis, E., broker, Hall of Commerce, Collins st west
Davis, Edgar, Canning st, Carl
Davis, Edward, furniture dealer, St. David st, F
Davis, Edward, Rosslyn st, W M
Davis, Emanuel, Burnett st, St K
Davis, F., 89 Otter st, E C
Davis, F. H., dairyman, 124 Gertrude st, F
Davis, G., and Co., timber merchants, Spencer st market
Davis, H. B., grocer, 35 Wellington st, E C
Davis, Hugh, Retreat inn, Nott st, San
Davis, Isaac, 120 Latrobe st east
Davis, Isaac, 3 Canning st, Carl
Davis, J., 149 Victoria parade, F
Davis, J., furniture dealer, 47 Gertrude st, F
Davis, J., 93 Chapel st, Pra
Davis, J., clothier and draper, 321 Elizabeth st
Davis, J., gardener, New st, Btn
Davis, J. F., boot and shoe dealer, High st, Pra

Davis, J., 172 Smith st, E C
Davis, J. G., 75 Bouverie st, Carl
Davis, James, moulder, 108 Latrobe st west
Davis, James, store, 24 Bridge road, Rd
Davis, John, 208 King st
Davis, John, grocer, Sydney road, Bk
Davis, John, 53 Brunswick st, F
Davis, John, 87 Napier st, Em H
Davis, Joseph, 90 Drummond st, Carl
Davis, Joseph, 149 Victoria parade, F
Davis, Joseph, dealer, 118 Latrobe st east
Davis, Joseph, Hoddle st, Rd
Davis, L. M., Surrey hotel, Lennox st, Rd
Davis, Levinson, gold broker, 95 Elizabeth st
Davis, Morris C., Barkly st, St K
Davis, Mrs. E., tailoress, 33 Franklin st west
Davis, Mrs., 139 Victoria parade, F
Davis, Mrs., Fawkner st, St. K
Davis, Mrs., Nott st, San
Davis, Mrs., 11 Montague st, Em H
Davis, P., Temple court, Collins st west
Davis, Peter S., barrister, Temple court, Collins st west
Davis, Peter, 3 Royal terrace, Nicholson st, F
Davis, R., 136 Eastern road, Em H
Davis, Robert, Fairie st, Young st, F
Davis, Robert, Berkeley st, Carl
Davis, Samuel, 133 Moor st, F
Davis, T. H., and Co., wine and spirit merchants, cellars Hall of Commerce
Davis, T. H., Wmn
Davis, Thomas, Vine hotel, 192 Bridge road, Rd
Davis, Wm., painter, 11 Peel st, Hot
Davis, Wm., grocer, Leicester st, Carl
Davis, Wm. J., 9 Henry st, F
Davis, Wm., Octavia st, St K
Davis, Wm., Greville st, Pra
Davis, Woolf, general dealer, 111 Russell st
Davison, G., storekeeper, Plenty road, Nth
Davison, Henry, Swan st, Rd
Davison, J., 59 Condell st, F
Davison, James and George, brassfounders, 76 Flinders lane east
Davison, Robert, grocer, Blackwood st, Hot
Davison, Wm., boot dealer, 136 Bridge road, Rd
Davy, Alfred Geo., acting secretary Northern Assurance, 105 Collins st west
Davy, George, 75 Drummond st, Carl
Davy, John, wine and spirit merchant, 247 Swanston st
Davy, T., Nth
Daw, David, 81 Cecil st, Wmn
Dawbarn, J., merchant, Moylan's buildings, Flinders lane west
Dawbarn, Seacombe, broker, &c., 76 Collins st west

Dawbarn, Wm., 181 Church st, Rd
Dawbarn, Wm. H., aerated water manufacturer, Bay st, San
Dawes, Mrs., dressmaker, 73 Lygon st, Carl
Dawkins, Mrs., draper, Hoddle st, E C
Dawson, A., 103 Argyle st, F
Dawson, A. J., 5 Westgarth st, F
Dawson, C. J., barrister, 36 Temple court, 75 Little Collins st west
Dawson, David, 122 Leicester st, F
Dawson, Francis, Derby st, E C
Dawson, H., 71 Kerr st, F
Dawson, James, carpenter, Hawdon st, Held
Dawson, James, 7 Bendigo st, Hot
Dawson, John, 45 Jeffcott st, W M
Dawson, M., Phoenix park, Bk
Dawson, M., 118 Johnston st, F
Dawson, Michael, 62 Swanston st
Dawson, Mrs., Commercial road, Pra
Dawson, Mrs., 75 Rose st, F
Dawson, Mrs., Williams road, S Y
Dawson, R. H., 35 Park st, Em H
Dawson, Richard, 35 Dorcas st, Em H
Dawson, T., 7 Carlton terrace, King William st, F
Dawson, Thomas, Sidney road, Bk
Dawson, W., Howard st, W M
Day, —, 160 Moray st, Em H
Day, Alfred, Argyle st, F
Day, C. R., 23 Brunswick st, F
Day, Cephas, bellhanger and gasfitter, Drummond st, Carl
Day, Charles, chemist, 27 Lonsdale st west
Day, Charles Robert, cab owner, 25 Leveson st, Hot
Day, F. J., Whitehall st, Fcy
Day, Henry, butcher, 206 Stephen st
Day, John, Millswyn st, S Y
Day, Mrs., draper, Drummond st, Carl
Daylesford Extension Gold Mining Company, 9 Elizabeth st
Dean, Lester, 1 Villiers st, Hot
Dean, Wm., importer of paints, paperhangings, &c., 67 Elizabeth st
Deans, Archibald, 32 Oxford st, E C
Dear, John, 31 Stanley st, W M
Dean, Christopher, Esplanade, St K
Deacon, Charles, Graham st, San
Deacon, Mrs., machine sewer, Graham st, San
Deaf and Dumb Institution, Commercial road, Pra
Deakin, Sam., architect, and C. E., 53 Dorcas st, Em H
Deakin, Wm., Domain st, Pra
Dean, B., grocer, Chapel st, Pra
Dean, George, Bay st, San
Dean, George, 37 Cremorne st, Rd
Dean, J., 7 Peel st, W M
Dean, Joseph, Capel st, Hot
Dean, Joseph, grocer, 225 Church st, Rd
De Beer, Samuel, ship broker, 1 Queen st

De Basto, Antonio, dining-rooms, 77 Flinders st west
De Beaumont, Madame, confectioner, 223 Bourke st east
Debeaux, A., pleasure gardens, Turnbull's point, S Y
De Blaquiere, G., signwriter, High st, St K, and Nelson st, Pra
Debney, George, currier, Flora bank
Decourtet, Madame, dress and stay maker, 90 Russell st
Dedman, James, 5 Macarthur place, Carl
Do Dollon, Allmant, colonial wine merchant and luncheon rooms, 45 Swanston st
Dee, W., 215 George st, F
Deeble, Henry J., corn and flour factor, 144 Smith st, E C
Deely, Thomas, 6 Pelham st, Carl
De Freitas, A., restaurant, 20 Bourke st east
Degraves, Wm., and Co., merchants, millers, and wool stores, 10 Flinders lane east, and Flinders st east ; and bonded stores, 1 Russell st
Degraves, Wm., M.L.C., 182 Collins st east
De Gruchy and Leigh, engravers and lithographers, 47 Elizabeth st
De Gruchy, Charles, Berkeley st, Carl
De Gruchy, Henry George, Domain road, S Y
De Gruchy, W., Argus agency, 205 Victoria parade, F C
Dehnert, Robert, 325 Victoria st, E C
Dehnert, Wm., hairdresser, 86 Victoria st, Rd
De Jacques, J., greengrocer, 3½ Stanley st, E C
De Lacey, Allen, Elgin st, Carl
De Lacey, Francis, 65 Drummond st, Carl
De Lagarde, Edward, watchmaker and jeweller, 53 Bourke st east
Delabonty, J., Punt Inn, Geelong road, Fcy
Delaney, Miss, dressmaker, 10a Lonsdale st west
Delaney, Miss, 9 Gloucester terrace, Fitzroy st, St K
Delaney, Mrs., 110 Lonsdale st west
Delaney, W. A., Fitzgerald st, Pra
Delbridge, Edward, sen., builder, 113 Kerr st, F
Delbridge, Edward, builder, 138 Moor st, F
Dell, George, gingerbeer manufacturer, Peel st, E C
Delves, Thomas, general dealer, Stanley st, E C
Demaine, Charles D., printer, 27 Market st and Nth
De Morton, R., 36 Market st, Em H
Dempsey, James, Beehive hotel, Blackwood st, Hot

Dempster, Andrew, plumber and gasfitter, 89 Russell st
Denby, J., dealer, Capel st, Hot
Denby, Mrs., Hoddle st, E C
Denehy, John, baker, Latrobe parade, Collins st east
Denham, Mrs., Victoria st, St K
Denham, Thomas, saddler, Moonee Ponds, Ess
Denham, W., Walsh st, W M
Denasm, Wm., 57 Leicester st, Carl
Denhorm, Wm., 10 Barry st, Carl
Denis Brothers, watchmakers and jewellers, 72 and 74 Bourke st east
Denis, W. H., Nth
Denison Plains Pastoral Company, Limited, 69 Bourke st east
Denler, Philip, store, Queensberry st, Carl
Denman, Reuben, 74 Victoria st, W M
Denne, M. E., clothing manufacturer, 31 Gertrude st, F
Denney, Samuel, Rowena parade, Rd
Denning, C. P., professor of dancing, 180 Little Collins st
Dennis, Alfred, Charles st, Prn
Dennis, Sullivan, Rock of Cashel Inn, 93 Little Lonsdale st east
Dennis, William, 51 Oxford st, E C
Denny, J. S., Rotherwood st, Rd
De Norton, R., 60 Dorcas st, Em II
Denston, Valentine, storekeeper, Bay st, Btn
Denton, James, coachbuilder, 7 Little Lonsdale st east
Denton, Mrs., William st north
Denton, W. P., founder, Franklyn st, W M
Denty, Mrs., dressmaker, 143 Smith st, F
De Olivera, D., 170 Madeline st, Carl
De Pass Bros. & Co., merchants, 40 Elizabeth st
De Pass, John, Darling st, Prn
De Pauw, Pierre, Garibaldi arms, 12 Little Collins st east
De Pietriche, Ferdinand, Turkish baths, Lonsdale st east
Derby, —, Illawarra st, Wmn
Dergie, Alexander, 39 Dryburgh st, Hot
Derham, Frederick, Palmerston st, Carl
Derham, John, Cavan hotel, Queensberry st, Carl
Derham, Wm., 52 Lygon st, Carl
Dernelly, —, butcher, Johnston st, E C
De Roman, Mrs., artificial flour manufacturer, 30 Latrobe st east
Derrett, Robert, bookseller and stationer, Bay st, San
Derrick, Anthony, 13 Victoria st, Carl
Derrick, John, 115 Fitzroy st, F
Derrick, Joseph, school, Brighton st, Rd
Derrick, Mrs., dressmaker, 69 Kerr st, F
Derrick, R., 156 Young st, F
Derrick, Wm., Kew
Derwent and Tamar Fire and Marine Assurance Co., 11 Little Collins st west

Desailly, F. W. and G. P., office, 107 Collins st west
Desailly, F. W., Btn
Desailly, G. P., East Btn
Deslanders, —, 48 Coventry st, Em II
Deslandes, Philip, Stawell st, W M
Detective Police office, 146 Little Collins st east
Dethridge and Benson, photographers, Bay st, San
Detmold, Wm., bookbinder, paper ruler, and account book manufacturer, 35 Collins st east, and 25 Little Collins st east
Deutch, Mrs., 65 King st, William st, F
Devaney, Thomas, cooper, 262 Smith st, E C
Devenish, Matthew, 53 Kerr st, F
Devenport, George, 22 Bridport st, Em II
Devenport, Thomas, wood and coal yard, 51 Napier st, Em II
Dever, J., Cecil st, Wmn
Deverell, Robert, Union st, Pra
Devereux, George, 8 Palmer st, F
Devereux, John, 16 Marian st, F
Devereux, Mrs., 48 Villiers st, Hot
Devernay, Wm., 9 Bouverie st, Carl
Devine, David, 27 Courtnay st, Hot
Devine, John, Britannia inn, 75 Queen st
Devine, John, grocer, 27 Leveson st, Hot
Devine, Mrs., 78 George st, F
Devine, Thomas, Miller st, W M
Devlin, Capt. Arthur, Wellington parade, E M
Devlin, Matthew, Prince Albert hotel, Argyle st, E C
Devonshire, —, 114 Swanston st
Devoy, Wm., Eagle hotel, Swanston st
Dewar, —, plumber, Gardiner's creek road, Pra
De Wardt, Thomas, 96 Hanmer st, Wmn
Dewey, C., 251 Church st, Rd
De Young, A. S., 5 Peel st, W M
Diamond, Joseph, Chetwynd st, Hot
Diamond, Thomas, Railway place, San
Dias, Daniel, letter carrier, 30 Little Lonsdale st east
Dias, Mark, Church st, Rd
Diason, R. B., Sydney road, Bk
Dibble, E., 71 York st east, Em II
Dick, Archibald, baker, Commercial road, Pra
Dick, G., bootmaker, Nicholson st, Carl
Dick, John, Abbotsford st, Hot
Dick, John, 36 Baillie st, Hot
Dick, Mrs., Wright's lane, Lonsdale st west
Dick, Russell, bootmaker, 77 Gertrude st, F
Dickason, Robert, coachbuilder, 173 Bridge road, Rd
Dickenson, E., butcher, 101 Victoria st, E C
Dickenson, Edward, accountant, Nelson st, Wr

Dickens, Jabez, carpenter, Elgin st, Carl
Dickenson, John, 111 Gertrude st, F
Dicker, Thomas, Alma st, St K
Dicker's Mining Record, 31 Collins st west
Dickie, John, plumber, 188 Bourke st east
Dickins, George, 112 Nicholson st, F
Dickins, Mrs., Hoddle st, E C
Dickins, Wm., Church st, Rd
Dickinson, C. B., solicitor, 67 Bourke st west
Dickinson, Edward, Nelson st, Pra
Dickinson, John, Hanover st, F
Dickinson, Paul, 3 Charles st, F
Dickinson, Rev. R. B., parsonage, Clarendon st, Em H
Dickmann, Hans A., Railway hotel, Swan st, Ild
Dickson, Charles, builder, Raglan st, San
Dickson, D., 92 Cardigan st, Carl
Dickson, Henry, Carlisle st, East St. K
Dickson, J., Roden st, W M
Dickson, James, carpenter, 36 Palmer st, F
Dickson, James, vinegar and blacking manufacturer, 9 Latrobe st east, and James st, Ild
Dickson, John, Yarra st, Fcy
Dickson, Mrs., 28 Napier st, F
Dickson, P., Argyle st, St K
Dickson, Peter, Twyford st, South Wmn
Dickson, Robert, carpenter, Gipps st, E M
Dickson, Robert, settler, Ascot vale, Flem
Dickson, Robertson, and Co., merchants, 23 Flinders lane east
Dickson, Thomas, accountant and mining agent, 66 Little Collins st west, and William st, 8 Y
Dickson, W. H., Howe crescent, Em H
Dickson, Wm., carpenter and joiner, Canning st, Carl
Dickson, Wm., Fitzroy st, F
Dickson, Wm., Prince of Wales hotel, Fitzroy st, St K
Dickson, Williams, and Co., merchants, 10 Queen st
Diener, J., 21 Lygon st, Carl
Dihm, E., tobacconist, 231 Lygon st, Carl
Dight, Wm. P, 112 Gore st, F
Dike, Norris W., coachbuilder, 16 Stephen street
Dikes, H., boarding-house, Flinders st west
Dill, George, Rotherwood st, Carl
Dillaway, Joseph, general dealer, Cremorne st, Rd
Dillet, J., Flemington road, Hot
Dillon and Burrows, confectioners, Latrobe st west
Dillon, D., 45 Napier st, F
Dillon, James, Preston
Dillon, Wm., blacksmith, Byron st, Hot
Dillon, Wm., 99 Westgarth st, F
Dillon, Wm. Henry, pastrycook, Latrobe st west
Dillon, Wm., tinsmith, Curzon st, Hot

Dingles, John, 11 Dover road, Wmn
Dinon, Maximilian, 76 Leicester st, Carl
Dinte, Hymen, tailor, 238 Bourke st east
Dinwoodie, J., Powlett st, E M.
Dirce, John, weaver, 66 Ann st, Wmn
Disher, Robert, New Bridge hotel, Gardiner's creek road, Pra
Disher, Samuel L., Pier hotel, Bay st, San
Dishington, Robert, grocer, Victoria st, Hot
Dismore, Charles, hairdresser, 29½ Bourke st west
Disney, J., Sir R. Nickle hotel, Haw
Diver, James, boot dealer, Chapel st, Pra
Divine, R., store, 121 Little Bourke st east
Diviney, Mrs., Smith st, E C
Dixon, Alexander, 123 Cremorne st, Rd
Dixon, Augustus, Shipwrights' Arms hotel, 92 Moray st, Em H
Dixon, Edward Francis, butcher, Dorcas st, and 37 Nelson st, Em H
Dixon, Edward, Lothian st, Hot
Dixon, Francis, Punt road, Rd
Dixon, F. B, Cornish Arms hotel, corner Latrobe and Stephen sts
Dixon, Henry, 24 Railway place, Wmn
Dixon, J., Punt road, Wr
Dixon, James, butcher, 152 High st, St K
Dixon, James, 28 Leveson st, Hot
Dixon, John, Gipps st, E M
Dixon, John, Wilson st, Pra
Dixon, Major, slater, 76 George st, F
Dixon, Mary, Church st, Rd
Dixon, Miss, George st, F
Dixon, Mrs., 110 Fitzroy st, F
Dixon, Philip G., aerated water manufacturer, 32 Rosslyn st, W M
Dixon, S. C., school, Queen st
Dixon, Thomas, 50 Osborne st, Wmn
Dixon, Wm., 58 Smith st, E C
Dixon, Wm., bookseller, 99 Little Collins st east
Dobb, John, Star and Garter hotel, 160 Bridge road, Rd
Dobbie, Andrew, 69 York st, Em H
Dobbin, Wm., Twyford st, Wmn
Dobbins, R. H., Miller st, Bk
Dobbs, Wm. W., Gardiner's creek road, S Y
Dobell, P., bootmaker, Hoddle st, E C
Doben, Josephine, greengrocer, Robe st, St K
Dobie, John, carpenter, Chapel st, Pra
Dobson, Frank S., barrister, 73 Little Collins st west
Dobson, James, estate agent, Inkerman st west, St K
Dobson, John, builder, Darby alley, off 9 Little Collins st east
Dobson, Joseph, carpenter and builder, off 9 Little Collins st east
Dobson, Josephine, greengrocer, Robe st, St K
Docker, E. W., High st, Pra

Dockyard, Government, Nelson place, Wm
Dodd and Thompson, merchants, 26 Queen street
Dodd, George, contractor, 18 Otter st, E C
Dodd, John, blacksmith, Flem
Dodd, R., shipwright, River side, South bank
Dodd, W. H., Claremont, Kew
Dodds, Samuel, Brighton st, Rd
Dodds, Thomas, 4 Palmer st, F
Doddy, John, 151 Cardigan st, Carl
Dodge, James, 83 Westgarth st, F
Dodgshun, Austin, and Co., warehousemen, 6 Elizabeth st
Dodgshun, James, Asling st, Bn
Dodgson, John H., merchant, 5 Bond st, Flinders lane west
Dodgson, Joseph, importer, 5 Bond st
Dodgson, Thomas, merchant, 5 Bond st
Dods, Alexander, Bridge road, Rd
Dods, B. H., Ferrars st, Em H
Dods, W., Sydney road, Bk
Dodson, G. E., machinist, 171 Victoria st, E C
Doe, Mrs., 214 Wellington st, E C
Doggett, Thomas, 35 Curzon st, Hot
Dogherty, C., Roose st, San
Doherty, J., 101 Bank st west, Em H
Doherty, J. D., Laurel hotel, Flem
Doherty, John G., stockade, Flem
Doherty, Wm., sculptor, 96 Queensberry st, Carl
Dolan, C., Adderley st, W M
Dolan, John, bootmaker, 160 Stephen st
Dolan, Patrick, grocer, 119 Faraday st, Carl
Dolding, Thos., chairman District Board, Pent
Dollchs, J., 115 Little Bourke st west
Dollard, Thomas, Phœnix hotel, corner of Clarendon and York sts, Em H
Don, C. J., 100 Oxford st, E C
Don, James W., chemist, Swan st, Rd
Donahoe, John, 35 Franklin st, W M
Donahoe, Patrick, Curzon hotel, 60 Curzon st, Hot
Donald, Charles, Richmond terrace, Rd
Donald, George, plumber, 91 Victoria st, Hot
Donald, James, tanner, Flem bank
Donald, Joseph, 37 Leveson st, Hot
Donaldson and Robertson, grocers, &c., Gardiner's creek road, Pra
Donaldson, C. A., 10 Franklin st west
Donaldson, D., 39 Moray place, Em H
Donaldson, David, 64 Arden st, Hot
Donaldson, George, 5 Barkly st, Carl
Donaldson, H. B., and Co., ship chandlers, Beach st, San
Donaldson, J., Gardiner's creek road, S Y
Donaldson, James, 67 Young st, F
Donaldson, James, shoemaker, 72 Stevedore st, Wm

Donaldson, James, Ivanhoe, Heid
Donaldson, John, Arden st, Hot
Donaldson, John, Ivanhoe, Heid
Donaldson, John, market gardener, Brown st, Heid
Donaldson, Miss, 101 Gertrude st, F
Donaldson, Mrs. E., 95 Raglan st, Em H
Donaldson, Mrs., 136 Gore st, F
Donaldson, Wm., Commercial road, Pra
Donaldson, W. H., and Co., upholsterers, &c., 71 Bourke st west, and 10 Franklin st west
Donaldson, W. H., 10 Franklin st west
Donelly, Peter, 20 Cardigan st, Carl
Donne, John, news agent and bookseller, Melbourne and Hobson's Bay United Railway Stations
Donne, Samuel, news agent, Domain road, S Y
Donnellan, Thomas, 116 York st, Em H
Donnelly, Abraham, Madeline st, Carl
Donnelly, John, 15 Greeves st, F
Donnelly, Peter, Chambers st, Pra
Donney, George, Leveson st, Hot
Donnolly, P. J., grain broker and auctioneer, Collins st west
Donlmn, Wm., draper, 32 Madeline st, Carl
Donohoe, Francis, Wreckyn st, Hot
Donohoe, John, Barkly st, Carl
Donohoe, Mrs., Dudley st, Wm
Donohoe, P., 62 Gore st, F
Donohoe, W. M., grocer and wine and spirit merchant, 187 Bourke st east
Donovan and Mulcahey, wholesale grocers, 28 Lonsdale st east, 179 Elizabeth st, and 6 Lonsdale st west
Donovan, J., greengrocer, Bedford st, Hot
Donovan, Margaret, Albert Park hotel, Moray st, Em H
Donovan, Michael, Hawke st, W M
Donovan, Mrs., 29 Cobden st, Em H
Donovan, P., 52 Market st, Em H
Donovan, Patrick, 179 Elizabeth st
Donovan, Stephen, Nicholson st, F
Doody, Dennis, tailor, 7 Fitzroy st, St K
Doody, W., baker, Miller st, W M
Doolan, B., blacksmith, Pres
Doolan, D., 107 Bank st west, Em H
Dooley, Martin, toll collector, Heidelberg road
Dooley, Michael, National hotel, Queensberry st, Carl
Dooley, Wm., Queensberry st, Hot
Dupping, Wm., Alma st, St K
Doran, Captain George, 6 Bank st west, Em H
Doran, W., 51 Stanley st, W M
Doreton, F., Carlisle st, St K
Doris, Wm., Barry st, Carl
Dorming, C., Flemington road, Hot
Dorrell, Charles, general dealer, 160 Little Collins st east
D'Orsay, —, Canning st, Carl

Dorrington, John, grocer, 284 Brunswick st, F
Dott, James, Stawell st, W M
Doubleday, Joseph, hairdresser and phrenologist, 118 Bourke st east
Doubleday, Miss, Courteney st, Hot
Douch, Henry W., baker and confectioner, 52 Nelson place, Wmn
Dougall, Joseph, 30 George st, F
Dougharty, J. G., Elwood
Dougharty, Michael, 25 Bonverie st, Carl
Douglas, B., 179 Fitzroy st, F
Douglas, Duncan, baker, Alfred place, Collins st east
Douglas, Elizabeth, boardinghouse, 143 Collins st east
Douglas, Gabriel, watchmaker, 15 Little Lonsdale st east
Douglas, George, brassfounder, 110 Flinders lane east and 125 Flinders st west
Douglas, George, hay and corn store, 17 Madeline st, Carl
Douglas, Henry, Nelson place east, Wmn
Douglas, J., 131 Gertrude st, F
Douglas, S. T., Barkly st, Carl
Douglas, Samuel, shipsmith, 24 Little Nelson st, Wmn
Douglas, W., architect, 6 Grattan st, Carl
Douglas, W. S., Millswyn st, S Y
Douglas, Wm., painter, 53 Cardigan st, Carl
Douglas, Wm., builder, Chetwynd st, Hot
Douglas, Wm., Dow st, San
Douglass, Alfred, merchant, 55 Little Collins st east
Douglass, J., 137 Gertrude st, F
Douglass, Samuel, shipsmith, Railway place, San
Douglass, Wm., Farie st, Young st, F
Doull, —, 29 Napier st, F
Doutch, Wm., Barkly st, Carl
Dove, Alexander, J.P., Essex st, Fey
Dove, W., 193 Raglan st, Em H
Dove, Wm., Elgin st, Carl
Dow, James, F., engineer, 41 Swanston st, and 154 Bourke st west
Dow, Mrs. George, 27 Dorcas st, Em H
Dow, Robert, 14 Montague st, Em H
Dow, Wm., 11 Church st, Em H
Dow, Wm., 20 Raglan st, Em H
Doward, Edward, Ballaarat
Dowd, —, 122 Kerr st, F
Dowden, E. A., Ralston st, S Y
Dowden, G., smith, 199 Stephen st
Dowdle, George, 3 Bouverie st, Carl
Dowdle, Miss, ladies' school, 30 Regent st, F
Dowdle, Thomas, 78 Bouverie st, Carl
Dowell, J., 16 John st, Wmn
Dowell, Ronald, shipmaster, 14 John st, Wmn
Dowling, Andrew, Kildare hotel, 19 Little Collins st east
Dowling, David, 96 George st, F

Dowling, F. M. B., surgeon, 114 Collins st east
Dowling, J., cabinet maker and carver, 135 Argyle st, F
Dowling, James, 19 Johnston st, E C
Dowling, Mrs., milliner, 90 Park st, Em H
Dowling, P., blacksmith, 29 Rose st, F
Dowling, Patrick, Crockford st, San
Dowling, Patk, Plough hotel, Bourke st west
Dowling, Philip, free stores and contractor, 116 Collins st west, and 109 Flinders lane west
Dowling, Samuel, commission agent, 90 Park st, Em H
Dowling, Thomas H., marine storekeeper, 230 Lonsdale st east
Down, James, Acland st, St K
Downer, Mrs. Isabella, Richmond terrace, Rd
Downes, F., Windsor castle hotel, St David st, St K
Downes, James, farmer, Flem bank
Downey, C., shoemaker, 55 Errol st, Hot
Downey, Miss, machine sewer, Victoria st, W M
Downie and Murphy, soap and candle works, River side
Downie, Charles, Australia Felix hotel, 121 Bourke st east
Downie, J. T., 70 Fitzroy st, F
Downie, John, 6 Erroll st, Hot
Downie, Thomas, baker, 191 Clarendon st, Em H
Downie, Walter, grocer, 1 Curzon st, Hot
Downie, Wm., grocer, &c., 50 Wellington st, E C
Downing, George, 83 St. David st, F
Downing, Henry, Old Lincoln inn, 73 Cardigan st, Carl
Downing, J. B., Palmerston place, Madeline st, Carl
Downing, Robert, 7 Brunswick st, F
Downing, W., St. Andrew st, Btn
Downs, John, bootmaker, 162 Little Lonsdale st west
Downs, Wm., produce dealer, 166 Wellington st, E C
Downward, J., Church st, Btn
Dowson, —, 112 Argyle st, F
Doyle, Frederick, 114 Little Lonsdale st east
Doyle, James, Abbotsford st, Hot
Doyle, James, Leveson st, Hot
Doyle, John, 19 Baillie st, Hot
Doyle, Laurence, Wexford hotel, 143 Little Lonsdale st east
Doyle, Michael, 131 Flinders lane west
Doyle, Mrs., Nott st, San
Doyle, Patrick, Dryburgh st, Hot
Doyle, Peter, Peel st, Pra
Doyle, T., schoolmaster, Edward st, Bk
Doyle, Wm., 137 King st
Doyles, James, grocer, Bridge st, Rd

Doyne and La Touche, civil engineers, 62 Collins st west
Doyne, W. T., Alma st, St Kilda
Drake, Joseph, 58 Grant st, Em H
Drake, John, schoolmaster, Yarra st, E C
Drake, Mrs., Graham st, San
Drake, S., dealer, 236 Johnston st, E C
Draper, H. J. M., pilot, Douglas parade, Wmn
Draper, Mrs., straw hat maker, Punt road, Pra
Draper, Thomas, bootmaker, Punt road, Pra
Draper, Walter, importer, 164 Elizabeth st
Draper, W., Garden st, Pra
Drayton, Mrs., butcher, Cole st, Wmn
Drayton, Mrs. E., 64 Nelson place, Wmn
Dreakford, Henry, 4 Wellington st, E C
Dredge, P., schoolmaster, Preston
Dredge, Theophilus, customs agent, Custom-house, and Union st, St K
Drew Brothers, grocers, Chapel st, St K
Drew, G., 134 Moor st, F
Drew, George Robert, baker, 24 Gertrude st, F
Drew, J., Carlisle st east, St K
Drew, Joshua, 187 Lygon st, Carl
Drew, Josh., cabinetmaker, Drummond st, Carl
Drew, T., Berkeley st, Carl
Drew, W., 144 Johnston st, F
Drigalski, Mrs., 4 Falkland terrace, Greeves st, F
Drinkmill, John, gardener, 131 Nicholson st, F
Driscoll, Daniel, 196 Roswell st
Driscoll, E., 98 York st, Em H
Driscoll, Miss, 102 Lygon st, Carl
Drogaish, H., bootmaker, 114 Little Bourke st west
Drohan, John, blacksmith, 63 Bourke st west
Drooey, Edward, shoemaker, Flem
Droop, J. F., Pickett st, Fcy
Droohet, Bradley, and Toché, importers, 39 Little Collins st west
Droohet, Justin, Bay st, Btn
Druce, Wm., 69 Cobden st, Em II
Druids (Order of), Grand Lodge, Bull and Mouth, Bourke st east
Drummond's Point, Globe, and Nightingale Quartz Mining Companies, and Raspberry Creek Gold Mining Company, 9 Elizabeth st
Drummond, Robert, tailor, 17 Thompson st, Wmn
Drummond, Wm., Cowper st, Fcy
Drury, John, blacksmith, 85 Lonsdale st east
Dry, D., and Co., builders, 84 Napier st, F
Drysdale, Eisentaedter, and Co., office, 32 Collins st west
Drysdale, James, bonecrusher, Flem Bank
Drysdale, John, 70 Dudley st, W M

Drysdale, John, Punt hill, S Y
Drysdale, T., Brunswick st, F
Drysdale, Thomas A., Brunswick st, F
Drysdale, Wm., miller, Flem Bank
Dubbledson, A., grocer and outfitter, Beach st, San
Duck, H., carpenter, Nth
Duckett, Edward, wholesale ironmonger, 24 Lonsdale st east, and Tennyson st, St K
Dudgeon, John, Dudley st, W M
Dudley, Carr, butcher, Church st, Rd
Dudley, John, watchmaker, High st, Pra
Dudley, Joseph, Hoddle st, E C
Duerdin, James, solicitor and notary public, 105 Collins st west
Duerdin, John, solicitor and notary public, Stephen st south
Duff, A., baker, Gardiner's creek road, Pra
Duff, Robert, 194 Cardigan st, Carl
Duffers, —, 21 Napier st, F
Duffett, Grant, and Woolcott, solicitors, &c., 83 Collins st west
Duffetts, J. G., llaw
Duffy, —, master mariner, 26 Church st, Em H
Duffy, W., shoemaker, Hodder st, Btn
Du Froeq and Booth, woollen drapers, 97 Swanston st
Du Frocq, T., 49 Hanover st, F
Duggan, Denis, 21 Baillie st, Hot
Duggan, M., storeman, 146 Bourke st west
Duguild, Alexander, Miller st, W M
Duhy, Philip, 13 Row st, F
Duigan, H. B., Albion st, Bk
Duius, George, 11 Napier st, Em II
Duit, —, 190 Kerr st, F
Duke, George, boatbuilder, 45 Ferguson st, Wmn
Duke, Joseph, house agent, &c., 125 Brunswick st, F
Duke, Mrs., fruiterer, 118 Bourke st east
Duke, Robert, 130 Madeline st, Carl
Duke, W. W., 58 Elizabeth st
Dumas, Alexander D., Domain road, S Y
Dumford, Mrs., 165 Spring st
Dummitt, Francis, Howard st, Hot
Dumville, Robert, Chetwynd st, Hot
Duocan, Alexander, confectioner, 10 and 12 Bourke st east
Duncan, Alexander, shoeing forge, 82 Johnston st, F
Duncan, Andrew, bootmaker, Howard, st, W M
Duncan, Christina, Bedford st, Hot
Duncan, George, baker, 47 and 49 Lonsdale st west
Duncan, George, storeman. Hoddle st, E M
Duncan, Gordon, Brunswick road
Duncan, James, Berkeley st, Carl
Duncan, James, Cardigan st, Carl
Duncan, James, blacksmith, Elizabeth st north

Duncan, James C., grocer, 88 Clarendon st, Em H
Duncan, John, Church st, Rd
Duncan, Mrs., pastrycook, 108 Swanston st
Duncan, Mrs. A., registry office, 19½ Lonsdale st west
Duncan, Mrs., 7 Royal terrace, Nicholson st, F
Duncan, Mrs., 9 Macquarrie st, Wmn
Duncan, Peter, Stoke st, San
Duncan, S., wood and coal yard, Hoddle st, E C
Duncan, Wm., coachbuilder, 76 York st, Em H
Duncan, Wm., 18 Twyford st south, Wmn
Duncombe, E. T., 106 Cardigan st, Carl
Dundass, C., 33 Dorcas st, Em H
Dunell, Wm., greengrocer, 145 Lygon st, Carl
Dunell, W., National hotel, Brunswick st, F
Dungate, W., dairyman, 116 Lonsdale st east
Dunger, Henry W., slater, 193 Stephen st
Dunkley, William James, boot and shoe manufacturer and importer, 55 and 57 Elizabeth st., 31 Bourke st, east
Dunlea, James, and Co., grocers, 107 Elizabeth st, and 54 Nelson place, Wmn
Dunlop and Edwards, drapers, Commercial road, Pra
Dunlop, John, 66 Dorcas st, Em H
Dunlop, John, Commercial road, Pra
Dunlop, Wm., produce dealer, 12 Western market, and Nth
Dunn, Allan, 18 Spencer st
Dunn, F., grocer, Cape st, Hotd
Dunn, F. A., Haw
Dunn, J., grocer, Dover road, Wmn
Dunn, J., shoe manufacturer, 4 Moor st, F
Dunn, J., 157 Little Lonsdale st east
Dunn, James, butcher, 129 King st
Dunn, James, Post Office hotel, 141 Elizabeth st
Dunn, James, 7 Rathdowne st, Carl
Dunn, John, 36 Montague st, Em H
Dunn, John, Chapel st, Pra
Dunn, M., Victoria st, W M
Dunn, Mrs., store, Berkeley st, Carl
Dunn, Mrs., Church st, E C
Dunn, Mrs., school, 50 Napier st, Em H
Dunn, Mrs., Free Scripture School, Sackville st, E C
Dunn, Mrs., 119 Moray st, Em H
Dunn, Peter, Johnston st, E C
Dunn, Richard, 62 Dudley st, W M
Dunn, Robert C., assistant registrar of shipping, Custom-house, Flinders st west, and 108 Little Lonsdale st west
Dunn, T., grocer, Pent
Dunn, Thomas, High st, Pra
Dunn, Thomas, tailor, 27 Lonsdale st east
Dunn, Wm., Darebin bridge hotel, Heidelberg road
Dunne, Mrs., 62 Raglan st, Em H

Dunn, Wilson, and Botterill, photographers, 41 Collins st east
Dunne, Wm., 167 Moray st, Em H
Dunnett, G. P., Henry st, Pra
Dunning, —, High st, Hot
Dunning, John, grocer, 112 Flinders lane east
Dunsford, Mrs., Wellington parade, F M
Dunstan, Mrs., dealer, 30 Swan st, Rd
Dunstan, Thomas, 61 Napier st, Em H
Dunston, John, 25 Rose st, F
Dunstone, James, 55 Cobden st, Em H
Dunstone, Thomas Oliver, chemist and druggist, 61 Bourke st east
Dunt, J., Pascoe st, Wmn
Dunwell, James, Inkerman st, St K
Durance, Mrs. Martha, draper and dressmaker, Bay st, San
Durham, R. G., electoral registrar, &c., Cape st, Held
Durrant, D., dairyman, Hampton st, Btn
Durrant, W., dairyman, Crescent, Btn west
Duthie, Wm., merchant, 122 Collins st west
Dutton, —, gingerbeer manufacturer, Derby st, E C
Dutton, H., wood and coal yard, Gore st, F
Davoy, J., Lennox st, Rd
Dwight, Henry Tolman, bookseller, 233 Bourke st east
Dwight, Richard W., grocer, 24 Coventry st, Em H
Dwyer, James, 29 King William st, F
Dwyer, John, 16 Stanley st, W M
Dwyer, John, Madeline st, Carl
Dwyer, John, 86½ Lygon st, Carl
Dwyer, John, 190 Lygon st, Carl
Dwyer, Mrs., school, 3 Osborne buildings, Napier st, F
Dwyer, Mrs., dressmaker, 24 Little Lonsdale st east
Dwyer, P. T., Dow st, San
Dwyer, T., boarding-house, 12 Latrobe st west
Dyal, John, 259 Fitzroy st, F
Dyer, Benjamin, carpenter, Ashurst st, Kew
Dyer, C. W., Garden st, Pra
Dyer, Charles, boot importer, 135 Swanston st
Dyer, E. D., Cliff st, Pra
Dyer, John, builder, Alphington, Held
Dyer, Mrs., nurse, 73 Lygon st, Carl
Dyer, Mrs, Rebe st, St K
Dyerman, C., currier, Elizabeth st extension
Dykes, James, Lygon st, Carl
Dykes, Samuel, dairyman, 42 Argyle st, F
Dymock, Walter, Curzon st, Hot
Dyner, Wm. L., Nelson st, Wmn
Dynon, John, glass and china dealer, 43 Lonsdale st west
Dyson, Arthur, nurseryman, seedsman, and florist, 15 Eastern Market

Dyson, W. R., Arthur st, Pra
Dyte, C., M.L.A., Parliament House

E

Eade, Joel, Hoddle st, E C
Eades, Henry, Jeffcott st, W M
Eades, J. C., Victoria st, St K
Eades, Richard A. M., M.B., physician, 164 Collins st east
Eades, Wm., Albert st, Pra
Eagan, P., Stewart st, Bk
Eager, Gerald F., Old Ship inn, Little Lonsdale st east
Eaglehawk Mining Association, 37 Market st
Eaglefield Pastoral Company, 115 Collins st west
Eagles, H. F., Roden st, W M
Earl, —, Whitehall st, Fcy
Earl, John, ironmonger, Graham and Stoke sts, San
Earl, John, greengrocer, 40 Cardigan st, Carl
Earle, Charles, optician, 100 Bourke st east
Earle, John, 20 Faraday st, Carl
Earle, Wm., Little Nelson st, Wmn
Earls, Thomas, tailor, 160 High st, St K
Early, Mark, Lancashire hotel, 71 Little Bourke st east
Earnell, Mrs. M., 62 Hanover st, F
Earnshaw, Charles, Foundry hotel, Hay st, San
Earnshaw, Samuel, machinist, Hay st, San
Easby, Ann, storr, Donverie st, Carl
Easdown, Miss, school, Hoddle st west, E C
Easson, Mrs., Fitzroy st, St K
East Collingwood Orderly room, Victoria parade, E M
East Melbourne Common School, Grey st, E M
Eastaway, George, Camberwell inn, Boroondara
Easton, Andrew L., 9 Jackson st, Wmn
Eastwood Brothers and Co., flock manufacturers, 31 a'Beckett st
Eastwood, Francis, Haw
Eastwood, Henry, baker, Clyde st, St K
Eastwood, Henry, Wellington hotel, 214 Wellington st, E C
Eastwood, Mrs., Baptist lane, 64 Little Collins st east
Eastwood, Mrs., Stanley st, E C
Eastwood, Wm., 32 a'Beckett st east
Easeby, Henry, Queensberry st, Hot
Eaton, W., Park st, S Y
Ebeinsteine, Mrs., 136 Gertrude st, F
Ebsworth, —, 100 Gore st, F
Ebsworth, Alfred, 56 Rowena parade, Rd
Eccles, Misses, school, 7 Apsley terrace, E M
Eckersall, T. S., Tyne st, Carl

Eckersall, Wm., Brunswick road
Eckersley, Charles, grocer, &c., 3 Wellington st, St K
Eckersley, Charles, Nelson st, Pra
Eckland, John, 57 Twyford st, South Wmn
Economist office, 99 Bourke st west
Ecroyd, Wm. J., Grey st, St K
Ecroyd, W. J., and Co., warehousemen, 1, 3, and 5 Flinders lane west
Eddington, Amos, Charles st, Pra
Eddie, James, carrier, Lothian st, Hot
Eddleston, John, Lothian st, Hot
Eddy, John, cab proprietor, 118 Kerr st, F
Eddy, Richard, George st, E M
Eddy, Wm., nursery and seedsman, 136 Elizabeth st, and Hartwell
Ede, John, gardener, Carpenter st, Bru
Edgar, Robert, importer of boots and shoes, 193 King st
Edgcombe, R. S., 78 Drummond st, Carl
Edges, A., 103 Smith st, F
Edgey, Edward, 30 Clarendon st, Em H
Edlen, Wm., 30 Clarendon st, Em H
Edmends, Wm., saddler, 253 Brunswick st, F
Edmonds and Behne, Beach st, San
Edmonds, Samuel, 218 Moray st, Em H
Edmonds, Thomas, 57 Osborne st, South Wmn
Edmoes, J. G., 260 Swan st, Rd
Edois, Robert, Dryburgh st, Hot
Edouin, Charles, Imperial hotel, corner Bourke and Spring sts
Edsall, Charles, dairyman, Robe st, St K
Edsell, F. S., Hampton st, Btn
Education office, Model Schools, Spring st
Edward, Mrs., Neptune st, St K
Edwards, Captain, Nott st, San
Edwards, E., Moreland road, Bk
Edwards, E., 40 Moor st, San
Edwards, E. D., Brewster st, Ess
Edwards, Edward, nightman, 41 Charles st, F
Edwards, Evan, 67 Jeffcott st, W M
Edwards, F. W., 5 Cardigan st, Carl
Edwards, G., Drummond st, Carl
Edwards, G. W., greengrocer, Commercial road, Pra
Edwards, George E., 42 Faraday st, Carl
Edwards, H., grocer, Hay st, San
Edwards, H. D., Capel st, Hot
Edwards, J., 46 Johnston st, F
Edwards, J., Albert st, Bk
Edwards, J., boatbuilder, Flinders st east
Edwards, J., Suffolk hotel, 49 Stanley st, E C
Edwards, J.C., Dover Castle hotel, Palmerston st, Carl
Edwards, James, 63 Kerr st, F
Edwards, John, Cole st, South Wmn
Edwards, John, Erroll st, Hot
Edwards, John, Williams road, Pra
Edwards, John, 32 Cardigan st, Carl

B

Edwards, John, greengrocer, 98 Stevedore st, Wmn
Edwards, John, parliamentary agent, 55 Bourke st west
Edwards, John, ropemaker, Spencer terrace, Little Bourke st west
Edwards, John, junior, M.L.A., solicitor, 55 Bourke st west, and 51 Brunswick st, F
Edwards, Joseph, 82 Bank st east, Em H
Edwards, Misses, milliners, 201 Swanston street
Edward, Mrs., 19 Cobden st, Em H
Edwards, Mrs., 138 Lonsdale st west
Edwards, P. E., Fitzroy st, F
Edwards, Richard, Prince of Wales hotel, Nelson place, Wmn
Edwards, T., 15 Perry st, E C
Edwards, Thomas, 112 Rose st, F
Edwards, W., Cochrane st, Bin
Edwards, W., engineer, 201 Swanston st
Edwards, W., Lennox st, Rd
Edwards, W., schoolmaster, 96 Cecil st, Em H
Edwards, Wm., gold and silver plate manufacturer, 85 Collins st east
Edwards, —, 67 Kerr st, F
Edyvean, M., 195 Gore st, F
Eeles, Henry, Sportsman's Arms hotel, 44 Little Bourke st west
Effy, Charles, upholsterer, Stephen st
Egan and Robertson, timber merchants, 152 to 162 Lonsdale st east
Egan, Dennis, New st, Bin
Egan, John, Highett st, Rd
Egan, Michael, Highett st, Rd
Egan, Mrs., Hoddle st, Rd
Egan, Mrs., 57 Lygon st, Carl
Egan, Mrs., 142 Moor st, F
Egan, P., Thomas st, Bin
Egan, Pk., farrier, 14 Little Lonsdale st west
Egan, Wm., Madeline st, Carl
Egerton, —, 55 Rathdowne st, Carl
Eggleston, Rev. John, Lonsdale st east
Eick, Anton, watchmaker and jeweller, 32 Collins st west
Eicke, George, 11 Lygon st, Carl
Eisenstaedter, Denis, merchant, 32 Collins st west, and corner of Grey and Burnett sts, St K
Eisert, G., upholsterer, 199 Russell st
Ekins, R. S., contractor, Grattan st, Carl
Ekman, R. A., furniture dealer, 18 Lonsdale st east
Elam, David, schoolmaster, Trinnian st, off High st, Prn
Elder, J., Lennox st, Rd
Elder, John, 240 Moray st, Em H
Elder, J., 9 James st, Wmn
Elder, Henry, watchmaker and jeweller, 63 Bourke st east
Elder, Mrs., laundress, 3 Derby st, E C
Eldershaw, G., 9 Twyford st, Wmn

Elderton, Charles, labour-office keeper, 86 Collins st east, 13 Bourke st west, and 279 King st
Eldon Chambers, Bank place, 77 Collins st west
Eldred, A., shoemaker, 161 and 163 Russell st
Eldridge, F., 20 Moray place, Em H
Eldridge, John, dyer, 108 Collins st east, and 42 Brunswick st, F
Eldridge, Thomas, Gardiner's creek road Tk
Eleanor, Mrs., 69 Young st, F
Electric Telegraph office, Exchange, Flinders lane west
Elkington, Albert, 105 William st
Ella, John, Fitzroy st, St K
Ellerker, John, commission agent, 49 Park st east, Em H
Ellery, R. L. J., director Melbourne Observatory, Botanical reserve
Ellemer, —, grainer, 56 Cardigan st, Carl
Elliott, Alfred, estate agent and money broker, 60 and 61 Temple court, Collins st west, and Nicholson st, F
Elliott, Andrew, coachbuilder, 86 Smith st, and 114 Wellington st, E C
Elliott, Andrew, Hanmer st, Wmn
Elliott, Benjamin, Perry st, E C
Elliott, G. H., cordial manufacturer, 160 Queen st, and corner of Queensberry and Drummond sts, Carl
Elliott, George, 210 King st
Elliott, James, plumber and gasfitter, Fawkner st, St K
Elliott, John, tailor, 3 King William st, F
Elliott, John, 19 Chetwynd st, W M
Elliott, Mrs., Garner st, St K
Elliott, Sisar, Arthur-seat road, Bin
Elliott, W., Hoddle st, E C
Elliott, W. H., cabinetmaker, High st, St K
Elliott, Wm., bootmaker, 29 Little Lonsdale st east
Elliott, Wm., 27 Hanmer st, Wmn
Elliott, Wm., 64 Greeves st, F
Ellis, Alexander, butcher, 189 Little Collins st east
Ellis, Angel, 2 Miami villas, Victoria parade, E M
Ellis, Charles, 62 Greeves, st, F
Ellis, Christopher W., house agent, 148 Bridge road, Rd
Ellis, Elias, 61 Cardigan st, Carl
Ellis, G. G., Acland st, St K
Ellis, George, St David st, Fcy
Ellis, J., Capel st, Hot
Ellis, J. C., and Co., coal importers, 81 Flinders st west, and 18 Bank st west, Em H
Ellis, James, 20 Bank st east, Em H
Ellis, James C., 18 Bank st west, Em H
Ellis, John E., china and glass dealer, 43 High st, and Octavia st, St K

Ellis, John, grocer, 160 Bourke st west
Ellis, Joseph, 11 Peel st, Carl
Ellis, J. L., 75 Smith st, F
Ellis, J. R., 35 M'Arthur place, Hot
Ellis, Louis, 44 Drummond st, Carl
Ellis, Mrs., 33 Young st, F
Ellis, Mrs., school, 104 Latrobe st west
Ellis, Peter, 113 Argyle st, F
Ellis, Samuel, butcher, Cliff st and Chapel st, Pra
Ellis, Thomas, portrait rooms, 45 Victoria parade, F
Ellis, W. E., jeweller, 104 Latrobe st west
Ellis, Wm., 12 Palmer st, F
Ellis, Wm., 1 Stevedore st, Wmn
Ellis, Wm. J., Nicholson st, F
Ellison, P., grocer, 241 Smith st, F
Ellitson, John, painter and paperhanger, Chapel st, and High st, Pra
Ellsworth John, 11 York st west, Em H
Elmes, Mrs., preparatory school, Barkly st, St K
Elms and Co., merchant tailors, 83 Elizabeth st
Elms, George, and Co., brewers, Clarke st, E C
Elms, George, Rose, Thistle, and Shamrock hotel, 176 Elizabeth st
Elms, Mrs., Oxford st, E C
Elms, T., Napier st, Em H
Elms, W., Barkly square, Rd
Elsasser, Charles, professor of music, 146 Collins st east
Elsey, James, fruiter, 86 Brunswick st, F
Elsum, J., baker, 53 Dover road, Wmn
Elvin, Gorney, Salwater river, Fcy
Elworthy and Dobbin, butchers, Beach st, San, and 51 Nelson place east, Wmn,
Elworthy, Richard, butcher, 23 High st, St K
Ely, C. W., Smith st, E C
Emanuel, J., professor of pianoforte, 11 Victoria parade, F
Embling, Thomas, surgeon, 31 Gore st, F
Emerald Hill, Sandridge, and St Kilda Building Society, Mechanics' Institute, Cecil st, Em H
Emerson, Alfred H., Yarra st, S Y
Emerson, George, Clarke st, E C
Emerson, Hugh, dairyman, Hotham st, E M
Emerson, M., bootmaker, 188 Little Collins st east
Emerson, Thomas, 50 Bridge rd, Rd
Emerson, Wm., Johnston st, E C
Emery, Henry, potter, Pres
Emery, J., 39 Young st, F
Emery, Michael, pottery, Pres
Emery, W., 81A Moor st, F
Emms, Stephen, Stoke st, San
Emmerson, James, Yarra st, Pra
Emmerton, Edward, farmer, 68 Drummond st, Carl
Emmett, John, 70 Bouverie st, Carl

Emmitt, Joseph, Cremorne st, Rd
Empey, Charles, butcher, Peel st, Pra
Emply, W., 121 Smith st, F
Empson, Wm., ironmonger, 81 Fitzroy st, F
Enault, Andre, bookbinder, 140 Latrobe st east
Energetic Gold Mining Company, 34 Queen street
Enes, Adolph Herman, 127 Bourke st east
England, Arthur, Charles st Pra
England, Edward, Clarendon road, Tk
England, S., signwriter, 145 Johnston st, F
English, Adam, New road, Bin
English, Andrew, 41 Cecil st east, Wmn
English, and Australasian Copper Company, 49 Flinders lane west
English, Daniel, Strand, Wmn
English, James, bookseller, 217 Swanston street
English, Mrs., fruiterer, Railway place, San
English, Scottish, and Australian Chartered Bank, 35 Elizabeth st ; branch, 29 Thompson st, Wmn
Enkson, Ankar, Inkerman st east, St K
Ennes, John, 70A Argyle st, F
Ennever, K., builder, 144 Moor st, F
Ennis, J., Wellington st, St K
Ensor, Mrs., 110 Gertrude st, F
Enticott, John, and Co., spouting manufacturers, 53 and 55 Flinders lane east
Entwistle, J., Lygon st, Carl
Equitable Loan and Investment Company of Victoria, 105 Elizabeth st
Erant, T., grocer, Palmerston st, Carl
Eresti, —, artist, Hoddle st, E C
Erichsen, C. F., tailor, 74 Elizabeth st
Erisin, Henry, Howard st, Hot
Ernest, Madame, Little Nelson st, Wmn
Erskine, G. W., Domain st, S Y
Erskine, James, plumber and gasfitter, 39 Swanston st
Erskine, John, 80 Bank st east, Em H
Erskine, Wm., painter, Barkly st, Carl
Ervine, Wm., draper, 141 Bourke st east
Esnouf, P., tinsmith, Peel st, W M
Escott, W. P., Rd
Escott and Lund, sharebrokers and legal managers, 3 Collins st west
Eskermil, Wm., Brunswick road, Bk
Esple, Mrs., boarding-house, 87 Collins st east
Esple, P., Walsh st, S Y
Ess, G., musician, 36 Smith st, F
Essex, A., 16 Greeves st, F
Ethel, D., brickmaker, Commercial road, Pra
Etherton, Mrs., Dow st, San
Ethridge, R., 54 Montague st, Em H
European Assurance Society, 74 and 76 Collins st west
Eva, John, painter, &c., 94 Collins st east
Evan, C., 50 Napier st, F

Evans, —, 14 Napier st, F
Evans, Aarons, chemist (P.O.), corner of Madeline and Queensberry st, Carl
Evans and Co., cabinetmakers, 38 A'Beckett st east
Evans Brothers, butchers, corner of Queensberry and Lygon sts, Carl
Evans, David, Lothian st, Hot
Evans, Edward, Peel st, Hot
Evans, Elisha, farmer, Pres
Evans, F. W., Gold st, E C
Evans, George, Royal Oak hotel, 160 Queen st
Evans, George, 265 Church st, Rd
Evans, Gordon, stock and sharebroker, Hall of Commerce, Collins st west, and Haw
Evans, H., watchmaker, 149 Little Bourke st east
Evans, Henry, Chetwynd st, Hot
Evans, Henry, 181 Swanston st
Evans, Henry, bootmaker, 145 Elizabeth street
Evans, Henry, bootmaker, 9 High st, St K
Evans, J., bootmaker, 17 Nelson place east, Wmn
Evans, J., Ferguson st, Wmn
Evans, J., 71 Clarendon st, Em H
Evans, J., Quarryman's arms, 48 Johnston st, E C
Evans, J., greengrocer, Chapel st, Pra
Evans, J. Davies, chemist, 198 Smith st, E C
Evans, J. H., bootmaker, 89 Victoria st, St K
Evans, J. W., 10 Princess st, F
Evans, J. W. and A., 86 Elgin st, Carl
Evans, James, Howard st, Hot
Evans, James, builder, 68 Napier st, F
Evans, James, auctioneer, &c., Gardiner's creek road, Pra
Evans, John, 3 Barkly st, Carl
Evans, John, 170 Eastern road, Em H
Evans, John, 56 Bailey st, Hot
Evans, John Clarke, importer and warehouseman, 27 Flinders lane west
Evans, John L., hide merchant and commission agent, 4 Orr's Buildings, Flinders lane west
Evans, Joshua, 63 Cambrige st, E C
Evans, Louis L., Clyde st, St K
Evans, Miss, Powlett st, E M
Evans, Mrs., 75 Rathdowne st, Carl
Evans, Mrs., Flem lid
Evans, Mrs., 12 Hanover st, F
Evans, R., fruiterer, 9 Western market
Evans, R., Albert st east, Bk
Evans, Richd., Charles st, F
Evans, Robert, 106 Stevedore st, Wmn
Evans, T., 3 Trafalgar place, Hot
Evans, T., 69 Gore st, F
Evans, Thomas, Barkly st, St. K
Evans, Thomas, estate agent, 19 Fitzroy st, St K

Evans, Thomas, tent and flag manufacturer, 4, 52, and 103 Bourke st west
Evans, Wm., contractor, 108 Johnston st, E C
Evans, Wm., 137 Moor st, F
Evans, Wm., Peel st, Hot
Eve, John Samuel, hairdresser and baths, 171 Bourke st east
Everard, John, Grey st, E M
Everard, John, and Co., tea brokers, 69 Collins st west
Everend, Mrs., 88 Young st, F
Everest, Henry, builder, Garden st, Pra
Everest, S. G., Haw
Everett, Isaac, boarding-house keeper, 143 Lonsdale st west
Everett, Mrs., 122 Raglan st east, Em H
Evershed, J., Osborne st, S Y
Evershed, R., 13 Dorcas st, Em H
Evett, W., gold and silver beater, 54 York st east, Em H
Eville, James, town clerk, 3 Dorcas st, Em H
Ewan, G., Union st, Bk
Ewart, Wm., 20 Coventry st, Em H
Ewart, Mrs. T., Carlton st, Carl
Ewin, John, Rowena parade, Rd
Ewing, Samuel, 38 Queensberry st, Hot
Ewing, Thomas A., chemist, 113 Brunswick st, F
Ewing, Wm., Peel st, Pra
Excell, W., Wellington st, St K
Excell, Walter, and Co., warehousemen, 6 Flinders lane west
Exchange, Flinders lane west and William st
Executive Council, Government House, Spring st
Exell, Mrs., confectioner and registry office, 93 High st, St K
Exhibition Building, William st
Exhibition of Fine Arts, 103 Collins st east
Exley, George, hay and corn store, Bridge road, Rd
Eyers, Daniel C., draper, Lang st, S Y
Eyre, D., 160 Eastern road, Em H
Eyre, Wm., broker, &c., 86 and 116 Collins st west, and 7 Eden terrace, St K
Eyres, D. C., 338 Swan st, Rd

F.

Faber, D., 1 Bath terrace, Faraday st, Carl
Fabern, George, Lennox st, Rd
Fabim, George, Goodwood st, Rd
Fadden, P., Blackwood st, Hot
Fagbery, Charles, grocer, 13 Stanley st, W M
Faggs, F., 35 Baillie st, Hot
Fairbairn, George, M.L.A., Parliament House
Fairbridge, J., butcher, Park st, Em H

Fairbridge, Robert, butcher, 166 Moray st, Em H
Fairchild, J., Dalgety st, St K
Fairchild, John, Hoddle st, Rd
Fairclough, Mrs., ladies' school, 65 Cremorne st, Ltd
Fairweather, J. F., Gardiner's creek road, S Y
Falconer, J., Orrong road, Tk
Falconer, John, builder, Napier st, F
Falconbridge, James, Grosvenor st, Pra
Falk, P., and Co., wholesale jewellers, 38 Little Collins st west
Falkner, George, Barkly st, St K
Falkner, Thomas, Heath st, San
Falls, James, Albert st, Fcy
Fallenstein and McKechney, merchants, 37 Flinders st west
Fallenstein, Isaac, Esplanade, St K
Falloo, John, general dealer, Peel st, E C
Falloon, John H., Oxford and Cambridge hotel, Rowena parade, Ltd
Falls, E. J., ship chandler, Beach st, San
Falvey, John, Rodes st, W M
Fanning, Nankivell, and Co., merchants, 5 and 7 Elizabeth st
Fanning, P. H., Vine st, Held
Fanning, Richard, Pra
Fannings, W., Curzon st, Hot
Farewell, Chas., Punt road, Rd
Farie, Claud, sheriff, William st, Pra
Farley, Henry, Greville st, Pra
Farley, John H., law stationer, 56 Little Collins st west, and Commercial road, Pra
Farley, Thomas, grocer, 49 Spencer st north
Farlow, Wm., Canning st, Carl
Farmer, George, Chapel st, Pra
Farmer, Henry John, solicitor, 6 Collins st east, and 358 Swan st, Rd
Farmer, Mrs., Webb st, F
Farmer, Thomas, Peel
Farmer, Thomas, Buckley st, Ess
Farmer's Journal office, 57 Elizabeth st
Farmer, Wm., Villiers st, Hot
Farquhar, J., Tyne st, Carl
Farquharson, J., 81 Napier st, Em H
Farrage, Wm, surgeon and accoucheur, 156 Collins st east
Farrance, George, storekeeper, 61 Bank st west, Em H
Farrance, Mrs. G., ladies' school, 61 Bank st west, Em H
Farrands, R. G., bootmaker, Royal lane, Bourke st
Farrant, J. C., blacksmith, 34 a'Beckett st, and Higbett st, Rd
Farrar, H. W., Commercial road, Pra
Farrar, H. W., and Co., merchants, 53 Little Collins st west
Farrar, John Wood, Williams road, Pra
Farrell, Frederick, Garden st, Pra
Farrell, J., Peel st, Hot

Farrell, J., leather warehouse, 7 Post Office place, and Rd
Farrell, John, bootmaker, 29 Lonsdale st west
Farrell, John, Ivanhoe, Heid
Farrell, Mrs., greengrocer, 134 Gertrude st, F
Farrell, Robert, 17 Wellington st, St K
Farrell, Stephen, Nott st, San
Farrell, Thomas, Ivanhoe, Held
Farrell, Thomas, bonecrusher, Flem bank
Farrell, Wm., 59 Dudley st, W M
Farrell, Wm., Ivanhoe, Held
Farrer, John, Barkly st, Bk
Farrington, John, Bay View hotel, Madeline st, Carl
Farrington, J., butcher, Inkerman st east, St K
Farrow, Wm., general storekeeper, 14 Flinders st west
Farwig, E. A., type founder and electrotyper, 19 Russell st south
Fatt, Edward C., 14 Church st, Em H
Faulkioer, Mrs., dyer, Bay st, San
Faure, Amelia, Albion hotel, Brunswick st, F
Fausset, Charles, solicitor, 41 Swanston st
Fawcett, Isaac R., tailor, 46 Gertrude st, F
Fawcett, J. W., 1 Alfred place, Victoria st, Carl
Fawcett, Thomas, Barkly st, St K
Fawkner, Hon. J. P., M.L.C., 226 Smith st, E C
Fawsett, Camillus, dentist, Caroline st, S Y
Fawssett, Mrs., 75 Collins st east
Fay, D., Dryburgh st, Hot
Fear, John, stationer, 44 Oxford st, E C
Fear, Z., grocer, Vera st, E C
Fearon, Luke, 18 John st, Wmn
Featherstone, Dr., deputy registrar births and deaths, Chapel st, Pra
Feddes, James, 14 Rosslyn st, W M
Feeban, Richard, City Arms hotel, 206 Elizabeth st
Feeny, Dennis, Carpentaria hotel, Lonsdale st west
Fegan, Thomas, 26 Palmer st, F
Fehon, Wm. M., assistant traffic superintendent V. R. S., Spencer st
Fehy, F., Dryburgh st, Hot
Feigl, Ignatius, draper, 195 Swanston st
Feinagle, Henry, Chapel st, S Y
Feldheim Brothers, importers, 63 Queen st
Feldheim, H., Grey st, St K
Fell, James, 219 George st, F
Fell, James, grocer, 217 George st, and 219 Gertrude st, F
Fellows, the Hon. T. H., M.L.C., barrister, 34 Temple court, Collins st west
Fellows, Rev. W., Orrong road, Tk
Felton, Alfred, wholesale druggist, 41A Swanston st
Female Refuge, Madeline st, Carl

Fenley, F., 109 Lygon st, Carl
Fenley, J., boarding-house, 68 Lonsdale st west
Fenton, Thomas, coachsmith, 3 Latrobe st west
Fenner, G. O., New st, Bk
Fennessy, Richard, seedsman and florist, Chapel st, Pra
Fenning, D., 19 Moray place, Em H
Fenton, James, hay salesman, Eastern Market, 185 Little Collins st east
Fenton, John, 48 Swan st, Rd
Fenton, John, 33 Fitzroy st, F
Fenwick Brothers, importers and warehousemen, 35 Flinders lane east, and 227 King st
Fenwick, David J., Barry st, Carl
Fenwick, F., 37 Franklin st, W M
Fenwick, Mrs., Miller st, W M
Fenwick, Robert, sewing machine maker, 38 Stephen st, and Chetwynd st, W M
Fenwick, Orlando, 227 King st
Fenwick, Pascoe, 227 King st
Fergie, H. P., notary public and conveyancer, 64 Little Collins st west
Ferguson and Urie, glass-stainers, plumbers, &c., 34 Curzon st, Hot
Ferguson, C., harbour master, Strand, Wmn
Ferguson, Elizabeth, grocer, 78 Errol st, Hot
Ferguson, Henry, Stanley hotel, Stanley st, W M
Ferguson, J., 66 York st west, Em H
Ferguson, J., 48 Bank st east, Em M
Ferguson, J., ironmonger, Gardiner's creek road, Pra
Ferguson, J., smith, Gardiner's creek road, Pra
Ferguson, J. M., Lang st, S Y
Ferguson, James, 34 Curzon st, Hot
Ferguson, James, bootmaker, 8 Rathdowne st, Carl
Ferguson, James, Flemington house, Flem
Ferguson, John, Scotchman's creek, Oakleigh
Ferguson, John, 77 Rosslyn st, W M
Ferguson, John, Chambers st, S Y
Ferguson, Mrs., Park st east, Em H
Ferguson, Thomas, 80 Gore st, F
Ferguson, Thomas, Heath st, San
Ferguson, Thompson, Artillery hotel, 19 Park st, Em H
Ferguson, W. R., Chambers st, S Y
Ferguson, Wm., watchmaker, corner Brunswick and Faris sts, F
Ferguson, Wm., tailor and clothier, 12 Clarendon st, Em H
Ferguson, Wm., Queensberry st, Hot
Ferguson and Mitchell, engravers, &c., 59 Collins st west, and Tk
Ferguson and Moore, general printers, 46 Flinders lane east

Ferguson, James, Gardiner's creek road, Tk
Fermoy Extended Gold Mining Company, Wood's Point, 99 Collins st east
Ferres, John, Government printer, Eastern hill
Ferrier, David, 82 Dorcas st, Em H
Ferris, James, Hoddle st, E C
Ferris, Mrs., boarding-house, 48 Cecil st, Wmn
Ferris, T. J., photographer, Chapel st, Pra
Ferris, W. H., Brighton st, Rd
Ferrier, James, Nicholson st, Carl
Fethle, John, Victoria st, Rd
Fettes, Mrs., boarding-house keeper, 116 Little Lonsdale st west
Fever, Wm., Preston
Fewins, —, 73 Wellington st, E C
Fidder, Mrs., 42 Coventry st west, Em H
Fidler, Richard, marine store, 236 King st
Field, Bryan, Perry st, E C
Field, J., musician, Bay st, Btn
Field, John, 143 Rose st, F
Field, T., Kent st, St K
Fielden, Rev. W. S. H., Victoria parade, F
Fielder, Charles, greengrocer, Queensberry st, Hot
Fielder, T., 17 Coventry st, Em H
Fieldhouse, J., Capel st, Hot
Fieldhouse, S., Capel st, Hot
Fielding and Beetchenow, butchers, 66 Smith st and 167 Wellington st, E C
Fielding, Richard, draper, Barkly st, Fry
Fielding, T., Waltham st, Hd
Fielding, Thomas, Sydney road, Bk
Fifeshire Prospecting Quartz Mining Co., Eldon chambers, Collins st west
Filhon, A., tobacconist, 120 Brunswick st, F
Filson, Caughey, and Dalzell, merchants, 64 William st
Filson, John, Flem
Finagle, H., Gardiner's creek road, Pra
Finch, E., Brighton st, Rd
Finchain, George, organ builder, Bridge road, Rd
Findlater, H., Cardigan st, Carl
Findlay, Francis, 157 Moray st, Em H
Findlay, J., Weston st, Bk
Findlay, John, 216 Clarendon st, Em H
Finlay, —, carpenter, Hanmer st, Wmn
Finlay, A., 52 Wellington st, E C
Finlay, C., Lothian st, Hot
Finlay, J., blacksmith, 322 Brunswick st, F
Finlay, J. H., 196 Lygon st, Carl
Finlay, James, 136 Rose st, F
Finlay, John, 24 Baillie st, Hot
Finlay, John, 75 Smith st, F
Finlay, H., Miller st, W M
Finlay, R., and Co., ship-builders, Yarra banks
Finlay, Wm., Duke of Rothsay hotel, 12 Elizabeth st

Finlay, Wm., tailor, 62 Collins st west, and Dow st, San
Finlay, Wm., 18 Little Oxford st, E C
Finlayson and Hutchinson, flock manufacturers and grain crushers, a'Beckett st west
Finlayson, George, Oxford st, E C
Finlayson, Graham, teacher, 16 Smith st, E C
Finlayson, J. R., 217 Victoria parade, E M
Finlayson, Matthew, 51 Rathdowne st, Carl
Finlayson, Mrs., Barry st, Carl
Finlayson, Peter, 16 Smith st, E C
Finlayson, Thomas, Darling st, S Y
Finn, Edward, 133 Leicester st, F
Finn, John, Carlisle st east, St K
Finn, John, Drummond st, Carl
Finn, John, tailor, 7 Victoria st, Rot
Finn, Michael, Southern Cross hotel, 165 Bourke st west
Finn, Rev. W. M., Heid
Finnerty, John, 269 Brunswick st, F
Finney, James, Barkly st, Carl
Finnimore, Mrs. D., Baillie st, Hot
Finnis, Mrs., Prince's st, F
Finnin, Wm., grocer, 92 Brunswick st, F
Fire Brigade and Engine Stations, Collins st west; Richmond terrace, Rd; Leveson st, Hot; Webb st, F; and Johnston st, E C
Firman, W. H., Smith st, E C
First and Second Netherlands India Fire and Marine Insurance Companies, 28 Queen st
First and Second Victorian Bowkett Building Society, Carl
First Victorian Bowkett Building Society, Grattan st, Carl
Firth, R. J., publisher, 53 Flinders lane west, and 45 Latrobe st west
Firth, Wm., mason, Swan st, Fcy
Fisch, Miss, Cobden st, Em H
Fischer, S., broker, 1 Queen st
Fish Market, Prince's bridge
Fish, Mrs., 42 Cobden st, Em H
Fisher, —, 117 Little Bourke st west
Fisher, —, teacher, Bay st, Btn
Fisher, Alexander, surgeon, 81 Stephen st
Fisher, Frederick, 94 Stevedore st, Wmn
Fisher, George, 99 Fitzroy st, F
Fisher, H., bootmaker, 190 Wellington st, E C
Fisher, H., maltster, Lennox st, Richmond terrace, Rd
Fisher, Harding, Argyle st west, St K
Fisher, Henry, Davis st, Pra
Fisher, Henry, shoemaker, 131 Little Collins st east
Fisher, James, 173 Lygon st, Carl
Fisher, John, Barkly st, Carl
Fisher, John, Capel st, W M
Fisher, John, grocer, Smith st, E C
Fisher, Joseph, 96 Little Collins st west

Fisher, Joseph, confectioner, 160 Bourke st east
Fisher, Mrs., Drummond st, Carl
Fisher, Wm. C., wine and spirit merchant, 47 Flinders lane west
Fisher, Wm., painter and glazier, 27 Nelson place, Wmn
Fisher, Wm., 62 Fitzroy st, F
Fishley, George Yeo, notary public, 18 Collins st east, and Cotham road, Kew
Fishley, P., 56 Bank st east, Em H
Fisk, Edward, confectioner, 19 High st, St K
Fisk, James, Drummond st, Carl
Fiske, Elizabeth, 199 Lonsdale st west
Fiskin, Thomas, Tennyson st, St K
Fitch, Ebenezer, builder, Barkly st, St K
Fitch, J., fruiterer, High st, St K
Fitch, Reuben A., oil merchant and drysalter, 99 Flinders lane east, and Nth
Fitts, John, 109 Gertrude st, F
Fitzgerald, David, tailor, 103 Queen st
Fitzgerald, David, Queensberry st, Hot
Fitzgerald, E. W., Howard st, Hot
Fitzgerald, J., Bouveria st, Carl
Fitzgerald, John, bill poster, 127 Little Collins st east
Fitzgerald, John, A.M., 18 Lonsdale st east
Fitzgerald, John, Prince of Wales hotel, 23 Dorcas st west, Em H
Fitzgerald, Mrs., 114 Cardigan st, Carl
Fitzgerald, Nicholas, M.L.C., Parliament House
Fitzgerald, Richard, timber merchant, &c, 140 Swan st, Rd
Fitzgerald, Thomas N., surgeon, 18 Lonsdale st east
Fitzgerald, Wm., carpenter, Mount Alexander road, Kew
Fitzgibbon, E. G., Town Hall, Swanston street
Fitzgibbon, J., Punt road, S Y
Fitzpatrick, James, 92 Elgin st, Carl
Fitzgibbon, John, Cremorne st, Rd
Fitzroy Market, Napier and Young sts, F
Fitzsimonds, John, 243 Smith st, F
Fiveash, E., Fitzroy st, St K
Flanagan, A., Queensberry st, Hot
Flanagan, J. P., grocer and coffee roaster, 260 Elizabeth st
Flanagan, James J., 26 Latrobe st west
Flanagan, Michael, Queensberry st, Hot
Flanagan, William A., sodawater manufacturer, 41 Little Lonsdale st east
Flannagan, J., sweep, 160 Little Collins st east
Flannagan, J., Stephen st
Flannagan, John, architect and surveyor, 5 Collins st east, and Studley Park
Flannagan, P., bootmaker, 170 Madeline st, Carl
Flannagan, Wm., blacksmith, 84 Little Bourke st west

Flannagan, Richard, a'Beckett st west
Flanner, Mrs. Hannah, Old White Hart hotel, 240 Bourke st east
Flannery, Mathew, bootmaker, Abbotsford st, Hot
Flannery, Owen, Geelong hotel, 202 Bourke st east
Flannery, Wm., Wreckyn st, Hot
Flarey, John, Greville st, Pra
Flatau, Samuel, importer of boots, &c., 209 Bourke st east
Flatman, Dennis, Chapel st, St K
Flatow, Joseph, jeweller, 189 Stephen st
Flaven, J., Arden st, Hot
Flaxman, C., Great Dandenong road east, St K
Fleeson, John, paperhanger, Commercial road, Pra
Fleetwood, Thomas P., solicitor, 82 Little Collins st west, and Church st, Rd
Fleming, Captain, 147 Moray st, Em H
Fleming, D., Rowena parade, Rd
Fleming, G., bootmaker, Maribyrnong st, Fcy
Fleming, Henry, greengrocer, Victoria st, Rd
Fleming, J., Graham st, San
Fleming, J. W., Union st, Bk
Fleming, John, Curzon st, Hot
Fleming, Robert, Ascot Vale, Flem
Fleming, Robert, McArthur place, Carl
Fleming, Thomas, Prince George hotel, 231 Swanston st
Fleming, W., Sydney road, Bk
Fletcher, C. H., Alphington
Fletcher, E., M.D., Sydney road, Bk
Fletcher, E., surgeon, 16 Grattan st, Carl
Fletcher, J. B., Gardiner's creek road, Pra
Fletcher, J., grocer, 57 Argyle st, F
Fletcher, John, hat maker and importer, 105 Bourke st east
Fletcher, John, grocer, Fitzroy st, St K
Fletcher, Joseph, wire worker, 15 Post Office place
Fletcher, Mrs., 48 Faraday st, Carl
Fletcher, Nell, provision store, 35 Post Office place
Fletcher, R. B., Kew
Fletcher, T., grocer, Argyle st, F
Flett, Peter, cooper, 21 Flinders lane east, and 32 Elgin st, Carl
Flett, J., Little Nelson st, Wmn
Flett, John, Perry st, E C
Flett, Peter, Keppel st, Carl
Fleury, Ann, repository, Swan st, Rd
Flexmore, J. H., Palmerston st, Carl
Flinder Copper Mining Company (S. A.), 55 Elizabeth st
Flinn, Michael, carrier, 115 Faraday st, Carl
Flinn, Mrs., Railway place, San
Flinn, Thomas, cooper, 224 Elizabeth st
Flinne, Mrs., school, Queensberry st, Hot
Flintoff, Thomas, 62 King William st, F

Flintoff, Thomas, and Co., British wine, vinegar and blacking manufactory, 97 Webb st, F; office, 18 Queen st
Flockhart, Andrew, currier, Flem bank
Flockhart, R., tanner and leather dealer, 172 Elizabeth st, and Hawthorn tannery
Flood, James, Railway place, San
Flood, James, 7 Baillie st, Hot
Floods, Thomas, 66 York st east, Em H
Florance, Mrs. W. H., boarding-house, 99 Flinders st west
Florance, Susannah, Royal Highlander hotel, Flinders st west
Florant, David, butcher, 35 Howard st, Hot
Florence, Anthony, surveyor and C. E., 52 Collins st east
Flower, Henry, flagmaker, 243 Smith st, F
Flower, Mrs., Wellington parade, E M
Flower, Mark, Moonee ponds
Flower, Wm., grocer, &c., corner of Smith and Otter sts, E C
Flynn, Mrs. Mary, 41 Franklin st west
Focker, Captain, 121 Park st west, Em H
Foden, J. C., Henry st, Pra
Fogan, J., 30 Rathdowne st, Carl
Fogan, Patrick, 17 Little Lonsdale st east
Fogarty Brothers, grocers, &c., Queensberry st, Hot
Fogarty, Rd., 15 Courteney st, Rd
Fogarty, Daly, and Co., wine and spirit merchants, &c., 196 Elizabeth st, and Peel st, Hot
Fogarty, James, Wellington st, Rd
Fogarty, Patrick, Wellington st, Rd
Fogarty, Patrick, 68 Fitzroy st, F
Fogis, C., Victoria st, Rd
Foley, J., Faraday st, Carl
Foley, Maliche, Hanksia st, Hcid
Foley, Michael, Malne st, Hcid
Foley, P., Howard st, Hot
Foley, Peter, Drummond st, Carl
Foley, Thomas, Arden st, Hot
Foley, W., tailor, 132 Lonsdale st east
Folk, Lewis, 27 Napier st, F
Folk, Lewis and Henry, 3 Apsley place, E M
Folk, Mrs. S., 3 Apsley place, E M
Follaml, John, estate agent, 16 Wellington st, St K
Follett, Mrs., school, Haw
Folley, P., 25 Baillie st, Hot
Fookes, Mrs., ladies' school, 15 Oxford st, E C
Foord, George, analytical chemist, 86 Elizabeth st, and Alma road, St K
Foot, John, Nicholson st, Carl
Foot, Robert, bootmaker, Bridge road, Rd
Foot, Robert, bootmaker, Chapel st, Pra
Foote, George, Stoke st, San
Footner, Robert, turner and cabinetmaker, 130 Brunswick st, F
Foott, Michael, M.L.A., Parliament house
Forbes, James, 39 Franklin st, W M

Forbes and Co., asphalters and tar distillers, 24 Collins st west, and River bank, south side
Forbes, James D., draper and clothier, 152 Smith st, E C
Forbes, John George, County court judge, Wellington parade, E M, and Melbourne Club, Collins st east
Forbes, Robert A., 193 Cardigan st, Carl
Forbes, Robert, builder, 95 Little Collins st east
Forbes, Wm., carpenter, Park st, S Y
Forbes, Wm., 7 St. David st, F
Force, F. B., Haw
Ford, Alfred, 3 Pelham st, Carl
Ford, Amos, bootmaker, High st, St K
Ford Brothers, clothiers, 421 King st
Ford, F., butcher, 65 Johnston st, E C
Ford, F. T. W., surgeon, &c., 4 M'Kenzie street
Ford, George, grocer, 140 Lygon st, Carl
Ford, H., Grey st, E M
Ford, John, Canning st, Carl
Ford, John S., 68 Napier st, Em H
Ford, Joseph, butcher, Bay st, Btn
Ford, Mrs., miscellaneous repository, Chapel st, Pra
Ford, Mrs. Elizabeth, 96 Johnston st, E C
Ford, Mrs., Royal Bath, Beach, St K
Ford, Thomas, Alphington
Ford, Wm., and Co., chemists and druggists, 67 Swanston st
Ford, Wm., Balaclava road east, St K
Ford, Wm., 36 Gore st, F
Ford, Wm., M'Kenzie st
Ford, Wm., 114 Fitzroy st, F
Forde, Jonathan, 19 Alma st, F
Forden, John, Curzon st, Hot
Fordham, Frank, manager of Victorian Jam and Pickle Company, William st, and 93 Park st, Em H
Fordham, Henry, grocer, Bay st, San
Fordham, S., tailor, 3 Hathdowne st, Carl
Fordred, George, painter, Barry st, Carl
Fordyce, A., 137 Clarendon st, Em H
Fordyce, Andrew, grocer, 118 Clarendon st and 7 Union st, Em H
Foreman, George, painter, Queensberry st, Carl
Foreman, J., machine sewer, 127 Clarendon st, Em H
Foreman, Mrs., 46 Hanover st, F
Foresters' Hall, Little Nelson st, Wmn
Foresters, Order of, Bush Inn, Elizabeth st
Forman, George, 137 Lonsdale st west
Forrest, A., cabinet maker, Canning st, Carl
Forrest, David C., 128 Collins st east
Forrest, Mrs., servants' registry office, 128 Collins st east
Forrester, Alexander, Walsh st, W M
Forrester, Charles, Metropolitan hotel, 117 William st
Forrester, Charles, 48 Rosslyn st, W M

Forrester, Mrs., Charles st, Pra
Forster, Charles, stock and share broker, 64 Elizabeth st, and Blessington st, St K
Forster, L. F., saddler and saddlery importer, 35 Post Office place
Forster, Luke, saddler, 29 and 31 Post Office place
Forster, R. P., High st, Pra
Forster, R. P., Charles st, Pra
Forster, Wm. Mark, merchant, &c., 31 Post Office place
Forsyth, A., Albert st, Pra
Forsyth, A., Dryburgh st, Hot
Forsyth, C., 98 York st west, Em H
Forsyth, David, 104 York st, Em H
Forsyth, James, butcher, 12 Swanston st
Forsyth, John, 18 Wellington st, St K
Forsyth, John, timber yard, 29 High st, St K
Forsyth, John, 170 Russell st
Forsyth, W., Holder st, Btn
Forsyth, W., 29 King William st, F
Forwood, Charles Rossiter, conveyancer, 6 Bourke st east
Forwood, Wm H., 125 Park st, Em H
Fosberry, J. W., Punt road, S Y
Fosey, Mrs., Graham st, San
Foster, E., saddler, 16 Johnston st, F
Foster, Edward, store, Albert st, Pra
Foster, George, coal and wood yard, 143 Clarendon st, Em H
Foster, James, cab proprietor, Pent
Foster, John, 73 Cobden st, Em H
Foster, John, Trinnian st, off High st, Pra
Foster, Mary, general store, Yewers st, Fcy
Foster, Mrs., Graham st, San
Foster, Mrs., grocer, 27 Little Collins st west
Foster, Mrs., 10 Palmer st, F
Foster, Mrs., Albert st, Pra
Foster, Oswald, 78 Bourke st east
Foster, T., Lennox st, Hd
Foster, Thomas, Henry st, Pra
Foster, Wm. Lett, Nelson st, Wmn
Fouch, Mrs., 46 Cremorne st, Hd
Foubister, Robert, Brighton st, Rd
Foulds, James, smith and wheelwright, 145 Little Lonsdale st east
Foulds, Mrs., Graham st, San
Foulds, Wm., 136 Fitzroy st, F
Fowler, Edwin, Darling st, S Y
Foulis, James E., produce dealer, 61 Wellington st, E C
Foulkes, J. Y., Alphington hotel, Heid
Fowler, Daniel, carpenter, 21 Young st, F
Fowler, E., 167 Lygon st, Carl
Fowler, Henry, 82 Cobden st, Em H
Fowler, J., Grant st, Em H
Fowler, J., Alma road, St K
Fowler, James, High st, St K
Fowler, John, Freemasons' hotel, 62 Dover road, Wmn
Fowler, Joseph, Nicholson st, F

Fowler, Mrs., 32 Argyle st, F
Fowles, James, 12 Coventry st, Em fl
Fox, Alexander, and Co., photographers, 75 Swanston st
Fox, Alexander, 41 King William st, F
Fox, Alfred Charles, 73 Little Collins st west, and Barkly st, St K
Fox, C., New st, Btn
Fox, Charles, Leicester st, Carl
Fox, Henry, painter and glazier, 208 Little Collins st east
Fox, James, 93 Bouverie st, Carl
Fox, Mrs., Murphy st, Pra
Fox, Thomas, poulterer and market gardener, 4 and 5 Eastern market, and 96 Swanston st
Fox, Thomas, Brunswick road, Bk
Fox, W., 9 Young st, F
Fox, W. B., Gore st, F
Foxall, J., 144 Kerr st, F
Foxcroft, John, engineer and machinist, corner Pelham and Berkeley sts, Carl
Foxcroft, Miles, carrier and commission agent, 22 Collins st east
Foxhall, James, Courtney st, Rd
Foxhead, J., 142 Kerr st, F
Foxwell, John, painter and decorator, 70 Young st, F
Foy, Hiram, 21 Queensberry st, Carl
Foy, James, 243 Albert st, E M
Foy, Rev. Joseph, Kew
Foy, Samuel, 29 King William st, F
Foyle flour mills, 301 Brunswick st, F
Frahm, Charles, dairyman, 42 Swanston st
Frame, Thomas, Spencer terrace, Little Bourke st west
Francis Brothers, merchants, 34 Flinders lane west, and 13 Hood st
Francis, Charles, sawyer, a Beckett st west
Francis, George, civil engineer, 77 Queen street
Francis, Henry, pharmaceutical chemist, 31 Bourke st east, and Albert st, Wr
Francis, Henry, carpenter, Graham st, San
Francis, J., Stanley st, E C
Francis, J. G., M.L.A., commissioner of trade and customs, 149 Albert st, E M
Francis, John H., Lennox st, Rd
Francis and McPherson, merchants, 26 King st
Francis, Mrs., 70 Nelson road, Em H
Francis, Mrs., 205 Lygon st, Carl
Francis, Robert, timber merchant, Geelong road, Fcy
Francis, Samuel, William st, Btn
Francis, Stephen, Ray st, Btn
Francis, W., 88 George st, E M
Franke, J. G., 95 Kerr st, F
Frankel, Jacob, 136 and 138 Russell st
Frankel, Louis, general dealer, 169 Swanston st
Frankenberg, S., importer and warehouseman, 69 Queen st, and Murphy st, S Y

Frankish, Thomas, Railway place, San
Franklin, Chas., stevedore, Strand, W'msn
Franklin, F., Rotherwood st, Rd
Franklin, Stephen, tailor, Lennox st, Rd
Franklin, T., 52 Cobden st, Em H
Franklyn, F. B., printers' broker, 20 Queen st, 42 Flinders lane west, and Brighton road, St K
Franks, L. T., jeweller, 13 Brunswick st, F
Franks, Mrs., store, Beach st, San
Franz, Christian, tobacconist, 89 Bourke st east
Franzen, John and Henry, watchmakers, 94 Little Lonsdale st east
Fraser, A., carpenter, 119 Moray st, Em H
Fraser, Alexander, M.L.C., Alma road, St K
Fraser, Angus, bookseller and stationer, 195½ King st
Fraser, A. W., Barkly st, St K
Fraser, C., 77 Moray st, Em H
Fraser, Charles, High st, Pra
Fraser, Caroline, Greyhound Inn, High st, St K
Fraser and Co., auctioneers, 33 Collins st west
Fraser, George, 64 Napier st, Em H
Fraser, Henry, Alma st, St K
Fraser, H. C., Argyle st, St K
Fraser, John, 112 Stevedore st, W'msn
Fraser, John, 51 Cardigan st, Carl
Fraser, Moses, lakerman st, East St K
Fraser, Mrs. E., Inkerman st, East St K
Fraser, Mrs., school, Fawkner st, St K
Fraser, Mrs. Jane, laundress, 90 Napier st, Em H
Fraser, Rev. Alexander, 93 Collins st east
Fraser, Robert, dyer and scourer, 83 Smith st, F
Fraser, H., Courteney st, Hot
Fraser, H. N., 33 Drummond st, Carl
Fraser, S., Regent st, F
Fraser, Walter, 47 Three-chain road, Em H
Fraser, Wm., Queensberry st, Hot
Fraser, J. A., Victoria st west, Bk
Frayne, George, Greville st, Pra
Frayne, John, grocer, &c., Peel st, Pra
Frazer, James, blacksmith, 3 and 15 York st, Em H
Frazer, Joseph, 77 Stanley st, W M
Frazer, Moses, commission agent, 13 Flinders lane west, and Inkerman st, St K
Frazer, Miss, Pelham st, Carl
Frazer, W., M.L.A., Gertrude st, F
Freak, B., Chapel st, Pra
Freame, Francis, Stoke st, San
Freame, H. G., solicitor, 6 Collins st east, and Goodwood st, Rd
Freame, J., bootmaker, Peel st, Pra
Freame, James, bootmaker, Railway place, San

Frear, J., grocer, Stanley st, E C

Frecher, Charles, Park st, S Y
Fredman, Jane, draper, 275 Brunswick st, F
Freeboth, F., John Knox's Church
Freeman, —, greengrocer, 56 Stanley st, E C
Freeman, Edmund, Wreckyn st, Hot
Freeman, G. W., builder, Richmond terrace, Rd
Freeman, Henry, 41 Lygon st, Carl
Freeman, J., surgeon, Arthur-seat road, Bm
Freeman, John, 234 Little Collins st east
Freeman, M., cooper, Ann st, Wmn
Freeman, Mathew, Lyons st, Wmn
Freeman, Mrs., Goodwood st, Rd
Freeman, Mrs., 76a George st, F
Freeman, Thomas, Osborne st, S Y
Freeman, Thomas, gardener, Ivanhoe
Freeman, Wm, 6 Yarra st, Em H
Freemantle, —, Roden st, W M
Freer, George, Barkly st, St K
Freer, W. H. and G., iron merchants, 191 Elizabeth st
Freer, W. H., 39 Rathdowne st, Carl
Frewth, Thomas, 45 Twyford st south, Wmn
Free Trade and Financial Reform League office, 12 Collins st east
French, A., 48 Lygon st, Carl
French, Benjamin, tailor, 50 and 60 Queen st, and Jolimont road, E M
French, Benjamin, 115 Moray st, Em H
French, George, cabinetmaker, Peel st, Pra
French, J. J., Kew
French, John, drayman, 100 Little Collins st west
French, Robert, shoeing smith, 100 Johnson st, F
Fretwell, J. O., 54 Roden st, W M
Frew, George, Albion st east, Bk
Frewin, Mrs. E., 20 Faraday st, Carl
Fribbs, Patrick, Courteney st, Hot
Frick, Charles, 171 Russell st
Fricker, Frank, dealer, Graham st, San
Friedlein, C. D. A., accountant, 49 Collins st west
Friendly Societies' Registrar's office, Government house, Spring st
Friends' Meeting House, 6 Russell st
Frisbee, C. H., wood engraver, Abbotsford st, E C
Frith and Co., bootmakers, 169 Little Bourke st east
Frith, Frederick, photographer and portrait painter, 7 Collins st east
Frith, Jessie, store, 73 Madeline st, Carl
Frith, W., Sydney road, Bk
Fritsch, Andrew, pottery, 45 Victoria st, E C
Frizzell, Mrs., 216 Cardigan st, Carl
Fromont, Henry, Union hotel, Union st, Bk

Frost, E. H., machinist and tool maker, 31 Little Collins st west
Frost, J., Albert st, Pra
Frost, John, Palmerston st, Carl
Frost, John, draper, 59 Erroll st, Hot
Frost, John, 52 Erroll st, Hot
Frost, J. P., 123 Argyle st, F
Frost, Mrs., midwife, Courteney st, Hot
Frost, Wm., carpenter, Derby st, E C
Frost, Wm., bootmaker, Sleight lane, 58 Little Collins st east
Frost, Wm, 17 John st, Wmn
Fry, H., corn store, Ferguson st, Wmn
Fry, Henry, Villiers st, Hot
Fry, James, Foresters' Arms hotel, corner Clarendon and Napier sts, Em H
Fry, James K., accountant and arbitrator, 114 Collins st west
Fry, John, Wellington st, Rd
Fry, Joseph, 135 Raglan st, Em H
Fry, W. A., Canning st, Carl
Fuge, H. R., Pelham st, Carl
Fuge, Robert, chemist, Burgundy st, Hdd
Fuhrmann, H., upholsterer, 86 Collins st east
Fulbrook, C., Levison st, Hot
Fulbrook, Wm., 26 Stanley st, W M
Fulford, Rev. H., Caroline st, S Y
Fulker, George, naturalist, 50 Lygon st, Carl
Fullar, R. S, boat builder, Flinders st east
Fullarton, John, 110 Madeline st, Carl
Fullarton, Mrs., 83 Cardigan st, Carl
Fuller, Edwin, grocer, 17 Gertrude st, F
Fuller, Francis, 205 Gore st, F
Fuller, Frederick, butcher, Queensberry st, Hot
Fuller, Frederick, Curzon st, Hot
Fuller, —, 41 Cremorne st, Rd
Fuller, Mrs., 2 Palmer st, F
Fuller, W., Rifleman's Arms, Chapel st, Pra
Fullerton, G., Baillie st, Hot
Fullerton, Robert, harbour master, Bay st, San
Fullerton, Thomas, coachbuilder, 81 Victoria st, E C
Fulton, Alexander, Cardigan st, Carl
Fulton, E. G., hay and corn dealer, 39 Howard st, Hot
Fulton, George, Middle st, Flem
Fulton, James, 155 Little Lonsdale st west
Fulton, J. F. W., Victoria Hydropathic Establishment, Greville st, Pra
Fulton, Robert, 430 King st
Fulton, Robert, 138 Leicester st, F
Fulton, Robert, Fulton st, St K
Fulton, Thomas, and Co., engineers and ironfounders, 137 Flinders st west
Fulton, Thomas, Rosslyn st, W M
Fulton, Wm, 84 Stanley st, W M
Furby, Thomas, grocer, 128 Little Lonsdale st west

Furlong, Mrs., Punt road, Rd
Furneaux, R., Osborne st, S Y
Furnim, John T., 49 Fitzroy st, F
Furse, C., machinist, 31 Little Collins st west
Fury, John, Miller st, W M
Fyfe, George, tinsmith, Little Latrobe st east
Fyfe, George, smith, Beach st, San
Fyfe, Mrs., 29 Napier st, Em H
Fyffe, George, 10 Cecil st, Wmn
Fyffe, John, Lothian st, Hot
Fyffe, Martha, Marine hotel, Little Nelson st, Wmn
Fysh, C. S., grocer, Haw
Fyvie, E., chemist, 130 Russell st

G.

Gabel, —, carpenter, Station place, San
Gabelds, Geo., gunmaker, 98B Bourke st east
Gabriel, Samuel H., solicitor, 69 Bourke st west, and Hothson st east, St K
Gacon, John, shoemaker, Flem bank
Gahan, John F., solicitor, &c., 78 Elizabeth st
Gahan, F., 52 Ferguson st, Wmn
Gain, F., Yarra st, E C
Galbraith, Wm., clerk, Powlett st, E M
Galby, Fidele, 18 Barkly st, Carl
Gale, A. F., dressmaker, 205 Swanston st
Gale, Anne, Brown st, Heid
Gale, Henry, general dealer, Bay st, San
Gall, J., Wellington parade, E M
Gall, R., contractor, St. Andrew st, Bto
Gall, Wm., blacksmith, Hanmer st, Wmn
Gallagher, D., 131 Lygon st, Carl
Gallagher, John, Fawkner st, St K
Gallagher, Michael, Carlisle st, East St K
Gallagher, P. M., cutler, 164 Brunswick st, F
Gallagher, Robert, baker, 27 Smith st, F
Gallagher, W., coalyard, Bay st, San
Callougher, Edward A., port gauger, 17 Market st
Galland, John, coachbuilder, 49 Victoria parade, F
Gallie, —, Abbotsford st, W M
Galloghy, John, bootmaker, Cremorne st, Rd
Gallogly, O. D., Civil Service Club hotel, 125 Collins st east
Gallop, Charles, blacksmith, 11 York st west, Em H
Gallop, James, Canning st, Carl
Gallop, Mrs., Pelham st, Carl
Galloway, J., 66 Fitzroy st, F
Gallpen, George, 23 Twyford st, Wmn
Galop, Charles, blacksmith, York st west, Em H
Galop, George, Bay st, San
Galt, A., Lyndhurst, Bk
Galt, David, 92 Cardigan st, Carl

Galvin, C., baker, 12 Howard st, Hot
Galvin, John, hatter, 73 Collins st west, and Yarra bank, South Melbourne
Galvin, John, 14 Little Lonsdale st east
Gamb, R., grocer, Station place, San
Gamble, Robert, 36 King William st, F
Gambling, —, carpenter, Church st, E C
Gameder, Thomas, Kew
Gamgre, Joseph, hairdresser, 9 Bourke st west
Gammie, J., 42 Park st west, Em H
Gamson, H., Esplanade, St K
Gamson, Thomas, Jolimont road, F M
Gane, John, 15 Dorcas st west, Em H
Gann, Patrick, 34 Little Lonsdale st east
Gant, G., 57 Cecil st, Em H
Gaol (chief), Russell st
Gapp, Thomas L., Arden st, Hot
Gapler, James, Chapel st, S Y
Garbett, Jos., Berkeley st, Carl
Garbutt, John, hame and chain maker, 2 Berkeley st, Carl
Garcie, E., Albert st, Pra
Gardener, J., grocer, 82 Moor st, F
Gardiner, Florence, produce merchant, High st, St K
Gardiner, Henry S., insurance and general agent, 1 Dorcas st west, Em H
Gardiner, Mrs., 42 Napier st, F
Gardiner, Mrs., Curzon st, Hot
Gardiner, N., Church st, Rd
Gardiner, Samuel, 13 Spring st south
Gardiner, W. and S., auctioneers, 26 and 28 Collins st east
Gardiner, Wm., Pent
Gardner, Andrew, butcher, Queensberry st, and Victoria st, Carl
Gardner, Charles, blacksmith, Chapel st, Pra
Gardner, E. W., Morton's hotel, Bourke st west
Gardner, F., furrier and skin dresser, 84 Collins st west
Gardner, John, Moreland st, Fey
Gardner, Mrs., grocer, Young st, F
Gardner, Mrs., 30 Napier st, F
Gardner, Mrs., provision dealer, 73A Gertrude st, F
Gardner, R., Illawarra st, Wmn
Gardner, R., upholsterer, 91 Park st east, Em H
Garen, John, Heath st, San
Garey, J., tailor, Gardiner's creek road, Pra
Garey, J., Davies st, Pra
Garland, A., builder, 42 Young st, F
Garland, T., Berkeley st, Carl
Garlay, John, 9 Barkly st, Carl
Garlick, W. S., solicitor, 49 Elizabeth st
Garlick, Wm. J., Acland st, St K
Garner, Mrs. William, High st, St K
Garrard and James, surgeons, 122 Collins st east
Garrett, John, 36A Rathdowne st, Carl

Garrett, Robert, and Co., corn factors, 205 Elizabeth st
Garrett, Robert, 13 Swan st, Rd
Garrick, —, 179 George st, F
Garrick, Alexander, storeman, 132 Little Bourke st west
Garriock, Mrs., Nicholson st, F
Garroty, P., Rowena hotel, Rowena parade, Rd
Garside, W. and J., copper and zinc workers, Bay st, San
Gartner, Wm., 107 Bourke st east
Garton, James, Garton's hotel, Swanston street
Gartshore, Robert, saddler and harness maker, 1 Victoria st east
Garvie, Martin, Gravesend, Fcy
Garvin, Richard, baker, Wellington st, Rd
Garwood, George, livery stables, 89 Flinders lane east
Gascard, A., restaurant, 107 Lonsdale st east
Gaskell, Joseph, bird and animal curator, 195 Bourke st east
Gaskin, R., hallkeeper, 10 Temple court
Gasparo, G., Italian and Swiss hotel, 232 Lonsdale st east
Gascoigne, G. C., McArthur place, Carl
Gass, Stewart, Grattan st, Carl
Gathercole, —, 57 Smith st, F
Gaston, J., Reilly st, F
Gates, C. E., Murphy st, S Y
Gates, Wm., Crockford st, San
Gatenby, Robert, saddler, 112 Queen st
Gatehouse, James, Gardiner's creek road, S Y
Gathergood, Jabez, Beach road, Bin
Gathing, G., 73 Roslyn st, W M
Gatland, Thomas, sexton, Little Collins st west
Gattrell, George J., Family and Colonial hotel, Little Bourke st east
Gann, John, photographer, 95 Swanston street
Gaunson, James, pilot, 27 Cecil st, Wmn
Gaunt, George, Carlisle st west, St K
Gaunt, John M., Argyle st, St K
Gaunt, Thomas, watch and clock maker, 5 Post office place
Gavin, John, Davis st, S Y
Gavey, J., High st, Pra
Gawn, W., grocer, 269 Brunswick st, and 131 Kerr st, F
Gay, Charles, contractor, Buckland st, Heid
Gay, George, hay and corn dealer, 72 Gertrude st, F
Gay, Samuel W., 103 Spencer st
Gay, W., 40 Bank st west, Em H
Gaynor, Wm., cab proprietor, 214 George st, F
Gaze, Wm., 14 Stanley st, W M
Gase, Wm., engineer, 113 Russell st

Geach, Edwin, manufacturer of bonnet fronts, 41 Swanston st
Geach, Thomas, confectioner, 63 Collins st west, and 54 King William st, F
Gear, James, Henry st, Pra
Gears, Thomas, 52 Latrobe st west
Geard, J., 51 Young st, F
Gearing, John, 56 Ann st, Wmn
Gearing, Mrs., Dover place, Wmn
Geary, Joseph, 5 Hoddle st, E M
Geddes, Charles, Capel st, Wmn
Geddes, Mrs., Lygon st, Carl
Geddum, G., Ireland st, Wmn
Gedge, Wm. E., Waltham st, Rd
Geeham, J., Castlemaine hotel, 9 Little Bourke st west
Geelong and Melbourne Lighterage Company, 37 William st
Geer, T., grocer, Punt road, S Y
Geggie, Wm., 236 Victoria st, ltd
Gell, —, solicitor, Arden st, Hot
Gell, C. S., 120 Raglan st, Em H
Gell, Francis T., solicitor and notary, 35 Queen st, and Abbotsford st, Hot
Gell, Margaret, Howard st, Hot
Gemmell, McCaul, and Co., auctioneers, 49 Collins st west
Gemmell, H. M. C., Carlisle st east, St K
General Post Office, 1 Bourke st east
Geoghagan, Philip, Highett st, Rd
George, C. S., George's hotel, Little Bourke st east
George, Ed., 5 James st, F
George, F. N., wood turner, Chapel st, Pra
George, Hugh, printer, 194 Victoria parade, E M
George, J., chemist, deputy-registrar and postmaster, Sydney road, Bk
George, J., Victoria st, E C
George, Joseph, George st, F
George, Mrs., library, 19 Oxford st, E C
George, R., 194 Wellington st, E C
George, Samuel, carrier, Flemington hill
George, Samuel, Argyle st, Pra
George, Wm., grocer, 110 Fitzroy st, F
Georges Brothers, drapers, 206 Smith st, E C
Georgeson and Co., boot and shoe warehouse, 7 Collins st east
Georgeson, Wm., Darling st, S Y
Georgy, Margt., boarding-house, 151 Latrobe st west
Geraghty, P., Rowena parade, ltd
German Association, 146 Collins st east
German Gymnastic Association, 200 Lonsdale st east
German Lutheran Church, Grey st, E M
Germania, German newspaper office, 95 Kerr st, F
Germany, J., Lygon st, Carl
Gerrand, Hamilton, 41 Nicholson st, F
Gerschel, L. C., 4 Osborne buildings, Napier st, F

Gerson, Jacob, importer of fancy goods, 133 Swanston st
Gessner, F. G., 124 Fitzroy st, F
Gessner, Francis D., Carlisle st, St K
Gessner, Wm., Clyde st, St K
Gettins, Cyrus, Acland st, St K
Gibney, O. A., 218 Napier st, F
Gibb, James, upholsterer, &c., 178 Church st, Rd
Gibbens, J., greengrocer, Cardigan st, Carl
Gibbes, C. B., St. David st, F
Gibbie, Jas., 118 Lygon st, Carl
Gibbins, Henry, grocer, Brighton st, Rd
Gibbins, M., Lennox st, Rd
Gibbons, John, 56 Stanley st, W M
Gibbons, John, ship builder and owner, Yarra bank, 49 King st, and 146 Latrobe st west
Gibbons, Wm. Sidney, analytical chemist, 5 Collins st east, and 6 Albert st, E M
Gibbs, —, auctioneer, Oxford st, E C
Gibbs, Edward M., Wellington parade, Rd
Gibbs, Edwin, Fleet st, Palmer st, F
Gibbs, G., druggist, Bay st, Btn
Gibbs, J., 45 Bank st east, Em H
Gibbs, J., 1 Gore st, F
Gibbs, James H., 101 Rosslyn st, W M
Gibbs, John, Adderley st, Wmn
Gibbs, John, Commercial hotel, 21 Thompson st, Wmn
Gibbs, H. and S., merchants, 19 Queen st
Gibbs, R. D., Alma st west, St K
Gibbs, Richard, 65 Rosslyn st, W M
Gibbs, Richard, Grey st, E M
Gibbs, Ronald, and Co. (in liquidation), merchants, 22 and 24 Queen st
Gibbs, S. M., Alma st west, St K
Gibbs, Wm., grocer, Church st, Rd
Gibbs, Wm., 39 Rosslyn st, W M
Gibson, Arthur, soft goods broker, &c., 18 Flinders lane west, and Windsor terrace, Wr
Gibson, Captain, 18 Bank st east, Em H
Gibson, D. and R., flour mills, 48 Leicester st, Carl
Gibson, D., Queensberry st, Carl
Gibson, G., joiner, Berkeley st, Carl
Gibson, G., 112 Stevedore st, Wmn
Gibson, Gavin, boot and shoe importer, 26 Collins st east, and Alma road, St K
Gibson, Jesse, storekeeper, Mount Alexander road, Ess
Gibson, James, surgeon, Flemington hill
Gibson, James, tailor, 77 Little Collins st east
Gibson, James, 11 Nicholas lane, Bourke st east
Gibson, Leon, confectioner, Rouse st, San
Gibson, Mrs., Pelham st, Carl
Gibson, Mrs., Waterloo st, St K
Gibson, Mrs., 88 Rowena parade, Rd
Gibson, R., stock salesman, 47 Bourke st west
Gibson, R., 31 Peel st, Hot

Gibson, Richard, Bourke st west
Gibson, Robert, Queensberry st, Carl
Gibson, Wm., Lennox st, Hel
Gibson, Wm., bootmaker, 150 Swan st, Rd
Gideon, Lewis, accountant, 63 Swanston st and 211 Bourke st east
Gidley, Robert, chemist, Commercial road, Pra
Gidney, Isaac, dealer, 41 Provost st, Hot
Gien, B., 112 Little Bourke st west
Gifford, J., carpenter, Carpenter st, Bmn
Gilbert, —, Prince's st, St K
Gilbert and Pustance, clothes cleaners, Victoria parade, E C
Gilbert, Edward, 49 Cecil st north, Wmn
Gilbert, F., 60 Market st, Em H
Gilbert, F. G., ticket writer, 33 Napoleon st, E C
Gilbert, George, Ferguson st, Wmn
Gilbert, James, sculptor, Latrobe parade, Collins st east
Gilbert, John, coachmaker, Bridge road, Rd
Gilbert, Wm., butcher, corner of Leicester and Berkeley sts, Carl
Gilbertson, John, circulating library, Swan st, Rd
Gilbertson, Wm., china and glass dealer, 104 Bridge road, Rd
Gilby, John, Hoddle st, F C
Gilchrist, D., 157 Lygon st, Carl
Gilchrist, J., 27 Oxford st, E C
Gilchrist, James and John, brassfounders, 161 Bouverie st, Carl
Gilchrist, Mrs., Cardigan st, Carl
Gilchrist, W. J., Brunswick road, Bk
Gilchrist, W. J., 43 George st, F.
Gilchrist, W. S., 61 William st
Gildersleve, S., fruiterer, 116 Lonsdale st east
Giles, Edward, 41 Smith st, F
Giles, Henry, carrier, High st, Pra
Giles, Joseph, boarding-house keeper, 166 and 168 Bourke st west
Giles, Mrs., J. E., seminary, High st, St K
Giles, T., smith, Wellington st, St K
Giles, W., builder, 116 Leicester st, F
Giles, W., painter, Elgin st, Carl
Gilham, Edwin, 43 Lothian st, Hot
Gill, —, 107 George st, F
Gill and Thorpe, importers, 36 Flinders lane west
Gill, Edwin, Neptune st, St K
Gill, Fowler, and Co., merchants, 13 Little Collins st west
Gill, James, 211 Albert st, E M
Gill, John, architect, 18 Collins st east
Gill, John, Dalgety st, St K
Gill, John, Illawarra st, Wmn
Gill, John R., Westbury st east, St K
Gill, John, 118 Stevedore st, Wmn
Gill, Mrs. J., milliner, 2 Bank st east, Em H
Gill, R., Carlton st, Carl

Gill, Samuel, 11 Argyle st, F
Gill, Samuel Thomas, artist, 56 Little Collins st west, and Lang st, S Y
Gill, W. B., Flem bank
Gill, Wm., Arden st, Hot
Gillam, Edwin, soap and candle works, Flem bank
Gillam, Mary Ann, Flem bank
Gillard, S., and Son, sisters, 160 Swan st, Rd
Gillard, Wm., grocer, 145 Bourke st west
Gillbee, Wm., surgeon, 113 Collins st east
Gillespie, —, 55 Flinders st west
Gillespie, John, 92 Dudley st, W M
Gillespie, Mrs., Barkly st, St K
Gillespie, R. W., dairyman, 67 Napier st, Em H
Gillet, Jonathan, Church st, Rd
Gillet and Harford, sign writers, &c., 85 Russell st
Gillett, E., 19 Napier st, F
Gillett, John, 85 Russell st
Gillett, Miss, Nicholson st, Carl
Gillibrand, Edward, dairyman, 98 Gore st, F
Gillies, Alexander, storekeeper, Flem hill
Gillies, D., M.L.A., 10 Victoria parade
Gillies, Wm., cooper, 9 Milton st, W M
Gilling, R., surgeon, Stephen st
Gillman, Francis, tailor, 256 Swan st, Rd
Gillman, John, Barry st, Carl
Gillman, John, 79 Curzon st, Hot
Gillon, James, 235 Smith st, F
Gillott, Samuel, 13 Brunswick st, F
Gillow, John, solicitor, 41 Swanston st, and 138 Napier st, F
Gillson, W., draper, 88 and 90 Brunswick st, F
Gilmore, Martin, Howard st, Hot
Gilmore, Mrs., Moor st, F
Gilmore, Wm., Wrecklyn st, Hot
Gilmour, John C., watchmaker, 53 Leveson st, Hot
Gilmour, S., 122 Moray st, Em H
Ginn, W., 78 Johnson st, E C
Ginney, John, 6 Marion st, F
Gipps, John, 16 Victoria st, Hot
Gipps Land Prospecting Association, 8 Little Collins st west
Gipps Land Steam Navigation Company, 97 Collins st west
Girand, L., confectioner, 189 Little Bourke st east, and 91 Bourke st east
Girdler, Joseph R., High st, Pra
Girdlestone, T. M., M.L.A., surgeon, 124 Bourke st west
Girdlestone, Wm., 241 Victoria st, E C
Girvin, James, sawmill and timber yard, and ironmonger, 71 and 73 Brunswick st, F
Gisling, —, Acland st, St K
Gillingham, C. F., tailor, Commercial road, Pra
Gissing, Geo., tailor, 75 Fitzroy st, St K

Gittins, Cyrus, grocer, Robe st, St K
Gittus, Thomas, umbrella maker, 90 Swanston st
Givens, W. S., 279 Moray st, Em H
Givan, A., Chapel st, Pra
Gladdin, Wm., Flem
Glaister, Thomas, and Co., contractors and stone merchants, Collins st west
Glaister, Thomas, Peel st, Hot
Glaister, Wm., Capel st, Hot
Glasgow Underwriters' Association, B. R. Mathews, agent, 33 Market st
Glass, Hugh, merchant, 20 a'Beckett st east, and Flem
Glassborow, T., 110 Johnston st, F C
Glasscock, G., 66 Napier st, F
Glassford, John R., Arthur st, Pra
Glassford, Mathew, Fulton st, St K
Glavin, John, Exploration hotel, 127 Little Lonsdale st east
Glaysher, Joseph, Williams' hotel, 109 Elizabeth st
Glazier, J., fancy repository, 62 Brunswick st, F
Gledhill, John, estate agent and broker, Bay st, San
Gledhill, Mrs., ladies' school, Bay st, San
Gledhill, Wm., Church st, Rd
Gleeson, C., builder, 128 Latrobe st west
Gleeson, J., Stanley st, W M
Gleeson, J., grocer, 203 King st
Gleeson, John, Heath st, San
Glen, A., stationer, Commercial road, Pra
Glen, James, Bay st, San
Glen, John, Brunswick st, F
Glen, T., pawnbroker, Fitzroy st, F
Glen, Wm. H., music warehouse, 103 Swanston st
Glenn, Miss Elizabeth J., ladies' seminary, 115 Collins st east
Glennon, John, bootmaker, 206 Russell st
Glew, E., Sydney road, Bk
Glew, G., Nth
Glew, J., Barkly st, Bk
Glew, S., Barkly st, Bk
Gloster, Alfred, printer, Cliff st, S Y
Gloster, James, 27 Franklin st, W M
Gloster, John, grocer, Victoria st, Rd
Glover, —, Williams road, Tk
Glover, —, 74 Wellington st, E C
Glover, —, Blessington st, St K
Glover, G., Williams road, Pra
Glover, Jabez, dairyman, 12 Bell st, F
Glover, John, Prince Albert hotel, Flem
Glover, Lawrance, 39 Fitzroy st, F
Glover, S., Church st, Bin
Glover, Thomas, butcher, Swan st and Church st, Rd
Glover, Thomas, upholsterer, 79 Clarendon st, Em H
Glynn, P., 51 Latrobe st east
Glynn, Robert, draper, 127 Swanston st and 121 Bourke st east
Goach, Mrs., 49 Cecil st, Wmn

Goble, George, 195 Cardigan st, Carl
Goble, George, George hotel, 48 Cecil st, Wmn
Goby, Charles A., coppersmith, 120 Lonsdale st east
Godber, Job, carpenter, 206 Lonsdale st east
Goddard, D., 138 Little Bourke st west
Goddard, J., nightman, &c., Little Collins st east and 29 Little Bourke st west
Goddard, Wm. H., Inkerman st, St K
Godden, J., 158 Little Bourke st west
Godfrey and Campbell, wine merchants, 109 Collins st west
Godfrey, George, Solicitor, 31 Collins st west
Godfrey, R., Peel st, Pra
Godfrey, Wm., 109 Collins st west
Godkin, James, 117 Moray st, Em
Godrich, Edward, Star hotel, King William and Fitzroy sts, F
Godso, Isaac, Flemington road, Hot
Godso, Wm., Canning st, Carl
Godwin, Geo., accountant, Garden st, Pra
Goebel, H., Derby st, E C
Goer, James, 20 King st, and Lygon st, Carl
Goermenann, J. Frederick, timber yard, 65 Latrobe st east
Goethe, Rev. Matthias, Gisborne st, E M
Goff, —, 63 Rose st, F
Goff, George, Nugget and Woolpack hotel, Pent
Goff, George, grocer, 86 Stevedore st, Wmn
Goggin, Thomas, boarding-house keeper, 144 Bourke st west
Gold, Mrs., ladies' nurse, 98 Oxford st, E C
Gold office, Custom house
Goldberg, Abraham, and Co., tobacconists, 68 Swanston st
Golden, Mrs., 91 Cecil st east, Wmn
Golding, Daniel, professor of singing, Paisley st, Fcy
Golding, M., Paisley st, Fcy
Golding, R., Crescent, Rin
Goldsbrough, John, grocer, Swan st, Rd
Goldsbrough, R., stock agent, Flem
Goldsbrough, R., and Co., wool brokers and stock and station agents, 105 Bourke st west
Goldsmith, —, hay and corn merchant, 246 Elizabeth st
Goldsmidt, J., chiropodist, 62 Collins st east
Goldsmith, Henry, china and earthenware dealer, 100 Brunswick st, F
Goldsmith, J., 27 Franklyn st, W M
Goldsmith, J. G., Barkly st, Carl
Goldsmith, Samuel, corn dealer, 241 Swanston st
Goldspink, David, glass and china dealer, 40 and 34 Lonsdale st west

Goldstein, Moses, pawnbroker, 147 Swanston st
Goldstein, Rev. Louis, 48 Lonsdale st west
Goldstraw, Charles, 85 Elgin st, Carl
Gonoin, M., 42 Villiers st, Hot
Gooch, W., 49 St David st, F
Good, —, schoolmaster, 75 Johnston st, E C
Good, Francis, grocer, 205 Clarendon st, Em H
Good Hope and Collingwood Mining Companies, Crooked River, Temple court Collins st west
Good, Mrs., 92 Drummond st, Carl
Good, Mrs., Brighton st, Rd
Good, Robert, 49 Franklin st west
Goodall, —, Palmerston place, Madeline st, Carl
Goodchild, Joseph, 91 George st, F
Goode, J., Punt road, S Y
Goode, Joseph, accountant, 114 Russell st
Gooleur, Charles, King st north
Goodfellow, Thomas, wheelwright, Nott st, San
Goodhiem, Sampson, cap manufacturer, 131 Spring st
Goodhind, Richard, and Co., malt and hop merchants and distillers, 21 Flinders lane
Goodlet, Alexander, broker, 80 Collins st west, and Delany's road, Haw
Goodliffe, Thomas K., importer of furniture, &c., 197 Brunswick st and 6 Moor st, F
Goodman, John, official assignee, 7 and 8 Eldon chambers, Collins st west
Goodrich, Henry M., pawnbroker, 95 Wellington st, E C
Goodrich, John, pawnbroker, 120 Young st, F
Goodridge, Thomas, Elgin st, Carl
Goodsier, J. D. C., Dow st, San
Goodson, Edwin, 120 Faraday st, Carl
Goodwin, J. W., Preston
Goodwin, Mrs, 99 Lygon st, Carl
Goodwin, Robert, Bridge road, Rd
Goodwin, Terrance E., 35 Barkly st, Carl
Goold, John, bootmaker, Gardiner's creek road, Pra
Goold, Thos., accountant, 42 Elizabeth st
Goolge, Samuel, grocer, Church st, Rd
Gordon, A., 31 Franklyn st, W M
Gordon, A, shipwright, River side south
Gordon, C., jun , Gordon st, Fcy
Gordon, C., boarding-house, 159 King m
Gordon, C., Gordon st, Fcy
Gordon, D., shoemaker, 12 Stanley st, E C
Gordon, D., Curzon st, Hot
Gordon, G., store, Arthur's Seat road, Din
Gordon, George, grocer, 50 Swan st, Rd
Gordon, Henry, Wreckyn st, Hot
Gordon and Gotch, news and advertising agents, 85 Collins st west
Gordon, J., South road, Din

Gordon, James, 24 Railway place, Wmn
Gordon, John, 2 Carlton st, Carl
Gordon, Mrs., store, 92 Leicester st, F
Gordon, Mrs., Blackwood st, Hot
Gordon, Peter, 60 Bank st east, Em H
Gordon, W., 40 Douglas parade, Wmn
Gordon, Wm., Napier hotel, 66 Stevedore st, Wmn
Gordon, Wm., Rotherwood st, Rd
Gorman, D., Canning st, Carl
Gorman, Mrs., 15 Peel st, Hot
Gorman, Robert, Villiers st, Hot
Gorman, John, Cape st, Heid
Gorrie, John, baker, 119 Little Bourke st west
Gosbell and Wilkinson, corn dealers, George st, F
Gosbell, H., Webb st, F
Gosden, J., baker, 161 Little Lonsdale st east
Gosling, Henry, butcher, corner of Gertrude and George sts, F
Gosman, Rev. A., Westbury st, St K
Gosnell, J., boot and shoe maker, 221 King st
Goss, David, Bond st, E C
Goss, George, builder, 44 Douglas parade, Wmn
Goss, Wm., Wellington st, Rd
Gossett, D. W., 16 Thompson st, Wmn
Gossett, Mrs., 108 Napier st, Em H
Gossett, Wm., emigration office, Wmn
Gotch, John S., 236 Albert st, E M
Gothorpe, Thomas, 68 Dover road, Wmn
Goudie, James, Whitehall st, Fcy
Goner, Thomas, Williams' road, Pra
Gough, Andrew, importer, 5 Market st
Gough, Alfred F., Studley st, E C
Gough, E., Grange road, Tk
Gough, J., and Co., maltsters, 150 Flinders lane east, and 123 Flinders st east
Gough, Jesse, Rowena parade, Md
Gough, Mark, greengrocer, 104 Lygon st, Carl
Gough, W., Prince of Wales hotel, Flem
Goulburn Valley Vineyard Company, 30 Queen st
Gould, Edward G., and Co., homeopathic chemists, 90 Collins st east
Gould, James, general store, 26 Coventry st, Em H
Goulding, M. J., tailor, 19 Lonsdale st east
Goulding, Thos., bootmaker, 67 Queensberry st, Carl
Goulter, C. E., photographer, 57 Collins st east, and 17 Corentry st, Em H
Goulter, H., 62 George st, F
Gourlay, John, 135 Moray st, Em H
Gourley, R., 142 Napier st, Em H
Gourly, J., 75 Nelson road, Em H
Govan, J., Bonverie st, Carl
Gover, Henry B., professor of music, 36 Grattan st, Carl
Government House, Spring st

Government Gazette and Government Printing office, Eastern hill
Government Shipping offices, Sailors' Home, Spencer st
Government Storekeeper's office, corner King and Bourke sts
Government Survey, &c., offices, Latrobe st west
Gow, James, Miller st, Bk
Gow, John, 243 Swan st, Rd
Gow, John, 130 Leicester st, F
Gowan, Andrew, clothier, 23 Collins st west
Gowan, J. D., Barkly st, St K
Gowland, Charles, toy maker, 139 Cardigan st, Carl
Gowling, Joseph M., Faraday st, Carl
Goyder, F. C., Hunt Club hotel, 71 Little Collins st east
Goyder, J., United States hotel, Bay st, San
Grace, J., toy warehouse, 98 Smith st, E C
Gracie, F., locksmith, 28 Little Bourke st west
Gracie, Hugh, George hotel, Victoria st west, Hot
Gracie, James, carpenter, 42 Arden st, Hot
Gracie, Thomas, 100½ Collins st east
Gracie, Thomas, 142 Brunswick st, F
Graeser, Frederick, cap maker, 71 Little Collins st east
Grady, James, 43 Park st, Em H
Grafton, Edward, watchmaker, &c., 63 Smith st, F
Graham, —, Waterloo st, St K
Graham, A., M'Kenzie st
Graham and Bergin, merchants and bonded and free store proprietors, 3 Flinders st west
Graham Brothers and Co., merchants, 91 Little Collins st east
Graham, Charles, 90 Dudley st, W M
Graham, Charles, Punt road, S Y
Graham, E., Capel st, W M
Graham, Edward, Balaclava road, St K
Graham, Edward, Westbury street, St K
Graham, Francis, oil and colourman, 70 Swanston st, and 22 Regent st, F
Graham, G., M.D., surgeon, 130 Swan st, Rd
Graham, J., 5 Flinders st west
Graham, James, hon. consul for Italy, Elibank house, S Y
Graham, James, Chapel st, Pra
Graham, James, Punt road, S Y
Graham, John, Clyde hotel, Elgin st, Carl
Graham, Mrs., 137 Kerr st, F
Graham, Peter, Southey st, St K
Graham, S. A., Elsternwick
Graham, Thomas, Victoria st, E C
Graham, Thomas, Queensberry st, Carl
Graham, Wm., sign writer, 13 Little Bourke st west

K

Grand Junction Mining Association, 37 Market st
Grandin, Andrew, 23 Market st, Em II
Grange, James, draper, 47 Cremorne st, Rd
Grant, A., 204 Gore st, F
Grant, Alexander, Simpson st, E M
Grant, Angus, storekeeper, Flem
Grant, Daniel, land and estate agent, 58 Elizabeth st, and Fitzroy st, St K
Grant, George, waggon builder, 44 Elizabeth st north, and Pent
Grant, George, 170 Queen st
Grant, George, Hope st, Bk
Grant, J. M'Pherson, President Board of Land and Works, Bm
Grant, James, Highland Chief hotel, Franklin st east
Grant, James, New Zealand tavern, 115 Swanston st
Grant, James, 116 Swanston st
Grant, John, Victoria st, Rd
Grant, John, 4 Ireland st, W M
Grant, John, Lothian st, Hot
Grant, John, Flem
Grant, Mrs., 131 Johnston st, F
Grant, Mrs., 85 Rose st, F
Grant, Mrs., fruiterer, Fitzroy st, St K
Grant, Peter, Byron st, Hot
Grant, R., 9 Stevedore st, Wmn
Grant, Wm., railway carriage works, 99 Little Bourke st west
Grant, Wm., Spencer st north
Grant, Wm., law agent and insolvency accountant, 55 Little Collins st east
Grant, Wm., Ireland st, W M
Grant, Wm., Queensberry st, Hot
Grant, Wm., carpenter, 108½ Latrobe st west
Grantham, George, Flem
Granton, John, general dealer, 152 Latrobe st west
Grasyfort, Ferdinand, restaurant keeper, 104 Elizabeth st
Gratton, Mrs., Arthur st, Pra
Grave, A., 13 Bridport st, Em H
Grave, Alfred, 19 Cobden st, Em H
Grave, Henry, solicitor, 82 Collins st west
Grave, W. G., ship chandler and sailmaker, 145 Flinders st west
Grave, W. G., mn., marine surveyor, 145 Flinders st west
Gravel-, D., 80 Argyle st, F
Graves, A., 193 Cecil st, Em H
Gray and Waring, coopers, 46 Little Bourke st east
Gray, Andrew S., surgeon and oculist, 155 Collins st east
Gray, Charles, Clyde st, St K
Gray, Charles, baker, 90 Queensberry st, Carl
Gray, F., George st, F
Gray, G., French polisher, 3 Drummond st, Carl

Gray, George, 240 Albert st, E M
Gray, George, 123 Park st west, Em H
Gray, J. P., Cardigan st, Carl
Gray, James, Drummond st, Carl
Gray, John, 4 Royal terrace, Nicholson st, F
Gray, John, 59 Electra st, Wmn
Gray, John, fruiterer, Eastern Market
Gray, John and Wm., butchers, 27 Wellington st, E C
Gray, Mrs., Nicholson st, Carl
Gray, Mrs., 58 Bank st west, Em H
Gray, R., cabinetmaker, 13 Cobden st, Em H
Gray, Richard, 28 Bouverie st, Carl
Gray, Richard, Drummond st, Carl
Gray, Richard, confectioner, 83 Bourke st east, and Drummond st, Carl
Gray, Robert, sign writer, 112 Little Lonsdale st east
Gray, W., Brunswick road, Bk
Gray, W., Drummond st, Carl
Gray, Wm., Lygon st, Carl
Gray, Wm., bootmaker, 112 Clarendon st, Em H
Gray, Wm., Wellington st, E C
Gray, Wm., 2 Bath terrace, Faraday st, Carl
Gray, Wm., Mac's hotel, 130 Smith st E C
Gray, Wm., bootmaker, Brunswick st, F
Grayham, H., musician, 139 Gertrude st, F
Grayshaw, Wm., 61 Oxford st, E C
Grayson, John, 78 Stanley st, W M
Grazebrook, Joseph, Pant road, S Y
Grear, —, Orrong road, Tk
Greathead, Alfred M., 22 Curzon st, Hot
Greathead, J. M., 84 Elgin st, Carl
Greathead, Joseph, chemist, Hoddle st, E C
Great Extended and Ouest Gold Mining Companies, 64 Elizabeth st
Great Tunnel Quartz Mining Company, 35 Little Collins st west
Great Western Quartz Mining Company, 52 Queen st
Greaves Brothers, drapers, 33 Collins st east
Greaves, F., 101 Kerr st, F
Greaves, Mrs., 20 Palmer st, F
Green, —, Orrong road, Tk
Green, —, Victoria st, E C
Green, Benjamin, Peel st, Pra
Green, C., bootmaker Cecil st, F
Green, Charles, 14 Raglan st, Em R
Green, E., greengrocer, 282 Brunswick st, v
Green, Edward, Lennox st, Rd
Green, Godfrey, outfitter, 163 Elizabeth st
Green, H., Sydney road, Bk
Green, Henry, Cardigan st, Carl
Green, Henry, 19 Palmer st, F
Green, J., Inverness hotel, Ireland st, W M

Green, J., 52 Lygon st, Carl
Green, J. R., farrier, 314 Gertrude st, F
Green, James, 80 Dudley st, W M
Green, John, chemist and druggist, 203 Bourke st east
Green, John, Patterson st, E C
Green, John T., carrier, Commercial road, Prn
Green, John T., share broker, &c., 32 Queen street
Green, Mrs., tobacconist, 85 Clarendon st, Em H
Green, Mrs., draper, 83 Victoria st, Carl
Green, Mrs., High st, Prn
Green, Mrs., Highett st, Rd
Green, Mrs., Fitzroy st, St K
Green, Mrs. E., 108 Albert st, E M
Green, Robert W., Highett st, Rd
Green, T., boarding-house, 28 Latrobe st east
Green, Thomas, livery stables, Green's lane, Little Lonsdale st east
Green, Thomas, 5 Twyford st, S Wmn
Green, Thomas S., plumber, painter, and glazier, 100 Cambridge st, E C
Green, W. R., 63 Punt road, Rd
Green, Wm., bootmaker, Bay st, San
Green, Wm., medical botanist, 229 Bourke st east
Green, Wm., 44 Dudley st, W M
Green, Wm., Cremorne st, Rd
Green, Wm., R, Punt road, Rd
Green, Wm., Kensington
Greenaway, Mrs., Ivanhoe
Greenaway, Thomas, bootmaker, 49 Little Nelson st, Wmn
Greenaway, Wm., Sir Henry Barkly hotel, Cape st, Held
Greene, Charles C., solicitor, 20 Collins st west, and Bin
Greene, John, Peel st, Prn
Greening, Benjamin, High st, Prn
Greenhill, Wm., solicitor, 147 Fitzroy st, F
Greenland, W. F., boatbuilder, Punt road, Rd
Greenlaw, Wm., Studley park, Kew
Greenlove, J., 211 George st, F
Greenough, John, 17 Palmer st, F
Greenshields, John, builder, &c., 191 Little Collins st east
Greenslade, Henry, tobacconist, Chapel st, Prn
Greenslade, Joseph, fruiterer and confectioner, 208 Elizabeth st
Greensmith, J., 16 Cross st, Hot
Greenway, Mrs., 1 Apsley place, Gisborne st, E M
Greenwood, James A., grocer and wine merchant, 55 Swan st, Rd
Greenwood, John, 1 and 2 a'Beckett st east
Greenwood, J., Thomas, Gipps st, E M
Greenwood and Leaver, corn store, Pent

Greenwood, Mrs., laundress, 7 Cobden st, Em H
Greenwood, Samuel, 60 Moray st, Em H
Greer, Mrs., 162 Victoria parade, E M
Greeve, J., boarding-house, 156 Bourke st west
Greeves, Augustus, F. A., M.L.A., surgeon, 205 Swanston st
Greg, Wm, 124 Queen st
Gregory, Charles, 84 Wellington st, E C
Gregory, David, Flowerdale hotel, 65 Bourke st west
Gregory, James, M.D., Lennox st, Rd
Gregory, Edward, boot and shoe dealer, 56 Errol st, Hot
Gregory, Edwin, Jolimont road, F M
Gregory, G. A, 135 Cecil st, Em H
Gregory, George, 57 Napier st, Em H
Gregory, George and Henry, timber merchants, 37 William st
Gregory, George, Domain road, S Y
Gregory, Henry, Walsh st, S Y
Gregory, Henry, Royal hotel, Flemington road, and Villiers st, Hot
Gregory, James, painter and grainer, 139 Little Collins st east
Gregory, John, grocer, 105 Queen st
Gregory, John, Dover road, Wmn
Gregory, John A., solicitor, 9 Elizabeth st, and Caulfield
Gregory, Mrs., Napier st, F
Gregory, Rev. J. H., Chapel st, St K
Gregory, Robert K., Church st, Rd
Gregory, T., Hope st, Bk
Gregory, Walter, bootmaker, 161 Brunswick st, F
Gregory's free stores, Stoke st, San
Greig, Edward D., Orrong road, Tk
Greig, J., Gardiner's creek road Prn
Greig, James, 60 Raglan st, Em H
Greig, James, Prahran st, S Y
Greig, John, Queensberry st, Hot
Greig, Miss, school, 49 Coventry st, Em H
Greig, Mrs., 21 Church st, Em H
Greig, Mrs., fancy repository, 144 Brunswick st, F
Greig and Murray, auctioneers, 50 Collins st west
Greig, Walter, confectioner, 113 Victoria st, Hot
Greig, William, importer of fancy goods, 36 Gertrude st, F
Greig, Wm., Gardiner's creek road, S Y
Greig, W. J., and Co., brokers, &c., 2 Hall of Commerce, 48 Collins st west
Grene, R., settler, Flem
Gresson, Robert C., solicitor, 81 Little Collins st west, and Koornong park, Kew
Greville and Bird, telegraphic and advertising agents, Hall of Commerce, 48 Collins st west
Greville, C., Park st, Bin

Grey and Brewer, bootmakers, 193 Little Collins st east
Grey, Mrs., Chapel st, St K
Grey, R., contractor, Brunswick st, F
Greystock, R., 30 Gore st, F
Grice, R., 59 Victoria parade, F
Grice, Sumner, and Co., merchants, 24 Flinders lane, and 17 Flinders st west
Grier, C., surgeon, 85 Parks st east, Em H
Grierson, Ed., 53 Stanley st, W M
Grierson, Mrs., 309 Victoria parade, E C
Grieve, James, engraver, 217 King st
Grieves, Wm., tailor, 7 Royal lane
Griffin, John, Star Inn, Chapel st, Pra
Griffin, Julin, Wellington st, Pra
Griffin, Joseph, surveyor, Trinian st, off High st, Pra
Griffin, Margaret, grocer, 152 Little Lonsdale st east
Griffin, Miles, cooper, Chapel st, Pra
Griffin, Mrs., 11 Dorcas st, Em H
Griffin, Mrs., Bedford st, Hot
Griffin, Mrs., Clyde st, St K
Griffin, T., Arden st, Hot
Griffin, T., 210 Gore st, F
Griffith, C., Cleveland House, Flinders lane east
Griffith, Charles, and Co., merchants, 20 Queen st
Griffith, D., Pres
Griffith, Evan, 3 Cole st, Wmn
Griffith, J., Perry st, E C
Griffith, Mrs., Capel st, W M
Griffiths, Cornelius, Commercial road, Pra
Griffiths, George, 16 Little Latrobe st, east
Griffiths, G., Marion st, F
Griffiths, John, Railway place, San
Griffiths, John, Villiers st, Hot
Griffiths, Joseph, Church st, Rd
Griffiths, Mrs., 45 Hanover st, F
Griffiths, Mrs., Hoddle st, E C
Griffiths, T., bootmaker, 120 Elgin st, Carl
Griffiths, Wm., 97 Stanley st, E C
Griffiths, Wm., Curzon st, Hot
Griffiths, Wm., 5 Hanover st, F
Grigg, Thomas, carpenter, Lothian st, Hot
Grimbly, Wm. H., Royal Terminus hotel, Beach road, Btn
Grimes, Edward, butcher, Arthur's seat road, Btn
Grimoldi, John, meteorological instrument maker, 81 Queen st
Grimwade, F. S, Fitzroy st, St K
Grimwood, Richard, Station place, San
Grimwood, S., musician, 32 Latrobe st west
Grimwood, Thomas, Victoria hotel, Hoddle st, E C
Grindlay, Mrs., grocer, Drummond st, Carl
Grindrod, W., Highett st, Rd
Grinrod, J., carpenter, Nth
Grogan, Daniel, Hoddle st, Rd

Grogan, Charles, bootmaker, 12 Lonsdale st west
Grogan, James, bootmaker, 190 Elizabeth street
Groom, Edward, 14 Cardigan st, Carl
Groom, Henry, contractor, 189 Smith st, E C
Groom, Joseph, 28 Little Lonsdale st, east
Groom, S. H., shipowner, 39 William st, and Haw
Grosse, Frederick, engraver on wood, 62 Collins st east, and Murphy st, S Y
Grout, James, New st, Btn
Grove, Mrs., preparatory school, Henry s., Pra
Grove, Wm., 16 Barkly st, St K
Grover and Baker, sewing machine makers, 80 Collins st east
Grover, R., Dryburgh st, Hot
Grover, Wm., Queensberry st, Hot
Groves, D. and J., grocers, 99 Stevedore st, Wmn
Groves, Edward, dealer, Hosier lane, off Flinders lane, east
Groves, G. W., 203 Cecil st, Em H
Groves, George, 15 Stevedore st, Wmn
Growley, H , 81 Rose st, F
Growley, Thomas, 83 Rose st, F
Gruber, E. E., chemist, 82 Wellington st, E C
Gruenert, O., Highett st, Rd
Grul, James, Twyford st, Wmn
Grum, Joseph, miller, Flem bank
Grundy, Joseph L., accountant and estate agent, Temple court
Grunsted, W. T., 35 Russell st
Grut, Thomas C., Park st, S Y
Grylls, G. W. F., Sydney road, Bk
Gubbin, Wm., bootmaker, Curzon st, Hot
Gudemann, R., accountant, Treasury, Spring st
Guerard, Eugene Voe, artist, Gipps st, E M
Guest and Ball, bakers, Alphington
Guest, George, fruiterer, Wellington st, E C
Guest, John, 207 Wellington st, E C
Guest, Samuel, butcher, Chapel st, Pra
Guest, Thomas B., and Co., steam biscuit bakers, 97 and 99 William st, and 199 Lonsdale st west
Guest, Wm. S., 21 Spencer st
Guiding Star Mining Company, 13 Swanston st
Guillaume, J. J., deputy registrar of births and deaths, &c., Gardiner's creek road, Tk
Guither, George, Station place, San
Guley, Mrs. Eliza, dressmaker, 30 Market st, Em H
Gullan, Wm., 151 Moor st, F
Gulland, Wm., 145 George st, F
Gullett, Edmund, 135 Rose st, F
Gummer, Job, grocer, Chapel st, Pra

Gummer, Thomas, Bignell's lane, Bourke st east
Gunn, Kenneth, plasterer, 120 Cardigan st, Carl
Gunn, George, store, Sydney road, Bk
Gunn, G., Gardiner's creek road, Pra
Gunn, G., stables, Commercial road, Pra
Gunn, Michael, Rialen st, Wmn
Gunniford, Mrs., Goodwood st, Bd
Gunning, Charles E., Westbury st, St K
Gunning, D., 129 Park st, Em H
Gunning, Joseph, grocer, Gardiner's creek road, Tk
Gunter, H., dyer, 88 Little Lonsdale st east
Gurner, Henry F., crown solicitor, 192 Collins st east
Gurner and Simms, dressmakers, Rowena parade, Rd
Gusheridge, Joseph, butcher, 78 Bridge road, Rd
Gutherle, H., 95 Bouverie st, Carl
Guthridge, H., Carlton st, Carl
Guthrie, Hugh M., 104 George st, E M
Guthrie, Jas., baker, 16 Dudley st, W M
Guthrie, John, Pelham st, Carl
Gutman, W., 43 Napier st, F
Goyatt, George, St. Edmond's road, Pra
Guyatt, Thomas, Richmond terrace, Rd
Gymnasium, Esplanade, St K
Gyton, R. J., Grange road, Tk

H

Haber, Wm., 13 Victoria st, E C
Hack, Benjamin, stationer, 225 Swanston street
Hacker and Son, painters and decoraters, 77 Fitzroy st, St K
Hackett, D. H., Yarra st, Heid
Hackett, C. P., police magistrate, Robe st, St K
Hackett, J., coachbuilder, 257 and 259 Brunswick st and Argyle st, F
Hackett, Martin, 52 Little Nelson st, Wmn
Hackett, Michael, Governor Bourke hotel, 122 Little Lonsdale st east
Hacking, Wm., greengrocer, 165 Little Collins st east, and 13 Eastern Market, Bourke st east
Hackward, J., Weston st, Bk
Hadden, John W., physician and surgeon, 10 Napier st, F
Haddon, R., Rowden st, W M
Haddow, Andrew, corn dealer, 47 Queensberry st, Hot
Haddrell, Jacob, 71 Condell st, F
Hadfield, John, schoolmaster, Peel st, Pra
Hadley, John, coachbuilder, 63 High st, St K
Hadley, Robert, Prince's st, F
Hadley, Thomas H., Beach road, Bmn
Hagerty and Wright, tinsmiths, 41 Post Office place

Hagarty, John, Baillie st, Hot
Hagg, John, 71 Johnston st, E C
Haggart, Henry, fancy repository, Sydney road, Bk
Haggett, D., Victoria st, Rd
Hagin, John, Nicholson st, Carl
Hagon, J., Arden st, Hot
Hague and Co., plumbers and baths, 63 and 65 York st, Em H
Hague, Wm., plumber, Chapel st, Pra
Haig, Wm., M.D., 48 York st, Em H
Haigh Bros., outfitters, 56 and 58 Collins st east
Haigh, Samuel, Pool road, S Y
Haiken, George B., 33 Nicholson st, F
Haines, J., Jackson st, St K
Haines, Thomas, 118 Victoria st, Rd
Hair, James, Wreckyn st, Hot
Haird, Joseph, Inkerman st, St K
Halbert, Wm., 130 Johnston st, F
Haldane, T., draper, 101 Wellington st, E C
Hale, W., Peel st, Pra
Haleman, John, 83 Moor st, F
Hales, G., bootmaker, 208 Wellington st, E C
Hales, S. W., Cremorne st, Rd
Hales, Wm., Queensberry st, Carl
Haley, C., 9 George st, F
Halfey, John, M.L.A., merchant, 144 Collins st west
Halford, Professor, 1 Royal terrace, Nicholson st, F
Halfpenny, D., grocer, 105 Cremorne st, Rd
Halifax, —, 213 Gore st, F
Halifax, C., High st, Pra
Hall, —, Barkly st, St K
Hall, —, 17s Cardigan st, Carl
Hall, —, farmer, Braend, Wmn
Hall, A. R., 33 Napier st, F
Hall and Gillespie, contractors, &c., Australian wharf, and Dryburgh st, Hot
Hall, C., plasterer, 126 Moor st, F
Hall, C., Wilson st, Un
Hall, David, iron worker and plumber, 69 Lygon st, Carl
Hall, E., plasterer, Grattan st, Carl
Hall, Edward, 127 Little Bourke st west
Hall, G., Court House hotel, 51 Cecil st, Em H
Hall, G., draper, 39 and 62 Nelson place, Wmn
Hall, G. W., Silver Gate hotel, Clarendon st, Em H
Hall, George, store, Arthur st, Pra
Hall, George Thomas, 34 Johnston st, E C
Hall, H., chimney sweep, Moor st, F
Hall, H., 28 Pelham st, Carl
Hall, Henry, chemist, 113 Bourke st east
Hall, Henry, Heath st, San
Hall, Henry, nightman, Faraday st, Carl
Hall, Henry, Twyford st, South Wmn
Hall, Hurtley, Kew

70　　　Hal　　　MELBOURNE　　　Han

Hall, J., Albert st east, Bk
Hall, James, carrier, 53 Cecil st, Wmn
Hall, James, Lygon st, Carl
Hall, John, butcher, 168 Smith st, E C
Hall, John, Carlisle st, East St K
Hall, John, machine sewer, Railway place, San
Hall, John, Swan st, Rd
Hall, John, 1 Villiers st, Hot
Hall, John, 109 Little Bourke st west
Hall, Joseph, tailor, 64 Collins st west
Hall, M., Chambers st, Pra
Hall, Miss, 35 Stanley st, W M
Hall, Mrs., 22 Church st, Em H
Hall, Mrs., 47 Brunswick st, F
Hall, Mrs., 191 Moray st, Em H
Hall, N., 61 Napier st, F
Hall, Nelliey, and Co., shipping agents, 81 Flinders st west
Hall of Commerce, 48 Collins st west
Hall, Richard, restaurant keeper, 215 Elizabeth st
Hall, S. W., 57 Napier st, F
Hall, T., Dover road, Wmn
Hall, T. W., grocer, 164 Bridge road, Rd
Hall, W., Church st, Bin
Hall, Wm., store, Stevedore st, Wmn
Hall, Wm., Strand, Wmn
Hall, Wm., 40 McArthur place, Carl
Hall, Wm., carpenter, 72½ Oxford st, E C
Hall, Wm. E., fruiterer, 180 Collins st east
Hallam, Joshua, Lennox st, Rd
Hallam, Wm., greengrocer, &c., 118 Cambridge st, E C
Hallenstein, O., and Co., tanners, 110 Swanston st
Hallenstein, J., 57 Rosslyn st, W M
Hallenstein, M., Barkly st, St K
Haller, F., and Co., merchants, 28 Queen street
Haller, Frederick, Clippe st, E M
Hallers, Henry, 85 Moor st, F
Hallett, Charles, draper, Chapel st, Pra, and High st, St K
Hallett, E., baker, 156 Smith st, E C
Hallett, George, South Melbourne hotel, Gardiner's creek road, Pra
Hallett, Mrs., midwife, 156 Smith st, E C
Halliburton, John H., importer of tweeds and wool broker, 19 Lonsdale st west
Halliburton, John H., 83 Nelson road, Em H
Halliday, D., Errol st, Hot
Hallion, P., Union st, Bk
Halliwell and Co., french polishers, 87 Gore st, F
Halliwell and Regan, french polishers, 74 Lonsdale st east
Halliwell, Henry, 138 George st, F
Halloran, Margaret, grocer, 145 King st
Hallows, Joseph, 58 Chetwynd st Hot
Hallum, —, greengrocer, Cambridge st, E C

Halpin, Richard, Queensberry st, Hot
Halstead, James, 111 Bonverie st, Carl
Halstead, Kerr, & Co., timber merchants, a'Beckett st
Halstead, R., confectioner, 19 Leicester st, Carl
Halstead, Thomas, Drummond st, Carl
Haly, Miss, dressmaker, Commercial road, Pra
Halyburton, Robert M., 13 Cecil st, Wmn
Ham, Cornelius J., house and estate agent, 45 Swanston st, and Grey st, E M
Ham, T. J., Grey st, E M
Hamalton, John, plumber and gasfitter, 15 Curzon st, Hot
Hambretch, O., 16 Drummond st, Carl
Hamel and Ferguson, engravers, &c., 85 Queen st
Hamel, Julius, High st, St K
Hamer, Louis, cutler, 57 Victoria st, Carl
Hamey, Wm., Nugget hotel, 39 Bonverie st, Carl
Hamford, T. W., Gore st, F
Hamilton, —, 63 Rosslyn st, W M
Hamilton, A., Moreland road, Bk
Hamilton, Daniel, Abbotsford st, W M
Hamilton, J., 132 Kerr st, F
Hamilton, James, Abbotsford st, Hot
Hamilton, James Smith, 211 Lonsdale st west
Hamilton, John, plumber and gasfitter, 15 Curzon st, Hot
Hamilton, John, 155 Cecil street, Em H
Hamilton, Mrs., infants' school, Cowper st, Fcy
Hamilton, Mrs., 124 Latrobe st west
Hamilton, Rev. R., 58 Napier st, F
Hamilton, Robert, Princess st, Flem
Hamilton, Robert, 17½ Victoria st, Carl
Hammersley, H., Lygon st, Carl
Hammill, Wm., Orrong road, Tk
Hammond, E. E., Victoria st west, Bk
Hammond, Henry G. S., saddler, Bay st, San
Hammond, H. T., Haw
Hammond, J., Cochrane st, Dta
Hammond, Mrs., dressmaker, 117 Russell street
Hammond, Richard, 140 Lonsdale st east
Hammond, R. K., Lower Crescent, Btn
Hampson, C., 210 Cardigan st, Carl
Hampson, R., engineer, 68 Dudley st, W M
Hamson, J., painter, Crescent, Btn
Han, Kee, grocer, 81 Little Bourke st west
Hanaway, Stephen, 49 Twyford st, South Wmn
Hanbury, O. I., solicitor, 87 Little Collins st west, and High st, Pra
Hancke, Miss, ladies' school, Victoria parade, E M
Hancock, David J., Wellington st, E C
Hancock, W. T., 77 Johnston st, E C
Hand, Selby, wire worker, &c., 29 Little Collins st west

Handasyde, Gilbert, Yarra Nurseries, S Y
Handasyde, M'Millan and Co., seedsmen, 60 Elizabeth st, and Yarra Nurseries, S Y
Henderson, Wm., Henry st, Pra
Handfield, Rev. Henry P., Gisborne st, E M
Handfield, Wm. H., Rowena parade, Rd
Handiford and Co., money brokers, 85 Temple court, and Chapel st, Pra
Handford, Edward, painter, lakerman st east, St K
Handford, Sarah, Punt road, Pra
Hangbome, F. K., Hotham Arms hotel, 19 Leveson st, Hot
Handren, John, Grattan st, Carl
Hands, Benjamin W., Jolimont, E M
Handsford, J., 68 Oxford st, E C
Handy, K., 2 George st, F
Handyside, F., 29 Coventry st, Em H
Hang Chao Hong, merchant, 65 Little Bourke st east
Hanily, M. J. P., Blessington st, St K
Hank, Foo and Co., Chinese merchants, 53 Little Bourke st east
Hanly and M'Donough, jun., tailors, 164 Johnston st, E C
Hanmer, Edward, 95 Wellington st, E C
Hann, Asher, Golden Gate hotel, 104 Clarendon st, Em H
Hann, F. B., butcher, 132 Ferrars st, and 68 Moray st west, Em H
Hann, P., 121 William st
Hannaford, M., Commercial road, Pra
Hannah, Mrs., Abbotsford st, W M
Hannah, Thomas, pilot, 2 Macquarie st, Wmn
Hannan, A., 125 Raglan st, Em H
Hannan, Denis, Galway Club hotel, 26 Little Bourke st east
Hannan, E., Moray place, Em H
Hannan, M., Dublin tavern, 162 Elizabeth street
Hanney, D., 2 and 4 Coventry st, Em H
Hannigan, P., Horse Market hotel, Flemington road, Hot
Hanning, Thomas, 6 Railway place, Wmn
Hannon, Robert, Marion st, F
Hannygton, Sarah, boarding-house, 144 Little Lonsdale st west
Hansard, John, 73 Clarendon st, Em H
Hansen, J. H., boarding-house, 72 Lonsdale st west
Hansen, N., coachbuilder, Hoddle st, E C
Hansen, Peter, Carlisle hotel, 147 Bourke st east
Hansen, Peter, restaurant and lodging-house keeper, 153 Bourke st east
Hansen, Wm., pilot, Gifford st, Wmn
Hansford, J., Tarrangower st, Fcy
Hansford, J., jun., Ovens st, Fcy
Hanslow and Sampson, tailors and outfitters, 101 Swanston st
Hanslow, James, Northcote

Hanslow, John, coach proprietor, 140 Victoria st, Rd
Hanslow, Peter, hay and corn dealer, 30 Victoria st, Rd
Hanson, Mrs., Charles st, F
Haphazard Gold Mining Company, 144 Elizabeth st
Happerfield, A. T., 66 Dudley st, W M
Harber, Thomas, 68 George st, F
Harbison, John, M.L.A., 103 Rosslyn st, W M
Harbison, W., Bay st, Bis
Harbottle, —, 43 Flinders lane west
Harbour, Mrs., 80 Victoria st, Rd
Harcoombe, Jehoiada, carpenter, 70 Moor st, F
Harcourt, A. J., manufacturer of asphalte, varnish, &c., 64 Flinders lane west, and Fcy
Harcourt, Ann, Wreckyn st, Hot
Harcourt, Durant, solicitor, 83 Swanston street
Harcourt, Rev. J., Cecil st, Em H
Harcourt, Robert, wholesale ironmonger, 64 Flinders lane west
Hard, Mrs., general dealer, 43 Cardigan st, Carl
Hardcastle, Wm., Church st, Rd
Hardcastle, Wm., woolbroker, 99½ Collins st west
Harden, Frederick, Stoke st, San
Hardess, George M., 135 Queensberry st, Hot
Hardie, Joseph, Avoca st, Fcy
Hardiman, David, Cremorne st, Rd
Harding, —, Chapel st, Pra
Harding, D., Pentridge
Harding, E., Union st, Bk
Harding, Ellen, draper, 143 Lonsdale st east
Harding, Frederick, Punt road, S Y
Harding, G., 2 Little Latrobe st east
Harding, John, bootmaker, 142 Cardigan st, Carl
Harding, John, 149 Cardigan st, Carl
Harding, John, bootmaker, Grattan st, Carl
Harding, Mrs., Jackson st, St K
Harding, Robert, 89 Barkly st, Carl
Harding, W. B., 133 Johnston st, E C
Harding, Wm., contractor, 41 Stanley st, E C
Harding, Wm., Kingston hotel, Highett st, Rd
Harding, Wm., 54 Madeline st, Carl
Harding, Wm. W., confectioner, 154½ Bourke st east
Hardingham, Joseph, Domain road, S Y
Hardman, D., 189 Cecil st, Em H
Hardress, —, 17 Kerr st, F
Hards and Laverett, saddlers, 30 Bourke st west
Hardwick, Wm., upholsterer, Chapel st Pra

Hards, Benjamin, S Y
Hardy, Alexander, Pelham st, Carl
Hardy, George, produce merchant, 25 Swan st, Rd
Hardy, James, Wellington parade, E M
Hardy, John H., Faulkner st, St M
Hardy, John, 19 Peel st, Hot
Hardy, William, Lyndhurst, Pent
Hardy, Wilson, and Co., produce merchants, 33 Flinders st west
Hare, —, Bay st, San
Hare, F. H., baker, 282 Victoria st, Rd
Hare, George, baker, 280 Victoria st, Rd
Hare, Mrs. H., school, corner Blackwood and Courtenay sts, Hot
Hare, Wm., grocer, 116 Latrobe st east
Harford, Wm., 28 Curzon st, Hot
Haren, James, grocer, 131 Little Bourke st east
Haren, Robert, Munster Arms hotel, 137 Little Bourke st east
Harford, T., bootmaker, Victoria parade, E C
Hargrave, Wm., master mariner, Station place, San
Hargreave, James, High st, St K
Hark, Mrs., Walter st, Fcy
Harker, George, M.L.A., 119 Victoria parade, F
Harker, John, Hoddle st, E M
Harkness, J., grocer, &c., 173 Bourke st east
Harley, Edward S., tea broker, 34 Queen st, and 1 Eden terrace, St K
Harley, Frederick, Chapel st, St K
Harman Brothers, clothing manufacturers, 62 Collins st east
Harmer, Henry, Haw
Harmstead, George, Banksia st, Hid
Harmsworth, John G., plumber, 54 Queensberry st, Carl
Harnett, David, Old Governor Bourke hotel, corner of Spring and Little Lonsdale sts
Harneman, J. C., produce store, 62 William st
Harnett, E., boarding-house, 8 Little Lonsdale st west
Harnwell, Wm., blacksmith, 243 Swanston st
Harper, —, carpenter, 29 Napier st, F
Harper, Alfred, accountant, 54 Queen st
Harper, G. G., Highett st, Rd
Harper, George, Chetwynd st, Hot
Harper, H., Hoddle st, E C
Harper, H., Berkeley st, Carl
Harper, H., Pelham st, Carl
Harper, Henry, 154 Madeline st, Carl
Harper, John, 24 Barkly st, Carl
Harper, Mrs., Perry st, E C
Harper, Robt., 15 Victoria parade, F
Harper, Robt., and Co., coffee roasters, 55½ Flinders lane east, and 15 Victoria parade

Harper, Robert, saddle and harness maker, 54 Elizabeth st extension
Harper, Wm., 47 Victoria st, Carl
Harper, Wm., bootmaker, 242 Swanston st
Harratt, Henry, Blackwood st, Hot
Harrigan, Thomas W., 59 Curzon st, Hot
Harrington, C. H., butcher, Pelham st, Carl
Harrington, D., greengrocer, 37 Victoria st, Carl
Harrington, John, 48 Stanley st, W M
Harrington, Patrick, saddler, 18 Elizabeth st
Harris, Abraham, pawnbroker, 3 Little Bourke st west
Harris, Abraham, boot and shoe dealer, 163 Little Lonsdale st east
Harris, Alfred, Dalgety st, St K
Harris and Co., locksmiths, &c., Chapel st, Pra
Harris and Heymanson, manufacturers, and boot importers, 2 Flinders lane east
Harris, G., broker, Chapel st, Pra
Harris, H., Pelham st, Carl
Harris, H., painter, 78 George st, F
Harris, Henry, accountant, 39 Franklyn st west
Harris, Isaac, confectioner, 66 Clarendon st, Em H
Harris, Jacob, 145 Collins st east
Harris, James, builder, Victoria st, E C
Harris, James, Sydenham hotel, Elizabeth st, off Hoddle st, Rd
Harris, James, builder, Nicholson st, Victoria st, E C
Harris, James, Chapel st, Pra
Harris, John, 167 Spring st
Harris, John, 95a Nicholson st, F
Harris, John, bootmaker, 36 Bridge road, Rd
Harris, Joseph, seedsman and florist, Punt road, S Y
Harris, Josiah, grocer, 97 Gore st, F
Harris, M., fancy repository, 162 Stephen street
Harris, Miss, 103 Victoria st, E C
Harris, Mrs., 38 Gore st, F
Harris, Nathaniel, and Co., office, 50 Collins st west
Harris, R., Miller st, W M
Harris, Thomas R., 71 Rosslyn st, W M
Harris, Thomas, storekeeper, 240 Napier st, F
Harris, Thomas, nightman, 41 Hanover st, F
Harris, Thomas, Flemington road, Hot
Harris, W., blacksmith, Barkly st, Bun
Harris, Walter H., dairyman, 197 Smith st, F
Harris, Wm. G., barrister, 73 Little Collins st west
Harrison, Captain H., 117 Cecil st, Em H
Harrison, C. J., Rising Sun hotel, Geelong road, Fcy

Harrison, Daniel, Gardiner's creek road, S Y
Harrison, Daniel W., Wilson st, Pra
Harrison, E. G., Haw
Harrison, George, fancy repository, 59 Gertrude st, F, and 75 Swanston st
Harrison, H., 99 George st, F
Harrison, Henry C., Gloucester hotel, Hoddle st, E C
Harrison, J. B., bootmaker, Commercial road, Pra
Harrison, John M., chemist, Gardiner's creek road, S Y
Harrison, L., 127 Moor st, F
Harrison, Mrs., 165 Victoria parade, F
Harrison, Mrs., Napier st, F
Harrison, Mrs., Fitzroy st, St K
Harrison, T., Sydney road, Bk
Harrison, Thomas, fishmonger, Bay st, San
Harrison, W., joiner, Gardiner's creek road
Harrison, Wm., Dudley st, W M
Harrison, Wm., furniture dealer, 14 Little Collins st east
Harrison, Wm., Wilson st, Pra
Harrison, Wm., store, Hoddle st, Rd
Harrison, Wm., wholesale grocer, wine and spirit merchant, 37 Flinders st east
Harvey, C., china dealer, 140 Brunswick st, F
Harston, A. W., Auburn road, Upper Haw
Harston and Co., law stationers, 77 Little Collins st west
Hart, Daniel, boot dealer, 223 Smith st, F
Hart, Edwin, 71 Faraday st, Carl
Hart, H., general dealer, 143 Little Lonsdale st east
Hart, H., 130 Moor st, F
Hart, Henri J., merchant, 73 Russell st
Hart, Henry, Westgarth st, F
Hart, Henry H., miscellaneous repository, 42 Collins st west
Hart, Hyam, Albert road, Fcy
Hart, J., 59 Dorcas st west, E H
Hart, John, Albert st, Pra
Hart, John, brickmaker, Chapel st, Pra
Hart, Jos., wood yard, Queensberry st, Carl
Hart, Moss H., general importer, 17 Little Collins st west
Hart, Mrs., wax florist, 66 Collins st east, and 51 Coventry st, Em H
Hart, Mrs., Barkly st, St K
Hart, Reuben, 29 Fitzroy st, St K
Hart, Reuben, grocer, &c., 246 Lonsdale st east
Hart, Robt., cab driver, 116 Little Bourke st west
Hart, S., toy manufacturer, 66 Collins st east, and 86 Cecil st, Em H
Hart, Samuel, 17 Grattan st, Carl

Hart, Walter, draughtsman and engraver on wood, 64 Little Collins st east
Hartlett, Wm., Supreme Court hotel, corner Russell and Latrobe sts
Hartley, —, bootmaker, High st, St K
Hartley, E., and Co., bonded store, Collins st west, corner King st
Hartley, Edward, Inkerman st, St K
Hartley, J., Chapel st, St K
Hartley, John, butcher, High st, St K
Hartley, Joseph, ironmonger, 151 Russell st, and 12 Pelham st, Carl
Hartley, Mrs., school, Inkerman st east, St K
Hartley, W., Bridge road, Rd
Hartley, Wm., Cole st, Wmn
Hartman, Mouritz, Rokeby st, E C
Hartnett, Richard, saddler, Whitehall st, Fcy
Hartnett, Wm., Moreland st, Fcy
Hartney, John, Capel st, Hot
Hartung, Nicholas, boarding-house, 96 Lonsdale st west
Hartwell, George, 152 Moray st, Em H
Harty, Thomas, Spencer st north
Harvey, H. and F., merchants, 17 Queen street
Harvey, J. F., turner, 47 Franklyn st
Harvey, James, bootmaker, 108 Fitzroy st, F
Harvey, John, Queensberry st, Hot
Harvey, John, Carlisle st, St K
Harvey, John, Queen st
Harvey, Mrs., High st, St K
Harvey, Mrs., school, Pres
Harvey, R. J., 49 Roden st, W M
Harvey, Richard, cork importer, 24 Little Collins st east
Harvey, Robert, tailor, 45 Lonsdale st west, and Balaclava road, Caul
Harvey, Thomas, builder, Pres
Harvey, Wm., agent Denison Plains Pastoral Company, 69 Bourke st west
Harvey, Wm., greengrocer, Beach st, San
Harvie, Montague, Docker st, Rd
Harving, Thomas, cabinetmaker, 60 Madeline st, Carl
Harwood, Henry, Grosvenor Arms hotel, High st, St K
Harwood, Mrs., Gardiner's creek road, S Y
Harwood, Wm., Telegraph hotel, Chapel st, Pra
Haselden, Herbert, oil and lamp importer, 36 Swanston st
Haskell, John, hairdresser, 172 Smith st, E C
Haskin, Wm., 239 Swan st, Rd
Haslam, James, tailor, 176 Drummond st, Carl
Haslam, Richard, Illawarra st, Wmn
Haslam, Thomas, Morris st, Wmn
Haslen, Mrs., Nott st, San
Harroy, Edward, Nicholson st, Carl

L

Hassel, Josias N., 98 Napier st, Em H
Hastie, D., Cardigan st, Carl
Hastings, James, 98 Leicester st, Carl
Hastings, Thomas, Charles st, F
Hastleton, James, Elgin st, Carl
Hatfield, George, blacksmith, Cremorne st, Rd
Hatt, J., general dealer, 98 Brunswick st, F
Hatton, Henry, butcher, Mount Alexander road, Ess
Haucke, Miss, school, 1 Elmbank terrace, Victoria parade, E M
Havaty, Jas. J., 45 Three chain road, Em H
Hawey, Ed., Nicholson st, Hot
Hawkers, W., 10 Rosslyn st, W M
Hawkers and Darbyshire, case makers, 94 Little Bourke st west, and 95 William street
Hawkins, Copeland, and Dailey, sharebrokers, 53 Queen st
Hawkins, Jeffrey, photographer, 20 Queensberry st, Carl
Hawkins, John, grocer, Nicholson st, Carl
Hawkins, M., butcher, Barry st, Carl
Hawkins, Mrs., 109 Argyle st, F
Hawkins, R., 11 Greeves st, F
Hawkins, Wm., Dalgety st, St K
Hawkins, Wm., shoemaker, Pres
Hawks, John, oyster dealer, 148 Little Bourke st east
Hawkshaw, Wm., 108 Rose st, F
Hawley, Joseph, 143 Moor st, F
Hawley, R., auctioneer, St Kilda st, Btn
Hawthorn, B., Nth
Hawthorn, Mrs., 22 Grattan st, Carl
Hay, J., 73 Cobden st, Em H
Hay, J. H, upholsterer, 120 Stephen st
Hay, James A., accountant, Garden st, Chapel st, S Y
Hay, W., Elgin st, Carl
Hay, Wm. T., 97 Derkly st, Carl
Hay, Wm. A., coffee roaster, Bridge road, Rd
Hayball, Robert, builder and ironmonger, New st, Btn
Haydn, F. A., 1 Cardigan st, Carl
Haydn, J. F., Cecil st, F
Hayes, Andrew, 31 Baillie st, Hot
Hayes, Dennis, Shannon hotel, Nth
Hayes, Edward, Provost st, Hot
Hayes, George, 24 Moor st, F
Hayes, Henry, 26 Moor st, F
Hayes, J., Hampton st, Btn
Hayes, James, Alma hotel, Chapel st, St K
Hayes, James, Blue Post hotel, 23 Little Collins st east
Hayes, John, dairy, 21 Little Latrobe st east
Hayes, John, 129 Rose st, F
Hayes, John, 174 Brunswick st, F
Hayes, Luke, Peel st, S Y
Hayes, Misses, ladies' seminary, Victoria st, Carl

Hayes, Miss, dressmaker, Pelham st, Carl
Hayes, Mrs., Loveron st, Hot
Hayes, Mrs., machine sewer, 7 Young st, F
Hayes, P., Saltwater river, Fcy
Hayes, Patrick, contractor, 1 Wellington terrace
Hayes, Patrick, merchant, Ess
Hayes, Robert, 21 Howard st, Hot
Hayes, T., 168 Kerr st, F
Hayes, T. R., upholsterer, 7 Young st, F
Hayes, Wm., 75 Queensberry st, Hot
Hayfield, —, fruiterer, 110 Smith st, E C
Hayhow, Henry, house decorator, 225 Lonsdale st east
Hayles, Mrs., Queensberry st, Hot
Hayman, Philip, and Co., importers of jewellery, 18 Collins st east, and 23 Burnett st, St K
Haymarket Theatre, 172 Bourke st east
Haynes, F., 29 Fitzroy st, F
Haynes, P., woodyard, 65 Faraday st, Carl
Haynes, Thomas, Leveson st, Hot
Haynes, Thomas, 73 Victoria st west, Hot
Hays, Miss J., Heath st, San
Hayson, Henry, Young st, F
Hayter, H. H., Margaret terrace, Bk
Haythorne, Frank, brickmaker, Flem bank
Haythorpe, George, 89 Napier st, Em H
Hayward, C. H., Denby road, Btn
Hayward and Co, commission merchants, 49 Flinders lane west
Hayward, H., cabinetmaker, 140 Collins st west
Hayward, Henry George, repository, 19 Coventry st, Em H
Hayward, J., Sarah Sands hotel, Bk
Hayward, John, 50 Ferguson st, Wmn
Hayward, Mrs., dressmaker, Rowena parade, Rd
Hayward, Mrs., 38 Victoria st, W M
Hayward, Rev. Rowland, Kew
Hayward, Robert, 142 Moray st, Em H
Hayward, W. G., bootmaker, 299 Victoria parade, E C
Hazleton, James M., jeweller, 85 Little Bourke st east
Hasleyrove, T., carpenter, Church st, Btn
Hazlehurst, Joseph, furniture broker, 282 Elizabeth st
Head, Joseph, 41 Stanley st, W M
Heal, Hy., Vere st, E C
Heale, Wm., Caroline st, S Y
Healea, Henry, carpenter, Flem
Heales, Mrs. H., 11 Nicholson st, F
Heales, R., 84 Oxford st, E C
Heales, R., 44 Wellington st, E C
Healey, Robert, bootmaker, High st, St K
Healing, George, bootmaker, 106 Bridge road, Rd
Healy, —, hay and corn store, Johnston st, E C
Healy, Charles, baker, Bouverie st, Carl

Healy, F., boarding-house, 121 Bourke st east
Healy, J., pawnbroker, 91 Clarendon st, Em H
Healy, James, Queensberry st, Hot
Healy, Michael, 13 Curzon st, Hot
Healy, Michael, Alma hotel, 161 King st
Healy, Miss, dressmaker and milliner, 174 Elizabeth st
Healy, Mrs., Barkly st, St K
Healy, Patrick, 26 Pelham st, Carl
Healy, Wm., 38 Jeffcott st, W M
Heape Brothers and Co., merchants, 11, 13, and 15 Flinders st west
Heape, Charles, Brighton
Heaps, J., Edward st, Bk
Heard Brothers, fishmongers, 50 Swanston st
Heard, Gideon, Argyle st, Pra
Heard, Henrietta, fruiterer, 9 and 10 Eastern Market
Heard, John, bootmaker, 208½ Bourke st east
Heard, Thomas, 83 George st, F
Heartfield, David, carpenter, Nelson st, Pra
Hearle, Wm., Williams road, Pra
Hearn, Josiah, High st, St K
Hearn, W. E., L.L.D., barrister, 73 Little Collins st west, and Melbourne University
Hearnden, John, Fulton st, St K
Heaslip, D., Bridge hotel, Bridge road, Rd
Heath, A. E., Bond st, E C
Heath, George, Ascot vale, Flem
Heath, Henry, oilman, &c., 104 Brunswick st, F
Heath, Joseph, Barney st, Rd
Heath, John, 219 Gore st, F
Heath, Joseph, and Co., wholesale grocers and wine and spirit merchants, 43 Swanston st
Heath, Joseph, 99 Moray st, Em H
Heath, Reuben, 66 Greeves st, F
Heath, R. R., South Audley st, E C
Heather, F., circulating library, 214 Eastern road, Em H
Heathcote, Howland, greengrocer, 38 Wellington st, E C
Heatherton, D., Weston st, Bk
Heaton, James, bootmaker, 89 Gore st, F
Heaton, John, White Horse hotel, Swan st, Rd
Hebbden, George, Gardiner's creek road, S Y
Hebblethwaite, R., 67 Rathdowne st, Carl
Hebrew Church and Schools, corner Stephen and Little Lonsdale sts
Hedderwick, A., 68 Argyle st, F
Hedderwick, Henry, Kew
Hedderwick, Robert, house and land agent, Brighton st, Rd
Hedges, Thomas, 36 Bank st west, Em H
Heelan, H., Kangaroo hotel, 84 Drummond st, Carl

Heelis, Ed. S., compositor, Grey st, E M
Heffernan, J., 20 Stanley st, W M
Heffernan, James, 134 Latrobe st west
Heffernan, James, 23 Victoria st, Hot
Heffernan, Mrs., Melbourne tavern, 104 Lonsdale st east
Hegarty, Mrs., 70 Raglan st, Em H
Hegarty's Baths, Beach, St K
Heickeh, S., 2 Falkland terrace, Greeves st, F
Heikcher, D., Charles st, Pra
Heinbecker, H., 81 Smith st, F
Heinecke, F. W., and Co., wholesale tobacconists, 59 Swanston st
Heintz, C., 96 York st, Em H
Heir, Mrs., Wreckyn st, Hot
Hellewell, Edward, whip maker, 3 Little Collins st west, and 33 Pelham st, Carl
Hellins, W., Btn
Hellor, J., Union st, Bk
Helm, Thomas, carver and gilder, 150 Bourke st east
Helms, Richard, tobacconist, 135 Bourke st east
Helmond, George, Capel st, Hot
Helton, J., Abbotsford st, W M
Hemert, Van J., 251 Smith st, F
Hemingway, John, Moray st, Em H
Hemmons, F. and J., druggists' sundrymen, Little Collins st east
Hemphill, C. E., Albert st east, Bk
Hems, Richard, Higbett st, Rd
Hemsford, G., Gore st, F
Hemsworth, Thomas, Barkly st, Carl
Henden, G., Cecil st, Wmn
Henden, Wm., Cecil st, F
Henderson, A., 36 Barry st, Carl
Henderson, Andrew, tinsmith and gasfitter, 76 Elizabeth st north
Henderson, Charles, grocer, 143 Queensberry st, Hot
Henderson, Edward, mechanical engineer, 63 Little Collins st west
Henderson, George, Baillie st, Hot
Henderson, George, 6 Dover place, Wmn
Henderson, Hewitt, dairyman, Smith st, F
Henderson, Hugh, blacksmith, Little Latrobe st
Henderson, J., crinoline manufacturer, 128 and 130 Spring st
Henderson, J., 23 Cardigan st, Carl
Henderson, James, store, 10 Bridge road, Rd
Henderson, James, Grey st, St K
Henderson, James, 172 Moray st, Em H
Henderson, James, 38 Argyle st, F
Henderson, J., 23 Cardigan st, Carl
Henderson, John, confectioner, 17 Little Latrobe st
Henderson, Joseph, 10 Condell st, F
Henderson, Mrs., 134 Nicholson st, F
Henderson, Mrs., 34 Bank st, Em H
Henderson, Mrs. Ellen, private boardinghouse, 5 Dorcas st, Em H

Henderson, P. E., civil and mining engineer, Glenlyon road, Bk
Henderson, Rev. A. M., Madeline st, Carl
Henderson, Robert, Elgin st, Carl
Henderson, Robert, draper, 53 Bank st west, Em H
Henderson, S., crinoline manufacturer, 130 Spring st
Henderson, Thomas, 179 Flinders lane east
Henderson, Thomas P., Haw
Henderson, Thomas, and Co., millwrights, Elizabeth st north
Henderson, W., 75 Webb st, F
Henderson, W., blacksmith, Gardiner's creek road, Pra
Henderson, Wm., Ralston st, S Y
Henderson, Wm., Dow st, San
Hendrick, Hugh, Richmond terrace, Rd
Hendy, John, greengrocer, Sackville st, E C
Hendy, George, Miller st, W M
Henger, Michael, cabinetmaker, 172 Lonsdale st east
Henkel and Patterson, tinsmiths, 30 Little Collins st east
Hennelle, G., 40 Moor st, F
Hennessy, J., 105 Kerr st, F
Hennessy, James, 62 Elgin st, Carl
Hennessy, James, Kerr st, F
Hennessey, Wm., fishmonger, 56 Swanston st
Henningham, R. M., Ralston st
Henriques, A., Victoria parade, F
Henriques, A. L., printing office, Angelo lane, 9 Bourke st east
Henriques, Mrs., 93 York st west, Em H
Henry, D., 45 Rathdowne st, Carl
Henry, David, jeweller and watchmaker, 31 Collins st east
Henry Jenkin, 104 Pelham st, Carl
Henry, Jenkin, 104 Cardigan st, Carl
Henry, Jos., 48 Latrobe st west
Henry, Mrs., 150 Bridge road, Rd
Henry, Mrs., 100 Kerr st, F
Henry, R., Village Belle Inn, Barkly st, St K
Henry, Thomas, surveyor, 5 Stephen st
Henry, Wm., Blue Bell hotel, 179 Little Collins st east
Henson and Broarly, saddlers, Elizabeth street
Henson, J., gunmaker, 62 Little Collins st east
Henty, Edward, Studley park
Henty, H. J., Hoxeth, Wellington st, Kew
Henty, Henry, Church st, Rd
Henty, Hon. James, M.L.C., Waltham st, Rd
Henty, Hon. S. G., M.L.C., merchant, 60 Collins st west and Kew
Henty, James, and Co., merchants, 11 Little Collins st west
Hepsey, J., Rathdowne st, Carl

Hepburn, Mrs., Elgin st, Carl
Hepburn, Robert, Auburn road, Haw
Hepburn, Wm., 100 York st, Em H
Hepinstall, Wm., Lygon st, Carl
Herald newspaper office, 9 Bourke st east
Herbert, Mrs., 45 York st west, Em H
Herbert, Mrs., 114 Latrobe st east
Herbert, Wm., butcher, Hallway place, San
Hercules Quartz Mining Company, 64 Elizabeth st
Herman, Ferd., Victoria parade, E M
Hermitage, G., 34 Elgin st, Carl
Heron, W. K., stationer, 116 Gertrude st, F
Herron, James, Marian st, F
Herring, Thomas, Richmond terrace, Hd
Herring, Wm. M., Henry st, Pra
Herrington, W. J., 3 Napier st, F
Hertogs, Mons., 4 Park terrace, Fitzroy st, St K
Hervey, Matthew, High st, St K
Hervey, Wm., Park st, S Y
Hess, F., musician, 147 Little Lonsdale st east
Hester, Thomas, general dealer, Nott st, San e
Hester, W., 233 Smith st, F
Hetherington, Charles, saddler, 8 Collins st west, and Jolimont terrace, E M
Hetherington, Rev. Irving, 91 Collins st east
Hevcran, J., Johnston st, E C
Hewet, George, cider manufacturer, 216 Moray st, Em H
Hewett, Joseph, general dealer, 142 Spring st
Hewett, Mrs., Lennox st, Rd
Hewitt, —, Elgin st, Carl
Hewitt, Cyrus, coach proprietor, 35 Bourke st east
Hewitt, J., Barkly st, Btn
Hewitt, James, accountant, 52 Collins st east
Hewitt, W., contractor, Day st, Btn
Hewlett, —, surgeon, Gertrude st, F
Hews, J., Hoddle st, E C
Hewson, —, saddler, 278 Elizabeth st
Hewson, Richard, Flemington road, Hot
Hewton, J., baker, 36 Coventry st, Em H
Heyde, Wm. Von der, 6 Walsh st, S Y
Heymanson and Co., warehousemen, 15 Flinders lane west
Heymanson, W., 8 Victoria parade, F
Heyne, E. B., 26 Swan st, Rd
Heywood, Captain, Jolimont place, E M
Hibberd, Alfred, Whitehall st, Fcy
Hibberd, Wm. George, hairdresser, Elizabeth street extension
Hi Chung, Chinese store, 61 Little Bourke st east
Hick, Benjamin, Forest hill, S Y
Hick, W. and D., merchants, 109 Collins st west

Hick, Wm., Grange road, Tk
Hickey, Donald, Berkeley st, Carl
Hickey, John, Errol st, Hot
Hickey, John, carver and gilder, 230 Bourke st east
Hickey, John, 28 Fitzroy st, F
Hickey, John, Davis st, Pra
Hickey, Mrs., 143 Bourke st west
Hickey, Peter, 82 Montague st, Em H
Hickey, Thomas, bookseller, &c., Elizabeth st
Hickford, James, sign writer, 83 Swanston st, and Sydney road, Bk
Hickinbotham, Wm., upholsterer, 27 Collins st east
Hickling, A., machine sewer, 219 Smith st, F
Hickling, Rd., 84 Rowena parade, Rd
Hickling, Samuel, greengrocer, 17 Cremorne st, Rd
Hickling, Wm., Caroline st, Pra
Hickling, Wm., 186 Drummond st, Carl
Hickmott, W., 117 Napier st, Em H
Hicks, A., plumber, 235 Lygon st, Carl
Hicks, Alfred, Glenlyon road, Bk
Hicks, F., Ascot vale, Flem
Hicks, Johnson, 233 Swan st, Rd
Hicks, Joseph, Gertrude st, Pra
Hicks, Mrs., greengrocer, Pelham st, Carl
Hicks, R. M., Albert st, Pra
Hickson Brothers, marine store, Derby st, E C
Hickson, L., marine yard, Franklin st
Hickson, Samuel, dealer, 2 Franklin st east
Hiddle, James, Morris st, Wmn
Hiddlestone, Wm., store, Leicester st, Carl
Hide, T., Bay st, San
Hide, W., 134 Nicholson st, F
Hieland, Henry, Gardiner's creek road, Tk
Higginbotham, Mrs., boarding-house, Clarendon st, Em H
Higginbotham, Thomas, 59 Gore st, F
Higginbotham, W., Waterloo st, St K
Higginbotham, Wm., hairdresser, 90 Brunswick st, F
Higginbotham, Wm., hairdresser, 234 Bourke st east
Higgins, Andrew, Burgundy st, Heid
Higgins, George, 86 Oxford st, E C
Higgins, J., dairyman, Wells st, Bru
Higgins, John, contractor, Ascot vale, Flem
Higgins, Mrs., Victoria st, St K
Higgins, Patrick, J.P., contractor, Ascot vale, Flem
Higgins, Thomas, Station place, San
Higginson, Rev. Henry, Gisborne st, F M
Higgs, Wm., Royal hotel, Punt road, Rd
Higham, Henry, Moor st, Fey
Highett, Wm., M.L.C., Bridge road, Rd
Higinbotham, George (Attorney-General) barrister, 73 Little Collins st west, and St. Kilda road, Bru

Higinbotham, Thomas, railway engineer-in-chief, Spencer st
Hildreth, J. A., 93 Lygon st, Carl
Hill, —, 36 Stephen st
Hill, Alexander, ironmonger, 129 Swanston st
Hill, Alfred, Church st, Rd
Hill, Charles, contractor, 20 Errol st, Hot
Hill, Charles, Highett st, Rd
Hill, David, Haw
Hill, G. H., ship chandler, 17 Nelson place east, Wmn
Hill, George, solicitor, 82 Collins st west, and Palermo st, Pra
Hill, George, watchmaker, Sydney road, Bk
Hill, Henry, Berkeley st, Carl
Hill, J., 81 Moray st, Em H
Hill, J. M., Union st, Pra
Hill, James, house decorator, 132 Collins st east
Hill, James S., Clarendon hotel, 203 Clarendon st, Em H
Hill, John T., hairdresser, 82 Swanston st
Hill, John W., baker, 22 Little Lonsdale st east
Hill, Joseph, undertaker and corn merchant, 75 and 77 Clarendon st, Em H
Hill, Joseph, Moor st, F
Hill, Joseph, Railway place, San
Hill, Mrs., 236 Swan st, Rd
Hill, Mrs., 60 Arden st, Hot
Hill, Mrs., baby linen warehouse, 63a Bourke st east, 19 Collins st east, and 7 Princes st, F
Hill, Mrs., Pelham st, Carl
Hill, Mrs., milliner and dressmaker, 211 Lygon st, Carl
Hill, Mrs., Argyle st, Pra
Hill, Mrs., dressmaker, George st, F
Hill, Mrs., school, 30 Coventry st, Em H
Hill, Mrs., Otago hotel, 93 Flinders st west
Hill, Rd., Templemore hotel, 35 Latrobe st west
Hill, Sarah, 10 Cross st, Hot
Hill, T., 7 Princes st, F
Hill, T. A., Inkerman st west, St K
Hill, Thomas, 54 Jeffcott st, W M
Hill, Walter, 1 King William st, F
Hill, Wm., 70 Drummond st, Carl
Hill, Wm., 11 Little Lonsdale st east
Hill, Wm., builder and contractor, 139 Latrobe st west
Hill, Wm., Sir Henry Barkly hotel, Westgarth st, F
Hill, Wm. Rowland, chemist and druggist, 63 Collins st east
Hill, Wm. C., Murphy st, S Y
Hills, Thomas, Inkerman st, St K
Hilliard, R. L., ferryman, River side south
Hillier, Edward, hatter, 55 Errol st, Hot
Hilligan, Patrick, Fawkner st, St K
Hillings, —, Gore st, F

Hilyard, E., 83 Bank st, Em H
Hilson, John, 63 Cardigan st, Carl
Hilson, John, store, Bay st, San
Hilton, Francis James, grocer and provision merchant, 207 Bourke st east
Hilton, Wm., 98 Cecil st, Em H
Himming, G., 35 Faraday st, Carl
Hinchliffe, George, smith, Kew
Hinchliffe, Wm., plumber, Stoke st, San
Hincks, J., muslin stamper, 116 Smith st, E C
Hinds, Wm., Ulster hotel, 61 Spring st
Hindson, John, 1 Fitzroy terrace, Clarendon st, E M
Hine, F. W., 36 Latrobe st west
Hine, Samuel, boarding-house, 204 Russell st
Hines and Sedgefield, solicitors, 60 Little Collins st west
Hines, J., Elsternwick
Hines, James W., 33 Gore st, F
Hines, John, Victoria st, Bk
Hinge, John, Wreckyn st, Hot
Hingston, J., and Co., law stationers, 76 Little Collins st west
Hingston, James, St K
Hinkins, John Thomas, Moonee Ponds
Hinkins, John Wm., Moonee Ponds
Hinkster, James, 259 Napier st, F
Hinton, Henry R., Wellington parade, E M
Hippesley, F., Rosslyn st, W M
Hippesley, Fredk., bootmaker, 61 Coventry st, Em H
Hipsworth, John, 125 Bouverie st, Carl
Hird, Joseph, cabinet maker, Franklyn st
Hislop, John P., master mariner, 51 Douglas parade, Wmn
Hislop, Mrs., 49 Wellington st, E C
Hitchcock, Wm., Henry st, S Y
Hoad, G., fruiterer, 29 Gertrude st, F
Hoar, Miss, grocer, Bridge road, Rd
Hobart, Alfred, 43 Victoria st, Hot
Hobart Town and Launceston Marine Insurance Company, 82 Collins st west
Hobbs, A., Chapel st, Pra
Hobbs, George, Capel st, Hot
Hobbs, James, Burnett st, St K
Hobbs, Mrs., Blackwood st, Hot
Hobbs, Stephen Kentley, cook and confectioner, 29 Collins st east
Hobson, Francis, 84 Hotham st, E M
Hobson, Mrs. S., 72 Cardigan st, Carl
Hobson, Robert, Vine st, Held
Hobson, Thomas, Hoddle st, E C
Hobson's Bay Soap and Candle Company, 78 Collins st west, and works corner of Latrobe and Adderley sts, W M
Hockin, Wm., Hockin's hotel, 185 Elizabeth st
Hocking, Francis, engineer and general smith, 274 Elizabeth st
Hocknell, Isaac R., Acland st, St K
Hockley, Louisa, school, Peel st, Hot

Hoddle, Robert, 223 Bourke st west
Hoddy, James, Illawarra st, Wmn
Hodge, J., hame and saddletree maker, 40 Bourke st west
Hodges, Henry George, photographer, 530 Brunswick st, F
Hodges, J., Union st, Bk
Hodgetts, G., Capel st, W M
Hodgins, Robert, Long st, Fey
Hodgkins, G., 12 Curzon st, Hot
Hodgkins, T., clothier, &c., 161 Bourke st east
Hodgkinson, Clement, assistant commissioner of lands and survey, Hotham st, E M
Hodgson, A., Argyle st, Pra
Hodgson, Alexander, 45 Faraday st, Carl
Hodgson, Alfred G., outfitter and draper, 13 Lonsdale st west
Hodgson, E., Wellington st, St K
Hodgson, Henry, butcher, 76 Swan st, Rd
Hodgson, Henry, Cecil st, F
Hodgson, John J., 13 Macquarie st., Wmn
Hodgson, John, 4 Argyle st, Pra
Hodgson, Mrs., miscellaneous repository, Chapel st, Pra
Hodgson, Richard, importer, 123 Lonsdale st west, and 143 Latrobe st west
Hodgson, W. P., painter, Faulkner st, St K
Hodson, Walter, Yarra hotel, 71 Flinders st west
Hodgson, Wm., 32½ Clarendon st, Em H
Hodgsons, Thomas, blacksmith, Durgancy st, Held
Hodnett, David, 24 Howard st, Hot
Hodnett, Wm., 97 Moray st, Em H
Hodson, Robert, Greville st, Pra
Hoelskin, Victor, confectioner, 167 Swanston st
Hoffman, C., tobacconist, 96½ Swanston st
Hoffmann, W. B., Em H
Hoffmann, Wm., Ess
Hogan, James, Prince's Bridge hotel, corner of Swanston and Flinders sts
Hogan, James, Robert Burns hotel, Smith st, E C
Hogan, John, Courtenay st, Hot
Hogan, Joseph, 44 Little Latrobe st west
Hogan, M., Park st, S Y
Hogan, Mrs., 22 Bank st west, Em H
Hogan, Mrs., Pelham st, Carl
Hogan, R., Thompson st, South Wmn
Hogan, Thomas, earthenware dealer, 202 Elizabeth st
Hogarth, Julius, chaser and goldsmith, 13 Bourke st west, and 66 Rosslyn s., W M
Hogarth, Wm., Darling st, S Y
Hogg, E. J., Grange road, Tk
Hogg, Mrs., 95 Gore st, F
Hogg, Mrs., Victoria parade, E C
Hogg, Peter, 85 Coventry st, Em H
Hogg, Thomas, Sydney road, Bk

Hogg, Wm., 44 Johnston st, F
Hoggre, James, 1 Chetwynd st, Hot
Holden, D., china dealer, Sydney road, Bk
Holden, Henry, Cremorne st, ltd
Holder, Henry, 10 Barkly st, Carl
Holder, James, 133 Westgarth st, F
Holder, ——, fishmonger, 64 Clarendon st, Em H
Holder, Mrs., 3 Pelham st, Carl
Holdoway, James, baker, 34 York st, Em H
Holdsworth, J. R., 166 Victoria st, Rd
Hole, James, Commercial road, Pra
Holgate, Enoch, grocer, 266 Victoria st, Rd
Holland, H., saw setter, 51 Smith st, F
Holland, Henry, Ess
Holland, W., paperhanger, Robe st, St K
Holland, W. H., Southey st, St K
Holland, Wm. C., Lothian st, Hot
Hollans, A., Nott st, San
Hollick, Mrs., Punt road, Rd
Hollick, Mrs., laundress, 90 Spencer st north
Holliday, Wm. H., butcher, 110 Moray st, Em H
Hollingworth, ——, 90 Moor st, F
Hollingworth, A., 160 Brunswick st, F
Hollis, Daniel, Bay st, San
Hollow, M., Bay st, Bra
Holloway, F., bootmaker, 46 Ferguson st, Wm
Holloway, J., Preston
Holloway, John, Lothian st, Hot
Holloway, Mrs., Robe st, St K
Holman, Jas., 35 Three-chain road, Em H
Holmen, R., 97 Fitzroy st, F
Holme, J. W., 2 Latrobe st west
Holmes, Abel, tailor, 25 Cardigan st, Carl
Holmes and Russell, merchants and ship owners, 8 Queen st
Holmes, C., Stoke st, San
Holmes, Captain, Dorcas st, Em H
Holmes, Edwin, 4 Nicholson st, F
Holmes, George, contractor, Ess
Holmes, J., bootmaker, Condell st, F
Holmes, J., John st, Bk
Holmes, J., Pelham st, Carl
Holmes, John, hawker, Latrobe parade, Collins st east
Holmes, John, Jolimont place, E M
Holmes, John, saddler, 70 Bridge road, Rd
Holmes, M., Bay st, Bra
Holmes, Mrs. S., dressmaker, 173 Russell street
Holmes, Thomas, 88 Leicester st, Carl
Holmes, White, and Co., merchants, 48 William st
Holmes, Wm., Nott st, San
Holmes, Wm., 86 Leicester st, Carl
Holroyd, Edward D., barrister, 16 Temple court, Collins st west
Holt, D., wheelwright, 173 Brunswick st, F

Holt, David, Roddle st, E C
Holt, Edward, Roddle st, E C
Holt, Richard (of Briscoe and Co.)
Holt, T., fancy repository, Chapel st, Pra
Holt, Wm., Kew
Holten, Richard, 19 John st, Wm
Holton, John, Grattan st, Carl
Holton, Thomas, tea and sugar sorter, corner Queen and a'Beckett sts
Home, John Walter, machine broker, and importer, corner Elizabeth and Latrobe streets
Homeward Bound Gold Mining Company, 9 Elizabeth st
Homewood, A., coppersmith, 33 Twyford st, South Wm
Homewood, Charles, 20 Gifford st, Wm
Hommel, T., Nth
Hommel, Theodor, and Co., tobacco manufacturers, 127 and 129 Lonsdale st west
Honden, Thomas, Dover place, Wm
Hood, A., manufacturing chemist, 59 Little Bourke st west
Hood and Co., manufacturing chemists, 160 Elizabeth st, 59 Little Bourke st west, and 78 Lonsdale st west
Hood, John, Chetwynd st, Hot
Hood, John, Richmond terrace, Rd
Hood, R., Church st, Rd
Hood, T., 183 Wellington st, E C
Hood, Thomas, rate collector, 49 Stanley st, E C
Hood, Wm., 2 Victoria terrace, Cardigan st, Carl
Hoof, Ann, boarding-house, 48 Stephen st
Hook, Mrs., 85 Westgarth st, F
Hooke, John B., Haw
Hooke, Thomas, blacksmith, Lonsdale st, and 39 Easy st, E C
Hooker, Henry, and Co., clothiers, hatters, and hosiers, 169 Bourke st east
Hopkins, Robert, Punt road, S Y
Hopkins, Robert, share and money broker, 20 Collins st east
Hoon, ——, 198 Gore st, F
Hooper, J., 12 Little Latrobe st east
Hooper, James, 46 Johnston st, E C
Hooper, Mrs., Little Nelson st, Wm
Hooper, Mrs., 135 Leicester st, F
Hope and King, importers of glass and china, 48 Collins st east
Hope, Arthur, Greville st, Pra
Hope, Charles, 38 Little Nelson st, Wm
Hope, D., bootmaker, 63 York st, Em H
Hope, James, Pra
Hope, Mrs., 46 Argyle st, F
Hopkins, C. F., Barkly st, Carl
Hopkins, Edward, Moreland st, Fcy
Hopkins, George, 39 Dryburgh st, Carl
Hopkins, Isaiah, Stevedore st, Wm
Hopkins, J. R., M.L.A., Parliament house
Hopkins, John, solicitor, 17 Eldon Chambers

Hopkins, Wm., grocer, 50 Madeline st, Carl
Hopkins, Wm., Faraday st, Carl
Hopkins, Wm., hairdresser, 71 Flinders st west
Hopkins, Wm. H., general dealer, 106 Brunswick st, F
Hopkinson, Samuel, 133 Bridport st, Em H
Hopwood, Thomas, outfitter, 5 Collins st east, and Kew
Hordern, Anthony and Wm., agents, 84A Russell st, and Nth
Hordern, W., 30 George st, F
Hore, George, 28 Baillie st, Hot
Hore, James, musician, 167 Lonsdale st east
Hore, Thomas, Illawarra st, Wmn
Horiball, J., 71 Rosslyn st, W M
Horigan, James, dairyman, 76 Cardigan st, Carl
Horley, A., Darling st, S Y
Horn, A., Johnston st, F
Horn, R., hairdresser, Cardigan st, Carl
Horn, W., 89 Rose st, F
Horncastle, H., Provost st, Hot
Horne, A., blacksmith, 199 Smith st, F
Horne, G. S. W., solicitor, 80 Collins st west
Horne, George, tailor, woollen draper, and outfitter, 1 Collins st east
Horne, H., 160 Young st, F
Horneman, Henry Alfred, Swan st, Fcy
Horneman, James C., produce dealer, 62 William st, and Yarra st, Fcy
Horner, Henry, secretary to the Australasian Financial Agency Company, Eldon Chambers, and Williams road, Tk
Horner, James, Albert st, Pra
Hornidge, J. P., Park st, Em H
Hornsby, F. K., Boden st, W M
Hornsby, J., tailor, 205 Napier st, F
Hornsfall, J., 40 Gore st, F
Horrell, Charles, C., High st, Pra
Horrown, W. H., Adderly st, W M
Hornsburg, David and Alexander, bootmakers, 85 Swanston st
Horsenail, Wm., lithographic printer, Heath st, San
Horsey, A. M., 79 Young st, F
Horsewell, Wm., Heath st, San
Horsfall, George, Hoddle st, Rd
Horsfall, J. A., draper, Gardiner's creek road, Pra
Horsfall, John, Murphy st, S Y
Horsley, —, 81 Kerr st, F
Horsley, Wm., Railway place, San
Horsebauld, 237 Swan st, Hd
Horticultural Society of Victoria, office, Haw
Horton, C., Elgin st, Carl
Horton, John N., grocer, 132 Spencer st north
Horton, Samuel, Commercial road, Pra

Horton, Joseph, woodyard, 69 Lygon st, Carl
Horwitz, H., 1 Victoria parade, F
Horwood, H., 106 Oxford st, E C
Horwood, E., Sawyers' Arms hotel, Ferry st, E C
Hose, F. W., Provost st, Hot
Hose, Wm., Jeffcott st, W M
Hosie, James, confectioner, 38 Bourke st east
Hosking, W. N., Park st, S Y
Hoskins, J., carrier, Flem
Hoskins, John, Crockford st, San
Hoskins, W. H., 63 Kerr st, F
Hoskins, Wm., 46 Hanover st, F
Hospital, corner of Lonsdale and Swanston sts; out-door patients' department, Little Lonsdale st east
Houghton, Henry, 9 Hanmer st, Wmn
Houghton, Mrs., laundress, 37 Cobden st, Em H
Houghton, Mrs., 46 Hanover st, F
Houghton, W. G., perambulator manufacturer, 6 Bridge road, Rd
Hourigan, John, Twyford st, South Wmn
House, Miss, milliner, 78 Brunswick st, F
House, S., Barkly st, St K
House, Samuel, and Co., corn and produce merchants, 264 Elizabeth st, and 17 Queen st
Houseley, N., Fitzroy hotel, Napier st, F
Houses of Parliament, Spring st
Houston, —, Palmerston st, Carl
Houston, Hugh, 17 Rosslyn st, W M
Houston, John, Beach road, Rtn
Houston, P., 94 Fitzroy st, F
Houten, Henry, drawing master, Garden st, Pra
Hovendon, F., 72 Napier st, Em H
How, —, steam chaff works, Gipps st, E C
Howard, —, Berkeley st, Carl
Howard, E. C., Wangaratta
Howard, G., 62 Stanley st, W. M.
Howard, H. F., 170 Lygon st, Carl
Howard, J., locksmith, 128 Gore st, F
Howard, Mrs., general store, 133 Victoria st, E C
Howard, Mrs., ladies' school, Gore st, F
Howard, Mrs. Edward, 15 Jeffcott st, W M
Howard, Wm., Palmerston st, Carl
Howard, Wm., carpenter, McKillop st. Bourke st west
Howarth, R., 54 Johnston st west, F
Howat, David, 21 Dorcas st, Em H
Howden, Charles, broker, 18 Queen st, and Albion st, S Y
Howe, John, 26 Railway place, Wmn
Howe, John, cigar manufacturer, High st, St K
Howe, R., bootmaker, 74 Brunswick st, F
Howe, Sarah, greengrocer, 71 Queensberry st, Carl
Howell, —, photographer, 47 Victoria parade, F

Howell, —, nurseryman, Chapel st, St K
Howell, Edward, 9 Baillie st, Hot
Howell, Edward, 17 King William st, F
Howell, G., 129 Kerr st, F
Howell, George T., 127 Kerr st, F
Howell, Thomas, fruiterer, 95 Bridge road, Rd
Howes, James A., 272 Brunswick st, F
Howes, James, 77 Moor st, F
Howes, W., butcher, South road, Btn
Howgate, Abraham, Yorkshire hotel, Wellington st, E C
Howie, Robert, draper, &c., 25 Bourke st east, and Barkly st, Carl
Howison, Alex., Stawell st, W M
Howitt, Godfrey, M.D., 196 Collins st east
Howitt, J., 111 Moray st, Em II
Howitt, W. G., surgeon, 153 Collins st east
Howlett, Mrs., Dover road, Wmn
Howlett, R., 219 Napier st, F
Howorth, Jeremiah, auctioneer and estate agent, 83 Collins st west
Howse and Blake, saddlers, 15 and 31 Bourke st west
Howse, W. B., tailor, Cremorne st, Rd
Howson, A., 9 Church st, Em II
Hoyt, Henry, coach proprietor and livery stable keeper, 90 Bourke st east
Hubbard, J., 30 Johnston st west, F
Huberts, John, Palmerston st, Carl
Hudson, C., Royal Dane hotel, Faraday st, Carl
Hudson, Charles, 184 Cardigan st, Carl
Hudson, J. G., draper, Chapel st, Pra
Hudson, Mark, Elgin st, Carl
Hudson, Mrs., machine sewer, 186 Wellington st, E C
Hudson, Mrs., Brighton st, Rd
Hudson, R. J., Marion st, F
Hudson, W., Abbotsford st, W M
Hudson, Wm., cattle salesman, Flem
Hudspeth, J., painter, Leicester st, Carl
Hudspeth, Mrs., 3 Woodland terrace, George st, F
Huesker and Krause, hay and corn dealers, 34 Little Lonsdale st east
Huggett, Wm., Victoria st, Rd
Huggins, John, house and land agent, 41 Swanston st
Hughan, John, steam saw and moulding mills, corner of Bourke and Spencer sts, and Moonee Ponds
Hughes, —, Leicester st, Carl
Hughes, A., 23 Ragion st, Em II
Hughes and Harvey, tinsmiths, 97 Little Bourke street east and 142 Lonsdale st east
Hughes, Charles, saddlers' ironmonger, Lonsdale st east and 142 Latrobe st west
Hughes, D., 63 Napier st, F
Hughes, Daniel S., provision merchant, 4 Lonsdale st east
Hughes, David T., barrister, 6 Temple court, Collins st west

Hughes, Edward, draper, &c., 144 Clarendon st, Em II
Hughes, George, blacksmith, 79 Moor st, F
Hughes, George, 35 Drummond st, Carl
Hughes, Hugh, manager Agra and Masterman's Bank, Union Club, Collins st west
Hughes, J., Carlisle st east, St K
Hughes, J., 13 Victoria parade, F
Hughes, James, 164 Napier st, F
Hughes, James, locksmith, 132 Little Bourke st east
Hughes, James, Sir Walter Scott hotel, 295 Elizabeth st
Hughes, James, pawnbroker, 45 Smith st, F
Hughes, James Vincent, hotel broker, 2 Flinders lane west, and Moray st, Em II
Hughes, Jos., 60 Bouverie st, Carl
Hughes, M., Noah's Ark hotel, Leicester st, Carl
Hughes, Mrs., 64 York st east, Em II
Hughes, Mrs., Chapel st, St K
Hughes, Mrs., dressmaker, 162 Collins st east
Hughes, Rev. E., 164 Johnston st, E C
Hughes, Richard, House st, San
Hughes, Samuel, Alma st, St K
Hughes, Thomas, 30 Grattan st, Carl
Hughes, W. H., furniture dealer, Victoria st, W M
Hughes, Wm., 89 Wellington st, Pra
Hugo, George, baker, High st, Pra
Hulbert, B., High st, St K
Hull, Henry N., commission agent, 13 Swanston st
Hull, Wm., M.L.C., Bridge road, Rd
Hull, Wm., Lothian st, Hot
Hull, Wm. Henry, receiver and paymaster, Treasury
Hulse, Thomas, 61 Roden st, W M
Hulston, Wm., Stephenson st, Fey
Hultgren, A., Hanover st, F
Humberston, Henry, 160 George st, F
Hume, H., Chetwynd st, W M
Hummerston, M., Commercial road, Pra
Hummerston, Michael, Lincoln hotel, Faraday st, Carl
Humphrey, —, nightman, 78 Smith st, E C
Humphrey, F., Pilgrim st, Fey
Humphrey, H., tailor, Gifford st, Wmn
Humphrey, J., Byron st, Hot
Humphreys, C., 118 Little Bourke st west
Humphreys, Captain H. W., Wellington road, F
Humphreys, George, cabinetmaker, 8 Cremorne st, Rd
Humphreys, Wm., carpenter, 175 Cambridge st, E C
Hung, Shing, Chinese chemist, 49 Little Bourke st east
Hunt, D., 19 Little Lonsdale st east
Hunt, E. H., importer of boots and shoes, 28 Flinders lane west

Hunt, Fredk., customs agent, Customhouse
Hunt, George, hatter, 148 Smith st, E C
Hunt, Henry, Kew
Hunt, J. J., painter, Black st, Bto
Hunt, J. W., Dryburgh st, Hot
Hunt, James, Stoke st, San
Hunt, John, poulterer, 52 Swanston st
Hunt, John, Rosslyn st, W M
Hunt, Joshua, hatmaker, 245 Bourke st east, and Palmerston st, Carl
Hunt, Mrs., 90 Dryburgh st, Hot
Hunt, Samuel, 37 Palmer st, F
Hunt, Wm., druggist, Pent
Hunt, Wm., restaurant, 17 Elizabeth st
Hunt, Wm. J., Odd Fellows' hotel, Webb st, F
Hunt, Wm., 28 Perry st, E C
Hunter, A., Gore st, F
Hunter and Co., blacksmiths, 73 Flinders lane east
Hunter, Daniel, 42 Cecil st, Em H
Hunter, E., Heidelberg road
Hunter, James, boot and shoe merchant, 159 Bourke st east
Hunter, John, tailor and clothier, 154 King st
Hunter, John, 32 Little Lonsdale st west
Hunter, John, 23 Little Lonsdale st west
Hunter, John, Argyle st east, St K
Hunter, Mrs., Franklin st west
Hunter, Mrs., 3 Reynold's terrace, George st, F
Hunter, Mrs., 1 Granite terrace, Gertrude st, F
Hunter, Robert, 178 George st, F
Hunter, Robert, surgeon, &c., 87 Cardigan st, Carl
Hunter, T. A., straw hat maker, 76 Lonsdale st east
Hunter, T. S., Argyle st, Pra
Hunter, Wm., Waterloo st, St K
Huntington, H. V., Drummond st, Carl
Huntsman, Benjamin, 90 Elgin st, Carl
Hurley, Thomas J., grocer, Cardigan st, Carl
Hurlston, A., miller, Pres
Hurlstone, P., miller, Union st, Dto
Hurren, John, bootmaker, 36 Swan st, Rd
Hurry, George, customs agent, 15 Market st, and Commercial road, Pra
Hurry, H., Commercial road, Pra
Hurry, John, auctioneer, 58 Elizabeth st, and Booroondara
Hurst, Robert, High st, St K
Hurst, Wm., commission agent, &c., Kirk's Bazaar, Bourke st west
Husband, J. F., and Co., importers, 74 Little Collins st west
Husband, Mrs., dressmaker, 72 Park st east, Em H
Husband, Wm., 192 Victoria parade, E M
Husband, Wm. H., solicitor, 99½ Collins st west

Hutchings, Charles, wholesale fruiterer, 8 Western Market, and St. Edmand's road, Pra
Hutchings, James, corner of William and Capel sts, W M
Hutchins, J., Canning st, Carl
Hutchins, James, 42 Wellington st, E C
Hutchins, Wm., 161 Fitzroy st, F
Hutchinson, L., carpenter, 9 Barkly st, Carl
Hutchinson, Matthew L., 64 Elizabeth st
Hutchinson, Mrs, 133 Cecil st, Em H
Hutchinson, R., Sydney road, Bk
Hutchinson, S., Hope st, Bk
Hutchinson, Thomas, Clarendon st east, Em H
Hutchinson, Thomas, 59 Bouverie st, Carl
Hutchinson, Wm., china and glass dealer, 114 Drummond st, Carl
Hutchinson, Wm., Station place, San
Hutchinson, Wm., Phoenix flour mills, Bay st, San
Hutchison, Alexander, compositor, Simpson st, E M
Hutchison, Andrew, cabinetmaker, 72 Smith st, E C
Hutchison, D., timber yard, Australian Wharf
Hutchison, J., Vere st, E C
Hutchison, J., Albion st east, Bk
Hutchison, James, Abbotsford st, Hot
Hutchison, Robert, Palmerston place, Madeline st, Carl
Hutchison, W., 22 Grattan st, Carl
Hutchison, W., machinist and smith, 16 Post Office place, and Baillie st, Host st
Huthwaite, Wm., store, Abbotsford st, Hot
Hutton, Charles D., house agent, 41 Swanston st, and 3 Cromwell st, E C
Hutton, James B., Hanmer st. Wmo
Hutton, Wm., 47 Cardigan st, Carl
Hutty, James, bootmaker, M'Grath place, Little Lonsdale st east
Hutty, Wm., 111 Victoria st, E C
Huxley, Parker, and Co., monumental sculptors, &c., 126 Little Collins st east, corner of Russell st
Huxtable, J., Moore st, Fcy
Huxtable, John Alfred, commission agent, &c., 133 Bourke st west
Huxtable, John, Caroline st, S Y
Huybers, Alfred, Barnett st, St K
Huybers and Wilkins, merchants, 31 Market st
Hyam and Co., 38 Elizabeth st
Hyama, H., bootmaker, 126 Little Bourke st east
Hyams, Nathan, Victoria Bazaar, 57 Swanston st and 27 Stephen st
Hyams, S., pawnbroker, 59 Elizabeth st
Hyde Brothers, produce merchants, 169 Brunswick st, F
Hyde, George, Labour in Vain hotel, corner Brunswick and Moor sts, F

Hyde, J., saddler, 20 Coventry st west, Em H
Hyde, R. and Co., marine store dealers, 11 Albert st, E M
Hyland, C., Burke and Wills hotel, Victoria st, E C
Hyland, Charles, butcher, 239 Victoria st, E C
Hyland, Mrs., Peel st, Prn
Hyland, W., Pelham st, Carl
Hyman, Mosely, 7 Mackenzie st
Hynde, Wm., 4 Jeffcott st, W M
Hyndman, J., Park View hotel, Punt road, S Y
Hyndman, Wm., gardener, 75 Rathdowne st, Carl
Hyne, James F., coachbuilder, Elizabeth st extension
Hyslop, Henry T., manufacturer and dealer in horse hair, 15 Latrobe st west

I.

Ibbotson, James, 50 Chetwynd st, Hot
Iddles, J., Graham st, Young st, F
Ievers, Daniel, furniture dealer, 122 Swanston st
Ievers, Wm., 101 Cardigan st, Carl
Ievers, Wm., jun., 99 Cardigan st, Carl
Iles, Samuel, Rowena parade, Rd
Illingworth, Frederick, fancy repository, 100 Spencer st
Illingworth, John G., hay and corn dealer, 245 Smith st, E C
Illman, George, Stanley st, W M
Ilsley, Samuel, High st, Prn
Illustrated Post office, 9 Bourke st east
Ilwraith, Thomas, William st north
Imes, C. G., druggist, 5 Madeline st, Carl
Immigrants' Aid Society, Collins st east, corner Swanston st; and Prince's bridge
Immigration Depôt, Little Collins st west
Immigration Hospital, 213 Bourke st west
Immigration Offices and Store, Latrobe st west, and 27 Thompson st, Wmn
Imperial Fire Insurance Company of London, 50 Elizabeth st
Impett, Jane, grocer, 34 Lygon st, Carl
Imri, W. W., Park st, Em H
Inch, George, 116 Elgin st, Carl
Ind, W., 99 Smith st, F
Independent Champion Gold Mining Co., 64 Elizabeth st
Industrial Building and Investment Society, 68 Gertrude st, F
Industrial Home, Punt road, S Y
Ingamells, Joshua, teacher, 166 Russell st
Ingham, N., Ewen st, Bk
Ingle, J. K., butcher, 51 Market st, Em H
Ingles, Adam, and Gresham, ship chandlers, &c., Beach st, San
Inglis, C. M., 3 Alexander terrace, Victoria parade, F
Inglis, Daniel, 33 Cecil st, Wmn

Inglis, Frank, baker, Cremorne st, Rd
Inglis, Rev. J. W., Bay st, Sno
Ingram, Arthur, 68 Ferguson st, Wmn
Ingram, Daniel, general dealer, 238 Johnston st, E C
Ingram, James, draper and outfitter, 137A King st
Ingram, John, 135 Westgarth st, F
Ingram, John D., 56 Bouverie st, Carl
Ingworth, Mrs., 58 Bridge road, Rd
Inkley, Wm., farrier, Carlisle st, St K
Inkpen, Henry F., carpenter, Acland st, St K
Inkson, James, Johnston st, E C
Inselmann, H., baker, corner Cambridge and Victoria sts, E C
Insolvency Weekly Register, 56 Little Collins st west
Insolvent Court, 56 Lonsdale st east
Inspector General of Penal Establishments' offices, corner Latrobe and William sts
Inspector of Distilleries' office, Latrobe st west
Inspector of Markets, Eastern Market, Stephen st
Inspector of Waterworks' office, Latrobe st west
Institution for Diseases of the Eye and Ear, 2 Albert st, E M
International Exhibition, Offices of, 64 Elizabeth st
Iredale, Andrew T., coal merchant, Spring street
Ireddale, Timothy, 195 Lygon st, Carl
Ireland, Charles, 3 Villiers st, Carl
Ireland, George, fancy repository and insurance agency, 183 Smith st, E C
Ireland, George, 1 Moor st, F
Ireland, George, 3 Bath terrace, Faraday st, Carl
Ireland, J., 173 Napier st, F
Ireland, Richard D., Q.C., barrister, 5 Temple court, Collins st west
Ireland, S., Sydney road, Bk
Ireland, W., 49 Nelson road, Em H
Ireland, Wm. J. A., seedsman and florist, 94 Smith st, E C
Irene Gold Mining Company, 3 Collins st west
Irish, Arthur, 39 Twyford st, South Wmn
Irish, John, Railway hotel, Bay st, Bln
Irons, John, contractor, 2 Hall of Commerce, Collins st west, and Hotham st, Em H
Irvine, —, 35 Meray place, E M
Irvine, E., Bank st east, Em H
Irvine, George, Graham st, Young st, F
Irvine, J. A., Milton st, St K
Irvine, James A., and Co., ale and porter bottlers and wine merchants, 69 Flinders st east
Irvine, Joseph, 56 Montague st, Em H
Irvine, Mrs., Wreckyn st, Hot

Irvine, Mrs. Ann, grocer, 211 Lygon and Faraday sts, Carl
Irvine, P., Oxford st, Hot
Irvine, Wm. F. D., chemist, 88 Queen st, and St K
Irving,—, 62 Park st east, Em H
Irving, A., 109 Argyle st, F
Irving, J. L., Howard st, Hot
Irving, James L., and Co., produce merchants, 278 and 280 Elizabeth st
Irving, Joseph, surveyor, Whitehall st, Fcy
Irving, Mrs. C., 74 Park st east, Em H
Irving, Mrs., 85 Leicester st, Carl
Irving, Wm., 38 Lothian st, Hot
Irwin, Andrew, Flem
Irwin, Catherine, 14 Dudley st, W M
Irwin, E., 13 Madeline st, Carl
Irwin, Wm., carrier, Queen st north
Isaac, James, 213 Swan st, Rd
Isaacs, A. M., 35 Stephen st
Isaacs, Abraham, dealer, 31 Little Lonsdale st east
Isaacs, B., and Son, London Tavern, 65 Elizabeth st
Isaacs, Benjamin, 147 Collins st east
Isaacs, Brothers, importers, 15 Lonsdale st west
Isaacs, G., 75 George st, F
Isaacs, Moss, pawnbroker, 203 Elizabeth street
Isaacs, Solomon, grocer, wine and spirit merchant, 202 Latrobe street east
Isaacs, W., 25 Stephen st
Isard, Wm., fancy repository, 107 Swanston st
Isbister, John, 161 Cecil st, F
Isbister, Mrs., Fitzroy st, F
Isherwood, E., tailor, 8 Alfred place, Collins st east
Isles, Nathan, 5 Baillie st, Hot
Israel, S., tailor, 32 Madeline st, Carl
Israelite Sanctuary, 111 Fitzroy st, F
Isworth, B., cab proprietor, Pres
Ives, W. J. B., undertaker, Punt road, Pra
Ivey, George Pearse, St Kilda st, Bzn
Izard, Henry J., shoemaker, 159 George st, F
Izard and Sons, bootmakers, 114a Wellington st, E C
Izod, John T., grocer, Commercial road, Pra

J.

Jack, Andrew and Richard, importers, 75 Flinders lane east
Jack, James, Barkly st, Carl
Jack, John, George st, F
Jack, Mrs., Simpson st, E M
Jack, Mrs., Wellington st, Rd
Jacka, George, 46 Berkeley st, Carl
Jackman, Thomas, gauger, 88 Collins st west

Jackman, Thomas J., Inkerman st, East St K
Jackson, A., commission agent, 151 Collins st east
Jackson, B., greengrocer, 251 Victoria parade, E C
Jackson, Charles J., engraver and lithographer, 79 Queen st
Jackson, Charles, tailor, 198 Little Bourke st east
Jackson, E., 5 King William st, F
Jackson, Edward, 110 George st, F
Jackson, F. W., British Lion hotel, Westgarth st, F
Jackson, G., 138 Kerr st, F
Jackson, H., baker, Nth
Jackson, Isaac, Chambers st, Pra
Jackson, J., bootmaker, 101 Westgarth st, F
Jackson, J., Peel st, W M
Jackson, J., Sydney road, Bk
Jackson, James, Footscray hotel, Albert road, Fcy
Jackson, James, 3 Charlotte terrace, Romlyn st, W M
Jackson, James, 11 Flinders lane west
Jackson, James, 33 Montague st, Em H
Jackson, John, Barkly st, Carl
Jackson, John, 17 Marian st, F
Jackson, Joseph, smith and waggon builder, Elizabeth st extension
Jackson, M., 47 St. David st, F
Jackson, Margaret, milliner and dressmaker, 151 Collins st east
Jackson, Mrs. K., Railway place, San
Jackson, Mrs., Moor st, F
Jackson, Rev. T. H., Strand, Wmn
Jackson, Robinson, engineer, 51 Ferguson st, Wmn
Jackson, Robert, dairyman, 81 Victoria st, Carl
Jackson, T., Grey st, E M
Jackson, Thomas, bootmaker, Cecil st north, Wmn
Jackson, Thomas, ironmonger, 81 Elizabeth st, and 6 Little Collins st west
Jackson, Thomas Wm., Prince's st, F
Jackson, W., letter carrier, 37 Pascoe st, Wmn
Jackson, W. B., warehouseman, 131 Bridport st, Em H
Jackson, Wm., Stoke st, San
Jacobe, Louis, butcher, 10 Arden st, Ho
Jacobs, Bernard, Canning st, Carl
Jacobs, Colman, Victoria st, St K
Jacobs, E., Esplanade, St K
Jacobs, H., cabinetmaker, 88 Napier st, F
Jacobs, Henry, 1 Union terrace, Cardigan st, Carl
Jacobs, L, Acland st. St K
Jacobs, Joseph, 30 Wellington st, E C
Jacobs, Lawrence, 49 York st west, Em H
Jacobs, Mrs. Arthur, 31 Johnston st, E C
Jacobs, Thomas, baker, &c., Pres

Jacobson, James, 31 Twyford st, Wmn
Jacobson, S. H., pawnbroker, 128 Russell street
James, Thos. Reynolds, manager electric telegraph, William st, corner of Little Bourke st
Jacomb, Robert E., official assignee, 11 and 12 Eldon chambers, Collins st west
Jaffray, W. R., 40 Bank st, Em H
Jager, E., cabinetmaker, Victoria st, Rd
Jago, J., Crockford st, San
Jago, Mrs., Richmond terrace, Rd
James, —, mason, Pelham st, Carl
James, —, Bendigo st, Hot
James, D., Albert st, Pra
James, Benjamin, 42 Barkly st, Carl
James, Charles, tailor, 15 Greeves st, F
James, Charles, boarding-house keeper, 139 Little Collins st east
James, Charles, Peel st, Pra
James, David, 143 Collins st east
James, E., contractor, Hoddle st, E C
James, Edmund, Nth
James, Edw., upholsterer, 62 Victoria st, Rd
James, F., 1 Clarendon terrace, Clarendon st, E M
James, G. P., Royal George hotel, Greville st, Pra
James, George, fancy repository, 63 Peel st, E C
James, George, blacksmith, Preston
James, Henry, Albert st, Wind
James, Henry, plumber, Pra
James, J., 50 King William st, F
James, J. C., Nott st, San
James, Jane, Earl of Zetland hotel, 13 Stanley st, E C
James, John, Hoddle st, E C
James, John P., Royal George hotel, Chapel st, Pra
James, Mary, boarding-house keeper, 132 Lonsdale st east
James, Mrs. Mary, 31 Moor st, F
James, Mrs., 1 Dover place, Wmn
James, Mrs., school, Barry st, Carl
James, S. W., Boundary hotel, corner Hotham and Hoddle sts, E M
James, T. H., 65 Kerr st, F
James, Thomas C., Nott st, San
James, Wm., S Y
Jameson, E., boarding-house, 150 King st
Jameson, E., 132 Little Bourke st west
Jameson, George, pawnbroker, 154 Russell st, and 139 Lonsdale st east
Jameson, Graham, storekeeper, Ess
Jamieson, Alexander, grocer, 151 Moor st, F
Jamieson, Alexander, Punt road, S Y
Jamieson, Captain S. G., 103 Napier st, Em H
Jamieson, David, tailor, M'Killop st, off Bourke st west
Jamieson, Francis, baker, Kew

Jamieson, George, and Co., wholesale warehousemen, &c., 4 Swanston st
Jamieson, J. P., Neptune st, St K
Jamieson, James, Preston Arms hotel, Pres
Jamieson, Miss, Lennox st, Rd
Jamieson, Mrs., 28 Smith st, E C
Janes, H., 25 Dover place, Wmn
Japp, John, boarding-house, Bay st, San
Jarman, Henry, cabinetmaker, 209 Lonsdale st west
Jarratt, R., grocer, 54 Smith st, E C
Jarratt, Thomas, Peel st, Hot
Jarrett, F. C., commission agent, 104 Collins st east, and Bk
Jarrett, Rev. W., Brunswick road, Bk
Jarrett, Thomas, farrier, Elizabeth st north, and Bouverie st, Carl
Jarrett, W. Henry, 38 Powlett st, E M
Jarvie, A., Brunswick road, Bk
Jarvie, W., Glenlyon road, Bk
Jarvie, Joseph, Princess hotel, 149 Smith st, F
Jayes, F., Gore st, F
Jeff. Davis Quartz Mining Company, 66 Little Collins st west
Jeffries, —, watchmaker, Swan st, Rd
Jeffries, George, Rowena parade, Rd
Jeffries, T. H., painter, 331 Fitzroy st, F
Jeffers, Mrs., 79 Kerr st, F
Jeffery, Alfred, Victoria parade, E M
Jeffery, Henry, grocer, 182 Clarendon st, Em H
Jeffery, Matthew, bootmaker, 61 Victoria parade, F
Jeffery, Robert, 83 Capel st, Hot
Jefferson, John, Lothian st, Hot
Jeffray, R. J., Grey st, St K
Jeffrey, —, grocer, 28 Otter st, E C
Jeffrey, D., 15 Drummond st, Carl
Jeffrey, J., Chapel st, Pra
Jeffrey, John, Park st, S Y
Jeffrey, R. J., secretary Eaglefield Pastoral Co., 115 Collins st west
Jeffrey, Samuel, farrier, Pres
Jeffreys, Charles, Railway place, San
Jeffreys, Joseph, Hoden st, W M
Jeffreys, Joseph, french polisher, 3 Church st, Em H
Jeffries, Henry, Hoddle st, E C
Jeffries, J., Richmond Brewery, Church st, Rd
Jeffs, Samuel, Hoddle st, Rd
Jellett, Mrs., 102 Fitzroy st, F
Jellie, J., Carpenter st, Btn
Jenkins, Lewis, Peel st, Pra
Jenkins and Halliam, pawnbrokers and auctioneers, 63 Errol st, Hot
Jenkins, Henry, carpenter, Peel st, Pra
Jenkins, James, 215 Gore st, F
Jenkins, John, saddler, &c., 49 Bourke st west
Jenkins, John, blacksmith, 60 George st, F
Jenkins, John, 55 Coventry st, Em H

Jenkins, John, saddler, Chapel st, Prn
Jenkins, Jos., pawnbroker, 13 Levison st, Hot
Jenkins, Thomas, builder, 65 Napier st, Em H
Jenkins, W., 93 Douglas parade, Wmn
Jenkins, Zachariah, blacksmith, 244 Johnston st, E C
Jenkinson, Mrs., 69 Cremorne st, Rd
Jenkinson, Samuel, carpenter and builder, 23 Little Collins east
Jenkinson, W., Hoddle st, E C
Jenkinson, Walter, Barry st, Carl
Jenman, Thomas, 87 Gore st, F
Jenner, C. J., M.L.C., iron merchant, &c., 47 Flinders lane east, and 53 Flinders st east
Jenner, Mrs., Coventry st east, Em H
Jenning, J., Cole st south, Wmn
Jenning, Joseph J., hon. sec. to Bible Society, 17 Swanston st, and S Y
Jennings and Coote, solicitors, 37 Queen st
Jennings, George James, builder, 6 and 8 Grattan st, Carl
Jennings, H., Kew
Jennings, Henry N., solicitor, 83 Swanston st, and Francis st, E C
Jennings, J. E., Walsh st, S Y
Jennings, James W., Ferguson st, Wmn
Jennings, James, 20 Rathdowne st, Carl
Jennings, John H., tea dealer and grocer, 105 Swanston st
Jennings, Mrs., 56 Moray st, Em H
Jennings, Samuel, bootmaker, High st, Prn
Jennings, Thomas, Blackwood st, Hot
Jennings, Thomas, 142 Lonsdale st west
Jennings, Thomas, undertaker, 128 Queen street
Jennings, W. T., 74 Moray st, Em H
Jenvey, Mrs., schoolmistress, 44 Moor st, F
Jenyns, J., tailor, 4 Madeline st, Carl
Jeremy, James, Wmn
Jeremy, John, traffic superintendent, Spencer street station
Jermann, W., 15 Dorcas st, Em H
Jervis, John, Hoddle st, Rd
Jervis, Mrs., Hoddle st, E C
Jerrems, T. C., Richmond terrace, Rd
Jessup, J., 12 Hanover st, F
Jessup, Thomas, 117 Elgin st, Carl
Jewell, J., carrier, Harcourt st, Hot
Joachimi, G., Gipps st, E M
Joblin, J. R., Station place, San
Jobson and Walland, furniture carters, 175 Napier st, F
Jobson, George, Pont road, S Y
Jobson, Thomas S., fruiterer, 54 Gertrude st, F
John, E., Lennox st, Rd
John Knox Free Church and Schools, Swanston st, corner Little Lonsdale st
Johns, Edward, Gipps st, E M

Johns, P., galvanized iron works, 81 Flinders lane east
Johns, Saml., 40 Curzon st, Hot
Johns, Wm., 32 Moor st, F
Johnson, —, Hoddle st, E C
Johnson, —, 93 Faraday st, Carl
Johnson, A., Barkly st, Bk
Johnson, Alfred J., Stoke st
Johnson and Co., importers of photographic goods, 28 Swanston st
Johnson, Annie, grocer, 106 Russell st
Johnson, Arthur E., architect, Furness terrace, Barkly st, St K
Johnson, C., 197 Cecil st, Em H
Johnson, C. J., 194 Moor st, F
Johnson, Frederick, Creswick st, Haw
Johnson, Frederick, Kew
Johnson, G., coal dealer, 43 Gertrude st, F
Johnson, G. A., cabinet maker, Grey st, E M
Johnson, G. F., 66 Napier st, Em H
Johnson, G. T., Nth
Johnson, G. and J., importers of fruit, &c., 39 William st
Johnson, George, 134 Westgarth st, F
Johnson, George, Nicholson st, F
Johnson, George, plumber and glazier, 6? Smith st, F
Johnson, H., Rowena parade, Rd
Johnson, Henry, conveyancer, 26 Temple court, Collins st west
Johnson, J., draper, 5 Nelson place, Wmn
Johnson, J., bandmaster, Prn
Johnson, J., wheelwright, Hay st, Bnn
Johnson, J., Weston st, Bk
Johnson, J., blacksmith, Bay st, Bnn
Johnson, J., 213 Gore st, F
Johnson, J. T., Esplanade, St K
Johnson, J. W., 4 Franklyn st, W M
Johnson, Jacob, Leveson st, Hot
Johnson, James, Johnston st, E C
Johnson, James, greengrocer, 168 Wellington st, E C
Johnson, James E., warehouseman, 37 Flinders lane east
Johnson, John G., Upper Northcote
Johnson, John, 73 Webb st, F
Johnson, John, greengrocer, 93 Napier st, F
Johnson, John, diningrooms, 118 Queen st
Johnson, John, 176 Victoria st, Rd
Johnson, John, 117 Westgarth st, F
Johnson, John, Union st, S Y
Johnson, Martin, 153 Moray st, Em H
Johnson, Mrs., Darling st, S Y
Johnson, Mrs., 108 Cardigan st, Carl
Johnson, Mrs., grocer, Little Lonsdale st east
Johnson, P., cooper, 147 Smith st, F
Johnson, Philip, solicitor, 34 Collins st west, and Clifton st, Rd
Johnson, R., 20 Oxford st, E C
Johnson, R., 51 Johnston st, F
Johnson, S., Thompson st, South Wmn

Johnson, B., Chetwynd st, W M
Johnson's Reef Gold Mines Company, 10 Elizabeth st south
Johnson, Richard, a'Beckett st east
Johnson, S. W., Royal Mail hotel, Wellington st, Pra
Johnson, T., Vale st, Hot
Johnson, T., gardener, Mill st, Bin
Johnson, T. G., Hoslyn st, W M
Johnson, Thomas, 186 Drummond st, Carl
Johnson, Thomas, Haw
Johnson, W. H., 108 Leicester st, Carl
Johnson, Wm., chemist, Punt road, and Nelson st, Pra
Johnson, Wm., Nicholson st, Fcy
Johnson, Wm., Barkly st, St K
Johnson, W. R., Bay st, Bin
Johnson, W. S., Heath st, San
Johnson, W., Post Office hotel, Chapel st, Pra
Johnson, Wm., 8 George st, F
Johnson, Wm., 194 Gore st, F
Johnston, Andrew, plumber and gasfitter, 9 a'Beckett st east
Johnston, Archibald, painter, Nicholas lane, 216 Bourke st east
Johnston, B. J., Elgin st, Carl
Johnston, D., Capel st, Hot
Johnston, D. and E., cabinetmakers, &c., 29 Latrobe st east, and Capel st, Hot
Johnston, E., Capel st, Hot
Johnston, E. C., 34 Latrobe st west
Johnston, Edward, 112 Young st, F
Johnston, George K., auctioneer and furniture warehouse, 118 Bourke st east, and Victoria cottage, Gipps st, E M
Johnston, Henry J., Robe st, St K
Johnston, J., Howard st, W M
Johnston, J., Stanley st, E C
Johnston, J. A., Station place, San
Johnston, James, goods and luggage store, 17 King st
Johnston, James A., bootmaker, 167 Clarendon st, Em H
Johnston, James E., St. Vincent's place, Park st west, Em H
Johnston, James, 54 Thompson st, Wmn
Johnston, Joseph, 233 Moray st, Em H
Johnston, Joseph R., 69 Park st, Em H
Johnston, Miss, dressmaker, 41 Madeline st, Carl
Johnston, Miss, dressmaker, High st, St K
Johnston, Mrs., 82 Ferrars st, E H
Johnston, Mrs. Jane, 17 Peel st, Hot
Johnston, Mrs. M., 11 Fitzroy st, F
Johnston, Mrs. M., fancy repository, 85 Rathdowne st, Em H
Johnston, O'Shanessy, and Co., photographic artists, 3 Bourke st east
Johnston, P., bootmaker, Rouse st, San
Johnston, R., sign writer, Sackville st, E C
Johnston, Rev. Kerr, San
Johnston, Robert, Brick st, Rd
Johnston, Robert, builder, Hotham st, E M

Johnston, Robert, 5 Alma st, F
Johnston, Samuel, 132 Bourke st west
Johnston, Thomas, 18 Dorcas st, Em H
Johnston, Thomas, 131 Little Bourke st west
Johnston, W., Bonverie st, Carl
Johnston, W. C., Geelong st, Fcy
Johnston, Waldron, Kew
Johnston, Wm., 7 Nicholas lane
Johnstone, H. J., Robe st, St K
Johnstone, Robert V., High st, Pra
Johnstone, S. P., Nott st, San
Jolliffe, —, cabinetmaker, Chapel st, Pra
Jolly, J., fruiterer, 31 Market st, Em H
Jolly, John, fruiterer, Bay st, San
Jolly, Thomas, carpenter, 98 Dryburgh st, Hot
Jolly, Thomas, carpenter, 16 Little Lonsdale st east
Jonas, John, bootmaker, Haw
Jonasson, Hermann, M.D., 174 Collins st east
Jones, A. B., Quarry hotel, Weston st, Bk
Jones and Guyatt, surgical instrument makers, 106 Lonsdale st east
Jones and Moses, boot and shoe warehouse, 292 Bourke st east
Jones and Thomas, bakers, High st, St K
Jones, Arthur Travor, carpenter, off Gisbourne st, E M
Jones, B., 125 Little Lonsdale st east
Jones, Benjamin, carrier, 73 Leveson st, Hot
Jones, Benjamin, and Co., wholesale glassware merchants, 101 Queen st
Jones, C., greengrocer, 27 Rathdowne st, Carl
Jones, C., Berkeley st, Carl
Jones, C., butcher, Graham st, San
Jones, Charles, Peel st, Pra
Jones, Chas. Edwin, M.L.A., Charles st, F
Jones, David, cabinetmaker, 3 Nelson place, Wmn
Jones, David, builder, Eleanor st, Fcy
Jones, David, 100 Dorcas st, Em H
Jones, David, Drummond st, Carl
Jones, David, Albert st, E M
Jones, E., 81 Little Oxford st, E C
Jones, E., bootmaker, 77 Wellington st, E C
Jones, F. B., 27 Moor st, F
Jones, Edward, 7 Hanmer st, Wmn
Jones, Edwin, Gertrude st, F
Jones, Edwin, Murphy st, S Y
Jones, Edwin, basket maker, 17 Johnston st, E C
Jones, F., Carlisle st east, St K
Jones, Francis, commissioner of audit, Jollmont terrace, E M
Jones, G., bootmaker, 8 Rathdowne st, Carl
Jones, Griffith, Little Hanover st, F
Jones, Henry, photographer, 19 Collins st east and 107 Elizabeth st

Jones, Henry, teacher, Palmerston st, Carl
Jones, Henry, Commercial road, Pra
Jones, Henry, 19 Cecil st, Wmn
Jones, H. S., Chetwynd st, W M
Jones, H. L., postman, Queen st north
Jones, Isaac H, sharebroker, 145 Elizabeth st
Jones, J., 62 Argyle st, F
Jones, J., 130 Moor st, F
Jones, J., 128 Cardigan st east
Jones, Jas., sharebroker, 145 Elizabeth st
Jones, James, Curzon st, Hot
Jones, J., Illawarra st, South Wmn
Jones, J., bootmaker, Victoria st, Hot
Jones, J., 43 Cecil st, Nsrth Wmn
Jones, J., dairy, Punt road, S Y
Jones, James, Highett st, Rd
Jones, J. M., Station place, San
Jones, J. P., 4 Little Latrobe st east
Jones, J. P., 343 King st
Jones, J. R., boatbuilder
Jones, J. T., Lennox st, Rd
Jones, John E., livery stables, 87 Gertrude st, F
Jones, John, Bouverie st, Carl
Jones, John, Fortune of War hotel, 203 Napier st, F
Jones, John, blacksmith, River side south
Jones, John, Stevedore st, Wmn
Jones, John, greengrocer, 55 and 57 Bank st west, Em H
Jones, John, grocer, Bouverie st, Carl
Jones, John, 106 Lonsdale st east
Jones, John, 222 Bourke st east
Jones, John, window-blind maker, 78 Lonsdale st east
Jones, John, 18 Marian st, F
Jones, John, 71 Little Nelson st, Wmn
Jones, John, 99 and 133 Leicester st. F
Jones, John C., chemist, Bridge road, Rd
Jones, John E., County Court hotel, a'Beckett st east
Jones, John M, grocer, Capel st, Hot
Jones, Joseph, Greeves st, F
Jones, L., 182 Russell st
Jones, Misses, school, Elgin st, Carl
Jones, Mrs., dressmaker, Palmerston st, Carl
Jones, Phillip F., reporter, Hanmer. st, Wmn
Jones, R., 3 John st, Wmn
Jones, R. D., 6 Studley park terrace, Victoria st, Pra
Jones, R. J., Heath st, San
Jones, Richard, accountant, 69 Collins st west, and Argo st, S Y
Jones, Robert, grocer, 335 Elizabeth st
Jones, Robert, Cole st, South Wmn
Jones, Robert, Junction hotel, Whitehall st, Fcy
Jones, Stephen, Elgin st, Carl
Jones, Stephen, Inkerman st east, St K
Jones, T. A., New Rising Sun hotel, Geelong road, Fcy

Jones, T. R., John st, Moor st, F
Jones, Thomas, Elgin st, Carl
Jones, Thomas, 5 Ferguson st, Wmn
Jones, Thomas, 34 Franklyn st, W M
Jones, Thomas, 53 Park st, Em H
Jones, Thomas H., Rifle Brigade and Jordan road hotel, Brunswick st, F
Jones, W., farrier, Barkly st, St K
Jones, W., land agent, Fcy
Jones, W., tobacconist, 158 Clarendon st, Em H
Jones, W., 39 Faraday st, Carl
Jones, W., 160 Moray st, Em H
Jones, W. W., painter and paperhanger, 228 Bourke st east
Jones, Wm., blacksmith, 160 Little Collins st east
Jones, Wm., grocer, Lennox st, Rd
Jones, Wm., horse dealer, 67 Argyle st, F
Jones, Wm., Howard st, Hot
Jones, Wm., land agent, Geelong road, Fcy
Jones, Wm., Nelson st, Pra
Jones, Wm., pilot, Osborne st, Wmn
Jones, Wm., produce merchant, Church st. Rd
Jones, Wm., Temple court Collins st west, and Whitehall st, Fcy
Jones, Wm., 9 John st, Wmn
Jones, Wm., 201 Lygon st, Carl
Jones, Wm., station master, 36 Bank st east, Em H
Jones, Wm., 20 Little Latrobe st east
Jones, Wm. B., lighterman and free store keeper, 149 Collins st west and 97 Flinders lane west
Jonnes, S. W., 39 Wellington st, St K
Jordan, Alexander, Macarthur place, Carl
Jordan, James, jam manufacturer, 21 Latrobe st west
Jordan, James, upholsterer, Parker st, Wmn
Jordan, John, mason, Brennan st, Em
Jordan, Mrs., Russell st
Jordan, W., 181 Little Lonsdale st east
Joseph and Co., watchmakers, &c., 55 Collins st east
Joseph, Henry, analytical chemist and assayer, 6 Collins st east
Joseph, Israel, clothier and draper, 69 Bourke st east
Joseph, Nathan, general importer, 21 Little Collins st east and 65 Swanston st
Josephs, Henry, 40 Nicholson st, F
Josephs, Joseph Solomon, merchant, 13 Elizabeth st, and Avoca st. S Y
Joshua Brothers, merchants, 46 William street
Joshua, J. M., Acland st, St K
Joshua, Moss, High st, St K
Joske, Alexander, Church square, St K
Joske Brothers, merchants, 2 Little Collins st west
Jouranneans, J., 44 Gore st, F

Jourdain, H. D., Yarra st, Hrid
Journal of Commerce office, 51 and 53 Flinders lane west
Jouvet, A., and Co., merchants, 3 Bond st
Jouvet, A., 204 Victoria parade, E M
Jor, Alfred, auctioneer, land agent, and hotel broker, 56 Little Collins st west
Joyce, —, builder, 110 Oxford st
Joyce, E. D., Bay st, San
Joyce, Edward, Station place, San
Joyce, John, 59 Drummond st, Carl
Joyce, R., bootmaker, Howard st, Hot
Joyce, Wm., Church st, Rd
Joynson, John, shoemaker, 265 King st north
Judd, J., Judd st, Rd
Judd, John, 45 Dover place, Wmn
Judd, Thomas, Kew
Jude, Ascher, watchmaker and jeweller, 79½ Bourke st east
Jorison, Charles, 142 Fitzroy st, F
Julians, E., contractor, corner of Clyde and Acland sts, St K
Juliff, James Charles, Sackville st, E C
Jupp, Wm., Albert st, Pra

K

Kabat and Lecky, stock and share brokers, Hall of Commerce, Collins st west
Kahl, F., cooper, Nott st, San
Kal, Schnism D., watchmaker and jeweller, 129 Gertrude st, F
Kalltow, Jns., Peel st, Hot
Kaines, C. and G., Duke of York hotel, High st, Pra
Kaiz, Mrs. S., grocer, 40 Little Latrobe st
Kasner and Moss, opticians, 17 Collins st west
Katzenstein, Isaac, merchant, 149 Collins st west, and Argyle st, St K
Katzenstein, J., Argyle st, St K
Kavanagh and Co., drapers, Queensberry and Leveson sts, Hot
Kavanagh, Francis P., 64 George st, F
Kavanagh, H., Shamrock hotel, Cardigan st, Carl
Kavanagh, Miss, dressmaker, Victoria st, Hot
Kaweran, F. F., 3 Apsley place, Gisborne st, E M
Kay, Andrew, Wilson st, S Y
Kay, Captain Joseph, Caroline st, S Y
Kay, J. H., Captain, R.N., clerk to Executive Council, government house
Kay, James, bootmaker, 35 Victoria st, Carl
Kay, James, painter, Kew
Kaye, —, draper, 166 Bridge road, Rd
Kaye, Butchart, and Co., cattle and sheep salesmen and commission agents, 56 Bourke st west
Kaye, Edward, farmer, Ess
Kean, Wm., Nicholson st, Carl

Keane, James, Yorkshire Stingo hotel, Hoddle st, E C
Keane, J. G., wood yard, 83 Faraday st, Carl
Keane, Wm., Victoria st, W M
Keane, Wm., Illawarra st, Wmn
Kearman, J., teacher, Pent
Keaney, John, Stevedore st, Wmn
Kearnan, —, teacher, Pent
Kearney, Arthur, Bull st, St K
Kearney, John, 43 Swanston st, and 58 Barney st, Rd
Kearney, P., school, Lothian st, Hot
Keating, J., Chetwynd st, Hot
Keating, James, 276 Smith st, F C
Keats, James, leather merchant, 281 Elizabeth st
Keay, Wm., 5 Jackson st, Wmn
Keobie, Samuel, general dealer, 184 Smith st, E C
Keedle, C., Sydney road, Bk
Keele, Henry, baker, Sackville st, E C
Keely, James, 144 Lonsdale st west
Keely, M., cabinetmaker, Murchison st, Nicholson st, Carl
Keen, G., painter, &c., Gardiner's creek road, Pra
Keenan, T., 94 Elgin st, Carl
Keene, Henry, grocer, 58 Errol st, Hot
Keene, James, surgeon and occulist, 127 Collins st east
Keens, John A., ironmonger, 161 Elizabeth st
Keep, Edward, wholesale ironmonger, 37 Elizabeth st, and Dandenong road
Keep and Waters, drapers and outfitters, 101 Stevedore st, Wmn
Keer, John, 20 Rosslyn st, W M
Kefford, R., 25 Oxford st, E C
Kelghery, J., bootmaker, Dover road, Wmn
Kelghery, —, shoemaker, Wellington st, E C
Keily, Josh., bootmaker, 86½ Swanston st
Keily, Michael, 93 Flinders st east
Keily, Thomas, bootmaker, 14 Flinders lane west
Keir, Richard, Franklin st, W M
Keith, Angustus, Temple court, Collins st west
Keith, C. F., upholsterer, 132 Cardigan st, Carl
Keith, Mrs., 138a George st, F
Kell, Wm., Highett st, Rd
Kelleher, Jeremiah B., Court House hotel, Grey st, St K
Kelleher, John, 80 Rose st, F
Kelleher, Robert, Albion hotel, corner Chapel and High sts, Pra
Kellett, Abraham, drayman, George st, E M
Kellett, Edward, grocer and corn dealer, Hoddle st, E C
Kellett, J., fruiterer, 38 Gertrude st, F

Kellett, Mrs., 279 Victoria parade, E C
Kellett, S., storekeeper, Kew
Kellett, Wm., Volunteer Arms hotel, 70 Montague st, Em H
Kelley, —, 143 Johnston st, E C
Kellock, J., 109 Oxford st, E C
Kelly, —, senior constable, police barracks, Fcy
Kelly, Alexander, cab proprietor, 116 Argyle st, F
Kelly and Co., coal merchants, 200 Elizabeth st north
Kelly, Anne, Madeline hotel, 47 Madeline st, Carl
Kelly, C., Dryburgh st, Hot
Kelly, Edward, draper, &c., 112 High st, St K
Kelly, F., Victoria parade, E C
Kelly, F., wigmaker, 237 Bourke st west
Kelly, G., surveyor, Stoke st, San
Kelly, H. L., C.E., 61 Napier st, Em H
Kelly, Hugh, 59 Victoria st, Rd
Kelly, J., 80 Kerr st, F
Kelly, James, Inspector of police, Fcy
Kelly, James, Brennan st, Ess
Kelly, James, Berkeley st, Carl
Kelly, James, Kelly's hotel, corner of Nott and Beach sts, San
Kelly, John, Government inspector, Fcy
Kelly, John, Punt road, S Y
Kelly, John, Station place, San
Kelly, John C., painter and paperhanger, 13 Church st, Em H
Kelly, M. J., Rathdowne st, Carl
Kelly, Michael, Reilly st, F
Kelly, Miss, ladies' school, Brunswick road, Bk
Kelly, Mrs., boarding-house, 123 Flinders lane east
Kelly, Mrs., 117 Argyle st, F
Kelly, Mrs., 119 Cecil st, Em H
Kelly, P., baker, 46 Napier st, F
Kelly, Patrick, Grosvenor st, Prn
Kelly, Patrick, Railway place, San
Kelly, Peter, contractor, 79½ Collins st east, and Newlands, Merri creek
Kelly, Peter, 19 Dorcas st, Em H
Kelly, Robert, Hoddle st, E C
Kelly, T., Victorian Pottery, Sydney road, Bk
Kelly, W., Miller st, Bk
Kelly, W. L., Stephen st
Kelly, W. L., jun., solicitor, 30 Swanston street
Kelly, Wm. Henry, 62 Moray st, Em H
Kelly, Wm. Henry, gas inspector, 46 Grey st, E M
Kelson, Edward, tailor and clothier, 175 Smith st, F
Kelson, Frederick, boot and shoe dealer, 99 Gore st, F
Kelson, J. H., Henry st, Prn
Kelson, W., builder, 132 Eastern road, Em H

Kemble, George, cabinetmaker, 63 William st
Kemp, Alex. and James, grocers and carpenters, 2 Macarthur place, Carl
Kemp, Owen, 35 Gore st, F
Kemp, Mrs., 6 Charles st, F
Kemp, Mrs., Barry st, Carl
Kemp, Mrs., 20 Napier st, F
Kemp, Mrs., stationer, Day st, San
Kemp, Samuel V., C.E. and architect, 62 Collins st west
Kemp, Thomas, news agent, 19 Queensberry st, Carl
Kemp, Wm., 11 Barkly st, Carl
Kemplen, Alexander, Henry st, Prn
Kempton, C. S., 27 Johnston st, F C
Kennelly, E. J., commission agent and broker, 59 Bourke st west
Kendall, J., Johnston st west, F
Kendall, J. B., Pent
Kendall, Thomas, 157 Little Collins st east
Kendall, Thomas, Thompson st, Wmn
Kendy, John, Arden st, Hot
Kenn, Wm., greengrocer, Chapel st, Prn
Kennard, Mrs., Bouverie st, Carl
Kennedy, A., 35 Young st, F
Kennedy, A. C., 45 Napier st, F
Kennedy, Alexander, tinsmith, 73 Gertrude st, F
Kennedy, Alexander, 55 Gertrude st, F
Kennedy, D., 191 Cecil st, Em H
Kennedy, D. S., Station place, San
Kennedy, Edward F., messenger, 61 Latrobe st east
Kennedy, George D., corn store, Hot
Kennedy, J., butcher, Fcy
Kennedy, James, plumber and gasfitter, 168 Elizabeth st
Kennedy, John, bootmaker, Church st, Rd
Kennedy, John, 139 Johnston st, F
Kennedy, John, grocer, 325 Brunswick st, F
Kennedy, John, 20 Cobden st, Em H
Kennedy, Joseph, butcher, Moreland st, Fcy
Kennedy, Michael, Caroline st, S Y
Kennedy, Morgan, Edinburgh Castle hotel, Courtney st, Hot
Kennedy, Mrs., 34 Smith st, E C
Kennedy, Mrs., 55 Brunswick st, F
Kennedy, Mrs., Trafalgar place, Hot
Kennedy, Owen, Inkerman st, St K
Kennedy, Patrick, butcher, Flem
Kennedy, Patrick, London hotel, Market street
Kennedy, Robert, Church st, Rd
Kennedy, Wm., Washington hotel, corner of Collins st west and William st
Kennedy, Wm., commercial traveller, 55 Little Collins st east
Kenneth, J. F., 20 Market st, Em H
Kennett, C. A., butcher, Station place, San
Kenney, G. E. A., saddler, 67 Stephen st

Kenney, Robert A., auctioneer, Arthur st, S Y
Kennison, James L., baker, corner Franklyn and Spencer sts
Kennon, Hugh, Black Eagle hotel, 161 Lonsdale st east
Kenney's Baths, beach, St K
Kenny, A. C., 56 St David st, F
Kenny, D., constable, 166 Russell st
Kenny, James, dairyman, 160 Ferrars st, Em H
Kenny, James, 90 Leicester st, Carl
Kenny, Michael, general store, Flemington road, Hot
Kenny, Mrs. F., 5 George st, E M
Kenny, R. A., saddler, Charles st, Pra
Kenny, Thomas, 33 Hoken st, W M
Kenny, Thomas, 28 Collins st west, and law
Kenrick, Michael, bootmaker, 227 Swanston st
Kent, D. S., Rowena parade, Rd
Kent, G., Edward st, Bk
Kent, J., Chapel st, Pra
Kent, W., Cecil st, F
Kentish, George, greengrocer, Bay st, San
Kenwood, Mrs., dressmaker, Curzon st, Hot
Kenworthy, Charles J., 2 Swan st, Rd
Keogh, E. and M., wholesale druggists, 11 Latrobe st east
Keogh, Joseph, 133 Nicholson st, F
Keogh, Michael, Fitzroy terrace, Clarendon st, E M
Keppel, Mrs., grocer, 153 Little Lonsdale st east
Ker, Robert, 10 Hall of Commerce, 46 Collins st west
Kerferd, G. B., M.L.A., 57 King William st, F
Kernohan, W. J., hardware merchant, 12 Bural st
Kerr and Co., timber yard, 30 Electra st, Wmn
Kerr, Andrew, Moor st, F
Kerr, Archibald, Barkly st, Carl
Kerr, David, 80 Cecil st, Wmn
Kerr, J., butcher, 41 Queen st
Kerr, James, Argyle st east, St K
Kerr, James, 83 Young st, F
Kerr, John, bootmaker, High st, Pra
Kerr, John, sailmaker, 10 Coventry st, Em H
Kerr, John, boarding-house, 107 Collins st west
Kerr, M., wood yard, 205 Lonsdale st west
Kerr, Mrs., 14 Perry st, E C
Kerr, Mrs., Octavia st, St K
Kerr, Mrs., Lennox st, Rd
Kerr, Mrs., Nathaniel, 6 Victoria st, W M
Kerr, P., Railway place, San
Kerr, Robert, estate agent, 10 Collins st west
Kerr, Thomas, saddler, Gordon st, Fcy

Kerr, Wm., Flem
Kerr, Wm., grocer, Capel st, Hot
Kerr, W., draper, 104 Wellington st, E C
Kerr, Wm., greengrocer, Hoden st, W M
Kerrison, James, bootmaker, 18 and 20 Elizabeth st extension
Kersey, H., 97 Park st, Em H
Kershaw and Co., agents, Swan st, Rd
Kershaw, R., grocer, Hoddle st, E C
Kershaw, Wm., naturalist, 142 Johnston st, F
Kersley, Robert, Grey st, St K
Kertland, W., 75 St. David st, F
Kesterton, W., Acland st, St K
Kestle, Mrs., 122 Elgin st, Carl
Ketin, Thomas, 16 Arden st, Hot
Kettels, David, Station place, San
Key, David, tailor, 23 Napier st, Em H
Key, Thomas, 91 Bridport st, Em H
Keyane, J., Flemington road, Hot
Keyburn, Edward, tinsmith, 234 Elizabeth st, and Btn
Keyburn, M., Leveson st, Hot
Keys, —, 204 Moray st, Em H
Keys, John, 18 Cross st, Hot
Keys, R., Keys' hotel, Arthur road, Btn
Keys, Wm., Yarra st, E C
Khun, A., dealer, 9 Little Lonsdale st west
Kibble, John, High st, Pra
Kidd, E., bonnet cleaner, Dorcas st, Em H
Kidd, Mrs., 81 Faraday st, Carl
Kidd, Mrs., 57 Erroll st, Hot
Kidd, Robert, builder, 231 King st
Kidd, Thomas, blacksmith, Moonee ponds
Kidd, W., 34 Church st, Em H
Kidd, W. and E., bonnet makers, Bay st, San
Kidner, George, butcher, Hyde st, Fcy
Kidner, J., timber yard, High st, St K
Kidney Bros., outfitters and tailors, 168 Smith st, E C, and 187a Elizabeth st
Kidney, Thomas, 3 Condell st, F
Kidney, Wm., 3 Condell st, F
Kidson, James, stationer, 5 Gertrude st, F
Kiel, John, Flemington road, Hot
Kierulf, John Palmer, merchant, 9 Elizabeth st
Kiessling, Gustave A., importer, 16 Flinders lane west
Kilbee, Charles, veterinary surgeon, Albert st, Pra
Kilburn, John, 46 Derby st, E C
Kilby, Thomas, Peel st, Hot
Kilgour, James, 31 Hammer st, Wmn
Killinghausen, E., jeweller, 105 Queen st
Kilmartin, Denis, Fcy
Kilmartin, Joseph, Twyford st, Wmn
Kilpatrick and Co., watchmakers and jewellers, 39 Collins st west
Kilpatrick, Captain, 182 Moray st, Em H
Kilwary, Mrs., 2 Dryburgh st, Hot
Kimber, F., Blackwood st, Hot
Kimber, W. T., poulterer and fruiterer, 8 Swanston st

Kimber, James, market gardener, Pra
Kimmance, Mrs., 33 Wellington st, E C
Kimpton, W. S., baker, 255 Brunswick st, F
Kimpton, Wm., baker, 101 Argyle st, F
Kinane, James, 26 Franklyn st, W M
Kinane, T., nurseryman, New st, Dto
Kinder, C., Albert st, Pra
Kinder, James, butcher, Peel st, Pra
Kinder, James, contractor, Wellington st, St K
King, —, hairdresser, Swan st, Rd
King, —, baker, 61 Condell st, F
King, —, Chetwynd st, W M
King, A., Charles st, Pra
King, A., St K
King, A., 96 Young st, F
King and Cunningham, stock and station agents, 67 Bourke st west
King and Parsons, warehousemen, 43 Collins st east
King, Andrew, Summerhill place, Wellington parade, E C
King, Arthur Septimus, Haw
King, Bernard, Catholic bookseller, 19 Lonsdale st east
King, Charles, Ferguson st, Wmn
King, Dennis, Patterson st, E C
King, E, professor of music, 75 Young st, F
King, Edward, Albert st, Pra
King, Emanuel, Fitzroy st, St K
King, Emanuel, umbrella and parasol maker, 41 Bourke st east
King, H. E., gingerbeer manufacturer, 260 Brunswick st, F
King, Henry, Lothian st, Hot
King, Jacob, Cole st, South Wmn
King, Jacob, store, Illawarra st, South Wmn
King, Jacob, Bay st, San
King, James, Church st, Rd
King, James, 62 Cobden st, Em H
King, Jesse, coachbuilder, 185 Smith st, F
King, John H., 72 Oxford st, E C
King, John C., manager Argus newspaper, 78 Collins st east
King, John, general store, Hoddle st, E C
King, John, Octavia st, St K
King, John, plumber and gasfitter, 94 Park st, Em H
King, John, Westbury st, St K
King, John, Haw
King, Joseph, Argyle st west, St K
King, Joseph, boot and shoemaker, corner of Sackville and Smith sts, E C
King, M., baker, Condell st, F
King, Mark L., M.L.A., Wellington parade, E M
King, Matthias, D., agent, Errol st, Hot
King, Mrs., dressmaker, 5 Wellington st, Pra
King, Mrs., pastrycook, 86 and 88 Swanston st

King, Robert W., straw hat manufacturer, 117 Brunswick st, F
King, Samuel, Cliff st, Pra
King, Samuel G., draper and outfitter, 64 Errol st, F
King, Thomas, butcher and baker, Alphington
King, Thomas, Railway place, San
King, W., 5 Wellington st, St Kilda
King, W., bailiff, 56 Little Collins st west
King, Wm., Essendon and Haw
King, Wm., 22 Pelham st, Carl
Kingsland, George, chemist, 139 Lonsdale st west
Kingsley, Mrs., school, Ascot Vale, Flem
Kingston, John, draper, Nelson place, North Wmn
Kingston, J. T., Provost st, Hot
Kingston, Mrs., fancy repository, 63 Nelson place, Wmn
Kingston, Wm., Brown st, Heid
Kinnmont, Rev. A. D., 7 Hawke st, W M
Kinkade, John, 123 Nicholson st, F
Kinna, M. T., Kinna's hotel, 217 Swanston st
Kinross, J., coachbuilder and importer of coachbuilders' materials, 214 Elizabeth street
Kinsella, Cashion, and Co., wine and spirit merchants, 43 Little Collins st west
Kinsella, Michael, farmer, Braybrook road, Ess
Kinsey, Mrs., dressmaker, 207 George st, F
Kinsley, M., Octavia st, St K
Kinsman, Nathaniel, auctioneer, 3 Moor st, F
Kinson, J., Fleet st, Palmer st, F
Kirby, Captain Thomas, 31 Barkly st, Carl
Kirby, James, greengrocer, 23 Leveson st, Hot
Kirby, Jeremiah, bootmaker, 50 Queensberry st, Carl
Kirby, Robert, Baillie st, Hot
Kirk, David, blacksmith, 46 Dudley st, W M
Kirk, G., Caroline st, S Y
Kirk, George, and Co., auctioneers, &c, 12 Bourke st west
Kirk, George, printer, 24 Park st east, Em H
Kirk, John, farmer, Ess
Kirk, Mrs. E., midwife, 22 Park st east, Em H
Kirkbank, T., bootmaker, 301 Elizabeth street
Kirkby, A., and Co., wine and spirit merchants, 9 Flinders st west
Kirkby, A., Williams road, Th
Kirkby, J., Chapel st, St K
Kirkham, George, Argyle st, St K
Kirkley, Mrs., 21 Bank st west, Em H
Kirkness, James, 106 Westgarth st, F
Kirkpatrick, A., grocer, Pent

Kirkus, Edward, Flem
Kirkwood, Mrs., 72 Nicholson st, F
Kirkwood, W., carpenter, Macquarie st, Wmn
Kirnan, Andrew, Dove hotel, Swan st, RJ
Kirwan, —, 50 Park st east, Em H
Kirwan, P. T., watchmaker, 79 Little Collins st east
Kirwood, Charles, draper, Kew
Kissling, A. U., 110 Fitzroy st, F
Kiswick, Wm., stock salesman, 47 Bourke st west, and North-park, Ess
Kitchen, J., and Sons, candle and soap makers, over Haglan st, San
Kitchen, John, sen., Waterloo st, St K
Kitchen, H. W., Royal Saxon hotel, Church st, Rd
Kitchingman James, 55 Queensberry st, Carl
Kiter, M., 3 Canning st, Carl
Kitt, —, Yarra st, off Hoddle st, E C
Kitt, James, secretary First and Second Howlett Building Society, Studley park, Abbotsford
Kitton, Charles, chemist, 126 Swanston st
Klausch, J. F., 37 Jeffcott st, W M
Klein, Brellus, and Co., merchants and commission agents, 28 Queen st
Klein, C., Grey st, St K
Kleisor, Anton, jeweller, 203A Bourke st east
Klingender, Charsley, and Liddle, solicitors, &c., Bank place, Collins st west
Klingender, E., Orrong road, Tk
Klose, J., store, Bridge road, Rd
Knaggs, Robert, surgeon, 137 King st
Knape, R., Brighton st, Rd
Knapman, George, blacksmith, Ivanhoe, Heid
Knarston, Captain, 126 Ferrars st, Em H
Kneale, J. P., shoemaker, 190 Cambridge st, E C
Knee, Ephraim, Dryburgh st, Hot
Kneen, Hugh, Young st, F
Kneller, Isaac, 227 Smith st, F
Knew, H., clothier, 103 Flinders st west
Knight, Andrew H., 111 Flinders lane west
Knight, C., medical galvanist, Foundry lane, Lonsdale st east
Knight, E. D., wholesale fruiterer, 10 Western Market
Knight, E. L., 59 Smith st, F
Knight, G., blacksmith, 44 King William st, F
Knight, G. G., Flem
Knight, George Henry, fruiterer, Western Market
Knight, J., locksmith, &c., 56 Queensberry st, Carl
Knight, J G., architect and C. E., secretary Intercolonial Exhibition, 54 Elizabeth st and 26 Collins st east
Knight, Josiah, 45 Victoria st, Hot

Knight, John, Somerset Arms hotel, Nicholson st, Carl
Knight, John, 3 Somerset cottages, Nicholson st, Carl
Knight, P., Edward st, Bk
Knight, Robert, Bay st, San
Knight, Samuel, Elgin st, Carl
Knight, W. M., whitesmith, Chapel st, Pra
Knight, Wm., ironmonger, 8 Franklyn st west, W M
Knight, Wm., painter and paperhanger, Cremorne st, Rd
Knight, Wm. F., Telegraph hotel, Ann st, Wmn
Knipe and Kyte, auctioneers, &c., 70 Elizabeth st
Knipe, J. H., Nelson st east, St K
Knock, Mrs., grocer, 91 Fitzroy st, F
Knockenhauer, C. E., tobacconist, 74 Flinders st west
Knoff, G., Webb st, F
Knoop, Wm. H., broker, 69 Collins st west
Knott, W., 66 Gore st, F
Knowell, James H., Blackwood st, Hot
Knowles, —, grocer, Gardiner's creek road, Tk
Knowles, Miss, milliner, 77½ Brunswick st, F
Knowles, Thomas, 24 Ferguson st, Wmn
Knox, —, 137 Moray st, Em H
Knox, George, 126 Lygon st, Carl
Knox, James, grocer, &c., High st, St K
Knox, Mrs., Neptune st, St K
Knox, T. W., Lennox st, Rd
Knox, Thomas, 45 Little Nelson st, Wmn
Knox, Wm., 62 Drummond st, Carl
Koch, Johann, dyer, Leaney st, Brighton st, Rd
Kofland, Peter, 65 Bouverie st, Carl
Köhler, F. A., outfitter, 45 and 47 Flinders st west
Kohng, S., Victoria st, St K
Kuhry, S. G., Haw
Kolling, Louis, 11 Little Latrobe st
Kolmetz, Alexander, engraver, Bignell's lane, Bourke st east
Kong Meng and Co, merchants, 96 Little Bourke st east
Koppen, Rudolph, wood and ivory turner, 22 and 25 Lonsdale st west
Korne, Captain, Fitzroy st, St K
Koss, Charles, bootmaker, 125 Little Collins st east
Kost, Samuel, Rose of Australia hotel, 126 King st
Kostadt, Henry, Blackwood st, Hot
Kraetzer, Leopold, manufacturing clothier, 28 Little Collins st west
Krakowski, Moses, pawnbroker, 86 King street
Kronberg, F., chaser, 117 Russell st
Kronheimer, Joseph and Co., tobacco importers and merchants, 21 Queen st
Kronheimer, Joseph, Nicholson st, F

Kruse, Adalbert, broker, Prussian consul, 60 Queen st
Kruse, John, manufacturing chemist, 96 Russell st and 119 Flinders st east
Kursteiner, Alfred F., architect and surveyor, 64 Collins st east
Kyle, Archibald, Queensberry hotel, corner Queensberry and Madeline sts, Carl
Kyle, Mrs., 132 Gore st, F
Kyte, Ambrose, M L.A., merchant, Commercial lane, Bourke st east
Kyte, Andrew, Douglas parade, Wmn

L.

Labdon, Mrs., Graham st, San
Labdon, Wm., Dow st, San
Labertouche, P. P., 61 King William st, F
Lacelive, Edwin, Franklyn st, W M
Lacey, H. W., Chapel st, Pra
Lacey, Nicholas, builder, 20 Lincoln square, Carl
Lacey, Patrick, grocer, 117 Little Bourke st east
Lacey, W., 31 Fitzroy st, F
La Chapelle, A., Rube st, St K
Lachmere, H., fruiterer, Davis st, Pra
Lackey, James, 24 Stevedore st, Wmn
Lachie, —, 183 Victoria parade, E C
Lacy, Michael, Coachmakers' Arms hotel, 115 Cardigan st, Carl
Lade, George, greengrocer, Spencer st
Lade, S., brickmaker, Victoria st west, Bk
Laden, Mrs., 53 Rosslyn st, W M
Laffan, Michael, grocery store, 77 Queenberry st, Hot
La Fonta, Richard, grocer, Church st, Rd
Laggen, J., High st, Rd
Laggett, Richard, 129A Johnston st, E C
Lagor, Wm. H., deputy registrar of births, &c., Rowena parade, Rd
Lagogiannis, Andrew, Chusan hotel, Beach st, San
Lahrmell, Wm., tailor, Bignell's lane, Bourke st east
Laidlaw, John, Provost st, Hot
Laidlow, W., Oxford st, Hot
Laighton, W., Howard st, Hot
Lain, H., 78 Bank st west, Em H
Laing and Webster, warehousemen, 16 Flinders lane east
Laing, James, general dealer, 253 Swanston st
Lainson, Alfred, 116 Faraday st, Carl
Lake, Wm., Quarries, Fcy
Lakeman, E. F., Globe hotel, corner of Swanston and Little Bourke sts
Lalor, D., Fcy
Lalor, J., boarding-house, 93 Flinders st east
Lalor, James, Beclive hotel, corner of Russell and Lonsdale sts
Lalor, P., M.L.A., Parliament House
Lalor, Peter, High st, Pra

Lamb, —, 3 Baillie st, Hot
Lamb, F. C., druggist, 84 Clarendon st, Em H
Lamb, Fred., merchant, 30 Queen st
Lamb, J., Caroline st, B Y
Lamb, J., 115 Rose st, F
Lamb, Jas., baker, 80 Stevedore st, Wmn
Lamb, John, Haw
Lamb, Mrs., store, Rouse st, San
Lamb, Mrs., 4 Cohden st, Em H
Lamb, Peter, 97 Cardigan st, Carl
Lamb, Wm., Cape st, Heid
Lamb, Wm., saddler, 130 Bridge road, Rd
Lamb, Wm., 153 Moor st, F
Lambard, John S., gunmaker, 114 Little Lonsdale st west
Lambert, Ann, 94 Drybargh st, Hot
Lambert, Henry, general dealer, 109 Fitzroy st, F
Lambert, J. C., 61 Gore st, F
Lambert, John, Patterson st, E C
Lambert, Louis, 88 Russell st south
Lambert, Mrs., Hoddle st, Hd
Lambert, Thomas, Kew
Lambert, Thomas, tanner and currier, 28 Lonsdale st east
Lambert, W. A., 117 Napier st east, Em H
Lambing, Wm., 4 Ann st, Wmn
Lamble, John, 10 Moor st, F
Lamble, T. and J., farriers, 2a Gertrude st, F
Lamble, Wm., blacksmith and farrier, 173 Little Bourke st east
Lamborn, W., Caulfield
Lamborn, Wagner, and Clarke, goldsmiths and jewellers, 42 Lonsdale st west
Lambourn, John, farmer, Fletcher st, Eas
Lambrick, John, Harcourt st, Hot
Lambrick, Nicholas, Harcourt st, Hot
Lambrick, Richard, Harcourt st, Hot
Lamborne, Wm., Chapel st, St K
Laming, Wm. F., store, 6 Nelson place, Wmn
Lamley, W., Swan st, Rd
Lamond, Mrs., 177 Moray st, Em H
Lamond, Wm. H., coal and produce merchant, 55 Flinders st east
Lamont, Edward H., broker, 66 Flinders lane west
Lamont, John, house and ship joiner, 79 Cecil st, Wmn
Lampes, George, upholsterer, 36 Little Lonsdale st east
Lancashire, Samuel, Court House hotel, Errol st, Hot
Lancaster, George, 82 Dorcas st, Em H
Lancaster, John, cab proprietor, 32 Argyle st, F
Lancaster, Mrs., milliner, Twyford st, Wmn
Lancaster, Mrs., school, Nicholson st, Fcy
Lancaster, Robert, 22 Macquarie st, Wmn
Lance, J., bootmaker, 96 Flinders lane east

Lan AND SUBURBS. Lat 95

Lancos. Mrs., school, Nicholson st, F
Land Mortgage Bank of Victoria, 28 Collins st east
Lander, John, 58 Chetwynd st, Hot
Lander, G. W., Argyle st east, St K
Landells, George, King st north
Landhall, C., 337 Victoria parade, E C
Landler, James, 60 a'Beckett st west
Landriggin, T., Arden st, Hot
Lands' Titles office, corner William and Lonsdale sts
Landsell, A., jeweller, 84 Flinders lane east
Landwehr, W., shoemaker, 58 Stanley st, E C
Landy, John, 8 Bendigo st, Hot
Landy, M. A., Bouverie st, Carl
Lane, Henry, saddler, Inkerman st east, St K
Lane, James H., Harvest Home hotel, corner of Flinders and Queen sts
Lane, M., Mexican terrace, Hoddle st, E C
Lane, Mrs., Berkeley st, Carl
Lane, Richard, Carlisle st east, St K
Lane, Wm., Alma st, St K
Lanett, Richard W., Haw
Lang and Co., lime merchants, 38 Queen street.
Lang, Andrew, grocer, 127 Little Bourke st west
Lang, G., 100 George st, E M
Lang, G. S., barrister, Temple court, Collins st west
Lang, J., Fitzroy st, St K
Lang, John, 18 Faraday st, Carl
Lang, L., Punt road, Rd
Lang, Ludwig, engraver, 60 Little Collins st east
Lang, Matthew, wine and spirit merchant, 83 Collins st west
Lang, W., Ashling st, Bru
Langan, P. J., market inspector, 144 Latrobe st west
Langdon, H., Westbury st, St K
Langdon, H. J., merchant, 8 Flinders lane west
Langdon, John, Flem
Langdon, P., post office, Inkerman st east, St K
Lange and Thoneman, merchants, 35 Market st
Lange, Charles, surgeon dentist, 64 Collins st east
Lange, F. C., Alma terrace, Chapel st, St K
Langford, J., Rowena parade, Rd
Langford, Mrs., midwife, 116 Lygon st, Carl
Langford, Richard, Railway hotel, Cecil st, Wmn
Langham, George, 8 Twyford st, Wmn
Langham, James, 61 Kerr st, F
Langhorn, George, grocer, 85 Coventry st, Em U

Langlands Brothers and Co., engineers, 141 Flinders lane west
Langlands, F., Brunswick road, Bk
Langlands, George, Swan st, Rd
Langlands, H. W., 37 Rathdowne st, Carl
Langlands, John, 63 Victoria parade, F
Langlands, Mrs., 503 Lygon st, Carl
Langlands, Thomas, Prince's st, F
Langley, John M., importer of glass, china, &c., 206 Bourke st east
Langley, Wm., 69 Queensberry st, Carl
Langridge, George D., general contractor, 72 Stephen st
Langridge, John, contractor, Perry st, E C
Langster, Mrs., Lennox st, Rd
Langstreth, E., grainer, 32 Madeline st, Carl
Langton, David E., butcher, 66 Brunswick st, F
Langton, Edward, accountant, &c., 12 Collins st west
Langton, Joseph, 3 Blackwood st, Hot
Langton, Mrs., 162 Moray st, Em H
Langtree, John, broker, 56 Little Collins st east
Langwill, Craig, and Co., ironmongers, 12 Collins st west
Langwill, Peter, Barnett st, St K
Lanigan, John, bootmaker, 31 Madeline st, Carl
Lanigan, Rev. —, 16 Cole st, Wmn
Lanman, O., china and glass warehouse, Chapel st, Pra
Lannigan, Stephen, Yarra st, Held
Lansby, Thomas, Haw
Lansdell, Stephen, glass case maker, &c., 81½ Flinders lane east
Lapthorne, H., 39 Coventry st, Em H
Larimer, Captain J., Westbury st, St K
Larkin, James, grocer, &c., 42 Cardigan st, Carl
Larkin, Michael, dairyman, 49 Park st west, Em H
Larkins, A., 149 Moor st, F
Larkins, Jas., bootmaker, 86 Chetwynd st, Hot
Larkins, W. S., Temple Court hotel, 49 Queen st
Larmar, M., bootmaker, 142 Brunswick st, F
Larmach, George, 32 Stanley st, W M
La Roche, Louis, house decorator, 4 Cole st, Wmn
Larrard, Alfred, Cremorne st, Rd
Larrett, H. W., Haw
Lascelles, Edwin, 10 Franklyn st, W M
Lassen, Laurity, oyster dealer, 170 Bourke st east
Lasson, D., 113 Kerr st, F
Last, H., 138 Elgin st, Carl
Latch, C., Nicholson st, F
Latham, Edward, 77 Berkeley st, Carl
Latham, John, Leicester st, Carl
Latham, W. J., 72 York st, Em H

Latimer, J. A., grocer, 56 Cambridge st, E C
Latimer, R., Builders' Arms hotel, James st, Wmn
La Trobe, F D., 63 Collins st west
Lattaca, Robert, Blessington st, St K
Lauder, John, Provost st, Hot
Laughton, B., Peel st, Hot
Laughton, James, P., 114 George st, F
Laughton, Joseph, ironfounder, &c., Vulcan Works, Latrobe st west
Laughton, N., Sobo Foundry, Franklyn st west
Laughton, T., Weston st, Bk
Launceston and Melbourne Steam Navigation Company, office, 23 Market st
Laurence, James, Station place, San
Laurens, J., storekeeper, 89 Spencer st
Laurenson, Arthur, Cremorne st, Rd
Laurenson, L., Stewart st, Bk
Lausen, Henry, restaurant keeper, Beach st, San
Lavers, Robert, curry powder manufacturer, 185 Swanston st
Lavers, Wm. D., bottle merchant, 185 Swanston st
Lavington Gold Mining Company, 3 Queen street
Law Brothers, upholsterers, 27 Collins st west
Law, F. F., Mount Gambier hotel, Palmer st, F
Law Institute of Victoria, 63 Temple court, Collins st west
Law, Mrs. Jane, dress and mantle maker, 19a Lonsdale st west
Law, P., 32 George st, F
Law, Sumner, and Co., seedsmen, 87 Swanston st
Law, Wm., Pra
Lawder, David, Abbotsford st, W M
Lawes, Henry, barrister, 13 Temple court, Collins st west
Lawes, Henry, Haw
Lawes, James, Elgin st, Carl
Lawler, John, cab proprietor, 67 Smith st, F
Lawler, P., Church st, Rd
Lawlor, James, Elizabeth st extension
Lawlor, H., 13 Railway place, Wmn
Lawlor, R., 15 Railway place, Wmn
Lawlor, Rd., Terminus hotel, Hanmer st, Wmn
Lawn, Thomas, photographist, 146 Swan st, Rd
Lawrance, James, ship auctioneer and broker, 95 Collins st west
Lawrance, Wm., broker, &c., 37 William st, Punt road, S Y
Lawrence, — 2 Pelham st, Carl
Lawrence and Adam, wholesale grocers and wine and spirit merchants, 198 Elizabeth st
Lawrence, Captain, Strand, Wmn

Lawrence, Charles, Flem
Lawrence, Edward, bootmaker, 141 Queensberry st, Hot
Lawrence, F. J., 149 Moray st, Em R
Lawrence, James, 13 Russell st
Lawrence, James, Dower place, Wmn
Lawrence, James B., Victoria buildings, Queen st
Lawrence, James, contractor, Victoria buildings, Queen st
Lawrence, John, upholsterer, &c., 158 Swan st, Rd
Lawrence, Mrs, Carlisle st west, St K
Lawrence, Samuel, bootmaker, a'Beckett st east
Lawrence, W. F., Station place, San
Lawrence, Wm., 32 Perry st, E C
Lawrence, Wm., broker, 37 William st
Lawrence, Wm.H., Inkerman st east, St K
Lawson, Andrew, 27 Bouverie st, Carl
Lawson, Charles G., grocer, 75 Drummond st, Carl
Lawson, F., Carson's cottages, 135 Collins st east
Lawson, J., 105 Bank st west, Em R
Lawson, John B., Charles st, Pra
Lawson, Matthew, slater, Dryburgh st, Hot
Lawson, Robert, 1 Cecil st, Wmn
Lawson, Wilfred H., 17 Regent st, F
Lawson, Wm., Clyde st, St K
Lawson, Wm. S., sewing machine maker, 101 Elizabeth st
Lawton, Madame, school, High st, Pra
Lawton, N., Peel st, W M
Lay, George, Station place, San
Lay, Mrs., Brighton st, Rd
Laycock, Wm., baker, 140 Johnston st, E C
Layton, John, greengrocer, Madeline st, Carl
Layzell, John C., carpenter, &c., 76 Little Collins st east
Lazarus, A., and Co., importers, 42 Elizabeth st
Lazarus Brothers, importers, 21 Little Collins st west
Lazarus, C., crinoline manufactory, 21 Lonsdale st west
Lazarus, J., 1 Alexander terrace, 113 Smith st, F
Lazarus, James, 63 Bouverie st, Carl
Lazarus, Joseph, 62 Baden st, W M
Lazarus, L., 80 Young st, F
Lazarus, Saml., Victoria buildings, Queen st north
Lazarus, Solomon, Victoria buildings, Queen st north
Lazarus, Thomas, ironmonger, 47 Little Collins st east
Lea, Wm., saddler, 46 and 48 Little Collins st east
Leaber, A., upholsterer, 116 Swanston st
Leach, Charles, Rathdowne st, Carl

Leach, Amram, draper and clothier, 151 Brunswick st, F
Leach, G. W., Curzon st, Hot
Leach, Nelson, Builders' Arms, Gertrude st, F
Leabeater, John, Capel st, W M
Leader office, 67 Elizabeth st
Leage, James, Domain road, S Y
Leahy, Wm. Henry, money broker, 79½ Collins st east
Leake, Richard, Flemington hill
Lear, F., 6 Palmer st, F
Lear, G. W., Nicholson st, Carl
Lear, Hugh, 138 Bridge road, Rd
Lear, W. H., 97 Faraday st, Carl
Learoyd, J., woolbroker, 76 Collins st west
Leary, George, butcher, 18 Dover place, Wmn
Leber, John, 39 Lygon st, Carl
Lechte, F., 117 Smith st, F
Leckenby, Thomas, hay and corn dealer, High st, Prn
Leckington, A., 176 Drummond st, Carl
Lecroisette, Thos., Latrobe st west
Lecky, Oliver R., 48 Collins st west
Le Clerc, Wm., 87 Argyle st, F
Le Compte, Louis, Forester's hotel, Fitzroy st, F
Le Cren, Charles, accountant sewerage department, Kew
Le Cren, Thomas, Argyle st, Pra
Leddio, Martin, broker and commission agent, 68 Flinders lane west
Ledger, Mrs., boarding-house, 30 Latrobe st east
Ledward, S. P., druggist, Bay st, Ein
Lee, Benjamin, ironmonger, 177 and 179 Bourke st east
Lee, C., 26 Brunswick st, F
Lee, D., professor of music, 32 Coventry st, Em H
Lee, Frank, 73 Swan st, Rd
Lee, James, Drummond st, Carl
Lee, James, grocer, 37 Provost st, Hot
Lee, John D., tobacconist, 49 Bourke st east
Lee, John, Carlisle st west, St K
Lee, Joseph S., Aavion st, Hot
Lee, Josh., bootmaker, 10 Gertrude st, F
Lee, Michael M., agent and broker, 18 Collins st east
Lee, Mrs. Emma, 147 Cecil st, Em H
Lee, Mrs. C., Powlett st, Em H
Lee, Mrs., tailoress, 15 Little Nelson st, Wmn
Lee, Oriel, Queensberry hotel, 53 Madeline st, Carl
Lee, Richard, 110 Gore st, F
Lee, Wm. L., medical galvanist, 95 Napier st, F
Lee, Wm., 20 Parker st, Wmn
Lee, Tick, merchant, 60 Little Bourke st east
Leech, J., Dorcas st, Em H

Leek, Charles, 63 Osborne st, Wmn
Lecke, H., E C
Leer, D., Bay st, San
Lees, Alexander, Walsh st, W M
Lees, F., saddler, Lothian st, Hot
Lees, John, 147 Queensberry st, Hot
Leeson, J., Lygon st, Carl
Leetch, Connolly, commission merchant, 41 Flinders lane east
Leftley, Mrs., dressmaker, Stoke st, San
Legg, John, 47 Ferguson st, Wmn
Leggan, James, Heath st, San
Legge, Samuel, Hobe st, St K
Leggett, Charles, 43 Rathdowne st, Carl
Lehrman, Wm., tailor, Bignell's lane, Bourke st west
Le Huray, James, 297 Fitzroy st, F
Leigh, Mrs., Alma st, St K
Leighton, David, Market st
Leighton, John G., pilot, 6 Macquarie st, Wmn
Leishman, Rev. W., Canning st, Carl
Leitch, A., grocer, 29 Coventry st, Em H
Leitch, George, Cremorne st, Rd
Leitch, Mrs., grocer, Nicholson st, F
Leith, Alex., Pelham st, Em H
Leith, Alexander, accountant and house factor, 26 Collins st west
Leith, James, veterinary surgeon, Darby alley
Lemmon, M., Berkeley st, Carl
Lemon, David, Powlett st, E M
Lemon, Wm., 130 Stevedore st, Wmn
Lempriere, Charles, M.D., surgeon, Burnett st, St K
Lempriere, Thomas Henry, auctioneer, sharebroker, &c., 79 Collins st west
Lempriere, W. G., Balaclava road, East St K
Lendrum, James, plumber, Moonee Ponds, Ess
Lennard, Mrs., Rouse st, San
Lennington, James, 107 Dover place, Wmn
Lennon, Hugh, blacksmith, Elizabeth st extension
Lennon, John, 175 Spring st
Lennox, Duncan, Moray st, Em H
Lenny, John, Prince's st, F
Leonnau, John, Brighton st, Rd
Leonard, J. W., grocer, Villiers st, Hot
Leonard, M., 23 and 25 Smith st, F
Leonard, Miss, Chetwynd st, W M
Leonard, Thomas, 65 Barkly st, Carl
Leonard, Thomas, draper, 173 Spring st
Leonard, Wm., 61 Rosslyn st, W M
Leopold, T., 91 Kerr st, F
Leopold, T., 8 Bell st, F
Leplastrier, H. H., Barkly st, St K
Leplastrier, J., High st, St K
Leplastrier, Louis H., Williams road, Pra
Leylin, George F., Queensberry st, Hot
Lequere, A., Punt road, Rd
Lerone, John, 178 Moray st, Em H

o

Leah, George Case, grocer, 143 Bourke st east
Leslie, David, 69 Courteney st, Hot
Leslie, Donald, Brunswick road, Bk
Leslie, R., 119 Napier st, Em H
Leslie, Wm., Stanley st, W M
L'Estrange, Joseph, solicitor, Brougham place, off Highett st, Rd
Letcher, E., 59 Cambridge st, E C
Letham, John, 115 Cardigan st, Carl
Letham, Mrs., milliner, 83 Gertrude st, F
Letheby, Joshua, powder magazine keeper, Whitehall st, Fcy
Lett, John, toy dealer, Bay st, San
Lett, R., brickmaker, 311 Victoria parade, E C
Letty, John, Abbot st, Hot
Levator, G., Carlisle st, St K
Lovene, James, greengrocer, 65 Wellington st, E C
Lever, Benjamin R., 56 Bouverie st, Carl
Lever, James, 76 Dudley st, W M
Leverett, George F., steel and brass cutter, 88 Napier st, Em H
Leverett, James, Boroondara
Leverett and Trantum, die sinkers, 29 Post Office place
Levey and Robson, printers' brokers, 9 Bourke st east
Levey, G. C., M.L.A., Bourke st east
Levi, Alfred, and Co., tobacco merchants, 78 Collins st west
Levi, Barnett, professor of music, 60 Cambridge st, E C
Levi, John, 2 Carlton terrace, King William st, F
Levi, Nathaniel, M.L.A., King William st, F
Leviathan Clothing Company, 68 Bourke st east
Levick, Robert, 58 King William st, F
Le Vierge, E., Clyde st, St K
Levinger, Bernard, broker and commission agent, 78 Collins st west
Levis, Mrs., Station place, San
Levitt, Samuel J., watchmaker, 59 High st, St K
Levy, Abraham, general dealer, 83 Stephen st
Levy, Abraham, Nicholson st, F
Levy, Abraham, boot and shoe warehouse, 79 Stephen st
Levy Brothers, importers of Birmingham and Sheffield goods, 24 Bourke st east
Levy, Goodman, Prince's st, St K
Levy, Henry, 124 Bourke st west
Levy, Jacob, 206 Russell st
Levy, John, 2 Carlton terrace, King William st, F
Levy, John, and Sons, Discount Bank, corner of Collins and William sts
Levy, Joseph, tobacconist, 243 Bourke st east
Levy, Lewis, 38 Elizabeth st

Levy, Lewis, 40 Nicholson st, F
Levy, Lyons, 129 Little Lonsdale st east
Levy, N., clothier, 157 Elizabeth st
Levy, S., 99 Napier st, F
Levy, Samuel, merchant, 61 Elizabeth st
Lewellen, E. G., chemist, Whitehall st, Fcy
Lewellin, J. H. H., surgeon, Chapel st, Pra
Lewer, Henry, Dryburgh st, Hot
Lewis, A. F., draper, 130 Bridge road, RJ
Lewis, Alf., draper, 68 Bridge road, Rd
Lewis and Tipping, dress and mantle makers, &c., 53a Russell st
Lewis, Arthur, Inkerman st, St K
Lewis, C., High st, St K
Lewis, Charles, and Co., ship brokers and commission agents, 4 Elizabeth st
Lewis, Charles, ironmonger, Chapel st, Pra
Lewis, Charles, 74 Barkly st, Carl
Lewis, Charles J., Williams road, Pra
Lewis, Daniel, plasterer, 35 McArthur place, Carl
Lewis, E., Peel st, Pra
Lewis, Edward, Chapel st, Pra
Lewis, Edward G., Inkerman st, St K
Lewis, G., bootmaker, 26 Bridge road, Rd
Lewis, George, Punt hill, S Y
Lewis, George, Vaucluse, Rd
Lewis, George, and Co., ship owners, &c., 141 Flinders lane west
Lewis, George, chemist and druggist, 5 Collins st east
Lewis, George, Punt road, S Y
Lewis, George, Haw
Lewis, James, 14 Carlton st, Carl
Lewis, James, 119 Nicholson st, F
Lewis, John, china and glass warehouse, Sydney road, Bk
Lewis, John, Greville st, Pra
Lewis, John, tailor, 10 Faraday st, Carl
Lewis, Joseph, restaurant keeper, 21 Bourke st west
Lewis, Joseph, Peel st, Pra
Lewis, Joseph, St K
Lewis, Julius, wine and spirit agent, 5 Grattan st, Carl
Lewis, Louis L., broker, 95 Collins st west
Lewis, Mrs., 73 Kerr st, F
Lewis, Mrs., midwife, 27 Queensberry st, Carl
Lewis, Mrs., High st, Pra
Lewis, P., inspector of police, 117 Fitzroy st, F
Lewis, Rev. W. R., Black st, Btn
Lewis, R. E., Victoria parade, F
Lewis, Richard, undertaker, 162 Young st, F
Lewis, Robert, dyer and scourer, 132 Clarendon st, Em H
Lewis, Robert, Mechanics' Arms Inn, 293 Little Collins st east
Lewis, Rose, dressmaker, 163 Little Collins st east

Lewis, Robert, 33 Victoria parade, F
Lewis, Samuel, pawnbroker, 164 King st
Lewis, Thomas, Capel st, Hot
Lewis, Wm., general dealer, 18 Swanston street
Lewis, Wm., painter, &c., 18 Macarthur place, Carl
Lewis, Wm., Canning st, Carl
Lewis, Wm., engineer, 1 Carson's cottages, Collins st east
Lewis, Wm., 161 Cambridge st, F
Lewis, Wm., Old England hotel, Buckland st, Heid
Lewis, Wm., tailor, 33 Dorcas st west, Em H
Leyden, Ellen, Newmarket hotel, 185 Bourke st east
Leyden, James, 104 Latrobe st east
Leyland, J., Hanmer st, Wmn
Leys, A., 45 Nelson road, Em H
L'llngenin, Dardell, importer, 8 Lonsdale st west
Liddall, Ann, Union st, S Y
Liddall, Thomas, baker and grocer, Rowena parade, Rd
Liddiard, J., butcher, Church st, Rd
Liddle, J., Westbury st east, St K
Lidstone, Wm., plumber and gasfitter, 131 King st
Lidwill, Robert A., Esplanade, Wmn
Lieson, Ellen, 47 Fitzroy st, F
Ligar, Charles W., Surveyor-General, 105 Bridge road, Rd
Liggins, Daniel, Union st, S Y
Lightbody, R., fruiterer, Spencer st
Lightfoot, Joseph, hairdresser, 52½ Clarendon st, Em H
Lightfoot, Robert, Flem
Lightfoot, Theophilus, mnr., Park st, Domain road, S Y
Lihou, Peter, Peel st, Pra
Lilburne, James, hay and corn merchant, 129 King st
Liley, Wm. T., river pilot, 16 Strand, Wmn
Lilienfeld, Bernard, M.D., 118 Collins st east
Lilley, Charles H., London tavern, Lennox st, Rd
Lilley, Wm., ironmonger, &c., 153 Swanston st
Lillie, Alexander, 107 Bridport st, Em H
Lilly, —, compositor, 48 Little Latrobe st east
Lilly, —, Carlisle st west, St K
Lilly, J., Fcy
Lilly, Henry, 74 Drummond st, Carl
Limond, Mrs., general dealer, 155 Clarendon st, Em H
Linacre, A., 135 Lygon st, Carl
Linahan, William, grocer, 193 Lygon st, Carl
Linard, B., King William st, F
Linch, Wm., 65 Faraday st, Carl

Lincker, John H., shipbroker, Hall of Commerce, Collins st west
Lincolne, Abraham, agricultural agent, 46 Bourke st west
Lindbloom, Schmidt, and Wang, tailors, 158 Russell st
Linda, G. C., bootmaker, 104 Victoria st, Rd
Lindemy, Mrs., Grey st, St K
Lindlay, Clement, 78 George st, E M
Lindley, H., steam saw mills, Argyle st, F
Lindner, Victor, upholsterer, 24 Russell st
Lindsale, —, hairdresser, 7 Gertrude st, F
Lindsay, Alexander, 39 Cecil st, Wmn
Lindsay, Alexander, draper, 184 Clarendon st, Em H
Lindsay, Captain S., George st, F
Lindsay, Edward, Canning st, Carl
Lindsay, George, Hosier lane, Flinders lane east
Lindsay, George, slater, Howard st, W M
Lindsay, George, Mill st, Hn
Lindsay, Henry L., C.E. and surveyor, 3 Little Collins st west
Lindsay, J., paperhanger, 289 Victoria parade, E C
Lindsay, James, 131 Victoria st, Hot
Lindsay, Joseph, Rowena parade, Rd
Lindsay, Wm., Byron st, Hot
Lindsell, C., hairdresser, 7A Gertrude st, F
Lindsey, Algernon, 9 Little Nelson st, Wmn
Lindsey, Edward, Faraday st, Carl
Lindsey, M., Crescent, Bln
Linegar, James, 61 Johnston st, F C
Lineker, John, saddler, 49 Smith st, F
Ling, Wm., 48 Market st, Em H
Lingham, Henry, 140 Moor st, F
Linsey, H., 57 Rose st, F
Linson, Walter, Rob Roy hotel, 61 Brunswick st, F
Linton, George, butcher, High st, Pra
Linton, George, 79 Lygon st, Carl
Linton, John, Flem
Linton, Thomas, 10 Stevedore st, Wmn
Lion and Royal Mail Gold Mining Companies, 64 Elizabeth st
Lipshut, John, tobacconist, 143 Elizabeth st
Liscomb, Wm., Jolimont square, E M
Lister, Charles, Clarendon st, Em H
Lister, Charles, Bendigo hotel, and wine stores, 196, 198, and 200 Bourke st east
Liston, James, Thompson st, S Wmn
Lithgow, Richard, bootmaker, 39 Cardigan st, Carl
Litolff, F., Rd
Little, J., draper, 250 Wellington st, E C
Little, John, undertaker, 72 and 74 Victoria st, Rd
Little, John, grocer, 34 Fitzroy st, F
Little, John More, 94 Johnston st, F
Little, Lambert, corner of Eastern road and Cobden st, Em H
Little B., bootmaker, Clyde st, St K

Little, Richard, merchant tailor, 41 Collins st east
Little, Wm., 14 Palmer st, F
Little, Wm., 86 Stanley st, W M
Littlejohn, James, Albert st west, Bk
Littlewood, John, painter, Peel st, Pra
Liverpool Association of Underwriters, B. R. Mathews, agent, 23 Market st
Liverpool and London and Globe Insurance Company, 9 Elizabeth st
Livesey, Benjamin, cabinetmaker, Bay st, Bto
Livesey, J., Moray place, Em H
Lively, John, gasfitter, 70 Gertrude st, F
Livie, David, 37 Cobden st, Em H
Living, Mrs., 9 Royal terrace, Nicholson st, F
Livingston, G. C., 113 Moray st, Em H
Livingstone, Daniel, modeller, 15 Queensberry st, Carl
Livingstone, James, 271 Fitzroy st, F
Livingstone, John, 51 Provost st, Hot
Livingstone, W. J., 137 Victoria st, W M
Lizar, Louis B., importer, 55 Elizabeth st
Lewellen, Mrs., Williams st north
Llewellyn, E. V., Chapel st, Pra
Lloyd, F., painter, &c., 54 Elizabeth st extension
Lloyd, George W., wood carver, 90 Gore st, F
Lloyd, H. H., clothier, 69 Bourke st west
Lloyd, John, farrier, Queensberry st, Carl
Lloyd, John, boarding-house, 43 Franklyn st west
Lloyd, John, Church st, Rd
Lloyd, John, 245 Albert st, E M
Lloyd, John, forge, 5 Berkeley st, Carl
Lloyd, John, wholesale grocer, 13 Swanston st
Lloyd, John, Corry st, Cardigan st, Carl
Lloyd, John C., insurance agent, &c., 34 Collins st west
Lloyd, John T., butcher, 89a Queen st
Lloyd, J. T., butcher, 173 Spencer st
Lloyd, Richard, Pelham st, Carl
Lloyd, Richard, boarding-house keeper, 142 Queen st
Lloyd, S., butcher, Haw
Lloyd, Thomas W., Jolimont square, E M
Lloyd, W., 81 Moor st, F
Lloyd, Wm., 31 Bridport st, Em H
Lloyd's Universal Veritas, 49 Collins st west
Lloyd's Underwriters' Association, B. R. Mathews and Son, agents, 23 Market street
Loader, Thomas, Inkerman road, St K
Loader, Thomas, and Co., wholesale saddlers and general merchants, 193 Elizabeth st
Loan, Lewis, 28 Bridge road, Rd
Lobascher, David, clothier, Beach st, San
Lobb, Wm. J., Hanmer st, Wmn
Loby, John, 86 Ferguson st, Wmn

Local Staff and Brigade Office of Volunteer Force, 45 Stephen st south
Loch, John D., Caroline st, S Y
Lochhead, John, Abbotsford st, W M
Lock, Wm. H., 46 Charles st, F
Locke, Charles, Chambers st, 8 Y
Locke, Charles, Brewster st, Ess
Locke, Charles, Millswyn st, 8 Y
Locke, J., potato dealer, 43 Flinders st west
Locke, J., Union st, 8 Y
Locke, James, Rouse st, San
Locke, Wm., Punt road, Rd
Locke, William, Gardiner's creek road, Pra
Locke, Wm., 25 Rathdowne st, Carl
Lockeyear, Alfred, hairdresser, 91 Bourke st east
Lockeyear, J. R., hairdresser, 87 Brunswick st, F
Lockhart, R., 116 Fichnlson st, F
Lockhart, Robert, Walsh st, W M
Lockington, Henry, Cardigan st, Carl
Lockhurst, John, wheelwright, Flem
Lockie, Bernard, 125a Kerr st, F
Lockwood and Tomlinson, bootmakers, 49 Thompson st, Wmn
Lockwood, J., Herald agency, High st, St K
Lockwood, James, 55 Osborne st, Wmn
Lockwood, N. H., Fitzroy st, F
Lockwood, Wm., bootmaker, Osborne st, Wmn
Logan, John, 43 Howard st, Hot
Logan, John, storekeeper, 21 Nelson place east, Wmn
Logan, Mrs., 177 Moray st, Em H
Logrie, J., sausage maker, Wellington st, E C
Loise, Alexander, 98 Flinders lane east
Lokey, F., Brunswick road, Bk
Loller, J., shoemaker, Halifax st, Btn
Lolly, Richard, 90 Oxford st, E C
Lomas, Charles, farrier, 37 Little Bourke st west
Lomax, S., butcher, Park and Cecil sts, Em H
London and Lancashire Fire and Life Insurance Company, 82 Collins st west
London and Melbourne Gold Mining Co., 54 Queen st
London and Oriental Steam Transit Insurance office, 5 Flinders st east
London Chartered Bank of Australia, 70 Collins st west
London Clubs Marine Insurance, 23 Market st
London and Colonial Company agent's office, 80 Collins st west
London Reef Amalgamated Gold Mining Company, 23 Post Office place
Loney, John, chaffcutter, Flem
Long and Son, chemists and druggists, 163 Bourke st east

Long, Charles, dairyman, 12 Little Latrobe st east
Long, Daniel Rutter, Wellington st, Pra
Long, Denis, mining agent, 3 Little Collins st west
Long, Henry J., 163 Bourke st east
Long, H. and J., chairmakers, Darkly st, Carl
Long, James, 120 George st, F
Long, John, grocer, 166 Ferrars st, Em H
Long, Jno. H., importer of kerosene lamps and oil, 166 Bourke st east
Long, John, 15 Cecil st north, Wmn
Long, M. L., 191 Spring st
Long, Miss, dressmaker, 15 King st
Long, T., 101 Oxford st, E C
Longley, Mrs., High st, Pra
Longmore, F., M.L.A., Hotherwood st, Rd
Longusbaye, Wm. E., Union st, Punt road, Wr
Lonie, W. and H., grocers, 146 Smith st, E C
Lonnen, James, boot and shoe maker, 178 Little Bourke st east
Lonsdale, Henry, undertaker and cabinetmaker, Ferguson st, Wmn
Looke, Charles, Milsywn st, Pra
Loomes, George, butcher, Little Latrobe st
Looney, Mrs. Mary, 102 Bank st west, Em H
Lopes, M. J., bottle merchant, Leicester st, Carl
Lord and Co., merchants, 126 Collins st west
Lord, J., 38 Cobden st, Em H
Lord, Mrs., milliner, 65 Cardigan st, Carl
Lord, R. P., draper, Pelham st, Carl
Lord, Samuel Perkins, Carlisle st west, St K
Lording, J. B., Railway hotel, Chapel st, Pra
Lorey, Wm., Hoddle st, Rd
Lorimer, James, 4 Fitzroy terrace, Clarendon st, E M
Lorimer, Marwood, and Rome, merchants, 48A William st
Loriot, John, bootmaker, 129 Victoria st, E C
Lormer and Co., bakers and confectioners, Gardiner's creek road, Pra
Lormer, Robert, biscuit manufacturer, 92 Spencer st north
Lorrie, Andrew, dairyman, Market street, Young st, F
Lorrie, John, Leveson st, Hot
Lory, James H., Harcourt st, Hot
Lostina, A., dining rooms, Flinders st
Lotherington, Joseph K., chemist, 16 Napier st, F
Lott, L., Nicholson st, F
Louden, John, builder, 121 Nicholson st, F
Loudon, James, boot and shoe dealer, 43 Queensberry st, Hot
Lough, E., bootmaker, 25 Coventry st, Em H

Lough, John, 119 Smith st, F
Loughlin, J., 17 Cross st, Hot
Loughman, Alfred, Flem
Loughman, D., produce merchant, 49 Flinders st west
Loughnan Bros., tobacco manufacturers, 147 Little Lonsdale st west
Loughnan, C., 127 Little Lonsdale st west
Loughnan, James, 145 Little Lonsdale st west
Loughnan, Richard, Little Miller st, Rd
Loughrey, W. J., 114 Nicholson st, F
Louis, Louis, Clyde st, St K
Louttitt, James, shipmaster, Little Nelson st, Wmn
Love, David, Lothian st, Hot
Love, J., grocer, corner Brunswick and Leicester sts, F
Love, James, wheelwright, Moonee Ponds, Ess
Love, R., Baillie st, Hot
Love, Thomas, fruiterer, Eastern Market
Love, W. McNaughton, Upper Haw
Love, Wm., Devonshire Arms, 21 Fitzroy st, F
Lovelace, Charles, 9 Wellington st, E C
Lovell, Wm., cabinetmaker, 93 and 95 Bourke st west
Lovering, Wm., 29 Smith st, F
Lovering, Wm., 107 Clarendon st, E M
Lovett, J., commercial traveller, Fcy
Lowcock, Henry, Charles st, Pra
Lowcock, Misses, ladies' school, Charles st, Pra
Lowden, Mrs., 23 Coventry st, Em H
Lowe, Captain, 195 Cecil st, Em H
Lowe, D., 43 King William st, F
Lowe, E., Union st, S Y
Lowe, G. E., Drummond st, Carl
Lowe, George Gregory, tobacconist, 32 Bourke st east
Lowe, James, Ivanhoe, Heid
Lowe, John, House st, San
Lowe, John, Charles st, Pra
Lowe, Joseph, 77 Drummond st, Carl
Lowe, Mrs., machine sewer, 45 Peel st, E C
Lowe, S. T., Rainbow hotel, corner Swanston and Little Collins st east
Lowe, Wm., 113 Leicester st, F
Lowing, Wm., Drummond st, Carl
Lowman, Joseph, 153 Fitzroy st, F
Lowrey, John, town clerk, Kew
Lowrie, John, 3 Hawke st, W M
Lowrie, John, boat builder, River bank
Lowrie, Mrs., working cutler, 98 Swanston st
Lowrie, Thomas, Gravesend, Fcy
Lyall and Co., merchants, 9 Market st
Lowry, Alexander, Faraday st, Carl
Lowry, James, 95 Cardigan st, Carl
Lowry, Mrs., 52 Pascoe st, Wmn
Lowry, Mrs., 59 Wellington st, E C
Lowry, Robert, Star of the West hotel, corner of King and Little Bourke sts

Loyd, Wm., 45 Cremorne st, Rd
Loyne, Mrs , milliner, 217 King st
Luby, James, 27 Pelham st, Carl
Lucas and Sons, confectioners, 88 and 82A Swanston st
Lucas, B., Cardigan st, Carl
Lucas, Benjamin, Church st, Rd
Lucas, C., Neptune st, St K
Lucas, Captain, 111 Park st west, Em H
Lucas, Charles, 4 Villiers st, Hot
Lucas, Charles James, Henry st, Wr
Lucas, H., 199 Cecil st, Em H
Lucas, H., Weston st, Bk
Lucas, J., Edward st, Bk
Lucas, J., 111 Bank st west, Em H
Lucas, John, 75A George st, F
Lucas, John, Market st, Em H
Lucas, Thomas, 47 York st, Em H
Lucas, Wm., Pelham st, Carl
Lucas, Wm. J., printer and stationer, 213 Swanston st
Lucey, Thomas, Courtenay st, Hot
Lucity, Frank, 25 Jeffcott st, W M
Luckman, Alfred, 56 Baillie st, Hot
Ludgater, Wm. G., 42 King William st, F
Ludman, —, 119 Moor st, F
Ludwick, Henry, Dudley st, W M
Ludwicke, C., Rouse st, San
Luffin, Michael, Provost st, Hot
Lugton, Alexander, engineer, 144 Little Lonsdale st east
Luke, David, Hotham st, Fry
Luke, Robert, 38 Cecil st, Wnn
Luke, Thomas, 3 Simpson st, E M
Lukey and Rimmer, ship brokers, &c., 48 Collins st west
Lukey, Captain, Mary st, Rd
Lulman, Augustus, Kew
Lumsden, Daniel, stationer and printer, 22 Swanston st
Lumsden, David, Hoddle st, E C
Lumsden, J., Fitzroy st, F
Lumsden, Robert, gardener, Grey st, E M
Lunatic Asylum, Yarra Bend
Lunam, Robert, Fitzroy st, St K
Lunch, Michael, baker, 97 Faraday st, Carl
Lund, R. W., E C
Lundborg, —, McArthur place, Carl
Lupson, G. T., 67 Cambridge st, F
Lupton, George, Williams road, Pra
Lush, George, 17 Perry st, E C
Lush, Joseph, Studley park
Lush, Mrs., Hotham st, E M
Lush, Mrs., 38 Palmer st, F
Lusher, Mrs., Brunswick hotel, Brunswick st, F
Lotheran Church, Gisborne st, E M
Lutroytch, Harold, Marian st, F
Luty, Wm., 102 Oxford st, E C
Luxmore, John, 64 King William st, F
Lyall, James, Courtenay st, Hot
Lyall, W. A., Nobe st, St K
Lyall, Wm., Carlisle st east, St K

Lyell and Brown, grocers, 100 Queen st
Lyell, Andrew, 48 Howe crescent, Em E
Lyell, J., 265 Victoria parade, E C
Lyell, George, Avoca st, S Y
Lyell, Mrs., Wellington parade, E M
Lyhane, James, 60 Arden st, Hot
Lying-in Hospital, Cardigan st, Carl
Lynan, J., Lothian st, Hot
Lynar, Rev. James, Heid
Lynch, —, grocer, Gipps st, E C
Lynch, Alfred, inspector of weights and measures, High st, Pra
Lynch, Dennis, 121 Napier st, Em H
Lynch, George, Victoria st, E C
Lynch, James, baker, 187 Cardigan st, Carl
Lynch, Michael, Haw
Lynch, Michael, Lynch alley, Post Office place
Lynch, P., 140 Nicholson st, F
Lynch, Patrick, Wicklow hotel, Bouverie st, Carl
Lynch, Wm., solicitor, 15 and 16 Eldon chambers, Collins st west
Lyne and Guthrie, shipsmiths, Nelson place, Wmn
Lyon, Henry, pawnbroker, 189 Bourke st east
Lyon, John, boarding-house, 68 King st
Lyon, Mrs., 6 Trafalgar place, Hot
Lyons, A., and Co., boat builders, River side south
Lyons, Abraham, tobacconist, 205½ Elizabeth st west
Lyons and Co., mining agents and share brokers, 5 Collins st west
Lyons, Cornelius, 4 Capel st, Hot
Lyons, Cornelius, 3 Villiers st, Hot
Lyons, D., Sydenham villa, Brighton road
Lyons, D., Murphy st, S Y
Lyons, E., Herald agent, 29 Queensberry st, Hot
Lyons, Isaac, and Co., auctioneers, 16 Collins st west
Lyons, J., Church st, E C
Lyons, J., Thompson st, South Wmn
Lyons, J., greengrocer, 92 Fitzroy st, F
Lyons, John, greengrocer, 10 Palmer st, F
Lyons, John, farmer, Fm
Lyons, Joseph, clothier and outfitter, 87 Elizabeth st
Lyons, Louis, 12 Victoria st, W M
Lyons, Robert, Davis st, S Y
Lyons, S. T., Murphy st, S Y
Lyons, Samuel, wine and spirit merchant, 53 Little Collins st east
Lyster and Cooke, stove manufacturers, &c., 192 Little Bourke st east
Lyttleton, Thomas H., Jolimont square, E M

M.

Mabbott, J. P., Kew
McAdam, G. R., schoolmaster, Flem

McAdam, Alexander, grocer and wine merchant, St. David st, St K
McAdam, W., 4 Rathdowne st, Carl
McAinsh, Wm., draper, Bay st, San
McAllister, —, Hoddle st, Rd
McAllister, E., Rowena parade, Rd
McAllister, Geo., 80 Montague st, Em H
McAllister, James, 108 Rose st, F
McAlpine, J. and C., coach builders, Bridge road, Rd
McAneny, Owen, 20 Cobden st, Em H
McAnuff, Hugh, Tankerville Arms hotel, Nicholson st, F
McAnuff, John, Osborne st south, Wmn
McAra, John, smith and wheelwright, 30 Bridge road, Rd
McArthur, A., Nott st, San
McArthur, Alexander, Heath st, San
McArthur, Capt., Hampton st, Bm
McArthur, D. C., Heidelberg road
McArthur, John, 104a Gore st, F
McArthur, Mrs., 8 Raglan st, Em H
McArthur, Mrs., ladies' seminary, Robe st, St K
McArthur, Sherrard, and Copeland, importers, warehousemen, and manufacturers, 30 and 32 Collins st east
McAskell, D., Stewart st, Bk
McAuley Brothers, grocers, 310 Bridge road, Rd
McAuley, Charles, storekeeper, Haw
McAuley, D., carpenter, 121 Brunswick st, F
McAuley, David, general store, Sydney st, Fcy
McAvoy, John, Sydney hotel, William st
McBean, Alexander, grocer, 93 Cardigan st, Carl
McBean, James, watchmaker and jeweller, 73 Elizabeth st
McBean, James, Barry st, Carl
McBean, John, Capel st, W M
McBean, Mary, dressmaker, 169 Lonsdale st west
McBride, J., 44 Howe crescent, Em H
McCaffey, Wm., Wellington st, Rd
McCall, Samuel, furniture broker, 112 Wellington st, E C
McCallum, A. K., Kew
McCallister, E. F., 20 Rowena parade, Rd
McCallum Brothers, importers, &c., 108 Collins st west
McCallum, D., 49 Rose st, F
McCallum, Daniel, marine surveyor, 37 Flinders st west
McCallum, J., Morris st, South Wmn
McCallum, Neill, and Co., merchants, 22 Flinders lane west
McCallum, Patrick, Kew
McCann, —, 3 Napier st, Em H
McCann, Daniel, Murris st, South Wmn
McCann, J., Bay View hotel, 159 Cecil st, Em H
McCann, Thomas, 168 Brunswick st, F

McCann, W. N., M.L.A., Parliament Houses
McCarthy, —, carpenter, 220 Johnston st, E C
McCarthy, —, Punt road, Pra
McCarthy, Charles, M.D., surgeon, 34 Lonsdale st east
McCarthy, D., 7 Little Latrobe st east
McCarthy, Dennis, Rose of Denmark hotel, Bedford st, Hot
McCarthy, James, 41 Rosslyn st, W M
McCarthy, M., 40 Lothian st, Hot
McCarthy, Timothy, 65 Young st, F
McCarthy, Wm., tailor, 59 Queensberry st, Hot
McCartney, M. C., New st, Bm
McCartney, S. H., 21 Cole st, Wmn
McCarty, J., Regent st, F
McCarty, Mrs., Arden st, Hot
McCathie, James, Powlett st, E M
McCaul and Campbell, grocers, 6 Faraday st, Carl
McCaul, G. J., Alma road, St K
McCaul, Mrs., Bony st, Carl
McCaul, R., 18 Gore st, F
McCauley, —, Princess st, St K
McCauley, Mrs., Dalgety st, St K
McCaw and Another, auctioneers and general commission agents, 48 Bourke st west
McCaw, M., Victoria parade, E M
McCean, Miss, milliner, Argyle st, St K
McCheane, E., 228 Moray st, Em H
McChesney, J., 205 Cecil st, Em H
McClean, Mrs., 83 Errol st, Hot
McClean, Samuel, Curzon st, Hot
McClean, Agnes, Chetwynd st, Hot
McClelland, J., Surrey hotel, 131 Johnston st, E C
McClelland, Samuel, 41 Little Bourke st east
McCloskey, Mrs., midwife, Johnston st, E C
McCluskey, Thomas, bootmaker, Queensberry st, Carl
McClure, Andrew, 23 Three chain road, Em H
McClure, John Leslie, Esplanade, Bm
McClure, Richard, grocer, 124 Smith st, E C
McClure, Valentine, and Co., wholesale grocers, wine and spirit merchants, 249 Elizabeth st
McColl, Alexander, 4 Rathdowne st, Carl
McComas, Francis, 8 Royal terrace, Nicholson st, F
McComas, John W., general agent, Temple court, Collins st west
McComas, Mrs., ladies' seminary, Cowper st, Fcy
McComas, W. R., Elgin st, Carl
McConaghy, Jas., Capel st, Hot
McConchie, —, draper, 70 Queensberry st, Carl

McConchie, Wm., bootmaker, Robe st, St K
McConkay, George, Palmerston st, Carl
McConnell, James, 22 Adderly st, W M
McConnell, James, Flem
McConnochie, John, coppersmith and brazier, 84 Queen st
McConnochie, John, and Co., grocers, corner of Pelham and Cardigan sts, Carl
McConochie, J., Berkeley st, Carl
McConochie, Wm., Argyle st, St K
McConky, James, 57 Stanley st, W M
McConville, John, Braybrook road, Ess
McCorkell, John, contractor, 95 Nicholson st, F
McCorkell, Samuel, Flem
McCormack, —, 136 Swan st, Rd
McCormack, Ander, 35 Bouverie st, Carl
McCormack, Mrs., 80 George st, F
McCormick, David, Greyhound inn, 52 Swan st, Rd
McCormick, M., 204 Bridge road, Rd
McCormick, P., Railway place, San
McCormick, S., watchmaker, 83 Swanston street
McCormick, Thomas, Railway place, San
McCormick, Wm., bootmaker, 67 High st, St K
McCowan, A., 44 Latrobe st west
McCoy, James, 94 Flinders lane east
McCracken, Peter, J.P., Ess
McCracken, Robert, Flem
McCracken, R., and Co., brewers, 110 Little Collins st west, and Flem
McCrae, Andrew, 4 Hoddle st, E M
McCrae, Captain A., Rotherwood st, Rd
McCrae, Farquhar, Rotherwood st, Rd
McCrae, George, 116 Flinders lane east
McCrae, Hon. John, M.L.C., Flint st, E M
McCraig, Alex., 7 Cecil st, Wmn
McCrea, George, 116 Flinders lane east
McCrea, John, 24 Market st, Em H
McCrea, Wm., chief medical officer, 132 Collins st east
McCree, James, 73 Stanley st, W M
McCree, John, 71 Stanley st, W M
McCrossan, Hy., 19 Market st, Em H
McCrum, Alex., 172 Stephen st
McCullam, Mrs., ferry, River side, south
McCubbin, Alexander, baker, 165 King st
McCubbin, Walter, 18 Ferguson st, Wmn
McCulloch, F., &c., musicseller, 59 Collins st west
McCulloch, Hon. James, Alma road, St K
McCulloch, Hugh, grocer, 15 Flinders lane west
McCulloch, Mrs., 141 Little Collins st west
McCulloch, Sellar, and Co., merchants, 31 Queen st; bonded stores, corner King and Little Collins sts
McCulloch, W. N., painter, Bench st, San
McCulloch, Wm., and Co., general carriers, 50 Elizabeth st
McCullough, J., Station place, San

McCullough, John, 7 Simpson st, E M
McCullum, D., Waterloo st, St K
McCully, John James, Flemington
McCutcheon, C., 134 Eastern road, Em H
McCutcheon, J., Capel st, W M
McCutcheon, Robert G., Victoria st, W M
McCurk, J., Rouse st, San
Mc Dermott, C., John st, F
McDermott, Malcolm, Domain st, S Y
McDonagh, James, Mac's hotel, 116 Stevedore st, Wmn
McDonald, —, 210 Napier st, Em H
McDonald, —, 64 Cambridge st, E C
McDonald, —, bookseller, 17 Oxford st, E C
McDonald, A. B., 1 Grattan st, Carl
McDonald, Alexander, grocer, 199 Swanston st
McDonald, Alex., Simpson st, E M
McDonald, Alexander, coach builder, 93 Queensberry st, Hot
McDonald, Archibald, photographic artist, St. George's Hall, Bourke st east
McDonald, C., grocer, 37 Howard st, Hot
McDonald, D., blacksmith, Pent
McDonald, Daniel, Charles st, F
McDonald, Donald, 79 Queensberry st, Carl
McDonald, Donald, 27 Little Nelson st Wmn
McDonald, Elizabeth, dressmaker, 139 Webb st, F
McDonald, F., builder, Nicholson st, Carl
McDonald, J., 10 Carlton st, Carl
McDonald, J., Douglas parade, Wmn
McDonald, J., 46 Hanover st, F
McDonald, J. B., 128 Spencer st north
McDonald, John, estate agent, 58 Little Collins st east
McDonald, John, Berkeley st, Carl
McDonald, John, Millswyn st, S Y
McDonald, John, 12 Carlton st, Carl
McDonald, John, 111 Queensberry st, Hot
McDonald, Miss, 202 Little Collins st east
McDonald, Mrs., 139 Victoria parade, F
McDonald, Mrs., Dorcas st, Em H
McDonald, P., Twyford st south, Wmn
McDonald, Peter, tailor, 108 Russell st
McDonald, R. A., M.D., Heidelberg road
McDonald, Rev. D., Dorcas st, Em H
McDonald, S., Weston st, Bk
McDonald, Thomas, Wellington st, Rd
McDonald, W., Roden st, W M
McDonald, Wm., seedsman, 128 Bourke st east
McDonnell, G., Franklyn st, W M
McDonnell, John, and Co., grocers, wine and spirit merchants, 85 Elizabeth st
McDonnell, John, Williams road, Tk
McDonnell, M. A., Murphy st, S Y
McDonnell, R., Charles st, Pra
McDonnell, S. M. C., Williams road, Tk
McDonnough, Patrick, boot and shoemaker, 55 Lonsdale st west

McDonoegh, Edward, jun., 164 Johnston st, E C
McDonough, J., Berkeley st, Carl
McDonough, James, Spencer st
McDonough, John, Queen st
McDonough, Joseph, Queen st
McDonough, Patrick, Lonsdale st west
McDougal, John F., Haw
McDougal, Robert, farmer, Ess
McDougal, Robert, Alma road east, St K
McDougal, Thomas D., accountant, &c., 13 Collins st west
McDougall, C., Sydney road, Bk
McDougall, Donald, restaurant, 18 Swanston st
McDougall, Dugald, Haw
McDougall, Duncan, Grey st, St K
McDougall, E., 79 Little Bourke st east
McDougall, J. W., 3 Studley Park terrace, Victoria st, Rd
McDougall, John, Raglan st, San
McDougall, John, printer, St Kilda Standard office, High st, St K
McDougall, Mrs. D., Simpson st, E M
McDougall, Robert, 146 Lonsdale st west
McDougall, Thomas W., Cliff st, Pra
McDowell, Alexander, Darkly st, St K
McDowall, J., Cochrane st, Btn
McDowall, J., grocer, 98 Johnston st, E C
McEachern, N., 144 Napier st, F
McElvoy, —, 28 Chetwynd st, Hot
McEmery, T. G., 113 Young st, F
McEustee, John, 126 Madeline st, Carl
McEvoy, James, Studley park
McEvoy, Peter, grocer, Brighton st, Rd
McEwan and Co., importers, and wine, spirit, and provision merchants, 23 Swanston st
McEwan, James, Merrivale st, St K
McEwan, James, Spencer st north
McEwan, James, and Co., wholesale and retail ironmongers, 79 and 319 Elizabeth st
McEwan, P., 94 Lygon st, Carl
McEwen, Alexander, bone crusher, Flem bank
McEwen, Alexander, Flem
McEwen, James, 74 Stanley st, W M
McEwen, James, Railway place, San
McEwin, James, Yarra st, Held
McFadzean and Lambert, hairdressers and perfumers, 41 Collins st east
McFadzean, Archibald, 88 Russell st
McFadzen, D., 5 Homer lane, Flinders lane east
McFarland and Sons, wholesale saddlers, 3 Lonsdale st west
McFarland, James, fellmonger, 101 Collins st west
McFarland, John, Cardigan st, Carl
McFarland, W., 3 Little Latrobe st east
McFarlane, Wm., house decorator, 106 Latrobe st east
McFarlane, —, Spencer st

McFarlane and Morris, tailors, 167 Bourke st east
McFarlane, Cunningham, watchmaker and goldsmith, 165 Elizabeth st
McFarlane, G., Albert st, E C
McFarlane, J., Whitehall st, Fcy
McFarlane, J. A., school, Wellington st, Btn
McFarlane, James, Punt road, Pra
McFarlane, James, 243 Moray st, Em H
McFarlane, John, 83 Leicester st, Carl
McFarlane, Mrs., 107 Albert st, E M
McFarlane, Snodgrass, 30 Cobden st, Em H
McFarlane, Thomas, Miller st, W M
McFarlane, Walter, Avoca st, Fcy
McGaffrey, Thomas, 3 Rosslyn st, W M
McGauran, T. F., surgeon, 213 Bourke st west
McGaw, Mrs., dressmaker, 184 Smith st, E C
McGee, H. J., 18 Elgin st, Carl
McGee, J., 134 Rose st, F
McGee, John, Nicholson st, F
McGee, John, Cochrane st, Btn
McGee, John, and Co., wholesale wine, spirit, and provision merchants, 189 Elizabeth st
McGee, R., 116 Victoria st, Rd
McGee, Wm., Princes st, F
McGee, Wm., Pelham st, Carl
McGenty, J., 63 Argyle st, F
McGeoch, A., Royal Standard hotel, William st north
McGie, James, Provost st, Hot
McGie, John, Victoria st, Carl
McGill, Frederick and George W., booksellers, &c., 127 Elizabeth st
McGill, Mrs. George, teacher of music and singing, Lang st, S Y
McGill, Richard F., Punt road, S Y
McGill, Wm, T., importer of iron pipes and machinery, 139 Collins st west
McGinley, J., Corkscrew hotel, King st
McGinty, J., bootmaker, 22 Gertrude st, F
McGirr, W. P., Gardiner's creek road, S Y
McGlone, J., police barracks, F
McGlone, James, storekeeper, 164 Smith st, E C
McGloe, W., 85 Argyle st, F
McGowen, James, Great Britain hotel, 109 Flinders st west
McGrath, —, confectioner, Rouse st, San
McGrath and Churchman, cemetery masons, corner Little Collins and Stephen streets
McGrath, James, Alfred place, Collins st west
McGrath, John, 196 Little Collins st east
McGrath, Michael, bootmaker, 237 Swanston st
McGrath, Patrick, Rouse st, San
McGraw, Robert, Elizabeth st extension
McGregor and Agnew, coachbuilders, 245 Swanston st

McGregor, —, Three chain road, Em H
McGregor, Daniel, bootmaker, Rowena parade, Rd
McGregor, Duncan, Bk
McGregor, John, 134 Cardigan st, Carl
McGregor, John, 80 Napier st, Em H
McGregor, Mary, Colonial Bank hotel, 2 Little Collins st east
McGregor, P., Park st, Pra
McGregor, P., 19 Dover road, Wmn
McGregor, R., teacher, Clarendon st, Em H
McGregor, Wm., 34 Elgin st, Carl
McGuigan, Henry, wine and spirit merchant, 176 Elizabeth st
McGuigan, John, bootmaker, 44 Collins st east
McGuiness, Mrs., Little Park st, S Y
McGuinness, J., Miller st, W M
McGuire, Mrs., 149 Fitzroy st, F
McGuirk, T., bootmaker, 33 Victoria st, E C
McHaffie, Mrs., Grey st, St K
McHaltie, G., shipwright, 33 Electra st, Wmn
McHarg, Andrew, Capel st, Hot
McHarg, Mrs., Pelham st, Carl
McHugh, John, 162 Ferrars st, Em H
McHutcheson, John, fancy repository, 255 Elizabeth st
McHutchison, Duncan, 109 Bank st west, Em H
McHutchison, T., 87 Bridport st, Em H
McIlreavy, W., mason, 245 Fitzroy st, F
McIlwraith, John, lead pipe manufacturer, 167 and 169 Little Collins st east
McIndoe, John B., grocer and wine merchant, Thompson st, and Cecil st, Wmn
McInerney, T., Dryburgh st, Hot
McInerny, M, 85 Lygon st, Carl
McInerny, Wm., 159 Queensberry st, Hot
McInnes, Duncan, greengrocer and blacksmith, 169 Clarendon st, Em H
McInnes, Mary, 200 Moray st, Em H
McIntosh, —, dairyman, 59 Dudley st, W M
McIntosh, —, Princes st, F
McIntosh, Alexander, wine, spirit, and provision merchant, 186 King st
McIntosh, Daniel, Alma st, F
McIntosh, David, Raleigh st, Fcy
McIntosh, D. H., 126 Fitzroy st, F
McIntosh, G., Wellington st, St K
McIntyre, A., grocer, 143 Cecil st, F
McIntyre, Abraham, 52 York st, Em H
McIntyre, D., grocer, 96 Oxford st, E C
McIntyre, H., tailor, 8 Latrobe st west
McIntyre, S., Robe st, St K
McIntyre, Stephen, 74 Argyle st, F
McIver, Donald, 18 Lincoln square, Carl
McIver, Duncan, Lincoln square, Carl
McIvor, John, 56 Bouverie st, Carl
McIvor, T., galvanist, Market lane, 141 Bourke st east
McJunkin, James, storekeeper, 11 King st

McKaige, Robt., commission agent, Whitehall st, Fcy
McKay, Captain, Roden st, W M
McKay, J., bootmaker, Spring st
McKay, J., Carlisle st, St K
McKay, J., Pent
McKay, John, plumber and coppersmith, 86 Collins st west
McKay, Mrs., 5 Palmer st, F
McKean, —, 43 Charles st, Pra
McKean, James, attorney, 49 Elizabeth st
McKean, John, 66 George st, F
McKeand, C., engraver, 41 Swanston st
McKeckney, Robert, William st, Gardiner's creek road
McKecknie, Donald, 175 Lygon st, Carl
McKecknie, John, crinoline manufactory, Bridge road, Rd
McKee, John M., 27 Gore st, F
McKee, Samuel, Osborne st, Pra
McKee, Wm., importer and commission agent, 75 Flinders lane east
McKeever, Bernard, Derby st, E C
McKeller, Alexander, blacksmith, 63 Lygon st, Carl
McKelsen, O., 164 Little Lonsdale st west
McKelvey, Elizabeth, 16 Raglan st, Em H
McKelvie, James, shipwright, Heath st, San
McKendrick, A., Spencer st
McKendrick and McEwan, cabinetmakers, 361 Spencer st, north
McKenna, A., Hampton st, Bru
McKenna, M., 32 Latrobe st east
McKenna, Wm., 158 Spencer st
McKenzie, A., bootmaker, Raglan st, Em E
McKenzie, —, Barkly st, St K
McKenzie, A., butcher, Roose st, San
McKenzie, A., bootmaker, Pent
McKenzie, Adamson, and Miller, coffee and spice merchants and general millers, 3 Queen st
McKenzie, Alex., carrier, Leveson st, Hot
McKenzie, Alex., Abbotsford st, W M
McKenzie, D., Dryburgh st, Hot
McKenzie, D., boarding-house, 109 Brunswick st, F
McKenzie, George, 93 Chetwynd st, Hot
McKenzie, J., High st, Pra
McKenzie, J. F., Union st, Rd
McKenzie, John, Burnett st, St K
McKenzie, John, 36 Nicholson st, F
McKenzie, Kenneth, grocer, 187 Little Lonsdale st east
McKenzie, Miss, boarding-house, 5 Franklyn st
McKenzie, R., Clyde st, St K
McKenzie, Roderick, Argyle st, St K
McKenzie, Roderick, undertaker, &c., 80 Clarendon st, Em H
McKenzie, Wm., High st, Pra
McKeogh, Daniel, 31 Rodney st, W M
McKeown, James, Wellington st, St K
McKernan, H., 17 Bouverie st, Carl

McKiernan, Richard, 170 Drummond st, Carl
McKillop, Mrs., 10 Church st, Em H
McKinlay, J., Barkly st, Bk
McKinlay, James, Berkeley st, Carl
McKinley, Mrs., midwife, 199 Wellington st, E C
McKinley, Robert, 215 Napier st, F
McKinnon, Henry, Great Britain hotel, Ferguson st, Wms
McKinnon, L., Tooronga
McKirby, J., Bell st, F
McKnight, George, Vice-Regal hotel, Church st, Hd
McKnight, W. A., chemist, Swan st, Rd
McLachlan, Capt. John, shipping agent, 16 Elizabeth st
McLachlan, Daniel, horse dealer, 49 Johnston st, E C
McLachlan, J., 57 Bridport st east, Em H
McLachlan, J., 19 King st
McLachlan, John, carver, &c., 11 Stephen street
McLachlan, Michael, 20 Bouverie st, Carl
McLaren, —, 116 Coventry st, Em H
McLaren, Alexander, 92 Madeline st, Carl
McLaren, George, 77 Stanley st, W M
McLaren, Mrs., 72 Nicholson st, F
McLaren, Mrs., Simpson st, E M
McLaren, Robinson, Glasgow Arms hotel, Elizabeth st
McLaren, Wm., 64 Raglan st, Em H
McLaughlan, —, 125 Little Bourke st east
McLaughlin, Charles, grocer, 91 Little Lonsdale st east
McLaughlin, Henry, grocer, 16 Cardigan st, Carl
McLaughlin, J., White Horse brewery, Johnston st, E C
McLaughlin, J., blacksmith, King st
McLaughlin, J., cordial manufacturer, Patrick st, Lonsdale st east
McLaughlin, John, tailor, Royal lane, Bourke st east
McLaughlin, P., Acland st, St K
McLay, C., Racecourse hotel, Flem
McLean, Angus, Flem
McLean, Captain, Roden st, W M
McLean, D., 59 York st west, Em H
McLean, D., hay and corn dealer, Chapel st, Pra
McLean, D. P., surgeon, Cecil st east, Wms
McLean, James, 21 Leveson st, Hot
McLean, John, shipmaster, William st
McLean, John, 5 Dover villas, Victoria parade, E C
McLean, John, Hawke st, W M
McLean, John, Buck's Head hotel, 15 Little Lonsdale st west
McLean, Joseph, 96 Lygon st, Carl
McLean, Mrs., George st, F
McLean, Neil, wine and spirit merchant, 11 Swanston st

McLean, Patrick, chemist, 131 Brunswick st, F
McLean, Peter, cabinetmaker, 79 Spring street
McLean, Peter, 16 Pelham st, Carl
McLehose, Mrs., 68 Hanover st, F
McLeish, J. P., 137 Little Bourke st west
McLeish, Wm., 27 Gifford st, Wms
McLellan, —, Hoddle st, E C
McLellan, —, carpenter, 193 Johnston st, E C
McLellan, Anthony, Hoddle st, E C
McLellan, D., 63 York st east, Em H
McLellan, J., baker, 13 a'Beckett st east
McLellan, John, nightman, 84 Latrobe st east
McLellan, Mrs., Wellington st, Pra
McLellan, Mrs., 25 Rathdowne st, Carl
McLellan, Robert, 60 Roden st, W M
McLellan, Wm., M.L.A., Parliament Houses
McLelland, James, Cardigan st, Carl
McLeod, Donald, 51 Young st, F
McLeod, J., shoemaker, Prahran
McLeod, John, 148 Lonsdale st west
McLeod, Mrs., ladies' nurse, 66 Cobden st, Em H
McLeod, Norman, sailmaker, Railway place, San
McLeod, Norman, 39 Stanley st, W M
McLinlock, John, Nicholson st, Carl
McLoy, James, fruiterer, Swan st, Rd
McLoon, James, 189 Little Lonsdale st east
McLoughlan, J., Pelham st, Carl
McLuckie, Robert, Heath st, San
McLuckie, T., Edward st, Bk
McMahon, Benjamin, greengrocer, Leveson st, Hot
McMahon, Captain Charles, office, Queen street
McMahon, F., Young st, F
McMahon, John, toy dealer, 9 Gertrude st, F
McMahon, Michael, Council hotel, 35 Johnston st, E C
McMahon, Mrs., 3 Cardigan st, Carl
McMahon, Patrick, Darling st, S Y
McMain, Peter, 71 Stephen st
McManus, A., Gardiner's Creek road, Pra
McMaster, James, 139 Little Collins st west
McMaster, Wm., grocer and confectioner, 69 Errol st, Hot
McMeckan, Blackwood, and Co., merchants, ship-owners, &c., 2 King st
McMerneoy, M., Bedford st, Hot
McMichael, Rev. I. C., 121 Gore st, F
McMichan, Captain, Hawke st, W M
McMillan, D., tailor, Cecil st, Em H
McMillan, G., 130 Napier st, Em H
McMillan, John, Howard st, Hot
McMillan, Richard, auctioneer and house agent, 86 Little Collins st west

McMillan, Thomas, Yarra st, S Y
McMillan, Wm., Union st, Hin
McMillan, Wm., butcher, Whitehall st, Fcy
McMillan, Wm. Henry, 2 Somerset place, Docker st, Hd
McMillin, John, tailor, Wellington st, St K
McMonican, —, Leveson st, Hot
McMuin, James, 85 Brunswick st, F
McMurtrie, David, builder, 6 Grattan st, Carl
McMurtrie, John, grocer, 148 King st
McNair, James, 239 Smith st, F
McNaly, John, ropemaker, 89 Little Lonsdale st east
McNamara, Edward, farmer, Ess
McNamara, James, Pascoevale road, Ess
McNamara, James, collar maker, 18 Little Latrobe st east
McNamara, John, boarding-house, 125 Little Bourke st west
McNamara, M., Dover road, Wmn
McNaughtan, Duncan, bootmaker, 21 York st, Em H
McNaughton, A., Barry st, Carl
McNaughton, D., ironmonger, 99 High st, St. K
McNaughton, John, bootmaker, 30 Madeline st, Carl
McNaughton, John, 138 Lonsdale st west
McNaughton, Love, and Co., warehousemen, 69 Flinders lane east
McNaughton, Wm., flaw
McNay, Thomas, farmer, Moonee Ponds, Ess
McNee, James, High st, Prn
McNee, John, shoemaker, 25 Johnston st, E C
McNee, Wm., blacksmith, 154 Little Bourke st west
McNeil, Hugh, 28 Bank st west, Em H
McNeil, J., Spencer st
McNeil, Mrs., 76 Elgin st, Carl
McNeill, —, 29 Clarendon st, Em H
McNeill and McDonald, plumbers and gasfitters, 75 Stephen st
McNeill, John, dyer, 108 Lonsdale st east
McNeill, John, 29 Church st, Em H
McNeill, L., Little Lonsdale st
McNevin, James, 45 Electra st, Wmn
McNicholl, Mrs., 125 Johnston st, E C
McNicol, Daniel, clothier and outfitter, 193 Bourke st east
McNield, Jane, 9 Thompson st south, Wmn
McNiles, Mrs., Carlisle st east, St K
McNish, Wm., boarding-house, 98 Queen street
McNulty, M., Bedford st, Hot
McPhail, Dugald, farmer, Braybrook road, Ess
McPhail, Wm., Nott st, San
McPhee, Donald, carrier, 73 Bourke st west

McPhee, John, Bunbury st, Fcy
McPherson, A., Berkeley st, Carl
McPherson, Arthur, Howard st, Hot
McPherson, Edwin, tailor and outfitter, 17 Beach st, San
McPherson, J. A., M.L.A., Parliament House
McPherson, J. A., Albion st, Bk
McPherson, James, hairdresser, 210 Smith st, E C
McPherson, James, carpenter, Flem
McPherson, James, draper, Bourke st east
McPherson, John, Nott st, San
McPherson, John, 19 Nicholson st, F
McPherson, Mrs., 59 Stanley st, W M
McPherson, Robert, Highett st, Rd
McPherson, Thomas, iron merchant, 203 Bourke st west
McQuade, J., 148 Moray st, Em H
McQuade, James, grocer, Railway place, San
McQualter, Thomas, 26 Faraday st, Carl
McQueen, George, wine and spirit merchant, 149 Napier st, F
McQueen, John, draper, Hoddle st, E C
McQueen, John H., 116 Bank st west, Em H
McQueen, Mrs. H., 6 Raglan st, Em H
McQueen, S. C., Cardigan st, Carl
McQueen, W., shipmaster, 27 James st, Wmn
McQuick, A., shipwright, 7 Cecil st, Wmn
McQuicken, John, Byron st, Hot
McQuinney, Alexander, Provost st, Hot
McQuirk, Michael, Robe st, St K
McRichie, J., 26 Clarendon st, Em H
McShain, A., 145 Drummond st, Carl
McShane, James, Pelham st, Carl
McShea, T., boarding-house, 176 Queen street
McSweeney, Peter, Three-chain road, Em H
McSymon, John, and Co, produce merchants, 286 Elizabeth st
McTaggart, Dl., 105 Faraday st, Carl
McTaggart, Mrs., milliner, Inkerman st west, St K
McTier, H., 18 Hanmer st, Wmn
McTurk, Charles, Blackwood st, Hot
McVean, Rev. A., Brunswick road, Bk
McVicar, Daniel, 114 Napier st, Em H
McWilliam, A., 47 Rosslyn st, W M
McWilliams, Henry, 191 Cardigan st, Carl
McWilliams, Mrs., milliner, 32 Wellington st, E C
Macadam, Mrs., Powlett st, F M
Macardy, A. H., 221 Swan st, Rd
Macardy, James, Williams road, Prn
Macarthy, Thomas, Swan st, Rd
Macartney, Arthur, 109 Albert st, E M
Macartney, the Very Rev. H. B., Dean of Melbourne, Grey st, E M
Macaulay, Wm., manager Asiatic Banking Corporation, at Collins st west

Macbain, James, M.L.A., Alma road, St K
Macdermott, J., solicitor, 50 Temple court, Collins st west
Macdonnell, E., barrister, 3 Temple court, Collins st west
Macdougall, A., and Co., printers, High st, St K
Macey, John, Wool st, F
Macey, Wm., blocking manufacturer, Moor st, F
Macfarlan, Alexander, and Co., commission merchants, 13 Flinders lane east
Macfarlae, D., money broker, &c., Neave's buildings, Collins st east
Macfarlan, Patrick, Hotham st, E M
Macfarland, James (H.M.C.), Thompson st, Wm
Macgibbon, John, printer and stationer, 49 Queensberry st, Hot
Macgregor and Henderson, solicitors, 57 Little Collins st west
Macgregor, J., M.L.A., Nicholson st, F
Macgregor, John, 18 Napier st, Em H
Macgregor, John M., commission agent, Hall of Commerce
Macgrotty, H., tailor, 13 Errol st, Hot
Macguiness, John, Park st, S Y
Mack, John, 146 Little Bourke st west
Mack, John, 41 Cobden st, Em H
Mackareth, James, Station place, San
Mackay, A., 13 Drummond st, Carl
Mackay, A., 30 Bouverie st, Carl
Mackay, F., 284 Victoria st, Rd
Mackay, George, LL.D., barrister, 23 Temple Court, Collins st west
Mackay, James, Nelson st, Pra
Mackay, M., Crockford st, San
Mackay, Miss, dress and mantle maker, 48 Russell st
Mackay, Mrs., 63 Madeline st, Carl
Mackay, Robert, bookseller and stationer 66 Elizabeth st
Mackay, R., Swan st, Rd
Mackennal and Scurry, architectural and figure modellers, 94 Russell st
Mackennal, J. S., Jolimont road
Mackenzie, Alexander, wholesale saddler, 63 Bourke st west
Mackenzie, D., tailor, 180 Little Collins st east
Mackenzie, D., Grey st, E M
Mackenzie, John, estate agent, 86 Collins st west
Mackey and Partridge, grocers, 44 Rosslyn st, W M
Mackey, F., Victoria st, Rd
Mackey, James, 46 Gertrude st, F
Mackey, Mrs., bonnet cleaner, 13 Clarendon st, Em H
Mackie, Alexander, mason, 7 Latrobe parade, Collins st east
Mackie, George, store, 111 Flinders lane east
Mackie, James B., 5 Napier st, Em H

Mackie, James B., hat and cap manufacturer, 5 Collins st west
Mackie, Mrs., 10 Brunswick st, F
Mackie, R., 138 Moray st, Em H
Mackie, Rev. George, Punt road, Pra
Mackie, Richard, shoemaker, Cape st, Hod
Mackie, Thomas, confectioner, 61 Victoria st, Carl
Mackinnon, L., Toorong
Mackintosh, A., baker, Elgin st, Carl
Mackintosh, John, Carlisle st east, St K
Mackintosh, John, builder, 118 Nicholson st, F
Mackintosh, Mrs., boarding-house, 94 Lonsdale st west
Mackle, Peter, bootmaker, 17 Flinders lane west
Macklin, W., 116 Moray st, Em H
Maclellan, John, store, 15 Market st, Em H
Macleod, David, marine surveyor, 11 Little Collins st west
Maclymont, J. G. M., schoolmaster, William st north
Macmelchan, James, and Co., Flemington Bone Mills
Macmillan, James, clothier, 26 Nelson place, Wm
Macnamara, John, Flemington road, Hot
Macnamara, John, merchant, 20 Collins st west
Macnamara, P., 184 Drummond st, Carl
Maconboy, James, solicitor, 92 Little Collins st west
Maconochie, P., slater, 55 Smith st, F
Macquay, S. W., electro-plater, Moor st, Fcy
Macquistan, A., contractor, &c., 201 and 199 Latrobe st west
Macredie, Wm., Domain road, S Y
Mactier, John, ironmonger, 4 and 6 Lonsdale st west and 177 Elizabeth st
Madden, D., 140 Little Lonsdale st west
Madden, David, Flem
Madden, Henry R., M.D., 90 Collins st east
Madden, James, bootmaker, 65 Wellington st, E C
Madden, James, 25 Hanmer st, Wm
Madden, James, 47 Cardigan st, Carl
Madden, James, Blacksmiths' Arms hotel, 250 Bridge road, Rd
Madden, John, solicitor, 33 Bourke st west
Madden, P., Freemasons' hotel, 166 Moray st, Em H
Madden, Timothy, general store, 118 Little Collins st west
Maddock, George, 60 Hanover st, F
Maddocks, Joseph, 26 York st east, Em H
Maddocks, Miss, school, 34 Barkly st, Carl
Maddocks, Mrs., grocery store, 96 York st, Em H
Maddox, Emma, 23 Lygon st, Carl

Maddox, Wm., butcher, 281 Brunswick st, F
Madeley, John, 61 Charles st, F
Maddigan, J. L., 4 Barkly st, Carl
Madigan, M., Howard st, Hot
Madigan, Mrs., dressmaker, Francis st
Magee, J., Victoria st, Carl
Magchie, C., 77 York st east, Em H
Magher, M., grocer, 37 Curzon st, Hot
Magness, Edward, baker, Flem
Magrath, Daniel, Flemington road, Hot
Magra, George, general dealer, 31 Errol st, Hot
Maggs, Mrs., milliner, 36 High st, St K
Maguire and Co., importers, 26 King st
Maguire, John, boot and shoe dealer, 114 Swanston st
Maguire, J. F., Orrong, Tk
Maher, James, boarding-house, 62 Latrobe st east
Maher, John, Byron st, Hot
Maher, Mary, 89 Dryburgh st, Hot
Maher, Patrick, butcher, 137 Little Lonsdale street east
Maher, Thomas, Victorian Railways hotel, 326 King st
Mahony, John, Wilson st, Pra
Mahon, Charles, grocer, Drummond st, Carl
Mahon, L., 19 Rathdowne st, Carl
Mahon, Mrs., 34 Pelham st, Carl
Mahon, Stephen, 115 Leveson st, Hot
Mahoney, Frederick, modeller, 194 Russell street
Mahoney, James, 109 Park st, Em H
Mahoney, John, Higbett st, Rd
Mahoney, John, Flem
Mahoney, John, Madeline st, Carl
Mahoney, Patrick, Flem
Mahoney, Timothy, 48 Perry st, E C
Mahoney, Wm., Waltham st, Rd
Mahony, Charles, grocer, 73 Victoria st, Carl
Mahony, T., hardware dealer, 159 Elizabeth st
Maidment, W. H., 151 George st, F
Mailer and Co., importers, 11 Flinders lane west
Mailer, Robert. Moreland road, Bk
Maillard, Fredk. Louis, Domestic Bazaar and Labour office, 122 Bourke st east
Maillard, W., butcher, Swan st, Rd
Main, Frederick, 30 Lothian st, Hot
Main, James, 105 Westgarth st, F
Main, J. P., 74 Leicester st, Carl
Main, Robert, 53 Osborne st, Wmn
Main, Thomas, engineer, George st, E M
Maine, Crawford, merchant, 113 Collins st west
Mair, Alexander, timber merchant, 10 Leicester st, Carl
Major, F., 104 Oxford st, E C
Major, John, 46 Park st, Em H
Maker, E. D., 104 Moray st, Em H

Malcolm, H., Ardeo st, Hot
Malcolm, J. F., builder, 135 Latrobe st east
Malcolm, J., bootmaker, 181 Clarendon st, Em H
Makepeace, John, Albion st east, Bk
Male, S., butcher, Wells st, Bta
Maline, James, 174 Swan st, Rd
Malinom, Alfred, 37 Brunswick st, F
Malleson, A. B., notary public, Blenheim House, F
Malleson and England, solicitors, &c., 36 Queen st
Mallett, C., 33 Johnston st, F
Mallet, David, Botanical hotel, Domain road, 8 Y
Mallett, James, ink and blacking manufacturer, Albert st, Pra
Mallett, Thomas, Charles st, Pra
Malley, Henry, public laundry, 8 Oxford st, E C
Mallinson, Bridget, 136 Queen st
Malmsbury and Taradale Gold Mining Company, 31 Collins st west
Malone, Stephen, Victoria st, Hot
Maloney, D., Thompson st, South V'mn
Maloney, Matthew, Leveson st, Hot
Maloney, Mrs., 127 Queensberry st, Hot
Maloney, Mrs., Roden st, W M
Maloney, Peter, boarding-house, 57 Little Bourke st west
Maltby, Miss, dressmaker, 123 Bourke st west
Manallack, T., Cornish Arms hotel, Sydney road, Bk
Manby, H. H., stationer, Elgin st, Carl
Manchester Unity Hall, Swanston st
Mandelberg, Nathan, general dealer, 46 Madeline st, Carl
Mangan, Michael, 22 Leicester st, Carl
Man, Wm., boarding-house, 95 Lonsdale st east
Man Shing, carpenter, 49 Little Bourke st east
Manihan, M., 41 Park st west, Em H
Mann, Frank, butcher, 177 Victoria st, E C
Mann, John, Alfred place, 101 Collins st east
Mann, John, nurseryman, High st, St H
Mann, Mrs., school, Halston st, S Y
Mano, Mrs., 43 Victoria st, Carl
Mann, S. F., Union st, S Y
Mann, Samuel, Freemasons' hotel, 9 Swanston st
Mannifield, Stephen, toolmaker, 121 Little Collins st east
Manning, G., coach proprietor, Wright's lane, Bourke st east
Manning, George, Grosvenor st, E C
Manning, George, butcher, Peel st, Pra
Manning, James, bootmaker, Berkeley st, Carl
Manning, John, Dover road, Wmn

Manning, Mrs., Easey st, E C
Mannings, John, 79 Gertrude st, F
Mannix, John, hairdresser, 204 Lonsdale st east
Manna, George, Robe st, St K
Manservgh, John C., 36 Little Bourke st west
Mansergh, Peter, veterinary surgeon, 19 Little Lonsdale st west
Mansfield, Mrs., 69 Stanley st, W M
Mansfield, Mrs., 40 Moor st, F
Manuel, Freeman, 58 Moray st, Em H
Manuel, H. W., road inspector, Flem
Manzies, H., 137 Gore st, F
Manskie, Wm., 11 Russell st
Maplestone, Charles, architect, Ivanhoe Lodge, near Heid
Maplestone, H., Berkeley st, Carl
Maplestone, Henry, timber merchant, 90 and 92 Elizabeth st extension
Mappin, W., High st, Pra
Maquay, Samuel W., Rennie st, Fcy
Maquay, Wm., electro plater and gilder, 3 Collins st west
Marcham, P. H., draper, 109 Cardigan st, Carl
Marchant, George F., tinsmith, 80 Bridge road, Rd
Marchant, James, 42 Little Latrobe st east
Margrie, George, undertaker, Rowens parade, Rd
Marine Yard, Ann st, Wmn
Mariners' Church, or Bethel, Beach st, San
Mariners' Reef Mining Co., 37 Market st
Mark, James, George hotel, Victoria st, Hot
Market Inspector's office, Eastern market, Stephen st
Markey, Thomas, Bouverie st, Carl
Markham, J., boarding-house, Latrobe st west
Markham, John, 88 Stanley st, W M
Marks, Adolphus, Acland st, St K
Marks, Benjamin, pawnbroker, 197 Elizabeth st
Marks, Caspar, merchant, 83 Swanston st
Marks, Edward, merchant, 118 Collins st west
Marks, Henry, pawnbroker, 131 Elizabeth st
Marks, Henry, general merchant, 117 Little Lonsdale st west
Marks, Joseph, wholesale grocer, 223 Elizabeth st
Marks, Julia, clothier and outfitter, 241 Elizabeth st
Marks, Lewis, tailor, 113 Little Lonsdale st west
Marks, Mark, tailor and clothier, 21 Bourke st east
Marks, Rev. H. D., 3 Richill terrace, W M
Marks, S., dairyman, Malvern

Marley, John G., Errol st, Hot
Marlow, Douglas, tailor, 147 Albert st, E M
Marmion, Peter, storekeeper, Fas
Maron, John, car proprietor, 31 Little Lonsdale st west
Maroney, James, bootmaker, 145 Russell street
Maroney, Patrick, Howard st, Hot
Marr, James, Chetwynd st, Hot
Marr, Thomas, Walsh st, W M
Marrett and Snlders, china, glass, and earthenware importers, 129 Russell st
Marrett, Wm., 106 Fitzroy st, F
Marriott, Sarah, 10 Little Latrobe st east
Marriott, Thomas, 51 Queensberry st, Carl
Marris, —, 270 Johnston st, E C
Marris, —, Clarke st, E C
Marris. H. M., 197 Gore st, F
Marris, Mrs. H., 36 Faraday st, Carl
Mars, Wm., Nott st, San
Marsden and Deacon, saw and tool makers, 213 Smith st, F
Marsden, F. W., accountant, 8 Eldon chambers, Bank place, Collins st west
Marsden, J., Barkly st, Bk
Marsden, John H., Charles st, Pra
Marsden, Stephen, Staffordshire st, Fcy
Marsh, B., 163 Lygon st, Carl
Marsh, Henry, Vaucluse, Rd
Marsh, Henry, and Co., warehousemen, 43 Elizabeth st
Marsh, Mrs., draper, Church st, Rd
Marsh, Samuel, Pembroke hotel, High st, St K
Marsh, W., coppersmith, Bay st, San
Marsh, W., and Co., painters and paperhangers, 2 Swanston st and Stephen st
Marshall, —, Lothian st, Hot
Marshall, Abraham, cabinetmaker, 12 Gore st, F
Marshall, B., Brighton st, Rd
Marshall, F., Weston st, Bk
Marshall, Frederick, 10 Stanley st, E C
Marshall, George, fancy repository and cricketing emporium, 57 Collins st east
Marshall, George, Brunswick hotel, Sydney road, Bk
Marshall, Henry, 229 Swan st, Rd
Marshall, J., Berkeley st, Carl
Marshall, J., Albert st, Bk
Marshall, J. J., and Co., commission merchants, 41 Flinders lane east
Marshall, James, solicitor, 6 Bourke st east
Marshall, James, William st north
Marshall, James, 20 Park st east, Em H
Marshall, James J. (vice-consul for Spain, and of Marshall and Co.), Kew
Marshall, John, Packington st, Kew
Marshall, John, Fawkner st, St K
Marshall, John, 3 Chetwynd st, Hot
Marshall, Mrs., Provost st, Hot
Marshall, Samuel, 2 Grattan st, Carl

Marshall, W., Charles st, Pra
Marshall, Wm., 84 Montague st, Em H
Marsham, J., Queensberry st, Hot
Marston, Carlingford, chemist and druggist, 159 Smith st, E C
Marshner, E., Commercial lane, 145 Bourke st east
Martelli, Alexander, architect, Carrara Marble Works, Latrobe st west
Martin, —, school, Chapel st, Pra
Martin, —, 168 Kerr st, F
Martin, —, 67 Victoria st, Carl
Martin's bonded store, corner William and Little Bourke sts
Martin, A., Stoke st, San
Martin, Alfred G., grocer, Villiers st, Hot
Martin and Hastings, grocers, 39 Little Lonsdale st east
Martin and Monash, general merchants, 19 Little Collins st west
Martin, Andrew, Australian hotel, 60 Bourke st west
Martin, Andrew, Perry st, E C
Martin, Capt. Septimus, Vaucluse, Rd
Martin, Charles, Bay st, San
Martin, Charles R., gold laceman and military embroiderer, 2 Flinders lane west
Martin, D., Lennox st, Rd
Martin, David, Garden st, Pra
Martin, Denis, Albert st, Em H
Martin, Edward, Pelham st, Carl
Martin, English, 116 George st, F
Martin, F., jun., Hope st, Bk
Martin, G., 18 Johnston st, E C
Martin, George, Brighton road east, St K
Martin, George, and Co., merchants and importers, 25 Market st
Martin, H., 15 Kerr st, F
Martin, J., bootmaker, Rouse st, San
Martin, J., Oxford st, Hot
Martin, J., dairyman, 155 King st
Martin, J., 115 Leicester st, Carl
Martin, J., photographer, High st, St K
Martin, James, bootmaker, 3 Little Latrobe st east
Martin, James, bootmaker, 8 Little Bourke st west
Martin, James, butcher, 88 Wellington st, E C
Martin, James, 20 Greeves st, F
Martin, James, 80 Johnston st, F
Martin, James, Lennox st, Rd
Martin, James, saddler, 22 Swanston st
Martin, James R., draper, Victoria st, Rd
Martin, James, 20 Greeves st, F
Martin, John, 87 Victoria st, Carl
Martin, John, 17 Kerr st, F
Martin, John, Moonee Ponds, Ess
Martin, John S., mining engineer, 66 Little Collins st west
Martin, Jos., and Co., merchant tailors, 185 Elizabeth st
Martin, Louis, Carlisle st, St K

Martin, Lawrence J., M.D., surgeon, 126 Collins st east
Martin, Mrs., 178 Victoria st, Rd
Martin, Mrs., ladies' nurse, 114 Napier st, F
Martin, P., bootmaker, High st, St K
Martin, Peter, John, brewer, 175 and 177 Flinders lane east
Martin, R., surgeon, Vine st, Heid
Martin, Rev. H., Haw
Martin, Richard, dairyman, 52 Madeline st, Carl
Martin, Robert, 89 Cardigan st, Carl
Martin, Robert W. K., barrister, 41 Temple court and Melbourne Club
Martin, S. R., draper, 22 Farday st, Carl
Martin, T., sen., Cumberland Arms hotel, Sydney road, Bk
Martin, Thomas J., Tivoli place, S Y
Martin, T. J., and Co., general commission and insurance agents, 82 Collins st west
Martin, T., junior, Hope st, Bk
Martin, T. W., baker, 195 Smith st, F
Martin, Thomas, 98 Leicester st, F
Martin, Thomas, 115 Raglan st, Em H
Martin, W., hay and corn dealer, 18 Gertrude st, F
Martin, W., Pelham st, Carl
Martin, Wm., 72 Errol st, Hot
Martin, Wm., cab proprietor, 122 Wellington st, E C
Martin, Wm., Park st, S Y
Martin, Wm. H., butcher, 194 Swan st, Bd
Martin, Wm., Hay and corn dealer, 5 Gore st, F
Martin, Wm., cooper, Commercial lane, Bourke st east
Martin, Wm., builder, Rosslyn st, W M
Martingley, Albert, Dryburgh st, Hot
Marum, John, tailor, Chapel st, Pra
Marwick, D., Queensberry st, Hot
Marwick, James, grocer, 20 Johnston st, E C
Marwood, Matthew, Caroline st, S Y
Mason, A., mattrass maker, a'Beckett st west
Mason, A., publisher, 51 Flinders lane west, and 49 Latrobe st west
Mason, A. P., 47 Latrobe st west
Mason, Cyrus, Octavia st, St K
Mason, F. H., Argyle st, Pra
Mason, H., grocer, Roden st, W M
Mason, J., M.L.A., Parliament house
Mason, James, J.P., 25 Drummond st, Carl
Mason, James, baker, 212 Wellington st, E C
Mason, John, general dealer, 224 Little Collins st east
Mason, John, 229 Clarendon st, Em H
Mason, Mrs. A., store, Abbotsford st, Hot
Mason, Thomas Williams, hat and cap manufacturer, 67a Collins st east
Mason, Thomas, auctioneer and commission agent, 64 Nelson place

Mason, Thomas, carpenter, Eas
Mason, Thomas C., Bay st, San
Mason, W., grocer, corner King and Haden sts
Mason, W., 207 Lonsdale st west
Mason, Wm., Provost st, Hot
Masonic Journal and Victorian Gazette, 26 Collins st east
Masons' Society, meet at Trades' Hall, Lygon st, Carl
Massey, George, hatter, Chapel st, Pra
Massey, John, 155 Cardigan st, Carl
Massie, J., blacksmith, 125 Wellington st, E C
Massina, A. H., 231 Swan st, Rd
Masson, Alexander, 59 Madeline st, Carl
Masson, David, professor of music, 135 Bridport st, Em H
Master in Equity, offices of, 51 Latrobe st east
Masterman, A. F., printer, Brunswick st, F
Masters, James, Cole st, South Wmn
Masters, Joseph, agent, 122 Bridge road, Rd
Masters, John G., haircutter, &c., 65 Collins st west
Masters, Thomas, hairdresser and tobacconist, 111 Elizabeth st
Masters, Wm., carpenter, 5 Nelson place, Wmn
Masterson, Mrs., 67 Clarendon st, Em H
Masterton, David, provision merchant, 25 and 34 Latrobe st east
Masterton, Wm., nightman, Punt road, Pra
Matear, Emma, Registry office, 81 Collins st east
Matier, James, Queensberry st, Hot
Matier, Thomas, Flem
Mather, George, poulterer, 6 Eastern Market
Mather, J., 94 Adderley st, W M
Mather, Mrs., 81 Cardigan st, Carl
Mather, W., Villiers st, Hot
Mather, Wm., hairdresser, 72 Elizabeth st
Matheson, Alexander, merchant, Elizabeth st
Matheson, J. (Bank of Victoria), Collins street
Mathew, James, Pent
Mathews and Tallerman, boot importers, 30 Lonsdale st east
Mathews, Barnard, 109 Albert st, E M
Mathews, B. H., and Son, commission merchants, and agents to Lloyds and Liverpool and Glasgow Underwriters' Association, 23 Market st
Mathews, B. R., Esplanade, Wmn
Mathews, J., Union st, Btn
Mathews, J., Commercial road, Pra
Mathews, John, general merchant, 27 Franklyn st
Mathews, John, 44 Faraday st, Carl

Mathews, John, 3 Berkeley st, Carl
Mathews, S., boot importer, 241 Bourke st east
Mathewson, Mrs., 216 King st
Mathewson, W., St. Andrew's st, Btn
Mathewson, W., Montague st, Em H
Mathieson, A., Waltham st, Rd
Mathieson, James, toolmaker, &c., 52 Bourke st west
Mathison and Co, commission merchants and forwarding agents, 61½ Little Bourke st east
Mathison, G. T., Fawkner st, St K
Mathison, James, Dudley st, W M
Mathes, John, pork butcher, 312 Brunswick st, F
Matthews Brothers, ironmongers, Nott st, San
Matthews, Edward, shipwright, Bay st, San
Matthews, Edwin, ironmonger, 121 Napier st, F
Matthews, J., butcher, Errol st, Hot
Matthews, J., Flemington road, Hot
Matthews, John Felix, architect and surveyor, 67 Swanston st
Matthews, Patrick, chemist, Robe st, St K
Matthews, Peter, carpenter, Brighton st, Rd
Matthews, Peter, architect and surveyor, 52 Collins st east
Matthews, S., Dock hotel, Morris st, Wmn
Matthews, Thomas, bootmaker, 117 Leicester st, F
Matthews, Wm., house decorator, 152 King st
Matthews, Wm., butcher, 48 Victoria st, Rd
Matthewson, J., 94 Kerr st, F
Matthewson, Mrs., 78 Stanley st, W M
Mattingly, A., schoolmaster, Errol st, Hot
Mattingly, C., schoolmaster, Cape st, Heid
Mattinson, John, Pelham st, Hot
Maule, Francis, bootmaker, Lennox st, Rd
Maume, E., bootmaker, Church st, Rd
Maver, J., plumber, 215 Swanston st
Mawhry, Henry, butcher, Kensington
Mawhinney, James, 63 Lygon st, Carl
Maxton, P., Osborne st, Pra
Maxwell and Co., surgical instrument makers, 95 Swanston st
Maxwell, Benjamin J., bootmaker, Gardiner's creek road, Pra
Maxwell, Henry, Curzon st, Hot
Maxwell, James, saddler, Moonee ponds, Ess
Maxwell, John, 80 Coventry st, Em H
Maxwell, W. H., draper, Kew
Maxwell, Wm., Pent
May, —, Plenty road, Nth
May, Alfred, Highett st, Rd
May, Elias, butcher, Robe st, St K
May, G., Cardigan st, Carl
May, George, chemist, 343 Elizabeth st

May, Henry E., 17 York place, off York st, Em H
May, J., and Co., salt merchants, 4 Spencer street
May, John, Hanover st, F
May, John, 10 Rosslyn st, W M
May, R. W., Carlisle st, St K
May, Sampson, Macarthur place, Carl
May, Thomas, 10 Rosslyn st, W M
May, Thomas, tailor, 6 Union lane, Bourke st east
May, W., butcher, Bay st, San
Maybelle, Joseph, fruiterer, Swan st, Rd
Mayes, H. J., Commercial Inn, 140 Little Bourke st east
Mayes, Robert, High st, Pra
Mayfield, Wm. G., wine and spirit merchant, 85 Queen st
Maynard, Frederick, wood dealer, 174 Drummond st, Carl
Maynard, J., Little Hanover st, F
Maynard, Philip, coachbuilder, 51 Hanover st, F
Maynard, Mrs., Perry st, E C
Mayne, James, wholesale grocer, &c., 114 Elizabeth st
Mayne, Mrs., St. David st, F
Mayston and Co., stationers, printers, &c., 178 Elizabeth st
Mayston, R, 3 Brunswick st, F
Mazeau, Mrs., Inkerman st, St K
Mead, T., butcher, 159 Victoria st. E C
Meaden, John W., 178 and 180 Wellington st, E C
Meagher, Wm., armourer, Eastern road, Em H
Meake, A., 29 Three-chain road, Em H
Mealmaker, Duncan, grocer, 57 Johnston st, F
Mealy, Mrs., 67 Kerr st, F
Meany, J. T., bootmaker, Bay st, San
Mearce, Miss, 16 Barry st, Carl
Meares, George, Barkly st, St K
Meares, George, and Robert S., drapers and outfitters, 119 and 121 Bourke st east
Mears, Eml., 36 Queensberry st, Hot
Mears, J. and A., herbalists, 138 Smith st, E C
Mears, J., bootmaker, Hoddle st, E C
Mears, John, Dryburgh st, Hot
Mears, Mrs., Walsh st, S Y
Mechanics' Institute, Melbourne, 81 Collins st east
Mechanics' Institutes—New st, Brighton; Chapel st, Pra; Electra st, Wmn; corner of Cecil and Dorcas sts, Em H; Napier st, Fcy, &c.
Medcalf and Hunt, importers of boots and shoes, 28 Flinders lane west
Medcalf, Charles, Derby st, E C
Medcalf, George, baker, 117 Little Lonsdale st east
Medhurst, Alfred and Frederick, carpenters, 17 Little Bourke st west

Medical Board of Victoria office, 178 Collins st east
Medical Society of Victoria office, Collins st east
Medley, John, blacksmith, Chetwynd st, Hot
Medlicott, H. A., Fitzroy st, St K
Meek, W. J., solicitor, 5 and 6 Eldon chambers, Collins st west
Meeks, Alfred, 222 Moray st, Em H
Meeks, Henry, 70 Leicester st, Carl
Meeks, Wm., bootmaker, 5 Queensberry st, Hot
Mehegan, Robert, 9 Leicester st, Carl
Meher, J., draper, 82 and 84 Brunswick st, F
Meikle, Robert, Simpson st, E M
Mehrtens, Herman, carrier, Elizabeth st extension
Meissner, G. Otto, tobacconist, 133 Bourke st east
Melbourne and Adelaide Steam Navigation; agents, McMeckan, Blackwood, and Co., King st
Melbourne and Geelong Steam Navigation; Wharf, Flinders st west, and 11 Market st
Melbourne and Hobson's Bay United Railway Company's stations and offices, Flinders st east and west
Melbourne and Launceston Steam Navigation; agents, Bayles and Co., Collins st west
Melbourne and Newcastle Miami Coal Company, 95 Collins st west
Melbourne and Sandridge United Carrying Company, Western Market
Melbourne and Suburban Building and Investment Society, 56 Little Collins st east
Melbourne and Williamstown Railway station, Spencer st
Melbourne Anglers' Society, 81½ Elizabeth st
Melbourne Banking Company, corner of Queen and Little Collins sts
Melbourne, Castlemaine, and Sandhurst Railway station, Spencer st
Melbourne Club, 137 Collins st east
Melbourne Deutscher Turn Verein, 200 Lonsdale st east
Melbourne Exchange, Hall of Commerce, Collins st west
Melbourne Exchange Company, 31 Queen street
Melbourne (City of) Gas and Coke Company, 9 Collins st west
Melbourne, Geelong, and Ballaarat Railway station, Spencer st
Melbourne Home, Flinders lane east
Melbourne Hospital, Lonsdale st east
Melbourne Ice Company's office, 60 Collins st west
Melbourne Orphan Asylums, Em H

Melbourne Jewish Philanthropic Society (collector), 7 Mackenzie st
Melbourne Loan and Discount Company, 90 Chancery lane
Melbourne, Mount Alexander, and Murray River Railway office, Spencer st
Melbourne Patent Stearine Candle Company, limited, 60 Queen st; works, Flem
Melbourne Prices Current office, 69 Bourke st west
Melbourne Public Library, Swanston st
Melbourne Punch, office, Collins st east
Melbourne Savings' Bank, Market st
Melbourne Total Abstinence Society, Hall, Russell st
Melbourne Typographical Provident Association, Mechanics' Institute, Collins st east
Melbourne, Warrnambool, Port Fairy, and Portland Steam Navigation Company; agent, S. G. Henty, 60 Collins st west
Melbourne Young Men's Association, Spring st
Melcher, W., brickmaker, Flockhart st, E C
Melcomb, Mrs., Lennox st, Rd
Melen, Edward, High st, Pra
Mellon, James, Wreckyn st, Hot
Mellon, S., greengrocer, Church st, Rd
Melody, Patrick, Cremorne st, Rd
Melville, A., Faraday st, Carl
Melville, Donald, Albion st west, Bk
Melville, Wm., Acland st, St K
Melvin, J., baker, 154 Wellington st, E C
Melvin, P., Oxford st, Hot
Mendes, George, pawnbroker, 39 Coventry st, Em H
Menos and Forsyth, boat builders, Nott st, San
Menser, Louis, fancy repository, 92 Swanston st
Menzies, Archibald, Menzies' hotel, 20 Latrobe st east
Menzies, Mrs., Acland st, St K
Mercer, J., store, Collins st, Bin
Mercer, Wm., coach painter, 269 Napier st, F
Merchant, Charles E., school, Ess
Merhant, F., Park st, S Y
Merfield, Wm., 8 Park st west, Em H
Merick, Charles, bootmaker, 248 Elizabeth st
Merick, Mrs., ladies' school, 134 Church st, Rd
Merifield, Wm., draper, 1 Wellington st, St K
Merker, F. W., Highett st, Rd
Merrall, E., wheelwright, Pres
Merrigan, J., grocer, 70 and 72 Spencer st
Merriman, Josiah, Tanner st, Rd
Merriman, Lewis A., Elizabeth st
Merriman, Wm., 32½ Clarendon st, Em H
Merritt, W. E., Times hotel, Clarendon st, Em H

Merry, Peter, draper, 35 Errol st, Hot
Merryweather, H., Abbotsford st, Hot
Merson, —, Fulton st, St K
Messenger, Francis, builder, Punt road, Pra
Messer, James, pastrycook, Commercial road, Pra
Messer, Mrs., fancy warehouse, Commercial road, Pra
Messerry, George, Chapel st, Pra
Messiter, Thomas, Lennox st, Rd
Messterer, John, 53 George st east, F M
Messiter, Josiah, builder, Rowena parade, Rd
Meston, J. C., 1 Kyte's buildings, Prince's st, F
Metcalf, T., draper, Haw
Metherell, E., grocer, Lygon st, Carl
Metropolitan and General Building, Investment, and Loan Society, 18 Collins st east
Metropolitan and Permanent Building and Investment Society, 18 Collins st east
Metropolitan Quartz-Mining Company, 31 Collins st west
Metters, James, bricklayer, &c., 76 Lonsdale st east
Metzger, E., professor of gymnastics, 17 Stephen st
Meyer, F., Union st, Rd
Meyer, F., 29 Dorcas st, Em H
Meyer, Francis, 45 York st east, Em H
Meyer, George, 196 Elgin st, Carl
Meyer, John, hay and corn store, Elizabeth st north
Meyer, Menk, and Co., importers, &c., 63 Queen st
Meyers, Abraham, Capel st, Hot
Meyl, H. L., hairdresser, 62 Bourke st east
Meynell, G., Malvern Hill
Meyring, Louis, Nicholson st, Carl
Meyring, Ludwig, chemist, 90 Swanston street
Michael, John, 145 Moor st, F
Michaelis, Boyd, and Co., merchants, 1 and 3 Elizabeth st
Michaelis, M., Esplanade, St K
Michel, J., 42 Jeffcott st, W M
Michel, Lewis J., Duke of Wellington hotel, 83 Flinders st east
Michie, Archibald, Minister of Justice, barrister, 73 Little Collins st west
Mickelbargh, J., greengrocer, St. David st, F
Mickelbargh, John, Peel st, Pra
Mickleborough, John, greengrocer, Greville st, Pra
Mickner, Louis, 84 Victoria st, Rd
Middlecoat, George, Richmond terrace, Rd
Middlemiss, Mrs., 105 Cardigan st, Carl
Middleton, D., saddler, Victoria st, Carl
Middleton, George, bootmaker, Pent

Middleton, Henry, 3 Sydney terrace, Wellington parade, E M
Middleton, J. W., 91 York st west, Em H
Middleton, James, 123 Little Bourke st west
Middleton, M., 6 Jeffcott st, W M
Middleton, M. F., Gardiner's creek road, Pra
Middleton, Mrs., Grey st, St K
Middleton, Thomas, Prince's st, St K
Middleton, Wm., Albert st, Pra
Mier, Barras, surgeon dentist, 77 Swanston st
Miers, Henry A., tobacconist, 23 Bridge road, Rd
Miers, Thomas H., baker and steam biscuit manufacturer, 22 Little Collins st east, and 2, 4, and 6 Brunswick st, F
Miles, Alfred, broker, 44 Brunswick st, F
Miles and Co., merchants, 99½ Collins st west
Miles, Charles, 272 Victoria st, Rd
Miles, Edward, Haw
Miles, Henry, shoemaker, 3 Thompson st, Wmn
Miles, John, 270 Victoria st, Rd
Miles, John E., Domain st, S Y
Miles, John R., teacher, Commercial road, Fey
Miles, Mrs., fruiterer, 177 Lonsdale st east
Miles, Thomas, boarding-house keeper, 179 Bourke st west
Mill, David, slater, 157 Little Lonsdale st east
Mill, Thomas, grocer, 167 Bourke st east
Mill, Wm., Thomson st, E C
Millar and Anderson, merchants, 7 Latrobe st east
Millar, J., grocer, 30 Elgin st, Carl
Millar, John, cooper, 13 Little Collins st east
Millar, Mrs., 63 Nelson road, Em H
Millar, Peter, Daylesford
Millar, Wm., Elsternwick
Millard, H., Union st, Bin
Millard, J. P., confectioner, 91 Flinders st east
Millard, Rev. J. G., 166 Victoria parade, E M
Millard, Wm., hat manufacturer, 78 Swanston st
Millbank, Mrs., 7 Jackson st, Wmn
Miller, A., Garden st, Pra
Miller, A., Cecil st, Em H
Miller, A. G., 121 King st
Miller, A. P., chemist, 222 Lonsdale st east
Miller, Alexander, Jolimont square, E M
Miller, Alexander, 7 Cremorne st, Rd
Miller and Douglas, ironmongers, &c., 32 Nelson place, Wmn
Miller and Gray, rope makers, 61 Flinders st west
Miller and Macquistan, wheelwrights, Spencer st

Miller and Johnston, agents for Nova Stearine soap and candle works, 35 Little Collins st west
Miller Bros., coachbuilders and importers, 80 Lonsdale st east
Miller, C., corn merchant, 104 Collins st west
Miller, E., 18 Little Lonsdale st west
Miller, Francis McDonald, cartridge manufacturer, Nicholson st, F
Miller, George, Wellington st, Rd
Miller, George, Union st, Rd
Miller, Henry, M.L.C., 5 George st, F
Miller, Henry, stock and share broker, 25 Collins st east
Miller, J., mattress maker, High st, St K
Miller, J. J., Victoria hotel, Fitzroy st, St K
Miller, J. S., Darling st, S Y
Miller, James, Dunsmure, Church st, Rd
Miller, James, bootmaker, Little Bourke st east
Miller, James, Park st, Em H
Miller, John, painter, Argyle st, St K
Miller, John, 106 Leicester st, Carl
Miller, John, Henry st, Pra
Miller, John, store and post office, Chapel st, Pra
Miller, John T., Darling st, S Y
Miller, Mars, secretary Melbourne and Suburban Building and Investment Society, 56 Little Collins st west
Miller, Mars, jun., Brighton st, Rd
Miller, Mrs. M., 3 Apsley place, Gisborne st, E M
Miller, R., Cremorne st, Rd
Miller, R., coachbuilder, 1a Latrobe st east
Miller, R., Victoria parade, E C
Miller, Rev. W. B., 45 Charles st, F
Miller, Richard, confectioner, 120 Bourke st east
Miller, Robt., bootmaker, 15 Little Bourke st west
Miller, Robert, corn store, 41 Wellington st, E C
Miller, Robert C., commission merchant, 104 Collins st west
Miller, S., Commercial road, Pra
Miller, T. S., Blessington st, St K
Miller, Thomas, solicitor, 64 Little Collins st east
Miller, Thomas, photographer, 98½ Swanston st
Miller, W., Peel st, Pra
Miller, W. M., Ess
Miller, Wm., Lennox st, Rd
Miller, Wm., baker, Commercial road, Pra
Miller, Wm., boarding-house, 57 Flinders lane east
Miller, Wm., shipmaster, 224 Moray st, Em H
Millership, W., 72 Kerr st, F
Milligan, T. D., 48 Park st, Em H
Millington, Samuel, Highett st, Rd

AND SUBURBS.   Mcf   117

Million, H., wood dealer, 3 Palmer st, F
Mills, A., draper, 256 Brunswick st, F
Mills, C., Gardeners' Arms hotel, Brighton st, Rd
Mills, Henry, timber merchant, Flinders lane west and King st
Mills, J., Emerald hotel, 48 and 50 Clarendon st, Em H
Mills, James, bootmaker, 59 Cardigan st, Carl
Mills, James, dealer, 96 Madeline st, Carl
Mills, John S., solicitor, 41 Swanston st, and Greeves st, F
Mills, R. S., 71 Bank st, Em H
Mills, Thomas, 68 Lygon st, Carl
Mills, W., engineer, &c., 14 a'Beckett st west
Mills, Wm., Punt road, S Y
Mills, Wm., tinsmith, 146 Little Lonsdale st east
Milne, —, Victoria st, E C
Milne, A., 80 Raglan st, Em H
Milne and Rankin, grocers, Barkly st, Carl
Milne, Charles, saddler, High st, St K
Milne, George, accountant, 30 Russell st
Milne, George M., 25½ Barkly st, Carl
Milne, J., ironmonger, 58 Brunswick st, F
Milne, James, 28 Johnston st, F
Milne, James, cabinetmaker, 33 Flinders lane
Milne, James, 19 Richmond terrace, Rd
Milne, Wm., 67 Collins st west
Milne, Wm. S., coppersmith and brazier, 47 Queen st
Milner, Wm., Church st, Rd
Milsham, Henry, Barkly st, Carl
Milson, Dr., Mission office, 98 Royal lane, Bourke st east
Milton, George, tailor, 225 Bourke st east
Milton, John B., Commercial road, Pra
Milton, John B., and Co., military tailors, &c., 54 Collins st east
Minahan, John, bootmaker, 74 Gertrude st, F
Minahan, Thomas, 63 Rathdowne st, Carl
Minchen, J., 80 Cohlen st, Em H
Minchin, Mrs., Cliff st, Pra
Minford, Thomas, 22 Raglan st, Em H
Minifie, Wm., oil and colour dealer, 77 Wellington st, E C
Mining Department offices, Queen st
Minns, J., Wells st, Dto
Minns, Rev. George, 3 Stephenson st, Rd
Minto, —, Electra st, Wmn
Minty, Wm. M., builder, 58 Park st, Em H
Mirams, Rev. James, 9 Grattan st, Carl
Mirko, George, lamp manufacturer and dealer, 152 Bourke st east
Miscamble, J., veterinary surgeon, Condell lane, Post Office place
Mitchell, —, office, 50 Temple court, Collins st west

Mitchell, A., gardener, Rotherwood st, Rd
Mitchell, A., restaurant, 259 Elizabeth st
Mitchell, Alexander, Station st, Fcy
Mitchell, Alexander, Victoria st, W M
Mitchell and Bonneau, merchants, 15 Elizabeth st
Mitchell and Co., brewers, Cremorne st, Rd
Mitchell, Archibald, Argyle st, St K
Mitchell, David, store and post office, Moreland st, Fcy
Mitchell, F., 17 Queensberry st, Carl
Mitchell, George, Railway place, San
Mitchell, J., 55 Market st, Em H
Mitchell, J., plumber and gasfitter, 55 Market st, Em H
Mitchell, James, store, Little Lonsdale st west
Mitchell, James, 7 Owen st, Nicholson st, Carl
Mitchell, James, Provost st, Hot
Mitchell, John, Gardiner's creek road, Tk
Mitchell, John, Hotham st east, E M
Mitchell, John, Hotham st, E M
Mitchell, John, Commercial road, Pra
Mitchell, John, dairyman, 64 Napier st, F
Mitchell, John, grocer and ironmonger, Commercial road, Pra
Mitchell, John, 44 Perry st, E C
Mitchell, John, tailor, Eleanor st, Fcy
Mitchell, M., 50 Bank st east, Em H
Mitchell, Mrs., Fcy
Mitchell, Mrs., Argyle st, F
Mitchell, Mrs., 7 Henry st, F
Mitchell, Mrs. Jane, dressmaker, Dorcas st, Em H
Mitchell, Peter, St. David st, F
Mitchell, R., Rotherwood st, Rd
Mitchell, S., Victoria hotel, Stevedore st, Wmn
Mitchell, T., butcher, Nth
Mitchell, Thomas P., Kew
Mitchell, Wm., Nicholson st, Fcy
Mitchell, Wm., collar maker, 255 Victoria parade, F C
Mitchell, Wm., watchmaker, 53 Errol st, Hot
Mitchener, Henry T., windowblind maker, &c., 64 Russell st, and Haw
Mixner and Campbell, lime merchants, 47 William st
Mixner, J. F., 61 Spring st
Moallar, Adolph, 72 Argyle st, F
Moate, George F., grocer, 62 Gertrude st, F
Moate, R., butcher, 130 Clarendon st, Em H
Model Training Schools, Spring st
Modral, J. J., Wilson st, Pra
Moeller, C., Mill st, Bin
Moeller, Philip, merchant, 63 Franklyn st west
Moer, James, 60 Little Nelson st, Wmn
Moffat, J., 218 Cardigan st, Carl
Moffat, S., Grey st, E M

Moffat, Wm. Turner, Lennox st, Rd
Moffatt, David, secretary Southern Insurance Company, 31 Queen st
Moffatt, G. R. G., Murphy st, S Y
Moffatt, John, M.L.A., Parliament House
Moffatt, W., 36 Kerr st, F
Moffatt, Wm., Goodwood st, Rd
Mohr, John, stock broker and mining agent, 3 Collins st west
Moir, John, 9 Provost st, Hot
Moir, Rev. Charles, Esplanade, St K
Moir, Richard, 57 Napier st, F
Molesworth, H., barrister, 22 Temple court, Collins st west
Molesworth, His Honor Judge, Haw
Moline, C., Haw
Moloney, Daniel, Exford hotel, 93 Little Bourke st east
Moloney, Daniel, Peel st, Pra
Moloney, John, 19 Arden st, Hot
Molony, James, bootmaker, 94 King st
Molrose, Charles, fancy box maker and bookbinder, 87 Little Collins st east
Molseed, Henry, Young Queen hotel, Madeline st, Carl
Monahan, E. J., 154 Stephen st
Monahan, James, High st, St K
Monahan, John, farmer, Pascoevale road, Ess
Monahan, Thomas, 19A Gore st, F
Monash, L., Dudley st, W M
Monck, Mrs., 3 Hotham terrace, Hotham st east, E M
Money, A., and Co., coopers, 46 Little Bourke st east
Money Wigram and Sons, line of packets, W. P. White and Co., agents, 10 Elizabeth st
Monk, A., St. Andrew's st, Bin
Monk, Joseph, carrier, Drewster st, Ess
Monk, Mrs., grocer, 149 Lonsdale st east
Monshin, Franco, Jolimont, E M
Monster Clothing Company, 21 Bourke st east
Montague, Alfred, 20 Hotham st east, E M
Montague, J., 192 Napier st, F
Mont de Piété Loan and Investment Co., 105 Elizabeth st
Montefiore, E. L., secretary Australasian Insurance Company, Collins st west
Monteith, —, 234 Napier st, F
Monteith, J. A., 34 Faraday st, Carl
Montgomery, Richd., corkcutter, 77 Smith st, F
Moodie, James D., shipwright, River-side south
Moody, Claude L., Haw
Moody, J. J., parliamentary and patent agent, 36 Collins st east
Moody, J. O., Haw
Moody, James, Pascoe st, W m
Moody, Leslie A., immigration agent and chief inspector of distilleries, Latrobe st west

Moody, Robert, Bell st, F
Moody, Robert, Dryburgh st, Hot
Moody, William, Condell st, F
Moon, Frederick, 3 Ann st, W m
Moon, George, 189 King st
Moon, John, ticket writer, Hoddle st, E C
Mooney, Daniel, grocer, 57 Spencer st north
Mooney, J., Preston
Mooney, J., Neptune st, st K
Mooney, James, 21 Chetwynd st, W M
Mooney, James, Royal hotel, Hobe st, St K
Mooney, Joshua, Liverpool Arms hotel, corner of Brunswick and Johnston sts, F
Mooney, Thomas, Little Nelson st, W m
Mooney, Wm., surgeon-dentist and chemist, 91 Elizabeth st
Moonie, Wm., Osborne st, South W m a
Moore, A. G., 90 Young st, F
Moore, Alfred, Spread Eagle Hotel, 312 Bridge road, Rd
Moore, Captain, Provost st, Hot
Moore, Charles W., watchmaker, Gardiner's creek road, Pra
Moore, David, M.L.A., Mooroefield, Merri creek
Moore, David, butcher, Pres
Moore, F., 59 Kerr st, F
Moore, F., Condell st, F
Moore, G., 5 Little Latrobe st east
Moore, George, bootmaker, 150 Lonsdale st east
Moore, George, 101 Napier st, Em H
Moore, George, medical practitioner, 40 Queensberry st, Hot
Moore, George W., judge's associate, Supreme Court
Moore, H., 134 Leicester st, Carl
Moore, H., and Co., merchants, 7 Latrobe st east
Moore, Hawthorn, and Co., merchants, 14 Queen st
Moore, Henry, stonecutter, 218 Eastern road, Em H
Moore, Hugh, 6 George st, E M
Moore, Isaac, Cardigan st, Carl
Moore, J., sign writer, 119 Smith st, F
Moore, J., Bay st, Bin
Moore, J., ticket writer, Hoddle st, E C
Moore, J., 109 Moor st, F
Moore, J., under secretary, Government House
Moore, J. S., Beach, Bin
Moore, J. V., Gardiner's creek road, Pra
Moore, James, Union st, Bin
Moore, James, official assignee, 10 Eldon chambers, Collins st west
Moore, John, iron merchant, 137 Bourke st west
Moore, John, Rowena parade, Rd
Moore, John H., Domain road, S Y
Moore, Joseph S., barrister, Temple court, Collins st west
Moore, Michael, farmer, Ess

AND SUBURBS. Mor 119

Moore, Michael, Peel st, Hot
Moore, Mrs., Victoria parade, E C
Moore, Mrs., 37 Young st, F
Moore, Mrs., Leonox st, Rd
Moore, Mrs., 20 Stanley st, E C
Moore, Mrs., 29 Lygon st, Carl
Moore, Richard, Staffordshire st, Fcy
Moore, Samuel, furniture carter, 74 Napier st, F
Moore, Samuel, fruiterer, 61 Collins st west
Moore, Samuel, furniture dealer, 39 Little Bourke st east
Moore, Thomas, saddle and harness manufacturer, 194 Elizabeth st
Moore, Wm., 46 Bank st east, Em II
Moore, Wm., wood and ivory turner, Peel st, E C
Moore, Wm. A., judge's associate, Supreme Court
Moorhead, David Johnston, stock and share broker, 69 Collins st west
Moorhead, James, Margaret st, Pra
Moorman, R. A., butcher, 225 and 250 Smith st, E C
Moore, Henry, Westbury st, St K
Moran, Anthony, 81 George st, F
Moran, J., Catholic schoolhouse, Fcy
Moran, James, Treasury hotel, 148 Queen street
Moran, M., Bay View hotel, Walsh st, W M
Moran, Michael, slater, 131 Gertrude st, F
Moran, Mrs., Punt road, S Y
Moran, Owen, Macarthur place, Carl
Moran, Roderick, grocer, 27 Little Lonsdale st east
Moran, T., 87 Montague st, Em II
Moran, T. J., Walsh in terrace, Rd
Moran, —, 4 Cardigan st, Carl
Morcombe, E. M., auctioneer, 124 Smith st, E C
Morcur, J., carpenter, Fawkner st, St K
Mores, H. J., Arden st, Hot
Morey, Ephraim, 9 Webb st, F
Morgan, —, 27 Fitzroy st, F
Morgan, —, baker, 36 Ferguson st, Wmn
Morgan and Mackintosh, squatters, 107 Collins st west
Morgan, Arthur, Lothian st, Hot
Morgan, B., 14 Brunswick st, F
Morgan, C., painter, &c., 9 Little Collins st east
Morgan, C. F., 84 George st, F
Morgan, Charles, 121 Johnston st, E C
Morgan, D., 14 Brunswick st, F
Morgan, G., Graham st, San
Morgan, G., hatter, 70 Clarendon st, Em II
Morgan, G. A., 74 Coventry st, Em II
Morgan, George, wood and coal yard, Cecil st, Wmn
Morgan, George, 22 John st, Wmn
Morgan, H., Weston st, Bk
Morgan, H. G., Peel st, Pra

Morgan, J., bootmaker, Commercial road, Pra
Morgan, J., outfitter, 4 Beach st, San
Morgan, J., and Co., shipping brokers, 34 Nelson place, Wmn
Morgan, John, Carlisle st, St K
Morgan, John, coppersmith, &c., Queensberry st, Hot
Morgan, John S., dairy farm, Pres
Morgan, John, Capel st, Hot
Morgan, Mrs., Graham st, San
Morgan, Mrs., Park st west, Em II
Morgan, O., 25 Smith st, F
Morgan, Patrick, cattle dealer, Flem
Morgan, R., South Yarra Club hotel, Gardiner's creek road, Pra
Morgan, R., 46 Lygon st, Carl
Morgan, Richard, off 58 Little Collins st east
Morgan, Robert, Arthur st, Pra
Morgan, Robert R., architect, 26 Collins st east
Morgue, The, Nelson place, Wmn
Morgan, Thomas, Cole st, Wmn
Moriarty, Jeremiah, tailor, 38 Little Collins st east
Moriarty, Patrick, 36 Elgin st, Carl
Moriarty, Jeremiah, Spring st, F
Morison, Alexander, grain store, 199 King street
Morison and Co., commission agents, 91 Flinders lane west
Morison, D., produce merchant, Westgarth st, F
Morison, G., Osborne st, Pra
Moritz, J., Neptune st, St K
Moritz, Solomon, merchant, 60 Elizabeth street
Morland, Wm., Wilson st, Pra
Morley and Carrick, general carriers, 14 Collins st east
Morley's Free Stores, Stoke st, San
Morley, Wm., grocer, Elgin st, Carl
Morley, Wm., Grattan st, Carl
Morley, Wm., Nott st, San
Morman, Ed. L., 5 Peel st, Hot
Mornay, A. A., M.D., Electra st, Wmn
Morne, Mrs., Cremorne st, Rd
Moroney, James, Carriers' Arms hotel, 211 Elizabeth st
Moroney, M., bootmaker, 99 Stephen st
Morphy, Mrs., 131 Lonsdale st west
Morrah, Arthur, Kew
Morrell, Frederick, Curzon st, Hot
Morrell, John, Clarence hotel, 2 Collins st east
Morricks, J., Prince's st, F
Morris, —, Railway place, San
Morris, D., 60 Queensberry st, Carl
Morris, David, 66 Raglan st, Em II
Morris, E., 50 Moor st, F
Morris, Edward, 105 Lygon st, Carl
Morris, Edward, Catherine st, Rd
Morris, George, Windsor st, Fcy

Morris, H., hotel broker, 114 Elizabeth st
Morris, Henry, gardener, Douglas parade, Wmn
Morris, Hugh, Swan st, Fcy
Morris, J., Kew
Morris, J., general dealer, Johnston st, E C
Morris, J. W., saddler, 115 William st
Morris, James, Rathdowne st, Carl
Morris, John, Nth
Morris, John, Robe st, St K
Morris, John, Albert st, Pra
Morris, John, and Roberts, J. S., commission agents, 21 Flinders lane west
Morris, Joseph, butcher, 79 Spencer st
Morris, Mrs., boarding-house, 199 Bourke st west
Morris, R., Brighton st, Rd
Morris, Richard, Hoddle st, Rd
Morris, Robt., Rosslyn st, W M
Morris, Samuel, 89 Flinders lane east
Morris, Thomas, butcher, 34 Madeline st, Carl
Morris, Thomas, Curzon st, Hot
Morris, Thomas A., Baptist lane, 64 Little Collins st east
Morris, W. E., 34 Gore st, F
Morris, W. J., 30 James st, Wmn
Morris, Wm., 24 Grattan st, Carl
Morrish, Frederick, French polisher, Mackillop st, 56 Bourke st west
Morrison, Mrs., ladies' school, Napier st, F
Morrison, A., carpenter, Gipps st, E M
Morrison, Alex, Oxford st, Hot
Morrison, Alex., merchant, 1 Western market, 209 King st
Morrison, Alexander (A.M.), principal Scotch College, Lansdowne st, E M
Morrison, Charles, Charles st, F
Morrison, George, Chambers st, S Y
Morrison, H., 395 Fitzroy st, F
Morrison, James, baker, Queensberry st, Hot
Morrison, Miss, Millswyn st, S Y
Morrison, Mrs., grocer, 81 Leveson st, Hot
Morrison, Peter, 266 Elizabeth st
Morrison, Robert, Curzon st, Hot
Morrison, Thomas, Davies st, Pra
Morrison, Wm., 5 Napier st, F
Morrow, J., Simpson st, E M
Morrow, John, Charles st, Pra
Morrow, Mrs., Nicholson st, F
Morrow, Robert, St. Andrew's hotel, Nicholson st, F
Morrow, Thomas, Morrow's hotel, High st, Pra
Mort and Watson, storekeepers, 91 Bourke st west
Mort, James, corner of Milton and Tennyson sts, East St K
Mortimer, E., Hoddle st, Rd
Mortimer, H. W., 3 Gertrude st, F
Mortimer, Henry, upholsterer, 187 Swanston st
Mortimer, Mrs. S. H., 25 Franklyn st west

Mortimore, T., Commercial lane
Mortley, Wm., Bond st, E C
Morton, Alfred, Polytechnic Café, Bourke st east
Morton, Charles, storekeeper, Flemington hill
Morton, George, bootmaker, 18 Rathdown st, Carl
Morton, James, butcher, Millswyn st, S Y
Morton, James, chemist, 112 Brunswick st, F
Morton, John, Haw
Morton, Mrs., 31 Lygon st, Carl
Morton, R., bootmaker, 131 Bourke st east
Morton, Thomas, 93 Leicester st, F
Morton, W. J., Grattan st, Carl
Morton, Wm., provision merchant, 78 Collins st west
Morton, Wm., Kew
Morton, Wm., draper, Haw
Morton, Wm. L., Walsh st, S Y
Morton, Wm., Criterion hotel, Collins st west
Mowley, Alfred, Madeline st, Carl
Moses, Hyam, clothier and outfitter, 115 Elizabeth st
Moses, John, draper, 247 Bourke st east
Moses, M., 228 Bourke st east
Moss, A., 36 Little Lonsdale st west
Moss, C., bootmaker, Church st, Rd
Moss, D., Queen st north
Moss, Edwin O., 32 Church st, Em H
Moss, George, 6 Capel st, W M
Moss George, tent and flag maker, Bourke st west
Moss, Henry, Bay st, San
Moss, Hugh, 20 Regent st, F
Moss, J., greengrocer, 99 Young st, F
Moss, James, news agent, Haw
Moss, James, Hanmer st, Wmn
Moss, John, 161 Little Collins st east
Moss, Mark, merchant, 64 Little Collins st west
Moss, Moton, provision merchant, 106 Flinders lane east
Moss, Peter, Howena parade, Rd
Moss, Rev. W., Commercial road, Pra
Moss, Reuben, 17 Collins st west
Moss, White, and Co., cigar manufacturers, 124 Queen st
Mossman, —, Prince of Wales hotel, Otter st, E C
Mossman, James, Norfolk hotel, Easy st, E C
Motherwell, James B., surgeon, 107 Collins st east
Mottram, Samuel, earthenware dealer, 180 Bridge road, Rd
Moust, Thomas, 10 York st east, Em H
Moubray, Lush, and Co., importers and drapers, 45 Collins st west
Moubray, Thomas, 5 Gloucester terrace, Fitzroy st, St K
Mould, C., Upper Haw

Mould, Charles, and Co., boot and shoe
 importers, 61 Swanston st
Moalder, George, Blandford st, Fcy
Moulder, Wm., Yarra st, Held
Moule, F. G., Bto
Moule, Wm., 125 Moor st, F
Moulton, Joseph, 17 Alma st, F
Moulton, Mrs., 129 Johnston st, E C
Mounser, C., Peel st, Pra
Mounsey, Mrs., 4 Bank st east, Em H
Mountain, —, Station place, San
Mountain Queen Quartz Mining Company,
 10 Elizabeth st
Mountain View Quartz Mining Company,
 55 Elizabeth st
Mounier, J., Park st west, Em H
Mourant, J. T., wood turner, 71 Oxford
 st, E C
Mournane, Mrs., 61 Nelson st, Em H
Mourilyan, Thomas, Argyle st, St K
Mouritz, G. A., coal merchant, 16 King st,
 Flinders st terminus, and Powlett st,
 E M
Mowbray, Mrs., greengrocer, 64 Ferrars st,
 Em H
Mowbray, William, Hoddle st, E C
Mowbray, Wm., painter and paperhanger,
 64 Ferrars st, Em H
Mowling, G., 29 Regent st, F
Mowling, George, importer of boots and
 shoes, 29 Bourke st east
Moxam, John, 37 Dryburgh st, Hot
Moxham, Edward, butcher, Stevedore st,
 Wms
Moxham, James, auctioneer, Stevedore st,
 Wms
Moxham, Wm. J., Caroline st, S Y
Moylan, Michael, Flemington road, Hot
Moylan, Thomas, 115 Little Lonsdale st
 west
Moyles, John, Weston st, Bk
Moyneham, Wm., greengrocer, Robe st,
 St K
Mucklow, John, wheelwright, Chapel st,
 Pra
Mudge, B. P., P.O., Malvern
Mueller and Co., ale and porter bottlers,
 Cremorne st, Rd
Mueller, F., Government botanist, Botanic
 gardens
Mueller, V. A., tobacconist, 104 Bourke
 st east
Muir, Cornelius, Caroline st, S Y
Muir, James, 34 Raglan st, Em H
Muir, James, 69 Osborne st, South Wms
Muir, James Henry, accountant, 34 Queen
 street
Muir, John, Heath st, San
Muir, Mrs., mantle maker, 31 Curzon st,
 Hot
Muir, Robert, grocer, Graham st, San
Muir, Stephen, 39 King William st, F
Muir, Wm. P., manager Land Mortgage
 Bank of Victoria, Gipps st, E M

Muir, Wm., accountant, &c., 41 Swan-
 ston st
Muir, Wm., grocer, 26 Little Lonsdale st
 west
Muirhead, James, poulterer, 66 Swanston
 street
Muirhead, James, 187 Lygon st, Carl
Muirhead, James, Flem
Muirhead, John, 94 Arden st, Hot
Mulcahey, Cornelius, 3 Bendigo st, Hot
Mulcahey, Edward, grocer, 55 Victoria st,
 E C
Mulcahey, P., Elizabeth st
Mulcahey, Thomas, Harp of Erin hotel,
 114 Queen st
Mulholland, Mrs., tobacconist, 44 Gertrude
 st, F
Mullan, John, 34 Rosslyn st, W M
Mallaly, John, customs agent, Custom-
 house, and 56 Clarendon st, E M
Mullen, John, Ralston st, Pra
Mullen, Samuel, bookseller and stationer,
 55 Collins st east
Muller, Mrs., straw bonnet maker, 27
 Lonsdale st east
Mullin, John, 231 Swan st, Rd
Mullinger, George, nightman, 23 Little
 Bourke st west
Mullins, Thomas, 186 Drummond st, Carl
Mullins, Timothy, grocer, 29 Young st, F
Mulready, W. J., cartage contractor, 74
 Westgarth st, F
Mulway, Robert, draper, Elgin st, Carl
Mumby, D., baker, Coventry st west, Em
 H
Mumby, Benjamin, baker, 13 Wellington
 st, St K
Mumby, Joseph, baker, 15 Wellington st,
 St K
Munce, Wm. R., Lothian st, Hot
Munday, Charles, Rosslyn st, W M
Munday, Charles, 109 Queensberry st, Hot
Munday, H., 105 Napier st, F
Munday, Mrs., Curzon st, Hot
Munday, Wm., boarding-house, 37 Russell
 street
Mundell, Mrs., 5 Granite terrace, Gertrudo
 st, F
Mundell, Sarah, 2 McKenzie st
Mundheng, John, storekeeper, Flemington
 hill
Municipal Council Chambers; Town Hall,
 Swanston st; New Court House, Btn;
 Court House, Sydney road, Bk; Court
 House, Johnston st, F C; Dorcas st
 west, Em H; Court House, Flem; Mar-
 ket square, F; Town Hall, Haw; Town
 Hall, Errol st, Hot; Athenæum, Kew;
 Town Hall, Chapel st, Pra; Bridge
 road, Rd; Graham st, San; Town Hall,
 St K; Court House, Wms
Municipal Delegates' Conference Office,
 56 Little Collins st east
Munkhouse, H., Station place, San

Munn, Henry, Peel st, Hot
Munro, George, tailor, 212 Victoria st west, W M
Munro, H. C., Latrobe parade, Collins st east
Munro, J., and Son, 193 Bourke st west
Munro, James, Wilson st, S Y
Munro, John, engineer, ironfounder, &c., 131 King st
Munro, John, 122 Cardigan st, Carl
Munroe, Donald, 92 George st, E M
Munroe, James, grocer, 54 Victoria st, Rd
Munroe, Hobert, Queensberry st, Hot
Munyard, J., turner, 63 George st, F
Munyard, John, 88 Bouverie st, Carl
Murdison, George, Simpson st east, E M
Murdoch, A., grocer, 8 Nelson place, N. Wmn
Murdoch, Alexander, grocer, 98 Dorcas st, Em H
Murdoch, Andrew, grocer, 46 Victoria st, Rd
Murdoch, Andrew, grocer, 63 Stanley st, E C, 155 Stephen st, and Johnston st, E C
Murdoch, J., grocer, Park st, Em H
Murdoch, James, grocer, 150 and 290 Brunswick st, F
Murdock, James, grocer, Raglan and Day sts, San
Murdock, James, fruiterer, 98 Drummond st, Carl
Murdock, James, grocer, Johnston st, E C
Murdock, R. J., Stoke st, San
Murphy and Leplastrier, wine and spirit merchants, 110 Collins st west
Murphy and Sutherland, milliners, Argyle st, St K
Murphy, Andrew, Murphy st, S Y
Murphy, Daniel, bootmaker, 137 Cardigan st, Carl
Murphy, Dennis, cab proprietor, Dryburgh st, Hot
Murphy, E., 51 Fitzroy st, F
Murphy, E. J., Kew
Murphy, Edward Joseph, 24 William st, and Orrong road, Tk
Murphy, H. M., M.L.C., Parliament House
Murphy, H. M., merchant, 67 Flinders st east
Murphy, Hon. Sir Francis, speaker Legislative Assembly, Church st, E C
Murphy, Hugh, Robe st, St K
Murphy, J., Happy Home hotel, Swan st, Rd
Murphy, James, blacksmith, Pent
Murphy, James, Leura, Tk
Murphy, John, Stoke st, San
Murphy, John, Quarry reserve, Fcy
Murphy, John, general dealer, 13 Queensberry st, Hot
Murphy, John D., Arden st, Hot
Murphy, Matthew, Kilkenny inn, 200 King st, corner of Lonsdale st

Murphy, M., trunk maker, 38 William st
Murphy, M., produce store, 65 William st, F
Murphy, M. D., The Reefers' hotel, corner of Stephen and Lonsdale sts
Murphy, Miss, Jackson st, St K
Murphy, Miss, 132 Queen st
Murphy, Mrs., Stoke st, San
Murphy, Mrs., Arden st, Hot
Murphy, P. G., solicitor, 95 Swanston st
Murphy, Patrick, 29A Bouverie st, Carl
Murphy, Patrick, grocer, 119 Bouverie st, Carl
Murphy, Patrick, Arden st, Hot
Murphy, Peter, coachbuilder, Gardiner's creek road, Tk
Murphy, Peter, 107 Bridge road, Rd
Murphy, Philip, Mahne st, Hcid
Murphy, Richard, Nth
Murphy, Thomas, 41 Rose st, F
Murphy, Thomas, greengrocer, Adelaide st, Fcy
Murphy, W., bootmaker, 31½ Bourke st west
Murphy, Wm., 87 Rose st, F
Murphy, Wm., 78 Lothian st, Hot
Murphy, Wm., 111 Cardigan st, Carl
Murphy, Wm., tailor, 162 Russell st
Murrall, Wm., river pilot, Stevedore st, Wmn
Murray, —, Leicester st, Carl
Murray, A., 23 James st, Wmn
Murray, Andrew, Domain road, S Y
Murray, Andrew, proprietor of The Economist, &c., 69 Bourke st west
Murray, Ann, Tam o' Shanter hotel, Lothian st, Hot
Murray, Brothers, tailors, &c., 21 Collins st east
Murray, C., 37 Jeffcott st, W M
Murray, D., Station hotel, Napier st, Fcy
Murray, D. W., wood and coal merchant, 16 Little Bourke st west
Murray, Darling, and Murrumbidgee River Steamers' Office, 100 Spencer st
Murray, F., 38 George st, F
Murray, Hugh, undertaker, Madeline st, Carl
Murray, J., painter, Blackwood st, Hot
Murray, J., New Constitution hotel, Lothian st, Hot
Murray, J. G., F
Murray, James, Sydney road, Bk
Murray, James, 22 Market st, Em H
Murray, James, Sackville st, E C
Murray, James, and Co., watch, clock, and chronometer makers, 107 Bourke st east
Murray, John, bootmaker, 63 Elizabeth st
Murray, John, 159 Queensberry st, Hot
Murray, Mrs., Chapel st, Pra
Murray, Mrs., 70 Kerr st, F
Murray, Mrs. A., Mac's hotel, 130 Smith st, E C

Murray, Mrs., 83 Chetwynd st, Hot
Murray, Mrs. M., Stoke st, San
Murray, P., Jeffcott st, W M
Murray, Peter, Flemington road, Hot
Murray, Robert, draper, Hobe st, St K
Murray, Thomas, 62 Cambridge st, E C
Murray, W. H., Faraday st, Carl
Murray, W. S. F., Pent
Murray, Walter, Bedford hotel, corner of Lonsdale and Swanston sts
Murray, Wm., bootmaker, 145 King st
Murray, Wm., Carlisle st east, St K
Murray, Wm., contractor, 49 Three-chain road, Em II
Murray, Wm., Station place, San
Murray, Wm., Harkly st, Carl
Murray, Wm., 91 Kerr st, F
Murray, Wm., 13 Stanley st, W M
Murray's Melbourne Prices Current office, 69 Bourke st west
Morrell, Wm., Ferguson st, Wmn
Murson, J., Ashing st, Bmn
Murtagh, Thomas John, Railway place, San
Museum of Art, at the Public Library, Swanston st
Museum of Natural History, Geology, Economic Geology, Agriculture and Mining, University, Carl
Musika, Fredk. W., baker and confectioner, 61 Nelson place, Wmn
Muskett, C., 78 Bourke st east, and 102 Brunswick st, F
Muspratt, J., Miller st, W M
Musson, J., Pent
Mutimer, Henry, butcher, Moonee ponds, Ess
Myatt, S., Peel st, Hot
Myer, G., grocer, Canning st, Carl
Myers, A., 11 Cardigan st, Carl
Myers and Zox, auctioneers and job warehousemen, 105a and 111 Elizabeth st
Myers, Edward, grocer, 25 Little Lonsdale st east
Myers, J., Station place, San
Myles, Harriet, fruiterer, 162 Bourke st east
Myles, Thomas, brewer, Sackville st, E C

N.

Nagle, —, 45 Lygon st, Carl
Nagle, G. F., registrar, 2 Franklyn st east
Nagle, James, 101 Faraday st, Carl
Nagle, Patrick, 56 Madeline st, Carl
Nairn, Robert, Lothian st, Hot
Nairne, James, 99 Queensberry st, Hot
Nalty, Henry, medical practitioner, 157 Little Bourke st east
Nand, R., Church st, Em II
Nangle, Patrick, cooper, 218 Elizabeth st
Nankervis, James, Harmsworth st, E C
Nankivell, T. J., High st, St K
Napier, John, grocer, 41 Victoria st, Carl

Napier, Thomas, J.P., Ess
Narracott, J., Pent
Nash, —, Provost st, Hot
Nash, A. S., insurance agent, 83 Swanston st
Nash, E., boarding-house, 50 Lonsdale st west
Nash, Henry, 14 Rathdowne st, Carl
Nash, Michael, 41 Faraday st, Carl
Natham and Durham, *Argus* and *Age* agency, and general store, Clarendon st, Em II
Nathan, B., cigar manufacturer, 80 Smith st, E C
Nathan, Bertram, money broker, 89 Swanston st
Nathan, John, 98 Latrobe st east
Nathan, L., Provost st, Hot
Nathan, Mrs. J., Spring st
Nathan, S. D., 49 York st, Em II
Nation, J., and Co., carpenters and cabinet makers, 50 Flinders lane east
National Bank of Australasia, 18 Collins st west
National Building Society, Bank place, Collins st west
National Hall, King William st, F
Naughan, R., painter, 60 Little Oxford st, E C
Naunton, W. B., baker, Charles st, F
Naylor, Jonas, American stables, 61 Victoria st, Carl
Naylor, Joseph, Bouverie st, Carl
Naylor, W., carpenter, Crescent, Btn
Naylor, Wm. H., auctioneers, 46 Collins st east
Neal, Wm., timber merchant, Ess
Nealer, James, Railway hotel, 119 Swanston st
Neare, R., 35 Napier st, F
Neave and Wiseman, woollen warehousemen, 45 Elizabeth st
Neave, Robert, Studley park road
Neck, Charles, 47 Moor st, F
Need, W., Wright lane, Lonsdale st west
Needham, John R., teacher of writing, Elizabeth st
Needham, Louisa, teacher of writing, 84 Elizabeth st
Needham, J. R., junior, teacher of writing, Brunswick st, F
Needle, E., grocer, Chapel st, Pra
Neeley, Henry, 99 Queensberry st, Hot
Neeson, Mrs. A., Butchers' Arms hotel, 97 Elizabeth st
Negus, E., Weston st, Bk
Negus, J., 21 York st, Em II
Neighbour, John, cattle dealer, Flem
Neighbour, H. S., 84 Drummond st, Carl
Neil, F. A., Brunswick road east, Bk
Neild, James E., M.D., 146 Collins st east
Neill, John, 7 Napier st, Em II
Neill, John, Argyle st east, St K
Neill, John, 19 Napier st, Em II

Neill, Pat., 68 York st, Em H
Neill, Robert, Inkerman st, St K
Neill, Robert, Inkerman road, St K
Neill, W., 140 Kerr st, F
Neill, Wm. Punt road, Pra
Neilley, W., secretary to Gipps Land Steam Navigation Company, 35 Bank st east, Em H
Neilson, E., 45 Cobden st, Em H
Neilson, J., 3 Elgin st, Carl
Neilson, Wm., 61 Barkly st, Carl
Nelder, C., coachbuilder, South Audley st, E C
Nelder, Charles, 9 Pelham place, Carl
Nelder, E., grocer, Hoddle st, E C
Nelson, —, 87 Napier st east, Em H
Nelson, E., general dealer, 293 Elizabeth street
Nelson, Horatio G., land and estate agent, 18 Swanston st
Nelson, James, bootmaker, 54 Bourke st west
Nelson, John, 51 Little Nelson st, Wmn
Nelson, John, 53 Baillie st, Hot
Nelson, John G., Rathdowne st, Carl
Nelson, M., Bouverie st, Carl
Nelson, Michael, hawker, 123 Little Bourke st west
Nelson, Mrs., Victoria parade, E C
Nelson, Philip, draper, 135 Little Collins st east
Nelson Reef Quartz Mining Company, 66 Little Collins st west
Nelson, Simon, clothier, 283 Elizabeth st
Nelson, Thomas, locksmith, &c., 118 High st, St K
Nelson, Wm., 31 Villiers st, Hot
Nesbitt, James Patrick, ironmonger, 247 Elizabeth st
Nesbitt, John, 92 Park st, Em H
Ness, Mrs. E., 5 Greeves st, F
Ness, Thomas, 78 Dudley st, W M
Ness, Wm., Rosalyn st, W M
Netherlands Consulate, 49 Collins st west
Nettleship, Wm., 16 Johnston st, E C
Nettleton, Charles, photographer, 19 Madeline and Bouverie sts, Carl
Nettleton, Peter, fellmonger, Victoria st, E C
Neven, J., Fitzroy st, St K
Neville, J. C., Nott st San
New Adventure Gold Mining Company, 9 Elizabeth st
New Alpine Gold Mining Company, 64 Elizabeth st
New Chum Mining Company, office, 37 Market st
Fish Market, corner of Flinders and Swanston sts
New Holland Gold Mining Company, 9 Elizabeth st
New, Rev. Isaac, Grey st, E M
New South Wales Marine Assurance Co., 80 Collins st west

New Wesleyan College, Punt road, 8 Y
New Zealand Insurance Co.'s Agency, 37 Flinders st west
Newberry, Charles, Chapel st, Pra
Newbigin, Edward, 97 Bridge road, Rd
Newbigin, J., 71 Wellington st
Newbry, F. E., Clyde st, St K
Newbury, Charles H., cab proprietor, 82 Coventry st, Em H
Newbury, W. H., bootmaker, Napier st, Em H
Newcome, Simon, Douglas parade, Wmn
Newell, A. H., Avoca st, S Y
Newell and Co., merchants, 28 King st
Newenham, Henry, 16 Dryburgh st, Hot
Newham, Thomas, and Co., land and estate agents, 22 Bridge road, Rd
Newhouse, Thomas, Franklyn st, W M
Newing, John, Pelham st, Carl
Newing, Thomas Robert, oil and colorman, 182 and 184 Bourke st east
Newlando, John, shipping agent, Cole's wharf
Newman, A., draper, 181 Wellington st, E C
Newman, Captain W. H., Morris st, South Wmn
Newman, Charles, Haw
Newman, Charles T., confectioner, 159 Brunswick st, F
Newman, Edward, 27 Regent st, F
Newman, George, 83 Barkly st, Carl
Newman, George, Railway place, San
Newman, George, bootmaker, 190 Church st, Rd
Newman, Henry, watchmaker and jeweller, 123 Elizabeth st
Newman, John, restaurant keeper, 31 Bourke st west
Newman, S. C., engineer, 151 Wellington st, E C
Newman, Wm. Henry, undertaker and furniture dealer, Bay st, San
Newman, Mrs., Waterloo st, St K
Newnham, George, butcher, Chapel st, Pra
Newport, Mrs., dressmaker, &c., 67 Gertrude st, F
Newson, James, Myross, Saltwater river
Newton, Hibbert, barrister, 84 Temple court, Collins st west
Newton, M., livery stables, Franklyn st east
Newton, Mrs., 68 Rowena parade, Rd
Newton, Thomas, 135 Raglan st, Em H
Newton, Thomas, 149 Little Bourke st west
Newton, Thomas, contractor, 66 High st, St K
Newton, Thomas, Miller st, Bk
Neylan, D., 240 Swan st, Rd
Niall, John, Nag's Hotel, Queen st
Niall, Peter, Limerick Arms hotel, Park st west, Em H
Niall, Peter, Punt road, Pra

Nichol, George, Studley park
Nichol, James, coachbuilder, 44 Latrobe st west
Nichol, R., 10 Lincoln square, Carl
Nichol, W., Reilly st. F
Nichol, Wm., 69 Clarendon st, Em H
Nicholas, Gregory. 16 Fitzroy st, F
Nicholas, H. C., music warehouse, High st, St K
Nicholas, James, 17 Drummond st, Carl
Nicholas, James, 43 Montague st, Em H
Nicholas, James, Dorcas st west, Em H
Nicholl, A., 88 Latrobe st east
Nicholl, Allan, Victoria st east, Bk
Nicholl, J., 86 Johnston st, F
Nicholl, John, 61 Rathdowne st, Carl
Nicholl, Robert, 6 Bank st east, Em H
Nicholls, Charles F., mining agent, 28 Collins st east
Nicholls, Charles, draper and P. O., Haw
Nicholls, George, 35 Thompson st, Wmn
Nicholls, George M., 136 Church st, Rd
Nicholls, Wm. T., Wellington st, Rd
Nichols, —, Wellington st, Rd
Nichols, —, Prince's st, F
Nichols and Cooper, bootmakers, Little Lonsdale st east
Nichols, Frederick W., Dudley st, W M
Nichols, George, bookseller, stationer, and news agent, 2 Bourke st west
Nichols, J., River bank
Nichols, Joseph, bootmaker, 197 Victoria parade, E C
Nicholson, Alexander, Haw
Nicholson, B. R., and Co., merchants and shipowners, 8 Elizabeth st
Nicholson, Benjamin B., Dalgety st, St K
Nicholson, D., Graham st, San
Nicholson, Durham, 26 Collins st east
Nicholson, Germain, grocer, 69 Collins st east
Nicholson, J. B., 62 Napier st, Em H
Nicholson, J., Elgin st, Carl
Nicholson, James, blacksmith, Hoddle st, E C
Nicholson, James, Arden st, Hot
Nicholson, Jeptha, Dow st, Sanh
Nicholson, John, 242 King st
Nicholson, Joseph, agricultural implement maker, 21 Bouverie st, Carl
Nicholson, Miss, 40 Argyle st, F
Nicholson, Neil, Eleanor st, Fcy
Nicholson, Richard, 202 Gore st, F
Nicholson, Sir A., Rowena parade, Rd
Nicholson, Wm., engineer, 60 Ann st, Wmn
Nicholson, Wm., 55 Thompson st, Wmn
Nicholson, Wm. H., Fulton st, St K
Nichus, Fritz, 138 Little Lonsdale st east
Nickin, Robert, Grange road, Tk
Nicol, John, Australia Felix hotel, 231 Lonsdale st west
Nicol, Walter, private boarding-house, 66 Flinders lane east

Nicol, Allan, broker, 26 Collins st east
Nicolas, Captain M., Nott st, San
Nicole, F., watchmaker, 133 Little Collins st east
Nicoll, Alex., tailor, 120, 122, and 124 Elizabeth st, and 86 and 88 Latrobe st east
Nicoll, Wm., Arden st, Hot
Nicolson, Charles Hope, superintendent of police, detective force, Little Collins st east
Nightengale, T., Hawke st, W M
Nightingale, Edward, carton maker, 94 Russell st
Nihill, Mary, Plough Inn, 123 King st
Nimmo, John, 69 Nelson road, Em H
Nimmo, Wm., Gurner st, St K
Ninnis, Thomas D., watchmaker, &c., 137 Bourke st east
Niven, D., and Co., iron and brass founders, 235 Victoria parade, E C
Niven, David, Chambers st, S Y
Niven, Wm., George st, E M
Nixon, J., Bay st, San
Nixon, James, 15 Dorcas st, Em H
Nixon, Thomas, 28 Coventry st west, Em H
Noall, Wm., stock and share broker, 34 Collins st west
Noar, Henry, bookseller and stationer, 59 George st, F
Noard, Wm., 55 Little Bourke st west
Nobbs, James, Hoddle st, E C
Nobbs, Wm., Miller st, Bk
Noble, A., 7 Queensberry st, Carl
Noble, John, store, Church st, Rd
Noble, Kay, Barry st, Carl
Noble, S. W., coffee roaster, 279 Elizabeth street
Noble, T., comedian, 145 Wellington st, E C
Noble, Thomas, auctioneer and land agent, 89 Clarendon st
Noble, Thomas, 13 Capel st, W M
Noble, W., 72 Moor st, F
Noel, Mrs., ladies' seminary, 123 Rathdowne st, Carl
Noel, Wriothesley B., chief commissioner of Insolvent estates, Studley park
Nolan, Luke, pottery, Bank road east, Bk
Nolan, John, Yorkshire Family hotel, Punt road, Pra
Nolan, Miss, Howard st, Hot
Nolan, Thomas C., solicitor, 55 Bourke st west
Noonan, James, Stanley st, W M
Noonan, James, contractor, 50 Dudley st, W M
Noonan, P., Clare Castle hotel, 84 Stephen st
Noone, —, 54 Bank st east, Em H
Noonen, Michael, dairyman, 18 Coventry st, Em H
Norman, Mrs., Nicholson st, Carl

126 Nor MELBOURNE O'Br

Norman, Mrs., 89 Bridport st east, Em H
Norman, W. J., cabinetmaker, carver, and gilder, 170 Elizabeth st
Norman, Wm. G., grocer, 75 Faraday st, Carl
Normoyle, J. J., Formosa terrace, St K
Norrie, John, Punt road, S Y
Norris, Christopher, butcher, 7 and 9 Little Bourke st west
Norris, James, 110 Fitzroy st, F
Norris, M., 166 Victoria parade, E M
Norris, Thomas, saddler, Elizabeth st
Norrish, John, 70a Young st, F
Norriss, Robert, Nicholson st, Carl
Norsworthy, J., butcher, Bay st, Bth
North China Insurance Co., 31 Queen st
North Grenville Mining Co., 122 Collins st west
North Melbourne Building Society, Errol st, Hot
North, Miss, Barkly st, St K, and Flem
North Specimen Hill Quartz Mining Co., 5 Collins st west
North, W., 184 Russell st
North, Wm., 133 Little Lonsdale st east
Northcott, John, bootmaker, 239 Elizabeth st
Northern Insurance Company, 105 Collins st west
Northmore, G., bootmaker, Church st, Rd
Norton, Charles, architect, 1 Spring st
Norton, Graham, and Co., lighter agents, 83 Flinders st west
Norton, H. E., Rowena parade, Rd
Norton, H. F., Haw
Noseda, Francis, japanner, 193 Little Collins st east
Norton, R., tailor, 500 Russell st
Norton, R. F., 89 Napier st, F
Norwood, Ed., 61 Drummond st, Carl
Notley, Charles, Notley's Toorak hotel, Gardiner's creek road, Tk
Notman, A., baker, 46 Clarendon st, Em H
Notman, Geo., coachbuilder, 29 Victoria st, Carl
Nott, E., butcher, Haw
Nott, Edwin, mattrass maker, Commercial road, Pra
Nott, J., Pelham st, Carl
Nott, James, carpenter, 81 Dorcas st, Em H
Nott, James E., Dow st, San
Nutt, Thomas, greengrocer, Peel st, Pra
Nott, Thomas H., confectioner, off 173 Little Bourke st east
Norwell, Robert, 41 Cecil st, Wmn
Nowlan, M., wood yard, 42 Stanley st, W M
Nowlan, Michael, Canning st, Carl
Nowlan, Patrick, Lothian st, Hot
Noyes and Reed, stock, station, land, and estate agents, 68 and 70 Queen st
Noyes, Arthur Ryder, Caroline st, S Y
Nudd, Edwin, 38 Johnston st, F

Nugent, John, 87 Coventry st east, Em H
Nugent, John H., boot and shoe dealer, 184 Smith st, E C
Nugent, John, 7 Bouverie st, Carl
Nugent, Martin, grocer, 24 Queensberry st, Carl
Nunn, Phillip Henry, 64 George st, E M
Nunn, Wm., Stoke st, San
Nutt and Murphy, solicitors, 24 William street
Nutt, Robert Wm., Caroline st, S Y
Nuttall, James, painter, 170 George st, F
Nuttall, James, Cape st, Hold
Nutting and Lewis, wholesale tinsmiths, japanners, &c., 15 Little Collins st east
Nutting, G., 52 Rosslyn st, W M
Nutting, Miss, dressmaker, 61 Elgin st, Carl
Nuttman, A., dealer, 155 Brunswick st, F
Nyberg Brothers, merchants, 40 Little Collins st west, and 6 Victoria buildings, Queen st
Nye, James, Abbotsford st, E C

O.

Oakford, Thomas, Wellington st, St K
Oakley, E., Roden st, W M
Oakley, G. H., Williams road, Pra
Oakley, John, glass importer, &c., 102 Lonsdale st east, 175 Swanston st, and Faraday st, Carl
Oakley, Mrs., 131 Victoria st, Hot
Oakley, R., Williams road, Pra
Oakley, Wm., 15 Johnston st, E C
Oakshott, St. John, 37 Gertrude st, F
Oastler, J., and Co., auctioneers, 25 Lygon st, Carl
Oaten, Charles, 124 Gertrude st, F
Oaten, J. P., grocer, Hoddle st, E C
Oaten, James, manufacturing saddler, 37 Lonsdale st west
Oaten, John, 75 Smith st, F
Oaten, Mrs., Victoria st, E C
Oates, —, teacher, Nth
Oates, J., Kerr st, F
Oates, Richard, Dryburgh st, Hot
Oates, Thomas, Vere st, E C
O'Brian, Patrick, 25 Victoria st, Carl
O'Brian, T., boarding house, 105 Lonsdale street
O'Brien and Gillott, solicitors, 114 Elizabeth st
O'Brien, Daniel, Flemington road, Hot
O'Brien, Henry, 22 Bouverie st, Carl
O'Brien, James, grocer, 116 Little Collins st west
O'Brien, John, Sleight's lane, 58 Little Collins st east
O'Brien, John, 93 Victoria st, Carl
O'Brien, John, 43 Park st west, Em H
O'Brien, Michael, 110 Latrobe st east
O'Brien, Mrs., greengrocer, 67 Bank st west, Em H

O'Brien, Mrs., Bedford st, Hot
O'Brien, P., schoolmaster, Cape st, Held
O'Brien, P., Vale st, Hot
O'Brien, P., 8 Bank st east, Em H
O'Brien, P. K., J.P., Haw
O'Brien, Patrick, Commercial lane, Bourke st east
O'Brien, R. G., Richmond terrace, Rd
O'Brien, Simon, Higlett st, Rd
O'Brien, Thomas, 55 St. Andrew st, F
O'Brien, Thomas, dairyman, McKillop st, Bourke st west
O'Brien, Thomas, Shamrock hotel, 81 Napier st, F
O'Brien, Thomas, police sergeant, Nott st, San
O'Bryan, C. Palmerston, Madeline st, Carl
Observer office, Smith st, F
Oberne, George, 32 Grant st, Em H
O'Callaghan and Swan, wholesale grocers, &c., 149 and 151 Bourke st east
O'Callaghan, Denis, Crown hotel, Lonsdale st west
O'Callaghan, O., 95 Faraday st, Carl
O'Callaghan, Thomas, Strangers' Home hotel, 163 Swanston st
Occleston, Thomas J., cork merchant, 8½ Little Collins st east
Occolowitz, Wm., and Co., watchmakers 58½ Bourke st east
Och, Martin, boot and shoe maker, 141 Flinders st west
O'Connell, M., 89 Lygon st, Carl
O'Connell, P., tailor, 32 Lonsdale st west
O'Connell, Richard, 23 Little Lonsdale st west
O'Conner, James, Young st, F
O'Conner, John, Madeline st, Carl
O'Conner, Martin, Dryburgh st, Hot
O'Conner, Murtough, Acland st, St K
O'Conness, Catherine, dressmaker, 138 Queen st
O'Connor, A., solicitor, 5 Neave's buildings, Collins st east
O'Connor, Anthony, 262 Collins st east
O'Connor, D. P., Fitzroy st, St K
O'Connor, Daniel Francis, auctioneer and estate agent, 55 Bourke st west
O'Connor, J., 84 Napier st, F
O'Connor, J., Bedford st, Hot
O'Connor, M., 16 Pelham st, Carl
O'Connor, Mrs., Peel st, Pra
O'Connor, Mrs., 14 Victoria st west, W M
O'Connor, Nicholas, chemist and druggist, Bridge road, Rd
O'Connor, P., Bedford st, Hot
O'Connor, T., bootmaker, Sydney road, Bk
O'Connor, Thomas, Lothian st, Hot
Odd Fellows, A. I. O., secretary, Commercial road, Pra
Odd Fellows G. U. O., secretary, 117 Staredore st, W win

Odd Fellows' Hall, (M.U.), 205 Swanston st, and Pascoe st, W nn
Ohlie, Richard, Burgundy st, Held
Oddy, Ezekiel, boot warehouse, 203 Swanston st
Oddy, Huston, fellmonger, 216 Elizabeth street
O'Dea, James, Franklyn st west, W M
Odell, Rev. Thomas, 122 Little Lonsdale st west
Odgers, Mrs., 143 Moray st, Em H
Odgers, W. H., secretary Civil Service Board of Examiners, Haw
Odon, Theodore, shoemaker, 161 Stephen street
O'Donnell, John, bootmaker, 95 Brunswick st, F
O'Donnell, P., Nott st, San
O'Donnell, P., 324 Brunswick st, F
O'Donnell, W., bootmaker, 127 Fitzroy st, F
O'Donohue, John, grocer, 122 Little Collins st west
O'Donovan, B. J., Moor st, F
O'Donovan, J., grocer, 69 Madeline st, Carl
O'Driscoll, Rev. J., Montague st, Em H
O'Dwyer, —, butcher, Pent
Oelrich, Augustus, undertaker, &c., 253 Church st, Rd
Oels, Louis, saddler, 90 Victoria st, Rd
O'Farrell, A., 56 Kerr st, F
O'Farrell, Hugh, George st east, F M
O'Farrell, John, Moreland st, Fcy
O'Farrell, M., 250 Johnston st, E C
O'Farrell, Mrs. E., Jolimont square, E M
O'Farrell, Patrick, Palmerston st, Carl
Offord, W., veterinary surgeon, Cremorne st, Rd
O'Flaherty, Martin, Sackville st, F C
O'Flannagan, C., 77 Franklyn st west, W M
Oftwinning, —, school, Bridge road, Rd
Ogbern, Mrs, Lygon st, Carl
Ogbourne, George, butcher, Kew
Ogbourne, Henry, Kew
Ogden E., Vine hotel, Moray st, Em H
Ogden, James, 242 Moray st, Em H
Ogden, John, 91 Lygon st, Carl
Ogden, John, Palmerston st, Carl
Ogg, Charles, chemist, Gardiner's creek road, Pra
Ogilvy, David, solicitor, Punt road, S Y
Ogilvy, John S., accountant, 65 Queen st
O'Gorman, —, draper, 110 Victoria st, Rd
O'Gorman, Cornelius, 218 Little Collins st east
O'Gorman, John, ironmonger, 32 Post Office place
O'Grady, Michael, M.L.A., manager Australian Alliance Assurance Co., 2 Collins st west
O'Grady, Thomas, contractor, 50 Drummond st, Carl

O'Hagan, —, house painter, Rouse st, San
O'Hagan, J., house painter, Bay st, San
O'Hagan, P. F., teacher, Lyons st, Wms
O'Halloran, —, bootmaker, 86 Bridge road, Rd
O'Halloran, D., Union st, Rk
O'Halloran, Denis, City hotel, Bourke st east
O'Halloran, Edward M. T., St K
O'Halloran, T., 186 Drummond st, Carl
O'Hanlon, Wm., carpenter, Palmerston st, Carl
O'Hara, P., potato dealer, Flemington rd, Hot
O'Haran, D., 155 Cambridge st, E C
O'Hare, Edward, grocer, Berkeley st, Carl
O'Hea, Rev. Charles, Pent
O'Hea, Wm. J., High st, Pra
O'Hoy, John, carriers' agent, 74 Little Bourke st east
O'Keefe, M. S., storekeeper, Yarra st, Held
O'Keiffe, Thomas, Inkerman st, St K
O'Kelly, Clarke and Brooks, mining agents and hotel brokers, 54 Bourke st east
O'Klee, Wm., Arden st, Hot
Oldfield and Lindley, timber merchants, 108 Nicholson st, F
Oldfield, Law, builder and contractor, 57 Elgin st, Carl
Oldfield, Robert, pottery works, Moreland st, Fcy
Oldfield, Wm., 163 Cardigan st, Carl
Oldham, G., Napier st, Em H
Oldham, James, 35 Leveson st, Hot
Oldham, John, solicitor, 49 Collins st west
Oldham, M. W., 93 Flinders lane east
Oldham, R., contractor, 39 Cecil st east
Olds, Wm., 121 Bouverie st, Carl
O'Leary, David, Wellington st, Rd
O'Leary, Dennis, cooper, 7 Little Lonsdale st west
O'Leary, L., 21 Pelham st, Carl
O'Leary, —, Ralston st, S Y
O'Leary, M. W., 93 Flinders lane east
O'Leary, Mary, 204 Little Collins st east
Olifant, Thomas, 19 Spencer st
Oliver, A., Haddle st, E C
Oliver, Charles, bootmaker, Chapel st, Pra
Oliver, James, ship and house joiner, 261 King st north
Oliver, Joseph, 12 Queensberry st, Carl
Oliver, R., butcher, Nth
Oliver, W., Star Inn, Wellington st, St K
Oliver, W., grocer, 14 Wellington st, E C
Ollard, H., solicitor, 11 Palmer st, F
Ollis, Eliza, Apollo hotel, 104 Flinders lane east
Olliver, A., timber merchant, Ireland st, W M
Ollivera, Jos., 12 Queensberry st, Carl
Olney, Robert W., Barkly st, St K
O'Loghlen, Brien, barrister, 4 Temple court, Collins st west

Olsen, F., bootmaker, 132 Spring st
Omand, John, Hotham st, E M
Omand and Miller, corn factors, 60 Bridge road, Rd
Omand, Peter, Villiers st, Hot
O'Mara, L., blacksmith, Vine st, Reid
O'Meara, M., tailor, 71 Bouverie st, Carl
O'Meara, Mary, fruiterer, 51 Lonsdale st west
O'Meara, P., Palmerston st, Carl
O'Meary, W., Clyde st, St K
O'Mullane, Mrs., 5 Wellington terrace, Wellington parade, E M
Omond, J., Kew
Omond, Robert, cooper, 261 Elizabeth st
O'Neal, —, Queen st
O'Neal, —, 189 Queen st
O'Neal, J., bootmaker, 27 Cardigan st, Carl
Onealy, Patrick, Pelham st, Carl
O'Neil and Co., shipwrights, &c., River side south
O'Neil, C., Union st, Bk
O'Neil, D., Union st, Bk
O'Neil, D., Darling st, Pra
O'Neil, H. J. P., North road, Dtn
O'Neil, J., Luscomb st, Bk
O'Nell, R., 51 Pelham st, Carl
O'Nelle, John, Abbotsford st, Hot
O'Nelle, Daniel, 28 Swanston st
O'Nelle, P., Canning st, Carl
O'Neill, Daniel, 9 Leveson st, Hot
O'Neill, Denis, Pent
O'Neill, J., 37 Elgin st, Carl
O'Neill, M., Barkly st, Carl
O'Neill, Mrs., 1 Leicester st, Carl
Opie, John, boot and shoe dealer, 133 Brunswick st, F
Oppenheimer and Co., merchants, Manchester lane, Collins st east
Ord, —, 7 Cundell st, F
Ord, R. J., grocer, Cremorne st, Rd
Ord, W. B., 7 Cundell st, F
Orchard, Mrs., 80 Ferrars st, Em H
Orderly Room, Royal Engineers, Lygon st, Carl
Orderly Rooms: Chapel st, Pra; Osborne st, Pra; Gisborne st, E M; Chetwynd st, Hot; Grattan st, Carl; Bridge road, Rd; Napier st, Fcy; and Gertrude st, F
O'Regan, C., clothes dealer, 79 Stephen st
O'Regan, James, butcher, 163 Little Lonsdale st east
O'Regan, James, 154 Russell st
O'Regan, Michael, butcher, 219 Elizabeth street
O'Regan, Thomas, 16 Bridport st, Em H
O'Reilly, Bernard, Canning st, Carl
O'Reilly, Mrs., Esplanade, St K
Organ, H., Berkeley st, Carl
Oriel, Thomas, Peel st, Pra
Oriental Bank Corporation, 13 Queen st
Oriental Rice Company; office, Eldon Chambers, Collins st west

Oriental Rice Mills, 5 Flinders st east
Orkney, James, Esplanade, St K
Orleman, Philip, Oxford st, Hot
Orme, Frederick, brewer, Chapel st, Prn
Orme, James, baker, 101 Coventry st, Em H
Orme, Rd., Berkely st, Carl
Ormiston, Wm., 121 Rosslyn st, W M
Ormiston, Andrew, Curzon st, Hot
Ormond, James, Esplanade, St K
Ormond, James, Erskine villa, Nth
Ormond, John, Prospect Hill hotel, Kew
Ormond, T., Kew
Ormond, Thomas, grocer, 173 Victoria st, E C
O'Rorke, J. R., Neptune st, St K
O'Rourke, Hugh, 37 Market st, Em H
O'Rourke, M., Fitzroy st, F
Orphan Asylums, Em H
Orr, J., 73 Napier st, F
Orr, J., M.L.A., Parliament house
Orr, John, 76 Victoria st west, W M
Orr, John, Esplanade, St K
Orrick, W., 51 Hanover st, F
Orton, J. W., Raglan st, st, Em H
Osborn, —, Hoddle st, Rd
Osborn, Cushing, and Co., importers and commission agents, 44 William st
Osborn, D. A., St K
Osborn, J., Davis st, Prn
Osborn, John Robert, accountant, Clark st, Abbotsford
Osborn, Mrs., 21 Cardigan st, Carl
Osborne, D., 7 Park st west, Em H
Osborne, James T., hairdresser and tobacconist, 23 Elizabeth st
Osborne, M. W., tea broker, Queen st, and Argyle st west, St K
Osborne, Thomas, corner Lonsdale and Spencer sts
Osborne, W., Highett st, Rd
Osborne, W., hairdresser, 60 Clarendon st, Em H
Osborne, Wm., 2 Trafalgar place, Hot
Osgool, R., Cardigan st, Carl
O'Shanassy, Hon. John, M.L.A., Haw
O'Shanassy, J., bootmaker, 18 Madeline st, Carl
O'Shanessy, F. F. R., Fitzroy st, St K
O'Shanessy, P., 398 Lygon st, Carl
O'Shannassy, Maurice, Hibernian hotel, 8 Little Lonsdale st east
O'Shannessy, Miles, Fitzroy st, St K
O'Shaughnessy, Patrick, Kew hotel, Kew
O'Shea, James, painter and decorator, 105 Queensberry st, Hot
O'Shea, G., Welsh Harp hotel, 116 King street
O'Shea, James, 28 Bank st east, Em H
O'Shea, John, painter, &c., 262 Elizabeth street
O'Shea, L., Eureka hotel, corner Victoria and Church sts, Rd
Osmond, O., Bay st, Bin

Osmond, Walter Ryle, compositor, 36 Moray place, Dorcas st, Em H
Ostler, James, Bay st, Btn
Ostler, Jas., auctioneer and commission agent, 81 Collins st east
O'Sullivan, J., Kerry hotel, corner King st and Flinders lane
O'Sullivan, Pat., butcher, 167 Bourke st west
Oswald and Inglis, ship chandlers, &c., 123 Flinders st west
Oswald, John, 155 Albert st, E M
Oswald, John, bootmaker, 122 Little Bourke st east
Oswald, R., Park st, Btn
Oswin, J., Kew
Oswin, Wm., Kew
Otago Marine Insurance Company, 82 Collins st west
Otago Steam Ship Company, agents' office, 16 Elizabeth st
O'Toole, Joseph, Palmerston st, Carl
O'Toole, P., Bridge Road hotel, 94 Bridge road, Rd
Otter, Robert, Greenhythe, Fcy
Otter, Wm., Greenhythe, Fcy
Ovens Gold Fields Water Company, 64 Elizabeth st
Ovens, Walter, baker, Moonee ponds, Ess
Ovenson, J., 36 Queensberry st, Hot
Overend, B., Sydney road, Bk
Ovran, Mrs. C., 6 Cobden st, Em H
Owen, Dudgeon, and Arnell, tobacco manufacturers, 159 Elizabeth st
Owen, E. F., Elgin st, Carl
Owen, Evan F., 75 Young st, F
Owen, H. Fountain, and Co., wine and spirit merchants, 29 Flinders lane west
Owen, J., Mount Erica, Prn
Owen, John, gardener, Moonee ponds, Ess
Owen, Mrs., 32 Leicester st, Carl
Owens, John, 123 Stevedore st, Wmn
Owston, Wm., and Co., merchants, 108 Bourke st west
Owston, W., Dalgety st, St K
Oxford, George, Marian st, F
Oxley, —, grocer, 230 Wellington st, E C
Oxley, A., Rowena parade, Rd
Oxley, Charles, Pelham st, Carl
Oxley, J., plumber, York st, Em H
Oxtoby, Charles C., Alma st east, St K

P.

Pablo Fanque, equestrian, Carson's cottages, 138 Collins st east
Pace, G. T., 36 Chetwynd st, H
Pacific Fire and Marine Insurance Company, 60 Collins st west
Packman, J., Sydney road, Bk
Packman, S., 39 Gore st, F
Padbury, John, carpenter, Kew
Page, E., cigar manufacturer, 58 Lygon st, Carl

Page, Henry Fleet, Palmer st, F
Page, James, Galloway Arms hotel, 90 Johnston st, E C
Page, James, 76 Johnston st, E C
Page, James, 78 Park st east, Em H
Page, James, 101 Rose st, F
Page, Martin, inspector of police, 57 St. David st, F
Page, R., Wmn
Page, Wm., Rennie st, Fcy
Pain, Charles Charlton, merchant, Condell's lane, Post Office place
Pain, George, Sydney road, Bk
Pain, Mrs., French laundress, Pelham st, Carl
Pain, W., 84 Rose st, F
Paine, H. E., 8 Berkeley st, Carl
Paine, Wm., Fail-Me-Never hotel, 131 Flinders st east
Painham, W. O., Church st, Rd
Painters and Paperhangers' Society, Trades' Hall, Lygon st, Carl
Paley, Edward, medical superintendent of Lunatic Asylum, Yarra Bend
Paling, Richard John, music seller and pianoforte importer, 35 Collins st east
Paliscini, Jos., wire-worker, Caroline st, S Y
Palk, Mrs., 107 Raglan st east, Em H
Palmer, —, 64 Montague st, Em H
Palmer and Hedderwick, solicitors, &c., 28 William st
Palmer, Charles, Dalgety st, St K
Palmer, D. C., Octavia st, St K
Palmer, Edward, High st, Pra
Palmer, George, 26 Loveson st, Hot
Palmer, H., Wellington st, St K
Palmer, H., bricklayer and plasterer, Rackville st, E C
Palmer, H. P., Alma st east, St K
Palmer, James, Barkly st, Fcy
Palmer, James, 115 Bank st west, Em H
Palmer, Mrs., Garden st, Pra
Palmer, S., Kew
Palmer, Sir James F., President Legislative Council, Haw
Palmer, T. W., judge's associate, Supreme Court
Palmer, Wm., Mercantile hotel, corner of King and Flinders sts
Palmer, Wm., dairy, Stoke st, San
Palmer, Wm., Kerr st, F
Palmer, Wm., printer and engraver, 41 Swanston st
Panama, New Zealand, and Australian Royal Mail Company, 4 Elizabeth st
Pannifex, Maximilian, insurance and advertising agent, 46 Elizabeth st
Panton, J. A., police magistrate, Alphington
Panrall, J., Grey st, E M
Paragelli, A., River bank, Rd
Parchum, Captain, 108 York st east, Em H

Panice, Charles Caygill, dentist, 79 Bourke st east
Parer and Arenas, restaurant keepers, 40 Bourke st east
Park, Andrew, 116 Johnston st, F
Park, James, Punt road, Rd
Parke, B., Wheatsheaf hotel, Brunswick st, F
Parker, Alex., 99 Cremorne st, Rd
Parker, B., Wheatsheaf hotel, 69 Rose st, F
Parker Brothers, Fitzroy brewery, Cecil st, F
Parker, Charles, and Co., grocers, 189 Clarendon st, Em H
Parker, D., Lennox st, Rd
Parker, G. K., 154 Bourke st east
Parker, Henry, 104 Johnston st, E C
Parker, Hugh, Caroline st, S Y
Parker, James, grocer, 79 Madeline st, Carl
Parker, James, contractor, 13 Smith st, F
Parker, James, Albert st, E M
Parker, John, Provost st, Hot
Parker, John J., bricklayer, &c., 90 Little Collins st west, and Blenheim st, St K
Parker, Mrs., Alphingstone
Parker, Mrs., draper, Sydney road, Bk
Parker, Mrs. J., Medway st, Fcy
Parker, Richard, carpenter, 120 Little Bourke st west
Parker, Thomas, baker, Hoddle st, E C
Parker, Thomas A., hatter, 210 Bourke st east
Parker, Thomas J., shipping agent and broker (Geelong Steam Navigation), 11 Market st
Parker, W., 82 York st, Em H
Parker, W., shipwright, Railway place, San
Parker, W. H., 20 Rathdowne st, Carl
Parkin, John, Oxford and Cambridge hotel, Rowena parade, Rd
Parkin, John A., Quarryman's Arms hotel, Church st, Rd
Parkin, R., 18 Oxford st, E C
Parkington, B. L., British hotel, 108 Queen st
Parks, J., 9 Victoria st, Hot
Parks, Thomas, corner of Elgin and Cardigan sts, Carl
Parlane, John, Illawarra st, Wmn
Parlett, C., 143 Johnston st
Parlon, L., Victoria st west, Bk
Parnecott, George, off 112 Little Lonsdale st west
Paroissien, C., painter, &c., Church st, Rd
Parr, D., Charles st, F
Parrey, George, Gipps st east, E M
Parrott, T. E., Bouverie st, Carl
Parry, —, Alma st west, St K
Parry, Charles, Moor st, Fcy
Parry, David, 49 Faraday st, Carl
Parry, Hugh, Highett st, Rd

Parry, John, joiner and builder, off 85 Little Collins st west
Parry, Mrs. D., Southampton st, Fcy
Parry, Thomas, 90 Lygon st, Carl
Parslow, Thomas, oil and colourman, 313 Elizabeth st
Parsons, Charles, Patterson st, E C
Parsons, G., St. Andrew st, Btn
Parsons, George, baker, 212 Church st, Rd
Parsons, George, blacksmith, Flem
Parsons, J., St. Andrew st, Btn
Parsons, James, Flem
Parsons, John, Chetwynd st, W M
Parsons, John, Bay st, San
Parsons, L., St. Andrew st, Btn
Parsons, S., tailor, 42 Victoria st, Rd
Parsons, Thomas, barrister, 27 Temple court
Parton and Hellins, solicitors, 28 Queen st
Parton, J., Alma st east, St K
Partridge, F. J., 90 Bank st west, Em H
Pascoe, John, 120 Johnston st, F
Paser, Julius, billiard table maker, 196 Little Bourke st east
Pash, George, 65 Cecil st, Em H
Pashley, G., Hugh st, St K
Pashley, G., Gasometer hotel, Smith st, E C
Pasker, J., 75 York st, Em H
Passmore, Joseph C., Devonshire hotel, New st, Btn
Paterson, Archibald and Wm., photographic artists, 5 Bourke st east
Paterson, E., 124 George st, F
Paterson, J. C., 76 Collins st east
Paterson, James, coal merchant, 139 Flinders st west
Paterson, John, grocer, 215 King st
Paterson, John, 50 Dorcas st, Em H
Paterson, Mrs. Emma, confectioner, 249 Bourke st east
Paterson, Ray, Palmer, and Co., warehousemen, 31 to 35 Flinders lane west
Paterson, Robert, 24 Curzon st, Hot
Paterson, Wm., photographer, 57 Bourke st east
Paton, Andrew, builder, 164 William st
Paton, J., ironmonger, 84 Queensberry st, Hot
Paton, James, 217 Albert st, E M
Paton, James, 25 Perry st, E C
Paton, John, 40 Rathdowne st, Carl
Paton, N., 57 Leveson st, Hot
Paton, Wm., 34 Lothian st, Hot
Patrick, Charles, cab proprietor, 111 Argyle st, F
Patrick, K., grocer, 2 Argyle st, F
Patrick, K., grocer, 233 Smith st, F
Patrick, Miss, Wellington st, St K
Patten, T., Pelham st, Carl
Patten, W., 119 Park st west, Em H
Patterson, Ann, storekeeper, Nicholson st, Fcy
Patterson, D., sailmaker, River-side south

Patterson, Donald, Villiers st, Hot
Patterson, Hugh, Barry st, Carl
Patterson, J., Nicholson st, Fcy
Patterson, J., storekeeper, Nicholson st, F
Patterson, James, 160 Moor st, F
Patterson, James, M.D., surgeon, Robe st, St K
Patterson, James, Lennox st, Rd
Patterson, Mrs., Barkly st, St K
Patterson, Mrs., 14 Bank st west, Em H
Patterson, Mrs., 3 Carlton st, Carl
Patterson, M., sailmaker, Clifford st, W mn
Patterson, W., Abbott st, W M
Patterson, W., Ashling st, Btn
Patterson, W., Corry st, Cardigan st, Carl
Patterson, W., 94 York st east, Em H
Patterson, Wm., Pelham st, Carl
Patterson, Wm., photographer, 66 Latrobe st east
Pattison, W., Peel st, Pra
Patton, David, draper, 315 Elizabeth st
Paul, J., 42 Chetwynd st, Hot
Paul, Mrs., Harcourt st, Hot
Paul, Rev. Arthur, Alma st east, St K
Paulett, T. A., Bond st, E C
Paulin, E., 123 Moray st, Em H
Paulin, James, greengrocer, 156 Clarendon st, Em H
Pausacker and Evans, portmanteau manufacturers, 117 Lonsdale st west
Pavey, Joseph, greengrocer, 87 Leveson st, Hot
Pavey, Thomas, solicitor, 60 Collins st west
Pawley, G., 93 Moor st, F
Paston, H., Ralston st, S Y
Paxton, Robert, 178 Moray st, Em H
Paxton, Wm., 62 Little Nelson st, W mn
Paydon, A., van proprietor, Swan st, Rd
Paynder, Robert, Austin st, Fcy
Payne, —, 35 Johnston st
Payne, Captain, Tennyson st, St K
Payne, Charles, Kew
Payne, Charles B., Dover road, W mn
Payne, Charles, Barry st, Carl
Payne, G., 168 Kerr st, F
Payne, G., 74 Johnston st, F
Payne, G. W., sign writer, 203 Victoria parade, E C
Payne, J., Bay st, Btn
Payne, J. W., painter and paperhanger, Sackville st, E C
Payne, John, Red Lion hotel, 104 Lonsdale st west
Payne, John, tailor, Barkly st, Carl
Payne, Lieutenant, 31 Dover road, W mn
Payne, Mrs., Gardiner's creek road, Pra
Payne, R., Chapel st, Pra
Payne, Robert, Fitzgerald st, Pra
Payne, S. J., Kew
Payne, S. W., tobacconist, 75 Gertrude st, F
Payne, Thomas, Gardiner's creek road, Pra

Payne, Thomas B., 35 Queen st
Payter, Henry, Cole st, Wmn
Peace, Joseph, bootmaker, 82 Elizabeth st north
Peach, Mrs., milliner, 197 Victoria parade, E C
Peach, Mrs., dressmaker, 10 Bridge road, Rd
Peachy, Mrs., dressmaker, 101 Rathdowne st, Carl
Peacock, Alex., Marine hotel, Nott st, San
Peacock, David, greengrocer, 111 Moor st, F
Peacock, George, Station place, San
Peacock, George, Twyford st, Wmn
Peacock, John, carpenter, 153 William st north
Peacock, Mrs., 38 Acland st, St K
Peacock, Robert, Queensberry st, Hot
Peacock, Robert, Spread Eagle hotel, Bridge road, Rd
Peacock, Samuel, 25 Moor st, F
Peacock, Thomas, bootmaker, 71 Madeline st, Carl
Peagram, W., timber yard, Charles st, Pra
Peak, H. and T., produce dealers, 37 Market st
Peake, John, master mariner, 159 Collins st east
Peake, John, shoemaker, 10 Johnston st, F
Peake, Mrs., ladies' school, 159 Collins st east
Peake, S., watchmaker, 192 Wellington st, E C
Peanian, D., Prospect Hill hotel, Kew
Pearce, Albert, Punt road, Pra
Pearce, Andrew R., operator, Hall of Commerce, 48 Collins st west
Pearce, H. E., Barkly st, Bk
Pearce, Isaac, 97 Jeffcott st, W M
Pearce, J., cabinetmaker, Barry st, Carl
Pearce, John, Ralston st, S Y
Pearce, Mrs., 197 Lygon st, Carl
Pearce, R. W., seminary, 16 Raglan st west, Em H
Pearce, Samuel, 111 Lygon st, Carl
Pearce, Stephen H., boarding-house keeper, 111 Little Lonsdale st west
Pearce, Thomas, general dealer, 153 Smith st, F
Pearce, Wm., 40 Stanley st, W M
Peardon, Solomon, Abbotsford st, Hot
Peardon, Solomon, leather merchant and tanner, 14 Bourke st east
Peardon, Solomon, pork butcher, Swanston st
Pearl, Mrs. C., boot and shoe dealer, 143 Brunswick st, F
Pearse, S., painter and paperhanger, 157 Clarendon st, Em H
Pearson, Charles, Williams road, Pra
Pearson, George, bottler, Condell's lane, Post Office place

Pearson, H. O., Cliff st, Pra
Pearson, J., Charles st, Pra
Pearson, J., Cochrane st, Bta
Pearson, John W., and Co., engravers, lithographers, and stationers, 67 Collins st east
Pearson, John, leather merchant, 94 Brunswick st, F
Pearson, Wm., Crown hotel, 44 Cecil st, Wmn
Pearson, Wm., M.L.A., Parliament House
Peart, Mrs., seminary, Grey st, St K
Peart, Robert, draper, 84 Stavedore st, Wmn
Pease, J. C., Haw
Peatt, T., Freemasons' hotel, Stoke st, San
Peck, Hugh, money broker and estate agent, 28 Collins st west
Peck, John M., auctioneer, Flem
Peddie, Cornelius, 25 Curzon st, Hot
Pedley, Edward, 28 Railway place, Wmn
Pedley, J., Miller st, Bk
Peebles, John, 18 Cole st, Wmn
Peebles, Wm., clothier and outfitter, 153 Bourke st east
Peebles, Wm., Jolimont, E M
Peebles, Wm., bootmaker, 31 William st
Peel, James, Albert st, Pra
Peel, James A., 10 Bank st west, Em H
Peel, S. R., engineer, 141 Latrobe st west
Peel, Wm., Williams road, Pra
Peers and Frew, tailors and outfitters, 54 Bourke st east
Peers, F. W., 149 Collins st east
Peers, Mrs., teacher of music, 149 Collins st east
Peers, Thomas, Crown hotel, High st, Pra
Pegg, Robert, Bankola st, Heid
Pegg, S. H., butcher, Chapel st, Pra
Pegler, John, Nelson st, Pra
Pegus, Wm. T., academy, Barkly st, St K
Pein, Wm., broker, 68 Flinders lane west
Peirce, James W., hairdresser and' tobacconist, 199 Elizabeth st
Peirce, John, Peel st, Hot
Peirce, Thomas, Capel st, Hot
Pellet, Wm., Garden st, Pra
Pelletier, Arthur, 189 Collins st east
Penal Establishments, offices of, corner of William and Latrobe sts
Pender, Michael, 134 Lonsdale st west
Pender, Wm., Ivanhoe, Heid
Pendegaast, A., Powlett st, E M
Pendrigh, Adam, Royal Park hotel, Queensberry st, Hot
Peninsular and Oriental Steam Navigation Company's Office, 5 Flinders st east
Penman, J. C., greengrocer, 196 Swan st, Rd
Penman, J. G., broker, 192 Swan st, Rd
Pennefeather, Frederick, 98 Little Bourke st west

Pennell, J. G., fruiterer, Nelson place, East Wmn
Penny, J., brewer, Cochrane st, Bin
Pennyfather, D., Cochrane st, Bin
Penrice, John, cabinetmaker, 147 Moor st, F
Pentland, Wm., solicitor, 51 Cecil st, Wmn
Pensholz, H., manufacturing jeweller, Angelo lane, 7 Bourke st east
Pepper, G., Charles st, Pra
Pepper, John, Darby hotel, 56 Gertrude st, F
Pepperd, Thomas, 27 Victoria st, Carl
Peram, George, Latrobe parade, Collins st east
Perchard, Thomas, builder, 129 Lennox st, Bd
Percival, M., Berkeley st, Carl
Percy, Charles E., schoolmaster, 28 James st, Wmn
Pereira, Luis A., Cecil st, Em H
Perew, Joseph, Highett st, Bd
Perkins, J. P., Brighton st, Bd
Perkins, James, baker, 182 Little Collins st east
Perl, M. M., importer, 78 Elizabeth st
Perraton, Wm., produce merchant, 54 Flinders st west
Perrett, Thomas, Heath st, San
Perrin, James, Marian st, F
Perrin, Rev. J. G., J.P., Haw
Perrin's Reef Mining Association, 85 Elizabeth st
Perris, Richard, Haw
Perrott, T. W., school, Lennox st, Rd
Perry, Alexander, greengrocer, Vere st, E C
Perry, Charles, Barclay st, Carl
Perry, Charles J. C., Stevedore st, Wmn
Perry, George, smith and springmaker, 170 Latrobe st east
Perry, George, Barkly st, St K
Perry, George W., photographer, 49 Elizabeth st
Perry, Henry, gunmaker and machinist, 15 Post Office place
Perry, J. and Co., coach painters, 188 Little Bourke st east
Perry, James, painter, 225a King st
Perry, James, Nott st, San
Perry, John, wheelwright and timber merchant, 165, 167, and 169 Russell st
Perry, Miss, seminary, Kew
Perry, Miss, school, Kew
Perry, Mrs., corner of Elgin and Cardigan sts, Carl
Perry, Richard, nurseryman, Heidelberg road
Perry, Right Rev. Charles, D.D., Bishop of Melbourne, Clarendon st, E M
Perry, Wm., auctioneer, 30 Collins st west
Perry, Wm., upholsterer, 51 Oxford st, E C
Perryman, F., Brighton st, Bd

Perugia, A., figure maker, 16 Latrobe st east
Peter, F., hairdresser, 4 Little Bourke st west
Peter, Mrs., Gurner st, St K
Peters, —, restaurant, Rouse st, San
Peters, Alfred, 6 Alma st, F
Peters, F., 25 Villiers st, Hot
Peters, James, farmer, Pres
Peters, John J., Gardiner's creek road, Pra
Peters, Thomas, boot and shoe dealer, 60 and 62 Smith st, E C
Peters, Thomas, Pelham st, Carl
Peters, Thomas, Leicester st, Carl
Peterson, Fredk., estate agent, &c., Junction, St K
Peterson, Henry, 184 Moray st, Em H
Peterson, John S., 21 Regent st, F
Peterson, Wm., and Co., merchants, 6 Queen st
Peterson, Wm., Westbury st, St K
Pethbridge, E., 136 Cardigan st, Carl
Pethbridge, Anthony, outfitter, 220 Elizabeth st
Pethbridge, Edward E., 220 Elizabeth st
Petherick, P. J., Studley Arms hotel, 206 Wellington st, E C
Petigrew, James, Punt road, Rd
Peto, Mrs., 141 Moray st, Em H
Petrie, John, tobacconist, Bay st, San
Petrie, Miss, private school, Bay st, San
Pett, James, draper, Hobe st, St K
Pett, Warwick, Grosvenor st, Pra
Pettard, G. U., 19 Barkly st, Carl
Pettet, John G., 39 Smith st, F
Pettett, Wm. H., M.L.C., contractor, Haw
Pettifer, Mrs., Hawke st, W M
Pettifer, S. W., Nth
Pettigrew, George Henry, 23 Robe st, St K
Pettigrew, James, Swan st, Rd
Pettit Bros., basket makers, 20 Post Office place
Petty, G., Hope st, Bk
Petty, George Wm., butcher, 205 Bourke st east, 217 Elizabeth st
Petty, John, Morland st, Fcy
Penglase, Elizabeth, Eglinton Castle hotel, 398 Brunswick st, F
Pewtress, Henry, 50 King William st, F
Pfeil, John F., grocer, &c., Chapel st, Pra
Pfiel, J., baker, 289 Victoria parade, E C
Pfund, James, Fawkner st, St K
Phaup, A., 17 Twyford st, Wmn
Phelan, Daniel, Pent
Phelan, Henry, 25 Napier st, Em H
Phelan, James, Domain road, Pra
Phelan, James H., Rowena parade, Rd
Phelan, K., corn store, 38 Coventry st west, Em H
Phelan, M., 83 Kerr st, F
Phelan, Martin, storekeeper, Haw
Phelan, Michael, Bouveris hotel, 47 Bouverie st west

Philharmonic Society, Mechanics' Institute, Collins st east
Philips, Constantine, Higheta st, Rd
Phillips, E. H., cabinetmaker, 65 High st, St K
Philips, Mrs., Franklyn st, W M
Phillips, A. B., Commercial road, Pra
Phillips and Davidson, oyster saloon, 91 Bourke st east
Phillips, C., bootmaker, Osborne st, South Wmn
Phillips, C. and F., hay and corn store, 40 Victoria st, Rd
Phillips, E., hairdresser, Madeline st, Carl
Phillips, Henry, grocer, Vere st, E C
Phillips, J., clothier, 6 Gertrude st, F
Phillips, J., china dealer, 49 Victoria st, E C
Phillips, J., painter, Derby st, E C
Phillips, J., tailor, Bay st, Sen
Phillips, James, pawnbroker, 224 Bourke st east
Phillips, James, 30 Stanley st, W M
Phillips, John, Flem
Phillips, John, surgeon, 29 Rathdowne st, Carl
Phillips, John, fruiterer, 18 Eastern market
Phillips, Myles, messenger, Australasian Insurance Company, 75 Collins st, west
Phillips, P., Flem
Phillips, Philip David, Warwick terrace, Drummond st, Carl
Phillips, Phineas S., china and glass warehouse, 136 Bourke st east
Phillips, Richard, Elgin st, Carl
Phillips, S., bootmaker, 151 Little Collins st east
Phillips, Samuel, 112 Kerr st, F
Phillips, Samuel, grocer, Sydney road, Bk
Phillips, T. D., Peel st, Pra
Phillips, Thomas, 33 Bell st, F
Phillips, Thomas T., boarding-house keeper, 98 Lonsdale st east
Phillips, W., Fitzroy st, F
Phillips, W., Derby st, E C
Phillipson, P., gold broker, 123 Elizabeth street
Philp, Margaret, Royal Oak hotel, Queen street
Philp, Thomas, 88 Franklin st west, W M
Philpott, Wm., ironmonger, Pent
Philpott, Wm., merchant, Hall of Commerce, 48 Collins st west
Phipps, Henry F., solicitor, 36 Collins st west
Picher, Stephen, 18 Pelham st, Carl
Pickard, Henry, 7a McArthur place, Carl
Picard, T., Berkeley st, Carl
Picken, Samuel, marine surveyor, 37 Flinders st west
Pickering, Arthur, grocer, Cremorne st, Rd

Pickering, J., nightman, Gardiner's creek road, Pra
Pickering, Mrs., Robe st, St K
Pickering, Thomas, contractor, 92 Gore st, F
Pickett, George, butcher, 127½ Brunswick st, F
Pickett, Margaret, Marlbyrnong st, Fcy
Pickles, E. and J., tinsmiths, 16 Little Latrobe st east
Pickles, J., blacksmith, 27 Station place, San
Picott, P. H., grocer, 149 Elizabeth st
Pidd, George, painter, 57½ Wellington st, E C
Pierce, —, carpenter, Church st, E C
Pierce, Mrs., 4 Napier st, F
Piesse, Charles A., 40 Otter st, E C
Pigdon, John, builder and contractor, 69 Faraday st, Carl
Pigott Brothers, merchants and commission agents, 45 William st
Pigott, E., general smith, 162 Little Bourke st east
Pigott, Henry Capel, Elsternwick
Pigott, James, Barkly st, Bk
Pigou, Louis John, Grey st, St K
Pigott, P. H., tea and coffee warehouse, corner Elizabeth and Little Bourke sts west
Piggot's veterinary forge, Stephen st
Pike, Benjamin, 40 Villiers st, Hot
Pike, John, Gardiner's creek road, Pra
Pike, Mrs., teacher, St. James' schools, Bourke st west
Pike, Robert, coachbuilder, Bay st, San
Pilliner, J., 46 Moor st, F
Pile, Mrs., dressmaker, 133 Lygon st, Carl
Pilkington, Mrs., professor of music, Princes st, F
Pillar, Thomas M., Albert st, Pra
Pilley, George, mining agent, 54 Collins st east
Pillinger, A. S., Bk
Pilot Board offices, Thompson st, Wmn
Pinkey, Samuel, bootmaker, 305 Victoria parade, E C
Pinn, Mrs., Marine hotel, New st, Bte
Pinner, Mrs., grocer, 93 Stephen st
Pinniger, John, butcher, Rowena parade, Hd
Pinnock, James Denham, Wellington parade, E M
Pinser, Joseph, Punt road, Rd
Pipe, Joseph, butcher, High st, Pra
Piper, Ellen, Crimean hotel, Moray st, Em H
Pirani, H. C., wine, spirit, and tea merchant, 9 Queen st, 92 Little Bourke st west
Pirani, James C., Barkly st, St K
Pitcher, Mrs. Sarah, general dealer, 227 Wellington st, E C
Pitches, George, carrier, Ess

Pitches, Joseph, Farmers' hotel, Ess
Pitches, Peter, Royal Saxon Hotel, 283 Elizabeth st
Pitchfork, S., Pilgrim Inn, Nth
Pitman, J., 44 Coventry st, Em II
Pitmann, Mrs., Garner st, St K
Pitt, C., 136 Leicester st, F
Pitt, Edward, 72 Douglas parade, Wmn
Pitt, G., storekeeper, 22 Johnston st, F
Pitt, R. G., Macarthur place, Carl
Pitt, Wm., Garrick's Head hotel, 173 Bourke st east
Pittard, Ed., Bridge road, Rd
Pittard, J., gardener, Pres
Pitts, Mrs. James, 7 Spring st
Plain, David, baker, 31 Dover place, Wmn
Plain, J., undertaker, Gipps st, E C
Plaisted, Arthur, 4 Woolf's cottages, Faraday st, Carl
Plaisted, Thomas, 48 Brunswick st, F
Plant, G., Peacock Inn, Nth
Plant, Mrs., dressmaker, 20 Ann st, Wmn
Planta, Mrs., 13 Little Nelson st, Wmn
Platt, James, Brunswick road, Bk
Platt, J., 204 Cardigan st, Carl
Platts, Rev. F. C., Bay st, San
Player, Thomas, bootmaker, 153 Spring st
Pleace, Mrs., Dorcas st, Em II
Pleasants, J., shoemaker, 212 Smith st, E C
Pleiades Gold Mining Company, 52 Collins st east
Pleuro Pneumonia Commission, Queen st
Plock, Adam, outfitter, 14 Collins st west, and High st, Pra
Plomer, John, Carlton Club hotel, Cardigan st, Carl
Ploos Van Amstel, J. W., and Co., merchants, 49 Collins st west
Ploos Van Amstel, John Wm., Consul-general for the Netherlands, 86 Hotham st, E M
Plowman, Robert, 26 Ann st, Wmn
Plommer, Andrew, surgeon and M.D., Bay st, San
Plummer, E. S., butcher, Sydney road, Bk
Plummer, James K. B., solicitor, 36 William st
Plunket, Charles T., chemist, 33 Lonsdale st east
Plunkett, George, 23 Franklyn st, W M
Plymin, Mrs., 233 Victoria parade, E C
Poat, R., Curzon st, Hot
Poat, S., 43 Cecil st, Em II
Podberry, F., grocer, Gipps st, E C
Podbury, Frederick, baker, 112 Smith st, E C
Podger, Charles, fruiterer, High st, St K
Podger, E., Alma st, St K
Pohlman, His Honour Judge, Punt road, Rd
Poile, Wm., Chambers st, Pra
Pointin, F. J., Cremorne st, Rd

Pokorny, J. J., mining and share broker, 69 Collins st west
Polak and Davis, money brokers, 81 Elizabeth st
Polak, N., Acland st, St K
Pole, J., Victoria parade, E C
Pole, Wm., 19 Stephen st
Poles, Wm., 241 Victoria parade, E C
Police Barracks, Russell st
Police Barracks, Mounted, Richmond road
Police Commissioner, offices of, 176 Collins st east
Police Courts (see Index)
Police Offices, Water, Nelson place, Wmn
Politz, Julius, cigar manufacturer, 99 and 101 Bourke st west
Pollard, E. A., broker, 69 Collins st west
Pollard, T., Vere st, E C
Polleykeit, H., Hoddle st, E C
Pollitt, J., Rowena parade, Rd
Pollock, J., dealer, 175 Stephen st
Pollock, John, butcher, 201 Wellington st, E C
Pollock, John, 97 Nicholson st, F
Pollock, Mrs., 35 Rosslyn st, W M
Pollock, Thomas, butcher, 118 Wellington st, E C
Polytechnic, 194 Bourke st east
Pond, W., Pelham st, Carl
Pontin, George, Lennox st, Rd
Poole, Ed., Junction hotel, Pres
Poole, George, hay and corn dealer, 266 Smith st, E C
Poole, Isaac, grocer, 77 Lygon st, Carl
Poole, J. C., Electra st, Wmn
Poole, John, pilot, Electra st, Wmn
Poole, Mrs., fruiterer, Bay st, San
Poole, Thomas, solicitor, 83 Swanston st
Poole, Wm., Abbotsford st, Hot
Poolman, H. K., manager of Victoria Sugar Company's Works, San
Pope, Edward, wheelwright and blacksmith, 7 Little Lonsdale st west
Pope, John, carpenter, Webb st, F
Pope, M. M., M.L.A., Duke of Rothsay hotel, Elizabeth st
Popham, John, Bouverie st, Carl
Popplewell, Benjamin, teacher, 65 Coventry st, Em II
Porrit, F., Church st, Rd
Porritt, Edmond G., 190 Johnston st, E C
Port, Jas., and Co. (John Wright, manager), timber merchants, corner Spencer and Bourke sts
Port Phillip and Colonial Gold Mining Company, 127 Flinders lane east
Port Phillip Farmers' Society's office, 46 Bourke st west
Porter, A. T., mining agent, 10 Elizabeth street
Porter, George Wallich, 2 Summerhill place, Wellington parade, E M
Porter, John Alfred, prothonotary of the Supreme Court, 22 Lonsdale st east

Porter, John, corner of Elgin and Cardigan sts, Carl
Porter, John J., Victoria st, Hot
Porter, John, tailor, 148 Little Lonsdale st east
Porter, Miss, 75 Napier st, F
Porter, Mrs., 43 Douglas parade, Wmn
Porter, Wm., contractor, Chapel st, Pra
Portland Steam Packet Company's office, 60 Collins st west
Ports and Harbours office, Nelson parade, Wmn
Portway, W., 26 Young st, F
Post Office (General), corner Bourke and Elizabeth sts
Postle, Mrs., registry office, Chapel st, Pra
Potter, John, Lord Raglan hotel, Hoddle st, Rd
Potter, Miss, school, 24 York st west, Em H
Potter, Rev. W., Cecil st, Em H
Potter, T., 201 Clarendon st, Em H
Potter, W. P., boot warehouse, 151 Swanston st
Potts, —, Marian st, F
Potts, John, Arden st, Hot
Potts, M., 222 Little Collins st east
Potts, Madame, accoucheuse, 25 Queensberry st, Hot
Poulter, E. J., 47 Dorcas st, Em H
Pound, J., blacksmith, 173 Brunswick st, F
Pound, John, carrier, Flem
Pounds, John, Faraday st, Carl
Pow, Francis, blacksmith, 102 Dorcas st, Em H
Pow, John K., accountant and auditor, 52 Collins st east
Powell, —, baker, Sindley st, E C
Powell, Giles, 38 Elgin st, Carl
Powell, J., Reilly st, F
Powell, H. T., 80 Cardigan st, Carl
Powell, J., and Co., bakers, 185 Wellington st, E C
Powell, James, 109 Victoria parade, F
Powell, John, watch and clock maker, 118 Russell st
Powell, John, bowling saloon keeper, 67½ Bourke st east
Powell, John, 14 Pelham st, Carl
Powell, L., Drummond st, Carl
Powell, Mrs. Maria, 24 Argyle st, F
Powell, Mrs., Flemington road, Hot
Powell, P., 79 George st, F
Powell, Stephen, 11 Flinders lane west
Powell, W. H., Whitehall st, Fcy
Power, H., Melbourne Club
Power, Hon. Thomas H., Haw
Power, James, 10 Palmer st, F
Power, Michael, gardener, Johnston st, E C
Power, Mrs., Gardiner's creek road hotel, Ralston st, Pra

Power, Robert, Boundary road, Tk
Power, Thomas, Palmer st, F
Power, Thomas, Marion st, F
Power, Wm., grocer and wine and spirit merchant, Clarendon st, Em H
Power, Wm., Gardiner's creek road, Pra
Powers, —, woodyard, Strand, Wmn
Powers, P. J., Sydney hotel, 141 Smith st, F
Powers, Rutherford, and Co., stock and station agents, 192 Queen st
Pownall, Thomas, 152 Spencer st
Pownceby, John, bookbinder, 132 Collins st east
Poynter, Mrs., Caroline st, S Y
Poynter, Robert, draper, 74 Smith st, E C
Pragget, G. W., civil engineer, manufacturer Hobson's Bay Soap and Candle Company, 205 Latrobe st west
Pratt, Palmer, coffee roaster and spice merchant, 90 Bourke st west
Pratt, Andrew, general ironmonger, 159 King st
Pratt, George C., printer, 98 Fitzroy st, F
Pratt, James, 37 Rosslyn st, W M
Pratt, John, Pelham st, Carl
Pratt, Joseph H., Grange road, Tk
Pratt, Mrs., 4 Pelham st, Carl
Pratt, Robert, Buckley st, Fcy
Pratt, Wm., gardener, Preston
Prebble, Thomas C., accountant, 35 Queen street
Prell, F. W., and Co., merchants, 33 Queen st
Prender, John, Rowena parade, Rd
Prendergast and O'Halloran, solicitors, 5 Eldon chambers, Bank place, Collins st west
Prendergast, Leonard, St K
Prendergast, P. F., Waverley hotel, Little Collins st west
Prendergast, W., 168 Madeline st, Carl
Preadivill, —, Union st, Bln
Prentice, A., 113 Little Bourke st west
Prentice, W., 8 Palmer st, F
Presbyterian Churches (see Index)
Prescott, Alfred, 3 Berkeley st, Carl
Presnell, —, shoemaker, 197 Wellington st, E C
Preese, —, 75 Wellington st, E C
Preswell and Goodson, dairymen, 58 Johnston st, F
Preswell, W., shoemaker, 89 Moor st, F
Prest, John, Osborne st, Wmn
Preston, George, Charles st, S Y
Preston, H., 47 Ross st, F
Preston, Mrs., Berkeley st, Carl
Preston, Robert, blacksmith, 58 Lothian st, Hot
Pretty, Wm., 21 Pelham st, Carl
Prevost and Deaslercs, hairdressers and perfumers, 96 Bourke st east
Prevôt and Co., cordial manufacturers, 120 Queen st

Prevôt, E. Joseph, Haw
Prewett, James, 72 Errol st, Hot
Price, Fred., engraver, 59 Swanston st
Price, J., Murphy st, S Y
Price, Mrs., hatmaker, 108 Victoria st, Rd
Price, Philip, Faraday st, Carl
Price, T., Chapel st, Pra
Price, T., Clarendon st, Em H
Price, Wm., 196 Gore st, F
Price, Wm., waiter, Royal lane, Bourke st east
Price, Wm., engraver and painter, 20 Little Collins st east
Prichard, C. A., grocer, Gipps st, E C
Prickett, Edward, solicitor, 57 Little Collins st east
Pridgeon, Thomas, Thompson st, Wmn
Pridham, Robert, butcher, Banksia st, Heid
Priest, E., carpenter, Church st, E C
Priestley, A. (accountant National Bank), Haw
Priestley, A. F., 222 Smith st, E C
Priestley, C., Union st, Windsor
Priestley, Samuel, 143 George st, F
Primitive Methodist Chapels (see Index)
Primrose, E. B., Haw
Primrose, E., Wilson st, Bru
Prince, Henry, 19 Regent st, F
Prince, James, Wellington parade, E M
Prince, Wm., blacksmith, 1 Mackenzie st
Princess Theatre, Spring st
Pringle, G. R. G., professor of music, 157 Collins st east
Prinn, W., Punt road, Pra
Prian, Wm., 30 Raglan st, Em H
Prior, J., carpenter, 58 Gore st, F
Prior, Mrs., 202A Cardigan st, Carl
Prior, W., Sydney road, Bk
Priston and Small, photographic chemists, 73 Little Collins st east
Pristoe, G. W., Charles st, Pra
Pritchard, E., York st, Bru
Pritchard, John, butcher, 271 Smith st, F
Pritchard, Osgood, Kew
Pritchard, P., 95 Leicester st, Carl
Pritchard, Wm., Peel st, Pra
Proctor, J., ironmonger, High st, St K
Proctor, John, store, Clinches st, Pra
Promall, T., 95 Rosslyn st, W M
Prosen, Robert, 161 Young st, F
Protestant Hall, corner Little Collins st east, and Stephen st
Prothonotary's Office, 22 Lonsdale st east
Proudfoot, James, 7 Howard st, Hot
Prouse, Charles, Albert st, Pra
Prowse, Henry, Pent
Prowse, Mrs., 63 Rose st, F
Prowse, W., Sydney road, Bk
Pruen, Charles J., and Keane, Wm., general carriers, corner of Elizabeth and Little Latrobe sts
Pryce, George, Argyle st east, St K

Pryce, Rev. C. S. Y., 33 Bridport st west, Em H
Pryde, George, importer, 10 King st
Prytherch, Wm., saddler, 24 Wellington terrace, E C
Public Library, Swanston st
Public Works Department Offices, Lonsdale st west, corner Queen st
Puckey, Thomas, 163 Fitzroy st, F
Puckle, Rev. E., Flem
Pugh, Wm. R., M.D., surgeon, 131 Collins st east
Pullan, Thomas W., brewer, Chapel st, Pra
Pullar and Co., coal merchants, 313 Elizabeth st
Pullar, D., 9 Mary st, Hot
Pullar, James, iron and coal merchant, 22 Lothian st, Hot
Pulle, S., Leveson st, Hot
Pullen, John, Hotham st, E M
Pullen, Mary, wharf contractor, corner of King and Rosslyn sts
Pullen, Thomas, Corry st, off Cardigan st, Carl
Pulling, Charles, Peel st, Pra
Pulver, Isaac, tobacconist, 99 Queen st
Pummeroy, Wm., plasterer, off 93 High st, St K
Punch, Michael, Fitzroy st, F
Punch office, 77 Collins st east
Punshon, Mrs., grocer, 156 King st
Punton, Andrew, baker, 184 Church st, Rd
Purcell, —, 89 Fitzroy st, F
Purcell, Alfred, 89 Fitzroy st, F
Purcell, Ann, Glasshouse hotel, Gipps st, E C
Purcell, Charles P., solicitor, 76 Elizabeth st
Purcell, George C., barrister, Temple court
Purcell, J., messenger, Royal Bank of India, 109 Collins st west
Purcell, James, Loughrea hotel, 106 Elgin st, Carl
Purcell, Martin, general store, 73 Bouverie st, Carl
Purcell, R., 106 Victoria st, Rd
Purchas, Albert, architect, civil engineer, and surveyor, 20 Temple court, Collins st east
Purday, Samuel, 28 John st, Wmn
Purdue, W., 37 Three chain road, Em H
Purdy, —, 214 Napier st, F
Purnell, Harriet, 117 Flinders st east
Purtill, John, timber merchant, Chapel st, Pra
Purssell, J., butcher, Commercial road, Pra
Purton, Edward, and Co., stationers, 106 Elizabeth st
Purvis, H. S., plumber, 107 Lygon st, Carl
Purvis, John, 57 Faraday st, Carl
Purvis, T., engineer, 49 Rosslyn st, W M
Puryer, R., Inkerman st, St K
Putman, H. M., 5A James st, F

T

Puttmann, Hermann, Hoddle st, Rd
Putts, T., Inkerman st east, St K
Pye, Mrs., chemist and druggist, 71 Drummond st, Carl
Pye, Samuel, Highett st, Rd
Pyle, Wm., Waltham st, Rd
Pyne, Booth and Co., warehousemen, 25 Flinders lane west
Pyne, Charles, 25 Flinders lane west
Pyne, John, Union st, S Y
Pynell, Alexander, Rouse st, San
Pyrke, John, and Co., stationers, Bridge road, and Church st, Rd (P. O.)
Pywell, H., grocer, &c., Rouse st, San

Q

Quail, Charles, 64 Lothian st, Hot
Quail, Wm., Hoddle st, E C
Quarrier, Thomas, Cole st, Wmn
Quedong Copper Mining Company, 9 Elizabeth st
Queen Insurance Co., 31 Queen st
Quick, F. G., 74 Coventry st, Em H
Quick, George, bottle merchant, Leicester st, Carl
Quigin, D., 198 Moray st, Em H
Quigley, Edward, Queen's Head hotel, 17 Cecil st, Wmn
Quigley, James, farmer, 108 Stevedore st, Wmn
Quigley, John, Prince Albert hotel, Douglas parade, Wmn
Quigley, Wm., Macqoarie st, Wmn
Quilty, Dennis, Wingfield st, Fcy
Quin, —, Abbotsford st, Hot
Quin, Daniel, Barkly st, Carl
Quin, Mrs., dealer, 114 Gore st, F
Quin, Patrick, Church st, Rd
Quinan, James, Raween parade, Rd
Quiney, Edward, toy and fishing tackle warehouse, 107½ Swanston st
Quinlan, Edward, Peel st, Hot
Quinlan, Francis, barrister, 15 Temple court, Collins st west
Quinlan, G., Waltham st, Rd
Quinlan, Jeremiah, Kilkenny hotel, Therry st
Quinlan, Michael, Flem
Quinlan, Michael, Glenmore hotel, Franklyn st, W M
Quinlan, Michael, 150 Spencer st
Quinlan, Thomas, Errol st, Hot
Quinn, J., Oxford st, Hot
Quinn, J. E., grocer, Cambridge st, E C
Quinn, James, Punt road, Hd
Quinn, Joseph, 3 York st, Em H
Quinn, Mrs., Barkly st, Carl
Quinn, Robert, provision store, Bay st, San
Quinn, T., fruiterer, Chapel st, Pra
Quion, Thomas, 116 Elgin st, Carl
Quirk, D., bootmaker, Church st, Pra
Quirk, James, 35 Rathdowne st, Carl

Quirk, Thomas, Kilkenny boarding-house, 64 Latrobe st east

R.

Radcliff, Charles, wood turner, 38 Little Bourke st west
Radcliffe, Wm., Bainbridge terrace, Bouverie st, Carl
Radden, Wm., 61 Dudley st, W M
Radden, Wm., Canning st, Carl
Rademacher, L., hat maker, 139 Moray st, Em H
Radford, 76 Napier st, F
Radford, Wm. John, earthenware dealer, 52 Queensberry st, Carl
Rady, James, 53 Rose st, F
Rae, Mrs., 40 Young st, F
Rae, R., 37 Lygon st, Carl
Rae, W., hay and corn store, Victoria st, Carl
Rae, Wm., Bouverie st, Carl
Raeby, John, 107 Leicester st, F
Rafferty, Thomas, farrier, Somerville road, Fcy
Raffine, David R., baker, 13 Little Lonsdale st west
Rafter, Jos., school, 16 Dover place, Wmn
Rahilly, Ellen, Olive Branch hotel, 111 Little Collins st west
Raid, John, 1 Highett st, Rd
Railway Department, Chief Engineer's office, Spencer st
Railway Department offices, William st
Raine, John, coachbuilder, 240 Napier st, F
Raine, John M., 36 Park st, Em H
Raine, T., Kew
Raine, Thomas, wholesale ironmonger, 5 Bourke st, east
Rains, Thomas, gardener, Dryburgh st, Hot
Rainsbury, Thomas, provision merchant, 243 Swanston st
Rainsford, John, grocer, 41 York st, Em E
Rainsford, John B., 216 Wellington st, E C
Rainson, Thomas, Johnston st, E C
Rake, Thomas, cook and confectioner, Thompson st, Wmn
Rakestraw, G., bootmaker, High st, St K
Rakowski, S., merchant, 37 Flinders st west
Raleigh, Michael, 40 Little Bourke st west
Raleigh, Walter, 156 Young st, F
Ralph, —, miller, Mill st, Bin
Ralph, R. J., 329 Fitzroy st, F
Ralph, Thomas S., surgeon, Kew
Ralston, John, Quarries, Fcy
Ramadge, S., grocer, Spencer st
Ramage, John, Abbotsford st, F
Ramage, Richard and George, tailors and clothiers, 79 Collins st east
Ramond, Mrs., 125 Fitzroy st, F
Ramsay, A., engineer, 26 Osborne st, Wmn

Ramsay, A , 15 Howard st, Hot
Ramsay, George, 64 Electra st, Wmn
Ramsay, John, M.L.A., 116 Fitzroy st, F
Ramsay, Rev. A. M., 96 Collins st east
Ramsay, Robert, Rowena parade, Rd
Ramsay, Robert, solicitor, 32 Queen st
Ramsay, W., Lincoln cottages, Bouverie st, Carl
Ramsay, W., 78 Raglan st, Em H
Ramsay, W. P., Stawell st, W M
Ramsdale, James, Berkeley st, Carl
Ramsden, J., Chetwynd st, W M
Ramsden, Samuel, Carlton flour mills, Leicester st, Carl
Ramsden, Samuel, 7 Fitzroy terrace, Clarendon st, E M
Ramsey, Mrs., milliner, 18 Little Nelson st, Wmn
Ramus, John, merchant, 9 Queen st
Randall, Mitchell, and Doward, solicitors, 109 Collins st west
Randall, T., Carlisle st east, St K
Randall, Thomas, 109 Young st, F
Randall, Thomas, Wilson st, Pra
Randell, J. W., and Co., drapers, 23 Bourke st east, and 125 and 127 Brunswick st, F
Randle, W., 24 Oxford st, E C
Raneleigh, Mrs., Baillie st, Hot
Raney, J., Pent
Rankin and Son, tailors, 239 Swanston st
Rankin, Dr., surgeon, High st, St K
Rankin, Henry, dealer, 10 Little Bourke st west
Rankin, James, cartage contractor, 149 Little Lonsdale st west
Rankin, James, Elgin st, Carl
Rankin, John, Kensington
Rasking, Wm., builder, 83 Darkly st, Carl
Rannard and Co., bootmakers, 186 Smith st, E C
Rannard, David, importer of boots and shoes, agricultural machinery, &c., 18 Elizabeth st
Ransie, Mrs., Berkeley st, Carl
Ransom, Isaac, Stoke st, San
Ransom, Thomas, Highbury Barn hotel, Haddle st, E C
Raper, John, Capel st, Hot
Raphael, —, 4 George st, F
Raphael, H., 121 Victoria parade, F
Raphael, J. S., 117 Flinders lane east
Rapson, J., Sydney road, Bk
Ratcliffe, J., High st, Pra
Ratcliffe, J., President Lincoln hotel, Bay st, San
Ratcliffe, James, 7 Macquarie st, Wmn
Ratcliffe, John M., Station place, San
Rattenbury, E., store, Dover road, Wmn
Rattray, Alex., contractor, 139 Little Bourke st west
Raven, J., Swan st, Rd
Raven, J., Victoria st, W M
Raven, Claudius J., Studley park

Raven, J. C., 70 Johnston st, F
Raven, John C., house painter, 131 Smith st, F
Raven, Joseph, Swan st, Rd
Raven, Wm., 140 Johnston st, F
Raven, Wm. G., undertaker, 143 Smith st, F
Ravenscroft, G., Berkeley st, Carl
Rawle, Wm., chemist and electoral registrar, Haw
Rawlings, James, 44 King William st, F
Rawlinson, Miss, draper, Kew
Rawlinson, Thomas George, C.E. and surveyor, 36 Queen st
Rawlinson, Wm., Clarendon st, Em H
Rawson, H., 1 Banbridge terrace, Bouverie st, Carl
Rawson, H., Wreckyn st, Hot
Ray, Briscoe, merchant, 31, 33, and 35 Flinders lane west
Ray, Henry N., Haw
Ray, James, Pent
Ray, Mrs., shopkeeper, Victoria lane
Ray, Robert, physician and surgeon, 105 Collins st east
Ray, T., 25 Dorcas st, Em H
Raybould, James, undertaker, Commercial road, Pra
Rayfield, John, Cecil st, Em H
Rayfield, W., 4 Raglan st, Em H
Rayment, Henry, 231 Moray st, Em H
Raymond, B., 149 Moor st, F
Raymond, James, 76 Coblen st, Em H
Raymond, John, Punt road, Rd
Raymond, Thomas, 17 Hanover st, F
Rayne, S., 65 Johnston st, F
Rayne, Thomas, Octavia st, St K
Rayner, Samuel, 84 Bouverie st, Carl
Raynor, W. H., Hull and London hotel, Bourke st east
Raynor, T. R., Carlisle st, East St K
Reayson, Harold, draper, 142 Clarendon st, Em H
Rayson, Walter, draper, 98 Spencer st north
Rea, Robert, Strand, Wmn
Read, Albert, solicitor, 59 Swanston st
Read, D., Vale st, Hot
Read, D., 54 Kerr st, F
Read, Henry, 150 Madeline st, Carl
Read, James, Grange road, Tk
Read, James, Cremorne st, Nd
Read, John, 101 Elgin st, Carl
Real, John, Illawarra st, Wmn
Read, John W., bootmaker, High st, St K
Read, Mrs., 65 Gore st, F
Read, Mrs., Darkly st, St K
Redford, Joseph, Nott st, San
Readshaw, R., 233 Gore st, F
Ready, Jeremiah, Clare hotel, 45 Little Bourke st west
Readle, John, Nicholson st, Carl
Really, G. F., 133 Kerr st, F
Reany, Joseph, 40 Latrobe st west

Reaney, Robert, saddler, 62 Bourke st west
Reaney and Roberts, machinists, 30 Post Office place
Reardon, Andrew, Dryburgh st, Hot
Reardon, Patrick, bootmaker, 35 Little Lonsdale st east
Reardon, Patrick, George hotel, corner of Cecil and Coventry sts, Em H
Reav, E. W., sailmaker, Little Nelson st, Wmn
Reay, Joseph, 87 Victoria st, Hot
Recliables, Order of, District Chambers, 119 Russell st
Redan Gold Mining Co., 85 Flinders st west
Reddan, Michael, bootmaker, Whitehall st, Fcy
Reddaw, Patrick, 35 Market st, Em H
Redden, Mrs, wood yard, Elgin st, Carl
Reddin, J., Newcastle hotel, 179 and 181 Stephen st
Redding, John, fishmonger, Whitehall st, Fcy
Redding, Thomas, furniture dealer, 85 Rathdowne st, Carl
Reddish, Richard, Curzon st, Hot
Reddish, Wm., pawnbroker, Queensberry st, Hot
Redman, Charles, wood yard, 65 Rathdowne st, Carl
Redman, Hannah, grocer, 56 Lothian st, Hot
Redman, Wm, 24 Dover road, Wmn
Redmond, Thomas, glass and earthenware dealer, 192 Elizabeth st
Reed and Barnes, architects and surveyors, 9 Elizabeth st
Reed, Daniel, 54 Kerr st, F
Reed, F., Caroline st, S Y
Reed, George, 166 Moray st, Em H
Reed, Henry, 231 Victoria st, E C
Reed, Joseph, Bay st, Bin
Reed, Joseph, bootmaker, Queensberry st, Hot
Reed, Richard, 105 Rosslyn st, W M
Reed, Robert, Carlisle st east, St K
Reed, Thomas, fancy repository, 49 Collins st east
Reed, Thomas, 24 King William st, F
Reedy Creek Gold Mining Company, 9 Elizabeth st
Reedy, J., 63 Raglan st, Em H
Rees, Benjamin, 91 Gore st, F
Rees, D., Queen st
Rees, Frederic, Rees's hotel, corner of High and Argyle sts, St K
Rees, John, 4 Parker st, Wmn
Rees, Rev. D., Gardiner's creek road, Pra
Rees, Wm. J., 152 Ferrars st, Em H
Reeve, H., 189 Victoria parade, E C
Reeve, John, iron foundry, Bay st, San
Reeve, R., dealer, Derby st, E C
Reeve, Wm., 75 Napier st, Em H

Reeves, Charles, Otter st, F C
Reeves, James, Highett st, Rd
Reeves, Samuel, 48 Charles st, F
Reffvm, —, baker, Little Lonsdale st west
Refuge, Female, Madeline st, Carl
Regan Brothers, locksmiths, &c., 6 Little Collins st east
Regan, James, Lang st, S Y
Regan, John, Emerald st, Em H
Regan, John, 138 Gertrude st, F
Regan, John, boatbuilder, Humse st, San
Regan, John, 8 Dover place, Wmn
Regan, John, 89 Moray st, Em H
Regan, Michael J., butcher, 319 Elizabeth street
Registrar General's office, Treasury, Spring st ; branch office, old Government House, William st
Registration Office for Births, &c., Prince's bridge
Registry Office for Diocese of Melbourne, 91 Little Collins st west
Regnert, Charles, Bay st, San
Reid, A., 89 Dorcas st east, Em H
Reid, Alexander, 3 Spencer terrace, Little Bourke st west
Reid, Charles, Kew
Reid, Charles, Carpenter st, Btn
Reid, D., Cardigan st, Carl
Reid, D., New st, Btn
Reid, George, 137 Latrobe st west
Reid, H. R., Electra st, Wmn
Reid, J., 69 Coventry st, Em H
Reid, J., bootmaker, 133 Little Bourke st east
Reid, J., 28 Barkly st, Carl
Reid, James, 70 Napier st, Em H
Reid, James, Gipps st, Rd
Reid, James, Howens parade, Rd
Reid, James W., sign writer, 35 Post Office place
Reid, James, 35 Daillie st, Hot
Reid, John, 18 Victoria st, Hot
Reid, John, Punt road, Rd
Reid, Mrs., fancy repository, High st, St K
Reid, Mrs., greengrocer, 173 Smith st, F
Reid, Mrs., post office, Pent
Reid, Mrs., feather cleaner, 108 Lygon st, Carl
Reid, Peter, grocer, 130 Ferrars st, Em H
Reid, Poole, and Co., merchants, 1 Queen st south
Reid, Robert, Punt road, Rd
Reid, Samuel, bootmaker, 15 Little Bourke st west
Reid, Thomas, baker, Blackwood st, Ho
Reid, Thomas, Illawarra st, Wmn
Reid, Wm., Bay st, San
Reily, James, Ivanhoe, Heid
Reily, W., teacher, Albert st, Bk
Reilly, J., 239 Victoria parade, E C
Reilly, John, Em
Reilly, Mrs., dairy, 60 Bank st west, Em H

Reilly, Mrs., laundress, 1 Cambridge st, E C
Reilly, T., butcher, Cardigan st, Carl
Reilly, Wm., grocer, Bridge road, Rd
Reitz, Frederick G., store, Church st, E C
Renard, Jules, wool broker, 20 Collins st west
Renehan, L. F., Clarke st, E C
Renison, George, 14 Pelham st, Carl
Renney, Mrs., Reilly st, F
Renshaw, Noah, 212 Wellington st, E C
Renton, James, Peel st, W M
Renwick, Samuel, Caulfield
Restorck, Mrs., dressmaker, 100 Flinders lane east
Rettwig, John, turner, 157 Russell st
Revley, J. J., Northcote
Reybarn, James, draper, 24 Curzon st, Hot
Reyleigh, Thomas, 146 Moray st, Em H
Reynolds, C. W., painter, Acland st, S Y
Reynolds, E., New st, Btn
Reynolds, Edward, solicitor, &c., 13 Bourke st west
Reynolds, Enoch, saddler, Haw
Reynolds, Frederick, 116 Madeline st, Carl
Reynolds, G., Carlisle st west, St K
Reynolds, H., Esplanade, St K
Reynolds, I., grocer, York st, Em H
Reynolds, J. N., seed merchants, 33 and 35 Swanston st
Reynolds, Samuel, 81 Johnston st, E C
Reynolds, Thomas, Station place, San
Reynolds, W., 15 Argyle st, F
Reynolds, Wm., 69 Victoria parade, F
Reynolds, Wm., 19 Douverie st, Carl
Reynolds, Wm., Bay View hotel, Beach st, San
Reynard, Charles G., photographer, 110 Elizabeth st
Rhimes, A., blacksmith, 201 Smith st, F
Rhind, Thomas, 127 Victoria st, Hot
Rhoado, Rd. D., Simpson st, E M
Rhoden, Charles, tin and copper smith, 350 Elizabeth st
Rhodes, Edward, Union st, Pra
Rhodes, F., Weston st, Bk
Rhodes, John, 253 Brunswick st, F
Rice, C., 117 Kerr st, F
Rice, James, 11 Thompson st, Wmn
Rice, Thomas, 119 Kerr st, F
Rice, Wm., 50 Charles st, F
Rice, Wm., 136 Kerr st, F
Rich, E., pawnbroker, 96 Brunswick st, F
Rich, Richard J., pilot, 29 Dover road, Wmn
Richards Brothers, grocers, High st, St K
Richards, Charles and Wm., grocers, Lygon st, Carl
Richards, David, Mechanics' Arms hotel, Cecil st, Em H
Richards, F., 72 Bridge road, Rd
Richards, J., grocer, Chapel st, Pra
Richards, J., Punt road, S Y

Richards, John, 30 Queensberry st, Carl
Richards, John, grocers, Miller st, W M
Richards, John, Villiers st, Hot
Richards, Jos., 42 Elizabeth st extension
Richards, Joseph, shoeing forge, 35 Victoria st, Carl
Richards, W., gunmaker, 105 Bourke st east
Richards, W., Blackwood st, Hot
Richards, Wm. W., 18 Faraday st, Carl
Richards, Wm., Electra st, Wmn
Richards, Wm., 176 Moray st, Em H
Richardson, —, 32 Brunswick st, F
Richardson, —, Clarendon st, E M
Richardson, Alexander, 30 Drummond st, Carl
Richardson, Edward, Ess
Richardson, J., M.L.A., Parliament House
Richardson, J., gardener, Carlisle st, St K
Richardson, J. H., hairdresser, 55 Errol st, Hot
Richardson, John, Inkerman st east, St K
Richardson, John Francis, bootmaker, 45 Queen st
Richardson, Jos. F., Gray st east, E M
Richardson, Joseph, estate agent, 28 Collins st east
Richardson, Joseph, Chapel st, Pra
Richardson, Joshua, 114 Leicester st, Carl
Richardson, M. A., house and land agent, High st, Pra
Richardson, Mrs., 63A Gore st, F
Richardson, Miss H., Johnston st, E C
Richardson, Mrs., ladies' seminary, Robe st, St K
Richardson, Mrs., Dalgety st, St K
Richardson, R., Tivoli place, Punt road, S Y
Richardson, Richard, American hotel, 243 Swanston st
Richardson, Robert, Nicholson st, Carl
Richardson, Robert, Faraday st, Carl
Richardson, T., Haw
Richardson, Thomas, 2 Sydney terrace, Canning st, Carl
Richardson, W., Faraday st, Carl
Richardson, W., corn store, Commercial road, Pra
Richardson, W. E., draper, Yarra st, Heid
Richardson, Wm., Caledonian hotel, Jeffcott st, W M
Richelieu, Robert, 127 Argyle st, F
Richie, Andrew, 38 Nicholson st, F
Richman, F., provision dealer, Latrobe st east
Richmond, George, Marion st, F
Richmond, V. W., surgeon, Cochrane st Btn
Richter, John, 48 Barkly st, Carl
Richter, L., bootmaker, 36 Little Bourke st west
Rickards, Charles, Peel st, Pra
Rickards, F., cabinetmaker, 72 Bridge road, Rd

Richards, John, Garden st, Pra
Ricketson, —, New st, Btn
Ricketson, Mrs., Darling st, S Y
Rickett, C., Cochrane st, Btn
Ricketts, Thomas, carpenter, Bay st, Dm
Ricketts, W., greengrocer and perambulator manufacturer, 56 Bridge road, Rd
Ridde, Wm., 30 Chetwynd st, Hot
Riddell, J. C., M.L.A., Melbourne Club
Riddell, Robert, Trinnian st, off High st, Pra
Ridding, Thomas, furniture dealer, Elgin st, corner Rathdowne st, Carl
Rider, A., bookbinder, 4 York st, Em H
Rider, Andrew, stationer and photographist, 53 Nelson place, Wmn
Rider, James, Lennox road, Rd
Rider, Jonathan, 50 Bouverie st, Carl
Ridler, Robert, butcher, 187 Bridge road, Rd
Ridley, George, 41 Wellington st, E C
Ridley, J., pilot, 44 Parker st, Wmn
Ridley, W., 13 Smith st, F
Ridoutt and Sons, oil and colour merchants, Commercial road, Pra
Riedy, Michael, Kildare Castle hotel, Queensberry st, Hot
Riemann, Bruno, publisher, 41 Swanston street
Rigby, Edward, Council Club hotel, corner of Lonsdale and Queen sts
Rigg, Anthony, 121 Swanston st
Rigg, George, 38 Drummond st, Carl
Rigg, Rev. —, Ann st, Wmn
Rigg, W., bootmaker, Cochrane st, Btn
Rigg, W. G., bootmaker, 13 Thompson st, Wmn
Rigley, —, milliner, 129 Cambridge st, E C
Riley, E., Jeffcott st, W M
Riley, Francis, Latrobe st west
Riley, Francis, 70 Rathdowne st, Carl
Riley, George, store, 178 Victoria st, Rd
Riley, J., 9 Lygon st, Carl
Riley, J., Addurley st, W M
Riley, J., 4 Miller st, W M
Riley, J. George, Seven Stars hotel, 12 Madeline st, Carl
Riley, James J., Graham st, San
Riley, John, Ess
Riley, John, Station place, San
Riley, John, Nott st, San
Riley, T., tobacconist, Beach st, San
Riley, Thomas, painter and paperhanger, 37 Lonsdale st west
Riley, Thomas, cabinetmaker, 288 Elizabeth st
Riley, Thomas, 182 Drummond st, Carl
Rillstone, Miss, dressmaker, Bridge road, Rd
Rimmer, Christopher, 233 Moray st, Em H
Rimmer, C. M., Octavia st, St K
Rimmington, Thomas, toy dealer, Greville st, off Chapel st, Pra

Rimpler, —, Moor st, F
Ring, Ed., Bridge road, Rd
Ring, P., Golden Cross hotel, corner King and Latrobe sts
Ring, R., 147 Johnston st, F
Rintel, Henry, Fitzroy st, F
Rintel, Rev. Moses, 13 Rathdowne st, Carl; school, Latrobe st east
Riordan, Dennis, 82 Bank st west, Em H
Riordan, Patrick, grocer, 31 Howard st, Hot
Ripley, Thomas, coachmaker, Bay st, San
Rippon and Phillips, solicitors, 8 Collins st east
Rippon, Charles, Nth
Rippon, Charles, 24 Johnston st, F
Rippon, Mrs., school, 24 Johnston st, F
Risk and Co., general carriers, 164 Elizabeth st
Rismondo, George, general dealer, 171 King st
Ritchie, Charles, joiner, 26 Little Bourke st west
Ritchie, David, 133 Cardigan st, Carl
Ritchie, Henry, office, 60 Elizabeth st
Ritchie, James, 83 Cecil st, Wmn
Ritchie, Mrs., 11 Cecil st, Wmn
Ritchie, Mrs., Peel st, Pra
Ritchie, S. N., wine and spirit merchant and importer, 4 Elizabeth st
Ritchie, W., bootmaker, 137 Latrobe st west
Roach, J., butcher, 96 Douglas parade, Wmn
Roach, Leonard, Queensberry st, Hot
Roach, Thomas, Graham st, San
Road, James, Cremorne st, Rd
Roads and Bridges Department offices, 191 William st
Robb, J., Barkly st, Bk
Robb, James, blacksmith, Flemington hill
Robb, W., Pont road, Pra
Robb, Wm., general broker, 21 Queen st
Robbins, Charles F., commission merchant, 49 Collins st west
Robbins, F., stevedore, Stoke st, San
Robbins, G. W., stevedore, Stoke st, San
Roberts, —, tailor, 201 Little Collins st east
Roberts, —, office, 18 Collins st east
Roberts, —, 24 Barkly st, Carl
Roberts, —, Dryburgh st, Hot
Roberts, —, 108 Rune st, F
Roberts and Co., blacksmiths, 35 Little Nelson st, Wmn
Roberts, Ann, laundress, 21 Little Latrobe st east
Roberts, B., Nott st, San
Roberts, B., gardener, Centre road, Btn
Roberts, C. F., 158 Victoria parade, E M
Roberts, Daniel, furniture dealer, 319 Victoria parade, E C
Roberts, Edward, sign writer and painter, Chapel st, Pra

Roberts, Edward J., butcher, 182 and 184 King st
Roberts, Frederick, watchmaker, 3 Thompson st, Wmn
Roberts, G., greengrocer, Church st, Rd
Roberts, George, fruiterer, Bay st, San
Roberts, Henry, 193 Napier st, F
Roberts, J., Chapel st, St K
Roberts, J., general dealer, 85 Wellington st, E C
Roberts, J., Haw
Roberts, J., Nth
Roberts, J., Fitzroy st, St K
Roberts, J., turner, Hoddle st, E C
Roberts, J., marble mason, Madeline st, Carl
Roberts, J. S., commission agent, Alma st, St K
Roberts, J. W., Rochester Castle hotel, Johnston st, F
Roberts, J. W., 18 Collins st east
Roberts, J. W., 124 Cardigan st, Carl
Roberts, J. W., Henry st, Pra
Roberts, J. W., butcher, 19 Thompson st, Wmn
Roberts, James, 12 Little Nelson st, Wmn
Roberts, James, 79 Capel st, Hot
Roberts, John, bootmaker, 219 Swan st, Hd
Roberts, John, hairdresser, 22 Post Office place
Roberts, John, Bay st, Btn
Roberts, John, 136 Napier st, F
Roberts, John, marble mason, 178 Faraday st, Carl
Roberts, John, 41 Leveson st, Hot
Roberts, K., Swan st, Rd
Roberts, Lydia, dressmaker, 138 Queen st
Roberts, Mr. and Mrs. William George, ladies' institute, Hotham st, E M
Roberts, Mrs., laundress, 14 Leicester st, Carl
Roberts, R. J., cabinetmaker, 140 Little Collins st east
Roberts, Richard, bootmaker, 317 Victoria parade, E C
Roberts, Richard, contractor, Fcy
Roberts, S., marble mason, 178 Madeline st, Carl
Roberts, Samuel, stationer, &c., 5 Nelson place north, Wmn
Roberts, Samuel H., signwritter, &c., 116 Swanston st
Roberts, Sarah Anne, South Park hotel, corner of Moray and Raglan sts east, Em H
Roberts, T. J., Berkeley st, Carl
Roberts, Thomas, 29 Illawarra st, Wmn
Roberts, W., 80 Moor st, F
Roberts, Wm., 51 Faraday st, Carl
Roberts, Wm., reaping machine maker, &c., 59 a'Beckett st west
Roberts, Wm., Punt road, Rd

Robertson, —, grocer, corner Stanley and Cambridge sts, E C
Robertson and Ferguson, coachbuilders and wheelwrights, 64 Bourke st west
Robertson and Jacques, tailors and outfitters, 25 Collins st east
Robertson and Moffatt, drapers, &c., 11 Bourke st east
Robertson, A., and Son, bakers, 97 Raglan st, Em H
Robertson, A. W., Castlemaine
Robertson, Andrew, Haw
Robertson, Andrew, Argyle st east, St K
Robertson, Ann, Clarendon Hotel, Punt road, Pra
Robertson, Charles, Scotch Pie shop, Bourke st east
Robertson, D., Woolpack hotel, corner of Queen st and Flinders lane
Robertson, Donald, 18 Curzon st, Hot
Robertson, Flora, 2 Fitzroy terrace, Clarendon st, E M
Robertson, Francis, Ess
Robertson, Francis, Kew
Robertson, G., Waltham st, Rd
Robertson, G., Grange road, Toorak
Robertson, George, Hoddle st, E C
Robertson, George, bookseller and stationer, 23 Collins st east, and 69 Elizabeth st
Robertson, George, 11 University st, Carl
Robertson, George, Stephen st
Robertson, George B., Blackwood st, Hot
Robertson, Gilbert, Palmerston st, Carl
Robertson, Hugh, blacksmith, High st, St K
Robertson, Hugh, Argyle st east, St K
Robertson, Isaac, Lonsdale st west
Robertson, J., butcher, Pelham st, Carl
Robertson, J. C., and Co., tea brokers, 32 Flinders lane west
Robertson, James, 156 Spencer st
Robertson, James, accountant, 73 Temple court, Collins st west
Robertson, James, Alma st west, St K
Robertson, James, Haw
Robertson, James, butcher, Barkly st, Carl
Robertson, James, Haw
Robertson, James, M.D., surgeon, Victoria st, Carl
Robertson, James M., architect and surveyor, Catherine st, Richmond hill
Robertson, James, Weinberg road, Upper Haw
Robertson, John, dyer and scourer, 78 and 89 Lonsdale st east
Robertson, John, hay and corn dealer, 219 King st
Robertson, John, blacksmith, Angelo lane, 7 Bourke st east
Robertson, John, 114 Madeline st, Carl
Robertson, John, 50 Cardigan st, Carl
Robertson, John, Faraday st, Carl

Robertson, John, grocery store, 53 Market st, Em H
Robertson, Joseph, corn dealer, 250 Brunswick st, F
Robertson, Miss J., 13 Young st, F
Robertson, Mrs., Alma st west, St K
Robertson, Mrs., Railway place, San
Robertson, Mrs. W., Darling st, S Y
Robertson, Oates, and Hallows, plumbers, 130 Collins st west
Robertson, Peter, Courteney st, Hot
Robertson, R., store, 149 Johnston st, E C
Robertson, Rev. A., William st north
Robertson, T., Robert, 19 Lygon st, Carl
Robertson, Robart, Miller st, W M
Robertson, Robert, watchmaker and jeweller, 19 Collins st west
Robertson, T., baker, Bay st, San
Robertson, T., 16 Electra st, Wmn
Robertson, T., Brunswick road, Bk
Robertson, Thomas, Reilly st, F
Robertson, Thomas, Queensberry hotel, Carl
Robertson, W., draper, 56 Gertrude st, F
Robertson, W., Heath st, San
Robertson, Wagner, and Co., coach proprietors, 35 Bourke st east
Robertson, Wm., farrier, 23 Little Collins st west
Robertson, Wm., 52 Dudley st, W M
Robertson, Wm., barrister, 39 Temple court
Robertson, Wm., Barry st, Carl
Robertson, Y., 6 Cardigan st, Carl
Robins, A. G., Nicholson st, F
Robinson, —, Moor st, F
Robinson, —, Napier st, Em H
Robinson, A., corner of Victoria and Nicholson sts, F
Robinson, A., schoolmaster, Black st, Btn
Robinson, Abraham, cartage contractor, &c., 29 Flinders lane west
Robinson, Blakiston, estate factor, Whitehall st, Fey
Robinson, C., Gardiner's creek road, Tk
Robinson, Chris., Borgondy st, Held
Robinson, Daniel, horse trainer, 206 Eastern road, Em H
Robinson, E., 156 Kerr st, F
Robinson, E. G., Vine st, Wr
Robinson, Francis, Hanmer st, Wmn
Robinson, F., machine sewer, 108 Brunswick st, F
Robinson, Hy., Lennox st, Rd
Robinson, J., 62 Dorcas st, Em H
Robinson, J., Rosslyn st, W M
Robinson, James, 26 Elgin st, Carl
Robinson, John H., 8 a'Beckett st
Robinson, John, wheelwright and smith, 24 Johnston st, E C
Robinson, Julia, 54 Latrobe st west
Robinson, Kate, store, 295 King st
Robinson, Leonard, draper, 37 Collins st east

Robinson, Miss, 20 Stevedore st, Wmn
Robinson, Mrs., Church st, Rd
Robinson, Mrs., grocer, 403 Lygon st, Carl
Robinson, Mrs., 69 Bridge road, Rd
Robinson, Mrs., 117 Raglan st east, Em H
Robinson, Robert, produce merchant, 39 Flinders st east
Robinson, Sydney Rudge, surgeon and dentist, Robe st, St K
Robinson, T., Commercial road, Pra
Robinson, T., 113 Gertrude st, F
Robinson, T., and Co., agricultural implement manufacturers and importers, 247 Elizabeth st
Robinson, Thomas, Spencer st
Robinson, Thomas, 101 Bouverie st, Carl
Robinson, Thomas, wheelwright and machine maker, Therry st, and Leicester st, Carl
Robinson, W., M.L.A., Parliament House
Robinson, W., Fitzroy st, St K
Robinson, W. F., Powlett st, E M
Robinson, W. F., Hotham st east, E M
Robinson, W. J., Elgin st, Carl
Robinson, Wm., 42 Dudley st, W M
Robinson, Wm. V., 5 Studley park terrace, Simpson's road, Rd
Robinson, Wm., Garden st, Pra
Robison Brothers and Co., plumbers and coppersmiths, 32 Flinders st west
Robison, J., Hoddle st, E C
Roble, Alex., Flinders st west
Robottom, Henry, gold chaser, 15 Post Office place
Robson, —, Bourke st east
Robson, Charles, 138 Lygon st, Carl
Robson, G. H., undertaker, 96 Brunswick st, F
Robson, John, Abbot st, Hot
Robson, Mrs., 34 Oxford st, E C
Robson, Richard, 146 Drummond st, Carl
Robson, Wm., 80 Cambridge st, E C
Rochard, J. W., 85 Cecil st, Em H
Roche, Francis, Errol st, Hot
Roche, Miss, school, 51 Queensberry st, Carl
Roche, Thomas, Post Office hotel, Pent
Roche, Thomas, Edinburgh Castle hotel, Bk
Rochfort, Benjamin, 72 George st east, E M
Rochford, L. J., Twyford st, Wmn
Rochford, Thomas, tailor, 18 Latrobe st east
Rochford, Wm., carpenter, 18 Latrobe st east
Rocke, Wm. H., Howe crescent, 50 Cecil st, Em H
Rockford, Thomas, 18 Latrobe st east
Rodd, Augustus W., storekeeper, Kew
Roddis, J. W., Pent
Roddick, Joseph, Wellington st, Rd
Rode, August, bootmaker, 37 Post Office place

Roden, M., 261 Victoria parade, E C
Rodger and Murray, grocers, &c., Ferguson st, W mn
Rodger, Thomas, 73 Cecil st, W mn
Rodgers, C., fruiterer, 151 Smith st, E C
Rodgers, David, 135 Little Bourke st west
Rodgers, G., and Co., general store, Bay st, San
Rodgers, Thomas, Bridport st west, Em H
Rodway, F., Dentist, 103 Collins st east
Roe, John, 269 Fitzroy st, F
Roebuck, J. P., chemist, Kew
Roff, Isaac, bill poster and tailor, 119 Little Collins st east
Rogan, M., grocer, 12 Lygon st, Carl
Rogan, Mark, 58 Latrobe st east
Rogers, D. H., ironmonger, 128 Smith st, E C
Rogers, Charles, saddler, 174 King st
Rogers, F., 36 George st, F
Rogers, F. H., photographer, Commercial road, Pra
Rogers, F. T., Gifford st, W mn
Rogers, George, 25 Twyford st, South W mn
Rogers, George, cooper, High st, Pra
Rogers, George, tailor and outfitter, 109 Bourke st east
Rogers, Henry, Canning st, Carl
Rogers, J., plumber, Bay st, Bm
Rogers, John, photographer, 150 Smith st, E C
Rogers, Miss Maria, schoolmistress, 13 Dover road, W mn
Rogers, Robert, carrier, Flemington hill
Rogers, Robert R., loan and share broker, and land agent, 3 Collins st west
Rogers, Thomas, 240 Napier st, F
Rogers, W. A., draper, 7 Gertrude st, F
Rogers, Wm., baker, Day st, San
Rogerson, Francis, farmer, Brennan st, Ess
Rogerson, Wm., Abbotsford st, W M
Rohlar, —, grocer, High st, St K
Roland, Charles, Morris st, W mn
Rolf, G. F., Goodwood st, Rd
Rolf, Mrs., Chapel st, Pra
Rolfe, —, 127 Raglan st, Em H
Rolfe and Bailey, merchants, 98 Bourke st west
Rolfe, Captain, High st, Pra
Rolfe, Charles, Rathdowne st, Carl
Rolfe, George, Carlisle st, East St K
Rolfe, George, jun., Regent st, F
Roll, J. B., Western st, Bk
Rolleston, Hugh, Walsh st, W M
Rollings, Wm., contractor, 96 Little Bourke st west
Rolls, B., and Son, boot importers, 14 Flinders lane west
Rolls, J., cab proprietor, 5 Young st, F
Romanis, John, house and land agent, Gardiner's creek road, Pra
Romanis, John, undertaker, Chapel st, Pra

Roman Catholic Chapels (see Index)
Ronald and MacBain, managers Australian Land and Finance Company, 22 and 24 Queen st
Ronald, B., Commercial road, Pra
Ronald, John, baker, 256 Brunswick st, F
Ronald, R. D., Gardiner's creek road
Ronalds, Nathaniel, nurseryman, Cremorne st, Rd
Ronke, Mrs., 123 Cecil st, Em H
Rooklidge, Thomas, and Co., saddlers, 60 Bourke st east
Rooklidge, Thomas, Waterloo st, St K
Rookwood, Miss, dressmaker, Chapel st, Pra
Rooney, M., Leitrim hotel, 119 Little Lonsdale st east
Rooney, Patrick, bootmaker, 89 Little Lonsdale st east
Roose, James, 15 Dover place, W mn
Rose, —, plumber, Charles st, F
Rose, A., Church st, Rd
Rose, Alexander, hay and corn store, 160 King st
Rose, Alex. O. G., judge's associate, Supreme Court
Rose, C., Stewart st, Bk
Rose, C. M., Argyle st, Pra
Rose, Henry, broker, &c., 53 Little Collins st east
Rose of Denmark Mining Company, 6 Collins st east
Rose, W., tailor, Darkly st, St K
Rosendale, Anthony, 127 Moray st, Em H
Rosengren, Gustaf, pianoforte manufacturer, 29 Lonsdale st east
Rosenthal, David, wholesale jeweller and importer, 2 Little Collins st west
Rosenthal, Julius, 133 Collins st east
Rosenwax, Elias, pawnbroker and salesman, 75 Elizabeth st
Rosewarne, Thomas, greengrocer, 90 Wellington st, E C
Rosie, Thomas, 27 Electra st, W mn
Rosier, James, W., gun maker, 45 Little Collins st east
Ross and Co., grocers, Gardiner's creek road, Pra
Ross and Smith, grocers, Grey st, St K
Ross and Smith, grocers, corner of Gertrude and George sts, F
Ross and Spowers, merchants, 31 Market street
Ross, Andrew, merchant, 29 Flinders lane east
Ross, C. S., and Co., timber and tobacco brokers and auctioneers, 60 Collins st west
Ross, Captain, High st, Pra
Ross, D., 10 John st, W mn
Ross, D., Queen st north
Ross, D. H., Lieutenant R.N., Charles st, F
Ross, David, blacksmith, Gardiner's creek road, Tk

U

Ross, Donald, 23 M'Arthur place, Carl
Ross, E., Gardiner's creek road, Tk
Ross, Francis, Trinnian st, off High st, Pra
Ross, G., Carlisle st, St K
Ross, H. F., 5 Raglan terrace, Robe st, St K
Ross, J., 94 Gore st, F
Ross, J., Turnbull's point, Punt road, S Y
Ross, J., bootmaker, 101 Victoria st, Carl
Ross, J. H., Hampton st, Btn
Ross, James, livery stable keeper, Flinders lane east
Ross, James, 36 Coventry st, Em H
Ross, John, 14 Little Nelson st, Wmn
Ross, John, 82 Leicester st, Carl
Ross, Mrs., 119 Gertrude st, F
Ross, Mrs., grocer, 201 Victoria parade, E C
Ross, Mrs., 17 Pelham st, Carl
Ross, P. F., wholesale saddler, 9 Lonsdale st west
Ross, R., tailor, Bourke st west
Ross, Robert, and Co., merchants, 110 Collins st west
Ross, Robert, tailor, 164 Bourke st west
Ross, W. B., bookseller, Chapel st, Pra
Ross, Wm., Kew
Ross, Wm. M., secretary Liverpool and London and Globe Insurance Company, 9 Elizabeth st
Rossen, ——, Bridge road, Rd
Rosser, C., Sydney road, Bk
Rosser, E., Sydney road, Bk
Rossiter, G. P., Richmond terrace, Rd
Rossiter, Miss, milliner, 221 Victoria parade, E C
Rossiter, T., grocer, Victoria and Swan st, Ild
Rostron, Laurence, jun., Kew
Rostron, Laurence, squatter, Ess
Rostron, P., Peel st, Pra
Rothwell, George, 89 Napier st, F
Rothwell, Wade, 22 Victoria st, Hot
Rough, C. E., grocer, Cambridge st, E C
Rough, W., Coventry st west, Km H
Roulston, Harvey, printer, Bridge road, Rd
Rourke, John, Drummond st, Carl
Rouse, F., l'entridge hotel, Pent
Rouse, John H., plumber and gasfitter, 16 Johnston st, F
Rouse, Wm., 75 Dorcas st, Em H
Row, Frederick, and Co., wool merchants, 64 Flinders st west
Rowan, Andrew, provision merchant, 78 Collins st west
Rowand, James, accountant, 149 Collins st west
Rowden Brothers, tinsmiths, 75 and 77 Russell st
Rowden, Charles, Napier st, F
Rowden, Frederick, pianoforte maker, 197 Stephen st

Rowden, Henry and John, 83 Russell st
Rowe, Brothers, butchers and grocers, 331 Church st, Rd
Rowe, B., Waltham st, Rd
Rowe, C., hay and corn store, Commercial road, Pra
Rowe, Dr., Gardiner's creek road, Tk
Rowe, Rev. James, Perry st, E C
Rowe, Thomas, land and commission agent, 93 Fitzroy st, F
Rowe, Wm. P., grocer, 132 Drummond st, Carl
Rowe, Wm., Flem
Howell, Wm., 2 Villiers st, Hot
Rowland, Henry, tinsmith, Kew
Rowlan and Cullen, shipping brokers, 58 Flinders st west
Rowland, J., nightman, 29 Little Bourke st west
Rowley, H., 6 Twyford st, Wmn
Rownie, J., Highett st, Rd
Rowsell, Mrs., 115 Cambridge st, E C
Roxburgh and Co., merchants, 20 Queen street
Roxburgh, George, Tivoli st, Punt hill, S Y
Roy, Charles, solicitor, 58 Little Collins st west
Roy, Jas., carpenter, McKillop st, Bourke st west
Roy, Mrs., Stoke st, San
Royal and Co., engineers, Barry st, Carl
Royal Bank of India, 109 Collins st west
Royal Society's Building, corner Stephen and Latrobe sts; secretary's office, 26 Queen st
Royce, Rev. James S. H., Pres
Roycraft, Mrs., 22 George st, F
Ruck, E. S., 59 Faraday st, Carl
Rucker, W. F. A., accountant and arbitrator, 35 Queen st
Rudall, James T., surgeon and oculist, 168 Collins st east
Rudd, Anthony P., cattle salesman, Ess
Rudd, Mrs., boarding-house keeper, 135 Collins st east
Ruddell Brothers, grocers, &c., 1 Eastern market
Ruddell, Joseph, 57 Queensberry st, Carl
Ruddle, Alfred, 425 King st north
Ruddle, James W., draper, Bay st, Btn
Rudduck, J. B., draper, Chapel st, Pra
Rudland, Wm., Rotherwood st, Hd
Rudman, John, builder, 89 Rathdowne st, Carl
Ruff, Abraham, soap and candle manufacturer, 41 Queensberry st, Hot
Ruff, James, Trinnian st, off High st, Pra
Ruffle, Mrs., 70 Dover road, Wmn
Ruglan, John, ship carpenter, River side, south
Rugless, Henry, 103 Collins st east
Rugley, ——, schoolmaster, New st, Btn
Rule, F., grocer, Henry st, Pra

Rule, Edward, grocer, Chapel st and High st, Pra
Rule, Frederick, bootmaker, Curzon st, Hot
Rule, John J., nurseryman, Church st, Rd
Rule, Joseph, Prince of Wales hotel, 136 Lonsdale st east
Rule, T., Osborne st, S Y
Rule, Thomas, 40 Stanley st, W M
Rumbell, Mrs. Isabella, midwife, 127 George st, F
Runting, W. J., 4 Bridport st, Em H
Runting, Wm., 71 Rathdowne st, Carl
Ruppio, F., cigar manufacturer, 27 Russell st
Rupprecht, Charles, Sabloniers hotel, corner Queen and a'Beckett sts
Rusden, G. W. (clerk of parliaments), Ashling st, Btn
Rusden, Henry, Tivoli place, Punt road, S Y
Rush, J., Berkeley st, Carl
Rush, Wm., tailor, High st, St K
Rushall, George, land agent, 46 Gertrude st, F
Rushall, Mrs., Fawkner st, St K
Rushton, John, Union st, Pra
Russ, George and Henry, butchers, Grey st, St K
Russell, —, school, 37 Osborne st, Wmn
Russell, A., Victoria st, Rd
Russell, A., 32 John st, Wmn
Russell, D., Bay st, San
Russell, E., produce merchant, 59 Flinders st west
Russell, F., Chambers st, S Y
Russell, F. G., Morland st, Fcy
Russell, G. P., timber yard, Crockford st, San
Russell, Henry, Hoddle st, E C
Russell, Henry, Inkerman st west, St K
Russell, J., printing office, 23 Church st, Em H
Russell, J., 175 Moray st, Em H
Russell, J., Hobe st, St K
Russell, James, baker, 77 Coventry st, Em H
Russell, John, mining manager and share broker, 33 Queen st
Russell, John J., painter, Gardiner's creek road, Pra
Russell, Mrs, 207 King st
Russell, Robert, architect and surveyor, 46 Elizabeth st
Russell, T., Calthorpe hotel, corner of Kerr and Brunswick sts, F
Russell, Thomas, 142A Latrobe st west
Russell, Thomas, 114 Latrobe st west
Russell, W., bootmaker, Nott st, San
Russell, W., 36 Barry st, Carl
Russell, Wm., corner of George and Powlett sts, E M
Russell, Wm., 21 Victoria st, E C
Russell, Wm., Palmerston st, Carl

Russell, Wm., Richmond terrace, Rd
Rutherford, James, 20 Lothian st, Hot
Rutherford, Mrs., 27 Palmerston st, F
Rutherford, Mrs. Sarah Ann, 86 George st, F
Rutherford, Thomas, Punt road, Rd
Rutherford, Wm., wood carver, 5 Franklyn st east
Rutherford, Wm., 17 Derby st, E C
Rutherwood, John, Abbotsford st, Hot
Rutledge, W., Gardiner's creek road, Pra
Rutter, George, stevedore, 30 Hanmer st, Wmn
Rutter, Robert, Peel st, Hot
Ruttledge, James, Peel st, W M
Ruxton, Mrs., Neptune st, St. K
Ryall, Henry, carpenter, Grosvenor st, Pra
Ryan, —, Cecil st, Wmn
Ryan and Hammond, stock agents, 57 Bourke st west
Ryan, Chas., St. Kilda road, Btn
Ryan, Dennis, Cowper st, Fcy
Ryan, Edwd., bootmaker, 84 Swanston st
Ryan, John, 13 Baillie st, Hot
Ryan, John, greengrocer, 19 Errol st, Hot
Ryan, John, Flemington rd, Hot
Ryan, John, 53 Faraday st, Carl
Ryan, John, Lalla Rookh hotel, Queensberry st, Hot
Ryan, John, blacksmith, Pickett st, Fcy
Ryan, John, Courtney st, Hot
Ryan, John, 35 Queensberry st, Carl
Ryan, Michael, tailor, 11 Lonsdale st east
Ryan, Miss, 9 Barry st, Carl
Ryan, Mrs., dressmaker, 111 Little Bourke st west
Ryan, Mrs., 36 Lygon st, Carl
Ryan, Mrs., 55 Pelham st, Carl
Ryan, P. J., Enniscorthy hotel, 38 Little Bourke st east
Ryan, Patrick, 10 Cecil st, Wmn
Ryan, Patrick, Latrobe parade, Collins st east
Ryan, Patrick, Abbotsford st, Hot
Ryan, Philip, Haymarket hotel, Blackwood st, Hot
Ryan, Robert, Longmore hotel, Peel st, Pra
Ryan, Rody, Canada hotel, Madeline st, Carl
Ryan, Stephen, Railway place, San
Ryan, T., 35 Barkly st, Carl
Ryan, Timothy, Ross's hotel, King st
Ryan, Thomas, 45 Park st, Em H
Ryan, W., furrier, Little Lonsdale st west, corner Queen st
Ryan, Wm., 76 Lygon st, Carl
Ryan, Wm., Yarra hotel, Cremorne st, Rd
Ryan, Wm., Shakespeare hotel, Dryburgh st, Hot
Ryan, Wm., Courteney st, Hot
Ryce, John, Union way, Bourke st east
Ryden, Michael, Berkeley st, Carl
Ryder, Geo. H., Arthur st, Pra

Ryder, R., Glenmore hotel, Franklyn st, W M
Ryland, James, Pelham st, Carl
Ryland, John, green grocer, Barry st, Carl
Ryland, John, 10 Pelham st, Carl

S.

Sabelberg, Jos., Punt hill, S Y
Sachs, John Gottlieb, wheelwright, &c., Elizabeth st extension
Sadden, W., Capel st, Hot
Sadler, J., store, Elgin st, Carl
Sadler, J. M., 172 Drummond st, Carl
Sadlier, John, Powlett st, E M
Sadlier, T., bootmaker, Wright lane, Lonsdale st west
Sagan, Robo., 23 Railway place, Wmn.
Sailors' Home, corner Spencer and Little Collins st west
Sainsbury, James, 117 Park st west, Em H
Sainsbury, James. 33 Nelson road, Em H
Salusbury, Miss, High st, Pra
Saint, Mrs., draper, 8a Victoria st, E C
Saker, George, Dover st, Wmn
Saker, Mrs., 113 Queen st
Salenger, Julius, 132 Collins st east
Salesberg, John, 9 Cobden st, Em H
Salisbury, Isaac, Rowena parade, Rd
Salkeld, Henry, 179 Punt rd, ltd
Salker, James, Argyle st, St K
Salmon, H., Graham st, San
Salmon, John, Rta
Salmon, Saul, 86 Johnson st, F
Salom, Isaac H., also writer, &c., 68 Courtney st, Hot
Salomon, J., jeweller, 17 Lonsdale st east
Salomon, M., importer, 60 Elizabeth st
Salter, H. P., accountant and mining agent, 64 Elizabeth st
Saltmash, Wm., Highett st, Rd
Salway, Benoni, 180 Madeline st, Carl
Sambrook, P., 172 Swan st, Rd
Sampford, Miss, 75 Spencer st
Sampson, D. B., 101 Swanston st
Sampson, George, 89 Oxford st, E C
Sampson, John, carrier, Elizabeth st north
Sampson, L., 38 Hanover st, F
Sampson, Mathew, 90 Arden st, Hot
Sampson, T. C., Palmerston st, Carl
Sampson, Wm., 109 George st, F
Samson, Horace, Kew
Samuel, E., and Co., general importers, 23 Little Collins st west
Samuel, Elias, 50 Nicholson st, F
Samuel, Elizabeth, confectioner, 76 Lonsdale st east
Samuel, Francis, dairyman, 98 Wellington st west
Samuels, A., Napier st, F
Samuels, James W., 128 Nicholson st, F
Samuels, Wm., baker, Bridge road, Rd

Samwells, —, Collins st east
Sanders, —, bootmaker, Hay st, San
Sanders, C. C., and Co., saddlers, 34 Bourke st west
Sanders, Henry, saddlers' ironmonger, 34 Lonsdale st east
Sanders, J., carpenter, High st, St K
Sanders, J., cab proprietor, Yarra st, E C
Sanders, John, Ralston st, Pra
Sanders, John. 18 Kerr st, F
Sanders, L., Nicholson st, F
Sanders, M., Nicholson st, F
Sanderson, George, Graham st, San
Sanderson, George, hatter, 22 Bourke st east
Sanderson, Henry, commission and mining agent, 34 Queen st
Sanderson, Isaac, engineer, Grey st, E M
Sanderson, J., 5 Victoria parade, E M
Sanderson, J., baker, Railway place, San
Sanderson, J., hat manufacturer and importer, 63 Collins st east
Sanderson, John, and Co., merchants, 34 Queen st
Sanderson, Joseph, Domain st, S Y
Sandford, Henry, tailor, 34 Nelson place, Wmn
Sandford, Robert, 5 Montague st, Em H
Sandford, S. G., 94 Cecil st, Em H
Sandham, Miss, Clyde st, St K
Sandilands, B. N., Cecil st, Em H
Sands and MacDougall, printers, stationers, &c., 46 and 48 Collins st west
Sands, G. J., M.L.A., Parliament House
Sands, Robt. Jas., greengrocer, 202 Johnston st, E C
Sandy Creek Poverty Reef Quartz Mining Company, 66 Little Collins st west
Sandy, Robert, 16 Macarthur place, Carl
Sangster, David, public baths, Swanston street
Sanguinetti, J. D., and Co., tailors, 30 Little Collins st east
Sanson, George, general dealer, 52 Little Bourke st west
Sargeant, D., draper, 85 Clarendon st, Em H
Sargent, G., store. Church st, Rd
Sargent, Henry, Railway place, San
Sargent, Henry, Nott st, San
Sargent, Mrs., Nott st, San
Sargood, King, and Sargood, warehousemen, 27, 29, and 31 Flinders st east
Sarjeant, James, muffin baker, 90 Gertrude st, F
Sarker, Mrs., Arden st, Hot
Sarsfield, J., 40 Latrobe st west
Satchell, James, 124 Raglan st, Em H
Saubrey, J. G., Henry st, Pra
Sault, Richard, Pra
Saunders, Chas. F., Grattan st, Carl
Saunders, Frederick, Perry st, E C
Saunders, John, Church st, Rd
Saunders, Lewis, 15 Spring st

Saunders, Mrs., school, High st, St K
Saunders, Mrs., school, Wellington parade, E M
Saunders, Richard J., 41 Fitzroy st, F
Saunders, W., Punt road, Pra
Saunders, W., Essex st, Fcy
Saunders, Wm., draper, 60 High st, St K
Saunders, Wm. H., shipmaster, 2 Prince's terrace, Fitzroy st, St K
Saubery, Ann, Chapel st, Pra
Savage, Richard, River-side south
Savage, Robert, High st, St K
Savill, A. M. J., 15 Palmer st, F
Savill and Tong, fruiterers, 4 Western Market
Savill, Thomas, Hoddle st, Rd
Saville, The Misses, ladies' school, 1 Victoria terrace, Napier st, F
Savings' Bank, Market st
Savings' Banks, Commissioners of, Market street
Sawbridge, W. H., Sandridge Inn, Bay st, San
Sawden, Wm., Kent st, Moor st, F
Sawdey, J. C., boarding-house, Bay st, San
Sawds, J. B., Highett st, Rd
Sawds, Jos., Chetwynd st, W M
Sawdy, Wm., butcher, Bay st, San
Sawell, Henry, Gipps st east, E M
Sawer, John, Fleet st, Palmer st, F
Sawers, R. W., 98 Moor st, F
Sawyer, John, 50 Wreckyn st, Hot
Sawyers, A., nursery, Pres
Sawyers, Mrs. Martha, Londonderry hotel, 190 Wellington st, E C
Sawyers, W., 18 Market st, Em H
Saxby, J. R., Railway place, San
Saxton, M., 37 Thompson st, South Wmn
Say, W. B., straw hat maker, Madeline st, Carl
Sayce and Co., chemists, Elizabeth st
Sayce, Edward, Wellington st, Dandenong road, Pra
Sayce, Lewis, 16 Gore st, F
Sayers, Alex., Davies st, Pra
Sayers, John N., letter-press printer, 218 Bourke st east
Sayers, Wm., produce merchant, Western Market
Scammell, George T., builder, Henry st, Pra
Scammell, William, Union st, Wr
Scanlon, Lawrence, 60 Arden st, Hot
Scanlan, Louis, bootmaker, 151 Victoria parade, F
Scanlan, Patrick, S., 75 Gore st, F
Scarborough, George, Ken
Scarborough, J., hootmaker, 180 Victoria st, Rd
Scarlet, George, bootmaker, 170 Johnston st, E C
Scarlett, T. Clifford, fruiterer, 233 Elizabeth st

Scarsdale Great Extended Gold Mining Co., 64 Elizabeth st
Schabel, C., 8 St. David st
Schabel, Charles, 181 Greeves st, F
Scheckell, Thomas, boot manufactory, 71 Spring st
Scheele, C., 168 Bridge road, Rd
Scheliger, C., 105 Gore st, F
Schemmel, — straw bleacher, 224 Lonsdale st east
Scherell, Frederick, 7 Palmer st, F
Schlerwagen, G., shoemaker, Commercial lane
Schild, John C. C., news agent, Hyde st, Fcy
Schilling, Joseph, watchmaker, 40 Little Bourke st west
Schlimmer, Wm., 65 Queensbury st, Carl
Schlnoerling, F. A., myall pipe manufacturer, 106 Bourke st west
Schleischer, C., 105 Gore st, F
Schlesinger, Mrs., Nicholson st, F
Schlesinger, Richard, mining manager, 37 Market st
Schlessinger, F., 79 Gore st, F
Schlobach, E., Alma road, East St. Kilda
Schlöstein, A. and Co., merchants, 38 Flinders lane west
Schlöstein, Adolph, Consul for Hamburg and Bremen, and Acting Consul for Hanover, 38 Flinders lane west
Schmidt, Francis, German cottages, Nicholson st, Carl
Schmidt, George, 72 Victoria st, N M
Schneider, George, bootmaker, Elgin st, Carl
Schobbert, L. F., hairdresser, 90 Bourke st east
Schober, A., 107 Kerr st, F
Schoenfield, Frederick, Faraday st, Carl
Schofield, Andrew, solicitor, 62 Collins st east
Schofield, George, bootmaker, 126 Clarendon st, Em H
Schofield, John, 112 Madeline st, Carl
Schofield, M., 110 Cecil st, Em H
Scholes, Mrs., 43 Jeffcott st, W M
Scholes, James, general dealer, 18 Bridge road, Rd
Scholtz, J., Yarra hotel, Johnston st, E C
Schoman, William, Morland st, Fcy
Schott, Augustus, 12 Young st, F
Schott, J., professor of music, 119 Collins st east
Schreiber, Henry, mathematical instrument maker, 110½ Queen st
Schreibers, Mrs., milliner, High st, St. K
Schubert, W., linguist, 108 Lonsdale st west
Schufor, Carl, grocer, Punt road, Pra
Schuler, Gustav, tobacconist, 45 Victoria parade, F
Schuhkraft, Wm., Grey st east, E M
Schwab, William, 7 Weyland's lane, F

Schyler, R., Station place
Seithers, G., 9 Elizabeth st
Seoff, Wm., Graham st, Young st, F
Scurfield, A., 138 Fitzroy st, F
Scotch Churches (see Index)
Scotch College, Lansdowne st, E M
Scotchmer, William M., 92 Young st, F
Scotland, Mrs. J., 149 Latrobe st west
Scots' School, 89 Collins st east
Scotson, John, 8 Gore st, F
Scott, —, 48 Adderley st, W M
Scott, —, Acland st, St. K
Scott, —, Pelham st, Carl
Scott, —, 109 Bouverie st, Carl
Scott, —, tailor, 190 Lygon st, Carl
Scott, —, dressmaker, 55 Napier st, F
Scott, A., Barry st, Carl
Scott, A., 60 Baillie st, Hot
Scott, Alexander, grocer, Berkeley st, Carl
Scott, Andrew, butcher, Bridge road, Rd
Scott, C., Peel st, Pra
Scott, D., 177 Dorcas st, Em II
Scott, Daniel, 24 Curzon st, Hot
Scott, Edwin, Scott's hotel, 107 Collins st west
Scott, Edward, Victoria parade, E M
Scott, G., blacksmith, 48 Johnson st, E C
Scott, George, 4 Church st, Em II
Scott, George, schoolmaster, Fent
Scott, George, engineer and millwright, 78 Young st, F
Scott, Hugh, Palmerston place, Madeline st, Carl
Scott, J., printer, New st, Bru
Scott, J., Raglan st, Em II
Scott, J., butcher, 11 Coventry st, Em II
Scott, J. A., shoeing smith, 36 Little Bourke st west
Scott, James, Thompson st, Wmn
Scott, James, bootmaker, 55 Bouverie st, Carl
Scott, James, solicitor, notary public, &c., 62 Little Collins st west
Scott, James, 7 Dorcas st, Em II
Scott, James, nurseryman, Haw
Scott, James, Elgin st, Carl
Scott, James, Arran st, Fcy
Scott, James, Miller st, W M
Scott, John, secretary City of Melbourne Gas and Coke Company, Collins st west
Scott, John, Spencer st
Scott, John, grocer, 137 Bouverie st, Carl
Scott, John, grocer, 47 Johnston st, E C
Scott, John, 54 Park st east, Em II
Scott, John, brickmaker, Flem
Scott, John, Flem
Scott and Co., coppersmiths and braziers, 113 Flinders st west
Scott, Jos., coach painter, 12 Lincoln square
Scott, M., Fitzroy st, St K
Scott, M. J., 130 Johnston st, E C
Scott, Mrs., dressmaker, 106 Lonsdale st east

Scott, Mrs., 93 George st, E M
Scott, Mrs., Waltham st, Rd
Scott, Mrs., 21 Rathdowne st, Carl
Scott, Mrs., boot dealer, 87 High st, St K
Scott, Mrs. A., boarding-house, 146 Lonsdale st west
Scott, Peter, butcher, 35 Coventry st, Em II
Scott, R., surgeon dentist, 239 Elizabeth st
Scott, R., 44 Swan st, Rd
Scott, Robert, baker, 84 Smith st, F C
Scott, Robert, Leviathan hotel, corner Napier and Gertrude sts, F
Scott, T., 214 King st
Scott, T., Miller st, W M
Scott, T., 31 Coventry st, Em II
Scott, T. H., 33 Gertrude st, F
Scott, Thomas, ship broker, 10 King st
Scott, Thomas R., 198 Eastern road, Em II
Scott, W., greengrocer, 68 Clarendon st, Em II
Scott, W. C., 239 Victoria parade, E C
Scottie, John, 11 Stanley st, W M
Scouller, John, 17 Young st, F
Scratton, Daniel, solicitor, 66 Latrobe st east
Screene, James, 17 Richmond terrace, Rd
Scripture Free Schools: 34 Little Bourke st west; 21 Smith st, F; 109 Little Bourke st east; 11 Cremorne st, Rd; Victoria st, Rd; Commercial road, Pra
Scriven, John, Greenhythe, Fcy
Scrivenor, T. L., 84 Young st, F
Scrivenor, F. W., 98 Argyle st, F
Scrivenor, Mrs., 84 Young st, F
Scuffian, C., Red Lion inn, Kew
Scully, E., 13 Victoria st, Carl
Scurry, J., Jollmont road, E M
Seaforth, H., 168½ George st, F
Seaker, Alfred, bootmaker, 97 Stephen st
Seamark, G., and Co., contractors, 57 Flinders lane east
Seamen's Church, corner Beach and Nott sts, San
Seamer, Mrs., 152 Kerr st, F
Search, Frederick, Flem
Searle, Edward, 36 Hanover st, F
Searle, James, butcher, 53 Queensberry st, Carl
Seath, Mrs., 135 Lonsdale st west
Seaver, Patrick, Argyle st, Pra
Sebastopol Lease Quartz Mining Company, 55 Elizabeth st
Sebire, Henry, 83 Johnston st, E C
Sebo, George, fruiterer, 131a Brunswick st, F
Secombe, John, 30 Lygon st, Carl
Second Richmond Building and Investment Society, Bank place
Second Union Building Society, 82 Collins st east
Second Victoria Building and Investment Society, 56 Little Collins st east
Seddon, Arthur, Twyford st, Wmn

Seddon, S., draper, Peat
Sedgcumbe, Mrs., 98 Oxford st, E C
Sedgefield, S. W., Howe crescent, Em II
Sedgwick, Henry, 106 Leicester st, F
Seekamp, C., 16 King William st, F
Seiele, Madam, 106 Lonsdale st west
Seidenschnur, H. H., 34 Stanley st, E C
Selby, George W., Avoca st, S Y
Selick, A., Brighton st, lld
Selkirk, F. T., 34 Clarendon st, Em II
Selkrig, Robert, 115 Gore st, F
Sellain, J., painter, Courtenay st, Hot
Sellar, Robert, Tennyson st, St K
Sellars, Robert, Tennyson st, St K
Selle, C. H., pewterer, Canning st, Carl
Sellers, C. H., Pelham st, Carl
Sellers, Thomas, Pelham st, Carl
Sellers, W., shoemaker, 327 Brunswick st, F
Sellers, Wm., Reilley st, F
Sellwood, Richard, Fitzroy st F
Semkina, W., carpenter, York st, Din
Semoonsum, P., 15 King William st, F
Senior, James, Hanmer st, Wmn
Senior, Thomas, Charles st, Pra
Serey, Frederick, Inkerman st east, St K
Sergeant, C. W., Chapel st, lld
Serle, F. W. D., Victoria hotel, Condell st, F
Serle, Henry, Lothian st, Hot
Serrell, Thomas, surgeon, 99 Victoria parade, F
Servais, Henry, piano maker, 4 Charles st, F
Service, James, and Co., merchants, 139 Bourke st west
Service, James, Carlisle st east, St K
Service, John, 96 Gore st, F
Service, Mrs., 60 George st, E M
Setford, James, sign writer and painter, 42 Bridge road, lld
Seward, J. M., Somerset park, Plenty road
Sewell, Isaac, wholesale grocer, 213 Elizabeth st
Sewell, J., Williams road, Pra
Sewell, Mrs., 137 Latrobe st west
Sewell, W., Cochrane st, Bin
Sewerage and Water Department Offices, 80 Lonsdale st west
Sexton, Daniel, Capel st, Hot
Seyfarth, Henry, tailor, 87 Russell st
Seyfried, J. B., watchmaker and jeweller, 150 Little Collins st east
Seymour, James, Hotham st, E M
Symour, John, carver, 214 Bourke st east
Seymour, Jos., David, carver, 230 Bourke st east
Seymour, Mrs., draper, 68 Wellington st, E C
Seymour, Wm., storekeeper, 23 Thompson st, Wmn
Shacklock, Peter, 6 Market st, Em II
Shade, W., ironmonger, Nth

Shade, Walter, carpenter, Nth
Shadforth, J., bootmaker, 31 Stanley st, E C
Shadwick, John, Flem
Shain, Alexander, 143 Drummond st, Carl
Shakespear, R. H., C.E. and surveyor, 69 Bourke st west
Shakespeare, Wm., hay and corn store, 112 Cambridge st, E C
Shall, J., Railway place, San
Shallvas, Henry, builder, 21 Leveson st, Hot
Shallow, Wm., Abbotsford st, Hot
Shanahan, James, baker, 53 Wellington st, E C
Shanahan, John, Mount Pleasant hotel, Lygon st, Carl
Shane, John, 133 Little Bourke st west
Shanks, Matthew, Abbotsford st, Hot
Shankly, John C., signwriter and painter, 107 Little Lonsdale st west
Shann, Richard, Bank of Victoria, Collins st east
Shannaban, D., blacksmith, Bedford st, Hot
Shannahen, M., Royal Australian hotel, Lygon st, Carl
Shannon, Edward, saddler, 45 York st, Em II
Shannon, John, 213 Clarendon st, Em II
Shannon, P., 61 Raglan st, Em II
Shannon, P. F., last modeller and bootmaker, 3 Collins st west
Shannon, Thomas, 46 King William st, F
Shappere, Solomon, Williamstown hotel, Thompson st, Wmn
Sharman, T., bootmaker, McGrath place, Little Lonsdale st east
Sharp, A., blacksmith, 90 Bridge road, Rd
Sharp, C., 16 Bank st, Em II
Sharp, Charles C., Ship hotel, Bay st, San
Sharp, Isaac, Clyde st, St K
Sharp, J., Jackson st, St K
Sharp, John, timber merchant, Collins st west
Sharp, Jos., 153 Nicholson st, F
Sharp, R. W., agent, 33 Queen st
Sharp, W., dealer, Chapel st, Pra
Sharp, Wm., blacksmith, Bridge road, Rd
Sharpe, Andrew, store, 70 Drummond st, Carl
Sharpe, Colman, 62 Bank st east, Em II
Sharpe, Henry L., flour factor, 13 Elizabeth st
Sharpe, J., 36 Clarendon st, Em II
Sharpe, J., Station place, San
Sharpe, Mrs., 26 Raglan st, Em II
Sharpe, Wm. Henry, stationer, 1 Barkly st, Carl
Sharples, Mrs., greengrocer, 188 Bridge road, Rd
Sharrel, Wm., 177 Lygon st, Carl
Sharwood, L. J., Darling st, S Y
Shaw, Charles, solicitor, 113 Stephen st

Shaw, Alfred, Ironmonger, 236 Elizabeth street
Shaw, G. and G., wholesale grocers, wine and spirit merchants, 36 Flinders st east
Shaw, Henry S., official assignee, 2 and 3 Eldon Chambers, Collins st west
Shaw, James, painter, Inkerman st east, St K
Shaw, James and John, gingerbeer manufacturers, &c., 20 Yorke st east, Em H
Shaw, James, Graham st, San
Shaw, John F., veterinary surgeon, 87 Flinders lane east
Shaw, Joseph, Carlisle st west, St K
Shaw, Mrs., 138 Brunswick st, F
Shaw, P., Cross st, Hot
Shaw, Thomas, oil importer, 99½ Collins st west
Shea, E. O., 5 Barkly st, Bk
Shea, G. W., 11 Peel st, W M
Shea, John G., solicitor, 90 Little Collins st west
Shenhan, F., 33 Cecil st, Em H
Sheahan, Patrick, and Co., produce merchants, 6 Western market
Shean, Wm., 71 Charles st, F
Shearer, J. and D., wine and spirit merchants, William st north
Shearwood, H., 4 Greeves st, F
Sheedy, John, Connell hotel, 204 Bridge road, Rd
Shehan, —, 291 Victoria st, E C
Shehan, P., 128 Madeline st, Carl
Shehan, Patrick, Harp of Erin hotel, 75 Madeline st, Carl
Sheehane, Mrs. J., 46 Cobden st, Em H
Sheedy, John, bootmaker, 207 Lygon st, Carl
Sheeky, W., Cooper's hotel, Little Lonsdale st east
Sheffield, J., Rowena parade, Rd
Shell, Patrick, general store, Elgin st, Carl
Sheldrake, J., 91 Gore st, F
Sheldrake, Jonathan, 7 Alma terrace, F
Sheldrick, George, Railway place, San
Shelley, W. W., North Richmond hotel, Victoria st, Rd
Shellow, Mrs., Arden st, Hot
Shelton, Henry, Domain st, S Y
Shephard, Mary, dressmaker, 32 Lonsdale st east
Shepherd, —, grocer, Studley st, E C
Shepherd, —, teacher, Pres
Shepherd, C., bootmaker, 70 Little Oxford st, E C
Shepherd, Albert, Pont road, Pra
Shepherd, Janet, confectioner, 249 Swanston st
Shepherd, Mrs., Chapel st, Pra
Shepherd, Thomas, Studley st, E C
Sheppard, A., 22 Collins st west
Sheppard, E., Swan st, Fcy
Sheppard, George, 31 Jeffcott st, W M

Sheppard, J., Rowena parade, Rd
Sheppard, John A., Eas
Sheppard, R., 136 Ferrers st, Em H
Sheppard, Sherborne, High st, St K
Sheppard, Thomas, Moore st, Fcy
Sheppard, Thomas, 44 Butler st, Em H
Sheran, F., Bouverie st, Carl
Sherry, C., Nicholson st, F
Sherer, Caleb, Old Diggers' hotel, corner of Smith and Sackville sts, E C
Sherer, D., Howard st, W M
Sherer, R., Peel st, Pra
Sheridan, J., 55 King William st, F
Sheriff, G., saddler, Johnston st, E C
Sherlock, W., York st, Em H
Sherrard, John S., fancy repository, 75 Victoria st, E C
Sherrard, Leslie James, Haw
Sherren, J. C., butcher, 166 Clarendon st, Em H
Sherrott, Edward, bootmaker, Hoddle st, E C
Sherry, John D., dealer in hides, 60 William st, River bank north
Sherry, Wm., fruiterer, Smith st, E C
Sherwin, J., M.L.A., Parliament House
Sherwin, Mrs., 1 Cambridge st, E C
Sherwood, Charles J., Baptist lane, Little Collins st east
Sherwood, George, nursery, Docklands st, Heid
Sherwood, Thomas, tailor, Franklyn st
Shiel, John, 140 Flinders lane east
Shiel, Patrick, 200 Cardigan st, Carl
Shields and Co., cornfactors, 343 Elizabeth st
Shields and Co., grocers, &c., 10 a'Beckett st east
Shields, E., Alma st, St K
Shiels, Margaret, ladies' school, Hotham st, E M
Shiels, Wm. J., Watt hotel, 79 Spencer st
Shier, Thomas, watchmaker, 124 King st
Shillinglaw, Henry, Richmond terrace, Rd
Shill, John, Hoddle st, E C
Shimells, E., 71 York st, Em H
Shine, Daniel, 137 Cardigan st, Carl
Shipp, F., bootmaker, 61 York st, Em H
Shipp, T., bootmaker, 74 Clarendon st, Em H
Shipp, Thomas, wireworker, 111 Little Bourke st west
Shippey, Henry, 143A Johnston st, E C
Shipping Office, Sailors' Home, Spencer st
Shirra, A., Cardigan st, Carl
Shoddock, C., bootmaker, Grosvenor st, Pra
Shoosmith and Curtis, Custom house agents, &c., 70 Flinders lane west
Short, Alex. E., Union Hotel, 369 Spencer street
Short Bros., photographers, 142 Smith st, E C

Short, David, 162 Moran st, Em U
Short, G., Commercial road, Pra
Short, Henry, Sir Charles Hotham hotel, 142 Flinders st west
Short, Michael, tailor, 232 Swan st, Rd
Short, Thomas, corner Roden and Adderley sts, W M
Short, W., 104 Nicholson st, F
Shortal, P., 25 Little Lonsdale st west
Shorter, James, 73 Curzon st, Hot
Shorthouse, Mrs. Ann, 90 York st, Em U
Shortt, Wm. C., chemist, 54½ Bourke st west
Shot, Richard, 28 Grattan st, Carl
Shotton, Richard, Grosvenor st, Pra
Showers, Robert, West of England hotel, Kerr st, F
Shubridge, John, 144 Queen st
Shudell, Charles, 14 Curzon st, Hot
Shults, H., boarding-house, 105 Little Bourke st east
Shurey, W., jun., pastrycook, 18 Gertrude st, F
Shurey, Wm., baker, corner of Gertrude and Fitzroy sts, F
Shuri, J., Miller st, W M
Shute, F., 90 Dorcas st east, Em U
Shuttleworth, F., solicitor, 231 Swanston street
Sierrap Lazarus, 45 Pelham st, Carl
Sibbald, H. Y., broker, 66 Collins st west
Sibering, E. U., 130 Collins st east
Sibkley, Wm., Elm Lodge, Kew
Sieman, F., Beach st, San
Sievwright, A., William st north
Sievwright, J., carpenter, Peel st, W M
Sievwright, M., solicitor, 51 Elizabeth st
Sigalski, D., 125 Flinders lane east
Signal Station, Nelson place, Wmn
Silktoe, Edwin, Errol st, Hot
Silk, H., 19 Dover place, Wmn
Silk, Robert M., grocer, Kew
Silsby, Joseph, Chetwynd st, Hot
Sill, Mark, gardener, Cape st, Heid
Sills, J. H., 19 Dover place, Wmn
Silver, John, Peel st, Pra
Silvester, Henry, 18 Greeves st, F
Sim, Wm. Geo., baker, 22 Little Bourke st west
Sime, D. and S., boarding-house, 48 Lonsdale st west
Simes, John, tailor, Madeline st, Carl
Simeon, J., 2 Granite terrace, Gertrude st, F
Simeon, Howard, agent, 79½ Flinders lane east
Simmers, James, grocer and ship chandler, 4 Nelson place, Wmn
Simmonds, John, 62 Drummond st, Carl
Simmonds, S. P., 81 Andrew's st, Btn
Simmons, J. G., Corry st, Cardigan st, Carl
Simmons, Joshua, pawnbroker, Franklyn st, St K

Simmons, James, Peel st, Pra
Simmons, Morris, dentist, 122 Bourke st east
Simmons, Mrs., 82 Douglas parade, Wmn
Simmons, Wm., tinsmith, 121 Brunswick st, F
Simons, J., 36 Church st, Em U
Simons, Wm. P., journalist, Greville st, Pra
Simons, Wm. V., analytical and operative chemist and lecturer, 25 Swanston st
Simpkins, J., 64 Ann st, Wmn
Simple, Peter, Bay st, San
Simpson, Alexander, Reilly st, F
Simpson, Fredk. W., baker, Johnston st, F C
Simpson, George, cordial manufacturer and merchant, 91 Little Bourke st west
Simpson, George, painter and paperhanger, 24 Errol st, Hot
Simpson, J., Miller st, W M
Simpson, John, Peacock hotel, Stephen st
Simpson, John J., greengrocer, Bedford st, Hot
Simpson, Miss, Grey st, St K
Simpson, Mrs., ladies' school, 126 Fitzroy st, F
Simpson, Mrs., 52 Coventry st, Em U
Simpson, Mrs. Fitzroy st, St K
Simpson, Mrs., Joseph, draper, 100 Moray st, Em U
Simpson, Robert, wholesale confectioner, Johnston st, F
Simpson, Robert, bootmaker, 84 Coventry st, Em U
Simpson, W., surgeon, &c., Whitehall st, Fcy
Simpson, William, Caroline st, S Y
Simpson, Wm., hay and corn dealer, 153 Bridge rd, Rd
Sims, —, 193 Smith st, F
Sims, Edward, Crockford st, San
Sims, G. W., 38 Moor st, F
Sims, Geo. John, solicitor, 18 Collins st east
Sims, George, 47 Wellington st, E C
Sims, H. C., Royal hotel, Clarendon st, Em U
Sims, Henry, timber and coal merchant, &c., Napier st, Fcy
Sims, J., draper, 181 Clarendon st, Em U
Sims, John, Madeline st, Carl
Sims, W., 83 Gore st, F
Simson, Robert, Gardiner's creek rd, Tk
Sinclair, —, Stoke st, San
Sinclair, Chas., Stoke st, San
Sinclair, D., Maribyrnong st, Fcy
Sinclair, George, 36 Young st, F
Sinclair, James, carpenter, 64 Little Bourke st west
Sinclair, John, baker, 84A Victoria st, Rd
Sinclair, John, engineer, &c., River side south
Sinclair, John, Jolimont road, E M

154   Sin   MELBOURNE   Smi

Sinclair, John, Palmerston place, Madeline st, Carl
Sinclair, Mrs. Eliza, 53 Nelson rd, Em H
Sinclair, P., hairdresser, 13 Little Bourke st west
Sinclair, Peter, 84 Bouverie st, Carl
Sinclair, Robert, 19 Twyford st, Wmn
Sinclair, Robert, 68 Greeves st, F
Sinclair, Thomas, 13 Montague st, Em H
Sinclair, W., 103 George st, F
Sinclair, William, builder, Farrady st, Carl
Sincock, William, accountant, 28 Collins st east
Singleman and Reidle, cabinet makers, 147 Lonsdale st east
Singer, J., Gardiner's creek road, Tk
Singleton, Robert, Domain road, S Y
Sin Kong Hap, merchant, 46 Little Bourke st east
Sinner, Thomas, 49 Little Bourke st west
Sinnet, Denis, 52 Jeffcott st, W M
Sinnock, J., bootmaker, Railway place, San
Sinnock, W., Wellington st, Pra
Sinnott, William, ship chandler, 23 York st, Em H
Sinnott, William, 27 Fitzroy st, F
Sircom, John, Bull st, St K
Sitch, Samuel, plumber, &c., Bridge road, Rd
Sivell, Abraham, 110 Argyle st, F
Skardon, Charles, surgeon dentist, Argyle st, St K
Skarratt, Charles, 4 Swiss terrace, Fitzroy st, F
Skarratt, Charles Carleton, Royal Mail hotel, 70 Bourke st east
Skeane, A. J., Barkly st, St K
Skeats, Chas., timber merchant and ironmonger, 161 Clarendon st, Em H
Skeen, J., tailor, 125 Bourke st east
Skews, Thomas, baker, Flem
Skidmore, Thomas, Albion st, Dk
Skilton, J., Chambers st, S Y
Skinner, —, 3 M'Arthur place, Carl
Skinner, F., crinoline manufacturer, 123 Russell st
Skinner, Fredk., Sandridge road
Skinner, George, Walsh st, W M
Skinner, George, 105 Farraday st, Carl
Skinner, J., carpenter, Park st, Bin
Skinner, J. W., Swan st, Fcy
Skinner, Jacob, Union st, Pra
Skinner, Mrs., 50 Hanover st, F
Skinner, Mrs., Alma st east, St K
Skinner, R., bootmaker, Railway place, San
Skinner, Samuel, Park st, S Y
Skinner, Thomas, Grey st, E M
Skirham, W., 39 Cecil st, Em M
Slack, Joseph Bragg, commission agent, 140 Queen st
Slack, Thos. Edward, Albert st, E M
Sladden, James, poulterer, 17 Eastern Market

Slade, —, bootmaker, 61 Clarendon st, Em H
Slade, Philip, 76 Johnston st, F
Slade, Wm., Gardiner's creek road, Tk
Sladen, Charles, M.L.C., Melbourne Club
Slater, James, grocer, Yarra st, E C
Slater, James, Lancashire Arms hotel, Yarra st, E C
Slater, John, Kew
Slater, Mrs. Geo., draper, 139 Cecil st, Em H
Slater, T., coffee roaster, Bay st, San
Slater, Thomas, 102 Spencer st
Slater, Walter, 17 Argyle st, F
Slater, William, Cardigan st, Carl
Slatford, Mrs., boot and shoe dealer, Chapel st, Pra
Slatterie, Apollos, printer, Haw
Sleight, Edwin, Highett st, Rd
Sleight, John, undertaker, 71 Collins st east
Sleven, Miss, machine sewer, 12 Gertrude st, F
Slip, Government Patent, Nelson place, Wmn
Slip, Wright's Patent, Nelson place, Wmn
Sloane, —, 75 York st west, Em H
Sloane, James, 67 Flinders st east
Sloane, Thomas, cooper, 15 Parker st, Wmn
Sloane, W., Waterloo st, St K
Sloane, W., and Co., merchants and commission agents, 115 Collins st west
Sloman and Son, furniture warehouse, 39 Queen st
Sloman, H., Peel st, Wr.
Sloman, Herman, 54 Little Latrobe st
Sloman, N., Inkerman st, St K
Slop, J., York st, Em H
Sly, Benjamin, 18 Rathdowne st, Carl
Sly, Benjamin, 69 Farraday st, Carl
Smale, A. W., Bay st, Bin
Small, T., draper, Victoria st, Rd
Small, Thos. Stephen, Church st, Rd
Small, W. E., Cecil st, F
Smart, —, 79 Raglan st, Em H
Smart, Charles W., 116 Johnston st, E C
Smart, G. J., professor of dancing, 139 Swanston st
Smart, Geo., 64 Young st, F
Smart, John, Rosslyn st, W M
Smart, Peter, bootmaker, Haw
Smart, Peter, 89 Victoria st, Carl
Smart, W., dairy, 172 Swan st, Rd
Smart, Wm., 19 Wellington st, E C
Smeaton, Thomas, fruiterer, 48 Swanston street
Smethers, H., builder, Lennox st, Rd
Smibert, Alex., Osborne st, Wmn
Smith, —, Graham st, San
Smith, —, 37 Argyle st, F
Smith, —, farrier, Carlisle st west, St K
Smith, —, grocer, Berkeley st, Carl
Smith, A., butcher, Commercial road, Pra

Smith, A., boarding house, 71 Flinders lane east
Smith, A., carpenter, 134 Raglan st, Em H
Smith, A. J., bookseller, &c., 30 Swanston street
Smith, A. K., Carlton foundry, 56 Leicester st, Carl
Smith, Adam, Suburban Railway hotel, Gardiner's creek road, S Y
Smith, Adam B., bootmaker, 110 Clarendon st, Em H
Smith, Alexander, bootmaker, Bay st, San
Smith, Alfred, brassfounder, 24 Post office place
Smith, Alfred, bookbinder, 4 Union way, Bourke st east
Smith, Alfred, tailor, 37 Stanley st, E C
Smith, Alfred L., Bank place, Collins st west
Smith and Banks, agents for Murray Steam Navigation Company, 100 Spencer st
Smith and Co., wholesale grocers, 23 Flinders lane west
Smith and Son, biscuit manufacturers, 71 and 73 Gore st, F
Smith and Stewart, bootmakers, 196 Swan st, Rd
Smith and Watts, surveyors, &c., Bank place, Collins st west
Smith and Willan, solicitors, 38 Collins st east
Smith, B., 100 George st, F
Smith, Benjamin D., 113 Park st, Em H
Smith, Brook, merchant, 8 Queen st
Smith, C., 19 Church st, Em H
Smith, C., 148 Swan st, Rd
Smith, Capt., Darling st, Pra
Smith, Captain W. H., Tennyson st, St K
Smith, Charles, general dealer, 76 Smith st, E C
Smith, Charles, Rotherwood st, Rd
Smith, Charles, 13 Spencer st
Smith, Charles and John, timber merchants, Albert st, E M
Smith, Christopher N., and Co., iron merchants, 147 Latrobe st west
Smith, D., 9 Stephen st
Smith, D., stoneworks, Bay st, San
Smith, David, 106 Spencer st north
Smith, E., accountant, 68 Temple Court, Collins st west
Smith, E., Peel st, Pra
Smith, E., draper, 4 Victoria st, Rd
Smith, Eliza, 4 Alma st, F
Smith, Elizabeth, tailoress, 46 Latrobe st east
Smith, F. L., barrister, Temple Court, Collins st west
Smith, F. L., Punt road, Pra
Smith, F. T., Union st, Pra
Smith, Francis, Reilly st, F
Smith, Francis G., manager Bank of Australasia, Barkly st, St K

Smith, Fredk. C., 66 Napier st, F
Smith, G., 43 George st, F
Smith, G., Railway place, San
Smith, G. F., Little Nelson st, Wmn
Smith, G. V., M.L.A., 110 Cardigan st, Carl
Smith, George, J., Church st, Rd
Smith, George, Nicholson st, F
Smith, George, earthenware pipe manufactory, Spencer st
Smith, George, 96 Smith st, E C
Smith, George, 66 Argyle st, F
Smith, George, Kew
Smith, George P., barrister, 13 Temple court, Collins st west
Smith, Gilbert, farrier, 36 Victoria st, Bd
Smith, H., Raglan st, Em H
Smith, H., High st, Pra
Smith, H. G., Wellington st, St K
Smith, H., J., 176 Carlton st, Carl
Smith, Harold S., accountant, merchant, &c., 122 Collins st west
Smith, Henry, grocer, 56 Bridge road, Rd
Smith, Henry, Spencer st north
Smith, Henry, surgeon, Abbotsford
Smith, Henry, hairdresser, 65 Stephen st
Smith, Henry, 29 Villiers st, Hot
Smith, Henry, gasfitter, 85 Lygon st, Carl
Smith, Henry, marine store, Curzon st, Hot
Smith, Hugh, blacksmith, 30 Park st, Em H
Smith, J., bootmaker, 212 Wellington st, E C
Smith, J., gardener, Mill st, Bto
Smith, J., 84 Dorcas st, Em H
Smith, J., 43 Nelson road, Em H
Smith, J., Dryburgh st, Hot
Smith, J., Canning st, Carl
Smith, J., builder, 13 King William st, F
Smith, J., Hoddle st, Rd
Smith, J., Blackwood st, Hot
Smith, J., oilman, 89 Brunswick st, F
Smith, J., 53 Bouverie st, Carl
Smith, J., 63 Gore st, F
Smith, J., 99½ Oxford st, F C
Smith, J., paperhanger, 54 Bridge st, Rd
Smith, J. B., Commercial road, Pra
Smith, J., C., J'nce
Smith, J. H., 145 Cecil st, Em H
Smith, J. J., and Co., leather merchants, 198 Elizabeth st
Smith, J. W., 23 Regent st, F
Smith, James, bootmaker, 118 Smith st, E C
Smith, James, 59 Cecil st, Wmn
Smith, James, engineer, Nott st, San
Smith, James, shoemaker, Thompson st, Wmn
Smith, James, 40 Young st, F
Smith, James, Bond st, E C
Smith, James, bootmaker, Queensberry st, Carl

Smith, James, Canning st, Carl
Smith, James, Errol st, Hot
Smith, James, Rose, Thistle, and Shamrock hotel, Pres
Smith, James, Leveson st, Hot
Smith, James A., Fitzroy st, St K
Smith, James, musician, 137 Gertrude st, F
Smith, James, 89A Queen st
Smith, Jesse, tailor, 197 Swanston st
Smith, John, 44 Jeffcott st, W M
Smith, John, hairdresser, 78 High st, St K
Smith, John, 77 Leicester st, F
Smith, John, tailor, Bay st, San
Smith, John, oil and colorman, 93 and 95 Smith st, F
Smith, John, plumber and gasfitter, 24 Little Collins st west
Smith, John, Nott st, San
Smith, John, Argyle st, Pra
Smith, John, 15 Nelson road, Em H
Smith, John, Chapel st, St K
Smith, John, junior, 50 William st
Smith, John M., fruiterer, 69 Swanston st
Smith, John M., bookseller and stationer, 235 Elizabeth st
Smith, John M., boot importer, 26 Little Collins st east
Smith, John Matthew, solicitor, 58 Little Collins st west
Smith, John Thomas, M.L.A., office, 41 Little Lonsdale st west
Smith, Joseph, wireworker, 43 Little Collins st east
Smith, Joseph J., 197 Lonsdale st west
Smith, Joseph, 85 Cobden st, Em H
Smith, L. F., Gardiner's creek road, Pra
Smith, Louis Lawrence, medical practitioner, 192 and 194 Bourke st east
Smith, M., 100 York st, Em H
Smith, Margery, fruiterer and confectioner, 53 Flinders st west
Smith, Mark, Roden st, W M
Smith, Mrs. Ann, 87 Napier st, F
Smith, Mrs., Granite terrace, Gertrude st, F
Smith, Mrs., Grattan st, Carl
Smith, Mrs., Little Latrobe st east
Smith, Mrs., Moor st, F
Smith, Mrs., 43 Lygon st, Carl
Smith, Mrs., 88 York st, Em H
Smith, Mrs., Little Nelson st, W mn
Smith, Mrs., 28 Young st, F
Smith, Mrs., 66 Napier st, F
Smith, Mrs., lace mender, 73 Collins st east
Smith, Mrs., 86 York st east, Em H
Smith, Mrs. Annie, Napier st, F
Smith, P., 148 Madeline st, Carl
Smith, P., 132 Little Lonsdale st west
Smith, P. W., Alphington
Smith, Peter, Spencer terrace, Little Bourke st west
Smith, Peter H., Grange road, Tk

Smith, R., gardener, New st, Btn
Smith, R., Barkly st, St K
Smith, R., tailor, Clarendon st, Em H
Smith, R. M., Wallace st, Tk
Smith, Rev. J. D., Bridge road, Rd
Smith, Richard, Chapel st, Pra
Smith, Robert, hairdresser, 7 Thompson st, Wmn
Smith, Robert, Cremorne st, Rd
Smith, Robert (electoral registrar for Carl), 129 Lygon st, Carl
Smith, Robert, and Co., merchants, 23 Flinders lane west
Smith, Robert Haden, Abbotsford
Smith, Samuel, Murphy st, S Y
Smith, Stanford, Carlisle st west, St K
Smith, Struelian, and Co., merchants, corner of Queen st and Collins st
Smith, Sydney, Darling st, S Y
Smith, Sydney W., C.E., Punt road, Pra
Smith, T., 12 Victoria parade
Smith, T., bootmaker, 131 Clarendon st, Em H
Smith, T., Capel st, Hot
Smith, T., printer, 68 Gertrude st, F
Smith, T., nightman, 102 Smith st, F
Smith, T., 121 Smith st, F
Smith, T., bootmaker, 73 Collins st east
Smith, T. D., stationer, Beach st, San
Smith, T. W., bootmaker, 33 Peel st, E C
Smith, Thomas, Inkerman st west, St K
Smith, Thomas, 6 Bell st, F
Smith, Thomas, grocer, &c., 21 Errol st, Hot
Smith, Thomas, 12 Victoria parade, Em H
Smith, Thomas, 107 Leicester st, F
Smith, Thomas G., greengrocer, 87 Victoria st, E C
Smith, Thomas H., Kew
Smith, Thomas H., 29 George st, F
Smith, Thomas Wm., 13 Argyle st, F
Smith, Thomas Y., Chetwynd st, Hot
Smith, Thomas, Governor Arthur hotel 27 Little Bourke st west
Smith, Thomas, baker, Sydney road, Lk
Smith W., 13 Stephen st
Smith, W., Wallis st, Tk
Smith, W., draper, 164 Clarendon st, Em H
Smith, W., Park st, S Y
Smith, W. A., boot and shoe merchant, 135 and 143 Brunswick st, F
Smith, W. C., William st north
Smith, W. F., 82 Blackwood st, Hot
Smith, W. G., Kew
Smith, W. H., White Horse hotel, 238 Bourke st east
Smith, W. H., 110 Little Lonsdale st west
Smith, W. H., 68 Kerr st, F
Smith, W. P., Curry st, Cardigan st, Carl
Smith, W. T., bootmaker, 60 Oxford st, E C
Smith, W. W., upholsterer and china dealer, Gardiner's creek road, Pra

Smith, Wm., National hotel, King William st, F
Smith, Wm., 202 Smith st, E C
Smith, Wm., Mill st, Btn
Smith, Wm., 137 Latrobe st west
Smith, Wm., hay and corn merchant, 31 Latrobe st east
Smith, Wm., restaurant keeper, 17 Bourke st west
Smith, Wm., 12 Victoria parade, E M
Smith, Wm., carpenter, Ascot vale, Flem
Smith, Wm., 35 Derby st, E C
Smith, Wm., Victoria st, E C
Smith, Wm., Twyford st, Wmn
Smith, Wm., ham curer, 100 Victoria st, W M
Smith, Wm., 43 Cecil st east, Wmn
Smith, Wm., Condell st, F
Smith, Wm., Star hotel, Swanston st
Smith, Wm., and Co., timber merchants, Therry st
Smith, Wm. H., shipowner, 29 Market st
Smith, Wm. H., junior, auctioneer and shipping agent, 29 Market st
Smith, Wm. Henry, painter, &c., 2 Carson's cottages, Collins st east
Smith, Wm. S., importer of oils, paints, glass, &c., 62 Elizabeth st
Smith, W. Villeneuve, barrister, 15 Temple court
Smithett, Wm. P., Little Bourke st west
Smithson, John, 126 Nicholson st, F
Smyth, H., Williams road, Prn
Smyth, Charles A., barrister, 40 Temple court, Collins st west
Smyth, G., 15 John st, Wmn
Smyth, G. E., tinsmith, 36 Cardigan st, Carl
Smyth, G. J., Nicholson st, F
Smyth, R. Brough, Office of Mines, Queen street
Smith, Rev. P., Bridge road, Rd
Smyth, Samuel, Sandhurst hotel, 46 Collst east
Smytherick, Wm. Cooper, 132 Wellington st, E C
Smythers, E. G. G., wine and spirit merchant, 41 Elizabeth st
Snadden, James, Albert st, Fcy
Snadden, Joseph, Buck's Head hotel, Napier st, F
Snaith, W. O., Nicholson st, Fcy
Snare, Richard, builder, Wilson st, Prn
Snare, Richard, Garden st, Prn
Snead, Mrs. Mary, dressmaker, 26 Coventry st, Em H
Snell, Henry, Walsh st, S Y
Snell, Horatio, furniture broker, 130 Young st, F
Snell, Mrs., Ralston st, Prn
Snellgrove, Charles, draper and outfitter, 17 Lonsdale st west
Snelling, W., chief clerk, penal establishment, Cotham road, Kew

Snelling, S., 15 Bouverie st, Carl
Snewin, Captain F., Avoca st, Prn
Sniddon, J., Albert st, Fcy
Sniders, Joseph, 96 Latrobe st west
Snilligrove and Son, drapers, Church st, Rd
Snodgrass and Co., 67 Queen st
Snodgrass, P., Chapel st, Prn
Snodgrass, P., M.L.A., 67 Queen st
Snook, Miss, 120 Napier st, F
Snow, Alfred, Southey st, St K
Snow, Charles, Berkeley st, Carl
Snow, G., goldsmith, Gardiner's creek road, Prn
Snow, John, 35 Pelham st, Carl
Snow, Packwood, and Co., carriers, 3 Little Collins st west
Snow, Richard, Barry st, Carl
Snowball, Joshua, commission merchant, Australian wharf
Snowden, A., St Hilliers st, E C
Snowden, Mrs. Caroline, 119 Park st west, Em H
Snowden, Mrs., 4 Courtney st, Hot
Snowden, John, Barry st, Carl
Sobee, G. W., 291 Lygon st, Carl
Sobey, Thomas, contractor, Pres
Societe Commerciale Belge (Antwerp), 20 Collins st west
Society of Mines, sec., 25 Flinders lane east
Soden, Henry, timber merchant, 139 Flinders st west
Soden, Joseph, watchmaker, Chapel st, Prn
Sohier, Philemoo, waxworks, 97 Bourke st east
Soleberg and Son, warehousemen, 71 Russell st
Solomon, Barnard, Waterloo st, St K
Solomon, Isaac, oyster saloon, 82 Gertrude st, F
Solomon, Isaac, and Co., hop and malt merchants, 1 Queen st
Solomon, J., 137 Leicester st, F
Solomon, J. S., Fitzroy st, St K
Solomon, J. S., and Co., outfitters, 91 Swanston st
Solomon, Joel, dealer, 108 Latrobe st east
Solomon, Joseph, 11 Grattan st, Carl
Solomon, Lewis, furniture broker, 148 Russell st
Solomon, M., draper, 196 Smith st, E C
Solomon, Morris, general dealer, 182 Smith st, E C
Solomon, Mrs., 45 and 47 Gore st, F
Solomon, S., and Co., furniture dealers and cabinetmakers, 118 and 130 Swanston st
Solomon, Saul, 251 Swanston st
Solomon, Saunders, dealer, 39 Post Office place
Solomon, Solomon, jeweller, 109 Collins st east

Solomon, Simon, 150 Russell st
Solomons, A., dealer, 177 Stephen st
Solomons, Abraham, outfitter, 103 Elizabeth st
Solomons, H., draper, 101 Stephen st
Solomons, H., fruiterer, High st, St K
Solomons, Lewis, 5 Queen st
Solomons, Lewis, furniture dealer, 41 High st, St K
Solomons, Louis, broker, 39 Little Lonsdale st east
Somers, Thomas, Edinburgh Castle hotel, Bk
Somerville, Samuel, dairyman, Gardiner's creek road, Pra
Somerville, Townsend, Ess
Somner, Wm., ltd
Soper, Wm., 119 Raglan st, Em H
Soues, E. L., Domain st, S Y
Sounners, Mrs., machine sewer, 239 King street
South Ajax Bolivia Reef Quartz Mining Company, 55 Elizabeth st
South Clunes Gold Mining Company, 122 Collins st west
South Crinoline Quartz Mining Company, 52 Collins st east
South Melbourne Building and Investment Society, 82 Collins st east
Southey, W. H., Latrobe st west
Southgate, Edward, bootmaker, 30 Bank st west, Em H
Sowtor, B., Miller st, W M
Spaight, Theresa, Union st, Pra
Spain, George, surgeon dentist, 114 Smith st, F
Spain, Wm., draper, 79 High st, St K
Spano, Edward, importer of watch materials, 94 Elizabeth st
Sparey and Bryant, galvanized iron manufacturers, 5 Latrobe st east
Sparey, M., 147 William st north
Spark, Henry, 97 Rosslyn st, W M
Sparkes, —, 97 Rosslyn st, W M
Sparkes, Mrs., 97 Cecil st east, Wmn
Sparling, Ellen, 101 Lonsdale st east
Sparrow, Francis, 154 Drummond st, Carl
Sparrow, G., livery stables, High st, St K
Sparrow, George, Sparrow's hotel, Fitzroy st, St K
Sparrow, Henry, 61 Jeffcott st, W M
Speakman, Edward, 178 Madeline st, Carl
Spear, Mrs., dressmaker, Sydney road, Bk
Spear, Richard, blacksmith, Charles st, F
Speculation Gold Mining Company, 9 Elizabeth st
Spence, Bros., and Co., merchants, 40 Flinders lane west
Spence, D., Avoca st, S Y
Spence, Francis, accountant and broker, 92 Collins st east
Spence, George, grocer, 41 Johnston st, E C
Spence, H., Arden st, Hot

Spence, James, Murphy st, S Y
Spence, James, Avoca st, S Y
Spence, John, Avoca st, S Y
Spence, Misses, dressmakers, 41 Napier st, F
Spence, Peter, 96 Moray st, Em H
Spence, Thomas, 82 Gore st, F
Spence, Wm., builder, 43 Johnston st, E C
Spencer, Edward, 53 Bouverie st, Carl
Spencer, James, 34 Kerr st, F
Spencer, Joseph, bootmaker, Drummond st, Carl
Spencer, Thos. Wm., schoolmaster, Flem
Spensley, Howard, Albert st, Pra
Spensley, James, ironmonger, corner of Brunswick and Moor sts, F
Spicer, Annie, grocer, 11 Rathdowne s, Carl
Spilding, James, Stawell st, W M
Spiker, Jacob, cigar maker, 53 Little Bourke st west
Spillor, Wm., Nott st, San
Spillers, Philip, Faraday st, Carl
Spink and Son, lapidaries, 100 Collins st east
Spink, Henry, grocer, 80 Flinders lane east
Spiro, F., Dalgety st, St K
Splatt, E. S., Studley park
Spollan, K., 9 Little Lonsdale st east
Spooner, Robert J., Flemington hill
Spooner, Samuel, Port Phillip Club hotel, 35 Flinders st east
Spottiswood and Son, builders, High st, St K
Spowers, Allen, 74 Collins st east
Spowers, J., Gardiner's creek road, Pra
Sprackiin, James F., 28 Wellington st, E C
Sprague, Edward, stock and share broker, 49 Collins st west
Spray, Henry, 71 Johnston st, F
Sprigg, George, secretary Acclimatisation Society, Royal park
Spriggs, W. G., importer, 8 Queen st
Spring, Francis, 15 Cecil st, Wmn
Spring, James, 32 Chetwynd st, Hot
Springthorpe, John, Westbury st east, St K
Sproule, Andrew, 19 Durras st, Em H
Spry, Alfred, 127 Latrobe st west
Spry, Joseph, cigar manufacturer, 37 Market st
Spurr, A., Henry st, Pra
Spyer, L. and S., merchants and commission agents, 30 Queen st
Squila, F., 49 York st east, Em H
Squire, —, George st, F
Squire, John, Henry st, Pra
St. Arnaud Silver Mines Company, 54 Elizabeth st
St. George, Frederick, livery stables, 16 Little Bourke st west
St. George's Hall, 73 Bourke st east

St. Helena Gold Mining Company, 5 Collins st west
St. James's Cathedral, Collins st west, corner of William st
St. John, A., dyer, 45 Moor st, F
St. John, Frederick, 3 Alma st, F
St. John, James, Railway place, San
St. Kilda and Prahran *Telegraph* office, Chapel st, Pra
St. Patrick's (R.C.) College and Schools, Lansdowne and Grey sts, E M
St. Patrick's Hall, 85 Bourke st west
St. Paul, A., dyer, 45 Moor st, F
St. Paul Brothers, manufacturing confectioners, 7 Collins st west; steam works, Elizabeth st north
St. Paul, G., Peel st, Hot
St. Paul, John, 3 Pelham st, Carl
St. Paul, Ralph, O'Connell st, Hot
St. Paul, W., O'Connell st, Hot
St. Paul, W. H., Peel st, Hot
St. Stephen's Church Schools, Richmond terrace, Rd
Stacey, Pease, and Co., wholesale ironmongers, 16 Little Collins st east
Stacey, W., bootmaker, 44 Little Bourke st west
Stacey, Wm. Robert, hairdresser, 212 Bourke st east
Stackpole, A., J.P., Haw
Staff, Chas., wax and paper flower maker, 91 Swanston st
Stafford, James, 131 Moray st, Em H
Stafford, James S., Church st, San
Stafford, Misses, seminary, Elgin st, Carl
Stafford, Wm., 17 Stanley st, E C
Stakeman, H. C., teacher of piano, Richmond hill
Staley, A., Court House hotel, Sydney road, Bk
Stamp, J., carpenter, Bay st, Bm
Stamp, Miles, grocer, New st, Bm
Stamp, Mrs., Domain st, Pra
Stampford, —, dairyman, Carpenter st, Bm
Standard office, High st, St K
Standeren, John, 14 Bell st, F
Standiford, E., Millswyn st, S Y
Stanesby, Geo. H., joiner and builder, 72 Fitzroy st, F
Stanford and Co., sewing machine importers, &c., corner of Bourke and Russell streets
Stanley and Nicholls, military tailors, 52 Collins st east
Stanley, E., egg and butter merchant, 7 Eastern Market, Bourke st east
Stanley, E., Cremorne st, Rd
Stanley, J., Railway place, San
Stanley, John, Gardiner's creek road
Stanley, R. S., Catholic bookseller, 9 Lonsdale st east
Stanway, John, china, earthenware, and glass importer, 175 Bourke st east

Staples, Miss, school, Ess
Stapleton and Taylor, slaters, Cardigan st, Carl
Stapleton, J. B., 127 Rathdowne st, Carl
Star of the Morning, the Riverina, and the Vulcan Amalgamated Companies, Wood's Point, 92 Collins st east
Star Reef Quartz Mining Company, 46 Collins st west
Stark, John, grocer, Napier st, F
Stark, Wm., Grey st, St K
Stark, Wm. E., secretary European Assurance Society, 74 Collins st west
Starr, R., fruiterer, 20 Lonsdale st west
Staughton, Mrs., 1 Prince's terrace, Fitzroy st, St K
Staughton, S. T., squatter, 17 Little Collins st west
Staunton, Captain, 131 Moray st, Em H
Staunton, Mrs., boarding house, 123 King street
Staveley, George, solicitor, 26 Queen st
Stawell, Sir Wm. F., Knt., Chief Justice, Studley park
Swabben, J., grocer, 76½ Smith st, E C
Stead Bros., fruiterers, poulterers, &c., 71½ Little Collins st west
Stead, James, Punt road, Rd
Stead, John, Punt road, Rd
Stead, T. and J., iron and timber merchants, 4 Park st east, Em H
Stead, Thomas, 92 Napier st, Em H
Steadman, Charles, nightman, 78 Coventry st east, Em H
Stealns, Mrs. G., 15 Smith st, F
Steam Navigation Board Offices, King st
Steane, —, Punt road, Pra
Stearn, E., tailor, Bignell's lane
Stearhouse, J., tailor, 88 Gertrude st, F
Stebbing, A., 267 Lygon st, Carl
Stedman, C., grocer, 365 Brunswick st, F
Stedman, Charles, Bay st, San
Stee, W., 10 Barry st, Carl
Steedman, John and Thos., tailors, 81 Russell st
Steel, Edwin, 52 Ann st, Wmn
Steel, James, Neptune st, St K
Steel, J. C., Leicester st, Carl
Steel, John, iron broker, &c., 137 Bourke st west
Steel, Mrs., Graham st, San
Steel, Robert, carpenter, Argyle st east, St K
Steel, Robert John, 41 Dryburgh st, Em H
Steele, David, baker, 305 Brunswick st, F
Steele, M., 69 Cobden st, Em H
Steele, R. C., Park st, Em H
Steele, Robt. C., and Co., butchers, 147 Flinders st west
Steele, Thomas, Queensberry st, Hot
Steele, Thos., Wreckyn st, Hot
Steiglitz Mining Company, 85 Flinders st west
Stelling, G. P., pottery, Church st, Rd

Stein, William, tailor, 22 Bourke st east
Steinock, A., 37 Wellington st, E C
Stollig, Charles, grocer, 21 Madeline st, Carl
Stenson, Joseph, Arthur st, Pra
Stent, E. J., grocer, Elgin st, Carl
Stenton, T., Rose st, F
Steny, R., store, Ashling st, Bru
Stephen, F. J. S., solicitor, 53 Little Collins st east
Stephen, J., plumber, Charles st, Pra
Stephen, James, bootmaker, Errol st, Hot
Stephen, James Wilberforce, barrister, 11 Temple Court, Collins st west
Stephen, James, Darling st, Pra
Stephen, Sir George, Knt., barrister, 11 Temple Court, Collins st west
Stephen, Wm. R., Inkerman st east, St K
Stephens and Delany, grocers, &c., Chapel st, Pra
Stephens, David, mason, Brennan st, Eas
Stephens, E., 200 Gore st, F
Stephens, Ells., Swan hotel, Church st, Rd
Stephens, Fredk., 236 Moray st, Em H
Stephens, G., bootcloser, 166 Albert st, E M
Stephens, James, Albert st, Pra
Stephens, Samuel, 63 Roden st, W M
Stephens, Stephen, solicitor, 65 Queen st
Stephens, Thomas, King's Arms hotel, Madeline st, Carl
Stephens, W., 71 Cobden st., Em II
Stephens, W., house decorator, 128 Moor st, F
Stephens, W. B., stores, Collins place, Collins st west
Stephens, W. B., bookseller and stationer, 15 Collins st west
Stephenson, D., Albert st., Bk
Stephenson, J., Hoddle st, E C
Stephenson, J., watchmaker, 13 Bourke st east
Stephenson, John, 22 Smith st, E C
Stephenson, P., Heidelberg road
Stephenson, Rev. F. E., Pres
Stephenson, Thomas, 134 Swan st, Rd
Storck and Shrimpton, hay and corn dealers, Chapel st, Pra
Sterck, Mrs., Claremont hotel, Commercial road, Pra
Sterling, W. L., solicitor, &c., 83 Swanston street
Stern, Philip, 203 Albert st, E M
Sterne, Samuel, solicitor, 3 Little Collins st west
Sterry, Wm., blindmaker, 134 Russell st
Stery, Wm., 116 Rose st, F
Stevens, —, 2 Carlton st, Carl
Stevens, Edward, bread and biscuit baker, Graham st, San
Stevens, G. P., grocer, Perry st, E C
Stevens, George, cabinetmaker, Chapel st, Pra
Stevens, George, Foundry hotel, King st

Stevens, George, 75 Coventry st east, Em II
Stevens, James, harness maker, 63 Smith st, F
Stevens, James, Robert Burns hotel, Courtney st, Hot
Stevens, John, blacksmith, Hot
Stevens, John, 203 Moray st, Em II
Stevens, John, carpenter, 271 King st north
Stevens, L., builder, 108 Park st, Em II
Stevens, W., High st, St K
Stevens, W., Oxford st, Hot
Stevens, Wm., bootmaker, 13 Derby st, E C
Stevenson, A., 106 Latrobe st west
Stevenson and Anketell, horse, brcd, and insurance agents, 13 Bourke st west
Stevenson and Elliott, coachbuilders and importers, 181 King st
Stevenson, George, Studley park
Stevenson, Henry, stock, station, and land agent, 90 Queen st
Stevenson, J., Westgarth st, F
Stevenson, John, Studley park, Kew
Stevenson, John, Wallis st, Tk
Stevenson, John, ironmonger, 80 Bourke st east
Stevenson, John, Nott st, San
Stevenson, L., and Sons, merchants and warehousemen, 14 Flinders lane east
Stevenson, R., 91 Nicholson st, F
Stevenson, T., 90 Queen st
Stevenson, T., 46 Latrobe st west
Stevenson, Thomas, heraldic painter, 46 Latrobe st west
Stevenson, Thomas, mayor, Ess
Stevenson, Thomas, Ascot vale, Flem
Stevenson, Thomas, land and estate agent, 46 Elizabeth st
Stevenson, Walter H., 170 Lygon st, Carl
Stevenson, Wm., Studley park, Kew
Stevenson, Wm., auctioneer, 48 Elizabeth street
Steward, F., hay and corn store, 30 Little Collins st east
Steward, F., sen., working jeweller, Bignell's lane, 161 Bourke st east
Steward, Henry W., importer of china, glass, earthenware, &c., 15 Flinders lane east
Stewart, A., Stewart st, Bk
Stewart, A., Grange road, Tk
Stewart, A., Victoria st, Hot
Stewart, Alexander, Capel st, Hot
Stewart, Alexander, Berkeley st, Carl
Stewart, Alexander, Ferguson st, Wmo
Stewart and Co., ship chandlers, Railway place, San
Stewart, C., 51 Coventry st, Em II
Stewart, Captain, Moray st, Em II
Stewart, Cornelius, surgeon, Church st, Rd
Stewart, E., Park st west, Em II

Stewart, F., hay and corn merchant, Little Collins st east
Stewart, George, japanner, 40 Post Office place
Stewart, H. W., 51 Hanover st, F
Stewart, Henry, blacksmith, 104 Douglas parade, Wmn
Stewart, J., Miller st, W M
Stewart, J., bootmaker, 50 Rosslyn st, W M
Stewart, J., furniture dealer, 27 High st, St K
Stewart, J., 36 Church st, Em H
Stewart, J. S., Swan st, Rd
Stewart, James C., Moor st, F
Stewart, James, 22 Dorcas st, Em H
Stewart, John, manager Oriental Bank, Alma road, St K
Stewart, John, blacksmith, Inkerman st west, St K
Stewart, John, general smith, 190 King st
Stewart, John, 212 King st
Stewart, Mrs., staymaker, 6 Wellington st, St K
Stewart, Mrs., Courtenay st, Hot
Stewart, Mrs., Lennox st, Rd
Stewart, Mrs., 45 Moray st, Em H
Stewart, Mrs., Darling st, S Y
Stewart, Mrs., school, Alma st east, St B
Stewart, Mrs. C., 95 Napier st, F
Stewart, Mrs. C., 16 Montague st, Em H
Stewart, O., Cardigan st, Carl
Stewart, P., 53 Dudley st, W M
Stewart, P., Maine st, Reid
Stewart, R., 25 Smith st, E C
Stewart, Robert, Walsh st, S Y
Stewart, T. W., carpenter, Hotham st, E M
Stewart, Thomas, Lyons st, Wmn
Stewart, W., Cardigan st, Carl
Stewart, W. S., Heidelberg road
Stewart, Wm., Buckley st, Fcy
Stewart, Wm., greengrocer, Clarendon st, Em H
Stewart, Wm., grocer, 45 Thompson st, Wmn
Stewart, Wm., tinsmith, Raglan st, San
Stubbs, Wm., cabinetmaker, Franklyn st west
Stickland, Francis, general smith, 137 Latrobe st east
Stidston, Wm., 8 Condell st, F
Stirling, G. P., potter, Bridge road, Rd
Still, W., 55 Leicester st, Carl
Stillman, Thomas, surgeon, Bridge road, Rd
Stillwell, J., 7 Carlton st, Carl
Stirling, G. P., 183 Bridge road, Rd
Stirling, George, draper, 190 Bridge road, Rd
Stirling, John, Curzon st, Hot
Stivey, John, carpenter, House st, San
Stock Exchange of Melbourne, Hall of Commerce

Stock, John W., 6 Carlton st, Carl
Stockdale, Benjamin, baker, Punt road, Pra
Stocks, Thomas, Henry st, Pra
Stockwell, E., herbalist, 199 Wellington st, E C
Stockwell, J., boot importer, Elgin st, Carl
Stodart, James, Chapel st, Pra
Stoddart, —, Gardiner's creek road, Pra
Stoddart, J., Gardiner's creek road, Pra
Stoddart, Matthew, 218 Victoria st, Pra
Stokes, C., Arden st, Hot
Stokes, Charles, Dryburgh st, Hot
Stokes, James, M.D., surgeon, Chapel st, Pra
Stokes, Robert, grocer, Condell st, F
Stokes, S., 380 Bridge road, Rd
Stokes, Thomas, die sinker and engraver, 100 Collins st east
Stokes, Wm., Kew
Stolworthy, Charles, 76 Brunswick st, F
Stombuce, A., 137 Johnston st, F
Stone and Zevenboom, brushmakers, Flinders lane east
Stone, D., 16 Errol st, Hot
Stone, C., Mill st, Bin
Stone, F., gardener, Hodder st, Bin
Stone, George, confectioner, 141 Brunswick st, F
Stone, George M., draper, 51 Peel st, E C
Stone, John, Barkly st, Carl
Stone, John, 117 Napier st, F
Stone, Mrs., Williams road, Pra
Stone, Mrs., 43 Victoria parade, F
Stone, R., Nor
Stone, R., bootmaker, 125 Gertrude st, F
Stone, H., carpenter, Mill st, Bin
Stone, R. H., surveyor, 121 Spencer st
Stone, Robt., bootmaker, 96 Fitzroy st, F
Stone, Robert, smith, 103 Little Bourke st east
Stone, Thomas, blacksmith, 45 Little Oxford st, E C
Stone, W. G., High st, Pra
Stone, Wm., Osbrone st, Wmn
Stone, Wm. A., Hyde st, Fcy
Stoneham, Wm., turner, 308 Elizabeth st
Stones, T., 26 Cobden st, Em H
Stonley, Stephen, Hoddle st, Rd
Stookes, George H., butcher, 139 Flinders st west
Stooke, John, butcher, Mill st, Bin
Storey, Edwin, Lothian st, Hot
Storey, —, teacher, Brunswick road, Bk
Storey, J., butcher, 183 Clarendon st, Em H
Storey, J., Swan st, Rd
Storey, John, butcher, 201 Moray st, Em H
Storie, G., Edward st, Bk
Storie, J., Edward st, Bk
Storr and Barnes, butchers, 64 Swan st, Rd

Story, Joseph, Artillery hotel, Elizabeth at north
Stott, George, corn store, Charles st, Pra
Stott, Henry, cabinetmaker, 93 Brunswick st, F
Stonckey, Frank, 10 Alfred place, Collins st east
Stow, Wm., carpenter, Gore st, F
Stow, Wm., carpenter, St. David st, F
Stracey, J., general agent, High st, St K
Stracey, John C., Inkerman st east, St K
Strachan, G., 10 Hanover st, F
Strachan, J., 4 Eden place, St K
Strachan, J. F., M.L.C., Queen st south
Strachan, James, horse dealer, 58 Argyle st, F
Strachan, John, boot and shoemaker, 170 Brunswick st, F
Strachan, Wm., (secretary Warrenheip Distillery Company) Acland st, St K
Straban, James, Barkly st, St K
Strange, G., Auburn road, Upper Haw
Stranger, Elijah, 119 Ross st, F
Stranger, Mrs. Eliza, 119 Ross st, F
Stranger, T., Barkly st, Bk
Stratford, W., 3 Swiss terrace, Fitzroy st, F
Stratton, A., 17 Dorcas st, Em H
Straubel, Bertrand, 27 Swan st, Rd
Straw, T., Sydney road, Bk
Street, James, boot store, 98 Clarendon st, Em H
Streeteman, —, Cecil st east, Wmn
Streeting, J., Union st, Pra
Strelt, Lewis, store, 33 Little Collins st west
Strettle, Abraham, and Co., stock and station agents, Bourke st west
Strickland, J., 42 Gertrude st, F
Strickland, L., coachbuilder, Stephen st
Strien, T., baker, 17 Brunswick st, F
Strode, T., Punt road, Richmond
Stronach, Wm., Murphy st, S Y
Strongman, Wm., Miller st, Rd
Stroud, J., Albert st west, Bk
Strudwicke, J. L., Halifax st, Bin
Stuart, John, Alma st, east St K
Stuart, Wm., Avoca st, S Y
Stub, O., mining agent, 13 Swanston st
Stubbs, Ann, fancy repository, 10 Lonsdale st west
Stubbs, John, William st, Rd
Stubbs, R., 147 Cardigan st, Carl
Stubbs, Thomas, auctioneer, 81 Collins st west
Stubbs, Thomas, printers' broker, 24 Latrobe st west
Stubbs, Wm., artist, 88 Argyle st, F
Stuckey, Mrs., refreshment rooms, Church st, Bin
Studdert, Rev. George, 2 Franklyn st west, W M
Studley, George, baker, Cape st, Heid
Stump, Richard, 206 Victoria parade, E M

Sturgess, Wm., 9 Miller st, W M
Sturman, J., herbalist, 248 Wellington st, E C
Sturt, Captain E. P. S., corner of Spencer and Dudley sts
Sturely, Henry O., solicitor, 62 Little Collins st west
Stutt, Wm., City Buffet cafe, Bourke st east
Stutlaford, A., 161 Collins st east
Stutlaford, Madame, professor of music, 161 Collins st east
Stuttor, Charles, draper, 137 Bourke st east
Stutzer, J. J., barrister, 25 Temple court, Collins st west
Sueur, Gustave, watchmaker, 111 Stephen street
Suffolk, E., Dow st, San
Suffren, Matthew M., watchmaker and optician, 48 Nelson place, Wmn
Sugars, W. C., York st, Em H
Sugden, Thomas, tanner, Flem
Sugden, W. J., Grand Junction hotel, High st, St K
Suhard, Louis, corner Grey and Simpson sts, E M
Sullivan, —, Cardigan st, Carl
Sullivan, D., Fountain Inn, Howard st, Hot
Sullivan, D. H., coachbuilder, 96 Gertrude st, F
Sullivan, Daniel, Ivanhoe, Heid
Sullivan, Isaac, 131 Leicester st, Carl
Sullivan, J., Kerry hotel, corner of King st and Flinders lane
Sullivan, J., builder, &c., Coromandel place
Sullivan, James F. (Minister of Mines), Victoria parade, E M, and Office of Mines, Queen st
Sullivan, John, 131 Raglan st, Em H
Sullivan, John, 61 Osborne st, Wmn
Sullivan, Joseph, Cock hotel, 163 Bourke st east
Sullivan, Martin, 35 Little Collins st east
Sullivan, Michael, 48 Faraday st, Carl
Sullivan, Michael, Baptist lane, Little Collins st east
Sullivan, Patrick, Spread Eagle hotel, Elizabeth st
Sullivan, T., Condell st, F
Sullivan, T., William st, Rd
Sullivan, Thomas, Vine st, Heid
Sullivan, Timothy, Australia Felix hotel, 221 Lonsdale st west
Sullivan, W. H., Parliamentary hotel, Spring st
Summerfield, Augustus, 55 Lygon st, Carl
Summers, C., sculptor, 105 Collins st east
Summers, J., Mrs. Bac., Oxon, 105 Collins st east
Summers, Henry, 25 Barkly st, Carl
Summers, J., Miller st, Bk

Summers, Joseph, Dudley st, W M
Summons, Isaac, grocer, 170 Stephen st
Sumner, T. J., Stony park, Merri creek
Sumner, Z., 10 St David st, F
Sung Chong Ou, merchant, 72 Little Bourke st east
San Choon Cheong, merchant, 55 Little Bourke st east
Sunday School Union of Victoria, 219 Swan st, Rd
Sundercombe, John, shoemaker, 20 and 34 High st, St K
Sunderland, Jos., Flem
Sunderland, Rev. J. P., Hoddle st, F M
Sunderland, T., Deputy Registrar-General, Haw
Sunderson, George, Boundary road, Tk
Sunhung, Cheong, butcher, 75 Little Bourke st east
Surmon, —, 157 Cecil st, Em H
Supple, G. H., barrister, 7 Temple court, Collins st west
Supreme Court, corner Latrobe and Russell sts
Sussmann, David, boot and shoe dealer, 191 Bourke st east
Sutcliffe, Alfred, wool sorter, 125 Bourke st west
Satcliffe, Richard, New st, Dtn
Suter, H., Mrs., Courtney st, Hot
Sutherland, —, accountant, Haw
Sutherland, Andrew, Barkly st, St K
Sutherland, Charles, and Co., merchants, 31 Queen st
Sutherland, Charles, Fawkner st, St K
Sutherland, James, Murchison st, Carl
Sutherland, John, 38 Young st, F
Sutherland, John, Heidelberg road
Sutherland, Mrs., 6 Cobden st, Em H
Sutherland, Mrs., Robe st, St K
Sutherland, Robert, Walsh st, W M
Sutherland, Roderick Allison, solicitor, 192 Collins st east
Sutor, O., 65 Young st, F
Sutton, John, Garden st, Pra
Sutton, Michael, 103 Little Bourke st west
Sutton, W., Osborne st, Wmn
Sutton, Wm., 42 Bank st, Em H
Suy Yick, merchant, 86 Little Bourke st east
Swain, John, 6 Peel st, W M
Swain, Mrs., 64 Bouverie st, Carl
Swainger, Thomas, bootmaker, Day st, San
Swale, G. A., 31 Smith st, F
Swallow and Ariell, ship bread and biscuit bakers, Stoke st, San
Swallow, James, butcher, 100 Clarendon st, Em H
Samger, Thomas, bootmaker, Day street, San
Swan, Charles, 11 George st, F

Swan, Isaac, butcher, 66 Wellington st, E C
Swan, Joseph, butcher, 7 Wellington st, St K
Swan, Margaret, 197 Albert st, E M
Swan, Mrs., 274 Fitzroy st, F
Swan, Robert, 17 Church st, Em H
Swan, S., Blackwood st, Hot
Swan, Thomas, watchmaker, High st, St K
Swan, W., 125 Faraday st, Carl
Swan, W., 56 Raden st, W M
Swan, Wm., butcher, 13 York st, Em H
Swan, Wm., 112 Coventry st, Em H
Swannell, James, butcher, Em
Swanson, —, Victoria st, W M
Swanson, John, furniture dealer, 64 Brunswick st, F
Swasey, J. D., merchant, 116 Collins st west
Sweatman, Charles, storeman, 164 Bourke st west
Sweatman, W., accountant, 122 Queen st
Sweeny, Mathew, Palmerston place, Madeline st, Carl
Sweet, H., ham curer, Pres
Sweetland, Stephen, Haw
Sweetman, James, 118 Leicester st, Carl
Sweetman, John, musician, 135 King st
Swetnam, Edmond, Hoddle st, E C
Swift, Charles B., Willow Tree hotel, Vere st, E C
Swift, Jas., accountant, 31 Queen st
Swift, Richard, 141 Cecil st, Em H
Swinborn, Mrs., corset maker, Gardiner's creek road, Pra
Swinbourn, James, steam saw mills and engineer, 163 Bourke st west
Swindell, John, dairyman, Commercial road, Pra
Swindley, S. J., South Audley st, E C
Swindley, Thomas, 210 Moray st, Em H
Switzer, E. H., bootmaker, 81 Little Collins st east
Sydenham, Walter, Peel st, Hot
Sydes, Edward, Grey st, St K
Syderff, John B., Gardiner's creek road, Pra
Sykes and Terry, boiler makers, River bank south
Sykes, Fred., Marian st, F
Syle, Robert, 230 Swan st, Rd
Syme, David, newspaper proprietor, 67 Elizabeth st
Syme, G., 127 Park st west, Em H
Symonds, C. H., Commissioner of Audit, 178 Collins st east
Symonds, E. S., Under Treasurer, Government office, Spring st
Symonds, Rev. J. C., Rathdowne st, Carl
Symons, J., Excelsior hotel, 231 Great Bourke st east
Synagogue, Jewish, 85 Bourke st west
Synot, M., Nth

T.

Tabb, David, Ivanhoe, Heid
Tahlik Vineyards Proprietary office, 70 Queen st
Tadgell, F. J., builder, 31 Provost st, Hot
Taegtow, Fred., tinsmith, 1 Parker st, W mn
Tait, Andrew, rate collector, 33 Macarthur place, Carl
Tait, Hugh, 135 Latrobe st west
Tait, John, Union st, Pra
Tait, Joseph, Commercial hotel, Nott st, San
Tait, Mrs., 94 George st, E M
Tait, W., greengrocer, 48 Hoddle st, E C
Tait, W. D., 46 Market st, Em H
Tait, Wm., 90 Stanley st, W M
Talbett, Mary, grocer, 134 Russell st
Talbot, Dr. H., Sydney road, Bk
Talbot, Edward, house and land agent, 2 Collins st east
Talbot, Miss, seminary, Sydney road, Bk
Talbot, T. W., draper, 85 Bourke st east
Talbot, Thomas, surgeon, Pent
Talbot, Wm., shoemaker, Webb st, F
Tallerman, D., commission merchant, 18 Collins st east
Tame, Thomas, bootmaker, 88 Gertrude st, F
Tankard, J., Tankard's Temperance hotel, 66 Lonsdale st west
Tankard, John, Albert st, Pra
Tanner, A. F., 38 Barkly st, Carl
Tapley, J., Bridge road, Rd
Taplin, W. M., house and land agent, 226 Napier st, F
Tapping, —, contractor, Reilly st, F
Tardy, James E., Arthur st, Pra
Tarrant, Edmund, Hobe st, St K
Tarrant, John, 39 Napier st, F
Tarratt, J., Sons, and Co., hardware merchants, 49 Collins st west
Tarry, John, bricklayer, Grosvenor st, Pra
Tartakover, Marcus, pawnbroker, 68 Smith st, E C
Tartakover, Mitchell, pawnbroker, 53 High st, St K
Tarver, James, iron foundry, Nott st, San
Tasmanian Fire Insurance Company, 62 Collins st west
Tasmanian Steam Navigation Company, 6 Elizabeth st
Tate, Archibald, 64 Hanover st, F
Tate, Frederick, customs agent, 13 Market street
Tate, W., greengrocer, 257 Victoria parade, E C
Tate, Walter, 303 Victoria parade, E C
Tawton, Wm., painter and paperhanger, 47 Coventry st, Em H
Tayler, Lloyd, architect and surveyor, 52 Collins st west

Tayler, Walter, 198 Russell st
Taylor, —, Lennox st, Rd
Taylor, —, 48 Napier st east, Em H
Taylor, —, Easey st, E C
Taylor, A. G., draper, High st, St K
Taylor, Alfred, Garden st, Chapel st, S Y
Taylor and Buckland, solicitors and notaries public, 71 Little Collins st west
Taylor, C., 18 Park st west, Em H
Taylor, C., bootmaker, 152 Russell st
Taylor, C. F., Rowena parade, Rd
Taylor, C. J., engineer sewerage department, Lonsdale st west
Taylor, Charles, 114 Lygon st, Carl
Taylor, Clement, professor of penmanship, 83 Elizabeth st
Taylor, Dr., Duver st, W mn
Taylor, E., gardener, Gardiner's creek road, Tk
Taylor, Edward B., stationer, Gardiner's creek road, Prn
Taylor, Enoch, importer of boots, &c., 57 Bourke st east
Taylor, F., Market lane, 143 Bourke st east
Taylor, George, 78 George st, F
Taylor, George, 51 Twyford st, South W mn
Taylor, George, bootmaker, Kew
Taylor, George, leather merchant, 2 Nicholson st, F
Taylor, George, butcher, 93 High st, St K
Taylor, George, Gore st, F
Taylor, George, Canning st, Carl
Taylor, George, bootmaker, 105 Lonsdale st east
Taylor, George H., solicitor, 22 Eldon chambers, Collins st west
Taylor, H., High st, Prn
Taylor, H., draper, 172 Clarendon st, Em H
Taylor, Henry, Waterloo hotel, 68 Little Collins st west
Taylor, Henry, Cardigan st, Carl
Taylor, Henry, 45 King William st, F
Taylor, J., 47 Market st, Em H
Taylor, J., 192 Gore st, F
Taylor, J. B., Octavia st, St K
Taylor, J. H., tailor, 115 Lygon st, Carl
Taylor, J. T., chemist, Stephen st
Taylor, James, Johnston st, E C
Taylor, Jas., gardener, 68 Johnston st, F
Taylor, James, Miller st, W M
Taylor, John, china dealer, 83 Brunswick st, F
Taylor, John, Hoddle st, Rd
Taylor, John, Arthur st, Pra
Taylor, John, bootmaker, 7 Cardigan st, Carl
Taylor, John B., 74 York st, Em H
Taylor, Joseph, and Co., merchants and importers, 114 Collins st west
Taylor, Joseph, Victoria st, St K
Taylor, M. W., Alma st west, St K

Taylor, Mrs., grocer, Inkerman st west, St K
Taylor, Mrs., 109 Queensberry st, Hot
Taylor, Mrs., Punt road, Pra
Taylor, Mrs., dressmaker, 165 Spring st
Taylor, Mrs., 53 Charles st, F
Taylor, Mrs. E., 135 Johnston st, F
Taylor, Mrs., 79 Faraday st, Carl
Taylor, R., dairy, Stanley st, E C
Taylor, R., carpenter, Church st, Bru
Taylor, Rev. James, George st, E M
Taylor, Rev. S., New st, Dtn
Taylor, Richard, Ferguson st, Wmn
Taylor, Samuel, dairyman, Studley st, E C
Taylor, Samuel, 59 Argyle st, F
Taylor, Samuel, boarding-house keeper, 16 Nelson place, Wmn
Taylor, Samuel, musician, Palmerston st, Carl
Taylor, T., butcher, 78 Bridge road, Rd
Taylor, T., bootmaker, 228 Lonsdale st east
Taylor, T. H., Acland st, St K
Taylor, Thomas, Station place, San
Taylor, Thomas, 323 Victoria st, E C
Taylor, Thomas, 131 Victoria st, E C
Taylor, Thomas, 140 Leicester st, F
Taylor, Thomas, Cremorne st, Rd
Taylor, Thomas, cheesemonger, Eastern Market
Taylor, Thomas, cheese factor and bacon curer, 33 Swanston st
Taylor, W., butcher, 103 Lonsdale st east
Taylor, W. R., painter and paperhanger, Greville st, Pra
Taylor, Wm., M.L.C., Melbourne Club
Taylor, Wm., Stoke st, San
Taylor, Wm., Wreckyn st, Hot
Taylor, Wm., 73 Faraday st, Carl
Taylor, Wm., Alma st, St K
Taylor, Wm. Henry, draper, corner of Cardigan and Queensberry sts, Carl
Teague, J., saddler, Pent
Teague, J. P., homœopathic physician, 160 Collins st east
Teale, Wm., builder, Queen st north
Teale's bonded stores, 105 to 109 William street
Tebbutt, James, Rowena parade, Rd
Tecke, B., cabinetmaker, 120 Gertrude st, F
Teerly, James, hairdresser, 221 Bourke st east
Teeson, D., grocer and draper, Moonee ponds
Tegethoff, B., professor of mathematics, Little Hanover st, F
Teis, Mrs. Margaret, 36 Stanley st, W M
Telegraph line of Royal Mail Coaches, 35 Bourke st east and 153 Elizabeth st
Telfer, A., ironmonger, Gardiner's creek road, S Y
Telfer, R. S., Cecil st east, Wmn
Telford, John, Fitzroy st, St K

Tell, Wm., Peel st, Pra
Tempany, George, 41 Barkly st, Carl
Tempany, Wm., wireworker, 33 York st, Em H
Temperance Hall, 112 Russell st
Tempest, S., bootmaker, 102 Clarendon st, Em H
Templeton, Hugh, teacher, Greeves st, F
Templeton, S., 22 Errol st, Hot
Templeton, W., P.M., Church st, Dtn
Tenant, John A., 22 Stanley st, W M
Tennant, Mrs., 2 Victoria parade, F M
Tennant, W. E., engineer, Victoria st, W M
Terlecki, F., carver, 191 Lygon st, Carl
Terlecki, P., Palmerston st, Carl
Terrey, John T., cabinetmaker, 94 Raglan st, Em H
Terry, Albert, Chapel st, Pra
Terry, Alfred, Houverie st, Carl
Terry, Alfred, 143 Cardigan st, Carl
Terry and Co., Victoria brewery, Chapel st, Pra
Terry, Captain, 4 Nelson place, Wmn
Terry, George, 150 Young st, F
Terry, George, 181 Victoria parade, E C
Terry, James, draper, 58 Gertrude st, F
Terry, Leonard, architect, 50 William st
Terry, R., 9 Wellington st, Pra
Terry, Hubert and Wm., grocers and spirit merchants, High st, St. K
Teutonic Gold Mining Company, 122 Collins st west
Tewdall, John, Drummond st, Carl
Tewsley, R., Chapel st, Pra
Thain, Alexander (Melbourne Loan and Discount Company), 90 Little Collins st west
Thallon, Henry, 205 Elizabeth st
Thames and Mersey Line of Packets, 48½ William st
Tharratt, W., Nth
Thatcher, Richard Henry, Izett st, Pra
Theatre Royal, 79 Bourke st east
Theis, H., 127 Rose st, F
Theobald, James, 14 Barkly st, Carl
Thibou, E. W. & S., furniture dealers, 257 Swanston st
Thibou, Samuel, Victoria st, E C
Thibow and Crabb, school, 66 Cardigan st, Carl
Third Union Building Society, 82 Collins st east
Third Victoria Building and Investment Society, 56 Little Collins st east
Thistlethwaite, Edward, grocer and wine merchant, 154 Clarendon st, E
Thistlethwaite, Mrs., dressmaker, 64 Park st east, Em H
Thistlethwaite, Wm., house and land agent, 37 Dorcas st east, Em H
Thom, J., 3 Macarthur place, Carl
Thom, R., plasterer, Charles st, Pra
Thom, W., 4 Dudley st, W M

Thomas, —, brickmaker, Duke st, E C
Thomas, —, Lennox st, Rd
Thomas and Mearcs, drapers, 178 Bridge road, Rd
Thomas and Rush, flour mills, Flem
Thomas, C. S., 7 Hanover st, F
Thomas, David, chemist, &c., Bay st, San
Thomas, David John, M.D., 172 Collins st east
Thomas, E., 203 Eastern road, Em H
Thomas, E., Wallis st, St K
Thomas, Ellis, shoemaker and boarding-house keeper, 9 King st and 221 Bourke st west
Thomas, F. H., architect and civil engineer, 83 Swanston st
Thomas, G., Heath st, San
Thomas, G., 28 Regent st, F
Thomas, G. B., 117 Nicholson st, F
Thomas, Geo. D., Chetwynd st, Hot
Thomas, Geo. F., M.D., 212 and 97 Loosdale st east
Thomas, George, Yarra st, Heid
Thomas, H., Grey st, St K
Thomas, Henry, printer, 75 Little Collins st west
Thomas, Herbert, Hotham st, E M
Thomas, Isaac, draper, Chapel st, Pra
Thomas, John, draper, 40 and 44 Clarendon st, Em H
Thomas, John, 14 Drummond st, Carl
Thomas, John, Cardigan st, Carl
Thomas, John, crane office, Australian wharf
Thomas, John, Royal George hotel, 132 Bourke st east
Thomas, Lewis, boot merchant, 25 Gertrude st, F
Thomas, Mrs., 159 Lygon st, Carl
Thomas, Mrs. Samuel, 66 King William st, F
Thomas, Patrick, 164 Russell st
Thomas, Paul, bootmaker, 3 Collins st east
Thomas, Stephen, bootmaker, 101 Elizabeth st
Thomas, Theophilus, draper, Chapel st, Pra
Thomas, Thomas, house carpenter, 3 Stevedore st, Wmn
Thomas, Thomas, 19 Stevedore st, Wmn
Thomas, W., Brunswick road, Bk
Thomas, W., 40 Elgin st, Carl
Thomas, W. C., 93 Dudley st, W M
Thomas, Wm., carrier, 108 George st, F
Thomas, Wm., fishmonger, Brunswick st, F
Thomas, Wm., engineer, 128 Little Lonsdale st east
Thompson, —, Commercial road, Pra
Thompson, —, Adderley st, W M
Thompson, A., Stoke st, San
Thompson and Son, painters and paperhangers, 212 Swan st, Rd

Thompson, A. C., Charles st, Pra
Thompson, Ann, crinoline manufacturer, 19 Gertrude st, F
Thompson Brothers, grocers, Nelson place east, Wmn
Thompson, C., 96 Cecil st, Em H
Thompson, C. W., 68 Bouverie st, Carl
Thompson, D., Lennox st, Rd
Thompson, D., Rouse st, San
Thompson, David, butcher, Bay st, San
Thompson, E., Bay st, Bru
Thompson, E., Peel st, Pra
Thompson, E., school, Grey st, St K
Thompson, Edward, money broker and estate agent, 92 Queen st
Thompson, Frederick, house and land agent, 75 Collins st east
Thompson, G., Wells st, Bru
Thompson, Hamilton, Punt road, Pra
Thompson, Henry, Royal hotel, Bay st, San
Thompson, J., Gardiner's creek road, Pra
Thompson, J., Bouverie st, Carl
Thompson, J., Macarthur place, Carl
Thompson, J., Railway place, San
Thompson, J., Hawarra st, S Wmn
Thompson, J., 111 Napier st, Em H
Thompson, J. A., Greeves st, F
Thompson, J. P., Gordon st, Fcy
Thompson, Jos., Arthur st, Pra
Thompson, James, livery stable keeper, 117 Queen st
Thompson, James, Wilson st, Bru
Thompson, James, 110 Nicholson st, F
Thompson, James A., 14 Young st, F
Thompson, John, draper, Haw
Thompson, John, 90 Cardigan st, Carl
Thompson, John, ironmonger, Flemington road, Hot
Thompson, John, 129 Kerr st, F
Thompson, John, greengrocer, 87 Little Lonsdale st east
Thompson, John, Elgin st, Carl
Thompson, John, 72 Nicholson st, F
Thompson, John, Dryburgh st, Hot
Thompson, John, Neptune st, St K
Thompson, John, Avoca st, S Y
Thompson, Joseph, Arthur st, Pra
Thompson, Joseph, Tattersall's hotel, 99 Bourke st east
Thompson, Joshua, engineer, 123 William street
Thompson, M. A., 146 Little Bourke st west
Thompson, Mark, Stoke st, San
Thompson, Miss, ladies' seminary, 60 Rosslyn st, W M
Thompson, Misses, ladies' college, Turnbull's point, S Y
Thompson, Mrs., 307 Victoria parade, E C
Thompson, Mrs. E., school, 15 Napier st, Em H
Thompson, Mrs., 72 Napier st, F
Thompson, Mrs., 72 Leicester st, Carl

Thompson, Mrs., Grey st, E M
Thompson, Mrs and the Misses, academy, Grey st, St K
Thompson, Ralph, accountant Union Bank, Alma road, St K
Thompson, Robert, accountant, 51 Elizabeth st
Thompson, Thomas, 265 Napier st, F
Thompson, Towers, Mac's hotel, Franklyn street
Thompson, W., tailor, Grattan st, Carl
Thompson, W. H., bootmaker, 164 Bridge road, Rd
Thompson, W. S., 145 Johnston st, E C
Thompson, Wm., bootmaker, 16 Leicester st, Carl
Thompson, Wm. H., Abbot st, Hot
Thompson, Wm., 70 George st, F
Thompson, Wm., boot importer, Clarendon st, Em H
Thompson, Wm., pocketbook maker, 132 Nicholson st, F
Thompson, Wm., M.D., surgeon, Gardiner's creek road, Pra
Thompson, Wm., 199 King st
Thompson, Wm., 45 Condell st, F
Thoms, George, 108 George st, F
Thomson, Alexander, Latrobe hotel, 90 Fitzroy st, F
Thomson, Alexander L., 26 Queen st
Thomson, Andrew, Whitehall st, Fcy
Thomson, Andrew, blacksmith, 32 Young st, F
Thomson, Andrew, blacksmith, Queensberry st, Hot
Thomson, Archibald, builder, 161 Cambridge st, E C
Thomson, Donald, Rose of Melbourne inn, corner of Hanover and Young sts, F
Thomson, Dr., Walsh st, S Y
Thomson, Edward, carrier, Ramsden st, E C
Thomson, H., bootmaker, 41 Errol st, Hot
Thomson, J., 30 Bank st west, Em H
Thomson, J., Chapel st, St K
Thomson, J. H., 101 Rathdowne st, Carl
Thomson, James, sexton, Gipps st west, E M
Thomson, James, Davis st, Pra
Thomson, James W., mining agent, 3 Little Collins st west
Thomson, John, grocer, 170 Smith st, E C
Thomson, John, M.L.A., Avoca st, S Y
Thomson, John, Nicholson st, Carl
Thomson, John, school, 98 Queensberry st, Carl
Thomson, John, 52 Rosslyn st, W M
Thomson, Joseph, 19A Cardigan st, Carl
Thomson, Mrs., dressmaker, 97 Cecil st, Em H
Thomson, Mrs., Dudley st, W M
Thomson, Mrs., Arthur st, Pra
Thomson, Mrs., Cardigan st, Carl
Thomson, Peter, livery stables, Therry st

Thomson, Peter, tailor and clothier, 16 Little Collins st west
Thomson, Ralph, Alma st east, St K
Thomson, Rev. James, Cardigan st, Carl
Thomson, W., tailor, Rathdowne st, Carl
Thomson, W. K., Greenfield, Elsternwick
Thoneman, Emil, Highett st, Rd
Thorley, J., 48 Market st, Em H
Thorley, Jabez, 80 Marian st, F
Thorn, Richard, bricklayer, Argyle st, Pra
Thorne, Charles, Caroline st, S Y
Thorne, James, professor of music, 3 Lansdowne st, E M
Thorne, Thomas, 65 Spring st
Thorney, F., bootmaker, 37 Napier st, Em H
Thorns, J., Union st, S Y
Thornton, J. C., 77 Argyle st, F
Thornton, Robert, 204 Eastern road, Em H
Thornton, Robert, 5 Pelham st, Carl
Thorp, Mrs., 119 Wellington st, E C
Thorp, R. T., gasfitter, 95 Little Collins st east
Thorpe, Henry, 66 Dover road, Wmn
Thorpe, Mrs. Leah, Bridge hotel, Marybyrnong st, Fcy
Thorpe, R. P., Fitzroy st, St K
Thorpe, Samuel, mining agent and salvage officer to the Fire Brigade, 49 Collins st west
Thorpe, Thomas, office, 49 Collins st west
Thresher, Henry, Exchange hotel, High st, St K
Thuner, C., and Co., cabinetmakers, 17 Little Lonsdale st west
Thurgarland, J., 129 Johnston st, F
Thurgood, W., confectioner, 209 Swanston st
Thurtell, A., Queen's Arms hotel, 25 Dorcas st west, Em H
Thwaites, G., and Co., cabinetmakers, 64 Little Collins st east
Thwaites, J. W., chemist, High st, St K
Thwaites, John, 74 Lygon st, Carl
Twaites, Thos. H., 64 Little Collins st east
Tickle, W. H., Rotherwood st, Rd
Tidd, Thomas, Pres
Tierney, Francis, 9 Victoria st, Hot
Tierney, Martin, 183 King st
Tierney, Mrs., tailoress, 11 Victoria st, E C
Tietzner, Henry, hay and corn merchant, 246 Elizabeth st
Tiffen, James B., picture dealer and printseller, 72 Brunswick st, F
Tiggins, C., dairy, 167 Victoria st, E C
Tighe, J., 132 Cecil st, F
Tillett, Alfred, pawnbroker, 16 Gertrude st, F
Tillett, George Wm., pawnbroker, 101 Brunswick st, F
Tilley, G., High st, Pra

Tilley, George, jun., contractor, Cliff st, Pra
Timbs, Henry, Nott st, San
Timbury, Charles J., commission agent, 68 Flinders lane west
Timbury, F. H., Rotherwood st, Rd
Timbury, John H., Haw
Timbury, W., Rotherwood st, Rd
Timewell, J., tailor, Hauk place, Collins st west
Timmins, J., Sydney road, Bk
Tims, G. W., 21 St. David st, F
Tindal, William, 18 Queensberry st, Carl
Tinning, J., Sydney road, Bk
Tipper, George H., Royal Haymarket hotel, Bourke st east
Tippel, Cornelius, wood turner, Highett st, Rd
Tippel, Mrs., Highett st, Rd
Toal, A., printer, 96 Moor st, F
Tobelman, W. G., 143 Russell st
Tobias, W., 122 George st, F
Tobin, J., Barry st, Carl
Tobin, M., Hawke st, W M
Tobin, Michl., 9 Cardigan st, Carl
Tobin, R., teacher, Nth
Toche, Paul, S Y
Tocknell, William, engraver, 41 Swanston street
Tod, Alexander, and Co., grocers, 114 Gertrude st, F
Tod, John, 36 Regent st, F
Todd, Alexander, 104 Leicester st, F
Todd, Hugh, baker, Bignell's lane, Bourke st east
Todd, John, 95 Bouverie st, Carl
Todd, John, 92 Leicester st, Carl
Todd, John, Caple st, Wmn
Todd, William, 107 Rose st, F
Toennies, Heinrich, boarding house, 31 Lonsdale st east
Tolhurst, J. E., butcher, Cardigan st, Carl
Tolhurst, J. K., Commercial road, Pra
Tolley, George, Millswyn st, Pra
Tolmie, Simon, tailor, 91 Flinders st west
Tomett, John, Goodwood st, Rd
Tomkin, John Hoyee, solicitor, 24 William st
Tomkins, James G., 135 Little Lonsdale st west
Tomlinson, John, sawmaker, 134 Little Bourke st east
Tompsitt, A., bootmaker, Chapel st, Pra
Tompson, G. H. D., 9 Elmbank terrace, Victoria parade, E M
Toms, Chas., Henry st, Pra
Toms, Charles, builder, 148 Smith st, E C
Toms, R., Coventry and Birmingham hotel, 48 Little Bourke st east
Toms, William, plumber, 138 Swan st, Rd
Tomson, C. E., 114 Moray st, Em H
Tondeur, O., and Co., merchants, 3 Flinders st east

Tong, W. S., corner of Napier and St. David sts, F
Tongue, James, perambulator maker, &c., Chapel st, Pra
Toole Brothers, grocers, 162 Bridge road, Rd.
Tooher, Thomas, boarding house, 134 Bourke st west
Toohey, M., Great Britain hotel, Clarendon st, Em H
Toohey, M., 4 Bendigo st, Hot
Toohey, Patrick, greengrocer, 287 Elizabeth st
Toohey, Thomas, and Co., merchants, 27 Latrobe st east
Toolin, Thos., tailor, 98 Little Collins st west
Toomey, James, 15 Cross st, Hot
Toon, John, Town Clerk of Hawthorn, Haw
Tope, Mrs. Ann, dressmaker, 154 Moray st, Em H
Tope, William, valuator, 65 Cobden st Em H
Topp, S., Ringwood, Caulfield
Topp, Samuel, and Co., importers, 9 Flinders lane west
Torpey, Danl., Old Lamb Inn, corner of Elizabeth and Franklyn sts
Torbin, M., 28 Johnston st, F
Torode, Peter, 106 Rose st, F
Torpey, Mrs., Catherine, 6 Henry st, F
Torrance, Andrew, painter and paperhanger, 72 Lonsdale st east
Torrance, Andrew, baker, Inkerman st east, St K
Torrance, Charles E., Punt road, Pra
Toslin, —, tailor, 38a William st
Tough, D., Sydney road, Bk
Tourdriner, James, stationer, High st, St K
Touzel, George, corner Carlisle and Chapel st east, St K
Torell, Charles J., surgeon, New st, Btn
Torey, Charles, 6 Hanover st, Wmn
Towell, Isaac, 129 Leicester st, F
Towers, George, carver and guilder, 73 Brunswick st, F
Towers, Thompson, Mac's hotel, Franklyn st east
Towers, Thompson, wheelwright, Franklyn st east
Town Hall, Swanston st
Towns, J. R. S., store, Cochrane st, Btn
Towns, R., and Co., merchants, 26 William st
Townsend, James, fruiterer, &c., 125 Elizabeth st
Tozer, —, 159 Victoria parade, F
Tozer, —, 64 Park st, Em H
Tozer, John, nautical instrument maker, Beach st, San
Tozer, Thomas, 7 Murchison st, Nicholson st, Carl

Tracey, John, tanner, Haw
Tracey, Wm., Pont road, Rd
Tracey, Wm., Marco Polo hotel, Grant st, Em H
Tracy, Richard T., M.D., surgeon, 189 Collins st east
Trades' Hall, Lygon st, Carl
Trail, William Charles st, Pra
Tranan, Joseph, greengrocer, 30 Ferguson st, Wmn
Trangmar, T., Brighton st, Rd
Trantum, Mrs., dressmaker, 73 Gertrude st, F
Trapp, H., Alma st., St K
Traisman, Caleb, grocer, 165 Little Lonsdale st east
Travers, Geo., Capel st, Hot
Travers, J., Capel st, Hot
Travers, John, Station place, San
Traynor, Patrick, general dealer, corner of Leveson and Dyron sts, Hot
Treacy, J., Railway hotel, Miller st, W M
Treacy, William Winter, auctioneer, 31 Bourke st west
Treacy, Wm., farrier, 14 and 20 Little Lonsdale st west
Treasury, The, Spring st
Trern, G., chemist, 170 Clarendon st, Em H
Treffry, John, Freemasons' hotel, corner of Smith and Gertrude sts, F
Tregarthur, Captain W., pilot, Dover road, Wmn
Treleaven, W., 18 Grattan st, Carl
Tremills, Henry, grocer, &c., 68 Moor st, F
Trenberth, Richard, coal merchant, 9 Rathdown st, Carl
Trenchard, John, solicitor, 69 Temple Court
Trenowan and Simpson, butchers, 5 Coventry st, Em H
Treneweth, J. and H., brickmakers, Victoria st west, Bk
Trentworth, Miss, school, 212 Moray st, Em H
Trescowthick, Henry, 40 Queensberry st, Hot
Tresider, W., wheelwright, Edward st, Bk
Trew, Edwin, Flem
Trewett, John, carman, George st, E M
Tribe, James, bricklayer, 27 Cobden st,

Trodd, Geo., dealer in treacle, Rouse st, San
Trodd, George, Graham st, San
Troedel, Charles, lithographic printer and engraver, 100 Swanston st
Trollope, Mrs., Wellington parade, F M
Tronson and Hill, manufacturers of flock, 35 Lygon st, Carl
Trott, W., 114 High st, St K
Trott, W., cabinetmaker, Argyle st west, St K
Trott, Wm., grocer, Spencer st
Trotter, B. H., Inkerman st west, St K
Trotter, G, 8 James st, F
Trotter, James, Napoleon III. hotel, corner of Bank and Ferrars sts, Em H
Trotter, Mark, 95 Victoria st, Carl
Trotter, Miss, schoolmistress, Pent
Trotter, R., grocer, 131 Brunswick st, F
Trottman, Thomas, 51 St David st, F
Trowell, J., 24 Bridport st, Em H
Trudgeon, William, 29 Johnston st, E C
Trudgeon, Wm. Hy., Marine st, F
Trumble, J., 22 Coventry st, Em H
Truss, Mrs., 7 King William st, F
Trust and Agency Company of Australasia, 56 Flinders lane west
Tryot, David, 19 Stevedore st, Wmn
Trythall, S., teacher, Hoddle st, F M
Tschentscher, Frederick, bootmaker, 123 Swanston st
Tucker and Browse, butchers, 55 Peel st, E C
Tucker, Francis, grocer, 61 Lygon st, Carl
Tucker, R. D., M.L.A., Temple Court hotel, Little Collins st west
Tuckett, Joseph R., merchant and broker, 20 Collin st west
Tuff, George, Errol st, Hot
Tuff, Mrs., 12 Bank st, Em H
Tulk, Augustus H. (public librarian), Hay st, Btn
Tullett, Henry, ironmonger, &c., Grey st, St K
Tullidge, Wm., money broker, 56 Little Collins st east
Tulloch, Capt. James, 40 Park st, Em H
Tulloch, David, engraver, 91 Cecil st, Em H
Tulloch, John, Avoca st, S Y
Tulloch, Wm., grocer, Cole st, S Wmn
Tully, Christopher, draper and outfitter, 159 Bourke st east

Turnbull, J., Chapel st, St K
Turnbull, James, 41 Howard st, Hot
Turnbull, Jane, 25 Johnston st, E C
Turnbull, John, baker and grocer, Nott st, San
Turnbull, John, Octavia st, St K
Turnbull, Mrs., Henry st, Pra
Turnbull, Mrs., 61 Stanley st, E C
Turnbull, P., 56 St. David st, F
Turnbull, Phipps, Alma st, St K
Turnbull, R. and P., and Co., merchants, 71 William st
Turnbull, Robert, 79 Rathdowne st, Carl
Turnbull, Robert, 49 Drummond st, Carl
Turnbull, Robert, M.L.C., William st
Turnbull, Robert, Alma st, St K
Turnbull, Wm., 30 Oxford st, E C
Turnbull, Wm., Cliff st, Pra
Turnbull, Wm., 71 George st, F
Turnbull, Wm.M., physician and surgeon, Russell st south
Turner, Alexander, Inkerman st east, St K
Turner and Gill, stationers, account book manufacturers, and paper rulers, 39 Flinders lane east
Turner, C., Commercial road, Pra
Turner, Caleb, Neptune st, St K
Turner, Dominic A., Prahran st, S Y
Turner, E., Neptune st, St K
Turner, Edward, Darling st, S Y
Turner, G., 38 Wellington st, E C
Turner, George, 6 Cardigan st, Carl
Turner, George, 1 Regent terrace, Faraday st, Carl
Turner, George, tinsmith, 88 Park st, Em H
Turner, H., 37 Raglan st, Em H
Turner, H., 3 Montague st, Em H
Turner, H. G., Robe st, St K
Turner, Henry, 93 Cecil st, East Wmn
Turner, Henry W., barrister, 57 Little Collins st east
Turner, J., Commercial road, Pra
Turner, J., 53 Dudley st, W M
Turner, J. C., Murphy st, S Y
Turner, J. E., boot store, 184 Bridge road, Rd
Turner, James, merchant, 80½ Little Collins st east
Turner, James H., wool scourer, 61 Flinders st west
Turner, James, artist and photographic colourist, 140 Gore st, F
Turner, John, and Co., manufacturers of oilmen's stores, Chapel st, Pra
Turner, John, ship and estate agent, 45 Flinders st west
Turner, John, Murphy st, S Y
Turner, John, carpenter, 36 Argyle st, F
Turner, John, Prahran st, S Y
Turner, John, 6 Lygon st, Carl
Turner, John, William st, Pra
Turner, Joseph, russia and morocco leather goods manufacturer, 48 Queen st

Turner, Matthew H., hairdresser, 132 Brunswick st, F
Turner, Mrs., bootmaker, Madeline st, Carl
Turner, Mrs., 31 Oxford st, E C
Turner, Mrs. J., Punt road, Pra
Turner, Mrs. J., professor of music, 49 Park st east, Em H
Turner, Phillip, Vaucluse, Rd
Turner, Rev. John, 43 Condell st, F
Turner, Richard, tinsmith, 200 Elizabeth street
Turner, W., Domain road, S Y
Turner, W., Trinnian st, Pra
Turner, W. B., 234 Swan st, Rd
Turner, W. H., Arthur st, Pra
Turner, Wm. F., 160 Victoria parade, E M
Turpie, J., whitesmith and bellhanger, 49 Cremorne st, Rd
Turton, W., 16 Dover place, Wmn
Turville, T., grocer, Railway place, San
Turville, T., Locomotive hotel, Railway place, San
Tutin, C., Rowena parade, Rd
Tweddale, Thomas, grocer, 230 Little Collins st east
Tweedel, Joseph, shipwright, River bank south
Twentyman, Edward, furniture dealer and carpenter, 81½ Queen st
Twentyman, George Osborn, seal, copper plate and die engraver, &c., 81½ Collins st east
Twentyman, R., importer, 11 Flinders lane east
Twentyman, Richard, 3 Prince's terrace, St K
Twentyman, Thomas, merchant, 25 Dorcas st, Em H
Twiddle, —, 50 Chetwynd st, Hot
Twiddlebridge, Wm., 58 Lothian st, Hot
Twigg, John, Moriand st, Fcy
Twinem, John, storekeeper, Flemington hill
Twitchell, Mrs., 20 Moor st, F
Twycross, James, and Sons, merchants, 19 Latrobe st east
Twycross, John, Toorak road
Twyford, Edward, fruiterer, 100 Smith st, E C
Tyas, Richard, butcher, Church st, Rd
Tydeman, James, Williams st, Pra
Tye, W., Prahran hotel, Chapel st, Pra
Tyler, J. C., collector customs, Wallace st, Tk
Tyler, James, nurseryman, Pres
Tyree, Peter, Walsh st, W M
Tyrell, Edwin, general dealer, Bridge road, Rd
Tyrer, John, carrier, Flem
Tyrie, Wm., hay and corn dealer, 31 Johnston st, F
Tyrrell, John, 10 Nicholas lane, Bourke st east

Tyrrell, Michael A., storekeeper, 7 Stevedore st, W mn
Tyrrell, Mrs., grocery store, Heath st, San
Tyrrell, Wm., boarding-house, 18 Little Lonsdale st east
Tyrrell, Wm., 11 Nicholas lane, Bourke st east
Tyson, Edward, Walsh st, S Y
Tyson, Thomas, merchant, 47 Elizabeth st
Tyson's Reef Quartz Mining, Crushing, and Pumping Company, 64 Elizabeth st
Tymen, G. H., accountant, Bank of N.S.W., Collins st west

U.

Uggles, Mrs. Sarah, Old Times hotel, 254 Elizabeth st
Ullathorne, Wm., and Co., manufacturers of shoe threads and grindery, 112 Swanston st
Umphelby, C. W., and Co., wine merchants, 60 Collins st west
Umphelby, Thomas, Hotham st, E M
Underwood, Henry, Illawarra st, W mn
Underwriters of France, 49 Collins st west
Undoubted Quartz Mining Company, Eldon chambers, Collins st west
Uniacke, M. A., store, Little Bourke st west
Unit, H., 42 Moor st, F
Union, A., 3 Moor st, F
Union Bank of Australia, 54 Collins st west
Union bonded stores, 61 William st
Union Building Society, 2nd ; Union Building Society, 3rd ; 82 Collins st east
Union Club of Victoria, 90 Collins st west
Union Gas Company's office, 82 Collins st east
Unitarian Church, Grey st, E M
United Fire and Marine Insurance Company, 26 Collins st west
United Friends Jewish Benefit Society; secretary, 201 Bourke st east
United Kingdom Temperance and General Provident Institute, 18 Collins st east
United Labourers' Friendly Society, meet at Trades' Hall, Lygon st, Carl
United Methodist Church, Chapel st, Pra
United Operative Bakers' Society, meet at Trades' Hall, Lygon st, Carl
Universal Marine Insurance Company, 40 Elizabeth st
Universal Traction Railway Patent Company, Eldon chambers, Collins st west
University of Melbourne, Carl
Unthank, G. F., tailor and draper, 197 Bourke st east
Unthank, J., draper, Hoddle st, E C
Unthlak, Thomas, Lennox st, Rd
Upson, Charles, 4 Marian st

Upper Murray Steam Navigation Company (Smith and Banks), 100 Spencer street
Ure, James A., Carlisle st east, St K
Ure, Robt., Westbank terrace, Hawthorne bridge
Urie, Young, and Co., starch and maizena manufacturers, 5 Market st
Urquhart, Alex., tinsmith, 10 Beach st, San
Urquhart, C. F. G., Builders' Arms hotel, Rowena parade, Rd
Urquhart, E., Simpson's hotel, 99 Victoria st, E C
Urquhart, George, Burnett st, St K
Urquhart, James, dairyman, 172 Wellington st, E C
Urquhart, John, Station place, San
Usher, Captain J., Macquarrie st, W mn
Usher, George T., and Co., upholsterers and mattress makers, 166 Lonsdale st east
Usher, Jas., 178 Madeline st, and 34 Grattan st, Carl
Uther, A. G., carpenter, Haw
Uther, F. K., Wellington parade, E M
Uther, Frederick, 2 Webb st, F

V.

Vail, Charles, tailor, York st, Em H
Vail, Edward Luke, solicitor, 8 Collins st east
Valantine, David Hood, 70 Lygon st, Carl
Vale, Edward, 102 Queensberry st, Carl
Vale, John, 118 Lygon st, Carl
Vale, John, 104 Spencer st
Vale, John, Westbury st, St K
Vale, W. M. K., M.L.A., Parliament House
Valentine, J., 128 Rose st, F
Vallet, Peter, Lothian st, Hot
Vallient, N., store, Ivanhoe, Heid
Van Berckelaer, —, photographer, High st, St K
Van Hemert, F. T., M.D., Grey st, St K
Vans, Mrs. B., Domain road, S Y
Vanguard, Zingari, and Wallace Deep Lead Mining Companies, Crooked River, Temple court, Collins st west
Vaughan and Webster, clothing manufacturers, 55 to 61 Russell st
Vaughan and Wild, brewers, Bedford st, E C
Vaughan, Benjamin, 124 Little Bourke st west
Vaughan, Henry, 15 Brunswick st, F
Vaughan, John, Horse and Jockey hotel, 144 and 146 Little Bourke st east
Vaughan, M., Wreckyn st, Hot
Vaughan, Moule, and Seddon, solicitors, &c., 71 Little Collins st west
Vaughan, S. B., Walsh st, S Y
Vaughan, Wm., Drummond st, Carl

172 **Vau** MELBOURNE **Wad**

Vaulcaden, J., Margaret terrace, Bk
Vautier, Joseph, Darkly st, St K
Vaux, James, Kew
Vaux, M., 133 Rose st, F
Veal, J. W., 87 Spencer st
Veal, John Wm., St. John's school, Latrobe st east
Veal, Thomas, grocer, Gipps st, E C
Veevers, R., 64 Argyle st, F
Veirth, J., Berkeley st, Carl
Veitch, Mrs., Commercial road, Pra
Velyer, J., Capel st, W M
Vent, Thomas, Nott st, San
Vent, Wm., 13 Grattan st, Carl
Verbrugge, Jacobus, store, Beach st, San
Verdon, George F. (Colonial Treasurer), Strand, Wnio
Verga, Thomas, printer and bag maker, 78 Russell st
Vergin, John, 73 Victoria st, Carl
Verity, W., butcher, 170 Bridge road, Rd
Vernon and Co., tanners and curriers, 204 Elizabeth st
Vernon, E., 118 Cardigan st, Carl
Vernon, John, tanner, Flem
Vernon, John, 4 Jollmont square
Vernon, John C., 20 Curzon st, Hot
Veris, Robert, 170 Johnston st, E C
Vibert, H., Pelham st, Carl
Vickers, Charles, architect, Kew
Vickers, Joseph, watchmaker, 14 Gertrude st, F
Vickers, Richard, hosier, 139 Bourke st east
Victoria and Riverine Pastoral Association, Limited, Collins st west
Victoria Coal Company, 117 Collins st west
Victoria Fire and Marine Insurance Co., 82 Collins st east. Agency, Eldon Chambers, Collins st west
Victoria Ice Company, office, 60 Collins st west
Victoria Life and General Insurance Co. and Savings' Institute, 82 Collins st east
Victoria Lime and Cement Company, Queen st
Victoria Railways Department Office, William st
Victoria Sugar Co.'s Offices, 12 Queen st, and Works, San
Victoria Trade Protection and Debt Recovery Association, 36 Collins st west
Victorian and New South Wales Gazetteers, office, 104 Collins st east
Victoria Grammar School, 95 Collins st east
Victorian Gymnastic Institution, 106 Flinders lane east
Victorian Institute of Architects, 49 Elizabeth st
Victorian Jam and Pickle Company, 1 William st

Victorian Manufacturing Association, 47 Bourke st east
Victorian Mining and Investment Association, 52 Collins st east
Victorian Permanent Building Society, Collins st east
Victorian Phonetic Society, Mechanics' Institute, Collins st east
Victorian Poultry Society. Secretary, 53 King William st, F
Victorian Railways Goods Depot, Spencer st
Victorian Rifle Association, officer, 63 Stephen st
Victorian Seamen's Mission, Hobson's Bay
Victorian Water Supply, Department of, 125 Lonsdale st west
Vieusseux, L., ladies' college, Clarendon st, E M
Vigurs, G. J., 37 Pelham st, Carl
Villers, T. C., 90 Rowena parade, Rd
Vincent, J., 276 Smith st, E C
Vincent, J. B., Brighton st, Rd
Vincent, John P., veterinary surgeon, 201 Lonsdale st west
Vincent, John J., grocer, 9 Vere st, E C
Vincent, Mrs., Pelham st, Carl
Vince, F., Punt road, Rd
Vines, J., baker, Commercial road, Pra
Vines, Michael, Trinnian st, Pra
Vipond, —, jeweller, 56 Cambridge st, E C
Virgo, Francis, Argyle st west, St K
Virgoe, Son, and Co., merchants, Collins place, Collins st west
Virgoe, Wm. Richard, junior, Bru
Visct, Mrs., 118 Elgin st, Carl
Volunteer Office, 45 Stephen st south
Von der Heyde, W., Walsh st, S Y
Von Geyer, Mrs., 46 Napier st, Em H
Von Reisen, Eliza, 115 Flinders st east
Von Reicke, Mrs., 104 Russell st
Vorwerg, Traugott, grocer, 12 Johnston st, F
Voss, T, farrier, 101 Moray st, Em H
Voyer, D., sweep, Bridge road, Rd

W.

Waddell, John, 90 Bouverie st, Carl
Waddell, Wm., Vallient st, E C
Waddington, J., cabinemaker, Hoddle st, E C
Waddle, John, 321 Brunswick st, F
Wade and Gowan, auctioneers and drapery salesmen, 20 Collins st west
Wade, James, Domain road, S Y
Wade, E. T., Church st, Rd
Wade, Thomas N., 39 Gore st, F
Wade, Wm., 93 Douglas parade, Wmn
Wade, Wm. Richard, secretary Tract Society, 17 Swanston st
Wadeson, L., gardener, Buckland st, Held

Wadeson, Herbert Temple, Wellington parade, E M
Wadley, E., 76 Napier st, Em H
Wadley, E. P., 201 Cecil st, Em H
Wade, Mrs., Stevedore st, Wmn
Wadsworth, J., Albatt st, Bk
Wadsworth, James, Howard st, Hot
Wadsworth, Robert, 93 Wellington st, St K
Waggon, J. T., 56 Elgin st, Carl
Wagner, F., tailor, Wright lane
Wagner, Leopold, Caulfield
Wagshore, Mrs., 78 Victoria st, Rd
Wagstaff, R., butcher, 138 Johnston st, E C
Wainwright, Mrs., Herald agency, 65 Stanley st, E C
Wainwright, Samuel, grocer, 187 Wellington st, E C
Waite, —, bonnet maker, 158 Smith st, E C
Waite, Thomas, 28 Brunswick st, F
Waite, Wm., High st, Pra
Wakefield, —, Argyle st east, St K
Wakefield, C., Charles st, F
Wakefield, Mrs., Caroline st, S Y
Wakeham, J., plumber, Queensberry st, Carl
Wakeman, John, wood yard, Church st, Rd
Walcot, J. B., Day st, Btn
Walden, James, dairyman, 21 Palmer st, F
Waldie, Miss, dressmaker, Cochrane st, Btn
Walding, T., Henry st, Pra
Walduck, Samuel, horse trainer, Ascot vale, Flem
Walduck, W. W., solicitor, 9 Elizabeth st
Wale, J., saddler, Inkerman st, St K
Walford, J., Inkerman st east, St K
Walkden, J., Easey st, F
Walker, A., Balaclava road, St K
Walker, Alfred, Darling st, S Y
Walker, B., Osborne st, Pra
Walker, B., Commercial road, Pra
Walker, Captain Joseph, 4 Powlett st, E M
Walker, David, 68 Rosslyn st, W M
Walker, G., Cochrane st, Btn
Walker, George, photographer and artist, 113 Queensberry st, Hot
Walker, George, Wellington st, St, K
Walker, George S., Chapel st, Pra
Walker, H., 67 York st east, Em H
Walker, Henry, Peel st, Pra
Walker, J., 43 Coventry st, Em H
Walker, J., 106A Fitzroy st, F
Walker, J., grocer, Canning st, Carl
Walker, J. F., schoolmaster, Punt road, Rd
Walker, John, 19 Pelham st, Carl
Walker, John, tailor, 104 Queen st
Walker, John, North British hotel, corner Bourke and Swanston sts

Walker, John, Chetwynd st, Hot
Walker, Joseph Henry, miller, 303 Brunswick st, F
Walker, Joseph, 189 Little Lonsdale st east
Walker, Joshua, Punt road, S Y
Walker, May, and Co., printers, stereotype founders, and electrotypists, 99 Bourke st west
Walker, Michael, butcher, 46 Rosslyn st, W M
Walker, Mrs., 3 Regent terrace, Moor st, F
Walker, Mrs. E., 87 and 89 Young st, F
Walker, Mrs. Elizabeth, 180 Moray st, Em H
Walker, Mrs., straw bonnet maker, 41 Lereson st, Hot
Walker, Mrs., Rosslyn st, W M
Walker, O. E., news agent, 7 Madeline st, Carl
Walker, Parker N., wool and tallow broker, 20 Collins st west
Walker, R., tallow factor, Victoria st, E C
Walker, R., Gifford st, South Wmn
Walker, Rev. —, Hoddle st, E C
Walker, Richard, 53 Baillie st, Hot
Walker, Robert, wholesale grocer, &c., 25 Swanston st, and 56 Flinders lane east
Walker, Samuel, bootmaker, 161 George st, F
Walker, T. H., Pres
Walker, T. J. S., druggist, Chapel st, Pra
Walker, Theodore, solicitor, 39 Swanston street
Walker, Thomas, wharf agent and cartage contractor, 1A Flinders st east
Walker, Thomas, Hanmer st, Wmn
Walker, W. F., 89 Young st, F
Walker, Wm., 103 Gertrude st, F
Walkerdon, H., brickmaker, Union st, Bk
Walkerdon, Joseph, brickmaker, Union st, Bk
Walkey, Jos., Capel st, Hot
Walkley, H., 77 Rathdowne st, Carl
Wall, George, Heidelberg road
Wall, George, purveyor to private parties, Blessington st, St K
Wall, Henry, Provost st, Hot
Wall, John, Charles st, Pra
Wall, Wm., 1 Woolf's cottages, Faraday st, Carl
Wallace, B., 2 Cross st, Hot
Wallace, E., blacksmith, Arthur's Seat road, Btn
Wallace, F., blacksmith, 179 Wellington st, E C
Wallace, J., baker, Blackwood st, Hot
Wallace, J., bookmaker, 118 Gertrude st, F
Wallace, John, 14 Adderly st, W M
Wallace, John C., Elmbank terrace, Victoria parade, E M
Wallace, Mrs., Stanley st, W M

Wallace, Mrs., 82 Victoria st west, W M
Wallace, Mrs., Madeline st, Carl
Wallace, Peter, baker and grocer, 32 Pelham st, Carl
Wallace, R., 34 Moray place, Em H
Wallace, William, 12 Condell st, F
Wallace, Wm., Nth
Wallach Brothers, furniture dealers, Elizabeth st
Wallen, R., Lennox st, Rd
Waller, Francis, Cremorne st, Rd
Walter, George, Carson's cottages, 13 Little Collins st east
Wallin, Frances, Waltham st, Rd
Wallis, George, 17 Lygon st, Carl
Wallis, J., carpenter, Albion st, Bk
Wallis, James, agent, 150 Lonsdale st west
Wallis, James, Bridge road, Rd
Wallis, James, timber merchant, Moonee Ponds
Wallis, John, bootmaker, 13 Gertrude st, F
Wallis, Mrs., laundress, 41 Franklyn st, W M
Wallis, R., wheelwright and blacksmith, 20 Elizabeth st extension
Wallis, Thomas, money broker and estate agent, 26 and 28 Collins st east
Wallis, Wm. J., publisher and linguist, 56 Little Collins st west
Walls, J., butcher, Grattan st, Carl
Walls, J., 147 Lygon st, Carl
Wallworth, Smith, hatter and army cap maker, 4 Bourke st east
Walsh, —, Adderly st, W M
Walsh, —, 86 Argyle st, F
Walsh, A., 44 Little Bourke st east
Walsh Brothers, watchmakers, jewellers, and silversmiths, 53 Collins st east
Walsh, C., George st, F
Walsh, D., gardener, Buckland st, Heid
Walsh, E., greengrocer, 171 Moray st, Em H
Walsh, Ellen, boarding house, 94 Lonsdale st west
Walsh, F., Haw
Walsh, Francis A., 37 George st, F
Walsh, Henry, tailor, 76 Little Collins st west
Walsh, Henry S., Haw
Walsh, J. J., 50 Condell st, F
Walsh, J. K., stationer, 52 Gertrude st, F
Walsh, James, 100 Queensberry st, Carl
Walsh, James, Monteagle hotel, Queensberry st, Carl
Walsh, James, Shannon and Shamrock hotel, Queensberry st, Hot
Walsh, James, 9 Victoria st west, W M
Walsh, John, tailor, 55 Errol st, Hot
Walsh, John, Rose of Denmark hotel, 193 Little Bourke st west
Walsh, Mrs., dairy, 101 Little Oxford st, E C

Walsh, R., bottle merchant, 45 Kerr st, F
Walsh, Patrick, contractor, Pres
Walsh, Thomas, sailmaker, 45 Bourke st west
Walsh, Thomas, 262 Smith st, E C
Walsh, Thomas, 51 Stanley st, W M
Walsh, Thomas, Stawell st, W M
Walsh, William, 67 Faraday st, Carl
Walshman, —, Tennyson st, St K
Walstab, George, auctioneer and estate agent, 72 Queen st
Walter, C., Bell st, F
Walter, F., cabinet maker, 6 Russell st
Walter, Frederick, Highett st, Rd
Walter, Thomas, merchant, 186 Flinders lane east
Walters, Brown, and Co., mining surveyors, Bay st, San
Walters, Captain, marine surveyor, Rouse st, San
Walters, James, 39 Franklyn st west
Walters, John, High st, Rd
Walters, Samuel, Lygon st, Carl
Walters, Thos., merchant, 9 Bond st
Walton and Sampson, dentists, 120 Collins st east
Walton Brothers, chemists and druggists, 48 Gertrude st, F
Walton, Denys, coffee merchant, &c., 31 a'Beckett st
Walton, J., 45 Bell st, F
Walton, J. T., Heath st, San
Walton, J. W., 73 Wellington st, E C
Walton, Hubert, 97 Lygon st, Carl
Wang, Schmdit, and Lindblom, tailors, 158 Russell st
Wann, Hy., 17 Barkly st, Carl
Warburton, Henry, Chapel st, Pra
Warburton, Joseph, confectioner, 19 and 21 Gertrude st, F
Warburton, Thos., galvanized iron warehouse, 23 Bourke st west
Warburton, W. J., grocer, 100 Wellington st, E C
Ward, —, Swan st, Rd
Ward, D., hairdresser, 92½ Bourke st east
Ward, Burnet, 20 Park st, Em H
Ward, C. S., 39 Rathdowne st, Carl
Ward, E., 60 Stephen st
Ward, Frederick, 16 Rathdowne st, Carl
Ward, Frederick William, surgical instrument maker, 44 Swanston st
Ward, George M., agent, 51 Spring st
Ward, J., Swan st, Rd
Ward, J., 20 Lonsdale st east
Ward, James, 73 Faraday st, Carl
Ward, James, 13 Cole st, Wms
Ward, James, 86 Napier st, Em H
Ward, John, Coventry st, Em H
Ward, John, 48 Thompson st, Wms
Ward, Lawrence, British hotel, Abbotsford st, Hot
Ward, Miss Mary, 47 Park st west, Em H
Ward, Mrs., Argyle st, St K

Ward, Mrs., milliner, High st, St K
Ward, Mrs., Rouse st, San
Ward, P., grocer, 19 Little Bourke st, west
Ward, P, Rouse st, San
Ward, Patrick, Union hotel, 118 Moray st, Em II
Ward, Patrick, bootmaker, Bay st, San
Ward, Robert, Arden st, Hot
Ward, Samuel, builder, 30 Young st, F
Ward, T., draper, High st, St K
Ward, T., draper, Octavia st, St K
Ward, W., Ann st, Wmn
Ward, Wm., 72 Little Nelson st, Wmn
Ward, Wm., hay and corn store, 211 King street
Warde, J., fruiterer, 97 Brunswick st, F
Wardell, Wm. Wilkinson, Inspector-General of Public Works, Public Works office
Warden, James, Derby st, E C
Warden, John, 65 Osborne st, Wmn
Warden, William, 175 Moray st, Em II
Wardill, R. W., Simpson st, E M
Wardill, S., sweep, 148 Little Bourke st east
Wardlaw, Jas., wheelwright, 169 King st
Wardlow, Alex., 70 Drummond st, Carl
Wardlesworth, A., bootmaker, Church st, Rd
Wardrop, A. B., M.L.A., accountant, Bank place, Collins st west
Wardrop, James, plumber and gasfitter, tin and copper smith, 4 Little Collins st east
Ware, Alfred, fruiterer, 20 Gertrude st, F
Ware, Edwin, 65 Victoria parade, F
Warein, —, painter, Smith st, E C
Warham, F., Napier st, F
Waring, E., 39 Hanover st, F
Waring, Mrs., dressmaker, Victoria st, Hot
Warman, James, registry office, 22 Little Collins st west
Warming, F., Albion hotel, Faraday st, Carl
Warmsley, Chas., 58 York st east, Em II
Warnass, Wm., Twyford st, Wmn
Warne, E. R., Commercial road, Fey
Warne, Henry, 135 Johnston st, E C
Warne, J., grocer, Beech st, San
Warne, John, restaurant keeper, Bay st, San
Warne, William, Cecil st, F
Warneford, Henry, grocer, 30 Barkly st, Carl
Warner, Ashton, Westgarth st, F
Warner, Charles F., 137 Raglan st, Em II
Warner, F., Fitzroy st, St K
Warner, George, Pentridge
Warner, Joseph, Wreckyn st, Hot
Warner, W. H., grocer, 119 Queensberry st, Hot
Warren, —, 12 Greeves st, F
Warren, A. G., Heath st, San

Warren, Ashton, Wellington st, Pra
Warren, G. H., 31 Rathdowne st, Carl
Warren, Hy., blacksmith, Latrobe parade, 132 Collins st east
Warren, James, Illawarra st, Wmn
Warren, James, Twyford st south, Wmn
Warren, Mrs., private boarding house, 23 Napier st, F
Warren, Mrs., Johnston st, E C
Warren, Robert, Whitehall st, Fey
Warren, Samuel, 8 James st, F
Warren, W., stationer, Bay st, San
Warren, William Henry, blacksmith, &c., 54 Post Office place
Warrenheip Distillery Company, office, 23 Queen st
Warrnambool, Belfast and Portland Steam Packet office, 60 Collins st west
Warrow, James, Illawarra st south, Wmn
Wartman, Lawrence H., pawnbroker, Chapel st, Pra
Warwey, Charles, 32 Faraday st, Carl
Warwick, Edward, undertaker, 21 Derby st, E C
Warwick, Henry, bootmaker, 35 Barkly st, Carl
Wassettine, H., painter, Fawkner st, St K
Washington, John, 251 Elizabeth st
Waschorn, T., Albert st, Pra
Waterhouse, Thos., cabinetmaker, Chapel st, Pra
Waterman, Isaac, picture-frame maker, 116 Elizabeth st
Waterman, J., Davis st, Pra
Waters and Co., patent agents, 58 Little Collins st east
Waters, E., Punt road, Rd
Waters, James, Stevedore st, Wmn
Waters, James, Albion st west, Bk
Waters, John, 240 King st
Waters, Miss, dressmaker, Raglan st, Em II
Waters, Samuel T., ship painter, River side south
Waters, T., butcher, Commercial road, Pra
Waters, Thomas, 247 Albert st, E M
Waters, Wm., insolvency accountant, 33 Hanover st, F
Waterstrom, George, engineer, Simpson st, E M
Watkin, Walter, Punt road, Pra
Watkins, F., butcher, 74 Clarendon st, Em II
Watkins, Wm., Carlton Club hotel, Gertrude st, F
Watkins, Wm., 213 Victoria st, E C
Watkinson, H. B., plumber, Cardigan st, Carl
Watkinson, Mrs., Garden st, Pra
Watson, —, stonemason, 51 Rose st, F
Watson, —, store, Pent
Watson, A., Woodville
Watson, A., 32 Swan st, Rd

Watson, A. S., Flem
Watson, Alex., 9 Peel st, E C
Watson, Alfred, Gardiner's creek road, Pra
Watson and Patterson, bacon curers, Prev
Watson, Benjamin, tailor, 13 Collins st east
Watson, C., Beach, Bin
Watson, Ch., 17 Errol st, Hot
Watson, Charles, wholesale grocer, &c., 19 Flinders lane west
Watson, David, carpenter, Inkerman st east, St K
Watson, E., Domain road, S Y
Watson, E. G., Glencoe, S Y
Watson, F., smith, Nth
Watson, F., stonemason, 172 Church st, Rd
Watson, G. B., Elphinstone, Fcy
Watson, George, cattle salesman, Kirk's bazaar, Bourke st west
Watson, George, Burnett st, St K
Watson, George, hairdresser, 131 King st
Watson, George, 8 Hanover st, F
Watson, George, and Co., slaters, &c., 174 Lonsdale st east
Watson, George Wm., chemist, 271 Brunswick st, F
Watson, J., 193 Cecil st, Em H
Watson, J., Byron st, Hot
Watson, J., Miller st, Bk
Watson, J. T., confectioner, 239 Bourke st east
Watson, James, grocer, corner Smith and Peel sts, E C
Watson, James, agent, 33 Argyle st, F
Watson, James, 197 Latrobe st west
Watson, James, 90 Latrobe st east
Watson, John, stock broker and insurance agent, 26 Collins st west
Watson, John, butcher, Chapel st, Pra
Watson, John, Bridge hotel, corner of Thompson and Osborne sts, Wms
Watson, John, Station place, Sau
Watson, Jos., corn dealer, &c., 161 Bourke st west and 14 Swanston st
Watson, McAuley, and Co., shipwrights, River side south
Watson, Mrs., 193 Latrobe st west
Watson, R., 84 Hanmer st, Wmn
Watson, Rev. J., Williams road, Pra
Watson, Robert, Bay View hotel, High st, St K
Watson, Samuel, Barkly st, Carl
Watson, Samuel W., Punt road, Pra
Watson, T. B., George st, F
Watson, Thomas, 20 Smith st, E C
Watson, Thomas R., conveyancer, notary public, and parliamentary agent, &c., 84 Little Collins st west
Watson, Wm., cooper, Gisborne st, E M
Watson, Wm., carpenter, 125 Latrobe st west
Watson, Wm., 175 Napier st, F

Watson, William, and Sons, warehousemen, 41 Little Collins st east
Watson, Wm., 2 Wellington terrace, Wellington st, St K
Watson, Wm., Victoria st west, W M
Watson, Wm., 58 Market st, Em H
Watson, Wm., Kensington
Watt, A., slater, 28 Faraday st, Carl
Watt, Archibald, grocer, 135 Queensberry st, Hot
Watt, Charles, 110 Albert st, E M
Watt, E. J., electro gilder, Rd
Watt, George, 120 Victoria st, Rd
Watt, James, 31 Victoria parade, F
Watt, James, River side south
Watt, John, 197 Flinders lane east
Watt, John, 41 Stephen st
Watt, Joseph, boot warehouse, 129 Elizabeth st
Watt, Mrs., ladies' nurse, Wellington st, Rd
Watt, Mrs., draper, 28 Faraday st, Carl
Wattinne, Fidele, wool broker, 99½ Collins st west
Watton, Edward, tinsmith, 311 Elizabeth street
Watton, Edward, 2 Prince's terrace, F
Watts, —, 21 John st, Wms
Watts, C., shoemaker, Pres
Watts, C. J., Hampton st, Bin
Watts, C. W., butcher, Cape st, Held
Watts, Edward, Alma st east, St K
Watts, Edwin, Domain road, S Y
Watts, George, 19 Johnston st, F
Watts, James, Drummond st, Carl
Watts, Jos., 45 Victoria st, Hot
Watts, Martha, china and glass dealer, Grey st, St K
Watts, Mrs., dressmaker, 191 Cambridge st, E C
Watts, Mrs., Hosier lane
Watts, Thomas, Cremorne st, Rd
Watts, Thomas, Caulfield
Wauchope, Andrew, Electra st, Wmn
Waugh and Hastle, modellers, 1 Little Oxford st, E C
Waugh Brothers, hay and corn store, 76 Rathdowne st, Carl
Waugh, J., 6 Cross st, Hot
Waugh, J., 48 Dudley st, W M
Waugh, James, 3 Owen and Nicholson sts, Carl
Waugh, James, hay and corn store, Elgin st, Carl
Waugh, John, 4 Bath terrace, Faraday st, Carl
Waugh, John, 77 Lygon st, Carl
Waugh, John and Robert, corn factory, 143 Swanston st
Waugh, R., 44 Lygon st, Carl
Waxman, Aaron, pawnbroker, 177 Swanston st
Waxwork Exhibition, 97 Bourke st east
Way, George, 138 Eastern road, Em H

Waymouth, Bryan, jun., broker and commission agent, 42 Elizabeth st
Waymouth, H., 89 Cecil st, Em H
Waymouth, Samuel, tailor, 149 Bourke st west
Weall, Benjamin, agent, 17 Swanston st
Wearing, R. W., Essex st, Fcy
Weatherhead, Robert, 39 Cecil st, Wmn
Weatherhead, Wm., builder, Heath st, San
Weatherley, Alfred, Union st, S Y
Weaver, Edward, 158 Church st, Rd
Weaver, J., 29 Jeffcott st, W M
Weaver, Mrs., Charles st, Pra
Weaver, R., grocer, Nth
Weaver, T. E., tobacconist, Greville st, Pra
Weaver, Wm., and Co., job warehousemen, 14 Elizabeth st
Weaver, Wm., Carlisle st east, St K
Webb, Alfred, bootmaker, Chapel st, Pra
Webb, Charles, architect, 102 Collins st east
Webb, Charles, 161 Spring st
Webb, Daniel, bootmaker, 55 Lonsdale st west
Webb, F., Church st, Pra
Webb, F. J., 75 St. David st, F
Webb, G. H. F., Government short hand writer and barrister, 1 Temple court, Collins st west
Webb, George, New st, Btn
Webb, H., oyster saloon keeper, 98A Bourke st east
Webb, H. Lawrence, Station place, San
Webb, John, schoolmaster, Mill st, Btn
Webb, John, 185 Cambridge st, E C
Webb, W. H., 73 George st, F
Webb, Wm., Parade hotel, Wellington parade, E M
Webb, Wm., 60 York st east, Em H
Webb, Wm., 21 Bell st, F
Webbe, Mrs., 4 Barkly terrace, Barkly st, Carl
Webber, B. L., Cliff st, Pra
Webber, S., Fitzroy st, F
Webber, Samuel, Leveson st, Hot
Weber, Albert, pianoforte maker, 77 Gertrude st, F
Webster, Alex., 12 Elizabeth st
Webster, Alex., 122 Drummond st, Carl
Webster Brothers, merchants, 29 Flinders lane west
Webster, D., Westbourne terrace, St K
Webster, Francis D., watchmaker, Bay st, Btn
Webster, J., 99 Kerr st, F
Webster, J., carpenter, Strand, Wmn
Webster, J., and Co., drapers, 283 Victoria parade, E C
Webster, J. T., watchmaker, 86 Clarendon st, Em H
Webster, John Campbell, Cotham road, Kew

Webster, John R., watchmaker, Smith st, F
Webster, Joseph, and Co., wholesale grocers, 30 Queen st
Webster, Joseph, Hartley Hall, Kew
Webster, Thomas D., 157 Cecil st, Em H
Webster, Thomas, 197 Cecil st, Em H
Webster, W., upholsterer, 161 Cardigan st, Carl
Webster, Wm., 17 Spring st
Weedon, Henry, Morning Star hotel, 154 Little Bourke st east
Weedon, J., grocer, Chapel st, Pra
Weedon, Wm., Palmerston st, Carl
Weekly Age office, 57 Elizabeth st
Weeks, H., Pelham st, Carl
Weeks, J., general dealer, Little Latrobe street
Wegner, Wm., 49 Napier st, F
Wehanck Bros., cabinetmakers, 16 Little Collins st east
Weighman, George, musician, 138 Little Lonsdale st east
Weinreuter, E., upholsterer, 117 Collins st east
Weir, Alexander, grocer, 227 Bourke st east
Weir, J., livery stables, Gardiner's creek road, Tk
Weir, Samuel, Perry st, E C
Weir, Wm., builder, 76 Oxford st, E C, and 25 Gertrude st, F
Welch, Henry P., Ashbourne, Tk
Welch, Joseph, halter, 66 Brunswick st, F
Welch, Stephen, Liverpool hotel, 211 Bourke st east
Welch, Wm., High st, Pra
Wellar, J., Union st, Btn
Wellard, J., Victoria st, Btn
Wellborne, George, boarding-house, 219 Bourke st west
Wellington Mining Association, 32 Collins st west
Wells, Arthur, C.E., William st north
Wells, C. J., grocer, Sydney road, Bk
Wells, J., Lennox st, Rd
Wells, James, Miller st, W M
Wells, R., Pelham st, Carl
Wells, Thos., 34 Bouverie st, Carl
Wells, Thos., High st, St K
Wells, W. J., Graham st, San
Wellsteed, George, grocer, 139 Brunswick st, F
Welsford, Samuel J., importer of fancy goods, 157 Swanston st
Welsh Chapel, Latrobe st west
Welsh, James, 250 King st
Welsh, Laurance, 65 Park st, Em H
Welsh, T., 78 Montague st, Em H
Welsby, Samuel, blacksmith, Church st Rd
Welton, John, Curzon st, Hot
Wenborn, W. A. J., George st, E M
Wenborne, C. F., 45 Drummond st, Carl

2 A

Wener, C., india-rubber manufacturer 139 Flinders st west
Wenk, A., 261 Fitzroy st, F
Wenzel and Ence, watchmakers and jewellers, 127 and 129 Bourke st east
Were, J. B., Alma st, St K
Were, J. D., and Son, stock and share brokers, and consulate-general of Portugal, Denmark, Norway, Chili, and Lubec, 22 Collins st west
Werner, John, 219 Moray st, Em H
Wernicke, A., cabinetmaker, 15 Victoria st, E C
Werth, C., tobacconist, 155 Wellington st, E C
Westlake, Mrs., 79 Cobden st, Em H
Wesleyan Home, Drummond st and Queensberry st, Carl
West, George, oyster dealer, 211 Swanston st
West, H., 35 Hanover st, F
West, H., wood turner, 227 Moray st, Em H
West, J., bootmaker, 39 Brunswick st, F
West, James, Victoria st, St K
West, James, 48 Johnston st, F
West, James, Prince Albert hotel, Chapel st, Pra
West, John, blacksmith, Ess
West, Richard, Edward st, Dk
West, Richard, Inkerman st, St K
West, Thomas, greengrocer, Chapel st, Pra
West, W., ironmonger, 136 Brunswick st, F
West, W. F., tobacconist, 157 Elizabeth st
West, Wm. H., Cremorne st, Rd
Westall, W. E., Lord Raglan hotel, Nott st, San
Westcott, G., 48 Johnston st, E C
West Melbourne Orderly room, corner of a'Beckett and Queen sts
Western Clubs Marine Insurance office, 23 Market st
Western Market, Flinders lane west and Market st
Westfield, Kennet, surveyor and cooper, 14 King st
Westhorp, Thomas, 43 Cecil st east, Wmn
Westley, Henry, solicitor and conveyancer, 26 Collins st west
Weston, J., greengrocer, Ferguson st, Wmn
Weston, Mrs., 24 Church st, E C
Weston, Thomas, butcher, Blackwood st, Hot
Weston, W., butcher, 201 King st, and Bn
Westwood, John A., 5 Owen st, corner of Nicholson st, Carl
Westwood, Samuel, Vere st, E C
Wetheridge, C., 4 Cross st, Hot
Weymark, M., dealer, 48 Cardigan st, Carl
Whaite, J., Abbotsford st, W M

Whalley, Charles, Wellington st, Fry
Whalley, James, Victoria st, E C
Whamond, Mrs., Twyford st, Wmn
Whan, John, blacksmith, 14 Queensberry st, Carl
Whannell, Thomas, 120 Rose st, F
Wharton, George, architect and surveyor, 24 Collins st west
Wharton, George, tailor, 78 Queen st
Wharton, Robert, and Co., commission merchants, 85 Flinders st west
Whatmuff, Mrs., school, 127 Johnston st, F
Whatmuff, Stephen, Hoddle st, E C
Wheatley, A., Park st, Em H
Wheatley, Mrs. Louise, midwife, 74 Fitzroy st, F
Wheelan, John, toll collector, Bridge road Rd
Wheeler, Ed., 19 Barkly st, Carl
Wheeler, F., 151 Cecil st, Em H
Wheeler, Henry, painter, plumber, and glazier, 35 George st, F
Wheeler, Henry, Hobs st, St K
Wheeler, J., tailor, 54 Cambridge st, E C
Wheeler, J. H., M.L.A., Parliament House
Wheeler, Jabez, Emu hotel, corner of Pelham and Bouverie sts, Carl
Wheeler, Mrs., 70 York st east, Em H
Wheeler, Mrs. W. J., straw hat maker, 35 Errol st, Hot
Wheeler, Mrs., school, 43 Smith st, F
Wheeler, Robert, 112 Napier st, F
Wheeler, Robert, Barkly st, Carl
Wheelhouse, J., 45 Little Latrobe st
Wheelhouse, John, machinist, 22 Post Office place
Whelan, Daniel, cabinetmaker, 249 Lonsdale st east
Whelan, James, Nott st, San
Whelan, P., contractor, 150 Bourke st west
Whelan, Peter, Curzon st, Hot
Whelehan, Michael, farmer, Ess
Whidgmore, —, master mariner, 33 York st west, Em H
Whipp, Mrs. S., 67 Nelson road, Em H
Whipp, Wm., Whipp's hotel, Bridge road, Rd
Whitaker, T., Brighton st, Rd
Whitby, A. L., Kew
Whitby, Edward, merchant, 25 Flinders lane east
Whitcomb, H., surgeon, 29 Stanley st, E C
White, —, 65 Moor st, F
White, A., grocer, 117 Flinders st west
White, A., 45 Moor st, F
White, Alex., grocer, corner of King and Flinders sts
White, Alexander, 168 Young st, F
White, Alfred, Custom-house agent, 17 Market st
White, Augustus F., chemist, Chapel st, Pra

White, Alfred, 111 Victoria st, Hot
White, B., boot and shoe dealer, 38 Bridge road, Rd
White, Benjamin, Provost st, Hot
White Brothers and Co., merchants, 3 Market st
White, C., 5 Park terrace, Fitzroy st, St K
White, C., brickmaker, Bay st, Btn
White, Captain, Strand, Wmn
White, Captain W., York st east, Em H
White, Charles, joiner, 3 Latrobe st east
White, D., 130 Fitzroy st, F
Wake, E., grocer, 81 Brunswick st, F
White, E., Stoke st, San
White, E. A., 63 Powlett st, E M
White, E. J., brewer, Cremorne st, Rd
White, F. D., Mitchell st, St K
White, F. K., Simpson st, E M
White, F. M., architect, 10 Elizabeth st
White, G., Dover road, Wmn
White, G., corn dealer, 179 Bridge road, Rd
White, George, and Co., brassfounders and gasfitters, 9 and 10 Albert st, E M
White, H., farrier, Flemington road, Hot
White, Isaac, Dryburgh st, Hot
White, Isaac, Cambridge Arms hotel, Cambridge st, E C
White, J., 130 Raglan st east, Em H
White, J., brickmaker, Bay st, Btn
White, J. C., Palmerston st, Carl
White, James, builder, 9 Park st west, Em H
White, James, Wellington st, Pra
White, James, merchant, rice mills, 5 Flinders st east, Dandenong road
White, James, 161 Lonsdale st west
White, James, parasol warehouse, 35 Madeline st, Carl
White, James, Dandenong road, Wr
White, James, 35 Madeline st, Carl
White, James H., and Co., shipping agents, 101 Collins st west, and Fulton st, St K
White, James, Stoke st, San
White, John, hay store, Bridge road, Rd
White, John, grocer, 112 George st, F
White, John, dairyman, Chatham st, Fcy
White, John, quarryman, Whitehall, Fcy
White, Jos, Shamrock hotel, 40 Lonsdale st west
White, Joseph, 3 Jackson st, Wmn
White, Joseph, 106 Russell st
White, Luke, Rouverie st, Carl
White, Mrs., dressmaker, Chapel st, Pra
White, Mrs., fruiterer and grocer, 79 Brunswick st, F
White, Mrs., Fitzroy st, St K
White, Mrs., Graham st, San
White, Mrs. Mary, 4 George st, E M
White, P., plumber and gasfitter, 5 Brunswick st, F
White, P. J., bookseller, &c., 5 Brunswick st, F
White, Patrick, Haw

White, Peter James, 225 George st, F
White, Richard C., 63 Cobden st, Em H
White, Robert, contractor, 112 Latrobe st west
White Star Line of Australian Packets; agent's office, 48a William st
White, Thomas, harness maker, Pres
White, Thomas, bootmaker, Barry st, Carl
White, Thomas, Haw
White, Thomas and Wm., wine and spirit merchants, 34 Flinders st east
White, W., 95 Lygon st, Carl
White, W. and G., ship builders and ship smiths, Nelson place, and coal-yard, Cecil st, Wmn
White, W. D., Victoria and Nicholson sts, F
White, W. J., Haw
White, W. P., and Co., merchants, 10 Elizabeth st
White, Walter, grocer, Dryburgh st, Hot
White, Wm. H., veterinary surgeon, Chapel st, Pra
White, Wm., 77 Capel st, Hot
White, Wm., land agent and surveyor, 81½ Collins st east
White, Wm., Haw
White, Wm., Simpson st, E M
Whitehead, Ed., Richmond terrace, Rd
Whitehead, Edward, 32 Gore st, F
Whitehead, Isaac, carver and gilder, 83 Collins st east
Whitehead, John, King st, W M
Whitehead, Joseph, 9 Young st, F
Whitehead, Miss, Williams road, Pra
Whitehead, Richard, Nicholson st, Carl
Whitehead, Richard, hall keeper, Hall of Commerce
Whitelaw, D., painter, Morny st, Em H
Whitelaw, James, Royal lane, Bourke st east
Whitelaw, Robert E., bootmaker, Simpson st, E M
Whiteley, Joseph, Ralston st, Pra
Whiteley, Mrs., greengrocer, 90 George st, F
Whiteley, P., Commercial road, Pra
Whitelow, Wm., 16 Howard st, Hot
Whitely, Thomas, 51 Cobden st, Em H
Whiteman, James, butcher, Chapel st, Pra
Whiteman, J. L., butcher, High st, Pra
Whiteman, John, farrier, off 56 Bourke st west
Whiteman, Mrs., Pelham st, Carl
Whiten, A., bookseller, 27 Stanley st, E C
Whitcoak, George, 151 Johnston st, E C
Whiterod, James, Cremorne st, Rd
Whiteside, James, bootmaker, 165 Little Bourke st east
Whiteston, P., Hotham st, E M
Whitfield, George, Capel st, W M
Whitfield, Joseph, working cutler, 17 Post Office place

Whitford, George T., Duke of Richmond hotel, Swan st, Rd
Whitford, Mrs., private boarding-house, 27 Russell st
Whitford, Robert, grocer, Lothian st, Hot
Whiting, A., bootmaker, 112 Nicholson st, F
Whiting, James, basket maker, 33 Post Office place
Whiting, J., 2 Webb st, F
Whiting, Wm., solicitor, 57 Little Collins st east
Whiting, W., 94 Leicester st, Carl
Whitlaw, David, baker, Peel st, Pra
Whitling, John, general dealer, 199 Little Collins st east
Whitman, Francis, wheelwright, Haw
Whitmore, Frederick, saddler, 71 Gertrude st, F
Whitmore, George, carpenter, 30 Little Bourke st west
Whitney, Chambers and Co., Ironmongers, &c., Collins st east, and 109 Flinders st east
Whitney, John, Tennyson st, St K
Whittaker, J. H., Dryburgh st, Hot
Whittaker, Mrs., 7 James st, F
Whittaker, Thomas, Little Hanover st, F
Whittenbury, Dr., New st, Bru
Whittingham Brothers, wholesale grocers, 7 Bond st, Flinders lane west
Whittle, J., bootmaker, Cremorne st, Rd
Whittle, John, 47 King William st, F
Whitton, F., 143 Cecil st, F
Whitton, George, printer, 101 Flinders lane east
Whitton, H. J., 6 Napier st, F
Whitton, Mrs., Hoddle st, E C
Whitton, Thos., hairdresser, &c., 9 Bourke st west
Whitty, A. L., Kew
Whitty, John, money and hotel broker, 60 Little Collins st east
Whomes, George, painter, 79 Hoslyn st, W M
Whyatt, J., grocer, Murchison st, Carl
Whyte, —, 50 Cobden st, Em H
Whyte, A., grocer, King st, and 117 Flinders st west
Whyte, D., grocer, 186 Smith st, E C
Whyte, James, Fulton st, St K
Whyte, John, store, Canning st, Carl
Whyte, Jas., Queensberry st, Hot
Whyte, Mrs., 76 Park st, Em H
Whyte, Mrs., Fitzroy st, St K
Whyte, Wm., builder and contractor, 85 Park st east, Em H
Whyte, Wm., 1 Errol st, Hot
Wiber, John, 63 Condell st, F
Wickham, John, Walsh st, W M
Wickham, Wm., shoemaker, Flem
Wicks, Edward, gardener, Esa
Wicks, Richard, 131 Little Lonsdale st west

Wicks, T. B., pocket book and manifold writer maker, 89 Little Collins st east
Widdicombe, John, draper, Chapel st, Pra
Widgery, John, solicitor, 43 Bourke st west
Wiegman, A., basket maker, 33 Post Office place
Wigg, H. S., Greville st, Pra
Wigg, Mrs., 4 Lygon st, Carl
Wiggin, Thomas, horse breaker, Lothian st, Hot
Wiggins, Wm., saddler, Swan st, Rd
Wigglesworth, J., surveyor, St Andrew's st, Bru
Wighan, John, plumber, Commercial road Bourke st east
Wight, E. H., Kensington
Wight, J., Edward st, Bk
Wight, J., wheelwright, Sydney road, Bk
Wight, Thomas C., printer, Simpson st, E M
Wightman, Peter, 69 Drummond st, Carl
Wigley, J., solicitor, Beach st, Sus
Wigmore, R. H., Bridge road, Rd
Wilcox, Edwin, Roxburgh Castle hotel, Chapel st, Pra
Wilcox, George, turner, 31 Napier st, F
Wilcox, Henry, Roxburgh brewery, Arthur st, Pra
Wilcox, John, coal and wood yard, 33 Palmer st, F
Wild, —, furniture broker, Swan st, RJ
Wild, Benjamin, butcher, 283 Brunswick st, F
Wild, Edward, 31 George st, F
Wild, Thomas, blacksmith, Pres
Wild, Wm., Elgin st, Carl
Wild, Wm., Kensington
Wildash, George, Young st, F
Wilden, Wm., nightman, Swan st, Rd
Wilder, D., share broker, commission agent, &c., 3 Collins st west
Wilding, Samuel, bootmaker, 158 Wellington st, E C
Wilkie, David F., M.L.C., physician, 105 Collins st east
Wilkie, Joseph, Caulfield
Wilkie, Kilner, and Co., pianoforte manufacturers, Queen st north
Wilkie, Webster, and Co., pianoforte and music warehouse, 15 Collins st east
Wilkie, Welch, and Co., agents, importers, and agricultural implement sellers, 32 King st
Wilkins, —, Twyford st, Wmn
Wilkins, Alfred, 31 Market st
Wilkins, Alfred, Harnett st, St K
Wilkins, Jacob, 160 Cardigan st, Carl
Wilkins, John, Cole st south, Wmn
Wilkins, John M. B., surgeon, Nelson parade, Wmn
Wilkins, John, Cole st, Wmn
Wilkins, Walter, surgeon, Bay st, San
Wilkinson, —, Chetwynd st, W M

Wilkinson, A., 18 Moray place, Em H
Wilkinson and Co., blacking manufacturers, 39 Dudly st, W M
Wilkinson Brothers and Co., merchants, 112 Collins st west
Wilkinson, Edward, 59 Elgin st, Carl
Wilkinson, Frederick, Master in Equity, 51 Latrobe st east
Wilkinson, Henry, Inkerman st west, St K
Wilkinson, Henry A., 24 Church st, Em H
Wilkinson, J., draper, 76 Brunswick st, F
Wilkinson, J., 189 King st
Wilkinson, James, Dudley st, W M
Wilkinson, John, Haw
Wilkinson, Miss, dressmaker, 26 Madeline st, Carl
Wilkinson, Miss Jane, artist, 174 Collins st east
Wilkinson, Mrs., 46 Adderly st, W M
Wilkinson, Mrs. W. A., professor of singing, 174 Collins st east
Wilkinson, Mrs., Powlett st, E M
Wilkinson, Rev. George, Nelson place, Wmn
Wilkinson, T., Sydney road, Bk
Wilkinson, Thomas, 35 Cobden st, Em H
Wilkinson, Thomas, agent Imperial Insurance Company, 39 Gore st, F
Wilkinson, Thomas, 4 Baillie st, Hot
Wilkinson, Wm., tailor and clothier, 186 Smith st, E C
Wilks, —, chemist, Wellington parade, E M
Wilks, C., Brighton st, Rd
Wilks, John, Millswyn st, S Y
Willan, Robert, Nicholson st, F
Willand, Thomas, 5 Palmer st, F
Willdridge, Richard, Haw
Willerson, H., general dealer, Rowena parade, Rd
Willet, J., 6 Henry st, F
Willett, Mrs., Russell st
Willey, George, grocer, High st, Pra
Willison, C. H., Crown hotel, High st, Pra
Willison, Charles R., Bunch of Grapes, Swanston st
Williams, —, 118 Raglan st east, Em H
Williams, —, Hanover st, F
Williams, —, Easy st, E C
Williams, —, 47 Rathdowne st, Carl
Williams, —, 35 Argyle st, F
Williams, Abraham, fruit importer, Western Market
Williams and Co., kerosene merchants, and importers of sewing machines, 31 Swanston st
Williams, B., M.L.C., 34 Bourke st west
Williams, Benjamin, Acland st, St K
Williams, Captain, 73 Raglan st, Em H
Williams, Charles, 26 Bank st east, Em H
Williams, David, mason, 136 Raglan st, Em H
Williams, Dr., Douglas parade, Wmn

Williams, Edward R., store, 131 Queensberry st, Hot
Williams, Evan, 1 McArthur place, Carl
Williams, F., dining rooms, 119 Flinders lane west
Williams, F., Heath st, San
Williams, F., 29 Baillie st, Hot
Williams, Francis, grocer, Chapel st, Pra
Williams, Francis, grocer, 5 Bouverie st, Carl
Williams, Fred., carpenter, Nott st, San
Williams, Frederick, Graham st, San
Williams, G., draper, Yarra st, Hedl
Williams, G., butcher, Faraday st, Carl
Williams, G. W., Chapel st, Pra
Williams, Henry, 191 Cardigan st, Carl
Williams, Henry, teacher, Pent
Williams, Henry, Elgin st, Carl
Williams, His Honor Judge, Punt road, S Y
Williams, J., 82 George st, E M
Williams, J., 75 Nelson road, Em H
Williams, J., 37 Cecil st, Em H
Williams, J., 7 Chetwynd st, Hot
Williams, J., Canning st, Carl
Williams, J., 94 Stanley st, W M
Williams, J., 47 King William st, F
Williams, J., Goodwood st, Rd
Williams, J., 69 Gore st, F
Williams, J. L., 134 Kerr st, F
Williams, James, Nicholson st, Carl
Williams, James, Flem
Williams, James, Naval Brigade hotel, Bay st, San
Williams, James, boarding-house keeper, 100 Lonsdale st east
Williams, James, butcher, 44 Ferguson st, Wmn
Williams, James Slope, bootmaker, 133 Gertrude st, F
Williams, James T., 134 Kerr st, F
Williams, John, Lamb inn, Little Latrobe st east
Williams, John, 82 Leicester st, Carl
Williams, John, 40 Little Nelson st, Wmn
Williams, John, butcher, Haw
Williams, John Joseph, 30 Johnston st, F
Williams, Margaret, Cliff st, Pra
Williams, Miss, dressmaker, 103 Napier st, F
Williams, Mrs., 32 Regent st, F
Williams, Mrs., dressmaker, Rowena parade, Rd
Williams, Mrs., 105 George st, F
Williams, Mrs., Registry office, 199 Victoria parade, E C
Williams, Mrs., midwife, 88 Elgin st, Carl
Williams, Mrs., 2 Bank st east, Em H
Williams, Owen, produce factor, 142 Collins st west
Williams, P. J., Barnett st, St K
Williams, Richard, 1 Canning st, Carl
Williams, Robert, wood, coal, and general store, 140 Ross st, F

Williams, R., 176 Moray st, Em H
Williams, Samuel, hay and corn dealer, 192 Lonsdale st east
Williams, Spiro, store, Nott st, San
Williams, T., Grange road, Tk
Williams, T., Brunswick st, Bk
Williams, T. H., 80 Alma st, F
Williams, Thomas, Grey st east, E M
Williams, Thomas, 138 Flinders lane east
Williams, Thomas S., photographic artist, 4 Collins st east
Williams, Thomas, hairdresser, 253 Elizabeth st
Williams, Thomas, Gurner st, St K
Williams, Thomas, Jackson st, St K
Williams, W., surgeon, Graham st, San
Williams, W., saddler, 221 Smith st, F
Williams, W., coachbuilder, 112 Johnston st, E C
Williams, W. D., 10 Queen st
Williams, W. H., 121 Lonsdale st west
Williams, Wm., railway and general carriage builder, Collins st west, and River Side north
Williams, Wm., 215 Albert st, E M
Williams, Wm., 185 Lygon st, Carl
Williams, William H., printer and label manufacturer, 23 Little Bourke st east
Williams, Wm., dyer, 138 Lonsdale st east
Williams, Wm., Caroline st, S Y
Williams, Wm., Wellington st, Bin
Williams, Wm., butcher, 108 Gertrude st, F
Williams, Wm., 142 Little Lonsdale st east
Williamson, B., timber yard, Gardiner's Creek road, Pra
Williamson, Charles, stock and share broker, and mining agent, Hall of Commerce, Collins st west
Williamson, Ed., tailor, High st, St K
Williamson, Geo., tailor and habit maker, 249 Elizabeth st
Williamson, John, and Co., curled hair manufacturers, 86 Elizabeth st north
Williamson, Mrs., 5 Roden st, W M
Williamson, Mrs., Wilson st, Pra
Williamson, R., 80 Victoria st, W M
Williamson, Thos., Wreckyn st, Hot
Williamson, Wm., Victoria hotel, Charles st, Pra
Williamson, Wm., Owen st, Nicholson st, Carl
Willis, G., 122 Johnston st, F
Willis, James B., Grosvenor st, Pra
Willis, N., Station place, San
Willis, Richard, London
Willis, Richard and Thomas, importers of clocks, jewellery, &c., 37 and 39 Little Collins st east
Willis, Samuel, ladies' bootmaker, 156 Bourke st east
Willis, T., 169 Victoria parade, E C
Willis, Thomas, dairyman, Highett st, Rd

Willis, Thomas, manufacturing jeweller, 39 Little Collins st east
Willis, Wm., blacksmith, 56 M'Killop st
Willis, Wm. L., general store, Leicester st, Carl
Williston, C. H., Builders' Arms hotel, Bridge road, Rd
Willman, Mrs., 263 Napier st, F
Willmott, George, oven manufacturer, 63 Little Collins st east
Willoughby, Howard, 201 Albert st, Em H
Willoughby, Mrs. C., 53 Cardigan st, Carl
Willoughby, T., butcher, Charles st, Pra
Wills, J., John st, Moor st, F
Wills, H. C., High st, St K
Wills, Thomas, Kew
Wills, W., 99 Cecil st, Em H
Wills, Wm., Castle inn, 104 George st, F
Wilmington, Mrs., 105 Victoria parade, F
Wilmot, H., ironmonger, a'Beckett st west
Wilmot, Henry, general dealer, 20½ Post Office place
Wilmot, William, ironmonger, 11 Eastern Market, Bourke st east
Wilmoth, Joseph, Hotham st, E M
Wilmott, Geo., colonial oven builder, 83 Little Collins st east
Wilms, C. A., and Co., ship chandlers, 13 Beach st, San
Wilshin and Leighton, merchants, 7 Market st
Wilshin, Daniel, Tivoli st, S Y
Wilson, —, House st, San
Wilson, —, Condell st, F
Wilson, —, plater, 183 Cambridge st, E C
Wilson, —, 33 Wellington st, E C
Wilson and Mackinnon, general printers and publishers, 78 Collins st east
Wilson, Benjamin F., Brighton st, Rd
Wilson Bros., butchers, Nicholson st, Carl
Wilson Bros., drapers, 125 and 127 Brunswick st, F
Wilson, Buchanan, and Co., merchants, 3 Queen st
Wilson, C., boarding house, 125 Collins st west
Wilson, C. F., hotel broker, 66 Little Collins st west
Wilson, Charles, tent maker, 343 Elizabeth st
Wilson, Crosbie and Co., merchants, 16 and 18 Flinders lane west
Wilson, D., Elgin st, Carl
Wilson, David, 49 Napier st, Em H
Wilson, David, 21 Rathdown st, Carl
Wilson, Donald, coachbuilder, Franklyn st east
Wilson, E., bootmaker, Brighton st, Rd
Wilson, Ed., accountant, 52 Queen st
Wilson, Edward, 74 Collins st east
Wilson, Edward, electro plater and gilder, 123 Little Collins st east
Wilson, Edward, M.D., surgeon, 132 Church st, Rd

Wilson, Edward, contractor, 170 Johnston st, E C
Wilson, George, saddler, Flem
Wilson, George, leather cutter, 89 Bridge road, Rd
Wilson, Geo., Richmond terrace, Rd
Wilson, George, Park st, S Y
Wilson, George, Pen
Wilson, George, Millswyn st, S Y
Wilson, H., machinist and smith, Barkly st, Carl
Wilson, Henry, Church st, Rd
Wilson, Henry, tinsmith, Chapel st, Pra
Wilson, Henry, miller, 140 Lonsdale st west
Wilson, Henry, plumber, 94 High st, St K
Wilson, Horatio F., carpenter, 117 Stevedore st, Wms
Wilson, Hugh, butcher, Bay st, San
Wilson, Hugh, Prendergast's hotel, Lonsdale st east
Wilson, J., Barkly st, St K
Wilson, J., 5 Courtney st, Hot
Wilson, J., jeweller, 76 Gertrude st, F
Wilson, J., grocer, 45 Little Lonsdale st east
Wilson, J., carpenter, McGrath's place
Wilson, J., blacksmith, Sydney road, Bk
Wilson, J., plumber, Gardiner's Creek rd, Pra
Wilson, J., bootmaker, 8 Beach st, San
Wilson, J., greengrocer, Leicester st east, F
Wilson, J., 23 Condell st, F
Wilson, J. H., Alphington
Wilson, J. N., Haw
Wilson, James, Railway place, San
Wilson, John, 3 Victoria st, Hot
Wilson, John, 84 Cambridge st, E C
Wilson, John, 13 Henry st, F
Wilson, Jos., Dover st, San
Wilson, Joseph, harness maker, 7 Carson's cottages, Collins st east
Wilson, M., hay and corn store, Chapel st, Pra
Wilson, M., china store, 64 Wellington st, E C
Wilson, M., 41 Moor st, F
Wilson, Miss, George st, F
Wilson, Miss, school, High st, Pra
Wilson, Monro W., barrister, Temple Court, Collins st west
Wilson, Mrs., 144 Little Bourke st west
Wilson, Mrs., 47 Napier st, F
Wilson, P. J., 65 Dudley st, Wms
Wilson, R., Barkly st, St K
Wilson, R., Dow st, San
Wilson, Robert, Simpson st, E M
Wilson, Robert, Admiral Napier hotel, Bridge road, Rd
Wilson, Robert, bootmaker, 193 Clarendon st, Em H
Wilson, T., bootmaker, 115 Russell st
Wilson, T., Bin

Wilson, T. N., produce merchant, Grey st, E M
Wilson, Thomas, Abbotsford st, E C
Wilson, W., 171 Victoria parade, F C
Wilson, W., grocery store, 27 Errol st, Hot
Wilson, W. M., barrister, 7 Temple Court, Collins st west
Wilson, Wm, Cardigan st, Carl
Wilson, Wm., greengrocer, 135 Cardigan st, Carl
Wilson, Wm., Victoria parade, F
Wilton, A., 59 Napier st, Em H
Wilton, Mrs., Berkeley st, Carl
Wilton, Wm., marine store, 8 Little Bourke st west
Wimble, N., Nth
Wincey, L., Fitzroy st, E
Winch, John, Twyford st, South Wms
Winder, John, cattle dealer, Flem
Winder, W. H., brickmaker, Ken
Winder, Wm., Flem
Windley, Alfred J., 174 Moray place, Em H
Windsor, A., George st, F
Windus, Charles, saddler, 59 Lygon st, Carl
Wines, S., 26 George st, F
Wing Chong, 59 Little Bourke st east
Wing, George, fruiterer, 174 Elizabeth st
Wing, H., Railway place, San
Wing, Joseph, share broker, &c., 1 Collins st west
Wing, Phillip, gold chain maker, Royal lane, Bourke st east
Wionell, John, smith, Haw
Winning, Alexander, 54 Hanmer st, Wms
Winsloe, Wm., tobacconist, 158 Bourke st east
Winter, Alfred, photographic artist, 172 Latrobe st east
Winter, S. V., Stevenson st, Rd
Winter and Gregory, grocers, 179 High st, St K
Winter, Charles, 52 Bouverie st, Carl
Winter, Conrad, House st, San
Winter, John, coal and wood yard, 41 Hanover st, F
Winter, Mrs., fancy repository, 96 Clarendon st, Em H
Winter, Richard, cabinetmaker, 172 Latrobe st east
Winter, Richard William, photographic artist, 172 Latrobe st east
Winter, W., grocer, 188 Bridge road, Rd
Winters, Charles, general store, 33 Little Bourke st west
Wintress, F., 37 Coventry st, Em H
Winwood, James, Wellington st, Rd
Wip Coon, 82 Little Bourke st east
Wiper, John, glass cutter, off 66 Little Collins st east
Wippell, J., Heidelberg road
Wisbey, A., Baillie st, Hot

Wise, A. J., 16 Young st, F
Wise, George Gordon, 16 Webb st, F
Wise, J. G., bootmaker, 71 Fitzroy st, St K
Wise, James, hairdresser, 29 Collins st west
Wise, Mrs. Jane, 64 Greeves st, F
Wiseheart, D., die sinker, &c., 25 Lonsdale st west
Wiseman, Arthur, 214 Napier st, F
Wiseman, Henry, coal yard, Nott st, San
Wisewould, James, Rockhill, S Y
Wisewould and Gibbs, solicitors, 16 Collins st west
Witchell, John, wheelwright, Chapel st, Pra
Witchell, Samuel, boarding-house, 50 Little Bourke st west
Witham, Wm., 63 Leicester st, Carl
Witheridge, F., Dover road, Wmn
Withers, A., draper, 71 and 73 Cecil st, Em H
Withers, F., Bridport st, Em H
Withers, Enoch, 54 Dorcas st, Em H
Withers, George, Steam Packet hotel, 7 Cole st, Wmn
Withers, J., Punt road, Rd
Withers, John R., solicitor, 17 Temple court, Collins st west
Withers, Wm., cooper, 3 Graham st, San
Withey, G., contractor, 72 Stephen st
Withy, Arthur, 92 York st, Em H
Witkowski, Julius, wholesale tobacconist, 11 Collins st west
Wolnarski, George, mining agent and share broker, 58 Elizabeth st
Wolf, J. Rudolph, engraver, 111 Little Bourke st
Wolfe, Edward D., master mariner, 57 Nelson road, Em H
Wolfe, J., engraver, 127 Little Lonsdale st east
Wolfenden, Wm., 91 Smith st, F
Wolff, Mrs., 99 Gertrude st, F
Wollaston, E., 68 Cardigan st, Carl
Wollaston, Rev. H., Powlett st, E M
Wolff, Marks, pawnbroker, 94 Swanston street
Wolmer, Mrs., 73 Cardigan st, Carl
Wolstenholme, E., ironmonger, 70 Brunswick st, F
Wolstenholme, John, 13 Lygon st, Carl
Wolstenholme, Mrs., tobacconist, 83A Brunswick st, F
Wood, —, dentist, 20 Russell st
Wood, A., Fitzroy st, F
Wood, A., Illawarra st, South Wmn
Wood and Cash, dairymen, 49 Little Lonsdale st east
Wood and Ware, brewers and spirit merchants, 82 Wellington st, E C
Wood, C., and Co., corn dealers, Franklyn st west
Wood, Captain, Gore st, F

Wood, David, Royal Sovereign hotel, 183 Smith st, F
Wood, David, photographer, 29 Bourke st east
Wood, E., jun., storekeeper and registrar of births and deaths, Pres
Wood, F., boot importer, 123 Bourke st east
Wood, Fredk., shoemaker, Moonee ponds, Ess
Wood, George, pastrycook, Chapel st, Pra
Wood, George, sailmaker, Nott st, San
Wood, Henry, greengrocer, 34 Lonsdale st west
Wood, J., 219 Swanston st
Wood, J., shoemaker, Carpenter st, Bta
Wood, J., coachmakers' ironmonger, Madeline st, Carl
Wood, J. R., Lennox st, Rd
Wood, J. W., 3 McArthur place, Carl
Wood, James, Capel st, Hot
Wood, James W., Swan hotel, 56 Gertrude st, F
Wood, James Williams, stock and share broker, &c., 35 Little Collins st west
Wood, James, Cardigan st, Carl
Wood, John, 4 Union terrace, Cardigan st, Carl
Wood, John, plumber, 76 High st, St K
Wood, John, corner Reilly and Brunswick sts, F
Wood, John, Dennistoun, barrister, 34 Temple court, Collins st west
Wood, John, 82 Wellington st, E C
Wood, John T., Sir R. Peel hotel, Peel st, E C
Wood, Jos., Cardigan st, Carl
Wood, Matthew, Osborne st south, Wmn
Wood, Miss, dressmaker, 92 Brunswick st, F
Wood, Mrs., 97 Gertrude st, F
Wood, Mrs., schoolmistress, Lennox st, Rd
Wood, Rev. Wm., Haw
Wood, Samuel, Rowena parade, Rd
Wood, Samuel, 207 Smith st, F
Wood, Sampson, Walsh st, S Y
Wood, T., grocer, Hoddle st, E C
Wood, Wm., 94 Young st, F
Wood, Wm., 49 Barkly st, Carl
Wood, Wm. J., blacking manufacturer, Gardiner's creek road, Tk
Wood, Wm., naturalist, 92 Brunswick st, F
Woodbridge, B., saddler, 29 Leveson st, Hot
Woodcock, Wm., Henry st, Pra
Woodcroft, W. J., 15A Young st, F
Woolfin, C. P., fancy repository, Clarendon st, Em H
Woodham, —, Peel st, Hot
Woodhead, Benjamin, dairyman, 144 Cecil st, F
Woodhead, D., 96 York st, Em H

Woodhouse and James, lithographers, print-sellers, &c., 95 Lonsdale st west
Woodhouse, Burns, and Co., merchants, off 53 Flinders st west
Woodhouse, E. A., and Co., ship and Insurance brokers, 85 Flinders st west
Woodhouse, H., Pelham st, Carl
Woodin, Robert, Hosier lane, Bourke st east
Woodroffe, L., Hoddle st, E C
Woodroffe, Mrs., 60 Electra st, Wmn
Woodrow, J. F., accountant, 173 Wellington st, E C
Woods, C., fellmonger, Ess
Woods, Ed., 139 Stephen st
Woods, Edward, Haw
Woods, F., boarding-house, Little Latrobe st east
Woods, Frederick G., 26 Rathdowne st, Carl
Woods, J., Batman's hotel, Spencer st
Woods, J., Ess
Woods, John, contractor, Argyle st, St K
Woods, Lieut. J. A., Morris st south, Wmn
Woods, Samuel, Greville st, Pra
Woods, W., Essendon hotel, Ess
Woods, Wm., 41 Baillie st, Hot
Woods, Wm. T., Lennox st, Haw
Woodsworth, Thomas, Parker st, Wmn
Woodville, J., Wellington parade, F M
Woodville, Jarrett, and Co., merchants, 50 Collins st west
Woodville, W. H., Wellington parade, E M
Woodward, —, Kew
Woodward and Co., potato salesmen, Eastern Market, Bourke st
Woodward, George, surveyor, Punt hill, S Y
Woodward, F., milliner, Charles st, Pra
Woodsworth, Thomas, Parker st, Wmn
Woodyard, Henry, 55 Argyle st, F
Woolcott and Turner, solicitors and proctors, 5 Collins st east
Woolcott, H., 68 Drummond st, Carl
Woolcott, John Spark, Gardiner's creek road, Tk
Woolcott, Mrs., Church st, Rd
Woolcott, R. R., Vaucluse, Rd
Woolcott, Wm. S., solicitor, 82 Collins st west
Wooldridge, Henry, surgeon, Avoca st, S Y
Wooley, John, 25 Grattan st, Carl
Wooley, H., contractor, Carlisle st west, St K
Woolf, —, tailor, 131 Little Lonsdale st east
Woolf Brothers, wine and spirit merchants, &c., 225 Elizabeth st
Woolf, F., Dalgety st, St K
Woolf, Henry, Travellers' Rest hotel, Nicholson st, F

Woolf, M. A., a'Beckett st west
Woolf, M. L., Victoria buildings, a'Beckett st
Woolf, P., 120 Fitzroy st, F
Woolf, P., bootmaker, 127 Little Lonsdale street east
Woolfe, C., bootmaker, Church st, Rd
Woolfe, E., Bay st, Bth
Woollatt, H. and F., butchers, Hoddle st, E C
Woolley, A., and Nephew, merchants, ship and insurance brokers, 10 Queen st
Woolley, Charles, Yarra st, Heid
Woolley, Charles, tailor, 168 Queen st
Woolley, Harwood, and Davies, solicitors, 14 Eldon chambers, Collins st west
Woolley, S. F., Fitzroy st, St K
Woolley, Septimus F., Fitzroy st, St K
Woolnough, Leander, Jolimont road, E M
Woolnough, R. H., Haw
Woolgato, H. W., 4 Swan st, Rd
Wootten, John, Pelham st, Carl
Wootton, Edward, Bay st, San
Wootton, G., carpenter, Church st, Rd
Wotton, F. K., Lothian st, Hot
Wordsworth, Ambrose, plumber and gasfitter, 149 Swanston st
Work, A., Fitzroy st, F
Work, W., grocer, 129 Leicester st, F
Worke, Mary, 29 Leveson st, Hot
Worley, G., Highett st, Rd
Worley, John, grocer, 141 Wellington st, E C
Wormald, F. G., chemist, 57 Latrobe st east
Worrall, J., tailor, &c., 130 Cardigan st, Carl
Worrall, J., Gardiner's creek road, Tk
Worrell, Mrs., Nicholson st, F
Worry, Robert, Church st, Rd
Worsley, Peter, gardener, Hobe st, St K
Worthington, George, barrister, 14 Temple court, Collins st west
Worthington, T., plumber, Ferguson st, Wmn
Wortley, V., grocer, Pent
Wortmann, Charles W. M., fruiterer, 161 Little Lonsdale st east
Wouldham and Samwells, coach-builders, 119 and 121 Flinders lane east
Woulfe, F., 103 Westgarth st, F
Woulfe, M., Cape st, Heid
Wragg, G., timber yard, Charles st, Pra
Wragge, George, chemist, 134 Collins st east
Wray, Peter, Pelham st, Carl
Wray, Thomas, Acland st, St K
Wray, Thomas Fawcett, accountant and broker, 55 Temple court, Collins st west
Wray, Wm., Union st, Pra
Wrede, Mrs., Church st, Rd
Wrigglesworth, Robert, 133 King st
Wright, —, 35 Young st, F
Wright, Andrew, contractor, Ess

2 B

Wright, Arthur J., manager Imperial Insurance Company, 4 Collins st west
Wright, Capt., Union st, Rd
Wright, Charles, Union hotel, Bourke st east
Wright, Charles, Heath st, San
Wright, Charles, Olive Branch hotel, 201 Stephen st
Wright, E., 60 Park st east, Em H
Wright, Edward J., draper, 84 Elizabeth street
Wright, Emanuel, Abbotsford hotel, 248 Johnston st, F C
Wright, George, Bay st, San
Wright, George, Bull and Mouth hotel, Bourke st east
Wright, George, 133 Queensberry st, Hot
Wright, Henry C., Bush inn, Commercial road, Pra
Wright, J., Bay st, San
Wright, J., 51 Flinders st east
Wright, J., outfitter, 7 Lonsdale st west
Wright, J. M., chemist, Bridge road, Rd
Wright, J. W., Inkerman st, St K
Wright, James, High st, Pra
Wright, James, Stevedore st, Wmn
Wright, James T., Capel st, W M
Wright, John, Spencer st
Wright, John, 18 Young st, F
Wright, R., 55 Cecil st, Wmn
Wright, R., shipbuilder, Nelson place, Wmn
Wright, R. M., 118 George st, F
Wright, Robert, 13 Peel st, Hot
Wright, T. Walne, importer, 3 Jeffcott st, W M
Wright, Thomas, grocer, &c., New st, Btn
Wright, Thomas, produce merchant, 243 Elizabeth st
Wright, Thomas, Albert st, E M
Wright, Thomas, artist, 236 Bourke st east
Wright, W. H., secretary Railways, Crown Lands offices, William st
Wright, Walter, Haw
Wright, Wm., engineer, 101 and 111 Little Bourke st west
Wright, Wm., general store, 268 Elizabeth street
Wrixon, H. J., barrister, 73 Little Collins st west
Wrixon, W. H., solicitor, 8 Collins st east
Wroe, Mrs., 125 Nicholson st, F
Wushman, L., Victoria st, Rd
Wustemann, Louis, Victoria st, Rd
Wuth, Adolph, gunmaker, 61 Bourke st west
Wyatt, Alfred, barrister, 32½ Temple court, Collins st west
Wyatt, G., Halfway place, San
Wyatt, J., bootmaker, 232 Wellington st, E C
Wyburn, T. J., solicitor, 62 Little Collins st west

Wyld, E., Park st, S Y
Wykeigh, G. T., commission agent, 58 Temple court
Wyley, Alexander, Adderly st, W M
Wyley, Vincent, Powlett st, E M
Wylie, Andrew, 12 Rosslyn st, W M
Wylie, David, 60 Arden st, Hot
Wylie, H. G., academy, 71 Napier st, F
Wymond, J. H., agent, 26 Collins st east
Wymond, T. H., Hed
Wymond, T. S., Chapel st, Pra
Wymons, F. S., 149 Cecil st, Em H
Wynfield, George, Robe st, St K
Wynn, Matthew, plumber, 80 High st, St K
Wynne, A., Oxford st, Hot

Y.

Yan Fatt, merchant, 53 Little Bourke st east
Yarra Yarra Gold Mining Company, 54 Elizabeth st
Yates, Benjamin, 130 Fitzroy st, F
Yates, G. G., 96 Queensberry st, Carl
Yates, George Joseph, miller, Merri creek
Yates, James, hairdresser, 160 Smith st, F C
Yates, Mrs., tailoress, 50 Cardigan st, Carl
Yates, Thomas, 9 Canning st, Carl
Yates, Thomas, 104 Elgin st, Carl
Yeaman, Andrew, 26 Lygon st, Carl
Yelland, George, hairdresser, 8 Bourke st east
Yencken, E. F., Hall of Commerce, Collins st west
Yeomans, Richard, 115 Lygon st, Carl
York, J., Victoria hotel, 162 Victoria st Rd
Yorke, Charles, Weston st, Fcy
Youl, J. R., draper, Clarendon st, Em H
Youl, John, 47 Cobden st, Em H
Youl, Richard, M.D., surgeon and city coroner, 111 Collins st east
Youlden, Edmund, butcher, 141 Swanston st, Post Office place
Young, A., Gore st, F
Young, A., goldsmith, 63 Stephen st
Young, A. F., 7 Peel st, Hot
Young and Martin, merchants, 117 Flinders lane west
Young and Potts, grocers, 216 Little Collins st east
Young, David, Gore st, F
Young, David, Fkm
Young, David, 77 Westgarth st, F
Young, G., Lennox st, Hd
Young, George, 90 High st, St K
Young, George, 90 Rosslyn st, W M
Young, George, Dow st, San
Young, George, grocer, Abbotsford st, E C
Young, Henry, hay and corn dealer, 9 Queensberry st, Carl

Young, Thomas, Kew
Young, J., Austin st, Fcy
Young, J. and J. C., merchants, 1044 Bourke st west
Young, J. F., 130 Bridge road, Rd
Young, James, Gipps st, E M
Young, Jas., coal and produce merchant, 93 Flinders st east
Young, James, Roden st, W M
Young, James, contractor, 3 Grattan st, Carl
Young, John, Dalgety st, St K
Young, John, grocer, 169 and 171 Spencer street
Young, John, port gauger, Villiers st, Hot
Young, John, contractor, Melbourne saw-mills, 163 Bourke st west
Young, John, medieval works manufacturer, 163 Bourke st west
Young, John, Hotham st, St K
Young, John, tailor, Flem
Young, Mrs., 7 Bridport st, Em H
Young, Mrs., 7 Peel st, Wmn
Young, Mrs., 52 Pascoe st, Wmn
Young, Mrs., 59 Raglan st, Em H
Young, Peter, wire worker, 12 Little Collins st west
Young, R., Stirling Castle hotel, 76 Smith st, E C
Young, Robert Morgan, 50 William st, and Kew
Young, Thomas, saddler, Gardiner's creek road, Pra

Young, W., and Co., woollen warehousemen, 36 Elizabeth st
Young, W. C. S., carpenter, Vine st, Heid
Young, Wm., Ivanhoe hotel, Ivanhoe, Heid
Young, Wm., Victoria Racing Club hotel, 24 Little Bourke st west
Younghusband and Co., merchants, 34 Elizabeth st
Younghusband, Isaac, Beach road, Bm
Youngman and Co., wholesale druggists and merchants, 125 Russell st
Youngman, Henry, Avoca st, S Y
Youngman, Jos., 63 Elgin st, Carl
Yuille, Wm. C., commission agent, Kirk's bazaar, 47 Bourke st west

Z.

Zaader, Cecile, bonded storekeeper, Highlander lane, 101 Flinders st west
Zeal, A. W., Gardiner's creek road, Tk
Zeal, W. A., M.L.A., Parliament house
Zelius, Martin, dining rooms, 5 William st
Zeplin, G., and Sons, professors of music, William st
Zevenboom, John, 26 Barkly st, Carl
Ziems, Henry, and Co., tobacconists, 80 Gertrude st, F
Zosky, W., 101 Lygon st, Carl
Zox, Ephraim, Robe st, St K
Zumstein, Herman, importer and Swiss Consul, 32 Collins st west

GEELONG ALPHABETICAL DIRECTORY.

1866-67.

A.

Adams, George, boarding-house, Corio st
Adams, Edward, hawker, Bellerine st
Ahern, Michael, builder, Bellerine st
Ah Sem, James, cabinetmaker, Little Ryrie st
Albert, John, labourer, Gheringhap st
Allan, Frederick, wire-worker, Union st
Allinson, James, saddler, Ryrie st
Alpin, James, builder, James st
Amiet, Louis, Peuston Suisse, James st
Anderson, Andrew, grocer, Victoria terrace
Anderson, Andrew, plumber, James st
Anderson, John, mining and general commission agent, Malop st
Anderson, James, draper and clothier, Malop st
Anderson, R., residence, Bourke crescent
Anderson, T. Y., and Co., drapers, Moorabool st
Anderson, William, boat-builder, Eastern Beach
Anderson, Wm., mason, Little Ryrie st
Anderson, —, residence, Yarra st
Anderson, W. S., wine and spirit merchant, Kardinia st
Andrews, Charles, warehouseman, Ryrie street
Andrews, Robert J., cabinetmaker, Moorabool st
Andrews, Samuel, coach-builder, Prospect place
Andrews, Wm., turnkey, Kilgour st
Andrews, R., draper, Moorabool st
Anstice, John, tailor, Ryrie st
Appleton, James, furniture warehouse, Little Ryrie st
Appleton, Mrs., confectioner, Moorabool street
Arbuckle, Thomas, tailor, Myers st
Argles, George, musician, Corio st
Armand, Mary, dining rooms, Moorabool street
Armstrong, Mrs., residence, Victoria terrace
Artillery reserve, Ryrie st
Ash, Mrs. C., schoolmistress, Bellerine st
Ashmore, Wm., furniture manufacturer, Moorabool st
Ashmore, Edward, cabinetmaker, Maude street
Ashmore, George, upholsterer, Maude st
Ashmore, J., upholsterer, Maude st
Ashton, James, sharebroker, Malop st
Atken, James N., watchmaker and jeweller, Moorabool st
Austin, C. H., bootmaker, Moorabool st
Austin, John, foundry, Mercer st
Australasian Insurance office; George Fraser, resident secretary, Yarra st
Australian Mortgage, Land, and Finance Co. (Limited); N. Bowes, manager

B.

Baddely, N., residence, Yarra st
Bailey, Thomas, detective officer, Moorabool st

Baird, John, blacksmith, Little Malop st
Baird, John, residence, James st
Baird, Thomas, residence, Fenwick st
Baker, Mrs., residence, Mundy st
Baker, R., tinsmith, Bellerine st
Ball, Mrs., grocer, Little Ryrie st
Baldock, Thomas, tinsmith, Moorabool st
Baldock, Thomas, tinsmith, Ryrie st
Balding, Robert, town surveyor, Bellerine street
Baldings, Robert, residence, Maude st
Band, Thomas, residence, Pevensey st
Bank of Victoria, Malop st ; Vincent W. Giblin, manager ; R. Gladstone, acting accountant
Bank of New South Wales, Malop st; W. J. M. Larnoch, manager
Bank of Australasia, Malop st; John R. Morris, manager ; John D. Coulston, accountant
Bannerman, John, butcher, Market place
Bannister, Henry, clerk, Maude st
Bannister, R. D., residence, Bellerine st
Bannister, Mrs., residence, Gheringhap st
Barber, Samuel, dealer, William st
Barbier, John, carrier, Malop st
Bardwell, E., solicitor, Moorabool st
Barnes, Robert, photographic artist, Union street
Barnes, Wm., tailor, Myers st
Bartlett, Edwin, draper, Moorabool st
Bartlett, G., cabinetmaker, Moorabool st
Bartlett and Brunton, saddlers, &c., Malop st
Bartlett, John, general store, Myers st
Bashla, Mrs., day school, Bellerine st
Baydon and Graham, soapworks, Corio st
Baylie, Mrs., residence, Yarra st
Baylie, Dr. W. R., surgeon, Moorabool st
Baxter, Wm., painter, Maude st
Beattie and Longloft, bootmakers, Mercer street
Beamond, Alfred, greengrocer, &c., Malop street
Beamond, Alfred, storeman, M'Killop st
Bean, Charles, bootmaker, Myers st
Beard, J., Manchester Arms, Malop st
Bedford, Mrs., Terminus hotel, Mercer st
Belcher, G. F., land officer, Moorabool st
Bell, James, wholesale and retail grocer, Moorabool st
Bell, Thomas, baker, Kilgour st
Bell, Wm., residence, Pevensey crescent
Bell, John, grocer and produce dealer, Malop st
Bennett and Son, pastrycooks, Malop st
Bennett's dining rooms, Eastern beach
Bent, A., Commercial hotel, Corio st
Bent's dining rooms, Corio st
Bentwith, Mark, residence, Victoria terrace
Bevan, —, pawnbroker, Union st
Bible Christian Chapel, Bellerine st
Biggs, —, residence, Pevensey st

Biggs and Co., china and earthenware dealers, Moorabool st
Birrell, James, residence, Myers st
Bird, David, grocer, Latrobe terrace
Binch, Wm., fisherman, McKillop st
Birch, —, drayman, Eastern beach
Blackney, George, fisherman, Prospect place
Blair, W., grocer, Corio st
Blake, Benjamin, bootmaker, Myers st
Blair, John, baker, Moorabool st
Blashki, Philip, watchmaker, &c., Moorabool st
Blashki, Philip, residence, Little Malop st
Bleuritt, Mrs., ladies' school, Maude st
Bohanna, Thomas, wheelwright, Little Myers st
Bolger, Martin, residence, Mercer st
Booth, Mrs., residence, Cavendish st
Borwick, Henry B., Western hotel, Mercer st
Botanical Gardens and the Agricultural and Horticultural Societies' reserve
Botanical Gardens hotel, Malop st
Bottomly, J., labour office, Ryrie st
Bourke, Thomas, grocer, Little Malop st
Bourke, Michael, produce merchant, Moorabool st
Bowen, J., jun., confectioner, Corio st
Bowen, —, warden of the gaol, Henry st
Bowen, Joseph, jun., confectioner, Moorabool st
Bowen, Joseph, male and female registry office, Moorabool st
Bowland, Edward, clerk, Myers st
Bowman, George, estate agent, Gheringhap st
Bowman, G. H., estate agent, Ryrie st
Box, Wm., shopman, William st
Brady, Owen, Freemasons' hotel, Malop street
Brady, Wm., grocer, Moorabool st
Bradley, George, watchmaker, Mercer st
Brazier, Chas., draper, Pevensey crescent
Brag, Mrs., milliner, Moorabool st
Bray, Joseph, tailor and outfitter, Moorabool st
Blearley Brothers, leather merchants, Malop st
Brehault, Thomas, carpenter, Swanston st
Brequet, Frederick, Little Malop st
Brennen, Edward, labourer, Corio st
Drew, Mary Ann, Ryrie st
Broadbent, George, collector, Little Malop street
Brodie, C., governor of the gaol, Myers st
Bright and Hitchcock, drapers, Moorabool st
Bright and Hitchcock's warehouse, Little Malop st
Brinkley, Mrs., residence, William st
Brinsley, Annie, dressmaker, Myers st
Brittian, Wm., carpenter, Latrobe st
Britter, Samuel, compositor, Bellerine st

Brod, Wm., saddler, Swanston st
Brodie, Charles, Geelong
Broderick, Patrick, produce store, Myers street
Brodie, Wm., carpenter, Corio st
Brook, Edward, veterinary surgeon, Bellerine st
Brooks, Zachariah, residence, McKillop st
Brown, Robert, painter, Garden st
Browne, Wm., grocer, Ryrie st
Browne, —, grocer, &c., Bellerine st
Brown, Mrs. Mary Ann, residence, Bellerine st
Brown, James, Thistle Inn, Corio st
Brown, Nathaniel, monumental mason, Ryrie st
Brown, Robert, painter, Myers st
Brown, James, grocer, Mercer st
Brown, Osborne, and Co., commission and forwarding agents, Mercer st
Brown, Warren H., draper, &c., Malop st
Brown, George, residence, Victoria terrace
Brown, Robert, paperhanger, Moorabool street
Brown, G., bootmaker, Bellerine st
Bryan, Thomas, labourer, Mundy st
Buckingham, H., butcher, Ryrie st
Buckingham, residence, Yarra st
Bull, Wm. J., chemist, Yarra st
Bullen, —, cooper, Ryrie st
Bullock, R. H., merchant, Little Malop st
Bullock, R. H., produce merchant, Little Malop st
Bampstead, S., labourer, Mundy st
Bunting, John, saddler, Prospect place
Burgess, George G., watchmaker, Myers street
Burgess, John, hawker, Sydney place
Burgess, G. G., watchmaker, Moorabool st
Burke Brothers, gentlemen's outfitters, Malop st
Burn, Mrs., residence, Fenwick st
Burns, Mrs., ladies' college, Gheringhap street
Burns, E., tailor, Ryrie st
Burns, John, Newmarket hotel, Little Malop st
Burns, Charles, cooper, &c., Yarra st
Burrows, Wm., residence, Ryrie st
Burrowes and Adamson, produce stores, Ryrie st
Burvill, Mrs., milliner, Moorabool st
Bushby, John, bootmaker, Latrobe terrace
Butler, Thomas, tailor, Bellerine st
Byrne, Michael, carpenter, Little Ryrie st

C.

Cakebread, Wm., coalyard, Little Malop street
Cakebread, Wm., cement store, Little Malop st
Calby, Philip McShane, residence, Little Malop st
Cameron, Gibson, and Co., grocers, wine and spirit merchants, Gheringhap st
Cameron, Hugh, merchant, Maude st
Cameron, Mrs., residence, Gheringhap st
Cameron, Donald, blacksmith, Latrobe terrace
Camp, —, coachbuilder, Little Myers st
Camp and Glenister, coachbuilders, Myers street
Campbell, James, residence, 81 Moorabool st; agent for the Australian Alliance Assurance, secretary for the Geelong and Western District Horticultural Society, and secretary Geelong Protestant Orphan Asylum
Campbell, John, baker, Kilgour st
Campbell, James, secretary to Horticultural Society, Moorabool st
Canny, Daniel, cabman, Little Malop st
Cannon, Thomas, French polisher, Little Ryrie st
Cantor, Benjamin, general dealer, Market place
Carr, J. G., auctioneer, Moorabool st
Carr, —, land agent, Ryrie st
Carr, Daniel, fruiterer, Ryrie st
Carr, D., greengrocer, Yarra st
Carley, John, labourer, Garden st
Caroe, John, sailmaker, Little Malop st
Carpenter, Wm., coachbuilder, Little Malop st
Carraway, J., carpenter, Prospect place
Carroll, W., butcher, Swanston st
Carter, Champion, Malop st
Cashan, Patrick, bootmaker, Kardinia st
Catholic Church, Yarra st
Catholic Parsonage, Yarra st
Cavanagh, Johana, residence, Latrobe terrace
Chalder, John, greengrocer, Mercer st
Chandler, Wm. Henry, postman, Little Myers st
Chapman, George, coachbuilder, Sydney place
Chiddle, James, carrier, William st
Christe, Arthur, clerk, Latrobe terrace
Christ Church Common School, Moorabool st; Mr. and Mrs. Macklan, schoolmaster and schoolmistress
Christ Church; Rev. George Goodman, Moorabool st
Clampett, Margaret, residence, Myers st
Clanchy, John, Brian Boru hotel
Clanchy, M., Queen's Head hotel, Ryrie st
Clare, J. and S., naturalists, Corio st
Clark Bros., grocers, Moorabool st
Clarke, Alfred, residence, Corio st
Clarke, Mrs., dressmaker, Myers st
Clarke, —, labourer, Bellerine st
Clarke, Michael, bootmaker, Myers st
Clarke, J., boot and shoe maker, Kardinia street

Clarke, Richard, 45 Market square
Clarkson, Wm., seedsman, Ryrie st
Clarkson, Wm., seedsman, Gheringhap st
Cloan, Michael, residence, Yarra st
Clements, James, labourer, Mundy st
Coade, Josiah, boot and shoemaker, Moorabool st
Cobb and Co.'s booking office, Malop st ; T. Stoneman and Co., proprietors
Cocks, David, produce dealer, Little Ryrie street
Cockerham, Charles, labourer, Myers st
Coirie, Wm., mason, William st
Colbert, Wm., greengrocer, Bellerine st
Cole, Edward H., wine and spirit merchant, Moorabool st
Coleman, William, Southey's hotel, Yarra street
Collingwood, Mrs., Prospect place
Collins, John, bootmaker, Ryrie st
Collins, John, bootmaker, Moorabool st
Collins, W. H., Kilgour st
Colonial Bank of Australasia, Malop st ; A. S. Park, manager; Wm. Tait, accountant
Colledge, Wm., chemist and druggist, Moorabool st
Coombe, Harvey, solicitor, Moorabool st
Common School : Miss Brew, schoolmistress, Ryrie st
Conway. Wm., upholsterer, Moorabool st
Cook, Charles, Napier, Bellerine st
Cook, Mrs., ladies' school, Victoria terrace
Cook, Thomas, jeweller, Gheringhap st
Copnay, A., fisherman, Bellerine st
Cordell, Henry, residence, Little Ryrie st
Corio Flour Mills, Gheringhap st
Cottell, O., labourer, Cavendish st
Cotton, Henry, compositor, Maude st
Corres, Thomas N., baker, Moorabool st
Cowle, James, residence, Garden st
Cowley's Dining Rooms, Kardinia st
Cox, Sarah, machinist, William st
Cox, —, tailor, Little Malop st
Craig, Alex., residence, Gheringhap st
Creed and Son, lock and gunsmith, Ryrie street
Cries, Martin, residence, Little Myers st
Crisp, Mrs., residence, Bellerine st
Croker, Joseph, butcher, Market place
Crook, Alfred, ironmonger, Ryrie st
Crook, Alfred, ironmonger, Latrobe terrace
Crouch, John, labourer, Garden st
Cunningham, —, iron bedstead manufacturer, Ryrie st
Cunningham, George, M.L.A., residence, Smythe st
Cunningham, William, carpenter, Mercer place
Cunningham, George, iron merchant, Malop st
Curle, Joseph, carrier, Cavendish st

Curle, Thomas, wine merchant, Ryrie st
Curnow, John, produce store, Ryrie st
Curnow, Wm., wheelwright, Little Ryrie street
Curron, Thomas, labourer, Little Ryrie st
Curry, Michael, labourer, Myers st
Curtain, Mrs., Little Ryrie st
Curtis, Robt., wheelwright, Little Ryrie st
Custom House, Eastern Beach
Cuthbertson, George, corn store, Gheringhap st
Cuthbertson, George, grocer, Myers st

D.

Dale, Henry, butcher, Maude st
Dalgety, Ibbotson, and Co., merchants, Moorabool st
Daniels, Thomas, residence, Kilgour st
Daniels, J., ironmonger, Moorabool st
Daniels, George, butcher, Little Ryrie st
Davey, Richard Peechee Lee, grocer, Moorabool st
Davey, Richard, grocer, Little Myers st
Davies, Henry, cabinetmaker, Myers st
Davies, Tudor, mariner, Cavendish st
Davies, H., cabinetmaker, Ryrie st
Davis, W., tailor and clothier, Malop st
Davison, John, Pevensey crescent
Davison, Edward, carpenter, M'Killop st
Davison, J., auctioneer, Little Malop st
Daws, Robert, storeman, Little Ryrie st
Dawson, Charles B., Princess of Wales hotel, Ryrie st
Day, Joseph, farrier, Ryrie st
Day, John, miner, Malop st
Day, Rev. Samuel, Baptist minister, Little Malop st
De Balk, E., photographic artist, Moorabool st
De la Hant, Wm., millwright and engineer, Cavendish st
Dellon, Henry, hairdresser and importer (next door to the Bank of Victoria), Malop st
Demillo, Xavier, Clare hotel, Bellerine st
Denmead, N., tinsmith, Little Malop st
Denny, Chas. J., residence, Victoria terrace
Dennys, C. J., woolmerchant, Victoria terrace
Dennys, C. J., and Co., woolbrokers, Moorabool st
Dens, Robert, glass and china warehouse, Market place
Dent, Mrs., dressmaker, Corio st
Descrimes, Peter E., upholsterer, Little Myers st
Dewar, John, labourer, Sydney place
Dick, Alex., residence, Victoria terrace
Dick, Alex., greengrocer, Malop st
Dickins, Edward, smith, Mercer st
Dickins, Edward, whitesmith, Smythe st
Dillon, Mrs., storekeeper, Little Myers st

Ditton, James, cutler, 23 Little Ryrie st
Dieancy, Mrs., residence, Bourke crescent
Dobinson, L., Presbyterian minister, Latrobe terrace
Docharty, Wm., storeman, Maude st
Domney, John, butcher, Dellerine st
Donelly, J., jun., Carriers' Arms, Corio st
Doogan, Matthew, blacksmith, Gheringhap st
Douglass, Alfred, proprietor *Geelong Advertiser* newspaper, Malop st
Douglass, Alfred, residence, Fitzroy st
Douglass and Co., Alfred, wool merchants, Victoria terrace
Dowling, Hy., carpenter, Latrobe terrace
Downie, Wm., printer, Kilgour st
Downie and Thompson, printers, Moorabool st
Downing, B. J., music teacher, Myers st
Ducker, W. F., private residence, Little Malop st
Ducker and Co., W. F., auctioneers, Little Malop st
Duffy, Michael, residence, Moorabool st
Duggan, Mrs., residence, Garden st
Duncan, Joseph, storeman, Kilgour st
Dunden, Edward, carpenter, Corio st
Dunning, John, greengrocer, Little Ryrie street
Dunthorne, George, carpenter Gheringhap st
Durran, John, carpenter, Kilgour st
Dupe, John, gunmaker, Ryrie st

E.

Earles, Edward, residence, Latrobe terrace
Eastwood, Edward, hatter, Moorabool st
Eastwood, Chas., hat manufactory, Little Malop st
Edddington, John, carter, Garden st
Edwards, Mrs., residence, Malop st
Electric Telegraph Office, Ryrie st
Elnor, Sarah, dressmaker, Little Ryrie st
Espinasse, Robert, ironmonger, Malop st
Etheridge, —, residence, Garden st
Evens, Wm., cabman, Mercer st
Excells, —, residence, Yarra st
Eyre, Thomas, residence, Corio st

F.

Fahey, Michael, bootmaker, Little Ryrie street
Fairbrother, James, residence, Corio st
Fallen, Michael, Farmers' hotel, Moorabool st
Farley, Peter, storeman, Smythe st
Farrell, Chas., accountant, Bank of Australasia, Malop st
Farrell, John, Court House hotel, Yarra st
Farrow, John, storeman, Kilgour st
Fawkner, —, residence, Malop st
Feehan, Mrs., residence, Bourke crescent

Fenton, Mary, grocer, Maude st
Ferguson, John, carriage builder, Ryrie st
Ferguson, John, coach builder, Myers st
Ferris, Mrs., straw hat manufacturer, Dellerine st
Field, Wm., sale yards, Ryrie st
Finch, Sophia, residence, Little Myers st
Fink, M. and H., wholesale grocers and provision merchants, Malop st
Fink, H., residence, Malop st
Fink, Henry, grocer, Myers st
Finn, Thomas, carter, Swanston st
Finnegan, Henry, labourer, Kilgour st
Firth, Joseph, butcher, Latrobe terrace
Fischer, Mr., jeweller, Kirk place
Fisher, Mrs., residence, Little Malop st
Fitchett, Alfred, residence, Little Myers street
Fitchett's Labour Mart, Malop st
Fitzgerald, David, wheelwright, Little Myers st
Fitzpatrick, John, labourer, Myers st
Fletcher, John, residence, Latrobe terrace
Floyd, Benjamin, furniture dealer, Little Ryrie st
Foot, Joseph, carpenter, 56 McKillop st
Forbes, Alex., Culloden Castle hotel, Latrobe terrace
Forbes, Mrs., residence, Garden st
Ford, George, labourer, Mundy st
Forster and Co., valuators and general agents, Moorabool st
Foster, Henry, mason, Mercer st
Fouracre, Thomas, cabinetmaker, Little Ryrie st
Fox, Henry, cabinetmaker, James st
Fox, Henry, cabinetmaker, Little Myers street
Fox, W., produce merchant, Moorabool st
Fox, Mrs., dressmaker, Myers st
Franks, Henry, bookseller, Ryrie st
Franks, Henry, stationer, bookseller, &c., Moorabool st
Fraser, S., Miss, dressmaker, Malop st
Fraser, Mrs., residence, Latrobe terrace
Fraser, Hugh, saddler, Maude st
Fraser, Mrs., residence, Munday st
Free Church and Common School, Little Malop st
Freeman, James, labourer, Gheringhap st
Freeman and Gaydon, tinsmiths, Malop street
Freeman, Wm., fruiterer, Market place
Friend, Mrs., boarding-house, Malop st
Friend, Samuel C., solicitor, Yarra st
Fyfe and Mackenzie, stock agents and wool brokers, Moorabool st

G.

Gabb, John, painter, Myers st
Gain, —, coachbuilder, Sydney place
Galletly, John, manager of London Chartered Bank of Australasia, Malop st

Gant, H. W., watchmaker and jeweller, Great Ryrie st
Garratt, John M., loan and share broker, house and land agent, Malop
Garratt, J. M., residence, Latrobe terrace
Gasborne, James, grocer, &c., Yarra st
Goalton and Chapman, coachbuilders, Ryrie st
Geelong Advertiser office; Alfred Douglass, proprietor, Malop st
Geelong Gaol, Swanston st
Geelong Gaol, Myers st
Geelong Hospital, Ryrie st
Geelong Savings' Bank; A. R. Reed, actuary
Gemeason, R., labourer, Victoria terrace
Gerratty, John, grocer, Yarra st
Gerrard, Charles, storeman, Kilgour st
Gibbins, J., cabinetmaker, Moorabool st
Gibbs, Ronald, and Co., wool merchants, Brougham place
Gibes, Thomas, watchmaker, Moorabool street
Giblin, Vincent W., manager, Bank of Victoria, Malop st
Gibson Brothers and Co., land, estate, and general agents, Yarra st
Gibson, George, grocer, Pevensey crescent
Gilbert, Mrs., residence, Fitzroy st
Gillies, Robert, tailor, William st
Gillis Henry, mariner, Corio st
Gladstone, R., acting accountant, Bank of Victoria, Malop st
Gladstone, Joseph, labourer, Kilgour st
Glen, —, labourer, Smythe st
Glenister, G., coachbuilder, Myers st
Glynn, —, residence, Garden st
Golden Horn Gold Mining Company; J. Inglis, manager, Little Malop st
Goldsmith, C., general dealer, Yarra st
Goodman, Rev. George, M'Killop st
Goodwin, George W., grocer, Moorabool street
Gosbell, James, grocer, Mercer st
Gosling, Richard, British hotel, Corio st
Gosney, James, carpenter, Mercer st
Gough and Sons, grocers, Latrobe terrace
Gough, W. J., Eureka hotel, Little Malop street
Goulden, N., moulder, Malop st
Goulton, W., coachpainter, Little Ryrie street
Goulston, John D., accountant, Bank of Australasia, Malop st
Graham, Patrick, carter, Myers st
Graham, Mrs., residence, Kilgour st
Graham, Olive, residence, Latrobe terrace
Grammar school, Yarra st
Grammar School, M'Killop st
Grant, —, labourer, Corio st
Grant, H. D., ornamental hairworker and jeweller, Ryrie st
Green, Thomas, brushmaker, Little Hyrie street

Greenwood, Rev. E., residence, Latrobe terrace
Griffiths Brothers, wine and spirit merchants, Little Malop st
Griffiths, V., wine and spirit merchant, Fitzroy st
Griffith, Frank, residence, Mercer st
Grigg, Tobias, baker, Ryrie st
Griggs, John, Preston's hotel, Ryrie st
Growden, Wm., builder, M'Killop st
Grundy, Wm., builder, Fenwick st
Guern, Auguste, Hotel de la Ville, Little Myers st
Gundry and Son, china and glass warehouse, Moorabool st
Guthrie, George, residence, Garden st
Guy, Arthur, solicitor, Yarra st

H.

Haney, G., restaurant, Moorabool st
Hackett, Wm., Royal Charter hotel
Hall, Charles, builder, Swanston st
Hall Brothers, drapers, Moorabool st
Hall, Benjamin, draper, Little Ryrie st
Hallifax, Joseph, fruiterer, Moorabool st
Halpin, C., compositor, Corio st
Hamilton, John, jeweller and engraver, Little Ryrie st
Handley, John, grocer, Ryrie st
Harbour Office, Eastern beach
Hare, Wm., bookseller, Mercer st
Hare, John, coachman, Swanston st
Hargraves, Mrs., residence, Bellerine st
Hargraves, Simon, wheelwright, Gheringhap st
Harmer, W., chimney sweep, Corio st
Harrington, T. M., manager, Bank of Australasia, Malop st
Harris, James, residence, Little Ryrie st
Harris, Wm., carpenter, Malop st
Harrison, James, *Geelong Register*, Kilgour st
Harrison, James, manager of *Geelong Register*, newspaper, Malop st
Harrison, Thomas, tailor, Corio st
Hartley, George, cowkeeper, Mundy st
Hartley, Allan, cowkeeper, Kilgour st
Hartly, M. J., collector for the hospital, Moorabool st
Hartnup, —, coachbuilder, Corio st
Harvey, Frederick, residence, Gheringhap street
Harvey, H. and F., produce merchants, Ryrie st
Hassell, Samuel, fruiterer, Moorabool st
Haslem, —, residence, James st
Haw, H. M., grocer, Yarra st
Hawkes Brothers, iron merchants, Malop street
Hawkes, Thomas, residence, Victoria terrace
Hawkesford, Wm. H., agricultural implement manufacturer, Ryrie st

2 c

Haworth, Edmund F., tanner and currier, Malop st
Hay Market, Myers st
Hayes, Captain, residence, Swanston st
Hayward, John, stevedore, Sydney place
Heade, Mrs. P., residence, Sydney place
Heady, John, grocer, Myers st
Heady, John, chaff mills, Myers st
Healy, Patrick, bootmaker, Yarra st
Hearle, Mrs., residence, Malop st
Heath and Cordell, general printers, Malop street
Heath, Edwin, fruiterer, Little Malop st
Heath, Mrs., residence, Corio st
Heath, Richard, dentist, Malop st
Henderson, Rev. James, Geelong
Hedrick, J., grocer, Little Ryrie st
Hendrick, John, and Co., grocers, and wine and spirit merchants, Malop st
Hendy, James, residence, Pevensey st
Hendy, James, loan and share broker, Malop st
Henry, James, dealer, M'Killop st
Henty, Jas., and Co., merchants, Brougham place
Hewitt, Alex., labourer, Bourke crescent
Hewitt, Wm., builder, Little Ryrie st
Higgins, W., solicitor, Yarra st
Higgins, John, bootmaker, Bellerine st
Hill, Mrs., registry office, Gherinhap st
Hillhouse, James, butcher, Myers st
Hinchcliff, John, residence, Swanston st
Hiscox, George, fishmonger, Moorabool st
Hitchins, Edward, residence, Kilgour st
Hobday, Joseph, pianoforte warehouse, Yarra st
Hocior, Mrs., residence, Latrobe terrace
Holden, —, grocer, Maude st
Holdsworth, Jos., builder, Little Malop st
Holland, —, junior, plumber, Bellerine st
Holland, Charles, mariner, Corio st
Holland, Andrew, junior, plumber, Bellerine st
Holland and King, paperhangers, Ryrie st
Holley, James, carpenter, Munday st
Holligan, Mrs., greengrocer, Moorabool st
Holman, John, grocer, Mercer st
Holmes, White, and Co., merchants, Gheringhap st
Holmes, White, and Co., merchants, Little Malop st
Holmes, Alfred, bootmaker, Yarra st
Holyoak, Frederick, cabinetmaker, Myers street
Hood and Co., coachbuilders, Little Malop street
Hooper, James, residence, M'Killop st
Hopkins, Mrs., residence, Mundy st
Hopton, T., Swan hotel, Fyansford
Horne, Miss, dressmaker, Bellerine st
Horeman, Wm., compositor, Swanston st
Hornsey, Fredk., residence, Sydney place
Hornsey Bros., paper merchants, Moorabool st

Hospital Reserve, Little Ryrie st
Hotchin, Robert, butcher, Gheringhap st
Hourigan, Denis, grocer, Moorabool st
Howard, —, bandmaster, Little Ryrie st
Howard, Robert, miner, Maude st
Howe, Joseph, confectioner, Kilgour st
Howe, Samuel, builder, Yarra st
Howell, Wm. S., auctioneer, Ryrie st
Howey, Wm., gingerbeer maker, M'Killop street
Hubbard, Eliza, ship inn, Yarra st
Huckin, residence, Eastern Beach
Hudson, Henry, Rising Sun hotel, Ryrie st
Hudson, John W., undertaker, Moorabool street
Huggins, Julius, compositor, Mundy st
Huggon, Thomas, compositor, M'Killop st
Hughes, M., tailor, Mundy st
Hughes, Josiah, ironmonger, Little Myers street
Humble and Co., foundry, Little Malop st
Humphries, H., hairdresser, Bellerine st
Humphrey, R., carpenter, M'Killop st
Hunt, A., mason, Bellerine st
Hunt, T. B., produce merchant, Ryrie st
Hunt, Alexander, tailor, Myers st
Hunt and Holmes, saddler, Malop st
Hunter, R., labourer, Gheringhap st
Hurst, Jacob, residence, Union st
Hutchins, Francis, carpenter, Gheringhap street
Hutchison, James, coachbuilder, William street
Hyde, Henry, labourer, Little Malop st
Hyman, Mrs., fancy goods merchant, Market place
Hynes, Mrs., Prince Albert hotel, Yarra st

I.

Icely, Robert, cooper, Mercer st
Imly, Mrs., residence, Corio st
Immigration Depôt, Ryrie st
Independent Chapel, Ryrie st
Industrial School, Swanston st
Inglis, Thomas, market inspector, Little Ryrie st
Irvine, John, bootmaker, Yarra st
Irvine, Henry, master mariner, Malop st
Isard, H. A., coal merchant, Moorabool st
Isely, Wm., broker, Latrobe terrace

J.

Jackson, residence, Eastern Beach
Jacobs, Morris, outfitter, Malop st
Jacobs, Hyam, outfitter and fancy goods merchant, Moorabool st
Jacobs, Morris, residence, Pevensey st
Jaffrey, Mrs., fancy repository, Moorabool street
Jane, Mrs., dressmaker, Moorabool st
Jeffray, Mrs., residence, Maude st
Jenson, James, residence, Bellerine st

Jen   DIRECTORY.   Mac   195

Jenkins and Bennett, undertaker, Moorabool st
Jenyngs, Thomas, hairdresser, Ryrie st
Jewish Synagogue, Yarra st
Johnson, Mr., residence, Malop st
Johnson, Mrs. J., grocer, Bellerine st
Johnson, James, butcher, Gheringhap st
Johnston, Thomas, greengrocer, Malop st
Johnston, Wm., labourer, Bellerine st
Johnston, John, saddler, Little Malop st
Johnston, Robert, saddler, &c., Malop st
Jones, F., hairdresser, Ryrie st
Jones, Chas., railway porter, M'Killop st
Jones, Wm., tailor, Mundy st
Jones, Wm., tailor, Myers st
Jones, Edward, labourer, Corio st
Joy, John, labourer, Bellerine st
Joyce, Robert, draper, Ryrie st
Julien, J., residence, Corio st
Julien, Mrs., dressmaker, Moorabool st
Just, Jacob, cabinetmaker, James st

K.

Keaman, Noble, grocer, Latrobe terrace
Keeble, Henry, naturalist, Moorabool st
Kernan, Thomas, labourer, Little Ryrie st
Krievman, Mrs., residence, Kilgour st
Kelly, Patrick, contractor, Latrobe terrace
Kelly, Thos., Crown hotel, Latrobe terrace
Kelsall, Mrs., residence, Corio st
Kennedy, Wm., bootmaker, Bellerine st
Kenny, Edward, grocer, Moorabool st
Keown, John, grocer, McKillop st
Kernot, W. A., chemist and druggist, Moorabool st
King, —, contractor, Gheringhap st
Kirkland, J., grocer, Malop st
Kirkwood, Alfred, draper, Latrobe terrace
Kitchen, Thos., grocer, Latrobe terrace
Kitchen, Robert, mason, Little Ryrie st
Kitchen, Thos., tailor, Latrobe terrace
Kitt, —, horse dealer, Swanston st
Kitz, Lewis, watchmaker, Moorabool st
Knight, Edward, Olive Branch hotel, Moorabool st
Knowlton, James, storekeeper, Moorabool street

L.

Ladies' Benevolent Asylum, McKillop st
Ladies' and Gentlemen's Baths, Eastern beach
Lake, John, tailor and outfitter, Malop st
Lambert, Mrs. J., Myers st
Lamble, E., blacksmith, Ryrie st
Landon, J., clerk of Petty Sessions Supreme Court
Lane, Wm., carter, Maude st
Langhorne, Edward, hay merchant, Little Myers st
Langhorne, Wm., shipping agent, Yarra st
Langhorne, Wm., residence, Malop st

Langley, Sarah, 47 Little Ryrie st
Larnach, W. J. M., manager Bank of New South Wales, Malop st
Laurence, J., Yarra st
Laurie and Tracy, slaters, Kardinia st
Lavenbarry, Matthew, produce store, Little Ryrie st
Lawrence, Samuel, bootmaker, McKillop street
Lawrence, J., dyer and cleaner, Little Malop st
Lawton, P., tobacconist, Malop st
Leckie, Mrs. John, grocer, Moorabool st
Leech, Alfred, labourer, Bellerine st
Leggitt, James, labourer, Kirk place
Lenan, John, labourer, Mundy st
Leon, S., pawnbroker, Kardinia st
Leonard, Serjeant, McKillop st
Le Patourel, Harbour office, Fitzroy st
Le Seur, James, tent maker, Ryrie st
Levien, H. G., seedsman, Moorabool st
Levey, A., Union st
Levy, Michael S., auctioneer, Ryrie st
Lewis, Joseph, Victoria hotel, Moorabool street
Linford, Alfred, miner, Myers st
Link, George F., schoolmaster, Pevensey crescent
Lockman, Mrs., residence, Garden st
Lockwood, Thomas, bootmaker, Swanston street
London Chartered Bank of Australasia, Malop st: John Galletly, manager; James Nichol, accountant
Loughlan, John, Royal Charter hotel, Yarra st
Love, Rev. A., McKillop st
Lowday, R., musician, Corio st
Lowe, Henry, carpenter, Maude st
Lowe, Isabella, Little Ryrie st
Lowe and McKenzie, butchers, Moorabool street
Lowry, Mrs., grocer, Malop st
Lucas, Wm., saddler, Latrobe terrace
Lugg, Mrs., residence, Fitzroy st
Lynch, John, labourer, Little Malop st
Lynch, M., labourer, Corio st

M

Macdonald, A. C., merchant, agent for the Imperial Fire Insurance Company, Australian Alliance Assurance Company, Equitable Mortgage Bank of Victoria, Ryrie st
Macdonald, —, residence, Victoria terrace
Mackefer, Victor, billiard room proprietor, Yarra st
Mackenzie, John, auctioneer, Victoria terrace
Mackie, Thos., mattress maker, Moorabool street
Mackie, Thomas, mattress maker, Little Ryrie st

Mackfin, H., schoolmaster, M'Killop st
Macpherson, —, carpenter, Bellerine st
Macnamara, Patrick, turnkey, Bourke crescent
Malcolm, Robert, carter, Smythe st
Malcolm, Thos, carpenter, Kilgour st
Maley, R., solicitor, Yarra st
Maley, Mrs., Little Malop st
Malloy, D., labourer, Corio st
Maloney, —, carrier, Swanston st
Manger, Mrs., residence, William st
Manger, Samuel, carpenter, Little Myers street
Mann, John, shipsmith and boiler maker, Eastern beach
Mansfield, Joseph, machinist, Cavendish street
Mansfield, John, baker and confectioner, Malop st
Marendaz, F., grocer, Moorabool st
Martin, David, residence, Bellerine st
Martin, Richard, watchmaker, Yarra st
Martin, B., and Sons, timber merchants, Ryrie st
Martin, James, shoemaker, Yarra st
Mason, T., candlemaker, Gheringhap st
Masonic Hall, Union st
Matthews Bros., butchers, Malop st
Matthews, Edward, chemist, Latrobe terrace
Matthews, James, bootmaker, Bellerine street
Matthews, John, farmer, Pevensey crescent
Maudsley, James, watchmaker, Eastern beach
McAllister, —, waterman, Malop st
McCallum, Mrs., residence, Malop st
McCallum, Nell, confectioner, Moorabool street
McCallum, Nell, confectioner, Maude st
McCallum, —, saddler, Malop st
McCallum, Nell, and Co., merchants, Brougham place
McCall, Andrew, baker, Myers st
McCarty, Thos., labourer, Kilgour st
McConbrie, John, baker, M'Killop st
McCullum, Mrs., residence, Latrobe terrace
McCure, Henry, boot and shoe warehouse, Moorabool st
McDonald, Allen, Caledonian hotel, Little Ryrie st
McDonald, Robert, chemist, Gheringhap st
McDonald, Patrick, wine and spirit merchant, Moorabool st
McDonald, R., New Drug Hall, Ryrie st
McDonald, P., and Co., wine and spirit merchants, Moorabool st
McDuff, P., brewer, Corio st
McEllroy, James, labourer, Bellerine st
McFarlane, Mrs., milliner, Malop st
McGee, Dick, and Co., general warehousemen, Moorabool st

McGouge, John, grocer, wine and spirit merchant, Moorabool st
McGregor, Thomas, carpenter, Kilgour st
McGregor, F., jeweller, Bellerine st
McKennon, Mrs., residence, Latrobe terrace
McKinnon, —, residence, Malop st
McIntosh, David, butcher, Little Ryrie st
McKiever, Phillip, residence, Little Ryrie street
McLanchlan, James, cabinetmaker, Little Malop st
McMullen, Jno., wine and spirit merchant, Little Ryrie st
McMullen, Wm., wine and general merchant, Ryrie st
McMullen, Alexander, cabman, Little Ryrie st
McMurrich, Mrs., Kilgour st
McNab, Wm., general store, Myers st
McNab, Wm., labourer, Smythe st
McNamara, Peter, greengrocer, Malop st
McNamara, J., merchant, Eastern Beach
McPherson, John, livery stables, Little Malop st
McPhillmy, Hugh, merchant, Victoria terrace
McWilliams, Andrew, architect, Moorabool st
McWilliams, Andrew, architect, Maude street
Meakin, Henry, Derby Arms hotel, Little Malop st
Mechanics' Institute, Ryrie st
Meldrom, —, limeburner, Sydney place
Melville, Mrs., labour office, Ryrie st
Mercer, George, bookseller and stationer, Malop st
Mercer, George, printer, Malop st
Metcalfe, Benjamin, plasterer, M'Killop st
Mildren, Edward, printer, Sydney place
Miles, Frederick Wm., tailor, Ryrie st
Miles, George, Excelsior clothing establishment, Moorabool st
Miles, George, draper and outfitter, Moorabool st
Milford, James, residence, Myers st
Miller, John, labourer, Fitzroy st
Miller, John, bootmaker, Maude st
Miller, James, Prince of Wales hotel, Little Malop st
Miller, J., Albion hotel, Little Malop st
Miller, Robert, mariner, Bellerine st
Mills, Edward, coachbuilder, Myers st
Milnes, George, coachbuilder, Malop st
Mingaye Syder, C. B., medical practitioner, Moorabool st
Mitchell, Mrs., residence, Latrobe terrace
Mitchell, James, residence, Corio st
Mooney, Thomas, hay and corn merchant, Little Malop st
Mooney, John, mason, Corio st
Montgomery, John, livery stables, Kardinia st

DIRECTORY.   197

Moore, W. S., blacksmith, Kardinia st
Moore, Rev. A., residence, M'Killop st
Moore, Wm., grocer, Gheringhap st
Moore, Benjamin, bootmaker, Little Ryrie street
Moore Brothers, produce dealers, Ryrie st
Moore, W. S., draper, Ryrie st
Markham, Wm., bootmaker, Moorabool st
Morris, Edward, bookseller, Gheringhap street
Morris, James, butcher, Little Malop st
Morris, John R., manager Bank of Australasia, Malop st
Morrison, Mrs., residence, M'Killop st
Moss, Hyam, merchant, Market place
Motteram, Joseph, blacksmith, Ryrie st
Mougher, James, gardener, Little Myers street
Mount, —, residence, Swanston st
Morton, Mark, sergeant of police, Bourke crescent
Madie, Mrs., residence, Myers st
Mulcahy, Patrick, carrier, Swanston st
Mulder, John F., hairdresser, Moorabool street
Mullen, Thomas, labourer, Cavendish st
Mulligan, John, hay and corn store, Little Malop st
Munro, Hugh, shoemaker, Bourke crescent
Munro, James, cabinetmaker, Ryrie st
Murphy, John, general merchant, Little Malop st
Murphy, Michael, mariner, Gheringap st
Murphy, Mrs., grocer, Bellerine st
Murray, Donald, labourer, Kilgour st
Murray, D., confectioner, Ryrie st
Murray, Wm., labourer, Swanston st

N.

Nash, Stephen, blacksmith, Ryrie st
Nash, Wm., painter, Mundy st
National Bank of Australasia: T. M. Harrington, manager; Charles Farrel, accountant, Malop st
Neal, Benjamin, signwriter, Ryrie st
Needham, John, writing master, Moorabool st
Nelson, Henry, Garden st
Nesbit, Wm., contractor, Maude st
Newman, Samuel, mariner, Latrobe terrace
Nicol, James, accountant of the London Chartered Bank of Australasia, Malop street
Nichol, J., grocer, Moorabool st
Nichols, John, Little Ryrie st
Nicholls, Thomas, and Co., wholesale and retail grocers and produce merchants, Ryrie st
Nicholson and Son, timber merchants, Ryrie st
Nickson, Mrs., Corio st
Nile, Cornelius, labourer, Kilgour st

Ninham, Thomas, cooper, Bellerine st
Noble, John, Corio st
Noble, Wm., grocer, Myers st
Noble, W. and Co., grocers, &c., Ryrie st
Noonan, J., Limerick Castle boarding-house, Corio st
Noonan, W. P., Royal Exchange hotel, Malop st
Noonan, James, labourer, Mundy st
Norman, James, contractor, Corio st
Norton, J., photographic artist, Malop st
Nott, Robert, builder, Myers st
Nott, B. G., painter, Myers st

O.

O'Brien, Thomas, Turf Club hotel, Malop street
Odgers, Elizabeth, draper, Myers st
Ogilvie and Robinson, auctioneers and shipping agents, Moorabool st
O'Halloran, Michael, dairyman, Little Ryrie st
O'Halloran, Andrew, Union st
O'Halloran, Michael, Red Lion inn, Moorabool st
O'Keene, John, tinsmith, Moorabool st
Ormerod, Lionel, photographic artist, Moorabool st
Ormerod, L., Eastern Beach
Ormond, Mary Ann, Kirk place
Osborne, G., hat manufacturer, Malop st
Osgen, John, mariner, Yarra st
Over, Henry, watchmaker, Union st
Owen, John, homoeopathic chemist, Ryrie street
Oxborough, Charles, George and Dragon hotel, Moorabool st

P.

Page, Frederick, Little Myers st
Pankhurst, Mrs., Moorabool st
Pardey, W. E., chemist, Moorabool st
Park, A. S., manager Colonial Bank, Malop st
Parker, Richard, ironmonger, Moorabool street
Parker, Chas., labourer, Kilgour st
Parkinson, James, storeman, Maude st
Parrott and Mills, carriage repository, Yarra st
Payne, John, carpenter, Bellerine st
Pasmore, Wm., gunsmith, 54 M'Killop st
Pasmore, Mrs., Yarra st
Passelaigue, Francis, Colonial Wine Depôt, James st
Paterson, Wm., collector, Maude st
Paterson, Lachlan, bootmaker, Latrobe terrace
Patton, Thomas, salesman, Little Ryrie st
Patterson, Elizabeth, greengrocer, Moorabool st
Patterson, Mrs., M'Killop st

Patterson, —, Bellerine st
Peak, Robert, coachtrimmer, Little Ryrie street
Prescott, Thos., carpenter, M'Killop st
Peters, J., slate merchant, Ryrie st
Peters, W., quarryman, M'Killop st
Pearose, Henry, fruiterer, Moorabool st
Phall, Chas., and Co., cabinetmaker, Gheringhap st
Pitman, Jacob, architect, Moorabool st
Pitman, J., Victoria terrace
Pittard, Wm., bootmaker, Gheringhap st
Police Court, Yarra st
Pool, Chas., coachbuilder, Little Malop st
Pontin, James, carter, Corio st
Portarlington hotel, Sydney place
Port, James, timber merchant, Little Ryrie street
Post Office, Ryrie st
Pounds, J. C., accountant, Union Bank, Yarra st
Powell, Geo., miller, Little Myers st
Powell, Thomas, brewer, Little Malop st
Powers, John, cooper, Malop st
Poynton, Edward O., chemist and druggist, Malop st
Pride, Henry, plasterer, Little Ryrie st
Prime, Richard, blacksmith, Little Malop street
Puffett, Thomas, Bush inn, Corio st
Purdue, E. G., warder, Swanston st

Q.

Quinan, James, deputy registrar of births, deaths, &c., Moorabool st
Quincy, —, Royal hotel, Malop st

R.

Rasdale, —, labourer, Bellerine st
Rashleigh, Mrs., teacher, Gheringhap st
Ray, James, plasterer, Bellerine st
Rea, Hugh, grocer, Mercer st
Reed, A. R., actuary Geelong Savings' Bank
Reedy, Timothy, Steam Packet hotel, Yarra st
Reeves Brothers, grocers, Moorabool st
Reeves, Robert, grocer, Myers st
Reeves, G., Corio st
Reid, James, cooper, Bellerine st
Reid, Alexander, produce merchant, Little Malop st
Reid, A. H., Moorabool st
Read, Charles, draper and tailor, Moorabool st
Reid, Mrs., Latrobe terrace
Reid, —, labourer, Malop st
Reid, Dr., surgeon, Ryrie st
Rendell, Mrs., Kilgour st
Reynard, —, restaurant, Malop st
Reyner, Walter, blacksmith, Little Malop street

Rice, George, Black Bull hotel, Malop st
Rich, Mrs., Kilgour st
Richardson, Mrs., music teacher, McKillop st
Richmond, Wm., painter, &c., Moorabool street
Ricketts, David, oven maker, Little Malop st
Rider, Thomas, wool merchant, Pevensey street
Riedy, Timothy, Steam Packet hotel
Rippon, George R., reporter, Moorabool st
Ritchie, C., bootmaker, Corio st
Ritchie, Peter, tailor, Moorabool st
Rix and Co, auctioneers and agents, Ryrie st
Rix, Thomas, auctioneer, Swanston st
Roach, Thomas, labourer, McKillop st
Roberts, Francis, labourer, Bellerine st
Roberts, Samuel, tinsmith, Malop st
Roberts, Walker, Moorabool st
Roberts, Jonah, photographic artist, Malop st
Robertson and Nash, painters and glaziers, Moorabool st
Robertson, John, City Saw-mill, Little Ryrie st
Robertson, Joseph, mason, Swanston st
Robertson, John, sawyer, William st
Robertson, James, bootmaker, Corio st
Robertson, Mrs., grocer, Corio st
Robinson, Sydney R., homœopathic surgeon, M.R.C.S.L. and L.S.A., Ryrie st
Roche, R., wheelwright and blacksmith, Moorabool st
Roche and Sons, blacksmiths, Moorabool street
Roffey, C., fishmonger and greengrocer, Malop st
Rogers, Patrick, labourer, Little Ryrie st
Rose, R. J., wheelwright, Yarra st
Rourke, Henry, contractor, Kilgour st
Rowden, Edward, French polisher, Myers street
Rowsein, Joseph, embroidery warehouse, Ryrie st
Roxburgh, Adam, draper, M'Killop st
Royce, Walter, baker, Little Myers st
Rudd, Mrs., draper, Moorabool st
Rush, Mrs., residence, Bellerine st
Ryan, Martin, Golden Age hotel, Gheringhap st
Ryan, Mrs., residence, Mundy st
Ryan, L., Builders' Arms, Malop st
Ryan, Patrick, labourer, McKillop st
Ryan, Mrs., dressmaker, Little Myers st

S.

Sach, Charles, residence, Myers st
Sander, Emil, tobacconist, Malop st
Sander, E., and Co., tobacconists, Malop street
Santley, E., bookbinder, Bellerine st

Sargeant, John, saddler, &c., Ryrie st
Sargeant, Benjamin, carpenter, Mercer place
Sasse, Edmund, drawing-master, Myers st
Saunders, E., residence, Victoria terrace
Schwab, Abraham, bootmaker, James st
Scotch Church, McKillop st
Scotch School, Little Myers st
Scotch School, Yarra st
Scott, Benjamin, agent, Moorabool st
Scott, James, engineer, Little Myers st
Scott Brothers, timber merchants, Corio street
Scott, Donald, timber merchant, Ryrie st
Seargeant, John, saddler, Mercer st
Searle, —, carter, Moorabool st
Searles, Robert, poultry merchant, Moorabool st
Sebastian, Robert, shipbuilder, Bellerine street
Seles, Hugh, carter, Gheringhap st
Sephenfelt, Frederick, labourer, Latrobe terrace
Sewell, Frederick, bootmaker, Ryrie st
Sharp, Wm., Pevensey st
Shaw, Wm., china and earthenware dealer, Moorabool st
Shaw, J. L., architect and surveyor, Yarra street
Shaw, Francis, boot and shoe maker, Moorabool st
Shaw, Dr. W., surgeon, Myers st
Sheckell, Thomas, basket manufacturer, Malop st
Sheedy, Patrick, mechanic, Mercer place
Sheehy, —, boatbuilder, Swanston st
Sheils, F., bootmaker, Corio st
Shepperd, Thomas, bootmaker, Moorabool st
Shepperd, Miss, ladies' seminary, Yarra st
Shepperd, Mrs., Latrobe terrace
Sherwood, —, general dealer, Little Myers st
Shirly, Richard, bootmaker, Gheringhap street
Short, John, produce dealer, Mercer st
Short, John, produce dealer, Latrobe terrace
Shugg, Thomas, mason, Maude st
Silders, Thomas A., Kent House and private hotel, Ryrie st
Sillett, S., London hotel, Moorabool st
Sims, James, livery stable keeper, Little Malop st
Sims, —, livery stable keeper, Malop st
Simson, James, official assignee, Yarra st
Simpson, Charles, fisherman, Smythe st
Sinclair, J., boatbuilder, Eastern beach
Skene, A. J., surveyor, Moorabool st
Skirving, Peter, Little Myers st
Skirving, Peter, tailor and outfitter, Moorabool st
Smith, J., gun and locksmith, Ryrie st
Smith, John, turner, Gheringhap st

Smith, Henry, turner, Mercer st
Smith, Ann, Little Ryrie st
Smith, Mrs., Myers st
Smythe, Mary, Myers st
Spalding, David, cabinetmaker, Kilgour st
Speedy, Henry, solicitor, Yarra st
Spence, D., horsedealer, James st
Spence, Mrs., grocer, Fitzroy st
Spriggins, Mrs., dressmaker, Mercer st
Solomon, E., greengrocer, Moorabool st
Staines, Wm., turnkey, McKillop st
Stainsby, Robert, draper, Bellerine st
Stanley, J., coach builder, Yarra st
Steedman, George, pianoforte maker and tuner, Yarra st
Stent, J., greengrocer, Malop st
Stevens, Wm., labourer, Swanston st
Stewart, Archibald, mason, Maude st
Stewart, James, draper, Kilgour st
Stock, Joseph, whitesmith and machinist Mercer st
Stokes, Benjamin, quarryman, Mundy st
Stirling, James, labourer, Corio st
Stone, Eliza, jeweller, Ryrie st
Stoneham, J., Temperance hotel, Yarra street
Stoneham, Samuel, cabman, Swanston st
Stoneman, Samuel, Gheringhap st
Stoneman, Thomas, coachbuilder, Latrobe terrace
Stoneman, Thomas, livery stables, Clare st, Malop st
Stoneman, Thomas, Union hotel, Malop street
Stoneman, Samuel, coachbuilder, Gheringhap st
Strachan and Co., bonded stores, Eastern beach
Strong, James, bootmaker, Mercer st
Stubart, Wm., carpenter, Swanston st
Sullivan, John, Britannia hotel, Yarra st
Sullivan, C., baker, Malop st
Sullivan, —, Swanston st
Summers, Wm., Australian hotel, Ryrie street
Superintendent's offices, Police, Little Myers st
Sutherland, Alexander, manager of Union Bank, Yarra st
Sutherland, A., bootmaker, Bellerine st
Sutton, Mrs., draper, Bellerine st
Swanston, Willis, and Co., merchants, Gheringhap st
Swift, Charles, clerk, 60 McKillop st
Sykes, John, carpenter, Gheringhap st
Synnot and Guthrie's wool stores, Clare st, Malop st

T.

Tait, John, timber merchant, Ryrie st
Tait, J., timber merchant, Swanston st
Tait, James, carpenter, Ryrie st
Tait, Joseph, Royal Mail hotel, Yarra st

Tait, Wm., accountant Colonial Bank, Malop st
Tait, Peter, boatbuilder, Eastern beach
Tann, Wm., bootmaker, Malop st
Tannock, Archibald, confectioner, Moorabool st
Tarbett, David, stoneman, William st
Taylor and Buckland, solicitors, Yarra st
Taylor, T., sweep, Little Malop st
Taylor, Richard, photographic artist, Ryrie st
Taylor, J. C., carpenter, Maude st
Taylor, Henry, cooper, Little Ryrie st
Taylor, James, carpenter, McKillop st
Taylor, Charles, saddler, Gheringhap st
Tempest, G. H., ironmonger, Ryrie st
Templeton, Andrew, cabinetmaker, Gheringhap st
Thacker, Henry, stationer, Ryrie st
Thacker, Henry, printer, Kirk place
The Geelong Gas Company, Little Malop st; G. G. Whalley, manager
The Geelong Grammar School, Moorabool st; J. B. Wilson, director
The *Geelong Register* newspaper office; James Harrison, manager
The Market Gardens, Little Malop st
The Police Court Reserve, McKillop st
The Police Station, Moorabool st
The Savings' Bank, Moorabool st
The Supreme Court, Myers st
The Troopers' Reserve, McKillop st
Theatre Royal, Malop st
Thomas, —, cabman, Mercer st
Thompson, Wm., printer, Ryrie st
Thompson, Wm., Latrobe terrace
Thompson, Thomas, paperhanger, Malop street
Thompson, Wm., bootmaker, Malop st
Thomson, W., ironmonger, Gheringhap st
Thorburn, Walter, carriage builder, Moorabool st
Thorburne, James, coachbuilder, McKillop st
Thorpe, W., bootmaker, Bellerine st
Tietgen, —, tailor, Pevensey crescent
Tolson, —, Eastern beach
Tomlinson, John, Ryrie st
Tool, Patrick, Star hotel, Myers st
Toole, James, wheelwright, Little Myers street
Toohey and Sons, blacksmiths, Union st
Tough, Robert, sailmaker, Moorabool st
Townsend, Nathaniel, bootmaker, Little Ryrie st
Tracey, Martin, brewer, Latrobe terrace
Trainer, Wm., bootmaker, Malop st
Treal, —, agent, Pevensey crescent
Trear, Miss, ladies' school, Bourke crescent
Trear, Wm., Mac's hotel, Eastern beach
Tremain, J., confectioner, Malop st
Trevena and Gabby, builders, &c., Malop street

Tuppin, J. H., seedsman, Little Malop st
Turnbull, W., McKillop st
Turner, Joseph, photographic artist, Moorabool st
Turner, J., photographic artist, Latrobe terrace
Tyler, Edward, tailor, Corio st
Tynes, Mrs., Latrobe terrace

U.

Ulrich, Charles, schoolmaster, Myers st
Union Bank of Australasia; Alex. Sutherland, manager; Joseph C. Poonds, accountant, Yarra st
United Presbyterian Church, Ryrie st
Upjohn, W., greengrocer, Malop st
Upjohn, W., grocer, Malop st
Upjohn, W., fruiterer, Market place
Upton, Wm., soap and candle manufacturer, McKillop st
Upwood, John, plasterer, Little Ryrie st
Ure, Agnes, teacher, McKillop st
Usher, Patrick, National hotel, Moorabool st

V.

Valentine, Francis, builder, McKillop st
Veitch, Thomas, wheelwright, Mundy st
Vey, James, watchmaker, Moorabool st
Victoria Lime and Cement Company, Little Malop st; — Parker, manager
Vile, James, water carrier, Little Ryrie st
Vines, Joshua, farm, station, and commission agent, Ryrie st
Volum, James, and Co., brewers, Corio st
Volunteer Orderly Room, Yarra st

W.

Wade, Wm., potato merchant, Yarra st
Wadelton, John, watchmaker, Ryrie st
Walden, Miss, teacher, Victoria terrace
Wale, G., draper, Moorabool st
Walker, Robert, labourer, Corio st
Walker, Roberts, and Co., grocers, Moorabool st
Walker, Samuel, labourer, Little Malop st
Walker, Wm., labourer, Ryrie st
Wall, Mrs., Phœnix hotel, Moorabool st
Wall, Robert, cabinetmaker, Yarra st
Wallace, Alexander, clerk, Fenwick st
Waldie, Mrs., baker, Kilgour st
Wallis, Dr., homœopathic doctor, Myers street
Walsh, John, carpenter, Little Myers st
Welsh, Mrs., dressmaker, Gheringhap st
Walshe, Dr., Ryrie st
Walters, Charles, grocer, Yarra st
Ward, George, labourer, Latrobe terrace
Ward, C., labourer, Bellerine st
Ward, Richard, wheelwright, Myers st
Ward, Mrs., dressmaker, Yarra st

Warden' Quarters of the Gaol, Little Myers st
Wane, W., coffee dealer, Little Malop st
Wane, Wm., coffee works, Union st
Warner, Joseph, bootmaker, Little Ryrie street
Warner, J. and R., bootmakers, Malop st
Warren, John, produce dealer, Moorabool street
Warr, Alfred, basketmaker, William st
Warr, Alfred, bootmaker, Moorabool st
Water Police Station, Eastern beach
Waters, Joseph, labourer, Little Ryrie st
Waters, Robt., Victoria terrace
Watt, James, Kilgour st
Watt, John, carpenter, Bellerine st
Watts, Mrs., storekeeper, Little Malop st
Watts, Wm., labourer, James st
Watts, Joseph, carpenter, Ryrie st
Waugh, Robt., Harbour Office, Mundy st
Weatheritt, Gerard, Myers st
Webb, Thomas, Corio st
Webber, John, cooper, Ryrie st
Webster, Lawrence, butcher, Moorabool st
Weeks, H., galvanist, Corio st
Welch, James, gasfitter, Little Malop st
Welch, —, grocer, Malop st
Wells, Robert, fruiterer, Ryrie st
Wesleyan Schools, Ryrie st
Wesleyan Chapel; Rev. W. L. Binks, Yarra st
Wesleyan Chapel and School, Little Ryrie street
Westacot, John, butcher, Mercer st
Whalley, G. G., manager, Geelong Gas Company, Little Malop st
Wheatland, Mrs., ladies' school, Kilgour street
Wheeler, James, labourer, Myers st
Whitchell, —, Eastern beach
Whitchell and Co., boot importers, Moorabool st
White, Michael, labourer, Garden st
White and Brockbank, agricultural implement manufacturers, &c., Ryrie st
Whitfield, John, agent, Maude st
Whitelaw and Co., grocers, Yarra st
Whitelaw, Charles, and Co., grocers, Malop street
Wigney, John, printer, Latrobe terrace
Wilcox, Charles, monumental mason, Little Ryrie st
Wilkins, Benjamin, chemist and druggist, Moorabool st
Wilkinson, L., Corio st
Wilkinson, Robert, ironmonger, Ryrie st
Wilks, Samuel, Farmers' hotel, Market square

Williams, James, Latrobe terrace
Williams, John, Latrobe terrace
Williams, T., bootmaker, Yarra st
Williamson, Henry, draper, Pyrie st
Williamson, Thomas, tailor, Bellerine st
Williamson, J., miner, Malop st
Whillie, Alexander, mason, William st
Wilmot and Key, photographic artists Malop st
Wilson, Wm., draper, Ryrie st
Wilson, J. B., director of the Geelong Grammar School, Moorabool st
Wilson, Buchanan, and Co., merchants, &c., Eastern Beach
Wilson and Moore, painters, Myers st
Wilson, Benjamin, dyer, scourer, and cleaner, Ryrie st
Wilson, Mrs., dressmaker, Myers st
Wilton, T., musician, Malop st
Wilton Edward, leather merchant, Moorabool st
Wilton, E., Corio st
Wise, George, Malop st
Wise, George, bookseller, Moorabool st
Witham, Charles, James st
Wood Brothers, timber merchants, Little Ryrie st
Wood Brothers, timber merchants, Myers street
Wood, J. S., Sir Charles Hotham hotel, Cavendish st
Wood, George, cabinetmaker and undertaker, Ryrie st
Wood, George, cabinetmaker, Gheringhap street
Wood, Mrs., 58 M'Killop st
Wood, W., J., baker, Latrobe terrace
Wood, Robert, grocery store, Myers st
Woods, James, labourer, Gheringhap st
Woods, George, coachbuilder, Ryrie st
Woodward, Thomas, coachbuilder, Little Malop st
Woodgatt, Thomas, veterinary surgeon, Ryrie st
Wook Yan (chinaman), Corio st
Woollard, John, bootmaker, Ryrie st
Woolley and Harwood, solicitors, Yarra street
Wray, Thomas, fancy repository, Moorabool st
Wright, Thomas, watchmaker, Malop st
Wyeth, Wm., gardener, Swanston st

Y.

Young, Andrew, grocer, Ryrie st
Young, C., carpenter, Bellerine st

SOUTH GEELONG ALPHABETICAL DIRECTORY.

1866-67.

Alexander, Henry Vanman, Lonsdale st
Allaston, Elizabeth, Bellerine st
Andrews, Wm., grocer, Moorabool st
Ashton, Wm., labourer, Yarra st

Badden, Thomas, butcher, Moorabool st
Ball, Benjamin, bootmaker, Moorabool st
Barnes, Robert, Lonsdale st
Bartlett, —, Young Queen hotel, Moorabool st
Batten, Thomas, butcher, Lonsdale st
Bedggood, Charles, plasterer, Fyans st
Blakestone, Mary, grocer, Fyans st
Bottrell, Wm., draper, Moorabool st
Bowyer, James, labourer, Little Fyans st
Boyd, Alexander, labourer, Fyans st
Butterworth, Thomas, Little Fyans st

Campbell, Donald, labourer, Bellerine st
Coleman, John, labourer, Little Fyans st
Comms Na Feinne grounds, Bellerine st
Connor, Thomas, carter, Fyans st

Davey Thomas, butcher, Moorabool st
Dent, Frederick, grocer, Moorabool st
Douglass, John, bootmaker, Fyans st
Doyle, James, policeman, Balliang st
Dupe, Wm., labourer, Barwon terrace

Eldridge, Wm., porter, Lonsdale st

Fagg Brothers, builders and ironmongers, Moorabool st

Female Goal, Yarra st
Fitzpatrick, Thomas, baker, Moorabool st
Flanders, Minnie, Yarra st
Flour Mill, vacant, Moorabool st
Fraser, Hugh, saddler, Moorabool st

Gates, John, Barwon Bridge hotel, Moorabool st
Geelong Pound
George, John, labourer, Foster st
Gibbs, William, engineer, Little Fyans st
Gideons, Henry, miller, Little Fyans st
Goodman, Mrs., Barwon terrace
Greenwood, Chas, Nelson's Victory hotel, Balliang st

Ham, Samuel, carpenter, Foster st
Hammond, Daniel, grocer, Fyans st
Hampson, George, tailor, Little Fyans st
Hardley, John, Yarra st
Hassett, John, blacksmith, Moorabool st
Hinchcliff, Matilda, Little Fyans st
Howard, Nathan, dealer, Bellerine st

Izod, Joseph, Esq., sheriff's officer, Fyans street

Jewell, Wm., farmer, Fyans st
Jewell, Elizabeth, Balliang st
Johnson, Alexander, labourer, Yarra st
Jones, James, general dealer, Moorabool st

Kitchen, Patrick, labourer, Little Fyans st

Lamble, Wm., grocer, Moorabool st
Lidgerwood, Margaret, Fyans st
Littlejohn, Isaac, carter, Fyans st
Laxmoor, William, town herdsman, Yarra street

Mackenzie, Roderick, labourer, Fyans st
Martin, George, butcher, Foster st
Martin, Richard, labourer, Lonsdale st
McClelland, William, horse dealer, Balliang street
McCracken, Joseph, policeman, Yarra st
McDonald, John, labourer, Bellerine st
McLaurin, Duncan, labourer, Balliang st
Miller, Margaret, Little Fyans st
Mills, Shannon, Little Fyans st
Mitchell, David, labourer, Fyans st
Monro, John, Bridge inn, Moorabool st
Morris, Henry, sawyer, Foster st

Nicholson, Peter, carpenter, Bellerine st

O'Neil, John, labourer, Bellerine st

Petitjean, Augustus Henry, watchmaker, Moorabool st
Power, George, rate collector, Lonsdale st

Price, Simeon, Balliang st
Purdue, Mrs., Barwon terrace

Rathleigh, Charles, schoolmaster, Balliang street
Robinson, Reynolds, miller, Fyans st

Sweeney, Thos., labourer, Little Fyans st
Scott, David, horse dealer, Foster st
Shaw, Markham, labourer, Bellerine st
Shepherd, Thomas, bootmaker, Foster st
Smyth, Peter, bootmaker, Moorabool st
South Geelong Pound, Bellerine st
Stewart, John, labourer, Fyans st
Stone, Frederick, draper, Moorabool st

Thomson, James, labourer, Little Fyans street
Towle, Dr., Yarra st
Turner, Hill, draper, Fyans st

Veitch, William, saddler, Moorabool st

Wade, Charles, labourer, Fyans st
Water Works, Moorabool st
Wesleyan Church and School, Balliang st
Wool, James, blacksmith, Moorabool st

ASHBY ALPHABETICAL DIRECTORY.

1866-67.

A.

Adams, George, engineer, Autumn st
Adams, John, miner, Albert st
Aitchison, John, drayman, Hope st
Alder, Henry, engine driver, Candover st
Alexander, Mark, letter sorter, Wheeler st
Allen, George, butcher, Packington st
Anderson, Alexr., squatter, Wellington st
Anderson, Geo., coach driver, Autumn st
Anderson, David, cokeman Wheeler st
Andrews, Chas., bricklayer, Spring st
Aram, Wm., carter, Anderson st
Archer, Reuben, farmer, Coronation st
Armour, Wm., Railway hotel, Hope st
Armstrong, Elizabeth, Autumn st
Arnott, Geo., bricklayer, Elizabeth st
Arthur, Ann, Coronation st
Ashby Common School, Wellington st; teacher, Thomas Targie
Ashton, James, sharebroker, Packington street
Atkinson, Samuel, gingerbeer manufacturer, Hope st
Atkinson, Matthew, labourer, Anderson st
Audsley, Thos. E., labourer, Catherine st

B.

Bailey, Isaac, bricklayer, Wheeler st
Bailiff, Jared, ironmonger, Packington st
Bannerman, John, butcher, Autumn st
Baptist Church, Aberdeen st
Barnett, Peter, storeman, Gertrude st
Bates, Richard, quarryman, Little Clarence st
Battersby, Thomas, bootmaker, Aberdeen street
Battle, Abraham, carter, Packington st
Baxter, John, carpenter, Clarence st
Baylis, Robert, labourer, Addis st
Beach, Richard, hawker, Villamanta st
Bean, Cornelius, baker, Waterloo st
Bean, Jonathan, tailor, Autumn st
Belfield, Joseph, bootmaker, Coquet st
Bell, Duncan, blacksmith, O'Connell st
Bell, Wm., hide and sheepskin merchant, Autumn st
Bemiet, Mary Ann, Autumn st
Bennett, Thomas, storeman, Villamanta st
Best, J. P., plasterer, Anderson st
Betts, Thomas, miner, Hope st
Birtrett, Joseph, sheep farmer, Autumn st
Bishop, James, salesman, Western st
Blackhall, Thomas, grocer, Hope st
Blackwell, Ebenezer, whitesmith, Aberdeen st
Blythe, Geo., brickmaker, King st
Bohn, Martin, bricklayer, Elizabeth st
Bond, Jonathan, railway porter, Autumn street
Bone, Mary, Hope st
Bonning, Theophilus, carter, Wellington street
Bonsford, John, builder, Wellington st
Bowen, Francis, marine stores, Keera st

Bowyer, —, storeman, Gertrude st
Boyle, R. W., Anderson st
Bram, Morris, labourer, Preston st
Bramsel, Joseph, labourer, Elizabeth st
Brash, Morris, general dealer, Western st
Brearly, Thomas, carpenter, Keera st
Brennan, Patrick, labourer, Britannia st
Brennen, Edward, blacksmith, O'Connell street
Brewster, David, gardener, Gertrude st
Bridge, James, labourer, Western st
Broadbent, George A., draper, Spring st
Brodie, Charlotte, Gertrude st
Brogan, Martin, cowkeeper, Spring st
Broomhead, Alfred, cabman, Wheeler st
Brown, Wm., gardener, King st
Brown, John, mason, Albert st
Brown, Louis, painter, Autumn st
Brown, John, butcher, Packington st
Brown, John, O'Connell st
Brown, Isaac, fireman, Autumn st
Brunger, George, storeman, Hope st
Buchanan, Robert, labourer, Autumn st
Buck, John, sen., carpenter, Church st
Buck, John, jun., labourer, Church st
Bunn, Wm., draper, Packington st
Bermobey, Mr., hawker, McDougal st
Burns, Mary, Britannia st
Burns, Garrard, Elizabeth st
Burr, Thomas, labourer, Albert st
Burr, Robert, labourer, Albert st
Burwell, Mrs., dressmaker, Packington st
Bushby, James, bootmaker, O'Connell st
Butt, John, mason, Addis st
Butters, John, draper, Preston st

C.

Campbell, Duncan, labourer, Wellington street
Canny, James, storeman, Wellington st
Carliler, David, schoolmaster, 73 Wellington st
Carmichal, John, carpenter, Autumn st
Carney, Wm., labourer, Britannia st
Carr, Joseph, tailor, Coronation st
Carr, Joseph, compositor, Gertrude st
Carroll, Thomas, policeman, Britannia st
Carson, John, fisherman, Spring st
Carter, Mr., Britannia st
Cary, James S., grocery store, Preston st
Cassdy, Thomas, carter, Spring st
Catterson, Wm., grocer, Villamanta st
Chalmers, Samuel, grocer, Autumn st
Chambers, George, Queen of the South hotel, Packington st
Charlton, John, carpenter, Autumn st
Charlton, Wm., gardener, Spring st
Chevalier, Francis, settler, Preston st
Chiselett, Joseph, labourer, Albert st
Clark, Samuel, butcher, Autumn st
Clark, David, labourer, Autumn st
Clarke, Richard, labourer, Albert st
Clarke, Richard, grocer, Aberdeen st

Clarke, John, wheelwright, Preston st
Clarke, Wm., blacksmith, Spring st
Clingan, Thomas, mason, Preston st
Cochrane, James, labourer, O'Connell st
Cohen, Morris, hawker, Western st
Colman, Patrick, labourer, Packington st
Colquhoun, Parline, contractor, Packington st
Collier, Leo, clerk, Autumn st
Collins, Wm., mason, Spring st
Collins, Thomas, labourer, King st
Commins, Daniel B., grocer, Spring st
Common School, Preston st
Congregational Church, Packington st
Connelly, John, wheelwright, Hope st
Cook, Stephen, gardener, Little Clarence street
Cook, Thomas, labourer, Ann st
Cook, J., hairdresser, Keera st
Cooke, James, labourer, Preston st
Corder, Wm., gardener, Wellington st
Corrigan, Samuel, wool merchant, Aberdeen st
Cottle, Robert, baker, Aberdeen st
Coxon, Mark P., butcher, Packington st
Corrin, Henry, blacksmith, Aberdeen st
Cow, Patrick, blacksmith, O'Connell st
Coy, John, engine driver, Hope st
Cranch, Wm., dealer in skins, Western st
Craven, Thomas, grocer, Packington st
Cripps, James, drill instructor, Villamanta st
Crook, Christopher, carpenter, Autumn street
Croker, Joseph, butcher, Aberdeen st
Crooks, Wm., blacksmith, Packington st
Crosby, John, labourer, Autumn st
Culzena, Susanna, day school, King st
Curle, Thomas, wine and spirit merchant, Aberdeen st
Curtis, Miss S., dressmaker, Packington street
Curtis, James, grocer, Packington st
Cuthbertson, John, grocer, Anderson st

D.

Dale, James, blacksmith, Villamanta st
Daniel, Wm. H., storeman, Wellington st
Dare, M. O., labourer, Autumn st
Davies, Frederick, labourer, Church st
Davies, James, mason, McDougal st
Dawe, Wm., labourer, O'Connell st
Dawson, Mr., Aberdeen st
Day School, Autumn st
Denmark, James, City of Norwich hotel, O'Connell st
Denals, Jane, day school, Autumn st
Denhan, John, hawker, Wellington st
Denny, Thomas, carpenter, Villamanta st
Dent, Wm., bootmaker, Packington st
Dick, Alexander, stonemason, Hope st
Dimelow, Joseph, grocery store, Autumn street

Dinelow, Joseph, grocer, Packington st
Dines, Wm., carter, Aberdeen st
Dobson, Elizabeth, Hope st
Docharty, Jane, nurse, Spring st
Dolarty, Martin, labourer, King st
Dolley, Ellen, King st
Dolley, Wm., butcher, Clarence st
Doolan, Thomas, labourer, King st
Dougheny, John, labourer, Autumn st
Douglass, Mrs. M., machinist, Spring st
Dovey, James, railway inspector, Anderson st
Doyle, Matthew, labourer, Packington st
Doyle, James, railway porter, Autumn st
Driver, Richard, gardener, Coquet st
Drummond, Stephen, Mrs., ladies' nurse, Candover st
Duffy, John, slipper maker, Spring st
Duncan, Alexander, butcher, Addis st
Duncan, George, mason, Spring st
Dunlop, Thomas, baker, Autumn st
Dunn, Richard, labourer, Spring st
Dunn, Miss, Addis st
Dunn, Peter, carpenter, Packington st
Dutton, Robert, joiner, Hope st
Dymmott, Alfred, butcher, Albert st

E.

Eades, Samuel, Clarence st
Eden, John, land agent, Villamanta st
Edwards, Frederick, builder, Coronation street
Elliott, Wm., labourer, O'Connell st
Elton, Mrs. Wm., Autumn st
Emery, George, mason, McDougal st
Estall, Wm. H., schoolmaster, Clarence st
Eustace, John, cowkeeper, Autumn st
Evans, Wm., blacksmith, Preston st
Everett, Charles, plasterer, Coquet st

F.

Fagan, Patrick, labourer, O'Connell st
Fallow, Andrew, engine driver, Wheeler street
Fairchild, —, painter, Wheeler st
Fargie, Thomas, schoolmaster, Villamanta street
Fargies, Jeanet, boarding-house, O'Connell st
Farr, James, carpenter, Addis st
Farrell, John, carrier, Hope st
Fenton, George, carpenter, Elizabeth st
Feltham, Henry, labourer, King st
Fewater, Wm., printer, Autumn st
Field, Margaret, Packington st
Fielder, Harry, stationer, Hope st
Fimmet, Jeremiah, labourer, Spring st
Finney, Peter, grocery store, O'Connell st
Fisher, Mrs., machinist and dressmaker, Autumn st
Fisher, George, baker, Wheeler st
Float, John, mangleman, Wheeler st

Ford, Michael, at the railway, Candover street
Ford, Robert, storeman, O'Connell st
Ford, Thomas, labourer, Autumn st
Foster, Henry, bootmaker and grocer, Packington st
Foster, Louisa, ladies' school, Villamanta street
Francis, John, contractor, Autumn st
Fraser, John, mason, Autumn st
Fraser, Thomas, tailor, Yuille st
Freud, John, practical gardener, John st
Fyoney, Wm., butcher, Packington st

G.

Gabally, James, cabman, Preston st
Gardner, James, storeman, Spring st
Garlic, Samuel, carpenter, Hope st
Gatehouse, Robert, clerk, Autumn st
Gatenby, John, painter, Britannia st
Geelong Fire Brigade branch station, Packington st
Gentil, Charles George, Aberdeen st
Giblin, Allan, tailor, Aberdeen st
Gilmore, John, labourer, Britannia st
Glereby, Isaac, butcher, Spring st
Glynn, Thomas, labourer, King st
Goff, W., tailor, Autumn st
Goff, John, grocer, Packington st
Goomey, George John, grocer, Spring st
Graham, Percival, schoolmaster, Coquet street
Green, Francis, labourer, Clarence st
Green, James, Spring st
Green, Fredk., grinder, Autumn st
Gregor, Alex., traveller, 45 O'Connell st
Grey, James Henry, labourer, O'Connell street
Grey, Thomas, labourer, Elizabeth st
Griggs, Isaac, Sir Wm. Wallace hotel, Autumn st
Grierson, James, mason, Wheeler st
Grundle, John, brickmaker, King st
Gubby, James, shoemaker, 67 Wellington street
Gubby, John, carpenter, Wellington st
Guest, John, engine driver, Wheeler st
Gullick, Thomas, grocery store, Wellington st
Gulliford, George, painter, Aberdeen st

H.

Hasson, John, labourer, Autumn st
Hackett, Wm., railway porter, Catherine street
Hackinson, Joseph, labourer, Clarence st
Hallaria, Michael, labourer, Spring st
Hagger, James, saddler, Spring st
Haines, John, clerk, Autumn st
Hair, John, engine driver, Coquet st
Hall, George, labourer, King st
Hall, George, schoolmaster, Autumn st

Hallman, Charles, blacksmith, King st
Hands, Edward, labourer, Spring st
Hannaford, Michael, Autumn st
Hardie, Peter, carpenter, Catherine st
Hardie, Peter, bootmaker, Gertrude st
Harding, Silas, Aberdeen st
Harkness, Wm., stonemason, Hope st
Harley, James, bootmaker, Aberdeen st
Harrick, Patrick, water carrier, Hope st
Harris, Richard, carter, Coronation st
Harrison, Daniel, Gertrude st
Harrison, John, labourer, King st
Harrison, James, carpenter, Western st
Harrison, H., bootmaker, O'Connell st
Harrison, John, carpenter, Western st
Hart, Henry, butcher, Elizabeth st
Harvey, Thomas, painter, Coronation st
Harvey, John, labourer, Spring st
Harvey, H. T., baker, Aberdeen st
Harvey, H. T., baker, Gertrude st
Harway, Alice, Wellington st
Hawkesford, Wm., cabinetmaker, Candover st
Haxton, John, carter, Hope st
Hayson, Wm., baker, Spring st
Hayward, Eliza, straw bonnetmaker, Gertrude st
Heasman, John, labourer, Clarence st
Heath, George, O'Connell st
Heath, Edwin, greengrocer, Aberdeen st
Heatherington, Charles, grocer, Ann st
Hedley, Robert, Globe inn, Packington st
Heenan, Wm., labourer, Autumn st
Henessy, Patrick, labourer, King st
Hewison, Lanslet, tailor, Hope st
Hewitt, Wm., tailor, Hope st
Hickinbotham, David, butcher, Spring st
Higgins, Alfred, railway porter, Gertrude street
Higgins, Rev. Wm., Villamanta st
Hilbert, George, mason, King st
Hill, John, engine driver, Hope st
Hill, Wm., hay and corn store, Packington st
Hill, Wm., botanical dispensary, Packington st
Hilson, George, grocer, Packington st
Hinsm, Ivay, labourer, Church st
Hitchcock, George, Aberdeen st
Hyatt, Joseph, labourer, Gertrude st
Hobbs, George, butcher, Hope st
Hobbs, Wm. S., butcher, Candover st
Hobson, John, mason, Autumn st
Hockley, Edward, labourer, Clarence st
Hockey, Mrs., dressmaker, Villamanta st
Holdsworth, Joseph, builder, Preston st
Hollow, Thomas, labourer, Wheeler st
Holmes, John, money broker, Gertrude st
Holmes, W., saddler, Aberdeen st
Homewood, Chas., coppersmith, Autumn street
Hooper, James, mariner, Preston st
Houlham, Mary, Autumn st
Howell, Dr., Packington st

Hoyle, Emanuel, engine driver, Little Clarence st
Horle, Wm., labourer, Gertrude st
Hurly, Mary, Packington st

I

Ince, John, grocer, Aberdeen st
Israelite Sanctuary, Spring st
Ives, —, gardener and florist, Aderdeen st
Ives, —, undertaker and cabinetmaker, Villamanta st
Ivison, Stephen, miner, Villamanta st

J

Jackson, Robt. William, compositor, Preston st
Jarman, Jane, Packington st
Jarrett, —, labourer, Gertrude st
Jeffs, Jonas, gardener, Autumn st
Jennings, John, tailor, Coronation st
Jennings, John, bootmaker, Coronation st
Jenkins, Wm., Wellington st
Jillet, John, draper, Hope st
Johnson, Edward, labourer, Albert st
Johnson, Margaret, Preston st
Johnson, W. H., bootmaker, Autumn st
Johnston, Jane, Spring st
Johnston, Mary, Candover st
Jones, Henry, butcher, King st
Jones, Wm., bricklayer, Albert st
Jose, James, miner, Spring st
Jose, Francis, bootmaker, Preston st
Joy, Wm., shopman, Candover st

K

Keating, Michael, coachman, Gertrude st
Kelly, John, contractor, Wheeler st
Kendall, John, brickmaker, King st
Kendall, Thomas, mason, Hope st
Kennedy, John, labourer, Autumn st
Kenshola, Samuel, tailor, Spring st
Kettle, Walter, butcher, Packington st
Kewley, Elizabeth, St. George's hotel, Packington st
Kewley, Thomas, miner, Yuille st
Kickey, Patrick, carrier, Clarence st
Kilhurn, Elizabeth, Packington st
Kingsbury, Amelia, Hope st
Kitz, Louis, Candover st
Kitchen, Thomas, Preston st
Kneebone, Fredk., farmer, John st
Kneebone, George, dairyman, Ann st
Knight, Thomas Edwin, carpenter, Aberdeen st

L

Lacey, Michael, labourer, Clarence st
Lamb, Jeanette, O'Connell st
Lamont, John, grocer, Hope st
Langton, Elizabeth, O'Connell st

Langdon, John, blacksmith, Packington street
Law, Rudolph, mariner, Wellington st
Lawrie, David, engineer, Aberdeen st
Leach, Misses, dressmakers, Villamanta street
Lenford, Elizabeth, Shearers' Arms hotel, Aberdeen st
Legg, Thomas, labourer, Anderson st
Leggett, Samuel, coachsmith, Wheeler st
Le Page, Nicholas, hawker, Albert st
Le Page, James, grocer, Britannia st
Le Page, Peter, hawker, Albert st
Lemmon, Robert, carrier, Britannia st
Lemmon, Eliza, Candover st
Lennan, E. R., schoolmaster, Aberdeen st
Lessels, John, engineer, Preston st
Le Sueur, James, tentmaker, Preston st
Leverich, Theodore, Coquet st
Lewis, Mrs., ladies' evening school, Packington st
Lowle, Samuel, farmer, Britannia st
Lowis, Thomas, labourer, Albert st
Le Liever, Isaac, wheelwright, Candover street
Linay, Fredk., Anderson st
Lions, Catherine, 55 Wellington st
Lishton, Garret, labourer, Britannia st
Lloyd, R. W., Villamanta st
Logan, Robert, bootmaker, Autumn st
Logan, Jane, Autumn st
Long, Sarah, Albert st
Longdon, John, blacksmith, Wheeler st
Longton, John, carter, Ann st
Lucas, Thomas, builder, Candover st
Lukey, Mary, Clarence st

M.

Macdonald, —, saddler, O'Connell st
Macdonald, John, labourer, Clarence st
Mardonell, John, lineman, &c., telegraph office, Spring st
Mack, Martin, labourer, King st
Maddern, Miss, dressmaker, Autumn st
Maher, Edward, bootmaker, Wheeler st
Maloney, Charles, farmer, O'Connell st
Mangen, James, labourer, Britannia st
Marriott, Wm., engraver, Aberdeen st
Marshall, George, greengrocer, Packington st
Marshall, James, carpenter, O'Connell st
Marshall, John, labourer, Clarence st
Marshall, Wm., carpenter, Gertrude st
Mason, Wm., bootmaker, Spring st
Matheson, John R., labourer, Packington street
Martin, Wm., builder, Wheeler st
Maughar, Daniel, labourer, Autumn st
McArthur, Margaret, Britannis st
McClelland, Thomas, storeman, Preston street
McCoy, James, labourer, Little Clarence street

McDead, Chas., labourer, Little Clarence street
McDiarmid, Peter, cabman, Clarence st
McDonald, Henry, soapmaker, Britannia street
McDonald, Edward, bootmaker, Britannia street
McEwen, John, mason, Spring st
McEwen, James, slater, Anderson st
McFarlane, Rammy, mason, O'Connell st
McGuire, Patrick, labourer, Elizabeth st
McGuire, Thomas, labourer, McDougal st
McGuire, James, blacksmith and wheelwright, Packington st
McKenna, James, labourer, Albert st
McKenzie, Mrs., dressmaker, Autumn st
McKenzie, John, labourer, Coronation st
McKinlay, Elizabeth, Autumn st
McKinnon, Angus, labourer, Clarence st
McKuen, Stephen, grocer, Wheeler st
McLane, John, railway guard, O'Connell street
McLauchlan, Roger, labourer, Autumn st
McLean, John, groom, Spring st
McLoughlan, Roger, grocer, Packington street
McMahon, John, labourer, Hope st
McMahon, Peter, Ashby hotel, Britannia street
McMullen, Isabella, Packington st
McMullen, John, miner, Spring st
McNeill, John, tailor, O'Connell st
McPherson, Wm., miner, Preston st
McRoy, Wm., mason, Catherine st
Meek, James, carpenter, Wheeler st
Mehan, John, labourer, Elizabeth st
Mekan, Patrick, labourer, Elizabeth st
Middleton, John, carter, Albert st
Millard, Edmond, blacksmith, Western st
Milligan, David, labourer, King st
Mirrielies, George, carrier, Ann st
Molyneux, John, painter, Autumn st
Molyneux, Henry, railway guard, Clarence street
Monahan, Robert, hawker, Britannia st
Moody, Charles, coachman, King st
Moore, Samuel, labourer, Albert st
Moore, Wm. Loth, blacksmith, Clarence street
Moore, Henry, draper, Yuille st
Moore, Ann, residence, Clarence st
Moore, Thomas, bailiff, Gertrude st
Moore, Daniel, carpenter, Gertrude st
Moore, James, painter, Preston st
Morgan, Charles, cook, Coquet st
Morgan, Wm., residence, Autumn st
Morgan, Wm., furniture broker, Autumn street
Morgerage, Edward, sawyer, Hope st
Morrison, Robert, general dealer, Autumn street
Morrison, Peter, grocer, Packington st
Morrow, James, labourer, Britannia st
Morton, —, bootmaker, Wheeler st

Moss, Mark, travelling hawker, Clarence street
Moss, John, labourer, Spring st
Mowbray, Joseph D., schoolmaster, Villamanta st
Mulhall, Wm., labourer, Clarence st
Munday, Samuel, residence, Coronation st
Mundy, Mary, Gertrude st
Murphy, Thomas, labourer, Clarence st
Murray, Phillip, carter, Wellington st
Murray, David, grocer, Clarence st

N.

Nangle, Martha, Hope st
Nangle, Ann, Wellington st
Napier, Thomas, labourer, Autumn st
Nash, Wm., bootmaker, Autumn st
Nelson, John, fisherman, Packington st
Nicholls, Thomas, grocery store, Autumn street
Nicholls, Wm., painter, Albert st
Nicholson, J. P., timber merchant, Villamanta st
Nicholson, Ward, blacksmith, Wellington street
Nixon, John, grocer, King st

O.

O'Bryan, Dennis, carter, Anderson st
O'Bryan, Cornelius, carrier, Church st
O'Bryan, Patrick, Argyle hotel, Aberdeen street
O'Connell, Thomas, policeman, O'Connell street
O'Connell, Thomas, policeman, Britannia street
O'Connor, Daniel, baker, Packington st
Oddy, James, grocer, Elizabeth st
O'Halloran, Alice, Britannia st
O'Honey, Patrick, carrier, Ann st
O'Kiefe, James, labourer, King st
O'Meara, Michael, O'Connell st
O'Meara, Michael, labourer, Britannia st
Orland, Mary, dairy, Little Clarence st
Ormond, Francis, Aberdeen st
Orr, John, mason, Elizabeth st
Osborne, Geo., hatter, Hope st

P.

Page, Harriet, Bunyip hotel, Spring st
Page, Margaret, Clarence st
Page, Wm., carpenter, Autumn st
Page, Wm., tailor, Coronation st
Parker, Cain, coachman, Coronation st
Parrott, Frederick, coachbuilder, Packington st
Parkinson, John, labourer, Autumn st
Parkinson, Robert, woolsorter, O'Connell street
Passmore, John, carpenter, Coronation st
Paterson, John, plumber, O'Connell st

Patterson, George, railway inspector, Britannia st
Patterson, James, mason, 82 O'Connell st
Pattison, John, labourer, Packington st
Pedder, Alfred, painter, Little Clarence st
Pelley, Joseph, Geelong and Ballarat hotel, Church st
Pembroke, Thomas, labourer, O'Connell street
Pendigast, Morris, labourer, Spring st
Peratt, Geo., labourer, King st
Phillp, Alexander, letter carrier, Coronation st
Phipps, Henry, platelayer, Clarence st
Pinch, P. J., violinist, Little Clarence st
Porter, Wm., labourer, Albert st
Porter, Robert, labourer, Autumn st
Poulson, Mary, Wellington st
Pound, Wm., grocer, Catherine st
Powell, Richard, brickmaker, King st
Powell, Thomas, butcher, Hope st
Powney, George, gardener, Gertrude st
Pratt, Mary Ann, Packington st
Primitive Methodist Chapel, Wheeler st
Protestant Free School, O'Connell st
Pulbrook, John, gingerbeer manufacturer, Autumn st
Purcel, James, labourer, Wellington st
Purcel, Michael, labourer, King st

R.

Radford, Maria Ann, Petrel hotel, Packington st
Raiment, Fredk., grocer, Addis st
Rammige, Captain John, Hope st
Rand, John, wheelwright, Wheeler st
Rankin, Robt., mason, Spring st
Rastrick, Geo. Thomas, Autumn st
Rastrick, Geo. Thomas, chemist, Packington st
Read, Charles, tailor and draper, Coronation st
Reeves Brothers, grocers, Packington st
Reid, Geo., bootmaker, Autumn st
Richardson, Thomas, bone merchant, Autumn st
Richardson, Wm., labourer, 30 Wellington street
Riley, Thomas, labourer, Little Clarence street
Robertson, Thomas, baker, Autumn st
Robertson, A. S., Aberdeen st
Robertson, Alex., labourer, Little Clarence street
Robins, Miss Gertrude, ladies' school, O'Connell st
Robinson, David, ship carpenter, Elizabeth st
Robinson, Thomas, carrier, Packington st
Rogers, John, labourer, Packington st
Rontley, Henry, butcher, Wellington st
Ruffin, Edwin, tallow chandler, Clarence street

Ruffin, Edward, bootmaker, Clarence st
Russell, James, cowkeeper, Britannia st
Ryan, Michael, carrier, Packington st
Ryan, Ellen, Autumn st
Rylah, Smith, mason, Gertrude st

S.

Salmon, Fredk., bootmaker, Packington street
Saunders, Wm., tinsmith, Hope st
Schofield, Mason, labourer, Western st
Sebe, Sarah, Clarence st
Seal, John, mason, Britannia st
Shackley, John, bootmaker, Aberdeen st
Shannon, Thomas, and Co., wheelwrights, Keera st
Sharp, Peter, brewer
Sharpley, Joseph, Hope st
Sharre, Robert, draper, Preston st
Shaw, Alex., quarryman, Autumn st
Shekell, Mrs. M., straw hatmaker, Autumn st
Shellman, Wm., Britannia st
Shepherd, Wm., bootmaker, Keera st
Sidley, Anna, Albert st
Sikes, Matthew, labourer, Preston st
Simmons, Ann, dressmaker, Wellington street
Simpkins, James, tailor, Spring st
Skews, Richard, farmer, Autumn st
Smith, Joseph, labourer, Ann st
Smith, Samuel, labourer, Little Clarence street
Smith, Joseph Jones, carpenter, Clarence street
Smith, Isaac, carpenter, Wheeler st
Smith, Wm., tailor, Hope st
Smith, Thomas, labourer, O'Connell st
Smith, John, labourer, Albert st
Smith, James, butcher, Spring st
Smith, John, Autumn st
Snell, James, bricklayer, Albert st
Snowden, J., house and sign painter, Packington st
Soap and Candle Factory (vacant), Preston st
Spellman, Wm., bootmaker, Packington street
Spicer, Henry, clerk, Hope st
Spriggins, George, farmer, Britannia st
Steel, Wm., labourer, Little Clarence st
Stent, John, grocer, Candover st
Stephens, Samuel, compositor, Spring st
Stephens, Joseph, labourer, Church st
Stephenson, Robert, carrier, Waterloo st
Stevens, Elizabeth, Spring st
Stevenson, David, bootmaker, Western st
Stewart, James, mason, Albert st
Stewart, Mary, grocer, Autumn st
Stirling, Wm., grocer, Spring st
St. James' Church of England School, Aberdeen st
Stoddart, Dr., Church st
Stone, James, coachsmith, Packington st
Stoneman, Wm., coachbuilder, Spring st
Strong, James, bootmaker, 71 O'Connell street
Summers, Josiah, bootmaker, Packington street
Syder, James, railway clerk, Packington street
Sykes, Louis, labourer, Britannia st

T.

Tainton, Philip, cowkeeper, Clarence st.
Tainton, Richard, labourer, Clarence st
Tainall, Samuel, labourer, O'Connell st.
Telegraph hotel (vacant), Packington st
Thewlais, Robert, labourer, Coquet st
Thomson, Charles A., shopman, Candover street
Thompson, Wm., draper, Wheeler st
Thompson, Elizabeth, Autumn st
Thompson, John, labourer, Elizabeth st
Thompson, Samuel, mason, Autumn st
Thompson, Wm., coachbuilder, Preston st
Thompson, Wm., tallow chandler, Hope street
Thorn, George, carpenter, Western st
Thorpe, Charles, Villamanta st
Timms, Mrs., Packington st
Tomlinson, Thomas, labourer, Britannia street
Toner, John, labourer, Ann st
Toohey, Michael, labourer, Autumn st
Townsend, John J., carpenter, Autumn st
Tulloch, J. M., draper, Packington st
Tullon, James, Spring st
Trainer, Mrs., Spring st
Tralt, Kyrn, grocer, Autumn st
Tracy, Lucinde, dressmaker, Antomn st
Trembling, George, builder, Hope st
Trendor, Charles, foreman at railway, Clarence st
Tretheway, Wm., dealer, Packington st
Trevena, Alfred, carpenter, Wellington st
Trickett, Wm., cabinetmaker, Spring st
Trotter, Joseph, contractor, Anderson st
Truscott, Wm., miner, Spring st
Truss, Robert, labourer, Spring st
Turnbull, Margaret, Spring st
Turner, John, grocer, Hope st

U.

United Methodist Free Church, Ann st

V.

Vance, Miss, dressmaker, Packington st
Vaughan, James, labourer, Wheeler st
Venneck, Alfred, sailmaker, off Preston street
Vickers, Alfred, bricklayer, Clarence st
Vines, Joshua, mail contractor, Villamanta street
Vines, Joshua, Packington st

W.

Walker, Wm., labourer, O'Connell st
Walls, Jennett, Hope st
Wamldni, —, painter, Gertrude st
Watt, Hugh, baker, Packington st
Watters, James, lybourer, Ann st
Watts, James, bricklayer, Packington st
Webster, Thomas, carpenter, O'Connell st
Welsh, Bernard, labourer, Clarence st
Wesleyan Chapel, Wellington st
Westaway, John W., cabman, Preston st
Wheelens, Wm., bootmaker, Aberdeen st
White, Robert, gardener, Wellington st
Wild, John, labourer, Albert st
Wild, Mary, McDougal st
Willet, James, engineer, Wheeler st
Williams, George, labourer, Coronation st
Williams, J. W., butcher, Villamanta st
Williams, Philip, mason, Coquet st
Williams, John, labourer, Albert st
Williams, Thomas, shipwright, Coquet st
Wills, Capt. John, Autumn st
Wilson, Christiana, Autumn st
Wilson, Geo., baker, Packington st
Winter, John, cabman, Clarence st
Wiseman, Benjamin, guard, Coquet st
Wood, James, mason, Autumn st
Wood, Geo., general store, O'Connell st
Wood, Edmund, grocer, Preston st
Woodward, Henry, draper, Aberdeen st
Wright, Geo., watchmaker, O'Connell st
Wright, Daniel, mason, Waterloo st
Wright, Elizabeth, Autumn st

Y.

Young, Thomas, grocer, Packington st
Young, Alexander, labourer, Clarence st
Young, John, mason, Coronation st

NEWTOWN AND CHILWELL DIRECTORY.

1866-67.

A.

Adamson, Moses, mason, Margaret st
Addams, Michael, draper, Barwon avenue
Akehurst, Arthur P., police magistrate, Noble st
Aldridge, Thomas, labourer, Skene st
Allan, Robert, draper, Virginia st
All Saints' Church, Noble st
Anderson, John, sharebroker, Virginia st
Andrews, Henry, Skene st
Anthony, Morris, watchmaker, Latrobe terrace
Armitage, Mrs., The Hermitage, Packington st
Arnold, Elizabeth, grocer, Fyans st
Asling, Richard, general dealer, Latrobe terrace
Aspinall, Richard, balter maker, Cumberland st
Atkins, Norcott, sheep manager, Marshall street
Austin, Wm., bootmaker, Skene st

B.

Backwell, Ebenezer, whitesmith, Clarendon st
Bade, Richard, gardener, Marvin st
Bailey, George, labourer, Sharp st
Baker, Wm., contractor, Skene st
Bales, Wm., tailor, Nicholas st
Ball, Stephen, bootmaker, Skene st
Hall, Wm., farmer, Leviens road
Bankhead, John, bootmaker, Noble st
Banks, John, quarryman, Clarke st
Barnard, John, labourer, Stephen st
Barnes, Wm., carpenter, Saffron st
Barr, Joseph M., carpenter, Park st
Barrs, Thomas, hatcher, Noble st
Bassett, George, labourer, Fyans st
Bassett, Thomas, carter, Clarendon st
Batten, James, general dealer, Chilwell court, Packington st
Bayley, Edward, carpenter, Clarendon st
Beard, Wm., cabman, Marshall st
Bendall, Wm., miller, Russell st
Bennett, Edward, whitesmith, Fyans st
Bennett, John, ropemaker, Russell st
Bennett, Elizabeth, Elizabeth st
Bennett, Frederick, turner, Margaret st
Bennion, Edwin, compositor, Sharp st
Bennett, Joseph, bricklayer, Bond st
Benson, Richard, labourer, Skene st
Best, James, cabman, Fyans st
Bible Christian Chapel, Bond st
Blair, Mrs., Charles st
Blaxall, Morris, grocer and baker, Fyans street
Bonnay, Mr., gardener, Skene st
Bonnett, John, painter and glasier, Austin terrace
Bonnett, George, labourer, Skene st
Bottroll, Wm., quarryman, Marvin st
Bowen, Nathan, Camden road
Bowey, Thomas, carter, West Melbourne road
Bran, Henry, cowkeeper, Bond st
Brew, —, carpenter, Latrobe terrace
Brewer, George, carpenter, Camden road
Briggs, Fletcher, fruiterer, Marshall st
Brimblecombe, Wm., mason, Sharp st
Brimblecombe, John, mason, Sharp st
Brockbank, John, ironmonger, Pleasant st

Brockwell, Richard, carpenter, Skene st
Brockwell, James, carpenter, Skene st
Brockwell, Wm., turner, Williams st
Brown, Wm., storeman, Clarendon st
Brown, Thomas, bootmaker, Clarke st
Brown, Nathaniel, monumental mason, Elizabeth st
Brown, James, blacksmith, Packington st
Brown, James, general dealer, Packington street
Brown, Thomas, bootmaker, Austin st
Bryon, Wm., Elizabeth st
Bruce, James, stonemason, Clarke st
Broffey, Dennis, Gold Diggers' hotel, Fyans st
Bruford, Eliza, ladies' school, Skene st
Bryant, Wm., labourer, Fyans st
Buck, Wm., tailor, Austin st
Buckland, Stephen, Packington st
Budd, John, carpenter, Clarke st
Bullock, R. H., Stephen st
Bunnet, John, painter, Latrobe terrace
Burch, Robert, mason, Bond st
Burke, Michael, labourer, Charles st

C.

Cade, John, carpenter, Charles st
Cakebread, Wm., lime and cement merchant, Austin st
Calder, David, labourer, Austin terrace
Capp, Robert, carter, Marshall st
Carpenter, Wm., coachbuilder, Packington street
Carr, Onesimus, fancy shop, Latrobe terrace
Carr, J. G., auctioneer, Skene st
Carrington, Walter, hawker, Clarendon st
Carter, Wm., gardener, West Melbourne road
Cathcart, Geo., West Melbourne road
Catholic Convent, Retreat road
Caton, Joseph, labourer, Bond st
Chafe, Richard, grocer, Bond st
Champion, Fredk., Pleasant st
Chant, Alfred, Skene st
Chappel, Jonathan, contractor, Marvin st
Chapple, Wm., carpenter, Fernly st
Chasholm, John, labourer, Fyans st
Chattel, Henry, Retreat road
Christopherson, Henry O., civil engineer, Retreat road
Child, Wm., baker, Latrobe terrace
Clarendon, Samuel, carrier, Fyans st
Clark, Charles, butcher, Skene st
Cleary, Wm., labourer, Russell st
Clutterbuck, W. G., carpenter, Noble st
Clydesdale, John, labourer, William st
Coady, Thomas, labourer, Austin st
Cocking, Elizabeth, Skene st
Cole, Thomas, labourer, Nicholas st
Coleman, John, labourer, Saffron st
Coleman, Henry, contractor, Mercer's hill
Colman, James, quarryman, Mercer's hill

Colenso, Edwin, undertaker, Nicholas st
Coles, Frank, labourer, Cumberland st
Collins, John, plasterer, Fyans st
Collins, Edward, carrier, Skene st
Comb, H. E., solicitor, Bloomsbury st
Common School, St. Peter's, Church of England, Marshall st
Connelly, John, carpenter, Noble st
Connell, Jerry, labourer, Sharp st
Coombs, J., turner, Noble st
Corbet, David, carter, George st
Cotton, Herbert, grocer, Russell st
Coulson, Henry, slater, Marshall st
Coy, Mark, ale and porter depôt, Saffron street
Creswell, Charles, confectioner, Clarke st
Crofts, Thomas, butcher, Clarke st
Croomer, Hy., carter, Marshall st
Cross, George, plumber, West Melbourne road
Cruickshank, James, gardener, Cumberland st
Cullen, John, Leviens road
Cuttle, Rev. —, George st

D.

Dale, Henry, butcher, Saffron st
Dallimore, Wm., carpenter, Marshall st
Daniel, Thomas, grocer and corn store, Saffron st
Daniels, Mark, stone cutter, Marvin st
Davidson, John, gardener, Skene st
Davis, John, boot and shoemaker, Marshall st
Davison, Chas., bricklayer, Russell st
Dawson, Mary, grocer, Latrobe terrace
Day, Rev. Samuel, Baptist minister, Bloomsbury st
Day, Caleb, draper, Marshall st
Denis, John, Latrobe terrace
Denmead, Nathaniel, tinsmith, Nicholas st
Dew, Wm., mason, Clarendon st
Dick, John, quarryman, Saffron st
Dickson, Edward, bootmaker, Upper Skene street
Dobson, James, sen., grocer, Packington street
Dobson, John, labourer, Noble st
Docherty, James, Clarendon st
Dodd, Samuel, tailor, Bond st
Dodds, Christiana, grocer, Bond st
Donaghay, Michael, ropewalk, Fyans st
Douglas, Hugh, quarryman, Saffron st
Drayton, Wm., labourer, Clarendon st
Drew, Wm., warder at the hospital, Austin terrace
Dun, Thomas, draper, Latrobe terrace
Dun, Thomas, saddler, Latrobe terrace

E.

Ebenezer Independent Chapel, Marshall street

214   Ebb   ALPHABETICAL   Hig

Ebbles, Wm., carpenter, Latrobe terrace
Eddy, Miss Mary Jane, dressmaker, Austin st
Edwards, —, plumber, Fyans st
Edwards, Wm., mason, Nantes st
Ellis, David, bootmaker, Fyans st
Elms, Charles, Barwon avenue
Fagar, Jane E., ladies' school, Skene st
Espinasse, Robt., ironmonger, Leviens road
Evans, Percival, cabman, Cumberland st
Evans, John B., law clerk, Upper Skene street
Eurn, Henry, labourer, Fernly st
Eyre, G. and J., bakers, Retreat road

F.

Fagg, Miss Elizabeth, Packington st
Fagg Brothers, timber merchants, Packington st
Fare, Robert, Duke of Wellington hotel, Packington st
Farrel, Patrick, labourer, Bond st
Folley, Ann, grocer, Retreat road
Fordham, Wm., Sawyers Arms' hotel, Noble st
Fowler, Richard, wholesale warehouse, off Bond st
Foy, James, bootmaker, Austin st
Podky, David, labourer, Saffron st
Ferguson, Wm., ropemaker, Russell st
Few, Edward, Bloomsbury st
Filae, Ebenezer, carpenter, Marshall st
Fisher, Henry, labourer, Bond st
Fitton, Wm., storeman, Saffron st
Fitton, James, Gold Diggers' hotel, Skene street
Fitzpatrick, Patrick, labourer, Clarke st
Fizzard, John, mangleman, Armitage road
Fletcher, Henry, labourer, Clarendon st
Fletcher, James, gardener, Nicholas st
Foster, Geo., blacksmith, Packington st
Fort, Wm., labourer, Fyans st
Fraser, Stewart, Packington st
Francis, Joseph, farmer, Sharp st
Frazer, Mackenzie, Austin st
Free Church of England, Latrobe terrace
Freer, Wm., coachmaker, Russell st
Friend, Robt., gardener, Fyans st
Fuller, Thomas, bootmaker, Skene st
Fuller, Charles, labourer, Austin terrace
Furnell, Robt., Skene st
Fynder, Thos., labourer, Woodstock st

G.

Gale, William, grocer, West Melbourne road
Gee, Edward, butcher, Sharp st
Geelong College, Skene st ; — Morrison, proprietor
Geoghegan, Samuel, Armitage road
Giblin, Vincent W., Noble st
Gilchrist, Archibald, tailor, Little Park st

Giles, Edmund, labourer, Fyans st
Gill, James, carter, Clarendon st
Gill, Henry, commission agent, Virginia street
Gill, Joseph, tailor, Noble st
Gillingham, Edwin, carrier, William st
Gilmore, Robt., labourer, Clarke st
Gorey, Joseph, butcher, Packington st
Grace, Dr., Skene st
Grant, Archibald, mason, Noble st
Grant, Elizabeth, Skene st
Grant, Wm., mason, Saffron st
Grave, Richard, stonemason, Virginia st
Gray, Alexander, miller, Latrobe terrace
Great Western hotel, West Melbourne road
Grecian, Geo., mason, Austin st
Grix, Benjamin, labourer, Nicholas st
Grix, John, labourer, Nicholas st
Grocll, James, tinsmith, Noble st
Groves, James, labourer, Clarendon st
Gunn, Barbara, dressmaker, Bond st
Guthrie, John, collector of customs, Latrobe terrace

H.

Hale, Wm., carpenter, Lawrence st
Hall, Edmond, printer, Latrobe terrace
Hamilton, James, grocer and carpenter, Clarke st
Hampton, Henry, baker, Sharp st
Harding, W., Latrobe terrace
Hardy, John, labourer, Woodstock st
Harper, William, bailiff, Fyans st
Harris, Thomas, ironmonger, Pleasant st
Harris, Edward, schoolmaster, Bloomsbury street
Harris, Wm., Retreat road
Harrison, Daniel, Elizabeth st
Harty, John, draper, Austin st
Harvey, Wm., butcher, West Melbourne road
Harvey, Thomas, mason, Russell st
Harwood, Thomas, solicitor, Skene st
Hawker, John, storeman, Skene st
Head, John H., gardener, Stephen st
Healey, James, grocer, Skene st
Healy, Jane, Packington st
Healey, John, grocer, Austin st
Heals, Wm., gardener, Bloomsbury st
Heard, James, plasterer, Bloomsbury st
Heath, John, carpenter, Cumberland st
Hebbard, Mrs., dressmaker, George st
Hebuirn, Thomas, carter, Saffron st
Hebuirn, Thomas, water-carrier, Nicholas street
Helm, C. O., schoolmaster, Austin st
Hendely, John, storeman, Clarendon st
Henderson, Rev. James, Armitage road
Henry, Thomas, grocer, Marshall st
Hickey, John, plasterer, Clarke st
Hicks, Matthew, quarryman, Saffron st
Higgs, Thomas, labourer, Fyans st

Hill, Mrs. John, schoolmistress, Upper Skene st
Hillman, Samuel, bootmaker, Noble st
Hillman, Edward, labourer, Williams st
Hislop, Wm., mason, Skene st
Hobbs, John, butcher, Skene st
Hochins, Joseph, ropemaker, Mercer's hill
Hodgson, Charles Alfred, Barwon avenue
Holdsworth, Thomas, contractor, Woodstock st
Hollen, John, labourer, Woodstock st
Hollow, Christopher, grocer, Skene st
Holmes, Maria, manglewoman, Little Park st
Holmes, Arthur, Fyans st
Horne, Thomas, paperhanger, Latrobe terrace
Horsey, Charles, carpenter, Skene st
Howarth, James, shoemaker, Nicholas st
Hunt, Henry, hawker, Margaret st
Hunt, Thomas B., baker, Latrobe terrace
Hunt, John, labourer, Bond st
Hurle, John, bootmaker, Skene st
Hutchins, Henry, coachman, Pleasant st
Hyatt, Moses, labourer, Skene st

I.

Ibboston, Charles, Stephen st
Ibboston's mill, off Fyans st
Irwon, T. W., teacher of singing, Skene street
Irving, David, mason, Noble st

J.

Jackson, John, labourer, Marshall st
James, Lucy Jane, schoolmistress, Blessington st
Jeffery, Thomas, New Town hotel, West Melbourne road
Jeffress, Wellington, gardener, Woodstock street
Jenkins, John, carter, Stephen st
Jenkins, John, mason, Upper Skene st
Jenkins, John, undertaker, Bloomsbury st
Jenkinson, Wm., water-carrier, Noble st
Johnson, Wm. W., carpenter, Retreat road
Johnston, James, labourer, Marshall st
Jones, Charles, carpenter, Bond st
Jones, Robert, plasterer, Clarke st
Jones, John, plasterer, Clarke st
Jones, Henry, contractor, Cumberland st

K.

Keenen, Patrick, policeman, Noble st
Kells, Henry, labourer, Skene st
Kennedy, Mary, Mercer's hill
Kinsella, James, gardener, Leviens road
Kernott, W. H., chemist, Latrobe terrace
King, Alfred, plumber, Marshall st
King, George, gardener, Marshall st
Knight, George, carter, George st

L.

Lane, H. B., Pleasant st
Lauchlan, Campbell, confectioner, Noble street
Lawrence, George, farmer, Latrobe terrace
Lee, Richard, blacksmith, Barwon avenue
Leach, Robert, labourer, Woodstock st
Levien, Benjamin G., Leviens row
Lewis, Wm., drapery store, Saffron st
London, John, West Melbourne road
Lowe, Robert, painter, Barwon avenue
Lowe, James, butcher, Russell st
Lowrie, Wm., labourer, Saffron st
Lowry, James, labourer, Austin st
Luttrell, Daniel, labourer, Marshall st
Lynch, Henry, sawyer, Bond st
Lynch, Lawrence, policeman, Pleasant st

M.

Macdonald, Ronald, sharebroker, Skene st
Macdonald, Jessie, Park st
Macdonald, Alex. C., auctioneer, Noble st
MacFarlane, Thomas, labourer, Cumberland st
Maddocks, Thomas, labourer, Saffron st
Malcolm, Michael, carter, Skene st
Malony, John, cowkeeper, Nicholas st
Marshall, Thomas, herdsman, West Melbourne road
Marsham, Robert, plasterer, Skene st
Martin, James, baker, Little Park st
Martin, Caleb, stonemason, Latrobe terrace
Martin, Thomas, mason, Marshall st
Martin, Henry, cabman, Clarke st
Martin, Wm., stonemason, Clarendon st
Martin, Richard, cabman, Noble st
Martin, Wm., mason, Latrobe terrace
Martin, Henry, carpenter, Lawrence st
Massie, John, labourer, Austin terrace
Mathews, Wm., wheelwright, Russell st
Matters, Joseph, painter and glazier, Russell st
Maxwell, Robert, Skene st
Mayes, John, labourer, Saffron st
McCallum, Peter, off Austin st
McCarty, John, farmer, Marvin st
McCullagh, R. M., Noble st
McClelland, Wm., plasterer, Bloomsbury street
McDonald, Michael, labourer, Marshall st
McDonald, Alex., mariner, Bond st
McDonald, Margaret, Bond st
McDonald, Angus, labourer, Saffron st
McDonald, Thomas, gardener, Clarendon street
McDermott, Michael, carter, Latrobe terrace
McFarlane, John, builder, Latrobe terrace
McInnes, Ronald, Cumberland st

McIntosh, John, labourer, Nicholas st
McKenzie, George, labourer, Elizabeth st
McLean, Hugh, limeburner, Park st
McLennan, Joseph, plasterer, Noble st
McMullen, W., Fernly st
McNaughton, John, miller, Latrobe terrace
McPherson, Captain, harbour master, Noble st
Meade, James, carpenter, Noble st
Meagan, Thomas, builder, Pleasant st
Merefield, Christopher, draper, Skene st
Mervil, Charles, tailor, Austin st
Metcalf, Joshua, Cremorne hotel, Packington st
Middlemiss, John, secretary to the Hospital, Austin st
Middleton, John Wm., coachbuilder, Austin st
Miles, George, teacher, Bloomsbury st
Miles, Wm., gardener, Noble st
Millard, Thomas, labourer, Marshall st
Miller, Wm., gardener, Fyans st
Mitchel, George, tailor, Camden road
Mitchel, Wm., labourer, Clarendon st
Moore, John, Camden road
Morall, John, gardener, Fernly st
Morris, James, labourer, Marshall st
Morris, Fredk., cabinetmaker, Noble st
Morrow, Charles S., squatter, Retreat road
Mulhern, Patrick, wheelwright, Saffron st
Mullen, Michael, labourer, Charles st
Murphy, Dennis, Little Park st
Murphy, Wm., carpenter, Park st
Murray, Daniel, confectioner, Park st
Musgrove, Wm., Noble st

N.

Nairn, Joseph, gardener, Skene st
Near, Samuel, carter, Bond st
Nelson, Henry, butcher, Fyans st
Newtown and Chilwell Fire Brigade, Packington st
Newtown Surveyor's office, Packington st
Newtown and Chilwell Police Court, Packington st
Newtown Police Station, Austin st
Nicholson, Donald, Williams st
Nokes, Thomas, stonemason, Skene st

O.

Oates, Wm., quarryman, Marvin st
O'Bryan, Daniel, labourer, Marshall st
O'Donoghue, Mary, grocer, West Melbourne road
O'Neil, Stephen, tailor, Little Park st
O'Neil John, tailor, Charles st
Osbourne, John W., bootmaker, Noble st

P.

Paine, John, carpenter, Russell st

Palmer, John, plasterer, Margaret st
Parker, Ann, general store, Skene st
Parker, —, limeburner, Saffron st
Parker, Richard, ironmonger, Retreat road
Parkinson, Wm., labourer, Marshall st
Parray, Thomas, labourer, Noble st
Passmore, Thomas, painter, Saffron st
Patterson, Wm., labourer, Sharp st
Pearson, Fredk., tanner, Latrobe terrace
Petch, Wm., carter, Bond st
Peters, John, carpenter, Marshall st
Phillips, Wm., labourer, Bond st
Piddle, George, gardener, Blessington st
Pigeon, Richard, butcher, Noble st
Pike, Robert, wheelwright, Russell st
Pile, James, stonemason, Fyans st
Pither, Henry, mason, Upper Skene st
Pittard, James, bootmaker, Bond st
Pistock, Jonathan, carpenter, Fyans st
Plummer, Wm., sawyer, Nicholas st
Pounds, Joseph, Packington st
Power, Charles, inspector of sheep, Skene street
Powell, Thomas, sawyer, Packington st
Preston, Wm., grocer, Skene st
Price, John, labourer, Clarendon st
Purnell, Wm., carpenter, Russell st

Q.

Quin, Michael, cowkeeper, Woodstock st
Quinan, James, registrar of births and deaths, Skene st

R.

Radcliff, John, gardener, William st
Rankin, James D., Commercial tavern, Leviens road
Robsamen, Madame, teacher of French, Skene st
Redman, John, carpenter, Upper Skene st
Reed, George, brickmaker, Skene st
Reeves, John, labourer, Clarendon st
Renault, Thomas, fruiterer, Saffron st
Rice, Joseph, Noble st
Richards, Wm., quarryman, Fyans st
Riddle, Thomas C., Skene st
Ricketts, James, wheelwright, Packington street
Ricketts, Wm., baker, Marshall st
Roach, Richard, wheelwright, Bond st
Roach, James, grocer, West Melbourne road
Roadknight, Thomas, Packington st
Roberts, John, carpenter, West Melbourne road
Robertson, Joseph, carpenter, Clarendon street
Robins, Thomas, labourer, Park st
Robins, Charles, carpenter, Clarendon st
Robinson, James, painter, Saffron st
Robinson, J. D., auctioneer, 7 Skene st

Robinson, Robert, labourer, Clarendon st
Rogers, Mary, Virginia st
Rolph, Nathaniel, hatmaker, Noble st
Ronald, R. B., Fernly st
Root, Wm., carpenter, Noble st
Rowand, Dr. Charles, Skene st
Roddock, Frederick, baker, Saffron st
Rutherford, Wm., carter, William st
Ryan, John, carter, Clarke st
Ryan, Patrick, labourer, Bond st
Ryan, Thomas, cowkeeper, Upper Skene street
Ryan, Timothy, cowkeeper, Russell st
Ryan, Timothy, labourer, Clarendon st

S.

Sadler, Edward, carter, Fyans st
Saffron, Edward, mason, Fernly st
Same, Harry A., Inspector of schools, Autumn st
Saunders, John, labourer, Marshall st
Sayers, Wm., tobacco stores, West Melbourne road
Sayers, W. Y., clerk, Newtown and Chilwell, Packington st
Scales, Mrs. Sarah, ladies' school, Packington st
Scott, Duncan, Fyans st
Scott, Charles, teacher, Nicholas st
Scott, James, timber merchant, Noble st
Seabrook, Robert, draper, Packington st
Searls, James, draper, Skene st
Seeley, Elijah, builder, Pleasant st
Seiver, John, upholsterer, Retreat road
Shashar, John, tanner, Fyans st
Shade, Andrew, Custom-house officer, Russell st
Shand, Wm., mason, Park st
Sharp, James, grocer, Packington st
Shaw, Joseph L., architect, Stephen st
Sheldrick, James, storeman, Blessington street
Shingfield, David, carpenter, Lawrence st
Shugg, Samuel, mason, Retreat road
Silk, James, tailor, Noble st
Simson, James, merchant, Skene st
Sinnott, Charles, labourer, Clarke st
Sladen, Charles, Esq., M.L.C., Packington street
Slammers, Miss Elizabeth, ladies' school, Pleasant st
Sleator, Samuel, rate collector, West Melbourne road
Smellie, Alexander, carpenter, Upper Skene st
Smith and Aitchison, general store, Elizabeth st
Smith, Hugh, dealer, Fyans st
Smith, John, butcher, Fyans st
Smith, John, stonemason, Clarendon st
Smith, George, labourer, Mercer's hill
Smith, Wm., labourer, Clarendon st
Smith, Joseph, cabman, Austin st

Smith, James, labourer, Noble st
Smith, James, Blessington st
South, Wm., Packington st
Spencer, James, ship steward, Margaret street
Spooner, Alfred, baker, Sharp st
Stephen, G. A., Stephen st
Stewart, Dr., surgeon, Fyans st
Stewart, Henry, mason, Margaret st
Stewart, John, bootmaker, Autumn st
Stewart, Matthew, sawyer, Bond st
Stock, Mark, builder and carpenter, Charles st
Stone, John, ship-builder, Park st
Stone, James, labourer, Fyans st
Stott, Benjamin, Life Insurance agent, West Melbourne road
Strange, Wm., Nicholas st
Stratford, Robert, cabinetmaker, Clarke street
Strickland, Rev. Frederick P., Skene st
Sullivan, John, grocer, Russell st
Sullivan, John, Cricket Club hotel, Latrobe terrace
Sutherland, Duncan, carter, Marshall st
Sweatman, Wm. J., sign-writer, Skene st

T.

Tappin, James, bookkeeper, Packington street
Taylor, Wm., carpenter, Saffron st
Taylor, John, gardener, Nicholas st
Telford, James C., Leviens road
Tempest, George, ironmonger, Autumn st
Thomas, Wm., bootmaker, Saffron st
Thomas, Wm., Nantes st
Thomas, —, chemist, Woodstock st
Thomas, Geo., wine and spirit merchant, Noble st
Thompson, Robert, labourer, Bond st
Thompson, Archibald, bootmaker, Russell street
Thompson, Thomas, baker, Park st
Thomson, Edward, plasterer, Skene st
Thorley, Wm., labourer, Charles st
Toogood, James, baker, Saffron st
Toole, James, wheelwright, Virginia st
Trenglove, John, coachsmith, Clarendon street
Trotman, Sanders, rate collector, West Melbourne road
Truman, Richard, stonemason, Packington st
Tweeddale, John, town inspector, Marshall st
Tweeddale, Wm., ironmonger, Latrobe terrace

V.

Vanstone, James, grocer, Clarendon st
Veal, Wm., labourer, Noble st
Vessey, Edward, compositor, Marshall st
Victor, Farbus, labourer, Sharp st

2 F

W.

Wade, Mrs. John, Clarke st
Walker, Henry, mariner, William st
Wallace, John, carpenter, Marshall st
Walter, Ellen Jane, day school, Austin st
Walters, Joseph, carpenter, Noble st
Walton, George, chemist, Skene st
Walton, Elijah, chemist, Saffron st
Warbaton, James, labourer, Noble st
Ward, Mary Ann, St. Allan's house, Retreat road
Ward, Alfred, painter, Blessington st
Warl, Wm., blacksmith, Marshall st
Watt, Wm., draper, Nantes st
Wase, Joseph, blacksmith, Russell st
Webber, George, boot and shoe maker, Bond st
Welch, James H., gasfitter, Noble st
Wells, Thomas, labourer, Skene st
Wesleyan Chapel, Noble st
Wesleyan School, Saffron st
Wheatland, Wm., carpenter, Fernly st
White, James, quarryman, Latrobe terrace
White, George, ironmonger, Austin st
White, James Charles, Noble st
White, Wm., stonemason, Latrobe terrace
White, John, bricklayer, Latrobe terrace
Whybrow, Philip, carter, Fyans st
Wigge, George A., bricklayer, Upper Skene st

Wilkinson, George B., Noble st
Wilkinson, Robert, ironmonger, Austin st
Williams, Wm., cook, Sharp st
Williams, Ralph, carter, Marvin st
Williams, Thomas, mariner, Austin terrace
Williams, Edward, butcher, Marshall st
Williams, Charles, labourer, Fernly st
Williams, George Thomas, cabman, Skene st
Williams, John, farmer, Packington st
Willmore, Mrs. Elizabeth, West Melbourne road
Wilson, Charles, labourer, Clarendon st
Wilson, John, merchant, Noble st
Willson, Mrs. Catherine, day school, Clarke st
Wright, Thomas, cabman, Skene st
Wright, Wm., Latrobe terrace
Wyatt, Joseph, carpenter and joiner, Skene st

Y.

Yates, Joseph, tollgate keeper, Clarendon street
Young, Robert, carrier, Marshall st
Young, John, architect, Leviens road
Young, John, postman, Russell st

Z.

Zoar Chapel, Noble st

THE WESTERN DISTRICT DIRECTORY,

INCLUDING

Winchelsea	Portland	Merino
Colac	Heywood	Digby
Birregurra	Dartmoor	Branxholme
Camperdown	Edenhope	Dunkeld
Terang	Harrow	Wickliffe
Mortlake	Balmoral	Ararat
Warrnambool	Cavendish	Beaufort
Woodford	Hamilton	Skipton
Koroit	Coleraine	Streatham
Belfast	Casterton	Meredith
Yambuk	Sandford	Steiglitz
Cressy	Lismore	Darlington
Framlingham	Purnam	Inverleigh.

1866-67.

A.

Abrahams, Isaac, tobacconist, Barkly st, Ararat
Adams, W., Victoria hotel, Mt. Cole, Beaufort
Adamson, Thomas, storekeeper, South Portland
Adamson, John, storekeeper, Steiglitz
Aitkin and Bostock, general storekeepers, Timor st, Warrnambool
Albert, J., Half-way house, Steiglitz
Allan, Thomas, butcher, Hurd st, Portland
Allan, J., and Co., timber merchants and ironmongers, Grey st, Hamilton
Allen, —, storekeeper, Skipton
Allen, Edward, bootmaker, Branxholme
Alliogham, John, draper, &c., Pleasant creek
Allitt, Wm., gardener, Otway st, Portland
Alexander, David, painter, South Portland
Ambler, Oliver, blacksmith, Dunced
Anderson, Thomas, Bentinck st, Portland
Anderson, George, Dunfern inn, Koroit
Anderson, David, saddler, Camperdown
Anderson, Geo., butcher, Winchelsea
Anderson, James, blacksmith, &c., Sandford
Andrews, Alexander, blacksmith, &c., Colac
Anthony, Wm., Royal hotel, Colac

Applegate, Wm., shoemaker, South Portland
Ararat Mining Board office, Barkly st, Ararat
Ararat Flour Mills. —, Forester, acc., Barkly st, Ararat
Archer, Wm., storekeeper, Colac
Archer, David, photographic artist, Colac
Armstrong, Robert, carpenter, Hurd st, Portland
Armstrong, T., bootmaker, Timor st, Warrnambool
Armstrong, P., draper, Timor st, Warrnambool
Arnold, John, saddler, Cox st, Belfast
Alberton, Mrs., fancy repository, Julia st, Portland
Atkinson, Edwin, town clerk, Otway st, Portland
Atkinson, Edwin, town clerk and borough treasurer, Portland
Atkinson, J. H., Apothecaries' Hall, Sackville st, Belfast
Austin, W. G., steam packet and general commission agent, Liebeg st, Warrnambool
Avery, W., painter, &c., Gray st, Hamilton

B.

Bachli, Frank, butcher, Barkly st, Ararat
Badnall, Chas. H., storekeeper, Heywood
Bailey, James, butcher, Hurd st
Bailey, George, hairdresser, Barkly st, Ararat
Baines, John, labourer, Camperdown
Balderson, Joseph, carrier, Cameron st, Portland
Balding, Henry, Hurd st, Portland
Ballis, Joseph, fruiterer, Timor st, Warrnambool
Barber, Geo., solicitor, Liebeg st, Warrnambool
Barber, R. W., coachbuilder, Liebeg st, Warrnambool
Barclay, Buros, superintendent of police, Coleraine
Barker, Thomas L., Royal hotel, Barkly st, Ararat
Barkley, Hugh Ross, superintendent of police, Portland
Barrett, Wm., town clerk, Belfast
Barsley, Edward, fruiterer and gardener, Julia st, Portland
Basch, Jacob, watchmaker, Barkly st, Ararat
Bateman, Wm., timber merchant, &c., Cox st, Belfast
Baylie, Chas., saddler and harness maker, Pleasant creek
Bayly, S. J., solicitor, commissioner for taking affidavits in the Supreme Court, &c., Princess st, Belfast

Bayne, Alexander, accountant, Bank Victoria, Liebeg st, Warrnambool
Bayne, Archibald, blacksmith, &c., Liebeg st, Warrnambool
Dageshawe, Ed., mining surveyor, Beaufort; agent for the Liverpool and London and Globe Insurance offices
Beams, Robert, carter, Percy st, Portland
Beath, David, storekeeper, Gray st, Hamilton
Beauvois, Hudson, agent, Gawler st, Portland
Beauvois, Hudson, county court bailiff, Portland
Beeson, James, gardener, Tyers st
Behrens, G., photographic artist, Barkly st, Ararat
Belcher and Co., storekeepers, wine and spirit merchants, Camperdown
Belfast Police Station, Cox st, Belfast
Bennett, Mrs., fruiterer, Sackville st, Belfast
Bennett, Thomas, tailor, &c., Bentinck st, Portland
Besley, Francis, coach painter, &c., Colac
Best, Jabez, general storekeeper and postmaster, Branxholme
Bevan, Geo., hotelkeeper, Bentinck st, Portland
Bevan, Geo., London hotel, Julia st, Portland
Bignell, Mrs., Royal hotel, Beaufort
Bilston, —, publican, Merino
Blair, James, police magistrate, Wellington road, Portland
Blair, James, police magistrate, Portland
Blair, David, grocer, Sackville st, Belfast
Blay, James, bootmaker, Percy st, Portland
Boffham, Thomas, bootmaker, Coleraine
Bond, John, storekeeper, Dunkeld
Bond, John, storeman, Blair st, Portland
Boardman, Robt., storekeeper, Steiglitz
Bourke, Garrett, tinsmith, View point, Ararat
Boyd, Thomas White, Swan hotel, Lismore
Boyle, James, storekeeper, Mortlake
Boylett, Benjamin, blacksmith and wheelwright, Mount Moriac
Bradley, Wm., Telegraph hotel, Colac
Bradshaw, Wm., woolwasher, Fern st, Portland
Bradshaw, Thomas, tailor, Julia st, Portland
Brady, James, tinsmith, Timor st, Warrnambool
Braham, F., postmaster and telegraph manager, Portland
Bramley, Wm., farmer, Colac
Brannely, Patk., bootmaker, Camperdown
Brebner, Isaac, tailor, Timor st, Warrnambool

Bracken, Francis, draper and clothier, Timor st, Warrnambool
Brewer, Henry E., surgeon, Richmond st, Portland
Brewster, Wm., bootmaker, Julia st, Portland
Bridger, Geo., tailor, Barkly st, Ararat
Briggs, J., draper, &c., Timor st, Warrnambool
Broadbent, Geo., Colac
Broadway, G., Boephey hotel, Framlingham
Bromfield, Astley, chemist, Liebeg st, Warrnambool
Bromfeld, W., Cricketers' Arms, Steiglitz
Bromley, John, bootmaker, Grey st, Hamilton
Brown, Joseph, baker, Timor st, Warrnambool
Brown Bros., butchers, Grey st, Hamilton
Brown, Wm., tailor, Grey st, Hamilton
Brown, John, storeman, Julia st, Portland
Brown, James, Manchester hotel, Barkly st, Ararat
Brown, James, saddler, &c., Grey st, Hamilton
Brown, Walter, baker, Percy st, Portland
Browning, John, boarding-school, South Portland
Browning, James, merchant, Percy st, Portland
Brownlies, J., undertaker and smith, Lingdale st, Hamilton
Brown's grocery and produce warehouse, Pleasant creek
Bruce, John, blacksmith, Wickliffe
Bruce, Neil, storekeeper, Palmer st, Portland
Bruce, Andrew, draper, Sackville st, Belfast
Buchhols, Louis, saddler, &c., Sackville st, Belfast
Buckle, Thos., Digby hotel, Digby
Buckley, Emma, Camperdown
Buglehole, Henry, stonemason, Blair st, Portland
Burbank, Ednot, teacher National School, Camperdown
Burgess, Nathaniel, blacksmith, Digby
Burkitt, R., hairdresser, Julia st, Portland
Burnett, Thos., Warrnambool hotel, Banyon st, Warrnambool
Barnett, James, painter, Henty st, Portland
Barrow, Thos., storeman, Henty st, Portland
Bye, Edmund H., gardener, Clarke st, Portland

C.

Cameron, James, blacksmith, Bentinck st, Portland
Cameron, John, saddler, Mortlake
Cameron, Mrs., Camperdown
Cameron, Donald, stock agent and auctioneer, Grey st, Hamilton
Cameron, Donald, settler, Bentinck st, Portland
Cameron, Neil, commission agent, Cox st, Belfast
Cameron, Angus, general storekeeper, Redruth
Cannon, William, labourer, Gawler st, Portland
Chadwick and Co., drapers, &c., Ararat
Challis, John, butcher, Winchelsea
Chambers, Henry, accountant Bank of Victoria, Cox st, Belfast
Chaffey, Philippa, Glenelg inn, Casterton
Camp hotel, ——, proprietor, Stawell
Campbell, Simon, blacksmith, Colac
Campbell, John, draper and outfitter, Grey st, Hamilton
Campbell, Wm. M., storekeeper, Hurd st, Portland
Campbell, James, secretary to the Mechanics' Institute, Barkly st, Ararat
Campbell, Mrs., dressmaker, Thomson st, Hamilton
Campbell, Gray, tobacconist, Pleasant creek
Candy and Batten, carpenters and undertakers, Pleasant creek
Carroll, John, shoemaker, South Portland
Carruthers, John, surveyor, Casterton
Carter, J., plasterer, &c., Drydan st, Hamilton
Carter and Brookman, blacksmiths, wheelwrights, &c., Mortlake
Catholic Church, Colac
Cave, James, hairdresser, Timor st, Warrnambool
Cavenagh, Geo., accountant, Bank of Australasia, Julia st, Portland
Chandler, ——, Britannia hotel, Julia st, Portland
Chandler, Thos., bootmaker, Grey st, Hamilton
Chapman and Butcher, butchers, Colac
Chapman and Butcher, bakers and confectioners, Colac
Chaponnel, John, watchmaker, &c., Pleasant creek
Charrett and Co., carpenters, builders, &c., Terang
Childe Bros., wine and spirit merchants, Pleasant creek
Christen, David, bootmaker, Timor st, Warrnambool
Church, Wm., Albion hotel, Barkly st, Ararat
Church of England; Rev. —— Pyne, clergyman, Camperdown
Clark, George, saddler, Beaufort
Clark, Miss, ladies' school, Gawler st, Portland

Clarke, Lindsay, surveyor, Henty st, Portland
Clarke, Peter, carpenter, Palmer st, Portland
Clarke, Thomas, tinsmith, Colac
Claridge, Geo., Percy st, Portland
Claridge, George G. P., Fern st, Portland
Clay, Richard, Palmer st, Portland
Clay, F. L., solicitor and commissioner for taking affidavits in the Supreme Court, Merino, and Gawler st, Portland
Clemes, Alfred B., chemist and druggist, Pleasant creek
Cleverdon, John, bookseller and stationer, agent for the London and Lancashire Fire and Life Insurance Companies, Warrnambool
Clough and Co., merchants, Grey st, Hamilton
Cannon, John, stationer and news agent, Darkly st
Coakley, Joseph, saddler, Timor st, Warrnambool
Cobb and Co.'s coach stables; J. Vines, proprietor, Colac
Cockman, Walter, general storekeeper, Liebeg st, Warrnambool
Codrington, John, painter, South Portland
Codrington, James, Tyers st, Portland
Colbert, Edmund A., surveyor, Percy st, Portland
Collin, Leopold R., teacher of music, Market square, Portland
Collins, Edwin, Royal Mail hotel, Dunkeld
Collins, —, solicitor, Camperdown
Collins, W., manager Cobb and Co.'s, Darkly st, Ararat
Collis, C. T., bootmaker, Grey st, Hamilton
Collard, Jeffray, tanner, Hurd st, Portland
Colstock, James, Liebeg st, Warrnambool
Common School, No. 187 ; —, schoolmaster, Duneed
Connor, John, auctioneer and commission agent, Colac
Constable, A. H., receiver and paymaster, Darkly st, Ararat
Coach, Mrs., storekeeper and fruiterer, Pleasant creek
Cook, Richard B., carpenter, Percy st, Portland
Cooke, Hervey, Prince of Wales hotel, Thomson st, Hamilton
Cooper, W., agent for the London and Lancashire Fire and Life Insurance Companies, Portland; *Portland Guardian* office
Cooper, W., general storekeeper, agent for the London and Lancashire Fire and Life Insurance Companies, post office, Steiglitz

Cope, Frederick Chas., clerk of courts, Darkly st, Ararat
Corney, Wm., South Portland
Cosser, Wm., labourer, Camperdown
Cox and Palmer, solicitors, Thomson st, Hamilton
Corstorphan, John, carpenter, Balmoral
Cotton, Albert, storekeeper, wine and spirit merchant, Chilwell and Danved
Court of Petty Sessions, Camperdown
Court of Petty Sessions, Darkly st, Ararat
Courtis, Edward C., general storekeeper, and agent for the London and Lancashire Fire and Life Insurance Companies, Casterton
Cowans, James, baker, Beaufort
Cowl, Wm., blacksmith, spring maker, and wheelwright, Terang
Craig, Samuel, coroner, Stawell shire, Stawell
Cramer, Chas. A., draper, Timor st, Warrnambool
Cramond and Dickson, drapers, Timor st, Warrnambool
Crick, James, Edenhope inn, Edenhope
Croker, Chas., merchant, Percy st, Portland
Cross, S., general storekeeper, Grey st
Cross, Samuel, draper, Hurd st, Portland
Crossley and Brown, ironmongers, Darkly st, Ararat
Crothers, W. and D., grocers and bakers, Pleasant creek
Cronch, Daniel, Travellers' Rest hotel, Casterton
Crouch, Edward, bootmaker, Darkly st, Ararat
Crouch and Co., bootmakers, Darkly st, Ararat
Crouch and Co., merchants, Percy st, Portland
Crough and Fethers, auctioneers, &c., Percy st
Cunning, Peter, turnkey, Palmer st, Portland
Cure, Joseph, boot and shoemaker, Colac
Curtis, Chas., gardener, South Portland
Cusson, M., general storekeeper, Merino
Cozens, James, storekeeper, Balmoral

D.

Dacomb, Edmund, merchant, Richmond st, Portland
Dahl, Murdoch C., accountant, Richmond st, Portland
Dalton, John, wheelwright and carriage-builder, Colac
Dane, James H., secretary Mechanics' Institute, Pleasant creek
Dane, Jas. Henry, accountant and agent to the London and Lancashire Fire Insurance Co., Pleasant creek

D'Arcy, Patrick, Shamrock hotel, Stawell
Darling, Wm., storekeeper, Woodford
Davidson, Alex., South Portland
Davis, Henry, auctioneer, stock and commission agent, Casterton
Davies, Richard, agent for the London and Lancashire Fire and Life Insurance Companies, Winchelsea
Davies, Thomas H., shoemaker, Bentinck st, Warrnambool
Davies, Daniel, bootmaker, Timor st, Warrnambool
Davies, Walter, bookseller, Timor st, Warrnambool
Davison, D. S., chemist and druggist, Pleasant creek
Dawson, P., photographer, Grey st, Hamilton
Dawson and Lee, grocers, &c., Barkly st, Ararat
Dawson, P., photographic artist, Liebeg st, Warrnambool
Day and Maclean, carriage builders, Percy st, Portland
Deacon, Henry, brickmaker, Clarke st, Portland
Denholm, John, farrier, &c., Grey st, Hamilton
Denney, John Thos., accountant, Glenelg st, Portland
Denny, J. T., accountant Union Bank of Australia, Julia st, Portland
Dent, James, bootmaker, Bank st, Belfast
Destree, Adolf, jeweller and watchmaker, Grey st, Hamilton
Deutscher, Carl T., refreshment house, between Hamilton and Coleraine
Dickman, Arthur, Travellers' Rest hotel, store and post office, Dirregurra
Dickson, Joseph, tinsmith, Pleasant creek
Digby, George, New Inn, Rosebrook road, Belfast
Dillon, Michael, bootmaker, Camperdown
District Survey Office, Clark Lindsay, district surveyor, Portland
Dix, Samuel, stonemason, Market square, Portland
Dobson, Henry, Picnic hotel, Barrenboet
Dodd, F. W., auctioneer and commission agent, Pleasant creek
Dogherty, —, Dogherty hotel, Cavendish
Dolman, Wm., butcher, Coleraine
Donaldson, B., Bunyip Inn, Cavendish
Doran, John, bootmaker, Beaufort
Douglas, Mrs., Berlin wool repository, Bentinck st, Portland
Douglas, Jas., saddler and harness maker, Coleraine
Douglas, James, watchmaker and engraver, Mortlake
Dudden, J., baker, Grey st, Hamilton
Duigan, John, postmaster and telegraph manager, Camperdown

Dunbar, Charles S., teacher, South Portland
Duncan and Saunders, blacksmiths, &c., Branxholme
Dunne, W., common school teacher, Steiglitz
Dunoon, George, tailor, &c., Colac

E.

Eager, Wm., chemist and druggist, Barkly st, Ararat
Eastick, Elijah, baker, confectioner, &c., Merino
Edgar, H., Spur hotel, Harrow
Edraich, Benjamin, Commercial hotel, Bentinck st, Portland
Edwards, Thomas, fancy bazaar, Timor st, Warrnambool
Edwards, John, wheelwright, Blair st, Portland
Ehinko, H., Princess Alexandra hotel, Liebeg st, Warrnambool
Ehrenberg, M., tobacconist, Barkly st, Ararat
Eiden, C. J., general storekeeper, Mount Moriac
Elder, A. M., post office and store, Skipton
Elliott, James, schoolmaster, Cavendish
Emmett, George, storekeeper, Smythesdale st, Hamilton
Emooe, Wm., butcher, Merino
Etheridge, T. S., accountant, Bank of Victoria, Pleasant creek
Evans, David, saddler and harness maker, Beaufort
Evans, David, tailor, Timor st, Warrnambool
Evans, Benjamin, blacksmith, &c., Pleasant creek
Evans, Martin, draper and clothier, Timor st, Warrnambool
Evans and Gleeson, livery stables, Liebeg st, Warrnambool
Everett, Chas., fruiterer, Liebeg st, Warrnambool

F.

Farley, Alfred T., auctioneer, Digby
Farnell, S. S., inspector of police, Camperdown
Farrell, Alexander, Hopkins' hotel, Wickliffe
Farrer, John, wheelwright and carpenter, Woodford
Fawthrop, Captain, harbour master, Portland
Fawthrop, James, harbour master, South Portland
Fedarb, Munro, and Co., glass, china, and furniture warehouse, Thomson st, Hamilton
Fender, Mrs., Winchelsea

Fenn, J., draper, &c., Julia st, Portland
Fenton, Michael, Timor st, Warrnambool
Ferguson and Wells, training stables, Grange creek, Hamilton
Ferguson, Duncan, sexton, Winchelsea
Ferguson, W., clerk of courts, Camperdown
Fidler, Thomas, butcher, Liebeg st, Warrnambool
Findlay, George, general storekeeper, Percy st, Portland
Finn, Thomas, Percy st, Portland
Finnigan, J., saddler and harness maker, Percy st, Portland
Finnigan, John, saddler, Gawler st, Portland
Firmin, Alfred, Kardinia hotel, Kardinia
Fisher, Sophia M., agent for the London and Lancashire Fire and Life Insurance Companies, Dunkeld
Fitzgerald, G., butcher, Mortlake
Fitzgerald, Bryan, tanner and currier, near the Immigration Depôt, Portland
Fitzpatrick, P. Albert, Excelsior hotel, Steiglitz
Flower, Horace, secretary to the shire, Belfast
Floyd, Wm., coachbuilder and wheelwright, Sackville st, Belfast
Foote, Wm., blacksmith and wheelwright, Liebeg st, Warrnambool
Forbes, John, bootmaker, Bank st, Belfast
Ford, Wm., bootmaker, Wickliffe
Ford, Frederick, general storekeeper, Merino
Fordham, Samuel, miller, South Portland
Foster, Wm., grocer and stationer, Barkly st, Ararat
Fox, Charles, stonemason, Bentinck st, Portland
Fraser, William, cooper, Percy st, Portland
French, R., bootmaker, Bentinck st, Portland
French, —, bootmaker, Gawler st, Portland

G.

Gaille, D. W., manager Bank of Australasia, Julia st, Portland
Gallin, John, furniture warehouse, Sackville st, Belfast
Game, George, fancy repository, Grey st, Hamilton
Gamon, Robert, wine merchant, Cox st, Belfast
Gamson, Frederick, druggist and chemist, Barkly st, Ararat
Gosling and Nugent, Gosling's hotel, Meredith
Gosney, James, carpenter and undertaker, Winchelsea

Gibbs and Cowell, butchers, Mortlake
Gibbs, Wm., plumber and paperhanger, Liebeg st, Warrnambool
Gibson, James, farmer, South Portland
Gilbert, John, bootmaker, Woodford
Giles, John, watchmaker, Barkly st, Ararat
Gilles, F. B., dressmaker and milliner, Coleraine
Gill, John, painter, Palmer st, Portland
Gillespy, M. A., Union Inn, Cox st, Belfast
Gilloch, James P., London tavern, Beaufort
Gleeson, F. and P., drapers, grocers, &c., Cox st, Belfast
Gleeson, Mrs., Victoria hotel, Colac
Goldsmith, Peter, fisherman, Tyers st, Portland
Goodwin, E. H., fancy repository and stationer, Pleasant creek
Gordon, John, tailor, Thomson st, Hamilton
Gorie, James, tailor, Liebeg st, Warrnambool
Gough, Wm., Branxholme hotel, Branxholme
Goulden, Benjamin, Victoria hotel, Steiglitz
Govett, Dr., Thomson st, Hamilton
Guion, Alfred, Temperance hotel, Sackville st, Belfast
Gunn, Wm., general storekeeper, Beaufort
Guthrie, Chas., accountant London Chartered Bank of Australia, Barkly st, Ararat
Gutllerrez and Co., storekeepers and wine and spirit merchants, Pleasant creek
Gracie, Thomas, draper, Beaufort
Grame, Hugh, cooper, Timor st, Warrnambool
Grant, J. S., agent for the London and Lancashire Fire and Life Insurance Companies, Sandford
Grant, John S., hotelkeeper, Palmer st, Portland
Grant, Patk., fruiterer and hairdresser, Sackville st, Belfast
Grant, John S., Caledonian Union hotel, Sandford
Grant, R. and G., Albion hotel, Carterton
Graves, J., general storekeeper and timber merchant, Beaufort
Graves, S., bootmaker, Grey st, Hamilton
Gray, John, baker, Colac
Gray, Isaac G., Black Horse Inn, Coleraine
Green, Chas., butcher, Cox st, Belfast
Greenham, Isaac, butcher, Sandford
Grieve and Benn, storekeepers, Mortlake
Grinham, C., Woodford inn, Dartmoor
Grubb, Wm., draper, Sackville st, Belfast
Gwyther, James, family hotel, Dunkeld

H

Haberkorn, Charles, brewer, Grey st, Hamilton
Haggaston, Joseph, storekeeper, Percy st, Portland
Haig, Chas., Western hotel, Wickliffe
Haley, Edward, bootmaker, Thomson st, Hamilton
Halley, Wm., stonemason, Finn st, Portland
Hamblin, Louis, Trawalla hotel, store, and post-office, Trawalla
Homes, J. T., baker, &c., Barkly st, Ararat
Hardie, John, stonemason, South Portland
Harrington, Rich., Dr., Liebeg st, Warrnambool
Harriott, George, postmaster, clerk of petty sessions, &c., Wickliffe
Harris, Edward, baker and confectioner, Beaufort
Harris and Troy, produce merchants, Beaufort
Harris, Richd. S., seedsman and fruiterer, Liebeg st, Warrnambool
Harris, H., bread and biscuit baker, Digby
Harris, J. H., boot and drapery mart, Steiglitz
Haslam, Thomas, printer, South Portland
Hassett, John, Eagle tavern, Furnim
Hawkes Bros., ironmongers, Beaufort
Hawkins, James, teacher, Percy st, Portland
Hawkins, Samuel P., Hurst st, Portland
Hay, James, cooper, Gawler st, Portland
Haynes, Geo., draper and storekeeper, Sackville st, Belfast
Hazledine, Samuel, poundkeeper, South Portland
Heath, Richard, Hermitage hotel, Harrow
Hemphill, C., accountant, Oriental Bank, Pleasant creek
Henderson, Hector, Fyans Ford hotel, Fyans Ford
Henderson, L., general storekeeper, wine and spirit merchant, Beaufort
Hendry, Wm., wheelwright and ploughmaker, Woodford
Henningsen, H. P., bookseller, stationer, and news agent, Beaufort
Henty, Edward, Bentinck st, Portland
Henty, S. G., and Co., merchants, Julia st, Portland
Herbert, Christopher, hairdresser, Beaufort
Herbertson, Robt., farmer, Julia st, Portland
Hickey, James, Bull and Mouth hotel, Pleasant creek
Hickin, —, agent National Bank of Australasia, Colac
Hide, John, coachbuilder, Timor st, Warrnambool

Hider, James, bookseller and stationer, Timor st, Warrnambool
Hill, Geo., blacksmith, Merino
Hill, John, teacher, Fitzgerald st, Portland
Hill, Robt., boot and shoemaker, Sackville st, Belfast
Hill, W. H., farrier, Pleasant creek
Hill, Wm., toll collector, Beaufort
Hill, John, bootmaker, Liebeg st, Warrnambool
Hodgson, Sholto D., storekeeper, Darlington, Elephant bridge
Hodgson, Thomas, storekeeper, Beaufort
Hoggeston, Joseph, general store, Percy st, Portland
Holfman, George, butcher, Barkly st, Ararat
Hollis and Peacher, butchers, Percy st, Portland
Holmer, Edwin F., baker, Palmer st, Portland
Holmes, Henry F., Tyers st, Portland
Holmes, John J., teacher, South Portland
Holmes, Edwin, storekeeper, Percy st, Portland
Holt, Isaac, Burnside's hotel, Pleasant creek
Hood, Alexander J., acting accountant Bank of New South Wales, Barkly st, Ararat
Hooper, E. G., View Point Dispensary, Ararat
Hopton, Edwin, Swan hotel, Fyans Ford
Horn, John, bootmaker, Terang
Howes, D. H., engineer to the Shire, Belfast
Hyland, Thomas Francis, Governor of the Gaol, Portland
Hughes, Edward F., printer, Henty st, Portland
Humpage, —, solicitor, Beaufort
Humm, George, butcher, Woodford
Hunt, H. R., surgeon, Casterton
Hutchison, J., Hamilton mills, Hamilton
Hutchinson, S., Victoria hotel, Percy st, Portland
Hutchinson, Samuel, general storekeeper, Gawler st, Portland
Hutton and Bulstrode, storekeepers, Sackville st, Belfast
Huxley, Edward, Forest Inn, Dulwarra, near Portland
Huxley, John, butcher, Tyers st, Portland

I

Iles, George, baker, Percy st, Portland
Illidge, George, Camperdown hotel, Camperdown
Ingram, James, bootmaker, Beaufort
Ingram, Edward, blacksmith, Coleraine
Ingram, Thomas, manager Bank of Australasia, Sackville st, Belfast

2 G

Inverarity, Henry, Dr., M.B., Cantab., public vaccinator and deputy registrar of births, deaths, &c., Merino
Irvine, Geo., Mortlake hotel, Mortlake
Isaacson, S., draper and clothier, Pleasant creek
Ison, George, tailor, Beaufort

J.

Jackson, John, baker and confectioner, Sackville st, Belfast
Jackson, Wm., Commercial hotel, Thomson st, Hamilton
Jacoby, S., draper, silkman, and clothier, Grey st, Hamilton
James, Wm., fruiterer, Timor st, Warrnambool
James, Mark, tinsmith, Mortlake
Jamieson and Co., general storekeepers, Koroit
Jamieson, W. W., ironmonger and grocer, Liebeg st, Warrnambool
Jarrett, Stephen, ironmonger, Percy st, Portland
Jarrett, George, coachbuilder and wheelwright, &c., Percy st, Portland
Jeffries, Thomas, carpenter, Kennedy st, Portland
Jenkins, David, Union hotel, East Woodford
Jenkins, Mrs., dressmaker, Barkly st, Ararat
Jennings, George, Western Turf hotel, Pleasant creek
Jennings and Co., photographic artists, Grey st, Hamilton
Jermyn, Dr., surgeon, Cox st, Belfast
Johnson, Henry J., Timor st, Warrnambool
Johnson, James L., F.B.S. Glasgow, doctor, Beaufort
Johnson, John, tailor, Barkly st, Ararat
Johnson, John, storekeeper, Beaufort
Johnson, J., blacksmith, Woodford
Johnson, Wm. H., tobacconist, Liebeg st, Warrnambool
Johnson, J. M., accountant Bank of Australasia, Sackville st, Belfast
Johnston, W., Oddfellows' hotel, Colac
Johnston, J. F., furniture warehouse, Barkly st, Ararat
Johnstone, John, farmer, Bridgewater road, Portland
Jones, A., Cressy hotel, Cressy
Jones, Daniel, clerk, Tyers st, Portland
Jones and Co., blacksmiths, &c., Liebeg st, Warrnambool
Jones, Wm., Western hotel, Balmoral
Jones and Arnot, farriers, Grey st, Hamilton
Jones, Geo., stonemason, Hurd st, Portland
Jones, John Henry, Clyde hotel, Clyde

Jones, John, stonemason, Julia st, Portland
Joyce, John, Hibernia hotel, Pleasant ck

K

Kannard, Mrs., View point, Ararat
Kaufmann, L., butcher, Grey st, Hamilton
Kavanagh, John, Bush inn, Putnam
Kay, David, ironmonger, Percy st, Portland
Kay, Rev. D., minister Presbyterian Church, Wickliffe
Kean, James, lighterman, Palmer st, Portland
Kean, Thomas, ship chandler, Gawler st, Portland
Keen, Rev. T. E., Camperdown
Keller, Thomas, confectioner, &c., Bentinck st, Portland
Kelley, Henry, secretary and treasurer, Stawell Shire, Stawell
Kelly, John, Union hotel, Julia st, Portland
Kelly, Matthew, Junction hotel, Erumbeet
Kelly, John, general storekeeper, Yambuk
Kelly, James, Yambuk inn, Yambuk
Kelly, Daniel, storekeeper, Koroit st, Warrnambool
Kendall, F. W., cabinetmaker and undertaker, Timor st, Warrnambool
Keeping, John, farrier, opposite Church of England, Percy st, Portland
Kerr, John, bootmaker, Sandford
King, Thomas, produce merchant, Liebeg st, Warrnambool
King, John, aerated water and cordial manufacturer, Lava st, Warrnambool
King, Wm, Milton st, Hamilton
Kistere, Wm., Balmoral hotel, Fyans ford
King, Carl, chemist and druggist, Gray st, Hamilton
Kofoed, John, brewer, Barkly st, Ararat
Knight, James, Knight's hotel, Sturt st, West Ballarat
Kruger, J. C. A., Commercial hotel, Timor st, Warrnambool
Kunnard, Mrs., storekeeper, Barkly st, Ararat
Kuntze, Mrs., fancy repository, Timor st, Warrnambool
Kucks, Wm., baker, Timor st, Warrnambool

L.

Laing, D. S., Warrnamblo hotel, Inverleigh
Laing, F. T. B., Terang hotel, Terang
Laity, Joseph, bootmaker, Dunkeld
Lamont, Herbert, solicitor, Barkly st, Ararat
Lanagan, Alfred, bootmaker, Timor st, Warrnambool

Lanen, George, plumber, &c., Liebeg st, Warrnambool
Landman, August, cabinetmaker, Timor st, Warrnambool
Lane, Albion S., Flying Buck hotel, Liebeg st, Warrnambool
Lane and Osborne, butchers, Gawler st, Portland
Lang, John, Squatters' Arms hotel, Balmoral
Langlands, J., agent for the London and Lancashire Fire and Life Insurance Companies, Horsham
Lavery, Patrick, blacksmith and farrier, Heywood
Laurie, Henry, town clerk, Timor st, Warrnambool
Law, Dr., Barkly st, Ararat
Lawrence, Dr., J.P., Camperdown
Layh, C., tobacconist, Gray st, Hamilton
Layley, Wm., bootmaker, Sandford
Laywell, W. A., stationer and postmaster, Pleasant creek
Lear, Elijah, fruiterer and seedsman, Julia st, Portland
Learmooth, Peter, Mary Burn mills, Hamilton
Learmonth, John H., settler, South Portland
Learmonth, J., auctioneer and commission agent, Grey st, Hamilton
Lee, John, storekeeper, Colac road, Modewarre
Lee, G. D., flour and produce dealer, Winchelsea
Lee, James, blacksmith, Winchelsea
Lemster, Christian, farrier and blacksmith, Colac
Lesser, Abraham, general storekeeper, Coleraine
Lesser's general store, Sandford
Levett, Francis F., settler, Gardens, Portland
Lightbody, Wm., Wesleyan minister, South Portland
Lincoln, Mrs., greengrocer, Sackville st, Belfast
Litchfield, Joseph, butcher, Mount Morlac
Littlejohn, J. B., manager London Chartered Bank of Australia, Barkly st, Ararat
Lockie, Andrew, saddler, Percy st, Portland
Loft, Wm., builder, Beaufort
Loftus, Wm., surgeon, Cox st, Belfast
London Chartered Bank of Australasia, Barkly st, Ararat ; A. B. Littlejohn, manager; Chas. Gothrie, accountant
Long, Wm., general storekeeper, Timor st, Warrnambool
Lord, Croaker, and Co., merchants, Percy st, Portland
Lord, Croaker, and Co., merchants, Grey st, Hamilton

Loni, Oscar, tailor and habit maker, Coleraine
Lowe, James, Heywood hotel, Heywood
Lowe, Joseph, storekeeper, Mortlake
Lucas, W. H., manager Bank of Victoria, Pleasant creek
Lay and Paterson, saddlers, Thomson st, Hamilton
Lymer, Thomas, undertaker, View Point, Ararat
Lyne and Aeschlmann, butchers, Barkly st, Ararat and Pleasant creek
Lyner, J. A., postmaster and telegraph manager, Bank st, Belfast
Lyon, John, farrier, &c., Beaufort
Lyon, Basil, general storekeeper and postmaster, Balmoral
Lyth, James, agent for the London and Lancashire Fire and Life Insurance Companies, Ararat

M.

Maccade, Edward, auctioneer, Barkly st, Ararat
Maconachie, J., saddler and harnessmaker, Pleasant creek
Mackwood, Thomas, Merino hotel, Merino
Maddock, Wm., bootmaker, Gawler st, Portland
Magners, G., general storekeeper, Stawell
Maitland, Wm., boot and shoe maker, Mortlake
Maloney and Johnson, carriage builders, blacksmiths, &c., Coleraine
Maltby, G., bread and biscuit baker, Sackville st, Belfast
Manning Ed., clerk of Petty Sessions, Hurd st, Portland
March, Mrs., general storekeeper, Sackville st, Belfast
Marriott, Joseph, draper, Julia st, Portland
Martin, Thomas, cooper, Liebeg st, Warrnambool
Mathieson, G. S., livery stables, Lingsdale st, Hamilton
McCallum, Donald, wheelwright, Digby
McCallum, A., wheelwright, blacksmith, &c., Beaufort
McCallum and Ainslie, drapers and outfitters, Pleasant creek
McCann, Snood, and Co., drapers, &c., Barkly st, Ararat
McCaskill, M., bootmaker, Coleraine
McClure, Valentine, and Co., storekeepers, Terang
McCollam, Alex., general smith, Beaufort
McConachy, Samuel, Lamb Inn, Percy st, Portland
McDonald, Alex., Mac's hotel, Mortlake
McDonald, Hector, tailor, Grey st, Hamilton
McDonald, Dr., Hamilton

McDonald, D. Allen, Winchelsea hotel, Winchelsea
McDonald, Mrs., Mac's hotel, Bentinck st, Portland
McDonald, D., Argyle Arms hotel, Grey st, Hamilton
McDonald, John, Mac's hotel, Buangor
McDougall, A. E., Grey st, Hamilton
McEdoo, M., baker, &c., Barkly st, Ararat
McEvoy, Thos., Sandford hotel, Sandford
McGell, A., High Park station, Cavendish
McGibbony, John, watchmaker and jeweller, Barkly st, Ararat
McGibbony, Henry, watchmaker, Barkly st, Ararat
McGoulgal, Stephen, Court House hotel, Steiglitz
McGowen, James, carpenter, Timor st, Warrnambool
McGuinness, Robert, stonemason, Gawler st, Portland
McGuinness, Thomas, lighterman, Hurd st, Portland
McIlwaine, Mrs., teacher Infants' School, Camperdown
McIntyre, Hector, butcher, Winchelsea
McKay, John, smith and wheelwright, Percy st, Portland
McKellar, D., wine, spirit, and provision merchant, Pleasant creek
McKenzie, Donald, tanner, Colac
McKenzie, —, general storekeeper, Grey st, Hamilton
McKillop, Alexander, Bentinck st, Portland
McKinnon, Charles, blacksmith, &c., Balmoral
McLaren, John, engineer Stawell Shire, Stawell
McLaughlin, John, hotelkeeper, Colac
McLaws, D., Koroit hotel, Koroit
McLean, Neil, timber merchant, Gawler st, Portland
McLean, Hector, engineer Shire Dundas, Hamilton
McLean, —, bootmaker, Branxholme
McLean, Daniel, blacksmith, Tyers st, Portland
McLeod, Angus, stonemason, Colac
McLennan, Wm., blacksmith and farrier, Steiglitz
McMahon, Robert, storekeeper, Bank st, Belfast
McMillan, R. and J., butchers, Terang
McMillan, Duncan, Camperdown
McMullen, Ed., livery stable keeper, Gawler st, Portland
McPhail, Hugh, bootmaker, Koroit
McPherson, Sandy Creek hotel, Sandy creek
McRae, Doorobin station, near Casterton; J. S. Murray, overseer
McRae, Duncan, Gawler st, Portland

McShechy, John, Koroit hotel, Coleraine
Mechanics' Institute ; James Campbell, secretary, Barkly st, Ararat
Mechanics' Institute ; James H. Dane, secretary, Pleasant creek
Melville, George, rate collector, Campendown
Mercer, John, storekeeper, Cavendish
Merchant, F. L., telegraph manager, Casterton
Merri Mills ; Aitkin and Bostock, proprietors, Merri st, Warrnambool
Meyler, Henry, Dr., deputy registrar of births, deaths, &c., and public vaccinator at Winchelsea and Mount Moriac, Winchelsea
Michael, J., draper, Thomson st, Hamilton
Michael, Isaac, general store, Percy st, Portland
Midgley, David, general storekeeper, Tacgery
Michael, Philip, Garibaldi hotel, Beaufort
Millar, Hugh, draper, South Portland
Miller, W., saddler, &c., Barkly st, Ararat
Miller, Wm., boarding-house keeper, Coleraine
Miller, Robert Charles, chemist and druggist, Mortlake
Milnes, Frank, carpenter, builder, and manufacturer of lever presses, Mortlake
Moffit, Mrs., storekeeper, Steiglitz
Molan, Maurice, Shamrock Inn, Koroit
Molloy, Michael, Lake Wallace hotel, Edenhope
Monegue, Thomas, butcher, Steiglitz
Moore, Wm. A., collector of customs, Hurd st, Portland
Moore, John, farmer, Colac
Monte, Joseph, grocer and wine and spirit merchant, Grey st, Hamilton
Moreland, Joseph, carpenter, Camperdown
Morgan, Wm., furniture and general store, Steiglitz
Morgan and Bird, blacksmiths, Winchelsea
Morgan, W., fishmonger, Barkly st, Ararat
Morris, Mrs., Camperdown
Morrison, John, Phœnix forge, Liebeg st, Warrnambool
Moutray, H. A., storekeeper, Yanbuk
Madden, J., Skipton hotel, Skipton
Martin, W., coachmaker, View Point, Ararat
Muerson, Francis, general storekeeper, Koroit
Muir, David, fruiterer, Beaufort
Muir, Walter, produce dealer, Pleasant creek
Mulcahy, C., Bull and Mouth hotel, Barkly st, Ararat
Mulla, John, Lady of the Lake hotel, Modewarre
Munro, Wm., Constitution hotel, Stawell
Murrew, Findon, storekeeper, Winchelsea

DIRECTORY.

Murray, Adam, Victoria hotel, Liebeg st, Warrnambool
Murray, E. L., postmaster and telegraph manager, Barkly st, Ararat
Muss, Thomas, merchant, Bentinck st, Portland

N.

Napthene, R. W., general storekeeper, post office receiving box, and electoral registrar, Terang
Napthene, R. W., general storekeeper, Woodford
National Bank; D. Macpherson, Thomson st, Hamilton
Nealy, Wm., Liverpool house, Stawell
Nelman, M., draper, &c., Sackville st, Belfast
Nevill, Barnard B., tinsmith, Julia st, Portland
Newson, Samuel, boot store, Steiglitz
Newton, F., Newmarket hotel, Barkly st, Ararat
Nolan, James, bootmaker, Beaufort
Norman, Chris., general storekeeper, &c., Koruit
Nicholls, George J., storekeeper, Percy st, Portland
Nicholson, Daniel, architect, South Portland
Nicholson, Daniel, town surveyor, Portland
Nickoll, Henry, Colemine hotel, Coleraine
Nickolls, John T., general storekeeper, Sandford
Nicol, John, settler, South Portland
Night, Miss, dressmaker, Barkly st, Ararat
Nunn, John, solicitor, Thomson st, Hamilton
Nurthen, George, fruiterer and general dealer, Percy st, Portland

O.

Oates, James, plumber, Barkly st, Ararat
O'Brien, Wm., Hibernia hotel, Koroit st, Warrnambool
O'Callaghan, —, Shamrock hotel, Barkly st, Ararat
O'Connell, D., general storekeeper, Coleraine
O'Connor, Patrick, general dealer, James st, Belfast
O'Conoothy, —, Lamb Inn, Percy st, Portland
O'Donnell, Francis, surgeon, Pleasant creek
O'Grady, Daniel, Travellers' Rest Inn, Woodford
Osan, Mrs., storekeeper, Streatham
O'Reilly, Owen, settler, Percy st, Portland

O'Reilly, Michael, proprietor of the Banner newspaper, Princes st, Belfast
Osborne, Wm., butcher, Percy st, Portland
Osborne, Richard, proprietor of the Examiner newspaper office, Timor st, Portland
Oswald, F. C., manager Bank of Victoria, Julia st, Portland
Owen, Mrs., registry office, Grey st, Hamilton
Owen, Fredk., commission agent, agent for the London and Lancashire Fire and Life Insurance Companies, Thomson st, Hamilton
Owen, Jane, Wickliffe
Oxenham, Robert, baker, Erumbeen

P.

Padwick, Wm., Hurd st, Portland
Pagan, John, Mortlake
Palmer, Edward, Timor st, Warrnambool
Parker, A. C., photographic artist, Warrnambool, Belfast, and Hamilton
Parker, John, veterinary and horse shoeing forge, Terang
Parker, George, boarding-house keeper, Camperdown
Parkes, John, undertaker and cabinetmaker, Cobac
Parr, Wm., lighterman, Percy st, Portland
Paterson, George, butcher, Woodford
Paterson, R. B., manager Bank of Victoria, Liebeg st, Warrnambool
Patience, James, bootmaker, Beaufort
Patience, George, tinsmith, Beaufort
Patience, Miss, dressmaker, Beaufort
Paton, John, manager Colonial Bank of Australasia, Camperdown
Patrick, Robert, blacksmith, Percy st, Portland
Peachey, John, Perseverance store, Casterton
Peake, Jos., storeman, Percy st, Portland
Peake, Wm., bootmaker, Harrow
Pearson, F. J., and Co., drapers, clothiers, &c., Beaufort
Penrose, Nicholas, blacksmith, Mortlake
Perel, E., draper, &c., Barkly st, Ararat
Perry, Wm. H., storekeeper, Borrumbeet
Phelan and Butler, produce dealers, Barkly st, Ararat
Phelan, Martin J., tanner, South Portland,
Philips, Henry, stonemason, Bentinck st, Portland
Phillip, —, schoolmaster, Grey st, Hamilton
Phillips, G., hairdresser, Thomson st, Hamilton
Pike, Chas., butcher, Camperdown
Pilven, Chas., Hamilton hotel, Lingsdale st, Hamilton

Pine, Rev. Alex., M.A., clergyman Church of England, Camperdown
Pitcher, Geo., butcher, Palmer st, Portland
Pitcher, John, wheelwright, Henty st, Portland
Plummer, Wm., J.P. and M.L.A., Timor st, Warrnambool
Police Station, Timor st, Warrnambool
Police Station ; Wm. Fogarty, trooper, Terang
Pooley, James, nursery and seedsman, Beaufort
Porter, Benjamin, furniture, bedding, and fancy repository warehouse, Gawler st, Portland
Portland Times newspaper office, Julia st, Portland
Post and Telegraph Offices, John Dorgan, postmaster and telegraph manager, Camperdown
Post and Telegraph Offices, E. Braham, postmaster and telegraph manager, Portland
Post and Telegraph Offices, E. L. Murray, postmaster and telegraph manager, Barkly st, Ararat
Powell, T., and Co., Corio brewery, Timor st, Warrnambool
Powell, Henry, draper, Timor st, Warrnambool
Powell, H. N., solicitor, Thomson st, Hamilton
Pyle, James, general storekeeper, Wickliffe
Packle, F. H., police magistrate, Camperdown
Panchard, John, timber merchant and ironmonger, Pleasant creek
Presbyterian Church, Colac
Presswell, John, solicitor, Barkly st, Ararat
Price, Thomas, Temperance hotel, Liebeg st, Warrnambool
Price, Wm. B., senior police constable, Casterton

Q.

Quigley, John, Wannon hotel, Redruth
Quinn, Wm., Commercial hotel, Terang

R.

Rackham, T. R., postmaster and telegraph manager, Timor st, Warrnambool
Radford, Caleb, surgeon, F.R.C.S., L.S.M., and coroner for the Casterton district, Casterton
Ramsay, Geo., bootmaker, Pleasant creek
Rea and Robertson, wine, spirit, and provision merchants, Colac
Reach, J. A., manager Oriental Bank, Pleasant creek

Read, Henry T., bookseller and stationer, Timor st, Warrnambool
Redford, Thomas, Bentinck st, Portland
Reed, Cornelius C., hawker, Hurd st, Portland
Reed, John, blacksmith and wheelwright, Koroit
Reeves, Wm., blacksmith, Birregurra
Renaison, Chas., watchmaker and jeweller, Grey st, Hamilton
Rentlers, Francis, Victoria hotel, Grey st, Hamilton
Revell, T. H., paperhanger, Belfast
Richie, David, tinsmith, Timor st, Warrnambool
Richie, T. T., acting accountant, London Chartered Bank of Australia, Pleasant creek
Richard, Thomas E., Otway st, Portland
Richardson, Joseph, grocer, and wine and spirit merchant, Pleasant creek
Richmond, James, teacher common school, Lake Wenmouth
Rickard, Arthur, draper, &c., Julia st, Portland
Ritter, Charles, restaurant, Grey st, Hamilton
Robertson, Roderick, storekeeper, Steiglits
Robertson, James, Percy st, Portland
Robertson, W. and J., Warraten Duffie Station ; Alexander McEdward, overseer, near Penola
Robinson, Thomas, labourer, Camperdown
Robinson, George, Spectator newspaper office, Grey st, Hamilton
Robinson, George, stationer and bookseller, Grey st, Hamilton
Rogers, Wm., blacksmith, Balmoral
Rogers, Joseph, plumber and glazier, Timor st
Roman Catholic Church, Camperdown
Rooke, William, wood cutter, Pleasant creek
Rosenbloom, H., storekeeper, Heywood
Ross, Hugh, Plough inn, Tower Hill Flat
Ross, George, Travellers' Rest hotel, Branxholme
Ross, Alexander M., architect, Bentinck st, Portland
Rout, B., draper and ironmonger, Colac
Row, John H., watchmaker and jeweller, Julia st, Portland
Rule, James H., plumber and painter, Timor st, Warrnambool
Rundel, Wm., Court House hotel, Barkly st, Ararat
Russel, James, general smith, View Point, Ararat
Russell, George, Eldersile station ; Wm. Thompson, overseer, near Apsley
Ryan, M., bootmaker, Barkly st, Ararat
Ryan, Miss, dressmaker, Grey st, Hamilton

S.

Salinger, H., Freemasons' hotel, Barkly st, Ararat
Salmon, Thomas and John, bootmakers, Percy st, Portland
Salmon, Thomas, shoemaker, Percy st, Portland
Salt, Henry, bootmaker, Bank st, Belfast
Sampson, Henry E., cabinetmaker, Hurd st, Portland
Sampson, Thomas, senior police constable, Wickliffe
Satchwell, Mrs., Elephant Bridge hotel, Darlington
Saunders, J. M., manager Bank of New South Wales, Barkly st, Ararat
Sayers, James, Winchelsea
Scharp, F. R., Beaufort hotel, Beaufort
Scheldon, John, clergyman Church of England, Winchelsea
Scherell, Robert, saddler and harness-maker, Timor st, Warrnambool
Scurer, Carl, hairdresser and perfumer, Pleasant creek
Schofield, James, woolwasher, Customs' Point, Portland
Scott, Philip, solicitor, Percy st, Portland
Scott, James, Steiglitz hotel, Steiglitz
Scott, R. D., district surveyor and land officer, Camperdown
Scott, John, Free Press newspaper office, Grey st, Hamilton
Scott, John, stationer, Grey st, Hamilton
Searle, Geo., Cricketers' Arms, Beaufort
Smith, Peter, tinsmith, Barkly st, Ararat
Seaton, David, miller, Palmer st, Portland
Seidel, A. F., boarding-house, Hamilton
Seaman, Henry Paul, surgeon, Lake Wenmouth
Seopold, John, Great Eastern store, Barkly st, Ararat
Shacklock, John, storeman, Glenelg st, Portland
Shadland, Charles E., grocer, &c., Barkly st, Ararat
Shannon and Co., land agents, Grey st, Hamilton
Shaw, G., hairdresser, Thomson st, Hamilton
Sheldrick, Walter, butcher, Liebeg st, Warrnambool
Sherwin, Mrs., confectioner, Thomson st, Hamilton
Sherville, Peter W., accountant, Bentinck st, Portland
Shields, R. W. H., butcher, Colac
Shrine, Charles, butcher, Harrow
Shirreff, J. I., carriage builder, blacksmith, and wheelwright, Pleasant creek
Silk, James, Farmers' hotel, Colac
Simmons, Richard, tailor, Palmer st, Portland
Simmons, W. G., butcher, Pleasant creek

Simmons, B., Great Eastern hotel, Barkly st, Ararat
Simpson, W. W., Criterion hotel, Grey st, Hamilton
Simpson and Francis, saddlers, &c., Merino
Simpson, Will, Forest Home hotel, Steiglitz
Simpson, W., storekeeper, Steiglitz
Sindall, John, accountant, Henty st, Portland
Singleton, Richard, clerk of court, Steiglitz
Slack, Miss, milliner and dressmaker, Timor st, Warrnambool
Sloley, Hugh, tinsmith, Sackville st, Belfast
Slous, George, produce merchant and commission agent, Warrnambool
Smith, Thos., general storekeeper, Branxholme
Smith, Mrs., storekeeper, Cox st, Belfast
Smith, John, Norfolk brewery, Beaufort
Smith, Jeremiah, Golden Age hotel, Beaufort
Smith and Osborne, proprietors of the Belfast Gazette newspaper, Cox st, Belfast
Smith, T., and Sons, tailors and habitmakers, Balmoral and Edenhope
Smith, James, actuary, Richmond st, Portland
Smith, Henry, wharfinger, Percy st, Portland
Smith, Thomas, storekeeper, Percy st, Portland
Smith, Wm. S., general storekeeper, Beaufort
Smith, Wm., butcher, Beaufort
Smith, T., tailor and habitmaker, Edenhope
Smith, Thomas, bootmaker, Pleasant creek
Smith, J., blacksmith, &c., Percy st, Portland
Smith, David, Commercial hotel, Bank st, Belfast
Smith, John, bootmaker, Steiglitz
Smith and Co., ironmongers, Barkly st, Ararat
Smith, Thomas, general store, Percy st, Portland
Smith, Jonas, wheelwright, Tyer st, Portland
Snellgrove Brothers, drapers, Grey st, Hamilton
Snow, Henry, butcher, Timor st, Warrnambool
Southcombe and Ireland, carpenters, Cox st, Belfast
Southern, Walter, livery stables, Grey st, Hamilton
Spencer, G. F., Good Woman hotel and storekeeper, Dartmoor
Spruce, John, blacksmith, &c., Burrumbeet

Spruhan, Jas., Western hotel and general storekeeper, Dunkeld
Stanworth, E. B., Stony Rises hotel, Stony Rise
Stelling Brothers, cabinetmakers and upholsterers, Timor st, Warrnambool
Steven, John C., butcher, Hurd st, Portland
Stevens, Robert, baker, Julia st, Portland
Stevens, F. P., and Co., produce merchants, Liebeg st, Warrnambool
Stevens, Mrs., registry office, Percy st., Portland
Stevenson, Moodie, and Miller, storekeepers, Camperdown, next door to Colonial Bank
Stewart, John, blacksmith and farrier, Casterton
Stichnath, D., uphosterer, Barkly st, Ararat
Stirling, James, Barwon hotel, Winchelsea
Stirling, Wm., storekeeper, Winchelsea
Stokes, W. A., manager Union Bank of Australia, Julia st, Portland
Stone, D. B., bootmaker, Heywood
Studt, Jacob, Crescent hotel, Beaufort
Sullivan, James, bootmaker, Sackville st, Belfast
Swinton, Wm., general storekeeper, Timor st, Warrnambool
Symonds, Stanley, cabinetmaker, Bentinck st, Portland

T.

Tallerman, J. and Co., storekeepers, Grey st, Hamilton
Tait, James, general storekeeper, Camperdown
Tate, John, Farmers' hotel, Woodford
Taylor, Mrs., Star of the West hotel, Sackville st, Belfast
Taylor, James Grant, warden, Barkly st, Ararat
Temple, George, grocer, &c., Barkly st, Ararat
The Bank of Australasia; D. W. Gallie, manager; George Cavenagh, accountant; Julia st, Portland
The Bank of Australasia, Sackville st, Belfast; Thomas Ingram, manager; J. M. Johnson, accountant
The Bank of Victoria, Cox st. Belfast: Wm. Young, manager; Hy. Chambers, accountant
The Bank of Victoria; F. C. Oswald, manager; F. L. Williams, accountant, Julia st, Portland
The Bank of Victoria: R. B. Paterson, manager; Alexr. Bayne, accountant, Liebeg st, Warrnambool
The Bank of Victoria: James Manson, manager; A. G. W. Scott, accountant, Beaufort

The Bank of Australasia; Edw. Palmer manager, Warrnambool
The Bank of New South Wales; J. E. Saunders, manager; Alexander J. Hox accountant, Barkly st, Ararat
The Bank of Victoria: W. B. Lucas, manager; T. S. Etheridge, accountant, Pleasant creek
The Bank of Victoria: D. Williams, manager, Grey st, Hamilton
The Banner newspaper office, Princes st, Belfast; Michael O'Reilly, proprietor
The Belfast Gazette newspaper office; Smith and Osborne, proprietors, Cox st, Belfast
The Belfast Brewery, Cox st, Belfast; Wm. Flattely, proprietor
The Bible Christian Church; Rev. T. E. Keen, minister, Camperdown
The Colonial Bank of Australasia; John Paton, manager, Camperdown
The Commercial hotel ; ——, proprietor, Pleasant creek
The Castlemaine hotel; ——, proprietor, Pleasant creek
The Court of Petty Sessions, Timor st, Warrnambool
The Examiner newspaper office; Richard Osborne, Timor st, Warrnambool
The Guardian newspaper office; Wm. Cooper, proprietor, also bookseller, stationer, &c., Gawler st, Portland
The London Chartered Bank of Australia, Pleasant creek; John S. Trew, acting manager; T. T. Ritchie, acting accountant
The National Bank of Australasia; ——Hicklin, agent, Colac
The Oriental Bank Corporation, Pleasant creek; J. A. Riach, manager; C. Hemphill, accountant
The Post Office and Telegraph Offices, T. R. Hackham, postmaster and telegraph manager, Timor st, Warrnambool
The Sentinel newspaper office; Davidson J. Burnie, proprietor, Koroit st, Warrnambool
Thesinger, Jacob, musician, Hurd st, Portland
The Star hotel, ——, proprietor, Pleasant creek
The Town Hall, Timor st, Warrnambool
The Union Bank of Australia; W. A. Stokes, manager; J. T. Denny, accountant, Julia st, Portland
The Western Times newspaper office; Patmore Gurney, proprietor, also bookseller and stationer, Julia st, Portland
Thomas, George, bootmaker, Barkly st, Ararat
Thomas, H., chemist, Timor st, Warrnambool
Thomas, W. D., carpenter, &c., Digby

DIRECTORY. 233

Thomas, Wm., brickmaker, West Suburbs, Portland
Thomas, Wm., stonemason, Palmer st, Portland
Thomson, M. R., tailor, Camperdown
Thompson, Andrew, watchmaker, Beaufort
Thompson, Buckle, and Black, Messrs., police magistrates, Terang
Thompson, G., and Co., general storekeepers, wine and spirit merchants, Edenhope
Thompson, A., and Co., general storekeepers and Ironmongers, Grey st, Hamilton
Thorn, John, galvanized ironworks, Sackville st, Belfast
Thron, S. W., gunsmith, Cox st, Belfast
Thurman, Wm., Richmond st, Portland
Thurman, Joseph, saddler and harness maker, Casterton
Thurman, Thomas W., Palmer st, Portland
Timor Baths ; L Rub, proprietor, Timor st, Warrnambool
Tobin and Co., grocers and produce dealers, Barkly st, Ararat
Tompkins, Joel, Camp hotel, Beaufort
Tooge, Wm., chemist and druggist, agent for the London and Lancashire Fire and Life Insurance Companies, Beaufort
Tooke, Joseph, Builders' Arms hotel, Percy st, Portland
Townsend, M., general storekeeper, Digby
Trainor, Wm., Racecourse hotel, Hamilton
Trangmar, C. M., storekeeper, Julia st, Portland
Trangmar, James, Julia st, Portland
Trangmar, G., storekeeper, Coleraine
Trew, Lennox, Stag hotel, Sackville st, Belfast
Trew, John S., acting manager London Chartered Bank of Australia, Pleasant creek
Trigg, Wm., Royal hotel, Timor st, Warrnambool
Tucker, James, Ripton hotel, Skipton
Tugby, Samuel, Yangery Prince hotel, Yangery
Tullogh, C., storekeeper, Harrow
Tulloch, Wm., accountant, Percy st, Portland
Turner and White, cabinetmakers, &c., Cox st, Belfast
Tuson, James, baker, Barkly st, Ararat
Tuson, James, Camp hotel, Barkly st, Ararat
Tytherleigh, John, Market square, Portland
Tytherleigh, Robert, blacksmith, Percy st, Portland

V.

Venner, Thomas, storekeeper, Barkly st, Ararat
Vine, Richard, Bentinck st, Portland
Volsey, Charles, watchmaker, &c., Sackville st, Belfast

W.

Wade, —, storekeeper, Steiglitz
Waldron, Edmond, saddler, Terang
Walker, Duncan S., Leura hotel, Camperdown
Walker, Mrs., general storekeeper, Cavendish
Walker, Thomas, agent, Percy st, Portland
Wall, Wm., Rising Sun hotel, Timor st, Warrnambool
Wall, John, Farmers' Inn, Sackville st, Belfast
Wallace, Hugh, Bank hotel, Sackville st, Belfast
Wallis, John, blacksmith, Camperdown
Walsh, Wm., Court House hotel, Colac
Walsh, H., watchmaker, &c., Timor st, Warrnambool
Wardell, Edward, Fern st, Portland
Warden's office ; James Grant Taylor, warden, Barkly st, Ararat
Wardle, Wm., solicitor, Timor st, Warrnambool
Warigoehs, Wm., hairdresser and naturalist, Gawler st, Portland
Warner, Richard, bootmaker, Harrow
Warren, Wm., baker, Colac
Watson, D., Mount Elephant hotel, Mount Elephant
Watson, W., currier, Grey st, Hamilton
Watson, Wm., tailor, Cox st, Belfast
Watson, Robert, blacksmith, Harrow
Watts, Henry, bootmaker, Liebeg st, Warrnambool
Watts, J. A., blacksmith, &c., Coleraine
Webb, Wm., Belfast shoeing forge, Sackville st, Belfast
Webb, Alfred R., accountant, Gawler st, Portland
Welch, Thomas, produce merchant, Beaufort
Wesleyan Church ; Rev. John Catterall, Colac
Weston, Wm., comptroller Savings' Bank, telegraph manager, and postmaster, Colac
Weston, James, chemist and druggist, Steiglitz
Wetzel, Frederick, baker and confectioner, Woodford
White, Thomas E., surgeon, Julia st, Portland
Whitehead, Thomas, grocer and produce dealer, Timor st, Warrnambool
Whyte, Charles, Woolpack Inn, Digby

Wiggins, John, Mount Shadwell hotel, Mortlake
Wild, John T., watchmaker, Sackville st, Belfast
Williams, Mary, dressmaker, Colac
Williams, Corrie M., auctioneer, Camperdown
Williams, Wm., Timor st, Warrnambool
Williams and Co., timber merchants, Timor st, Warrnambool
Williams, Leo, accountant, Hurd st, Portland
Williams, F. L., accountant Bank of Victoria, Julia st, Portland
Williamson, D., Grey st, Hamilton
Wilson, George, chemist and druggist, Julia st, Portland
Wilson and Meats, general store, Wickliffe
Wilson, Rev. Francis R. M., Presbyterian minister, Camperdown
Wilson, James Y., Julia st, Portland
Wilson, Wm. S., storekeeper, Palmer st, Portland
Wilson, —, storekeeper, Thompson st, Hamilton
Wilson, George, chemist, Julia st, Portland

Witton, John, general storekeeper, Inabok
Withers, Charles, draper, Barkly st, Ararat
Womersley, Samuel, smith, &c., Dunkeld
Wood, George, storekeeper, Timor st, Warrnambool
Wood, John, saddler, Barkly st, Ararat
Woodhead, Samuel, storekeeper, wheelwright, &c., Dunkeld
Worrall, John, solicitor, Timor st, Warrnambool
Wortham, F., agent for the London and Lancashire Fire and Life Insurance Companies, Smythesdale
Wotherspoon Brothers, and Co., wholesale wine, spirit, and provision merchants, Beaufort
Woutrick, Alfonse, fruiterer, Steiglitz
Wyat, Wm., Streatham hotel, Streatham
Wyly, Dr., Grey st, Hamilton

Y.

Young, Andrew, saddler, &c., Koroit
Young, Stephen, blacksmith, Barkly st, Ararat
Young, Wm., manager Bank of Victoria, Cox st, Belfast

SANDHURST ALPHABETICAL DIRECTORY.

1866-67.

A.

Aarons, David, labour office Williamson street
Abbot, Joseph H., New Times Boot Mart,
Abell, Thomas, fruiterer, Williamson st
Adams, Alfred, railway porter, Quarry hill
Adler, R. G., carter, Rowan st
Ah Git, storekeeper, Golden square
Aitken, James, produce merchant, Bridge street
Albin, John, miner, Myrtle st
Aldworth and Co., agents for Murray Fishing company, Pall Mall
Aldworth, Alfred, Williamson st
Aldworth, Frank, butcher, Howard place
Alexander, —, tailor, Little Bull st
Alexander, Alfred, Bull st
All Saints' Boys' Day School; W. Willis, master, View Point
All Saints' Girls' Day School; Mrs. Barker, mistress, View Point
Allsop, Thomas, carter, Myrtle st
Allday, S. C., storekeeper, Mitchell st
Allingham and Moore, grocers and drapers, Golden square
Allen, Edwd., Williamson st
Allan, Jas., Chinese store, Golden square
Amblin, Wm., miner, Wattle st
Ambrose, Mrs., Bull st
Amos, Wm., Golden square
Anderson, Wm., Golden square
Andrews, John, collector, Quarry hill
Andrews, Richard, manager Bendigo Gas Company, Beehive chambers, Pall Mall
Anderson, A. W., manager Oriental Bank, View Point
Anderson, Arthur, clerk and draughtsman, View Point
Anderson, Joseph, Mundy st
Andrews, Richard, Quarry hill
Anderson, John, miner, Golden square
Anderson, James, miner, Lucan st
Anderson, John, engineer, Bancroft st
Anderson, James, cattle dealer, Lucan st
Anderson, Wm., tailor, Myers st
Ankel, Chas., bootmaker, High st
Armitage, John, grocer, View Point
Armstrong, Wm., puddler, Dowling st
Armstrong, John, oyster rooms, Williamson st
Arnold, Miss, Hargreaves st
Arthur, Arthur, blacksmith, Bridge st
Askew, John, publican, Lyttleton terrace
Aspinall, George, butcher, Bridge st
Ashley, Wm., engineer, Wattle st
Atherton, George, greengrocer, High st
Atkinson, John H., chemist and druggist, View Point
Atkinson, H. L., Dr., View Point
Avard, R., storekeeper, Dowling st
Aughterson, Otto, Williamson st

B.

Bacon, Joseph, brickmaker, Barnard st
Baderston, T., livery stables, McCrae st

236 Bal ALPHABETICAL Bra

Baird, Wm., hide and skin merchant, Dowling st
Baird, John, storekeeper, Myrtle st
Baird, Samuel, cab driver, Dowling st
Bailey, Mrs., King st
Bailey, J. R., Mitchell st
Bales, Henry, tobacconist, Bull st
Baker, Mrs., View Point
Baker, Wm. J., fruiterer, Bridge st
Balsillie Bros., drapers, Pall Mall
Balsillie, W., McLaren st
Ball, Mrs., widow, Short st
Ball, Thomas, bootmaker, High st.
Balmer, Robert, master National School, Golden gully
Bannerman, Andrew, gold broker to Bank of New South Wales, View Point
Bannerman, Wm., manager Bank of New South Wales, View Point
Bannerman, Andrew, gold broker, Bank of New South Wales, Wattle st
Banfield, James, Bull st
Bank of Victoria—George Valentine, manager, View Point
Bank of Australasia—John Lawford, manager, Pall Mall
Bank of New South Wales—Wm. Bannerman, manager, View Point
Banson, Joseph, Royal Oak hotel, McIvor street
Banfield, John, carpenter, Forest st
Baptist Chapel, Hargreaves st
Barrett, Thomas, miner, Bridge st
Barnett, Adol., M.D., London, M.R.C.S.E., L.S.A.—J.P. for Colony of Victoria, Rowan st
Barker, Mrs., mistress All Saints' Day School, View Point
Barlow, Squire, McCrae st
Barry, David, baker, High st
Barrick, Joseph, saddler, Barkly place
Bartrop, George, clerk of courts, Camp hill
Barkley, J., teacher, McCrae st
Barlow, George, labourer, Hargreaves st
Barnett and Coates, Temple court
Barnett, —, town crier, Dowling st
Bartlett, Steve, sign painter, and ticket writer, Bull st
Barlogy, Joseph, labourer, Bernal st
Bartlett, A. S., painter, Lucan st
Barker, George, wheelwright, Vine st
Barkley, John, master St. Killian's Common School, McCrae st
Bashford, Henry, Williamson st
Bass, Wm., fruiterer, Bridge st
Batchelder, D. P., photographic artist, Pall Mall
Batten, H. T., Glasgow Beef hotel, High street
Bates, —, tinsmith, Bernal st
Baumno, Picard, butcher, Bridge st
Bayne, Alexander, Myrtle st
Baxter, James, Rowan st

Beaver, Henry B., M.D. and surgeon, Bridge st
Beaver, Samuel, wood carter, Dowling st
Beaver, Dr., McCrae st
Beaglehole, H., Golden square
Beaglehole, Wm., fruiterer, High st
Begley, John, quarryman, McCrae st
Bell, Catherine, boarding house, Myrtle st
Bendigo Advertiser office, Hargreaves st
Bendigo Gas Company; Richard Andrews, manager, Beehive Chambers, Pall Mall
Bendigo Independent, Mitchell st
Bendigo Evening News, Williamson st
Bendigo Gas Works, Bridge st
Bennett, R. M., builder, Rowan st
Bennett, Wm., bootmaker, Howard place
Benevolent Asylum, Barnard st
Benson, C., auctioneer, Bancroft st
Benson, Thos., auctioneer and sharebroker, Pall Mall
Beuson and Co., auctioneers, Mundy st
Bentley, Robert, draper, View Place
Bentley, —, miner, Forest st
Bentwich, Isaac, tobacconist, Pall Mall
Berges, John A., baker, View Point
Betham, John, surgeon, View Point
Betham, John, M.R.C.S., and L.S.A., London, View Place, Rowan st
Bignell, Tom, tailor, Temple Court, Pall Mall
Bignell, S., coachbuilder, Bancroft st
Bignell, George, Bull st
Bill, Richard Hawker, Barnard st
Birch, Henry, reefer, View Place
Bird, Wm., reefer, Rowan st
Birtweasel, —, stonemason, Little Bull st
Birthisel, George, labourer, Arnold st
Biessel, Henry, hairdresser, Mundy st
Bitters, —, labourer, Bernal st
Blake, James, farmer, Back creek
Blackham and Co., proprietors *Bendigo Independent* newspaper, Mitchell st
Black, S., reefer, Myers st
Blair, Eliz., boarding house, McLaren st
Blackham, W. G., Mollison st
Blackwell, John, engineer, Wattle st
Blunt, Edward, baker, Myers st
Bockelman, H., Hamburgh hotel, High st
Bock, Herman, saddler, Bridge st
Bock, Charles, storekeeper, Nolan st
Boffey, Thomas, butcher, McIvor st
Boin, John, carpenter, Williamson st
Bolton Bros., butchers, Williamson st
Booth, J., refreshment rooms, Lacan st
Bohr, George, baker, Mitchell st
Bondy, Conrade, miner, Forest st
Bowman, Joseph, engineer, Barkly place
Bowman, Joseph, bootmaker, High st
Boulter, Chas., bootmaker, Barnard st
Bourke, P. F., Bourke's hotel, Bridge st
Boulger, Eliza, widow, Back creek
Bowles, Henry, blacksmith, Wattle st
Bragg, John, cab driver, Dowling st
Brasher, Thomas, fruiterer, Bernal st

Bracher, Henry, News agent, Lucan st
Bradley, Wm., watchmaker, High st
Branan, Michael, Mitchell st
Brandon, Joseph, fancy repository, Pall Mall
Branch, E., timber merchant, High st
Brenan, Stephen, miner, McCrae st
Backnall, Wm., auctioneer, Mundy st
Bridges, Samuel, blacksmith, High st
Bridges, Samuel, Forest st
Bridle, Thomas, tinsmith, Forest st
Bridges, Chas. J., grocer, View Point
Brierly, James, Mundy st
Briggs, Philip, wood turner, Rowan st
Briggs, Wm., saddler, Lyttleton terrace
Brigham, Dexter, restaurant, High st; residence, Forest st
Broadfoot, Mrs., ladies' seminary, Forest street
Brodie, Henry, solicitor, Quarrie hill
Brockley, John, printer and stationer, Bridge st and Lyttleton terrace
Brockevell, Thos., malster, Lucan st
Brown, Chas., accountant and commission agent, Pall Mall
Brown, C. J., accountant, Wattle st
Brown, James, Golden square
Brown, Edward, miner, Back creek
Brown, McDuff, storekeeper, Barnard st
Brown, Mrs., nurse, Vine st
Brown, John, blacksmith, Golden square
Brown, Mrs., Hargreaves st
Brown, Mungo, miner, Dowling st
Brown, John, miner, Dowling st
Brown, John, blacksmith, Golden square
Brown, John, miner, King st
Brown, Joseph, storekeeper, Kangaroo flat
Browne, J., storekeeper, Pegleg gully
Browning, Matthew, grocer, View Point
Bruce, W., and Co., aerated waters and cordial manufacturers, Sandhurst and Eaglehawk
Bucknall Bros., auctioneers, and estate agents, Mundy st
Bucknall, W. A., auctioneer, View Point; residence, Mackenzie st
Buckley, John, miller, McIvor st
Buckley, J., miller, Myers st
Buchan, D., registrar births and deaths, View Point
Budden, Wm., coffee and spice merchant, Williamson st
Bud, Miss, preparatory school, High st
Budden, Wm., Bull st
Burnside, James, sharebroker and agent, Temple Court, Pall Mall
Burrell, Peter, horse dealer, Lyttleton terrace
Burrowes, Wm., reporter, *Bendigo Independent*, Forest st
Burrowes, Wm., Myrtle st
Burrowes, W. N., traveller, Quarry hill
Burrowes, E. D., Royal hotel, High st
Burns, Martin, butcher, McIvor st

Burns, John, farmer, McIvor st
Burdick, Samuel, carpenter, Wattle st
Burke, John, baker, McCrae st
Burton, H., publican, High st
Bush, Albert, grocer, and hay and corn dealer, Williamson st
Burchall, William, bricklayer, Hargreaves street
Butcher, Benjamin, horse dealer, Hargreaves st
Butler, John, miner, Bridge st
Butterworth, Robert, stonemason, King st
Butt, Thomas, bricklayer, King st
Butwistle and Flun, Mitchell st
Boyd, James, M.D., L.S.A., Licentiate of the Faculty of Physicians and Surgeons, View Point
Byrne, Robert, printer, Mackenzie st
Byrne, Morice, Williamson st
Boyd, Hugh, M.D., L.R.C., S.E.L.R.C.P.E., View Point

C.

Cahill, Benjamin, storekeeper, Golden sq
Cahill, Thos., bootmaker, Hargreaves st
Cahill, James, blacksmith, Williamson st
Cahill, John, bootmaker, View Point
Cahill, Cornelius, restaurant, McIvor st
Cairncross, George, draper, Short st
Calder, John, accountant, McLaren st
Caldwell, J. T., quartz reefer, Forest st
Callahan, John, carter, Bernal st
Calvert, Henry, chemist and druggist, View Point
Cameron, Alexander, refreshment room, Mitchell st
Cameron, Denis, commission agent, Mitchell st
Campbell, C. A., bailiff, McLaren st
Campbell, Robert, saddler, &c., High st
Campbell, Alex., labourer, Wattle st
Campbell, H. C., mining surveyor, Rowan street
Campbell, J., carriage inspector, Myers st
Canning, John M., restaurant, Golden sq
Cardus, Jos., accountant, Williamson st
Carey, Michael, refreshment house, Lyttleton terrace
Carinduff, Andrew, tobacconist, Bridge st
Carmichael, James, commercial salesman, King st
Carmody, Thos., High st
Carnes, John, watchmaker, Mitchell st
Carney, Patrick, restaurant, Bernal st
Carpenter, Charles, miner, Mitchell st
Carr, Patrick, bootmaker, Bridge st
Carr, —, horsebreaker, Little Bull st
Carss, Joseph W., bookbinder and stationer, Mitchell st
Carstairs, John, Bricklayers' Arms hotel, McIvor st
Carter, William, painter, McLaren st
Carter, Henry, dentist, Pall Mall

Carter, John J., commercial traveller, Wattle st
Casey, J. J., barrister, Temple Court chambers
Casey, Wm., bookseller and stationer, Mitchell st
Casey, Wm., miner, Wattle st
Casey, Edward, storekeeper, Bernal st
Catholic Church, Bernal st
Central Bank of Western India.—John Hasker, agent, View Point
Chambers, Miss, Hargreaves st
Chandler, Edward, furniture dealer, View Point
Charmer, Edward, soap maker, Bridge st
Chassaud, G. W., teacher, Forest st
Cherry, James, blacksmith, McLaren st
Cherry and Spinks, farriers, Hargreaves street
Chevalier, Thos., photographer, Pall Mall
Chomley, H. M., superintendent of police, Camp hill
Church of England.—Rev. W. R. Croxton, minister, Forest st
Church of England, Kangaroo flat
Church, George, miner, McCrae st
Clackson, Mrs., dressmaker, Forest st
Clancy, M., Bernal st
Clapperton, Adam, Golden square
Clay, Daniel, bootmaker, Wattle st
Clarke, John, Back creek
Clark, Mrs., Bridge st
Clark, Robert, Golden square
Clark, Ann, storekeeper, Barnard st
Cleary, Ellen, refreshment rooms, Lucan street
Clegg, James N., Allies hotel and restaurant, Bull st
Clegg, Halstead, grocer, Bull st
Cleugh, James, wheelwright, Lyttleton terrace
Coates, Rosanna, Myrtle st
Cobb and Co., coach factory, Mundy st
Cobb and Co., coach office, Williamson st
Cockerill, Richard, bootmaker, Mitchell st
Code, Edward, Haymarket dining rooms, Williamson st
Cohn, Julius, brewer, residence, Bancroft street
Cohn Brothers, Bridge st
Cohn, Jacob, brewer, Barkly place
Cole, Wm., brickmaker, Arnold st
Cole, Sydney G., traveller, King st
Colonial Bank of Australasia: Malcombe Tolmie, manager, Pall Mall
Coleman, William, carpenter, McCrae st
Collie, Mrs., labour office, McCrae st
Collier, C. H., compositor, Myrtle st
Collcutt, Edwin, grocer, Williamson st
Collopy, Thomas, dairyman, Arnold st
Combes, H., tinsmith, Kangaroo flat
Common School: — Richards, master, Golden square
Commander, M. and E., grocers, Mundy st

Conelly, Thomas, miner, McIvor st
Corneilly, Thomas, labourer, Bramble st
Connelly, J., puddler, Dowling st
Connelly, Thomas J., ironmonger, High st
Connelly, Thomas, Barkly place
Conway, Joseph, bootmaker, Hargreaves street
Conroy, Patrick, general store, McCrae st
Conroy, John, wheelwright, Lucan st
Congregational Church, Quarry hill
Congregational Church, Forest st
Cook, Wm., roofer, Mackenzie st
Cooper, John, timber merchant, Bridge st
Cooper, Miss, dressmaker, Bull st
Cooper, Mrs., Beehive hotel, Mitchell st
Connoughton, James, refreshment rooms, Golden square
Corbett, Daniel, miner, Dowling st
Costello, Mrs., refreshment rooms, Kangaroo flat
Cotton, Charles R., solicitor, &c., Bull st
Court of Petty Sessions, View Point
Coutts, Franklin, McCrae st
Cove, Charles, bootmaker, Bridge st
Cowper, John, carpenter, McLaren st
Cox, G. S., solicitor's clerk, Bancroft st
Coyle, Peter, farrier, McCrae st
Craven, Elijah, confectioner, High st
Crawford, Charles, Ship Inn, Back creek
Crawford, Abraham, draper, Pall Mall
Craig, George N., sharebroker, View Point
Craig, James, draper, View Point
Craig, George N., mining manager, Forest street
Creswick, George, McIvor st
Cremins, Michael, miner, McIvor st
Crew, Wm., goldsmith, Forest st
Crimins, John, puddler, Dowling st
Crowson, John, Blue Bell Inn, High st
Crowley, Mrs., milliner and wax flower maker, Williamson st
Croxton, Rev. Wm. R., minister of Church of England, Forest st; residence, View Point
Croft, —, carpenter, Barnard st
Croft, John D., sharebroker, View Point
Crowe, J., British Queen hotel, Bridge st
Crump, Thomas, miner, McIvor st
Cruikshank, Dr., surgeon, Lyttleton terrace
Cullen, James J., house painter, &c., Mitchell st
Cullinger, Thomas, Robert Burns hotel, Mitchell st
Cully, Thomas, Imperial hotel, High st
Cunneeo, Peter, store and produce dealer, Bridge st
Cunningham, W., coachmaker, Dowling st
Cunningham, Frederick, grocer, Williamson st
Curtain, Patrick, miner, Back creek
Curnegan, Wm., plasterer, Bernal st
Currie, Robert, draper, Bridge st

Curtin, Patrick, labourer, Back creek
Cutten, C. E., Bramble st
Cutten, C. F., solicitor, Beehive chambers, Pall Mall
Cuthbert, David, refreshment room, Bridge st

D.

Daley, Charles, carpenter, Mitchell st
Darby, Edmund, tinsmith, Barnard st
Darcey, John, storekeeper, McCrae st
Davidson, Wm., timber merchant, Mitchell st
Davies, Robert, gasfitter, McCrae st
Davis, John Thomas, draper, Pall Mall
Davis, David, mason, Barnard st
Davis, Wm., fruiterer, High st
Davis, Samuel, wheelwright, Dowling st
Davis, Edwin Thos., compositor, King st
Davison, Nathan, bootmaker, High st
Dawbarn, —, Golden square
Dawbarn, John, bookseller and stationer, View Point
Daws, Francis, restaurant, McIvor st
Deeham, Patrick J., Black Swan hotel, McCrae st
Degraves and Co., Wm., merchants, Williamson st
Dehn, Henry, baker, High st
Dempsey, Alex., quarryman, Myers st
Dempter, Wm., peddler, Mitchell st
Dennison, Joseph, brickmaker, McLaren street
Denovan, W. D. C., sharebroker, Pall Mall
Donovan, Mary Ann, storekeeper, Barnard st
Derham and Son, Hall of Commerce, Mundy st
Derham, T. P., draper and outfitter, Pall Mall
Derham, T. P., draper, McLaren st
Devereaux, James, miner, McCrae st
Deverell, Spencer R., manager telegraph office, Mitchell st
Devine, Sackey, miner, Dowling st
Dick, James, Barnard st
Dick, Robert, butcher, Dowling st
Dickson, Miss, ladies' school, Rowan st
Dickson, David, sharebroker, Pall Mall
District Survey Office, View point
Donnelly, John, mail guard, Vine st
Donohue, Rody, labourer, Mollison st
Donolly, Julia, laundress, Barnard st
Donovan, Patrick, cab driver, Hargreaves street
Dooley, John, bootmaker, Kangaroo flat
Doran, Joseph, schoolmaster, Lyttleton terrace
Douglas, C. W., clerk, Bramble st
Dew, Timothy, dairyman, Mitchell st
Dowers, George, bootmaker, Lucan st
Dowling, —, miner, Hargreaves st
Downey, Mrs., refreshment room, Bridge street

Doyle, James, ironmonger, Mitchell st
Dravis, J. T., draper, Barkly place
Dresher, Phillip, watchmaker, Bridge st
Drew, Wm., Bernal st
Drew and Conway, tinsmiths, Mundy st
Drought, Wm., police sergeant, Camp hill
Drury, John, Williamson st
Duncan, J. C., clerk railway department, Quarry hill
Duncan, George, Mitchell st
Dunn, Daniel, Williamson st
Dunnington, Robert, saddler, Lyttleton terrace
Dulrichie, Jas., bootmaker, Golden square
Duven, Thomas J., restaurant, Mundy st
Duxbury, John, blacksmith, Myers st
Duxbury, John, farrier, Hargreaves st
Dwyer, John, London and Dublin hotel, Mitchell st
Dwyer, Patrick, contractor, Arnold st
Dwyer, Mary, teacher, Back creek

E.

Eadie, Dr., Forest st
Eadie and McIntyre, chemists and druggists, High st
Ebsworth, Wm., hatter, Dowling st
Egan, Patrick, McCrae st
Egan, Thomas, peddler, Arnold st
Egan, Patrick, farrier, McCrae st
Engel, Nicholas, German bandmaster, Bridge st
Ennis, Bernard, sergeant of police, Camp hill
Elliott, George, brewer, Golden square
Elliott, A., brewer, Golden square
Ellis, Samuel, Supreme Court hotel, Howard place
Ellis, Frederick, clerk, Quarry hill
Ellison, Henry, clerk, Williamson st
Esterhank, Eaglestone, and Co., cattle salesmen, Williamson st
Evans, Mrs., Hargreaves st
Ewart, Robert B., engineer, Quarry hill
Ewington, Wm., farrier, Back creek

F.

Fairchild, Joseph, pianoforte maker, Williamson st
Fairley, M., librarian and stationer
Farman, B. and W., carpenters, Kangaroo flat
Farrington, Wm., brickyards, Back creek
Farrell, James, Barkly place
Fasherly, —, miner, Barnard st
Faul, Francis G., builder, Hargreaves st
Fawn, James, London brewery, Golden square
Fay, Mrs., laundress, Myers st
Fealey, W. H., letter carrier, Dowling st
Featherstone, J. E., High st
Ferguson, Robert, puddler, Dowling st

Ferguson, John, blacksmith, Kangaroo flat
Ferrand, Mrs., widow, Mackenzie st
Field, David, plumber, Mitchell st
Findlay, John, grocer, High st
Finlay and Co., drapers, View point
Finn, Peter, mason, Dowling st
Finster, Arthur, professor of music, Little Bull st
Fire Brigade Depôt, High st
Fisher, John, clerk, Barnard st
Flack, F. P., painter, Dowling st
Flegg, W. M., solicitor, Short st
Flegg, Wm. M., solicitor, Beehive chambers, Pall Mall
Flood, Patrick, bootmaker, Bridge st
Flood, Patrick, wheelwright, Bridge st
Fletcher, Edmund, butcher, Mundy st
Fletcher, G. A., town clerk, Bramble st
Fletcher, Albert, Williamson st
Fletcher, Albert, butcher, McLaren st
Flemming, Mary, boarding-house, Mitchell street
Flemming, George, mason, Quarry hill
Follen, Patrick, draper, Lucan st
Foley, Denis, labourer, Bernal st
Foley, Michael, miner, McCrae st
Forbes, —, miner, Forest st
Forbes, Thomas, Golden square
Ford, John, puddler, Bramble st
Ford, Mrs., High st
Forest Street Common School : Daniel Kennedy, master
Foreman, Thomas, butcher and storekeeper, Kangaroo flat
Fosdyke, G., draper, Forest st
Fosdyke, Gardner, draper and outfitter, Pall Mall
Forsdyke, Gardner, draper, Howard place
Forsyth, James, Mitchell st
Foulger, John, Star and Garter inn, Mitchell st
Fox, Michael, labourer, Bramble st
Fox, Robert Thomas, general storekeeper, Melvor st
Foy, Francis, wholesale produce store, McIvor st
Francis Brothers, importers and general merchants, Pall Mall
Francis Brothers, Beehive stores, Hargreaves st
Francis, Richard, Mundy st
Fraser, James, quartz reefer, Myrtle st
Fraser, Hugh, blacksmith, Bridge st
Fraser, Lachlan, baker, Lyttleton terrace
Fraser, Alexander, cab-driver, McCrae st
Free Library and Reading Rooms, View point
Freemason hotel livery bait stables, Mundy street
Frew, David, grocer, Williamson st
Friedman, Rev. Isaac, Jewish minister, Dowling st
Frost, Mrs., Mundy st

Frost, Frederick, mattress maker, Wattle street
Frost, Charles, draper and outfitter, Pall Mall
Fuall, James, McCrae st
Fuller, —, tailor, Melvor st
Fyson, Cecilia, widow, Williamson st

G.

Gabriel, John, blacksmith, Mollison st
Gabriel, J., coachbuilder, Hargreaves st
Gabriel and Bull, butchers, Mitchell st
Gale, C., governor of gaol, Camp hill
Galding, John, miner, McIvor st
Gallagher, Daniel, produce merchant, High street
Gambetti, Chas., William Tell inn, Golden square
Garber, John, miner, Bridge st
Gardner, John, general store, High st
Garsed, Edward, chemist and druggist, Howard place
Gay, Wm., fruiterer, Pall Mall
Gay, Wm., Hargreaves st
Gengnogel, Charles, baker, High st
Gerson, Hyman, boot and clothing store, Bridge st
Gibbie, James, banker, View place
Gibbs, Henry, storekeeper, Dowling st
Gibson, George, refreshment rooms, Back creek
Gibson, Thomas, carpenter, Vine st
Gill, W. H., quartz miner, Rowan st
Gissinge, R. M., chemist and druggist, Bridge st
Gittins, W. D., butcher, Williamson st
Gladwin, Richard, blacksmith, Kangaroo flat
Glinnon, John, refreshment room, Bull st
Goddard, Job, storekeeper, High st
Goddard, Charles F., Waterloo hotel, Bridge st
Gold Office of Bank of New South Wales. —Andrew Bannerman, gold broker, View point
Gollmick, Wm., professor of music and languages, Barkly place
Golightly, Wm., carpenter, Quarry hill
Gooda, Wm., brickyards, Back creek
Goode, John, painter, Short st
Goode, J., painter and glazier, Forest st
Goodwin, James, produce merchant, View point
Gordon, Joseph, miner, Myrtle st
Gorman, Francis, miner, King st
Gosson, Richard, professor of music and pianist, Little Bull st
Goudge and Sibley, tanners and curriers, Bull st
Gowan, James, Limerick Castle hotel, Williamson st
Grange, Mrs., Hargreaves st
Grant, J. C., confectioner, Barkly place

Grant, John Charles, confectioner, Pall Mall
Grant, Wm., baker, High st
Gray, Thomas, blacksmith, Lyttleton terrace
Gray, Robt., tobacconist, High st
Gray, Samuel, Golden square
Greasley, Henry, butcher, Golden square
Green, Wm., bootmaker, Back creek
Green, Henry, Rifle Brigade hotel, View Point
Greives, Mrs., refreshment room, High st
Griffin, Mrs., draper and haberdasher, View Point
Gripes and Co., Francis, engineers and ironfounders, Wattle st
Gripe, Francis, ironfounder, Mackenzie st
Grovening, Julius, chemist, High st
Groome, Mrs., dressmaker, Mitchell st
Grosman, F. A., View Point hotel
Guitler, August, bootmaker, High st
Guldon, Fanny, laundress, Bernard st
Gulloch, Thomas, View Point
Gunn, Wm., Glasgow Arms hotel, Kangaroo Flat

H.

Hackett, Pat., storekeeper, Charlston road
Haday, Thomas, miner, McCrae st
Hadley, John C., Bendigo hotel, Bridge st
Hall, Joshua, tinsmith, Bridge st
Hall, J., storekeeper, Kangaroo Flat
Hall, James, news agent, Forest st
Hall, Thomas, American boarding house, Hargreaves st
Hallas, Nathaniel, musician, Bramble st
Halliger, Henry, furniture warehouse, View Point
Hallins, Mrs., High st
Hamble, —, reefer, Williamson st
Hamilton, James, stationer, Williamson street
Hancock, Rd., Bakers' Arms, Bridge st
Hands, Edward, butcher, Forest st
Hannan, Denis, carter, Dowling st
Hansen, C., saddler, Dowling st
Harkness and Gray, grocers, High st
Harrison, E., journalist, Mackenzie st
Harris, James, carpenter, Myers st
Harlow, John, Crescent hotel, Bridge st
Harrison, Robert, bootmaker, Golden square
Harvey, Thomas, butcher, McCrae st
Harris, Thomas, Crown hotel and dining rooms, Hargreaves st
Hartley, —, compositor, Wattle st
Harper, Wm., tentmaker, Bridge st
Hardll, James, watchmaker and jeweller, High st
Harding, B., foreman of works, Bancroft street
Harcourt, J. M., proprietor of Bendigo Evening News, Williamson st

Harris, W. J., storekeeper, Back creek
Harrison, Mrs., day school, Mitchell st
Hart, George, Bridge st
Harris, Mrs. John, Mundy st
Harper, George, corn factor, Lyttleton terrace
Hart, G. W., Beehive chambers
Hart, James, engineer, Wattle st
Harper, Wm., Globe hotel, Bridge st
Hassell and Daly, contractors and builders, Hargreaves st
Hasker, John, official agent, Sandhurst mining district
Hassell, John, builder, McLaren st
Hatty, David, Golden square
Hawkins, James, Terminus hotel, Mitchell street
Hawkins, Mary Ann, dressmaker, Mitchell st
Hawley, John, miner, McCrae st
Hawkins, Geo., paperhanging warehouse, View Point
Hawkesworth, Alf., saddlers' ironmonger, Mitchell st
Hawkins, Otto, accountant, Capel court, Pall Mall
Hawkins, George, paperhanger, Forest st
Hayes, Patrick, grocer, Bridge st
Hayes, James Bernard, Dean, St. Killian's Church, McCrae st
Haynes, Joseph, bakery, Arnold st
Hayes, P., Bridge st
Hayes, John Thomas, baker, Hargreaves st
Haynes, James, Locan st
Haynes, Richard, blacksmith, Myrtle st
Haynes, J. G., confectioner, Pall Mall
Hayes, Rev. J. B., D.D., Catholic Church, Bernal st
Heaney, Michael, tailor, Back creek
Hearse, J., veterinary surgeon, McCrae st
Heffernan, Michael, Albert hotel, McCrae street
Heffernan, Wm., Lyceum Theatre hotel, Pall Mall
Heffernan, Wm., Shamrock stables, Williamson st
Heffernan and Crawley, Shamrock hotel, Pall Mall
Heffernan, Jeremiah, Victoria hotel, Pall Mall
Heffernan, Wm., Union hotel, Williamson street
Heire, Daniel, greengrocer, Bridge st
Helm, J. A. C., barrister, Hall st
Helm, J. A. C., barrister, View Point
Hemming, Wm., grocer, Forest st
Hemming, Wm., grocer, View Point
Henderson, R., carpenter, Wattle st
Heon, Charles A., compositor, Barkly place
Hennessy, Michael, restaurant, Mundy st
Henson, Thomas, carpenter, Quarry hill
Henright, Patrick, miner, Arnold st

2 i

Henry, Miss, dressmaker, View Point
Henry and Co., hay and corn dealers, High st
Hermann, F. J., dyer, Bridge st
Hickey, John, miner, Bernal st
Hickey, James, Harp and Shamrock hotel, Mundy st
Hickman, Henry, hairdresser, Williamson street
Hilderman, C., watchmaker, Bridge st
Hill, Frederick, butcher, Bridge st
Hill, Moore, commission agent, Lyttleton terrace
Hill, Captain Moore, Bull st
Hoad and Co., tailors and outfitters, Pall Mall
Hoad, Henry, draper, View place
Hoaresley, Edwd., barrister, Gould's buildings, Bull st
Hobson, Mrs., Bridge st
Hodgson, W., plumber, Myers st
Hogan, Patrick, puddler, Bernal st
Hogan, Thomas, refreshment room, Back creek
Hogg, Ann, widow, Dowling st
Hogg, S. P., auctioneer and sharebroker, View Point
Hoggins, Park., residence, Golden square
Holahan, James, Bendigo livery stables, Williamson st
Holdsworth, John, chemist and druggist, Pall Mall
Holdsworth, John, wholesale druggist, Williamson st
Holland, Alfred, wheelwright, High st
Holland, Wm., brickmaker, Arnold st
Holloway, B., labourer, Wattle st
Holmes, G. and J., ironmongers, McCrae street
Holton, Edward, boot and shoe warehouse, Pall Mall
Holmes, J. and W., lithographers, McCrae street
Holmes, Mr., Forest creek
Hopkins, —, Kangaroo flat
Hopper, O. J., assistant borough clerk, Quarry hill
Horbury and Smithurst, iron, tin, and zinc workers, Mitchell st
Horn, Robert, hairdresser, Bridge st
Horner and Boswick, brickmakers, Back creek
Horsfall, John, coachmaker, Quarry hill
Horsfall, Fredk., labourer, Golden square
Horton, J. W., M.R.C., veterinary surgeon, Hargreaves st
Horwood, J., and Sons, ironfounders and engineers, Vine st
Horwood, J., ironfounder, Mackenzie st
Hoskins, John, storekeeper, Quarry hill
Hoskins, James, blacksmith, High st
Hosking, W., engineer, Wattle st
Hourigan, James, Metropolitan hotel, corner Bull and Hargreaves sts

Houston, Robert, sexton Sandhurst Cemetery
Howard, J. J., storekeeper, McIvor st
Howard, Miss, ladies' seminary, Myers st
Howe, G. A., Fleece hotel, Charleston st
Howler, Frederick, tobacconist, View point
Hoyle, John, carter, McIvor st
Hughes, Edward, timber merchant, View place
Hughes, Wm., grammar school, Williamson st
Hughes, James, baker, Kangaroo flat
Holbert, Henry, High st
Hull, George, storekeeper, Rowan st
Hulley, Joseph, grocer, Mundy st
Hunt, Wm., bricklayer, McLaren st
Hunter, Joseph, miner, Dowling st
Hunter, J., miner, Dowling st
Hurst, Ambrose, wheelwright, Mitchell st
Hutchison, Mrs., Bancroft st
Huxtable, Edmund, watchmaker, Pall Mall
Hyndman, David, Australian hotel, Bridge street

L

Irvine and Co., J., engineers and founders, Shamrock st
Isaacs, Samuel, general dealer, Bridge st

J.

Jackson, Henry, ironmonger, Forest st
Jackson, W. G., hide merchant, Back creek
Jackson, Henry, ironmonger, View point
Jackburn, Thomas, confectioner, Hargreaves st
Jackson, Henry, bullion and discount offices, View point
Jacobs, John, bootmaker, Howard place
Jacobs and Solomon, boot and clothing store, Bridge st
Jacobs, S., jeweller, Myers st
Jalland, G. J., Hobson's hotel, Bridge st
James, Charles, labourer, Mitchell st
James, Rev. Thomas, Wesleyan minister, Forest st
Jamieson, Mrs., Bull st
Jennings, W., nurseryman, Kangaroo flat
Jennings, George, cordial maker, McIvor street
Jenson, Frederick, Prince of Wales hotel, High st
Jervis, J. P., Sandhurst
Johns, John, mason, Short st
Johnson, Robert, Freemason's hotel, Pall Mall
Johnson, John, butter merchant, Lucan st
Johnson, William, carpenter, McIvor st
Johnson, W. K., Sandhurst hotel, Lyttleton terrace
Johnson, Mrs., Hargreaves st
Jones, A. J., Mundy st
Jones, Ralph, produce dealer, Golden sq

Jones, Abel, brickmaker, Back creek
Jones, A. J., Anchor brewery, McCrea st
Jones, John, bootmaker, Barnard st
Jones, Richard E., butcher, McIvor st
Jones, Henry W., greengrocer, Bridge st
Jordan, Dr., Forest st
Joseph and Co., jewellers, Pall Mall
Juler, Jacob, tobacconist, Bull st
Jung, Philip, National hotel, Bridge st
Junge, August, tobacconist, High st

K

Kalm, Henry, miner, Dowling st
Kane, Patrick, Mitchell st
Kealey, Peter, engineer, Mitchell st
Kensley, F., boarding house, Short st
Keller, John, tailor, High st
Kelly, Denis, restaurant, McIvor st
Kelly, James, Full and Penty hotel, Bull street
Kelly, Wm., residence, Golden square
Kelly, James, engineer, High st
Kelly, A., labourer, McLaren st
Kelly, John, Back creek
Kennedy, Mrs., Bridge st
Kennedy's Niagara hotel, corner Mundy and McCrae sts
Kennedy, James, miner, Mitchell st
Kennedy, John, labourer, Barnard st
Kennedy, James, labourer, Wattle st
Kenny, W. A., merchant, Mundy st; residence, View st
Kenworthy, Joseph, refreshment room, Williamson st
Keppler, Charles, baker, View Point
Kerr, John, plumber and gas fitter, Bull st
Kerr, Wm., refreshment rooms, High st
Kerr, Charles H., draper, Pall Mall
Kershaw, H., miner, Myrtle st
Kessler, Hendrick, bootmaker, Mitchell st
Kilborde, Peter, contractor, Back creek
Killberg, Gilbert, carpenter, Back creek
Kilden, Martin, Brian Boru hotel and general store, McIvor st
Kincelle, Michael, wheelwright, Vine st
Kilgour, Mrs., Mitchell st
King, H., oil and kerosene store, McIvor street
King, Robert, bricklayer, Forest st
King, Adam, assayer, Forest st
King, Samuel, assistant market inspector, Dowling st
King, Henry, paperhanger and stainer, Pall Mall
King, John, refreshment room, Golden sq
Kitchen, Solomon, Argyle hotel, Lyttleton terrace
Kitchen, Solomon, Alexander hotel, Mundy st
Kirkby, G. W., cordial maker, High st
Kleeberger, Julius, labourer, Arnold st
Kleeberger, Hugo, wine and spirit merchant, Bridge st

Kleinsgarn, Anton, bootmaker, High st
Klemm, F. C., wine and spirit merchant, Mundy st; residence, Mollison st
Kneese, Otto Henry, miner, Lucas st
Knight, Wm., saddler, Pall Mall
Knight, Chas., bricklayer, Arnold st
Knight, Wm., saddler, Myers st
Kofford, Mrs., McCrae st
Kuhl, Peter, tinsmith, Golden square

L

Lambert, T., leather merchant, Mundy st
Lambert, Chris., butcher, Williamson st
Landsell, George, soap and candle manufacturer; residence, Forest st
Landvoight, Dr., Forest st
Lane, —, miner, Quarry hill
Langton, A., sub-treasurer, Camp hill
Langton, Samuel, Bull st
Lange, John, coach painter, Barnard st
Lansell, Wm., chandler, McIvor st
Lansell, Geo., soap and candle manufacturer, View Point
Latham, Wm., hairdresser, View Point
Latham, John, reefer, Mollison st
Lawden, J., bricklayer, Myers st
Lawler, John, Kangaroo flat
Layes, C., bootmaker, Mundy st
Lawford, John, manager Bank of Australasia, Pall Mall
Leahy and Meagher, storekeepers, McIvor street
Legg, Mrs., day school, Mitchell st
Lev, J. B., Builders' Arms hotel, Mitchell street
Lee, Geo., The Butts hotel, Williamson st
Leech, Frederick, musician, Bramble st
Leeds, Michael, sharebroker, Beehive Chambers, Pall Mall
Leggatt, J., tinsmith, Bridge st
Lemmon, J., refreshment rooms, High st
Lenahan, Thomas, labourer, Back creek
Lewis, Samuel, hairdresser, Myers st
Lewis, Samuel, hairdresser, Bull st
Lewis, Leon W., tobacconist, Pall Mall
Levi, Samuel, Bull st
Leyboase, Ed., fancy repository, High st
Liddle and Hunter, brewers, King's bridge, Bridge st
Ligee, William, refreshment room, Bridge street
Lionett, John, Williamson st
Litzenberger, Jerkol, baker, Golden sq
Little, R., boot salesman, Paddy's gully
Lloyd, L., coachmaker, Lyttleton terrace
Lloyd, A. M., cattle inspector, Charleston road
Loch, Daniel, carpenter, Mollison st
Lockhart, John, general storekeeper, McIvor st
Lockyer, Margaret, householder, View place
Longbottom, Charles B., Mitchell st

Lohmann, John, tobacconist, High st
Long, Francis, baker, Barnard st
Loridan, Jean Baptiste, corn merchant, High st
Lotherington, J. K., bookkeeper, Barnard street
Love, Robert A., architect, &c., Pall Mall; residence, Ironbark
Lovell, Mrs., restaurant, High st
Lovell, —, Mitchell st
Lovett, John, miner, Back creek
Lowden, John, Lowden's hotel, McCrae st
Lucas, Mrs., ladies' seminary, Barkly place
Lunn, Wm., cabinetmaker, Bull st
Lupton, J. E., deputy sheriff, Camp hill
Lutheran Church, Mackenzie st
Luxton, James, Devonshire Arms hotel, Kangaroo flat
Lyceum Theatre; Varley and Hoskins, lessees, Pall Mall
Lyon, Frederick, paperhanger, Bridge st
Lyons, Philip, general dealer, Bull st

M.

Macartney, J. W., Quarry hill
Macartney, John N., *Argus* agent, Pall Mall
McDonald, Angus, general store, High st
McDonald, Mrs., Williamson st
Machin, Robert, printer, Myrtle st
McIndoe, R., blacksmith, Barnard st
Mackay and Co., *Daily and Weekly Advertiser* office, Hargreaves st; and agents for the *Riverine Herald*, Echuca
Mackay, Wm., railway porter, Quarry hill
Mackay, Angus, printer, McLaren st
McKinney, Mrs., refreshment room, Bridge st
McKinley, Mrs., refreshment room, High street
Mackins, Mrs., refreshment room, Golden square
Macord, Samuel, commercial dining rooms, Hargreaves st
McPherson, L., and Co., auctioneers and cattle salesmen, Pall Mall
McPherson and Co., cattle salesmen, Hargreaves st
Madden, Merton, Golden square
Magee, Arthur, storekeeper, Lucan st
Magee, James, miner, King st
Mager, Arthur, timber merchant, Bridge street
Mahaffy, James, bootmaker, Williamson street
Mahon, Mrs., McIvor st
Mahony, Daniel, puddler, High st
Mailer, James, bootmaker, Mitchell st
Malone, B., McCrae st
Malone, R., produce merchant, McIvor st
Malone, Anthony, restaurant, McIvor st

Mann, George H., Bull st
Mansfield, John, carpenter, Mitchell st
Mappin, T., cutler, Hargreaves st
Marrinon, —, butcher, McIvor st
Martell, W., butcher, High st
Martin, George, carpenter, Myrtle st
Martin, Mrs., laundress, Dowling st
Marwick, —, contractor, Myrtle st
Marks, Henry, Hargreaves st
Marks, Henry, auctioneer, Bull st
Marquart, Herman, tailor, Mackenzie st
Marshall, David, secretary Mechanics' Institute, McCrae st
Marshall, Joe. Golden square
Martley, M., Beehive chambers
Martley, James F., barrister, Bull st
Masonic Hall, Myers st
Mason, Thomas, horsedealer, Short st
Masdyke, John, engineer, Wattle st
Mathieson, Duncan, refreshment rooms
Matherson, Johanna, High st
Matson, Henry, restaurant, High st
Matcer, John, butcher, Forest st
Matthews, J., bootmaker, McIvor st
Mawdsley, John, painter, Golden square
Max, —, hairdresser, Forest st
Max, S., hairdresser, Pall Mall
Maxwell, Edwin Stanford, M.D., M.R.C.S. Lon., Kangaroo flat
Maynard, Hy., Rowan st
McArthur, John Carter, Bridge st
McColl, Hugh, storekeeper, Sheepwash road
McCarthy, Con., miner, Williamson st
McCling, —, fitter, Vine st
McCleeland, J., storekeeper, Bridge st
McCulloch, Alexander, commission agent, Mollison st
McCullum, Mrs., Williamson st
McDevitt, Hugh, produce salesman, Myers st
McDonald, C. C., sodawater manufacturer, McCrae st
McDonald, Mary Ann, refreshment room, Mitchell st
McDonald, —, bone merchant, Mitchell st
McDonald, Alex., carpenter, Mitchell st
McDonnell J., and Co., grocers, Golden square
McDougall, Donald, Mundy st
McDougall, D., agent for Australian Insurance Co., Beehive chambers, Pall Mall
McEwen, Margaret, widow, Barkly place
McGee, —, Golden square
McGrath, Patrick, Bull st
McGrath, Edward, grocer, High st
McGrath, Thomas, compositor, Forest st
McGregor, Mrs., refreshment room, Williamson st
McIntyre, John, mayor, Barnard st
McIvor, John, tinsmith, Bridge st
McKee, —, miner, Forest st
McKee, R. H., drover, Wattle st

McKenzie, —, Quarry hill
McKenzie, D., tailor, Barnard st
McKinnon, Wm., storekeeper, Mollison st
McLachlan, Lachlan, police magistrate, View Point
McLachlan, John, storekeeper, Rowan st
McLachlan, L., police magistrate, Bancroft st
McLaggen, James, baker, McCrae st
McLean and Bruce, cabinetmakers, High street
McLennan, Alexander, fancy bread and biscuit baker, McCrae st
McLeod, James, confectioner, Mitchell st
McLevy, —, Mundy st
McLoughlin, Mrs., laundress, Dowling st
McLoy, John, restaurant, Mitchell st
McMahon, Patrick, puddler, Bridge st
McManning, Thomas, miner, Barnard st
McMaster, Alexander, labourer, Williamson st
McMichael, Wm., printer and stationer, Pall Mall
McMichael, D., engineer, Wattle st
McMickan, James, Mitchell st
McMillin, W., clerk, Kangaroo flat
McNamara, Jas., blacksmith, Hargreaves street
McNamara, James, blacksmith, Bernal st
McNamara, Thomas, blacksmith, Bramble st
McPherson, —, carpenter, Quarry hill
McVey, John, general blacksmith and farrier, High st
Meader, W., Albion hotel, View Point
Meagher, Thomas, puddler, Lucan st
Meagher, Michael, Temple Court hotel, Pall Mall
Meakin, Benjamin, Golden square
Mechanics' Institute; David Marshall, secretary, McCrae st
Medlin, T., tailor, Wattle st
Melrose, John, jeweller and dentist, Bridge st
Merrigan, Andrew, refreshment rooms, Golden square
Merrill, Busza, and Densley, steam saw mills, Back creek
Meyer, Michael, miner, McCrae st
Michael, John, refreshment rooms, Kangaroo flat
Mier, Mrs., Golden square
Mills, T., Bull st
Mills, Alfred J., cooper, Lucan st
Miller, W. C., painter, Vine st
Miller, James, draper, Golden square (Post office receiving box)
Miller, Philip, baker, Myrtle st
Miller, Adam, engineer, Barnard st
Miller, John, reefer, Mackenzie st
Miller, —, Quarry hill
Miller, Wm., blacksmith, Back creek
Milne, Edward, carpenter, Barnard st
Milward, C., bricklayer, Forest st

Minter, James, storekeeper, Back creek
Minty, Wm., fruiterer, Bridge st
Mitchell, John, blacksmith, Mundy st
Mitchell, J., blacksmith, Myers st
Mitchell, John, shoemaker, Hargreaves st
Mitchell, Madame, vocalist, Barnard st
Molle, L., bootmaker, Mackenzie st
Molloy, J. T., Bath hotel, Bridge st
Mollison, Crawford, warden, Camp hill
Monahan, Mary, refreshment rooms, Bernal st
Montgomery, James, solicitor, Forest st
Montgomery, James, solicitor, Bull st
Moody, Joseph, jeweller and watchmaker, View Point
Moody, Mrs., Short st
Mooney, Denis, cattle dealer, Bancroft st
Mooney, James, labourer, Barnard st
Moore, —, Bull st
Moore, Mary, dressmaker, Bridge st
Moore and Co., F., carriers, Williamson st
Moore, Thompson, Kangaroo flat
Moore Brothers and Co., storekeepers, Kangaroo flat
Moore, Frank, carrier, Forest st
Moorhead, Robert, wine and spirit merchant, High st
Moran, Matthew, swimming baths, Mitchell st
Moran, Charles A., bootmaker, Hargreaves st
Moran, Charles, shoemaker, Williamson street
Moran, Maurice, printer, Hargreaves st
Moran, W., bootmaker, McIvor st
Morey, B., saddler, Myers st
Morey, Barnard, saddler, Williamson st
Morris, Philip, general dealer, Bull st
Morley, Samuel, gardener, Nolan st
Morris, C., collector, McLaren st
Morrack, G. P., teacher, Kangaroo flat
Morton, John, carpenter, Wattle st
Morton, John, Mitchell st
Morton, Mrs., Short st
Morrison, Rev. —, clergyman, Barnard st
Moss, Wm., cabinetmaker, High st
Motteram, John P., solicitor, McCrae st
Moulden, Thomas, brewer, Barkly place
Mowley, Cornelius, miner, Arnold st
Moyle, Thomas, painter, Barnard st
Mulconry, James, Town Hall hotel, Lyttleton terrace
Mulfeny, John, contractor, Myers st
Mulligan, James, Mitchell st
Mulvall, D., restaurant, McIvor st
Mumford, John T., miner, Dowling st
Mundy, Neil, miner, Arnold st
Munro, Duncan, tailor, View Point
Murphy, Phillip, general store, McIvor st
Murphy, Wm., builder, Forest st
Murphy, Peter, labourer, Quarry hill
Murry, Catherine, boarding house, Williamson st
Murray Fishing Company, Pall Mall

N.

Nadin, Mrs., laundress, Williamson st
Napier, Wm., Williamson st
Nott, Mrs., dressmaker, High st
Nolan, Keron, Mitchell st
Norton, Joseph, stoker, Quarry hill
Norworthy, J. N. W., butcher, Mitchell st
Neale, W. H., agent, Back creek
Nelson, Timothy, butcher, McCrae st
Nelson, Harriet, restaurant, Myers st
Nelson, Mrs., Mundy st
Nestved, J. J., blacksmith, High st
Newton, cab driver, Little Bull st
Nish, Rev. J., clergyman of the Presbyterian Church, Myers st
Nixon, Fred. H., general store, McIvor st

O.

O'Brien, Timothy, puddler, Mackenzie st
O'Brien, Patrick, International hotel, Kangaroo flat
O'Brien, John, labourer, McCrae st
O'Brien, Terence, Hibernian hotel, Golden square
O'Brien, Morgan, chemist, High st
O'Connor, Wm., Bull st
O'Connell, Hannah, laundress, Myers st
O'Connor, Patrick, puddler, McIvor st
O'Connor, Wm., hay and corn dealer, Hargreaves st
O'Connell, Mrs., Hargreaves st
Oda, Miss, Mundy st
O'Dea, Gilbert, labourer, Back creek
O'Donoghue, Mrs., laundress, Dowling st
O'Driscoll, Michael, puddler, Forest st
O'Dwyer, Rev. Augustine, Catholic Church, Bernal st
O'Gorman, Michael, contractor, Bramble street
O'Grady, Thomas, Telegraph hotel, Mitchell st
O'Keefe, Edward, Commercial hotel, Pall Mall
O'Keefe, Francis, storekeeper, Short st
O'Keefe, Edward, Hargreave st
O'Keefe, Francis, general second-hand store, High st
O'Lochlin, —, Mitchell st
Oliver, Mrs., Dowling st
O'Meara, —, sergeant drill instructor, Forest st
O'Neill, Henry, general store, Bridge st
Orth, Henry, baker, Bridge st
Orr, James, manager Union Bank of Australia, View point
Orme, Frederick, grocer, Bridge st
Oriental Bank Corporation ; A. W. Anderson, manager, View point
Osborne, C., butcher, Kangaroo flat
Osborne, Sydney, moulder, Wattle st
Osborne, Joseph, Temperance hotel, Bull street

Osborne, Robert, storekeeper, Back creek
Owen, George, painter, Mitchell st

P.

Pagendorf, Henry, refreshment rooms, High st
Palwick, Mary Ann, refreshment rooms, Quarry hill
Palmer, Henry, law stationer, Temple court, Pall Mall
Palmer, Henry, Noah's Ark hotel, Mundy street
Pannel, Richard, carpenter, King st
Parker, Michael, reeler, Barnard st
Parker, Samson, hatter, Capel court, Pall Mall
Patten, Robert, storekeeper, Williamson street
Patterson, John, draper, Back creek
Paul, Wm., storekeeper, King st
Paxton, John, Railway hotel, Dowling st
Payne, Miss, day school, Bull st
Pearman, Phillip, saddler, Kangaroo flat
Pearce, John, storekeeper, Bridge st
Pearson, Jonas, ironmoulder, Myrtle st
Peel Brothers, cordial manufacturers, King st
Pellatt, George, bricklayer, Forest st
Penistan, James, sharebroker, Quarry hill
Penistan, James, sharebroker, Pall Mall
Pendleton, James, grocer and fruiterer, Mitchell st
Penberthy, Wm., grocer, High st
Pepper, Matthew, miner, Arnold st
Perry, Daniel, storekeeper, Barnard st
Perry, George, coach trimmer, Hargreaves street
Perl, Marcus, general dealer, Myers st
Petersen, Christian, Old Prince of Wales hotel, High st
Pettigrew, Robert, saddler, Pall Mall
Petrick, H., refreshment room, McIvor st
Petrie, Charles, letter carrier, Myrtle st
Pfau, P., bootmaker, Bridge st
Phelan, Michael, restaurant, Mundy st
Phillips, A., cordial manufacturer, Locus street
Phillips, —, bailiff, Dowling st
Phillips, George, baker, Bridge st
Phillips, John, carter, Back creek
Phillips, John, tailor, Forest st
Pile, D., bootmaker, Kangaroo flat
Pitman, George, solicitor, View place
Pitman, George J., solicitor, Bull st
Platt, Wm., miner, Arnold st
Platt, T., gingerbeer merchant, McCrae street
Player, E., storekeeper, Mitchell st
Player, A. E., bootmaker, Short st
Player, Alfred E., Britannia boot mart, Pall Mall
Pleuss, James, blacksmith, Wattle st
Plumbe, Henry, butcher, Mitchell st

Plummer, Charles, carpenter, Arnold st
Police Station ; Patrick Ryan, constable, Golden square
Pounds, Dr. J. B., coroner and Government vaccinator, &c., View Point
Poulson, Paul, coachbuilder, Myers st
Poulson, Paul, coachbuilder, Hargreaves street
Powell, —, fruiterer, Williamson st
Powell, Edwin, cooper, McCrae st
Powson, Honora, restaurant, Kangaroo flat
Powers, Rutherford, and Co., stock and station agents, Williamson st
Power, Mrs., refreshment room, High st
Power, Wm., grocer and wine dealer, Bridge st
Power, John, grocer, Bridge st
Powder Magazine, off Cemetery road
Presbyterian Church, Myers st
Pritchard, —, Golden square
Prior, Jacob, bootmaker, View point
Prior, J. M., baker, View place
Pritchard, Wm., produce merchant, Golden square
Proctor, George, waiter, Short st
Pulfer, Wm., moulder, Wattle st
Punch, John, Golden square
Punch, Charles A., Punch's hotel, High street
Purnell, Joseph, slaughterman, Back creek
Purves, J. K., Five Lions hotel, View point

Q.

Quinn, Timothy, refreshment room, High street
Quinn, Peter, stonemason, Forest st
Quinn, Wm., butcher, High st

R.

Ramsay, W. A., ironmonger, Vine st
Ramage, Rd., cutler, Dowling st
Rankin, Mrs., boarding house, Lyttleton terrace
Rashleigh, Wm., fancy repository, View Point
Raymond and Hall, grocers, seedsmen, wine and spirit merchants, Pall Mall
Reah, John H., brickmaker, Arnold st
Read, Chas. H., butcher, High st
Rea, James, law clerk, Forest st
Redding, Mrs., refreshment room, High st
Redrobe, R., compositor, Myers st
Reed, John, timber merchant, Quarry hill
Regan, John, bricklayer, Wattle st
Registry Office for Births and Deaths; D. Buchan, registrar, View Point
Renwick, John, produce merchant, Hargreaves st
Renstraw, James, dyer, View Point
Rex, Richard, Butchers' Arms inn, Mundy street

Reynolds, Albert, hairdresser, View Point
Reynolds, Wm., miner, View Point
Richards, Mark, labourer, Wattle st
Richardson, Mrs., Kangaroo flat
Richardson, Isaac, Myrtle st
Mealy, John, bootmaker, Mundy st
Richardson, Mrs., Williamson st
Richardson, Cornelius, gas worker, Bridge street
Richdele, George, salesman, Mitchell st
Richards, —, residence, Golden square
Rigby, Wm. H., lawyer, Forest st
Riley, Patrick, bootmaker, High st
Rismo, Mrs., Hargreaves st
Robshaw, J. K., stationer and printer, Pall Mall
Robshaw, J. K., Short st
Robathan and Stevens, military tailors, Pall Mall
Robinson, Wm., miner, Myrtle st
Robinson, Henry, builder, Mitchell st
Robinson, Wm., refreshment room, Mundy st
Robinson, Geo., moulder, Lacus st
Robinson, P., draper, Myers st
Roberts, Abraham, blacksmith. Short st
Robertson, John S., plumber, Mitchell st
Roberts, Alexander, Caledonian hotel, and blacksmith, Golden square
Roberts and Sons, Wills st
Roberts, W., blacksmith, Wills st
Roche, Dr., surgeon, Golden square
Roden, Philip, refreshment rooms, Golden square
Rogers, Abraham, storekeeper, Kangaroo flat
Rogers, George, saddler, golden square
Rogan, Daniel, carter, McIvor st
Rogers, George, Golden square
Robs, Peter, Belvidere hotel, Wattle st
Roman Catholic Church, Kangaroo flat
Ronald, J. S., bank messenger, King st
Rosetta, Johanna, refreshment rooms, Bernal st
Rose, Peter, Belvidere hotel, Barnard st
Rothwell, Edward C., mercantile agent, Quarry hill
Rotheram, John, Golden square
Rowcliff, J. W., Durham Ox hotel, and Union store, Back creek
Row and Co., Edward, cattle salesmen, Pall Mall
Row and Co., Edward, stock and station agents, Williamson st
Row, Edward, McLaren st
Rudd, Mrs., Mitchell st
Rutherford, Miss, Williamson st
Ryal, Robert, commission agent, Lyttleton terrace
Ryan, Robert, commission agent, Charleston road
Ryan, Hammond, and Co., commission agents, Bull st
Ryan, Matthew, miner, Lucan st

Ryah, James, market inspector, Back creek
Ryan, Patrick, constable, police station, Golden square
Ryan, Bartholomew, United Kingdom hotel, cordial manufacturer, Golden square
Rymer, John S., solicitor, Harker's buildings, Pall Mall

S.

Sackleford, Henry, miner, Arnold st
Samuel, Morris, pawnbroker and jeweller, High st
Sam Kwong Bow, storekeeper, Golden square
Sanders, John T., Wattle st
Sandhurst and Inglewood Tannery Co., Beehive chambers; Joshua P. Gray, secretary
Sandhurst Cemetery, R. Houston, sexton
Sandhurst Hospital, Arnold st
Sandhurst Hospital, Lucan st
Sanger, E. C., accountant, Short st
Sartori, Francis, tailor, Williamson st
Sartori, Francis, tailor, Mitchell st
Saunders, John T., clerk Petty Sessions, View point
Saunders, Henry, Golden square
Savory, George, cattle dealer, Bancroft st
Savoren, Wm. C., storekeeper, Bridge st
Savage, Michael, miner, Dowling st
Savings' Bank, Hargreaves st
Sayer, Thomas, undertaker, Bridge st
Sayer Brothers, brewers, Bridge st
Scanlan, Mrs., storekeeper, High st
Scales, Wm., storekeeper, Lucan st
Scols, Joseph, reefer, Bernal st
Scott, Alex. M., Rainbow hotel, Sandhurst
Scott, David, confectioner, Lucan st
Scott, David, confectioner, Bridge st
Scott, Mrs., Forest st
Scheienberger, Geo., baker, Bridge st
Schroder, C. W., butcher, Dowling st
Schlomm, Charles, tobacconist, Pall Mall
Schultiers, Chas., grocer and baker, High street
Schow, L. P., bootmaker, High st
Scott, G., carpenter, King st
Scott, Geo., bootmaker, Williamson st
Scott, Alexander, Rainbow family hotel, Hargreaves st
Schallstad, John, bootmaker, High st
Seague, Henry, bricklayer, Quarry hill
Sexler, Phillip, butcher, High st
Selwood, Jesse, blacksmith, Barnard st
Sengelman and Riedle, furniture dealers, View Point
Saville, Wm., Daniel O'Connell hotel, High st
Seymour, Isaac, blacksmith, Myrtle st
Sewell, Wm., bootmaker, Hargreaves st

Seward, Geo., storekeeper, Forest st
Shalland, Miss, ladies' school, Mitchell st
Sharp, Mrs., refreshment rooms, Bridge street
Shirras, Wm., assayer and practical chemist, Pyke st, Quarry hill
Sheppard, Wm., bootmaker, Myers st
Sibley, J. W., M.D., Bath dispensary
Sibley, R. B., tanner and currier, Forest street
Simpson, Walter, clerk, Barnard st
Simpson, A. J., bootmaker, Bridge st
Simpson, Joseph, mason, Rowan st
Simpson, Gavin, draper, Bridge st
Simeon, Jonathan, mason, Rowan st
Sinclair, John, grocer and produce merchant, Golden square
Sin Hon Con, storekeeper, Bridge st
Sin Won Goon, storekeeper, Kangaroo flat
Skeary, Henry, warden's clerk, Camp hill
Skillicorn, Thomas W., storekeeper, Kangaroo flat
Skilberk, Thomas, labourer, Myrtle st
Slarke, Thomas R., carter, Lyttleton terrace
Slattery, J. B., cordial manufactory, McCrae st
Slattery, Christopher, refreshment rooms, Bridge st
Slattery, Mrs., Lucan st
Slocombe, Mrs., Wattle st
Slocombe, John, wheelwright, McKenzie street
Smallwood, T., bricklayer, Wattle st
Smethells, Mrs., High st
Smith, J. K., chemist, Forest st
Smith, Wm., architect, Rowan st
Smith, Henry, painter and paperhanger, Mitchell st
Smith, R. O., stock and sharebroker, View point
Smith, Alfred A., Williamson st
Smith, John, Quarry hill
Smith, R. O., sharebroker, Forest st
Smith, Mrs., Hargreaves st
Smith, W., architect, Forest st
Smith, Wm., fruiterer, Kangaroo flat
Smithers, Joseph, paperhanger, McCrae st
Smith, Wm., carpenter, High st
Smith, Wm., wheelwright, Bridge st
Smith, —, mason, Dowling st
Smith, George, coachbuilder, McCrae st
Smyth, C. W., hatter, Pall Mall
Snow, Mrs., High st
Snow, Francis F., saddler, Mundy st
Somers, James, miner, Barnard st
Southern, Thomas C., bookkeeper, Barnard st
Southan, Mrs., Wattle st
Sparkman, George, Golden square
Spinks, —, veterinary surgeon, Williamson street
Stanton, Geo., Newmarket hotel, Charlton road

DIRECTORY. 249

Startup, Stephen, salesman, Waterloo st
Stanley, —, Bull st
Stewart, Robert, carpenter, Quarry hill
Stevenson and Powell, general storekeepers, View point
Stewart, James, miner, King st
Stewart, John, bootmaker, Pall Mall
Stewart, John, Bull st
Stewart, James, bootmaker, Mollison st
Stewart, D., View point
Stephens, W., timber yard, Bernal st
Stephens, Wm., timber merchant, McCrae street
Stevenson, Richard, Mitchell st
Sterpe, Michael, butcher, McIvor st
Stead Brothers, fruiterers, Pall Mall
Stephenson, James, storekeeper, Kangaroo flat
Steel, Mrs., fancy repository, High st
Steele, Mrs., Hargreaves st
Stevenson, Richard, produce dealer, High street
Stabbings, F., cook, King st
Stabbings, —, carpenter, Little Bull st
Stein and Holm, painters, Lyttleton terrace
Stilwall, Robert, commercial traveller, Williamson st
St. Killian's Church; James Bernard Hayes, dean, McCrae st
St. Killian's Common School; John Barkly, master, McCrae st
St. Patrick's Benefit Society's Hall, McCrae st
Stohr, W. B., miner, Dowling st
Stokes, Joseph, fruiterer, Mitchell st
Strickland Brothers, brewers, High st
Stranghman, John, basket maker, Bridge street
Stredwick, J. W., fruiterer, &c., Golden square
Strode, Thomas, carpenter, Williamson street
Strong, J. T., civil engineer, Back creek
Stretton and Sims, brickmakers, Back creek
Stoffers, Emil, draper, Bramble st
St. John's Common School, Lucan st
Sullivan, Jeremiah, refreshment rooms, McCrae st
Sullivan, Wm., carpenter, Bernal st
Summers, James, bootmaker, McCrae st
Sant, John, engineer, Bancroft st
Sweny, Mary, housekeeper, Lyttleton terrace
Swift, Thomas, watchmaker, McCrae st
Symonds, Joseph, wine merchant, Mundy street
Symonds, Joseph, Criterion hotel, Mundy street
Symonds and Co., family wine merchants, Pall Mall
Symonds, Joseph, Bull st
Symons, Oliver, carpenter, Short st

T.

Taite, James, carpenter, Dowling st
Tamplin, Edward, carpenter, Mollison st
Tardiff, George, saddler, &c., Pall Mall
Taylor, Samuel, brickyards, Back creek
Taylor, William, refreshment rooms, High street
Taylor, Rev. T., minister Baptist Chapel, Hargreaves st
Taylor, Henry, wheelwright, Kangaroo flat
Taylor, J., stonemason, Mitchell st
Taylor, Rev. Thomas, Baptist minister, Barkly place
Taylor, John Hamlet, government surveyor and land officer, commissioner of crown lands, captain Bendigo rifles, View point
Telegraph Office, Mitchell st
Temperance Hall, View point
Terry, George, carter, Short st
Thom, Miss, Rowan st
Thomas, Mrs., widow, Dowling st
Thomas, Lewis, miner, Dowling st
Thomas, George, draper, Bernal st
Thompson, James, grocer, Mitchell st
Thompson, P., carpenter, King st
Thompson, Hope, refreshment room, Hargreaves st
Thoms, Miss, ladies' school, Rowan st
Thunder and Co, Lucan st brewery
Thunder, A., Barnard st
Timony, T., Howard place
Tipper, J., tentmaker, Myers st
Tipper, J. and W., tent and bedding manufacturers
Tippey Brothers, View point
Tolmie, Malcolm, manager Colonial Bank of Australasia, Pall Mall
Tolmie, Malcolm, Hargreaves st
Tonhill, James, butcher, Golden square
Toohey, Patrick, miner, McCrae st
Toohey, Thomas, miner, McCrae st
Toobey, John, dairyman, Lucan st
Torrens, Wm., cattle salesman, Barnard street
Touzeau, John F., miner, Myrtle st
Trabinger, Frederick, butcher, McCrae st
Trapp, L., furniture warehouse, View point
Trotter, George, boarding-house, High st
Trulove, James, baker, Kangaroo flat
Truelove, Henry, Wheatsheaf hotel, Golden square
Tucker, Peter, bricklayer, Quarry hill
Tully, James, refreshment rooms, Quarry hill
Tully, —, Mitchell st
Turnbull, Wm., carpenter, Myrtle st
Turner, Alfred G., bootmaker, Wattle st
Twigley, E., court crier, Camp hill
Tyrrell, Myra, widow, Wattle st
Tyson, Mrs., Mundy st

2 K

U.

Union Bank of Australia; James Gibby, manager, View point

V.

Vahland, W. C., architect, Barkly place
Vahland and Getzschmann, architects, Harker's buildings, Pall Mall
Vahland, P. D. F., teacher, Quarry hill
Valentine, George, manager Bank of Victoria, View point
Varley and Hoskins, lessees Lyceum theatre, Pall Mall
Veale, David, bootmaker, Mitchell st
Vicary, —, storekeeper, Myrtle st
Virgo, Francis, lawyers' clerk, Barnard st

W.

Wagner, John, coach proprietor, Forest st
Walker and Co., G. F., timber merchants, Hargreaves st
Walker, James C., View point
Walker, George F., tentmaker, Lyttleton terrace
Wall, James, bootmaker, High st
Waller, John, news agent and stationer, Bridge st
Wallis, Robert, confectioner, Mundy st
Walsh, Patrick, Limerick hotel, McCrae st
Walter, George F., draper, Upper View place
Ward, Noll, saddler, &c., McIvor st
Ward, Barnard, grocer, McCrae st
Warden's Office, Camp hill
Wardill, Ann, housekeeper, Lyttleton terrace
Warne, Mrs., straw hat manufacturer and dyer, View point
Warren, John, builder, Hargreaves st
Wat A Chee, government interpreter, Lucan st
Waimough, Edward, draper, Mundy st
Watson, G., hide, skin, and potato merchant, Lyttleton terrace
Watson, Richard, commission agent, Hargreaves st
Watson, J. C., draper, Barnard st
Watson, Mrs., fancy repository, View point
Watson, Darnton, produce dealer, Bridge street
Watson, Mrs., grocer, Williamson st
Watts, Joseph, engineer, Wattle st
Watts, James, engineer, Wattle st
Webb, Samuel, tailor, Pall Mall
Webb, Arthur, Bull st
Webb, George, tailor, Short st
Webb, Wm., cattle salesman, Forest st
Webb, W. and A., storekeepers, Pall Mall
Webb, Wm., carpenter, Barnard st
Welch, Wm., greengrocer, Bridge st
Welch, Wm., compositor, Barnard st
Welldon, Mrs., boarding-house, Mundy st

Wen Loong, tea dealer, Bridge st
Wesleyan Chapel, Golden square
Wesleyan Church, 1863, Bridge st
Wesleyan Church and School, Kangaroo flat
Wesleyan Church, Forest st
Wetherspoon, John, upholsterer, Barnard street
Wheaton, Samuel A., butcher, Bridge st
White, David, storekeeper, Dowling st
White, Thomas, labourer, Bramble st
White, James, actuary Savings' Bank, Hargreaves st
White, David, land surveyor, Myers st
Whitelock, John, tailor, Wattle st
Whitelock, John G., tailor, View point
Whitmarsh, J. M., quartz reefer, Mackenzie st
Widtsing, Wm., marine store dealer, McIvor st
Whyte, David, grocer, Mitchell st
Wickam, J. F., Harp of Erin hotel, High street
Wicklam, John, boardinghouse, Dowling street
Wilde, Charles, fancy repository, Bridge st
Wilkins, Richard, miner, McCrae st
Williams, Henry, confectioner, Mundy st
Williams, Thomas J., salesman, Quarry hill
Williams, Wm., miner, Back creek
Williamson, Richard, butcher, View Point
Willis, W., master All Saints' day school, View Point
Willis, Thomas, bootmaker, Mitchell st
Wills, Wm., Mitchell st
Wilson, Robert, Government engineer, Forest st
Wilson, Geo., clerk, Forest st
Wilson, James, tobacconist, Bridge st
Wilson and Phillips, fishmongers, Pall Mall
Wilson, Thomas, miller, Mollison st
Witt, Frederick, Commercial dining rooms, Howard place
Wolstencroft, John, brickmaker, Back creek
Wolstencroft, J. and W., brickmakers, McIvor st
Wood, Wm., Yorkshire hotel, High st
Wood, Wm., butcher, High st
Wood, Charles, hairdresser, Mitchell st
Woolf, Abraham C., watchmaker, Bridge street
Woolfe, Patrick, dairyman, Williamson st
Womack, W. E., baker, Bridge st
Wormold, Chas., greengrocer, Mollison st
Wotherspoon, John, mattress maker, Wattle st
Wright, Wm., teacher, Back creek
Wrigley, Thomas, builder, Mitchell st
Wrixon, Edward, solicitor, Pall Mall
Wrixon, Edward, solicitor, Forest st
Wycherley, George, miner, Arnold st

Y.

Young, Edwin, butcher, View Point
Young, Mrs., View place
Young, Thomas, cordial manufacturer, Myers st
Young, Edward, butcher, Back creek

Young, James, Golden square

Z.

Zahringer, C., jeweller, Pall Mall
Zinklar, Frederick, butcher, Bridge st

SANDHURST DISTRICT ALPHABETICAL DIRECTORY.

1866-67.

A.

Abbott, W., publican, Sailors' gully
Abbott, W., blacksmith, Sailors' gully
Abernethy, W., Sailors' Gully hotel, Sailors' gully
Abernethy, Rev. James McClurg, Presbyterian minister, Eaglehawk
Abel, Andrew, refreshment room, Pegleg
Albert, —, reefer, Long gully
Alexander, Joseph, White Horse hotel, Californian gully
Allison, Alex., baker, Pegleg
Anderson, Miss, assistant teacher, common school, Eaglehawk
Andrews, R. H., agent Bank of Victoria, Eaglehawk
Anderson, James, Camp hotel, Eaglehawk
Andrews, George, White hills
Argus Company (registered); J. Harris, manager
Ashley, James, blacksmith, Ironbark
Avery, G., butcher, Eaglehawk

B.

Baird, John, storekeeper, Eaglehawk
Baptist Church; Rev. Mr. Henny, minister, White hills
Barry, John, constable, Eaglehawk
Barrell, Thos., publican, Eaglehawk
Bank of Victoria, Eaglehawk
Baron, Adolph, storekeeper, Long gully
Baylee, James, White hills
Bell, Wm., blacksmith, White hills
Bennett, George, cab driver, Ironbark
Beyer, A., storekeeper, Ironbark
Bible Christian Chapel, White hills
Bible Christian Chapel, Sailors' gully
Blackburn, Mrs., White hills
Blake, Wm., quartz miner, Californian gully
Bodilly, Nicholas, storekeeper, Long gully
Bond, Joseph, carpenter, Long gully
Bond, E., refreshment rooms, White hills
Booth, E., bootmaker, Californian gully
Borne, Dr., Eaglehawk

Botanical Gardens, White hills
Boyle, Miss, mistress Common School 123, Californian gully
Bray, —, Pegleg
Brazier, Rev. A., Sailors' gully
Briggs, Wm., saddler, White hills
Britten, J., draper, Raglan st, White hills
Brook, Thomas, engine driver, Ironbark
Brown, W., engineer, Pegleg
Brown, Thomas, commercial traveller, White hills
Brown, Matthew, storekeeper, Ironbark
Bruce, Charles, engineer, Sailors' gully
Bruce, W. and Co., cordial manufacturers, Eaglehawk and Sandhurst
Buckland, J., butcher, White hills
Burt, W. H., London tavern, Eaglehawk
Burns, James, builder, Ironbark
Burrage, Albert, baker, White hills
Bust, Miss, ladies' seminary, White hills
Bye, Henry, engineer, White hills
Byers, Wm., coachbuilder, White hills

C.

Caldwell, J. T., reefer, Sailors' gully
Carden, John, draper, Eaglehawk
Carrington, —, cab driver, Pegleg
Case, James, miner, Pegleg
Cavenagh, Wm., constable, Eaglehawk
Chalk, T. P., refreshment rooms, Epsom
Chambers, Jonathan, blacksmith and wheelwright, Ironbark
Chapman, Jos, Sailors' gully
Chapple, J., contractor, White hills
Cheyne, Dr., Government vaccinator, Epsom
Christian, E., blacksmith, Californian gully
Church of England, Eaglehawk
Clifton, Wm., Anchor store, Sailors' gully
Clothier, Benjamin, Pegleg
Clothier, S., timber merchant, Pegleg
Colenso, Jonathan, builder, Long gully
Coke, Mrs., day school, White hills
Coke, W., saddler, Raglan st, White hills
Collie, John, timber merchant, Long gully
Collins, Henry, bootmaker, Ironbark
Common School (Roman Catholic), Epsom
Connell, Thomas, baker, Long gully
Cook, Wm., Franklin hotel, Sailors' gully
Copewell, Wm., boot warehouse, Epsom
Cory, Charles, fruiterer, Eaglehawk
Corkadale, Ann, storekeeper, Eaglehawk
Corlass, Jas., carpenter, Californian gully
Counsell, Samuel, storekeeper, Pegleg
Cox's crushing machine, Long gully
Cox, Robert, blacksmith, White hills
Cullman, Philip, miner, Long gully
Creeth, George, storekeeper, Long gully
Croaker, Mrs., storekeeper, Eaglehawk
Crowther, D. H., clerk, White hills

D.

Daniels, —, builder, Huntly
Denis, John S., blacksmith, Long gully
Derham, John, blacksmith, Sailors' gully
Derham, T. P., draper, Eaglehawk
Dickson, Joseph, tailor, Eaglehawk
Doddrell, Robert, cabman, Epsom
Doran, Daniel, labourer, White hills
Dower, —, gardener, White hills
Dowker, James, miner, Epsom
Drysdale, John, miner, Californian gully
Dunlop, A. McBride, miner, Eaglehawk

E.

Eastwood, John, miner, Sailors' gully
Edston, Francis, labourer, Sailors' gully
Edwards, Wm., miner, Californian gully
Egan, Lawrence, puddler, White hills
Elliott, —, painter, &c., Sailors' gully
Elwood, J., reefer, Californian gully
Evans, Albert, musician, White hills
Evans, Rice, refreshment rooms, Californian gully
Eyre, Thomas, reefer, Pegleg

F.

Fawcett, Richard, master Common School 123, Californian gully
Fawcett, Miss, teacher, Common School 123, Californian gully
Fogarty, Matthew, draper and grocer, Epsom
Fognelil, Andrew, bootmaker, Long gully
Foot's hotel, Epsom
Francis, John, storekeeper, Pegleg
Fraser, J., storekeeper, Californian gully
Freeman, Peter, miner, Eaglehawk
French, W. H., Manchester Arms, Long gully
Fricker, T., painter, White hills
Frost, —, reefer, Californian gully
Fulson, W., baker, Sailors' gully

G.

Gaffney, Patrick, Robin Hood hotel, White hills
Gibbins, Mrs., widow, Ironbark
Gibbs, Wm., miner, Ironbark
Gilbert, John, blacksmith, Californian gully
Giles, John, blacksmith, Epsom
Gilbert, Thomas, storekeeper, White hills
Glasson, George James, engineer, White hills
Gleeson, Michael, puddler, White hills
Goldsmith, W., tinsmith, White hills
Gorvine, Wm., reefer, Ironbark
Goyne, Francis, storekeeper, White hills
Graham, James F., painter, Eaglehawk
Green, Wm., carpenter, White hills
Grieve, Robert, storekeeper, Eaglehawk
Grovener, Henry, Eaglehawk hotel
Guy, Benjamin, miner, White hills

H

Hagger, George, storekeeper, Pegleg
Hale, Frank, miner, California gully
Hanken, John, mason, Sailors' gully
Harris, John, Specimen Hill hotel, Pegleg
Harris, Joseph, Sailors' gully
Harris, Wm., miner, White hills
Hart, E., and Co., storekeepers, Long gully
Hart, G. W., surveyor, Ironbark
Harden, Henry, stonecutter, White hills
Hasker, J., Specimen hill, Long gully
Hay, Alexander, draper, Eaglehawk
Hearder, Wm., Commercial hotel, Long gully
Heath, Charles, Ironbark
Hefill, John, Eaglehawk dining rooms
Hegarty, Daniel, reefer, Sailors' gully
Hegarty, Eugene, reefer, Sailors' gully
Herdegen, Andrew, miner, Pegleg
Hickey, Robert, reefer, Sailors' gully
Hills, Samuel, refreshment rooms, Californian gully
Hill, W., timber merchant, White hills
Hill, J. G., Catherine Reef hotel, Pegleg
Hilson, Govan, bootmaker, Pegleg
Hobbs, Thomas, butcher, California gully
Hockings, —, nursery, Epsom
Hodgson Brothers, storekeepers, California gully
Hodgson, J. W., storekeeper, Sailors' gully
Hodges, Frederick, schoolmaster, Sailors' gully
Hogg, James, Fifeshire store, Ironbark
Hogan, and Cantwell, wheelwrights and blacksmiths, White hills
Hogan, Daniel, wheelwright, Epsom
Holles, Samuel, quartz miner, Eaglehawk
Hope, John, blacksmith, Eaglehawk
Holdsworth, John, chemist, White hills
Hoskens, Jas., greengrocer and fruiterer, White hills
Hoskens, James, fruit garden, White hills
Howe, John, puddler, White hills
Howe, J., miner, California gully
Howe, —, bricklayer, California gully
Howard, W. H., storekeeper, California gully
Huggard, Alexander, chemist, White hills
Hoghes, Joseph, contractor, Epsom
Hunter, Millar, and Co, shoers and blacksmiths, Epsom
Hunter, John, storekeeper, Epsom
Hyett, James, carpenter, White hills

I.

Inglis, James, storekeeper, White hills

J.

Jack, David, White Hills hotel
Jackson, W., hairdresser, &c., Eaglehawk
Jackson, — stock driver, White hills
Jackson, Samuel, blacksmith, Pegleg
James, R. H. and F., bootmakers, Pegleg
Jamison, Wm., watchmaker, Ironbark
Jamieson, W., watchmaker, Sailors' gully
Jeffrey, Rolfe, blacksmith and timber merchant, Eaglehawk
Jenkins, John, blacksmith, Epsom
Johnson, John, butcher, Sailors' gully
Johnston, W. J., Prince of Wales hotel, Sailors' gully
Jopling, James, iron and brass founder, Ironbark

K

Kelly, W., tinsmith, Eaglehawk
Keiran, Thomas, M.D., California gully
King, Wm., bootmaker, Pegleg
Kneebone, Wm., miner, White hills
Knight, J. G., storekeeper, Epsom
Knott, Samuel, painter, Pegleg

L.

Lambert, Christopher, Ironbark
Langham, Rev. J., minister, Primitive Methodist Church, Eaglehawk
Langon, J. H., draper, &c., Pegleg
Lawrence, John, storekeeper, Pegleg
Lawry, R. P., carpenter, California gully
Layzell, Frank T., watchmaker and jeweller, Eaglehawk
Lester, James, butcher, Pegleg
Letheby, C., chemist and druggist, Eaglehawk
Lewis, Wm., proprietor, Equity crushing machine, Epsom
Lake, —, refreshment rooms, Ironbark

M.

Maller, N., bootmaker, Eaglehawk
Makens, P., baker, Sailors' gully
Marks, Samuel, carpenter, White hills
Murdoch, Wm., butcher, Sailors' gully
Marmion, J., Staff hotel, Great Staff bakery and general store, White hills
Mann, J. Raven, auctioneer, &c., Eaglehawk
McCrea, Miss, fancy repository, Pegleg
McCeig, Hugh, puddler, White hills
McDonald, John, storekeeper, Long gully
McGauran, Bernard C., Town Hall hotel, Eaglehawk
McGregor, Mary, Star Reef hotel, Pegleg
McGivern, Thomas, miner, White hills
McLeer, John, blacksmith, Long gully
Meehan, P., baker, Sailors' gully
Mills, Edward, miner, White hills
Mitchell, Mrs., dressmaker, White hills
Mirow, H., butcher, White hills
Moore Bros., Geelong store, Long gully
Moore, Wm., engineer, Sailors' gully
Moore, Martin, miner, Sailors' gully
Moorhead, D., storekeeper, Sailors' gully
Morgan, Elizabeth, bookseller and stationer, Eaglehawk

Morris, John, storekeeper, Ironbark
Mowley, J., miner, White hills
Muir, Wm., cab proprietor, White Hills
Mulberon, James, inspector of nuisances, Eaglehawk
Mumby, James, hairdresser, Eaglehawk
Muronit, Wm., agent Bank of Victoria, Epsom
Murdoch, D., butcher, Sailors' gully

N.

Nankarrow, —, miner, Pegleg
Nash, E., library, White hills
Neal, Jonathan, Long gully
Nelson Mining Company, California gully
Newton, C. J., Pavilion hotel, Sailors' gully
Newton, C., sharebroker, Eaglehawk
Nicholas, Wm. H., miner, Long gully
Nicholson, Timothy, saddler and harnessmaker, Eaglehawk
Nicholson, Dr., Sailors' gully

O.

Orben, Oswald, miner, Ironbark
Oriental Bank Corporation, Eaglehawk

P.

Pabst, Joseph, butcher, White hills
Palmer, Geo., storekeeper, Sailors' gully
Palmer, R. S., storekeeper, Job's gully
Pascoe, James, California gully
Pascoe's crushing machine, White hills
Pearson and Co., coffee rooms, Eaglehawk
Pearsall, R., tinsmith, Eaglehawk
Pearse, J. A., boarding-house keeper, Pegleg
Pentreath, N., hay and corn store, Long gully
Pentreath, P., storekeeper, Long gully
Perseverance Crushing Company, Long gully
Phillips, Ralph, Epsom
Philpot, Walter, shoer and general blacksmith, Long gully
Pierce, Thomas, sawyer, Pegleg
Police Station, Long gully
Police Station, Eaglehawk
Polglase, John, Lord Nelson hotel, Job's gully
Primitive Methodist Church, Eaglehawk

Q.

Quinn, John, Shamrock hotel, Huntly
Quinn, Patrick, constable, Eaglehawk

R.

Raye, Wm., saddler, &c., Long gully
Reads, George, agent Oriental Bank Corporation, Eaglehawk

Reid, Patrick, accountant, Oriental Bank Corporation, Eaglehawk
Reid, John, agent Bank of New South Wales, Eaglehawk
Renney, Rev. Mr., Baptist Church, White hills
Richards, R., manager North Specimen Hill Company, Sailors' gully
Richards, Sergeant, acting clerk of Petty Sessions, and Commissioner for Affidavits in Supreme Court, Eaglehawk
Richardson, Robert, railway time keeper, White hills
Rider, Thomas, miner, Ironbark
Roach, Paul, blacksmith, Sailors' gully
Roper, —, master Common School, California gully
Roper, H., Turf tavern, Epsom
Rorke, Joseph, miner, White hills
Roseware, Henry, miner, White hills
Rosaow, Theodore, British and American hotel, Ironbark
Rowe, Henry J., Rose of Australia hotel, Long gully
Rule, John, blacksmith, Pegleg
Ryan, Matthew, Junction hotel, White hills

S.

Sagasser, Antonas, quartz miner, Ironbark
Saunders, Edward, miner, White hills
Saunders, Charles, miner, White hills
Scanlon, John, refreshment room, Eaglehawk
Schmidt, Hermann, bootmaker, Ironbark
Schleiger, Charles, butcher, White hills
Scott, Patrick, carpenter, Sailors' gully
Sexton, Thomas, Quartz Miners' Arms and store, Ironbark
Shalder and Laird, blacksmiths and wheelwrights, Ironbark
Sharpe, Robert, chemist and druggist, Epsom
Sibley, James Wm., physician and surgeon, Long gully
Sickman, Wm., gardener, White hills
Sim, A., baker, Epsom
Simms, Richard, miner, Sailors' gully
Simpson, W., storekeeper, Eaglehawk
Simson, Geo., butcher, Epsom
Skepper, Wm. G., butcher, California gully
Skurrie, Archibald, tinsmith, Eaglehawk
Skurrie, G., baker, Epsom
Slade, J., master, Church of England school, Long gully
Smith, M., dressmaker, White hills
Smith, C. L., gold broker, Epsom
Sorley, Henry, physician, Eaglehawk
Stanley, Alexander, Silver Miner hotel, Long gully
Star Reef Quartz Mining Company crushing machine, Pegleg

Staumbal, W., Admiral hotel, Long gully
Steel, John, carpenter, Eaglehawk
Stevens, James, storekeeper, Long gully
Steward, James, brewer, Sailors' gully
Stoops, John, miner, California gully
Stopplebein, Christian, tinsmith and zinc worker, Long gully
St. Lawrence, Margaret, Wellington hotel, White hills
Stringer, Henry, miner, Long gully
Stroom, Philip, baker, Long gully
Stromb, L., butcher, Eaglehawk
Sutton, Daniel, boot and shoe warehouse, Eaglehawk
Swift, Alfred, master, Wesleyan day school, Ironbark
Sydney, Orlando, Dr., author, discoverer of auriferous quartz in Australia, &c., Sailors' gully

T.

Tabb, Wm., miner, California gully
Taylor, —, master common school, Eaglehawk
Taylor, J., in charge of police station, Long gully
Thatcher, J. H., Napier st, White hills
Theisen, James, Railway store, White hills
Thirlwell, James, miner, California gully
Thorpe, James, storekeeper, Eaglehawk
Thomas, John, miner, Pegleg
Thorpe, Frederick, Johnson's reef hotel, California gully
Tidy, Thomas, railway overseer, White hills
Tolhurst, R. E., architect, Pegleg
Toomey, Mrs., storekeeper, White hills
Town Hall, Eaglehawk
Treacy, M., refreshment rooms, California gully
Tregove, Richard, carter, White hills
Trounson, Thomas R., carpenter, Pegleg
Trewtheway, Richard, storekeeper, Pegleg
Trewhella, Chris, joiner, White hills
Trevine, —, miner, Pegleg
Tuck and Son, tinsmiths, Pegleg
Tuck, T. J., pastrycook, Eaglehawk
Tupper, —, miner, White hills
Turpin, Mrs., greengrocer, Long gully

W.

Wakeman, Eliza, storekeeper, Epsom
Wall, J. E., surgeon, White hills
Walker, F., tentmaker, White hills
Walker, A. M. C., town clerk, Eaglehawk
Wall, W. P., tailor, White hills
Walsh, Michael, butcher, Long gully
Webb, John, Fountain hotel, White hills
Webb, Henry, miner, Sailors' gully
Webster, Graham, police magistrate, Eaglehawk
Webster, John, miner, Epsom
Weddell, James G., manager Star Reef Quartz Mining Company, Pegleg
Weller, Henry, butcher, Long gully
Wernet, Esther, storekeeper, Sailors' gully
Wesleyan Church, California gully
Wesleyan Day School, Ironbark
Wesleyan Church, Pegleg
Wetherston, George, blacksmith, Pegleg
Wheeler, Benjamin, bootmaker, White hills
Whiteing, J., bootmaker, Epsom
White, C., painter, &c., Eaglehawk
White, T., watchmaker, White hills
White, J., bootmaker, White hills
White, T., refreshment room, Ironbark
White and Spier, painters, Eaglehawk
Whitham, James, butcher, Pegleg
Whyte, J. H., carpenter, Epsom
Whyte, David, farrier and blacksmith, Eaglehawk
Williams, Wm., miner, Pegleg
Williams, John, nurseryman, seedsman and florist, White hills
Williams, John William, J.P., Eaglehawk
Williams, T. G., miner, California gully
Williams, J. W. and G., storekeepers, Eaglehawk
Williams, John, boarding house, Pegleg
Wiseman, A., reefer, Sailors' gully
Wood, Ely, storekeeper, California gully
Wright, C. H., storekeeper, White hills
Wylie, Wm., carpenter and wheelwright, Sailors' gully

V.

Vine, Edward, miner, Ironbark

Y.

Young, Alex., quartz miner, Ironbark
Young, E. W., hay and corn store, Long gully
Young, Henry, baker, Eaglehawk
Young, Thomas, Eaglehawk
Young, Ann, storekeeper, Eaglehawk

Z.

Zoller, J., bootmaker, White hills

CASTLEMAINE ALPHABETICAL DIRECTORY.

1866-67.

A.

Aaron, Solomon, optician, Market square
Abbott, Alf., Shamrock hotel, Barker st
Adams, W., auctioneer, agent, &c., Lyttleton st
Aitken, David, miller, Graves st, Castlemaine
Alce, Wm., restaurant, Forest st
Alderson, Chas., produce merchant, Wesley hill
Andrew, R., timber merchant, Mostyn st
Andrew, Mrs. V., dressmaker, Mostyn st
Anderson, George, timber merchant, Mostyn st
Anderson, Caleb, Templeton st
Anderson, Craig, and Co., wine and spirit merchants, Templeton st
Archibald, A., hairdresser, Hargreaves st
Armstrong, Mrs., greengrocer, Mostyn st
Ash, Mrs., fruiterer, Barker st
Ash, Wm., blacksmith, Graves st
Attenborough, J., and Co., wheelwrights, coachbuilders, and general smiths, Mostyn st
Attenborough, J., Mostyn st
Audibirt, A., tobacco manufacturer, Chewton

Bagot, Henry Wm., Coachbuilders' Arms, Wesley hill
Balloy, Joseph, storekeeper, Doveton st
Baker, Wm., mining and share broker, Hargreaves st
Baker's Temperance hotel, Hargreaves street
Bale, Wm. D., contractor, Norwood Lodge, Doveton st
Ballard, T. R., Mystery hotel, Barker st
Ball, Joseph, manager Colonial Bank of Australasia, Mostyn st
Baldwin, Wm., grocer, Hargreaves st
Bank of Victoria, Market square
Bank of New South Wales, Market square
Bank of Australasia, Market square
Bannister, Thomas, Bedford hotel, Forest street
Barber, —, hairdresser, Chewton
Barwick, Mrs., fruiterer, Forest creek, Castlemaine
Barrett, —, plumber, &c., Barker st
Barker, W., chemist and druggist, Chewton
Barnes, Thomas S., furniture and ironmongery store, Forest st
Beckingsale, T. and J., grocers, Forest st
Beddard, Francis, vineyard, Dudleigh
Behrmann, Henry, watchmaker, Barker street
Bell, Joshua, storekeeper, Forest creek road
Biddick, John, bootmaker, Barker st
Billis, John, butcher, Elizabeth st
Bisset and Co., bakers and grocers, Barker st

Blackwell, Richard, actuary of Savings' Bank, Hargreaves st
Bolger Brothers, stock and sharebrokers, Barker st
Bond, J., Mount Alexander hotel, Chewton
Booch, Wm., day school, Chewton
Boundy, Chris., storekeeper, Wesley hill
Bourne, Miss, ladies' school, Hargreaves street
Boarne, Abraham, Hargreaves st
Bonsfield, Wm., hairdresser, Lyttleton st
Bowden, John Henry, Prince of Wales hotel and general store, Wesley hill
Boyce, John, carter, Forest creek road
Boyce, Mrs., general store, Forest creek road
Bradbury, Samuel, hay and corn dealer, Graves st
Braithwaite, Mrs., greengrocer, Mostyn st
Brandt Brothers, importers of boots and shoes, Market square
Brown, Samuel, bread and biscuit baker, Graves st
Brown, T. L., mining surveyor, Lyttleton street
Bryant, Mrs., refreshment room, Wesley hill
Bull, J. R. N., police magistrate
Bullock, Mrs., laundress, Forest st
Bundesen, Peter, Golden Hope hotel, Chewton
Burley, Mrs., storekeeper, Chewton
Burnill, Fredk., refreshment rooms, Chewton
Burnett, J. W., agent of Liverpool and London Fire and Life Assurance Company, Forest st
Burgess, H., butcher, Forest creek road
Button, Wm. H., butcher, Chewton
Butler, S. W., bacon factor and general storekeeper, Chewton
Bythell, Wm. R., iron merchant and ironmonger, Market square

C.

Cairnes and Co., undertakers, Barker st; residence, Lyttleton st
Cairnes, W. B., undertaker, Lyttleton st
Callaway, Alf., Templeton st
Callaway, Alfred, boot and shoe warehouse and clothier, Market square
Callander, Alexr., undertaker, Chewton
Caldwell, Miss, Templeton st
Campbell, Wm., Templeton st
Campbell and Co., A., timber and lime merchants, Barker st
Carbarns, John, storekeeper, Forest creek road
Card, David, watchmaker, Market square
Card, Mrs., Hargreaves st
Castlemaine Gas Company's Works; Edward Martin, secretary, Forest st

Castlemaine Co-operative Grocers' Co.; Samuel Myring, manager, Mostyn st
Castlemaine Market, Mostyn st
Castlemaine Grammar School; R. N. Hobart, principal, Barker st
Catholic Church, Hargreaves st
Caulfield, Hugh, Clydesdale hotel, Kennedy st
Chatfield, Henry, baker, Mostyn st
Chaplin, Newton, hay and corn dealer, Mostyn st
Chapman, George, gunsmith and general blacksmith, Barker st
Chewton Market
Chewton Court House
Chewton Town Hall
Chiltern, Mrs., dressmaker, Hargreaves st
Christie, John, Templeton st
Christopher, Henry, accountant, and agent for Australasian Insurance Co., Frederick st
Christmas, Edmund, Diggers' hotel, Forest creek road
Church of England Common School, Forest st
Church, Robert J., Horse and Jockey hotel, Lyttleton st
Church's Five Flags hotel, Campbell's creek
Clark, Hugh, bootmaker, Forest creek road
Clark, John, potato salesman, Mostyn st
Clough, John, printer, Barker st
Cockrem, John H., sign writer, Lyttleton street
Collier, Charles, peddler, Chewton
Colonial Bank of Australasia, Mostyn st
Common School; James Fanagan, schoolmaster, Chewton
Coombes, John, watchmaker, Johnston st
Cook, Charles, pastrycook and confectioner, Barker st
Cook, Thomas, storekeeper, Chewton
Cook, Michael, saddler, &c., Chewton
Corbet and Rogers, corn and flour factors, Market square
Corbet, David, bootmaker, Graves st
Cornish, John, colour merchant, Chewton
Cornish, A., market inspector, Castlemaine
Cousens, John, fishmonger, Mostyn st
Coachman, Thomas, surveyor, Hargreaves street
Courtier, Edmund, Great Centre hotel and dining room, Mostyn st
Crawford, Rev. Archibald, minister of Church of England, Mostyn st
Cramer, Rev. H. S., minister of Baptist Church, Templeton st
Crawford, Abram, draper, Market square; residence, Campbell st
Crawcour, Samuel, tobacconist, Market square
Crocker, —, fancy repository, Mostyn st

2 L

Crow, Henry, produce merchant, Barker street
Criterion hotel, Mostyn st
Cubit, —, town councillor, Castlemaine
Cullen, Mrs., fruiterer, Forest creek road
Cunnack, —, town councillor, Castlemaine
Cuthbert, Wm., tailor, &c., Chewton

D.

Dale, W., and Co., butchers, Barker st
Darby, Mrs., Hargreaves st
Davies, Wm., bootmaker, Wesley hill
Davie, Joseph, bootmaker, Chewton
Davis, Wm. B., O'Hara Burke hotel, Mostyn st
Davis, T., town clerk, Castlemaine
Davis, John, tobacconist, Chewton
Dawson, Henry, chemist, Hargreaves st
Dawson, Wm., iron merchant and ironmonger, Market square
Day, Rev. Edwin, minister of Congregational Church, Lyttleton st
Deakin, —, solicitor, Lyttleton st
Dent, Wm., watchmaker, Chewton
Deneill, Andrea, general dealer, Hargreaves st
Desreaux, John, farrier and blacksmith, Elizabeth st
Dick, Miss, ladies' school, Chewton
Doherty, Joseph, fruiterer, Lyttleton st
Downe, W. B., town surveyor; office, Market square
Dowling, John, master Common School No. 166, Lyttleton st
Drennan, Wallace, grocer, Graves st
Dunster, Mrs., Hargreaves st
Dunstan, Wm., coachbuilder, Wesley hill
Dunstan, Wm., blacksmith, Chewton
Dunedon, Alfred Thos., butcher, Chewton
Durant, T., grocer and wine and spirit merchant, Barker st

E.

Eddes, Miss, and Chubb, Mrs., Minerva House educational establishment for young ladies, Barker st
Edwards, Norval, Mount Alexander hotel, Mostyn st
Edwards, James, baker and storekeeper Chewton
Electric Telegraph office, Barker st
Elliott, George, baker and confectioner, Mostyn st
Elliott, T. and J., and Co., produce merchants, Doveton st
Emery, Francis, Templeton st
English, Scottish, and Australian Chartered Bank, Market square
Evans, George, quartz reefer, Templeton street

F.

Farnsworth, Henry, compositor, Templeton st
Farren, John, manager Bank of New South Wales, Market square
Farrell, James, mayor, Castlemaine
Farroll, George, watchmaker, Market square
Featherby, N., Miners' Arms, Chewton
Fisher and Jackman, butchers, Barker st
Fitzgerald, Edward, Mostyn st
Fisher, Mrs., Forest st
Fitzgerald, Edward, solicitor, Lyttleton st
Fitzgerald, Nicholas, Castlemaine brewery, Elizabeth st
Five Flags store, Campbell's creek
Flemming, Wm., tinsmith, Mostyn st
Formby, Robert, sodawater manufacturer, Templeton st
Fagan, Hugh, Railway hotel, Graves st
French, Joseph B., chemist and druggist, Hargreaves st
Froomes, W., bootmaker, Market square
Froomes, W. and H., drapers, Market square

G.

Garot, A. L., watchmaker and jeweller, Mostyn st
Gellert, Soren, Gellert's hotel, Urquhart street
Gingell, Frederick, Lyttleton st
Glass, Charles E., proprietor of Our Daily News, Market square
Glass, G. W., druggist, &c., Market square
Glendenning, John and George, wholesale and retail butchers and cattle dealers, Mostyn st
Gleeson, Michael, rag and metal merchant, Templeton st
Glover, Robert, storekeeper, Chewton
Gordon, Catherine, fruiterer, Forest st
Goodwin, Wm., pastrycook and confectioner, Barker st
Granata, G. B., land agent, Barker st
Graham, Thomas, storekeeper, Graves st
Gravier, J. B., Lion soap and candle works, Elizabeth st
Green, Henry W., news agent, Barker st
Greenhill, G., slater, roofs repaired and slates for sale, Barker st
Green, David, wheelwright and blacksmith, Forest st
Green, Wm. J., acting manager Union Bank of Australasia, Mostyn st
Grover, Miss, dressmaker, Hargreaves st
Grover, Charles, tinsmith, Barker st
Grubb, Edward R., baker, Barker st
Guthrie, Marp, teacher, Lyttleton st

H.

Hall, John, bootmaker, Wesley hill
Hallandall, George, butcher, Chewton

Hammond, John, bootmaker, Hargreaves street
Harris and Co., Vineyard reef, Wesley hill
Hargetz, George T., storekeeper, Graves street
Hardy, Dr. J. H., dispensary, Chewton
Harvey, Henry, hairdresser, Graves st
Harding, Charles, master common school, Chewton
Harris, Louis, Albion hotel, Wesley hill
Harrington, Charles, Barker st
Harper, G. G., manager Bank of Australasia, Market square
Hasler and Granger, tailors and hosiers, Barker st
Hatch, John D., baker and storekeeper, Castlemaine
Heard, Robert, bootmaker, Graves st
Heley, Charles, tinsmith, Market square
Henry, J. and W., general merchants, Forest st
Hickling, F. W., accountant Bank of Australasia, Market square
Hill, Rev. Wm., visiting minister, Wesleyan Church, Chewton
Hobart, R. N., principal of the Castlemaine Grammar School, Mechanics' Institute, Barker st
Hodson, Henry, miner, Hargreaves st
Hodgson, A. T., bookseller and stationer, Market square
Holmes, Chas., bootmaker, Templeton st
Holmes, C. A., rate collector, office, Market square
Honeyman, Mrs., labour office, Barker st
Horn, Mrs., Hargreaves st
Hudson, James, storekeeper, Graves st
Hughes, J. D., assistant clerk Petty Sessions, Castlemaine
Hunter, Geo., oil and colour merchant, Barker st
Hyman, Maurice, bookseller and stationer, Chewton

I.

Iredale, Peter, paperhanger, Barker st
Isaacs, Henry, agent English, Scottish, and Australian Chartered Bank, Market square
Isaacs, G. and H., Lyttleton st
Ives, Mrs., Queen's hotel, Kennedy st

J.

James, Mrs., Hargreaves st
Jeffreys, Thomas, baker, Chewton
John, John, tailor, Forest st
Johnson, Benj., bootmaker, Chewton
Johnston, Wm., storekeeper and butcher, Graves st
Johnston, John, Carriers' Arms hotel, Elizabeth st
Johns, —, farrier, &c., Chewton
Jones, Mrs. E. W., restaurant, Elizabeth street
Jones, Thomas W., mason, Hargreaves st
Jones, Wm., saddler, Graves st
Jones, John Ashton, bootmaker, Chewton
Joynes, Thomas, refreshment rooms, Chewton
Juniper, Joseph, coachbuilder, Chewton

K.

Kerrigan, Michael, storekeeper, Chewton
Kearney, James, storekeeper, Chewton
Kedslie, George, bread and biscuit baker, Chewton
Kegan, —, town councillor, Castlemaine
Keegan, Lawrance, butcher and baker, Graves st
Kennedy, C. C., coffee dealer, Hargreaves street
Kendell, Wm., Bignell's hotel, Mostyn st
Kentish, N. L. S., clerk Petty Sessions
Keogh, Patrick, Metropolitan hotel, Mostyn st
Kerrigan, —, general storekeeper, Campbell's creek
Kerr, Alexander, manager Oriental Bank Corporation, Market square
Kerr, George H., bootmaker, Barker st
Khoong Soon, storekeeper, Forest creek road
Kibble, T. F., Barker st

L.

Langford, Wm., surgeon, Hargreaves st
Lang Brothers and Brock, nursery and seedsmen, Talbot nursery, Barker's creek
Lansdale, John, tailor, Chewton
Lane, Henry, Foresters' Arms, Hargreaves street
Lawrence, Thomas, hairdresser, Chewton
Lay, W. D., house furnishing rooms, Barker st
Leech, George C., barrister-at-law, Lyttleton st
Lenne and Co., nursery and seedsmen, Lyttleton st
Lewis, John, Victoria hotel, Urquhart st
Lillycrap, Henry, blacksmith, Urquhart st
Lindsay, Jas., saddle and harness maker, Mostyn st
Lippeigoes, Julius, musician, Mostyn st
List, Charles, bootmaker, Chewton
Lock, John, Cornish hotel, Mostyn st
London and Lancashire Fire and Life Insurance Companies; A. Poole, agent, Lyttleton st
Low, Wm., Red Hill hotel, Chewton
Lucas, W. H., sub-agent Oriental Bank Corporation, Chewton

M.

Mahon, Wm., Forest creek hotel, Chewton
Mackintosh, John, quartz reefer, Templeton st
Macdougall, John, Templeton st
Macque, —, Barker st
Mackay, Dr., Hargreaves st
Maguire, John, Albion hotel, Mostyn st
Maloney, Wm. James, Caledonian hotel, Elizabeth st
Manifold and Co., coachbuilders and blacksmiths, Hargreaves st
Manifold, John, blacksmith and wheelwright, Forest creek road
Martin, Edward, secretary Castlemaine Gas Company, Forest st
Marks, Barrea, pawnbroker and general dealer, Forest st
Mason, John R., butcher, Hargreaves st
Masson, Geo., Barker st
Matthewson, John, grocer, wine and spirit merchant, Barker st
Matthews and Co., proprietors of the *Mount Alexander Mail*, Mostyn st
Maunder, Wm. M., accountant, commission agent, and broker, Lyttleton st
McBride and Co., brewers, Campbell's creek
McCabe, John W., ironmonger, Barker st
McCarthy, —, tinsmith, Forest st
McClelland, Michael, grocer, &c., Market square
McCrae, James, postmaster, Chewton
McDonnell, Wm., bootmaker, Barker st
McGrath, Dr., Hargreaves st
McGregor, Wm., livery stable keeper, Mostyn st
McInnes, A., draper and outfitter, Barker street
McKenzie, J., millwright, &c., Lyttleton street
McLaren, A. J., chemist and druggist, Mostyn st
McLean, C., Niagara hotel, Elizabeth st
McMillan, John, storekeeper, Chewton
McMillan, Mrs., storekeeper, Chewton
McMillan, Anthony, grocer, Market square
McNaught, Wm., pump manufacturer, tinsmith, &c., Chewton
McPherson and Cunnack, tanners and curriers, Barker st
Mecking, Chas., master Common School No. 670, Wesley hill
Mechanics' Institute, Barker st; Eric Finlason, secretary
Merrifield, George, solicitor, &c., Lyttleton st
Meredith, Thomas, Chewton gardens, Chewton
Metcalfe, Charles, Exchange hotel, Forest street
Miller, Mrs., greengrocer, Graves st
Millar, Wm. S., cooper, Lyttleton st
Millar, James, confectioner, Scotch pie house, Mostyn st
Miller, Christian T., fruiterer and confectioner, Mostyn st
Mills, J. M., bricklayer, Templeton st
Mitchell, R., grocer, Chewton
Mitchell, Mrs. Geo., storekeeper, Chewton
Montgomery, W., Lyttleton st
Mooney, Richard, general store, Elizabeth street
Morement, Wm., musicseller, Hargreaves street
Morley, Robert, Freemasons' hotel, Mostyn st
Morris, Joseph E., china warehouse, Mostyn st
Mudge, Charles, farrier and blacksmith, Elizabeth st
Murdoch, Campbell, farrier and blacksmith, Graves st
Murphy, Lawrence, Castlemaine hotel, Hargreaves st
Murray and Christie, millers, Forest st, Castlemaine
Myring, John, coachbuilder, Forest st
Myring and Halford, importers, wine, spirit, and general merchants, Forest st

N.

Newcombe and Laver, timber merchants, Barker st
Newlands, William H., stationer, Lyttleton st
New Times store, Campbell's creek
Nicholls, Thos., compositor, Templeton st
Nicholson, Charles W., sharebroker, Lyttleton st
Neibuhr, W., cabinetmaker, Market square
Nugent, Mrs., fruiterer, Barker st

O.

Oates, Philip, bootmaker, Graves st
O'Connell, Daniel, tailor, Hargreaves st
O'Connell, Daniel, military tailor, Market square
Oddfellows' hall, Chewton
Omeara, Martin, carpenter, Hargreaves st
Orderly room, C.V.R.C., Lyttleton st
Oriental Bank Corporation, Market sq
Oriental Bank Corporation, Chewton
O'Seen, James, Mechanics' Arms, Barker street
Ottery, Robert, butcher, Chewton
Our Daily News office, Market square

P.

Pascoe, Isaac, butter dealer, Chewton
Paton, J., clerk, Post-office
Paynter, F. E., solicitor, Lyttleton st
Paynter, Francis, solicitor, Lyttleton st
Perry, Edward, fishmonger, Mostyn st and Forest creek road

Peterson, John, grocer, Barker st
Peterson, Louis, dealer, Mostyn st, Mount Alexander
Pett, Alfred, produce dealer, Mostyn st
Pickett, J., haircutter and perfumer, baths, &c., Mostyn st
Piesing, James, painter, Lyttleton st
Pike, Mary, grocer and fruiterer, Forest street
Police Court, Lyttleton st
Poole, Alfred, agent and broker, Lyttleton street
Post-office (The), Lyttleton st
Power, John, bootmaker, Market square
Presbyterian Church, Mostyn st
Preshaw, Wm. F., J. P., coroner and public vaccinator, Lyttleton st
Price, —, town councillor, Castlemaine
Price, John, Builders' Arms, Hargreaves street
Primitive Methodist Church, Chewton
Purnell, George, bootmaker, Chewton

Q.

Quillinan, Wm., Barkly Bridge inn, Barker st
Quong Fat, Chinese store, Forest st

R.

Raisbeck, Joseph, miner, Chewton
Ramsay, David, tinsmith, Mostyn st
Randall, Alfred, storekeeper, Forest creek road
Raymond, Samuel, Hargreaves st
Redd, F. A. S., superintendent of police, Templeton st
Reid, Robert, Wesley hill bakery, Wesley hill
Richards, Wm. E., auctioneer and commission agent, Lyttleton st
Richardson, David, bootmaker, Mostyn st
Roberts, Henry, bootmaker, Market sq
Roberts, H., and Co., bootmakers, Barker street
Roberts, A. W., general carrier, Templeton street
Robertson, Wagner, & Co., coach factory, Barker st
Robertson, Wagner, and Co., Cobb and Co.'s booking office, Hargreaves st
Robinson, Mrs., Templeton st
Robinson, John H., butcher, Mostyn st
Rogers, John, Criterion hotel, Market sq
Ross, Donald, saddler, Market square
Ross, Joseph, Hotel de l'Europe et Pension Suisse, Mostyn st
Ross, Daniel, cabinetmaker, Graves st
Ross, Wm. H., draper, Market square
Rowse, D., storekeeper, Chewton
Rowe, Wm., coachbuilder, Wesley hill
Rowe, Chas. S., registry office, Barker st

Royal hotel, Market square
Rule, H., painter and grainer, Barker st
Russell, Miss, Hargreaves st
Russell, Thos., produce merchant, Barker street
Ryland, George, draper, Market square
Ryan, J. W., Market square

S.

Sampson, Francis H., bootmaker, Lyttleton st
Savings' Bank, Hargreaves st
Schroeder, E., tobacconist, Mostyn st
Scott, Wm., blacksmith and wheelwright, Johnstone st
Sevier, M. M., fancy repository, Market square
See, Beck J., hay and corn store, Chewton
Sharp, W., surgeon, Chewton
Shaw, Angus, coach painter, Graves st
Shaw, James, painter, Forty-foot hill, Saint st
Shepherd, Richard, traveller, Templeton street
Sicker, Chas., cabinetmaker and upholsterer, Barker st
Siddell and Ryan, Crown brewery, Winter's flat
Sidebottom, Wm., F., ironmonger, Lyttleton st
Simpson, Robert, ironmonger, Graves st
Sin Gee Shing, Chinese storekeeper, Forest creek road
Slattery, John, Supreme Court hotel, Hargreaves st
Sloman, D., tobacconist, Market square
Smyth, Thomas, bootmaker, Barker st
Smyth, George, barrister-at-law, Lyttleton street
Smith, George, Hargreaves st
Spence, L. H., coach painter, Mostyn st
Stevens, Francis, Volunteer tavern, Market square
Stewart, J., confectioner, Barker st
Stewart, Miss, educational establishment, Hargreaves st
Stobo, Jas., tailor; residence, Hargreaves street
Stobo, James, tailor and woollen draper, Mostyn st
Stoiart, E. H., postmaster, Lyttleton st
Stoddart, John, Templeton st
Suen, James, greengrocer, Graves st
Summerland, J., carpenter and joiner, Doveton st
Summers and Webb, butchers and cattle dealers, Mostyn st
Sun War Kee, Chinese store, Forest st
Sun Quong Yat, Chinese store, Forest st
Supreme Court, Lyttleton st
Survey Land office, Hargreaves st
Swan, Mrs., Hargreaves st
Sweeny, J. F., Hargreaves st

T.

Tait, John T., tailor, Barker st
Tather, George Alexander, corn dealer, Elizabeth st, Tarrangower road
Taylor and Gosling, drapers and clothiers, Barker st
Taylor, E. W., butcher, Wesley hill
Temple, John, butcher, storekeeper, Wesley hill
Theatre Royal, Market square
The *Mount Alexander Mail* office, Mostyn street
The Sir Henry Barkly Quartz Crusher —Fairburn, proprietor
Thiselton, John, bootmaker, Johnstone st
Thompson and Co., millers, corner of Kennedy and Parker sts
Thorburn, Henry C., commission agent, Barker st
Tillman, Henry, hairdresser, Barker st
Tilt, H. R., clerk, Post-office
Tott, John, Tott's hotel, Barker st
Tulloch, Wm., general store, Mostyn st
Tulloch, Wm., Lyttleton st
Tulloch, Archibald, storekeeper, Forest creek road
Turner, John, carrier, Doveton st
Turner, Mrs., milliner and dressmaker, Doveton st
Tracy, C. W., dentist, Hargreaves st
Treasury (The), Barker st
Treasure, John, baker and storekeeper, Forest creek road

U.

Union Bank of Australia, Mostyn st
Uphill, Chas. G., draper, Market square
Upson, John P., general dealer, Chewton
Ustick and Co., produce dealers, Chewton

V.

Vale, Mrs., bookseller, Mostyn st
Vincent, Geo., Coliban hotel, Elizabeth st
Vincent and Co., dyers and scourers, Barker st
Vivian and Co., ironfounders, Mostyn st

W.

Wait, —, Chewton
Wallace Daniel, auctioneer, Market sq
Wallace's Horse Repository, Lyttleton st
Warley, George, Goldsmiths' hotel, Market square
Watkin, Rev. E. J., visiting minister, Wesleyan Church, Chewton; residence at Campbell's creek
Watson and Co., butchers, Barker st
Watson, Faulder, Imperial hotel, Lyttleton street
Watson, Mrs. Joseph, Cumberland inn, Barker st
Watson, Walter, baker, Hargreaves st
Welch, Miss Emmeline, assistant teacher Common School No. 670, Wesley hill
Wells, Mrs., dressmaker, Templeton st
Wesleyan Chapel, Chewton
Wesleyan Methodist Church, Forest st
Wheeler, Joseph, photographic artist, Market square
Wheeler, Mrs., Forest creek road
Wherrett, Chas., photographer, Barker st
Wherrett, Chas., photographer, Hargreaves street
White, Richard, coachbuilder and blacksmith, Hargreaves st
Whitby, George H., bookseller and stationer, Barker st
Wilkins, William, bootmaker, Barker st
Williams, David, and Son, blacksmiths and shoeing smiths, Forest st
Williams, F., grocer and provision merchant, Mostyn st
Williams, David, storekeeper, Chewton
Williams, T., Temperance boardinghouse, Chewton
Wilson, Thomas, carpenter, Barker st
Winborg, Frederick, storekeeper, Forest creek road
Winks, Henry, clothier, Market square
Wood, Mrs., laundress, Elizabeth st
Wragge, Henry, veterinary surgeon and livery stable keeper, Hargreaves st
Wright, Joseph, tanner and currier, Market square
Wright, Joseph, tanner and currier, Elizabeth st

Y.

Young, Thomas, manager Bank of Victoria, Market square
Young, Robert, grocer, Wesley hill

ECHUCA ALPHABETICAL DIRECTORY.

1866-67.

A.

Alexandre, Dr., surgeon, dentist, and aurist, High st
Allen, Robert, engineer, High st
Amos and Co., timber merchants, Hare st
Andrews, Thomas, tailor and draper, High street

B.

Balfour, John, police constable, Dixon st
Bank of New South Wales, High st
Bank of Victoria, High st
Barker, Wm., M.D., Justice of the peace, Echuca
Benson, James, dining rooms, Nish st
Boddy, Thomas, soda water and cordial manufacturer, Dixon st
Bonded Warehouse (The), High st
Borough Council Chambers, High st
Bourke, David, bootmaker, High st
Brooks, George, Limerick Castle hotel, Hare st
Brown, John, furniture and bedding warehouse, High st
Brown, Thomas, carpenter, Percy st
Bruce, A. W., goods clerk, Echuca station
Burchart, Rev. Mr., minister Wesleyan Church, Echuca
Burgess, James, clerk and bookkeeper Manning's stores, Fish st
Burke, John, bootmaker, Moama
Burton's Echuca timber yard, Heygarth st
Burton, Robert, timber merchant and paperhanger, Hare st
Berit, W. F., M.A., principal of select academy, and conductor of Civil Service and University training classes, Anstruther st
Butcher, H. G., hay and corn dealer, Anneely st
Butler, George, maildriver, Anstruther st

C.

Carpenter, Alfred, bookseller and news agent, High st
Chambers, Robert, baker, Anstruther st
Chisholm, John, carpenter, Anstruther st
Church of England, Hare st
Cleary, Sergeant, inspector of nuisances, Echuca
Clemens, Johanna, storekeeper, Anstruther st
Clipperton, George, accountant Bank of Victoria, High st
Clough's warehouse and wharf; — Riddell, agent, Hare st
Cobb and Co.'s booking office, at Iron's Bridge hotel; R. Payne, agent
Cobb and Co.'s livery stables, Dixon st
Connell, W. H., master Common School No. 208, Hare st
Connell, Mrs., assistant teacher Common School No. 208, Hare st
Corven, Thomas, farrier and blacksmith, High st

Court of Petty Sessions, Dixon st
Crabtree, Thomas, tinsmith, Hare st
Crossen, Dr., Echuca dispensary, High st
Crossen, Dr., Percy st
Cumming and Watson, bakers, High st
Custom House, Hare st

D.

Daniel, John, contractor, Hare st
Dawbarn, James, butcher, Annesly st
Dennis, Miss, Percy st
Dewar, D., cook and confectioner, High st
Disher, W. J., Hare st
District Survey Office, High st
Dodd, Frank, wheelwright, Anstruther st
Doel, Richard, Wiltshire Arms, Annesly street

E

Easterby, Richd., reporter *Riverine Herald* office, High st
Echuca Road Board Office: Hall of Commerce, High st
Edelman, Henry, Murray River hotel and dining rooms, High st
Elliot, Edmund, grocer and storekeeper, Sturt st
Engelbert, Henry, hotelkeeper, Hare st

F.

Farmers, Charles, storekeeper, High st
Faust, Wm., Chief Ranger Foresters' Court Hearts of Oak No. 3996
Faust and Wilson, wheelwrights and blacksmiths, Anstruther st
Ferguson, —, Darling st
Fitzgerald, John M., Locomotive restaurant, Hare st
Fleming, J. H., Full and Plenty boardinghouse, Heygarth st
Forbes, D. W., manager post and electric telegraph office, Hare st
Ford, A. R., compositor, Dixon st
Forest, Anthony H., Steam Packet hotel, Hare st
Fulcher, James, bricklayer, Hare st

G.

Gellatly, Peter N., painter, High st
Gibson, Hugh, Dixon st
Gibson, Wm., Percy st
Gibson, Wm., horse bazaar and livery stables, High st
Gilles, E., treasurer borough council, High street
Gilles, Edmund F., manager Bank of Victoria, High st
Gannon, Thos., senior constable, Moama
Glass, Robert J., J.P., Echuca
Goodwin, Joseph, greengrocer, High st
Graham, Wm P., Shamrock hotel, High st
Gray, Oswald, Hare st
Green, Mrs., nurse, Heygarth st

H.

Hall, Thomas W., cabinetmaker, Hare st
Hanson, Theodore, butcher, High st
Hand, John, labourer, Moama
Harvey, Wm., saddler, High st
Hatfield, Charles A., hairdresser and tobacconist, High st
Hatt, Wm., carpenter and joiner, Percy street
Hayes, James, Alma hotel, Annesly st
Hayward, Henry S., storekeeper, Hare st
Hayward, H., storekeeper, Moama
Hill, James, butcher, Hare st
Hogarth, F., draper and clothier, High st
Hogarth, Finlay, store and post office, Moama
Hogarth, F., storekeeper, Hare st
Homan, Edwin, storekeeper, Annesly st
Homan, Edwin, general merchant, High street
Hopwood's Bridge, Campaspe; William Heilley, collector
Hopwood, H., auction room, Hare st
Hopwood, Henry, Dixon st
Hopwood's Vineyard, off Connelly st
Hopwood, Henry, proprietor of punt and pontoon bridge, River Murray, and proprietor of Campaspe bridge
Hoiks, H., secretary to Freemasons' office, Redman's Commercial hotel, High st
Hunt, Joseph, puntman, Hare st
Hutchings, Alexander, veterinary surgeon, chemist and druggist, Hare st

I

Iron, James, Bridge hotel, High st and Warren st
Ivey, Charles, butcher, Nish st

J.

Jago, Thomas, Anstruther st
Jenkins, J., restaurant, Maude st
Jewison, Mrs., school, Annesly st
Johnson, Job, storekeeper, Hare st
Jones, P., carrier, Moama
Jones, Edward, wheelwright, High st

K

Kenyon and Scott, bootmakers, High st
Kynaston, Edward, surveyor, Moama

L.

Lahey, John, Harp and Shamrock hotel, High st
Langford, George, Dixon st
Langford, George, district surveyor, High street
Lenoard, Henry, shipbuilder, Moama
Lewen, R. G., ironmongery and crockery warehouse, High st

DIRECTORY. Sim 265

Lewers, Thomas, manager Bank of New South Wales, High st
Lewis, Hugh C., draper, Melbourne House, High st
Long, Osborne, dining rooms, Hare st
Lyons, Eugen, contractor, Annesly st

M.

Mace, Captain, master of the *Lady Darling* steamer, Anstruther st
Major, Henry, secretary to Forester's Court Hearts of Oak No. 3996; office at Hedman's Commercial hotel
Mallam, B. W., refreshment room, railway station
Manning's Noah's Ark livery stables and produce stores; entrance, Hare st
Mansell, George, clerk of courts, Moama
Manning, Edward, livery and bait stables, produce merchant, and general storekeeper, Nish st
Markam, George, driver, Anstruther st
Matthews Brothers, ironmongers, Hare st
Matholomew, George, carpenter, Anstruther st
Mayne, Andrew, manager Melbourne grocery company's store, High st
McCulloch, W., and Co., general carriers, Annesly st
McDonnell, S. W., police constable and inspector of slaughteryards, Dixon st
McKee, Wm. D., telegraph clerk, Echuca station
McLeod, Donald, Riverine hotel, Sturt st
McNamara, Michael, carter, Darling st
McNamara, John, carter, Darling st
Melville, George, Caledonian Family hotel, near railway station, Hare st, Echuca
Milledge, Charles, ironmonger, Hare st
Mitchell, Thomas, residence, Hare st
Mitchell, John, Echuca hotel, High st
Moama Custom House; Charles E. Gordon, sub-collector
Moore, Walter W., builder and timber merchant, High st
Moore, Walter, High st
Munro, —, plumber, Anstruther st
Murray Fishing Company, High st
Murray Fishing Company, new premises, High st

N.

Nesbit, Robert, tailor, High st
Newbould, Dr., Heygarth st
Newman, Charles, butcher, Moama
Nedd, Thomas, Jolly Waggoner hotel, Annesly st
Noble, Wm., blacksmith and farrier, High street
Nolan, Philip, Victoria hotel, and produce stores, Hare st

O.

O'Brien, D. J., assistant manager, Post and Electric Telegraph office, Hare st
O'Connell, Owen, butcher, Darling st
O'Connell, Owen, Hopwood's Old House, Hare st
O'Neil, Peter, police constable, Dixon st

P.

Parr, Frederick, carrier, Moama
Pascoe, Charles E., town clerk and municipal surveyor, office, High st
Payne, Fredk., auctioneer and commission agent; agent for R. Goldsbrough and Co., Australian Alliance Assurance Company, Bird Island Company, Murray river steamers; and Custom House agent, High st
Payne, Wm., solicitor to Echuca borough council, High st
Payne, R., agent for Cobb and Co., High street
Pearce, Thomas, bootmaker, Maude st
Phemister, James, bootmaker, High st
Post Office and Electric Telegraph Office, D. W. Forbes, manager, Hare st
Powell, —, detective office, Percy st
Powell, Henry, Bendigo hotel, and agent for Edinburgh brewery
Pulling, Alexander F., chemist and druggist, High st

R.

Ralston, —, Dixon st
Redman, George, Commercial hotel, High street
Reilly, Wm., collector, Hopwood's Campaspe bridge
Reese, Charles, watchmaker and jeweller, High st
Riddle, Samuel, agent, Hare st
Riverine Herald office, Mackay and Co., proprietors, High st
Roberts and Ferguson, coachbuilders, High st
Robertson, Wagner, and Co., forwarding agents, railway station
Rogers, W. J., tinsmith, plumber, and zinc worker, High st
Rogers, W. J., tinsmith, Hare st

S.

Schlestedt, Julius, furniture dealer, High street
Shackell, James, residence, Hare st
Shackell, James, and Co., auctioneers, valuators, and Customs' agents, commissioners of court of New South Wales, Hall of Commerce, High st
Simmons, Wm., bootmaker, near railway station

2 M

Simonds, J. L., chemist and druggist, High st
Smith, Wm., engineer, Anstruther st
Snead, J. R., watchmaker and jeweller, Hare st
Standard Brewery, J. W. Disher, proprietor, Hare st
Stead, J. C., station master, Echuca railway station
St. George's Hall, James Irons, proprietor, Hare st
Strutt, Charles E., M.D., resident police magistrate, coronor, and guardian of minors
Sutton, George, baker, Hare st

T.

Taylor, Henry, Dixon st
Taylor, H. P., solicitor, High st
Taylor, Wm., carpenter, Hare st
Templeton, Burnett, clerk of courts, commissioner of Supreme Court for taking affidavits, Echuca
Toal, Joseph, constable, Echuca
Turner, Frank, fruiterer, High st
Turner, Edward, butcher, Heygarth st
Towle and Co., drapers, High st

Twigge, F. H., *Riverine Herald* office, High st
Towle, Thomas, draper, Heygarth st
Tuycross, Samuel, butcher, Hare st

V.

Vahland and Getzschmann, architects, High st

W.

Walton, George carrier, Moama
Warman, —, chief officer, Custom House, Hare st
Warwick, Humphrey, saddler and harness maker, Darling st
Watt, James, Junction hotel, Moama
Wesleyan Chapel, Piercy st
Wharpanila Vineyards, property of Mr. Robert J. Glass
White, Wm., labourer, Anstruther st
Wilson Wm., carpenter, Hare st
Wood, Charles, boarding-house, Hare
Wigram, A., bricklayer, Anstruther st

Y.

Young, G. E., Caledonian hotel, Anstruther st

BALLARAT AND BALLARAT EAST DIRECTORY.

1866-67.

A.

Aaron, Henry, hawker, Eureka st
Aaron, Herman, hawker, Victoria st
Abbott, —, wheelwright, Raglan st
Abbott, Henry, tailor, Mair st
Abbott, Henry, carter, Eureka st
Abbott, Henry, tailor, Dana st
Abel, A. T., mineralogist, Wills st
Abernethy, W. T., painter, Dawson st
Abram, George, miner, Sebastopol
Abrahams, George, painter, Macarthur st
Abrahams, Isaac, messenger police court, Ascot st
Abrahams, Hyam, news agent, Raglan st
Abramorwitch, Isaac, bootmaker, Main road
Ackroyd, James, miner, Talbot st
Ackroyd, F. W., miner, Pleasant st
Acreman, R., messenger, Lydiard st
Adeney, Rev. H. W. H., Sturt st
Adair, R., brickmaker, Peel st
Adams, E., miner, Brown hill
Adams, Mrs., nurse, Lydiard st
Adams, James, bootmaker, Raglan st
Adams, John, carter, Lyon st
Adams, —, Dawson st
Adams, James, labourer, Armstrong st
Adair, Thomas, surveyor, Sturt st
Adams, John, bootmaker, Creswick road
Adamson, James, mason, Eyre st
Adamson, Mrs., dressmaker, Windermere street

Ade, Stephen, labourer, Humffray st
Agnew, Wm., carrier, Errard st
Agnew, T. C., collector Star, Seymour st
Ah Coon, Chinese interpreter, Young st
Ah Chow, Chinese interpreter, Clayton st
Ahern, Jeremiah, draper, Wills st
Ahern, Patrick, car proprietor, Grant st
Ah Fow, carpenter, Clayton st
Ahrens, John, Exchange hotel, Bridge st
Ainley, F., brewer, Victoria st
Akehurst, A. P., solicitor, Lydiard st and Wendouree parade
Akins, Edgar, joiner, Eyre st
Aldred, Thomas, coach builder, Mair st
Alexander, Raphal, baby linen warehouse, Bridge st
Alexander, Andrew, carpenter, Drummond st
Alexander, John, mason, Eureka st
Alexander, S., milliner, Bridge st
Alexander, W., contractor, Skipton st
Aley, J. J., labourer, Main road
Algre, J., miner, Drummond st
Allan and Donn, saddlers, Creswick road
Allchin, Alfred, saddler, Main road
Allchin, Mrs., milliner and dressmaker, Main road
Allchin, Alfred, saddler, Sebastopol
Allen, George, blacksmith, Urquhart st
Allen, J., draper, East st
Allen, Abraham, blacksmith, Eyre st
Allen, Wm., nightman, Dawson st
Allen, James, miner, Grant st

Allen, Wm., carpenter, Dawson st
Allen, George, and Co., blacksmiths, Mair street
Allanby, Rev. C. G., Brown hill
Allording, Robert, carter, Victoria st
Allingham, Mrs., confectioner and fruiterer, Sturt st
Allison, Cuthbert, miner, Eyre st
Allison, Misses, day school, Victoria st
Alman, M., tobacconist, Main road
Alroe, Peter, miner, Main road
Alston, D., collar maker, Main road
Alsworth, J., miner, Main road
Amies, Mrs., Doveton st
Anderson, Neil, coach driver, Skipton st
Anderson, Alex., bootmaker, Skipton st
Anderson, A., boot importer, Bridge st
Anderson, A., boot importer, Victoria st
Anderson, J., tailor, Main road
Anderson, J., miner, Dawson st
Anderson, James, Ripon st
Anderson, Joseph, carpenter, Mair st
Anderson, Wm., carter, Humffray st
Anderson, James, contractor, Humffray st
Anderson, Wm., miner, Dood st
Anderson, Mrs., Eureka st
Anderson, Mrs., Doveton st
Anderson, George, clerk, Doveton st
Anderson, Henry, carpenter, Yuille st
Anderson, W., miner, north of municipal boundary
Anelly, W., miner, Lexton st
Andrews, J., miner, Burnbank st
Andrews, —, Cobblers
Andrews, Joseph, miner, Lal Lal st
Andrews, Thomas, blacksmith, Lydiard st
Andrews, Solomon, Woodman hotel, Lydiard st
Andrews, Henry, Barley Sheaf hotel, Barkly st
Andrews, J., miner, Esmond st
Angus, W., traveller, Ligar st
Angus, John, mason, Eyre st
Angwin, Justin, miner, Rowe st
Angwin, Benjamin, engineer, Lydiard st
Angwin, Benjamin, miner, Brougham st
Ansell, Wm., miner, Rowe st
Anstis, Charles, miner, Esmond st
Anthony, —, miner, Main road
Anwyl, J., draper, Sebastopol road
Appo, Mrs., store, Lydiard st
Appow Chtong, Chinese interpreter, Clayton st
Archer, James, hairdresser, Armstrong st
Archer, John, hairdresser, Dana st
Archer, J., labourer, Little Bendigo
Archer, Thomas, labourer, Sturt st
Archibald, Edward, Stock Exchange hotel, Lydiard st
Ardagh, John, bootmaker, Main road
Ardagh, Patrick, bootmaker, Main road
Ardagh, Thomas, bootmaker, Main road
Armes, Alfred, bootmaker, Queen st
Armitage, Mrs., Doveton st

Armstrong, E., clerk, Armstrong st
Armstrong, —, bookbinder, Eyre st
Armstrong, S., miner, Sebastopol
Armstrong, George, Camp hotel, Sturt st
Armstrong, J., horsebreaker, Doveton st
Armstrong, George, labourer, Brougham street
Armstrong, Walter, moulder, Raglan st
Arnold, Mrs., teacher, Sturt st
Arnold, W., Carriers' Arms, Creswick road
Arthur, H. H., moulder, Armstrong st
Arthur, Wm., Armstrong st
Arthur, Miss E. L., school, Armstrong st
Ash, Mrs., Scott's parade
Ash, Joseph, miner, Wendouree parade
Ashley, Thomas, miner, South st
Ashley, John, ticket writer, Grenville st
Ashley, John, smith, Albert st
Ashmore, Joseph, miner, Doveton st
Askew, Thomas, smith and wheelwright, Creswick road
Askwith, Mrs., Doveton st
Ashton, E., butcher, Ligar st
Ashworth, Thomas, labourer, Grant st
Asquith, Robert, brickmaker, Havelock street
Atkins, F., undertaker, Bridge st and Main road
Atkins, F., upholsterer, Main road
Atkins, George, bootmaker, Clayton st
Atkins, —, miner, Errard st
Atkins, Mrs., school, Humffray st
Atkinson, Frederick, sharebroker, Creswick road
Atkinson, Thomas, carpenter, Macarthur street
Attwood, Charles, carpenter, Mair st
Austin, Charles, miner, Pleasant st
Austin, Edward, labourer, Howard st
Avery, John, miner, Queen st
Avery, Mrs., nurse, Ripon st
Axford, Wm., carpenter, East st
Ayers, Wm., fruiterer, Wills st
Ayers, G. W., painter, Grant st

B.

Bade, Martin, tobacconist, Sturt st
Badham, Charles, miner, Dana st
Bagshaw, Abraham, sharebroker, Lydiard street
Bagshaw, A., sharebroker, Dawson st
Bain, Angus, machinist Star, Peel st
Bain, John, hawker, Victoria st
Bain, Roderick, Havelock st
Baines, John, Macarthur st
Baines, John, carpenter, Barkly st
Baines, Edward, painter, Macarthur st
Bailey, Charles, china and earthenware dealer, Sturt st
Bailey, Christopher, china and earthenware dealer, Doveton st
Bailey, Mrs., Sturt st

Bailey, Martin, miner, Clyde st
Bailey, Thomas W., labourer, Peel st
Bailey, Simeon, miner, Cobblers
Bainbridge, F., Cosmopolitan hotel, Eyre street
Baird, J. K., oil and colour merchant, Bridge st
Baird, J. K., Mair st
Baird, S., town surveyor, Drummond st
Baird, Mrs., Creswick road
Barkley, James, storekeeper, Clayton st
Baker, James, carter, Black hill
Baker, James, sharebroker, Sturt st
Baker, F., miner, Brougham st
Baker, James, sharebroker, Eyre st
Baker, Henry, stonemason, Doveton st
Baker, —, miner, Bond st
Baker, Fred., builder, Nell st
Baker, Wm., storekeeper, Eyre st
Balhausen, D., miner, Grant st
Balhausen, E., miner, Barkly st
Balhausen, —, miner, Lyons st
Ball, Alfred, gardener, Eyre st
Ball, Wm., confectioner, Main road
Ball, Wm., storekeeper, Humffray st
Ballantine, J. B., miner, Ascot st
Ballantine, James, mason, A 1 st
Ballarat Fire Brigade, Barkly st
Ballarat West Fire Brigade, Sturt st
Ballarat East Police Station, Barkly st
Ballingall, Alexander, Dawson st
Balmer, George, clerk, Main st
Baldam, Noah, smith, Clarendon st
Balmain, James, painter, Seymour st
Banaby, Henry, carter, Humffray st
Barber, H., storekeeper, Skipton st
Barber, Charles, miner, Eyre st
Barberry, John, bootmaker, Bridge st
Barcelone, Hugh, miner, Dana st
Barklay, Wm., billiard table keeper, Dana st
Bargn, J., produce store, Creswick road
Barlow, John, carter, Dawson st
Bannister, G. C., carpenter, Armstrong st
Barckiam, Mrs., laundress, Armstrong st
Bardwell, Wm. H., miner, Dana st
Bardwell, Wm., photographer, Sturt st
Barker, Wm., contractor, Doveton st
Barker, Wm., wheelwright, Creswick road
Barker Brothers, wheelwrights, Creswick road
Barkley, Mrs., Dutch Harry hotel, and butcher, Sebastopol
Barnes, James, miner, Sebastopol
Barnes, John, labourer, Macarthur st
Barnes, J. F., draper, Victoria st
Barnes, George, cabinetmaker, Ripon st
Barnes, W. H., clerk, Lyons st
Barnett, Thomas, miner, Sebastopol
Barnett, M., tobacconist, Bridge st
Barnett, Mrs., dressmaker, Talbot st
Barr, Joseph, bricklayer, Armstrong st
Barrel, Samuel, miner, Lyons st

Barrett, James, butcher, Main road
Barrett, Mrs., Victoria st
Barrett, George, mason, Dawson st
Barrett, J., upholsterer, Armstrong st
Barrie, Samuel, ironmoulder, Errard st
Barrow, Wm. H., mason, Mair st
Barrow, John, butcher, Mair st
Bartlett, Samuel, accountant, Lydiard st
Bartlett, John, cabinetmaker, Humffray street
Bartlett, George, miner, Doveton st
Bartlett, A. H., horse dealer, Macarthur street
Barry, Mrs., Lexton st
Barry, Wm., produce dealer and coach proprietor, Sebastopol
Barry, Mrs., boardinghouse keeper, Ascot street
Barry, Andrew, miner, Humffray st south
Bartholomew, Alexander, compositor, Humffray st south
Barvil, Walter, plasterer, Seymour st
Baskerville, E. A., tobacconist, Main road
Bason, Charles, car driver, Main road
Bassy, James, mason, Havelock st
Bate, J. H., porter, Main road
Batiste, Andrew, cabinetmaker, Peel st
Bateson, A., miner, Eureka st
Batten, W. H., secretary Mechanics' Institute
Batten, Mrs., Talbot st
Batten, Edward, miner, Talbot st
Battle, Mrs., laundress, Lydiard st
Battimer, Robert, bootmaker, Victoria st
Batty, Samuel, miner, Grant st
Batty, George, Grant st
Baurdel, Eugene, Imperial diningrooms, Armstrong st
Bawden, Edward, miner, Little Bendigo
Baxter, John, dairyman, Skipton st
Baylee, S., commercial traveller, Drummond st
Bean, Angus, Peel st
Bear, August, gardener, Nightingale st
Beauchamp, —, miner, Lal Lal st
Bearpark, Miss, school, Raglan st
Beard, Henry, grocer, Doveton st
Beard, James, bootmaker, Eyre st
Bearment, George, carpenter, Main road
Beasley, Misses, school, Dana st
Beaufort, —, miner, Black hill
Beaumont, James, miner, Humbank st
Beaven, G. F., miner, Urquhart st
Beaven, Thomas, carpenter, Errard st
Beavis, John, bootmaker, Armstrong st
Beck, John, carpenter, Sturt st
Beckingham, George, rag merchant, Armstrong st
Beeson, Samuel, blacksmith, Creswick road
Beeton, Rorie, miner, Main road
Begg, David, carpenter, Ripon st
Bell, John, saddler, South st
Bell, Peter, compositor, Sturt st

Bell, Samuel, gardener, Errard st
Bell, John, miner, Drummond st
Bell, John, timber merchant, Armstrong street
Bell, Thomas, labourer, William st
Bell, John, tentmaker, Humffray st
Bell, A., butcher, Eyre st
Bell, Wm. Edward, miner, Dana st
Bell, Henry, builder, Seymour st
Bell, Wm., miner, Burnbank st
Bell and Wright, timber merchants, Market square
Bellair, Thomas S., Rainbow hotel, Sturt street
Benjamin, Joshua, Drummond st
Bennett, William, watchmaker, Bridge st
Bennett, Isaac, miner, Neil st
Bennett, W., miner, Dawson st
Bennett, H., produce broker, Armstrong street
Bennet, W., watchmaker, Macarthur st
Bennett, James, lace store, Barkly st
Bennett, James, miner, Barkly st
Benoit, —, seedsman, Market st
Benson, Wm., architect, Mechanics' Institute Chambers
Benson, Wm., architect, South st
Benson, Philip, gardener, Peel st
Benson, Henry, plasterer, Armstrong st
Berkell, Highoven, miner, Scott's parade
Bernjahn, Henry, jeweller, Grenville st
Bernstein, John, military tailor, Bridge street
Bernstein, John, tailor, Wills st
Bernstein, Solomon, and Co., outfitters, Main road
Berry, Wm., miner, Seymour st
Berry, Jacob, brickmaker, Albert st
Berry, Godfrey, tailor, Wills st
Berryman, Miss, seamstress, Grant st
Berryman, Andrew, miner, Grant st
Berryman, —, painter, Windermere st
Berryman, James, miner, Victoria st
Berryman, D., miner, Barkly st
Bertison, James, miner, Skipton st
Best, Charles, carpenter, Barkly st
Bettridge, John T., joiner, Main road
Beveridge, Chas., miner, Sebastopol
Beynon, James, miner, Barkly st
Bibby, James, Lancashire Arms, Black hill
Bibby, Thomas, miner, Humffray st
Bibby, James, clerk, Yuille st
Bicknell, F., storeman, Ligar st
Diggs and Shopjaw, china and earthenware dealers, Bridge st
Bignell, Wm., Union hotel, Sturt st
Bignell, Wm., Rainbow hotel, Sturt st
Bignell and Duffy, George hotel, Lydiard street
Bilney, Charles, miner, Rowe st
Binder, Robert, blacksmith, Grant st
Binder, Benjamin, builder, Ligar st
Binder, Mrs., school, Ligar st

Binney, J., baker and confectioner, Main road
Binstead, Mrs., fancy repository, Sturt st
Bird, Richard, mason, Otway st
Bird, Thomas, miner, Havelock st
Bird, J., Errard st
Birtchnell, L. S., accountant, Mechanics' Institute chambers
Birtchnell, L. S., accountant, Ligar st
Bisgrove, Mrs., laundress, Humffray st
Bishop, J., and Co., Soho Works, Dana st
Bishop, D. H., dairyman, Humffray st
Bishop, W. R., lithographic printer, Armstrong st
Black, John, surveyor, Victoria st
Black, Donald, miner, Ligar st
Black, —, reporter
Black, —, importer, Raglan st
Black, James, carter, Barkly st
Blachford, Edward, painter, East st
Blackburn, J., miner, Macarthur st
Blackett, Thomas, Cumberland and Durham hotel, Bridge st
Blade, Henry, miner, A 1 st
Blake, Chas., Junction hotel, A 1 st
Blair, J., miner, Barkly st
Blair, Lewis, bootmaker, Rowe st
Blaney, Edward, quarryman, Ascot st
Blanchard, Thomas, compositor, Lyons st
Blanford, John, office keeper, Sturt st
Blase, John, miner, Little Bendigo
Bleckly, G. W., compositor, Peel st
Blemy, J., miner, Main road
Blight, Peter, carpenter, Barkly st
Blood, —, miner, Barkly st
Bloore, J. W. C., chemist, Skipton st
Blundell, John, Ligar st
Blythman, Francis, miner, Young st
Boarse, John, miner, Ascot st
Bonvard, J., baker, Drummond st
Bodycombe, J., pattern maker, Doveton st
Bock, Alfred, jeweller, Main road
Bolan, J., Lady of Lake hotel, Armstrong street
Bolimer, J., hairdresser, Main road
Bolter, Henry, brewer, Eureka st
Bolster, James, bookbinder, Eyre st
Bolster, Mrs., milliner, Eyre st
Boncolas, Nicholas, confectioner, Main rd
Bond, Sampson, mason, Skipton st
Bone, Henry, miner, Humffray st
Bonella, A., miner, Drummond st
Booley, Robert, coachsmith, Ligar st
Doonsha, Tyrned, carter, Pleasant st
Booth, Wm., miner, Little Bendigo
Booth, R. F., carpenter, Creswick road
Booth, Ernest, carpenter, Main road
Borialse, John, miner, Brown hill
Boswell, Mrs., fruiterer, Main road
Bower, Thomas, labourer, Doveton st
Bowden, Henry, miner, Humffray st
Bowman, Thomas, gasman, Mair st
Bowman, Jonathan, gasman, Macarthur street

Bowner, James, hairdresser, Dana st
Bowles, Jeremiah, grocer, Bridge st
Boxall, Wm., butcher, Armstrong st
Boxall, Mrs., sempstress, Armstrong st
Boxhorn, Joseph, jeweller, Sturt st
Boulton, —, carpenter, Main road
Boundy, J., tanner, Pleasant st
Bourke, Wm., bootmaker, Main road
Boyd, Charles, printer, Sturt st
Boyd, Wm., publican, Mair st
Boyd, Samuel, manager Turkish baths, Armstrong st
Boyle, James, Rainbow hotel, Grant st
Brace, J. W., Oriental hotel, Wendouree parade
Bracher, Wm., carpenter, Sturt st
Bradbury, T., dairyman, Nightingale st
Bradbury, Francis, builder, Dawson st
Braddock, James, engineer, Burnbank st
Bradford, W., baker, Macarthur st
Bradley, John B., storeman, Lydiard st
Bradley, Patrick, miner, Grant st
Bradley, E., sharebroker, Sturt st
Bradley, E., and Co., sharebrokers, 6 Eldon chambers, Lydiard st
Brady, O. C., surgeon, Eyre st
Brady, John, miner, Raglan st
Brailey, William, produce dealer, Creswick road
Braithwaite, Thomas, Cricketers' Arms, Cricket Ground
Brammell, Albert, engineer, Dana st
Brandon, Robert, tailor, Lydiard st
Bransions, Mrs., Dana st
Brasburger, Jacob, bootmaker, Main road
Bray, John, miner, Little Bendigo
Bray, William, Victoria hotel, Sebastopol
Bray, Charles, miner, Barkly st
Bray, William, miner, Doveton st
Bray, Josiah, storekeeper, Victoria st
Bray, James, engineer, Creswick road
Breeden, J., miner, Doveton st
Breen, Mrs., Dyte's parade
Breeze, Mrs., dressmaker, Young st
Bremner, J., storekeeper, Victoria st
Brennan, John, constable, Peel st
Brennan, Patrick, Raglan st
Brennan, B., labourer, Humffray st
Brennan, Thomas, miner, Grant st
Brewer, Mrs., Dyte's parade
Brewer, Mrs., greengrocer, Princes st
Brewer, Henry, labourer, Burnbank st
Brewster, George, labourer, Drummond st
Brewster, James, gardener, Ripon st
Brewster, Alex., compositor, Wills st
Briant, George, baker, Seymour st
Bridges, Wm., artist, Plank road
Bridges, Wm., carter, King st
Bridget, Thomas, butcher, Peel st
Bridgewater, Thomas, bootmaker, Victoria street
Bright, —, clerk, Clarendon st
Britton, John, builder, Victoria st
Broadbent, Thomas, miner, Burnbank st

Broadbent, James, Eureka st
Broadbent and Co., carriers, Bridge st
Broadbent, W., carrier, Barkly st
Broadbent, Peter, carpenter, Barkly st
Brock, John, musician, Victoria st
Brockenshire, James, miner, Ligar st
Brooks, —, miner, Little Bendigo
Brook, W. F., compositor, Brougham st
Brooks, F., tinsmith, Main road
Brooks, Julian, miner, Humffray st
Brooks, Alex., carter, Eamond st
Brooks, Chas., boatbuilder, Peel st
Bromage, J., straw hat manufactory, Dawson st
Brookes, G., building surveyor, Dana st
Broadhurst, George, carter, Mair st
Bromley, J. W., Mair st
Brophy, Francis, tailor, Peel st
Brophy, D., Atlantic hotel, Skipton st
Brose, Mrs. M., dressmaker, Clayton st
Brosnan, Maurice, bootmaker, Main road
Brown, Miss, dressmaker, Creswick road
Brown, J., labourer, Creswick road
Brown, —, miner, Malakoff st
Brown, Francis, miner, Main road
Brown, Mrs., dressmaker, Main road
Brown, Charles, blacksmith, Main road
Brown, John, engine driver, Urquhart st
Brown, Chas., painter, Sturt st
Brown, W., Earl of Zetland hotel, Bridge street
Brown, And., moulder, Main road
Brown, Fred., mattress maker, Wills st
Brown, Wm., labourer, East st
Brown, Alex., carpenter, Grant st
Brown, W. A., wireworker, Grant st
Brown, Geo., mason, Doral st
Brown, Paul, labourer, Peel st
Brown, W. M., Armstrong st
Brown, Andrew, draper, Raglan st
Brown, Mrs., Lyons st
Brown, Harry, mason, Errard st
Brown, Mrs., Drummond st
Brown, Henry, Bath Arms, Dana st
Brown, Henry, store, Dana st
Brown, Wm., miner, Eyre st
Brown, Samuel, hairdresser, Mair st
Brown, Thomas, stationer, Mair st
Brown, Mrs., dressmaker, Mair st
Brown, John, blacksmith, A 1 st
Brown, W., chemist and druggist, Sebastopol road
Brown, J. J., Stork hotel, Armstrong st
Brown, J., engine driver, Seymour st
Brown, J. G., miller, Mill st
Brown, James, miner, Brougham st
Brown, A. J., teacher, north of Boundary street
Brown, J., Wendouree parade
Brown and Osborne, forwarding agents, Armstrong st
Browne, Mrs., Errard st
Browne, A. V., law clerk, Brougham st
Browne, D., mason, Peel st

Browne, John, labourer, Peel st
Brownley, G., post-office clerk, Errard st
Bruce, —, carpenter, Armstrong st
Bruce, James, tailor, Sturt st
Bruce, James, miner, Talbot st
Brudie, W., miner, Eyrie st
Brudenell, J., hairdresser, Bridge st
Brudie, Wm., miner, Eyrie st
Brugless, James, store, Dawson st
Brumby, Robert, miner, Main road
Brun, James, labourer, Dawson st
Bruton, R., standpipe keeper, Main road
Bruton, Mrs., dressmaker, Ripon st
Bruun, L. E., oil and color merchant, Bridge st
Bryant, Edward, miner, Peel st
Bryant, Wm., labourer, King st
Bryant and Stallard, sharebrokers, Sturt st
Bryant, Edwin, sharebroker, Mill st
Bryce, J., miner, Young st
Bryce and Chalmers, grocers, Bridge st
Brymer, Mrs., laundress, Eyrie st
Buchacker, —, teacher, Eureka st
Buchan, Wm., miner, Pleasant st
Buchanan, James, miner, Pleasant st
Buchanan, George, Temperance hotel, Bridge st
Buchanan, A., painter, Sebastopol
Buchanan, J., painter, Barkly st
Buckinghamshire, S., miner, Errard st
Buckle, J., tailor, Victoria st
Buckle, John, tailor, Humffray st
Buckle, James, waiter, Wills st
Budds, Mrs., Ligar st
Budge, Wm., carter, Wills st
Bugden, Wm., miner, Eyre st
Buley, James, builder, Dawson st
Bull, James, engineer, Eyre st
Bull, Edward, engineer, Dana st
Bull, R., car proprietor, Esmond st
Bull, James, livery stables, Armstrong st
Bull, James, livery stables, Doveton st
Bull, Thomas, miner, Dawson st
Bull, Wm., Red Bull hotel, Humffray st
Bullen, George, clerk, Raglan st
Bullen, Thomas, miner, Drummond st
Bullock, Wm., miner, Humffray st
Bultrees, Joseph, coachbuilder, Lygar st
Bumblecombe, G., miner, Little Bendigo
Bunce, Dr., Dawson st
Bunce, Mrs., professor of music, Lyons st
Burbidge, Wm., engine driver, Dana st
Burch, Robert, smith, Main road
Burden, T., produce merchant, Main road
Burgess, John, wheelwright, Doveton st
Burgess, George, miner, Scott's parade
Burgoyne and Co., grocers, Sturt st
Burke, John, labourer, Talbot st
Burke, —, law clerk, Dana st
Burke, Michael, car proprietor, Dana st
Burke, L., Golden Gate hotel, Victoria st
Burke, J., Bakery Hill hotel, Humffray st
Burke, Mrs., Errard st
Burns, Thomas, engineer, Dawson st

Burns, Michael, dairyman, Wendouree parade
Burns, —, miner, Ascot st
Burns, Wm., miner, Talbot st
Burns, R. W., contractor, Creswick road
Burns, Thomas, tinsmith, Main road
Burns, James, miner, Scott's parade
Burns, Joseph, labourer, Havelock st
Burns, James, miner, Emax st
Burns, Mrs., teacher, Seymour st
Burridge, G., brickmaker, Scott's parade
Borrows, Thomas, blacksmith, Dana st
Borrows, Mrs., dressmaker, Dana st
Borrows, John, cattle dealer, Lyons st
Borrows, C., store, Young st
Borrows, James, carter, Creswick road
Borrows, W., carter, Burnbank road
Bursch, L., tailor, Main road
Burton, F., Barkly st
Burton, Thomas, miner, South st
Burton, W. H., carpenter, Main road
Busfield, Henry, cardriver, Armstrong st
Bush, Wm., painter, Humffray st
Bush, Matthew, carrier, Holmes st
Bushley, Joel, Plank Road hotel, Main road
Butcher, Geo., miner, Scott's parade
Butler, W. H., miner, Victoria st
Butler, —, carrying agent, Skipton st
Butler, Patrick, storekeeper, Main road
Butler, J. W., Eldon chambers, Lydiard street
Butler, J. W., agent, Raglan st
Butler, Mrs., Raglan st
Butler, Mrs., sempstress, Doveton st
Butler, John, carpenter, South st
Batson, Isaac, miner, Wills st
Button, E., carpenter, Main road
Butter, John, miner, Little Bendigo
Byers, Robert, labourer, Dana st
Byron, Miss, milliner, Raglan st
Bywater, Wm., minor, Malakoff st

C.

Cadell, Wm., miner, Humffray st
Cadigan, Joshua, labourer, East st
Cadwallader, Oliver, inspector of railway, Humffray st
Cahill, Cornelius, miner, Victoria st
Cail, J., storekeeper, Bridge st
Cairns, F., miner, Queen st
Cairns, J., carter, Wills st
Cairns, Thomas, tailor, Victoria st
Cain, David, Neil st
Cain, John, miner, Raglan st
Calcott, Thomas, miner, Sturt st
Calcott, T., miner, Sturt st
Calcott, Arthur, miner, Dana st
Calcott, Edwin, Stag hotel, Bridge st
Caldwell, J. W., carter, Armstrong st
Callahan, John, miner, Drummond st
Callan, Joshua, labourer, Humffray st
Calder, Robert, miner, Peel st

Calder, James, miner, Peel st
Callinan, Patrick, Review hotel, Skipton street
Callinan, —, hotel keeper, Victoria st
Calero, Henry, butcher, Esmond st
Campbell, Wm., miner, Bond st
Campbell, James, engineer, Dana st
Campbell, Thomas, labourer, Clyde st
Campbell, Alexander, engineer, Dana st
Campbell, Alexander, miner, Sebastopol
Campbell, John, miner, Skipton st
Campbell, Hugh, chemist, Main road
Campbell, J., miner, Sebastopol
Campbell, F. E., compositor, Ligar st
Cameron, John, miner, Mair st
Cameron, Duncan, miner, Webster st
Cameron, James, carpenter, Peel st
Cameron, A., coachdriver Seymour st
Cameron, Wm., miner, Errard st
Cameron, Wm., Skipton st
Cameron, Donald, groom, Ligar st
Cameron, Donald, miner, Ligar st
Canning, Peter, clerk, Burnbank st
Cannavan, Miss, dressmaker, Sturt st
Cant, —, tinsmith, Humffray st
Cantor, Edward, butcher, Main road
Cantyclaar, J., dyer and scourer, Main road
Capes, John, clerk, Drummond st
Carpenter, George, labourer, Havelock st
Carpenter, H., leather cutter, Main road
Carpenter, Thomas, French polisher
Carnell, —, miner, Grenville st
Carney, Mrs., laundress, Eureka st
Carey, J., hawker, Peel st
Carey, M., teacher, King st
Cargin, M., market inspector, Sturt st
Carver, J. S., auctioneer, Lydiard st
Carver, Lawrence, and Hitchins, sharebrokers, Lydiard st
Carlisle, Robert, engineer, Queen st
Carlyon, James, carter, Esmond st
Carlile, John, miner, Humffray st
Carlile, H., engineer, Queen st
Carr, George, blacksmith, Scott's parade
Carr, Mrs., Windermere st
Carr, John, brickmaker, McArthur st
Carr, William, hawker, Doveton st
Carr, G., smith and wheelwright, Creswick road
Carr, —, miner, Raglan st
Carrol, A., Garry Owen hotel, Victoria st
Carrol, B., bricklayer, Humffray st
Carrol, Robert, blacksmith, Peel st
Carrol, P., carter, Victoria st
Carrol, James, railway porter, Armstrong street
Carrol, John, warder, Doveton st
Carrol, James, labourer, Eureka st
Carrol, R., off Mair st
Carrol, Mrs., Windermere st
Carrol, James, miner, Bridge st
Carrol, J., miner, Black hill
Carmichael, coachdriver, Queen st
Carrick, Thomas, bootmaker, Bridge st

Cartwright, R., boiler maker, Raglan st
Cargeeg, J., produce and general store, Creswick road
Carlton, Martin, carter, Errard st
Carter and Co., Phoenix foundry, Armstrong st
Carter, John, Golden Fleece hotel, Mair st
Carter, Richard, engineer, Eureka st
Carter, J., plasterer, Ripon st
Carter, J., Golden Fleece hotel, Skipton st
Carter, Henry, miner, Skipton st
Carter, G. A., Garrick's Head hotel, Sturt street
Carter, R., and Co., Phoenix foundry, Doveton st
Carstairs, David, clerk, Barkly st
Carstairs, Mrs., dressmaker, Wendouree parade
Casell, H. R., architect, Sturt st
Casey, Mrs., King st
Casey, John, painter, Victoria st
Casey, Peter, contractor, Lyons st
Casey, John, John o'Groat's hotel, Main road
Cass, B., Horse Bazaar hotel, Main road
Casserly, M., quarryman, Drummond st
Cassidy, F., constable, Camp reserve
Casson, Henry, carter, Errard st
Cater, John, miner, Armstrong st
Cathcart, J. B., law clerk, Esmond st
Cathie, J., porter, Neil st
Catton, A., coachdriver, Ascot st
Cairon, Wm., carter, Al st
Catron, Wm., carter, Howard st
Cathel, John, miner, Talbot st
Cavanagh, Malachi, storekeeper
Cavan, Edward, carter, Drummond st
Cave, John, gardener, Wendouree parade
Cawa, James, Mair st
Cawley, Patrick, miner, Black hill
Cayley, Peter, traveller, Malakoff
Cazaly, H., Mining Exchange
Cecil, Thomas, miner, Main road
Chalmers, Mrs., Young st
Chalmers, —, hawker, Eyre st
Chalmers, H. B., merchant, Webster st
Chalmers, —, dairyman, Humffray st
Chalmers, Wm., carpenter, Bridge st
Chalmers, J., grocer, Grenville st
Chalmers, H., miner, Sunny corner
Chalk, Alfred, law clerk, Webster st
Chalken, Wm. W., miner, Queen st
Challenger, J. W., hotelkeeper, Main road
Chambers, Isaac, miner, Lyons st
Chamberlain, Geo. F., chemist, Main road
Chamberlain, E. W. G., clerk, Victoria st
Chamberlain, Charles, carter, Lydiard st
Chapman, Henry, clerk, Armstrong st
Chapman, Geo., clerk, Lyons st
Chapple, Richard, confectioner, Raglan st
Chapple, W., grocer, Eyre st
Charles, Wm., miner, Bond st
Charlesworth, E., miner, Barkly st
Charlton, Thomas, miner, Eyre st

2 N

Charlton, Edward, miner, Dana st
Charley, Phillip, coachmaker, Dawson st
Charles, George, bricklayer, Howard st
Cherry, John, painter, Ligar st
Cherry, Henry, Victoria hotel, Armstrong street
Chong, Pong Nang, minister, Young st
Chiswick, Joe, bellman, Lyons st
Chisholm, George, blacksmith, Sebastopol
Chisholm, James, carter, Black hill
Chisholm, Chas., miner, Wendouree parade
Chisholm, James, miner, Howard st
Childs, James, butcher, Humffray st
Chisel, Charles, miner, Esmond st
Chipnell, John, miner, Albert st
Cheeney, Wm., Chinese interpreter, Young st
Chown, H. C., Freemasons' hotel, Eureka street
Christy, D., electoral registrar, Errard st
Christie, L. N., and Co., drapers, Sturt st
Chumley, Edward, foundryman, Armstrong st south
Churchill, Wm., carter, Scott's parade
Churchett, George, cordial manufacturer, Dawson st
Clancy, P., miner, Scott's parade
Clague, Thomas, storeman, Errard st
Clauwell, John, miner, Wendouree parade
Clapp, Robert, carter, Wills st
Clapham, George, hawker, Ligar st
Clark, P., carpenter, Grant st
Clark, Isaac, miner, Dyte's parade
Clark, Perry, musician, Scott's parade
Clark, F. S., carter, Clayton st
Clark, John, carter, East st
Clark, W. D., miner, Raglan st
Clark, John, law clerk, Lydiard st
Clark, Robert, Raglan st
Clark, Wm., miner, Raglan st
Clark, Wallace, cooper, Victoria st
Clark, Thomas, butcher, Armstrong st
Clark, Thomas, miner, Dana st
Clark, John, labourer, Dana st
Clark, John, miner, Humffray st
Clark, Thomas, grocer, Dana st
Clark, Thomas, grocer, Victoria st
Clark, Benjamin, soap and candle manufacturer, Wendouree parade
Clark, John, labourer, Doveton st
Claxton, F. M., grocer, Webster st
Claxton, F. M., grocer, Armstrong st
Claxton, Richard, shoemaker, Humffray street
Clay, Charles, moulder, Grant st
Clay, J., painter, Armstrong st south
Clayton, — James, refreshment rooms, Wendouree parade
Cleary, Patrick, carter, Clayton st
Cleary, J., storekeeper, Sturt st
Clegg, James, labourer, Raglan st
Clegg, Thomas, grocer, Sturt st
Clegg, —, hatmaker, off Victoria st

Clelland, James, gardener, Webster st
Clemm, W., hatter, Sturt st
Clemence, Samuel, blacksmith, Howard st
Clemence, Richard, engineer, Doveton st
Clendenning, Dr., coroner, Humffray st
Cline, John, labourer, Main road
Cluse, —, labourer, Wendouree parade
Coates, Wm., blacksmith, Main st
Cobbett, Wm., storeman, Ligar st
Cock, —, Eldon chambers, Lydiard st
Cocks, Henry M., carter, Skipton st
Cocks, E., draper, Ascot st
Cockin, Elijah, hotel keeper, Wills st
Cockburn, Wm., miner, Young st
Cockle, John, carter, Otway st
Code, Wm., labourer, Dawson st
Cole, Walter, carter, Dawson st
Codlin, Charles, Sturt st
Coe, Arthur, baker, Urquhart st
Cogden, Oliver, plumber, Howard st
Cohen, Michael, bricklayer, Raglan st
Cohen, Simon, ironmonger, Sturt st
Cohen, David, fruiterer, Main road
Cohen, S., miner, Wills st
Coker, W. H., miner, Ligar st
Colahan, Wm., miner, Havelock st
Coleny, James, miner, Ascot st
Cole, J., carter, Scott's parade
Collie, J., bricklayer, Raglan st
Collis, Edmund, miner, Dana st
Collins, Franklin, British American hotel, Esmond st
Collins, Thomas, plasterer, Peel st
Collins, John, saddler, Main road
Collins, F., miner, Lal Lal st
Collins, John, miner, Little Bendigo
Collins, Wm., miner, Little Bendigo
Culliver, Arundell, miner, Peel st
Collett, James, miner, Grant st
Collett, Charles, blacksmith, Eureka st
Colgrave, Edwin, miner, Armstrong st
Comb, T., newspaper proprietor, Webster street
Comb, Joseph, town clerk, Sturt st
Combe, Matthew, barrister, Lydiard st
Commins, P., Main road
Compton, John, compositor, Eureka st
Condon, Jonathan, miner, Little Bendigo
Condon, Morris, miner, Drummond st
Condy, W. L., carpenter, Doveton st
Condy, James, labourer, Clyde st
Condy, Peter, fruiterer, Humffray st
Conifer, —, miner, Ebden st
Conolly, J., miner, Sebastopol
Connoly, Henry, contractor, Webster st
Conlin, Patrick, miner, off Victoria st
Cowlson, J., mason, Armstrong st south
Conway, P., Speedwell hotel, Little Bendigo
Conway, Henry, contractor, Webster st
Conway, Michael, miner, Drummond st
Cook, Miss, dressmaker, Raglan st
Cook, Isaac, brickmaker, A 1 st
Cook, Henry, miner, Humffray st

Cook, Robert, carpenter, Humffray st
Cook, Walter, carter, Humffray st
Cook, Robert, butcher, Sturt st
Cook, George, Sebastopol hotel, Sebastopol
Cookson, E., contractor, Macarthur st
Cookson, Matthew, contractor, Macarthur street
Cooney, M., blacksmith, Victoria st
Cooney, Patrick, miner, Humffray st
Cooney, John, bootmaker, Eureka st
Cooper, John, carrier, Armstrong st
Cooper, Mrs., Drummond st
Cooper, Christopher, carpenter, Windermere st
Cooper, Wm., engineer, Dana st
Cooper, Owen, carpenter, Windermere st
Cooper, Edward, bootmaker, Barkly st
Cooper, John, hat and bonnet maker, Humffray st
Cooper, S., blacksmith, Urquhart st
Cooper, James, miner, Armstrong st
Cooper, Thomas, labourer, Holmes st
Cooper, Augustus, miner, South st
Cooper, David, blacksmith, Errard st
Copeland, J., sharebroker, Drummond st
Copeland, H., miner, Drummond st
Corbould, Wm., tailor, Sturt st
Cordukes, Misses, stationers, Sturt st
Cordukes, H., secretary Benevolent Asylum, Doveton st
Cormack, Alexander, carpenter, Sturt st
Cornish, John, miner, Dyte's parade
Cornish, H., miner, Princes st
Cornish, John, merchant, Mair st
Cornish, Edwd, storeman, Main road
Cornish, Thomas, sharebroker, Sturt st
Corbett, James, miner, Dana st
Corbett, Patrick, miner, Dana st
Corbett, Wm., miner, Dyte's parade
Corbett, Patrick, draper, Barkly st
Corbett, Wm., store, Seymour st
Corbett, Wm., miner, Essex st
Corkhill, Robert, grocer, Armstrong st
Corrigan, J., bandmaster, Wills st
Cortessos, E., store, Bridge st
Costin, John, carpenter, King st
Costin, —, ironmonger, Bridge st
Costin, H., timber merchant, Main road
Costain, John, miner, Pleasant st
Cott, Wm., miner, Errard st
Cottar, James, miner, Errard st
Cottar, Pearce, Ascott st
Cottier, T., baker, Barkly st
Cottle, J., engine driver, Victoria parade
Cottle, Henry, store, Eureka st
Coulsell, John, bricklayer, Talbot st
Coutts, Alexander, Creswick road
Coutts, D., and Sons, bakers and grocers, Humffray st
Coutts, —, clerk, Armstrong st
Cown, James, plumber and painter, Sturt street
Cowan, John, blacksmith, Macarthur st

Cowan, Thomas, mining surveyor, Sturt street
Coward, Henry, blacksmith, Victoria st
Cowdell, Thomas, bootmaker, Peel st
Cowall, John, bricklayer, Lyons st
Cowly, Joseph, carpenter, Eyre st
Cowly, John, storeman, Camp reserve
Cowland, W., builder, Peel st
Cox, Thomas, tailor, Main road
Cox, Frederic, bootmaker, Sturt st
Cox, James, Western hotel, Creswick road
Cox, James, miner, Humffray st
Cox, Samuel, carter, Creswick road
Cox, W., stonemason, Armstrong st
Cox, W. M., Common School teacher, Soldiers hill
Cox, George, bootmaker, Dana st
Cox, W. M., schoolmaster, Neil st
Cox, Amos, schoolmaster, Raglan st
Craddock, J., baker and grocer, Victoria street
Craig, Walter, Craig's hotel, Lydiard st
Craig, Alexander, hotel keeper, Sturt st
Crampton, James, nightman, Dana st
Crampton, M., labourer, Howard st
Cramen, —, carter, Clayton st
Cranston, Thomas, carpenter, Lyons st
Crane, Wm., manager, Creswick road
Crane, James, tailor, Peel st
Crannige, Charles, miner, Humffray st
Crapps, M., miner, Brougham st
Crawford, James, butcher, Humffray st
Crawford, Thomas, carpenter, Sebastopol
Cray, John, waiter, Raglan st
Craik, Jemie, Scottish hotel, Dana st
Cray, W., post office clerk, Errard st
Creber, W., carpenter, Sturt st
Creblin, Charles, miner, Doveton st
Crees, John, butcher, Sturt st
Crees, John, slaughterman, Creswick road
Cressy, George, miner, Windermere st
Croft, R., schoolmaster, Brougham st
Creighton, M. H., oil merchant, Mair st
Creighton, M. H., oil merchant, Brougham street
Creston, W., accountant, Seymour st
Cripps, H., coachmaker, Ligar st
Crisp, John, painter, Victoria st
Critchley, R., miner, Sturt st
Critchley, R., miner, Armstrong st south
Critchley, B., miner, Sturt st
Cressand, J., cordial manufacturer, Doveton st
Crouch, George, salesman, Victoria st
Crouch, J., sharebroker, Sturt st
Crough, Mrs., laundress, South st
Crompton, Thomas, bootmaker, Creswick road
Crook, W. F., carpenter, Victoria st
Cross, George, contractor, Brougham st
Cross, Robert, miner, Eyre st
Cross, F., miner, Talbot st
Crossbie, Miss, Esmond st
Crossdale, Stephen, constable, Main road

Creadale, P., constable, Barkly st
Crosaly, J., contractor, Mair st
Crotty, James, miner, Young st
Crow, Alexander, hotelkeeper, Lydiard st
Crow, James, mason, Humffray st
Crowley, Thomas, bootmaker, Eureka st
Crowley, Patrick, King st
Croughey, James, miner, Princes st
Crowther, John, Newington post office
Crowther, Miss, Doveton st
Crook, W. H., cattle salesman, Skipton st
Cronk, W., greengrocer, Victoria st
Cronk, H., butcher, Victoria st
Croyle, J., sharebroker, Windermere st
Cullin, J., engineer, Seymour st
Cullinan, Patrick, miner, Sebastopol road
Cummins, R., miner, Sturt st
Cummins, Rev. Robert, Victoria st
Cummins, Robert, carter, Lydiard st
Cummins, J., Regatta Club hotel, Wendouree parade
Cummings, M., boarding-house, Errard st
Cummings, —, Drummond st
Cummins, timber merchant, Main road
Curl, M., miner, Pleasant st
Curlaw, J., miner, Skipton st
Curley, James, Railway hotel, Neil st
Curnic, George, refreshment rooms, Wendouree parade
Currant, W., smith, Barkly st
Curran, Matthew, miner, Dana st
Corran, James, mason, Humffray st
Currie, James, carpenter, Bridge st
Curry, Miss, Drummond st
Curry, John, labourer, Otway st
Curnow, J., miner, Urquhart st
Curnow, Wm., miner, Black hill
Curnow, Peter, miner, Brown hill
Curnow, Andrew, Sunny corner
Curtis, Thomas J., engineer, Otway st
Curtis, Patrick, miner, Urquhart st
Curtis, Edwin, produce dealer, Peel st
Curtis, James, printer, Mair st
Curtis, James, printer, Victoria parade, Wendouree lake
Curtis, Wm., carpenter, Mair st
Curwin, sharebroker, Sturt st
Coolas, P., miner, Victoria st
Cuthbert, Charles D., architect, Lignar st
Cuthbert, Charles D., architect, Sturt st
Cuthbert, H., solicitor and procter, Lydiard st
Cuthbert, H., Sturt st
Cuttance, W. L., miner, Barkly st
Cutter and Laidlaw, livery and bait stables, Sturt st
Cutter, J., engineer, Eyre st
Cotter, Henry, baker, Errard st
Cutter and Lever, coachbuilders, Armstrong st

D.

Daglish, H., engine driver, Main road
Daglish, H., engine driver, Sturt st
Daisey, J., carrier, Drummond st
Dallas, Alex., coach driver, Eyre st
Dale, John, carpenter, Dawson st
Dale, Samuel, miner, Barkly st
Dale, Christian, miner, Sebastopol
Dale, John, miner, Talbot st
Dallimore, J., foundryman, Urquhart st
Daly, Edward, bootmaker, Eureka st
Dalzel, Frank, miner, Talbot st
Danis, Joseph, wheelwright, Armstrong street
Daniel, Rev. G., Wesleyan minister, Barkly street
Dangrs, Matthew, miner, Main road
D'Augri, N., miner, Sturt st
Dangerfield, Alexander, City hotel, Lydiard st
Daneyger, George, ironmonger, Main road
Dances, J., labourer, Sturt st
Dances, J., labourer, Main road
Dasset, George, miner, Barkly st
Davenport, Joshua, labourer, Lal Lal st
Darley, Miss, Grenville st
Darwin, Richard, bootmaker, Main road
Davis, F., tentmaker, Victoria st
Davis, George, miner, Barkly st
Davis, John, miner, Eureka st
Davis, Mrs., hat cleaner, Eureka st
Davis, James, miner, Macarthur st
Davis, George, miner, Little Bendigo
Davis, D., carpenter, Sebastopol
Davis, Wm., draper, Sebastopol
Davis, John, Prince of Wales hotel, Cobblers
Davis, Wm., miner, Cobblers
Davis, Thomas, miner, Cobblers
Davis, Thomas, plasterer, Lydiard st
Davis, David, bootmaker, Sebastopol
Davis, F., draper, Victoria st
Davis, J. C., miner, Urquhart st
Davis, Thomas, miner, Lyons st
Davis, —, blacksmith, Talbot st
Davis, John, grocer, Mair st
Davis, E., contractor, Urquhart st
Davis, Thomas, miner, Urquhart st
Davis, James, miner, Armstrong st south
Davis, James, tentmaker, Bridge st
Davis, Isaac, pawnbroker, Main road
Davis, Richard, bootmaker, Main road
Davis, Miss, Main road
Davis, Wm., carman, Otway st
Davis, —, bawker, Dyte's parade
Davis, R., miner, Seymour st
Davis, Joseph, clerk, Clarendon st
David, B., engine driver, Humffray st
Davison, John, miner, Lyons st
Davison, Robert, surveyor, Lyons st
Davison, H., cabinetmaker, Humffray st
Davidson, Robert, mining registrar, Camp reserve
Davey and Co., engineers, Armstrong st
Davey, Thomas, engineer, Mair st
Davy, Thomas, carter, Victoria st
Davy, John, labourer, Humffray st

Davy, Wm., ironmonger, Lydiard st
Davy, Edward, carter, Victoria st
Davy, Thomas, miner, Bond st
Davy, Charles, carter, Armstrong st south
Davy, Joseph, plasterer, Princes st
Davy, Thomas, engineer, Lyons st
Daw, Henry, butcher, Dana st
Daw, Wm., carter, Victoria st
Dawling, James, miner, Little Bendigo
Daws, —, upholsterer, Doveton st
Dawson, Alexander, engineer, Armstrong street
Dawson, R. G., grocer, Urquhart st
Dawson, J., merchant, Sturt st
Dawson, H., cabinetmaker, Humffray st
Dawson, J., dealer in building materials, Sturt st
Dawson, Benjamin, soap and candle manufacturer, Sturt st
Dawkins, James, outfitter, Talbot st
Day, Thomas, cabinetmaker, Raglan st
Day, Henry, carter, Bond st
Deal, F., miner, Bond st
Dean, John, auctioneer, Doveton st
Dean, Alex., mason, Eyre st
Deas, Mrs., laundress, Esmond st
Deas, Robert, miner, Young st
Debrow, —, miner, Skipton st
Deeble, Mark, miner, Humffray st
Deeble, Samuel, auctioneer, Sturt st
Deburst, George, butcher, Little Bendigo
Dehogard, Mrs., oculist, Drummond st
Dempster, S., gasfitter, Main road
Dempster, Alexander, miner, Cobblers
Demner, Edward, miner, Humffray st
Denholm, George, blacksmith, Barkly st
Denham, P., blacksmith, Talbot st
Denman, Geo., miner, Sturt st
Dennis, John, turner, Nell st
Denny, Alfred, miner, Errard st
Denier, Alfred, wheelwright, Windermere street
Dermoody, James, miner, Talbot st
Devison, J., miner, Little Bendigo
De Saxe, S., dentist, Bridge st
Dent, Anthony, miner, Mair st
Dent, Mrs., Royal George hotel, Lydiard street
Devison, Geo., miner, Little Bendigo
Diamond, Joseph, miner, Talbot st
Dibden, Thomas, fruiterer, Main road
Dickson, J. M., miner, Sebastopol
Dickson, Mrs., fancy repository, Sturt st
Dickson and Forsyth, grocers, Armstrong street
Dickson and Turnbull, Lydiard st
Dickens, Samuel, miner, Black hill
Diakinson, R., slaughterman, Cobblers
Dickinson, Samuel, miner, Clayton st
Dietrich, Dr., surgeon, Eureka st
Diggins, T., North Grant hotel, Bridge st
Diggins, Robert, draper, Grant st
Dillon, Dennis, carter, Raglan st
Dilges, J. M., blacksmith, Sebastopol road

Dilpratt, Samuel, miner, Skipton st
Dimant, Samuel, miner, Wills st
Dimelow, J., schoolmaster, Raglan st
Dimock, Dr., surgeon, Dawson st
Dimock, Fredk., sharebroker, Brougham street
Dimock and Letcher, sharebrokers, Sturt street
Dimond, Wm., traveller, Lyons st
Dimsey, Wm., gardener, Albert st
Dingle, John, bootmaker, Skipton st
Dingle, R., bootmaker, Eyre st
Diney, Mrs., Lyons st
Dines, Wm., draper, Windermere st
Disney, Charles, carter, Wendouree parade
Ditchber, John, Mining Exchange
Ditchburn, John, sharebroker, Lydiard st
Ditchburn, Robert, miner, Eyre st
Dix, Wm., miner, Lal Lal st
Dixon, Mrs., laundress, Lyons st
Dixon, Geo., miner, Humffray st
Dixon, R., hawker, Mair st
Dixon, W., Haymarket hotel and dining rooms, Mair st
Dixon, M., miner, Humffray st
Dixon, John, tanner, Sturt st
Doane, J. A., architect, Mechanics' Institute chambers, Sturt st
Doane, J. A., architect, Seymour st
Dobb, Charles, carter, Armstrong st south
Dobbie, David, carpenter, Macarthur st
Dobson, Wm., blacksmith, Sturt st
Dobson, Robert, Lyons st
Docarell, Henry, wheelwright, Main road
Dodd, Robert, miner, Clyde st
Dodds, Robt., salesman, Barkly st
Dodds, James, Buck's Head hotel, Bridge street
Duig and Cant, tinsmiths, Bridge st
Duig, J., tinsmith, Wills st
Dolland, Michael, miner, Talbot st
Donald, Peter, blacksmith, Urquhart st
Donald, —, engineer, Dawson st
Donald, Samuel, bootmaker, Humffray st
Donovan, Dennis, labourer, Eureka st
Donnavon, Jerry, carter, Humffray st
Donoghue, Patrick, labourer, Eureka st
Donoghue, P., labourer, Princes st
Donnolly, P. J., and Co., grain and commission agents, Dawson st
Donaldson, Thomas, miner, Drummond st
Doran, James, baker, Lal Lal st
Dormer, Thomas, miner, Drummond st
Dorman, M. J., carpenter, Ripon st
Douglas, Wm., labourer, Ascot st
Douglass, D., Windermere st
Douglas, R., miner, Macarthur st
Douglas and Lagg, blacksmiths, Eureka street
Douglas, Thomas, blacksmith, Eureka st
Doulan, —, blacksmith, Ascot st
Dow, Robert, storeman, Princes st
Dow, Isaac, miner, Skipton st

Dow, Wm., storekeeper, Armstrong st
Dow, E. J., teacher, north of boundary
Dow, James, miner, Albert st
Dow, James, miner, Little Bendigo
Dow, Isaac, miner, Skipton st
Doward, E., solicitor, Dana st
Dowdney, Edward, editor, Eureka st
Dowlan, M., blacksmith, Lydiard st
Dowlan, M., blacksmith, Edgar st
Downing, Josiah, clerk, Macarthur st
Downing, John, miner, Grant st
Downing, James, miner, Grant st
Downing, Robert, miner, Bond st
Downes, F. C., sharebroker, Sturt st
Downes, John, miner, Humffray st
Downes, Mrs., milliner, Humffray st
Downes, F. A., sharebroker, Victoria st
Doyle, John, railway porter, Barkly st
Drake, Ezra, traveller, Lyons st
Drake, Z., stonemason, Dana st
Draisy, —, carter, Sturt st
Draper, R., furniture dealer, Bridge st
Drew, Edward, carter, Wendouree parade
Drew, Edward, miner, Little Bendigo
Drew, Alfred, bootmaker, Victoria st
Drummond, D., miner, Cobblers
Drummond, P., miner, Black hill
Drummond, J., miner, Drummond st
Drury and Wright, ironmongers, Bridge street
Drury, W. L., ironmonger, Webster st
Duffy, Michael, store, Eureka st
Duffy, John, dairyman, Wendouree parade
Duffy, Mrs., Little Bendigo
Duffy, Michael, labourer, Princes st
Duggan, —, carpenter, Victoria st
Dugian, Janice, telegraph office, Raglan st
Dalhousie, Mrs., Raglan st
Duke, John, miner, Errard st
Duke, C. E., saddler, Eyre st
Dumelow, Edward, store, Victoria st
Dunn, Thomas, builder, Victoria st
Dunn, Charles, shoeing forge, Main road
Dunn, H., railway labourer, Scott's parade
Dunn, Wm., blacksmith, Esmond st
Dunn, R., and Co., merchants, Lydiard st
Dunn, Wm., blacksmith, Main road
Duberlin, H. H., bootmaker, Armstrong street
Dunberg, Andrew, miner, Princes st
Dunce, Andrew, slater, Balaclava st
Dunk, Mrs., Dunk's hotel, Grenville st
Duncan, Forbes, butcher, Macarthur st
Duncan, Gilbert, Edinburgh Castle hotel, Armstrong st
Duncan, James, nurseryman, Wendouree parade and Sturt st market
Duncombe, J. A., commission agent, Neil street
Dundon, James, railway porter, Wills st
Dungey, E. V., miller, Drummond st
Dunnet, Edward, miner, Main road
Dunning, Thomas, tailor, Sturt st

Dunston, Hugh, miner, Queens st
Dunstan, Thomas, miner, Rowe st
Dunston, Thomas, carter, Lexton st
Dunstan, James, carter, Lexton st
Dunstan, John, mason, Drummond st
Dunstan, W., miner, Esmond st
Dunstan, Peter, carpenter, Grant st
Dunstan, Thomas, miner, Main road
Dupel, F., carpenter, Albert st
Durack, Patrick, miner, Victoria st
Dance, Robert, miner, Skipton st
Dwight, Elijah, shoemaker, Brown hill
Dwyer, T., soap and candle manufacturer, Eureka and Mair sts
Dwyer, Phillip, labourer, off Victoria st
Dwyer, M., baker, Neil st
Dwyer, Mrs., dressmaker, Neil st
Dyke, D., store, Eyre st
Dyer, G., cloister, Yuille st
Dyte, Charles, M.L.A., Main road

E

Eady, —, miner, Bond st
Earl, Mrs., dressmaker, Main road
Earl and Co., builders, Main road
Eathrowl, Mrs., nurse, Wills st
Earthrowl, John, grocer, Wills st
Earton, John, bootmaker, Main road
Easton, B., carter, Doveton st
Easton, H., musical instrument maker, Doveton st
Eastwood and Cummins, produce and timber merchants, Main road
Eastwood, C., produce dealer, Lydiard st
Eaves, Wm., cornfactor, Armstrong st
Eaves, Wm., cornfactor, Lyons st
Ebworthy, Richard, Creswick road
Eddy, James, miner, Peel st
Eddy, —, clerk, Webster st
Eddy, George, builder, Brougham st
Edgerton, James, miner, Burnbank st
Edmonds, E., clerk, Clarendon st
Edwards, Charles, mason, Princes st
Edwards, James, storekeeper, Sebastopol
Edwards, Mrs., dressmaker, Princes st
Edwards, James, boatbuilder, Wendouree parade
Edwards, Thomas, plumber, Lyons st
Edwards, Owen, tentmaker, Humffray st
Edwards, Owen, tentmaker, Main road
Edwards, John, mason, Otway st
Edwards, Samuel, baker, Main road
Edwards, Thomas, miner, Young st
Edwards, Thomas, miner, Bond st
Eggerton, W., engine driver, Nightingale street
Eldridge, John, miner, Little Bendigo
Eldridge, Thomas, store, Eyre st
Elijah, Richard, groom, Clarendon st
Elford, John, miner, Humffray st
Ellard, James, miner, Little Bendigo
Ellery, James, miner, Bond st
Ellingsworth, J., coachsmith, Raglan st

DIRECTORY. 279

Elliott, Walter, sheep dealer, Nell st
Elliott, M., Bank of Australasia, Lydiard street
Elliott, F. M., miner, Drummond st
Elliott, George, carpenter, Drummond st
Elliott, James, miner, Skipton st
Elliott, F., blacksmith, South st
Elliott, Cameron, butcher, Esmond st
Elliott, Mrs., Wills st
Ellis, Mrs., laundress, Nell st
Ellis, W. H., carpenter, Lydiard st
Ellis, J., Bristol hotel, Raglan st
Ellis, Thomas, turner, Humffray st
Ellis, J., horse dealer, Yuille st
Ellis, Charles, carter, Wills st
Ellis, Edward, miner, Wills st
Ellis, Thomas, miner, Little Bendigo
Ellis, Mrs., store, Grant st
Elsmore, Henry, clerk, Eyre st
Elshringham, Thomas, miner, Macarthur street
Embling, W. H., Sturt st
Embleton, Thomas, carter, Wills st
Emerson, John, miner, Sturt st
Emerson, Wm., cabinetmaker, A 1 st
Emery, Augustus, carpenter, Main road
Emery, J. W., Washington hotel, Skipton st
Empson, J. E., cabinetmaker, Windermere st
Endey, Walter, miner, Barkly st
Endus, P., wheelwright, Malo road
Engelhardt, —, carpenter, Mair st
England, George, plumber, Lal Lal st
English, John, miner, Sebastopol road
English, J., grocer, Grant st
Errington, Wm., engineer, Raglan st
Eskop, R. H., bank clerk, Sturt st
Esmond, W., blacksmith, Dana st
Esmond, John, miner, Ferwood st
Esos, Robert, tailor, Wills st
Eve, John, miner, Ripon st
Eva, Peter, miner, Ripon st
Eva, Mrs., Ripon st
Evan, Evan, pattern maker, Armstrong st south
Evans, James, miner, Wills st
Evans, George, mason, Sturt st
Evans, Mrs., dressmaker, Sturt st
Evans, James, miner, Sebastopol road
Evans, Thomas, tailor, Sebastopol road
Evans, Morgan, miner, Sebastopol road
Evans, Mrs., midwife, Grant st
Evans, James, miner, Grant st
Evans, Edward, tailor, Grant st
Evans, Joshua, carpenter, Peel st
Evans, J., labourer, Ligar st
Evans, Rev. W. M., Lyons st
Evans, W., stonemason, Lyons st
Evans, Thomas, miner, Errard st
Evans, R., cabinetmaker, Ascot st
Evans, Charles, miner, Talbot st
Evans, Jeremiah, Dana st
Evans, Mrs., Dana st

Evans, Charles, traveller, Dana st
Evans, J., miner, Eyre st
Evans, Mrs., Victoria st
Evans, Charles, Britannia boardinghouse, Armstrong st
Evans, Peters, north of boundary
Evans, Lewis, miner, Barkly st
Everdale, J., collar maker, Wills st
Everleigh, Essex, ironmonger, Nell st
Everingham, F., auctioneer, Raglan st
Everingham, F., auctioneer, Lydiard st
Ewart, George, grocer, Sturt st
Ewart, Wm., engine driver, Pleasant st
Ewart, Richard, miller, Pleasant st
Ewins, Josiah, bookseller, Sturt st
Eyles, F., tailor, Ripon st
Eyles, George, labourer, Lyons st
Eyres Brothers, ironmongers, Sturt st
Eyres, Wm., ironmonger, Clarendon st

F.

Fabricius, Jacob, miner, Lyons st
Ferguson, Wm., miner, Skipton st
Ferguson, Joseph, miner, Sebastopol
Farley, James, china dealer, Bridge st
Farley, Wm., miner, Nightingale st
Farquhar, Wm., grocer, Mair st
Farr, Rev. J., Nell st
Farr, Thomas, carpenter, Dawson st
Farr, Thomas, carpenter, Eyre st
Farr, James, miner, Macarthur st
Farrel, James, butcher, Grant st
Farrell, John, miner, Drummond st
Farrell, Wm., plasterer, Humffray st
Farren, Matthew, miner, Victoria st
Fawcett, Mrs., nurse, Ligar st
Faulks, Wm., Errard st
Fayll, James, plumber, Urquhart st
Feans, Wm., miner, off Victoria st
Featherstone, G., miner, Ripon st
Fenning, —, bank clerk, Dawson st
Fenton, John, miner, Webster st
Fenton, A. R., drill instructor, Howe st
Ferguson, Donald, carpenter, Lydiard st
Fern, Henry, miner, Skipton st
Fern, John, miner, Windermere st
Fern, Daniel, miner, Skipton st
Fennie, Wm., carpenter, Raglan st
Ferris, Theophilus, miner, Albert st
Fewster, Joseph, labourer, Dana st
Fidler, Robert, miner, Victoria st
Field, James, miner, Esmond st
Field, Alfred, painter, Main road
Field, Thomas, miner, Little Bendigo
Fielding, Enoch, carter, Grant st
Fife, James, carpenter, Grant st
Figg, Wm., tailor, Humffray st
Figgis, S., manager of gasworks, Black hill
Fincham, G. R., leather merchant, Main road
Finlay, John, teacher, Main road
Finly, David, storekeeper, Victoria st

Finlayson, J., miner, Dana st
Finlayson Brother, blacksmiths, Armstrong st
Finlayson, James, draper, off Victoria st
Finlayson, John, draper, off Victoria st
Finlayson, W., tailor and clothier, Bridge street
Finlayson, Alfred, gardener, Sturt st
Finn, Mrs., Wills st
Finn, —, barrister, Lydiard st
Finnegan, James, Mallow hotel, Skipton street
Finnis, G. F., newspaper publisher, Raglan st
Finster, Guido, pianist, Skipton st
Firth, Mrs., bonnet maker, Skipton st
Fishburn, J., carter, Macarthur st
Fisher, James, miner, Grant st
Fisher, Wm., miner, Skipton st
Fisher, W. W., grocer, Sturt st
Fisher and Kerr, grocers, Sturt st
Fisher, J., dairyman, Princes st
Fisher, Robert, miner, Clyde st
Fisher, John, Errard st
Fisher, Mrs., Dana st
Fishwick, James, carpenter, Doveton st
Fitchett, W. H., labour mart, Mair st
Fittall, Wm., compositor, Peel st
Fitzgerald, R., labourer, Lydiard st
Fitzgerald, J., hawker, Bridge st
Fitzherbert, J., clerk, Humffray st
Fitzmaurice, Miss, school, Lyons st
Fitzpatrick, Wm., clerk, Neil st
Fitzpatrick, P. C., mining registrar, Victoria st
Flanders, George, storeman, Clyde st
Flannagan, E., Shamrock hotel, Main road
Fleming, J., engineer, Dana st
Fleming, J., engineer, Armstrong st
Fleming, F., miner, Drummond st
Fletcher, John, miner, Humffray st
Fletcher, E., miner, Humffray st
Fletcher, J. F., clerk, Creswick road
Fletcher, Henry, carpenter, Skipton st
Flint, M. W. C., Venetian blind maker, East st
Flintoff, Thomas, photographer, Sturt st
Floyd, Wm., lay reader, Clayton st
Floyd, Wm., labourer, rear of Armstrong and South sts
Flora, Mrs., King st
Fogherty, Mrs., laundress, Queen st
Foley, Timothy, hotelkeeper, Armstrong street
Foley, Timothy, Plough and Harrow, Mair street
Folland, Phillip, bootmaker, East st
Foord, John, storekeeper, Eureka st
Forbes, W., veterinary surgeon, Sturt st
Forbes, A. J., mining manager, Victoria street
Forbes, Thomas, miner, Lexton st
Foreshaw, Joseph, miner, Mair st
Ford, John, miner, Wills st

Foden, Joseph, miner, Dana st
Ford, W. H., Southern Cross hotel, Sturt street
Ford, James, miner, Pleasant st
Ford, James, miner, Windermere st
Ford, James, labourer, Peel st
Ford, Michael, baker, Peel st
Fordyce, T., gunsmith, Dana st
Foreman, J., carter, Victoria st
Forshaw, —, miner, Lyons st
Fortune, H., painter and decorator, Victoria st
Foster, Wm., labourer, Queen st
Foster, —, bank clerk, Sturt st
Foster, H. B., carpenter, Sebastopol
Foster, H. B., miner, Sebastopol
Foster, J., bootmaker, Doveton st
Fotheringham, Wm., painter, Soldiers' hill north
Fothergill, Wm., carpenter, Ripon st
Foulk, Geo., carpenter, Eureka st
Fowell, Jane, fruiterer, Humffray st
Fowler, Joseph, saddler, Armstrong st
Fox, H. B., miner, Lydiard st
Fox, Catherine, St. Nicholas hotel, Main road
Fox, John, Limerick City hotel, Victoria st
Fox, Wm., miner, Skipton st
Foyer, James, engineer, Ripon st
Frampton, Jacob, miner, A 1 st
Francis, W. H., clerk, Barkly st
Francis, Thomas, miner, Barkly st
Francis, Mrs., registry office, Armstrong street
Francis, J. S., joiner, Lydiard st
Franklin, —, Suburban hotel, north of boundary
Franklin, Edward, carter, Humffray st
Franklin, James, carpenter, Victoria st
Franklin, Joseph, Errard st
Franklin, Michael, miner, Sebastopol
Franklin, Ebenezer, miner, Sebastopol
Franklin, —, miner, Sebastopol
Franks, James, engineer, Dana st
Franks, Samuel, hawker, Main road
Franks, Nathan, hawker, Main road
Franz, Carl, tinsmith, Main road
Franzen, H., blacksmith, Little Bendigo
Fraser, Jason, bricklayer, Queen st
Fraser, Rev. D., Seymour crescent
Fraser, Samuel, draper, Webster st
Fraser, J., miner, Talbot st
Fraser, W., bricklayer, Queen st
Fred., Thomas, waiter, Wills st
Frielayer, J. G., bootmaker, Albert st
Frigg, Henry, miner, Humffray st
Fries, Mrs., Humffray st
Frost, Wm., carter, Raglan st
Fry, Richd., labourer, A 1 st
Fry, James, blacksmith, Wills st
Fryer, James, miner, Little Bendigo
Fuller, Thomas, draper, Skipton st
Furguson, John, miner, Barkly st
Furguson, Alfred, gardener, Sturt st

Furners, W. H., miner, Drummond st
Fussell, —, provision dealer, Main road
Futcher, James, tinsmith, A 1 st

G.

Gabbett, B., Imperial hotel, Humffray st
Gaff, James, engine driver, Humffray st
Gaff, Daniel, miner, Young st
Gail, Joseph, carter, Main road
Gainsbury, Mrs., Victoria st
Gainsborg, Aaron, hotel, Main road
Gajin, —, clerk, Raglan st
Gale, Mrs., Malakoff st
Gale, H. J., carpenter, Main road
Galland, Constant, wine vaults, Mair st
Gallagher, F., constable, Humffray st
Galt, D., hatter, Bridge st
Galt, D., hatter, Barkly st
Galt, A., miner, Soldiers' hill
Galvin, Timothy, contractor, Bridge st
Gannet, Mrs., school, Ascot st
Gardner, Miss, dressmaker, Raglan st
Gardner, —, tailor, Raglan st
Gardner, C., coach proprietor, Dawson st
Gardner, Wm., bricklayer, Scott's parade
Gardner, Mrs., Main road
Gardner, N., miner, Little Bendigo
Gardner, Henry, labourer, Victoria st
Gardner, Thomas, miner, Wendouree parade
Gardner, Robert, miner, Burnbank st
Gardner, Thomas, miner, Gnarr st
Garnham, B., bricklayer, Scott's parade
Garth, Ralph, bootmaker, Main road
Garvey, Mrs., Dawson st
Garvey, P., miner, Drummond st
Gaskell, G. E., bookseller, Bridge st
Gasser, Xavier, jeweller, Bridge st
Gasson, J., miner, A 1 st
Gates, R., butcher, Armstrong st
Gates, Henry, fruiterer, Peel st
Gauni, Joseph, miner, Eyre st
Gavin, Wm., sharebroker, Sturt st
Gavin, Wm., sharebroker, Dana st
Gay, Phillips, Koh-i-noor hotel, Eyre st
Gear, Samuel, miner, Dana st
Gedlin, J., miner, Sebastopol
Gellatly, James, saddler, Doveton st
Genest, George, mason, A 1 st
George, Wm., bootmaker, Lyons st
George, James, miner, Eureka st
George, Mrs., midwife, Eureka st
George, J., Golden Lion hotel, Grant st
George, Mrs., seamstress, Hood st
George, J., hawker, Little Bendigo
George, James, dairyman, Little Bendigo
George, Matthew, miner, Little Bendigo
George, Joseph, bootmaker, Armstrong st
George, J., cooper, South st
Gerretti, J., carpenter, Doveton st
Getting, George, engineer, South st
Gibb and Co., engineers, Mair st
Gibbs, J., engineer, Webster st

Gibbings, Richard, livery stable keeper, Sturt st
Gibbings, Richard, Windermere st
Gibbs, R. B and S., merchants, Sturt st
Gibbs, R. B., merchant, Victoria st
Gibbs, James, carrier, Victoria st
Gibbs, John, draper, Macarthur st
Gibson, James, moulder, Urquhart st
Gibson, Mrs., restaurant, Main road
Gibson and Scott, bootmakers, Bridge st
Gibson, Wm., carpenter, Wills st
Gibson, C. W., clerk, Dawson st
Gibson, Thomas, carpenter, Ascot st
Gibbert, Duncan, miner, Little Bendigo
Gibbert, J., miner, Ascot st
Gibbert, James, miner, Sebastopol
Gibbert, Mrs., Victoria st
Gibbert, Alfred H., miner, Armstrong st
Gibbert, Charles, miner, Esmond st
Gilbert, Thomas, miner, Havelock st
Gilbert, Edwd., clerk, Lyons st
Giles, Wm., carpenter, Raglan st
Giles, Mrs., milliner, Ripon st
Giles, Wm., butcher, Victoria st
Gillespie, Alex., carter, Macarthur st
Gilgam, Michael, miner, Lyons st
Gill, Mark, Britannia hotel, Bridge st
Gill, Mrs., dressmaker, Armstrong st
Gill, John, saddler, Eureka st
Gill, Benjamin, miner, Little Bendigo
Gillander, James, moulder, Urquhart st
Gillard, Edwd., carter, Victoria st
Gillender, F., moulder, Doveton st
Gillingham, W., labourer, Rowe st
Gills, Thomas, carpenter, Ascot st
Gilmore, W. H., miner, Raglan st
Gilmore, Wm., miner, Windermere st
Gilmore, J., miner, Balaclava st
Gimblett and Hambly, bootmakers, Main road
Gingell, George, carpenter, Armstrong st
Gisbon, J., blacksmith, Main road
Glasscock, James, miner, Eureka st
Glasgow, Thomas, Victoria st
Glasgow, J., miner, Black hill
Glasson, Richard, butcher, Humffray st
Glasson, Wm., miner, Humffray st
Glasebrook, J., miner, Victoria st
Glennan, Andrew, bellman, Wills st
Glennie, Wm., bootmaker, Sturt st
Glennister, Henry, engineer, Peel st
Glennister, —, engine driver, Neil st
Glenn Brothers, store, Main road
Gleeyas, James, miner, Pleasant st
Glover, Robert, contractor, Errard st
Glover, James, miner, Red Lion st
Glover, Joseph, Foundry hotel, Yuille st
Goddard, Philip, carpenter, Lyons st
Goddard, Geo., miner, Wills st
Goddard, P., brickmaker, Rowe st
Goddard, J., carpenter, Howard st
Goddard, Andrew, labourer, Creswick road
Godden, George, bootmaker, Sebastopol

2 o

Godfrey, John, Humffray st south
Golding, W., carter, Skipton st
Goldstein, Alex., hawker, Main road
Goldstucker, —, forwarding agent, East street
Goldsworthy, J., miner, Skipton st
Goldsworthy, Josias, miner, Skipton st
Goldsworthy, Thomas, engineer, Raglan street
Golony, Ily., bricklayer, Burnbank st
Gondy, Edward, compositor, Rowe st
Goode, Benjamin, bill poster, Lydiard st
Good, Thomas, Prince of Wales hotel, Humffray st
Goodall, Matthew, miner, Doveton st
Goodall, John, miner, Eyre st
Goodfellow, Richd., clerk, Dana st
Gordon, George, miner, Queen st
Gordon, Alex., butcher, Eureka st
Gordon, Mrs., storekeeper, Eureka st
Gordon and Engelhardt, saddlers, Armstrong st
Gordon, Samuel, carpenter, Lyons st
Gore, Wm., carpenter, Raglan st
Gore, Chas., painter, Drummond st
Gorman, —, constable, Humffray st
Gorman, James, miner, A 1 st
Gostall, J., Sturt st
Gotty, Wm., engineer, Sturt st
Goujon, Samuel, sharebroker, Sturt st
Goujon, James, carter, Humffray st
Goulding, Robert, storekeeper, Brougham street
Gowan, Thomas, miner, Armstrong st
Gowring, H., fruiterer, Main road
Grace, J., carpenter, Peel st
Grace, James, carpenter, Drummond st
Graham, W., clerk, Raglan st
Graham, F., bootmaker, Talbot st
Graham, David, engineer, Dana st
Graham, J., moulder, Dana st
Graham, W., clerk, Mair st
Graham, Geo., Botanical Gardens
Graham, James, miner, Darkly st
Graham, James, miner, Skipton st
Graham, Thomas, miner, Skipton st
Graham, James W., miner, Creswick road
Graham, Wm., blacksmith, Main road
Grant, F., confectioner, Peel st
Grant, Wm., butcher, Dana st
Grant, James, storekeeper, Sturt st
Grant, James, Clyde hotel, Sturt st
Grant, Isaac, butcher, Sebastopol
Grant, J. T., miner, Urquhart st
Grant, James, store, Main road
Grassden, Edwd., engine driver, Eyre st
Gratton, Herbert, traveller, Peel st
Gray, Ebenezer, ironmonger, Eyre st
Gray, Francis, storekeeper, Eyre st
Gray, Ralph, carter, Armstrong st
Gray, Ebenezer, ironmonger, Armstrong street
Gray, James, boot salesman, Armstrong street

Gray, J. W., produce salesman, Yuille st
Gray, J., miner, Lyser st
Gray, Thomas, St. George U. G. M. C., Lydiard st
Gray, George, miner, Lyons st
Gray, David, porter, Dawson st
Gray, Mrs., Drummond st
Gray, Hugh, analytical chemist, Drummond st
Gray, Robert, miner, Drummond st
Gray, Wm., blacksmith, Drummond st
Gray, Andrew, baker, Eureka st
Gray, Thomas, baker, Eureka st
Gray, James, moulder, Grant st
Gray, Thomas, labourer, Creswick road
Gray, J., Scott's parade
Greaves, Mrs., storekeeper, Scott's parade
Greaves, James, brickmaker, Black hill
Greaves, H. M., and Co., drapers, Lydiard street
Green, Wm., miner, Victoria st
Green, James, tailor, Esmond st
Green, Mrs., dressmaker, Armstrong st
Green, George, miner, Lyons st
Green, J., carter, Main road
Green, F., clerk of sessions, Drummond st
Green, F., jun., Drummond st
Green, J., bootmaker, Humffray st
Greenfield, A. M., bank accountant, Raglan st
Greenley, J., mason, Queen st
Greensborough, Aaron, tailor, Esmond st
Greenland, Mrs., dressmaker, Humffray st
Greenaway, Wm., miner, Main road
Greenwood, Thomas, miner, Little Bendigo
Greenwood, J., clerk, Errard st
Greenwood, Richd., tea merchant, Dana street
Greig, Nicholas, labourer, Esmond st
Gregory, Jabez, main layer, Grenville st
Grey, Wm., Nag's Head hotel, Main road
Gribble, Benjamin, miner, Queen st
Gribble, J., miner, Talbot st
Gribble, E. V., miner, Urquhart st
Griffin, Miss, school, Peel st
Griffiths, Edwd., coach trimmer, Eyre st
Griffiths, James, miner, Esmond st
Grimbley, Wm., Victoria baths, Greenville street
Groat, Charles, miner, Little Bendigo
Grollet, Julian, fruiterer, Peel st
Grose, Nicholas, bootmaker, Eyre st
Grose, John, tanner, Sussex st
Grose, Thomas, miner, Mair st
Grout, J., furniture dealer, Humffray st
Grout, Charles, miner, Little Bendigo
Grundy, J. R., tobacconist, Main road
Guest, George, miner, Esmond st
Gudge, G., confectioner, Armstrong st
Guibarra, Fredk., miner, Mair st
Guon, Arthur, letter carrier, Esmond st
Guon, George, miner, Lexton st
Guon, Mrs., nurse, Raglan st

Gunn, Robert, mason, Ascot st
Gunn, Wm., painter, Ascot st
Guan, Wm., tailor, Dana st
Gunn, J., fruiterer, Main road
Gunter, Fredk., bailiff, Lyons st
Gunter, Thomas, labourer, Albert st
Gunyon, J., carpenter, Sebastopol
Guthrie, H., miner, Drummond st
Guthrie, —, labourer, Humffray st

H.

Haggerty, C., water carter, Creswick road
Hague, J., moulder, Peel st
Haigh, Samuel, Miners' Support hotel, Lyons st
Haines, J., Dana st
Haines, Lowther, carpenter, Eureka st
Hale, Edward, painter, Mair st
Hall, N., miner, King st
Hall, —, King st
Hall, Thomas, miner, Brougham st
Hall, James, miner, Esmond st
Hall, W., store, Grant st
Hall, J., miner, Humffray st south
Hall, R., bootmaker, Creswick road
Hall, Mrs., dressmaker, Creswick road
Hall, J., miner, Sebastopol
Hall, B., Farmers' hotel, Creswick road
Hall, James, miner, Talbot st
Hall, James, miner, Burnbank st
Hallam, Stephen, carpenter, Eureka st
Hallas, Wm., miner, Cobblers
Halley, Rev. J., Ligar st
Halliway, Mrs., Peel st
Halliday, J. F., bootmaker, Sturt st
Halliday, Wm., coach driver, Doveton st
Halls, W. T., beer bottler, Raglan st
Hake, J., carpenter, Lyons st
Halse, Edwin W., smith, Lyons st
Hamburger, Simon, pawnbroker, Humffray st
Hamber, Chas., miner, Doveton st
Hambly, Wm., bootmaker, Grant st
Hamer, Henry, tailor, Seymour st
Hames, Arthur, carter, Drummond st
Hamilton, Mrs., store, Victoria st
Hamilton, C., saddler, Neil st
Hamilton, Chas., saddler, Lydiard st
Hamilton, D., bank clerk, Webster st
Hamley, John, miner, Grant st
Hammer, Michd., miner, Rowe st
Hammett, Wm., clerk, Humffray st
Hammond, J., bookseller, Main road
Hammond, J., bookseller, Sturt st
Hammond, Wm., miner, Young st
Hammond, J., miner, rear of Armstrong street
Hancock, James, miner, Dana st
Hancock, Fredk., tailor, Drummond st
Hancock, J., blacksmith, Main road
Hancock, N., carpenter, north of boundary
Hancock, Charles, carman, Skipton st

Hancock, W., painter, Wills st
Hancock, Henry, car proprietor, Victoria street
Handley, Thomas, miner, Barkly st
Handlow, Patrick, carpenter, Victoria st
Hannah, H., miner, Creswick road
Hannon, Robert, detective, Lyons st
Hanson Brothers, marble masons, Creswick road
Hardie, Wm., bootmaker, Armstrong st
Hardy, Chas., miner, Urquhart st
Hardy, L. O. and J., solicitors, Lydiard st
Hardy, L. O., solicitor, Armstrong st
Hardy, Thomas, plasterer, Dawson st
Harding, H., watchmaker, Main road
Harding, W., chairmaker, Mair st
Harding, Thomas, Mair st
Harding, George, carpenter, Dawson st
Hardyman, Patrick, labourer, Mair st
Hardsfield, Samuel, miner, East st
Hargraves, Robt., Boundary hotel, Creswick road
Hare, D., miner, Lyons st
Harley, Patk., miner, Neil st
Harper, Samuel, tailor, Ascot st
Harrington, Edward, tinsmith, Victoria st
Harrington, H. A., hawker, Victoria st
Harris, Wm., miner, Dana st
Harris, Mrs., laundress, Dana st
Harris, Chas., printer, Barkly st
Harris, Wm., miner, Armstrong st
Harris, Henry, Peel st
Harris and Hintler, solicitors, Lydiard st
Harris, John, solicitor, Wendouree parade
Harris, Geo., carter, Raglan st
Harris, Thomas, saddler, Mair st
Harris, James, fruiterer, Creswick road
Harris, Lazarus, fancy repository, Main road
Harris, Wm., Eglington hotel, Main road
Harris, John, miner, Skipton st
Harris, M., miner, off Victoria st
Harris, W., miner, Nightingale st
Harris, Henry, miner, Bond st
Harris, John, cook, Wills st
Harrison, G. W., clerk, King st
Harrison, J., timber merchant, Main road
Harrison, J., engineer, Eyre st
Harrison, J., miner, Barkly st
Harrison, Wm., carpenter, Macarthur st
Harrison, F., miner, Humffray st
Harrison, James, bacon curer, Armstrong street
Harrison, Thomas, blacksmith, Raglan st
Harrison, Thomas, clerk, Errard st
Harrison, Henry, engineer, Mair st
Harrison, Mrs., dressmaker, Mair st
Harrison, Mrs., boot warehouse, Mair st
Harry, J., miner, Humffray st south
Harry, Richard, miner, Seymour st
Hart, James, grocer, Grant st
Hart, R. greengrocer, Grant st
Hart, D., miner, Little Bendigo
Hart, Thomas, P. O. clerk, Skipton st

Hart, Charles, slaughterman, Brougham st
Hartly, Robert, miner, Drumwood st
Hartley, Samuel, carpenter, Burnbank st
Hartley, Mrs., school, Burnbank st
Hartley, George, cooper, Skipton st
Hartridge, Wm., carter, Dana st
Hartland, S. D., clerk, Wills st
Harvey, John, miner, Skipton st
Harvey, John, miner, Humffray st
Harvey, Richard, law clerk, Ligar st
Harvey, Wm., miner, Sunny corner
Harvey, Wm., miner, Bond st
Harvey, Wm., miner, Black hill
Harwood, —, wheelwright, Peel st
Haskell, James, blacksmith, Victoria st
Hassel and Moncton, millers, Wendouree parade
Hassel, B. S., miller, Wendouree parade
Hassel, W. J., M.R.C.V.S.L., Lyons st
Hassel, Geo., Watermen's hotel, Wendouree parade
Haswell, D., bootmaker, King st
Hatton, Wm., grocer, Eyre st
Hauser, P., carter, Main road
Haviland, John, storekeeper, Main road
Haviland, J., Dunmore Flitch hotel, Main road
Hawken, John, mason, Victoria st
Hawken, Mrs., dressmaker, Victoria st
Hawkins, Thomas A., clerk, Victoria st
Hawkins, Thomas, carman, Main road
Hawkins, Wm., carter, Seymour st
Hawkins, Thomas, miner, rear of Armstrong st south
Hawkins and Copeland, sharebrokers, Lydiard st
Hawthorn, John, labourer, Peel st
Hayden, F., grocer, Victoria st
Haydon, Frank, foundryman, Errard st
Hayes, Wm., grocer, Wills st
Hayes, J., telegraph clerk, King st
Hayes, Edward, compositor, King st
Hayes, —, miner, Wills st
Hayles, Samuel, butcher, Eyre st
Hayson, Alfred, Golden Fleece, Victoria st
Hazel, John, tailor, Humffray st
Hazelhurst, S. J., miner, Humffray st
Hazeman, Charles, smith, Talbot st
Heacon, Michael, labourer, Barkly st
Headdy, E., Lydiard st
Headley, John, moulder, Doveton st
Healey, Mrs., seamstress, Lyons st
Healm, —, carter, Ascot st
Heaney, Wm., labourer, Eureka st
Heard, Wm., carpenter, Eureka st
Heath, Thomas, clerk, Dawson st
Heath, Geo., bookseller, Main road
Heath, Charles, salesman, Urquhart st
Heathcote, H., carter, Little Drummond st
Heathorn, Thomas, confectioner, Bridge st
Heise, Dr., Webster st
Helis, Wm., miner, Skipton st
Henderson, Robert, miner, Peel st
Henderson, James, labourer, Peel st

Henderson, John, slater, Lydiard st
Henderson, J., manager of Colonial Bank, Lydiard st
Henderson, Rev. W., Lydiard st
Henderson, J., engineer, Lyons st
Henderson, Jane, miner, Talbot st
Henderson, Samuel, miner, Howard st
Henderson, Wm., labourer, Clyde st
Henderson, James, carpenter, Clyde st
Henderson, Wm., storekeeper, Main road
Henderson, Wm., mining agent, Sturt st
Henkell, H., Phoenix hotel, Barkly st
Henning, F., carpenter, Talbot st
Henning, Patrick, labourer, Armstrong st
Hennessey, M., Newgrove hotel, Victoria street
Henessy, J., painter, Barkly st
Henry, A., plumber, Victoria st
Henry, John, miner, Errard st
Hepburn and Leonard, auctioneers, Lydiard st
Hepburn, Benjamin, auctioneer, Drummond st
Hepburn, James, ironmonger, Main road
Herbert, James, carrier, Raglan st
Herbert, D., nurseryman, Lyons st
Herbert, James, miner, Humffray st
Herd, James, miner, Esmond st
Herler, James quarryman, Ascot st
Herman, Rev. S., Barkly st
Herman, F., miner, Skipton st
Herring, Mrs., school, Eyrie st
Herring, F., fruiterer, Main road
Herving, Charles, Lydiard st
Hervey, Charles, miner, Sturt st
Hewitt, John, blacksmith, Ascot st
Hewitt, George, fruiterer, Main road
Hewitt, —, soap and candle manufacturer, Mair st
Heycock, J. W., bank manager, Neil st
Hickman, J., boiler maker, Yuille st
Hickman, J., and Son, engineers, Mair st
Hicks, Francis, miner, Mair st
Hicks, Richard, miner, Neil st
Hickens, James, miner, Brougham st
Highfield, Mrs., school, Peel st
Higgins, Thomas, engine driver, Greaville street
Higgins, Mrs., school, Eureka st
Higgins, Michael, soapmaker, Wills st
Higgins, Joseph, carter, Doveton st
Higgins, Mrs., milliner, Doveton st
Higgins, Joseph, miner, Drummond st
Higgins, James, miner, Lydiard st
Higgins, F., miner, Lydiard st
Hill, H., superintendent police, Lydiard st
Hill, Josiah, carter, Humffray st south
Hill, J. R., boiler maker, Yuille st
Hill, Alfred, carter, Humffray st south
Hill and Jones, blacksmiths, Creswick road
Hill, Thomas, carter, Barkly st
Hill, Isaac, builder, Victoria st
Hill, Edwin, engine driver, Lydiard st

Hill, David, carter, Lydiard st
Hill, William, miner, Little Bendigo
Hill, A., hat manufacturer, Sturt st
Hill, Miss, dressmaker, Main road
Hill, R., tailor, Ebden st
Hillas, T., surgeon, Sturt st
Hillas, T., surgeon, Sebastopol
Hillman, Josiah, blacksmith, Skipton st
Hind, Josiah, carpenter, South st
Hindman, Charles B., carpenter, East st
Hindmarsh, James, engineer, Mair st
Hine, Edwin, miner, Pleasant st
Hiney, Claude, miner, Skipton st
Hirdsford, W., bricklayer, Doveton st
Hirst, Henry, butcher, Lyons st
Hirst, William, brickmaker, Peel st
Hirst, Robert, brickmaker, Peel st
Hirt, J. G., tailor, Humffray st
Hiscock, Mrs., storekeeper, Lydiard st
Hitchings, J. H., hairdresser, Lydiard st
Hitchins, F., auctioneer, Doveton st
Hitchins, William, miner, Humffray st
Hoare, Charles, clerk, Dawson st
Hoban, Pierce, miner, Little Bendigo
Hoblin, Miss, dressmaker, Yuille st
Hobson, William, moulder, Peel st
Hockey, miner, Pleasant st
Hocking, John, carpenter, Dana st
Hocking, James, brewer, Doveton st
Hocking, Jacob, miner, Skipton st
Hocking, James, miner, Skipton st
Hocking, Richard, miner, Skipton st
Hocking, Thomas, miner, Skipton st
Hockins, Thomas, storekeeper, Havelock street
Hockley, Edward, solicitor, Lyons st
Hodge, James, carter, Burnbank st
Hodge, George, miner, Grant st
Hodgson, Ralph, miner, Gnarr st
Hodgson, Edward, watchmaker, Bridge street
Hodgson, William, miner, Macarthur st
Hodgson, Edward, watchmaker, Eyre st
Hodgson, James, miner, Burnbank st
Hofferman, James, mason, Burnbank st
Hoffmeister, G., butcher, Lydiard st
Hoffman, Louis, draper, Eureka st
Hogan, Michael, bootmaker, Eureka st
Hogan, Daniel, labourer, Victoria st
Hogg, George, compositor, Dawson st
Hogg, George, miner, Howard st
Holder, R., ironfounder, Doveton st
Holding, Richard, carpenter, Lydiard st
Holland, Thomas, miner, Lydiard st
Holland, Miss., school, north of boundary
Holland, John, labourer, Scott's parade
Holland, Henry, miner, Scott's parade
Hollis, Rev. J., Macarthur st
Holloway, Edward, labourer, Eureka st
Holloway, George, tinsmith, Doveton st
Holmes, Stone & Co., leather merchants, Bridge st
Holmes, Charles, leather merchant, Lyons street

Holmes, White & Co., merchants, Lydiard street
Holmes and Salter, solicitors, Lydiard st
Holmes, George, stonemason, Peel st
Holmes, John, carpenter, Macarthur st
Holmes, Francis, groom, Errard st
Holmes, —, solicitor, Webster st
Holmer, F., carter, Grant st
Holmes, Thomas, miner, Sebastopol
Holmes, Thomas, carter, Grant st
Holmes, J., bookseller, Bridge st
Holmuth, R., butcher, Main road
Holt, William, carter, Drummond st
Holt, Thomas, bookkeeper, East st
Holthouse, Dr., Eyre st
Holyoak, Wm., butcher, Esmond st
Honeycomb, James, miner, Sturt st
Hook, Thomas, labourer, Soldiers' hill
Hook, C. J., carpenter, Blain road
Hoolahan, Patrick, miner, Otway st
Hoolahan, —, labourer, Otway st
Hoolahan, Miss, Camp reserve
Hooper, John, miner, Brown hill
Hootan, Mrs., Raglan st
Hopkins, Samuel, miner, Humffray st
Hopkins, John, miner, Macarthur st
Horne, Joseph, carter, Barkly st
Hornden, J., wheelwright, Sturt st
Horr, J. C., coach proprietor, Ligar st
Hornington, James, car proprietor, Ligar street
Hosken, Rev. W. H., Armstrong st
Hosken, Peter, miner, Little Bendigo
Hosken, R., miner, Little Bendigo
Hoken, W., miner, Little Bendigo
Hotchin, W. H., stationer, Sturt st
Haugh, M., Eastern hotel, Main road
Houston, John, miner, Havelock st
Houston, —, miner, Raglan st
Howatt, Alex., miner, Windermere st
Howatt, Wm., blacksmith, Dana st
Howe, Mrs., nurse, Ripon st
Howe, C., gardener, Black hill
Howell, Edward, miner, Peel st
Howell, J. R., tinsmith, Main road
Howle, James, blacksmith, Grant st
Howley, R., paperhanger, Eyre st
Hubner, Gerhard, jeweller, Eureka st
Hudson, —, detective, Ligar st
Hudson, Dr., Sturt st
Huggett, J., tinsmith, Grant st
Huggins and Carr, blacksmith, Wills st
Huggins, R., blacksmith, Humffray st
Hughes, Evan, mason, Clarendon st
Hughes, —, miner, Humffray st
Hughes, Douglas, clerk, Dawson st
Hughes, George, compositor, Dawson st
Hughes, Wm., storekeeper, Ligar st
Hughes, Wm., wheelwright, Albert st
Hughes, James, miner, Cobblers
Hughes, Thomas, miner, Sebastobol
Hughes, D., baker, Sebastopol
Hughes, Mrs., Wills st
Hughes, Thomas, miner, Wills st

Hughes, Emma, Wendouree parade
Hughes, Thomas, miner, Sebastopol
Hulett, Mrs., seamstress, Raglan st
Hull, Joseph, bootmaker, Humffray st
Humphreys, J., blacksmith, Main road
Humphreys, W., engine driver, Lydiard st
Humphries, Cabel, engineer, &c., Armstrong st
Hunt, Thomas, carpenter, Humffray st
Hunt and Opie, Victoria foundry, Armstrong st
Hunt, James, engineer, Doveton st
Hunt, Miss, dressmaker, Eyre st
Hunt, Charles, miner, Victoria st
Hunt, Thomas R., Eastern Station hotel, Humffray st
Hunt, James, engineer, Esmond st
Hunt, Thomas, miner, Main road
Hunt, Ebenezer, draper, Errard st
Hunt, George, bricklayer, Ligar st
Hunter, David, miner, Barkly st
Hunter, J., builder, Eyre st
Hunter, R., and Co., law writers, Lydiard street
Hunter, James, miner, Skipton st
Hunter, John, miner, Skipton st
Huntington, J., miner, Armstrong st south
Huntley, John, cabinet maker, Lyons st
Hurks, Thos., Tam o' Shanter hotel and produce store, Creswick road
Hurle, D., engineer, Drummond st
Hurley, Thomas, teacher, Windermere st
Hurling, James, fruiterer, Sturt st market
Hurly, Patrick, labourer, Howard st
Horst and Paine, grocers, Victoria st
Hussey, Mrs., Windermere st
Hutchinson, H., woodsplitter, Clyde st
Hutchinson, Alfred, bootmaker, Main road
Hutchinson, Alfred, bootmaker, Peel st
Hutchinson, Wm., miner, Humffray st
Hutley, Wm., blacksmith, Mair st
Huthnance, W. H., carter, Macarthur st
Hutson, Samuel, tinsmith, Mair st
Hutson, Samuel, tinsmith, Howard st
Hutson, George, letter carrier, Dana st
Hutton, R., miner, Malakoff st
Huyghue, S. D. L., warden's clerk, Sturt street
Hyams, John, gardener, A 1 st
Hyams, John, and Co., opticians, Sturt st
Hyams, James, miner, Humffray st south
Hyde, John, bootmaker, Humffray st
Hyde, Thomas, carter, Clayton st
Hyland, R., detective, Barkly st
Hylton, J., clerk, Eyrie st
Hynam, D., miner, Dana st

I.

Ibbotson, Henry, cooper, Main road
Iferty, Edward, grocer, Skipton st
Inch, Charles, cooper, Pleasant st
Incry, John, labourer, Creswick road
Ingulby, J., carter, Howard st

Ingolsby, John, carter, A 1 st
Ireland, Andrew, storekeeper, Macarthur street
Ireland, Andrew, miner, Havelock st
Irving, Glover, and Co., contractors and timber merchants, Sturt and Raglan streets
Irving, Thomas, bootmaker, Grant st
Irving, John, saddler, Sturt st
Irving, Geo., Family hotel, Sturt st
Irving, Wm., carpenter, Sturt st
Irving, I., contractor, Raglan st
Irving, Robert, miner, Skipton st
Irvine, Matthew, labourer, Clyde st
Irwin, Alex., confectioner, Bridge st
Irwin, William, Provincial hotel, Lydiard street
Irwin, Wm., railway guard, Lydiard st
Irwin, Fredk., carpenter, Dana st
Isabell, Geo., mason, Mair st
Isbill, James, Family hotel, Sturt st

J.

Jacks, Mrs., laundress, Humffray st
Jacks, William, Jack's hotel, Sturt st
Jackson, John, Farmers' Return hotel Creswick road
Jackson, Geo., Bridge st
Jackson, John, north of boundary
Jackson, Miss, dressmaker, Dana st
Jackson, Mrs., Eyre st
Jackson, J., carter, Victoria st
Jackson, James, painter, Mair st
Jackson, Richard, miner, Mair st
Jackson, J., Black hill
Jackson, —, builder, Bridge st
Jackson, H. A., butcher, Bridge st
Jackson, James, smith, Wills st
Jacobs, Solomon, clothier, Main road
Jacobs, James, Raglan st
Jacobs, —, carter, Doveton st
Jaygu, George, produce dealer, Humffray street
Jago, Francis, bootmaker, Skipton st
Jakils, Martin, miner, Sebastopol
James, James, Brownhill
James, James, miner, Scott's parade
James, Wm., bricklayer, Errard st
James, J., wheelwright, Grant st
James, James, carter, Bond st
James, G. W., coachdriver, Albert st
James, Edward, architect, Brougham st
James, Joseph, miner, Barkly st
James, Thomas, miner, Ligar st
James, John, miner, Drummond st
James, William, bootmaker, Drummond st
James, Wm., labourer, Talbot st
James, Wm., carpenter, Victoria st
James, Edward, architect, Sturt st
James, A., miner, Eyre st
James, John, miner, Humffray st
James, John, miner, Humffray st
James, John, miner, Armstrong st

James, Wm., miner, Doveton st
Jamison, Peter, tailor, Dana st
Jamison, Blair, storekeeper, Creswick rd
Jane, H., labourer, Bond st
Jansen, Antonia, Little Bendigo
Jansen, John, miner, Humffray st
Jansen, Maurice, miner, Macarthur st
Jardise, Thomas, clerk of petty sessions, Drummond st
Jarvise, James, greengrocer, Humffray st
Jarvis, Walter, miner, Macarthur st
Jeffries, Thomas, miner, Macarthur st
Jeffries, James, Australia Felix hotel, Eureka st
Jeffrey, John, miner, Barkly st
Jeffrey, Wm., plumber, Doveton st
Jekyll, John, watchmaker, Eureka st
Jelbart, John, miner, Eyre st
Jenkes, —, engineer, Ascot st
Jenkins, Nicholas, engine driver, Ascot st
Jenkins, Thomas, miner, Drummond st
Jenkins, Edward, labourer, Burnbank st
Jenkins, Henry, labourer, Eureka st
Jenkins, Wm., mason, Drougham st
Jenkins, W. W., butcher, Eureka st
Jenkins, —, produce dealer, Eureka st
Jenkins, Wm., bootmaker, Armstrong st
Jenkins, —, refreshment rooms, Sebastopol
Jenkins, Evan, miner, Cobblers
Jenkins, James, miner, Little Bendigo
Jenkins, J. H., hardware dealer, Urquhart st
Jenkins, Wm., fruiterer, Skipton st
Jenkinson, Andrew, miner, Urquhart st
Jenkinson, Hugh, miner, Black hill
Jewel, Henry, butcher, Sebastopol
Jewell, Thomas, painter and glazier, Eureka st
Jewell John, miner, Humffray st south
Jewell, Edward, painter, Eyre st
Jewkes, —, engineer, Ascot st
Jinks, John, shoemaker, Barkly st
Johns, Thomas, miner, Eureka st
Johns, Thomas, carter, Drummond st
Johns, Henry, miner, Windermere st
Johns, John, miner, Sturt st
John, Nicolas, bootmaker, Victoria st
Johns, James, miner, Humffray st
Johns, Thomas, miner, Humffray st
Johns, J. S., taxidermist, Lydiard st
Johns, Thomas, miner, Sturt st
Johns, John, miner, Albert st
Johns, Humphrey, miner, Grant st
Johns, Wm., miner, Grant st
Johnson, James, store, Eureka st
Johnson, James, miner, Bond st
Johnson, Thomas, labourer, Macarthur st
Johnson, John, miner, Grant st
Johnson, Thomas, carter, north of boundary
Johnson, James, miner, Young st
Johnson, John, bottle merchant, Talbot st
Johnson, Thomas, miner, Lyons st

Johnson, —, baker, Talbot st
Johnson, James, miller, Sussex st
Johnson, Mrs., Pleasant st
Johnson, Thomas, hairdresser, Bridge st
Johnson, Thomas, labourer, Dana st
Johnson, Geo., farmer, Creswick road
Johnson, Jones, miner, Errard st
Johnson, Henry, miner, Humffray st
Johnston, John, miner, Windermere st
Johnston, R., woodsplitter, Humffray st
Johnston, Wm., builder, Sturt st
Johnston, Chas., gardener, Webster st
Johnston, Francis, carpenter, Dana st
Johnston, George, carpenter, Neil st
Johnston, M., labourer, Drummond st
Johnston, P., miner, Raglan st
Johnston, H. W., compositor, Rowe st
Johnston, James, miner, Urquhart st
Johnston, Wm., labourer, Havelock st
Johnston, H., carpenter, Clarendon st
Johnston, J., brickmaker, Clarendon st
Johnston, William, carpenter, Clarendon street
Johnston, Wm., gardener, Clarendon st
Johnston, James, engineer, Eyre st
Jones, Hugh, miner, Barkly st
Jones, H. R., miner, Wendouree parade
Jones, F. C., baker, Macarthur st
Jones, Isaac, law clerk, Macarthur st
Jones, Mrs., Ascot st
Jones, Joseph, coffee roaster, Dana st
Jones, Wm., miner, Errard st
Jones, Wm., miner, Drummond st
Jones, W. H., boatbuilder, Drummond st
Jones, John, miner, Windermere st
Jones, Thomas, miner, Mair st
Jones, Owen, miner, Mair st
Jones, D., and Co., drapers, Sturt st
Jones, Mrs., store, Humffray st
Jones, Joseph, miner, Eyre st
Jones, John, ironmonger, Eyre st
Jones, Edward, Pacific hotel
Jones, Thomas, restaurant, Victoria st
Jones, Wm., miner, Armstrong st
Jones, Chas., gardener, Doveton st
Jones, John, smith, Doveton st
Jones, Mrs., strawbonnet cleaner, Doveton street
Jones, M., miner, Essex st
Jones, George, tinsmith, A 1 st
Jones, Thomas, Neil st
Jones, D. W., carter, Ligar st
Jones, E. Welsh Harp hotel, Lydiard st
Jones, Evan, carter, Raglan st
Jones, W., coach proprietor, Raglan st
Jones, Alexander, fishmonger, Wills st
Jones, W., carpenter, East st
Jones, Wm., engine driver, Princes st
Jones, Evan, miner, Scott's parade
Jones, James, miner, Scott's parade
Jones, Thomas, grocer, Rowe st
Jones, E., miner, off Victoria st
Jones, H., Victoria hotel, Main road
Jones, Joseph, miner, Black hill

Jones, Lewis, miner, Little Bendigo
Jones, Richard, miner, Black hill
Jones, James, miner, Little Bendigo
Jones, —, miner, Little Bendigo
Jones, Richard, miner, Sebastopol road
Jones, Evan, miner, Cobblers
Jones, Edward, miner, Cobblers
Jones, Coleman, carter, Sebastopol
Jones, Henry, miner, Young st
Jones, Joseph, coffee roaster, Bridge st
Jones, Edward, chemist, Main road
Jones, J. H., architect, Camp st
Jones, Wm., blacksmith, Urquhart st
Jones, James, butcher, Skipton st
Jones, James, carter, Nightingale st
Jones, Edward, miner, Nightingale st
Jordon, Thomas, labourer, Howard st
Jordan, Edward, engineer, Eyre st
Josephs, Henry, Australia Felix hotel
Joseph, John, bootmaker, Sebastopol
Joseph, Joseph, outfitter, Bridge st
Joseph and Co., fishmongers and poulterers, Bridge st
Joseph, Lewis, fishmonger, Main road

K

Kall, Mrs., Pleasant st
Kane, John, labourer, Talbot st
Kane, John, miner, Pleasant st
Kant, M., miner, Sebastopol
Kappe, Charles, miner, Eyre st
Kay, Archibald, bootmaker, Sturt st
Kay, J. A., bootmaker, Raglan st
Keane, Wm., labourer, Peel st
Keane, Thomas, bootmaker, Peel st
Keane, H., moulder, Urquhart st
Keane, James, miner, Skipton st
Keany, Edward, miner, Nightingale st
Kearns, Martin, miner, Ripon st
Kearn,o Thomas, carter, Eyre st
Keast, Sampson, mathematical instrument maker, Bond st
Keast, George, coachdriver, Grant st
Keast, George, smith, Ebden st
Kelham, C., sheriff's officer, Armstrong st
Kellet, D., bricklayer, Lignr st
Kelly, John, miner, Windermere st
Kelly, James, carpenter, Wills st
Kelly, A., engineer, Armstrong st south
Kelly and Preston, blacksmiths, Main road
Kelly, P., blacksmith, Humffray st
Kelly, James, labourer, Doveton st
Kelly, John, clerk, Errard st
Kelshaw, John, painter, Ascot st
Kelt, Wm., miner, Sturt st
Kelt, James, miner, Black bill
Kemble, Mrs., Victoria st
Kemp, Wm. S., billiard table keeper, Ascot street
Kemp, F., labourer, Wills st
Kemp, —, Talbot st
Kenahan, P. R., Kilkenny and Dublin hotel, Skipton st

Kendall, W. P., storekeeper, Barkly st
Kendall, Richard, carter, Little Bendigo
Kennedy, Thomas, miner, Windermere st
Kennedy, James, moulder, Barkly st
Kennedy, Charles, clerk, Dana st
Kenny, J., druggist, Grant st
Kent, Mrs., nurse, Humffray st
Kent, Richard, teacher, Victoria st
Kent, Patrick, miner, Rowe st
Kent, Richard, master of Common School, Barkly st
Kenyon, John, mason, Drummond st
Kernick, J., miner, Humffray st
Kernick, Edward, miner, Humffray st
Kermaan, Wm., miner, Errard st
Kermode, Thomas, miner, Dana st
Kermode, Wm., miner, Dana st
Kerr, Lawrence, painter, Barkly st
Kerr, George, moulder, Dawson st
Kerr, A. C., ironmonger, Armstrong st
Kerr, Wm., miner, Cobblers
Kerr, John, carpenter, Brougham st
Kerse, M., miner, Ascot st
Kerswick, —, miner, Raglan st
Kettle, James, carter, Scott's parade
Ketto, James, miner, Sturt st
Keynoeh, John, Lal Lal st
Keys, E., labourer, South st
Keys, Dennis, Shamrock hotel, Victoria street
Kibble, —, Creswick road
Kidd, Thomas, road contractor, Eureka st
Kidd, J., clerk, Dana st
Kiddle, Andrew, tailor, Sturt st
Kiene, Henry, painter, Humffray st
Kisner, Dr., surgeon, Mair st
Kilburn, Joseph, stoker at gasworks, Dana street
Kildah, Mrs., teacher, Clarendon st
Kilmister and Purdue, saddlers, Mair st
Kilpatrick, Robert, miner, Bond st
King, H. J. Newton, postmaster, Humffray street
King, A. H., ironmonger, Dawson st
King, John, miner, Windermere st
King, J., labourer, Humffray st south
King, L. T., draper, Blair st
King, R., farrier, Victoria st
King, John, bootmaker, Sturt st
King, A. H., ironmonger, Bridge st
King, Arthur, solicitor, Sturt st
King, Samuel, miner, Rowe st
King, James, carpenter, Wills st
King, F., carter, Holmes st
King, R., veterinary surgeon, Humffray street
King, Thomas, professor of music, Grant street
Kington, Walter, sharebroker, Sturt st
Kington, W., sharebroker, Lydiard st
Kington, Samuel, miner, Eyre st
Kingshot, —, Wendouree parade
Kinnear, Kennedy, labourer, South st
Kinney, James, miner, Main road

Kibble, —, law clerk, Creswick road
Kipps, Wm., miner, Lyons st
Kirchness, John, miner, Drummond st
Kirk, James, commission agent, Lydiard street
Kirkness, Wm., miner, Skipton st
Kirley, Charles, miner, Ripon st
Kirton, Edmund, bootmaker, Dana st
Kissock, Mrs., butcher, Clarendon st
Kitchen, Miss, fancy repository, Mair st
Kitchen, Miss, fancy repository, Bridge st
Kith, James, miner, Sturt st
Kleim, Adam, woodcarter, Lal Lal st
Klog, Chas., miner, Errard st
Klog, Wm., carpenter, Windermere st
Knight, Rev. S., Lydiard st
Knight, R., blacksmith, Dawson st
Knight, H., lemonade maker, Red Lion st off Mair st
Knight, James, Junction hotel, Sturt st
Knight, John, foundryman, Armstrong st
Knoll, A. R., saddler, Grant st
Korn, F. A., architect, Sturt st
Kroyle, C. J., miner, Dana st
Kyle, Wm., draper, Sebastopol
Kyle, Alex., miner, Sebastopol
Kyle, Samuel, miner, A 1 st

L

Label, Thomas, baker, Main road
Lable, Alphonse, carpenter, Drummond st
Lable, Madame, dressmaker, Windermere street
Lacey, Mrs., nurse, Drummond st
Lach, Wm., pianoforte tuner, Neil st
Laelett, W., bricklayer, Lyons st
Lafon, Louis, butcher, Peel st
Laidlaw, Thomas, livery stable proprietor, Raglan st
Laidlaw, J., nurseryman, Wills st
Lake, Robert, carter, Urquhart st
Lake, John, collector, Dana st
Lakeland, Wm., grocer, Victoria st
Lakeland, John, carter, Victoria st
Laland, C., butcher, Esmond st
Lamb, Jacob, butcher, Victoria st
Lamb, James, miner, Sturt st
Lamb, R., butcher, Creswick road
Lamber, Mrs., laundress, Raglan st
Lambert, Joseph, draper, Main road
Lambert and Herd, rag merchants, Main road
Lambert, R., carpenter, Boundary st, Soldiers' hill
Lambert, Mrs., laundress, Ligar st
Lampshire, John, miner, Doveton st
Lampshire, Wm., miner, Doveton st
Lander, Joseph, carpenter, Skipton st
Lane, Timothy, Port Phillip hotel, Sturt street
Lane, E. J., saddler, Ynille st
Lane, Henry, painter, Eureka st
Lane, D., cooper, Doveton st

Lane, Henry, painter, Havelock st
Lane, Mrs., Little Bendigo
Lane, Wm., store, Brown hill
Laing, A. D., steam chaffcutting machine, Creswick road
Lang, Thomas, and Co., seedsmen and florists, Bridge st
Lang, Charles, seedsman, Eyre st
Lang, James, Wendouree parade
Lang, John, lamplighter, Barkly st
Lang, Robert, storekeeper, Doveton st
Langdon, John, miner, Sturt st
Langdon, John, cattle dealer, Webster st
Langdon, James, miner, Seymour st
Langdon, James, miner, Sturt st
Laugdon, Joseph, miner, Dawson st
Langley, James L., carter, Albert st
Langton, J., carter, Skipton st
Lansdell, Robert, miner, Drummond st
Larkins, E. W., tailor, Lydiard st
Larkin, John, mason, Raglan st
Largeen, A. T., blacksmith, Main road
Large, Thomas, nurseryman, Albert st
Larner, —, sergeant, Barkly st
Latham, Joseph, miner, Black hill
Lattimore, Thomas, coach painter, Neil st
Lathlan, F. J., miner, Humffray st
Law, David, carpenter, Wills st
Law, J., ironmoulder, Urquhart st
Lawler, James, miner, South st
Lawlor, M., quarryman, Pleasant st
Lawrence, Wm., miner, Drummond st
Laurie and Tracy, slaters, Lydiard st
Lawson, D., miner, Young st
Lawson, —, Brougham st
Leach, —, carter, Windermere st
Leaman, John, boarding house keeper, Ascot st
Leatherman, Charles, hawker, Humffray street
Lebalastrier, John, bandmaster, Ascot st
Le Bins, Mrs., Raglan st
Lecras, John, builder, Raglan st
Leckie, James, miner, Cobblers
Ledger, Thomas, plasterer, Doveton st
Ledwidge, Peter, butcher, Seymour st
Ledwidge, Simon, butcher, Neil st
Lee and Hull, brewers and bottlers, Ripon street
Lee, Morgan, miner, Dana st
Lee, Edward, porter on railway, Victoria street
Lee, Parkyn, miner, Victoria st
Leech, H., fruiterer, Main road
Leech, H. F., produce dealer, Armstrong street
Leech, H. F., produce dealer, Doveton st
Legg, James, carpenter, Esmond st
Legg, James, plasterer, Wills st
Lekage, Peter, engine driver, Wills st
Lemon, Thomas, bricklayer, Wills st
Lent, Chas., Lydiard st
Leonard, James, Royal Mail hotel, Cobblers

2 P

Leonard, Wm., auctioneer, Seymour st
Lepels, James, engineer, Sturt st
Lewels, J., engineer, Victoria st
Letcher, John, miner, Barkly st
Letcher, W., miner, Little Bendigo
Levit, Wm., coachbuilder, Armstrong st
Levine, Alfred H., watchmaker, Dana st
Levine, A., watchmaker, Bridge st
Levine, Israel, tobacconist, Main road
Levinson, Hyman, jeweller, Sturt st
Levinson, Hyman, jeweller, Victoria st
Levinson, Joseph, jeweller, Dawson st
Levy, J., hawker, Main road
Lewell, W., bootmaker, Clayton st
Lowell, John, engineer, Humffray st
Lewis, Lewis, miner, Clayton st
Lewis, Edward, miner, Sebastopol
Lewis, Thomas, miner, Sebastopol
Lewis, H., miner, Sebastopol
Lewis, John, baker, Drummond st
Lewis, John, miner, Drummond st
Lewis, Charles, ironmonger, Humffray st
Lewis, J., mason, Wills st
Lewis, E. F., proctor and conveyancer, Lydiard st
Lewis, Thomas, bootmaker, Lydiard st
Lewis, Wm., miner, Ascot st
Lewis, Jenkin, storeman, Talbot st
Lewis, Edward, tinsmith, Barkly st
Lewis, Henry, miner, Barkly st
Lewis, Wm., miner, Victoria st
Lewis, Aaron, miner, Humffray st
Lewis, Mrs., school, Humffray st
Lewis, E. F., solicitor, Lyons st
Lexton, Maurice, carter, Raglan st
Liddle, Alexander, baker, Humffray st south
Liddle, H., carpenter, Peel st
Liddy, J. J., Dawson st
Light, Charles, tailor, Sturt st
Lilburne, Wm., clerk, Drummond st
Lilly, George, storekeeper, Humffray st
Lilley, Reuben, miner, Albert st
Lilley, Ebenezer, miner, Albert st
Lincoln, Edward, carter, Errard st
Linell, Richard, miner, Mair st
Ling, Henry, miner, Humffray st
Linnian, P., miner, Victoria st
Linsey, Thomas, smith, Humffray st
Linstead, Chas., surveyor, Clayton st
Lister and Angel, provision merchants, Sturt st
Lister and Angel, fruiterers, Bridge st
Liston, Alexander, miner, Urquhart st
Litchhorn, John, carter, Macarthur st
Little, John, toy and fancy repository, Bridge st
Little, Wm., estate agent, Raglan st
Little, Edith, Lyons st
Little, Edward, store, Dana st
Little, Edward, compositor, Dana st
Little, John, carter, Boundary st, Soldiers' hill
Little, George, fruiterer, Sturt st market

Little, G., miner, Boundary st, Soldiers' hill
Livermore, James, labourer, Dawson st
Livermore, Mrs., nurse, Drummond st
Livingston, W., clerk and keeper of pound, Sturt st
Livingston, Arthur, clerk and keeper of powder magazine, Sturt st
Livingston, J., storekeeper, Victoria st
Lloyd, Benjamin, carpenter, Scott's parade
Lloyd, Henry, butcher, Peel st
Lloyd, W., labourer, Macarthur st
Lockett, George, reporter, Victoria st
Loft, John, miner, Armstrong st
Lofven, J. H. S., storekeeper, Little Bendigo
Logan, —, baker, Humffray st south
Logan, James, watchmaker, Humffray st
London Chartered Bank, Main road
Loney, James, bootmaker, Mair st
Long, Mrs., laundress, Victoria st
Long, Wm., baker, Esmond st
Long, Mrs., dressmaker, Bond st
Long, A. J., baker and confectioner, Main road
Longhand, —, Wills st
Longmore, Wm., bank clerk, Victoria st
Longwell, John, compositor, Ligar st
Longwell, Wm., car driver, Shipton st
Longstaff, Joseph, chemist, Bridge st
Longstaff, Joseph, chemist, Wills st
Lonnins, George, builder, Raglan st
Lopas, Antonio, hairdresser, Main road
Lord, G., fruiterer and confectioner, Main road
Lord, F., labourer, Eyre st
Lorden, Stephen, miner, Barkly st
Lorenzo, Charles, miner, Wendouree parade
Lorrick, John, miner, Havelock st
Loughnan, W., miner, Scott's parade
Love, Patrick, labourer, Barkly st
Lovell, Wm., builder, Raglan st
Lovelock, R., grocer, Wills st
Lovie, John, miner, Eyre st
Lovitt, George, grocer, Shipton st
Lovitt, George, grocer, Doveton st
Lowe, James, miner, Dana st
Lowe, Wm., contractor, Doveton st
Lowe, J., Sir William Wallace hotel, Wills st
Lowle, James, ironmonger, Humffray st
Lowther, J., master Common School, Errard st
Lucan, Thomas, cook, Main road
Ludbrook, George, carpenter, Main road
Lugg, Wm., miner, Scott's parade
Lugg, Wm., draper, Main road
Lugg, George, miner, Little Bendigo
Lugg, B. H., carpenter, Grant st
Luke, Richard, miner, Mair st
Lumley, Wm., moulder, Drummond st
Luth, S., store and timber merchant, Sebastopol

Lates, S., miner, Main road
Latherwood, J., labourer, Wendouree parade
Latwa, James, draper, Neil st
Lyall, E. B., sub-inspector police, Camp
Lye, Wm., labourer, Black hill
Lyle, Thomas, tailor, Dana st
Lyle, —, carter, Dana st
Lynch, H., carter, Princes st
Lynch, —, miner, Sebastopol
Lynn, A. L., solicitor, Lydiard st
Lynn, Adam L., solicitor, Drummond st
Lyons, James, miner, Windermere st
Lyons, Thomas, painter, Skipton st
Lyons, Francis, Kerry hotel, Main road
Lyons, Charles, engine driver, Scott's parade
Lyte, Charles, baker, Main road

M.

Macaulay, Stewart, miner, Bond st
Macfarlane, Dr., surgeon, Sturt st
Macgillivray, Mrs., school, Lyons st
Mackay, Henry, carpenter, Seymour st
Mackie, Alexander, miner, Princes st
Macrae, Daniel, draper, Bridge st
Macree, Wm., carpenter, Doveton st
Macree, Peter, sheep dealer, Clarendon st
Madama, C., boat builder, Wendouree parade
Madden, James, miner, Sunny corner
Madden, Wm., miner, Little Bendigo
Madden, Wm., labourer, Grant st
Madden, W. H., miner, Brougham st
Madley, Miss, store, Mair st
Mafiny, Mrs., teacher, Victoria st
Magills and Coghlan, brewers, Dana st
Magor, Mrs., dressmaker, Lyons st
Magor, John, mason, Dawson st
Magore, Thomas, miner, Esmond st
Mague, James, miner, Grant st
Maguire, James, miner, Errard st
Mahar, John, carter, Burnbank road
Maher, Patrick, miner, Scott's parade
Mahon, Joseph, rate collector, Rowe st
Mailarch, J., bootmaker, Main road
Maldment, John, miner, Humffray st
Main, Dugald, carpenter, Scott's parade
Main, David, publican, Lyons st
Main, John, carter, Ascot st
Maitland, Alexander, carman, Skipton st
Major, Edwin, gardener, Main road
Major, Charles, fruiterer, Creswick road
Major, James, bootmaker, Sebastopol
Major, J., miner, Sebastopol
Major, John, miner, Barkly st
Makray, Miss, boarding-house, Doveton street
Malcolm, J., miner, Esmond st
Malcolm, James, ironmonger, Mair st
Malcolm, Robert, wheelwright, Main road
Malcolm, Robert, wheelwright, Sturt st
Malcolm, James, carpenter, Seymour st

Mallon, James, carter, Armstrong st
Mallet, Mrs., Errard st
Malony, John, carter, Doveton st
Malony, Patrick, miner, Victoria st
Malony, J., constable, Camp reserve
Malony, Dr., surgeon, Main road
Malone, Mrs., Wills st
Manelark, Thomas, moulder, Nell st
Mancefield, J., constable, Camp reserve
Manderson, James, engineer, Sturt st
Manchester, J., ironmoulder, Macarthur street
Manchester, Misses, school, Macarthur st
Manderson, John, engineer, Sturt st
Mann, Henry, miner, Mair st
Mann, Samuel, solicitor, Armstrong st
Manne, William, boots, Scott's parade
Mann, Robert, greengrocer, Humffray st
Manning, John, policeman, Armstrong st
Manship, George, carpenter, Burnbank st
Manway, —, labourer, Bond st
Marchant, Mrs., nurse, Windermere st
Marks, George, butcher, Creswick road
Markillie, Jacob, Creswick road
Marratt, Josiah, watchmaker, Wills st
Marooney, Mrs., Armstrong st
Marrow, M., lime and cement merchant, Doveton st
Marsh, W. H., Doveton st
Marsh, D., store, Urquhart st
Marshall, William, butcher, Eureka st
Marshall, —, draper, Sturt st
Marshall, R., butcher, Humffray st
Marshall, Evans, miner, Sebastopol
Marshall, J., grocer, Sturt st
Marshall, S. H., grocer, Doveton st
Marshall, Alexander, accountant, Lydiard street
Marshall, Mrs., draper, Sturt st
Marshall, Mrs., nurse, Nell st
Marshall, William, rate collector, Lyons street
Marshall, Alexander, mining manager, Raglan st
Marshall & Co., *Evening Post*, Mair st
Marshall, George, newspaper proprietor, Dana st
Martin, John, hawker, Main road
Martin, Michael, boarding-house keeper, Main road
Martin, James, miner, Main road
Martin, William, warehouseman, Sturt st
Martin, J., tailor, Sturt st
Martin, George, compositor, Wills st
Martin, William, labourer, Princes st
Martin, William, clerk, Lydiard st
Martin, —, Lydiard st
Martin, M., Phœnix Park hotel, Lydiard street
Martin, William Parker, North Star hotel, Lydiard st
Martin, T., foundryman, Windermere st
Martin, —, plasterer, Dana st
Martin, Charles, teacher, Doveton st

Martin, Mrs., teacher, Doveton st
Martin, William, engine fitter, Doveton street
Martin, John, tailor, Sturt st
Martin, W. H., wheelwright, Eureka st
Martin, George, miner, Eureka st
Martin, Thomas, miner, Eureka st
Martin, J., miner, Main road
Martin, D., carpenter, Bond st
Martin, James, miner, Bond st
Martin, —, clothier, Main road
Mason, Thomas, blacksmith, Eureka st
Mason, James, labourer, South st
Mason, —, miner, Main road
Mather, John, brewer, Webster st
Mather, Andrew, Scotch hotel, Mair st
Mather, W., tinsmith, Main road
Mather, Thomas, Mair st
Matthews, Andrew, miner, Doveton st
Matthews, George, labourer, Boundary st, Soldiers' hill
Matthews, Peter, engineer, Cobblers
Matthews and Son, butchers, Main road
Matthews, S., butcher, Mair st
Matthews, F. G., labourer, Talbot st
Matthews, William, miner, Ascot st
Matthews, —, brewer, Drummond st
Matthews, John, miner, Havelock st
Matthews, John, builder, Neil st
Matthewson, James, mason, Doveton st
Matthewson, John, tailor, Ligar st
Maule, Margaret, Rose of Denmark hotel, Creswick road
Maule, M., store, Creswick road
May, James, miner, Eyre st
May, Samuel, miner, Webster st
May, Silas, miner, Wendouree parade
Mayne, John, labourer, north of municipal boundary
McAllister, J., blacksmith, Lydiard st
McAllister, Thomas, quarter-master, Camp st
McBride, Robert, miner, Skipton st
McCallum, A., miner, Main road
McCallum, Neil, and Co., merchants, Doveton st
McCann, Miss, store, Eureka st
McCann, —, sharebroker, Raglan st
McCann, T., produce and timber merchant, Skipton st
McCann, David, carter, Humffray st
McCarty, James, standpipe, Humffray st
McCarty, Benjamin, store, Eureka st
McCartney, James, miner, Little Bendigo
McCartney, F., coach builder, Mair st
McCartney and Aldred, coach builders, Armstrong st
McCaul, D. B., cooper, Barkly st
McClennan, O., coachsmith and wheelwright, Creswick road
McClean, —, greengrocer, Grant st
McClellan, James, baker, Drummond st
McClellan, Andrew, carpenter, Raglan st
McClintock, W., miner, Little Bendigo

McClymont, Robert, butcher, Main road
McConnel, John, carter, Princes st
McCormack, P., carpenter, Scott's parade
McCormack, Mr., solicitor, Raglan st
McCormack, N. H., solicitor, Lydiard st
McCoy, Robert O., Ballarat College
McCrossen, John, rag merchant, Main road
McCullock, Wm., carpenter, Pleasant st
McCullock, R. V., turner, Peel st
McDermott, F. M., barrister, Lydiard st
McDermott, F. M., barrister, Drummond street
McDonald, Alexander, miner, Drummond street
McDonald, J. G., mason, Drummond st
McDonald, James, slater, Eyre st
McDonald, Colin, miner, Dawson st
McDonald, Alex., storekeeper, Neil st
McDonald, R. D., Albion hotel, Sturt st
McDonald, James, storekeeper, Lydiard st
McDonald, Miss, boarding house, Doveton street
McDonald, John G., storekeeper, Lydiard street
McDonald, —, miner, Essex st
McDonald, Miss, mistress in Common School, Eureka st
McDonald, J. J., plumber, Sturt st
McDonald, Mrs., dressmaker, Sturt st
McDonald, James, Crown hotel, Creswick road
McDonald, J. and G., plumbers, Sturt st
McDonald, Mrs., Sturt st
McDonald, R. D., Albion hotel, Main road
McDonald, —, nurse, Albert st
McDowall, R., miner, Lydiard st
McDowall and Gray, produce dealers and salesmen, Market square
McElliott, —, hawker, Armstrong st
McElroy, Patrick, labourer, Macarthur st
McElroy, E., chimneysweep, Talbot st
McElroy, E., coachbuilder, Mair st
McEwan, —, needlewoman, Errard st
McFail, Alexander, miner, Eyre st
McFarlane, —, carpenter, Little Bendigo
McGeary, James, hammerman, Talbot st
McGhee, —, miner, Black hill
McGill, James, miner, Skipton st
McGill and Co., sharebrokers, Sturt st
McGill, —, traveller, Lyons st
McGowan, Samuel, clerk, Dawson st
McGowan, David, hawker, Clayton st
McGowan, Alex., teacher, Esmond st
McGowan, Robert, miner, Grant st
McGrath, Miss, dressmaker, Sturt st
McGrath, James, labourer, Brougham st
McGreggor, Richard, miner, Eureka st
McGreggor, James, carter, Humffray st
McHannah, Thomas, gardener, Brown hill
McIlatty, —, blacksmith, Main road
McIlatty, John, labourer, Mair st
McIlatty, James, blacksmith, Victoria st
McIlenry, Wm., miner, Ascot st

McKenzie, Malcolm, miner, Eyre st
McKenzie, T., miner, Mair st
McIntosh, A.
McIntosh, Wm., bootmaker, Urquhart st
McIntosh, L., miner, Clayton st
McIntosh, Alex., bootmaker, Yuille st
McIntosh, J., carpenter, Grenville st
McIntosh, Alex., bootmaker, Yuille st
McIntosh, Charles, miner, Raglan st
McIntosh, James, carpenter, Peel st
McIntyre, George, carter, Dyte's parade
McIver, M., tailor, Urquhart st
McIver, —, teacher, Queen st
McKay, Thomas, blacksmith, Princes st
McKay, Archibald, quarryman, Ascot st
McKay, Donald, platelayer, Neil st
McKay, James, miner, Brougham st
McKay, David, storekeeper, Macarthur st
McKay, —, quarryman, Ascot st
McKay, Wm., miner, Grant st
McKay, —, teacher, Grant st
McKay, Angus, carpenter, Albert st
McKeown, Henry, hawker, Doveton st
McKercher, John, blacksmith, Lydiard st
McKercher, David, tailor, Skipton st
McKechnie, D., mason, Queen st
McKinlay, Thomas, mason, Doveton st
McKinnon, James, miner, Humffray st
McKinney, Jacob, storekeeper, Little Bendigo
McKinney, Franklin, blacksmith, Armstrong st
McKenzie, Hugh, miner, Main road
McKenzie, D., miner, Main road
McKenzie, John, carpenter, Humffray st
McKenzie, James, miner, Wills st
McKenzie, Alex., quarryman, Wills st
McKenzie, Nicholas, road overseer, Ascot street
McKenzie, Elizabeth, Talbot st
McKenzie, —, miner, Dana st
McKenzie, Alexander, gardener, Armstrong st
McKenzie, James, miner, Sebastopol
McKissock, James, butcher, Lydiard st
McKissock, A., butcher, Urquhart st
McLaren, Mrs., storekeeper, Talbot st
McLarty, Archibald, stonemason, Doveton street
McLaughlin, Mrs., North Ballarat school, Brougham st
McLeod and Lethbridge, cattle agents, Raglan st
McLean, Robt., Emu hotel, Armstrong st
McLean, —, Talbot st
McLean, Hugh, Neil st
McLean, Allan, bootmaker, Bridge st
McLean, Neil, shoemaker, Mair st
McLean, —, miner, Armstrong st
McLean, Alex., grocer, Doveton st
McLeoly, Wm., carpenter, Creswick road
McLenan, Henry, miner, Queen st
McLeod, C., Lydiard st
McLough, —, miner, Dana st

McLyell and Co., sharebrokers, Sturt st
McManamney, —, Victoria st
McManamney, Thomas, carter, Grant st
McManamney, —, Mack's hotel, Victoria street
McMill, Wm., miller, Havelock st
McMorin, Robt., miner, Creswick road
McNab, D., miner, Pleasant st
McNab, John, mason, Windermere st
McNail, Hector, carter, Albert st
McNally, P., constable, Humffray st
McNamara, Martin, miner, Windermere street
McNamara, P., labourer, Peel st
McNamara, James, restaurant, Victoria street
McNamara, James, labourer, Humffray st
McNash, James, carter, Urquhart st
McNee, Mary, storekeeper, Barkly st
McNee, Marjory, Salutation store, Errard street
McNeil, James, carpenter, Esmond st
McNeil, Neil, mason, Victoria st
McPherson, D., carpenter, Victoria st
McPherson, Colin, storekeeper, Macarthur street
McPherson, D., china and glass dealer, Main road
McQuie, J. B., accountant, Sturt st
McQuie, James, accountant, Wills st
McQuie, John, miner, Eyre st
McSparrow, Malcolm, blacksmith, Errard street
McSpooraw, Matthew, blacksmith, Skipton st
McSwarm, Neil, carter, Lyons st
McTaggart, —, miner, Humffray st
McTaggart, Duncan, miner, Armstrong street
McWhae, Alex. B., miner, Lyons st
McWhae, Peter, miner, Lyons st
McWhae, Andrew B., mason, Doveton st
Mead, S. L., Bird in hand hotel, Victoria street
Meade, E. T., Commercial hotel, Sturt st
Mead, E. F., Coomora hotel, Main road
Meade, —, carpenter, South st
Meadden, Thomas, miner, Grant st
Meadway, P. J., miner, Esmond st
Meyre, Mrs., Skipton st
Mechin, James, labourer, Eyre st
Medoxon, —, miner, Talbot st
Meigin, L. B., coach proprietor, Lyons st
Melrose, Mrs., Barkly st
Melrose and Splitter, Main road
Melverton, J., carpenter, Macarthur st
Melverton, Richd., carpenter, Macarthur street
Melvin, D., miner, Windermere st
Melvin, Archibald, carpenter, Dawson st
Menagh, J., constable, Camp reserve
Menzies, Alfred, bootmaker, Humffray st
Menzies, Robert, storeman, Ascot st
Mercer, Wm., ironmonger, Webster st

294　Mer　　ALPHABETICAL　　Moo

Mercer, W., labourer, Peel st
Meredith, Mrs., milliner and dressmaker, Creswick road
Merlin, Thomas, blacksmith, Sebastopol
Merritt, John, bootmaker, Doveton st
Merritt, Thomas, horse dealer, Eureka st
Merry, Richard, miner, Neil st
Merson, James, secretary of the Temperance League, Urquhart st
Messenger, John, engine driver, Raglan st
Metcalf, F. C., clerk, Sturt st
Metcalf, J. C., clerk, Sturt st
Metcalf, J., miner, Young st
Mewburn, Thomas, brickmaker, north of Municipal Boundary
Miall, Mrs., dressmaker, Wills st
Michan, R. A., baker, Sebastopol
Michell, Henry, butcher, Skipton st
Michell, Joseph, miner, Armstrong st
Michell, T. J., butcher, Mair st
Middleton, J., mining surveyor, Ligar st
Middleton, J., mining agent, Sturt st
Middleton, W., miner, Sturt st
Middleton, James, mining agent, Main rd
Middleton, —, rag merchant, Main road
Middleton, John, labourer, Camp reserve
Middleditch, W., miner, Sturt st
Midlin, J., miner, Skipton st
Midlin, Thomas, miner, Humffray st
Miliani, D., miner, Sturt st
Miles, Robt., storekeeper, Cobblers
Mills, Wm., miner, Humffray st south
Mills, Wm., miner, Little Bendigo
Mills, Thomas, carter, Humffray st
Mills, Mrs., laundress, Humffray st
Mills, John, saddler, Creswick road
Mills, A. D., bookbinder, Lyons st
Millay, John, miner, Mair st
Miller, Gilbert, blacksmith, Errard st
Miller, Thomas, storeman, Victoria st
Miller, —, telegraph office, Raglan st
Miller, Samuel, miner, Lyons st
Miller, James, storekeeper, Sturt st
Miller, James, miner, Doveton st
Miller, Geo., miner, Doveton st
Miller, Ann, storekeeper, Doveton st
Miller, John, schoolmaster, Essex st
Miller, Montague, carpenter, off Webster street
Miller, J., bootmaker, Sturt st
Miller, J., manager, Scott's parade
Miller, Thomas, carpenter, Scott's parade
Miller, James, miner, Clayton st
Miller, James, storekeeper, Sturt st
Miller, R. F., traveller, Skipton st
Millet, James, miner, Little Bendigo
Millson, Thomas, cabinet maker, Lydiard street
Milne, D., fruiterer, Main road
Milner, William, furniture dealer, Main road
Milner, William, furniture dealer, Sturt st
Minchin, Lewis, miner, Sturt st
Minogue, John, carter, Scott's parade

Minton, Wm., painter, Main road
Minton, Mrs., nurse, Windermere st
Minton, Benjamin, painter and glazier, Victoria st
Mitchell, James, miner, Drummond st
Mitchell, D., Prince of Wales hotel and butcher, Eyre st
Mitchell, John, miner, Dawson st
Mitchell, John, miner, Pleasant st
Mitchell, James, miner, Dana st
Mitchell, Alfred, solicitor, Lydiard st
Mitchell, —, miner, Mair st
Mitchell, John, miner, Doveton st
Mitchell, John, miner, Brougham st
Mitchell, James, miner, Barkly st
Mitchell, Wm., horse dealer, Eureka st
Mitchell, James, miner, Eureka st
Mitchell, F., clerk, Sturt st
Mitchell, Richd., miner, Humffray st
Mitchell, Samuel, carter, Humffray st
Mitchell, J., miner, Main road
Mitchell, R. S., Creswick road
Mitchell, James, miner, Humffray st south
Mitchell, Stephen, miner, Grant st
Mitchell, T. W., brickmaker, Black hill
Mitchell, Wm., constable, Albert st
Mitchison, R. F., auctioneer and official assignee agent, Lydiard st
Mitchison, Wm., miner, Mair st
Mitton, Geo., miner, Sebastopol
Mobbs, James, miner, Creswick road
Mobley, Thomas, butcher, Doveton st
Moffat, Wm., brickmaker, Pleasant st
Moffatt, Mrs., dressmaker, Urquhart st
Moffy, J. C., teacher, Victoria st
Moir, Thomas, miner, Grant st
Moir, Miss, confectioner, Sturt st
Morzer, James, miner, Sebastopol
Molrooney, M., miner, Ascot st
Mols, Geo., bootmaker, Wills st
Moky, J. C., teacher, Victoria st
Molony, James, labourer, Victoria st
Momle, Julius, clerk, Neil st
Monachan, Miss, dressmaker, Victoria st
Monarch, Mrs., Bond st
Moncton, Robt., miller, Windermere st
Montgomery, F., coachpainter, Peel st
Montgomery, John, hairdresser, Main road
Montgomery, John, clerk, Lydiard st
Montague, Peter, miner, Ebden st
Monteith, Samuel, miner, Pleasant st
Mooney, John, Bond st
Mooney, Peter, bootmaker, Eureka st
Moody, R., storeman, Dawson st
Mooney, Miss, teacher of music, Sturt st
Moore, Francis, miner, Errard st
Moore, S., mining engineer, Drummond street
Moore, Wm., carpenter, Eyre st
Moore, John, mining manager, Eyre st
Moore, Geo., ironmonger, Lyons st
Moore, G., collector for hospital, Lyons street

Moore, Wm., carpenter, Lyons st
Moore, —, Lydiard st
Moore, W. J., painter, Doveton st
Moore, Maurice, plasterer, Seymour st
Moore, Wm., carrier, Barnbank st
Moore, James, miner, Barkly st
Moore, W., gardener, Little Bendigo
Moore, Mrs., dressmaker, Little Bendigo
Moore, Edwd. C., Sturt st
Moorhead, W., farmer, Nightingale st
Moorhouse, D., confectioner, Main road
Moorhouse, B., confectioner, Sturt st
Moorhouse, C. J., carpenter, Urquhart st
Moorabed, James, miner, Barkly st
Moran, James, miner, Scott's parade
Moran, James, miner, Victoria st
Morgan, Wm., carter, Windermere st
Morgan, Geo., grocer, Dawson st
Morgan, —, miner, Pleasant st
Morgan, Joseph, ironmonger, Lydiard st
Morgan, —, accountant, Lydiard st
Morgan, Henry, accountant, Doveton st
Morgan, S. J., fish and poultry store, Sturt street
Morgan, James, carpenter, Humffray st
Morgan, Wm., blacksmith, Humffray st
Morgan, John, Wills st
Morgan, Thomas, carter, Armstrong st
Morgan, P., miner, Little Bendigo
Morgan, Noah, miner, Cobblers
Morgan, Morgan, miner, Cobblers
Morrel, Hamilton, carter, Ripon st
Morrel, R., market gardener, Creswick rd
Morrel, J., coachbuilder and wheelwright, Grenville st
Morris, Maurice, Grapes hotel, Grant st
Morris, J., foundryman, Sturt st
Morris, Chas., miner, Little Bendigo
Morris, J., miner, Little Bendigo
Morris, N., miner, Clyde st
Morris, Geo., contractor, Brougham st
Morris, Richd., labourer, north of boundary
Morris, C., undertaker, Sturt st
Morris, C., Humffray st
Morris, Arthur, Ascot st
Morris, James, painter, Pool st
Morris, Thomas, clerk, surveyor's office, Eyre st
Morris, John, bricklayer, Ascot st
Morris, R., carpenter, Lydiard st
Morrison, A., plasterer, Havelock st
Morrison, M., National Bank of Australasia, Lydiard st
Morrison, R., traveller, Armstrong st
Morrison, James, carter, Barkly st
Morrison, J., baker, Sturt st
Morrison, Duncan, railway porter, Humffray st
Morrison, James, broker, Sturt st
Morrison, Andrew, grocer, Main road
Morrison, James, carter, Howard st
Morrows, Henry, miner, Brown hill
Morrow, —, storekeeper, Armstrong st

Morrow, —, lime and cement merchant, Doveton st
Morton, Daniel, storekeeper, Barkly st
Morton, D., produce dealer, Main road
Morton, Matthew, contractor, Skipton st
Morton, George, mariner, Creswick road
Mortimer, John, chimney sweep, Ascot street
Morwitch, Lyons, traveller, Ligar st
Morwitch, A., Great Britain hotel, Main road
Morwitch, S., theatre, Main road
Moss, Wm., tinsmith, Armstrong st
Moubery, Mrs., laundress, Rowe st
Mounsberry, E., Yong st
Mounsey, Launcelot, miner, Sebastopol
Mounsey, James, miner, Sebastopol
Mounsey, Isaac, miner, Sebastopol
Moyes, Thomas F., carpenter, Ligar st
Moyle, John, miner, Wills st
Moyle, Thomas, miner, Grant st
Muggerity, John, slaughterman, Pleasant street
Muir, Wm., plasterer, Victoria st
Mair, Andrew, miner, Dana st
Mulser, F., tobacconist, Sturt st
Mulder, T., Duke of York hotel, Humffray st
Mulder, F., hairdresser, Sturt st
Mullen, —, miner, Talbot st
Mullen, Mrs., nurse, Black hill
Mullen, Thomas, forwarding agent, Nell street
Muller, F., Sturt st, Ballarat
Muller, Thomas, carpenter, Webster st
Mulligan, J., miner, Little Bendigo
Mulligan, P., miner, Little Bendigo
Mumby, W. C., gunmaker and bellhanger, Sturt st
Munday, Harry, blacksmith, Humffray street
Mumford, F., carpenter, Scott's parade
Munroe, G. G., merchant, Errard st
Munroe, P., blacksmith, Eyre st
Munroe, John, miner, Dawson st
Munroe, Richard, saddler, Lydiard st
Munroe, Mrs., Lydiard st
Munroe, Robt., saddler, Armstrong st
Munroe, John, carpenter, Doveton st
Munroe, Mahony and Ballantine, sharebrokers, Sturt st
Munroe, J., bootmaker, Sturt st
Murch, George, carpenter, Peel st
Murfett, W., bricklayer, Nightingale st
Murfett, James, bricklayer, Pleasant st
Murphy, E., butcher, Creswick road
Murphy, Patrick, labourer, Creswick road
Murphy J., miner, South st
Murphy, C., blacksmith, Main road
Murphy, Mrs., laundress, Scott's parade
Murphy, Neil, labourer, Princes st
Murphy, John, Specimen hill hotel, Eureka
Murphy, B., labourer, Ligar st

Murphy, James, Railway Terminus hotel, Armstrong st
Murphy, John, wheelwright, Windermere street
Murphy, Miss, storekeeper, Main road
Murray, Chas., miner, Errard st
Murray, John, carpenter, Victoria st
Murray, Matthew, miner, Eyre st
Murray, W., labourer, Armstrong st
Murray, F. J., miner, Webster st
Murray, Wm., compositor, Wills st
Murray, John, mason, Wills st
Murrray, H. R., Bridge st
Morton and Leggo, brewers, Creswick rd
Musgrove, Richd., clerk, Dawson st
Myles, —, master of Hebrew school, Barkly st
Myers, A., miner, Eureka st
Myer, Sydney, cigar manufacturer, Main road
Myller, Edward, carter, Eureka st

N.

Nancarroll, Wm., miner, Barkly st
Nancarrow, Wm., miner, Grant st
Nanceton, Wm., carter, Barkly st
Nankervis, J., miner, Armstrong st south
Nash, W. H., coach painter, Doveton st
Nash, Henry, painter, Skipton st
Naylor, W. H., carpenter, Seymour st
Neal, John, bootmaker, Talbot st
Neal, D., dairyman, Humffray st
Neep, Wm., miner, Princes st
Nell, Robt., carter, Clyde st
Nell, Thomas, miner, Eureka st
Nell, Thomas, labourer, Rowe st
Neilson, Mrs., Holmes st
Neish, Geo., labourer, Windermere st
Nelve, James, produce merchant, Lyons st
Nelkira, Joseph, tobacconist, Bridge st
Nellthorp, Alfred, butcher, Errard st
Nelson, John, mathematical instrument maker, Raglan st
Nettle, R., gratemaker, Barkly st
Nettle, R., turner, Barkly st
Nettleship, Wm., jeweller, Eureka st
Neville, Peter, miner, Skipton st
New, D., miner, Dana st
Newey, F., carpenter, Sturt st
Newey, F., carpenter, Sturt st
Newhall, Wm., carpenter, Peel st
Newman, Mrs., store, Eureka st
Newman, Henry, painter, Lyons st
Newman, Wm., carpenter, Peel st
Newman, James, engineer, Mair st
Newman, Wm., plasterer, Lal lal st
Newman, Robt., clerk, Victoria st
Newport, J., carter, Scott's parade
Newsome, Henry, miner, Ai st
Newton, John, mason, Burnbank st
Newton, Mrs., Dana st
Neylan, James, miner, Humffray st
Nicholas, Henry miner, Seymour st

Nichols, James, produce merchant, Armstrong st
Nicholls, Thomas, carpenter, Doveton st
Nicholls, John, carpenter, Doveton st
Nicholl, Mrs., dressmaker, Doveton st
Nicholls, R. W., nurseryman and seedsman, Bridge st
Nichols, John, carter, Burnbank st
Nicholls, Andrew, miner, Humffray st south
Nicholl, Robt., draper, Victoria st
Nicholl, F. P., butcher, Peel st
Nicholls, R., nursery, Peel st
Nicholls, Richard, carpenter, Peel st
Nicholls, H. W., engineer, Lydiard st
Nicholls, Henry, editor, Errard st
Nicholls, Robert, engineer, Armstrong st south
Nicholls, Henry, miner, Armstrong st south
Nicholls, Wm., butcher, Armstrong st south
Nicholls, James, miner, Young st
Nicholls, R., carter, Humffray st
Nicholls, Thomas, miner, Humffray st south
Nicholson, Robt., mason, Sussex st
Nicholson, Wm., fruiterer, Main road
Nicholson, Geo., grocer, Sturt st
Nicholson, Matthew, miner, Armstrong st south
Nicholson, Geo., doctor, Sturt st
Nicholson, Chas., bricklayer, Humffray street
Nicols, James, boot salesman, Armstrong street
Ninham, —, law clerk, Armstrong st
Ninnis, Miss, Bridge house, Skipton st
Niven, F. W., lithographer, Seymour st
Nixon, Wm., sharebroker, Webster st
Nixon, R., hatter, Raglan st
Nobbs, John, cooper, Eyre st
Noble, Wm., miner, Ascot st
Noblett, Geo., publican, Main road
Nolan, John, labourer, Scott's parade
Nolan, Peter, Exchange hotel, Sebastopol
Nalt, Geo., publican, Humffray st
Norman, Geo., engineer, Wills st
Norman, —, engine driver, Wills st
Norrie, David, storekeeper, Sturt st
Norrie, Daniel, storekeeper, Sturt st
North, John, miner, Victoria st
North, James, miner, Sebastopol
North, James, miner, Dyte's parade
Northy, Thomas, miner, Wills st
Northy, Robt., miner, King st
Northy, John, miner, Scott's parade
Norton, Henry, miner, Talbot st
Nott, Geo., Scandinavian hotel, Main road
Nuckey, Hugh, engineer, Creswick road
Nugent, H., professor of dancing, Sturt street
Nums, John, miner, Armstrong st
Nurthle, James, miner, Humffray st south

Nuttal, Thos., cabinet maker, Macarthur street

O.

Oatley, Thomas, bootmaker, Main road
Oats, Wm., miner, Eyre st
Oats, Thomas, miner, Humffray st
O'Brien, Miss, needlewoman, Sturt st
O'Brien, John, Victoria st
O'Brien, Phillip, miner, Victoria st
O'Brien, Terence, labourer, Victoria st
O'Brien, J. J., teacher, Sturt st
O'Brien, Miss, teacher, Sturt st
O'Brien, John J., teacher, Sturt st
O'Brien, M., miner, Essex st
O'Brien, James, baker, Eureka st
O'Brien, Patrick, miner, Brown hill
O'Brien, David, carter, Howe st
O'Brien, James, brickmaker, Black hill
O'Brien, D., labourer, Black hill
Ochiltree, B. N. S. W., Lydiard st
O'Connor, Owen, British dining rooms, Lydiard st
O'Connor, D., inspector weights and measures, Lydiard st
O'Connor, Miss, ladies' school, Lydiard st
O'Connor, —, Windermere st
O'Connor, Dennis, bricklayer, Sturt st
O'Connor, Miss, milliner and dressmaker, Sturt st
Oddie, James, and Co., auctioneers and valuators, Dana st
Odger, James, grocer, Victoria st
Odium, Robert, hairdresser, Wills st
O'Donold, D., sodawater manufacturer Victoria st
O'Farrell and Son, horse bazaar, Doveton street
O'Farrell, M., auctioneer, Doveton st
O'Farrell and Son, cattle salesmen, Armstrong st
O'Farrel, H. J., produce dealer, Creswick road
Ogleby, James, law clerk, Armstrong st south
O'Hallaran, James, miner, Dyte's parade
Oheir, D., Western hotel, Bridge st
O'Keef, Patrick, bootmaker, Eureka st
O'Key, Wilmot, Excelsior hotel, Eyre st
O'Larensbed, Charles, contractor, Sturt st
Olden, O. S., Mining Exchange
Oldfield, Stephen, store and post office, Peel st
Oldham, Wm., sharebroker, Sturt st
Oldham, James, teacher, Dana st
Oldman, Richard, miner, Urquhart st
Olcey, Charles, fruiterer and greengrocer, Creswick road
O'Meara, M., shoemaker, Humffray st
O'Meara, James, Limerick Castle hotel, Bridge st
O'Neil, Peter, labourer, Eureka st
O'Neil, Mrs., Drummond st
O'Neil, Wm., miner, Creswick road

O'Neil, J., miner, Albert st
Opie, Thomas, miner, Bond st
Opie, Tristan, engine fitter, Armstrong st
Opie, John, engineer, Nell st
Opie, James, engineer, Nell st
Opie, Thomas, miner, Scott's parade
Opie, James, miner, Grant st
Orchard, J., minister, Lyons st
Ordets, R., horse dealer, Wills st
Orenshard, John, carter, Pleasant st
Orme, Edward, agent, Eyre st
Ormond, W., labourer, Creswick road
Orr, Wm., tanner, Sturt st
Orr, George, carpenter, Sturt st
Orr, Matthew, miner, Humffray st south
O'Shaughnessy, M., constable, Mair st
Osborne, Wm., carter, Ascot st
Osborne, Alfred, tailor, Mair st
Osborne, Edward, manager of Golden Well Gold Mining Company, Mair st
Osborne, Edward, clerk, Macarthur st
Osborne, John, miner, north of municipal boundary
Osborne, J., bootmaker, Sturt st
Osborne, Wm., agent, Peel st
Osborne, Frank, storekeeper, Ligar st
Osborne, George, labourer, Creswick road
Osborne, J., general store, Sebastopol
Osborne, Wm., contractor, Bond st
O'Toole, Thomas, constable, Camp reserve
Owen, James, miner, Sebastopol
Owen, Owen, bootmaker, Main road
Owen, Edward, tent maker, Dyte's parade
Owen, Thomas, miner, Drummond st
Owen, Roland, miner, Mair st
Oxley, E., paperhanger and painter, Dana street
Oxley, Mrs., dressmaker, Dana st

P.

Padden, J., miner, Cobblers
Paige, E. A., miner, Windermere st
Painter, —, solicitor, Sturt st
Paisley Thomas, miner, Humffray st
Pallamountain, S., miner, Little Bendigo
Pallamountain, W., miner, Little Bendigo
Palmer, George, draper, Bridge st
Palmer, J., fruiterer and storekeeper, Main road
Palmer, Joseph, miner, Drummond st
Palmer, F., cooper, Main road
Palmer, James, engineer to water commission, Wills st
Palmer, John, labourer, Boundary st
Pamphilon, Edwin, grocer, Eyre st
Park, miner, Little Bendigo
Park, Wm., blacksmith, Errard st
Parke, Robt., carpenter, Rowe st
Parker, J. W., grocer, Skipton st
Parker, James, chemist, Main road
Parker, James, shoemaker, Peel st
Parker, Wm., carpenter, Lyons st
Parker, James, labourer, Windermere st

Parker, Anthony, storeman, Wills st
Parker, Miss, dressmaker, Ripon st
Parnell, Wm., plasterer, Lydiard st
Parr, Edward, engraver, Lydiard st
Parr, E., Ascot st
Parr, D., painter, Lydiard st
Parry, Florence, straw hat manufacturer, Armstrong st
Parry, Robert, gunsmith, Victoria st
Parsons, Robert, butcher, Clayton st
Parsons, Mrs., Pleasant st
Partridge, D. S., bootmaker, East st
Pascoe, —, labourer, Eureka st
Pascoe, James, agent, Howe st
Pascoe, Richard J., tailor, Sturt st
Pask, Lambert, labourer, Ligar st
Pateman, Mrs., teacher, Humffray st south
Paterson, Mrs., grocer, Bridge st
Paterson, James, butcher, Bridge st
Paterson, James, butcher, Sturt st
Pathick, Samuel, carpenter, Dawson st
Patience, D., bootmaker, Creswick road
Patman, W., miner, north of municipal boundary
Paton, Mrs., Dana st
Paton, Robt., Lyons st north
Patrick, George, miner, Burnbank st
Patten, Joseph, labour mart, Mair st
Patten, Mrs., labour mart, Humffray st
Patterson, T., miner, Humffray st south
Patterson, Thomas, miner, Skipton st
Patterson, J. D., hairdresser, Lydiard st
Patterson, —, car proprietor, Errard st
Patterson, James, carpenter, Errard st
Patterson, G. W. F., clerk of petty sessions, D. E., Drummond st
Patterson, D., carpenter, Victoria st
Pattie, James, labourer, Burnbank st
Pattinson, Timothy, miner, Dana st
Pattinson, J. H., draper, Main road
Passmore, Wm., gunsmith, Victoria st
Paul, J. R., butcher, Creswick road
Pawsey, John, salesman, Eyre st
Payne, John, miner, Sebastopol
Payne, Mrs., Princes st
Payne, David, butcher, Eureka st
Pazanan, fireman on railway, Doveton st
Peach, Wm., jeweller, Sturt st
Peak, Wm., miner, Barkly st
Peake, W. H., miner, Bond st
Pearce, Richard, fruiterer, Skipton st
Pearce, Samuel, miner, Otway st
Pearce, George, labourer, Lyons st
Pearce, Thomas, Lintons carrier, Raglan street
Pearce, Wm., miner, Pleasant st
Pearce, Thomas, miner, Eyre st
Pearce, Edwin, carpenter, Doveton st
Pearce, Wm., carpenter, Doveton st
Pearce, John, labourer, Doveton st
Pearce, W., engine driver, Little Bendigo
Pearce, Henry, miner, Barkly st
Pearce, Thomas, miner, Barkly st
Pearmain, William, bootmaker, Bridge st

Pearmain, W., bootmaker, Albert st
Pearce, James, miner, Wills st
Pearson, F. G., clerk, Ascot st
Pearson, Joseph, miner, Grant st
Pearson, D., miner, Ascot st
Peasnell, Thomas, china dealer, Humffray street
Peart, Joseph, miner, Sebastopol
Peasnell, W., hawker, Scott's parade
Peebles, J., miner, Skipton st
Peirce, W. E., registry office, Armstrong street
Peirce, W. E., registry office, Lydiard st
Peirce, W. E., agent, Dawson st
Peirce, James, pattern maker, Doveton st
Pell, Joseph, hawker, Little Bendigo
Pemberton and Co., Evening Post office, Mair st
Penall, Wm., miner, Armstrong st
Penhall, Thomas, labourer, Armstrong st
Penhall, Jane, butcher, Armstrong st
Penhalluriack, Joseph, miner, Eureka st
Penhalluriack, Miss, dressmaker, Humffray street
Penhalluriack, Pierce, miner, Princes st
Penny, Charles, miner, Humffray st
Penny, Mrs., Main road
Penshorn, G. F., painter, Sturt st
Perkins, Stephen, baker, Talbot st
Perrie, George, blacksmith, Humffray st
Perrie, Thomas, butcher, Humffray st
Perry, Thomas, gun and locksmith, Bridge street
Perry, James, miner, Esmond st
Perryman, Thomas, labourer, Doveton s-
Pescud, James, butcher, Main road
Pescud, Henry, butcher, Dawson st
Peters, W., professor of music, Errard st
Peters, Thomas, carter, Grant st
Peters, Absolom, miner, Pleasant st
Petrie, George, engineer, Windermere st
Petrie, Robert, miner, Eyre st
Pickford, Mrs., sempstress, Humffray st south
Picking, Alfred, carpenter, Barkly st
Pickup, James, miner, Ascot st
Picton, —, law clerk, Grant st
Pierson, Isaac, paper ruler, Webster st
Pierse, Mrs., boarding house, Raglan st
Pike, John, miner, Urquhart st
Pilgrim, James, labourer, Queen st
Pillow, Samuel, blacksmith, Peel st
Pimm, C., Northumberland Arms, Sturt street
Pimm, Charles, blacksmith, Sturt st
Pinch, William, mason, Raglan st
Piper, E. J., professor of music, Dawson street
Pitfield, Robert, moulder, Raglan st
Pitt, Henry, miner, Urquhart st
Pitt, Henry, miner, Armstrong st south
Pizzie, George, Hit or Miss hotel, Nell st
Pizzie, George, collar maker, Nell st
Phair, —, wheelwright, Errard st

Phelan and Butler, produce dealers, Main road
Phelan, Joseph, labourer, Peel st
Philip, Edmund, butcher, Eyre st
Phillip, Samuel, miner, Brown hill
Phillips, Samuel, fruiterer, Young st
Phillips, William, miner, Humffray st south
Phillips, W. J., miner, Sebastopol
Phillips, W., carter, Skipton st
Phillips, J., and Co., produce dealers, Main road
Phillips, W. H., All Nations hotel, Armstrong st south
Phillips, Henry, hawker, Main road
Phillips, Mark, bootmaker, Raglan st
Phillips, Joseph, labourer, Raglan st
Phillips, Mrs., laundress, Talbot st
Phillips, Richard, saddler, Victoria st
Phillips, Joseph, store, Humffray st
Phillips, W., miner, Humffray st
Phillips, Joseph, produce dealer, Humffray street
Phillips, Thomas, miner, Doveton st
Phillips, Richard, saddler, Clarendon st
Phillips, J., miner, Barkly st
Phillips, J., cooper, Barkly st
Phillipson, David, miner, Essex st
Phillipson, E., miner, Talbot st
Philps, Wm., miner, Little Bendigo
Philps, Benjamin, porter, Peel st
Piace, Thomas, tinsmith, Victoria st
Plant, Miss, school, Sturt st
Plant, John, miner, Wendouree parade
Platt, Thomas, miner, Brougham st
Pleydell, Wm., builder and contractor, Lydiard st
Pleydell, W. F., Lord Nelson hotel, Main road
Pheppard, Henry, stonemason, Burnbank street
Plover, Alphonse, carter, Sturt st
Plummer, J., butcher, Clayton st
Plummer, Joseph, butcher, Errard st
Polkinghorn, J., engineer, Burnbank st
Pollard, Octavius, wheelwright, Princes st
Pollard, Mrs., laundress, Lal Lal st
Pomroy, Wm., bootmaker, Bond st
Pool, Mrs., Wills st
Poole, F., fruiterer, Main road
Pooley, W., registrar of births, deaths, and marriages, and manager of Savings' Bank, Sturt st
Porter, W., bootmaker, Main road
Porter, James, bricklayer, Drummond st
Porter, Wm., bootmaker, Dana st
Porter and Co., wholesale grocers, Armstrong st
Porter, T., wholesale grocer, Doveton st
Portenus, Robert, labourer, Doveton st
Portlock, James, miner, Skipton st
Potter, Thomas, teacher, Brown hill
Poster, Rev. J., Lydiard st
Potter, —, miner, Sussex st

Potts, Geo., storekeeper, Humffray st
Potts, Miss, dressmaker, Humffray st
Powell, Isaac, carter, Holmes st
Powell, Thomas, hawker, Havelock st
Powell, Mrs., dressmaker, Lyons st
Powell, Wm., bricklayer, Lyons st
Powell, Thomas, moulder, Mair st
Power, David, miner, Lyons st
Power, Mrs., storekeeper, Drummond st
Power, Patrick, miner, Ascot st
Power, David, miner, Ascot st
Powers, Josiah, miner, Brown hill
Powrie, A., plumber, Armstrong st south
Powrie and Henry, plumbers, Armstrong street
Powson, George, labourer, Clyde st
Praed, Thomas, miner, Sebastopol
Pratt, Thomas, produce store, Creswick road
Preedy, J., miner, Cobblers
Preece, George, labourer, Eureka st
Preisig, Mrs., Barkly st
Preisig, F., upholsterer, Humffray st
Presley, Henry, miner, Drummond st
Preston, John, blacksmith, Ascot st
Preston, Thomas, miner, Holmes st
Pribble, Edward, labourer, Victoria st
Price, —, fruiterer, Humffray st south
Price, Mrs., laundress, South st
Price, J., cooper and mining mechanic, Main road
Price, Evan, mason, Rowe st
Price, Mrs., dressmaker, Raglan st
Price, E., storekeeper, Lyons st
Price, Evan, miner, Ascot st
Prieton, James, miner, Main road
Priestley, —, storekeeper, South st
Pritchard, W., bailiff, Armstrong st south
Pritchard, D. B., engineer, Black hill
Pritchard Brothers, basket makers, Main road
Proctor, Wm., carriage builder, Sturt st
Proctor, John, quarryman, Pleasant st
Proud, Joseph, City of London hotel, Mair st
Proudfoot, Chas., blacksmith, Eureka st
Prout, Thomas, car driver, Peel st
Prout, Samuel, miner, Wills st
Proven, John, miner, Bond st
Proven, David, miner, Bond st
Pruddle, Robert, gardener, Scott's parade
Prunty, Patrick, miner, Wills st
Pryde, Andrew, draper, Lyons st
Pryor, John, miner, Little Bendigo
Pryor, J., miner, Grant st
Punshorn, G. F., painter, Sturt st
Purday, W., labourer, Doveton st
Purdie, J., storekeeper, Doveton st
Purdon, W., miner, Humffray st
Purdue, W., saddler, Lyons st north
Purnell, Joseph, cabinetmaker, Doveton street
Pyne, James, miner, Queen st

Q

Quall, John, miner, Ripon st
Quall, Thomas, miner, Bond st
Querre, Geo., miner, Urquhart st
Quick, Israel, miner, Peel st
Quick, Patrick, miner, Victoria st
Quick, Paul, produce dealer, Eureka st
Quick and Jenkins, produce dealers, Eureka st
Quick, R. N., miner, Little Bendigo
Quilliven, Patrick, carter, South st
Quilliams, John, miner, Windermere st
Quinn, Richd., baker, Sturt st
Quinlane, Neil, ironmonger, Webster st
Quinlan and Forsyth, ironmongers, Armstrong st
Quinn, Thomas, miner, Barkly st
Quong Loy Guon, storekeeper, Main road

R

Raby, John, blacksmith, Bond st
Rae, John, miner, Ascot st
Rae, Thomas, baker, Eureka st
Rae, John, labourer, King st
Radley, Wm., plasterer, Ascot st
Rail, Richd., miner, Esmond st
Raleigh, Thomas, Pallas Green hotel, Victoria st
Ralph, Francis, stonemason, South st
Ralph, Mrs., Armstrong st south
Ralph, Edwin, butcher, Drummond st
Ralston, Robert, miner, Dana st
Ramenidge, Adam, miner, Wills st
Ramsey, John, teacher, Dawson st
Ramsey, John, miner, Skipton st
Ramsey, Robert, salesman, South st
Rand, Edwd., chemist, Sturt st
Rand, —, clothier, Bridge st and Main road
Randall, Mitchell, and Doward, solicitors, Lydiard st
Randall, Charles, solicitor, Sturt st
Randall, Thomas, solicitor, Doveton st
Rankin, Thomas, miner, Albert st
Rankin, Thomas, miner, off Victoria st
Rankin, Miss, Sturt st
Ransom, Henry L., miner, Drummond st
Ratt, F., miner, Main road
Rattray, James, auctioneer, Lydiard
Ratz, Conrad, miner, Sebastopol
Raymond, George, plasterer, Humffray st
Rayner, Alfred, miner, Little Bendigo
Rawlings, James, miner, Sebastopol
Rawlins, Henry, miner, Dawson st
Reardon, —, railway porter, Humffray st
Reccord, Thomas, Globe hotel, Victoria st
Reddall, George, carter, Burnbank st
Redpath, —, miner, Little Bendigo
Redmond, John, bootmaker, Albert st
Redmond, Miss, school, Clayton st
Reece, J., miner, Main road
Resid, Thomas, carter, Young st

Reeves, Charles, wine merchant, Doveton street
Reeves, W. S., surveyor, Doveton st
Rees, Wm., tailor, Raglan st
Rees, Edwd., miner, Cobblers
Reid, Wm., mining manager, Raglan st
Reid, John, carter, Dawson st
Reid, James S., miner, Drummond st
Reid, Paul, clerk, Victoria st
Reid, J., ironmonger, Webster st
Reid, Alex., carpenter, Macarthur st
Reid, Evander, miner, Wendouree parade
Reid, Thomas, miner, Brougham st
Reid, Mrs., East st
Reid, John, miner, Clayton st
Reid, John, New York bakery, Main road
Reid, Richd., miner, Main road
Reid, H., engineer, Armstrong st south
Reid, Andrew, carpenter, Brown hill
Reid, Joseph, miner, Esmond st
Reid, James, wheelwright, Greaville st
Reid, Robt., stonemason, Grant st
Reisky, John, confectioner, Sturt st
Renouf, David, miner, Drummond st
Renton, Geo., engineer, Armstrong st south
Retallack, Michael, blacksmith, Greaville street
Retchford, Thomas, salesman, Urquhart street
Rewman, Henry, greengrocer, Armstrong street
Reynolds, Peter, plasterer, Talbot st
Reynolds, Henry, plasterer, Talbot st
Reynolds, Geo., grocer, Lyons and Urquhart sts
Reynolds, W., labourer, Black hill
Rhodes, John, produce dealer, Clayton st
Rhodes, W., produce dealer, Clayton st
Rhodes Brothers, produce dealers, Main road
Rice, Josiah, brickmaker, Rowe st
Rich, Chas., miner, Dana st
Richards, Samuel, accountant, Peel st
Richards, Thomas, hawker, Peel st
Richards, Jabez, market inspector, Lyons street
Richards, Archibald, miner, Lyons st
Richards, Thomas, bricklayer, Lyons st
Richards, James, quarryman, Ascot st
Richards, Edwd., miner, Ascot st
Richards, Richd., butcher, Victoria st
Richards, Enoch, sharebroker, Sturt st
Richards, Enoch, sharebroker, Victoria st
Richards, Wm., tailor, Victoria st
Richards, Thomas, miner, Mair st
Richards, Thomas, horse dealer, Humffray street
Richards, John, miner, Humffray st
Richards, F., cabinetmaker, Armstrong st
Richards, Martin, miner, Barkly st
Richards, Morgan, Fire Brigade hotel, Barkly st
Richards, Thomas, engineer, East st

Richards, Josiah, miner, Scott's parade
Richards, Thomas, miner, Main road
Richards, Mrs., nurse, Armstrong st
Richards, J. W., miner, Little Bendigo
Richards, M., miner, Little Bendigo
Richards, David, miner, Sebastopol
Richards, Wm., miner, Sunny corner
Richards, J., miner, Cobblers
Richards, Ellis, miner, Cobblers
Richards, W., miner, Grant st
Richards, H., miner, Grant st
Richards, J., miner, Humffray st south
Richards, J., miner, Albert st
Richardson, Samuel, carpenter, Mair st
Richardson, David, Webster st
Richardson, J., carver and gilder, Wills st
Richardson, Peter, miner, Queen st
Richardson, J., Sportsmen's Arms hotel, Main road
Richardson, J., miner, Brown hill
Richardson, James, miner, Ikod st
Rickett, George, tripeman, Creswick road
Richmond, J., millwright, Wendouree parade
Ridley, Alex., gardener, Drummond st
Rigglewood, Jacob, carter, Lal Lal st
Riley, Thomas, labourer, Ligar st
Riley, J., bootmaker, Wills st
Millstone, John, blacksmith, Neil st
Rimmington, W., butcher, Sturt st
Rimmington, John, miner, Humffray st
Rippon, Edwin, miner, Bond st
Rishworth, R., storekeeper, Burnbank st
Ritchie, D., tinsmith, Eyre st
Ritchie, William, miner, King st
Ritchie, ——, miner, Barkly st
Roach, William, bootmaker, Grenville st
Robbie, William, miner, Doveton st
Roberts, John, miner, Burnbank st
Roberts, M., moulder, Wendouree parade
Roberts, Robert, miner, Otway st
Roberts, John, carpenter, Parker st
Roberts, John, draper, Main road
Roberts, John, miner, Black hill
Roberts, John, miner, Little Bendigo
Roberts, Duncan, Brown hill
Roberts, Henry, miner, Cobblers
Roberts, John, miner, Grant st
Roberts, William, labourer, Peel st
Roberts, Mrs., nurse, Peel st
Roberts, Edwin, pattern maker, Ascot st
Roberts, H. T., butcher, Dana st
Robertson, George, carpenter, Peel st
Robertson, Edwin, painter, Ligar st
Robertson, William, manager Bank of Victoria, Lydiard st
Robertson, D., brewer, Raglan st
Robertson, J., architect, Ascot st
Robertson, David, miner, Eyre st
Robertson, W. V., secretary Trade Protection Society, Lydiard st
Robertson, W., traveller, Wills st
Robertson, Peter, carter, Howard st
Robertson, Mrs., seamstress, Barkly st

Robins, Patrick, Windermere st
Robins, E., furniture manufacturer, Creswick road
Robins, E., furniture manufacturer, Armstrong st
Robinson, J. C., miner, Sebastopol
Robinson, Peter, miner, Black hill
Robinson, Mrs., Brougham st
Robinson, T., law clerk, Doveton st
Robinson, John, bootmaker, Dana st
Robinson, A., moulder, Ascot st
Robinson, J., pattern maker, Ascot st
Robinson, J., blacksmith, Lyons st
Robinson, Andrew, bootmaker, Peel st
Robinson, Peter, labourer, Peel st
Robinson, Thomas, Stock Exchange
Robson Thomas, painter, Sturt st
Robson Thomas, Adelphia hotel Sturt st
Robson, William, carpenter, Eureka st
Robson, R., Windouree parade
Rochester, Charles, fruiterer, Victoria st
Rockliff, William, engineer, Macarthur st
Rockshaw, A., bootmaker, Sebastopol
Rodd, John, clerk, Lyons st
Roddoway, J., miner, Skipton st
Rodger, D., carrier, Clyde st
Rodier, W. B., town clerk M.E., Wills st
Rodier, John, miner, Raglan st
Roff, I. and J., outfitters, Main road
Roger, W., Miner, Barkly st
Rogers, Mrs., dressmaker, Grenville st
Rogers, W., miner, Essex st
Rogers, George, carter, Doveton st
Rogers, Thomas, draper, Dana st
Rogerson, John, bootmaker, Wills st
Rollo, A., bootmaker, Sturt st
Roland, ——, miner, Sebastopol
Root and Gray, wheelwrights, Main road
Roscoe, Mrs., upholsterer, Talbot st
Rose, W., carter, Eureka st
Rose, John, Painter, Urquhart st
Rose, Edward, miner, Sebastopol
Rose, Miss, teacher, Urquhart st
Rosenon, A., dyer, Main road
Rosenblum, E. J., teacher, King st
Ross, Hugh, carter, Main road
Ross, Alexander, carpenter, Young st
Ross, Robert, salesman, Queen st
Ross, Donald, carpenter, Humffray st
Ross, Henry, guard, Doveton st
Ross, Donald, carter, Brougham st
Ross, D., storekeeper, Ligar st
Ross, D., City of York hotel, Ligar st
Ross, R., bank clerk, Lydiard st
Ross, Peter, miner, Drummond st
Rosser, Thomas, carter, Armstrong st
Rotheram, William, Victoria st
Rourke, James, North British hotel, Main road
Rouse, James, miner, King st
Round, W. S., compositor, Lyons st
Round, W., Cosmopolitan chain works, Lyons st
Round, E., patent chain maker, Dawson st

Rowan, James, storekeeper, Skipton st
Rowen, J., cabinetmaker, Webster st
Rowand, C., inspecting engineer of roads and bridges, Sturt st
Rowe, A. F., ironmonger and grocer, Main road
Rowe, W., engineer, Rowe st
Rowe, John, carter, Armstrong st
Rowe, James, miner, Doveton st
Rowlands, —, miner, Dawson st
Rowland and Lewis, gingerbeer manufacturers, Sturt st
Rowland, —, Dawson st
Roxburgh, A., traveller, Eyre st
Royal, Thomas, miner, Peel st
Rudd, Mrs., babylinen warehouse, Sturt st
Rudge, Mrs., Sturt st
Ruffin, E., tallow chandler, Eureka st
Rule, —, miner, Grant st
Rush, Mrs., boarding house, Victoria st
Rush, W., tailor, Dana st
Rushall, W., engineer, Sebastopol road
Rushbrook, E., coachdriver, Armstrong st
Rushton, Henry, carpenter, Armstrong st south
Rushton, Emanuel, carpenter, Brougham street
Russ, Wm., store, Victoria st
Russell, Albert, compositor, Raglan st
Russell, C., coach proprietor, Dawson st
Russell, J., brickmaker, Mair st
Russell, Mrs., dressmaker, Mair st
Russell, James, miner, Humffray st
Russell, James, labourer, Armstrong st
Russell, James, labourer, Clyde st
Russell, —, labourer, Eureka st
Russell, Robert, carrier, Main road
Russell, Peter, carpenter, Urquhart st
Russell, Wm., carpenter, Armstrong st
Rushworth, Wm., foundryman, South st
Rutland, Robt., greengrocer, Sturt st
Rutter, John, miner, Humffray st
Rutter, —, solicitor, Main road
Ryal, E. B., inspector, police barracks, Lydiard st
Ryan, Edward, miner, Lydiard st
Ryan, —, teacher, Victoria st
Ryan, Robt., car driver, Victoria st
Ryan, M., labourer, Eureka st
Ryan, M., miner, Humffray st
Ryan, Timothy, contractor, Eureka st
Ryan, Mrs., laundress, Scott's parade
Ryan, Dennis, carter, Sussex st
Ryan, Robt., car proprietor, Lal lal st
Ryan, James, quarryman, Urquhart st
Ryan, James, miner, Sebastopol road

S.

Sach, John, carpenter, Victoria st
Saddler, James, bank clerk, Little Drummond st
Sage, Abel, engineer, Wills st
Sainsbury, James, miner, Barkly st
Salkeld, Wm., engineer, Raglan st
Salter, Wm., engine driver, Lyons st
Salter, Charles, solicitor, Dana st
Salter, G. W., clerk, Eyre st
Sampson, Wm., miner, Lal lal st
Sandford, James, cook, Peel st
Sandford, James, carter, Peel st
Sandry, John E., miner, Scott's parade
Sanderson, Sarah, teacher, Barkly st
Sarah, Nicholas, miner, Brown hill
Sargeant, —, plasterer, Yuille st
Sass, Herman, miner, Macarthur st
Saunders, James, baker, Errard st
Saunders, Chas., bricklayer, Humffray st
Saunders, Chas., miner, Armstrong st south
Saunderson, James, gardener, Ligar st
Saunderson, James, clerk, Ligar st
Savage, Tobias, miner, South st
Savage, Samuel, painter, Main road
Sawkins, Wm., upholsterer, Dana st
Sawyer, James, bricklayer, Barkly st
Sawyer, John, bricklayer, Barkly st
Saxon, Thomas, oil merchant, Eyre st
Sayers, A., and Co., land and estate agents, Lydiard st
Sayers, Alfred, sharebroker, Raglan st
Sayers, Mrs., Raglan st
Sayer, Alfred, carter, Main road
Scaleton, Mrs., midwife, Grenville st
Scammell, Mrs., milliner, Sturt st
Scarlett, James, carter, Scott's parade
Scates, Chas., tinsmith, Humffray st
Scatcherd, J. A., miner, Peel st
Scharrer, John, clothier, Main road
Schmedling, H. A., Dutch Harry hotel, Main road
Schofield, Thomas, slater, Seymour st
Schræder, Samuel, musician, Eureka st
Schriever, A., storekeeper, Sebastopol
Scoles, Mrs., Little Bendigo
Scople, Chas., draper, Errard st
Scott, John, stonemason, Nell st
Scott, Petter, confectioner, Nell st
Scott, Thomas, carpenter, Raglan st
Scott, Geo., carpenter, Lyons st
Scott, Henry, carpenter, Errard st
Scott, Thomas, quarryman, Ascot st
Scott, Richard, miner, Ascot st
Scott, Mrs., Talbot st
Scott, —, bootmaker, Peel st
Scott, Joseph, Mair st
Scott, John, miner, Clyde st
Scott, Robert, carter, Clyde st
Scott, Martin, miner, A 1 st
Scott, John, car driver, Barkly st
Scott, Geo., miner, Brougham st
Scott, Richd., barman, Grant st
Scott, James, miner, Skipton st
Scott, Abraham, jeweller, Bridge st
Scott, Robert, saddler, East st
Scruse, Edwin, brewer, Mair st
Screen, Thomas, tanner, Sturt st
Seacombe, John, carpenter, Grant st

Seagrave, John, messenger, Grant st
Searle, James, draper, Ligar st
Searle, James, miner, Raglan st
Searle, W., baker, Main road
Sebo, W., butcher, Eureka st
Sever, W., produce dealer, Humffray st
Seely and Bradbury, builders, Dawson st
Seeley, Wm., builder, Dawson st
Seeley, Thomas, contractor, Grenville st
Seffert, Louis, miner, Drummond st
Sefton, Mrs., dressmaker, Clarendon st
Selby, James, miner, Sebastopol
Sell, Wm., carpenter, Raglan st
Sellars, Mrs., fruiterer, Main road
Sellars, Mrs., laundress, Yuille st
Semple, Thomas, butcher, Dana st
Semple, —, Victoria st
Sergeant, —, sharebroker, Sturt st
Sergeant, R. M., sharebroker, Sunny corner
Sexton, Michael, miner, Otway st
Seymour, Henry, tripeman, Humffray st
Sewell, T., Queen's Head hotel, Humffray street
Shand, Mrs., hairdresser, Main road
Shanks, Henry, engineer, Drummond st
Shannahan, Thomas, produce dealer, Armstrong st
Shannon and Jones, grocers, Eureka st
Shannon, James, miner, Eureka st
Shannon, George, grocer, Sturt st
Sharp, D., Macarthur st
Sharp, Robt., miner, King st
Sharp, James, engineer, Eureka st
Sharp, C. W., butcher, Sturt st
Sharkey, Thomas, billiard table manufacturer, Dana st
Shaw, R., butcher, Sturt st
Shaw, John, carpenter, Humffray st
Shaw, J. R., government contract surveyor, Errard st
Shaw, —, bailiff, Errard st
Shaw, Wm., engineer, Armstrong st
Shaw, Archibald, labourer, Grant st
Shaw, D., carter, Humffray st south
Shaw, Edward, labourer, Creswick road
Shaw, John, miner, Little Bendigo
Shaw, Chas., cabinet manufacturer, Main road
Shawn, R., miner, King st
Shean, Patrick, labourer, Wills st
Sheara, John, Lyons st
Shears, Wm., carpenter, Raglan st
Sheen, Luke, miner, Ripon st
Shelan, D., miner, Barkly st
Sheldon, Joseph, labourer, Lydiard st
Shellack, R., labourer, Bond st
Shelly, J., Manchester Arms hotel, Eureka street
Shepard, J., miner, Ligar st
Sheppard, W. H., chemist, Sturt st
Shepheard, Mrs., seamstress, Errard st
Shepherd, Henry, butcher, Main road
Shepherd, Wm., miner, Humffray st

Sheppard, W. G., decorator, Peel st
Sherrard, C. W., warden, Dawson st
Sherlock, Rev. F. S., Main road
Shirra, John, Brewery hotel, Drummond street
Shirra, John, brewer, Sturt st
Sherridan, Walter, architect, Ligar st
Sherry, Terry, carter, Macarthur st
Skewring, J. H., warden, Eyre st
Shiel, Rev. Dr., Victoria st
Shields, Moses, miner, Sebastopol
Shields, Joseph, miner, A1 st
Showman, J., pawnbroker, Bridge st
Shoten, W., carter, Grant st
Shoulder, G., carter, Albert st
Shrumpton, Thomas, King st
Shudall, A., Brewery hotel, Drummond st
Silk, Miss, Wills st
Sillman, Thomas, miner, Windermere st
Silverlock, photographer, Main road
Sim, John, miner, Howard st
Sim, R., saw mills, Humffray st
Sim, W., produce dealer, Haymarket
Simms, John, musician, Humffray st
Simms, W., timber merchant, Ligar st
Simms, W., engineer, Wendouree parade
Simms, Richd., miner, Macarthur st
Simms, S. W., tinsmith, Otway st
Sincock, G. E., road overseer, Armstrong street
Sincock, Samuel, carpenter, Howard st
Simmonds, Mrs., Raglan st
Simmonds, Wm., blacksmith, Lyons st
Simmonds, John, cattle salesman, Lyons street
Simmonds, J., picture frame maker, Peel street
Simmonds, A. M., carver and gilder, Main road
Simmonds, Moses, hawker, Main road
Simkin, Joseph, miner, Nightingale st
Simpson, F., hawker, Eureka st
Simpson, W., carpenter, Howard st
Simpson, Thomas, traveller, Armstrong st
Simpson, John, walter, Eyrie st
Simpson, Thomas, labourer, Havelock st
Simpson, John, engineer, Dawson st
Sinclair, John, tailor, Eyre st
Sinclair, James, miner, Little Bendigo
Sin Ler Cheong, storekeeper, Clayton st
Singleton, John, plasterer, Scott's parade
Singleton, Mrs., Victoria st
Sin Ye War, storekeeper, Main road
Sirrell, Hughes, miner, Humffray st
Skardon, W., bootmaker, Main road
Skelton, Walter, miner, Sebastopol
Skelton, John, clerk, Wills st
Skewes, John, miner, Dana st
Skewes, Samuel, miner, Pleasant st
Skewes, Andrew, miner, Dana st
Skidmore, Wm., miner, Burnbank road
Skillern, Edwd., carter, Dyte's parade
Skoglind, August, baker, Little Bendigo
Sladen, A., miner Humffray st south

Slack, Mrs., laundress, Eyre st
Skoglund, Oscar, and Gurtaf, storekeepers, Little Bendigo
Slater, Henry, miner, Williams st
Slater, Samuel, fish and poultry dealer, Bridge st
Sleep, Wm., carpenter, Humffray st
Sleep, J. F., jeweller, Lydiard st
Sleigh, John, cabinet maker, Pleasant st
Slowman, —, carpenter, Windermere st
Smallie, —, labourer, Ripon st
Smart, John, miner, Drummond st
Smart, Miss, dressmaker, Young st
Smillie, Gordon, overseer of roads and bridges, Drummond st
Smidth, J. G., carter, Lydiard st
Smith, W. D., car driver, Humffray st
Smith, James, sharebroker, Lydiard st
Smith, Henry, carrier, Raglan st
Smith, James, timber merchant, Lyons st
Smith, James, miner, Drummond st
Smith, John, miner, Windermere st
Smith, Daniel, miner, Windermere st
Smith, Wm., miner, Ascot st
Smith, James, mason, Ascot st
Smith, E., bootmaker, Pleasant st
Smith, Geo., carter, Havelock st
Smith, Thomas, labourer, Ripon st
Smith, Mrs., nurse, Ripon st
Smith, James, carpenter, Ripon st
Smith, Miss, dressmaker, Dana st
Smith, Geo., miner, Victoria st
Smith, Wm., compositor, Victoria st
Smith, Wm., car proprietor, Victoria st
Smith, Mrs., dressmaker, Muir st
Smith, George, miller, Sturt st
Smith, W. C., auctioneer, Sturt st
Smith, Bros., timber merchants, saw mills, Ballarat west
Smith, Mrs., Union hotel, Sturt st
Smith, Wynne, and Wynne, discount bank, Sturt st
Smith, John, miner, Seymour st
Smith, A. H., miner, Clarendon st
Smith, Geo., seedsman, Armstrong st
Smith, Geo., sordsman, Barkly st
Smith, Adam, timber merchant, Doveton street
Smith, John, baker, Doveton st
Smith, Alex., slaughterman, Soldier's hill, beyond boundary
Smith, W. H., boat proprietor, Wendouree parade
Smith, W. P., manager Bank of Victoria
Smith, W. H., boat proprietor, Victoria st
Smith, W. H., gardener, Eureka st
Smith, George, nursery, Albert st
Smith, Wm., miner, Humffray st south
Smith, Wm., school, Humffray st south
Smith, Henry, miner, Young st
Smith, Robt., mason, Bond st
Smith, James, miner, Little Bendigo
Smith, Joseph, Turf hotel, Creswick road
Smith, F., hotel, Main road

Smith, A. V., photographer, Main st
Smith, J. Henry, restaurant, Main st
Smith, Henry, draper, Main road
Smith, George, miner, Ebden st
Smith, James, car proprietor, Main st
Smith, Henry, butcher, Wills st
Smith, Alexander, grocer, Wills st
Smith, James, labourer, Otway st
Smith and Kersley, Main road
Smithwhite, W., blacksmith, Wendouree parade
Smyth, James, Cricket Club hotel, ... street
Smyth, R., fellmonger, Parker st
Smythe, R., storekeeper, Barkly st
Snelling, J., carpenter, Eyre st
Solder, Samuel, carpenter, Doveton st
Snow, Mrs., storekeeper, Main road
Soloman, Phillip, Barkly st
Solomon & Bardwell, photographers, Sturt street
Solomon, Morris, accountant, Victoria st
Soldiers hill police station, Armstrong st
Somergill, Thomas, miner, Havelock st
Somerville, Alexander, carter, Doveton st
Sommers, William, miner, Eyre st
Sonnenberg, P., fancy repository, Bridge street
Southall, Enoch, bootmaker, Ligar st
Southall, William, butcher, Ligar st
Southall, William, miner, A 1 st
Southey, Henry, miner, Doveton st
Southward and Sumpton, grocers, Sturt street
Southwick, T., carpenter, Scott's parade
Spackham, J., bricklayer, Drummond st
Spain, W., bank clerk, Wendouree parade
Spaniuske, J. H. F., Union hotel, Humffray st
Spargo, Nicholas, engineer, Neil st
Spargo, James, labourer, Ripon st
Spargo, —, Armstrong st
Sparkman, Henry, draper, Princes st
Spear, W., miner, Dyte's parade
Spedding, W., carpenter, Drummond st
Spence, John, miner, Victoria st
Spielcoogel, N. F., Bridge st
Spiers, James, miner, Havelock st
Springer, Charles, cook, Grant st
Sprout, —, moulder, Dawson st
Spruhan, Lawrence, miner, Dawson st
Spurgeon, J., miner, Macarthur st
Stainer, James, storekeeper, Barkly st
Stallard, W., Ballarat Grammar School, Doveton st
Stamp, John, pattern maker, Ascot st
Stan, W., labourer, Brougham st
Stanger, Geo., tailor, Dana st
Stansfield, L., painter, Doveton st
Stanton, Mrs., confectioner, Sturt st
Star, Mrs., Howard st
Stark, M., miner, Dana st
Steabbin, Short, and Co., drapers, Bridge street

Steel, Joseph, baker, Barkly st
Steinle, J., cabinet maker, Wills st
Steinfeld, E., cabinet maker, Bridge st
Steinfeld, E., cabinet maker, Peel st
Stephens, M., miner, Little Bendigo
Stephens, Henry, miner, Little Bendigo
Stephen, John, bootmaker, Skipton st
Stephen, Edward, miner, Sebastopol
Stephens, Henry, carpenter, Victoria st
Stephens, Wm., Windermere st
Stephens, J. F., plumber and painter, Drummond st
Stephens, Robert, miner, Dawson st
Stephens, G., and Son, coachbuilders, Peel street
Stephenson, William, miner, Brown hill
Stephenson, Jonathan, labourer, Drummond st
Stevens, Harry, labourer, Humffray st
Stevens, Misheck, painter, Lyons st
Stevens, Wm., miner, Errard st
Stevens, Wm., miner, Windermere st
Stevens, Wm., miner, Pleasant st
Stevens, J. B., bootmaker, Eureka st
Stevens, Thomas, miner, Ebden st
Stevenson, Thomas, boiler maker, Clyde street
Stevenson, Wm., painter, Lydiard st
Stevenson, Wm., Unicorn hotel, Sturt st
Steward, J., news agent, King st
Steward, John, miner, Errard st
Stewart, Jas., M.D., Ballarat
Stewart, J., miner, Scott's parade
Stewart, W., traveller, Doveton st
Stewart, D., Armstrong st
Stiland, J., carter, off Victoria st
Stillman, W., Butchers' Arms, Black hill
Stirdie, James, miner, Main road
Stocks, F., Otway st
Stock, Robert, miner, Barkly st
Stock, Samuel, miner, Talbot st
Stocks, J. D., mining agent, Victoria st
Stoddart, Mrs., Wills st
Stoddart, John, carter, Scott's parade
Stoddart, James, miner, Sebastopol
Stokes, James, chemist, Armstrong st
Stokes, John, gardener, Howard st
Stone, Joseph, engineer, Humffray st
Stone, Joseph, miner, Little Bendigo
Stone, Mrs., laundress, Nell st
Stoney, B. A., boarding house, Lydiard st
Stoney, B. A., dining rooms, Sturt st
Stoney, B. A., Royal Mail hotel, Lydiard street
Storey, Benjamin, plasterer, Black hill
Stoten, Robert, miner, Wills st
Stothard, Henry, carpenter, Clyde st
Strachan and Co., merchants, Lydiard st
Strachan, —, merchant, Dana st
Stradley, Thomas, miner, Sunny corner
Strands, T. A., hardwareman, Main road
Strange, James, miner, Otway st
Strassford, W., agent, Haglan st
Stratton, D., miller, Ripon st

Stray, J., butcher, Grant st
Street, John, miner, Windermere st
Strickland, E. J., hide and wool salesman, Lydiard st
Strickland, E. J., fellmonger, Melbourne road
Stringer, Robert, bootmaker, Bowe st
Strutt, John, miner, Skipton st
Stubbs, J. R., joiner, Lyons st
Stuck, Wm., blacksmith, Wills st
Sturley, John, butcher, Armstrong st
Stulze, Ludwig, carpenter, Main road
Styles, John, mason, Humffray st
Sullivan, Neil, blacksmith, Talbot st
Sullivan, Elizabeth, laundress, Havelock street
Sullivan, John, plasterer, Havelock st
Sullivan, —, brickmaker, Brougham st
Sullivan, James, labourer, Princes st
Sully, J., miner, Brown hill
Sullivan, Mrs., Nell st
Summers, F., grocer, Eyre st
Summers, F., china and hardware dealer, Armstrong st
Summers, John, miner, Eureka st
Sun Ching Cheong, store, Main road
Surridge, John, butcher, Main road
Surtees, Morrison, mason, Doveton st
Surtees, Morrison, mason, Macarthur st
Susenbeth, Carl, cabinetmaker, East st
Sutherland, Dr. Humffray st
Sutherland, Alex., mason, Barkly st
Sutherland, Alex., compositor, Mair st
Sutton, R. H., musicseller, Main road
Sutton, Rev. W., Lyons st
Suttrick, —, blacksmith, Camp reserve
Swain, Henry, agent, Doveton st
Swain, Samuel, carter, Burnbank st
Swaine, Alex., miner, Cobblers
Swallow, Mrs., Main road
Swan, James, tailor, Eureka st
Swann, Andrew, bootmaker, Humffray st
Swanston, Thomas, bootmaker, Main road
Sweaton, James, carter, Barkly st
Sweeney, Peter, contractor, Victoria st
Sweeney, Daniel, slaughterman, Soldiers' hill
Swindells, James, draper, Wendouree parade
Syme, John, miner, Bond st
Symon, —, miner, rear of Armstrong st south
Symons, Chas., salesman, Grant st
Symons, H., butcher, Wendouree parade

T.

Tabel, Peter, storekeeper, Ligar st
Tannock, James, upholsterer, Mair st
Tannock, James, upholsterer, Lydiard st
Tapper, John, carpenter, Queen st
Taplin, —, ironmonger, Sturt st
Tates, James, bootmaker, Eureka st
Tarte, J. V., produce broker, Hay Market

2 R

Tarte, J. V., produce broker, Doveton st
Tarte, J. V., produce broker, Lydiard st
Tarrant, Isaac, miner, Skipton st
Tarrant, Wm., bootmaker, Drummond st
Tart, George, butcher and storekeeper, Sebastopol
Tatham, F. W., miner, Cobblers
Tattersall, John, butcher, Humffray st
Taylor, David, miner, Peel st
Taylor, Eli, cabinetmaker, Peel st
Taylor, J., upholsterer, Peel st
Taylor, Wm., carter, Ligar st
Taylor, Alex., horse dealer, Raglan st
Taylor, J., baker and storekeeper, Dana street
Taylor, J. G., furniture dealer, Sturt st
Taylor, —, bricklayer, Sturt st
Taylor, Wm., miner, Macarthur st
Taylor, James, butcher, Sturt st market
Taylor, Wm., bricklayer, Barkly st
Taylor, Andrew, carter, Eureka st
Taylor, Robert, store, Eureka st
Taylor, J., miner, Humffray st
Taylor, W., brickmaker, Humffray st
Taylor, Thomas, car proprietor, Otway st
Taylor, Ralph, miner, Scott's parade
Taylor, Mrs., sempstress, Dyte's parade
Taylor, Robert, waiter, Urquhart st
Taylor, John H., tinsmith, Creswick road
Taylor, Alex., miner, Sebastopol
Taylor, J., miner, Esmond st
Teague, Mrs., butcher, Brown hill
Teasdale, Jonathan, carpenter, Eiden st
Telford, W. J., car proprietor, Doveton st
Telford and Co., confectioners, Bridge st
Tenley, Geo., miner, Bond st
Tench, James, mason, Dawson st
Teach, James, miner, Talbot st
Tenney, J., carter, Humffray st
Thackeray, Thomas, mason, Ligar st
Thiemeyer, Henry, cabinetmaker, Sturt street
Thomas, J., miner, Barkly st
Thomas, S. G., storekeeper, Barkly st
Thomas, Jonas, Criterion store, Armstrong st
Thomas, John, miner, Doveton st
Thomas, Richd., miner, Sturt st
Thomas, Phillip, miner, Sturt st
Thomas, J., miner, Humffray st
Thomas, David, cooper, Humffray st
Thomas, —, miner, Humffray st
Thomas, Jacob, engineer, Urquhart st
Thomas, Jacob, engineer, Eyre st
Thomas, Benjamin, miner, Sebastopol
Thomas, Benjamin, engineer, Cobblers
Thomas, J., miner, Esmond st
Thomas, Geo., miner, Esmond st
Thomas, Henry, miner, Esmond st
Thomas, David, miner, Bond st
Thomas, J., traveller, Mair st
Thomas, Wm., butcher, Dana st
Thomas, David, butcher, Lyons st
Thomas, Edwd., miner, Ascot st

Thomas, Mrs., Wills st
Thomas, Nicholas, miner, Dyte's par[ade]
Thomas, Benjamin, miner, King st
Thomas, David, Yarrowee hotel, [Creswick] road
Thomas, James, miner, Parker st
Thomas, —, miner, Grenville st
Thomas, Edwd., miner, Urquhart st
Thomas, John, carpenter, Skipton st
Thomas, Richd., mason, Nightingale s[t]
Thomas, W., saddler, Armstrong st so[uth]
Thomas, David, miner, Sebastopol
Thompson, J. T., Garrick's Head, St[urt] street
Thompson, Chas., miner, Peel st
Thompson, Henry, groom, Havelock st
Thompson, David, engineer, Nell st
Thompson, —, miner, Doveton st
Thompson, R., fruiterer, Sturt st market
Thompson, W., secretary water commission, Lyons st north
Thompson, Jonathan, miner, Humffray st
Thompson, Wm., china and glass dealer, Victoria st
Thompson, Robert, greengrocer, Victoria street
Thompson, Thomas, architectural and cabinet carver, Mair st
Thompson, Wm., miner, Lexton st
Thompson, Mrs., laundress, Lyons st
Thompson, Wm., carpenter, Dawson st
Thompson, —, foundryman, Errard st
Thompson, W. H., produce merchant, Main road
Thompson, George, painter, Armstrong st south
Thompson, John, miner, Sebastopol
Thompson, Wm., miner, Sebastopol
Thorne, Joseph, brewer, Mair st
Thorne, C., wheelwright, Doveton st
Thorne, Thomas, miner, Little Bendigo
Thornton, James, builder, Victoria st
Thorpe, John, carpenter, Lyons st
Thurling, Robt., Tasmanian dining rooms, Armstrong st
Thursfield, Thomas, smith, Talbot st
Thurston, Geo., carpenter, Main road
Thurtell, —, tinsmith, Esmond st
Tickell, James, miner, Cobblers
Timmerman, Wm., Seymour st
Timmins, Wm., blacksmith, Dawson st
Timms, John, tailor, Humffray st
Tinkler, John, boiler smith, Clarendon st
Tinworth, Charles, miner, Main road
Tinsley, Henry, boiler maker, Grant st
Tippett, Cornelius, contractor, Skipton st
Tippett, Thomas, miner, Little Bendigo
Tiplin, James, miner, Barkly st
Tiplin, Miss, school, Barkly st
Tisher and Co., soap and candle works, Barkly st
Tobias and Marks, fishmongers, Main road
Tobin, James, labourer, Nightingale st

Todd, John, bricklayer, Humffray st
Todd, Thomas, grocer, Humffray st
Todd, Alex., carpenter, Dana st
Todd, Thomas, cutler, Wills st
Tolley, Samuel, carter, Dyte's parade
Tomkin, Alfred, tinsmith, Main road
Tomkins, Mrs., Humffray st
Tomline, J., miner, Mair st
Tongue, J., miner, Little Bendigo
Tonkin, Wm., miner, Rowe st
Tonkin, Thomas, miner, Bond st
Tonner, James, miner, Talbot st
Toomey, Michael, store, Lydiard st
Tough, Mrs., boarding house, Lyons st
Toussan, J., miner, Sebastopol
Towl, Edward, chemist, Sturt st
Townson, Thomas, compositor, Eureka st
Toy, Richard, engineer, Doveton st
Tozer, J., miner, Queen st
Tozer, Wm., miner, Eyre st
Tozer, Henry, miner, Eureka st
Tracey, Wm., miner, Sebastopol
Tracey, Benjamin, fruiterer, Wills st
Trahar, Richard, foundry, Dana st
Trainor, James, painter, Ligar st
Trecarilie, —, miner, Ascot st
Tregaskis, Richard, engineer, East st
Tregaskis, Mrs., ladies' school, East st
Tregenza, Wm., bricklayer, Wills st
Tregoosing, Henry, miner, Clayton st
Triglone, John, miner, Esmond st
Trench, R. Le Poer, barrister, Lydiard st
Trench, R. Le Poer, barrister, Creswick road
Trenery, Edwin, miner, Dana st
Tregenza, —, professor of music, Barkly street
Trengrove, John, blacksmith, Humffray st
Trengrove, Thomas, veterinary surgeon, Bath st
Trengrove, Wm., engineer, Humffray st
Trese, Wm., blacksmith, Armstrong st
Tresselear, Edward, miner, Esmond st
Tress, Geo., produce dealer, Main road
Trelize, Joseph, miner, Ripon st
Trelize, Thomas, miner, Barkly st
Treshall, Walter, miner, Grant st
Trevaskis, —, butcher, Little Bendigo
Trevarrow, —, miner, Little Bendigo
Trevithar, Josiah, mailman, Bond st
Trevithick, Wm., dairyman, Doveton st
Trevena, Josiah, fruiterer, Main road
Trimbath, Wm., miner, Ligar st
Trimbath, Richard, miner, Ligar st
Trimbath, James, miner, Brougham st
Trotman, Wm., miner, Esmond st
Troop, J. W., locomotive fireman, Doveton street
Trower, J., miner, Creswick road
Trudgan, Wm., miner, Brougham st
Tucken, J. S., plasterer, Windermere st
Tuckett, Geo., billiard table proprietor, Esmond st
Tugwell, John, accountant, Sturt st

Tugwell, John, accountant, Mair st
Tullock, McLaren, and Co., merchants, Lydiard st
Tulloch, Wm., merchant, Errard st
Tunbridge, R., timber merchant, Doveton street
Tunbridge, R., timber merchant, Dawson street
Tunnicr, Richard, constable, Victoria st
Tunks, —, miner, Grant st
Tung Cheong, tailor, Main road
Turnbull, James, carpenter, Sturt st
Turnbull, Wm., butcher, Burnbank st
Turner, Samuel, miner, Barkly st
Turner, Marmaduke, draper, Barkly st
Turner, James, labourer, Macarthur st
Turner, Thomas, gardener, Armstrong st
Turner, Mrs., registry office, Armstrong street
Turner, Henry, engineer, Dana st
Turner, John, wine cooper, Dana st
Turner, A. T., professor of music, Lyons street
Turner, Edwin, butcher, Main road
Turner, Thomas, miner, Creswick road
Turner, Charles, butcher, Little Bendigo
Turner, S., Prince Alfred hotel, Cobblers
Turnhill, J., tailor, Barkly st
Turpie, D., produce dealer, Humffray st
Tuxen and Co., wine and spirit merchants, Main road
Tweedie, Wm., bailiff, Doveton st
Tweedie, D., miner, Armstrong st
Twentyman & Stamper, outfitters, Bridge street
Twigg, John, miner, Esmond st
Tyack, W. H., miner, Essex st
Tyler, James, labourer, Lydiard st
Tyler, John, miner, Ascot st
Tynan Brothers, blacksmiths, Sturt st
Tynan, Edward, blacksmith, Mair st
Tynan, Wm., blacksmith, Talbot st
Tynan, James, blacksmith, Dana st
Tyrill, James, stock and share broker, Sturt st

U.

Unthank, Wm., labourer, Scott's parade
Unwin, Charles, butcher, Main road
Unwin, James, mailman, Camp reserve
Upjohn, E., nightman, Doveton st
Uran, Mrs., Eyre st
Urio, Wm., miner, Ascot st
Urwin, Thomas, miner, Barkly st
Urwin, Jane, dressmaker, Barkly st
Usher, J. F., chemist, Creswick road
Uwins, W., miner, Humffray st

V.

Vail, Wm., tailor, Dana st
Vale, W. M. K., bookseller, Lydiard st
Vallance, James, miner, Albert st
Valley, George, miner, Doveton st

Vallentine, S. G., inspector of cattle yards, Clarendon st
Vanbeuren, M., coach trimmer, Main road
Vaose, W. B., bank clerk, Wendouree parade
Varcoe, Benjamin, miner, Humffray st
Varcoe, Wm., miner, Drummond st
Varcoe, Benjamin, miner, Armstrong st south
Varren, J., carter, Wills st
Vasey, Henry, dairyman, Wills st
Vasey, John, smith, Errard st
Venn, F., carter, Clayton st
Veal, Wm., miner, Humffray st
Vercoe, Benjamin, miner, Wills st
Vercoe, Mrs., Ripon st
Vetts, William, labourer, Albert st
Vetts, Chas., M.R.C.V.S.H., Mair st
Viant, Henry, miner, Cobblers
Vickers, Isaac, miner, Sebastopol
Vickers, M., sempstress, Main road
Vickery, J. S., soap and candle manufacturer, Humffray st
Victor, John, Ballarat Collegiate School, Holmes st
Vigours, Charles, carman, Humffray st
Vince, Louis, grocer, Main road
Vince, Louis, grocer, Wills st
Vincent, Thomas V., miner, Wills st
Vincent, Thomas, miner, Dyte's parade
Vippond, Richd., jeweller, Lydiard st
Vite, F., carpenter, Barkly st
Voight, Chas., tailor, Victoria st
Vowles, George, carter, Yuille st
Vowles, J., Parade hotel, Wendouree parade

W.

Wade, John, miner, Doveton st
Wagg, Mrs., Windermere st
Wainwright, James, labourer, Creswick road
Wainwright, William, dairyman, Main road
Wakefield, Dr., surgeon, Humffray st
Walburton, Thomas, miner, Sussex st
Waldock, Simon, carter, Creswick road
Walford, Wm., carpenter, Hond st
Walker, Alfred, tailor, Humffray st
Walker, D., labourer, Armstrong st
Walker, James, labourer, Doveton st
Walker, W. J., carpenter, Clarendon st
Walker, George, miner, Eureka st
Walker, John, miner, Black hill
Walker, John, tailor, Skipton st
Walker, James, hatter, Bridge st
Walker, Charles, pastrycook, &c., Bridge street
Walker, Wm., hairdresser, Main road
Walker, Wm., traveller, Ligar st
Walker, John, miner, Eyre st
Walker, John, stonecutter, Neil st
Walker, John, moulder, Eyre st
Walker, Dugald, tailor, Dana st
Walker, Samuel, sharebroker, Sturt st
Walker, Samuel, sharebroker, Lyons st
Walker, Rev. R. T., Drummond st
Walker, James, labourer, Dawson st
Walker, John, store, Dana st
Walker, John, furniture dealer, Dana st
Walker, John, groom, Albert st
Wall, John, carpenter, Sturt st
Wall, Wm., carpenter, Sturt st
Wallace, —, miner, Cobblers
Wallace, Major, sheriff, Camp st
Wallace, Peter, miner, Lyons st
Waller, George, carter, Talbot st
Wallis, —, miner, Humffray st
Wallis and Dobson, timber merchants, Sturt st
Wallis, Wm., timber merchant, Lyons st
Wallis, Robt., miner, Barkly st
Walsh, Patrick, Hand of Friendship, Victoria st
Walsh, Michael, sharebroker, Lyons st
Walsh, R., barrister, Lydiard st
Walsh, R., barrister, Lyons st
Walsh, Charles, miner, Drummond st
Walsh, Samuel, storekeeper, Sturt st
Walter, Wm., carpenter, Main road
Walters, Thomas, miner, Seymour st
Walters, John, miner, Sturt st
Walters, James, carpenter. Main road
Walters, John, plasterer, Albert st
Walters, Joseph, carter, Black hill
Walton, Wm., Windermere st
Walton, Alfred, cardriver, Main road
Walton, —, miner, Drummond st
Walton, Thomas, miner, Wendouree parade
Ward, James, butcher, Sturt st
Ward, John, engineer, Windermere st
Ward, James, Royal Saxon hotel, Sturt st
Ward, Sampson, blacksmith, Windermere street
Ward, J. H., greengrocer, Main road
Ward, Robt., miner, Ripon st
Ward, Wm., fruiterer, Main road
Ward, L. H., Beaufort hotel, Eyre st
Ward, A. G. C., Sturt st
Warde, Cornelius, actor, Eureka st
Wardle, Henry, sawyer, Dana st
Wardrop, John, moulder, Errard st
Warmald, James, labourer, Ligar st
Ware, Wm., miner, Skipton st
Ware, Samuel J. D., miner, Eyre st
Ware, John, miner, Grant st
Ware, James, carter, Seymour st
Wareham, James, miner, Wendouree parade
Waring, James, tallow chandler, Sturt st
Warne, Richd., miner, Ebden st
Warner, Henry, chemist, Armstrong st
Warrell, Edward, miner, Humffray st
Warren, Wm., coach proprietor, Webster street
Warren, Robt., miner, Wendouree parade
Warren, Nicholas, Ebden st

Warren, Wm., butcher, Dana st
Warren, J. T., stonemason, Peel st
Warren, Mrs., Lyons st
Warrener, Eli, Cornwall Arms, Main road
Warton, Thomas, miner, Lexton st
Warwick, James, bricklayer, Queen st
Wasley, Josiah, Engine driver, Errard st
Waters, Samuel, miner, Victoria st
Waters, Wm., carter, Lyons st
Waters, Samuel, painter, Sturt st
Waterman, George, tailor, Armstrong st south
Waterson, Mrs., Black hill
Waterson, Philip, miner, Bond st
Watkins, Geo., miner, Dawson st
Watkins, Phillip, miner, Albert st
Watmore, Edwd., fruiterer. Main road
Watson, John, carpenter, Main road
Watson, Wm. Henry, Town Hall hotel, Armstrong st
Watson, John, miner, Clyde st
Watson, James, carter, Macarthur st
Watson, John, bootmaker, Dana st
Watson, Aaron, miner, Goarr st
Watson and Thorne, brewers, Ascot st
Watson, Wm., brewer, Creswick road
Watson, Geo., miner, Brougham st
Watson, Mrs., nurse, Talbot st
Watson, John, miner, Esmond st
Watson, E., blacksmith, Armstrong st south
Watson, Mrs., Victoria st
Watts, W., Sturt st
Watts, Albert, engineer, East st
Watt, James, saddler, Lyons st
Wayne and Brind, chemists, Bridge st
Wayne and Brind, chemists, Sturt st
Weaver, Richd., labourer, Barkly st
Weaver, Edwd., wheelwright, Peel st
Weatherstone, Geo., bootmaker, Peel st
Weber, Mrs., laundress, Windermere st
Weber, Emil, Dana st
Webb, John, dairyman, Ascot st
Webb, Geo., carpenter, Ascot st
Webb, Mrs., Ascot st
Webb, Richd., miner, Eureka st
Webb, James, labourer, A 1 st
Webster, Wm., carter, Boundary st
Webster, Wm., miner, Barkly st
Webster, Wm., butcher, Skipton st
Webster, Thomas, wood turner, Eyre st
Weeks, —, tanner, Creswick road
Weetch, John, turner, Grenville st
Welch, Geo., traveller, East st
Welch, Benjamin, agent, Barkly st
Welch, Mrs., confectioner, Main road
Weldon, Robt., letter carrier, Dawson st
Wells, James, miner, Errard st
Welsh and Surplice, estate agents, Armstrong st
Welsh, Patricius, estate agent, Webster street
Welsh, Edward, butcher, Barkly st
Welsh, Wm., solicitor, Lydiard st

Wenman, Samuel, salesman, East st
Were, J. H., Camp st
Wesley, Wm., miner, Grant st
West, Geo., Western hotel, Armstrong st
West, Thomas, blacksmith, Main road
West, Chas., labourer, Drummond st
Westerngreen, —, miner, Clyde st
Westgarth, Chas., miner, Eyre st
Wharton, John, wheelwright Talbot st
Wheeler, J., french polisher, Victoria st
Wheeler, Joseph, confectioner, Drummond street
Wheeldon, Isaac, miner, Eyre st
Whelan, James, bootmaker, Eureka st
Whelan, John, miner, Nell st
Whellan, —, Lyons st
Whitburne, Edward, engine driver, Princes street
White, J. W., Lydiard st
White, Thomas, carman, Humffray st
White, John, carter, Doveton st
White, James, miner, Barkly st
White, Patrick, miner, South st
White, John, watchmaker, Main road
White, James and William, stationers, Sturt st
White, John, carter, Wills st
White, Thos., draper, Nell st
White, Thomas, mason, Grenville st
White, G. T., joiner, Dawson st
White, John, moulder, Dawson st
White, Thomas, miner, Drummond st
White, Geo., miner, Drummond st
White, James, miner, Eyre st
White, Wm., miner, Victoria st
White, Thomas, bank clerk, Mair st
Whitehead, Henry, draper, Sturt st
Whitehead, James, labourer, Macarthur st
Whitehead, W., miner, Pleasant st
Whitehouse, James, British Queen hotel, Bridge st
Whitelaw, Mrs., store, Creswick road
Whitelaw, Thomas, painter and glazier, Sturt st
Whitelaw, Thomas, painter and glazier, Yuille st
Whitesides, Miles, tailor, Drummond st
Whitford, Cornish, carpenter, Burnbank street
Whitford, Mrs., Talbot st
Whitford, M. K., grocer, Victoria st
Whitford, M. K., butcher, Victoria st
Whitney, Joseph, coachsmith, Mair st
Whitley, James, carpenter, Ebden st
Whitrick, Robt., miner, Ligar st
Whitten, E. T., bootmaker, Bridge st
Whitten, E. T., bootmaker, Main road
Whitten, James, miner, Main road
Wicks, Geo., sharebroker, Sturt st
Wicks, Geo., sharebroker, Victoria st
Wickett, Wm., quarryman, Pleasant st
Widdy, Chas., labourer, Nell st
Wigney, F., compositor, Barkly st
Wilbank, Geo., bootmaker, King st

Wilcock, James, teacher, Barkly st
Wilcock, Joseph, miner, Sussex st
Wilcox, James, carter, Al st
Wilkie, John, miner, Drummond st
Wilkie, Wm., miner, Lydiard st
Wilkie, —, carter, Clayton st
Wills, Thomas F., saddler, Sturt st
Wills, Thomas, miner, Little Bendigo
Wilmot, Edward, ironmonger, Bridge st
Wilmot, J., miner, Macarthur st
Winsley, Geo., miner, Eyre st
Witkowski Bros., tobacconists, Bridge st
Whitten, Joseph, clerk, Skipton st
Whittington, J., baker, Brougham st
Whittle, James, chemist, Creswick road
Whitty, Geo., painter, Mair st
Wilson, Wm., mason, Drummond st
Wilson, Adam, storekeeper, Drummond street
Wilson, Smith, carpenter, Drummond st
Wilson, James J. A., dentist, Sturt st
Wilson, Miss, sempstress, Dana st
Wilson, Mrs., sempstress, Sturt st
Wilson, S., miner, Humffray st
Wilson, —, musician, Humffray st
Wilson, John, labourer, Doveton st
Wilson, Robert, storekeeper, Wendouree parade
Wilson, David, miner, Cobblers
Wilson, Alex., miner, Cobblers
Wilson, Wm., miner, Black hill
Wilson, Rev. J. G., Sebastopol
Wilson, —, miner, Sebastopol
Wilson, James, blacksmith, Sebastopol
Wilson, Wm., painter, Peel st
Wilson, John, telegraph repairer, Neil st
Wilson, Mrs., sempstress, Neil st
Wilson, J. B., groom, Raglan st
Wilson, Thomas, carpenter, Raglan st
Wilson, J., miner, Errard st
Wilson, Wm., groom, Albert st
Wilson, Geo., miner, Humffray st south
Wilson, E., Guiding Star hotel, Sebastopol road
Wilson, Wm , miner, Lal lal st
Wilson, James, car driver, Clayton st
Wilson, James, carpenter, Scott's parade
Wilson, Samuel, storeman, Lyons st
Winsor, Henry, wheelwright, Humffray street
Wishart, Wm., carpenter, Clarendon st
Withers, W. B., reporter, Lyons st
Witte, Albert, store, Albert st
Wilkins, W. G., grocer, Drummond st
Wilkins, Thomas, bootmaker, Macarthur street
Wilkins, Thomas, bootmaker, Mair st
Wilkins, —, clerk, Lydiard st
Wilkinson, Robt., standpipe keeper
Wilkinson, Geo., standpipe keeper
Wilkinson, Joseph, labourer, Peel st
Wilkinson, Thomas, compositor, Wills st
Wilkinson, G., wheelwright, Scott's parade

Wilkinson, Edward, miner, Ripon st
Wilks, Walter, blacksmith, Boundary st
Winchcombe, Stephen, miner, Barnhust street
Windover and Davis, saddlers, Lydiard st
Windover and Davis, saddlers, Main road
Windover, James, saddler, Dawson st
Windover, Wm., butcher, Sturt st
Windle, John, newspaper proprietor, Errard st
Wine, J. A., chemist and store, Eyre st
Wingate, W., surveyor, Humffray st south
Wingrove, Thomas, miner, Eureka st
Winkin, Thomas, miner, Scott's parade
Winsor, Charles, miner, Rowe st
Williams, Mrs., school, Ligar st
Williams, Thomas, carpenter, Ligar st
Williams, Philip, Olive Branch hotel, Lydiard st
Williams, Richd., Raglan st
Williams, James, foundryman, Dawson st
Williams, John, miner, Errard st
Williams, Thomas, miner, Errard st
Williams, John, carpenter, Errard st
Williams, John, bootmaker, Grant st
Williams, Mrs., dressmaker, Creswick rd
Williams, Thomas, engine driver, Lal lal street
Williams, E., Wendouree hotel, Wendouree parade
Williams, Alfred, miner, Skipton st
Williams, J., miner, Skipton st
Williams, Miss, dressmaker, Skipton st
Williams, Wm., miner, Skipton st
Williams, Alfred, billiard rooms, Sturt st
Williams, Robert, teacher, Sturt st
Williams, Matthew, engine driver, Wills st
Williams, J., miner, Wills st
Williams, Wm., miner, King st
Williams, Griffith, miner, Rowe st
Williams, Wm., miner, Bond st
Williams, James, miner, Bond st
Williams, James, miner, Drummond st
Williams, P., miner, Ripon st
Williams, —, bricklayer, Dana st
Williams, —, miner, Eyre st
Williams, Wm., carrier, Victoria st
Williams, David, miner, Mair st
Williams and King, grocers, Armstrong street
Williams, David, merchant, Yuille st
Williams, John, labourer, William st
Williams, David, miner, Cobblers
Williams, Mrs., Black hill
Williams, Joseph, miner, Little Bendigo
Williams, Thomas, carpenter, Sebastopol
Williams, David, surgeon, Sebastopol
Williams, Mrs., Sebastopol
Williamson, James, manager Union Bank, Lydiard st
Williamson, John, Errard st
Williamson, John, miner, Dana st
Willis, James, fruiterer, Main road
Willen, John, blacksmith, Ligar st

Willey, Samuel, Dana st
Wood, Sampson, mason, Howard st
Wood, —, foreman timber yard, Creswick road
Wood, Mrs., laundress, Havelock st
Wood, Thomas, inspector for Council, Errard st
Wood, Thomas, foundryman, Grant st
Wood, Edward, miner, Humffray st south
Wood, Andrew, labourer, Bond st
Wood, Harvey, chemist, Windermere st
Wood, Francis, miner, Ripon st
Wood, Harris, clerk of the Mining Board, Lydiard st
Wood, Geo., bootmaker, Victoria st
Woodrow, J. F., law clerk, Humffray st
Woodward, W. J., brewer, Eureka st
Woodward, Walter, miner, Sebastopol
Woolcock, James, teacher, Barkly st
Woolcock, John, carter, Howard st
Woolcock, Wm., blacksmith, Wills st
Worcestershire, Chas., labourer, Eureka street
Worrall, Wm., miner, Peel st
Worrell, Thomas, miner, Wills st
Worsley, Thomas, clogmaker, Humffray street
Worth, Wm., carpenter, Dawson st
Worthington, Wm., bellman, Young st
Wren, James, bricklayer, Barkly st
Wright, W., billiard table keeper, Sturt street
Wright, W., billiard table keeper, Doveton st
Wright and Rowson, butchers, Humffray street
Wright, Alex., gardener, Clyde st
Wright, Thos., timber merchant, Clarendon st
Wright, Walter, miner, Boundary st
Wright, Theodore, gardener, Belaclava st
Wright, Isaac, carpenter, Sturt st
Wright, John, carter, Clayton st
Wright, John, miner, Raglan st
Wright, Henry, farmer, Dawson st
Wright, James, miner, Ripon st
Wright, Mrs., boarding house, Ripon st

Wright, —, ironmonger, Dana st
Wright, J., Hope and Anchor hotel, Victoria st
Wright, Donald, engineer, Mair st
Wrigley, Richd., ironmonger, Mair st
Wrigley, Richd., ironmonger, Lydiard st
Wyatt, Robt., bank messenger, Mair st
Wylie, Thomas, miner, Windermere st
Wynne, John, bank manager, Sturt st
Wynne, G. A., Lyons st
Wynne, Robt., rate collector, Drummond street

Y.

Yarra, James, engineer, Sturt st
Yates, Chas., tent maker, Peel st
Yates, Alfred, grocer, Humffray st
Yates, W., carter, Armstrong st
Young, Rev. W., Grant st
Young, Fredk., miner, Esmond st
Young, Yost, miner, Sebastopol
Young, H., coach smith, Creswick road
Young, J., butcher and produce store, Skipton st
Young, A., Rising Sun hotel, Main road
Young, W., *Argus* agent, Chamber of Commerce, Sturt st
Young, Mark, White Hart hotel, Sturt st
Young Brothers, wheelwrights, Clayton street
Young, Andrew, store, Skipton st
Young, Edward, carter, Clayton st
Young, Mrs., store, Clayton st
Young, George, bootmaker, Wills st
Young, R., woodcutter, north of municipal boundary
Young, John, brickmaker, Boundary st
Young, Thomas, sawyer, Humffray st
Young, Thomas, Bricklayers' Arms, Victoria st
Younger, James, baker, Skipton st
Younger, Andrew, miner, Burnbank st

Z.

Zachariah, Isaac, hawker, Princes st
Zahnluter, Andrew, miner, Humffray st

BUNINYONG ALPHABETICAL DIRECTORY.

1866-67.

Allan, Robert, gentleman, Forest st
Allan, R., gentleman, Warrenheip st
Andrew, Wm., brickmaker, off Warrenheip st
Arkins, P. R., postmaster, &c., Warrenheip st
Ashburner, T. and W., booksellers, Warrenheip st
Avender, —, jeweller, Learmonth st
Bardon, Mrs., Warrenheip st
Bardon, John, miner, Warrenheip st
Batchelor, Wm., labourer, Warrenheip st
Bardon, Thomas, miner, Warrenheip st
Barry and Co., wine and spirit merchants, Warrenheip st
Baxter, Mary, store, Learmonth st
Beeton, James, gardener, Warrenheip st
Berry, Andrew, bootmaker, Learmonth st
Berry, George, settler, Forest st
Bishop, John, saw mills, Learmonth st
Blackburn, G., publican, Learmonth st
Bloxam, —, labourer, Warrenheip st
Bolton, Leonard, farmer, Learmonth st
Bradshaw, Edward, butcher, Learmonth street
Bradshaw, W., baker, Learmonth st
Bradley, Jacob, grocer, Warrenheip st
Brayshaw, D., draper, Learmonth st
Brew, John, labourer, Simpson st
Briggs, Robert, labourer, Forest st
Borrough, J., butcher
Boyd, —, road engineer, Warrenheip st
Brown, J., butcher, Learmonth st

Bronen, P., woodcutter, Warrenheip st
Bryden and Hedrick, storekeepers, Learmonth st
Burns, Miss, dressmaker, Warrenheip st
Calder, Thomas, labourer, Learmonth st
Cammins, —, labourer, Yuille st
Campbell, Dugald, painter, Scott st
Capes, Wm., lay reader, Warrenheip st
Casey, Dr., surgeon, Warrenheip st
Clark, John, gardener, Forest st
Coyle, Geo., manager of tannery, Learmonth st
Craven, Ernest, currier, Learmonth st
Croul, labourer, Warrenheip st
Croul, gardener, off Warrenheip st
Culloway, —, mason, Warrenheip st
Davis, Andrew, tanner, Learmonth st
Davis and Sons, tanners, Learmonth st
Davison, Andrew, saddler, Warrenheip st
Donoghue, Martin, carpenter, Warrenheip street
Doyle, Robt., teacher, Warrenheip st
Drayman, D., undertaker, Warrenheip st
Drynan and Harris, ironmongers, Learmonth st
Drynan, Henry, ironmonger, Forest st
Eason, Wm., butcher, Warrenheip st
Eason, —, gardener, off Warrenheip st
Fasham, Thomas, blacksmith, Learmonth street
Field, J., carter, Warrenheip st
Forest, —, labourer, Warrenheip st
Fowler, P., carter, Simpson st

Francis, James, brickmaker, off Warrenheip st
Franklin, —, woodcutter, off Warrenheip street
Fredl, Theophilus, carter, Simpson st
Galligan, Geo., rate collector, Simpson st
Gardener, Miss, dressmaker, Warrenheip street
Gardener, F., farmer, Warrenheip st
Gillespie, R., bank manager
Gleeson, James, road contractor, Simpson st
Good, T., printer, Warrenheip st
Goode, S., town clerk, Warrenheip st
Graham Brothers, bootmakers, Warrenheip st
Greaves, H. M., draper, Learmonth st
Hardacres, W. and T., drapers, Warrenheip st
Hardie, R. M., surgeon, Forest st
Harris, Arthur, ironmonger, Learmonth st
Harrison, —, carpenter, Yuille st
Harrison, J. T., grocer, &c., Learmonth st
Hastie, Thomas, clergyman, Learmonth st
Hebb, Timothy, shoemaker, Learmonth st
Hedrick, Peter, wholesale grocer, &c., Learmonth st
Hervey, P. M., surveyor, Scott's st
Higgins, J., draper, Warrenheip st
Hughes, Matthew, miner, Warrenheip st
Jackson, carpenter, Warrenheip st
Johnson, Robert, mason, Warrenheip st
Jones, F. H., fruiterer, Learmonth st
Jones, Robt., medical assistant, Learmonth st
Kennedy, John, wood carter, Learmonth street
Killminster, —, tanner, Warrenheip st
Lane, John, labourer, Simpson st
Lindsey, Mrs., seamstress, Warrenheip st
Marshall, John, labourer, Learmonth st
Martin, Wm., draper, Learmonth st
Martin, John, carpenter, Warrenheip st
Martin, Wm., car driver, Warrenheip st
Matheson, Geo., bootmaker, Learmonth st
McCrae, James, carpenter, Warrenheip st
McLaren, James, tailor, Scott's st
McLaren, Wm., miner, Scott's st
McDonald, Alex., shoemaker, Warrenheip st
McKenzie, H., gardener, Warrenheip st
McKenzie, —, labourer, Learmonth st
McKissock, Donald, miner, Yuille st
McKitchen, Benjamin, tailor, Learmonth street
McMahon, P., carrier, Warrenheip st
McNee, —, overseer in sodawater manufactory, Forest st
McPherson, James, dairy, Warrenheip st
Miller, Archibald, publican, Warrenheip street
Minhinnick, H. H., Exchange hotel, Learmonth st
Mitchell, Geo., labourer, Yuille st

Morgan, J. T., Warrenheip st
Moss, T., fruit garden, Warrenheip st
Mulligan, Wm., Court House hotel, Learmonth st
Munroe, Miss, teacher, Warrenheip st
Mullet, Mrs., laundress, off Warrenheip st
Mitch, R., ironmonger, Learmonth st
Nettle, E., surveyor, &c., Scott's st
Newman, E., chemist, Warrenheip st
Nook, Henry, brickmaker, Warrenheip st
Nussy, Joseph, publican, Warrenheip st
Oliver, —, labourer, Yuille st
Oliver, D., gentleman
Parsons, Wm., saddler
Pocknee, John, baker, Learmonth st
Pollack, Wm., baker, off Warrenheip st
Porter, James, blacksmith, Learmonth st
Purves, Thomas, chemist, Learmonth st
Reese, Thomas, wheelwright, Warrenheip street
Remington, John, labourer, Warrenheip st
Rogers, —, judge, Simpson st
Rowbottom, Isaac, baker, Learmonth st
Russell, J., C. E. clergyman, Warrenheip street
Saunders, Wm., sodawater manufacturer, Learmonth st
Scott, G., plumber, Warrenheip st
Sellack, Geo., Crown hotel, Learmonth st
Sergeant, —, labourer, Yuille st
Seymour, Geo., wood carter, Warrenheip street
Shepherd, Thomas, brewer, Simpson st
Simpson, Robt., blacksmith, Learmonth st
Sinclair, Miss, dairy, Warrenheip st
Sleman, John, baker, &c., Learmonth st
Smith, —, labourer, Learmonth st
Smith, James, gardener, off Warrenheip street
Smith, C., general store, Warrenheip st
Smith, —, labourer, Yuille st
Sowlee, T., plumber, &c., Learmonth st
Stafford, John, carter, Simpson st
Stephen, Geo., and Son, blacksmiths, Warrenheip st
Stork, Joseph, tailor, Warrenheip st
Tallor, —, jockey, Warrenheip st
Thomas, Chas., woodcutter, Warrenheip st
Thomas, John, labourer, Warrenheip st
Tompkins, Wm., tanner, Warrenheip st
Topp, —, cider manufactory, Warrenheip street
Turner, Henry, baker, Warrenheip st
Ward, Ralph, baker and librarian, Warrenheip st
Watson, John, shoemaker, Warrenheip st
Webb, Miss, fruit garden, Warrenheip st
Webb, John, butcher, Learmonth st
Williams, Wm., tanner, Warrenheip st
Wilson, R. S., storekeeper, Learmonth st
Wilson, John, baker, &c., Learmonth st
Wilson, Joe, labourer, Warrenheip st
Wyatt, Henry, car proprietor, Simpson st
Young, Conrad, Warrenheip st

BROWNS ALPHABETICAL DIRECTORY.

1866-67.

Ah Chum, gardener
Ah Yin, storekeeper
Alexander, Chas., miner
Archer, Mrs., dressmaker
Bentley, miner, off the main street
Bickett, James, mining manager
Bodden, Thomas, mining manager
Brown, John, Crow Club hotel
Calan, Daniel, miner
Craddock, Thomas, confectioner
Crow, George, miner
Davis, John, miner
Firth, James, miner
Formby, Thomas, Watson's Hill hotel
Gadson, Mrs., storekeeper
Gartside Brothers, storehouse
Gartside Brothers, storekeepers
Granger, Wm., baker and storekeeper
Hall, Wm., teacher P. S.
Hall, Mrs., teacher P. S. Smythes
Harris, Wm., miner
Hauser, Phillip, grocer
Hepburn, Geo., shoemaker
Hill, —, miner
Hobelen, Patrick, hawker
Hoffman, —, tailor

Hodson, Michael, Washington hotel
Kirby, John, baker
Kitchen, Mrs.
Laundon, Wm., carter
Lumsley, John, miner
McGee, —, baker and storekeeper
Middleton, Richd., miner, off the main st
Mitchell, Daniel, miner, off the main st
Mitchell, James, miner, off the main st
Neville, Geo., blacksmith
Oman, W., hay and corn dealer
Pearce, H. W., Crow Club hotel
Pearcey, Richd., miner
Russel, Richd., miner
Sanders, Mrs., washerwoman
Smith, Wm., miner, off the main st
Spew, Michael, miner
Spivey, John, bootmaker
Tench, John, miner, off the main st
Thompson, Henry, general fruit store
Thompson, Moses
Twining, Chas., butcher
Wade, Mary Ann, cloth shop
Waite and Craddock, blacksmiths
Waite, Wm., blacksmith
Wilkinson, John, miner

SCARSDALE ALPHABETICAL DIRECTORY.

1866-67.

Ackman, E., storekeeper
Aisbitt, M., miner
Aisbitt, M. and J., butchers
Albert, —, miner
Allen, James, Morton and Leggo's agent
Allenbury, Chas., carpenter
Allison, Isaac, tinsmith
Armstrong, Geo., miner
Ash, Robt., timber merchant
Bailey, Wm., Union hotel
Bangay, Dr.
Barrett, Edwd., Grey Horse hotel
Bassett, Geo., carpenter
Bate, Wm., miner
Bell, Alex., carter
Bell, John, miner
Bell, Robt., miner
Bell, Wm., miner
Benney, Richd., bootmaker
Blackburn, Joseph, sexton
Blake, David, miner
Blackwell, Isaac, Luck's All hotel
Bleakey, John, blacksmith
Brangh, Wm., miner
Briggs, Abel, miner
Bryam, Patrick, Scarsdale Foundry hotel
Broadwood, Thomas, miner
Brown, James, miner
Brown, Thomas, baker
Brown, John, engine driver
Bulotti, F., miner
Burke, Joseph, miner
Caldwell, Robt., store and baker

Calvert, Wm., miner
Campbell, Walter, schoolmaster
Carnegie, Wm., blacksmith
Carr, Thomas, miner
Chappell, Isaac, Pound hotel
Chapman, Thomas, miner
Chibnall, C. C., hotel keeper
Chinney, John, miner
Clark, James, storekeeper
Clarke, Alex., blacksmith
Clarkson, —, miner
Clarkson, John, miner
Clowes, Martin, miner
Clyoe, Fredk., miner
Comb, Wm., miner
Creighton, James, miner
Cross, Wm., Club hotel
Croy, James, miner
Croy, Peter, bootmaker
Cummings, Richd., miner
Davidson, Joseph, miner
Davis, Joseph, miner
Davy, Thomas, miner
Davy, J. Z., miner
Deans, John, miner
Dean, Wm., blacksmith
Denham, Wm., miner
Denny, John, miner
Dixon, Joseph, engineer
Donaldson, Joseph, miner
Drury, J., miner
Duchar, Alex., baker
Duncan, John, miner

Dundower, Wm., miner
Evans, Wm., store
Evans, W., soap and candle manufacturer
Ellison, James, miner
Fairless, J., miner
Farrell, Thomas, carter
Fisher, George, farmer
Foster, J., baker
Fraser, John, smith
Fraser, John, fancy repository
Funcke, Charles, Black Hill tannery
Gardoni, Vincent, farmer
Garner, James, blacksmith
George, Isaac, miner
German, John, carter
Graham, John, miner
Graham, Joseph, miner
Gray, John, miner
Grime, James, storekeeper
Hain, Richard, carpenter
Hals, Charles, saddler
Hale, John, miner
Hamilton, Daniel, miner
Hamilton, Wm., draper
Hanley, Peter, boarding house
Hargreaves, John, miner
Harrison, J., miner
Hansom, James, miner
Hardcastle, Wm., foundryman
Hardy, James, miner
Hart, Dean, Foresters' Home hotel
Hawkes, W. H., draper
Healey, John, miner
Henderson, Thomas, miner
Hillard, Mrs., fruiterer
Hiscott, George, All Nations hotel
Hodges, James, miner
Hogg, Bennett, miner
Hoolan, James, miner
Hopkins, Wm., miner
Hopkins, James, carpenter
Hudson, Wm., miner
Hunter, James, miner
Howell, J., miner
Ingles, George, produce store
Irons, John, blacksmith
Irvine, Wm., miner
Jackson, Thomas, engine driver
Jackson, Edward, chemist
Jefferson, Wm., carter
Jefferson, Joseph, carter
Jennings, Jabez, miner
Jenkins, Jacob, Garibaldi restaurant
Jobblin, Matthew, miner
Johnson, George, draper
Johnson, Thomas, bootmaker
Johnson, Miss, dressmaker
Jones, John, miner
Kidd, Thomas, engine driver
King, Wm., labourer
Kinnear, Robert, painter
Kirk, David, clerk
Knight, J. H., store
Knight, John, miner

Knights, Edmund, stationer
Laidlaw, Wm., engineer
Lanrygan, John, miner
Larkins, Wm., miner
Lechie, Peter, miner
Lee, John, miner
Lightfoot, George, miner
Lippratt, Samuel, miner
Lloyd, Richard, restaurant
Lodge, John, miner
Longley, E. F., manager National Bank
Lorndon, —, miner
Lyons, J. S., gold broker
McCullugh, Mrs., dressmaker
McCraig, John miner
McGeathen, John, miner
McGeathen, Hugh, miner
McGrath, Patrick, miner
McHugh, Mrs.
McIntosh, Thomas, miner
McIntosh, Daniel, miner
McKanlon, produce store
McKenzies, George, produce store
Macfie, Alexander, Bute hotel
McKindes, James, miner
McLean, George, miner
McLean, Wm., bootmaker
McLeish, John, miner
McQuitty, John, miner
McTagg, —, miner
Maddison, Edward, miner
Manners, Wm., miner
Marks, Richard, miner
Martin, James, foundryman
Martin, James and Charles, foundry
Matthews, —, miner
Matthews, Wm., miner
Matthewson, Henry, miner
May, David, miner
Mercer, Alex., miner
Merrin, Edward, ironmonger
Miller, Conrad, Royal Exchange hotel
Miller, James, miner
Miller, John, painter
Millender, —, miner
Minayer, Richard, miner
Mitchell, F., miner
Mooney, Andrew, Foundry hotel
Moore, James, miner
Morrison, H., carter
Murton, David, butcher
National Bank, E. F. Longley, manager
Neuss, James, miner
Newton, John, miner
O'Brien, Mrs., laundress
Orams, Josiah, blacksmith
Overend, James, carpenter
Parker, Sarah, Black Swan hotel
Peart, James, miner
Pollock, James, miner
Porter, —, hawker
Prentice, M., storekeeper
Presbyterian Church
Price, J. and W., ironfounders

Prentice, Geo., miner
Primitive Methodist Chapel
Raddenbury, John, fruiterer
Ramsey, James, miner
Reynolds, Geo., miner
Richards, John, miner
Roberts, J. P., general store
Ross, Thomas, miner
Ross, John, miner
Rutherford, John, town clerk
Sanger, Dr.
Saunders, Henry, labourer
Saunders, Henry, poundkeeper
Scott, Thomas, boarding house
Seaton, Wm., brickmaker
Sharp, Edward, miner
Shepherd, Mrs., draper
Shinall, John, miner
Simpson, John, miner
Sinclair, James, miner
Skelton, Walter, draper
Skinner, Robert, miner
Skinner, Mrs., ladies' school
Skinner, John, miner
Smith, Chas., carpenter
Smith, Edward, wheelwright
Smith, Edward, tailor, &c.
Smith, Wm., store
Smith, John, miner
Smith, James, miner
Smith, James, draper, &c.
Smith, F., miner
Smith, Owen, miner
Somerfield, Richard, dairyman
Southward and Sumpton, grocers
Spikin, John, butcher

Stannix, Wm., draper
Stanford, —, engineer
Stoker, Robert
Sullivan, James, bootmaker
Syme, Wm., tinsmith and plumber
Switzer, George, miner
Tempest, —, miner
Tennent, John and James, store
Thompson, John, miner
Tonkin, James, miner
Treverton, Edward, miner
Trevor, Joseph, tobacconist
Tulloch, —, miner
Tweedle, Wm., miner
Varty, Josiah, miner
Vincent, Mrs.
Waif, Robert, miner
Walker, Wm., miner
Walker, Alex, miner
Walker, James, miner
Walker, —, miner
Wallace, Wm., miner
Warne, Wm., miner
Watson, John, miner
Webb, Chas., butcher
Wesleyan Church
Wesleyan Church, Newtown
Whitpaine, Richard, Scarsdale hotel
Wieram, J. H. A., hairdresser
Wilkinson, David, miner
Williams, John, seedsman, &c.
Wellington, —, miner
Wilson, Wm., miner
Woodall, Rev. W., Wesleyan minister
Young, James, tanner
Young, Rutherford, miner

CRESWICK ALPHABETICAL DIRECTORY.

1866-7.

A'Beckett, W. G., surgeon, Albert st
Adams, John, storeman, Cambridge st
Andrew, Richard, blacksmith, Clunes road
Anderson, Geo., carter, Victoria st
Anthony, T. W., Anthony's hotel, Albert street
Antin, James, miner, Clunes road
Archibald, Joseph, constable, Raglan st
Ayres, W. H., merchant, Cambridge st
Ayres, William, carter, rear Melbourne road
Baitly, Agnes, storekeeper, Albert st
Banks, John, miner, Victoria st
Bank of New South Wales, A. Lowers, manager
Bank of Australasia, H. B. Chomley, manager
Barclay, Mrs., fruiterer, Albert st
Beckerlig, James, miner, Clunes road
Beckerley, Richard, miner, Clunes road
Billing, W., storekeeper, Melbourne road
Birch, George, barman, Hall st
Birt, James, miner, Clunes road
Blaney and Hoole, blacksmiths and wheelwrights, Spring Hill road
Boam, Henry, miner, Clunes road
Body, John, miner, Victoria st
Booty, Elijah, blacksmith, Albert st
Borough Council Chambers, Albert st; Joseph Reid, town clerk
Brickley, John, labourer, Melbourne road
Brien, F., carpenter, Melbourne road
Broadhurst, James, carpenter, Clunes rd
Burch, Wm., gardener, rear Melbourne rd
Burton, R. A., solicitor, Napier st and Albert st
Bush, —, painter, Cambridge st
Butt, Thomas, miner, Melbourne road
Bygrave, Green, White Swan hotel, Melbourne road
Cannon, Wm., ostler, Victoria st
Cannon, Geo., painter, rear Melbourne rd
Carpenter, Misses, school, Albert st
Carr, John, Ballarat road
Carry, Mrs., Victoria st
Carthews, Thomas, miner, Clunes road
Carthew, Wm., hotelkeeper, Clunes road
Catholic Church, Napier st
Catty, Peter, miner, Clunes road
Church of England, Napier st; Rev. J. Pollard
Cole, Geo., ginger beer manufacturer, Spring hill road
Colwell, Geo., miner, Clunes road
Common School, Albert st; P. Harrington, master, Mrs. Harrington, mistress
Common School, Napier st; J. Fairball, master
Common School, Victoria st; J. Nicholas, master, Miss Ferguson, mistress
Common School, Clunes road
Cooper and Walton, drapers, Albert st
Cooper, Thomas, sharebroker, Albert st
Coults, Mrs., Ballarat road
Court House, Raglan st; G. L. Hutchinson, clerk

Cox   DIRECTORY.   Lan   319

Cox, Wm., miner, North parade
Creswick and Clunes Advertiser office, Albert st
Croft, F. T., draper, North parade
Crougie, Nicholas, miner, Clunes road
Curley, John, miner, Melbourne road
Curtis, Wm., miner, Clunes road
Datson, Isaiah, miner, Victoria st
Davies, Wm., Bridge hotel, North parade
Davis, J. Moore, reporter, Melbourne rd
Davies, Edward, bootmaker, Albert st
Dectrow, Chas., pianist, Melbourne road
Dennis, P., coach proprietor, North parade
Dickenson, Thomas, wheelwright, Melbourne road
Divers, S. L., bootmaker, Albert st
Divers, J., bootmaker, Raglan st
Donoghue, Patrick, miner, Raglan st
Dunn, Thomas, W., miner, Clunes road
Dunt, —, miner, Melbourne road
Dunstan, Thomas, storekeeper, Albert st
Durose, Thomas, draper, Albert st
Dusantboy, Thomas, miner, Clunes road
Dowling, C. C., warden, Camp hill
Ebrington, G. H., labourer, Camp hill
Edwards, F., chemist, Albert st
Edwards, Wm., miner, Victoria st
Edwards, James, carter, Napier st
Ellis, Wm., miner, Raglan st
Ellis, James, bootmaker, Napier st
Ellis, John, carpenter, Napier st
Elworthy, J., labourer, rear Melbourne road
Fair, A. E., bootmaker, Fraser st
Fairhall, John, teacher, Napier st
Faull, W. H., miner, Victoria st
Faulknor, James, contractor, Albert st
Few, James, miner, Clunes road
Filling, W. H., cooper, Cambridge st
Fisher, Fredk., baker, Albert st
Fitzgerald Bros., general store, Albert st
Fitzgerald, Rd., produce merchant, Napier street
Fleming, Richard, miner, Clunes road
Flinn, Thomas, labourer, Albert st
Fox, —, tailor, North parade
Frazer, Geo., watchmaker, Albert st
Gardiner, Wm., draper, Albert st
Garrett, James, miner, Clunes road
Garton, James, miner, Melbourne road
Gaylor, John, carter, Melbourne road
Germans, John, coach proprietor, Raglan street
Geeling, —, miner, Clunes road
Goad, Thomas, miner, North parade
Goad, Thomas, store, North parade
Goad, Elisha, miner, Clunes road
Golding, Geo., slaughterman, Clunes road
Gray, F., storekeeper, Clunes road
Gribble, Joseph, miner, Clunes road
Grover, Wm., Church hill
Grover, W., baker, Church hill
Gunn, John, miner, Raglan st
Girr, Geo., carpenter, Melbourne road

Hammon, Henry, merchant, Melbourne rd
Hancock, Mrs., Melbourne road
Hanson, —, miner, Napier st
Harman, —, miner, Napier st
Harrington, P., stationer, Albert st
Harris, Joseph, fruiterer, Albert st
Haslem, Robert, miner, Raglan st
Hassell, Thomas, ironmonger, Cambridge street
Hay, Archibald, contractor, Melbourne rd
Hearman, J., tobacconist,
Herbertson, J., saddler, Albert st
Herring, M. D., Camp hill
Hin Wah, storekeeper,
Hock, J., mason, Clunes road
Hockley, Edward, solicitor, Raglan st
Hodge, John, miner, Melbourne road
Hodge, John, miner, Clunes road
Hogg, William, carter, rear Melbourne rd
Holley, Robt., livery stables, Albert st
Hoole, Wm., wheelwright, North parade
Hoole and Blaney, blacksmiths and wheelwrights, Spring Hill road
Hooper, Benjamin, miner, Clunes road
Hospital, R. C. Lindsay, resident surgeon
Hutchinson, G. L., clerk court, Hall st
Iles, Wm., bootmaker, Albert st
Inch, Geo., miner, Raglan st
James, W., miner, Clunes road
James, James, miner, Clunes road
James, Joseph, miner, Clunes road
James, Joseph, blacksmith, Clunes road
Jansen and Co., grocers, Albert st
Jebb, John Thomas, draper, Albert st
Jenkins, Athanasius, miner, Victoria st
Johnson, Mrs. B. K., teacher, Napier st
Jones, Wm., saddler, Albert st
Jones, Thomas, bootmaker, Melbourne rd
Jones, John, miner, North parade
Jope, J., miner, Clunes road
Jordan, S., brickmaker, rear Melbourne road
Jury, Simon, mason, Clunes road
Kay, Henry, Chinese interpreter, rear of Melbourne road
Kean, William, miner, Victoria st
Keast, John, miner, North parade
Kelly, J., Diggers Rest, Albert st
Kelly, James, McGill and Coglan's agent, Cambridge st
King Bros., butchers, Fraser st
King, Thos., miner, Clunes road
King, W. M., grocer, Victoria st
Kinsman, S., miner, Raglan st
Knapman, James, miner, Victoria st
Knight, Geo., blacksmith, rear of Melbourne road
Knowles, James, butcher, Albert st
Kurvis, Wm., miner, Clunes road
Laby, Thomas J., miller, Albert st
Laby, Thomas J., miller, Cambridge st
Laity, Geo., miner, North parade
Lambert, W. J., bricklayer, Albert st
Lang, Thomas, dairyman, Camp hill

320　Lan　ALPHABETICAL　Rob

Langey and Thoneman, grocers, Albert st
Leake, Rice, general store, Albert st
Leake, Rice, storekeeper, Napier st
Lees, W. B., chemist, Albert st
Lewers, A., bank manager, Albert st
Lindair, W., produce store, Clunes road
Lindsay, R. C., surgeon, Albert st
Longstaff, Newark, carpenter, Raglan st
Low, Henry, carter, Raglan st
Lokowsky, Carl R., tinsmith, Albert st
Lyons, Alexander, blacksmith, Albert st
Lyons, Wm., blacksmith, Cambridge st
Lyall, Wm., carpenter, Cambridge st
McCrae, Alexander, sheep dealer, rear of Melbourne road
McCarthy, J., Robinson's hotel, Albert st
McCormack, Matthew, produce store, Albert st
McCulloch, M., storekeeper, Albert st
McKinnon, James, surveyor, rear of Melbourne road
Mader, P., sodawater maker
Mader, Geo., confectioner, Albert st
Main, Mrs., Cambridge st
Mandley, W., miner, rear of Melbourne road
Mann, James, dairyman, Melbourne road
Mann, James, blacksmith, Melbourne rd
Marks, Richd., miner, rear of Melbourne road
Markett, J. A., commission agent, Albert street
Marriage, John, carpenter, rear of Melbourne road
Marshall, J., draper, Albert st
Martin, J., gardener, Melbourne road
Martin, David, Camp hill
Martin, Wm., constable, Napier st
Martin, F. M., printer, Hall st
Matthews, Geo., mason, Melbourne road
Maudsley James, clerk, rear Melbourne rd
May, Richd., miner, Clunes road
May, Benjamin, miner, Clunes road
May, Isaac, baker, Melbourne road
Mechanics' Institute, Albert st
Meyer, Wm., carpenter, rear Melbourne road
Miller, Thomas, miner, Raglan st
Minfall, W., miner, Raglan st
Mitchel, P., carter, Napier st
Mitchell, James A., store, Victoria st
Mitchell, Edwd., produce store, Melbourne road
Moller, Henry, coach proprietor, Ballarat road
Molesworth, M., dressmaker, Melbourne road
Moore, —, traveller, Hall st
Moore —, Sergeant, drill instructor, Cambridge st
Moore Bros., bootmakers, Albert st
Morgan, John Thomas, fruiterer, Albert street
Morgan, Wm., painter, Melbourne road

Morton, —, storeman, Hall st,
Moyle, Samuel, engineer, Cambridge st
Moyle and Crowell, manufacturers aerated waters, ginger beer, &c., Cambridge st
Moyle, Wm., bootmaker, Albert st
Mollanky and Georgehan, drapers
Munroe, James, bootmaker, Albert st
Murray, Mrs., Raglan st
Marion and Leggo's depot, Albert st
Mancarrow, —, miner, Victoria st
Neal, Richard, miner, Raglan st
Nicholson, Joseph, teacher, Cambridge st
Nicklers, Edwd., miner, Raglan st
Ninnis, Richd., miner, Clunes road
O'Dee, T. P., barrister, Napier st
Opie, Thomas, mason, Cambridge st
Organ, J., saddler, Albert st
Orr, James, storekeeper, Albert st
Orr, Archibald, slaughterman, Clunes rd
Osborn, Phelim, Clunes road
Oxley, Edwd., carter, Napier st
Pale, Phelim, miner, Clunes road
Parramin, Richd., gardener, rear Melbourne road
Pascoe, Anthony, timber merchant, Albert st
Pascoe, Lewis, miner, Clunes road
Patching, Henry, watchmaker, Albert st
Patterson, E., Melbourne road
Paul, James, carpenter, North parade
Paul, James, miner, Raglan st
Peacock, James Henry, tailor and outfitter, Albert st
Pearce, Samuel, miner, Albert st
Pearce, W. J., contractor, Melbourne road
Pemberton, W., carter, Melbourne road
Penglase, Samuel, miner, Clunes road
Penrose, S. P., carter, Raglan st
Phillips, Stephen, miner, Victoria st
Pickles, G. F., restaurant, Albert st
Pickles, G., blacksmith, Raglan st
Pollard, M., store, Melbourne road
Pollard, Rev. G., Episcopal
Polkinghouse, Richard, miner, Napier st
Popjoy, —, revenue officer, near Melbourne road
Postlewaite, Diana, dressmaker, Albert st
Post Office, John Twaites, postmaster
Prysen, Matthew, carpenter, Napier st
Pruning, Hermain, tobacconist, Albert st
Presbyterian Church, Ballarat road
Prohasky, Wm., merchant, Albert st
Prout, Lawrence, store, Albert st
Quinn, Mrs., Albert st
Reid, Joseph, town clerk, Napier st
Reid, James, miner, Victoria st
Reis, J. A, hairdresser, Albert st
Richards, Thomas, miner, Clunes road
Raan, James, miner, Clunes road
Roberts, Wm., builder, Albert st
Roberts, M., Talbot hotel, Melbourne road
Roberts, Joseph, carter, Raglan st
Robins, Thomas, miner, Raglan st

Robins, Robt., dairyman, Camp hill
Rogers, Wm., miner, Raglan st
Rogers, James, British hotel, Albert st
Roose, Joseph, wheelwright, Albert st
Roose, J., storekeeper, Raglan st
Rowell, Thomas, cabinetmaker, Albert st
Roycroft, John, news agent, Albert st
Sampson, John, miner, Melbourne road
Saunders, James, carpenter, Albert st
Searle, John, miner, Clunes road
Sedon, Richard, fruiterer, Albert st
Seton, Richard, blacksmith, Melbourne road
Semton, Geo., blacksmith, Victoria st
Sendair, Wm., produce dealer, Clunes road
Sevreing, J. H., storekeeper, Creswick rd
Schwambach, P., miner, Raglan st
Scott, J. C., baker, Albert st
Shagwin, Wm., carter, Raglan st
Shearer, J. S., Commercial hotel, Victoria street
Short, Chas., bootmaker, Spring Hill road
Shurnooth, John, miner, Raglan st
Skehan, —, Rev., Napier st
Skewse, Matthew, cooper, Raglan st
Simmonds, S., Talbot hotel, Melbourne road
Simons, Wm., wheelwright, Clunes road
Slater, Henry, brickmaker, rear Melbourne road
Sleep, Thomas, miner, Victoria st
Slocum, Henry, coachdriver, Melbourne road
Smith, J., hotelkeeper, Creswick road
Spargo, James, miner, Clunes road
Spargo, Luke, miner, Clunes road
Spence, Archibald, plumber, Raglan st
Spanner, Wm., bootmaker, Albert st
Staley, Mrs., fruiterer, Albert st
Stahamer, Henry, cabinetmaker, Albert st
Steele, Dr., Albert st
Stephens, R., Star hotel
Stevens, Martin, miner, Napier st
Stevenson, James, surveyor, Albert st
Stevenson, James, surveyor, Napier st
Storey, Henry, Temperance dining rooms, Albert st
Sutcliffe, John, miner, Melbourne road
Tenterfort, J., miner, Melbourne road
Titheridge, Henry, tailor, Albert st
Thomas, James, miner, North parade
Thorne, G. T., watchmaker, Albert st
Thorl, —, miner, Clunes road
Transton, Lillus, fruiterer, Albert st
Treglowan, Thomas, storekeeper, Clunes road
Treglowan, John, miner, Clunes road
Treuathle, Thomas, miner, Clunes road
Truscott, Thomas, miner, Clunes road
Turner, H. C., carter, Napier st
Tyett, Stephen, miner, Raglan st

Vague, Wm., carter, Clunes road
Wade, —, miner, Spring hill road
Waghs, A., musician, Melbourne road
Wallace, Jas., carpenter, Melbourne road
Wallish, Robert, miner, Clunes road
Ward, B., Harvest Home hotel, Creswick road
Warden, Wm., dairyman, Clunes road
Watkins, A., butcher, Albert st
Watson, Wm., butcher, Raglan st
Watson, Wm., miner, rear Melbourne road
Watson, Peter, miner. Ballarat road
Weller, James, photographer, Albert st
Welsh Chapel, Clunes road
Wesleyan Chapel, Clunes road
Wesleyan Chapel, Victoria st
Whalley, J., Temperance boarding house, Ballarat road
Whan, Isaac, storeman, Melbourne road
Whan, Samuel, storeman, Melbourne road
Whatman, W. J., Court House hotel, Raglan st
Whitton, Robert, miner, Cambridge st
Whiffin, C., blacksmith, Melbourne road
White, —, sexton, Clunes road
Wilkinson, —, miner, Napier st
Wilkinson, John, compositor, Melbourne road
Willan, Wm., fruiterer, Melbourne road
Wickett, George, miner, Clunes road
Williams, James, carter, Albert st
Williams Bros, butchers, Albert st
Williams, Geo., china and fancy dealer, Albert st
Williams, W., miner, Clunes road
Williams, —, miner, Clunes road
Williams, Colin, miner, Clunes road
Williams, Joseph, miner, Clunes road
Williams Bros., storekeepers and produce dealers, Clunes road
Williams, Joseph, produce dealer, Clunes road
Williams, Robt., miner, Raglan st
Williams, Thomas, carpenter, Napier st
Williams, Rev. G., Wesleyan minister, Napier st
Williams, H. G., butcher, Victoria st
Willis, John, bootmaker, Napier st
Wilson, George, butcher and store, Albert street
Wilson, Wm., bootmaker, Raglan st
Wood, Thomas, miner, Clunes road
Wood, Wm., miner, Spring hill road
Woodland, Geo., brickmaker, Camp hill
Woodland, Mrs., dressmaker, rear Melbourne road
Worth, J. B., compositor, Albert st
Vine, M., storekeeper
Ziele, Conrad, painter, Albert st
Zanzeen, H., and Co., agents for the Victorian Fire and Life Insurance Company

2 T

SMYTHESDALE ALPHABETICAL DIRECTORY.

1866-67.

Aldous, Emma, fancy repository, Brooke street
Allsen, Edward, cooper, Brooke st
Allen, —, constable, Camp
Armstrong, Thomas, miner, Brooke st
Bagshaw and Blackburn, share brokers, Brooke st
Baird and Paton, ironmongers, Wills st
Ballard, Benjamin, photographer, Burke street
Bang, Gernand, butcher, Brooke st
Bang and Pfeiderer, butchers, Brooke st
Bangay, Richd., surgeon, Brooke st
Bank of Australasia; Thomas W. Burke, manager, Brooke st
Barnett, Dr., surgeon, Brooke st
Barr, Robt., storekeeper, Brooke st
Battridge, Charles, fruiterer, Ireland st
Bell, Caleb, miner, Brooke st
Best, J., boot and shoemaker
Bishop, Charles, carter, Ireland st
Blanche, Andrew, Reservoir hotel, Brooke street
Blanch, Robt., Surprise hotel, Brooke st
Blackwell, Mrs., Wills st
Brerton, James, fruiterer, Brooke st
Brown, Rev. J. M., P. M. minister, Ireland st
Bruce, Mrs., Brooke st
Buck, —, senior constable, Camp st
Burns, James, carpenter, Wills st
Cameron, John, dairyman, Brooke st
Catholic Church, Ireland st
Cawley, J., share broker, Brooke st
Church of England, Rev. S. Walker, Brooke st
Clapperton, J. F., bank manager, Brooke street
Clements, W. P., miner, Wills st
Cohen, E. A., auctioneer, Brooke st
Cole, James, saddler, Brooke st
Common School, Burke st, T. F. Matthews, master, Mrs. Orr, mistress
Corinaldi, H. A., chemist, Brooke st
Corinaldi, H. A., hotelkeeper
Council Chambers, Burke st, R. Kelland, town clerk
Cox, Solomon, Junction hotel
Creed, Edward, store, Brooke st
Daley, Peter, detective, Ireland st
Dalton, John, bootmaker, Brooke st
Dalton, John, bootmaker, Burke st
Duncan, F., bricklayer, Wills st
Dunlop, John, carrier, Brooke st
Elder, J., grocer, Brooke st
Elvine, Mrs., ladies' school, Brooke st
Foreman, Joseph, blacksmith, Brooke st
Goman, L., boot and shoe maker
Good, Henry, fruiterer, Brooke st
Good, Robert, carpenter, Burke st
Gordon, Peter, miner, Brooke st
Gow, Rev J., Presbyterian, Wills st
Gowdie, James, carpenter, Brooke st
Grenville Advocate office, Wills st
Hackridge, —, storeman, Ireland st
Ham, D., sharebroker, Brooke st

Hamilton, J., P.M. and warden, Camp
Hamilton, Henry, miner, Brooke st
Hammond, James, dairyman, Brooke st
Hanson, Mrs., Burke st
Harris, Matthew, blacksmith, Brooke st
Harris, Matthew, fruiterer, Brooke st
Harris, William, enginedriver, Wills st
Harris, Thomas, miner, Ireland st
Hart, D., soda and cordial manufacturer, Burke st
Hawkins, Joseph, reporter, Loader st
Herd, Thomas, carter, Ireland st
Hinds, Mrs., Brooke st
Hinks, James, carter, Brooke st
Hollewon, —, merchant, Brooke st
Hollewon and Alpen, grocers, Brooke st
Holly, Jeremiah, saddler, Brooke st
Hore, John, miner, Wills st
Hoskins, W., store, Burke st
Howlands, James, miner, Brooke st
Hudson, Thomas, draper, Burke st
Hughes, Thomas, Ayrshire hotel, Wills st
Jackson, John, miner, Brooke st
Johnson, Thomas, grocer, Brooke st
Jones, Geo. G., printer, Brooke st
Juler, Wm., watchmaker, Brooke st
Keith, John, store, Brooke st
Kelland, Richd., town clerk, Burke st
Kendall, Thomas, miner, Brooke st
Kelyon, James, miner, Brooke st
Lamotty, David, Court House hotel, Brooke st
Lamond, A., tailor, Loader st
Lathbury, James, storekeeper, Brooke st
Lawson, Thomas, painter, Brooke st
Lawson, James, painter, Burke st
Lee, Wm., carpenter, Brooke st
Lemp, James, bootmaker, Brooke st
Lemp, Gernande, bootmaker, Brooke st
Le Page, Peter, miner, Brooke st
Lewin, James, Bull Inn, Ballarat road
Lock, R. H., Reservoir hill
Loft, Charles, bank messenger, Brooke st
Lutheran Church, Brooke st
Lyons, J. S., sharebroker, Brooke st
McDonald, M., Surprise hotel, Brooke st
McGill and Coglan, brewers, Brooke st
McGowan, Wm., clerk, Burke st
McPhae, J., miner, Wills st
Mansfield, —, miner, Brooke st
Marsh, J., bricklayer, Ireland st
Mechanics' Institute, Brooke st
Milne, Charles, Banner of War hotel, Ballarat road
Mitchell, Wm., miner, Brooke st
Mooney, Andrew, carter, Loader st
Morris, Robt., carter, Burke st
Morris, W. T., draper, Brooke st
Mortenson, Edwd., chemist, Burke st
Mosley, James, Foresters' Arms, Brooke street
Morley, J., blacksmith, Brooke st
Monssell, Jane, boarding house, Burke st
Mouser, J., carpenter, Ballarat road

Murphy, J., carpenter, Ireland st
Neville, G., smith and farrier, Brooke st
Newring, —, miner, Wills st
Nicholson, W. B., clerk of court, Ireland street
Norris, J., miner, Brooke st
O'Connor, J., seedsman, Brooke st
O'Brien, W., and Son, coach builders, Brooke st and Burke st
Paine, J., Wills st
Papenhagen, Paul, merchant, Burke st
Parker, Ebenezer, miner, Brooke st
Parker, Mrs., draper, Brooke st
Pascoe, Wm., miner, Brooke st
Paton, R. R., ironmonger, Brooke st
Pinney, Augustus, baker, Loader st
Potts, E. A., miner, Ireland st
Potts, Edward, miner, Burke st
Post Office; John Nicol, postmaster
Power, H. A., Royal hotel, Brooke st
Power, H. A., hotelkeeper, Loader st
Price, J. and W., ironmongers, Brooke st
Price, W., ironmonger, Brooke st
Price, J., ironmonger, Ireland st
Primitive Methodist Chapel, Ireland st
Puryer, P. H., blacksmith and livery stable keeper, Brooke st
Quong Coon Choong, store, Brooke st
Rawlings, Thomas, draper, Brooke st
Rankin, Joseph, clerk, Burke st
Reid, James, Diggers' Arms, Brooke st
Reitz, Henry, butcher, Burke st
Reitz and Hind, butchers, Burke st
Reynolds, Wm., bricklayer, Wills st
Robb, Wm., painter, Brooke st
Robertson, J., carter, Brooke st
Scadden, Wm., bootmaker, Brooke st
Schwartz, Chas., tinsmith, Brooke st
Scruse and Ainley, brewers, Brooke st
Searle, Richd., baker, Brooke st
Shackleton, Edward, store, Burke st
Sheridan, F., store, Brooke st
Simpson, Wm., gardener, Brooke st
Stedman, Chas. E., solicitor, Burke st
Stedman, Chas. E., solicitor, Ireland st
Stoddart, Geo., Nugget hotel, Brooke st
Stockson, J., carpenter, Burke st
Stoker, J. G., solicitor, Brooke st
Stoney, Isaac, inspector police, Ireland st
Tolliday, J., blacksmith, Ireland st
Union Bank; J. F. Clapperton, manager, Brooke st
Upton, Squire, miner, Burke st
Vale, R. T., bookseller, Brooke st
Veal, Matthew, livery stables, Brooke st
Veitch, Andrew, carpenter, Burke st
Walker, Rev. S., Church of England, Ireland st
Walsh, Were and Moore, sharebrokers, Brooke st
Ward, Stephen, clerk, Wills st
Warnecke, Edward, draper, Brooke st
Warne, Mrs., school, Brooke st
Weighbridge, Creed E., clerk, Brooke st

Wesleyan Church, Ireland st
Williams, Chas., newsagent, Burke st
Williamson, H., sub-treasurer, Brooke st
Williamson, C., Market House hotel, Burke street
Willson, Mrs., laundress, Burke st
White, A., surveyor, Brooke st
Wood, Edward, carpenter, Burke st
Woods, —, miner, Ireland st
Woodhouse, Geo., chemist, Brooke st
Wortham, F., sharebroker, Brooke st
Wortham, Mrs., boarding school, Brooke street
Wrathall, R., Oddfellows' hotel, Brooke st
Wrathall, Henry, coach proprietor and blacksmith, Brooke st
Wrathall, Henry, Royal Mail hotel, Brooke st
Wright, J., bootmaker, Brooke st
Wright, Edward, miner, Brooke st
Young, Adam, hotel, Brooke st
Young, Adam, blacksmith, Brooke st

CLUNES ALPHABETICAL DIRECTORY.

1866-67.

Allan, Ann, storekeeper, Fraser st
Allen, Nicholas, store, Fraser st
Allen, Robt., carpenter, Camp st
Allen, R. A., carpenter, Camp st
Angove, Thomas, miner, Fraser st
Angove, William Hy., miner, Templeton street
Angove, Thomas, miner, Templeton st
Angus, Henry, miner, Ligar st
Annear, Joseph, miner, Beckwith st
Appleby, Wm., lessee of gasworks
Armstrong, John, miner, Camp st
Ashninth, D., miner, North Clunes
Baker, J., plasterer, Camp st
Baldry, J., Farmers' hotel, Service st
Balfour, James, miner, Templeton st
Barber, John, miner, Purcell st
Barker, Jane, Crown Inn, Service st
Barwell, J., plasterer, Camp st
Barwell, Mrs., Talbot st
Bates, Richard, miner, North Clunes
Bawden, Thomas, miner, Creswick road
Baylis, James, miner, Fraser st
Beard, Joseph, miner, North Clunes
Bewley, John, miner, Beckwith st
Beck, John, groom, Pratt st
Bell, Henry, tailor, Fraser st
Bennett, Joseph, miner, Ligar st
Bennett, Thomas, miner, Service st
Bernard, Alex., miner, North Clunes
Berryman, A., miner, Pratt st
Birch, William, smith, Bailey st
Birch, William, miner, Creswick road
Blackband, William, hairdresser, Fraser street
Blake, Robert, miner, Fraser st
Blanchard, J., miner, Ligar st
Blanchard, C., Telegraph hotel, Bailey st

Blanchard, William, miner, Turello st
Bland, R. H., manager of Port Phillip Company's station
Bolger, Moses, constable, Camp st
Bone, Thomas, miner, Turello st
Boney, Chas., tinsmith, Fraser st
Bond, Thomas, miner, Creek crescent
Bond William, miner, Pratt st
Bostick, Chas., butcher, Camp st
Boulter, Henry, draper, Fraser st
Brandon, A., dressmaker, Fraser st
Breer, George, contractor, Pratt st
Broad, Philip, miner, Creswick road
Broad, John, miner, Turello st
Brown, Geo., miner, Creswick road
Brown, J., miner, Beckwith st
Brown, Thomas, carpenter, North Clunes flat
Brown, Chas., miner, Creek Crescent
Bruce, James, miner, Camp st
Brunt, James, miner, Ligar st
Buchanan, Mrs., milliner, Fraser st
Buckham, James, labourer, Camp st
Bullen, James, miner, Creswick road
Burke, P., miner, Purcell st
Burke, E., miner, Ligar st
Burns, Wm., miner, Camp st
Burns, P., miner, Ligar st
Butler, James, miner, Ligar st
Caley, Geo., blacksmith, West parade
Carroll, Wm., miner, Hannah st
Carter, Wm., Red Lion hotel, North Clunes
Cass, B., draper, Fraser st
Cassidy, J., carpenter, Templeton st
Catholic Chapel, Bailey st
Cearley, J., miner, North Clunes
Circle, Robert, miner, North Clunes
Chadwick, Abraham, miner, Pratt st
Chalmers, Alex., blacksmith, Fraser st
Champion, J., miner, Creswick road
Chatwin, C. H., printer, George st
Clark, Christopher, miner, North Clunes flat
Clemenson, Christopher, miner, North Clunes
Clements, John, miner, North Clunes flat
Clemente, Mark, miner, Ligar st
Clunes Gazette office, Fraser st
Corking, Wm., miner, Creswick road
Collier, J. L., postmaster, Bailey st
Collier, —, store, Creswick road
Common School; P. Kempson, master; Mrs. Kempson, mistress
Connell, Mrs., grocer, Fraser st
Cook, Alfred, miner, Camp hill
Cooper, Samuel, foundryman, Bailey st
Corry, Stephen, miner, North Clunes
Coundon, Ralph, Bull and Mouth hotel, Fraser st
Cowley, Edwd., miner, Purcell st
Crane, Henry, miner, Camp st
Crane, John, miner, Creswick road
Creary, Simon, miner, Creswick road

Cronin, Patrick, miner, North Clunes
Croteb, Wm., miner, Creswick road
Cullen, Nicholas, miner, Service st
Cullis, W. E., Nag't Head hotel, Fraser st
Custance, J., miner, North Clunes flat
Dale, Edwd., Kent hotel, Fraser st
Dargaville, J. M., bank manager, Fraser street
Darl, Mrs., Service st
Davenport, Jonas, miner, Creek crescent
Davidson, A., bank manager
Davis, D., engine driver, Fraser st
Davis, J., miner, Bailey st
Davis, James, mason, Purcell st
Davis, John, miner, West parade
Davis, Henry, miner, Service st
Davis, Rees, engineer, Paddock
Dawson, Alfred, storekeeper, Service st
Deegan, P., and Son, merchants, North Clunes
Degruit, Martin, miner, Creswick road
Desmond, John, labourer, Templeton st
Dixon, James, grocer, Fraser st
Dixon, Wm., baker, Purcell st
Dockery, Anthony, merchant, Fraser st
Dodds, Wm., Prince Albert hotel, Bailey street
Dougan, Mark, draper, Bailey st
Donaldson, Charles J., and Co., drapers, Fraser st
Douglas, James, carter, North Clunes
Downs, Rev. —, Presbyterian minister, Service st
Druce, Henry, carpenter, Beckwith st
Duncan and Johnston, builders and timber merchants, Bailey st
Duncan, H. W., Templeton st
Dunn, John, miner, George st
Durick, —, constable, Camp st
Earl, John, tinsmith, Fraser st
Edwards, J., grocer, Bailey st
Edwards, Thomas, engine driver, Creswick road
Edwards, —, miner, Creek crescent
Edwards, James, produce dealer, Ligar st
Elder, Robt. M., Criterion hotel, Fraser st
Elliott, Chas., sharebroker, Fraser st
Ellis, John, miner, Creek crescent
Etheracy, James, teacher, Fraser st
Etheracy, Mrs., teacher, Fraser st
Ewart, Wm., miner, Ligar st
Fair, Alfred, bootmaker, Beckwith st
Fairhead, J., miner, North Clunes
Finch, James, butcher, Fraser st
Finnegan, —, miner, Fraser st
Forbes, John, engine driver, Talbot road
Foirer, Joseph, fruiterer, Fraser st
Foster, Joseph, miner, Camp hill
Frampton, Wm., miner, Camp st
Francis, James, miner, Creek crescent
Franklin, J., gas manager, Pratt st
Frawley, Peter, miner, North Clunes
Fry, James, miner, George st
Ferguson, Peter, miner, North Clunes

Gainsborough, Nell, miner, North Clunes
Gardner, Nelson, miner, Ligar st
Gass, Wm., carpenter, Bailey st
George, John, blacksmith, Talbot road
George, John, hotel keeper, Talbot road
Gilbert, John, engine driver, Turello st
Gill, H. F., miner, Turello st
Goodman, Arthur, Clunes hotel, North Clunes
Gordon, Dr., Fraser st
Gordon, Wm., miner, North Clunes
Gordon, Chas., Port Phillip hotel, Paddock
Gray, W. J., agent
Gray, Dr., miner, Ligar st
Gray, Nichol, miner, North Clunes
Gray, Benjamin, miner, North Clunes
Gray, Wm., miner, North Clunes
Gray, Alex., engine driver, Fraser st
Greaves, Richd., hairdresser, Fraser st
Greenfield, Abel, miner, Service st
Greenfield, Henry, miner, Service st
Gribbin, John, Farmers' hotel, Service st
Gribble, James, miner, Ligar st
Gribble, James, miner, Purcell st
Gribble, Henry, miner, Service st
Gribble, James, miner, Service st
Griffiths, John, Robert Burns hotel, Fraser st
Griffiths, —, miner, North Clunes
Griffiths, James, brickmaker, Service st
Grimwood, Edwin, miner, George st
Gripe, Wm., miner, Creswick road
Halliwell, Sylvester, miner, North Clunes
Hamilton, John, miner, North Clunes
Hancock, Samuel, miner, North Clunes flat
Hannah, Robert, miner, North Clunes
Hansen, P. C., tinsmith, Fraser st
Harden, John, carpenter, Talbot road
Harris, James, livery stables, Fraser st
Harrison, Henry, miner, North Clunes
Harrison, Wm., livery stables, Bailey st
Harvey, C. J., manager Clunes Company Paddock
Hawkins, Geo., miner, Ligar st
Hearn, Miss, dressmaker, Bailey st
Heath and Cooper, foundry, Purcell st
Heath, Wm., engineer, Hannah st
Heath, George, miner, North Clunes
Heather, Chas., miner, North Clunes
Henner, James, miner, Creswick road
Hick, Thomas, miner, Ligar st
Hickey, John, miner, North Clunes
Hickmot, —, miner, North Clunes
Hickox, F. P., accountant, Bailey st
Hicks, Daniel, carpenter, Fraser st
Highmarsh, Isabella, Northumberland hotel, North Clunes
Hitchins, John, carpenter, Bailey st
Holmer, Peter, miner, Creswick road
Holler, Wm., miner, Creswick road
Hood, Thomas, Robert Burns hotel, Fraser st

Hopkins, Wm., stampman, Camp st
Horner, James, miner, North Clunes
Hotchin, Edwin K., draper, Fraser st
Howard, John, miner, Ligar st
Howard, Jason, miner, Purcell st
Howrie, John, stampman, Camp st
Hudson, James, carpenter, Bailey st
Hugo, Charles, miner, George st
Hunter, Mark, miner, North Clunes
Hyman, L., tobacconist, Fraser st
Jackson, John, blacksmith, Camp st
James, Thomas, miner, Camp st
Jarvis, Geo., miner, Ligar st
Jelf, J. Thomas, draper, &c., Albert st
Jeffrey, James, miner, George st
Jenkins, Luke, Freemasons' hotel, Bailey st
Jenkins, D., miner, Pratt st
Jessop, Benjamin, solicitor, Camp hill
Jewell, W. H., miner, Alliance st
Johns, Wm., wheelwright, Fraser st
Johnson, Wm., draper, Service st
Jones, John, miner, Pratt st
Jones, John, miner, Templeton st
Jones, Ellis, bootmaker, Fraser st
Jones, Thomas, grocer, Fraser st
Jones, Thomas, and Son, wine and spirit merchants, Fraser st
Jones, Owen, miner, Fraser st
Kelly, J., commercial agent, Cambridge st
Kenney, M., miner, North Clunes
Kenworthy, Wm., smith, Service st
Kenworthy, Wm., blacksmith, Fraser st
Kent, Richd., miner, Beckwith st
Kidd, John, miner, Turello st
King, George, butcher, North Clunes
King Brothers, butchers, Fraser st
Kinsman, —, miner, Creswick road
Klemson, John, miner, North Clunes
Knox, John, carpenter, Service st
Knuckey, James, store, Service st
Lamble, Mrs., Hannah st
Lane, James, carpenter, Service st
Lanyon, Thomas, miner, Templeton st
Lavers, James, miner, Pratt st
Lavers, Thomas, miner, Ligar st
Lawler, M., miner, Camp st
Lawrence, A., Factory hotel, Purcell st
Lain, Wm., store, Templeton st
Lean, John, Templeton st
Lees, John, engine driver, Turello st
Leary, C., stampman, Camp st
Lomas, John, miner, Creek crescent
Longstaff, Ralph, timber merchant, Fraser street
Lochraft, John, Commercial hotel, Fraser street
Luff, Wm., miner, Talbot st
Lugg, Henry, All Nations hotel, North Clunes
Luke, John, miner, Creswick road
Lyall, John, miner, North Clunes
Lyall, John, miner, Service st
McAllister, James, miner, North Clunes flat

McColl, Misses, dressmakers, Fraser st
McDonald, John, miner, Camp st
McDonald, —, miner, North Clunes flat
McDonald's station
McIntosh, Hugh, blacksmith, Service st
McKenzie, Dr., Service st
McLeod, Geo., miner, Purcell st
McMurchies, Alex., baker, Fraser st
Maas, Mrs., ladies' school, Dalley st
Manning, Thomas, miner, Creswick road
Marks, Edwd., miner, Beckwith st
Marks, Jane, store, Service st
Marks, E., miner, Camp st
Marshall, J., Royal hotel, Fraser st
Martin, Michl., store, Fraser st
Martin, Wm., miner, Creswick road
Martin, Wm., blacksmith, Ligar st
Mason, A. F., fruiterer, Fraser st
Masonic Hall, Camp st
Mather, Robert, accountant, Camp hill
Matthews, F. J., carrier, Fraser st
Mayberry, —, miner, North Clunes
Merrifield, Samuel, miner, Smeaton st
Merry, John, miner, George st
Milne, David, engineer, Templeton st
Mitchell, James, miner, Creswick road
Mitchell, Wm, miner, George st
Mitchell, Mrs., Service st
Mitchell, J., store, Fraser st
Mitchell, John, miner, North Clunes
Mister, E.
Moffitt, John, draper, Fraser st
Monk, Alex., miner, North Clunes
Moody, M., store, Fraser st
Morgan, John, miner, Service st
Morgan, —, stampman, Camp st
Moritse, —, carpenter, Creswick road
Morris, John, miner, North Clunes
Morrison, R., tobacconist, Fraser st
Mortimer, Wm., miner, Templeton st
Moser, Herman, Exchange hotel, Fraser street
Mulcahey, John, bootmaker, Service st
Mulcahey, John, bootmaker, Fraser st
Munday, John, miner, Paddock
Murry, Geo., miner, North Clunes flat
Myers, John, miner, Ligar st
Naser, Traste, miner, North Clunes
Nancivall, John, miner, Creswick road
National Bank, Fraser st; Alexander G. Davidson, manager
Neil, High, engine driver, Camp hill
Nelson, Adolphe, miner, Bailey st
Nichol, R., miner, Fraser st
Nichol and Wallace, timber merchants, Fraser st
Nichols, Andrew, store, Ligar st
Nicholls, Richard, miner, Beckwith st
Nicholson, Nick, miner, Fraser st
Nightingale, James, miner, Camp st
Nisbett, John, miner, North Clunes
Noble, Edward, store, Fraser st
Noon, Miss H., boarding house, Fraser st
Oates, Wm., miner, Creswick road

Oates, James, miner, Creswick road
Olrich, Christopher, miner, North Clunes
Olman, Henry, miner, Creswick road
O'Neil, John, carpenter, West parade
O'Toole, James, miner, North Clunes
Pascoe, Joseph, miner, Creswick road
Pascoe, J., miner, George st
Patience, John, Caledonian hotel, North Clunes
Payne, Thomas, gasman, Creek crescent
Pearce, William, miner, North Clunes
Pearce, James, Ligar st
Pearce, William, miner, Ligar st
Pearce, Peter, miner, Camp st
Perry, Thomas, miner, George st
Perry, George, miner, George st
Peters, F., miner, Fraser st
Peters, John, miner, Beckwith st
Phillip, John, saddler, Fraser st
Phillips, James, coach driver, Ligar st
Phillips, Henry, carter, Purcell st
Phillips, Thomas, lay reader, Service st
Phillips, John, miner, Creek crescent
Pickford, J., store, Camp st
Pitcher, Josiah, butcher, Fraser st
Pollard, W., boardinghouse, Fraser st
Presbyterian Church, Service st
Proctor, George, Camp hotel, Bailey st
Purday, Simon, miner, North Clunes
Rankine, William, bootmaker, Fraser st
Rapson, William, miner, Service st
Rane, Richard, carpenter, North Clunes flat
Reid, John, miner, Ligar st
Reynolds, F., miner, Service st
Richards, R., miner, Fraser st
Richards, —, carter, Creswick road
Richards, Stephen, miner, Templeton st
Richards, John, miner, Service st
Richards, James, miner, Camp hill
Richardson, Wm., boarding house, Fraser street
Riley, Thomas, miner, Creek crescent
Roberts, D., Victoria hotel, Fraser st
Roberts, Owen, wheelwright, Fraser st
Roberts, James, blacksmith, Fraser st
Roberts, Isaac, miner, Camp st
Roberts, John, miner, Camp st
Roberts, Samuel, miner, Creswick road
Roberts, John, miner, Ligar st
Roberts, Joseph, miner, Ligar st
Roberts, John C., miner, Camp Hill
Robinson, Dr., Fraser st
Robinson, Wm., miner, George st
Robson, Joseph, stamp captain, Paddock
Rodley, William, miner, North Clunes
Rofe, John, reporter, Bailey st
Rogers, Jonathan, blacksmith, Fraser st
Roland, George, miner, Beckwith st
Rosales, —, miner, North Clunes
Rose, Wm., bootmaker, Fraser st
Ross, —, miner, North Clunes
Rothwell, Charles, miner, North Clunes
Rowe, F., fruiterer, Fraser st

Rowe, George, miner, Ligar st
Saunders, —, stampman, Paddock
Schmidt, Dr. R. W., Fraser st
Schooley, Joseph, miner, Fraser st
Schaffenorth, Richard, fancy repository, Fraser st
Schroder, C. R., Schroder's hotel
Scott, W. G., Scott's villa
Scott, William, miner, Service st
Scott, Charles, miner, North Clunes
Shaw, Charles, miner, Creswick road
Shawbrear, Robert, labourer, Ligar st
Shenaw, —, miner, Creswick road
Sheppherd, James, miner, North Clunes
Sheridan, Wm., carpenter, Templeton st
Shiels, F., bootmaker, Fraser st
Showl, Thomas, miner, Camp hill
Shrigley, J. A., chemist, Fraser st
Shuts, —, miner, Creswick road
Sincox, James, miner, Purcell st
Simmonds, Thomas, butcher, Fraser st
Simmonds, Walter, miner, Alliance st
Simmonds, John, engine driver, Turello st
Simons, Edwin, miner, Creswick road
Simpson, Hugh, miner, Templeton st
Skeldon, Mrs., Purcell st
Slade, Leonard, stamperman, Fraser st
Sloan, John, bootmaker, Fraser st
Sloan, J., bootmaker, Camp st
Slocomb, Robert, stampman, Fraser st
Smidt, George, miner, Bailey st
Smith, Alexander, watchmaker, Fraser st
Smith, John, miner, Creswick road
Smith, Robert, miner, Service st
Smith, J. H., town clerk, Camp hill
Southward and Sumpton, merchants, Fraser st
Spark, Hugh, miner, North Clunes
Stanton, Thomas, miner, Camp hill
Stead, James, wheelwright, Fraser st
Stead, James, wheelwright, Camp st
Steel, Gilbert, miner, North Clunes
Stephens, John, miner, North Clunes
Stephens, J., Seven Stars hotel, Fraser st
Stevenson, Wm., miner, Camp st
Stewart, Charles, stampman, Fraser st
Strail, Edward, miner, Creswick road
Street, William, miner, North Clunes
Stubbs, Joseph, draper, Service st
Sutherland, C. T., miner, North Clunes flat
Symes, George, miner, Ligar st
Tanner, Richard, engineer, Alliance st
Tarnoe, S. W., painter, Purcell st
Tarrant, Samuel, miner, Creek crescent
Tarrant, Benjamin, fruiterer, Fraser st
Taylor, John, carpenter, Camp st
Thomas, Henry, Clunes foundry
Thomas, D., Exchange hotel, Fraser st
Thompson, H. A., miner, Paddock
Thompson, —, mason, Creswick road
Treloar, Thos., butcher, Fraser st
Trentar, Thomas, miner, George st
Trenery, Joseph, miner, Bailey st

Tremerick, Henry, miner, Creswick road
Trevan, John, miner, George st
Trevan, William, miner, Creswick road
Trounce, Charles, miner, Creswick road
Truscott, Edward, miner, Creswick road
Truscott, Richard, miner, Creswick road
Truscott, William, miner, Creswick road
Union Bank, Fraser st, J. M. Dargaville, manager
Uran, V., miner, Creswick road
Usher, John, engine driver, Camp st
Vaughan, Charles, miner, Creswick road
Verney, John, miner, Beckwith st
Vincent, Samuel, miner, Turello st
Vivian, Wm., miner, Creswick road
Vivian, James, miner, Beckwith st
Wakefield, Thomas, miner, Creswick road
Wallace, Wm., miner, Camp st
Wallace, Peter, carpenter, Bailey st
Wallace, Henry, carpenter, Bailey st
Wallace, William, miner, North Clunes flat
Walton, Edward, chemist, Fraser st
Walton, John, miner, Camp st
Wansley, John, engine driver, Camp st
Ward, John, bootmaker, Fraser st
Watts, Thomas, engine driver, Talbot st
Watts, Mrs., North Clunes
Webb, John, miner, Creswick road
Weichhardt, Johannes, tinsmith, Fraser street
Weickhardt, J. C., baker, Fraser st
Wesleyan Church, Service st
White, Wm., miner, Ligar st
White, Edward, miner, North Clunes flat
White, Charles, contractor, Camp hill
Whitfield, John, miner, North Clunes
Whittleson, John, miner, North Clunes
Wiles, Griffin, Washington hotel, Fraser street
Wilks, Wm., engine driver, Fraser st
Williams, Morgan, stoker, Fraser st
Williams, Jane, Bailey st
Williams, David, miner, Templeton st
Williams, George, miner, North Clunes
Willis, Matthew, miner, Camp st
Willis, James, engine driver, Camp st
Wills, James, miner, North Clunes
Wilmot, Henry C., accountant, West parade
Winchester, Eric, produce dealer, Fraser street
Wingate, Walter, Albion hotel, Fraser st
Winnett and Jennings, bootmakers, Fraser street
Winning, Paul, painter, &c., Fraser st
Wilson, James, engine driver, Talbot road
Woodford, Richard, miner, Fraser st
Woolcock, John, miner, North Clunes flat
Youlton, John, blacksmith, Turello st
Young, John, painter, Fraser st
Young, James, miner, North Clunes
Zornig, Henry, miner, Fraser st
Zornig, Mrs. A., school, Fraser st

KYNETON ALPHABETICAL DIRECTORY.

1866-7.

Abbey, Thomas, tinsmith, Piper st
Abbey, Thomas, tinsmith, High st
Abell, Mrs., Lauriston st
Aiken, —, farmer, Jennings st
Alexander, Mrs., Family hotel, Piper st
Anderson, David, mason, Bodkin st
Apperly, John, secretary of the shire, Wedge st
Argyle, Edward, farmer, Mount Alexander road
Armstrong, Oliver G., Jennings st
Arnold, Wm., bootmaker, Piper st
Attwood, Samuel, haircutter, Piper st
Bailey, Thomas, labourer, Bodkin st
Baines, Thomas, farmer, Piper st east
Baldwin, Edwin, dealer in earthenware, stationery, and fancy goods, High st
Bank of New South Wales, Piper st—Henry B. Stiles, manager; Frederick Millidge, accountant
Baptist Chapel—Rev. G. Rickerby, pastor, Piper st
Barkin, Alfred, butcher, High st
Beates, Wm., High st
Begg, Robert, Yaldwin st
Bennett, J. T. H., sharebroker and commission agent, Piper st
Bennett, James T. H., Ebden st
Bethell, Isaac, carpenter, Mitchell st
Bethell, Isaac, wheelwright, Piper st
Blair, Wm., mason, Donnithorne st
Blair, W. J., manager Colonial Bank of Australasia, High st

Bland, —, mason, Simpson st
Blencowe, Nathaniel, Jeffrey st
Blundell and Hurry, solicitors, Ebden st
Bodkin, Miss, day school, Bodkin st
Booker, George, solicitor, Piper st
Booth, —, farmer, Mount Alexander road
Boulton, F. H., Jennings st
Boyle, Christopher, labourer, Ebden st
Braithwaite, Wm., Victorian hotel, Campaspe bridge, Mount Alexander road
Brockett, Wm , farmer, Welch st
Brocklebank, T., bootmaker, Piper st
Bromley, Paul J., carpenter, Lauriston st
Brown, Edward, Powlett st
Bull, Richard, Albion hotel, Mollison st
Bunn, Miss, dressmaker, Mount Alexander road
Burge, Wm., Simpson st
Burt, Michael, labourer, Begg st
Burton, Thomas, timber merchant and paperhanging warehouseman, Baynton street
Cameron, carpenter, Lauriston st
Cantwell, Wm., labourer, Powlett st
Carolin, John, collector to the Kyneton Hospital, Beauchamp st
Carroll, John, labourer, Mount Alexander road
Carroll, John, labourer, High st
Carter, Wm., quarryman, Powlett st
Carter, Joshua, Simpson st
Casey, Mrs., widow, Yaldwin st
Castles, Thomas, carpenter, Simpson st

Castles, James, carpenter, Simpson st
Castilla, Frederick, miller, Piper st
Charles, James, quarryman, Yaldwin st
Charles, Mrs., Wedge st
Charles, Wm., carter, Yaldwin st
Charles, John, quarryman, Hutton st
Charles, Philip, joiner, Hutton st
Charles, Philip, labourer, Jennings st
Chester, John, plasterer, Jennings st
Christie, George, baker, High st
Church of England, Piper st
Cleary, J., Court House hotel, Hutton st
Clinton, Mrs., ladies' school, Baynton st ; Miss Sheridan, assistant
Cockburn, Alexander, blacksmith, Powlett street
Colonial Bank of Australasia; W. J. Blair, manager ; John Robertson, accountant, High st
Common School No. 343, Baynton st; R. Cox, schoolmaster; Mrs. Cox, schoolmistress
Common School No. 355, Yaldwin st ; Robert Begg, schoolmaster; Mrs. Begg, schoolmistress
Conway, Jas., deputy registrar of births, deaths, &c., Yaldwin st
Conway, —, labourer, Bodkin st
Cook, Robert, grocer, High st
Coughlan, Timothy, clothier, High st
County Court, Hutton st
Cox, Ross, Simpson st
Crawford, Isaac, saddler, Mollison st
Crawford, George, labourer, Simpson st
Crow, Henry, brickmaker, Beauchamp st
Cuddy, —, labourer, Simpson st
Cullen, Patk., labourer, Mount Alexander road
Dalton, Mary, teacher, Epping st
Daniels and Adair, drapers
Davey, Thomas, compositor, Lauriston st
Degraves, W., and Co., millers, Mount Alexander road
Dellin, Peter, labourer, High st
Dericot, Margaret, greengrocer, Piper st
Dickson, Henry, draper, High st
Ditman, —, carter, Epping st
Dodds and King, tanners and curriers, Mount Alexander road
Donohoe, Timothy, miller, Mitchell st
Donnely, John, police constable, Mitchell street
Donovan, Patrick, Farmers' hotel, Mount Alexander road
Dougan, Thomas, labourer, Bodkin st
Dowling, Thomas, draper, Piper st
Doyle, Thomas, College hotel, Piper st
Dubourg, Rev. Charles, Ebden st
Duffie, James, farmer and chaff cutter, Mount Alexander road
Dufty, Francis H., photographic artist, Piper st
Dwyer, Dennis, labourer, Ebden st
Earl, Mrs., Mount Alexander road

Edmund, Charles, painter, High st
Ellerton, John, blacksmith, Mount Alexander road
Ellis, Wm., Royal hotel, Piper st
Fagan, Wm., farmer, Mount Alexander road
Fahey, Wm., bootmaker, Mollison st
Ferris, Mrs., widow, Piper st east
Ferris, George, Harvest Home hotel, Mount Alexander road
Fleck, Mrs., ladies' school, Wedge st
Fleck, Gabriel, engineer and surveyor, Wedge st
Foley, Patrick, bootmaker, High st
Foley, Daniel, bootmaker, Hutton st
Fowler, Henry, gingerbeer manufacturer, Begg st
Gardner, Thomas, labourer, High st
Geary, Dr. H., coroner, Baynton st
Gibson, Hugh, Lauriston st
Gilbert, Edward, labourer, Bodkin st
Giles, Alfred J., boarding house, High st
Glenny, Henry, photographic artist, Mollison st
Gloster, James, wine, spirit, and provision merchant, Piper st
Gourlay, Thomas, inspector of weights and measures, High st
Graham, Wm., grocer, High st
Grant, Mrs., draper, High st
Grant, Richard, bricklayer, Yaldwin st
Gratwicke, Joseph, labourer, Bodkin st
Gray, Andrew, quarryman, Welch st
Green, Reginald, superintendent of police, Police paddock
Green, Wm. H., Hutton st
Green, John, labourer, Epping st
Green, Wm., china and glass warehouse, Piper st
Gregory, Thomas M., Kyneton hotel, Piper st
Gresson, Robert C., solicitor, Hutton st, and Chancery lane, Melbourne
Grice, George, labourer, Begg st
Grimley, Wm. C., agent for the London and Lancashire Insurance Company, and general commission agent, Baynton street
Groves, G. F., postmaster and telegraph manager, Mollison st
Gullick, Elizabeth, fruiterer, High st
Hagley, Geo., contractor, High st
Hall, Robt., St. Agnes' hotel, Mount Alexander road
Hall, Thomas W., general furnishing warehouse, Mollison st
Hamilton, John, bootmaker, High st
Hamilton, Henry, residence, Begg st
Hanigen, Margaret, dressmaker, High st
Hansby, Fredk., Collegiate School, Wedge street
Hardie, Alex., ironmonger, Piper st
Hargreave, Thomas, Royal Oak hotel, High st

Harold, John, furniture warehouse, Mollison st
Harrington, Luke, labourer, Bodkin st
Harris, Wm. H., day school, Wedge st
Hart, Michael, drill instructor, Simpson st
Hart, J. C., wheelwright, Welch st
Hayward, John, bootmaker, High st
Henderson, Rev. R., minister of the Presbyterian Church; residence. Ebden st
Higgins, Peter, carpenter, Wedge st
Hill, Geo., carpenter, Beauchamp st
Hobbs, Abraham, soda water manufacturer, Beauchamp st
Hoctor, Thomas, labourer, Simpson st
Hollis, Chas., saddler, Mollison st
Holt, Edwd., carriage builder, Welch st
Hutchinson and Walter, agricultural implement manufacturers, Welch st
Independent Church; Rev. J. Hutchinson, minister, Hutton st
Jacobs, —, farmer, Piper st east
Jarman, Wm., fruiterer, Piper st.
Jarrett, Edwd., butcher, Mitchell st
Jarrett, Henry, butcher, Piper st
Jarrett, Wm., wholesale and retail grocer
Jennings, John, residence, Jennings st
Johnson and Cock, brewers, Beauchamp st
Johnson, G. W., grocer, wine and spirit merchant, Piper st
Johnson, Wm., blacksmith and wheelwright Baynton st
Johnston, Isaac, carpenter, Wedge st
Jones, John, bootmaker, Yaldwin st
Kearney, M., Railway hotel, Baynton st
Kelleter, Thomas, Volunteer hotel, High street
Kelley, M., blacksmith, Hutton st
Kelly, Dr., Baynton st
Kelly, Samuel, letter carrier, Simpson st
Kennedy, Richard, Harp of Erin hotel, Piper st
Kenworthy, Benjamin, storekeeper, Baynton st
Kelkey, Michael, carpenter, Welch st
King, Thomas, labourer, Mount Alexander road
Kinnar, Mrs., widow, Piper st east
Kinniard, Thos., Lauriston st
Kirk, James, gardener, Mount Alexander road
Kyneton Hospital, Simpson st
Kyneton Gas Works, Ebden st
Kyneton Savings' Bank, Piper st ; Frank Robertson, actuary
Kyneton Volunteer Orderly Room ; Wm. Roberts, secretary, Piper st
Labey, John, fruiterer, Piper st
Laird, James, grocer, Epping st
Langenbach, Joseph, watch and clock maker, Piper st
Larter, Geo., Baynton st
Lemaitte, Chas., carpenter, Simpson st
Lesori, Nicholas, miner, High st
Letch, Mrs., Lauriston st

Lillis, John, Weighbridge hotel, High st
Linklater, Jacob S., mason, High st
Lister, Thomas, baker, Piper st
Lloyd, Richard, carrier, High st
Lockhart, Robert, saddler and harness maker, Piper st
Loughlen, Edmond, cooper, High st
Love, Daniel, blacksmith, Epping st
Lowery, Mrs., dressmaker, High st
Lowes, Thomas, draper, Donnithorne st
Lowther, Joseph, baker and confectioner, High st
Lugton, Geo., wheelwright, Mitchell st
Lynes, Mrs., Epping at
Macasey, —, labourer, Beauchamp st
Macdonald, John, builder, Mollison st
Macarthy, Patrick, bootmaker, Mullison st
Macuurn, —, labourer, Begg st
Major, James, butcher, High st
Mann, W. J. E., grocer, Baynton st
Manning, William, carpenter, Simpson st
Maplebach, Geo., labourer, Bodkin st
Marshall, Wm. W., lessee of the Kyneton Gas Works, Mitchell st
Masterton, Alex., contractor, Simpson st
Mathers, James, High st
Maxwell, John, grocer, wine and spirit merchant, High st
Maxwell, John, surveyor, Wedge st
Mayfield, Edward, carrier, Beauchamp st
McAlpin, James, tailor, Ebden st
McArthur, John, labourer, Beauchamp st
McClure, Thomas, grocer, Piper st
McGill, James, engineer, Bodkin st
McGrath, John, brewer, Donnithorne st
McGuire, John, police constable, Piper st east
McKenna, Martin, Champaspe brewery, Ebden st
McKenna, James, tailor, Piper st
McLauglan, Thomas, Piper st east
McLeod, A., storekeeper, Mount Alexander road
McMillan, T. L., surgeon, Bodkin st
McNeill, Sarah, dressmaker, Piper st
McPherson, Daniel, carriage painter, Piper st
Meagher, Patrick F., Criterion hotel, Piper street
Mechanics' Institute ; Wm. C. Grimley, secretary, Baynton st
Meber, Miss, dressmaker, High st
Mehew, Matthew, labourer, Bodkin st
Menzies and Co., corn factors and chaff cutters, High st
Metcalfe, Robt., bootmaker, Baynton st
Middleditch, Geo., carrier, High st
Miles, Thomas, draper, High st
Millidge, Geo., ironmonger, High st
Millidge, Fredk., accountant, Bank of New South Wales, Piper st
Millidge, Fredk., High st
Moodie, J., and Co., millwrights and agricultural machinists, Piper st

Moodie, James, engineer, Mitchell st
Moodie, Miss, ladies' school, Mollison st
Montgomery, —, Bodkin st
Moresby, Miss, ladies' school, High st
Morris, Joshua, carter, Begg st
Morrall, Geo., carpenter, High st
Murphy, Mrs., storekeeper and restaurant, Mollison st
Murphy, Patrick, storekeeper, High st
Murray, Wm., bread and biscuit baker, High st
Neal, W. F., news agent, Mollison st
Nicholas, David, labourer, Bodkin st
Noonan, James, boarding house, Piper st
Norman, Matthew, cabinet maker and upholsterer, High st
Olding, Thos., mason, Epping st
Oraphcrton, Thos., miner, Mount Alexander road
Ousey, Miss, teacher of music, Piper st
Parker, Henry G., draper, Piper st
Parkes, John, butcher, Begg st
Paterson, John, dairyman, Simpson st
Pennington, James, farmer, Piper st
Perkin, J., house, sign, and decorative painter, &c., Mollison st
Perkin, J., Bodkin st
Perkin, C. and F., grocers, High st
Perkins, E., chemist and druggist, High st
Perkins, E., chemist and druggist, Piper street
Pescell, Dr. James, Welch st
Pettit, James, painter, &c., Powlett st
Piggins, Geo., builder, Piper st east
Pike, John, miner, Wedge st
Police camp; Reginald Green, superintendent, Ebden st
Post and Telegraph offices; G. E. Grooves, postmaster, and telegraph manager, Mollison st
Powell, H. J., corn merchant, High st
Powles, John, gardener, Ebden st
Powles, Geo., carter, &c., Begg st
Prebble, Chas., watchmaker and jeweller, Piper st
Presbyterian Church; Rev. H. Henderson, minister, Yaldwin st
Pride, Martin, labourer, Simpson st
Purdue, Alfred, teacher, Mollison st
Quick, James, fishmonger, High st
Ramsdale, James, contractor, Lauriston st
Rattray, Wm., plumber, High st
Reid, —, dairyman, Piper st east
Reano, Wm., residence, Jeffrey st
Richardson, Geo., boot and shoe manufacturer, High st
Riordan, John, labourer, High st
Riley, Michael, gardener, Mount Alexander road
Robertson, Frank, bookseller, stationer, and news agent, Piper st
Robertson, Frank, Ebden st
Robertson, John, accountant, Colonial Bank of Australasia, High st

Robson, John, saddler, Piper st
Rock, James, labourer, Powlett st
Rogers, Alex., mason, Mitchell st
Rogers, Mrs., High st
Rogers, Peter, tailor, Mollison st
Rogers, Thomas, and Co., drapers, High street
Roman Catholic Church, Ebden st
Rosel, A., and Co., tobacconists, High st
Rosel, Augustus, sharebroker and mining agent, and agent for the Australian Mutual Provident Society (Life Assurance), High st
Rye, Stephen, carpenter, Lauriston st
Sandford, Wm., labourer, Powlett st
Servaes, Charles, carter, Epping st
Sharpe, Robert, farmer, Mount Alexander road
Shawcross, John, grocer, Mollison st
Sheen, Daniel, mason, Jennings st
Sheen, James, mason, Lauriston st
Sheen, Richd., labourer, Mount Alexander road
Shirlock, Robt., labourer, Beauchamp st
Skidmore, Thomas, painter, Piper st east
Smith, C. H. J., surveyor, Epping st
Smith, James, brewer, Mitchell st
Smith, Miss, ladies' school, Epping st
Spence, J. H., chemist and druggist, High street
Stead, Chas., miner, Donalihorne st
Steinmeyer, G. A., tobacconist, Piper st
Stewart, William H., engineer, Simpson street
Stoppa, Jesse, labourer, Powlett st
Storey, John, teacher under Board of Education, Greenhill, by Kyneton
Stiles, Henry B., manager Bank of New South Wales, Piper st
Sturt, —, Wedge st
Styles, Geo., sign painter, &c., Mount Alexander road
Summerville, Chas., boat builder, Dutton street
Sunderland, Wm., Simpson st
Surman, Maria, Ebden st
Swanwick, Wm., wine and spirit merchant, High st
Swinton, Mrs., Junction hotel, Mollison st
Symington, J., Creighton hotel
Tanner, Charles, farrier and veterinary surgeon, Piper st
Taylor, James, blacksmith, Piper st
The Kyneton Guardian newspaper office, High st; M. K. Armstrong, proprietor
The Kyneton Observer newspaper office, Ebden st; H. F. Neal, proprietor
The Queen Insurance Co., Piper st; Geo. Booker, agent
The London and Lancashire Insurance Co.; Wm. C. Grimley, agent, Baynton street
Thirkettle, William J., builder, Yaldwin street

Thompson, Ann, Epping st
Thompson, John C., Donnithorne st
Thompson, Thomas, labourer, Simpson st
Thomson, John B., butcher, High st
Thorne, Chas., wheelwright, Powlett st
Thornton, James, fishmonger, Piper st
Tolmie, James, mason, Powlett st
Tonks, Geo., carpenter, Lauriston st
Toobey, John, Jeffrey st
Trainor, Owen, draper, Epping st
Torphy, Samuel, Mount Alexander road
Turphy, John, blacksmith, Piper st
Turner, Alfred, cabinetmaker, Piper st
Turner, Chas., blacksmith, Piper st
Vail, Daniel, labourer, Mitchell st
Vance, Rev. George O., Ebden st
Vardy, Wm. S., solicitor, Hutton st
Veale, A. J., blacksmith, Powlett st
Walker, John, blacksmith, Welch st
Wallis, Thomas M., seedsman, Piper st
Walters, Thomas, Jennings st

Weaver, Thomas, butcher, Lauriston st
Wedgwood, E. H., Queen's Head hotel, High st
Welgall, Henry, clerk of courts; residence, Donnithorne st
Wells, Joseph J., chemist and druggist, Mollison st
Wells, Mrs., Powlett st
Wesleyan Church, Ebden st; Rev. Charles Dubourg, minister
White, John S., contractor, Hutton st
White, John, Freemasons' hotel, Yaldwin street
White, Luke, carpenter, Lauriston st
White, Mrs., day school, Hutton st
Willis, J. L., assistant clerk of courts; residence, High st
Wilson, Robert, blacksmith, High st
Winchcomb, —, labourer, Bodkin st
Wood, Alexander, baker, Welch st
Young, Charles, auctioneer, &c., Piper st

MALMSBURY ALPHABETICAL DIRECTORY.

1866-67.

Adams, David, bootmaker, Mollison st
Adamson, F. E., Urquhart st
Adamson, F. E., and Co., brokers and corn agents, Mollison st
Allen, Walter, manager, Malmsbury Brewery Company, Mollison st
Armstrong, Dr. James J., Mollison st
Amlett, Wm., Family hotel, Mollison st
Bank of Victoria, Orr st ; Robert Hyndman, agent

Bank of New South Wales ; William H. Metcalfe, agent, Mollison st
Bethane, Geo., labourer, Clowes st
Blythman and Pitt, mining agents, Mollison st
Blyth, James, Orr st
Blyth and Co., millers, Mollison st
Booker, Geo., solicitor, Mollison st
Boundy, Wm., Bennett st
Brayley, H., carpenter, Mollison st

Brasch, Stern, and Co., general storekeepers, Mollison st
Bringham, Geo., carter, Mollison st
Calcutt, Geo., blacksmith, Mollison st
Cameron, Robt., miner, Mollison st
Carroll, Lawrence, storekeeper, Mollison street
Chambers, John, Mollison st
Church of England; Rev. H. C. Watson, clergyman, Mollison st
Coghlan, John, Junction hotel, Mollison st
Common School No. 4x0, Mollison st; Wm. Wade, schoolmaster; Mrs. Wade, schoolmistress
Cook, Michael, saddler, Mollison st
Court of Petty Sessions
Cullen, Thomas, traveller, Mollison st
Davy, Edwd., chemist and druggist, Mollison st
Degruchy, John, carpenter, Mollison st
Dell, George J., chemist, Mollison st
Dougall, James, Commercial hotel, Mollison st
Eastham, James, quarryman, Urquhart st
Egan, Denis, farmer, Urquhart st
Essery, Jane, boarding house, Mollison st
Evans, W. S., Malmsbury hotel, Mollison street
Field, Richd., blacksmith, Mollison st
Flemming, David H., watchmaker, Mollison st
Fraser, John, postmaster and telegraph manager, Mollison st
French, Isaac L., National hotel, Mollison street
Gillard, Henry, saddler, Mollison st
Good, Wm., labourer, Mollison st
Grant, Alex., storekeeper, Mollison st
Green, Geo. F., Mollison st
Green and Lee, stock and share brokers, Mollison st
Hall, Edwd., trooper, Police camp
Harvey, James H., Clowes st
Henry, J. and W., wine and provision merchants, Mollison st
Hollyman, Wm., pork butcher, Mollison street
Holmes, Wm., senior constable, Police camp
Hook, John W., wheelwright, Clowes st
Hockey, John, butcher, Mollison st
Hooppell, Samuel E., timber merchant, Mollison st
Hubbard, John, miner, Urquhart st
Hunter, Robt., Orr st
Hyodman, Robt., agent Bank of Victoria, Orr st
Irving, Geo., labourer, Clowes st
Jackson, Matthew, contractor, Mollison st
Johnson, Daniel, labourer, Drake st
Johnson, Matthew, brewer, Clowes st
Jones, Thomas, mason, Clowes st

Jones, John, miner, Urquhart st
Keller, Phillip, baker, Mollison st
Kennedy, J. P., Railway hotel and general storekeeper, Orr st
Ladbury, F. C., station master, Railway station
Lipplegoes, Julius, Coliban hotel, Mollison st
Lynch, John, farmer, Clowes st
Macredie, John, labourer, Clowes st
Maher, John, butcher, Mollison st
Malmsbury Brewery Company; Walter Allen, manager, Mollison st
Markham, Edwd., miller, Clowes st
Meagher, Cornelius, Urquhart st
McGreggor, Duncan, blacksmith, Mollison st
McKenna, Michael, Travellers' Rest hotel, Mollison st
Metcalfe, Wm. H., agent Bank New South Wales, Mollison st
Miller, Alex., carpenter, Urquhart st
Morgan, Joseph, labourer, Clowes st
Mossip, James, carpenter, Urquhart st
O'Hanlin, Terrence, baker, Urquhart st
O'Neil, Edwd., fruiterer, Mollison st
Oswin, John, miller, Urquhart st
Parkin, T., carpenter, &c., Orr st
Perkin, Thomas, blacksmith, Mollison st
Pengergrass, John, labourer, Clowes st
Pettigrew, Daniel, bootmaker, Mollison st
Planche, F. C., haircutter, Mollison st
Pleasants, Geo., Duke of Kent hotel, Mollison st
Pook, Thomas, tailor, Mollison st
Post and Telegraph offices; John Fraser, postmaster and telegraph manager, Mollison st
Richardson, John, Clowes st
Rose, Wm., carter, Mollison st
Russell, Alex., engineer, Drake st
Ryan, Daniel, Racecourse hotel and storekeeper, Mollison st
Scott, —, carpenter, Urquhart st
Shepherdson, J. B., timber merchant, Bennett st
Short, Wm., carpenter, &c., Clowes st
Simpson, Mrs., ladies' school, Clowes st
Smith, Henry V., quarryman, Mollison st
Stanley, Wm., miner, Clowes st
Stinger, Joseph, miner, Urquhart st
Toohey, J. T., and Co., brewers, Mollison street
Tyson, John, J.P., Clowes st
Vardy, W. S., solicitor, Mollison st
Wade, Wm., schoolmaster, Common School, Mollison st
Waite, Wm., miner, Orr st
Webb, John S. G., Clowes st
Welaford, Geo., bootmaker, Mollison st
Wilson, Alfred, general storekeeper, Mollison st

TARADALE ALPHABETICAL DIRECTORY.

1866-67.

Allen, John, labourer, Davy st
Andrews, Geo., manager Bank of Australasia, High st
Angove, Samuel, miner (suburban)
Archibald, Henry, surveyor, town clerk, borough treasurer, and deputy curator of Intestate estates for the Castlemaine District, High st
Arnold, Edward, miner (suburban)
Auld, Andrew, blacksmith, Patterson st
Austin, J. L., solicitor, &c., and commissioner for taking affidavits, &c., Faraday st
Atkin, Wm. B., surgeon and government vaccinator, High st
Baird, Alexander, miner (suburban)
Banks, —, miner (suburban)
Beckwith, Wm. J., coach, cart, and waggon builder, High st
Bell, Thomas, stationer, High st
Benbow, C. A., accountant, Bank of Australasia, High st
Berry, Godfrey B., storekeeper, High st
Billett, Martin, miner (suburban)
Bilsbury, Robt., farmer, Lyall st
Bliss, Wm. A. R., Oddfellows' Arms
Boorues, Peter, carpenter, High st
Bowman, John, Temperance boarding house, Lyall st
Branch, Benedict, blacksmith, Patterson st
Bray, John H., miner (suburban)
Broad, Wm., carpenter, High st
Brown, George W., Viaduct hotel (suburban)
Brown, Thomas, blacksmith (suburban)
Buckley, Benjamin, Victoria hotel, High street

Budd, W. J., manager National Bank of Australasia, High st
Buhl, John, hairdresser, High st
Bullimore, James, baker, High st
Bunderson, Mrs., Taradale hotel, High st
Calanchini, P., Prince of Wales hotel, High st
Callcott, Robt., miner, High st
Clair, Mrs. (suburban)
Cocking, Thomas, jun., miner (suburban)
Cocking, Thomas, miner (suburban)
Cocking, Wm., miner (suburban)
Colonial Bank of Australasia; Geo. Andrews, manager; C. A. Benbow, accountant
Common School, High st; John Wilson schoolmaster; Catherine Renny, schoolmistress
Corrie, Wm., storekeeper, High st
Cox, Mrs., High st
Cumming, Stephen, miner, High st
Cunningham, Wm. H., High st
Cunningham, Wm. H., tinsmith, High st
Curnow, John, miner, Davy st
Dadlow, Jonathan, miner, High st
Dalves, James, High st
D'Arcy, Garrott, Rose, Shamrock and Thistle hotel, High st
Daw, —, miner (suburban)
Dawson, Wm., ironmonger, High st
Deery, Joseph, carpenter, High st
Dinner, Peter, miner, High st
Donald, James, miner (suburban)
Dorgan, Wm., miner (suburban)
Dorman, Stephen, agent for *Our Daily News* newspaper, High st
Dunbar, John, tailor, High st
Dunn, Thomas, carpenter, High st

Dunstan, James, carter, High st
Edwards, John, miner, Lyall st
Ellis, Henry, postmaster and telegraph manager, High st
Ellis, Joseph W., lamplighter, High st
Erskine, James, miner, High st
Foster, Geo., bailiff, High st
Fothergill, Thomas F., fancy bread baker High st.
Gambell, Henry, carpenter, Patterson st
Garden, John, Castle hill
Garden, Wm., merchant, High st
Gibbs, Matthew, farmer, Taradale
Giles, Mrs. (suburban)
Glandfield, John, builder, Patterson st
Gluth, Wm., miner, High st
Goosey John, miner, Patterson st
Gordon, Wm. G. S., broker, High st
Graham, Wm., butcher, High st
Grant, Geo. H., jeweller, Patterson st
Graydon, Chas., secretary Odd Fellows' society, Patterson st
Griffiths, John, High st
Ham, Wm. (suburban)
Hannon, Thomas, miner, Davy st
Harris, Elizabeth, ladies' school, High st
Harris, James, miner, Patterson st
Heard, Wm., bootmaker, High st
Heffernan, Thomas, Lyall st
Henwood, Henry, miner (suburban)
Heritage, John, builder, High st
Hickey, Patrick, miner (suburban)
Higgins, William, miner (suburban)
Hill, A. T., accountant National Bank of Australasia, High st
Hindmarsh, John, miner (suburban)
Holbrook, Geo., miner (suburban)
Humphrey, James, Patterson st
Jackson, Thomas, storekeeper, High st
Jago, Henry, miner (suburban)
Jones, —, labourer (suburban)
Kerr, Mrs., dairykeeper, High st
Kennedy, Wm., miner, Lyall st
Kestle, John, miner (suburban)
Kewley, Thomas, timber yard, High st
King, Catherine, dressmaker, High st
Knowles, Richd., miner (suburban)
Kroeger, Fredk., upholsterer, High st
Lancashire, Wm., engineer, High st
Lamb, Louis A., William Tell inn, High st
Laurie, Henry, miner, High st
Leak and Gordon, mining agents, High st
Leek, — (suburban)
Leigh, James, teacher, Davy st
Lemmack, Wm., miner, Patterson st
Lerew, John, chemist and druggist, High street
Lewellen, William, produce merchant, High st
Lyons, James, miner (suburban)
Macarthy, Jeremiah, Patterson st
Macpherson, —, carpenter, High st
Mackinson, Chas., High st
Manning, Samuel, miner, High st

Manual, Thomas, miner, Patterson st
Martin, William, Martin's hotel, High st
Maskiell, Chas., greengrocer, High st
Mason, Richard E., United Kingdom hotel, High st
May, Samuel, miner, Lyall st
McCaulay, Geo., hay and corn dealer, High st
McDonald, James, miner, High st
McLachlan, Wm. R., saddler, &c., High st
McLaghlan, Wm., Davey st
McKensie, Mrs. (suburban)
McNamara, James, miner, Lyall st
Meyer, Hy., tobacconist, High st
Mill, Wm., miner (suburban)
Mitchell, James, bootmaker, High st
Morris, John, miner, High st
Morrison, David, miner, High st
Munro and Sullivan, bootmakers, High st
Murray, Thomas A., miner, High st
National Bank of Australasia; W. J. Budd, manager, High st; A. T. Hill, accountant
Nelson, Robert, miner, High st
Newman, John, miner (suburban)
Nicholson, Geraldine, Commercial inn, High st
O'Connor, Michael, sawyer, Davy st
Orwin, Thomas, mining and commission agent, High st
Orwin Bros., butchers, High st
O'Toole, Edward, police constable (suburban)
Peaty, Stephen, miner, High st
Pemberton, Wm., draper, High st
Pemberton, brickmaker, High st
Penberthy, James, miner (suburban)
Perry, John, Albion hotel, High st
Phemister, John, miner, High st
Plowright, Thomas, Freemasons' hotel, High st
Popple, John, bootmaker, High st
Porter, Wm., miner (suburban)
Post and Telegraph offices; Henry Ellis, postmaster and telegraph manager, High st
Postell, Benjamin, printer (suburban)
Powell, Alice, Court House hotel (suburban)
Presbyterian Church; Rev. — Anderson, minister, High st
Priddeth, Chas., miner (suburban)
Prout, Thomas, miner (suburban)
Reynolds, Wm., J.P., High st
Richie, Alex., miner, Patterson st
Rigby, Geo. Owen, physician and surgeon, Davy st
Riley, John, labourer, Davy st
Rodda, Stephen, National hotel, High st
Rogers, Thos., blacksmith, High st
Rodman, James, painter, &c., Patterson street
Rutledge, Mrs. (suburban)
Ryan, Patrick, miner (suburban)

Sayers, Wm., cooper, High st
Shrimpton, Geo., store and hotelkeeper, High st
Sims, Samuel, miner, Patterson st
Sinclair, James, blacksmith and wheelwright, High st
Singleton, John, Golden Age hotel, High street
Smith, John, carpenter (suburban)
Smith, Thomas, miner, High st
Spencer, J. C. and S., general storekeepers, High st
Stephens, Wm., Great Britain hotel, High street
Stavens, —, miner, Lyall st
Strickland, Robt., mining registrar, High street
Stubbins, —, Railway hotel (suburban)
Symon, Bernard, legal manager and mining agent, High st
Symons, John, miner, High st
Teague, —, butcher, High st
The Church of England; Rev. Henry Watson, clergyman (suburban)
The Court of Petty Sessions (suburban)
The New Court of Petty Sessions, Faraday st
The Odd Fellows' hall; Chas. Graydon, secretary, High st
The Police Station (suburban); Sergeant J. Brown, senior constable
The Taradale Express newspaper office, High st; John Janson, proprietor
Thomas, John, builder, High st
Thureau, Julius, miner, High st
Thureau, Wm., miner, Patterson st
Tibbs, Geo, miner (suburban)

Timbey, —, miner (suburban)
Timmins and Robottom, blacksmiths, High st
Trevaskes, John, miner (suburban)
Treverton, James, miner, High st
Trodgen, W. H., miner (suburban)
Turner, Thomas, mining surveyor, High street
Vicary, Geo., mining broker, High st
Waller, John, brickmaker, High st
Walmsley, Richard J., mining broker, High st
Ward, Wm., Royal Mail hotel, High st
Warren, Charles, carpenter, High st
Watson, Rev. H. (suburban)
Wells and Flemming, drapers, High st
Wells, Henry, draper (suburban)
Wells, James, miner (suburban)
Westwood, John, bootmaker, High st
Wherry, Wm., miner, Lyall st
White, Wm., blacksmith, High st
Whitty, Derick, miner, High st
Whylan, Wm., miner, Lyall st
Wicking, John, timber merchant and ironmonger, High st
Wilby, Wm., miner Patterson st
Williams, Wm., miner, Patterson st
Williams, John, miner, High st
Williams, James, miner, Patterson st
Williams, Thomas B., miner (suburban)
Williams, Margaret, High st
Wilson, John, schoolmaster, Common School, High st
Wilson, Daniel, draper and general storekeeper, High st
Wright, William, miner (suburban)

LAURISTON ALPHABETICAL DIRECTORY.

1866-7.

Blackwell, John, blacksmith
Bradley, Thomas, bootmaker
Crymble and Stringer, Kent hotel and general storekeepers
Golterdy, Mrs.
Hamblin, Geo., carpenter
Hill, Ralph, manager Lauriston Gold Mining Company
Holton, Geo., Great Britain store
Jordon, Chas. E., Hit or Miss notel
Lauriston Common School; Edwin Sinnatt, schoolmaster
McNee, Peter, miner
Oxnam, Richd., miner
Pearce, John, miner
Pope, Matthew, miner
Sanderson, John, miner
Sheppard, A., Lauriston hotel
Sinnatt, Edwin, master Common School
Stembridge, Elizabeth, boarding house
The Abraham Lincoln Gold Mining Company; Thomas Hargreaves, manager
The British Empire Quartz Gold Mining Company; John Stringer, manager
The Comet Gold Mining Company; A. Rosel, manager

The Dalhousie Gold Mining Company; G. F. Green, manager, Malmsbury
The Duke of Kent Gold Mining Company; G. F. Green, manager, Malmsbury
The General Wyndham Quartz Gold Mining Company; F. G. Lavender, manager
The Glengower Gold Mining Company; A. Pardue, manager
The Hit or Miss Gold Mining Company; Ralph Hill, manager
The Last Chance Gold Mining Company; S. O. Oliver, manager
The Lauriston Gold Mining Company; —, Hill, manager
The North Wyndham Quartz Gold Mining Company; A. Rosel, manager
The Pemberley Gold Mining Company; John Stringer, manager
The Prince Christian Gold Mining Company; John Stringer, manager
The Wellington Gold Mining Company; F. Lavender, manager
Uran, Wm., miner
Veall, Edmund J., blacksmith
Welch, Thomas, storekeeper
Wilkinson, Thomas

BEECHWORTH ALPHABETICAL DIRECTORY.

1866-67.

Abbott, Mrs., ladies' seminary, Beechworth
Alderdice, Alex., clerk, Camp st
Allsopp, J. F., butcher, High st
Ambrose, J. F., builder, Camp st
Ansell, Edwin, confectioner, Camp st
Atkinson, Robinson, and Correll, coachbuilders, Camp st and High st
Athenæum (The), Loch st
Bacon, James, Loch st
Balfour, Adam, carpenter, William st
Baldwin, Mark, Victoria hotel, High st
Bank of New South Wales ; Chas. Stewart, manager, Ford st
Bank of Australasia ; Edward Morah, manager, Ford st
Bank of Victoria, Ford st ; A. K. Sheppard, manager
Barker, Chas., storeman, Ford st
Batchelor, C. John, news agent, Last st
Bashgate, Thos., labourer, William st
Beechworth Gaol, Sydney road ; J. B. Castilan, governor
Beechworth Grammar School ; John H. Cuzner, principal Church School
Belton, Edward James, billiard marker, Ford st
Berry, Geo. R., receiver and paymaster, Camp st
Bishop, Jos. E., wheelwright, New Town
Booking office Melbourne coaches ; H. W. Peel, agent, Ford st
Borcham, Francis, gunsmith, Camp st

Bowman, J. J., barrister, Finch st
Bradney, Rev. M. W., minister Independent Church, Last st
Bradstick, Thos., High st
Brett, Josiah, veterinary surgeon, Black Springs
Brett, W. G., sheriff, Sydney road
Bromley, Geo., Imperial hotel, High st
Brooke, Edward, chemist and druggist, Ford st
Brown, John, hairdresser, &c., Ford st
Bunster, Wm., clerk, Ford st
Burcham, Anstin, miller, New Town
Carew, John, shoemaker, Camp st
Carroll, Wm., wardsman, Church st
Cassidy, John, labourer, New Town
Clark, David, constable, Finch st
Clarke, John S., Star Commercial hotel, Ford st
Clark, Robert, grocer and wine and spirit merchant, Ford st
Clark, Robert, carpenter, High st
Cleary, Michael, labourer, High st
Clemenger, Henry, storekeeper, Ford st
Clifford, James, carpenter, Last st
Coe, John, architect and surveyor, Last st
Collier and Lawrence, saddlers, Ford st
Common School No. 94 : Wm. Austen, master ; Mrs. Austen, mistress ; Joseph Maloney, assistant teacher
Common School, Loch st
Concannon, Henry, carpenter, Loch st
Coulsbee, John, butcher, Ford st

Connolly, J., Shamrock hotel, Camp st
Connolly, Michael, coach proprietor, Finch street
Constitution office, Camp st
Cope, Judge, Kars st
Cost, J., proprietor of saw mills, High st
Craddock, Francis, constable, Last st
Crawford, Nain, coach proprietor, Ford st
Crouch, Joseph, miner, High st
Crawford and Connolly, coach proprietors and livery stable keepers
Cronsligham, Robt., Loch st
Cuningham, James, ironmonger, Carrick vale
Cunningham, W., butcher, High st
Cunningham, R. L., ironmonger, Ford st
Cuzner, J. H., Belle Vue House, Church street
Davidson, Andrew, carpenter, Kars st
Davis, Richd., assistant master Beechworth Grammar School, Last st
Davis, —, miner, Finch st
Dalton, Joseph P., baker, Finch st
Dalziel, Thos., surveyor, William st
Dammian and Raicke, tobacconists, Ford street
Dawson, James, draper, Ford st
Deutschman, J., and Co., importers, High street
Devonshire, Richard, carpenter, William street
Dodd, Matthew, farmer, New Town
Donovan, Timothy, labourer, Church st
Dooley, Richard, mason, Church st
Douglas, Richard, tinsmith, High st
Douglas, Richard, tinsmith, Ford st
Doyle, —, *Ovens and Murray Advertiser* office, Beechworth
Doyle, John, stonecutter, Finch st
Drung, Patrick, constable, Last st
Drury, Arthur, clerk of courts office, Ford st
Drury, Arthur, clerk, Finch st
Duff, Kennedy, mail guard, Finch st
Duncan, Gordon, storekeeper, Ford st
Duncan, —, ironfounder, New Town
Duncan, Wm., painter and paperhanger, Ford st
Dunn, Wm., tailor, Ford st
Dunn, James, labourer, Ford st
Dunn, E. H., Loch st
Durnam, Patrick, labourer, Last st
Dwyer, Patrick, mail guard, Loch st
Dyer, Alfred, brewer, Church st
Dyer, Wm. H., brewer, Camp st
Edwards' mill, William st
Edwards, Henry, Ovens brewery, Last st
Electric Telegraph office, Ford st ; R. B. Hodson, manager
Evans, Henry, storekeeper, Camp st
Evans, Henry, grocer, Loch st
Eveleigh, J. J., storekeeper, Camp st
Fawkner, Geo., baker and confectioner, Ford st and New Town

Fairbank, James, labourer, Last st
Ferguson, Mitchell, clerk, Lorb st
Fiddes, Donald, contractor, Finch st
Fiddes, James, carpenter, Ford st
Fiddes, Donald, builder and contractor, Ford st
Finch, Richard, clothier and outfitter, Ford st
Fitzgerald, Martin, publican, Church st
Fisher, J. D., Commercial hotel, Ford st
Fletcher, Donald, M.R.C., High st
Fletcher, John, bootmaker, High st
Flood, Charles, tailor, Camp st
Foreman and Co., ironmongers, Ford st
Foster, W. H., Prince of Wales hotel, High st
Fox, Henry Tregellis, surgeon, Camp st
Gammon, Geo., druggist, Ford st
Gorrod, Geo., waiter, Camp st
Garnett, John Cope, newspaper editor, Last st
Grant, W. H., warden, Ford st
Gannt, W. H., police magistrate, Camp st
Geddes, Wm, chemist, Last st
Geddes, Wm., chemist and druggist, Camp st
Giffard, Edward, miner, High st
Gilman, John, tailor, Ford st
Gill, Christopher, Wooragee hotel
Gillan, John, tailor, Finch st
Gladon, Charles, bootmaker, Camp st
Glen, John, engineer, Finch st
Glover, William, boot and shoe maker, Camp st
Glass, —, bootmaker, Finch st
Goodwin, Geo., watchmaker, Ford st
Goodman, Chas., watchmaker and jeweller, Ford st
Graham and Wilson, produce merchants Ford st
Gray and Co., H., auctioneers, Ford st
Gregory, John, storeman, Last st
Greig and Wilson, contractors and builders, Finch st
Gregory, John, turnkey, Last st
Grennis, John, boot and shoe maker, New Town
Griffiths, Louis, contractor, Finch st
Grogan, Patrick, stonemason, Ford st
Gruber, Robt., storekeeper, Camp st
Haig, Alex., gardener, Finch st
Haig, Thomas, saddler, Ford st
Haines, —, drover, Last st
Hall, Alzerno, photographer, Ford st
Hamel, James, carpenter, High st
Hamill, James, cooper, High st
Hamilton, Wm., Finch st
Hanzard, Bamber, gardener, Finch st
Hancen, Thomas, carpenter, High st
Harper, Edward W., plasterer, Finch st
Hartnell, Timothy, trooper, Finch st
Haynes, Mrs., ladies' seminary, Finch st
Henderson, Mrs., William st
Higgins, Chas., saddler, Loch st

Higgins, A., grocer, Finch st
Higgins, —, storekeeper, Camp st
Hodson, R. B., manager electric telegraph, Ford st
Hogg, Richard, gardener, Loch st
Hoskins, J. H., New Town
Howard, W. C., bookseller and stationer, Ford st
Hughes, John, Church st
Hughes, Alexander, miner, Ford st
Hughes, J. K, accountant, Church st
Hume, Edward, carpenter, Finch st
Hunt, Thomas, nurseryman, gardener, and seedsman, Ford st and High st
Hunter, Roger, carpenter, High st
Hyndman, W. M., agent Oriental Bank Corporation, Ford st
Ingram, James, bookseller, stationer, and seedsman, Camp st
Independent Church, Loch st ; Rev. W. M. Bradney, minister
Jones, J. H., carpenter, High st
Keane, Timothy, Exchange hotel, High street
Kingston, Henry, quartyman, Finch st
Koch, August, butcher, Camp st
Kyle, James, contractor, Loch st
Kyle, James, undertaker, Ford st
Lahey, Nicholas, mason, Loch st
Lampitt. Chas., engineer, Loch st
Leahy, Nicholas, stonemason, Loch st
Lee, James, labourer, Finch st
Lent, Thomas, Loch st
Lemme, Frederick, New Town hotel
Littlewood, H. and J., drapers, Ford st
Lyon, Geo., tobacconist and news agent, Ford st
Manson, John, tailor, Ford st
Manwaring, Wm., detective, Last st
Marshall, H. S., grocer, Ford st
Martin, Patrick, tinsmith, High st
Martin, George C., carrier, Last st
Mason, Geo., carpenter, William st
Masterton, Hamilton, & Co., storekeepers, Ford st
Matthew, Wm., law stationer, Ford st
Mayhew, Geo., compositor, Loch st
Malosch, Catherine, butcher, New Town
Melrose, —, Loch st
Melman, John, upholsterer, Ford st
Merton, Richard H., Metropolitan hotel, Camp st
McCleery, Alex., commercial traveller, Finch st
McDonald, R. W., baker and flour merchant, New Town
McKee, Hugh, bricklayer, Loch st
McKenzie, Robert, storekeeper, New Town
McLean, Alexander, coach builder, Ford street
McMillan, Alex., clerk, Loch st
Middlemiss, Mrs., Finch st
Miller, J. G., groom, Ford st
Moore, Wm., courtkeeper, Kars st

Morrah, F. W., manager Bank of Australasia, Ford st
Morris, Henry, district surveyor, William street
Morrison, A. M., and Co., grocers, New Town
Morris, David, secretary to Hospital, Kars street
Morton, Frederick, solicitor, Church st
Muirhead, George, tailor, Finch st
Murray, John, labourer, Last st
Nankervis, Thomas, coach driver, Finch street
Nelson, F., Finch st
Nenber, W. H., school, Finch st
Newson, Wm., Empire hotel, Camp st
Newton, J., bootmaker, Finch st
Nixon, Hugh, commission agent, Sydney road
Noble, Mrs., fancy repository, Ford st
O'Brien, Joseph, wardsman, Church st
O'Brien, Frederick, draper's assistant, Ford st
O'Connor, Felix, trooper, Last st
Oke, Charles, printer, Last st
O'Keef, Michael, engine driver, Last st
O'Neill, Peter, labourer, Last st
Oriental Bank Corporation; W. M. Hyndman, agent, Ford st
Ovens Tannery Company; Todd and Hallahan, Ford st
Ovens Hardware Company, general ironmongers, Ford st
Ovens and Murray Advertiser office, Ford street
Ovens Hospital, Church st
Palmer, Alex. S., bank clerk, Finch st
Paton, Ninin, ironmonger's assistant, Ford street
Peterson, Mrs., Loch st
Phelan, John, messenger, High st
Phillips, Wm., Temple Bar hotel
Police Court and Police Station, Ford st
Post Office, corner Ford st
Pratten, Thos., storekeeper, New Town
Proctor, Frederick A., clerk, Loch st
Presbyterian Church, Sydney road ; Rev. J. K. McMillan, minister
Ramsay, P. D., wine and spirit merchant, Ford st
Ransom, Robt., Albion hotel, Ford st
Raphael Brothers, tobacconists, Ford st
Rath, T., blacksmith, Camp st
Ray, Franklyn B., clerk, Camp st
Rees, Geo., publican, Camp st
Renehan, Joseph, bootmaker, High st
Richmond, John, draper, Ford st
Richter, Augustus, watchmaker and jeweller, Ford st
Robinson, George, painter and glazier, Ford st
Robinson, Henry, coachbuilder, High st
Roche, Jeremiah, labourer, Church st
Rogers, Alex., iron and brass founder

Rogers, Edward, publican, High st
Row, Wm., contractor, Last st
Ruddach, Wallace H., Sportsman's Arms, Ford st
Rundle, Sydney H., draper and outfitter, Ford st
Russom, E. J., sodawater and cordial manufacturer, Loch st
Rutledge, Adam, constable, Finch st
Rutherford, John R., contractor, Last st
Ruxton, Henry W., professor of music, Last st
Ryan, Bridget, storekeeper, Ford st
Sawer, Charles, tailor, Camp st
Salet, Charles, watchmaker, Camp st
Schlichtweg, Wilhelm, tailor and wine grower, Ford st
Scaborne, Harry, clerk, Last st
Searle, Geo., newspaper editor, Last st
Sengleman and Riedle, furniture warehouse
Shedden, John, carpenter, Last st
Sheppard, A. K., manager Bank of Victoria, Ford st
Slater, Alvara L., surgeon, Church st
Smith, Mrs., laundress, Loch st
Smith, Sydney, manager of Homeward Bound Quartz Mining and Crushing Company, Rocky Point
Smith, Agnes, storekeeper, Camp st
Smith, Wm., cattle dealer, Finch st
Soulby, W. T., London tavern, Camp st
Spearing, James H. B., bookkeeper, Commercial hotel, Ford st
Spencer, Edwd., miner, New Town
Spiers, Robert B., carpenter, New Town
Steed, R. H., draper, Last st
Steel, Wm., boot and shoe maker, Ford st
Stephen, George Milner, barrister, Camp st
Straughair and Duncan, Beechworth Foundry, New Town
Stevens, John, builder and contractor, Finch st
Stevens, Mrs., laundress, Loch st
Stewart, Charles, manager Bank of New South Wales, Ford st
Stewart, Alex., draftsman, Camp st
St. George's Hall; proprietor, W. T. Soulby
Stillard, James, carter, High st
St. Leger, F., clerk, Ford st
Summerville, Mrs., Loch st
Taylor, R., and Co., wine and spirit merchants, Ford st
Taylor, J., storekeeper, Last st

Taylor, John, crockery and furniture warehouse
Telford, Wm., auctioneer, Ford st
Thomson, Wm. J., wholesale confectioner, Camp st
Thomson, Alexander, Oriental hotel, New Town
Thornton, Robt., restaurant, Camp st
Tierney, R. W., Catholic Presbytery, Finch st
Tilsley, James, engineer, William st
Todd, J., groom, Finch st
Townsend, A. M., dentist, Camp st
Tozé, Hung, government Chinese interpreter, Finch st
Turner, Wm., watchmaker and jeweller, Camp st
Turner, A. M., William st
Tyrer, J. H., clerk Warden's office, Ford street
Van Orton, Francis, timber merchant, High st
Warner, Thomas, butcher, Camp st
Warner, James, butcher, Camp st
Warren, John, Loch st
Warren, Richard, printer, Ford st
Warden's office, Ford st
Watts, J., plumber and glazier, Ford st
Waugh, Thomas, Harp of Erin hotel, Church st
Webster, —, water carrier, Last st
Webster, James, traveller, Camp st
Welch, —, superintendent; residence, High st
White, Mrs., William st
Whitenay, M. E., dressmaker, Finch st
Williams, A. P., draper, Ford st
Williams, A. P., Finch st
Wilson, Robt., messenger, Ford st
Wilson, David, carpenter, Last st
Williams, Craven, baker, Finch st
Witt, O. K., hay and corn store, New Town
Witt, Wm., chemist and druggist, and insurance agent, Ford st
Woollecke, Charles, cabinetmaker, New Town
Wright, Thos. H., clerk, Last st
Young, Robt., boot and shoemaker, Camp street
Young, J., boot and shoemaker, Camp st
Young, Thomas, solicitor, Ford st
Younger, Geo., house steward (hospital), Church st
Zincke and Martin, solicitors, Camp st

KILMORE ALPHABETICAL DIRECTORY.

1866-67.

Abbott, Geo., grocer, Sydney st
Ambrose, Mrs., near racecourse, Gibb st
Anderson, Robt., labourer, George st
Arcus Bros., grocers, Sydney st
Arcus, —, storekeeper, Albert st
Arkler, Joseph, quarryman, Clark st
Ballie, J., coachdriver, Sydney st
Baker, Thomas, carpenter, Gibbs st
Ball, John, mason, Sydney st
Barfoot, Henry, stationer and confectioner, Sydney st
Barnett, James, miller, Victoria st
Barry, —, clerk of court; residence, Hamilton st
Barrett, Wm., baker, Sydney st
Batterbury, Edwin, labourer, Powlett st
Barkley, Donkin, labourer, George st
Beavan and Stillman, chemists and druggists, Sydney st
Beagan, James, bootmaker, Albert st
Bert, Henry, labourer, Albert st
Biddle, Joseph, bootmaker, Sydney st
Biers, Henry, Powlett st
Bindley, Frank L., surgeon, Powlett st
Boroughs, M., stonemason, Victoria st
Bossence, Thos., undertaker and cabinetmaker, Sydney st
Botanical Gardens, suburbs
Brady, John, labourer, Gibbs st
Branigan, Rev. Michael, Sutherland st
Brenan, Jeremiah, labourer, Union st
Brien, Cornelius, labourer, George st
Bristow, H. B., postmaster, Powlett st

Bruce, M. J., Golden Padlock Ironmongery store, Sydney st
Bryant, —, coach painter, Hamilton st
Buckland, Jas., Sutherland st
Canlin, Mrs., Hamilton st
Canlin, James, labourer, Hamilton st
Carr, —, blacksmith, Gibbs st
Carroll, E., hairdresser, Sydney st
Catholic School; John C. Hayes, master, Miss Hayes and Miss Reilly, assistant teachers
Catholic Church, Sutherland st
Cavine, Edward Moore, land agent, Victoria st
Clack, Joseph, labourer, Bourke st
Cleak, Jonathan, carpenter, Powlett st]
Clark, Lucy, Powlett st
Clare, Joseph, Fitzroy st
Coghill, Thos., town crier, Victoria st
Colonial Bank of Australasia; Matthew Hayes, manager, Sydney st
Cole, Hannah, crockery and fancy store, Sydney st
Collard, J. S., miller, Bourke st
Collins, Mrs., Sydney st
Common School, Powlett st; J. W. Kerr, master
Cook, Geo., blacksmith, Melbourne st
Cook, Fredk., coachbuilder; residence, Hamilton st
Corry, Michael, labourer, Powlett st
Council Chambers and Town Clerk's Office, Sydney st

Court House, Powlett st
Couston, James, bootmaker, Sydney st
Crabtree, Henry, tinsmith, Powlett st
Crane, Thos., carrier, Powlett st
Craine, S., carrier, suburbs
Crewin, P., dairyman, Sydney st
Cuttletoo, R., near Racecourse
Davis, Mrs., Fitzroy st
Day, Patrick P., Kilmore flour mills, Sydney st
Deane, Thos., storeman, Albert st
Dobinson, W. P., draper, &c., Sydney st
Duffy, Wm., Victoria st
Duff, —, bootmaker, Sydney st
Dumphy, L., Kilmore restaurant, Powlett street
Dunbar, Wm., labourer, Union st
Dwyer, Wm., blacksmith, Sydney st
Dwyer, Edward, boarding house, Sydney street
Dwyer, Mrs., Gibbs st
Easdale, Robt., wheelwright, Albert st
Edgar, Robt., plumber and tinsmith, Sydney st
English, John, labourer, Mitchell st
Fahay, Richd, wigger, Sydney st
Fitzpatrick, James, farmer, Sutherland st
Flanaghan, John, labourer, Albert st
Fleury, James, architect, Sydney st
Flynn, —, suburbs
Fox, —, bricklayer, Sydney st
Fraser, John, labourer, Union st
Franklyn, Richd., labourer, Union st
Franklyn, Thomas, shepherd, Victoria st
Fraser, C. R. W., Oriental Bank, Sydney street
Free Press office; Thomas Hunt, printer and publisher
Freer, John, Victoria st
Fyun and Co., maltsters and brewers, Sydney st
Gibbins, Wm., civil engineer, Mitchell st
Gibbons, John, labourer, Albert st
Gibbons, —, engineer, Albert st
Gilman, John Hill, Albert st
Glover, Peter, bootmaker, Sydney st
Grace, —, solicitor, Sydney st
Grant, —, Sydney st
Green, John, storekeeper, Powlett st
Griffin, John, publican, Sydney st
Hall, Rev. O. F., pastor Methodist Church, Bourke st
Hamilton, George, carter, Andrew st
Hammond, J., livery stables, Sydney st
Hammond, John, Victoria st
Hanlan, S., carpenter, Gibbs st
Harris, H. P., and Co., storekeepers, Sydney st
Hartnell, Wm., storekeeper, Somerset house, Sydney st
Hatton, Richd., carrier, suburbs
Helms, Chas., tobacconist, Sydney st
Heron, Robt., governor of gaol
Heron, Mrs., matron of gaol

Hickey, Patrick, bootmaker, Sydney st
Holding, Henry, gardener, Andrew st
Howden, John, blacksmith, Hamilton st
Hodges, James, tailor, Sydney st
Hudson, Geo., Melbourne st
Hudson, Geo., hay and corn store and general provision merchant, Sydney st
Hume, Mrs., Albert st
Hunt, Ann, Sydney st
Hunt, John, cooper, Sydney st
Hunt, Thomas, general printer, Sydney st
Hunt, John, turnkey of gaol
Jamieson, Robt., farmer, Sutherland st
Keeton, —, constable, Victoria st
Kelley, Matthew, Kilmore inn, Sydney st
Kennedy, Geo., blacksmith, Sydney st
Kenrick, John, storeman, Sydney st
Kerr, Wm., contractor, Fitzroy st
Keys, J. B., and Co., chemists and druggists, Sydney st
Keys, J. B., Dalhousie hotel
Kilmore Hospital, near the Reservoir
Kilmore Gaol, Sutherland st
Kinnear, Geo., saddle and harness maker, Sydney st
Kilmore Water Reserve and Dam, Camp hill
Kyle, Wm., butcher, Sydney st
Lansley, Geo., smith, farrier, and wheelwright, Sydney st
Lansley, Thomas, blacksmith, Victoria st
Lee, James, brickmaker, Albert st
Leahy, Michael, blacksmith, Sydney st
Linton, —, Albert st
Lord, Thomas, cutler, Albert st
Lucas, Samuel, brickmaker, Sydney st
Lyons, James, contractor, Hamilton st
Macarthy, Rev. Francis, Sutherland st
Maguire, Patrick, labourer, Sydney st
Malkin, —, labourer, Victoria st
Maloney, Edwd., storekeeper, Powlett st
Martin, Thomas, labourer, George st
Masterton, James, labourer, Victoria st
Matches, Henry, Gibbs st
Maxwell, Mrs., Manse, Fitzroy st
McClellan, P., Dunrobin Castle hotel, Sydney st
McCloud, Mrs., widow, George st
McCloud, —, labourer, Victoria st
McDonald, Mrs., Fitzroy st
McDonald, Patrick, labourer, George st
McDonnell, Murdock, labourer, Sutherland st
McDonnell, John, carrier, Sutherland st
McGregor, Donald, watchmaker, Sydney street
McKay, A. M., resident magistrate; office, Camp hill
McKay, Margaret, Albert st
McKenzie, John, draper, Albert st
McKenzie, John, squatter, Sydney st
McKenzie, John, draper, Sydney st
McKey, Wm., hotel keeper, Sydney st
McLeod, Kenny, quarryman, Clark st

McMahon and Kyle, butchers, Powlett st
McMann, Thomas, labourer, Lonsdale st
Meade, Thomas de C., solicitor, Sydney st ; residence, Sutherland st
McWeney, —, mail guard, Hamilton st
Mechanics' Institute, Powlett st
Methodist Church, Bourke st
Miller, Robert, carrier, Sutherland st
Milligan. —, carpenter, Victoria st
Moodie, James, Powlett st
Moore, Thomas, chief turnkey of gaol
Morgan, Richard, Red Lion hotel, Sydney street
Morrissey, Bryan, butcher, Fitzroy st
Morrissey, Thomas, farmer, Sydney st
Moyle, Granville B., gardener, Gibbs st
Mulcahey, J., bootmaker, Sydney st
Munro, Hector, schoolmaster, Piper st
Murphy, Julia, storekeeper, Powlett st
Murray, Matthew, Royal Oak hotel, Sydney st
Murray, Alex., mason, Albert st
Nelson, Mrs., Albert st
Nelson, Eliza, widow, Powlett st
Newton, Edward, Fitzroy st
Nicholas, W., Police office, Camp hill
Nicholson, Dr., coroner, Victoria st
O'Brien, Patrick, clerk, Powlett st
O'Connor, Maurice, labourer, Gibbs st
O'Connor, John, solicitor, Sydney st
O'Connor, Patrick, contractor, Union st
O'Dea, J., labourer, suburbs
Office of Survey and Lands, suburbs
O'Grady, P., tobacco manufactory, Sydney st
O'Meara, Mrs., Hamilton st
Osborn, James W., auctioneer, Sydney st
Ostian, Thomas, labourer, Victoria st
Parker, Geo., engineer and brass founder, Powlett st
Pateos, James, labourer, George st
Payne, —, hawker, Sydney st
Percival. Wm., labourer, Bourke st
Perrett, Wm., engineer, Clarke st
Post office, Powlett st
Poulton, John, saddler, Melbourne st
Presbyterian Church, Hamilton st
Proudfoot, James, mason, George st
Rawdon, Mrs., laundress, Sydney st
Rawlings, John, engineer, Melbourne st
Reilly, John S., Sydney st
Reddy, M., labourer, Sydney st
Roberts, Thomas F., brewer, Sydney st
Rohde, H., fruiterer and tobacconist, Sydney st
Richards, —, Fitzroy st
Ruthven, James, carrier, Victoria st
Ryan, Charles, labourer, Fitzroy st

Ryan, John, draper, Sydney st
Sawell, W. L., auctioneer, Sydney st
Scudamore. George, painter, Fitzroy st
Seymour, Jerry. labourer, Union st
Shadwick, —, carter, Fitzroy st
Shea, Mrs., Lonsdale st
Shee, Catherine, Powlett st
Singleton, Rev. Wm., Church of England minister, Church st
Skane, —, Fitzroy st
Smeaton, Wm., blacksmith, Piper st
Smith, Thomas, labourer, Fitzroy st
Soraghan, Francis, Coach and Horses hotel, Powlett st
Stafford, Wm., turnkey of gaol
Staines, John, carpenter, Sydney st
Stapleton, M., boarding house, Powlett st
Stewart, Alexander, carpenter, Andrew st
Stewart, Mrs., Fitzroy st
Stewart, Geo., contractor, Fitzroy st
Stillman, Arthur, chemist, Fitzroy st
Stimson, Leonard, grocer, Sydney st
Sugden, Alfred, tanner, Sydney st
Sutherland, farmer, suburbs
Taylor Brothers, drapers, Sydney st
Telegraph office, Powlett st
Thomas, James, Bull and Mouth hotel
Thomas's stables and corn store, Sydney street
Todd, J., boarding house, Sydney st
Tracy, Dennis, labourer, Sydney st
Trainor, John, Hibernian hotel, Sydney st
Turnbull, Mrs., dressmaker, Sutherland st
Twigg and Connor, solicitors, Sydney st
Twigg, James W., solicitor, Fitzroy st
Tyre, —, constable, Camp hill
Usher, Rev. Mr., Wesleyan minister, Piper st
Valentine, —, farmer, suburbs
Vanbeerns, H., timber merchant and ironmonger, Sydney st
Wakelan, —, Lonsdale st
Warren, James, watchmaker and pawnbroker, Sydney st
Welland and Sons, grocers, Sydney st
Whelan, John, labourer, Gibbs st
Whitelaw, John, contractor, Hamilton st
Wiesel, John P., undertaker, Sydney st
Williams, Alexander, boarding house, Sydney st
Wilson, Henry, carter, Victoria st
Wilson, John, labourer, Albert st
Wood, Mrs., Sydney st
Woodward, Edward, proprietor *Kilmore Examiner*, residence, Gibbs st
Woodwood, E., *Kilmore Examiner* office, Sydney st
Young, Thos. B., storekeeper, Powlett st

WANGARATTA ALPHABETICAL DIRECTORY.

1866-67.

Abbott, Wm., miller, Ely st
Adams, Robt., labourer, Murphy st
Aitken, John, banker, Faithfull st
Allen and Baldry, Wangaratta flour mills, Templeton st
Allen, Joseph, labourer, Murphy st
Ashworth, Samuel, carpenter, Murphy st
Amery, Thomas, carpenter, Templeton st
Bailey, Thos., constable, Reid st
Baldry, Chas., miller, Templeton st
Bank of New South Wales; Thos. Bently, manager, Faithfull st
Banks, John, sawyer, Baker st
Barr, Abraham, tinsmith, Murphy st
Barrow, Joseph, brickmaker, Warby st
Batchelor, Edmond, farmer, One Mile
Bayly, Albert Chas., auctioneer, Murphy street
Bell, James, labourer, Rowan st
Bentley, Thomas, Wangaratta
Bevan, Thos., sawyer, King st
Derrigen, Patk., blacksmith, Ryley st
Bickerton, Wm., commission agent, Murphy st
Blake, James, publican, Ryley st
Boyd, Wm., tanner, Templeton st
Boyd and Lelshinan, tanners, Templeton street
Bradley, Richd., groom, Rowan st
Brett, James, farmer, Murphy st
Brockman, Wm., miller, Ryley st
Bullwant, Thomas G., saddle and harness maker, Murphy st

Burke, Edmond, butcher, Murphy st
Burrows, John, North Wangaratta flour mills, North Wangaratta
Burrows, Fredk., baker and confectioner, Murphy st
Burton, J. W., veterinary forge, Roy st
Caher, James, labourer, Mackay st
Cavanagh, Hugh, general storekeeper, Murphy st
Constable, Wm. W., grocer, Templeton st
Colvin, Andw., horsebreaker, Templeton
Coombes, Wm., brickmaker, suburbs
Crowley, John, tailor, Murphy st
Crisp, Amos, horsebreaker, Templeton st
Cusack, Michael, butcher, suburbs
Cusack, Thos., publican, Murphy st
Crock, Henry, farmer, North Wangaratta
Crockett, Walter H., farmer, North Wangaratta
D'Abel, Geo., carpenter, Faithfull st
Dale, Wm., butcher, Murphy st
Daley, Patk., labourer, Templeton st
Day, Joseph T., carpenter, Gray st
Deware, David, carpenter, Ford st
Dispatch office ; John Rowan, publisher
Dives, Wm., labourer, Reid st
Dixon, James, general storekeeper, Ryley street
Dobbyn, Wm. A., surgeon and coroner.
Duncan, Chas., fruiterer, Murphy st
Dunlop, Robt., storekeeper, Murphy st
Duchatel, J. C., Shakespeare hotel, Faithfull st

Dunkley, John, farmer, North Wangaratta
Dunkley, Thos., farmer, North Wangaratta
Dunn, Patk., farmer, North Wangaratta
Edmondson, Geo., publican, Faithfull st.
Edwards, Wm., Australasia hotel, North Wangaratta
Electric Telegraph office, and Post office; Wm. Shields, manager, Murphy st
Evans, D. H., miller, residence, Roy st
Evans, D. H. and Co., Victorian steam mills, Murphy st
Federal Standard office; Wm. Bickerton agent, Murphy st
Fennell, Louis, wheelwright, Murphy st
Ford, Chas., chemist, Murphy st
Gibson, A. M., general storekeeper, Murphy st
Gill, James, farmer, North Wangaratta
Gillen, Rev. Geo., Catholic minister; residence, South Wangaratta
Grant, Duncan, farmer, North Wangaratta
Grant, John, builder and timber merchant, Murphy st
Grey, James, schoolmaster, Faithfull st
Good, James, labourer, Ryley st
Goring, Ed., labourer, Ryley st
Gammage, Thomas, farmer, North Wangaratta
Hall, John, butcher, Murphy st
Hall, John, Dewdrop Inn, Three-mile ck
Hallett, Dr., Ryley st
Harris, Geo., groom, Reid st
Harrison, Wm., bailiff, Ovens st
Heach, Frank, butcher, Murphy st
Horsefall, Abraham, farmer, North Wangaratta
Howard, Ed. C., coach proprietor, Murphy street
Hughes, Wm., wheelwright, North Wangaratta
Isset, David, butcher, Murphy st
Jarvis, Robt. W., labourer, Ovens st
Johnstone, John, labourer, Templeton st
Jones, John, farmer, North Wangaratta
Jones, Henry, boot and shoemaker, Murphy st
Kantor, Simon, storekeeper, Murphy st
Kelloe, Thomas, labourer, Gray st
Kelley, Francis, farmer, North Wangaratta
Kerr, John, farmer, North Wangaratta
Ketz, Henry, Royal hotel, Murphy st
Koch, Frank, brickmaker, North Wangaratta
Larkings, Thomas, storekeeper, Rowan st
Laffin, Nicholas, policeman, North Wangaratta
Lean, Gilbert, labourer, Ovens st
Leigh, Henry B., clerk, North Wangaratta
Leishman, Thomas, tanner, Templeton st
Lomas, Benj., surveyor, Templeton st

Lucas, Edward, general storekeeper, Albion house, Reid st
Maloney, Patrick, labourer, Rowan st
McCullum, John, gardener, Docker st
McDonald, Wm., farmer, North Wangaratta
McDonald, Patrick, Wangaratta hotel, North Wangaratta
McDonald, James, labourer, North Wangaratta
McMullin, Dr. J. K., surgeon, Murphy st
McKenna, Patrick, publican, North Wangaratta
McEntrum, James, publican, North Wangaratta
Meyers, Charles, labourer, North Wangaratta
Mitchell, Frank, Royal Victoria hotel, Faithfull st
Millard, Thomas, carter, Faithfull st
Montgomery, James, labourer, Ryley st
Moody, Wm., carter, Templeton st
Moore, John, farmer, suburbs
Mottershead, Joseph, carpenter, Ryley st
Munro, Anne, bookseller and stationer, Reid st
Murdoch, Wm., Commercial hotel, Murphy st
Norton, John, solicitor, Reid st
Norton, Samuel, vinegrower, Roy st
Noonan, Mitchel, labourer, Ovens st
O'Halloran, Patrick, farmer, North Wangaratta
O'Neill, Daniel, labourer, Docker st
Osbaldiston, Samuel, general storekeeper, Murphy st
Ovens and Murray Advertiser office, Murphy st
Ovens Bridge Toll; Patrick Naughten, collector
Painter, William, Sydney hotel, Templeton street
Palpy, Wm., hairdresser, Murphy st
Patterson, Geo., labourer, Templeton st
Philips, Joseph, farmer, One Mile
Pierce, Isaac, groom, King st
Police Station, Murphy st
Ponchard, Francis, butcher, Gray st
Porter, Ladock, town clerk, Murphy st
Powell, G. T., bootmaker, Faithfull st
Rowan, John, printer and publisher, Reid street
Rundle, Charles A., chemist and druggist, Murphy st
Ryley, Francis, engineer, Ovens st
Sales, Thos., blacksmith, Murphy st
Salisbury, S., farmer, suburbs
Savage, Patrick, solicitor, Murphy st
Sayer, Benjamin, Council Club hotel, Wangaratta
Shadforth, Robt. W., police magistrate, Murphy st
Shaw, Joseph, bricklayer, King st
Sheppard, Thos. C., baker, Murphy st

Shields, Wm., postmaster and manager electric telegraph, Murphy st
Sloam, James, accountant, South Wangaratta
Smith, William, butcher, Murphy st
Snelling, W. M., watchmaker and tobacconist, Murphy st
Steel, Daniel, labourer, Cusack st
Stead, Joseph, sawyer, King st
Sutton, Wm., carter, Cusack st
Swan, Andrew, farmer, Faithfull st
Swan, James, blacksmith, Faithfull st
Tate, W. P., bootmaker, Hoy st
Thomson, Wm., bootmaker, Hoy st
Thompson, J. P., carpenter, Murphy st
Tutty, John, Shamrock hotel and store, North Wangaratta
Tripp, Joseph, labourer, Cusack st
Walles, John, storekeeper, Murphy st
Wall, John, tailor, Templeton st
Ward, Louis McDermot, brewer, Templeton st
Ward, Wm., gardener, North Wangaratta
Wheeler, Richard, bootmaker, Murphy st
White, Albert, brickmaker, Cusack st
White, Wm., labourer, Docker st
Whitlock, Henry, Baker st
Whitlock, Miss, ladies' seminary, Baker st
Williams, James, carter, One Mile
Willis, W'm., saddler, Murphy st
Wilson, Wm., newsagent, Murphy st
Woodhead, Joseph B., tailor and draper, Reid st

ALBURY ALPHABETICAL DIRECTORY.

1866-7.

Atkins, James, Smollett st
Austin, Thomas, Townsend st
Babbington, Geo., Townsend st
Babbington, Daniel, Townsend st
Badior, Albert, Townsend st
Baier, John, Kiewa st
Ballantyne, David, Smollett st
Bank of New South Wales; John Wm. Jones, manager
Barber, Henry, Kiewa st
Beddington, Dunn, blacksmith, Townsend street
Blackmore, Samuel F., Dean st
Bonsfield, Wm., Dean st
Brooks, Geo., printer, Dean st
Bullock, Thomas, Dean st
Burnes, Wm. Hume, drug store, Townsend st
Burnes, Wm., Townsend st
Campbell, James, Townsend st
Carolan, Patrick, Townsend st
Carolan, Wm., Townsend st
Chant, Henry, Townsend st
Clarke, Edward, Townsend st
Costin, Robt., Kiewa st
Curran, Ernest A., Kiewa st

Daniels, Nicholas, Townsend st
Darby, Geo. J., Royal hotel, Albury
Davies, Isaac, Townsend st
Day, Geo. P., Albury flour mills, Albury
Day, Geo. P., Dean st
Dayley, Dennis, Kiewa st
Deverill, R. W., Dean st
Donevan, Timothy, Townsend st
Dunn, Samuel, Townsend st
Edmonson, Wm. M., Townsend st
Eisenhardt, Henry, Kiewa st
Evans, Alfred, general store, Dean st
Evans, Edwin, Kiewa st
Evans, Joseph, Smollett st
Evans, Wm. B., Townsend st
Fallon, James Thomas, storekeeper, Kiewa st
Farmer, Chas., Smollett st
Field, Thos., Horse and Jockey hotel, Townsend st
Fleming, Geo. T., Dean st
Flynn, Patrick, Smollett st
French, Wm. B., Kiewa st
Gader, Thomas B., Townsend st
Gible, Joseph, Townsend st
Girdler, Richard P., Townsend st
Gray, John C., Kiewa st
Green, Wm., Townsend st
Groman, Theodore, Townsend st
Halbert, John, Kiewa st
Hall, Norton, Medical Hall, Kiewa st
Hily, Patrick, Townsend st
House, Chas., Kiewa st
Hosing, Fredk., watchmaker and jeweller, Kiewa st
Jennings, John, Kiewa st
Jones, Wm., Dean st
Jones, John Walker, manager Bank New South Wales, Townsend st
Jones, Lewis, Exchange hotel, Townsend street
Justice, Matthew, tailor, Dean st
Keatinge, Jeffrey J., medical practitioner, Townsend st
Kennedy, Alexander J., Townsend st
Kilfoil, John, Imperial hotel, Townsend st
King, Thomas, butcher, Townsend st
Kralgen, Chas., Dean st
Langeschwordt, August, butcher, Townsend st
Lane, Samuel, fancy repository, Townsend st
Lovett, Geo., Kiewa st
Mackie, Peter, Townsend st
Marden, John, Kiewa st
Mate, J. H., and Co., wholesale store, Townsend st
Mason, Samuel, baker, Townsend st
McCowan, Thomas, Fruit market, Townsend st
McDonald, Hector, Kiewa st
McGinn, Daniel, Townsend st
McGuffin, Elizabeth, milliner, Townsend street

McLennan, Kenneth, storekeeper, Kiewa street
Meighan, John, Kiewa st
Metcalfe, Thos. J., Townsend st
Meyer, Fredk. John, Kiewa st
Mills, Mary Ann, storekeeper, Townsend street
Miller, Walter M., Kiewa st
Mott, G., and Co., Border Post office, Townsend st
Moffitt, John Thomas, Townsend st
Moffitt, Hugh, storekeeper, Kiewa st
Morgan, Thomas, Kiewa st
Morgan, John, Kiewa st
Morgan, Joseph, Kiewa st
Mudge, Samuel, Dean st
Murphy, Charles, boot and shoe warehouse, Kiewa st
Negro, Clement, Empire hotel, Townsend st
Nichols, John, Rose Inn, Kiewa st
Nichols, Robert, Kiewa st
North, Samuel C. V., Kiewa st
O'Brien, Peter, Townsend st
O'Brien, Daniel, Kiewa st
Owen, Robt., Dean st
Paine, John H., Smollett st
Parker, Robt., Kiewa st
Peard, Francis, Dean st
Peard, John, Dean st
Peard, John, Townsend st
Pearce, Wm., Smollett st
Petzold, Alfred, saddler, Townsend st
Poole, John, Kiewa st
Quick, John, Kiewa st
Ran, Henry, Kiewa st
Reinhard, Geo., Townsend st
Robson, Geo., Townsend st
Ross, Alexander, Townsend st
Ross, James, Townsend st
Routh, Joseph, Dean st
Shelling, John, Townsend st
Sherry, Simon, Kiewa st
Simmons, Thomas, Dean st
Skerman, Thomas, Kiewa st
Smith, Edward, Townsend st
Solomon, Lewis, Townsend st
Spurr, Edmonson, Dean st
Stewart, Alexander, Townsend st
Stewart, Hugh, Dean st
Stewart, Wm., Dean st
Stilger, Caspar, Dean st
Stone, Thos. H., Kiewa st
Thomson, Robt., saddler, Townsend st
Thorold, Geo. C., Kiewa st
Toer, Wm., Kiewa st
Waite, Wm., Townsend st
Walker, Arthur, Globe hotel, Kiewa st
White, Aveline, milliner, Townsend st
White, James, Townsend st
Wilkinson, Henry, Kiewa st
Wilson, James, tailor, Townsend st
Wise, Wm., Townsend st
Woods, John, Kiewa st
Wursch, Christian, Dean st

OVENS DISTRICT ALPHABETICAL DIRECTORY,

INCLUDING

Avenel
Beveridge
Broadford
Benalla
Chiltern
Corowa
Donnybrook
Euroa
Heathcote
Pentridge
Pyalong
Rutherglen
Stanley
Seymour
Tallarook
Tarrawingee
Violet Town
Wallan Wallan
Wadonga
Wahgunyah
Yackandandah

1866-67.

AVENEL.

Avenel hotel
Fenton, Samuel, storekeeper
Shelton, Esau, Royal Mail hotel and provision store

BEVERIDGE.

Fletcher, Niel, storekeeper and postmaster

BROADFORD.

Armstrong, Julius
Adams, Francis, squatter, Sunday creek
Burston, Samuel, farmer
Cameron, Donald C., Junction hotel
Duffy, John, farmer
Duffy, James, farmer
Fitzgerald, John, farmer
Ferrel, Joseph M., poundkeeper, Sugar Loaf creek
Hammersley, Wm. E., farmer
Keagle, James, farmer
Maxfield, James, Broadford flour mills
McKenzie, David, farmer
McKenzie, John, farmer
McKay, Duncan, farmer
Purrier and Woolnough, general storekeepers, post office
Ross, Chas., Junction store
Vinge, George, Sunday Creek hotel

BENALLA.

Alkemade, P. and A., storekeepers
Banfield, James, Liverpool Arms
Hoyburd, Geo., brickmaker
Brown, James, farmer
Browne, Edwin
Burns, Wm., bootmaker
Byrne, John, storekeeper
Cain, Daniel, bootmaker
Cain, John, bootmaker
Cherry, Moses

Chiffers, Miss
Clarke, Samuel, storekeeper
Clark, Richard, Black Swan hotel
Clark, Richard, steam flour mills
Cobham, —, superintendent of police
Corp, Thomas
Craven, Marcus, storekeeper
Emes, Robert, butcher
Fawkes, Geo., butcher
Feehan, Daniel, assistant surveyor
Fields, James, labourer
Fleming, Thomas, butcher
Foley, Thomas, labourer
Fraser, J., hay and corn store
Freeman, Rev. John, Church of England minister
Gascoigne, John, painter
Gascoigne, Henry, painter
Gawne, Thomas, bootmaker
Goldburg, Thomas, tailor
Gorden, Wm., saddler
Gorwell, John, storekeeper
Henry, Dr., Medical Hall
Hoskins, —, Royal hotel
Kissick, Evan, bootmaker
Larkin, Mrs.
Low and Martin, Benalla hotel
Lamsden, Thomas, Benalla Dispensary
Lymer, George
Macarthy, Wm., assistant operator electric telegraph
McNally, Matthew, general store
Mann, Richard, plumber and coppersmith
Mason, Robt.
Middleton, Henry, general store
Montford, W. B., clerk Police station
Moorhead, —, storekeeper
Morey, Wm.
New Court House
Nixon, W., Survey Office
O'Leary, Cornelius, bakery
O'Shea, Patrick, lockup keeper
O'Shea, James, bootmaker
Papers, Wm., P.M.
Ride, W., hay and corn store
Sharp, Geo., Commercial hotel
Telegraph Office
Toll bar, W. Stanton, keeper
Whelan, Henry, constable, Police station

CHILTERN.

Bank of Victoria; W. A. Longuehay, agent
Bank of Australasia; J. P. Spence, agent
Beach, John, boot and shoemaker
Beggs, John, Royal hotel
Bennett, John, secretary Athenaeum
Berrigen, Patrick, Empire hotel
Black, James, New Ballarat bakery
Brown, J. K., draper
Bramle, H., boot and shoe store
Bruen, N., shoemaker
Busse, Fredk., Albion hotel

Cameron, Lachlan, miner
Chiltern Athenaeum, Connees st
Crum, Robert, tinsmith
Damm and Haacke, tobacconists
Donelly, J., hairdresser
Duffy, Jane, Telegraph hotel
Ferrier, J. H., ironmonger
Gale, —, tailor
Graham, Robert, bootmaker
Gleeson and Co., butchers
Henry and Co., butchers
Houston, S., bootmaker
Hunter, W. C., bookseller
Hyenga, Wm., storekeeper, Allan's flat
Jager, Adolph, German store
Jones, W., fruiterer
Kavanagh, John, storekeeper
Keller, Geo., storekeeper
Kerr, Adam, saddler
Kilgour, Henry, blacksmith
Laing, David, baker
Lanenstein, H., tailor and draper
Loftus, James, baker
Manson, John, draper
Marum, Thomas, chemist
Maxwell, Wm., draper
McCape, Arthur H., gunmaker
Mein, Thomas K., auctioneer
Mitchell, Henry, storekeeper
McLaughlin, H., furnishing undertaker
Morgan, A., blacksmith
Moss, Joseph, Crown hotel
Murphy, John K., blacksmith
Nicholson, Edward, general storekeeper, &c., Cumberland House
Oreus Hardware Company; C. G. Darvall
Peel, Thomas, Royal Mail hotel and livery stables
Powell, J. Thomas, Golden Ball hotel
Ralph, Geo., butcher
Reese, David, butcher
Rhodes, Daniel, general storekeeper
Roberts, J. S., draper
Robinson, David, Albion hotel
Rogers, Edward, carpenter
Rogers, Mrs. Edward, registry office
Ruppio Brothers, Hotel de Paris
Sheffield and Dunn, carpenters
Smith, Montague George, solicitor
Smith and Houston, timber merchants and builders
Turner, J. W., storekeeper
Weil, James T., assistant storekeeper
Wilberforce, J., Golden Age hotel
Williams, J. H., stationer and seedsman
Williams, Fredk., Commercial hotel

COROWA.

Carr Brothers, general storekeepers
Copeland Brothers, blacksmiths
Elliott, Wm., wheelwright
Hynes, John, Corowa bakery
Martin, W. J., Royal hotel

Stead, Thomas, saddler
Underwood, Henry, Steamboat hotel
Weir, James W., wholesale and retail wine and spirit merchant

DONNYBROOK.

Crichton, John, baker and general storekeeper, Sydney road
Fairley, John, coachbuilder and wheelwright, Sydney road

EUROA.

Benton, Wm., Pilgrim inn
Brockhurst, J., bootmaker
Corran, James, labourer
Deboos, J., Seven Creeks hotel
Maginnis, Hugh, blacksmith
Williams, Edward, Royal Oak hotel

HEATHCOTE.

Adamson, W. G., solicitor, High st
Adams, Edwin, chemist, High st
Borough Chambers, High st
Bolton, Henry, and Co., brewers, Heathcote
Brady, Edward, Emu hotel, High st
Bridget, Mrs., High st
Cameron, Allen, publican, High st
Campbell, James, agent Oriental Bank Corporation, High st
Carkeet, Dr., High st
Catholic Church (St. Mary's), High st
Chapman, J. E., chemist, High st
Clayton, Fanny, High st
Coache, —, trooper, High st
Common School No. 300 ; C. Lawson, master
Connell, James, The Thistle, High st
Connolly, Mrs., High st
County Court, High st
Cox, Richard, contractor, High st
Craven, John, Northumberland Arms, High st
Craven, Thomas, steam sawmills, High st
Crawley, Charles, butcher, High st
Crawley, Mrs., milliner and dressmaker, High st
Cromack, Rev. John, United Methodist Free Church minister, High st
Crowle, James, timber merchant and furnishing ironmonger, High st
Cunningham and Co., Shamrock hotel, High st
Currie, Robert, baker, High st
Dale, Joseph, draper, High st
Dearman, Thomas, revenue inspector, High st
Dougall, John, stationer, High st
Drewett, Thomas, baker, High st
Duncan, Mrs., fancy bazaar, High st
Dunn, —, constable, Heathcote

Emson, John B., miller, Heathcote
English Church ; Rev. Mr. Budd, High st
Etheridge, Chas. E., Lake hotel, High st
Farley, John, Union hotel, High st
Ferguson, J. D., storekeeper, High st
Foam, Daniel, McIvor inn, High st
Ford, Peter, carpenter, Heathcote
Foyster, Robert Geo., High st
Fubbard, Wm., hairdresser, High st
Goddard, Benjamin, storekeeper, High st
Gordon, Henry F., painter, High st
Grant, Alexander, tinsmith, High st
Grant, John, blacksmith, High st
Grundy, Martin, wheelwright and blacksmith, and Globe hotel, High st
Hall, J., bootmaker, High st
Hall and James, general storekeepers, High st
Hanson, Henry, butcher, High st
Halstead, Wm., butcher, High st
Harding, Wm., coffee house, High st
Hawridge, James, bootmaker, High st
Hay, James, Heathcote hotel, High st
Hill, Frank, Criterion hotel, High st
Hodgson, Henry, general store, High st
Inch, Alexander, storekeeper, High st
Jackson, W., Victoria hotel, High st
Jones, John, storekeeper, High st
Keene, Daniel, draper, &c., High st
Kennedy, John
King, Mrs., milliner, High st
Lewis, Wm. E., stationer, High st
Matheson, D. M., Matheson's hotel, Sandhurst road, Heathcote
McDonald, George H., blacksmith and wheelwright, High st
McDonald, Charles, bootmaker, High st
McEvilly, Michael, Hibernian hotel, High street
McIvor Times office, High st ; Robert G. Foyster, publisher
Maloney, John, tinsmith, High st
Mansfield, —, constable, High st
Marshall, John, contractor, High st
Masonic Hall, High st
Millette, Johu, attorney, High st
Minter, Henry G., miner, High st
Moore and Co., general storekeepers, High street
Morris, A. H. R., Mount Ida hotel, High street
Nicholson, Daniel, blacksmith, High st
O'Dwyer, Mrs., storekeeper, High st
O'Meara, Patrick, miner, High st
O'Neil, —, Police office, High st
Oriental Bank Corporation ; Jas. Campbell, agent
O'Sullivan, Patrick, saddler, High st
Parker, James, storekeeper, High st
Pilling, Edward, saddler, High st
Police Camp, High st
Police Court, High st
Post Office and Electric Telegraph Office, High st ; James McLachlin, manager

Preston, Abraham, carpenter, High st
Presbyterian Church, High st
Prior, —, constable, High st
Robinson, Wm., sodawater and cordial manufacturer
Robinson, Wm., M.R.C.S., High st
Rodgerson, D., stationer and hairdresser
Reid, P., accountant, Oriental Bank Corporation, High st
Runge, Wm., hotel keeper, High st
Sangster, Wm., blacksmith, High st
Sexton, Samuel W., Argyle hotel, High street
Shervon, M., non-commissioned officer police force, High st
Sims, Daniel, butcher, High st
Smith, Wm., High st
Stephen, Wm., baker and confectioner, High st
Stewart, James, baker, High st
Strong, J. P., engineer, High st
Strong, J. T., surveyor and mining registrar, High st
Spreadbury, James, gingerbeer store, High st
Spreadbury, Charles, bootmaker, High street
Tierney and Co., brewers and cordial manufacturers, High st
Townsend, Wm., butcher, High st
Trevaskis, Wm., High st
United Methodist Free Church
Walker, Edwin, butcher, High st
Walsh, Laurence, watchmaker, High st
Wardell, W., manager Bank of Victoria, High st
Ward, P., saddler, High st
Whalley, Horace, schoolmaster, High st
Wilson, —, superintendent police force, High st
Winhold, Frederick, butcher, High st
Winters, —, trooper, High st
Wollaston, Wm. E., warden's clerk, High street
Young, Walker, High st
Young, David, miller, High st

PENTRIDGE.

Crawford, R. F., New Golden Fleece hotel, Pentridge
Flanaghan, F., Volunteer Arms hotel
Hunt, Wm., chemist and druggist
Kirkpatrick, Adam, crockery and grocery store
McFoyle, John, Pentridge hotel
Prowse, Henry, butcher
Wortley, Valentine, wine, spirit, and provision merchant

PYALONG.

Bebb, Stephen, storekeeper
Cooke, Patrick, White Hart hotel
Doogan, Hugh, Pyalong hotel
Leeson, Robert, storekeeper

RUTHERGLEN.

Arnoldi, C., carpenter
Badewits, Julius, tobacconist
Benjamin, Samuel, Cricketers' Arms
Booth, Wm., Rutherglen hotel
Boyd, Wm., Royal Standard hotel
Braun, Nathan, shoemaker
Connor, John, storekeeper
Cooper, George, draper
Croft, B. W., saddler
Dadds, James Wm., draper
Devers, Christian, butcher
Douglas, Thomas, Golden Age
Erber, Adam, shoemaker
Fisher, Benjamin, fruiterer
Friend, Mrs., billiard saloon
Gablenz, Francis, Lordship larder
Gibbons, W. T., fruiterer
Graham, John, produce merchant, hay and corn store
Gardner, Robt., storekeeper
Grant, James, tailor
Grimer, P., tobacconist
Ilsig, Alexander, saddler
Haluswelin, Henry, artist and photographer
Hunter, George, storekeeper
Jacobs, John, boot and shoemaker
Johnstone, Geo., baker
Kelly, John, Empire hotel
Kruger, Bernard, furniture warehouse
Logan, Duncan, storekeeper
Lodlo, L., draper
McLenan, Alexander, blacksmith
McLary, —, merchant
Murray Hardware Company, Shenstone and Audley
Obbinson, Thomas, chemist and druggist
Oriental Bank; Richard Page, manager
Orr, John, bookseller and stationer
Pasteria, Carlo, tailor
Reynolds, J., Sydney hotel
Risby and Jobing, blacksmiths and wheelwrights
Roberts and Buskell, drapers
Salomonson, Victor, importer of earthenware and china
Schwengel, Chas., Victoria hotel
Shroder, Fredk., Crown hotel
Thorpe, Wm., Star hotel
Toban, Michael, shoemaker
Vorbert, Herman, storekeeper
Worthington, S. C., chemist
Worthington, A. C., bailiff

2 z

SEYMOUR.

Bennett, —, butcher
Blay, Wm., saddler
Cole, James, carpenter
Deaney, —, sergeant of police
Egan, Patrick, bootmaker
Gilbertson, Rev. Jas., Church of England minister
Guild, Alex., Royal hotel
Guild, —, general storekeeper and butcher
Harris, W., blacksmith and wheelwright
McKay, Hugh, bootmaker
McNally, Patrick
O'Neill, James, teacher Common School
Orr, Peter, manager Electric Telegraph Office
Peacock, Thomas
Perron, Clement, general storekeeper
Redford, Richard, blacksmith
Shadwick, —, blacksmith
Stubbs, Rev. Albert, minister Wesleyan Church
Walton, W. R., Prince of Wales hotel
White, Thomas, baker

STANLEY.

Allan, Alex.
Atkinson, James
Augustine, Joseph
Bainbridge, John, boot and shoe maker
Bennett, Thomas
Benson, Alfred
Black, John
Blake, Robert
Brandon, George
Brinstidt, Hendrick
Brooke, Alex.
Bunning, Wm.
Castro, Joseph de Salvs
Clough, Charles
Conarty, Thomas
Collins, Joseph
Crampton, John
Davis, David
Davies, Thomas
Donnohue, Michael
Don, John
Donn, Alexander
Dunn, John
Duane, Patrick
Durkan, Patrick
Dyring, Charles, brewer
Elvers, John
Field, Frederick
Finnie, John
Flinn, John
Foster, Alfred Lucas, Vine hotel
Fraser, Thomas
Fraser, David
Geary, Wm.
Glaves, Wm.
Gripps, Daniel

Hammer, Louis A.
Harris, Hugh
Harris, Thomas
Haworth, George, storekeeper
Hedley, Thomas
Hill, Charles W.
Hill, Alexander
Hohn, Frederick
Holt, Edward
Houston, Wm.
Hughes, Arthur, storekeeper
Holme, Edward
Kennedy, Thomas, storekeeper
King, Alexander
Krenger, Adolph
Lang, John and Alexander, butchers
Lacey, James
Lee, Wm.
Little, Thomas, Full Moon hotel
London, Robert
McIntosh, David
McGeehan, Edward
McGalnes, Neil
McLachlan, James
McQuilton, Alexander
Maison, Simon Von
Manton, Wm. H., storekeeper
Marsden, Evan
Matthews, George
Matthiesen, Y. and J., general storekeepers
May, John B.
Mencker, Auguste, storekeeper
Muter, James, baker
Newton, Wm., storekeeper
Olderog, John
O'Reilly, John
Palmer, Henry, schoolmaster
Pettigrew, Wm., Son hotel
Robinson, Samuel, Live and Let Live hotel and store
Seckleman and Hammer, storekeepers
Scopes, Thomas, carpenter
Smith, Campbell, blacksmith
Walker, Henry, boot and shoe maker
Wright, Samuel W., Star hotel

TALLAROOK.

Fox, Thomas, Tallarook hotel

TARRAWINGEE.

Brown, Andrew, miller, Seymour steam mills
Devery, B., Red Lion hotel
Ladson, Thomas, post office and store
Nolan, Hopton, Plough Inn

VIOLET TOWN.

Hobson, James, storekeeper
Keane, Patrick, Rose, Shamrock, and Thistle hotel
Williams, Henry, Commercial hotel

WALLAN WALLAN.
Middleton, James, general storekeeper

WADONGA.
Brown, —, National School
Brownrigg, Capt. R.N., P.M.
Buck Brothers, storekeepers
Chauncy, W. S., superintendent of roads
Coverdale, James, postmaster and manager of electric telegraph
Dumbrell, Wadonga flour mills and hotel
Ileam, J. P.
Loom, Geo., wheelwright
Mackay, A., Border hotel
Mason, Samuel, baker
Nicholson, John, grocer

WAHGUNYAH.
Bridge, R. B., chemist and druggist, Foord street
Hayes, Mary Ann, Union hotel
Foord, John, miller
Jillet, J. D., storekeeper, Foord st
Lowes, R., stock and station agent, Foord street
Marshall, J., Endeavour hotel, Foord st
Rau, Camille, Empire hotel, Foord st
Sandrall, Prosper, storekeeper, Foord st
Scott, James, Wahgunyah hotel, Foord st
Simpson Brothers, boot and shoemakers, Foord st
Smith and Harris, agents for Murray and Jackson's steamers
Turner, Robert, butcher, Foord st

YACKANDANDAH.
Allen, Fredk., Star hotel
Bank of Victoria; W. A. Tonguelaye
Catholic Church
Caldwell, James, miner
Cole, James M., Commercial hotel
Costa, Bernardo, storekeeper
Cunningham, Oliver, carpenter
Cunningham, Thomas, storekeeper
Dobson, Jonathan, blacksmith
Frazell, John G., draper

Freeman, Fredk., general storekeeper
Haig, John, baker and confectioner
Hattersley, John, sodawater and cordial manufacturer
Henry and Co., butchers, High st
Isaacs, A., tailor
Keller, J., vineyard
Keppel, A., bootmaker
Kong Hi, storekeeper
McDermott, —, fruiterer
Miller, Thomas, draper
Muller, D., vineyard
Muller, A., surgeon
Nell, —, woodman
Perry, Francis, tobacconist and general merchant
Perrotett, —, secretary Shire Council
Power, Gilbert, Clarence hotel
Ramsay, —, miner
Raphael Brothers, watchmakers and jewellers
Reichardt, Charles, saddler
Reid, —
Rigney, Anthony A., family chemist
Roper, Walter H., merchant
Spence, R. J., Bank of Australasia
Stewart, —, drapery store
Stiles, F. W., bookseller and stationer
Walrond, Edwin, clothier
Wesleyan Chapel
Wilkinson, —, news agent
Young S., solicitor

CHRISTMAS TOWN.
Ashdown, James, Rising Sun hotel

STONEY CREEK.
Herbert, Nicholas, Coach and Horses hotel

EVERTON.
Hodge, George, Golden Ball hotel

DUCK PONDS.
Wheeler, John, Royal hotel

WOORAGEE.
Gill, Christopher, Wooragee hotel

GIPPS LAND ALPHABETICAL DIRECTORY.

1866-67.

A.

Abbott, T. B., sharebroker, Ligar st, Grant
Abraham, Alfred, Rose and Crown hotel, Daley st, Grant
Adams, John, carpenter, Davies st, Grant
Adams, Henry, bootmaker, Pearson st, Sale
Adams, Wm., Royal hotel, Gertrude st, Grant
Ahier, Thomas Francis, Jungle hotel, Grant road
Aitkin, James, squatter, North Gipps Land
Ake, James, miner, Happy-go-Lucky
Alberton Council Chambers, Bridge st, Tarraville
Alexander, Edwd., postmaster and storekeeper, Happy-go-Lucky
Albury, Robt., miner, Ligar st, Grant
Albrecht, C. D., mining engineer, Happy-go-Lucky
Alexander, Robt., Raymond st, Sale
Allis, John, cabinetmaker, Foster st, Sale
Allinson, Henry, shoemaker, Tyers st, Stratford
Alldridge, Henry, wheelwright, Yarram
Allen, Alex., sawyer, Rosedale
Allen, Wm., carpenter, Rosedale
Alley, Mansell, storekeeper, Happy-go-Lucky, and Butler st, Bald hills
Allerdice, John, farmer, Tanamba
Allerdice, Wm., Maffra road
Allen, John, miner, Stringer's creek
Alsey, A. F., Alberton
Alpine Quartz Gold Mining Company; P. H. McArdell, manager, Stringer's creek
Alford, John, farmer, Alberton, Gipps Land
Amy, John, Alberton
Andrews, Richard, labourer, Reeve st, Sale
Annand, J., baker, Oakleigh
Annis, Chas., miner, Stringer's creek
Anna, Henry, Reeve st, Sale
Aneissner, T. A. & Co., tobacconists, Daley st, Grant
Anderson, Wm., labourer, Marley st, Sale
Antievcich, Nicolo, Mull Hem hotel, Grant road
Anderson, Andrew, carpenter, Palmerston
Anderson, Thomas, miner, Dandenong
Andrews, John, miner, Happy-go-Lucky
Anderson, Alfred H., Foster st, Sale
Anderson, E, watchmaker, Foster st, Sale
Armstrong, Wm., draper and clothier, Daley st, Grant
Armstrong, W. E., Mount Pleasant, Grant
Armstrong, John, mechanic, Victoria reserve
Ashton, John, Commercial inn, Tarraville road

Ashton, Peter, miner, Happy-go-Lucky
Atkinson, Edward G., York st, Sale
Attwood, James, butcher, Happy-go-Lucky
Atkinson and Lees, solicitors, Raymond st, Sale
Austen, James, miner, Happy-go-Lucky
Avery, John, carpenter, Palmerston

B.

Baker, Rev. Henry, Wesleyan minister, Thompson st, Sale
Baker, John, coachman, Dandenong
Bailey, Hugh, packer, Toongabbie
Baines, Joseph, accommodation house, Rosedale
Ballintine, —, Junction hotel, Grant road
Baller, Henry, plumber and glazier, Happy-go-Lucky
Balley, Geo., miner, Happy-go-Lucky
Ball, Wm. E., Anchor brewery, Stringer's creek
Ball, John, woodsplitter, Sale
Bamford, Wm., butcher, Thompson st, Sale
Bank of Victoria, York st, Sale
Bangray, Geo., storekeeper, Berwick
Bank of Australasia, D. Trail, manager, Raymond st, Sale
Bank of Victoria, Stringer's creek: D. B. Liddell, agent
Barr, James, clerk to the Petty Sessions, Oakleigh
Barben, Robt., Oakleigh hotel
Barker, Robt., accountant, Dickson st, Stratford
Barker, Robt., Shepherds' hotel
Barlow, Thomas, mailman, Yaram
Bargery, R. J., storekeeper, Tarraville road, Yaram
Barnet, Wm., labourer, Maffra
Barnes, Wm., miner, Happy-go-Lucky
Barber, Ephraim, blacksmith and wheelwright, Macalister st, Sale
Bartlett, Wm., Dandenong
Barker, Thomas H., chef de cuisine, Merton, Rosedale road
Bassett, Jonathan, storekeeper and carrier, Tarraville
Bath, John, squatter, Alberton
Bates, —, farmer, North Gipps Land
Batty, Mrs., widow, Yaram Yaram
Boyliss, Edwd. Wm., squatter, Merton, Rosedale road
Bayles, —, squatter, Alberton, Gipps Land
Bayles Bros., carriers, Stratford road
Beard, Albert, carrier, Rosedale
Beard, Henry, commission agent, Sale
Bearpark, James, cooper, Foster st, Sale
Bearpark, Wm., bootmaker, York st, Sale
Bear, Geo., miner, Happy-go-Lucky
Beech, Thomas, builder, Grant

Beech, Solomon, storekeeper, Grant
Beck, Philip, miner, Stringer's creek
Belcher, W. R., collector of customs, Port Albert
Belcher, James, carrier, Elgin st, Sale
Bell and Rigby, chemists and druggists, Stringer's creek
Bennett, John, miner, Stringer's creek
Benson, Chas., Oakleigh
Betty, Thomas, farmer, Yaram Yaram
Bines, John, miner, Stringer's creek
Biggs, D., watchmaker, Ligar st, Grant
Bishop, Thomas, wheelwright, Oakleigh
Bisset, David, butcher, Macallster st, Sale
Black, Henry, storekeeper, Reeves st, Tarraville
Black, Henry, farmer, Alberton
Black, Hulbert, Happy-go-Lucky
Black, Wm., sawyer, Happy-go-Lucky
Blacker, Thomas, squatter, North Gipps Land
Blackie, Robt., miner, Stringer's creek
Bland, Abraham, storekeeper, Yaram Yaram
Bland, John, ironmonger, Foster st, Sale
Blose, Thomas, farmer, Tanamba
Blose, Daniel, farmer, Tanamba
Blose, Robt., farmer, Tanamba
Blose, James, cattle dealer, Tanamba
Blyth, David, carrier, Marley st, Sale
Bodman, H., Trenton Valley, Yaram
Boggy Creek, Lime Works, Woodside
Bogan, Patk., bushman, Butler st, Bald Hills
Borgwardt, P., tinsmith, Foster st, Sale
Boldner, Leman, Strathfield
Bolton, John, miner, Stringer's creek
Bolton, Francis, carter, Wellington st, Port Albert
Bomford, J. and J., drapers and outfitters, Reeves st, Tarraville
Bond, Edwin, boarding house, Happy-go-Lucky
Booth and Co., cabinetmakers, Foster st, Sale
Borain, James, stock driver, Rosedale road
Bourke, Michael, Latrobe hotel
Bourke, Wm., labourer, Pakenham
Bowen, Joseph, hairdresser, Dawson st, Grant
Boylew, Mary, widow, Reeves st, Sale
Bowden, —, squatter, Alberton
Bowman, J., Gipps Land hotel, Pakenham
Bowman, W. Alexander, Bridge hotel, Dandenong
Bowman, John S. H., schoolmaster, Stratford, Tyers st
Bray, Wm., Pearson st, Sale
Bradly, Samuel, labourer, Taralgon
Broadfoot, J. G., Belle Vue House, Tarraville

Braggs, John, miner, Happy-go-Lucky
Braithwaite, Wm., Foresters' Arms hotel and store, Oakleigh
Bray, John, miner, Sale
Bray, Wm. H., saddler, Foster st, Sale
Bredel, H., general store, Dawson st, Grant
Brisbane, W. and W. G., storekeepers, Berwick
Brides, Richard, sawyer, Tyers st, Stratford
Brackloff, —, tobacconist, Ligar st, Grant
Brooks, Charles, miner, Stringer's creek
Brown, Nicol, Drovers' Rest, Rosedale road
Brown, John, farmer, Alberton
Brown, Matthew, bushman, Toongabbie
Brown, James, letter sorter, Bald Hills
Brown, W., harbour department, Wellington st, Port Albert
Brown, Mary, widow, Merrick st, Stratford
Brown, Francis, sawyer, Grant road
Brown, Peter, miner, Stringer's creek
Brown, John, farmer, Alberton
Brown, Wm., farmer, Berwick
Bruckmar, W. H., cordial manufacturer, Davis st, Grant
Bruce, —, prospector, Toongabbie
Bryant, Wm., Sale school
Brunt, Ralph, farmer, Berwick
Bryant, W., bakery and boarding-house, Sale
Byrne, Robert, farmer, Alberton road
Buckley, Wm., squatter, Alberton
Buckley, Abraham, miner, Stringer's creek
Buckley, P. C., squatter, Alberton
Buckley Brothers (Thomas and John), farmers, Port Albert
Buckley, Samuel, farmer, Alberton road
Bullock, F. Thomas, registrar of births and deaths, and public vaccinator, Dixon st, Stratford
Bull and Sons, saddlers, Blackburn st, Stratford
Burley, James, packer, Bald Hills
Butler, Henry, solicitor, Foster st, Sale
Butler, Michael, farmer, Berwick
Butler, Alfred, Sale
Butler, —, squatter, North Gipps Land
Buchanan, Isaac, squatter, North Gipps Land
Bull, Wm. Gay, harness maker, Sale
Butterworth, Joseph, saddler, Rosedale
Bustine, Wm., cattle drover, Taralgon
Burrows, Thomas, deputy registrar births and deaths, Port Albert
Burns, John, labourer, Sale
Burgoyne, Thomas, carpenter, Maffra
Burns, Robert, Tarraville road
Burrows, Thos., auctioneer and valuator, Wharf st, Port Albert
Bushe, Robert, Cunningham st, Sale

Bushe, Robert, solicitor and conveyancer, Foster st, Sale
Byles, J. H., cordial manufacturer, Daley st, Grant
Burton, James, labourer, Sale
Burrows, Wm., brickmaker, Berwick
Byrne, John, storekeeper, Bald Hills

C.

Cabaizer, Christian, bootmaker
Cadden, Wm., storeman, Toongabbie
Cadden, Benjamin P., storekeeper, Toongabbie
Caesar, Augustus, sawyer, Grant road
Cahill, Patrick, shoemaker, Tyers st, Stratford
Cairns, —, bushman, Rosedale
Callon, Wm., storekeeper, Stringer's creek
Callagan, Chas., farmer, Alberton, Gipps Land
Caldon, A., Union bakery, Daley st, Grant
Campbell, Michael, saddler, Raymond st, Sale
Campbell, Robert, mason, Pearson st. Sale
Campbell, Duncan, squatter, North Gipps Land
Cameron, Thos., miner, Happy-go-Lucky
Campbell, Duncan, Taralgon hotel
Campbell, Duncan, storekeeper, Taralgon
Camp, James, storekeeper, Daley st, Grant
Campbell, Dominick, bullock driver, Toongabbie
Campbell, S. Morison, storekeeper, Maffra
Cant, Samuel, labourer, Berwick
Cansick, Paul, Rosedale hotel
Carberry, John, miner, Stringer's creek
Carr, James, miner, Happy-go-Lucky
Carroll, James, Union hotel, Daley st, Grant
Carron Timber and Iron yard, J. Law and Co., proprietors, Raymond st, Sale
Carpenter, Mrs., schoolmistress, Raymond st, Sale
Carden, —, constable, police station, Bridge st, Tarraville
Cary, James, blacksmith, Tyers st, Stratford
Carter, Francis, miner, Stringer's creek
Carter, T., carrier, Bridge st, Tarraville
Carter, Wm., bootmaker, Tarraville road
Cary, J. W., hairdresser, Raymond st, Sale
Cary, Emil E., draper, Macalister st, Sale
Carver, Saml., Exchange hotel, Stringer's creek
Carpenter, John, squatter, Alberton
Carpenter, John, Yarram
Carpenter, James, farmer, Yarram
Carpenter's bridge (erected 1864), Toongabbie
Carhill, James, Toongabbie

DIRECTORY. 359

Castle Rosso Quartz Mining Company, Happy-go-Lucky
Cassidy, James, gaoler, Sale
Caty, W. T., barman, Albion hotel, Raymond st, Sale
Catchpole, W., Tarraville hotel, Lefton st, Tarraville
Catholic Church; Father O'Keane, minister, Bridge st
Cavanagh, Mrs., teacher, Rosedale
Cawly, Francis, cabman, Alberton
Charlesworth, H., labourer, Sale
Charlewood, George, miner, Happy-go-Lucky
Chandler, John, miner, Lefton st, Tarraville
Chance, Elsie, miner, Stringer's creek
Clappey, John, sawyer, Toongabbie
Chester, Wm., carrier, Tanamba
Chewn, Charles, bricklayer, Rosedale
Christinson, Neil, storekeeper, Victoria reserve
Christinson, S., baker and confectioner, York st, Sale
Christianson, C., baker, Stringer's creek
Church of England, Raymond st, Sale
Church of England, Dandenong
Clark, Mrs., Turf hotel, York st
Clarke, Francis, accommodation house, Stockyard hill, Happy-go-Lucky
Clark, Thomas, packer, Toongabbie
Clark, John J., mail contractor, Butler st, Bald Hills
Clark, Henry, miner, Stringer's creek
Clements, Robert, carter, Woodside
Clements, Peter, packer, Butler st, Bald Hills
Clements, John, bootmaker, Foster st, Sale
Cleugh, George, coachmaker, Stringer's creek
Cliff, George, packer, Toongabbie
Cliff, Richd., packer, Toongabbie
Clowes, John, overseer, Tanamba
Coates, James, postmaster, Spring Vale
Coalgate, —, carpenter, Rosedale
Coates, James, storekeeper
Coates, James, Spring Vale
Cobano, John, wine and spirit merchant, York st, Sale
Cobb and Co.'s booking office, Foster st, Sale
Cocks, Thomas, bushman, Rosedale
Collins, Charles, bushman, Rosedale
Collier, Wm., Raymond st, Sale
Collins, James, bootmaker, Yarram
Collins, John, squatter, Alberton
Collis, George, beer house, Victoria reserve
Colvin, John, labourer, Palmerston
Coleman, Charles, packer, Toongabbie
Cole, John, carrier, Elgin st, Sale
Coleman, Thomas, Halfway House, junction of Sale and Rosedale roads

Collins, John, Woodside hotel, Gipps Land
Collins, John, labourer, Palmerston
Coleman, E. J., gaoler, Palmerston
Cole, Martin, Castle Burns hotel, Grant road, junction of the two roads to Stringer's creek
Common School No. 596, Stratford
Common School No. 615; J. G. Broadfoot, master, Tarraville
Combs, Henry, surveyor, Grant road
Conard, Wm., carpenter, Stringer's creek
Connelly, David, miner, Happy-go-Lucky
Connor, —, Tarwan hotel, Dandenong road
Connor, Thomas, miner, Happy-go-Lucky
Connor, David, Bunyip hotel, Dandenong
Connor, David, farmer, Bunyip
Connolly, Jeremiah, produce store, Daley st, Grant
Connelly, Dennis, Dargo hotel, Grant road
Cooper, C. C., carpenter, Grant road
Council Chambers, Foster st, Sale
Cosmopolitan hotel stables, Toongabbie
Costello, Pietro, farmer, Alberton
Copper Mines, Happy-go-Lucky
Cooper, James, labourer, Reeves st, Tarraville
Court House, Foster st, Sale
Coughton, bushman, Rosedale
Cousen, Tom, miner, Happy-go-Lucky
Cowen, John, packer, Toongabbie
Cowell, James, miner, Rosedale
Cox, Thos., hotelkeeper, Stringer's creek
Cragg, George, copper miner, Happy-go-Lucky
Crane, James, carter, Stewart st, Tarraville
Crane, Robert, carrier, Prince st, Rosedale
Crane, Martha, widow, Reeves st, Tarraville
Craik, James, gardener, Berwick
Crawford, Francis, accommodation house, Grant road
Crighton, Alexander, butcher, Berwick
Crisp, William B., hotel, Maffra
Cromb, John, contractor, Tarraville
Crompton, B. P., storekeeper, Yarram
Cross, Wm., farmer, Maffra road
Crossley, E. W., ironmonger, Reeves st, Tarraville
Crouch, Simon, labourer, Alberton road
Crouch, John, Tarraville
Cudy, Daniel, carrier, Stratford road
Cullam, Margaret, Palmerston
Cullam, James, blacksmith and wheelwright, Reeves st, Tarraville
Callam, Samuel, carrier, Palmerston
Cummins, Edward, farmer, Maffra road
Cunningham, W. B., J.P., squatter, North Gipps Land
Cupid, George, carrier, Sale
Curran, Thomas, bushman, Rosedale

Curran, John, bushman, Stringer's creek
Curtin, J., bootmaker, Oakleigh
Currie, Thomas, Royal Mail hotel, Daley street
Cutting, Charles, accommodation house, Rosedale road
Cullin, Charles, bushman, Rosedale

D.

Daget, Louisa, dressmaker, Ligar st, Grant
Daley, John, miner, Stringer's creek
Dalton, Richard, storekeeper, Ligar st, Grant
Dampsey, John, Exchange hotel, Daley st, Grant
Darlow, —, squatter, residence, Oakleigh
Dargan, Thomas, carpenter, Tyers st, Bald Hills
Davey, James and Co., drapers and storekeepers, Foster st, Sale
Davidson, Thomas, farmer, Berwick
Davidson, James, farmer and carrier, Rosedale
Davies, Wm., Café Cuisine, Happy-go-Lucky
Davies, George, farmer, Maffra road
Davies, Henry, storekeeper, Butler st, Bald Hills
Davies, James, farmer, Maffra road
Davies, James, stockrider, Rosedale road, Merton
Davies, —, farmer, Alberton
Davies, George, carpenter, Tarraville
Davis, Richard, Bridge inn, Longford, Gipps' Land
Davies, G., and Smith, D., blacksmiths, Reeves st, Tarraville
Dawson, Samuel, secretary to Avon Road Board, York st, Sale
Daws, Frederick, Reefers' hotel, Daley st, Grant
Day school, York st, Sale
Day, Jas., copper miner, Happy-go-Lucky
Deakin, J. G., storekeeper, Rosedale
Deakin, John G., storekeeper, Happy-go-Lucky
De Hong, farmer, Stratford road
Delaney, Richard, teacher, Grant road
Dessent, Charles, carrier, Palmerston
DeShong, John, Thompson st, Sale
Devonshire, Charles, gardener, Yarram
Dixon, John, commercial traveller and agent for new publications, collector for Wood's Point and Gipps Land Directory, 1866; Melbourne address, 197 Smith st, Fitzroy
Dick, George, bootmaker, Dandenong
Dickins, H., Shakspeare hotel, Stratford
Dickson, Thomas, overseer, Rosedale
Diddens, Samuel, brickmaker, Sale
Dickinan, —, storekeeper, Oakleigh
Dight, J. F., butcher, Reeves st, Tarraville

Digney, James, blacksmith, Daley st, Grant
Disher, Thomas, surveyor, Raymond st, Sale
Disher, W. H., storekeeper, Reeves st, Tarraville
Dobshere, John, miner, Happy-go-Lucky
Dobbinson, Rev. Launcelot, Presbyterian minister, Tarraville
Dobson, H., postmaster and electoral registrar, Dandenong
Doherthy, John, farmer, Yarram
Dolan, Wm., packer, Bald Hills
Dole, John, gardener, Marley st, Sale
Donohan, Richard, miner, Happy-go-Lucky
Donoghoe, D., farmer, Alberton
Doran, Francis, storekeeper, Oakleigh
Dowett, Wm., miner, Stringer's creek
Drew, J. J., tinsmith, York st, Sale
Dragveitar, Jacomb, miner, Red hill
Driver, Thomas, sawyer, Toongabbie
Dudman, W., View Point hotel, Stringer's creek road
Duncan, David, storekeeper, Wharf st, Port Albert
Duncan, George, merchant, residence, Macallister st, Sale
Dun, James, carrier, Pearson st., Sale
Dunbar, J., Dandenong hotel
Dunphy, Brothers, storekeepers, Daley st, Grant
Dunn, John, farmer, Alberton
Duff, John, accommodation house, Carpenter's bridge, Thomson's River
Duncan, D. and T., wine and spirit merchants, and storekeepers, York st, Sale
Duncan, D., Electoral Registrar, Port Albert
Duke, Robert R., packer, Rosedale
Duke, Thomas, farmer, Yarram
Duvall, —, postmaster, Stringer's creek
Dyer, Wm., contractor, Woodside road
Dyer, Wm., Latrobe bar, near Sale

E.

Eastway, Henry, bushman, Yarram
Eastlake, John, carpenter, Pearson st, Sale
Edger, James, miner, Happy-go-Lucky
Edmonds, John, labourer, York st, Sale
Edwards, George, tinsmith, York st, Sale
Edwin, Edmund, miner, Lefton st, Tarraville
Egan, W. C., farmer, Alberton
Eggleton, Thomas, miller, Berwick
Elliot, Richard, baker, Stringer's creek
Elliott, Andrew, packer, Toongabbie
Ellis, E. D, general storekeeper, Dandenong
Elwin, —, farmer, Berwick
Emerson, J. D., solicitor, Dawson st, Grant

DIRECTORY.

Eng   Gly   361

English, John James, residence, Dessally street
Enright, James, Shamrock hotel, Grant
Eona, Thos., miner, Happy-go-Lucky
Ewen, Robert, market gardener, Alberton road
Exchange hotel stables, Stringer's creek

F.

Fermaner, David, harbour master, Port Albert
Faris, T., brickmaker, Alberton road
Farran, F. J., manager National Bank of Australasia, Sale
Farley, Joseph, bushman, Rosedale
Felley, Michael, constable, Stratford
Fellcon, Mitchell, miner, Stringer's creek
Fenned, James, sawyer, Toongabbie
Fennon, Wm., storeman, Butler st, Bald Hills
Fenwick, Wm., miner, Happy-go-Lucky
Fennen, Wm., miner, Happy-go-Lucky
Fergulson, Wm., brewer, Tanamba
Ferguison, Peter, brewer, Tanamba
Ferris, Jacob, postmaster and manager of electric telegraph, and bookseller, &c., Port Albert
Fidler, Valentine, miner, York st, Sale
Finch, Joseph, miner, Happy-go-Lucky
Finch, John, miner, Happy-go-Lucky
Fisher, Edward, farmer, North Gippsland
Fish, Mary, Star hotel, Grant road
Flanner, James, storekeeper, Tarraville road
Finely, Thomas, pie shop, Dawson st
Flint, James, wharfinger, Woodside road
Flinn, Bernard, miner, Stringer's Creek
Florance, Hubert, miner, Stringer's Creek
Florance, Henry, Lord Howe inn, Grant road
Flynn, Jas. M., farmer, Alberton
Forster, Wm., Commercial hotel, Grant
Forbes, Wm., surgeon, residence, Dawson st, Grant
Foreman, Wm., farrier, Tarraville
Foreman, Thos., fisherman, Palmerston
Forbes, Wm., residence, York st, Sale
Ford, Matthew, farmer, Alberton
Foster, W. H., police magistrate of Rosedale and Sale
Foster, Sarah, widow, Sale
Foster, William, squatter, Stratford
Foakes, M., packer, Toongabbie
Foymbie, Samuel, editor, Elgin st, Sale
Foy, Wm., Yarram hotel, Yarram
Fox, M., dairyman, Tyers st, Bald Hills
Fox, Edward, farmer, Yarram
Frankenberg, S., wine and spirit merchant, Grant and Stratford
Frawley, Michael, former, Berwick
Francis, H., bootmaker, Foster st, Sale
Fraser, John, wheelwright, Rosedale
French, Geo., Club hotel, Sale

French, Geo., carrier, Tarraville road
Frencham, W., printer, Guardian, Port Albert
Frendenshal, D., Exhibition house, Daley st, Grant
Frost, J. P. B., schoolmaster, Palmerston
Frost, R. B. H., Alberton road
Fryer, Thomas, brickmaker, Dessally st, Sale
Fry, George, sawyer, Woodside
Futcher, Jas., tinsmith, Davies st, Grant
Fyers, E. F., police magistrate, Alberton road
Fyffe, David, Royal Exchange hotel, Foster st, Sale

G.

Gadd, Thomas, storeman, Stringer's creek
Gairdner, Wm., J.P., Stringer's creek
Galvin, —, farmer, Alberton
Gallagher, Wm., miner, Stringer's creek
Galloway, Richard, blacksmith, Blackbourne st, Stratford
Gaol, Palmerston; E. J. Coleman, keeper
Garner, Ed., blacksmith, Dandenong
Garnar, Thos., miner, Stringer's creek
Garland, Rosanna, widow, Palmerston
Garvey, Patrick, labourer, Maffra
Gasson, Edward, carpenter, Woodside
Gatland, Thomas, baker, Dandenong
Gates, James, Cranbourne
Geddes, Robt., carpenter, Sale
Gerrard, James, chemist and druggist, Foster st, Sale
Gee, R., accommodation house, Grant road
Gibson and Knox, farmers, Chute st, Bald Hills
Gibbs, John, labourer, York st, Sale
Gibbs, James, farmer, Berwick
Gibbs and Co., Robt., blacksmiths, &c., Dessally st, Sale
Gibney, Jas., general storekeeper, Maffra
Gibbott, Wm., carrier, Palmerston
Gibney, James, Macalister hotel, Maffra
Gibb, G., boarding house, York st, Sale
Giulim, Battista, butcher, Grant road
Gillion, John, Port Albert hotel, Wharf st, Port Albert
Gilles, Simon, Iguana Creek hotel, Grant road
Ginty, John, dairyman, Berwick
Gippsland Hardware Company, Port Albert
Glass, John, Raymond st, Sale
Gland, A., Yarram
Glass, John, blacksmith, Raymond st, Sale
Glynn, James, farmer, Tanamba
Gleeson, Thomas, blacksmith, Chute st, Bald Hills
Glee, Richard, miner, Stringer's creek
Glynn, John, farmer, Alberton
Glynn, James, stockrider, Rosedale road, Merton

3 A

Glynn, Robert, carrier, Marley st, Sale
Goodwin, Geo. E., carrier, Wellington st, Port Albert
Gordon, Chas., coachdriver, Reeves st, Sale
Gordon, Richard, miner, Happy-go-Lucky
Goldie, Dr., Lefton st, Tarraville
Goss, Fredk., Spring Hill hotel and store, Grant road
Gowan, Chas., labourer, Berwick
Goy, Matthew, carpenter, Alberton road
Goy, Richard, farmer, Yaram
Graham, Geo., miner, Happy-go-Lucky
Graham, John, Mountain Queen hotel and livery stables, Happy-go-Lucky
Grant, Robt., wheelwright, Berwick
Grant, Edward J., Half-Way house, Woodside
Greaves, James, butcher, Dandenong
Gregory, J. C., teacher, Rosedale
Gregory, J., Rosedale
Green, Robt., carrier, Pearson st, Sale
Greenwood, Mrs. Wm., widow, York st, Sale
Green, George, carrier, York st, Sale
Greenaway, Richard, labourer, York st, Sale
Gregory, James, labourer, Alberton
Griffiths, Thos., miner, Happy-go-Lucky
Griffiths, John, farmer, Alberton
Griffiths, John, miner, Bald Hills
Griffith, —, painter, Alberton road
Gallmaine, Rev. M., Dandenong
Guthridge, Nehemiah, timber and ironmerchant; office of the Colonial Insurance Company, Foster st; residence, York st, Sale
Guthridge, Wm., Aurora flour mills, York st, Sale

H

Haddon, Dr., Main st, Stringer's creek
Hadley, Joseph, woodsplitter, Victoria st, Port Albert
Hall, Alexander, chemist and druggist, and electoral registrar, postmaster, &c., Reeves st, Tarraville
Hall, Joseph, blacksmith, Stringer's ck
Hallor, Geo., draper and clothier, Dawson st, Grant
Hall, Joseph, miner, Stringer's creek
Halls, John, bakery, Happy-go-Lucky
Haller, Chas., carpenter, Ligar st, Grant
Halliday, Jos., packer, Tarambs
Hamlin, Thos., squatter, Redbank
Hanning, James, miner, Happy-go-Lucky
Hanley, Charles, carrier, Desailly st, Sale
Hansford, Hy., miner, Stringer's creek
Hanna, John, baker, Raymond st, Sale
Happerley, Wm., bootmaker, Tarraville road
Hanton, Ed., carrier, Rosedale
Harrison and Co., general storekeepers, Daley st, Grant

Harris, Walter H., dairyman, Smith st, Fitzroy, Melbourne
Harlestone, P., miller, Dandenong
Hardy, John, woodsplitter, Maffra road
Harvey, Matthew, toll collector, Dandenong
Hardy, Joseph, Bulgoback hotel, Grant rd
Hardwicke, Ed., solicitor, Alberton
Hara, W. O., farmer, Maffra
Harvey, Mrs., widow, York st, Sale
Harris, —, constable, Tyers st, Bald Hills
Hargreave, Brennan, and Co., storekeepers, Sale
Hardwidge, William, labourer, Stratford road
Haslet, Rebecca, Blackburn st
Hawkins, Chas., farmer, Yaram
Hawkins, Thomas E., carpenter, Sale
Hawkins, Mrs., boarding and day school, Thompson st, Sale
Hayes, Henry, miner, Happy-go-Lucky
Hayes, John, plasterer, Pearson st, Sale
Hayes, Henry J., butcher, Butler st, Bald Hills
Hayes, Wm., storekeeper, Alberton
Hayward, Joseph, dairyman, Reeves st, Tarraville
Hedley, Dr., consulting rooms, Raymond st, Sale
Henderson, F., whip manufacturer, Dandenong
Henderson, J. B., engineer, Tarraville rd
Hemmings, Alfred, schoolmaster, Dandenong
Hemmings, John, carpenter, Dandenong
Hender, John, Dandenong
Hennessy, Michael, Emmerring hotel, Berwick
Hepburn, Wm., ostler, Reeves st, Tarraville
Herbert, H. T., watchmaker and jeweller, Davis st, Grant
Herbert, G., farmer, Alberton
Hester, Samuel, mining smith, Cyclops forge, Stringer's creek
Hester, S. L., secretary Mariner's Benefit Association, Stringer's creek
Hetherington, John, miner, Happy-go-Lucky
Hetherington, W., miner, Happy-go-Lucky
Hetherington, Thomas, miner, Happy-go-Lucky
Hewitt, C., booking-office, Dandenong
Heywood, John, engineer, Stringer's ck
Hibby, W., carter, Stewart st, Tarraville
Hickey, Mrs., Rosedale
Hickey, John, carrier, Rosedale
Hickey, Michael, miner, Happy-go-Lucky
Hiem, James, builder, Desailly st, Sale
Hiho, Richard, farmer, Yaram
Hilliard, Wm., carrier, Rosedale
Hill, James, miner, Stringer's creek
Hill, Henry, cabinetmaker, Sale
Hill, Benj., blacksmith, Toongabbie

Himmell, James, carrier, Macalister st, Sale
Hindel, Samuel, carpenter, Yaram
Hobson, Edward, contractor, Tarraville rd
Hobbs, James Joseph, accountant, Tarraville road
Hobson, Henry, bushman, Yaram
Hoddinott, Uriah, squatter, Alberton
Hodson, F., sharebroker, Dawson st, Grant
Hogans, Timothy, Rosedale
Hogan, Timothy, packer, Tanamba
Hogg, Geo., squatter, Alberton
Holland, Mary, storekeeper, Grant road
Holmes, Peter, Stringer's creek
Hollinsworth, A., carpenter, Toongabbie
Hopkins, Agnes, La Bloera hotel, Ligar st, Grant
Hopkins, Chas., Pearson st, Sale
Hopgood, John, miner, Happy-go-Lucky
Hood, John, Victoria st, Port Albert
Hood, John, merchant, Wharf st, Port Albert
Hood and Co., merchants and general agents, Port Albert
Horton, Philip, butcher, Toongabbie
Horne, Charles, sawyer, Tyers st, Bald Hills
Horsedale, Chas., blacksmith, Maffra
Hoskin, Wm., carrier, Raymond st, Sale
Howe, Philip, farmer, Rosedale
Howden, Wm., Victoria st
Hudson, David, miner, Happy-go-Lucky
Hughes, David, miner, Stringer's creek
Hughes, Thomas, carrier, Palmerston
Hughes, Wm., miner, Stringer's creek
Hughes, —, barrister-at-law, Dawson st, Grant
Hull, John, carter, Elgin st, Sale
Humphrey, John, miner, Stringer's creek
Hunter, Thomas, sharebroker, Daley st, Grant
Hunton, —, carpenter, Rosedale
Huntingdon, Geo., labourer, Yaram
Hunt, G., storekeeper, Oakleigh
Hurley, Arthur, miner, Gertrude st, Grant
Hutchison Brothers, wholesale wine and spirit merchants, York st, Sale, and Grant
Hutchison, John, stonemason, Alberton road
Hutchison, Henry, gardener, Alberton road
Hutchison, —, wine and spirit merchant, Ligar st, Grant
Hutchison, Wm., storeman, Palmerston
Hyde, Edward, labourer, Foster st, Sale
Hyms, James, bricklayer, Pearson st, Sale

I.

Inch and Robertson, Halfway House, Anderson's Track, Grant road

Inder, Jacob, contractor, Stewart st, Sale
Inglis, John, M. B. C., storekeeper, Tarraville
Iredale, David, toll collector, Mulgrave
Irwin, James, constable, Stringer's creek
Irson, Henry, miner, Happy-go-Lucky
Irwin, Thomas, Mulgrave Arms, Mulgrave
Irwin, Gilbert, storekeeper, Berwick

J.

Jacobs, H., carrier, North Gipps Land
James, John, builder and lime merchant, Dennily st, Sale
James, W., clerk, Victoria st, Port Albert
Jamison, Geo., sawyer, Happy-go-Lucky
James, Wm., clerk, Alberton road
James, —, Diggers' Rest hotel
Jardin, Wm., labourer, Alberton road
Justice, —, carpenter, Alberton road
Jeff, Wm., farmer, Yaram
Jenson, Louis, builder, York st, Sale
Jenkins, John, miner, Happy-go-Lucky
Jerome, —, packer, Toongabbie
Jessop, James, farmer, Alberton
Job, Thomas, carter, Tarraville road
Johnstone, T., and Co., provision merchants; office of Gipps Land Lakes Navigation Company, Raymond st, Sale
Johnstone, T., and Co., accommodation house, Grant road
Johnston, George G., office at Reefers' Arms hotel, Stringer's creek
Johnston, Thomas, brickmaker, Victoria reserve
Johnson, Thomas, labourer, Reeves st, Sale
Johnston, John, squatter, Tanamba
Johnston, J. W., painter, Dawson st, Grant
Johnson, John, prospector, Bald Hills
Johnston, J. W., Medical Dispensary, Dawson st, Grant
Johnston, John, squatter, Newbourne park, Bald Hills
Johnston, Rosina, widow, Sale
Jones, John, prospector, Stringer's creek road
Jones, John, carrier, Grant road
Jones, Wm., carpenter, Sale
Jones, Mrs. M. A., Fulham station, North Gipps Land
Jones, John, blacksmith, Stringer's creek
Jones, Henry, squatter, Alberton
Jones, G. T., mining agent, Dawson st, Grant
Jones, Edward, Reefers' Arms hotel, Stringer's creek
Jones, George, bushman, Toongabbie
Jones, T., butcher, Oakleigh
Jang Sing, carrier, Sale

K.

Kampf, W. D., general store, Daley st, Grant
Keighley, Gregory, bootmaker, Dandenong
Kelly, Wm., Victorian hotel, Darling st, Grant
Kelly, Richard R., draftsman, Survey office, Palmerston
Kelly, Richard D., surveyor, Wellington st, Port Albert
Kelsall, Captain, Alberton road
Kelsall, E., clerk of courts, Palmerston
Kenna, James, bootmaker, Reeves st
Kempble, John C., miner, Happy-go-Lucky, Tarraville
Kennedy, John, miner, Stringer's creek
Kennedy, M., farmer, Alberton
Kennerbry, Daniel, miner, Raymond st, Sale
Kenewin, Thomas, packer, Bald Hills
Kenerch, Gostey, miner, Stringer's creek
Kenyon, Taylor, Oakleigh
Kennle, Augustus, miner, Ligar st, Grant
Kerr, Wm., labourer, York st, Sale
Kerwin, Wm., dairyman, Berwick
Kidd, Robert, blacksmith, Dandenong
King, A. Peter, Racecourse hotel
King, John J., miner, Happy-go-Lucky
King, John, squatter, North Gipps Land
King, George, sawyer, Grant road
Kine, John, sen., miner, Stringer's creek
Kingswell and Becher, livery stables and store, Daley st, Grant
Kine, John, jun., miner, Stringer's creek
Kinder, Robert, miner, Happy-go-Lucky
Kitchen, D. H., shoeing forge, Foster st, Sale
Knight, Stephen, farmer, Reeves st, Sale

L.

Langridge, Charles, Pioneer hotel, Daley st, Grant
Latham, George, butcher, Tyers st, Stratford
La Trobe, tollgate, Woodside road
Lambert, Michael, labourer, Grant road
Lamb, John, farmer, Alberton
Lang, Thomas, Royal hotel, Reeves st, Tarraville
Larkins, Wm., labourer, Foster st, Sale
Lawley, John, miner, Stringer's creek
Law, Joseph, and Co., Carron timber and iron yard, Raymond st, Sale
Lear, Isaac, refreshment house (12-mile yard), Rosedale road
Lear, John J., saddler and harness maker, Reeves st, Tarraville
Leary, Wm., miner, Stringer's creek
Leary, W., miner, Stringer's creek
Leary, John, miner, Stringer's creek
Lee, Thomas P., miner, Happy-go-Lucky

Lee, John, accommodation house, Grant road
Lee Brothers, produce store, Ligar st, Grant
Lee, Charles, produce merchant, Grant
Leeson, J. D., watchmaker, goldsmith, and bookseller, stationer, and telegraphic agent, &c., Foster st, Sale
Leslie, James, engineer and blacksmith, Raymond st, Sale
Lethbridge, Robert, cattle dealer, Rosedale; residence, Sydney cottage, Rosedale
Lewis, George, miner, Happy-go-Lucky
Lighoone, Wm., sawyer, Daley st, Grant
Linney, James, carrier, Stratford
Linney, John C., draper, Prince st, Rosedale
Lind, Marcus, carrier, Raymond st, Sale
Liston and Vize, aerated water manufacturers, Raymond st, Sale
Liston, J. F., Flooding Creek Dispensary, Raymond st, Sale
Liverpool and London Insurance Company's office; Wm. Patten, agent, Desailly st, Sale
Lloyd Brothers, storekeepers and Post office, Tyers st, Stratford
Lloyd, Thomas, packer, Toongabbie
Lockhurst, Elizabeth, widow, Wellington st, Port Albert
Logue, Thomas, saddler and harness maker, Raymond st, Stratford
Lonsdale, Mrs., Elgin st, Sale
Lovell, Elizabeth, laundress, Desailly st, Sale
Lowrie, Francis, miner, Stringer's creek
Lucas, John, packer, Toongabbie
Lucas, Joseph, packer, Toongabbie
Lucas, Wm., packer, Toongabbie
Lucas, Chas. Thomas, refreshment house, Rosedale road, Merton
Luke, Henry, storekeeper and postmaster, Prince st, Rosedale
Lynch, Patrick, farmer, Victoria reserve
Lynch, Lawrence, miner, Stringer's creek
Lynch, Morris, miner, Stringer's creek
Lyons, David, miner, Happy-go-Lucky
Lyons, Walter, miner, Happy-go-Lucky
Lyons, Patrick, packer, Chute st, Bald Hills

M.

Maccachairo, Archibald, Raymond st, Sale
Mackintosh, Murdock, storekeeper, Grant road
Mackerrin, Geo., Desailly st, Sale
Mackenzie, Duncan, carrier, Reeves st, Sale
Macalister, Matthew, squatter, North Gipps Land
Mackenzie, John, farmer, Victoria reserve
Mackay, John, farmer, Alberton

Macphail, John, squatter, Alberton
Macdonald, John, Halfway House hotel, Grant road
Macallister, Catherine, York st, Sale
Mackintosh, Donald, York st, Sale
Maclean, Donald, carpenter, Desailly st, Sale
Macallister, Dr., Raymond st, Sale
Macdonald, Henry, storekeeper, Reeves st, Tarraville
Mackenzie, Roderick, miner, Stringer's ck
Mackenzie and Ross, general storekeepers, Raymond st, Sale
Mackey, Richard, broker, &c., Foster st, Sale
Macleod, —, J. P., Rosedale
Maddocks, Edward, miner, Toongabbie
Magendie, John R., packer, Toongabbie
Mackenzie's Academy, Woolside
Mallett, Frederick, carpenter, Macallister st, Sale
Manderhausen, M., Chef Nationals hotel, Daley st, Grant
Manual, Wm., blacksmith, Dawson st, Grant
Marnall, Richard, accommodation house, Grant road
Marshall, C., boarding house, Bald Hills
Martin, C., M.D., public vaccinator, Oakleigh
Marrell, Richard, sawyer, Pearson st, Sale
Marr, Thomas, farmer, Berwick
Martin, Mrs., widow, Dandenong
Martin, Edward, Back Creek hotel, Bald Hills
Martin, Robert, miner, Bald Hills
Martin, Donald, miner, Stringer's creek
Martin, Francis, Niagara hotel, Daley st, Grant
Martin, Jacob, labourer, Alberton
Mark, Thomas H., restaurant, Carpenter's bridge, Happy-go-Lucky
Marr, Thomas, farmer, Berwick
Mark's Cottages, Alberton road
Mark, —, carpenter, Wharf st, Port Albert
Mark, T. H., engineer, Toongabbie road
Marshall, John, Pretty Boy hotel, Grant road
Mason, W. H., master Common School No. 693, Yaram
Mason, Wm., shoemaker, Yarram
Mathison, Arthur, miner, Stringer's creek
Matthews, Thomas, Royal hotel, Sale
Matthewson, John, sawyer, Tyers st, Stratford
Matthews' Medical Hall, Ligar st, Grant
Mangham, Michael, farmer, Stratford road
Maxwell, James, saddler, Maffra
May, John, farmer, Yarram
McAlpine, Wm., packer, Toongabbie
McCantee, Patrick, miner, Happy-go-Lucky

McCarthy, John, carrier, Tarraville road
McCarthy, Timothy, storeman, Wharf st, Port Albert
McCloud, H. F., farmer, Alberton
McCauly, —, bootmaker, Sale
McCole, Wm., butcher, Desailly st, Sale
McCole, Duncan, ironmonger, &c., Desailly st, Sale
McCole, John, carrier, Marley st, Sale
McCole, Duncan, M. D. C., Desailly st, Sale
McCloud, Wm., farmer, Alberton
McCoy, Mrs., farm, Alberton
McDonald, —, barrister-at-law, Gertrude st, Grant
McDonald, C., storeman, North Gipps Land
McDonald, S., Palmerston
McDonald, Peter, sawyer, Reeves st, Sale
McDonald, —, Digger's Rest Inn, Toongabbie
McElgunn, John, constable, Alberton
McElgunn, Patrick, trooper, Palmerston
McFayden, Donald, shoemaker, Maffra
McFarlane, John, labourer, Foster st, Sale
McFarlane, Malcolm, farmer, Tanamba
McGlond, Henry, miner, Happy-go-Lucky
McGrath, Patrick, Commercial Inn, Reeves st, Tarraville
McGulness, M., restaurant, Grant road
McGhee, Daniel, M.B.C., Raymond st, Sale
McIntyre, carrier, North Gipps Land
McIntyre, Charles, Harbour Department, Wellington st, Port Albert
McIlsin, D., farmer, Berwick
McKenna, Patrick, miner, Happy-go-Lucky
Mackenzie, Patrick, labourer, Grant road
Mackensie, Arthur, Reeves st, Sale
Mackensie and Ross, storekeepers, Sale
Mackay, James, woodsplitter, Maffra road
Mackearney, Michael, miner, Happy-go-Lucky
Mackelpin, Don, farmer, Alberton
Mackenzie, Donald W., Ship Inn, Tarraville road
Macloughlin, Joseph M., builder, York st, Sale
Macloughlin, Patrick, bakery, Dixon st, Stratford
Macloughlin, John, carpenter, Rosedale
Macloughlin, John, squatter, Tanamba
Macmann, John, carrier, Rosedale
Macmaster, John, miner, Reeves st, Sale
MacNieb, Mrs., milliner, &c., Reeves st, Tarraville
Macphail's stockyard, Merryman's creek
Macphail's cattle yards, Woodside
Macphail, John, Merryman's Creek hotel, Sale and Woodside roads
Mechanics' Institute, Foster st, Sale

Meekin, George, engine driver, Happy-go-Lucky
Meikell, Daniel, miner, Stringer's creek
Merritt, John, miner, Happy-go-Lucky
Mergo, James P., coach proprietor, Macalister st, Sale
Merryman's Creek bridge (erected 1865), Rosedale road
Merry, Wm., farmer, Maffra
Miller, Andrew, farmer, Victoria reserve
Miles, Josiah, Swamp Inn, Woodside
Millar, Henry, Retreat hotel, Moe
Miller, George, farmer, Berwick
Milton, Wm., farmer, Yarram
Mitchelson, Samuel, watchmaker, Desailly st, Sale
Mitchell, Mrs., day school, Elgin st, Sale
Mitchell, Albert, bootmaker, Sale
Mitchel, Frederick, bricklayer, Dixon st, Stratford
Mitchelson, John, painter, &c., York st, Sale
Mitchelmore, Samuel, carpenter, Foster st, Sale
Moudie, Andrew, carpenter, Toongabbie
Mulphy, Michael, Star hotel, Sale
Monkey creek, Woodside
Montgomerie, Wm., J.P., squatter, North Gipps Land
Monaghan, Thomas, sawyer, Woodside
Moore, Michael, farmer, Alberton
Moore, Wm., carpenter, Rosedale
Moore, Wm., farmer, Alberton
Moore, Wm., miner, Happy-go-Lucky
Mooney, John, labourer, York st, Sale
Morris, John, sawyer, Yarram
Morris, Richard, miner, Stringer's creek
Morrisby, Alfred, miner, Stringer's creek
Morgan, David, labourer, Stratford road
Morton, Lockhart, copper mines, Happy-go-Lucky
Morris, Thomas, butcher, Happy-go-Lucky
Monger, Wm., timber merchant, Raymond st, Sale
Morgan, John, carrier, Grant road
Muldoon, John, squatter, North Gipps Land
Muldoon, Daniel, squatter, North Gipps Land
Mulroy, James, labourer, Alberton road
Munday, Wm., butcher, Rosedale
Murrey, Power, miner, Stringer's creek
Murphy, Cornelius, Shamrock hotel, Pearson st, Sale
Murphy, Luke, carrier, Stringer's creek
Murray, Wm., accommodation house, Grant road
Murray, J., and Co., clothiers, &c., Raymond st, Sale
Murray, Colin, Pearson st, Sale
Murray, Colin, wine and spirit merchant, Sale
Murray, —, farmer, Berwick
Murphy, John, miner, Happy-go-Lucky

N.

Nairn, Wm., farmer, Alberton road
Napper Brothers, farmers, Alberton
Napper, Simeon, butcher, Reeves st, Tarraville
National Bank of Australasia ; F. J. Farran, manager, Foster st, Sale
Nash, George, butcher, Happy-go-Lucky
Nelson, Charles, miner, Stringer's creek
Nelson, Jessie, Woodgate park, Tarraville road
Neilson, James, blacksmith, Maffra
Neptune Quartz Gold Mining Company, Stringer's creek
Newton, E. T., Alberton road
Newman, John, wood splitter, Raymond st, Sale
Newton, Frank, carrier, Marley st, Sale
Newport, Michael, farmer, Alberton
Newson, Thomas, butcher, Stringer's creek
Nicholl, John, farmer, Alberton
Nicholson, Donald, storekeeper, Ligar s, Grant
Nice, Thomas, tailor, Tarraville road
Nichols, Edward, harness maker, Dandenong
Nicol, Wm., Royal Mail hotel, Grant rnd, Dargo flat
Noble, Wm., letter sorter, Tarralgon
No. 2 North-east Happy-go-Lucky ; John Hall and Co., proprietors
Noolan, P., farmer, Alberton
Nolan, John, coachman, Alberton road
Norwood, James, Collingwood store, Gertrude st, Grant
Norman, Susan, Palmerston st, Sale
Norwood, James, Court House hotel, Gertrude st, Grant

O.

Oates, Robert, barman and chef de cuisine, Toongabbie
O'Brien, Daniel, Limerick Arms
O'Brien, J., baker and confectioner, Raymond st, Sale
O'Brien, Denis, packer, Toongabbie
O'Connor, —, constable, Rosedale
O'Donnell, Cornelius, miner, Stringer's creek
Odell, Thomas, Camp hotel, Daley st, Grant
Odell, John, Omeo restaurant, Davies st, Grant
Office of the *Gippslander* and *Sale Express* newspapers ; Edward E. Atkinson, proprietor, York st, Sale
Office of North Gipps Land Steamboat Company, Raymond st, Sale
Office of the Lilydale Amalgamated Quartz Mining Company, Happy-go-Lucky ; Alfred Lee, manager
Office of the Berwick Road Board

Oghill, James, miner, Stringer's creek
O'Halloran, Stephen, Victorian bakery, Dawson st, Grant
O'Halloran, Morris, Alberton
O'Keane, Rev. Father, Bridge st, Tarraville
O'Keane, Rev. Father, Stratford road
O'Malley, Geo., prospector, Bald Hills
O'Mara, M. O., farmer, Alberton
O'Niel, John, farmer, Victoria reserve
O'Rourke, Thomas, labourer, Reeves st, Tarraville
Orchard, Daniel, Bridge Inn, Blackbourne st, Stratford
Osler, Wm., Toongabbie
Osborne, Michael, farmer, Bald Hills
Osborne, Mosbeck, farmer, Maffra road

P.

Pack, James, miner, Happy-go-Lucky
Packett, Richard, butcher, Macalister st, Sale
Page, J., bootmaker, York st, Sale
Pakenham Bridge, erected 1865
Parker, Samuel, miner, Toongabbie
Parker, W. F., house painter, Foster st, Sale
Parrott, Robert, bushman, Yarram
Parrott, Robert, miner, Happy-go-Lucky
Pardom, Thomas, carrier, York st, Sale
Parr, Wm., manager Bank of Victoria, Port Albert
Patterson, Thomas, miner, Stringer's creek
Patten, Wm., solicitor, Desaily st, Sale
Patten, James, packer, Tyers st, Stratford
Pearson and English, stock and commission agents, Foster st, Sale
Pearl, Geo., gardener, Alberton road
Pearson, Wm., M.L.A. and J.P., North Gipps Land; manager copper mines, Happy-go-Lucky
Pearson, Alex., J.P., squatter, North Gipps Land
Peck, Mrs., widow, Marley st, Sale
Peers, Melbourne Hunt hotel, Oakleigh
Pentridge, Farmer, farmer, Maffra road
Penifold, Henry, miner, Happy-go-Lucky
Pendlebury, James, sharebroker, Bald Hills
Pepper, Wm., teacher, Alberton
Peterson, James, miner, Stringer's creek
Pettet, James, builder, Reeves st, Sale
Peterson, Charles, Cosmopolitan hotel, Stringer's creek
Pettet, Macarthur, and Co., horse, cattle, and commission agents, Raymond st, Sale
Pettit, J. H., office, Raymond st, Sale
Phelp, James, miner, Stringer's creek
Phillips, Henry, bushman, Rosedale
Phillips, Geo. H., Government pilot, Wellington st, Port Albert

Phill, Wm., ostler, Wellington st, Port Albert
Pickett, Richard, butcher, York st, Sale
Piera, Fritz, sawyer, Stewart st, Tarraville
Platchek, Branch, and Co., drapers and storekeepers, Foster st, Sale
Plough, Thomas, coach driver, Sale
Plough, Sarah, dressmaker, Sale
Podesta, John, miner, Stringer's creek
Police Station, Bridge st, Tarraville
Police Station, Michael Feely, constable, Tyers st, Stratford
Police Station, W. Smyth, trooper, Taralgon
Police Station, Foster st, Sale
Police Station, Main st, Toongabbie
Po Nini, bakery, Rosedale
Pope, Thos., Freemason's Arms, Reeves st, Tarraville
Porter, Wm. O., legal manager Alpine Gold Quartz Mining Company, Stringer's creek
Pope, David, Esq., Dandenong
Pope, Hy., Mount Pleasant hotel, Dawson st, Grant
Porch, Enoch, sawyer, Rosedale
Port Albert General Cemetery. — Kelly, secretary, Alberton road
Post Office, Prince st, Rosedale
Post Office and Telegraph Office, Raymond st, Sale
Post Office, Dandenong
Post Office, Moe
Post Office, Oakleigh
Post Office, Pakenham
Post Office, Spring Vale
Potter, Wm., butcher, Dandenong
Powell, Geo., packer, Bald Hills
Powell, Henry, butcher, Prince st, Rosedale
Powell, Thos., packer, Bald Hills
Power, Geo., accommodation house, Grant road
Power, Thomas, miner, Stringer's creek
Price, Thomas, brickmaker, Sale
Price, Richard, sawyer, Bridge st, Tarraville
Presbyterian Church, Dandenong
Presbyterian Church, Berwick
Proser, Daniel, joiner, Sale
Pucklefort, W. J., brickmaker, Desaily st, Sale

Q.

Quinlan, R., clerk of courts, Rosedale and Sale

R.

Ramsay, J., tobacconist, Daley st, Grant
Randall, —, farmer, Alberton
Randall, John, labourer, Berwick
Rapel, Edward, miner, Stringer's creek

Ratcliffe, Robert, carrier, Reeves st, Tarraville
Rawson, Geo., miner, Stringer's creek
Ray, Charles, carrier, Elgin st, Sale
Rayan, John, packer, Tanamba
Read, Richard, miner, Stringer's creek
Reaves, Andrew, farmer, Berwick
Reeve, Edmund, miner, Happy-go-Lucky
Reeves Brothers, farmers, Alberton
Reeves, John, carrier, Tyers st, Stratford
Regan, Jeremiah, carrier, Yaram
Reeves, James, Reeves st
Reid, John, sawyer, Reeves st, Sale
Reid, Wm., bootmaker, Grant
Reeves, Frederick, carrier, Tyers st, Stratford
Rentall, James, farmer, Rosedale
Rentall, Geo., blacksmith, Rosedale
Rentall, Thomas, packer, Rosedale
Rentall, Geo., Rosedale
Rentall, Henry, bushman, Rosedale
Rice, James, general storekeeper and wine and spirit merchant, Stringer's creek
Rice, J., bootmaker, Foster st, Sale
Rice, Arthur, miner, Stringer's creek
Rice, Mark, miner, Stringer's creek
Richardson, Wm., engineer, Stringer's creek
Richardson, Robt., labourer, Berwick
Ricketts, —, squatter, Alberton
Ridge, Robt. L., Sydney cottage, Rosedale road
Riely, John, shoemaker, Alberton road
Rindall, Samuel, farmer, Yaram
Ritchie, A. H., blacksmith, shoeing smith, and coachbuilder, Foster st, Sale
Roader, Fredk., cooper, York st, Sale
Roach, Daniel, labourer, Reeves st, Sale
Roach, Edward, packer, Tanamba
Roberts & Duvall, storekeepers, Stringer's creek
Robinson, Abraham, miner, Ligar st., Grant
Robinson, Robt., saddler, Rosedale
Roberts and Gadd, Post Office and storekeepers, Russell creek
Roberts, Robt., contractor, Foster st, Sale
Robertson, Andrew M., contractor, Macalister st, Sale
Roberts, John L., draper, Tarraville road
Robertson, Henry, carpenter, Davies st, Grant
Roder, Fredk., cooper, York st, Sale
Rogers, James, miner, Stringer's creek
Rogers, James, carrier, Alberton road
Roman Catholic Church; Rev. Father Shiok
Ronne, Bridget, Mount Pleasant house, Stringer's creek road
Rooke, John, squatter, Alberton
Rose, Walter, farmer, Tanamba
Ross, Geo., Cunningham st, Sale
Ross, Geo., bootmaker, Rosedale
Ross, Thomas, miner, Stringer's creek
Ross, James, farmer, Alberton road
Rosedale hotel stables, Rosedale
Rossles, Hy., mining engineer, Stringer's creek
Rotherwell, Geo., saddler, Sale
Rowley, John, carrier, Rosedale
Rowland, Geo., wheelwright and blacksmith, Victoria st, Port Albert
Royal hotel, H. Luke, proprietor, corner of Lyons st, Rosedale
Runey, Thomas, farmer, Victoria reserve
Ruck, Robt., tailor, York st, Sale
Russell, J., squatter, North Gipps Land
Ruddock, Samuel, storekeeper, Dandenong
Rumpff, Peter, contractor, Pakenham
Rumpff, Chas., storekeeper and wine and spirit merchant, Bald hills
Ryan Brothers, printing office, Daley st, Grant
Ryan, Martin, miner, Happy-go-Lucky

S.

Salter, H. W., Royal Mail hotel, Woodside
Sale Brewery; Richard Jamieson, proprietor, Dawson st, Sale
Sayer, Daniel, saddler, &c., Foster st, Sale
Sayers, David, blacksmith, Happy-go-Lucky
Scarf, John, miner, Happy-go-Lucky
Scanlon, Sergeant E., Sale
Scoulin, Sergeant, Raymond st, Sale
Schneider, Gustave, timber merchant, Thompson st, Sale
Scott, Thomas, bricklayer, Pearson st, Sale
Scott, Wm., farmer, Yaram
Scott, Wm., farmer, Alberton
Scott, Wm., butcher, Maffra
Scutts, Geo., farmer, Alberton
Scutts, Geo., butcher, Victoria st, Port Albert
Sewell, John, horse bazaar and livery stables, and auctioneer, Foster st, Sale
Seymour, W. M., farmer, Alberton
Searle, Hy., blacksmith, Berwick
Shauley, A. J., Albion hotel, Raymond st, Sale
Shanklin, Robt., chemist and druggist, Raymond st, Sale
Shanklin, M., seedsman, Raymond st, Sale
Shadbroke Police Station; John Smallman, trooper, Woodside
Sherwood, Fredk., accommodation house, Happy-go-Lucky, Toongabbie road
Sheppard, Wm. A., bushman, Rosedale road, Merton
Sheer and Co., provision store, Dawson st, Grant
Sherwood, Henry, farmer, Alberton
Sherwood, Frederick, carrier and livery stable keeper, Happy-go-Lucky

Shink, Rev. Father, Stratford road
Sibbold, C. R., manager Bank of Victoria, York st, Sale
Silvester, —, farmer, Maffra road
Silverton, Wm., butcher, Maffra
Sims, Thomas, carrier, Rosedale
Simmons, Edward L., M.D., J.P., and public vaccinator, Rosedale
Sladen, James, miner, Stringer's creek
Slater, Stephen, Freemasons' Arms, Dawson st, Grant
Slade, Captain, superintendent of police, Sale
Slater, James, carrier, Yarram
Smallpage and Co., mining agents, Grant
Smallman, J., Shadbroke Police Station
Smart, Richard, bootmaker, Stringer's creek
Smith, Lancett, miner, Reeves st, Sale
Smith, James, miner, Happy-go-Lucky
Smith, J. D., J.P., squatter, North Gipps Land
Smith, David, blacksmith and storekeeper, Reeves st, Tarraville
Smith, J., blacksmith, Oakleigh
Smith, Geo., bushman, Rosedale
Smith, James H., labourer, Berwick
Smith, T. H., Gipps Land store, Lefton st, Tarraville
Smith, W. H., draper and outfitter, Foster st, Sale
Smith, D. B., butcher, Stringer's creek
Smith, John, bootmaker, Alberton
Smith, F. S., Forest hotel, Grant road
Smith, John, miner, Tarraville road
Smith, Peter, carpenter, Tarraville road
Smith, George, butcher, Tarraville road
Smith, R., draper, Raymond st, Sale
Smith, Wm., miner, Happy-go-Lucky
Smith, John, miner, Happy-go-Lucky
Smith, Charles, farmer, Alberton
Smith, Fredk., miner, Stringer's creek
Smith, T. J., saddler, &c., Foster st, Sale
Smithson, Sydney, merchant and gold broker, Dandenong
Snowdon, Jacob, contractor, Lefton st, Tarraville
Sothern, John, surveyor, Raymond st, Sale
South Gipps Land Quartz Mining Company, Stringer's creek
Sprod, W. T., York st, Sale
Spring, Captain, Tarraville road
Spearing, Chas., miner, Happy-go-Lucky
Survey Camp, Main st, Toongabbie
Sunderman, —, contractor, Rosedale
Stacin, James, Harbour Department, Palmerston
Stagg, John, gardener, Rosedale road
Stanley, Robt., carrier, Rosedale
Stanway, George, Temperance hotel, Port Albert
Staples, John, miner, Happy-go-Lucky
Stears, Samuel, miner, Stringer's creek

Steady, George, engineer, Stringer's creek road
Stead, Hy. W., M.B.C., wine and spirit merchant, Ligar st, Grant; residence, Raymond st, Sale
Stewart, Alex., miner, Happy-go-Lucky
Stenner, Wm., carpenter, Berwick
Stephens, J., carpenter, Desailly st, Sale
Steward, Alex., miner, Happy-go-Lucky
Stewart, Walter, farmer, Berwick
Stewart, Robt., carpenter, Maffra
Stewart, D. C., carpenter, Bald Hills
Stewart, Alex., labourer, Tarraville road
Stewart, N., bootmaker, Daley st, Grant
Stevenson, Richd., M.D., Berwick
Stone, John, Victoria reserve
Stretch, Rev. J. T. C., Church of England minister, Stewart st, Tarraville
Strange, John, miner, Dandenong
Stubbs, J., butcher, Grant
Stuart, Chas., candle manufacturer, Raymond st, Sale
Swan, Samuel, Blackbourne st, Stratford
Swirl, Henry, blacksmith, Berwick
Sweeney, —, farmer, Alberton
Swering, Chas., mining engineer, Gertrude st, Grant

T.

Targett, Fred., tailor, York st, Sale
Tasling, Richd., labourer, Tarraville road
Tait, Wm., miner, Happy-go-Lucky
Tait, Lawrence, miner, Stringer's creek
Talbot, Doyle, carrier, Sale
Tanner, Samuel, packer, Toongabbie
Tapping, Robt., secretary Mechanics' Institute, Sale
Tapley, Geo., miner, Stringer's creek
Tanger, John, miner, Stringer's creek
Tarraville bridge, erected 1862
Tate, John, labourer, Maffra
Taylor, James, squatter, Alberton
Taylor, Geo., Stockyard hotel, Grant road
Taylor, John, labourer, Alberton
Taylor, S., mining manager, Stringer's creek
Taylor, John, packer, Bald Hills
Taylor, Joseph, miner, Happy-go-Lucky
Taylor, John, labourer, Alberton
Taylor, S., manager South Gipps Land Quartz Mining Company, Stringer's creek
Taylor, Benjamin, farmer, Taralgon
Taylor, Henry, bushman, Toongabbie
Tyrrell, Thomas, Junction hotel, Dawson st, Grant
Thatcher, Samuel, mariner, Wellington st, Port Albert
Thewen, Fred., miner, Stringer's creek
The Go-Lucky Quartz Mining Company; Joseph Coates, manager, Happy-go-Lucky
Thompson, —, farmer, Alberton

3 B

370　Tho　　ALPHABETICAL　　Whi

Thompson, Richard, boarding school, Reeves st, Tarraville
Thomson, John, Foster st, Sale
Thompson, John, Daley st, Grant
Thompson, James, packer, Toongabbie
Thompson, Wm., miner, Stringer's creek
Thompson, —, carpenter, Berwick
Thompson, John, baker, Stringer's creek
Thomas, N. W., storekeeper, Thompson st, Sale
Thomas, Edwd., Brewery Arms hotel and Alpine brewery, Grant road
Thomas, John, Harbour Department, Wellington st, Port Albert
Thomas, James, miner, Ligar st, Grant
Thoms, Captain, Stewart st, Tarraville
Thomas, John, Alpine hotel, Daley st, Grant
Tiernan, W., shoemaker, Berwick
Toole, J., labourer, Bridge st, Tarraville
Tollgate, Mulgrave
Topping, Robert, saddler, &c., Raymond st, Sale
Town Hall, Foster st, Sale
Town Clerk's office, Foster st, Sale
Thorp, Francis, shoemaker, York st, Sale
Traills, Alex., accommodation house, Grant road
Traill, D., manager Bank of Australasia, Sale
Travers, James W., butcher, Raymond st, Sale
Travers, Wm., Macalister st, Sale
Travis, Chas., miner, Happy-go-Lucky
Tricks, W. J., accountant, Raymond st, Sale
Trenand, Edwd., miner, Stringer's creek
Troud, John, tobacconist, office of Gippslander and Express, Foster st, Sale
Tuchfield, Rev. Jas. W., Wesleyan minister, Tarraville road
Tucker, Thomas, contractor, Lofton st, Tarraville road
Turnbull, Howden, and Co., merchants, Wharf st, Port Albert
Turnbull, David, Victoria st, Port Albert
Turner, Thomas M., Palmerston st, Palmerston
Turnbull, John, J.P., Rosedale
Turnbull, J., J.P., Taralgon
Turton, Wm., government surveyor, Palmerston
Turnbull and Henderson, squatters, North Gipps Land
Turnbull, Howden, and Co., merchants, Daley st, Grant
Turner, T. M., clerk and landing waiter H.M. Customs, Port Albert
Turton, J. F., and Co., Victoria bakery, Daley st, Grant
Tusk, Daniel, woodsplitter, Grant road
Tyers, C. J., police magistrate, Palmerston

V.

Vanston, James Turpin, United Bakers, Grant
Vesper, Wm., carrier, Taralgon
Vickery, Henry, miner, Stringer's creek
Vincent, Wm., shoemaker, Rosedale
Vize, W. H., photographer, Raymond st, Sale
Vos, Chas., farmer, Yaram

W.

Wait, John, carrier, Prince st, Rosedale
Walker, Chas., farmer, Rosedale
Wallworth, John, carpenter, Tarraville road
Walton, —, farmer, Berwick
Walsh, John, storekeeper, Tarraville road
Walker, Chas., blacksmith, Toongabbie
Walhalla Gold Mining Company (Registered); Hy. Rossles, manager, Stringer's creek
Wallace, Ferguson, mailman, Bald Hills
Waldock, W. W., solicitor and conveyancer, Victoria st, Port Albert
Walker, F. Alfred, mining engineer, Ligar st, Grant
Warton, John, shoemaker, York st, Sale
Warren, B. K., surgeon and accoucheur, Raymond st, Sale
Wastel, W. H., general store, Oakleigh
Watts, Wm., farmer, Rosedale
Watson and Abbott, officers, Gertrude st, Grant
Watson, Edwd., farmer, North Gipps Land
Watts, Martha, accommodation house, Tanamba
Waters, Joseph, bricklayer, Sale
Watson, Thos., farmer, Wharf st, Port Albert
Weaver, —, carpenter, North Gipps Land
Weaver, F. M., miner, Happy-go-Lucky
Webster, Robt., accommodation house, Grant road
Webb, John R., York st, Sale
Weldon, Joseph, labourer, Woodside
Welch, M., farmer, North Gipps Land
Weighbridge, Reeves st, Tarraville
Wellington Church, Spring Vale
Werner and Klus, Gipps Land soap and candle works, Foster st
Were, Mrs., Rosedale
Wesleyan Church, Oakleigh
Westwood, Ellen, Royal hotel, Mulgrave
Wesleyan Church, Rev. Henry Baker, minister, Raymond st, Sale
Wesleyan Chapel, Berwick
Whalley, John, ostler, Taralgon
White and Co., general store and Albion hotel, Dawson st, Grant
White, Thomas, maildriver, Foster st, Sale

White, J. C., miner, Happy-go-Lucky
White, Joseph, ostler, York st, Sale
White, Alex., carpenter, Toongabbie
White, Thomas, miner, Happy-go-Lucky
Whitworth, Joseph, labourer, Alberton
White and Co., Albion hotel, Dawson st, Grant
Whittle, Henry, restaurant keeper and parker, Toongabbie
Wickes, Harlo, musician, Stringer's creek
Wideson, James, farmer, Rosedale
Widor, Samuel, carrier, Yaram
Wilford, Alfred, storeman, Grant road
Williamson, Wm., boarding house, Woodside
Williams, Robt., carrier, Berwick
Williamson, Ramsay, bootmaker, Lefton st, Tarraville
Williamson, Wm., surveyor, Sale
Williams, John, draper, Rosedale
Williams, Richard, Merriman's Creek house, Rosedale road, Merton
Williamson, J., junior, farmer, Maffra rd
Williamson, J., senior, farmer, Maffra rd
Williamson, W., cattle dealer, Maffra rd
Williamson, A., farmer, Maffra rd
Williams, Thomas, sawyer, Rosedale
Williams, Fredk., farmer, Alberton
Williams, John, miner, Stringer's creek
Williams, David, bushman, Yaram
Williams, John, farmer, Maffra road
Wilmot, J. G. W., district surveyor, Ligar st, Grant
Wilson, Henry, Berwick hotel, Berwick
Wilson, Henry, labourer, Dandenong
Wilson, Catherine, widow, Yaram
Wilson, John, miner, Stringer's creek
Wilson, J., squatter, North Gipps Land
Wilson, Thomas, farmer, Alberton
Wilson, Isaac, engine driver, Happy-go-Lucky
Wilson, John, general storekeeper, Tyers st, Bald Hills

Wilson, Thomas, carpenter, Yaram
Willis, John, carrier, Reeves st, Tarraville
Willis, Thomas, farmer, Alberton
Willis, Wm., farmer, Alberton
Wilks, Henry, labourer, Victoria reserve
Wilton, Wm., farmer, Yaram
Willmartin, John, labourer, Pearson st, Sale
Wilkinson, John, Palmerston st, Palmerston
Winden, Edward, sawyer, Rosedale road
Windom, John, carpenter, York st, Sale
Winch, Benj., farmer, York st, Sale
Wise, Fredk., sawyer, Toongabbie
Wise, Fredk., Rosedale road
Wishart, John, Sir Henry Barkly hotel, Wondelde; post-office, John Wishart, postmaster
Woodhouse, Wm., Alberton road
Woodside bridge, erected 1865
Wood, Geo., painter, decorator, and paperhanger, and boarding house and restaurant, Raymood st, Sale
Wood, Chas., miner, Happy-go-Lucky
Wood, Wm., carter Victoria st, Port Albert
Wood, Chas., farmer, Yaram
Wood, W.'B., Gipps Land Hardware Company, Wharf st, Port Albert
Wood, Francis, farmer, Yaram
Wright, James, chef de cuisine, Bald Hills
Wrigglesworth, John, carpenter, Macalister st, Sale

Y.

Yates, Wm., bushman, Rosedale
Yates, Wm., carter, Grant road

Z.

Zerpheur, Le Sexes, boatman, Grant

WOOD'S POINT ALPHABETICAL DIRECTORY.

1866-67.

A.

Abraham, Chas., miner, View Point, Gaffney's creek
Abraham, Mrs., milliner and dressmaker, View Point, Gaffney's creek
Acheron river and bridge
Adcock, W. E., bookseller and stationer, View Point, Gaffney's creek
Akehurst, A. P., police magistrate and warden, Ellery st, Wood's Point
Alexander, —, boot and shoe warehouse, Main road from Wood's Point to Jamieson
Albert Davies and Co., general storekeepers, Raspberry ck, and at Bridge st, Jamieson
All Saints' Church; Rev. Thos. B. Vipont, minister, Gaffney's ck
All Saints' School; Rev. Thos. B. Vipont, master, View Point, Gaffney's ck
Allen, Thomas, carter, Jamieson river
Allen, Thomas, Ten-Mile house, Main rd from Wood's Point to Jamieson
Allen, Wm., Emerald Reef hotel, High st, Matlock
Alport and Co., drapers and outfitters, Jordan st, Matlock
Alport and Co., drapers and clothiers, Wood's Point
Anderson, Henry Wood, actuary and manager Union Bank of Australasia, High st, Matlock

Andrews, James, butcher, Nicholson st, Healesville
Andrews, Wm., postmaster and manager, Telegraph and Post office, Bank st, Jamieson
Angrove, Thomas, mining manager, Gaffney's ck
Aughter, S. Edward, chemist and druggist, High st, Matlock
Ansier, W., accommodation house, Main road from Wood's Point to Jamieson
Answorth, A. B., mining surveyor, Butler st, Wood's Point
Arkley, Robt., miner, View Point, Gaffney's ck
Arthur and Payne, house decorators, Scott st, Wood's Point
Arthur, J., carpenter, facing the Goulburn, Wood's Point
Arkwith, R., bootmaker, Drysdale's flat
Aulberg, John, miner, vicinity of the hospital, Wood's Point
Ayrling, Mrs., Globe hotel, Scott st, Wood's Point

B.

Baber, —, sergeant of police, Jamieson
Badger, Thomas, draper and milliner, Hurley st, Wood's Point
Bailey, Richd., mining agent, Hurley st, Wood's Point
Ball room; John Holland, Healesville

Bamford, Geo., tailor, Chenary st, Jamieson
Bank of Victoria, Bridge st, Wood's Point; Gerald Pendlebury, manager
Barry, Wm., bootmaker, Jordan st, Matlock
Barker, A., mining manager, McDougall st, Wood's Point
Baker, Wm., Bewfer's hotel, Raspberry creek
Bayoe, Fred., solicitor, Perkin st, Jamieson
Beaven, J., and Co., coach office and livery stables, Scott's st, Wood's Point
Beaven, J., and Co., booking office, Main road from Wood's Point to Jamieson, and Bank st, Jamieson
Beal, Fredk. J., mining manager, Jordan st, Matlock
Bealem, W., Wood's Point
Bell, Chas., butcher, Bridge st, Wood's Point
Bell, Thomas M., Yarra Flat hotel, Yarra track
Benjamin and Rappiport, merchants, Bridge st, Jamieson, and Scott st, Wood's Point
Bennett, John, miner, Rising Sun gully
Berger, H. A., J.P., M.B.C., chemist and druggist, Bridge st, Jamieson
Bew, Henry, George hotel, Scott st, Wood's Point
Bidgr, Michael, blacksmith, Bank st, Jamieson
Billson, G., London tavern, Butler st, Wood's Point
Black, Andrew, carpenter, Marysville
Black, S., Segel, Royal Mail hotel, Scott st, Wood's Point
Blake, John, carpenter, Main road from Wood's Point to Jamieson
Blein, James, M.B.C., merchant, Gray st, Jamieson
Blair, H. Hugh, surveyor, Drummond Point, Gaffney's creek
Blether, Edw., mining manager, Morning Star hill
Bloomer, Matthew, mining manager, facing the Goulburn, Wood's Point
Boobier, James, Great Britain hotel, High st, Matlock
Boobier, W. J., vicinity of the Hospital, Wood's Point
Boocher, J., miner, Scott st, Wood's Point
Bower, Mrs., widow, facing the Old Bridge, Jamieson
Box, James, mining engineer, Raspberry creek
Box, Henry, accommodation house, Glen Watts
Bond, Wm., Hit or Miss, Rose st, Fitzroy
Boyne, John, facing the Goulburn, Wood's Point
Boyle, Samuel, storekeeper, Fernshaw

Branch, John, mining agent, High st, Matlock
Brady, Wm., miner, Main road, from Wood's Point to Jamieson
Braan, John, miner, High st, Matlock
Breen, John, blacksmith, Main road from Wood's Point to Jamieson
Brennan, Edward, town crier, Hurley st, Wood's Point
Brew, John, labourer, Fernshaw
Brown and Townsend, storekeepers, High st, Matlock
Brown, L. James, Castle hotel, Raspberry creek
Brice, George, Criterion hotel, Bridge st, Jamieson
Brown, Thomas B., timber merchants, High st, Matlock
Bruen, Bartholomew, Reefers' hotel, Jordan st, Matlock
Brown, Thomas, jun., blacksmith, Jordan st, Matlock
Brown, Thomas, sen., blacksmith, Jordan st, Matlock
Brown, Thomas, coach driver, Chenery st, Jamieson
Brown, Thomas, miner, High st, Matlock
Brown, Charles, miner, Main road from Wood's Point to Jamieson
Brown, James L., Castle hotel, Castle Point, Raspberry creek
Bruce, Geo., storekeeper, Fernshaw, Watt's bridge
Brockman, Henry, accommodation house, Mount Arnold
Burrell, John, carrier, Bank st, Jamieson
Bushby, James, painter and glazier, Fitzroy
Burgett, Henry, American hotel, Scott st, Wood's Point
Butler, J. E., mining agent, architect and surveyor, and general mining manager, &c., Hurley st, Wood's Point
Butler, James, Morning Star hotel, Hurley st, Wood's Point
Butler, J. E., mining manager, Raspberry creek
Butler, Thomas, bootmaker, High st, Matlock

C.

Cadden, Patrick, butcher, Raspberry creek
Cahill, J. T., bank clerk, Colonial Bank of Australasia, Wood's Point
Caldwell, Andrew, town clerk, engineer, estate and commission agent, Chenery st, Jamieson
Calcutt, Bedelia, Club House hotel, Wood's Point
Callaghan, Patrick, miner, facing the Goulburn, Wood's Point
Cameron, Ewen, Tri Bhean hotel and general store, &c., Glen Watts

Cameron and Barton, butchers, Marysville
Campbell, Miss, assistant teacher, View Point, Gaffney's creek
Campbell, John Collin, court bailiff, Nash st, Jamieson
Campbell, Alex., accommodation house, Main road from Wood's Point to Jamieson
Campbell, Thomas, miner, Gaffney's creek
Cape, —, bushman, Nicholson st, Healesville
Carson, Joseph, mining agent, Hurley st, Wood's Point
Carthner, Arthur, miner, Jamieson river
Castllo, Patrick, miner, Gaffney's creek
Cashle, Charles, labourer, Fernshaw
Casey, —, miner, Morning Star hill
Cassidy, Patrick, labourer, Jamieson river
Cauldwell, —, clerk, Raspberry creek
Cavanagh, John, miner, Harper's creek, Matlock road
Cawthorn, Thomas, mining manager, Morning Star hill
Chapman, Wm., sawyer, Chenery st, Jamieson
Chapple, W., B C. mining manager, Raspberry creek
Church of England ; Rev. W. H. Cooper, minister, McDougall st, Wood's Point
Clarke, W., and Sons, sharebrokers and mining agents, Bridge st, Wood's Point
Clarke, Charles E., mining manager, Bridge st, Wood's Point
Clark, John, dairyman, Chenery st, Jamieson
Clayton, Henry, storekeeper, Bank st, Jamieson
Cleave, Frank, miner, Main road from Wood's Point to Jamieson
Cliff, David, carpenter, Nash st, Jamieson
Clifford, Timothy, Hit or Miss, Healesville
Coats, Edward, A 1 bakery, Bank st, Jamieson
Cobham, F. M., superintendent of police, Jamieson
Cock, John, carpenter, Main road from Wood's Point to Jamieson
Cohen, John, Court House hotel, Drummond's Point, Gaffney's creek
Cohen, Wolfe, baker and confectioner, Scott st, Wood's Point
Cohill, L. L, manager Colonial Bank of Australasia, Raspberry creek
Coidler, Edward, butcher, Donaldson st, Matlock
Collogan, Wm., miner, Drysdale's flat, Wood's Point
Colonial Bank of Australasia, Hurley st, Wood's Point ; J. McCoy, manager
Colonial Bank of Australasia ; J. Chapman, acting manager, High st, Matlock

Collou and Co., Wood's Point Lands office
Colters, Daniel, engineer, Harper's creek, Matlock road
Condray, J. C., storekeeper, Main road from Wood's Point to Jamieson
Connell, Joseph, bricklayer, Jamieson river
Connelly, Michael, surveyor, High st, Matlock
Connell, W., miner, Drysdale's flat
Common School ; J. C. Wilton, schoolmaster, High st, Matlock
Cook, John, Colonial Bank hotel, High st, Matlock
Cook, Henry, saddler, Bank st, Jamieson
Cooper, Alfred, Junction hotel, Bank st, Jamieson
Cooper, Wm., packer, Healesville
Corbett, D., sawyer, Hurley st, Wood's Point
Corbett, J., sign writer and painter, Hurley st, Wood's Point
Cormick, Joseph, lock-up keeper, Nash st, Jamieson
Coster, W. Frederick, Hurley st, Wood's Point
Courtenay, Rev. P. A., Hurley st, Wood's Point
Coulls, Joseph, journalist, facing the Goulburn, Wood's Point
Court House, Nash st, Jamieson
Court House, Ellery st, Wood's Point
Cowan, James, blacksmith, Nicholson st, Healesville
Cox, Jas., mining manager, Drummond's Point, Gaffney's creek
Cue, Henry, cabinetmaker, Chenery st, Jamieson
Cummins, Hugh, constable, Drummond's Point, Gaffney's creek
Cunningham, Patrick, miner, High st, Matlock
Crane, Samuel, miner, Harper's creek, Matlock road
Crawford, Samuel, accommodation house, Main road from Wood's Point to Matlock
Crawford, Thomas, Spring Vale hotel, The Springs
Creed, Jeremiah, Bridge hotel, Bridge st, Wood's Point
Crighton, Andrew, restaurant, Bank st, Jamieson
Crisp and Co., law writers and stationers, Hurley st, Wood's Point
Crisp, Edward, secretary Wood's Point Cricket Club
Croin, Patrick, market gardener, Main road Wood's Point to Jamieson
Cronin, Michael, miner, Harper's creek, Matlock road
Cronin and O'Callaghan, wine and spirit merchants, High st, Matlock

Cronin, Timothy, miner, Harper's creek, Matlock road
Crole, Wm., labourer, Blackspur
Cross, Charles, clerk, Chenery st., Jamieson
Croy, Alexander, accommodation house, Main road from Wood's Point to Matlock
Currie, James W., Family hotel, Healesville

D.

Dallas, John, saddler, Nicholson st., Healesville
Daly, Wm., storeman, Raspberry creek
Daly, Timothy, miner, vicinity of the Hospital, Wood's Point
Danver's, Frank, miner, Drysdale's flat
Dargaville, J. M., bank manager, Perkins st., Jamieson
Davidson, Mrs., Halfway House, Main road from Wood's Point to Matlock
Davies, Alfred, merchant, Perkins st., Jamieson
Davies, Joseph, merchant, Bridge st., Jamieson
Davies, Samuel, general storekeeper, Bridge st., Jamieson
Davies, S., Royal Mail hotel, Big river
Davies, Chas., house decorator, Raspberry creek
Davies, John, miner, Main road from Wood's Point to Jamieson
Davies, John, miner, Raspberry creek
Dawkin, —, livery stable keeper, facing the Goulburn, Wood's Point
De Jordan, —, brewer, Scott st., Wood's Point
Deakin, Chas., miner, Glen Watts
Dearlove, —, miner, Drysdale's flat
DeBeer, S., draper and outfitter, Perkins st., Jamieson
Dean, —, miner, vicinity of the Hospital, Wood's Point
Deonery, Henry, packer, Jamieson river
Delaney, Patrick, blacksmith, Chenery st., Jamieson
Dellar and Taylor, packers, Jamieson river
Dermott, Fitzherbert, Matlock
Dighbey, Frederick, miner, facing the Goulburn, Wood's Point
Diggins, John, miner, View Point, Gaffney's creek
Dilles, George, packer, Main road from Wood's Point to Jamieson
Dockendorff, C., merchant, High st., Matlock, and Drummond's Point
Dolter, Dennis, Commercial hotel, Bank st., Jamieson
Donoghue, James, carter, Jamieson river
Donoghan, Daniel, miner, Huricy st., Wood's Point

Donovan, Cornelius, Shamrock hotel, High st., Matlock
Doran, James, sawyer, Hurley st., Wood's Point
Downing, William, mining agent and civil engineer, Hurley st., Wood's Point
Duncan, James, miner, Gaffney's creek
Duockly and Hockins, mining agents and share brokers, facing the Goulburn, Wood's Point
Dermott, Dr., surgeon, Jordan st., Matlock
Drummond, Richard, miner, Rising Sun gully
Drysdale, Eisenstadter, timber merchant, Scott st., Wood's Point

E.

Edwards, Geo., Goulburn hotel, Bridge st., Jamieson
Egan, John, blacksmith, facing the Goulburn, Wood's Point
Eidstaentear, Dennis, Scott st., Wood's Point
Ellenoir, Henry, carpenter, Main road from Wood's Point to Jamieson
Ellerton, John, accommodation house, Nicholson st., Healesville
Ellery, John, miner, Morning Star hill
Easson, James, boot and shoemaker, Rose st., Fitzroy
Ellis, Henry, sharebroker, facing the Goulburn, Wood's Point
Emerson, A. H., solicitor, Bank st., Jamieson
Evans, Evan, miner, High st., Matlock
Embling, Jas., acting agent, Union Bank of Australasia, Wood's Point
England, Joseph, miner, facing the Goulburn, Wood's Point
Everat, Thomas, carpenter, Fernshaw
Evans Brothers, printers, stationers, &c., Bridge st., Wood's Point

F.

Fahn, James, accommodation house, Black Spur
Fehring, John, Travellers' Rest hotel, Big river
Fall, Gabriel, mining manager, Rising Sun gully
Farrell, Robert, carpenter, Healesville
Farrell, Patrick, miner, Drysdale's flat
Fenner, Harry, View Point, Gaffney's creek
Felix, John, commercial traveller, facing the Goulburn, Wood's Point
Finn, Daniel, general storekeeper and wine and spirit merchant, Hibernia brewery, Jamieson
Fisher, Frederick, Fisher's hotel, Fisher's creek

Fisher, Samuel, boot and shoe warehouse, Bridge st, Jamieson
Fishorck, John, carter, Jamieson river
Fitzgibbons, Patrick, miner, Main road from Wood's Point to Jamieson
Fitzmorris, John, miner, Gaffney's creek
Fletcher, —, mining manager, Morning Star hill
Foos and Oat, Reefers' hotel, Scott st, Wood's Point
Foos and Oat, livery stables, Scott st
Foreman, Robert, miner, Raspberry creek
Fox, Joseph, packer, Chenery st, Jamieson
Framur, James, packer, Jamieson river
Frewne, H., mining manager, Bank st, Jamieson
French, Daniel, miner, Main road from Wood's Point to Jamieson
Frenchman, Robt., miner, High st, Matlock
Furlong, John, stonemason, Nash st, Jamieson
Fuller, Fredk., butcher, Wood's Point

G.

Gabriel, D. R., general storekeeper, Scott st, Wood's Point
Gall, Charles, musician, Donaldson st, Matlock
Garrett, John, gardener, Main road from Wood's Point to Jamieson
Geary, Henry, mining agent, Bridge st, Wood's Point
Gibbs, George, mining manager, Raspberry creek
Giggin, John, trooper, Marysville
Gilbert, Margaret, Royal Highlander hotel, Scott st, Wood's Point
Gleeson, Hugh, miner, Drysdale's flat
Gleeson, Peter, M.B.C., Gray st, Jamieson
Gochin, E., hairdresser and tobacconist, Bridge st, Wood's Point
Godfrey, Honora, accommodation house, Main road from Wood's Point to Jamieson
Godwin, Horman, law clerk, Nash st, Jamieson
Godwin, —, solicitor, Perkin st, Jamieson
Good, Henry, gardener, Main road from Wood's Point to Jamieson
Goodier, Charles, butcher, Fernshaw
Gordon, —, carrier, High st, Matlock
Goulding, Alfred, printer, Perkin st, Jamieson
Gough, Lewis W., farmer, Main road from Wood's Point to Jamieson
Gray, Walter, Big river
Green, Richard, miner, Gaffney's creek
Gormanl, Augustus, store, Chenery st, Jamieson
Gutheil and Bottner, medical dispensary, Scott st, Wood's Point

H.

Hall, Wm., veterinary shoeing forge, Nicholson st, Healesville
Hall, John, butcher, Marysville
Hall, Joseph, ship carpenter, Nicholson st, Healesville
Hallenstein and Co., merchants, Melbourne and Jamieson; residence, Mary st, Jamieson
Halton and Quin, mining agents and sharebrokers, High st, Matlock
Hames and Ashbee, Marysville hotel
Hammond, James, Thistle and Shamrock hotel, Drummond's Point, Gaffney's creek
Hargreaves, Ewen, accommodation house, Cumberland creek
Harlow, —, mining manager, Raspberry creek
Harold, Dr., consulting room at Parker's Wood's Point dispensary
Harris, J., carpenter, Drysdale's flat
Harrison, Captain, police magistrate and warden, Jamieson
Hart, Herbert, draper and outfitter, High st, Matlock
Hart, Wm., general storekeeper, Bridge st, Jamieson
Hargreaves, Charles E., hotel and restaurant, Cumberland creek
Harty, John, miner, Gaffney's creek
Hartigan, M., miner, High st, Matlock
Harker and Ellis, mining agents, Scott's st, Wood's Point
Harker, Calvert, mining agent, Morning Star hill
Hayes, Jas., Morning Star hill
Hayes, J., portrait rooms, facing the Goulburn, Wood's Point
Hedger, Frank, butcher, Jordan st, Matlock
Hennissy, Simon, farmer, Chenery st, Jamieson
Herwood, Walter, restaurant, Main road from Wood's Point to Jamieson
Heydicke, Augustus, cooper, Chenery st, Jamieson
Hiller, Frederick, butcher, Scott st, Wood's Point
Higgins, Thomas, miner, Morning Star hill
Hobday, Thomas, blacksmith, Chenery st, and Bank st (corner), Jamieson
Hodson, W., Black Spur inn, Black Spur
Hogan, Wm., miner, Rising Sun gully
Holland, Jane Annie, Royal Mail hotel, Jordan st, Matlock
Holland, John, Royal Mail hotel, and store, Nicholson st, Healesville
Hooper, James, miner, Main road from Wood's Point to Jamieson
Hope, Edward, carpenter, vicinity of the hospital, Wood's Point

Horne, Theodore M., Frenchman's restaurant, Main road from Wood's Point to Jamieson
Horner, Thomas, butcher, Healesville
Horman, H. F., warden's clerk, Ellery st, Wood's Point
Hornbuckle, A. B., clerk Petty Sessions, Ellery st, Wood's Point
Horton and Williamson, mining agents, Hurley st, Wood's Point
Hoskin, Wm., farmer, Jamieson river
Hoskins, Richard, dairyman, Kelly's
Hoskins, Thomas, butcher, Hurley st, Wood's Point
Howard, Elizabeth, The Howard house, Scott st, Wood's Point
Hutchison, J., restaurant, Gaffney's creek
Hutchison, Charles, miner, Scott st, Wood's Point
Hyninson, —, carpenter, Drysdale's flat

L

Islа, Dr., surgeon, J.P., Scott st, Wood's Point
Islа, Dr., consulting rooms, and at Gothic and Buttner's dispensary
Iram, Wm., sawyer, Fisher creek
Irwin, Patrick, miner, Gaffney's creek
Irwin, Charles, miner, Gaffney's creek

J.

Jackson, H., boarding house, Hurley st, Wood's Point
Jeanings, John, miner, Rising Sun gully
Jenkins, John, miner, Morning Star hill
Jefferson, Matthew, Watts Bridge inn, Fernshaw
Jolly, James, Albion hotel, Drummond's Point, Gaffney's creek
Jolly, M. J., mining manager, Gaffney's creek
Jolliffe, William, storeman, Jamieson river
Johnson, H. William, Reefers' hotel, Fernshaw
Johnson, George, miner, High st, Matlock
Johnson, Peter, miner, Fernshaw
Jones, M. John, general store, Scott st, Wood's Point
Jones, James, John, carter, Mary st, Jamieson
Jones, Hugh, miner, Main road from Wood's Point to Jamieson
Jones, William, miner, Main road from Wood's Point to Jamieson
Jones, Samuel, miner, Main road from Wood's Point to Jamieson
Jones, Timothy, boot and shoe warehouse, View Point, Gaffney's creek
Jones, James, labourer, Jamieson river
Jones, George, miner, Drysdale's flat
Jurkart, Charles, butcher, Rasberry creek
Justice, R. G., Beehive hotel, Bridge st, Jamieson

Justice Brothers, merchants, Perkin st and Gaffney's creek; and general storekeepers and wine and spirit merchants, Raspberry creek

K.

Kaeppel, Julius, Bank st, Jamieson
Kairwen, William, Junction hotel, Marysville
Keinhardt, C., mining manager, Matlock
Kelloch, John, carpenter, Main road from Wood's Point to Jamieson
Kelley, Thomas, Commercial hotel, Main road from Wood's Point to Jamieson
Kelly, John, Homeward Bound hotel, Drummond's Point, Gaffney's creek
Kelly, Patrick, accommodation house, Main road from Wood's Point to Jamieson
Kelly, John, miner, Morning Star hill
Kelly, John, Alpine restaurant, Kelly's
Kelson, J. H., M.B.C., Court House hotel, Perkin st
Keppel, Maurice, Australian hotel, Marysville
Kennedy, David B., M.B.C., Niagara hotel, junction of Hurley, Butler, and Ellery sts, Wood's Point
Kennedy, Ellen, Thorny hotel, Scott st, Wood's Point
Kennisgasser, Henry, mining manager, Matlock
Kirtland, Richard, miner, Main road from Wood's Point to Jamieson
Kirkland, James, brewer, Bank st, Jamieson
Kirkpatrick, Henry, miner, Gaffney's creek
Kitts, John, carpenter, Drysdale's flat
Klien, Gustavus, hay and corn store, Marysville
Klim, Charles, miner, High st, Matlock
Kopman, Christoph, musician, Jordan st, Matlock
Kopman, Charles, musician, High st, Matlock
Korburn, Frederick, bootmaker, Scott st, Wood's Point
Koehler and Schulz, Mount Arnold hotel
Kirkpatrick, George C., mining manager, Jordan st, Matlock

L.

Laby, John P., mining manager, Gaffney's creek
Lambert, John, miner, Raspberry creek
Lamprall, George, quarryman, Fernshaw
Laneley, Jonas, shoemaker, Nicholson st, Healesville
Lawlor, Martin, Union hotel, High st, Matlock
Lawlor, Patrick, restaurant, Drysdale's flat

Langbley, Adolphus, miner, Jamieson river
Leary, Edwin, clerk, Marysville
Leader, Thomas, bushman, Glen Watts
Ledger, John, sawyer, Gaffney's creek
Lee, William, miner, Gaffney's creek
Lee, J. Lewis, general storekeeper, Drummond's Point, Gaffney's creek
Lee, Abraham, general storekeeper, Raspberry creek
Legge, Thomas, confectioner, Scott st, Wood's Point
Lewis, William, miner, Main road from Wood's Point to Jamieson
Lewis, F. D., mining manager, Gaffney's creek and Raspberry creek
Loughrey, Andrew, schoolmaster, Nash st, Jamieson
Ludlow, B. Frederick, sharebroker and mining agent, Reefers' hotel, Raspberry Point, Main road from Wood's Point to Jamieson
Lunnies, E. E., Albion hotel, Scott st, Wood's Point
Lynch, Thomas, miner, Chenery st, Jamieson

M

Maclean, D. and A., grocers and ironmongers, Jordan st, Matlock
Macdonald, John, sawyer, Marysville
Maggin, Brothers, general storekeepers, Scott st, Wood's Point
Mahan, James, tin and coppersmith, Scott st, Wood's Point
Malone, John, packer, Jamieson river
Maloney, Patrick, accommodation house, Acheron
Marusorich, Mattor, Chef Imperial, Scott st, Wood's Point
Martin, J. C., mining manager, Gaffney's creek
Martin, Peter, accommodation house, Fernshaw
Martin, Daniel, miner, Gaffney's creek
Martin, Michael, billiard marker, High st, Matlock
Marcarath, Bartholeman, All Nations hotel, Morning Star hill
Mason, John, storekeeper, Fernshaw
Mason, Phillip, draftsman, Drummond's Point, Gaffney's creek
Mason, Cyrus, mining agent and sharebroker, Bridge st, Wood's Point
Mason, Cyrus, sharebroker, Morning Star hill
Matthewson, William, Junction hotel, View Point, Gaffney's creek
Mather, J. W., and Johnson, Healesville hotel, Healesville
Matthews, Robt., "Willie, we have missed you" hotel, The Springs
Maxwell, W. C., Alps hotel, Drysdale's flat
Maxwell, Robert, carpenter, Raspberry creek
Mayne, Robert, storekeeper, Marysville
Mayne, Robert, postmaster, Marysville
McCormick, Charles, carpenter, Marysville
McCaig Brothers, butchers, View Point
McCann, Edward, carpenter, Jordan st, Matlock
McCoy, J., manager Colonial Bank of Australasia, Wood's Point
McDonald, David, Junction restaurant, Kelly's
McDonald, —, Morning Star hill
McDougall, J. C., receiving store, Grey st, Jamieson
McDonald, John, packer, Main road from Wood's Point to Jamieson
McDonald, —, carpenter, vicinity of the Hospital, Wood's Point
McDermott, Edward, Wood's Point
McEwen, James, Star hotel, Bridge st, Jamieson
McEwen, John, packer, Chenery st, Jamieson
McEwan, —, musician, facing the Goulburn, Wood's Point
McFarland, John, carpenter, Drysdale's flat
McFarland, —, barrister-at-law, Butler st, Wood's Point
McGarth, Patrick, miner, Gaffney's creek
McIntosh, John, builder, facing the Goulburn, Wood's Point
McIntyre, —, butcher, High st, Matlock
McKean, Arthur, road overseer, Marysville
McLean, Archibald, depôt store, Chenery st, Jamieson
McClure, Mark, miner, Reefers' hotel, Main road from Wood's Point to Jamieson
McLaren, Alexander, general storekeeper, High st, Matlock
McMaine, James, schoolmaster, Nash st, Jamieson
McMaine, Wm., miner, Drysdale's flat
McNiel, —, bootmaker, High st, Matlock
Mel'herson, John, restaurant, Main road from Wood's Point to Jamieson
Mel'herson, Angus, miner, facing the Goulburn, Wood's Point
McWaters, —, fancy repository, Scott st, Wood's Point
Mead, Wm., sawyer, Hurley st, Wood's Point
Miller, James, M.B.C., merchant, Bridge st, residence, facing the Goulburn, Wood's Point
Meldrum, Norman, tailor, Scott st, Wood's Point
Miller, Frank, mining manager, Bank st, Jamieson
Mills, Wm., bricklayer, Jamieson river

Merick, George, engineer, Gaffney's creek
Mitchel, John, storekeeper and baker, Main road from Wood's Point to Jamieson
Monte, Richard, Retreat inn, Main road from Watson's creek, Wood's Point, to Jamieson
Monk, Adolphus, miner, Chenery st, Jamieson
Montgomery, R. T., miner, Gaffney's creek
Montefiore, Sydney, postmaster, McDougall st, Wood's Point
Montgomery, W. E., commission agent, Bridge st, Jamieson
Moor, Wm., brewers' assistant, Jamieson river
Morgan, Henry, sawyer, Drysdale's flat
Morgan, S. D. Ralph, mining agent, facing the Goulburn, Wood's Point
Morrison, Hugh, baker, Nicholson st, Healesville
Morris, Luke, Raspberry creek
Mountford and Co., Mountain brewery, View Point, Gaffney's creek
Mountford and Co., Bridge inn and store, Bridge st, Wood's Point
Mountford, Hill, and Co., general storekeepers, View Point, Gaffney's creek
Mowday, Henry, sawyer, Main road from Wood's Point to Matlock
McDermott, Edward, Hurley st, Wood's Point
Mosquito Creek bridge, Glen Watts
Mullen, John, Morgan's Cornish hotel, Scott st, Wood's Point
Munro, John, miner, Harper's creek, Matlock road
Murphy, Jeremiah, accommodation house, Bridge st, Wood's Point
Murphy, James, sawyer, Drysdale's flat
Mitchell, Edward, miner, Rising Sun gully

N.

Napier, Charles, carpenter, Nicholson st, Healesville
Nash, Wm., brewer, Jamieson river
Nash, Andrew, M.D., J.P., M.B.C., M.R.C.S., physician and surgeon, Bridge st, Wood's Point
National School ; — Hounslaw, teacher, Butler st, Wood's Point
Naumberg, Edward, general merchants, Scott st, Wood's Point
Nelson, John, miner, Harper's creek, Matlock road
Newbound, Wm., jun., carpenter, Scott st, Wood's Point
Newbound, Wm., sen., carpenter, Scott st, Wood's Point
Newman, R. U., mining manager, High st, Matlock
Nichols, Frederick, labourer, Fernshaw

Nicholls, S., mining manager, Raspberry creek
Nicholson, Moses, bootmaker, Nicholson st, Healesville
Nicholson, J., implement maker, Bouverie st, Melbourne
Nicholson, John, J.P., M.D., M.R.C.S., public vaccinator, &c., Bridge st, Jamieson
Nimmo, Mary, storekeeper, Fernshaw
Nolan, Wm. Frederick, Shamrock hotel, Nicholson st (river crossing), Healesville
Nolan, Daniel, mining manager, Gaffney's creek
Norris, Wm., M.D., surgeon, Gaffney's creek
Norris, Wm., mining manager, Gaffney's creek
Nugent, Honora, Hibernia hotel, Scott st, Wood's Point

O.

Oat, J., facing the Goulburn, Wood's Point
Oats, Richard, engineer, Raspberry creek
O'Connor, Thomas, miner, Gaffney's creek
O'Connor, Owen, labourer, Jamieson river
O'Donnell, John, carrier, Cobham st, Jamieson
O'Day, John, miner, Gaffney's creek
Office of the *Wood's Point Times and Mountaineer*, Bridge, Scott st, Wood's Point
O'Leary, Wm., miner, Harper's creek, Matlock road
Oliver, Albert, watchmaker and jeweller, Scott's st, Wood's Point
O'Neil, H., surveyor, Bank st, Jamieson
O'Reardon, Richard, mining agent and sharebroker, Hurley st, Wood's Point
O'Reilly, Edward, Wood's Point bakery, Hurley st, Wood's Point
Orenshaw, Edward, baker, Marysville
Ottorose, John, tobacconist, Scott's st, Wood's Point
Owen, John, miner, Donaldson st, Matlock

P.

Palling, Henry, McIvor hotel, Scott st, Wood's Point
Palling and Co., cordial manufactory, facing the Goulburn, Wood's Point
Palmer and Hewitt, mining agents and sharebrokers, Main road from Wood's Point to Jamieson
Parr, Charles, miner, Fernshaw
Pardy, Robert, carpenter, Scott's st, Wood's Point
Parker, Thomas, Wood's Point Dispensary, Hurley st

Parry, John, Parry's Royal hotel, Jordan st, Matlock
Patton, John, M.B.C., butcher, Bridge st, Jamieson
Patterson, A. S., Golden Age hotel, Main road from Wood's Point to Jamieson
Pawlemore, H. Christian, packer, Jamieson river
Payne, W., Cornish Arms, Ellery st, Wood's Point
Pearson, T. W. B., warden's servant, Ellery st, Wood's Point
Percy, J. H., mining manager, High st, Matlock
Pendlebury, Gerard, manager Bank of Victoria, Wood's Point
Perry, Ebenezer, prospector, Raspberry creek
Perry, John, miner, facing the Goulburn, Wood's Point
Perry, John, Coach and Horses hotel, Yarra Track
Perry, Charles, Main road from Wood's Point to Jamieson
Perkins and Co., Alpine brewery, facing the Goulburn, Wood's Point
Perkins, James, M.B.C., Jamieson
Perkins, Patrick, Drysdale's flat, Wood's Point
Peters, Peter, carrier, Chenery st, Jamieson
Petty, Henry, accommodation house, Belle creek, near Mount Arnold
Phillipi, Wm., packer, Healesville
Philips, F., bootmaker, Bridge st, Wood's Point
Pitt, Wm., Star hotel, Scott's st, Wood's Point
Pitchimor, Charles, tinsmith, Bridge st, Jamieson
Plenis, James, miner, Harper's creek, Matlock road
Palmer, Charles, contractor, Scott's st, Wood's Point
Police Station, Drummond's Point, Gaffney's creek
Police Station, Nash st, Jamieson
Post-office ; postmaster, Sydney Montefiore, McDougall st, Wood's Point
Police Station Reserve, Hurley st, Wood's Point
Pollock, Chas., miner, Gaffney's creek
Post-office; C. Dankendroft, postmaster, Drummond's Point, Gaffney's creek
Post-office ; J. W. Currie, postmaster, Nicholson st, Healesville
Post-office ; M. Jefferson, postmaster Fernshaw
Power and Blain, produce merchants, Perkin st, Jamieson ; and Goulburn brewery, Jamieson river
Power, Thomas, miner, Morning Star hill
Power, W. E., mayor, M.B.C., Jamieson

Presbyterian Church, Ellery st, Wood's Point
Prongan, Jacob, miner, facing the Goulburn, Wood's Point
Prusser, H., bootmaker, Scott st, Wood's Point
Prym, Jacob, miner, Morning Star hill
Pudleck, Wm. McGrant, restaurant, near Ligar
Purcell, Chas., solicitor, vicinity of the Hospital, Wood's Point
Purcell, P. Chas., solicitor, Scott st, Wood's Point

Q

Quin, P. J., chemist and storekeeper, Wood's Point

R

Radford, Sydney, musician, Hurley st, Wood's Point
Raebery, Chas., carpenter, Jamieson river
Randall, Richd., labourer, Fernshaw
Rapiport, flour, M.B.C., Nash st, Jamieson
Raphael, Maurice, M.B.C., government auctioneer, Perkin st, Jamieson
Rawlins, Mackintosh, and Co., bakers, High st, Matlock
Read, Alexander, miner, Morning Star hill
Reardon, John, miner, vicinity of Hospital, Wood's Point
Ree, Wm., miner, Drysdale's flat
Regan, John, blacksmith, facing the Old Bridge, Jamieson
Reginemus, T. Vincent, hairdresser, Bridge st, Jamieson
Reisrnaner, Emiel, packer, Cobham st, Jamieson
Reinhardi, Carol, butcher, High st, Matlock
Renshaw, Joseph, mining agent and sharebroker, View Point, Gaffney's creek
Rev. P. A. Courtney, Nash st, Jamieson
Richards, Thomas, confectioner, Chenery st, Jamieson
Richardson, Robt., miner, Nash st, Jamieson
Riley, Edward, clerk, Marysville
Riley, John, miner, Drysdale's flat
Robson, John, Acheron Bridge hotel, Acheron
Robinson, John, auctioneer, Morning Star hill
Robinson, Emma, store, Chenery st, Jamieson
Robinson, Mary, Scott st, Wood's Point
Robinson, John, auctioneer and broker, Scott st, Wood's Point
Robson, Jane, hotel, High st, Matlock
Roberts, —, farmer, Marysville
Robertson, Archibald, packer, Parkin st, Jamieson

Robertson, Archibald, carrier, Main road from Wood's Point to Jamieson
Robertson, Jas., Commercial hotel, Bridge st, Wood's Point
Ross, John, bootmaker, Bridge st, Jamieson
Roman Catholic Church ; Rev. F. Courtany, Donaldson st, Matlock
Roman Catholic Church, Nash st, Jamieson
Ronghan, Patk., miner, Gaffney's creek
Rort, Thornton, bushman, View Point, Gaffney's creek
Rosser, Alfred, town clerk, Scott st, Wood's Point
Rosser, Thomas, miner, Gaffney' creek
Rogers, Bernard, draper and storekeeper, Bridge st, Wood's Point
Rogers, Joseph, miner, Chenery st Jamieson
Russell, J. W. Chas., civil engineer and mining surveyor and registrar, Jordan st, Matlock
Russell, Wm., miner, Gaffney's creek
Russell, Wm., miner, Raspberry creek
Ryan, John, French bakery, Scott st, Wood's Point
Ryan, John, miner, Drysdale's flat

S.

Sadistrom, John, labourer, Hurley-st, Wood's Point
Sanderson, A. Wm., bootmaker, View Point, Gaffney's creek
Saunders, J., general store, Drysdale's flat
Saunders, Samuel, carpenter, Fernshaw
Scanlan, Garrett, miner, Gaffney's creek
Scoase, John, blacksmith, Scott st, Wood's Point
Scott, Robert, M.B.C., Scott st, Wood's Point
Scott, Joseph, Royal Mail hotel, Nicholson st, Healesville
Strulz, Chas., Mount Arnold
Scott, Jonathan, Garibaldi restaurant, Fisher's creek
Scott, H., miner, Morning Star hill
Selby, John, miner, Harper's creek, Matlock road
Sergeant, W. Charles, blacksmith, Marysville
Shakespere, Joseph, mining manager, Gaffney's creek
Sharples, Robt., Richmond hotel, Nicholson st, Healesville
Sharp, Geo., draper and outfitter, Hurley st, Wood's Point
Sharkey, —, wood splitter, vicinity of Hospital, Wood's Point
Shaw, John, brewer, facing the Old Bridge, Jamieson
Shearer and Tait, Victoria store, High st, Matlock

Sherick, Alonzo, butcher, Drummond's Point, Gaffney's creek
Shepard, John, storekeeper, Nicholson st, Healesville
Shehan, Cornelius, miner, Main road from Wood's Point to Jamieson
Shortall, Philip, Flour-bag hotel, Main road from Wood's Point to Jamieson
Simes, James, labourer, Glen Watts
Simpson, Geo., commission agent, Bank st, Jamieson
Sinclair, Emma, Sinclair's hotel, Jordan st, Matlock
Singleton and Ashman, Kilmore store Jordan st, Matlock
Smallman, Thos., C.P.S., clerk of Court of Mines, Jamieson
Smith, Thomas, Half-way house, Cumberland creek
Smith, T. C., watchmaker and jeweller, Scott st, Wood's Point
Smith, Villeneuve, barrister-at-law, Butler st, Wood's Point
Smith, Rev. Fredk., Nash st, Jamieson
Smith, Louis, View Point hotel, Gaffney's creek
Smith, Geo., blacksmith, Healesville
Smith, Geo., sawyer, Hurley st, Wood's Point
Smith, Wm., miner, Raspberry creek
South, Louis, stonemason, Nicholson st, Healesville
Spiers, John, miner, Harper's creek, Matlock road
Stack, Patk., miner, Drysdale's flat
Star hotel stabling, Cobham st, Jamieson
Stevens, Chas., Gaffney's creek
Steers, James, miner, Gaffney's creek
Stewart, Robt., miner, Main road from Wood's Point to Jamieson
Stoffers, Henry, tobacconist, stationer, &c., Jordan st, Matlock
Sullivan, Henry, miner, facing the Old Bridge, Jamieson
Sullivan, James, packer, Main road from Wood's Point to Jamieson
Survey Office, High st, Matlock
Swan, Wm., store depot, Cobham st; residence, Nash st, Jamieson

T.

Taylor, R. John, packer, Main road from Wood's Point to Jamieson
Tendwill, Richard, carpenter, Raspberry creek
Temporary gaol, Hurley st, Wood's Point
Thompson, F. Wm., brickmaker, Jamieson river
Thompson, Samuel, saddler, Bridge st Jamieson
Thompson, Thomas, government surveyor survey office, Matlock

Thomson and Croke, mining agents and sharebrokers, Harley st, Wood's Point
Thomson, Arthur, carpenter, High st, Matlock
Thomas, H. F., warden's clerk, Ellery st, Wood's Point
Times and Mountaineer office, Wood's Point
Tisas, Daniel, wine and spirit and general storekeeper, Bridge st, Jamieson
Todd, Joseph, carter, Chenery st, Jamieson
Tindale, —, Gaffney's creek
Tomlinson, Chas., *Times and Mountaineer*, Wood's Point
Toogood, Wm., brewer, Fernshaw
Toomey, John, Water's hotel, Morning Star hill
Toomey, Daniel, miner, Morning Star hill
Tracagey, Dr., M.D., Bridge st, Jamieson
Treseder, Thos., Sir Charles Napier hotel, Scott st, Wood's Point
Tripp, Upton Wm., solicitor, Harley st, Wood's Point
Turner, —, draper, Morning Star hill

U.

Union Bank of Australia; James Emhling manager, Scott st, Wood's Point
Union Bank of Australia; H. W. Anderson, acting manager, High st, Matlock
Union Bank of Australia; J. M. Dargaville, manager, Parkin st, Jamieson
Union Bank of Australia; Henry E. Young, manager, Raspberry creek
Uper, —, Watt's bridge, Fernshaw

V.

Vanroe, Henry, *chef de cuisine à Paris*, Main road from Wood's Point to Jamieson
Veen, Theodore, gingerbeer manufacturer, Jordan st, Matlock
Vern, John, Alpine bakery, Scott st, Wood's Point
Verling, John, mining manager, Matlock
Vickery, R. Samuel, mining surveyor, Bridge st, Jamieson
Vipont, Rev. Thomas D., View Point, Raspberry creek
Vipont, Miss, assistant teacher, Raspberry creek

W.

Walton, Charles, chemist and druggist, View Point, Gaffney's creek
Walter, Samuel R., mining agent, facing the Goulburn, Wood's Point
Walker, Charles, storekeeper, Nicholson st, Healesville
Warlow, George L., mining agent and sharebroker, High st, Matlock
Warve, John, miner, Fernshaw
Waterhouse, Thomas, miner, Rising Sun gully
Weatherhead, John, Globe hotel, Raspberry creek
Webb, James Cole, forwarding agent, Grey st, Jamieson
Webb, John, restaurant, Gaffney's creek
Webster, —, carpenter, Ellery st, Wood's Point
Wheeler and Turner, outfitters, Scott st, Wood's Point
Weley, Thomas, miner, facing the Goulburn, Wood's Point
Wreford, John, solicitor, Ellery st, Wood's Point
West, E. H., carpenter and builder, Chenery st, Jamieson
Wheeler, Francis, packer, Main road from Wood's Point to Jamieson
Whitfield, W. Robt., storekeeper, Marysville
Whitelaw, John, government auctioneer, and mining agent, Scott st, Wood's Point
Whitelaw, John, Ellery st, Wood's Point
Whitehouse, Joseph, carpenter, Chenery st, Jamieson
Whitfield, W. Robert, fancy repository, Jordan st, Matlock
White, Wm., woodsplitter, Bank st, Jamieson
Williams, Mrs., restaurant, Drysdale's flat
Williams, Jane, restaurant, Scott st, Wood's Point
Williams, William, restaurant, Bank st, Jamieson
Williams, Griffiths, miner, High st, Matlock
Wilson, Charles, Bank st, Jamieson
Wilson and Taylor, forwarding agents, Bank st, Jamieson
Wilson, Wm., Gaffney's creek
Wilson, Robt., storekeeper, Nicholson st, Healesville
Wilson, William, veterinary surgeon and blacksmith, Marysville
Wilmot, Wm., storekeeper, Nicholson st, Healesville
Wilkes, Clement, road engineer, Marysville
Wolster, John, carpenter, High st, Matlock
Woolf, Philip A., fancy bread and biscuit baker, View Point, Gaffney's creek
Wood, Charles, labourer, Marysville
Wood, Henrie, Ellery st, Wood's Point
Wood's Point Brewery Company (limited)
Wood's Point Times and Mountaineer office, Scott st, Wood's Point
Wood's Point Leader, Collon and Co., The Bridge, Wood's Point
Woodward, Job, gardener, Cobham st, Jamieson

Wormall and Co., general storekeepers, Scott st, Wood's Point
Wright, Andrew, butcher, Scott st, Wood's Point
Wright, George, Stevenson hotel, Marysville
Wright, Henry, butcher, facing the Goulburn, Wood's Point
Wright, Richard, mining manager, Main road from Wood's Point to Jamieson
Wright and Cunningham, carriers, Healesville

Y.

Young, Mrs., butchery, Hurley st, Wood's Point
Young, John, tinsmith, Bridge st, Wood's Point
Young, Wm., miner, Harper's creek, Matlock road

Z.

Zochlo, F., hairdresser and perfumer, The Bridge, Wood's Point

LODDON, WIMMERA, AND RODNEY

DISTRICTS

COMMERCIAL DIRECTORY,

INCLUDING

Inglewood
Huntley
Tarnagulla
Avoca
Dunolly
Maldon
Newstead
Runnymede
Bet Bet
Rushworth

Green Gully
Blanket Flat
Whroo
Goornong
Murchison
Lamplough
Woodstock
Bong Bong
Mount Blowhard
Newbridge

Jones' Creek
Ascot
Aredale
Bealiba
Elmore
Rochester
Ravenswood
Kingower, &c.

1866-67.

INGLEWOOD.

Anderson, James, baker, Brooke st
Attwood, S., miner, Brooke st
Bambridge, —, miner, Brooke st
Bank of New South Wales; T. K. Johnstone, manager, Brooke st
Bank of Victoria; J. D. Mills, acting agent, Brooke st
Bastor, Wm., merchant, Brooke st
Beard, J., carpenter, Brooke st
Bergrie, J., miner, Brooke st
Biddle, Charles, blacksmith, Brooke st
Bird, James, bootmaker, Brooke st
Boag, James, boutmaker, Brooke st
Bowme, Edwin, seedsman, Brooke st

Bradburn, Thomas, corn merchant, Brooke street
Brazin, Thomas, tailor, Brooke st
Breese, T. S., saddler, Brooke st
Bruntley, Mrs., Brooke st
Bruse, T. S., hairdresser, &c., Brooke st
Campbell, Thomas, tailor, Brooke st
Chapman, R., brickmaker, Brooke st
Church of England; Rev. W. Chalmers
Coleman, G. S., hairdresser, Brooke st
Common School; T. Thomson, master
Cotton, Isaac, fruiterer, Brooke st
Couchman, W. G., mining surveyor, Brooke st
Crosland, George, M.D., M.R.C.S., public vaccinator and registrar, Brooke st

Cronin, J. T., bootmaker, Grant st
Davies, Thomas, watchmaker, Brooke st
Denny, S., M.D., L.R.C.S.P., Brooke st
Desandes, John, photographic artist, Brooke st
Dunn, J. S., butcher, Brooke st
Durston, Thomas, baker, Brooke st
Farmer, W., undertaker
Farquhar, McPherson, butcher, Brooke st
Field, Francis, hotel keeper
Ford, George, Ford's hotel, Brooke st
Furvent, Thomas, miner, Brooke st
Gardner, J. R., acting manager London Chartered Bank of Australia, Brooke street
Garland, Josiah, mason, Brooke st
Gibbins, John Geo., storekeeper, Brooke street
Golden, Thomas, fruiterer, Brooke st
Grieve, James A., solicitor, Brooke st
Gunst Brothers, slaughtermen, Brooke st
Gunst, Wm., Albion hotel, Brooke st
Hamilton, E., refreshment rooms, Brooke street
Hamen, H., butcher, Brooke st
Harbottle and Porch, drapers, Brooke st
Hardy, —, clerk of courts, Brooke st
Harper, W. J., inspector of weights and measures, Tarnagulla road
Hays, Robert, shoemaker, Brooke st
Heldritser, Nicholas, cabinetmaker, Brooke st
Holden, E., storekeeper, Brooke st
Hornblower, J. G., printer and stationer, Brooke st
Howard, Thomas, historian, Brooke st
Inglewood Hospital; D. Radcliff, surgeon, Grant st
Inglewood Advertiser office, Brooke st; J. G. Hornblower, proprietor
Isaac, C., coach proprietor, Brooke st
Jennings, Wm., storekeeper
Jewhurst, F., draper, Brooke st
Kean, J. F., news agent, Charlie Napier hotel, Brooke st
Kirwan, John, storekeeper, Brooke st
Lamont, Herbert, attorney, Grant st
Landry, Wm., storekeeper, Brooke st
Levey, J., hay and corn store, Brooke st
Longstone, J., miner, Brooke st
Lowther, O. McD., police magistrate, Brooke st
Lyle, James, butcher, Grant st
Lyons, Patrick, Shamrock hotel
McClelland, R., grocer, Grant st
McCrae, John, bootmaker, Brooke st
Mack, Michael, baker, Brooke st
Munro, Dondan, and Co., ironmongers, Brooke st
Nixon, George, grocer, Brooke st
North, George, Adelphi hotel, Brooke st
Paget, Mrs., dressmaker, Brooke st
Peppermill, Henry, Court House hotel, Grant st

Pentrock, John, confectioner, Brooke st
Peyton, L. O., postmaster and telegraph manager, Grant st
Philips, Thomas, chemist, Grant st
Pigot, George, Pelican hotel, Brooke st
Plant, Thomas, watchmaker, Brooke st
Pole, Joseph, butcher, Brooke st
Police Station; Sergeant Acton, Grant st
Porch, J., draper, Brooke st
Plomstead, A. G., Niagara billiard saloon, Brooke st
Presbyterian Church; Rev. J. Baird
Pratt, J. M., auctioneer and sharebroker
Pyle, Benj., blacksmith, Grant st
Raddock, Thomas, tinsmith, Brooke st
Radcliffe, H. H., M.R.C.S.E. and L.A.U.L. coroner, Brooke st
Roff, James, storekeeper, Brooke st
Roberts, Albert, Harp of Erin hotel, Brooke st
Robertson, J. S., J.P., Grant st
Roman Catholic Church; Father Shanahan
Rose, R., contractor and builder
Ross, Charles, hay and corn store, Brooke street
Savage, Wm., Western bakery, Brooke street
Shaw, Benj., wheelwright, Grant st
Slattery, James, miner, Brooke st
Smart and Creed, painters, Brooke st
Smellie, Charles, butcher, Brooke st
Smith, W. M., Empire State hotel, Brooke street
Soy, Thomas, sawyer, Brooke st
Speedy, Graham, storekeeper, Grant st
Stewart, A., boot and shoe warehouse, Brooke st
Stock, C. W., mining and literary agent, Brooke st
Strudwick, John, billiard marker, Brooke street
Sutcliffe, Wm., miner, Brooke st
Tatchill, Henry, miner, Brooke st
Thornton, George, bootmaker, Brooke st
Tivey, Joseph, general store, Brooke st
Valentine, Mrs., dressmaker, Brooke st
Vivian and Co., ironfounders, Brooke st
Walls and Flent, blacksmiths
Ward, Martin, bookseller
Webb, G. H., miner, Brooke st
Western, Joh, storekeeper, Brook st
Wilson, Isaac, ironmonger, Brooke st
Wilson, James, J.P., Grant st
Wingfield, James, saddler, Brooke st

MINING COMPANIES.
The Old Inglewood Reef
Poverty Reef
The Morning Star Reef
The Yeldham Reef
The Great Colombian Reef
The Nil Desperandum
The Bendigo Reef

3 D

The Leicester Reef
The March Reef
The Unity Company's Claim
The Independent Quartz
The Reality Reef
The Jersey Reef
The Victoria
The Maxwell Reef
The Concord Reef
The Great Extended Maxwell's Reef
The Dreadnought Reef
The Kentish
The Garibaldi and Kentish United
The Surface Hill Quartz
The Ophir
The Trafalgar
The Nairnshire Quartz
The Enterprise
The South Trafalgar

HUNTLEY.

Atkinson, Wm., storekeeper, Whipstick store, Huntley
Austin, —, storekeeper, Lower Huntley
Britt, F., proprietor of the Monitor Alluvial Claim
Cartmell, R. F., postmaster and storekeeper, Main st
Cerdnini, Peter, butcher, Huntley
Coakley, John, butcher, Main st
Cole, Geo., storekeeper, Lower Huntley
Freeman, George, miner
Frost, John Wm., Camp hotel, Lower Huntley
Harleman, George, blacksmith
Hoskins, Cole, Whitely, and Co., Huntley sawmills
Hinde, Richard, Shamrock and Thistle hotel
Kenetle, Otto, publican, Lower Huntley
McGauchey, Wm., storekeeper, Bagshot
Macneece, J. M., surgeon, Lower Huntley
Matchell, John, Belfast general store, Lower Huntley
Mitchell, —, miner, Lower Huntley
Nunsloeffer, F., miner, Lower Huntley
Nolan, J. P., storekeeper, Huntley and Raywood
O'Dwyer, John F., storekeeper
Pratt, Thomas, contractor
Rogers, James, blacksmith
Rouch, Chas., storekeeper, Lower Huntley
Ryan and Co., Deep Lead hotel
Slade, Jno., baker
Sproy, John, bootmaker
Tilburn, J., miner
Timewell, James, Telegraph hotel
Treasider, Wm., wheelwright
Waits, Wm. W., Victoria hotel
Yuille, J., carpenter

TARNAGULLA.

Arnold, David, Halfway House hotel
Barlow, James
Beynon, John, miner
Binney, Josiah, miner
Bristol, Robt., miner
Bowman, Gen., baker
Brown, —, miner
Cameron, J., tailor and clothier
Chalmers, Rev. R. W., Church of England
Christopher, James, chemist, &c.; post office receiving box
Clay, A. B., George hotel
Clark, Andrew, miner
Clark, James, storekeeper
Council Chambers, Commercial road
Common School, Commercial road
Colonial Bank; A. H. Willis, manager
Crimp, Wm., reporter
Davies, Walter, miner
Davis, J. W., miner
Davies, W. M., manager Cambrian Company
Eady, John, restaurant keeper
Ellis, Samuel, Victoria hotel
Fenton, John, cabinetmaker
Foskett, George E., miner
Grant, C. J., surgeon, public vaccinator and registrar
Griffiths, Wm., miner
Griffith, Henry, hairdresser
Grisoldi and Williams, blacksmiths, &c.
Grisold, Thomas, Commercial road
Gunn, Mrs., midwife
Hargreave's sawmills, Commercial road
Harper, Wm., head master Common School
Harvey, George, baker
Herd, Wm., general store
Hayward, W. L., miner
Hogg, Wm., fruiterer
Hull, Stephen, miner
Irvine, Thomas, collector
James, James, miner
Jenkins, Wm., miner
Johnson, Wm., shoemaker
Johnson, —, general store
Jones, Thomas, miner
Jones, Samuel, miner
Jones, Edward, miner
Jordan, James, draper
Joseph, John, bootmaker
Joseph, Wm., tobacconist
Kelly, James, draper
Kerr, Charles A., draper
Kerr, James, saddler
Lane, J. S., money broker
Leonard, J. P., compositor
Lewin, Frank, Golden Age hotel
Llewellen, Wm., miner
Lord, Thomas, miner
Lown, Abijah, miner

Madden, —, miner
Manuel, R., gold broker
Martin, J., miner
Masters, P., cabinetmaker
Maunder, George, shoemaker
McBride, —, ironmonger
McMillan, —, surveyor
McMillan, Reservoir and Powder Magazine keeper
McPherson, —, miner
Mitchell, James, miner
Moore, C., miner
Moneymant, R., miner
Myles, David, storekeeper
Newman and Barstall, butchers
Nicholl, Wm., miner
Northwood, John
Order of Forresters' Court ; W. Doherety, secretary
Order of Odd Fellows, M.O.I.F.; T. Whitford, N.G.
Ousley, Jacob, blacksmith
Page, Thomas, bookseller and stationer
Parker, H., miner
Patterson, Mrs., laundress
Pierce, John, storekeeper
Police Station; Constable Kelly in charge
Presbyterian Church ; Rev. T. A. Hamilton
Primitive Methodist Chapel ; Rev. — Brawell, pastor
Pulck, John, miner
Raddock, R., miner
Ramsey, Robert, accommodation house
Ray, James, and Co., drapers, &c.
Ray, James, mayor
Reece, Wm., Criterion store
Rees, Wm., miner
Renshaw, D., miner
Roman Catholic Church ; Rev. Fathers Finlay and Shannan
Ross, Robert, miner
Saxe, De S., visiting dentist
Scantlebury, John, blacksmith
Scholfield, Wm., miner
Sheppard, Wm., boot and shoe warehouse
Smale, James, miner
Small, Mrs., milliner and dressmaker
Smith, Thomas, miner
Smith, John, builder
Smith, J. H., Temperance restaurant
Tarnayalla Courier office ; T. Page, proprietor
Thomas, Wm., miner
Thorpe, Joseph, miner
Thomas, Evan, miner
Thompson and Co., drapers, &c., Commercial House
Thomson and Comrie, Exchange store
Tingley, George, miner
Titus, John, miner
Treloar, W. H., blacksmith
Turner, Jane, dressmaker
Turnbull, Mrs., Tarnagulla hotel

Turnbull, Mrs., storekeeper
Union Bank ; H. S. Hooke, manager
Vanables, John, miner
Waller, Charles, coach proprietor
Warren, Mrs. C. E., private school
Webb, John, miner
Webb, George H., blacksmith
Wesleyan Church ; Rev. A. Woodall
Willersdoff, J. C., baker and storekeeper
Williams, Andrew, miner
Williams, Robert, miner
Williams, L., blacksmith
Williams, Thomas, miner
Williams, Wm., miner
Williams, Mrs., Creswick store
Williams, John, bootmaker
Wilson, Rev. S., Ebenezer Chapel
Woodall, —, Wesleyan minister
Wylie, J. P., compositor
Yates, James, miner
Yeomon, John, storekeeper

AVOCA.

Allanson, W. H., saddler
Avoca Mail; G. F. Patten, proprietor
Bacon, J. Bailey
Bank of Victoria; L. Ogilby, manager
Basbal, Felix, storekeeper
Bostock, Peter, butcher
Brennan, James, miner
Brookes, H., hairdresser
Brown, George, tailor
Bryant, R. C., bairdresser
Campbell, Neil, Union hotel
Chellen, John, watchmaker
Church of England, Rev. — Yateman
Clasen, John, cabinetmaker
Coghlan, J., farmer
Coke, M., solicitor
Common School, G. R. McAdam
Dance, Wm., miner
English, —, mining surveyor
Goodshaw, Wm., chemist and druggist
Green, Charles, brickmaker
Hall, H., secretary Shire Council
Healey, Cornelius, constable
Henry, T. W., bootmaker
Holland, T., produce merchant
Hughes, Thomas, miner
Jennings and Co., J., blacksmiths
Johnstone and Steel, timber merchants
Kay, John, blacksmith and farrier
Kearney, John, wheelwright
Kelly, J. F., draper
Keihl, R. A., butcher
Kilpatrick, James, storekeeper
King, Peter, baker
King, T. C., sign painter
Lange and Thornman, merchants
McDonald and Steel, carpenters
McLean, D., draper and storekeeper
Miles, Henry, gingerbeer and cordial manufacturer

388 ALPHABETICAL

Nicholls, Mrs.
Overs, H., hay and corn dealer
Parrington, E., market gardener
Paten, J. F., stationer, &c.
Pearson, C. K., watchmaker
Police Station ; Superintendent Mason
Post-office and Telegraph station ; J. Woodward, manager
Powers, Henry, baker
Rosbach, J. H., bootmaker
Smith, J. B., Avoca hotel and livery stables
Snell, Edmund, storekeeper
Sulliff, Wm., draper and outfitter
Sumner, Z., tinsmith
Sweet, Francis, butcher
Town Hall; H. Hall, clerk
Trevena, Wm., Victoria hotel
Trevithick, H., Commercial hotel
Wesleyan Church, Rev. Mr. Fitchell
Whitley, Wm., carpenter
Wise, W. M., auctioneer

DUNOLLY, MALDON, &c.

Allen, John H., tobacco manufacturer, Newstead
Ali, Isaac, storekeeper, Runnymede
Alexander, H., druggist, Dunolly
Amonah, F., hot het store, Bet Bet
Anstead, James, puddler, Chinaman's flat, Rushworth
Ansaldi, D., restaurant, Green gully
Atkinson, James, blacksmith, Runnymede
Babidge, James, Bridge Inn, Cobbinabbin
Band and Hazely, storekeepers, Balaclava hill, Whroo
Banderbile, Wm., storekeeper, Blanket flat
Barnett, A. R., academy, Goorong
Barratt, Wm., blacksmith and farrier, Murchison
Barrett, —, farmer, Runnymede
Barrow, Mrs. E. M., farmer, Runnymede
Bayly, John, butcher, Newbridge
Bell, James, merchant, Dunolly
Belt, —, farmer, Runnymede
Benbow, Thomas W., manager Bank of Victoria, Rushworth
Berthon, F., farmer, Runnymede
Blair, Robert, bootmaker, Newstead
Blyth, John, miller, Newstead
Bonin, A., linendraper, Newstead
Brasher, Mrs. M., Imperial hotel, Rushworth
Brewer, A. G., nurseryman and seedsman, Dunolly
Briton, James, miner, Lamplough
Brice, G. G., butcher, Rushworth
Broderick, M. A., storekeeper, Maldon
Buckley and Bridge, millers, Newbridge
Burke, Michael, Old Junction Inn, Woodstock

Burrell, W. T., watchmaker, Rushworth
Butler, James, tailor, Newstead
Calder, Thomas, Ironmonger and timber merchant, Maldon
Callander, Wm., bootmaker, Maldon
Carrol, Thomas, boarding house, Beng Bong
Carter, John H., teacher Common School, Whroo
Cartwright, G., Clare Castle hotel, Lamplough
Carver, F., blacksmith, Mount Blowhard
Catlin, James, butcher and baker, Runnymede
Chapman, C. W., butcher, Maldon
Clark, L., farmer, Runnymede
Clark, John, blacksmith, Runnymede
Clark, Wm., merchant, Newstead
Connell, A., bootmaker, Newbridge
Cosgrove, Wm., Eddington
Cowle, C. T., manager Bank of New South Wales, Maldon
Coy and Anderson, blacksmiths and wheelwrights, Rushworth
Cracknell, George, baker, Rushworth
Craggie, F., farmer, Runnymede
Crossley, J., baker, &c., Maldon
Cummins, John, bootmaker, Lamplough
Cannecu, M., farmer, Runnymede
Dabb and Cop, produce merchants, Maldon
Darley, Wm., Rushworth hotel, Rushworth
Davison, Thomas, seedsman, Maldon
Day, Robert, brewer, Newbridge
Day, Joseph, butcher, Newstead
Dean, Henry, farmer, Runnymede
Dean, Jabez, Shakespeare hotel, Maldon
Degraves, W. E., squatter, Runnymede
Denny Brothers, bootmakers, Maldon
Derrick, Wm., miner, Jones creek
Devereux, John, wheelwright, Bangaree
Digby, Thomas, Golden Deer, Ascot
Drake, P., Campaspe hotel, Axedale
Duggen, P., Rose of Australia hotel, Glendarnell
Dunstan, John, carpenter, Axedale
Eastman, Alexander, publican and storekeeper, Goornong
Easton, Frederick, restaurant, Lyons st. Newstead
Evans, Edward, carpenter and wheelwright, High st, Maldon
Ellis, E. M., storekeeper, Bong Bong
Ellis, Edward, Kangaroo hotel, Maldon
Erwin, Henry, London hotel, New Bridge
Eyes, Charles, storekeeper, Spring flat, Bong Bong
Farrar, Frederick A. G., postmaster and electric telegraph manager, Maldon
Farrow, W., miner, Lamplough
Ferguson, J., farmer, Runnymede
Ferguson, John, bootmaker, Main st, Maldon

Fitzgerald and Co., brewers, Newbridge
Fish, W., sawyer, Lamplough
Fogarty, Patk., storekeeper, Lamplough
Franklin, Henry, bootmaker, Main st, Maldon
Gadsby, Wm., Waggon and Horses hotel, Mount Blowhard
Gamble, Thomas, Australasian hotel, Maldon
Grant, Donald, Bet Bet hotel, Bet Bet
Griffin, James, Runnymede
Griffin, Lawrence, and Co., forwarding and commission agents, Runnymede
Gobbett, Edward, storekeeper, Maldon
Guerrero, Joseph, Miners' Arms, Main st, Maldon
Ham, Ann, storekeeper, Main st, Maldon
Hannah, Milten, Criterion hotel, Rushworth
Heasey, Thomas, bookseller and news agent, Main st, Maldon
Harley, John, storekeeper, Whroo
Hayes, Thomas, farmer, Runnymede
Healey, Dr., Rushworth
Hicks, Henry, saddler, registrar of births and deaths, bailiff of County Court, Rushworth
Hicks, John A., chemist and druggist, Main st, Maldon
Higgins, P. and J., Cornelia Creek station, Cornelia Creek, Rochester
Holder, Henry, baker, &c., Newbridge
Honnens, A., gold smelter, jeweller, and proprietor of glue manufactory, Springs, Maldon
Howieson, Tate, and Co., printers and publishers, High st, Maldon
Ibbotson, John, saddler, Newstead
Irving, James, saddler, Ascot
Ison, Henry, butcher, Dunolly
Izat, Wm., saddler, Newbridge
Jackson, Henry, farmer, Runnymede
Jones, John, station master, Runnymede
Joyce, George, Junction hotel, Newstead
Kean, Wm., blacksmith, Newbridge
Keay, George, hairdresser, Main st, Maldon
Kennedy, Hugh, tailor, Broadway, Dunolly
Kirsley, Francis, draper, Dunolly
Langton, John, storekeeper, Goornong
Leeburch, Henry, clerk of court, Rushworth
Lewis, John Thomas, reefer, Whroo
Lindsey, John, bootmaker, Main st, Maldon
Locke, George Wm., physician, High st, Maldon
Lucas, Thomas, farmer, Runnymede
Mackenzie, Hugh, storekeeper, Maldon
Maddocks, Frederick, Criterion hotel, Maldon
Maher, Thomas, head master Common School, Murchison

Marsden, Thomas, hotelkeeper, Green Valley
Marsden, Eliza, Newstead hotel, Newstead
Martin, Frederick, Newbridge hotel, Newbridge
Marwick, John, Ravenswood hotel, Ravenswood
Matheson, John, Moora hotel, Moora
Mathieson, Joseph, storekeeper, Newbridge
Matthews, Wm., plumber and painter, Maldon
Matthews, James, Woodstock Inn, Woodstock
McArthur, George, baker, Main st, Maldon
McFarlane, John, Albion hotel, Newbridge
McFarlane, John James, outfitter, &c., High st, Maldon
McIntosh, Robert, Murchison
McKenna, James, and Co., Broadway, Dunolly
McMahon, John, farmer, Runnymede
McMillan, Neil, M.D., Castle Hill, Murchison
Millar, Thomas Roberts, coachbuilder, Rushworth
Millgate, Henry, miner, Bung Bong
Milne, Charles Henry, ironmonger, Broadway, Dunolly
Milton, Hannah, Criterion hotel, Rushworth
Morgan, J. W., storekeeper, Maldon
Morris, Francis Freeman, general agent, Maldon
Moss, George, tailor, Rushworth
Murphy, Patk., farmer, Runnymede
Nalor, J., miner, Lamplough
Neill, Robert, boot and shoe maker, Main st, Maldon
Newington, Joel, storekeeper and postmaster, Newbridge
Nicholas, Henry Boyne, mining surveyor, Rushworth
Nicholson, Joseph, storekeeper, Bung Bong
Noell, Wm., tobacconist, main st, Maldon
Nomens and Scheel, timber merchants and storekeepers, Lyon st, Newstead
Nottage, John C., Farmers' Arms hotel, Newbridge
O'Brien, M., farmer, Runnymede
Ogilvy, J. T., storekeeper and publican, Ascot
O'Neill, —, baker, Lamplough
O'Neill, John, M.D., High st, Maldon
Padley, William, iron merchant, Maldon, Daylesford, and Melbourne
Page, Robert, Royal hotel, Maldon
Partridge, A., butcher, Bung Bong
Papengoth, Carl Emil, cabinetmaker, High st, Maldon
Pearson, Hugh, general store, Newbridge
Pile, —, farmer, Runnymede

Phillips, Joseph, watchmaker, &c., Broadway, Dunolly
Phillips, Mark, Caledonian hotel, Murchison
Pincott, John, bootmaker, Broadway, Dunolly
Post Office; J. Newington, postmaster, Newbridge
Potter, Thomas, farmer, Runnymede
Presbyterian Church and School, Rushworth
Primitive Methodist Church; Rev. T. Bracewell
Raven, Thomas, storekeeper, &c., Rushworth
Raven, M., farmer, Runnymede
Raven, Henry, miner, Jones' creek
Rattery, Wm., farmer, Runnymede
Reid, George M., and Co., chemist and druggist, High st, Maldon
Reydsted, Charles, travelling photographer
Reynolds, Edward, solicitor, High st, Maldon
Roberts, C. T., storekeeper, Bung Bong
Roberts, John Henderson, storekeeper, Rushworth
Robinson, John, High st, Maldon
Roger, Morgan, blacksmith, High st, Rushworth
Rowe, Dr., squatter, Runnymede
R———, Rudolph, British American hotel, Maldon
Rule, Oliver Richard, watchmaker and jeweller, High st, Maldon
Salas, Frederick, butcher, Murchison
Salter, Wm., Maldon
Sands, John, wholesale and retail tinsmith, High st, Rushworth
School, National, Mr. Lowther, Runnymede
Scott, George, Railway hotel, Runnymede
Seake, Jonathan B., hotelkeeper, Runnymede
Seward, Thomas, Seward's hotel and post office, Rochester
Seymour, A. and H. C., Lounge hotel, High st, Maldon
Shlach, James, bootmaker, Rushworth
Shottes, ——, farmer, Runnymede
Simpson, George, Bendigo hotel, Dunolly
Simpson, James, miner, Lamplough
Skelton, James, Beehive hotel, Main st, Maldon
Smith, Hugh, physician and surgeon, Newstead
Smith, Thomas Heathorn, chemist and druggist, High st, Rushworth
Solsbey, George, miner, Jones' creek

Sparling, C., Scotch pie shop, Broadway, Dunolly
Steake, J., Runnymede
Steele, James T., draper, Maldon
Steer, J., and Son, blacksmiths, Axedale
Strohouse and Greig, storekeepers, Maldon
Sternberg, Alexander, storekeeper, Rochester
Stewart, John G., storekeeper, Rushworth
Stewart, Charles Haggart, store and post office, Murchison
Sutherland, Wm., Newstead biscuit manufactory, Newstead
Swindale, ——, farmer, Runnymede
Telegraph Station; Henry Jennyings, Runnymede
Thompson, George, Albert hotel, Whroo
Thorne, Robt., seedsman and storekeeper, Newbridge
Timothy, Michael, mounted constable in charge of police station, Murchison
Tidswell, Wm., saddler, Broadway, Dunolly
Tragonniny, Joseph, storekeeper, Loddon valley
Trocke, Wm., news agent and tobacconist, Main st, Maldon
Turner, Jesse, miner, Jones' creek
Trucbridge, Catherine, dressmaker, Main st, Maldon
Toohy, Hannorah, storekeeper, Rushworth
Tyrer, Thomas, tobacconist and job ironmonger, Broadway, Dunolly
Vaughan, J., butcher, Fryer's creek
Wade, Bridget, general storekeeper, High st, Maldon
Waltran, William Charles, storekeeper, secretary Mechanics' Institute, Rushworth
Wales, Alexander, saddler, High st, Maldon
Warner, Joseph, bootmaker, Rushworth
Warnock Brothers, merchants, Maldon
Warren, Samuel, bootmaker, Main s, Maldon
Weekes, Samuel Thomas, builder and undertaker, Broadway, Dunolly
Whittle, John, butcher, High st, Maldon
Wigg, Walton, brewer, Rushworth
Williams, John, miner, Lamplough
Wilson, David, hotel and post office, Mount Blowhard
Wood, James, and Co., grocers and wine and spirit merchants, Maldon
Wright, John, officer in charge of police station, Axedale
Zanazco, Adolph, store and post office, Sneaston

BOURKE, EVELYN, & MORNINGTON DISTRICTS COMMERCIAL DIRECTORY,

INCLUDING

Essendon
Heidelberg
Templestowe
Lilydale
Gap
Gisborne
Little Swamp
Keilor
Bungaree
Bacchus Marsh

Dowling Forest
Warrenheip
Ballan
Melton
Sunbury
Diggers' Rest
Gordon
Eltham
Queenstown
Woodend

Moorabool
Broadmeadows
Flemington
Moonee Ponds
Spring Creek
Franklinford
Springfield
Myrniong
Aitken's Gap
&c., &c., &c.

1866-67.

Armstrong, Alfred, mining surveyor, Eltham
Armstrong, Thomas, farmer, Yarra flats
Artis, Henry, Commercial hotel, Lilydale
Baker, Mr., farmer, Sunbury
Baker, Edward, farmer, Gap
Balfour, James, tailor, Aitkins st, Gisborne
Barling, J., schoolmaster Common School, registrar of births and deaths, Sunbury
Beavan, Alfred Sparzheim, postmaster, Gisborne
Beed, Thos., publican and farmer, Plough inn, Little Swamp
Beer, Jacob, cooper, Gisborne
Beeton, David, storekeeper, Keilor

Bentley, S. J., hotelkeeper and farmer, Lee creek, Bungaree
Blair, Robert, farmer, Lilydale
Bostwood, James, baker, Bacchus Marsh
Bourke, John, Lilydale
Bourke, Michael, Manchester hotel, Gap
Bourke, Michael, Junction hotel, Dowling Forest
Brennand, Robert, blacksmith, Warrenheip
Britt, Patrick, Carriers' Arms, Black hill, Moorabool
Brown, Matthew, farmer, Inglis st, Ballan
Brown, W., Bacchus Marsh
Bruce, Alexander, farmer, Lilydale
Bryce, Henry, farmer, Lilydale

Buckland, Charles, labourer, Templestowe
Bull, John, Barley Sheaf hotel, Miners' Rest
Butler, G. S. C., M.D., J.P., Heidelberg
Cahill, John, Morning Star hotel, Warrenheip
Burman, James, Caledonian hotel, Queenstown
Callaghan, Edward, hotelkeeper, Bacchus Marsh
Cameron, —, butcher, Queenstown
Carew, Michael, shoemaker, Melton
Carr, John, M.L.A., J.P., Gisborne
Carter, W., store, Pentridge
Castella, Paul de, farmer, Lilydale
Castella, Hubert de, farmer, Lilydale
Casser, George, general storekeeper, Ardlie st, Broadmeadows
Chambers, Luke, Mount Macedon hotel, Gisborne
Cherry, Edward, Aitken st, Sunbury
Child, —, farmer, Lilydale
Choumara, —, post office, Gordon
Clarke, Charles, Monmouthshire hotel, Diggers' Rest
Clark, David G., schoolmaster, Eltham
Drummond, T. D., clerk of police court, Eltham
Common School, Queenstown, Robert Alice, master
Cook, Alex. Thomas, smith and wheelwright, Essendon
Cooke, Henry, blacksmith, Ballan
Cousens, Moses, butcher, Inglis st, Ballan
Cousens, Henry, butcher, Pike flat
Cricket Club, W. B. Andrew, secretary, Eltham
Cunningham, Cornelius, blacksmith, Inglis st, Ballan
Dorricutt, John, builder, Bacchus Marsh
Day, James, storekeeper and postmaster, Aitken's Gap
De Castella, Hubert, vineyard, St. Hubert, Lilydale
Dendy, Henry, flour mills, Eltham
Denham, Thomas, saddler, Moonee Ponds
Dolamore, W. J., draper, Woodend
Dorriant, John, Bacchus Marsh
Dorrington, Wm. Josh., saddler, Gordon
Dowling, Philip, master Common School, Lilydale
Duncan, Walter, Ballan
Dyke, Richard, storekeeper, Woodend
Eagling, John, hotelkeeper, Keilor
Wallis, B. O., Eltham hotel, Eltham
Elr, James, shoemaker, Lilydale
Evans, John, Railway hotel, High st, Woodend
Evans, Thomas, miner, Queenstown
Ewings, George, Eltham
Fay, James, Farmers' hotel, Moorabool
Feild, Julia, hotelkeeper, Ballan
Ferris, George, Harvest Home hotel, Boggy creek

Field, James, postmaster, Templestown
Field, William, druggist, Hamilton st, Gisborne
Fisher, Allan, farmer, Lilydale
Fitzsimmons, Thos., Sydney hotel, Woodend
Fletcher, Geo., farmer, Yarra flats
Flyn, Peter, miner, Queenstown
Foster, W., miner, Queenstown
Fraser, Donald R., blacksmith, Ballan
Furlong, Alexander, Railway inn, Keilor
Gandion, Nicholas, farmer, Lilydale
Gardner, John, storekeeper, Eltham
Garlick, Rev. F. B., Church of England minister, Gisborne
Gilmore, William, blacksmith, Broadmeadows
Glennon, James, farmer, Lilydale
Glover, John, Prince Albert hotel, Flemington
Glover and Cooper, butchers, Woodend
Gosling, Wm., butcher, Inglis st, Ballan
Goudre, Matt, hotelkeeper, Keilor
Gray, Gilbert, farmer, Lilydale
Greeves, Wm. Hunter, chemist and druggist, deputy registrar of births and deaths, Woodend
Haine, John, farmer, View hill, Yarra flats
Haines, Richard, storekeeper, Gisborne
Hamilton, T. F., J.P., Gisborne
Hammerton, Thos., baker, Woodend
Hand, Thomas, farmer, Lilydale
Haniford and Macroidden, butchers, Eltham
Harding, Daniel, wheelwright, Eltham
Harman, Robert, Crown hotel, Lilydale
Harper, John, Butchers' Arms, Flemington road
Hawke, Wm., labourer, Sunbury
Hart, Henry, miner, Queenstown
Henkins, J. T., Moonee Ponds
Herbert, Wm., farmer, Point Pleasant, Yarra flats
Hewish, James, farmer, Templestowe
Hewish, James, hotelkeeper, Templestowe
Higginbotham, W., storekeeper, Woodend
Hill, Wm. Henry, Victoria hotel, Broadmeadows
Hill, Wm., baker, Gisborne
Hill, Frederick, draper, Gisborne
Hinkins, John Thos., postmaster, Moonee Ponds
Horoeil, Charles L., bootmaker, Calthorpe st, Gisborne
Hullis, Rev. Josiah, parish church, Eltham
Hunniford, Thomas, postmaster, Eltham
Hussey, Henry, storekeeper, Gisborne
Ibbotson, Alice, Cumberland Inn, Woodend
Ireland, R. D., Templestowe
Jackson, Williamina, dressmaker, Moonee Ponds
Jarrol, Wm., gardener, Eltham
Johnston, A., storekeeper, Woodend

Joiner, M., farmer, Lilydale
Jones, Edward, hotelkeeper, Bacchus Marsh
Jopling, John, surgeon, &c., Tyne cottage

Keating, John, butcher, Woodend
Kenny, John, Springfield hotel and post office, Springfield
Kent, Robert, farmer, Templestowe
Kerr, Issic, bakery and general store, Eltham
Kerr and Black, farmer, Lilydale
Kerr, Wm., storekeeper, Woodend
Kincblac, Thomas, farmer, Lilydale
Kings, Richard T., butcher, Lilydale
Kings, T. C., butcher, Alphington
Knoll, John C., postmaster and storekeeper, Queenstown
Koe, W. Bacchus Marsh
Lacey, James, farmer, Templestowe
Lacey, Frederick, postmaster and storekeeper, Green gully
Leonard, Anthony, bootmaker, Gisborne
Lishder, A., Lilydale
Lithgow, David, Lilydale hotel, Lilydale
Lithgow, John, farmer, Lilydale
Loran, P., Roma hotel, Spring Creek
Lutrell, Edmond, Woodend hotel, High st, Woodend
Macintyre, Gilbert B., farmer, Lilydale
Macintyre, Thomas, farmer, Lilydale
Mackay, Samuel, farmer, Lilydale
Major, J., storekeeper, Gordon
Manningham, Patk., farmer, Lilydale
Morand, Daniel, boot and shoe manufactory, Gisborne
Martelli, A., farmer, Lilydale
McBride, Robert, shepherd, Rockbank station
McGregor, Angus, deputy registrar, cemetery, Aitken st, Sunbury
McIlraith, Wm., farmer, Lilydale
McIntyre, G. B., Lilydale
McIntyre, Michael, Mac's hotel, Ballan
McKay, Alexander, Anderson's Creek post office, Lilydale
McKee, Henry, trooper in charge Broadmeadows police station
McKenzie, Alfred, London and Liverpool Arms, Woodend
McPherson, James, farmer, Yarra flats
McPherson, Duncan, saddler, Gisborne
Merlot, Robt., farmer, East Ballan
Millett, George, Bald Hills hotel, Aitken's Gap
Minouge, Martin, storekeeper, Franklinford
Mongovan, John, Warrenheip hotel, Warrenheip
Mongovan, John, post office, Leigh Creek
Monti, Angelo Bartalome, storekeeper, Springfield
Matershaw, Wm., bootmaker, High st, Woodend

Munby, Hugh, hay and corn factor and farmer, Woodend
Murphy, John, dining rooms, Aitken's Gap
Murphy, Denis, farmer, Lilydale
Murrell, W., Melbourne road, near Ballarat
Musgrave, Anthony Thomas, solicitor, Ballan
Nicholson, Mrs. W., farmer, Lilydale
Nottingham, James, carpenter, Lilydale
O'Hanlon, Terence, baker, Hamilton st, Gisborne
Ovens, Walter, baker, Moonee Ponds
Page, Charles, bootmaker, Woodend
Panton, J. A., P.M., Eltham
Paterson, Thomas, miller, Woodend
Paul, Henry, farmer, Lilydale
Pearson, John, Eltham
Perrin, Henry, postmaster, Lilydale
Persse, S. R., Grand Junction hotel, Melbourne road
Peterson, Peter, fruiterer, High st, Woodend
Petty, James, postmaster, Yarra flats
Police Station, Eltham ; Senior Constable Lawlor in charge ; Mounted Constable Mills
Police Station, Gisborne ; Sergeant Hall, constable
Police Station, Queenstown ; Constable James Lindsay in charge
Pool, Edward, Junction hotel, Preston
Presbyterian School, Templestowe
Prismall, Daniel, baker, Inglis st, Ballan
Pritchard, David Thomas, saddler and harness maker, High st, Woodend
Pullbrook, John, farmer, Lilydale
Pury, Samuel De, farmer, Lilydale
Quadri, A. D., Yarra Flats hotel, Yarra flats
Quick, Walter James, Commercial hotel, Blanket flat
Quinland, Timothy, storekeeper, Moonee Ponds
Rae, Wm., surgeon, J.P., and coroner, Bacchus Marsh
Rass, Daniel, storekeeper, Melton
Reid, James, blacksmith and wheelwright, Bacchus Marsh
Renny, John, Springfield
Richardson, Abraham, Plough inn, Gisborne
Riley, John, publican, Flemington
Robbie, Wm, bootmaker, Woodend
Robinson, W., J.P., Gisborne
Robinson, Robert, hotel keeper, Gordon
Ross, Daniel, Melton
Rouget, John, farmer, Lilydale
Rourke, John, Lilydale
Rourke, Denis, farmer, Lilydale
Russell, Josiah, Highland Chief hotel, Springfield
Ryan, Michael, storekeeper, Melton

Sampson, Wm. Thomas, Victoria hotel, Woodend
Saunders, John, storekeeper, Bacchus Marsh
Scott, Henry F., minister, Parsonage, Ballan
Sefton, John, hotel keeper, East Ballan
Shaw, John, hotel keeper, Ballan
Shibler, Augustus, storekeeper, Melton
Smith, James, Irishtown, Plenty road
Smith, James, storekeeper, Smyth's gully, Queenstown
Smith, John, butcher, Templestowe
Smith, Thomas Pybus, draper, Gisborne
Smith, John, farmer, Lilydale
Smith, Richard J., brewery, Queenstown
Smith, James, butcher, Aitken st, Gisborne
Smith, W. C., tailor, Woodend
Stead, Wm., joiner, Lilydale
Stebbings, George, Eltham
Stevens, R., butcher, Hamilton st, Gisborne
Stooke, Henry, Rose hill, Eltham
Strachan, Mary, storekeeper, Woodend
Stubbs, George, Moorabool hotel, Moorabool creek
Suman, James, Queenstown
Summers, John, farmer, Providence place, Eureka
Sutellery, T. H., storekeeper, Queenstown
Sutton, Henry, Mount Macedon hotel, Woodend
Sutherland, John, Broomfield
Swannell, John, hotel keeper, Myrniong
Swift, J. D., sawmills, Lilydale
Telford, Robert, hotel keeper, Ballan

Tenniel, James, Beach Tree hotel, Tullamarine
Thompson and Brown, storekeepers, Moonee Ponds
Thornton, Patrick, Campbellfield beerhouse, Gisborne
Tooley, John, farmer, Lilydale
Toy, Edward, farmer, Calton estate, Templestowe
Trew, Marian, hotelkeeper, Eltham
Upton, Charles, farmer, Lilydale
Walker, Alexander, farmer, Templestowe
Wallace, Wm., farmer, Lilydale
Wallis, B. O., Eltham hotel, Eltham
Walters, James, farmer, Yarra flats
Walton, W., labourer, Sunbury
Warmoll, Eliza, storekeeper, Flemington
Watts, Wm., bootmaker, Bacchus Marsh
Webb, Henry, farmer, Lilydale
Webbe, N. P., storekeeper, Myrniong
Whale and Brown, greengrocers and fruiterers, Bacchus Marsh
Wheeler, B., Shamrock hotel, Carlsruhe
Whllan, Edward, solicitor, Gisborne
White, John, Commercial hotel, Gisborne
White, John, farmer, Lilydale
Williams, John, blacksmith, Aitken st, Gisborne
Wilson, John, Gordon
Wilson, Sarah, storekeeper, Moonee Ponds
Wingrove, Charles, road surveyor, Eltham
Wipple, Walter, storekeeper, Eltham
Woods, P., Broadmeadows
Young, Thomas, baker, Queenstown
Younger, Thomas, farmer, Lilydale
Younger, Thos., and Co., farmers, Lilydale

TALBOT, RIPON, GRENVILLE, & DALHOUSIE

DISTRICTS

COMMERCIAL DIRECTORY,

INCLUDING

Talbot	Kingston	Majorca
Maryborough	Smeaton	Coomoora
Daylesford	Vaughan	Joyce's Creek
Carisbrook	Gap	Franlinford
Amherst	Learmonth	Springs
Guildford	Miners' Rest	Glenlyon
Yandoit	Lexton	Coghill's Creek
Fryers Town	Hepburn	Burrambeet, &c.

1866-67.

A

Abberton, Patrick, Talbot store, Glenlyon
Adamson, Mal, storekeeper, Maryborough
Albritch, Frank, butcher, Talbot
Alexander, H. M., Daylesford
Allan, Robert, saddler, Learmonth
Allan, Robert, wheelwright, Kingston
Allan, James, miner, Fryers Town
Allison, Edward Wm., builder and ironmonger, Kingston
Amherst Hospital; F. B. Salmon, secretary; D. C. Dixon, house surgeon
Anderson, James, manager London Chartered Bank, Maryborough
Anderson, James, butcher, Fryers creek
Anderson Brothers, millers, Smeaton
Anderson, Mrs., Lexton
Andrew, J., watchmaker, Carisbrook
Andrew, John, farmer, Smeaton
Armstrong, Wm., Smeaton
Armstrong, Henry, butcher and storekeeper, Yandoit
Arnold, J. F., storekeeper, Majorca

B.

Bach, Antoine, butcher, Talbot
Bagot, S., hairdresser, Maryborough
Ball and Bandbox, drapers, Vaughan
Bank of Australasia; M. J. Whiton, Talbot
Bank of Victoria, Crescent, Camp st, Talbot; M. Tong, manager
Banner, W., bootmaker, Vaughan

Barber, Wm., postmaster, Gap
Barberis, Joseph, Prince of Wales hotel, Vincent st, Daylesford
Barnes, Thomas C., storekeeper, Learmonth
Bateman, J. E., proprietor of *Talbot Leader*, Talbot
Baugh, Henry, labourer, Miners' Rest
Bear, George, miner, Fryers Town
Beckingsale, Thomas and George, storekeepers, Vincent st, Daylesford
Bedolo, M., Spring Creek hotel, Spring Creek
Bell, James, restaurant, Maryborough
Bell, R. B., family grocer, Talbot
Bellot, John, Junction hotel, Vaughan
Bennet, Mrs., Bridge Inn, Amherst
Bennetts, Elizabeth, fruiterer, Camp st, Talbot
Bentley, Henry, saddler, Fryers Creek
Bertrand, A. J. S., bootmaker, Ballarat st, Talbot
Bey, Peter, ironmonger, &c., Talbot
Biaggi, Carlo Andrea, publican, Guildford
Blackwell, Thomas, timber, lime, and colour merchant, Burke square, Howe and Vincent sts, Daylesford
Blakeney, T. S., Vincent st, Daylesford
Blanchard, John, saddler, Amherst
Blight, John, hotel keeper, Sulky gully, near Ballarat
Blundell, Frank Freeman, photographer, Camp st, Talbot
Bond, Frederick James, publican, Vaughan
Bonn, Thomas, White Swan hotel, Jones's Creek
Borland, Hugh, bootmaker, High st, Maryborough
Boros, A., brewer, Daylesford
Boyle, Henry, publican, Fryers Town
Bradshaw, Charles, Albion hotel, Creswick road
Brent, Mrs. A., Lallah Rookh, Majorca
Bridgewater, Thomas, bootmaker, Learmouth
Brightwell, Felix, carter, Kingston
Broadbent, Mary, Stag hotel, Kingston
Broadfoot, Mary, storekeeper, Ballarat st, Talbot
Brodie, Mrs., news agent, Carisbrook
Brown, Frederick, miller, Kingston
Brown, Elliot, Brown's Family hotel, Talbot
Brown, L., butcher, Amherst
Brown, James, carter, Talbot
Browne, Charles Townley, Criterion hotel, Vincent st, Daylesford
Browne, Edward, clog and patten maker, Argyle st, Talbot
Browne, James U., hotel keeper, Coomoora hotel, Coomoora
Buchanan, Thomas, saddler, Maryborough
Burke, Mrs. A., store, Fryers Creek
Busell, John, miner, Fryers Town

Burton and Co., general merchants, Hepburn
Bustelli, Joseph, working jeweller, Vincent st, Daylesford
Butler, George, farmer, Middle creek, Morlock
Butler, John S., sen., wool sorter, Joyce's Creek
Butler, John S., jun., farmer, Joyce's Creek
Butterly, Matthew, Spring hotel, Gap

C.

Cambridge, George Henry, merchant, Carisbrook
Cameron, C., draper, Maryborough
Camp, Talbot ; Sergeant Bell in charge
Campbell, Angus, storekeeper, Glenlyon
Campbell, A., miner, Ballarat st, Talbot
Card, Edward, carpenter, Coomoora
Cardinal, Henry, Liverpool Arms, Amherst road
Carisbrook Post and Telegraph office ; James A. Bennie Smith, manager
Carter, W. H., bootmaker, Majorca
Carr, Dr., Talbot
Carroll, Charles, grocer, Vincent st, Daylesford
Carter, George Levi, boot manufacturer, Fryers Town
Cattle and Co., reefers, Fryers Town
Christian and Co., Maryborough
Church of England, High st, Amherst
Church of England, Argyle st, Talbot ; Rev. — Barker
Church of England, Fryers Town ; Rev. — Holt
Church of England, Miners' Rest ; Rev. — Powell
Clark, Samuel Hawkins, publican, Fryers Town
Clarke, Mary, restaurant, Majorca
Clayton, John, blacksmith and wheelwright, Westmoreland hotel, Fryers Town
Cohn Brothers, Talbot brewery, Ballarat st, Talbot
Cole, Daniel, butcher, Fryers Town
Colles, James, postmaster and Telegraph office, Camp st, Talbot
Collier, Wm., storekeeper, Fraser st
Colquhoun, Henry, storekeeper, Shepherd's flat, Hepburn
Common School ; Mr. Gannon, head master
Common School, Miners' Rest
Common School ; John Coutts, teacher, Gap
Cooke, William, Nag's Head hotel, Carisbrook
Cowell, Thomas, miner, Daylesford
Council Chambers, Kingston ; H. Macey, secretary

Court House, Camp st, Talbot
Court of Petty Sessions, Fryers Town;
— Townsend, clerk
Cox, Joseph, Showyard hotel, Smeaton
Cox, Thomas, chemist, Majorca
Coyle and Dargan, storekeepers, Fryers Creek
Craddock & Walker, blacksmiths, Brown's diggings
Crawcoor, Isaac, pawnbroker, Vincent st, Daylesford
Creelman, John Auchterlonie, L.R.C.S.E., district coroner, Learmonth
Cribbes, Wm., blacksmith, Fryers Town
Cromble, —, sharebroker, Talbot
Crooks, John, leather merchant, Talbot
Cross, Andrew, grocer, Howe st, Daylesford
Culimore, John, miner, Fryers Town
Culley, Benjamin, draper, Commercial road, Talbot
Curtin, Patrick, farmer, Smeaton
Corthoys, Joseph, mining agent, Vincent st, Daylesford
Cushen, George, Union hotel, Albert st, Daylesford

D.

Daly, John, Talbot
Davenport, J., painter, Fryers Creek
Davidson, George Wemyss, hotel keeper, Smeaton
Davis, David, watchmaker and jeweller, Vincent st, Daylesford
Daws Brothers, seedsmen and storekeepers, Kingston
Daws, W., butcher, Carisbrook
Day, John, fruiterer, Majorca
Dennis, —, shoemaker, High st, Amherst
Dethmer, Wm., publican, Yandoit hotel, Yandoit
Dickson, Thomas, labourer, Smeaton
Dimsey, David, farmer, Franklynford
Dixon, George, Franklin hotel, Yandoit
Dobson, Catherine, Yandoit
Done, A., bookmaker, Argyle st, Talbot
Doolittle, F. W., M.D., hospital, Daylesford
Douglas, Patrick, general storekeeper, Amherst
Dohuan, John, draper, Guildford
Downing, A., accountant, Ballarat st, Talbot
Dow, Dr., coroner, Ballarat st, Talbot
Down, J. W. F., confectioner, Castlemaine st, Fryers Town
Draper, Ambrose, news agent, Daylesford and Yandoit
Draper, W. M., baker, High st, Amherst
Duncan, Francis, Wallaby hotel, Connqors
Dundon, David, storekeeper, Yandoit

E.

Eastwood, Archibald, Argyle st, Talbot
Eddy, Matthew, publican, Vincent st, Daylesford
Edwards, J. B., stationer, &c., High st, Amherst
Edwards, J. B., goldsmith and jeweller, Talbot
Edwards, James F., mining agent, Old Race Course, Hepburn
Edwards, Robt., seedsman, Daylesford
Egglesso, C. E., town crier, Talbot
Elder, Wm., saddler, Argyle st, Talbot
Elder, Wm., Camp hotel, Talbot
Elliot Brothers, storekeepers, Yandoit
Elvish, James, fruiterer, Vincent st, Daylesford
Elvish, Thos., fruiterer, Howe st, Daylesford
Elworthy and Froom, produce store, Majorca
English, Isabella, Carlsruhe
Evans, Thomas, draper, High st, Amherst

F.

Fabean, —, bootmaker, Maryborough
Fairlie, Walter, and Co., butchers and storekeepers, Lexton
Farmer, Joseph, Coghill's Creek
Farmer, Robert Ward, chemist and druggist, Maryborough
Farrell, Samuel, Enterprise hotel, Glenlyon road
Fenton, James, solicitor, Maryborough
Fenton, John, Separation hotel, Fryers Town
Ferguson, D., sheep dealer, Fryers Town
Finlay, David, Commercial hotel, Guildford
Finlayson, N. J. A., blacksmith, post office, Miners' Rest
Fisher and Co., storekeepers, High st, Amherst
Fisher's brick yards, High st, Amherst
Fisher, Thomas, merchant, High st, Amherst
Fitzgerald, John, Lady of the Lake hotel, Learmonth
Fitzgerald, N., storekeeper, Howe st, Daylesford
Fleischer, Geo., blacksmith and wheelwright, Yandoit
Fletcher, Geo., bootmaker, Kingston
Flewin, Geo., brickmaker, Miners' Rest
Flynn, J., teacher, Camp st, Talbot
Flynn, Patrick, storekeeper, Talbot
Forester's Hall, High st, Amherst
Fostevin, John, blacksmith, High st, Amherst
Fowler, John, hawker, Lexton
Frampton, —, High st, Amherst

Fraser, James, hairdresser, Commercial road, Talbot
Fryers Town Academy, Cornelius Gladwin, proprietor, Fryers Town
Furbur, John, All Nations hotel, Argyle st, Talbot

G.

Galtress, C., dairyman, Fryers Town
Gammon, M., head master Common school, Yandoit
Glamboin, —, bootmaker, Guildford
Gibton, —, commissioner for taking affidavits, Camp st, Talbot
Gilbart, Frederick, Koroobeang hotel, Castlemaine hotel
Gillard, Walter John, saddler, Kingston
Gillilong, Edward, agent Bank of Victoria, Vaughan
Gladwin, Cornelius, Fryers Town
Glashen, F., farmer, Coghill's Creek
Glenny, G. and S. S., general storekeepers, Glenlyon
Goldspring, Charles, boot and shoe maker, Argyle st, Talbot
Gordon, Thomas, bootmaker, Argyle st, Talbot
Gracie, Henry, storekeeper, White hills, Maryborough
Graham, David, storekeeper, White hills, Maryborough
Graham, Geo., senior, contractor Miner's Rest
Grandjean, Eugene, Vineyard hotel, Glenlyon road
Grashen, Thomas, miner, High st, Amherst
Grasse, Pietro, chemist, Old Racecourse, Daylesford
Gray, —, bootmaker, Coghill's Creek
Gray, D., blacksmith
Grayling, R., miner, Lexton
Green, Henry, butcher, Kingston
Greenwood, Chas., saddler, Smeaton
Griffiths, James William, druggist, Burke square, Daylesford
Guilart, M., Maryborough
Gutheil and Buttner, chemists, Vincent st, Daylesford

H

Hackett and Co., general storekeepers, Amherst
Hall, Wm., miner, Amherst
Halpin, James, storekeeper, post office receiving box, Coomoora
Hamilton, David, bookseller and stationer, Vincent st, Daylesford
Hamilton, E., fancy repository, Talbot
Harbottle and Porch, drapers, Talbot
Harbottle and Porch, drapers, High st, Maryborough
Hardigan, W., tobacconist, Maryborough

Hardy, T. D., produce dealer, Ballarat st, Talbot
Harken, John, storekeeper, Maryborough
Harlinge, M., coach factory, High st, Amherst
Harris, Robt., butcher, Majorca
Harrison, J., Gap
Harrison, W. G., farmer, Springs
Harrison, —, tobacconist, Majorca
Hauser, Jacob, bootmaker, Fryers Town
Haynes, Thomas, miner, accommodation house, Coomoora
Hays, G. H., Carisbrook
Heales, John, Kingston
Hedley, Robert, tinsmith, High st, Amherst
Helliwell, J., West of England hotel, Albert st, Daylesford
Hently, Charles Fredk., storekeeper, Glenlyon
Heppner, Henry, bootmaker, Talbot
Hill, Archibald, hotelkeeper, Smythe's creek road
Hill, James, storekeeper, Camp hotel, Carisbrook
Hill, James, fruiterer, High st, Maryborough
Hilton, Wm., miner, Fryers Town
Hinks, J. Wesley, Imperial hotel, Ballarat st, Talbot
Hodge, Harriet, Metropolitan hotel, Daylesford
Hogg, Geo., wheelwright, Fryers Town
Hotchins, A., store, Carisbrook
Holland, John, miner, Fryers Town
Holmes, Grace, Belle Vue hotel, Fryers Town
Holmes, Jas., Golden Age hotel, Ballarat st, Talbot
Hooper, Geo., taxidermist, &c., Ballarat st, Talbot
Horsfield, Henry, Pioneer hotel, Yandoit
Hoskins, H. H., solicitor, Camp st, Talbot
Howard, John, mailman, Argyle st, Talbot
Huong Chooy Goon, merchant, Talbot
Hutton, Henry F., watchmaker, Vincent st, Daylesford
Hunter, John, saddler and harness maker, Green st, Carisbrook
Hurle, Robert, butcher, Maryborough
Husband, W. J., slaughterman, Gap

I.

Ingram, John, watchmaker, High st, Maryborough

J.

Jacobs, Henry, blacksmith and wheelwright, Smeaton
James, Joseph Alfred, stationer, Guildford
James, W. E., photographer, Talbot

Jamieson, Neil, blacksmith, Kingston
Janker, —, bootmaker, Dunolly.
Johnston, Chas., Horse and Jockey hotel, High st, Amherst
Johnston, Samuel, livery and bait stables, Talbot
Jolly, J. W., blacksmith, Camp st, Talbot
Jones, James, carrier, Lexton
Jones, James, accommodation house, Coomoora
Jones, H. L., stationer, Majorca
Jowett, Frederick, butcher, Commercial st, Talbot

K

Kaye, Wm., fruiterer, Maryborough
Kelly, Mrs. O., Bridge Inn, Carisbrook
Kemp, G. S., farmer, Coghill's Creek
Kemp, J. and G., Junction hotel, Glenlyon road
Keoff, C., London hotel, Majorca
Kewley, Thomas, hotelkeeper, Bungaree
Kersley, F., draper, Maryborough
Kershaw, J. C. C., bootmaker, Camp st, Talbot
King, Wm., saddler, Guildford
Kirk, Wm, Talbot coach factory, Talbot
Kitto, F., miner, Fryers Town
Klein, T. G., Union hotel, Ballarat st, Talbot
Knapp, Henry, Bungaree
Knight and Waddington, blacksmith, Majorca
Kourtland, L., cabinetmaker, Ballarat st, Talbot
Krauley, T. E., publican, Kingston

L

Ladd, Thomas, storekeeper, Talbot
Lammin, Joseph, wheelwright, Coghill's Creek
Lanes, F., Green gully
Lange, L., Prince of Wales theatre, Maryborough
Langhem and Co., coffee roasters, Daylesford
Lansdown, John, hotelkeeper, Creswick road
Lavazzolo, John, Victoria hotel, Vincent st, Daylesford
Lawrence, R. J., Daylesford
Layland, H., dairyman, Fryers Creek
Lee, J. B., blacksmith, Vaughan
Legg, Edward James, Commercial hotel, Maryborough
Lembecke, John, tobacconist, Commercial road, Talbot
Lerew, David, grocer, Vincent st, Daylesford
Lesman, A., surveyor, Ballarat st, Talbot
Lewin, James, Ball Inn, Smythesdale road
Lewis, Mrs., ladies' school, High st, Amherst

Lewis, John, miner, High st, Amherst
Lightly, John, Excelsior hotel, Vincent st north
Lincoln, David, Variety store, Amherst
Lisle, J. H., Talbot
Little, Charles J., storekeeper, Miner's Rest
Little, C. J., J.P., Coghill's Creek
Lloyd, Mrs., accommodation house, Ballarat st, Talbot
Lockhart, James, blacksmith, High st, Amherst
Logan, A. C., Maryborough
London Chartered Bank of Australasia, Talbot; manager, J. Fowler
London Chartered Bank of Australia, Majorca; manager, J. Makinson
Long, Thomas, cabinetmaker, Raglan st, Daylesford
Longford, T., saddler, Majorca
Look, Elisha, tinsmith, Howe st, Daylesford
Lowe, Thomas, baker, Learmonth
Lowenstein, Alexander, tobacconist and gold broker, High st, Maryborough
Logg, Samuel, Majorca
Lugg, W. M., blacksmith and wheelwright, Learmonth

M.

Mack, S., butcher, Kingston
Mackey, G., miner, Yandoit
Malnon, C., tobacconist, Vincent st, Daylesford
Makinson, Charles, solicitor, Fryers Town
Malcolm, Jas. Burn, medical practitioner, Vaughan
Malne, Joseph, storekeeper, Yandoit
Mann, Peter, miller, Smeaton
Manning, Wm., carpenter, Ballarat st, Talbot
Maguire, James, grocer, Howe st, Daylesford
Marks, Joseph, gardener, Lexton
Marriott, Arabella, hotelkeeper, Majorca
Marshall, Wm., fruiterer, High st, Amherst
Marston, Josiah, painter, Chapman st, Talbot
Martin, W., cobbler, Gap
Martin, Michael, farmer, Smeaton
Martin, Thomas, carter, Lexton
Maslow, Robert James, storekeeper and wholesale fruiterer, Amherst
Mason, William Rutherford, storekeeper, Vaughan
Masson, J., bootmaker, Gap
Muther, Robert, farmer, Smeaton
Matthews, Wm., Coghill's Creek
May, Garland, storekeeper, Maryborough
McCann, P. E., Banner of War hotel, Smythe's creek road
McClelland, —, North British hotel, Talbot

McCormick, Patk., accommodation house, Coomoora
McCracken, Jas., shopkeepers, Coomoora
McCrae, Charles, Miners' Rest hotel, Miners' Rest
McCrae, Duncan, Dowling Forest hotel, Miners' Rest
McCullock, W. G., and Co., stores, Maryborough
McDermott, —, solicitor, Talbot
McDonald, Wm., Lexton hotel, Lexton
McDonough, Mrs., general store, Kingston
McDule, storeman, High st, Amherst
McFarlan, James, storekeeper, Glenlyon
McGillivray, John, saddler, Vincent st, Daylesford
McGlashan & Cumming, machine makers, Lake Learmonth
McGrath, Edward, blacksmith, Burrumbeet
McKay, Wm., postmaster and storekeeper, Learmonth
McKell, J., plumber and gasfitter, Vincent st north, Daylesford
McKenzie, J. L., registrar of births and deaths, Vaughan
McKenzie, J. M., Stag hotel, Learmonth
McKenzie, Roderick, miner, Amherst
M'Lean, Andrew, hotelkeeper, Learmonth
McNeil, Allen, blacksmith, Coghill's Creek
Mellas, —, Dowling hotel
Meadows, Isaac, High st, Amherst
Mechanics' Institute, Kingston; secretary Ed. Dawson
Mechanics' Institute, Talbot; secretary J. Fletcher
Medcraft, —, blacksmith, Carisbrook
Mercer, Wm., medical practitioner, postmaster, public vaccinator, registrar of births and deaths, and electoral registrar, Fryers Town
Meredith, Joseph, Fountain hotel, Vincent st, Daylesford
Merrifield, Christopher, Ocean Child hotel, Burrumbeet
Meriga, Antonio Giovanni, Athens hotel, Raglan st, Daylesford
Moriton, Geo., Imperial hotel, Majorca
Merrett, Fredk., Bellevue hotel, Gap, Mount Bolton
Michael, James Phillip, cabinetmaker, Albert st, Daylesford
Middleton, James Philpott, storekeeper, Vaughan
Millar, Wm., Australian bakery, Majorca
Millar and Anderson, general merchants, Vincent st, Daylesford
Miller, John, blacksmith, Fryers Creek
Miller, Jacob, wheelwright, Smeaton
Mills, Edwin, painter, High st, Amherst
Mills, Robert, grocer, Vincent st, Daylesford
Minster, Charles, hotelkeeper, Smeaton
Mitchell, Wm., general store, Talbot

Molony, Thos., United States hotel, Talbot
Meriga, Antonio Giovanni, farmer, Leetcher creek, Daylesford
Monton, S. E., tinsmith, Carisbrook
Moore, Samuel, miller, Smeaton
Moore Bros., general merchants, Fryers Town
Moore, Wm., blacksmith, Springs, Mount Bolton
Morgan, Wm., Carriers' Arms, Miners' Rest
Morris, Wm., storekeeper, Talbot
Morse, Robert, stonemason, Argyle st, Talbot
Mosely, B. P., watchmaker, Majorca
Murphy, James, blacksmith, Talbot
Murphy, T. F., High st, Amherst
Murphy, Wm., Farmers' hotel, Lexton
Murray, James, Waverley hotel, Majorca
Murray, —, blacksmith, &c., Coghill's Creek
Murrell, Wm., licensed victuallers, Melbourne road, Ballarat
Murro, Margaret, Caledonian hotel, Dowling Forest
Myers, John, tinsmith, Fryers Creek

N.

Nairn, John, storekeeper, Daylesford
Naples, Thomas, baker and confectioner, Albert st, Daylesford
Nagel, Fredk., tobacconist, Vincent st, Daylesford
Neale, Wm., baker, Carisbrook
Nekke, Louis, Lake View hotel, Burrumbeet
Newman, James, general storekeeper, Guildford
Nicol, Wm., bootmaker, Yandoit
Niven, Hugh, bootmaker, High st, Amherst
Nobblett, Geo., aerated water manufacturer, Ballarat st, Talbot
Noble, Geo., blacksmith, Coghill's Creek
Noble, Mrs. Geo., storekeeper, Coghill's Creek
Norton, M. A., billiard saloon, Majorca

O.

O'Brien, Wm., hotelkeeper and farmer, Learmonth
O'Brien, Martin, farmer, Burrumbeet
Ockilman, J. P., carpenter, Ballarat st, Talbot
Odd Fellows' Hall, M.U.I.O.O.F., Commercial road, Talbot
O'Fee, Mary, Glasgow Arms hotel, Majorca
Office of Exploring Gold Mining Company, Commercial road, Talbot
Office of Princess Alexandra Company, Ballarat st, Talbot

Office of Union Gold Mining Company, Ballarat st, Talbot
O'Grady, Peter, American hotel, Old Racecourse, Hepburn
Orde, T. T., butcher, Glenlyon
Oxley, Geo., Wright, tailor, Talbot
Owen, Robert, storekeeper, Majorca
Owens, Mrs., publican and storekeeper, Barker's creek

P.

Padley and Co., ironmongers, Daylesford
Pairman, Thos., Pyrenees hotel, Lexton
Parker, Lucy, ladies' school, Argyle st, Talbot
Parker, Richard, mining agent, Vincent st, Daylesford
Parker, Henry, bootmaker, Vincent st, Daylesford
Parker, Isabella, confectioner, Maryborough
Parry, Emma, Court House hotel, Camp st, Talbot
Pascoe, James, farmer, Kingston
Paul, James Melvin, chemist and druggist, Talbot
Pearson, John, M.R.C., corn dealer, Talbot
Pearson, J., carrier, Gap
Peddington, James, Carisbrook hotel
Pensom, Edwin Bellinger, whitesmith and bellhanger, Vincent st, Daylesford
Perry, J. K., gas manufacturer, Argyle st, Talbot
Pettegrove, A., bootmaker, Maryborough
Phillips, John, Farmers' Arms hotel, Raglan st, Daylesford
Phipps, James, hotelkeeper, Vincent st, Daylesford
Pierce, Thomas, wine and spirit merchant, Ballarat st, Talbot
Pitcher, Josiah, butcher, Smeaton
Pittman, Lambrook, saddler, Howe st, Daylesford
Pincke, Daniel, ironmonger and boot dealer, High st, Maryborough
Police Station, Coghill's Creek; Constable Michael Kennedy in charge
Police Station, Lexton; Sergeant Buckman
Police Station, Gap; James Dowling in charge
Police Station, Smeaton; mounted constable H. Wilkinson in charge
Porte, La D., M.D., surgeon, Argyle st, Talbot
Post office, Lexton; George Watson, postmaster
Pozzi, Alexander, interpreter, Vincent st, Daylesford
Preshaw, David Ogilvy, chemist and druggist, Carisbrook
Presbyterian Church, High st, Amherst

Presbyterian Church, Lexton; Rev. — Adams
Presbyterian Church, Miners' Rest; Rev. — Smyth
Presbyterian Church, Fryers Town
Primitive Methodist Chapel, Talbot; Rev. — Adams
Prohasky, Wm., merchant, corner Albert and Bridport sts, Daylesford

Q.

Quick, Robert, saddler, Learmonth
Quick, W. J., Commercial hotel, Blanket Flat
Quinlan, A. R., solicitor, &c., Talbot

R.

Rainers, J. C., Royal hotel, Vincent st, Daylesford
Reasley, Thomas Edward, publican, Kingston
Ready, W., chemist (Argus agent), Maryborough
Richmond, Alexander, draper, Vincent st, Daylesford
Road Board, Fryers District, Fryers Town; J. N. Amos, secretary
Robinson and Liddle, wheelwrights and blacksmiths, Talbot
Rodda, Thomas, Vaughan
Rose, Wm., carpenter, Coghill's Creek
Rooke, James, carter, Argyle st, Talbot
Rooke, Thomas, contractor, Argyle st, Talbot
Rooney, James, accommodation house, Coomoora
Ross, Wm. Henry, carpenter, Exchange hotel
Rossell, Thomas, storekeeper, Main st, Kingston
Rowles, T. R., baker and confectioner, Talbot
Ryan, James, shoemaker, Kingston
Ryan, Matthew, Camp hotel, Learmonth

S.

Sadler, W. B., accountant, Ballarat st, Talbot
Salmon, F. D., tobacconist, High st, Amherst
Samuel, Samuel, solicitor, Maryborough
Sanders, H. J., and Co., ironmongers
Sault, Ann, Theatre Royal, Talbot
Schmidt, R. W., surgeon, M.M.D.V., Talbot
Schroeder, Christian, butcher, Yandoit
Schulze, Carl, farmer, Springs, Mount Bolton
Scudamore, George, Vaughan
Searle, F. J., chemist and druggist, Talbot

3 F

Sebastian, C., butcher, Vincent st north, Daylesford
Serjeant, Thomas Woolcock, B.A., clergyman, Lake Learmonth
Settle, Jonathan, wheelwright, Yandoit
Shaw, John, carpenter, Fryers Creek
Shearer, Theodore, miner, Fryers Town
Shears, Josiah, London hotel, Talbot
Simper, Charles, Old House at Home hotel, Carngham
Sinclair, Arthur, bootmaker, Howe st, Daylesford
Sinclair, Mrs. G., Brewers' Arms, Majorca
Sinclair, John, and Co., drapers, &c., Anfers st, Guildford
Skillan, James, grocer, Vincent st north, Daylesford
Small, D., store, Majorca
Small, David, grocer, Talbot
Smart, Henry, miner, Fryers Town
Smith, Alexander, storekeeper, Talbot
Smith, E. G., hotel keeper, Hill and East sts, Daylesford
Smith, James, constable, Lexton
Smith, Joseph, mining surveyor and registrar, Talbot
Smith, Thomas, storekeeper, Gap
Smith, Walter, auctioneer and commission agent, Burke square, Daylesford
Smith, W. J., Kingston
Smyth, Samuel Wilson, mining agent, Vincent st, Daylesford
Solomon, Bernstein, and Co., Majorca
Soloman, Bernstein, and Co., outfitters, Talbot
Sparling, David, butcher, Vaughan
Sprinks, H. T., barman, Ballarat st, Talbot
Staley Brothers, storekeepers, Yandoit
Stavely, David, store, Majorca
Steers, F., store, Gap
Stein, A., tentmaker, Talbot
Stephens, Ed., Telegraph hotel, Maryborough
Stephenson, James, Liverpool Arms, Glenlyon road
Sterling, Wm., draper, Maryborough
Steward, Henry, watchmaker and jeweller, Gap
Stiles, John, blacksmith, Fryers Town
Stillings, Edwin, dispensing chemist, Vincent st, Daylesford
Sully, James, Diggers' Rest hotel, Diggers' Rest

T.

Tait, Mary, Derby hotel, Miners' Rest
Talbot Leader office; Messrs. Bateman, Clark, and Co., proprietors, Talbot
Tangy, Thomas, store, Majorca
Tatcher, Thomas, gingerbeer factory, Argyle st, Talbot
Tate, Robert Wm., fancy repository, Fryers Town
Taylor, D., store, Maryborough
Taylor, David, farmer, Smeaton
Taylor, Jacob E., greengrocer, Vincent st north, Daylesford
Tennant, C., Carriers' Arms, Howe and Raglan sts, Daylesford
Thomas, Allen, clothier, Howe st, Daylesford
Thomas, Joshua, teacher, Kingston
Thomas, Wm. H., ironmonger, Howe st, Daylesford
Thompson, H., Commercial road, Talbot
Thompson, John, storekeeper, Coomoora
Thompson, Henry, ironmonger, Talbot
Thornton, George, publican, Miners' Rest
Thornton, George, miner, Talbot
Toe, E., saddler, Talbot
Toulth, —, miner, High st, Amherst
Tozer, Edgar. butcher, Ballarat st, Talbot
Traversi, Carlo, Traversi's hotel, Howe st, Daylesford
Tranter, Mrs. J., Majorca
Trowt, Robert, butcher, High st, Amherst
Tweedale, W., chemist and druggist, Amherst
Twining, James, Mill hotel, Vincent st, Daylesford

V.

Vale, R. T., news agent, Burke st
Vercy, Henry, tailor, Vincent st, Daylesford
Victor, George, draper, Vincent st, Daylesford
Virtue, Peter, grocer, Maryborough
Vorwerg, Miss Mary, storekeeper, Coomoora

W.

Walder and Co., storekeepers, Chapel st and Nuggetty hills, Fryers Creek
Walsh, J. D., bootmaker, Majorca
Walsh, Thomas, Harp of Erin, Majorca
Wanless, James Wm., wheelwright and blacksmith, Glenlyon
Wark, A., Foresters' Home, Majorca
Warne, Alfred, White Hart, Gap
Watson, George, J.P., Lexton
Watts, Charles, butcher, Hepburn
Weatherley, Wm., publican, Ballarat st, Talbot
Wells, Joseph Fredk., Red Lion hotel, Vincent and Raglan sts, Daylesford
Wesley, John, Imperial hotel, Ballarat st, Talbot
Wesleyan Church, High st, Amherst
Wesleyan Church, Gap; Rev. W. Kaze
Wesleyan Methodist Chapel, Commercial road, Talbot
Wesleyan Church, Camp st, Talbot

Wesleyan Chapel, Lexton
Westwood, Julius Peter, boot and shoe store, Vincent st, Daylesford
Whatman, James, builder, Coomoora
Whatmore, Richard, seedsman, &c., Kingston
Whear, T., Blacksmiths' Arms, Fryers st, Guildford
Whittaker, Wm., storekeeper, Argyle st, Talbot
Widdowson, George, Farmers' hotel, Coghill's Creek
Wilkinson, Robert Wood, druggist and seedsman, Talbot
Williams, C., Majorca
Williams, Frederick, storekeeper, Nuggetty gully, Tarnagulla
Williams, George, miner, Fryers Town
Williams, John Shields, publican, Auction Mart hotel, Vincent st, Daylesford
Williams, John, baker, Vaughan
Williams, Sarah, Talbot hotel, Harcourt

Wilson, D., Mount Blowhard hotel, Mount Blowhard
Wilson, W. C., McIvor hotel, Maryborough
Winch, Mrs., ladies' school, Camp st, Talbot
Wiseman, Richard, tailor and habitmaker, Albert st, Daylesford
Wisewould and Gibbs, solicitors, Camp st, Talbot
Wissing, Frederick, tobacconist, Vincent st, Daylesford
Wood and Knight, booksellers, High st, Amherst
Wood, Wm., deputy registrar births and deaths, Ballarat st, Talbot
Worsley, J. H., carpenter, Majorca
Wright, Mrs., ladies' school, High st, Amherst
Wright, Robert, miner, High st, Amherst
Wrigley, T. D., Commercial hotel, Talbot
Wyatt, J. W., general store, Yandoit

DENILIQUIN ALPHABETICAL DIRECTORY.

1866-67.

Allet, Jonathan, wheelwright
Atkinson, John Olbory, Hill Plain Inn, Deniliquin road
Barbour, John, carpenter
Beel, Alex.
Beggs, James, warder
Bennett, Edward, fruiterer, &c.
Birch, Chas., labourer
Bullock, David, watchmaker
Bree, Wm., bricklayer
Broughton, John Archer, clerk of petty sessions
Burton, Henry, Redbank hotel, Mathoura (Deniliquin road)
Cameron, Donald, tailor, Cressy st
Campbell, Duncan Wm., accommodation house, Mathoura (Deniliquin road)
Carpenter, Alfred, stationer and news agent, End st
Carne, Thomas Broughton, commission agent, End st
Crawford, Oliver, printer
Crutchley, Herbert, cattle drover
Davidson, J. H., inspector of police
Dixon, John, hawker
Dowling, Edwin
Dugan, Rev. John, Roman Catholic minister
Edmondson, John, Bridge hotel, George street
Edwin and St. Vens, pastrycooks and confectioners, Cressy st
Elliot, Chas., brickmaker

Evans, Joseph, watchmaker, Cressy st
Fidler, Wm., fruiterer, End st
Filson, R. D., and Co., merchants, End st
Gibson, John, publican, George st
Giles, James, P.M.
Gill, Robt., gardener
Gillespie, John, butcher
Goldsack, Geo., civil engineer
Graham, John Ryrie, innkeeper, Moira inn
Graves, Harry Gorden, agent
Harper, Rev. Samuel S., Church of England minister
Harrison, Chas., solicitor
Harrison, Anne, charwoman
Harrison, Chas., secretary Mechanics' Institute
Heavyside, Anthony, storekeeper
Hodgkins, Henry, storekeeper
Hooper, Wm. Henry, bookkeeper
Jefferson, Thomas, photographer, news agent, and fancy repository, End st
Jeffery, Geo. Abbitt, attorney, solicitor, and conveyancer
Jefferson, Mrs., ladies' school, Cressy st
Jones, David Griffiths, proprietor *Pastoral Times*
Jones, John, bootmaker, End st
Kelly, Elizabeth, charwoman
Kelly, M. H., manager electric telegraph station
Larnach, Albert, manager Australian Joint Stock Bank, End st

Laitimer, Geo., hospital wardsman
Loban, James, compositor
McCarter, Hanus, midwife
Macartney, Ross, agent for Robertson, Wagner, and Co., and A. W. Robertson and Co.
McCulloch, Wm., and Co., carriers
Mahoney, John, groom
McKenzie, Wm., commission agent
McKenzie, Roderick, tailor, End st
McLaurie, R., squatter
Mann, James, agent for Ettershank, Eaglestone, and Co., Kaye, Butchart, and Co., and Dalmahoy Campbell and Co.
Mann, John, cattle agent
Manser, Richard, labourer
Martley, Wm., bootmaker, End st
Marshall, Frederick, St. George hotel, St. George st
Mayger, James Fredk., proprietor *Deniliquin Chronicle*, George st
Mayne, John W., tin and copper smith, End st
Middlemas, Robt., bullockdriver
Miller, Samuel King, teacher of National School
Miller, John, carter
Millin, Robt., labourer
Miller, George, manager Bank of New South Wales
Miller, Walter Moore, solicitor, End st
Moore, E., squatter
Mort and Watson, merchants (Melbourne and Deniliquin)
Nettleton, Henry, clerk
Nissen, Peter, labourer

Noyes, Alfred Wm. Finch, surgeon, End street
O'Shanassy, John, squatter, Moira station
Perry, Wm., Exchange hotel, End st
Phillips, John, squatter, Mathoura station
Reynolds, John, cabinetmaker
Roberts, John Joseph, Highlander hotel, End st
Robertson, Thos., solicitor
Robertson, L. and T., storekeepers, North Deniliquin
Robinson, James, storeman
Roper, Ashton, wheelwright
Rosenfield Brothers, drapers, End st
Roth, Max, storekeeper, End st
Saloshin, Henry, auctioneer and commission agent
Sanders and Son, seedsmen and fruiterers, End st
Simpson, Wm.
Simpson, Joseph, blacksmith and wheelwright, Cressy st
Smith, Daniel, cook
Smith, George, carpenter
Stewart, Mary, dressmaker
Sullivan, Thomas, saddler, End st
Sullivan, John, tailor
Sweeny, George, brickmaker
Taylor, James, bootmaker, End st
Taylor, John, Royal Family hotel, End st
Taylor, John, butcher and baker
Trist, Thos., carter
Walker, Thos., bricklayer
Walker, George James, draper, Cressy st
White, George M., postmaster
Whitney, Robt., butcher
Wren, Erasmus, physician, End st

ALTERATIONS AND ADDITIONS

RECEIVED TOO LATE FOR PROPER INSERTION.

Admans, Geo., Australian hotel, Queenscliff
Appleby, Hamlet, publican, Epsom
Barnard, Charles, miner, Plumridge st, White Hills
Barrett, John, Shamrock hotel, Epsom
Baglan, Peter, Criterion hotel, Esplanade, Echuca
Bayes, Wm., Echuca hotel, High st, Echuca
Blair, Alex., contractor, Anstruther st, Echuca
Bottomley, John, fruiterer, High st, Echuca
Bourke, John, bootmaker, Moama
Bryans, Hugh, Lissie st, Queenscliff
Burnett, T., Court of Petty Sessions, Echuca
Burney, F. G., clerk, Hare st, Echuca
Capewell, Wm., bootmaker, Broadway, Epsom
Church of England; Rev. — McCausland, Echuca
Clements, Johanna, storekeeper, Anstruther st, Echuca
Coleman, S., Wallington, Queenscliff road
Ellis, H., labourer, Hare st, Echuca
Ellison, Mary Ann, Sir Charles Hotham hotel, White Hills
Evans, Wm., butcher, Napier st, White Hills
Ferguson, Wm., saddler, Darling st, Echuca
Ford, Wm., butcher, High st, Echuca
Gibson, Thomas, station master, Echuca
Gleeson, Bridget, Limerick Castle hotel, Hare st, Echuca
Groves, H. M., butcher, High st, Echuca
Harvey, Wm., Vine hotel, Moama
Hayes, J., Victorian Terminus hotel, Annesley st, Echuca
Henley and Co., A. H., Queenscliff
Herlitz, Herman, German Town, near Queenscliff
Hogarth, Finlay, storekeeper, Moama
Huggard, Alexander, Charles Napier Arms, White Hills
Kendall, George Henry, photographer, High st, Echuca
Knight, Isaac Hodgson, storekeeper, Broadway, Epsom
Lackington, Alfred, labourer, Echuca
Leahy, John, Harp and Shamrock hotel, High st, Echuca
Lelby, W., Royal hotel, Queenscliff
Leys, Robert, produce merchant and livery stables, Neish st, Echuca
Linthorne, Walter, storekeeper, Annesley st, Echuca

Long, Eugene Theodore, Bell Rock hotel, Esplanade, Echuca
Marrison, John, baker and publican, White Hills
Mayne, Andrew, and Company, grocers, wine and spirit merchants, High st, Echuca
McMajor, Henry, Bunt hotel, Echuca
Mitteram, J. P., solicitor, High st, Echuca
Nash, Wm., squatter, Torrumbarry
Newman, Chas. H., butcher, Moama
Nisbet, Robert, tailor, High st, Echuca
Norman, Charles, bootmaker, Heygarth st, Echuca
Palmer, Charles, sailmaker, High st, Echuca
Reid, Duncan, blacksmith, High st, Echuca
Roberts, Broughton, and Co., engineers, tinsmith, and general smiths, High st, Echuca
Roberts, James, butcher, White Hills
Robinson, Wm., Robin Hood hotel, White Hills
Schakell, J., J.P., High st, Echuca
Sharp, Robert, chemist and druggist, Epsom
Simpson, John Lionel, Freemasons' hotel, Annesley st, Echuca
Simpson, C. C., chemist, &c., Heuse st, Queenscliff
Stephenson, Joseph, hotel keeper, Esplanade, Echuca
Stewart, George, Avenel hotel, Avenel
Stubbs, J., and Co., drapers and clothiers, High st, Echuen
Sunstrom, Albert, storekeeper, High st, Echuca
Thompson, Lawrence, Moolap hotel, Queenscliff road
Trainor, John, J.P., Moama
Tryll, Adam, tailor, Radcliff st
Turner, Edwin, butcher, High st, Echuca
Waltham, Thomas, butcher, Neish st, Echuca
Walker, George E., outfitter, High st, Echuca
Ward, Charles, hotel, Hare st, Echuca
Watmoogh, G. G., Watmough's family hotel, Queenscliff
Watt, James, Junction, Moama
Webster, John, store, Epsom
Williams, John, Queenscliff
Williams, Renault, brewer, Echuca and Moama
Wilson, Benjamin, blacksmith and farrier, Anstruther st, Echuca
Young, William Henry, tailor, Heygarth st, Echuca

SQUATTING DIRECTORY,

AND

GENERAL INFORMATION.

SQUATTING DIRECTORY.

VICTORIA.

1866.

A.

Adams, Robert, St. Enoch's, Ararat
" " Mount Elephant, Warrnambool
Adams, J. S., Baila Baila, Melbourne
Adams, Francis, Sunday Creek, A. Gisborne
Adeney, Wm., Chorolyn, Warrnambool
Affleck, James, Yanac-a-yanac, West Wimmera
Affleck, David, Pleasant Banks "
Affleck, William, Rose Bank "
Affleck and Broughton, Lemon Springs "
Airey and Nicoll, Warranooke, East Wimmera
Airey and Ker, Killingworth, Gisborne
Aitken, James, Mosquito Point, Settled Districts
Aitken, J. C., Acheron, Gisborne
" " Thornton "
Alexander, Robert, Genoa, North Gipps Land
Allen, Benjamin, Kirkenong "
Allen, James, Merrimingo "
Allen, Wm. Wilson, Colanith, Warrnambool
Amey, John, Jack Rivulet, Settled Districts
Anderson, Alex., Boryalloch North, Warrnambool
Anderson, Alex., Bangal, Ararat
Anderson, David, Waterloo Ck., East Wimmera
Anderson, Caleb, Wooragee, A. Beechworth
Anderson, William, Boryalloch South, Warrnambool
Anderson and Shaw, Woorinyrolte "
Anning, C. C. S., Mount Pleasant, Echuca
Archibold, George, Duldo, Swan Hill
" " Ross Plains "
Archbold and Son, Brimin or Nipo, Swan Hill
Armstrong, William, Tittibong "
" " Parwin, or Mt. Shadwell, Warrnambool
Armytage, Charles H., Fulham, No. 1 and No. 2, West Wimmera
Atkinson and Pepper, Heath, West Wimmera
Austin, B. and Albert, Ellyor, Warrnambool
Austin, James, Yor, Grant
Austin, John, Green Hills, A. Warrnambool
Austin, J. and J., Greenvale, Ararat
Austin, S. and J., Waterloo Plains, Grant

B.

Bacchus, W. H., Pewcorth, Ballaarat
Bacchus, W. H., Combajak, Ballaarat
Bagot, E. Meade, Lindsay Island, Swan Hill
" " Woolwooiwa "
" " Lower Caloine "
" " Lower Cullulerain "
" " Watermeite "
Bagot, F. N., Cameron's Run, Gisborne
Baird, M. H. and S., Mount Hute, Ballaarat
Bakewell, John, Manton's or Tooraddin, Melb.
Baker, W. H. C., Six Mile Creek, West Wimmera
Bakewell, John, Red Bluff, Melbourne
Bakewell and Lyall, Great Swamp, Melbourne
Ballantine, Duncan, Summerlee, North Gipps Land
Bank of Australasia, Goorambat, Benalla
" " Mokoan "
Barber, C. H., Gundowring, Beechworth
Barbour, Robert, Bullengarooke, Gisborne
Barclay, John, Greenvale, Portland
Barker, William, Mount Alexander, Castlemaine
Barker, John, Cape Schanck, Melbourne
Barker, John, Cape Schanck and another, Settled Districts
Barnett and Brascombe, Holcombe, Castlemaine
Barrett, John, Paignle, Swan Hill
Batchelor, Jas., Richmond, Portland
" " Fitzroy River, Portland
" " Tangarty, Gisborne
" " Worrialock, Melbourne
Bath, Robert, Cherry-tree Flat, Settled Districts
Bathe, J., Axedale, Castlemaine
Bathe, Jas., Toomah, Melbourne
Baylee and Headlam, Upper Moira, Benalla
Bayliss, Henry, Bremia, Beechworth
Baynton, Thomas, Darlington, Gisborne
Bayth, E. W., Merton, South Gipps Land
Beat, T. H., Kotupna, Benalla
Bear, John F., Norongorong, Beechworth
Bear and McMahon, Turrick Terrick Plains, Echuca
Bear and McMahon, Bungil and Keolong, Beechworth
Bear and McMahon, Mitta Mitta, No. 2 do.
Beggs, Francis, Bushy Creek, Warrnambool
Beggs, Charles, Yabba Yabba, Benalla
" " Benalla "

G

Begg, G. and F., Enrembern or Mt. Cole, Ararat
Bell, John, Warrambine, Ararat
Bell, Jas., Golf hill, East Grant
Bell, Messrs. Gulph, Settled Districts
Bell, Robert Lewis. Mount Mercer Cattle Station, Ballaarat
Bell and Armstrong. Gulph No. 2, Melbourne
Bennett, Robert, Merri Jig, Swan Hill
" " Japparit "
" " Keria "
" " Poopsindle "
" " Tallarook "
" " Bennett's Run "
" " King "
" " Belfield, East "
" " " West "
Benjison, Richard, Mount Wellington, North Gipps Land
Beveridge, Andrew, Tyntindie, Swan Hill
" " Lowan Flat "
Beveridge, M. K., Mount Myall "
Beveridge, G. N. and P., Eureka "
Beveridge Brothers, Piangill "
" " Burra Burra "
Birch, Edward, Bullarook, Castlemaine
Black, George, Tarwin, West and East, Settled Districts
Black, Neil & Co , Gleecormiston, Warrnambool
" " The Sisters "
" " Liberton Bank "
" " Warrangs, Portland
Black, Neil, Sections, Glenelg, Warrnambool
Blair, James, Clunie, West Wimmera
Blake and Parker, Borrombeta, Ballaarat
Blackwood and Buckley, Tyralgoon, West, North Gipps Land
Bolen, A. V. et Lux, Aunt Heath, Portland Coreyaue
Bosman, Henry, Trenton Valley, Settled Districts
Bolden, Lemuel, Strathfieldsaye, North Gipps Land
Box and M'Kenzie, Malintangoon West, Benalla
Box, J. and W., Miller's Ponds "
" " Godaur "
Box, John, Wappan "
Bond, Thomas, Upotipotpon, "
" " Stony Creek "
Bond, E. M., Degamero, Beechworth
Booth and Holloway, Tragowell or Lower Lake, Echuca
Bourke and Neville, Minton's Creek, Melbourne
Bovid, Joseph, Hooraham. Beechworth
Bowki Brothers, Gooramadda "
Bowler, Samuel, Mitta Mitta, No. 1, Beechworth
Bowler, Samuel T., Magura "
Bowles, Ambrose, Lamplough, A., Castlemaine
Bowring, Edwin, Lyne, Portland
Box, Richard, Barwidgee, Beechworth
Boyd, M'Naught and Boyd, Comeraighip, Ballaarat
Boyd, M'Naught and Boyd, Dereel. Ballaarat
Bradey and Dumphey, Wandiligong & Fortpunha, Beechworth
Bramwell, J., Quamintock East. Castlemaine
" " Quamitatook West, Swan Hill
" " Reedy Lake, Castlemaine
" " Springfield, "
Brereton, John, Fanwick, Omeo
Brock, A., Torpicben, Castlemaine
Brook, Thomas Colliet, Worrough, Benalla
" " Tallarook, Gisborne

Brock and Brookman, Tallygaroopna, Benalla Mundonsa
Broughton, J. B., Moren Kathia, West Wimmera
Broughton, R. B., Second East Narin, West Wimmera
Brown, R., Wonga Wonga, Settled Districts
Brown, Charles, Gravels, Omeo
Brown, Thomas, jun., Yallock Vale, Grant

Brown and Rutherford, Strathmerton East, Benalla
Brown and Hillier, Scrubby Forest, South Gipps Land
Bryant, M. and W., Cairn Curran, Castlemaine Muckleford
Buchanan, J., Roseneath, North Gipps Land
Buckley and Mason, Chillington, Omeo
Buckley, F. C., Benambra, Beechworth
" " Coady Vale, South Gipps Land
" " Coady Vale, bettled Districts
" " Bole Bole "
" " Nroyang, North Gipps Land
" " Maryville, North Gipps Land
" " Getambly, Omeo
Bucknell, E. G., Roxborough Vale, Castlemaine
Budd, H. F. H., Tarcombe, Benalla
Burchett, H. and Alfred, St. Germaine, Echuca
Bullen, F. and G. F., Chin Chin, Benalla
Barnett, W. T. Y., Wirnborchep, East Wimmera
Butchart, J., Bushy Park, North Gipps Land
" " Eagle Vale "
" " Stratford "
Butler, Thomas, Deighton "

C.

Cain, Peter, Rosehill, Benalla
Caldwell, Robert, Solitude, Melbourne
Callanan, Michael, Long Warren "
Calder, Robert, Polkemmet, West Wimmera
Cameron, Alexander, Mount Sturgeon Plains Warrnambool
Cameron, Alexander, Morgiana, Portland Lower Crawford "
Cameron, A. and A., Rutledge "
Cameron, Duncan, Bligay, West Wimmera
Cameron, D., Meran. Castlemaine
Cameron, D., exers. of, Violet Creek, Portland
Cameron, Duncan, Spring Hill, West Wimmera Heath Hill "
Cameron, A. and J., Ghemaulin, No. 1, Portland
Cameron, George, Doenlong Creek "
Cameron, Christina, Narrawong "
Cameron, Donald, Ultima, Swan Hill
Cameron, Alexander, Nigretta, West Wimmera
Campbell, John, Gleecoa, South Gipps Land
Campbell and Co., Essay of Windermere, Omeo
Campbell and Elms, Chetwynd, West Wimmera
Campbell and Messer, Eumeralla, West, Portland
Cantwell, R., Glenbyan, Ballaarat
Carfrae and Jervis, Woolliworm, West Wimmera
Carfrae and Jervis, Zochiel, West Wimmera Black Heath, West "
Carmichael, W., Grassmero, Warrnambool
Carmichael, William, Blackfellow's Creek, Portland
Carmichael, W., Harton Hills, Warrnambool
Carmichael, W. and J., Refuge, Portland
Carmichael, W. and G. Helvest, West Wimmera
Carmichael and Russell, Aberfoyle, Castlemaine Serpentine, Echuca
Carter and Sons. Rowbrook, West Wimmera
" " Glenisia, North and South "
" " Wortook "
Carter, Charles, Brim Spring "
Carwither and Stewart, Glenalbyn, North Gipps Land
Catin, John, Catio's Run, Castlemaine
Cay, Robert, Lockico Plains "
Chalmers, J., Elizabeth Island, Melbourne
Chambers, H., Sydenham, North Gipps Land
Champ, W. T. N., Dardalwarrah, Great
Chenery, A., Deintin, Benalla
" " Loyola "
Chirnside, J. B., West Charlton, East Wimmera Lake Woromook "
Chirnside, T. and A., Kenilworth, South, West Wimmera

Chirnside, Thomas, Barton, West Wimmera
Chirnside, Andrew, Carambalac, Warrnambool
" Carngog "
Chirnside, T. and A., Mount William, Ararat
Chirnside, T. & A., Markanger, West Wimmera
" Victoria Lagoon "
Chirnside, F. and Logan, Elephant North, Warrnambool
Chirnside and Logan, Elephant South
" Burrumbeep, Ararat
" Tattyoon "
Chisholm, J. W., Myrhee, Benalla
Clapham, J. G. and R. Sinclair, East, Portland
Clairperton, T., Amphitheatre, East Wimmera
Clarke, W. J. T., La Rose Mokepillie, and Lexington, West Wimmera
Clarke, W. J. T., Lockhart, West Wimmera
" Morny, West "
Clarke, David, Pigeorvet, West, Ballaarat
" Biddle, No. 2 "
Clarke, M. N., Avoca or Wycherproof, East Wimmera
Clarke, Thomas, Salisbury Plains, Echuca
Clarke, William, Owens Crossing Place, Benalla
Clarke and Maclaine, Surettie's Dale, Swan Hill
Clarke, John T., and Maclaine, John J., Capvera, Swan Hill,
Clarke, John T., and Maclaine, John J., Strathmore or Gibson's Well, Swan Hill
Clement, Thomas Nixon, Maskery, Echuca
Clutton, David, Harjarg, Benalla
Clough, J. H. and Co., Darbalary, Beechworth
" Lamphugh, Castlemaine
" Woodstock "
" Bandaramongree, Omeo
" Knighton, Swan Hill
" Lansdowne "
" Pine Ridge, East "
" Pine Ridge, West "
" Towns "
" Drumbanagher, West Wimmera
" Touristania, Gisborne
" Longlands, Swan Hill
" Maiden Hills, Castlemaine
Coghill, George, Woodstock, South Gippsland
" Glenderwel, Castlemaine
Coldham, John, Grassdale, Portland
Coldham, George, Enermeele "
Cole, Nicholas, West Cloven Hill, Warrnambool
Cole, F. and E., Darlington,
Collins, John, Snugtarough, South Gippsland
Colonial Bank of Australasia, Mount Napier Portland
Conolly, J., Kangaroo, Melbourne
" Ovens "
Conolley, J., Summerside, Warrnambool
Connolly, Joseph, Koowee-rup, Melbourne
Connor, P. and T., Merimerrabong, Beechworth
Cook, Cecil Tybus, Lake Condon, Portland
" Whittlebury "
Cook, Wm., Ayrey's Inlet, Settled Districts
Cooke, William, Moplanicaam, Hallaarat
Coppock, John, Albacutya, West Wimmera
" Outlet, Lake Hindmarsh "
Cooper, D. E., Warrapingue, Ararat
Cortett, E., Kilmore, Melbourne
Coutis, J. and G., Coyarah Springs, Castlemaine
Coutts, Brothers, Ballorbuyk, Swan Hill
Coutts, Messrs., Pilgrimage Richmond
Coutts, J. G. and D., Brebanah, Castlemaine
Craig, Angus, Eddington, Warrnambool
Crawford and Co., Campaspe, Gisborne
Creswick, Henry, St James, Benalla
Crooke, Edward, Holey Plains, South Gippsland
Crooke, Edward, Lucknow, North Gippsland
Crosswell, R., Erinsera, Settled Districts
Crowe, Joseph, Talonga, Beechworth
Crosier, John, Pollya, Swan Hill
" Kidd's Station "

Crosier, John, Outer Cullullerane "
" Upper Cullullerane "
" Tarackna "
" Cuinine Upper "
" Owens "
Curdle, Daniel, Tandercook, Warrnambool
Cumming, J., Terrinallum
Cumming, John, Stony Point
Cumming, G. and W., Mount Fyans, Warrnambool
Cunningham and M'Credie, Glenelg, Portland
" Greenwich "
" Dederaag, Beechworth
Cunningham and M'Credie, Wilderness, South Gippsland
Cunningham and M'Credie Berremboke, Grant
Cumingham, A., Ellangowan "
" Kittrick "
" St. Helen's "
Cunningham, H., Sand Hills, Swan Hill Stratford
Currie, J. L., Geelengia, or Lara, Warrnambool
" West Elephant, No. 1 "
Currie and Lowa, Biddle, No. 1, Ballaarat
Currie, Scott, and Co., Kaaritnba, Benalla
Currie, Scott, and Dufrayer, Strathmerton West Benalla
Curtain, M., Nelson, Warrnambool
" Yallook "

D.

Dalgety and Co., El Dorado East, Beechworth
Dalgety and Ibbotson, Concongella, West Wimmera.
Dalton, C., Black Forest, Gisborne
Dancy, J. E., Tooram, Warrnambool
Daniels, Samuel, Changue, Benalla
Darcy, Michael, Marvego or Dempsey's, Benalla
Darlot, J. M. and H. K. H., North Brighton, West Wimmera
Dance, J. E., Beckley's Creek, Settled Districts (late Stanhope), Sections
Davidson, S. J., Allenvale, or Sinclair's, West Wimmera
Dawson and Mitchel, Kangatong, Warrnambool
Dawson, G. J., Glenfern, Settled Districts
Degraves, William, North and South Woodlands, East Wimmera
Degraves, William, Woodside, South Gippsland
DeLittle, R. and H., Caramut, Warrnambool
DeLittle, Douglas, and De Little, Ledcourt, West Wimmera
Dal'ace, M., Spring Creek and Wild Duck Plains, Gisborne
Denniston, Harbern H., Wattle Station, Benalla
Dennis Brothers, Carr's Plains, East Wimmera " Robertson's "
Dennilly, Edwin, King Vale, North Gippsland
Daveling, H., Sections, Unbo, Settled Districts

Dewing, F., Paraparap, Grant
Dick, G. C., Glenmore, Omeo
Docker, Joseph, Busthorambo Plains, Beechworth
Donald, W. M., Banyeyong East, East Wimmera
Donald, J. S., Corack, East Wimmera
Donyan, Thomas, Munboik, Settled Districts
Donyan, Rerry, and Jenning, Tarbarlan, Settled Districts
Douglass and De Little, Banyeus Plains, East Wimmera
Dowling, Thomas, Jellalabad, Warrnambool
Duff, Robert, Thogolong, Beechworth
Dumphy and Brady, Puripunk, Beechworth
Duncan, H., Jun., Deighton East, North Gippsland
Dundas, James, Nog-Nog-Wa, North Gippsland

Dunlop, J. K., Kadnook, West Wimmera
Dunlop, J. H., Buckle Kuppie, West Wimmera
Dun, G. K., Katandra, Benalla
Dunn, C. C., Bolwarra, Ballaarat
Dunsford, W. H., Langerfield, Gisborne
Dyott, Eleanor, French Island, Melbourne

E

Eddington, John, Dallangeich, Warrnambool
Eddington and Son, Drysdale
Edgar, David, Pine Hills, West Wimmera
Edols, J. and T., Inglestone, Grant
Edols, Thomas, Donegar, West Wimmera
  "   Upper Regions, West Wimmera
Egan, John, Greenwald No. 2, Portland
  "   Cortnella, Castlemaine
Egan, James, Major's Line, Gisborne
Elder, John, and Son, Burrumrue, Ballaarat
Ellerman, H. C., Antwerp, West Wimmera
Elsaille and Strachan, Jingellao, Beechworth
Evans, G. B. and J. R., Morrison's, Grant
Evans, John, Whitefield, Benalla
Evans, D. H., Wabonga, Beechworth
Ewbank, G., Swanwater North, East Wimmera

F

Faithful, W. P., Edi, Beechworth
Fallon, T., Boglara, Portland
Feehan, Richard, Wild Cattle Run, Settled District
Freeban, Richard, Wild Cattle Run, South Gipps Land
Felstead, John, Sertious, Monroolbark, South Gipps Land
Fen ton, Frederick, Ravenswood or Mount Alexander, Castlemaine
Fenton, John, Richmond Plains, Castlemaine
  "   Spring Hill
Ferguson and Symons, Raymond Island, North Gipps Land
Ferguson, D., Flowerdale, Gisborne
Ferrell, J. M., Northwood,
Firebrace, R. T., Hayfield, South Gipps Land
Fiskin, A., Lal-Lal, Ballaarat
Fitzgerald, James, Lake Monemia, Ararat
Fitzgerald and Co., Mullagh, West Wimmera
Flanner, James, Sandy Point, Settled Districts
  "   Sunday Island
Fletcher, Miles, Tullick, Portland
Flint, B., Mount Haddbead, North Gipps Land
Flower, Lydiard and Co., Nareb-Nareb, Warrnambool
Forsyth, J. and R., Maintongoon East, Benalla
Forsyth, Robert, Munnatollaka,
Foster, John, Glenfalloch, A., North Gipps Land
Foster, John, Boisdale, South Gipps Land
  "   Tangel,
  "   Durgo, North Gipps Land
  "   Castleburn,
Fraser, Robert, Lillirie, Ararat
Fraser, A., Stratherick, Omeo
French, Aebrwen, Monivae, Portland
Fryer, Peter, Molka, Benalla
Forlonge, W., Euroa
  "   Salnfield,
  "   Croppers,
  "   Honeysuckle, Sth.,
  "   Faithful's Creek
  "   Mangaloro,
  "   Strathbogie,
  "   Springs, A.
  "   Wombat Hill
  "   Balle's Hill,
  "   Seven Creeks

G

Gardiner, B., Wrandron, Melbourne
Gavan, Emily, Sunday Creek, Gisborne
  "   Mount Piper

Gibb, Matthew, Patrick's Day, Warrnambool
Gibbs, Ronald and Co., Mount Emu, Ararat
Gibbs, Ronald and McBain, Fern Hills, Benalla
Gibbs, Ronald and Ronald, Coogbool, West Wimmera
Gibbs, Margaret, Glenvale, Settled Districts
Gibson, T. L., Lake Bringalbart, West Wimmera
Gill, J., Mallas, Swan Hill
Glass, Hugh, Bullock Creek Plains, Castlemaine
  "   Bullock Creek   "
  "   Noorilim, Benalla
  "   Lower Coliban, Castlemaine
  "   Glengower,   "
  "   Torumbarry, East, Echuca
  "   Torumbarry, West,   "
  "   Torumbarry, Middle,   "
  "   Glenhope,   Gisborne
  "   Mount Macedon Ranges   "
  "   Steel's Creek,   "
  "   Nelly Yallock, Castlemaine
  "   Mount Hope Creek, Echuca
  "   Weddikar or Myer's Creek, Castlemaine
Glass, Hugh, Wabrignan, Gisborne
  "   Moyreisk or Bathacar, East Wimmera
Glass, Hugh, Avoca Forest, East Wimmera
  "   Castlemaine
  "   Plains of Thalia, East Wimmera
  "   Mt. Sturgeon, Nos. 1, 2, 3, 4, West Wimmera
Glass, Hugh, Towaninnie, Swan Hill
  "   Niagaroo, Gisborne
  "   Riverdale, Nos. 1 and 2, Gisborne
  "   Killeen, or Five Mile Crk., Benalla
  "   Meering Lake, or Combatook, Castlemaine
Glass, Hugh, Avoca Forest, Castlemaine
  "   Stratford Lodge,   "
  "   Tahilk, Benalla
  "   Wharparella, Echuca
Godfrey and McKinnon, Kilkunda, Settled Districts
Godfrey, M., Roort, Castlemaine
Goldsbrough and Parker, Borodomanan, North Benalla
Goldsbrough and Parker, Borodomanan, South Benalla
Goldsbrough and Parker, Junction, Benalla
Goldsbrough, Richard, Arebdale, Castlemaine
  "   Danolly,
  "   Sandy Creek,
Goldsbrough, Richard, Cooltorna, East Wimmera
Gordon, James, Newlands, West Wimmera
  "   Murudara,   "
  "   Ganoo-Ganoo   "
  "   The Gums, Warrnambool
Gould, H., Gould's Run, Beechworth
Graham, E., Glencairne, North Gipps Land
Grant, Robert, Switzerland, Benalla
Grant, G., Pentland hills, Gisborne
Grattan, Humphrey, Canlarobo, Gisborne
  "   Gowangardie
Gray and Palmer, Dalham Hill, Gisborne
Gray, J. H. G., and W. Telford, Dandongadale, Beechworth
Green, E. R., Greenvale, Benalla
  "   Kellawarra,
Green, Ann, Oxley Plains, Beechworth
Grice, Sumner and Co., Maryvale, West Wimmera
Grier, Sumner and Co., Ulswater, West Wimmera
Grice, Sumner and Co., Navarre, East Wimmera
Grice, Sumner and Co., Lake Wallace, West Wimmera
Grice and Sumner, Edgar's Plains, Castlemaine
Griffith and Green, Mount Hope and Mount Pyramid, Echuca

Griffith and Grews, Glenmore, Grant
Griffin, Frederick, Preston, Benalla
Grover, G., Colbinabin, South, Echuca
Gobarcup.
Gulliver, James, Lilliput, Beechworth
Gundry, Joseph, Iron Bark Ranges, Settled Districts
Guthrie, H. M., Glenvale, Gisborne

H.

Hadden, Wm., Lodge Park, Benalla
" South Benalla
Haley, C. S., Diamond Creek, Settled Districts
Hall, A. W., Glenalbyn, Castlemaine
Hallet, Andrew, Devon, South Gipps Land
Halkiay, William, Merino Plains, East Wimmera
Halkiay, William, Spring Bank, East, Castlemaine
Halkiay, William, Spring Bank, West, East Wimmera
Halkiay and Richmond, Glenice, West Wimmera
Hamilton, Robert, Morella, West Wimmera
Hamilton, L.G., Buangor, Ararat
Hamilton, Thomas, Mount Haw Haw, South Gipps Land
Hamilton, Thomas, Mount Juliet, South Gipps Land
Hamilton, William, Glenaroua, Gisborne
Hampton, W. J., Mount Franklin, South Gipps Land
Hampton and Waits, Langwarry, South Gipps Land
Hampton and Wetts, Tarwen, South Gipps Land
Hancock, Theodore, Allerton, Grant
Hanson and Wheeler, Adjie, Beechworth
Hardie, H. and J., Glenburn, Gisborne
Harney, John, Barnedown, Castlemaine
Harpham, W. T., Dean Station, Gisborne
Hasler and Co., Cherry-tree Hill, Grant
Hassell, James, Koorongwootong, East, West Wimmera
Hastie, John, Panpundal, Warrnambool
Hawkins, S. P., Melville Forest, West Wimmera
Hay, William, Pine Lodge, Benalla
Henderson, John, Sections, Cape Liptrap, Settled Districts
Henderson, John, River Tyers, South Gipps Land
Henderson, John, River Tyers, North, South Gipps Land
Henderson, John, Pennebanuewar, Gisborne
Henry, C. F., Pasty Guru-Guru, Melbourne
Hensleigh, John b., Deddick, North Gipps Land
Henty, Edward, Connell's Run, West Wimmera
Henly, Edward, Muntham, West Wimmera
Henty, Francis, Merino Downs, Portland
Henty, S. G., Mount Sturgeon Plains North, or Warrayure, Warrnambool
Henty, S. G., Mount Sturgeon Plains South, Warrnambool
Henty, S. G., Strathfillan, East Wimmera
" Tallangoer. West Wimmera
Harvey, Matthew, Long Beach, Settled Districts
" Tongeomoogic, Omeo
" Hindi
" Hunomongic
Herbert, W., Virtue Hall, Settled Districts
Hick, J., Mt. Eccles and Lake Gorrie, Portland
Hick, John, Ardonachie, Portland
" Grafton
Higgins, John, Gibbo, Omeo
Hughett, William, Maindample, Benalla
Hill, W., Running Creek, Settled Districts
Hipos and Harurs, Ranges, East Wimmera
Hines, F. P., Newhapper, West Wimmera
Hindmagh, William, Yambuk, Warrnambool
Hislop and Agnew, Mariben, East Wimmera

Hore, John, Bethanga, Beechworth
" Talgarno, "
Hoddinott, Uriah, Mundy Creek, South Gipps Land
Hoddinott, Uriah, Sanville, South Gipps Land
" Warrigal Creek, A, South Gipps Land
Hoddinott, Uriah, Warrigal Creek, No. 1, Settled Districts
Holland, William, Cairnmine, Swan Hill
" Annefield, A, "
" Annefield, B, "
" Annefield, C, "
" Annefield, D, "
Holmes and Campbell, Lorquon, West Wimmera
Holmes, White and Co., Glendhu, East Wimmera
Hood, John, Clifton Plains, A, Swan Hill
" Clifton Plains, B, "
" Clifton Plains, C, "
" Clifton Plains, D, "
" Clifton Plains, E, "
Hood, J., Hollywood, A, B, and C, West Wimmera
Hopkins, Arthur, Mount Hesse, Grant
Houston, George, Gunbower, Echuca
Houston, Joshua, and J. B. Dennell, McKenzie Springs, or Worrall, West Wimmera
Hume, Elizabeth, Yarrowonga, Benalla
Huon, William, Wodonga, Beechworth
Hurst, Edward, Emmerill East, Portland
Hutchison, Peter, Glen Roland, Warrnambool
Hutchison, John, Mount Strum, Portland
Hutchison, J., Runnymede, "
Hutton, David, Purdert. Warrnambool
Hyland, J., Shadwell South, A, "

L.

Ibbotson and Buckley, Goomalibee, Benalla
Ibbotson, Charles, Tawonga, Beechworth
Ibbotson and Blackwood, Warrnambayne, Benalla
Inglis, Peter, Warrcubeip, Ballarat

J.

Jack, W. C., Mount Wills, Omeo
Jackson, S. and W., Sandford, Portland
Jamieson, E., Boise Plains, Warrnambool
Jamieson, H. and R., Irymple and Mildura, Swan Hill
Jamieson, H. and R., Beardook, Swan Hill
Jarrett, H. and J., The Den, Gisborne
Jenkins, John, Winterregh, Beechworth
Jeffreys, Henry C., Burnewang, East and West, Echuca
Jellie, James, Tortibnurruck, Melbourne
Johnston, John, Hurdle Creek, Beechworth
Johnson, Henry, Eglintoun, Benalla
Johnson, John, Newburn Park, South Gipps Land
Johnson, John, Swan Reach, North Gipps Land
Johnson, John, Kilmorie, North Gipps Land
" Allendale, "
" Illewarra, "
Johnson, G. W., Woodside, Gisborne
Johnson, A., Bambang, Swan Hill
Joyce, Alfred, Norwood, Castlemaine
Joyce, George, Plaistowe, "
Jones, Highway, Yan Yip, West Wimmera
" Tattyara, "
" Yan Yip, North "
Jones, Henry, Kriz Vale, South Gipps Land
Jones, R. D., Bourville, Beechworth
Jones, Eliza, Towong, Omeo
Jones, H. and D. O., Tallagiers, West Wimmera
Jones, H. and D. O., Tallagiers, North, West Wimmera
Jones, Lloyd, Avenel, Benalla
Jones, J. W., Fulham, South Gipps Land

DIRECTORY.

K

Kaye and Butchart, Yarraberb and Myer's Creek, Echuca
Kaye and Butchart, Bullock Creek, Open Plains and Tandarra, Echuca
Kaye and Butchart, Sandy Creek, North Gipps Land
Kaye, Butchart and Co., Neilfeera, Benalla
Kennedy, David, Union, Warrnambool
Keys, C., Brellana, Dandenong, Settled Districts
Kichington, George, Thillagallanga, Beechworth
Kidd and Brickett, Jallandoon, Beechworth
King, W. E. and A. N., Wingelgoodhin, Omeo
King, John Co., Rosedale, South Gipps Land
  " Kearea, "
  " Haake's Bridge, "
King, John, Mulagong, Beechworth
Kinnear, R. H., Conover, Castlemaine
  " Conover and Spring Bank, East Wimmera
Kinnear, R. H., Lower Moira, Benalla
Kyles, William, Sections, Tooroowrang, Settled Districts

L

Lane, McDonald and White, Clunes, Castlemaine
Lane, McDonald and White, Clunes, Benalla
Leag, A. and G., Yangher, Warrnambool
Lavender, J. S., Kiewllamore, South Gipps Land
Lawson, Charles, Benlock, North Gipps Land
Leake and McLachlan, Monheong, Portland
  Kenilbrush, "
  " Settled Districts
  Monheong, "
Learmonth, William, Fitzroy L'Estrange, Portland
Learmonth, William, Tahara, Portland
  " St. Helen's, Settled Districts
Learmonth, J. and T., Buninyong, Ballarat
Lett, J. S. and W., Sutton Forest, Settled Districts
Levey, G. C., Towland, Portland
Lewis, Richard, Sandy Water Holm, Portland
  " Pleasant Hills, "
  " Hills Downs, "
Lewis, W. H. and J. A., Merrigum, Echuca
  " Arilpatrick, or Cooma, Echuca
Liddle, Robert, Springs, Benalla
Lincoln, Abraham, Darfold, Gisborne
Lindsay, William, Quamby, Warrnambool
Lintott, Wheatley, and Garrett, Baci-Baci, Swan Hill
Little, D., Heath Springs, West Wimmera
Lloyd, J. F., Emu Hill, No. 1, Ballarat
Lloyd, Frederick, Mountain Glen, South Gipps Land
Lock, J. A., Bushy Park, Settled Districts
Lord, Thomas, Mount Misery, Melbourne
Ludlow, George, Quail Island, Melbourne
Lynch, Thomas, Mount Barnbett, Ararat
Lyon and Ferrier, Ballance, Gisborne
  Morwklong, "
  " Narraport, East Wimmera

M

McArthur, P., and Gilbert, Lauvency, Warrnambool
McArthur, P., Meringorott, Warrnambool
McBean, D., Old Crossing Place, Echuca
McCallum, Alexander, Youngera, Swan Hill
McCallum, Duncan, Ardgarton, Portland
  Ardno, East "
McCallum, E., Ardno, West "
McCartney, J. A., Warrooley, Beechworth
McClellan, —, Cape Wrath, Portland

McColl, James, Yal Nai, West Wimmera
McCrae, A. J., Mount Useful, South Gipps Land
McCulloch, James, Dhurroap, Beechworth
McCulloch and Sellar, Emu Station, Benalla
  " Springs Station, Benalla
  " Yerring, Melbourne
  " Tatong, Benalla
McDonald, Alexander, Armidale, South Gipps Land
McDouncil, John, Yrinia, Benalla
McDowell, J. W., Newchurch, Warrnambool
McEachern, A. and M., Strathdownie, West, Portland
McEachern, H., Heathfield, Portland
McEachern, W. and A., Strathdownie, East Portland
McEachern, D. and A., Kangaroo, Portland
McFarlane, M., Glenafsloch, North Gipps Land
McFarlane, J. and P., Island, Gisborne
McFarlane, James, Glenmaggie, South Gipps Land
McFarlane, J. A., Sections, Yan Yean, Settled Districts
McGill, A., Hyde Park, West Wimmera
McGillivray, Alexander, Cargerie, Grant
McGuinness and Bell, Corong, Swan Hill
  Mimpree, "
  " Lake Wilhelmina, Swan Hill
McIlaffle, W. and J., Philip Island, Melbourne
McIntosh, Alex., Glendinning, West Wimmera
  " Muorieng, "
  " Spring Bank, "
McIntyre, D. and A., Snizart, Portland
McKay, G. E., Tarrawingee, Beechworth
  " Yackandandah, "
McKay and Kerr, Waranga Park, Echuca
McKellar, Thomas, Croxton, Portland
  " Kanawalla, West Wimmera
McKellar, William, Nauaria, Benalla
  " Lima, "
McKellar and Flower, Kuchworth, Portland
McKenzie, Alex., Hardy Creek, Gisborne
  " Banning Creek, "
McKenzie, Donald, Mount Pleasant, Benalla
McKenzie, J. M., Choobinane, Benalla
McKerney, J., Kenilworth North, West Wimmera
McKinlay, Andrew, Polockdale, Ararat
McKinnon, Collin, Mountain Creek, East Wimmera
McKinnon, D., Maryde Yallock, Warrnambool
McKinnon, John, Koruit, West Wimmera
McKinnon, Malcolm and D., Kalabro, or Bokeby, Portland
McKnight and Hamilton, Dunmore, Warrnambool
McLachlan, J. R., Rich Avon East, East Wimmera
McLean and McLeod, Sections Fitz Roy River, Settled Districts
McLean, Donald, and Co., Lalbert, Swan Hill
McLean Bros., and Gilles, Glenaladale, North Gipps Land
McLeish, Duncan, Muddy Creek, Gisborne
McLeiland, William, Happy Valley, Gisborne
McLennan, S., Tamboon, North Gipps Land
McLennan, A. and D., Grimble, West Wimmera
McLellan, D. and N., Cove "
McLeod, H., Lewisrdory, Gisborne
McLeod, H. L. Reaye, West Wimmera
McLeod, J. C., Orhoat, North Gipps Land
McLeod, John N., Castlemaddie, Portland
  " Mount Clay, "
McLeod, N. R., Normella, or Lockend, North Gipps Land
McLeod, N. R., Balmsdale, North Gipps Land
McLoughlin, John, Delickmora, "
McMillan, Archibald, Glenwyllan, East Wimmera
McMillan, Archibald, Irrewarra, West Wimmera

McMillan, Archibald, Sheep Hills, East Wimmera
McMillan and McDonald, Leaghur, Castlemaine
McMillan, Angus, Culgmundle, North Gipps Land
McMillan, Angus, Tabbarabbara, North Gipps Land
McMillan, John, Hazlewood, South Gipps Land
McNab, D., Lake Bolac, Ararat
Mr Naught and Boyd, Mindie, No 2, Ballarat
Mr Naughton, J., Dutson, South Gipps Land
McNicol, D., Bullen Merri, Warrnambool Kilngamite
McNicoll, John, Bassett's, Portland
McNicol, P. and W., Kenyang South, Warrnambool
McNicol and McKinnon, Duncon, Warrnambool
McNicoll and Smith, Fox Hall, Portland Borongorong, West Wimmera
McPhail, John, Meadows, South Gipps Land
McPherson, Dugald, Nulli, West Wimmera Bungletap West, Grant
McPherson, James, Nerrin Nerrin, Warrnambool
McPherson, James, Yarra Glen, Settled Districts
McPherson, John, Wilderness, West Wimmera
Mr Pherson, William, Nangeela, Portland
McPherson, Thomas, Lowlands, South Gipps Land
McVean, J. B., Danach Forest, Castlemaine
McWilliam, W. H., Crawford, Portland
Macalister and Morgan, Miboat, North Gipps Land
Mackay and Sons, Lal-lal West, Ballarat
" Mount Mercer Cattle Station, A, Ballarat
Mack, J. G., Gnarkeet, Warrnambool
" Germoyemerraga, "
Macredie and Turnbull, Bunjeyong, West, East Wimmera
Macredie, G. Cunningham, Morton Plains, East Wimmera
Macredie, G. Cunningham, Watcham, East Wimmera
Manifold, J. and P., Purrambete, Warrnambool
Mason, R., Fifteen-mile Creek, Benalla
Matches and Duncan, St. Margaret's Island Settled Districts
Matheson, John, Moranghurk, Grant
Matthews, J. H., Little Portland, Beechworth
Maxwell and Drew, Yanakie, Settled Districts
Mayne, James, Mulla Mullane, Benalla
Meighan and Gray, Cassills, Omeo
Mercy Brothers, Deighton, West, North Gipps Land
Messer, W. C., Bongmire, West Wimmera
Mickle, Bakewell and Lyall, Yulloch, Melbourne
Miller, Alexander, Murindinda, East, Gisborne " Murindinda, West, "
Miller, Henry, Mount Elgin, West Wimmera
" Davis Plains, West Wimmera
" Laneyiran, Ararat
" Brim, West Wimmera
Miller and Matthewson, Westdown Plains, W., Echuca
Miller, John and David, Murrabit, Castlemaine
Miller, James, Nicerilim, East, Benalla
Milne, Robert, junr., Merriang, Beechworth
Mitchell, D., Steel's Flat, Melbourne
Mitchell, Thomas, Tangamhalanga, Beechworth
Moffatt, Robert, Bichavon, West, East Wimmera
Moffatt, R., Glenloth, Castlemaine
Moffatt, John, Hopkins' Hills, Warrnambool
Mogg, V. N., Swan Water, South, East Wimmera
Mollison, W. T., Pyalong, Gisborne
Montgomery, William, Heart, North Gipps Land
Montgomery, William, Mountain Creek, North Gippsland

Moody, John, Wando Dale, West Wimmera
Moore, Charles, Wagra, Beechworth
Moore, Frederick Thomas, Lareby, Benalla
Morrison, Hugh, Burbosegyhurk, East, Grant
Morrow, C. S., Bangal, Grant
" Morcep, "
Mulcahy, John, Mount Pleasant, Melbourne
Mullins, Charles, Moyolemby, Benalla
Murchison, John, Kerrisdale, Gisborne
Murray, Andrew, South Stoney Rises, Warrnambool
Murray, Andrew, Irrewillips, Grant
Murray, Hugh, Illmioryte, "
" Gnorareet, "
Murray, James, Gleasmpile, Settled Districts
" Ghim Ghim Bean, Melbourne
Murray, William, Deanrubin, Portland
Mast, Thomas, Argyle, Portland
" Mepunca, West Wimmera
" Park Hill, Portland
" Brisbangle, West Wimmera
Myers, John, St. Germain's, Melbourne

N.

Nankervilio and Calvert, Parisyallork, Warrnambool
Nankerville and Calvert, Forest, Warrnambool
National Bank, Gamawarre, Echuca
Nell, H. J., Ardaey, Portland
Nicholas, R., Tolrech, Gisborne
Nicholson, W., Dairy, Melbourne
" Parambool, Melbourne
" View Hill, "
" Woulisade, "
Nicholson and Conz, Mount Disappointment, Gisborne
Nixon Hugh, Buffalo, East, Beechworth
Nolan, Wm., Glenmiro, West Wimmera
Noonan, Daniel, Lamplough, B, Castlemaine
Norrie, David, Cudgiewa, Beechworth
Nugent and Whitebread, Cowper's Heifer, Beechworth

O.

O'Brien, John, Buffalo Heifer Station, Beechworth
O'Connor, M. J., Mount Bunisyong, Ballarat
O'Dea, Patrick, Cornella Creek, Echuca Tongala, "
" Residowa Plains, East, Echuca
Officer, C. M. and S. H., Lingmer, West Wimmera
Officer, C. M. and S. H., Mount Talbot, West Wimmera
Officer, Robert J., Yat Nat, A, West Wimmera
Ogilvy, J. S., Bungbulme, Settled Districts
O'Neil, William, Beggary, Omeo
O'Reilly, B., Alidorf, Beechworth
O'Reilly, Owen, Wando, West Wimmera
" Steep Bank Rivulet, West Wimmera
O'Reilly, Owen, Cashmere, West Wimmera
Ormond, F., jun., Horyalork East, Warrnambool
Orr, J. and F., Yawong, East Wimmera
" Yawong Springs, Castlemaine
" Yawong Springs, Castlemaine
Osborne, J., sen., Yackandandah West, Beechworth
Osborne, J. and H., Kergunis, Reid's Hill, Beechworth
Osborne, John, Bungletap East, Grant

P.

Palmer, Murphy and Henty, Peerhelbe, Benalla
Palmer, T. W., Ancora, North Gipps Land
" Burk Springs, "
" Windermere, Omeo
" Derwentwater, "
Parker, Hugh, Redbank, East Wimmera

Parslow and Meighan, Coburgra, Omeo
Paterson, J. H., exors. of, Kimbolton, Gisborne
" Langwarner,
Patterson, Myles, Pine Grove East, Echuca
" Pheninny Creek, or Kama-
rooka, Echuca
Paton, A. and Sons, Yabba, Beechworth
Paul, James, Cropper's Creek "
Pearce, J. W., Arcadia, Benalla "
Pearce, Thomas, Angahook, Settled Districts
Pearson, John, Glenorchy, Portland
" Rifle Range
Pearson, William, Kilmany Park, South Gipps
Land
Pearson, William, Forest Hill, South Gipps
Land
Pearson, William, Moondara, South Gipps
Land
Peppin, G. H., and Sons, Rwoothal, Benalla
Phillips, Henry, Tarrone, Warrnambool
Philpott, W., Mount Ararat, Melbourne
Power and Ainslie, Campania, Swan Hill
" Sand Mount,
Power and Ainslie, Salt Lake, Swan Hill
" Spectacle Plains, Swan Hill
" Pine Plains
Power and Davenport, Louth, Portland
" Compton Creek
" Major Mitchell's Creek,
Gisborne
" Broom Hill, Swan Hill
" Broom Hill, South "
" Chaves Plain, East "
" Chaves Plains, West "
" Corenha "
" Mainmarra, "
" Snusel, "
" Werrengoart, Portland
Power, R., Pine Hills, or Loxdon, Echuca
Power, T. H., Terrick Terrick, East, or Prairie,
Echuca
Prendergast, J. and J., Omeo, A, Omeo
Purvis, James, Toolgerook, Melbourne
Pyers, George, Lawler, East Wimmera

Q.

Quarterman, J., Glenmona, Castlemaine
Quarterman and Rutherford, Wonwondah, West
Wimmera
Quin, James, Glenmore, Tenalla
Quin, Johnson, Marramomate, Beechworth

R.

Ray and Morrison, South Corner Inlet, South
Gipps Land
Ray and Morrison, Mount Singapore, Settled
Districts
Read and Younger, Wahgunyah, Beechworth
Ready and Hook, Minton's Creek, or Conoial,
Melbourne
Reid, David, Barnawartha, Beechworth
Ray and Morrison, Mount Singapore, Settled
Districts
Ready and Hook, Minton's Creek, or Conabal,
Melbourne
Read and Younger, Wahgunyah, Beechworth
Reid, D., Barnawartha, Beechworth
Reid, William James, Woodhurne, Grant
Reid Brothers, Carraragarmonger, Beechworth
Richardson, James, Gorrin, Ararat
Richardson and Ayres, Kenyang North, Warr-
nambool
Riddle, John, Geftingal, Omeo
Riddle and Hamilton, Cairnbill, Gisborne
" Turritable,
Ritchie, Daniel, Blackwood, Warrnambool
Ritchie, John, Fiery Creek, Ararat
" View Lake,
Ritchie, Simon, Woodbourne, Warrnambool
Roadknight, W., sen., Stony Rises, Warrnam-
bool

Roadnight, Thomas, Gerangamete, Grant
Roadknight and Stirling, Lake Tyen and
Snowy River, Settled Districts
Robertson, A. S., Little Corangamite, Warrnam-
bool
Robertson, D., Englefield, West Wimmera
" Gringengirona,
Robertson, Alexander, Saltmer, "
" Mira Lake, "
Robertson, George, Warrock, "
Robertson, J. V., Konarwarren, Warrnambool
Robertson, Thomas, Campaspe River, Echuca
Robertson, W. and J., Wando Vale, West Wim-
mera
Robertson, R. T., Cherrington, Gisborne
" Mount Campbell, Echuca
Robertson, Wm., Wooling, Gisborne
" Ondit, Grant
Robertson, Wm. and John, Niruan, Portland
Robertson, W. H. and J. H., Moorabbee, Echuca
" Pine Grove West,
Echuca
Robertson, Brothers, Woodford, Portland
" Kinkell,
" Mount Mitchell, Castle-
maine
Robertson, T. J. J. and T., Victoria Valley,
West Wimmera
Robertson, J. G. and T., Moora-Moora, West
Wimmera
Robertson, Messrs., Wannon, Ararat
" Yarram Yarram, Ararat
" East Loddon, Castlemaine
Rogers, John, Churchill Island, Melbourne
" Sandstone Island,
Roper, W. H., Mullindollingong, Beechworth
Ross, John, Mount William Plains, Ararat
Ross Brothers, Eldorado, West Wimmera
Rosborough, Thos., Myrtle Creek, Beechworth
Roston, L., Tottington, East Wimmera
" Hambottom,
Rourke, C., Wooloogoorang, Omeo
Rourke, E., Nugnan Haggan,
Rourke, James, Brodhen Creek, South Gipps
Land
Rourke, John, Little River, North Gipps Land
Rourke, William, Brodribb,
Rowe, R., Long Corner, Beechworth
Rowe, J. P., Terrick Terrick, Echuca
Rowe, William, Gnarkret, East, Warrnambool
Rowe and Son, Glenfine, Ballarat
Ruffy, W. J., Sandabuilla, Benalla
" Dropmore,
Russell, Alex., Slawballfork, Ararat
Russell, Phillip, Carngham, Ballarat
Russell, Geo., Elderslie, West Wimmera
" Upper Leigh, Grant
Russell, Messrs., Wardy Yalloch, Ballarat
Russell, T. and Co., Allen's House, Grant
" Mount Hebrews,
" Long Water Holes, Grant
Russell, Aitken and Co., Langi Willie, or Lian-
jamie, Ararat
Ryan, John, Powlett's Plains, Castlemaine
Ryan, L., Lawlott, West Wimmera
" Bunyip, "

S.

Sanders, J., Ronald Kirk, Swan Hill
Sanderson, J., Piccorvet, East, Ballarat
Sanderson and Co., Sprrill-burril, Warrnambool
Schlesinger, Richard, River Tyers South, South
Gipps Land
Scott Brothers, Canual, West Wimmera
Scott and Sons, Warrenknabel,
Scott, Hugh, Jancourt, Warrnambool
Scott, Daniel, Deloine, North Gipps Land
Shanahan, Martin, Marno, East Wimmera
" York Plains, "
Shaw and Forge, Table Top, Benalla
Shields and Horsley, Totara, Swan Hill
Short, John, Louttit Bay, Settled Districts

Simpson, John, Westway, Melbourne
Simson, John, Hurdy Gurdy, „
    „   „   Trevallo, Ararat
Simson, Robert, Mount Rose, Ararat
    „   „   Langi Kal-Kal,
Simson, D. C., Exors. of, Charlotte Plains, Castlemaine
    „   „   Janevale, Castlemaine
    „   „   Langi Coori,
Simsons and Ralston, Dergholm, Portland
    „   „   Roseneath,
Sinclair, William, Wyuna, Echuca
Skene, William, Plains, West Wimmera
Skene, William and Co., Burrowye, Beechworth
Sloane, William and Co., Woodaga, or Wooragee, Beechworth
Sloane, William and Co., Thowgala, Omeo
    „   „   Narong, Swan Hill
    „   „   Pine, „
    „   „   Mount Teddington, East Wimmera
    „   „   Portacle, Portland
Smith, A. J., Langley Vale, Gisborne
    „   „   Borbapeyghark West, Grant
Smith, John and Elizabeth, Cow, Swan Hill
Smith, J. D. and A., Girrard, Settled Districts
    „   „   Lindenow, North Gipps Land
Smith and Wynne, North Boundary, No. 1 Swan Hill
Smith and Wynne, North Boundary, No. 2 Swan Hill
Smith and Wynne, Red Bluff Well, West Wimmera
Smith and Wynne, South Boundary, West Wimmera
Snodgrass, Peter, Doogalook, Gisborne
Snodgrass, W., Tarawell, „
Speed, W., Derrimal, „
Stanbridge, W. E., Lake Boga, Swan Hill
Stanbridge, W., Astley's, or Tyrrell, Swan Hill
Stanhope and M'Cradden, Buckley's Creek, Warrnambool
Staughton, Simon, exors. of, Brisbane Ranges, Grant
Steiglitz, A. W., Tullives, West Wimmera
Stephens, Thomas, Curyo North, Swan Hill
Stevens, Thomas, Nautngbool, Ballarat
Stevenson, John, Wangerbill, North Gipps Land
Stephenson, Henry, Glenburnie, Gisborne
Stephenson, P., Toolamba, Echuca
    „   „   Wannala,
Stewart, Gideon, Habbie's Howe, Benalla
    „   „   Glenlyon,
    „   „   Rocky Passes, „
Stratton, Ricard and Co., Sections, Alberton, Settled Districts
Street, Frederick, Baraninda, Beechworth
Strettle, A., Paripa, Warrnambool
    „   „   Bangonia, Beechworth
Sumner and Bene, Coolort, Melbourne
Sutherland, R., Native Creek, Grant
Swan, William, Kuwrongwootong West, West Wimmera
Swan, D., Spring Vale, West Wimmera
Swanston, C. L., Meurve,
Synnott, Monckton, Brighton South, West Wimmera

T.

Tait, Henry, Spring Creek, Settled Districts
Taylor, John and A., Breakfast Creek, Portland
Taylor, James, Warrigall Creek, No. 2, Settled Districts
Taylor, James, Warrigall Creek, South Gipps Land
Taylor, James, Oammen Creek, South Gipps Land
Telford, J. C., Swinton, West Wimmera

Thom, Archibald, Kiklon, or Dickson's, Benalla
Thomas, Charles, Howqua Hills,
Thomas and Another, Goulburn Downs, „
Thomson, John, Shadwell South, E, Warrnambool
Thomson, John, Snake Island, Settled Districts
    „   „   Kellambete, Warrnambool
Thomson and Cunningham, Red Grass Hills, South Gipps Land
Thomson and Cunningham, Hill End, South Gipps Land
Thomson and Cunningham, Tangel Hills, South Gipps Land
Thomson and Cunningham, Clyde Bank and Marley Point, North Gipps Land
Thomson and Cunningham, Clyde Bank and Marley Point
Thomson, George, Challkeum, Ararat
Tolmie, M. and W., Limestone Ridge, Portland
Tolmie, E., Deneran, Benalla
    „   „   Holland's Creek, „
Torry, J. S., Benalla, Castlemaine
Tower, Francis, Junction of Hopkins and Black Rivers, Warrnambool
Trust and Agency Co., Rockwabanyule, Castlemaine
Trust and Agency Co., Rolleston, Echuca
    „   „   East Charlton, Castlemaine
    „   „   Narrewillock, „
    „   „   Trappyer „
    „   „   Terrick Terrick West, Echuca
    „   „   Wyrbetella, Castlemaine
    „   „   Yeungroon, „
    „   „   Duck Swamp, Echuca
    „   „   Buchan, Omeo
    „   „   Western Allamatya, Swan Hill
    „   „   Barbision, Swan Hill
    „   „   Kenmare, „
    „   „   Blackrose, „
    „   „   Dunmore West, Warrnambool
    „   „   Bushy Creek, Warrnambool
    „   „   Squattleseamers, Warrnambool
    „   „   Cobram, Benalla
    „   „   Evergreen, West Wimmera
    „   „   Glanmire, West Wimmera
    „   „   Pine Hills, Lake Hindmarsh, West Wimmera
Tucket, W. H., Spring Bank, Portland
Turnbull, J. F., Lowyang, South Gipps Land
    „   „   Travignon East,
Turnbull, Thomas, Kmo Plains, Benalla
    „   „   Broken Creek,
Turnbull, George, Bulangum, East Wimmera
    „   „   Carron East, „
    „   „   „ West,
Turnbull and Son, Winalburn, Portland
Turnbull, Thomas, Honeysuckle North, Benalla
Turnbull and Co., Sections, Settled Districts
Turnbull, Philps, „
    „   „   Lara, East Wimmera
    „   „   Witchipool, „
Turnbull, R. and P., Mangrove, South Gipps Land
Turner, W. J., Coolay, West Wimmera
Twomey, John, senr., Old Stockyard, Portland
Twomey, John, Kotor, Warrnambool

U.

Underwood and Pickering, Muddy Creek, A, Gisborne
Urquhart, George, Gayfield, or Mulknyus, Swan Hill

Urquhart, George, Mournpool, Swan Hill
" Ballarook, West Wimmera
" Nurnurnemal, Swan Hill
" Ouyen, "
" Rash, "
" Yellampip, "

V.

Vaughan and Wild, Tuerong, Melbourne Bunnyip.
Vicary, T. W., Cape Otway, Settled Districts
" Yan Yan Gart, Grant
Vicary, George, Dean's Marsh, Grant
Vine, Richard, Woolborne, West Wimmera

W.

Waddle, W., vxors of, I Y U, Melbourne
Walker, Alexander, Dallamoung, East Wimmera
Walker, W. G., Tam Groggin, Omeo
" Omeo B, Omeo
Wall, R., Stainsforth, Gisborne
Wallace, William, Nicary, South Gipps Land
Wallace, John, Ballark, No. 1 and 2, Grant
Waller, W. W., Bureep Bureep, South Gipps Land
Waller and Hazell, Merton Rash, South Gipps Land
Walsh and O'Brien, Mount Ararat Creek, Melbourne
Warby, Benjamin, junr., Taminick Plains, Benalla
Ware, Joseph, Minjah, Warrnambool
" Muston's Creek No. 2, Warrnambool
Ware, Joseph, Spring Byrne, Portland
" Sinclair West, "
Ware, John, Green Hills, Warrnambool
Ware, J. G., Koorkmiaong, or Cloven Hill, Warrnambool
Ware, J. G. and J., Yalla-y-poora, Ararat
Warren, Richard, Mount Typo, Beechworth
Watson, Andrew, Nangwarry, Portland
Watson, N. G., Wurmatong, Beechworth
" Tintaldra, Beechworth
" Jerrimal, Beechworth
" Cunyong, Omeo
" Walwa, Beechworth
Watson, W., Corinawarrabel, Settled Districts
Watts, J., Moray East, West Wimmera
Webster, John, Shadwell North, Warrnambool
Webster, M'Kinnon, and Wright, Mount Battery, Benalla
Wedge, H., Sections, Eumemmerring, Settled Districts
Wheeler, Arthur, Upton, Benalla
Wheeler, Charles, Nariel, Beechworth
Wheeler, Henry, Wangambetan, Benalla
White, James, Briebong Hill, Portland
White, T. W., Hogshot Heath, Swan Hill
Whitehead, Robert, Spring Creek, Warrnambool
Whitehead, Thomas, Wabba, Beechworth
Whittaker, J. and J., Longlands, West Wimmera
Whittaker, William, Tibbutt, North Gipps Ld.
Williams, J., Sutton Grange, Castlemaine
Williams, F. J., Curyo South, Swan Hill

Williamson, C., Junction or Gleniogie, East Wimmera
Williamson, C., Dennmerron, East Wimmera
Willan, F. C., Kingorera Creek, Castlemaine
" Kingower
Willis, Charles, Tea Tree Creek, Warrnambool
Willis, K., Koolmeert, West Wimmera
Willis, T., Sections Plenty, Settled Districts
Willis, William, Wellatt, West Wimmera
Wilson, Alexander, Vectis
" Wyn-wyn
" Murkindar
" Arapiles
" Darragan
Wilson, David, Bryan O'Lean, Warrnambool
Wilson, John, Christmas Hills, Melbourne
Wilson, Thomas, Dowling Forest, Ballarat
Wilson, George, Wonga Lake, Swan Hill
Wilson and Lesce, St. Mary's Lake, West Wimmera
Wilson, James, Tallangatta, Beechworth
" Kangaroo Ground
Wilson, Samuel, Narmbool, Ballaarat
Wilson and Elder, Yarlam, Grant
Wilson Brothers, Green Hills, East Wimmera
" Kirkwood
" Marma Downs
" St. Helen's
" Walmer and Tulganny, West Wimmera
Wilson Brothers, Kewell, West Wimmera
" Blackheath, East "
" Longerenong, East Wimmera
" Ashens "
" Avon or Mallee Plains "
Wilson, Crosbie and Boyd. Mathkia, Benalla
Winter, John, Stewart's Plains, Echuca
" Caragarac
" Colbinabia "
" Corop
" Ranshaw, Ballarat
Winter, Samuel Pratt, Muredah or Spring Valley, Portland
Winter, J. and W., Colbinabia North, Echuca
Winter Brothers, Burrambool, Kehuca
Withers, Jason, Ultima, Beechworth
" Eldorado West
Wood Brothers and Kirk, Punial Island, Swan Hill
Wood Brothers and Kirk, Gerahmin
" South Tyrrell "
Woodside, John, Happy Valley Creek, Beechworth
Woodside, John, Kiewa, Beechworth
Worster, Mary, George and Thomas, Byrnemonger, Omeo
Wright, C. K., Lake Catherine, Warrnambool
" Sherbrook
Wyelaskir, J. D., Nanapimselap, Ararat

Y.

Youl, Ebenezer, St. Kitts, Warrnambool
Young, Thomas, Newington, West Wimmera
Young, William, Dundas
" Mount Korolt
Younger George, Bochara "

Z

Zealily, Robert, South Beach, Settled Districts

GENERAL INFORMATION.

COLONY OF VICTORIA.

Victoria has an area of 86,831 square miles (55,571,840 acres), or 2,813 square miles less than that of England, Scotland, and Wales united. Its greatest length from east to west is about 480 miles, with an average breadth of about 150 miles. It is separated from South Australia on the west, by an incorrectly-marked boundary line along the supposed 141st meridian, from the sea coast to the river Murray; from New South Wales on the N. and N.E. by the river Murray to its principal source; thence by an imaginary boundary line E.S.E. to Cape Howe. From Cape Howe, which is on about the 150th meridian, west to the 141st meridian, it is bounded on the south by Bass's Straits and the Pacific Ocean. The most southerly points of Victoria and of the continent of Australia are at Wilson's Promontory (39 deg. 8min. south latitude), and at Cape Otway (38 deg. 51 min.). The most northerly point is at the north-west angle of the colony (about the 34th parallel of south latitude).

A main range or watershed extends from east to west throughout nearly the whole length of the colony, giving rise to rivers, which flow northwards towards the Murray River, and south to the ocean. The climate is generally excellent; but with the whole breadth of Australia on the north, and the wide Pacific Ocean on the south, there are occasionally great fluctuations in the temperature, caused chiefly by changes in the atmospherical currents.

In the year 1803 New South Wales made an attempt to form a convict settlement near the Heads of Port Phillip; but on the 27th of January, 1804, the party abandoned the region in great haste, characterising the territory as an "unpromising and unproductive country." For thirty years nothing further was done, until the Messrs. Henty settled at Portland Bay, in about the year 1833. In the year 1834, the private enterprise of some Tasmanian colonists led to the establishment of the Colony of Victoria. The following correct historical dates are derived from a blue book of the British House of Commons: The late Mr. John Bateman first arrived on the 26th of May, 1835. On the 15th of August, 1835, Mr. J. P. Fawkner's party arrived, and on the 10th of October following he himself reached Port Phillip. The first census was taken on the 25th of May, 1836. There were then in the new colony 142 males and 35 females—in all 177 souls. On the 7th of April, 1861, the total population numbered 540,322, or 328,651 males and 211,671 females. On the 31st of March, 1865, according to the estimate of the Registrar General, there were in the colony 351,023 males and 259,870 females, in all 610,893 souls.—Extracted from *Bradshaw's Guide.*

GOVERNMENT OF VICTORIA.

EXECUTIVE COUNCIL.

His Excellency the Officer Administering the Government and Commander of Her Majesty's Forces in the Australian Colonies — Brigadier-General George Jackson Carey, C.B.
Private Secretary — Capt. and Brevet-Major D. W. Tuyper, 50th Regiment.
Chief Secretary—The Hon. James McCulloch.
The Minister of Justice—The Hon. Arth. Michie.
The Attorney-General—The Hon. George Higinbotham.
The Minister of Finance, or Treasurer—The Hon. George Frederick Verdon.
The President of the Board of Land and Works and Commissioner of Crown Lands and Survey—The Hon. James Macpherson Grant.
The Commissioner of Trade and Customs—The Hon. James Goodall Francis.
The Minister of Mines—The Hon. James Forrester Sullivan.
The Hon. Henry Miller, without office.
Clerk to Executive Council—J. H. Kay, Esq.

PARLIAMENT OF VICTORIA.

N.B.—Members of the Legislative Council and the Speaker of the Legislative Assembly take the title of "Honorable."

LEGISLATIVE COUNCIL.

Composed of Thirty Members—Six Provinces, containing 16,061 Electors.
President—The Hon. Sir James F. Palmer, Knt.
Chairman of Committees—The Hon. David Wilkie.

Retire	Name	Province	Town Address
1868	A'Beckett, Thos. Turner	Central	91 Little Collins street west
1864	Anderson, Robert Stirling	Eastern	91 Little Collins street west
1868	Bear, John Pinney	Southern	Victoria Parade
1872	Black, Neil	Western	Melbourne Club
1873	Campbell, William	North Western	Melbourne Club
1872	Clarke, Wm. John Turner	Southern	Collins street and Queen street
1870	Cole, George Ward	Central	Cole's Wharf
1870	Degraves, William	Southern	97 Flinders lane east
1874	Fawkner, John Pascoe	Central	Smith street, Collingwood
1871	Fitzgerald, Nicholas	North Western	Union Club
1868	Fraser, Alexander	North Western	33 Collins street west
1871	Fellows, Thomas Howard	Central	34 Temple Court
1873	Henty, James	South Western	11 Little Collins street west
1864	Henty, Stephen George	Western	91 Market street
1870	Highett, William	Eastern	Melbourne Club
1874	Lowe, John	South Western	Parliament Houses
1868	Hull, William	Central	Richmond
1866	Jenner, Caleb Joshua	South Western	Collins street west
1870	McCrae, John	South Western	Albion House, Nicholson st
1874	Miller, Henry	Western	43, Collins street west
1870	Mitchell, William Henry Fancourt	North Western	Melbourne Club
1874	Murphy, Henry Morgan	Eastern	Parliament Houses
1870	Palmer, Sir James Frederick	Western	Parliament Houses
1874	Pettett, William Henry	Southern	Parliament Houses
1868	Sladen, Charles	Western	Melbourne Club
1866	Strachan, James Ford	South Western	Queen street south
1868	Taylor, William	Southern	Melbourne Club
1872	Turnbull, Robert	Eastern	William street
1868	Williams, Benjamin	Eastern	24 Bourke street west
1868	Wilkie, David	North Western	108 Collins street east

THE LEGISLATIVE ASSEMBLY.

Composed of 78 Members.   49 Districts, containing 165,485 Electors.
Speaker—The Hon. Sir Francis Murphy.   Chairman of Committees—Peter Lalor.

☞ *The figures denote the number of Members for the District.*

Name.	District.	Town Address.
Aspinall, Butler Cole	Portland 1	29 Temple Court
Baillie, Wm. Gray	Castlemaine 3	49 Collins street west
Balfour, James	East Bourke 2	11 Little Collins street west
Bayles, William	Villiers and Heytesbury 2	Collins street west
Blackwood, Samuel Henry	Castlemaine 3	Temple Court
Blackwood, John Hutcheson	West Melbourne 3	King street
Bowman, Robert	Maryborough 2	Parliament Houses
Bunny, Brice Frederick	St. Kilda 2	21 Temple Court
Burrowes, Robert	Sandhurst 2	Parliament Houses
Burtt, John Goulson	North Melbourne 2	Mechanics' Institute
Byrne, Robert	Crowlands 2	40 Collins street east
Casey, James Joseph	Mandurang 2	Parliament Houses
Connor, Joseph Henry	Polworth & South Grenville 1	Parliament Houses
Cope, Edward	East Bourke Boroughs 1	101 Little Collins street
Cunningham, George	Geelong East 2	Parliament Houses
Davies, Benjamin George	Avoca 2	Carlton Club, Gertrude st
Dyte, Charles	Ballarat East 2	1 Bank place, Collins street west
Edwards, John	Collingwood 3	Brunswick street, Fitzroy
Embling, Thomas	Collingwood 3	26 Gore street, Fitzroy
Evans, Gordon Henry James	Belfast 1	13 Hall of Commerce
Farrell, James	Castlemaine 3	Parliament Houses
Foott, Nicholas	Geelong West 2	Parliament Houses
Francis, James Goodall	Richmond 2	28 King street
Fraser, William	Creswick 2	Parliament Houses
Gillies, Duncan	Ballarat West 2	10 Victoria Parade
*Grant, James Macpherson	Avoca 2	89 Collins street west
Halfey, John	Sandhurst 2	54 Collins street west
Hanna, Patrick	Murray Boroughs 1	120 William street
Harbison, John	North Melbourne 2	155 Rosslyn st., West Melbourne
Heath, Richard	Geelong West 2	Menzie's Hotel
Henty, Henry	Grenville 2	11 Little Collins street west
*Higinbotham, George	Brighton 1	Crown Law Offices
Hopkins, John Rout	South Grant 2	Union Hotel
Ireland, Richard Davies	Kilmore 1	6 Temple Court
Jones, Charles Edwin	Ballarat East 2	Cor. Charles & Gore sts., Fitzroy
Karford, George Briscoe	Ovens 2	Spencer street Station
King, Mark Last	West Bourke 3	16 Collins street west
Lalor, Peter	South Grant 2	Parliament Houses
Langton, Edward	East Melbourne 2	12 Collins street east
Levey, George Collins	Normanby 1	"Herald" Office, Bourke street
Levi, Nathaniel	East Melbourne 2	Collins and William streets
Longmore, Francis	Ripon and Hampden 1	149, Collins street west
Love, Andrew	Crowlands 2	Parliament House
Macgregor, John	Rodney 1	87 Chancery Lane
MacBain, James	Wimmera 1	24 Queen street
Macpherson, John Alex.	Dundas 1	19 Nicholson street
McCann, William Nelson	South Grant 2	Parliament Houses
McCaw, Matthew	East Bourke 2	Bourke street west
*McCulloch, James	Mornington 1	Queen street
M'Kean, James	Maryborough 2	Elizabeth street south
McLellan, William	Ararat 2	Parliament Houses
McMahon, Charles	West Melbourne 3	Melbourne Bank Company
Moore, David	Sandridge 1	16 Queen street
Murphy, Sir Francis	Grenville 2	Parliament Houses
O'Grady, Michael	South Bourke 2	2 Collins street west
Orr, John	Murray 1	Parliament Houses
Pearson, William	Gipps Land North 1	Melbourne Club
Plummer, Wm.	Warrnambool 1	1 Lansdown ter., Lansdown st
Ramsay, John	Maldon 1	115 Fitzroy street, Fitzroy
Reeves, Isaac Godfrey	Collingwood 3	Parlt. II., or Victoria Crescent
Richardson, John	Geelong East 2	Parliament Houses
Riddell, John Carre	West Bourke 3	Melbourne Club
Sands, George John	Dalhousie 1	Temple Court Hotel
Smith, George Varney	Ovens 2	67 Faraday street, Carlton
Smith, John Thomas	West Bourke 3	Town Hall
Smith, Geo. Paton	South Bourke 2	13 Temple Court
Smyth, Fred. Leopold	Villers and Heytesbury 2	40 Temple Court
Snodgrass, Peter	Gipps Land South 1	67 Queen street
Snowball, Joshua	St. Kilda 2	Melbourne U. R. Station
*Sullivan, James Forrester	Mandurang 2	Victoria Parade
Tucker, Robert Braithwaite	Kyneton Boroughs 1	Temple Court Hotel
Vale, Wm. Mountford Kinsey	Ballarat West 2	Parliament Houses
*Verdon, George Frederick	Williamstown 1	Treasury
Watkins, William	Evelyn 1	Carlton Club Hotel
Wardrop, Archibald Baird	Richmond 2	1 Bank place
Wheeler, James Henry	Creswick 2	Temple Court Hotel
Whiteman, John	Emerald Hill 1	Bourke street west
Wilson, William	Ararat 2	16 and 18 Flinders street west

GENERAL INFORMATION.

OFFICERS OF PARLIAMENT.

Clerk of the Parliaments, G. W. Rusden.
Legislative Council.—Clerk, G. W. Rusden. Assistant Clerk, C. L. Comyns Usher, A. A. C. Le Souef. Clerk of the Papers, Edmund Finn. Reader, James Weare. Housekeeper, Henry Madden. Six Messengers.
Legislative Assembly.—Clerk, John Barker. Clerk Assistant, A. G. Dumas Sergeant-at-Arms, W. G. Palmer. Clerk of Committees, A. Warner. Clerk of the Papers, T. G. Atkinson. Assistant Clerk of the Papers, S. M. Gill. Clerk of Private Bills, G. H. Jenkins. Reader, George M. Hardesa. Housekeeper, G. E. Pearse. Six Messengers.
Library.—Librarian, James Smith. Assistant Librarian, W. Dopping. Clerk, F. Sinclair. Chief Messenger, R. Church, and two Messengers. The Library contains about 13,000 volumes, and is always open to members.
Government Shorthand Writer—J. H. Webb.
Comptroller of Refreshment Rooms and Stables—W. G. Palmer. Contractor for Refreshment Rooms, E. H. Gregory.
Orders to the Galleries are obtained from Members of each House. To the Body of the Council, outside the Bar, from the President. To the Assembly, Speaker's Gallery, from the Speaker.
Enrolled Parliamentary Agent.—J. J. Moody, 38 Collins street east.

GOVERNORS OF OTHER AUSTRALIAN COLONIES.

New South Wales—Sir John Young.
New Zealand—Sir George Grey.
Queensland—Sir George Bowen.

South Australia—Sir Dominic Daly.
Tasmania—Colonel Thomas Gore Browne.
Western Australia—Dr. J. S. Hampton.

DEPARTMENTS UNDER THE HON. THE CHIEF SECRETARY.

Chief Secretary—The Hon. James McCulloch, M.L.A. Under Secretary, J. Moore, J.P. Offices, Government House, Spring street.
Audit Office.—Commissioners, Chas. H. Symonds, A. J. Agg, and F. Jones. Office, Collins street east.
Board of Examiners for the Civil Service.—W. E. Hearn, M.A., LL.D., Capt. Kay, R.N., F.R.S., W. W. Wardell, and A. W. Chomley. Sec., W. H. Odgers. Government House, Spring street.
Registrar-General—Wm. Hy. Archer, J.P., Government house, Spring street.
Police.—Chief Commissioner, Frederick C. Standish. Paymaster, W. Mair. Inspecting Superintendent, P. H. Smith. Chief Clerk, Henry Moors. Offices, Collins street east. Melbourne Police District.—T. H. Lyttelton, Sup.-in-charge. Office, Police Court, Swanston street. No. 1 Division, Inspector Sadlier, Sub-Inspector Dobson, Russell street, Melbourne. No. 4 Div. and Water Police, Inspector Beaver, Williamstown Station. Co. Bourke and Depôt District.—Inspector Hare, Sub-Insp. McNamara, Police Depôt, Richmond. Detective Police.—Central Office, Little Collins street east, near Eastern Market, Melbourne. Inspector Nicolas. Resident Clerk, James D. Scott.
Gaols.—Claud Faris, Sheriff. Melbourne, G. Wintle, Governor.
Patents.—Chief Secretary's and Registrar-General's Offices.
Penal.—Inspector-General of Penal Estab., W. T. N. Champ. Visiting Justice Gaols and Stockades, R. Youl, M.D. Visiting Justice Hulks, F. Call. Chief Clerk, W. Snelling. Accountant, J. Stone Pentridge Penal Establishment, Sup., M. H. Smith. Inspector and Sup. of Hulks, H. W. Blachford. Offices, corner of William and Latrobe streets.
Medical.—Chief Medical Officer, William M'Crea, M.B. Chief Clerk, T. R. Wilson. Offices, 178 Collins street east.

GENERAL INFORMATION.

Health Officer, Queenscliffe, Alex. P. L. Robertson, M.D. Res. Surgeon Pentridge Stockade, J. Reed, M.D.

Central Board of Health.—President, W. M'Crea, M.B. Members: R. Youl, M.D., W. M. Bell; J. T. Smith, M.L.A.; W. W. Wardell. Secretary, T. R. Wilson. Superintendent, Inspector J. N. Hassall.

Anatomy, School of, Melbourne University.—Licensee to practice Anatomy, Professor Halford. Inspector, W. M'Crea, M.B.

Medical Board of Victoria.—President, W. M'Crea, M.B. Members: Dr. G. Howitt, E. Barker, Dr. Motherwell, Dr. R. Youl, Dr. D. J. Thomas, Dr. W. M. Turnbull. Secretary, T. R. Wilson. Office, 178 Collins street.

Lunatic Asylum, Yarra Bend.—Medical Superintendent, E. Paley. Resident Surgeons, Alexander J. Paterson, and L. Dick.

Receiving Hospital for the Insane.—Royal Park. Resident Surgeon, W. L. Gordon, M.D.

Friendly Societies.—Certifying Barrister, F. S. Dobson; Registrar, J. Lascelles. Office, at Chief Secretary's Office.

Board of Education.—Sir J. F. Palmer, Church of England; W. H. Archer, Roman Catholic; James Balfour, Presbyterian; T. J. Sumner, Wesleyan; and Isaac Hart, Jewish Community. Inspector-General, R. H. Budd. Secretary, Benjamin F. Kane. Organising Inspectors, J. Geary, and G. W. Brown. Inspectors, H. Venables, H. A. Same, J. Sircom, A. Gilchrist, J. Main. Accountant, T. Tester.

Botanical Gardens.—Government Botanist, Dr. Mueller, F.R.S., Knight Legion of Honor, Knight Order Dannebrog; assistant, Carl Wilhelmi.

Board of Agriculture.—President, J. C. Riddell, M.L.A. Chairman of the Council, P. McCracken, J.P. Secretary, J. M. Matson. Offices, Old Treasury, Queen st.

National Museum. — At University. Director, Professor M'Coy.

Experimental Farm, near Flemington.—Secretary, J. M. Matson.

Central Board Appointed to watch over the Interests of the Aborigines.—T. J. Sumner, W. Macredie, T. Embling, Hon. S. G. Henty, M.L.C., J. Mackenzie, and R. Brough Smyth. Mr. Brough Smyth acts as Secretary. Offices, Queen street, Melbourne.

Board to consider Claims for Rewards and Premiums for New Manufactures and Industries.—Hon. J. G. Francis, M.L.A., Hon. R. S. Anderson, M.L.C., S. H. Bindon, M.L.A., J. Harrison, W. Lyall, J. G. Reeves, J. C. Riddell, M.L.A., J. Sherwin, and J. J. Stutzer. Secretary, C. Greville.

Inspectors of Sheep.—Chief Inspector, E. M. Curr. District Inspectors—Melbourne District, J. Riley, Offices, Queen street, Melbourne. East Wimmera, J. M. Allen, St. Arnaud. Echuca, W. Sperling, Taradale. Geelong, C. Peever, Skene street, Geelong. Gipps Land, R. Wedge, care of Inspector of Police, Sale. Glenelg, J. H. Kerr, Coleraine. Mortlake, D. McRae, Warrnambool. Portland, J. F. Shaw, Hamilton. Wangaratta, R. Perry, Cain Cottage, Benalla. West Wimmera, R. Stirling, Horsham. Benalla, F. Mackenzie, Kilmore.

NAVAL DEPARTMENTS.

Royal Navy.—Admiralty and Colonial Survey.—Additional of H.M. ship "Curaçoa," for Surveying Service. Commander, H. L. Cox, R.N., Commanding; T. Bourchier, Master, R.N.; J. G. Boulton, 2nd Master, R.N.; S. S. Crispo, Writer; P. H. McHugh, Draughtsman.

Naval Training Ship.—Commander, Lieutenant G. A. Woods. Sub-Lieutenant, F. O. Handfield.

DEPARTMENTS UNDER THE HON. THE TREASURER.

Minister of Finance.—The Hon. George F. Verdon, M.L.A. Under-Treasurer, E. S. Symonds. Accountant, R. Undemann. Treasury, Spring street.

Receivers and Paymasters.—Travelling Receiver and Paymaster, J. Hall; Ararat, A. H. Constable; Avoca, A. Meyrick; Ballarat, W. H. Barnard; Beechworth, G. R. Berry; Belfast, P. Nicholson; Castlemaine and Maldon, C. Megson; Daylesford, J. Fisher; Geelong, G. F. Belcher; Grant, H. C. Staveley; Inglewood, S. Wyman; Melbourne, W. H. Hull; Maryborough, A. Reynell; Port Albert, W. R. Belcher; Portland, W. A. Moore, Sandhurst, A. Langston; Warrnambool, A. W. Musgrove; Dunolly, J. W. Butt; Hamilton, W. Sewell; Smythesdale, H. Williamson; St. Arnaud and Landsborough, H. G. Bennett; Talbot, H. E. Jenkins; Wood's Point, G. J. Rumley; Stawell, G. W. Fitzsimons.

Stores and Transport.—Secretary to Tender Board and Inspector of Stores, F. F. Moore. Assistant Secretary to Tender Board, G. Lane. Assistant Inspector of Stores, J. Peirce.

Government Printing Office.—Eastern Hill.—John Ferres, Government Printer; S. J. Walker, Accountant; C. Baker, Overseer.

MILITARY.

Staff.—Brigadier-General Carey, Commanding the Forces. Brevet-Major Tupper, 50th Regiment, A.D.C. Captain W. Heywood, 14th Regiment, Major of Brigade.

Commissariat.—Deputy Commissioner-General G. Horne, Comptroller of Army Expenditure. Deputy Assistant Commissioner-General, H. R. A. Middleton, J.P., Military Chest and Store Accountant.

Medical Staff.—Staff Surgeon, R. Lewins, M.D. Staff Assistant Surgeon, H. Scott. *Purveyor's Department.*—W. Robertson, Purveyor's Clerk-in-charge.

Royal Artillery.—No. 2 Battery, 7th Brigade—Captain and Brevet-Lieutenant Colonel C. H. Smith, Commanding. Lieutenants: W. H. Graham, A. L. C. Smithett, and C. Boyd.

Offices.—Staff and Commissariat Offices, New Military Barracks, Princes Bridge. Colonial Barrack-master, Major C. H. Hall.

VOLUNTEER FORCE.

General Staff.—Colonel Commandant of Volunteers, W. A. D. Anderson. Sup. of Local Military Store Department, Major C. H. Hall. Staff Captain Prince of Wales V. V. Light Horse, O. S. Burton. Staff Captain R. V. V. Artillery, W. H. Snee. Staff Captain Naval Brigade, C. R. Payne. Brigade Sergeant-Major, J. Fahey. Brigade Quarter Master Sergeant, E. Riley. Office, 45 Stephen street.

DEPARTMENT UNDER THE HON. THE MINISTER OF MINES.

Minister of Mines.—Hon. J. F. Sullivan, M.L.A. Secretary, R. Brough Smyth, F.G.S.L. Chief Clerk, Richard Francis.

Mining Surveyors.

Ararat—Ararat, C. J. W. Bussell. Barkly and Pleasant Creek, J. D'Alton. Beaufort, J. Templeton.

Ballarat.—No. 1 Division, R. Davidson. 2, P. C. Fitzpatrick. 3, T. Cowan. 4, M. O'Malley. Buninyong, R. R. Harvey. Smythesdale, J. Lynch. Creswick, J. Stevenson. Steiglitz, T. Woolgrove. Gordon, T. Cowan. Blackwood, E. G. Magnus.

Beechworth.—Beechworth Division, A. McKay. Yackandandah, T. G. Kennan. Chiltern, R. Arrowsmith. Morse's Creek, R. H. Stone. Matlock, J. Uaher, junior. Gaffney's Creek, 1, St. H. Blair. Jamieson, S. K. Vickery. Wood's Point, A. B. Ainsworth. Donnelly's Creek, J. G. Peers.

Grant, Crooked River, A. F. Walker. Enoch's Point, Big River, P. Nevins.

Castlemaine.—Castlemaine Division, T. L. Brown. Fryer's Creek, R. L. M. Kitto. Taradale, T. Turner. Kyneton, J. Maxwell, senior. Maldon, R. Nankivell. Daylesford, A. Johnson. St. Andrew's, West and South, G. Francis. St. Andrew's, Central, A. Armstrong.

Maryborough.—Maryborough Division, D. O'Leary. Avoca, R. English. Talbot, J. Smith. Redbank, W. Byrne. Inglewood, W. G. Couchman. Dunolly, R. J. McMillan. St. Arnaud, J. Phillips. Sandhurst—Sandhurst Division, T. Forbes, G. W. Hart, C. E. Barker, J. W. Raby. Kilmore, G. Francis. Heathcote, J. T. Strong. Rushworth, H. B. Nicholas. Heywood, J. Ryan.

Keepers of Powder Magazines.—Ballarat, A. Livingstone. Creswick, P. Dowling. Castlemaine, M. M'Craith. Maldon, J. Greer. Maryborough, W. Britt. Avoca, M. Conniff. Dunolly, R. J. Webb. Inglewood, W. Acton. Talbot, J. Boyle. Ararat, F. C. Cope. Pleasant Creek, H. H. Roberts. Sandhurst, A. Dunlap. Beechworth, J. B. Castisan. Heathcote, R. Carkeet. St. Arnaud, C. F. Moran. Tarnagulla, H. A. McMillan. Daylesford, L. Whelan. Sale, E. Stanton. Eaglehawk, P. Quin.

DEPARTMENTS UNDER THE BOARD OF LAND AND WORKS.

Board of Land and Works.—President, Hon. J. M. Grant, M.L.A. Members: C. W. Ligar, J. Stevenson, W. W. Wardell, C. Hodgkinson.

Lands and Survey.—Surveyor-General, C. W. Ligar. Assistant Commissioner to Lands and Survey, C. Hodgkinson. Chief Clerk, A. Morrah. Accountant, E. J. Agg. Clerk-in-Charge of Land Occupation Office, C. H. Fletcher. Chief Correspondent Clerk, J. Lewis. Clerk-in-Charge of Parliamentary Papers, J. Christie. Chief Draftsman, R. Counsel. Head office, Latrobe st. west.

Land Officers (Sec. 15, Land Act).—Ararat, G. R. Rorry. Ballarat, J. Hall. Beechworth, W. H. Barnard. Belfast, P. Nicholson. Benalla, W. Piper. Camperdown, R. D. Scott. Castlemaine, J. A. Panton. Dunolly, J. W. Butt. Echuca, G. Langford. Geelong, O. F. Belcher. Hamilton, E. Wrixon. Inglewood, J. M. Gaunt. Kilmore, E. M. Cairnes. Maryborough, A. Reynell. Melbourne, A. Morrah. Port Albert, W. R. Belcher. Portland, W. A. Moore. Sale, J. Le Merchant Carey. Sandhurst, A. Langston. Warrnambool, A. W. Musgrove.

Solicitors Empowered to Grant Certificates of Titles.—R. E. Lewis, M. W. Taylor, E. Charsley, J. Liddle, J. Mac-

GENERAL INFORMATION.   vii.

bury, R. C. Greeson, J. Smith, R. Willan, J. K. B. Plummer.

Public Works Department.—Inspector-General of Public Works, &c., W. W. Wardell. Accountant and Chief Clerk, A. Galt. Clerks of Works and Draftsmen, S. H. Merrett, F. Kawerau, C. Maplestone, A. T. Snow, W. H. Steel, T. A. Eaton, C. Barrett, H. A. Williams, T. J. Clarke, A. E. Johnson, H. Mosely. Office-keeper, M. Madden.

Sewerage and Water Branch.— Accountant and Chief Clerk, C. Le Cren. Valuator, F. Stephens. Engineer, C. Taylor. Assistant Engineer and Draftsman, E. Lange. Chief Turncock, S. Bannon. Resident Inspector Yan Yean, W. Bell. Rate Collectors: De Burgh D'Arcy, A. McHarg, W. Eckersall, T. Brocklebank, R. C. White, O. Cockburn. Offices, Lonsdale street west.

Roads and Bridges.—Acting Commissioner of Roads and Bridges, Hon. J. F. Sullivan, M.L.A. Assistant Commissioner, John Stevenson. Secretary, P. P. Labertouche. Treasurer, R. C. Carr. Inspector-General, R. W. Larritt. District Engineers—Melbourne, J. Crawley, William street; Ballarat, C. Rowand; Wangaratta, F. Riley.

Victorian Railways.—Acting Commissioner of Railways, Hon. J. G. Francis, M.L.A. Secretary, W. H. Wright. Accountant, A. Mathison. Chief Clerk, J. J. Hewitt. Offices, William st. Engineer-in-Chief, T. Higinbotham. Traffic Superintendent, J. Jeremy. Assistant Traffic Superintendent, W. M. Febon. Travelling Inspector, W. A. Tetley. Office, Batman's Hill. Board meet every Wednesday, at 11 a.m.

Geological Surveyor.—Director of Mining and Geological Surveys, A. R. C. Selwyn.

DEPARTMENTS UNDER THE HON. THE COMMISSIONER OF TRADE AND CUSTOMS.

Commissioner of Trade and Customs—Hon. J. G. Francis, M.L.A. Inspector-General of Customs, J. Guthrie. Chief Clerk, C. Greville. Chief Clerk, Audit Branch, H. J. Leplastrier. Custom House, Flinders street west.

Melbourne. — Collector, J. Chatfield Tyler. Chief Clerk—Donald Munroe. Senior Landing Surveyor—Richard Down. Junior Landing Surveyor — H. M. Guthrie. Senior Landing Waiter—J. MacFarlane. Assistant Registrar of Shipping, R. C. Dunn. Warehouse keeper— G. Bagyertz.

Williamstown.—Landing Surveyor and Tide Inspector—D. W. Gossett. Clerk—G. Ashton.

Geelong.—Collector, J. Guthrie. Chief Clerk, S. S. Rennie. Senior Landing Waiter, H. B. Lane.

Shortland's Bluff (Queenscliff).—Tide Surveyor, H. E. Browne.

Portland—Collector, W. A. Moore.

Port Fairy—Collector, Peter Nicholson.

Warrnambool—A. W. Musgrove.

Port Albert—Collector, W. R. Belcher.

Wahgunyah — Coast Waiter, J. G. Jackson.

Belvoir—Coast Waiter, J. Chapman.

Swan Hill—Coast Waiter, B. Beaver.

Cowans—Coast Waiter, T. D. Gorden.

Narung—Coast Waiter, J. Blackwood.

Echuca—Collector, W. H. Willock.

Government Shipping Office.—Shipping Master and Registrar of Seamen, J. J. Shillinglaw. Office, Sailors' Home, Spencer st. At Sandridge—G. Terry, Clerk-in-charge. At Williamstown — W. C. Rees, Harbor Office, Clerk in charge.

Ports and Harbors. — Chief Harbor-master of Victoria, Charles Ferguson, J. P. Assistant-Harbor-master, D. J. M'Pherson. Clerk, W. C. Rees. Superintendent of the Marine Yard, D. Elder. Melbourne Harbor-master, A. Campbell; Assistant H. M., G. Doran; Geelong Harbor-master, W. Nicholson; Portland Harbor-master and Pilot, J. Fawthrop; Warrnambool, F. Helpman; Belfast Harbor-master and Pilot, J. B. Mills; Port Albert Harbor-master, D. Fermaner. Offices,—Nelson Parade, Williamstown. Government steamer, *Pharos*, R. Fullarton, master. Lightship, west channel, J. Liddle, master. Geelong Light-ship, J. Watt, master. Light-ship Keeper, Gellibrand's Point, W. Richards. Lighthouse Keeper, Shortlands Bluff and Swanspit, William Foy. Lighthouse Keeper, Cape Otway, W. R. Ford. Gabo Island, G. Tapp. Wilson's Promontory, J. Liberton. Cape Schanck, R. Bowie.

Pilot Board.—Office at Williamstown. C. Ferguson, J.P. (Chief Harbor Master), President. Members: J. T. Mason, A. Devlin, G. A. Stephen, A. Sutherland.

Steam Navigation Board.—Chairman, C. Ferguson, J.P.; B. R. Matthews; G. A. Stephen; A. Sutherland; A. Devlin. Secretary—W. C. Rees. Engineer-Surveyor—A. Wilson. Examiners—G. W. Groves, Navigation; W. H. Smith, Seamanship; A. Wilson, Steam and Engineers.

Powder Magazines.—Footscray: J. R. Keays. Geelong: J. Fitzsimmons. Portland: E. Wardell. Port Fairy: H. E.

GENERAL INFORMATION.

Hollick. Warrnambool: A. C. Farquharson.

Inspectors of Distilleries.—Chief-Inspector, Lesley A. Moody. Messrs. P. Le P. Bookey, P. H. Smith, T. H. Littleton, W. A. P. Dana, E. Slade, Winch, Mason, Purcell, Nicholson, F. A. & Reid, G. Heath, H. R. Barclay, H. M. Chomley, W. K. Nicolas, J. Falconbridge, J. Hart, T. Hurley, J. Watson.

Immigration.—Immigration Agent and Principal Emigration Officer for the Colony of Victoria, Lesley A. Moody. Williamstown—Emigration Officer, D. W. Cossett; Assistant Emigration Officers, A. G. Branford, T. Roch, A. Ross, T. D. Hammond. Officers for carrying out the Chinese Act: Medical Inspector, D. P. McLean, M.D., J.P.; Surveyor, S. Picken. Geelong—Assistant Immigration Agent, Collector of Customs; Queenscliff—Assistant Immigration Officers, A. Robertson, M.D., and H. E. Brown. Portland—Assistant Immigration Agent, Collector of Customs. Belfast—Assistant Imm. Agent, Coll. of Customs. Port Albert—Assistant Immigration Agent, Collector of Customs. Warrnambool—Assistant Immigration Agent, Collector of Customs. Officers for carrying out the Passengers' Act, Immigration Officers at the different ports, as above.

DEPARTMENTS UNDER THE POSTMASTER-GENERAL.

Deputy Postmaster-General—William Turner. Inspector of Postal Service, H. P. Bance. Accountant, B. Waymouth. Sup. of Mail Branch, Adolphus Sievwright. Chief Clerk, T. W. Jackson. Controller of Money Order and Savings Bank Branch, W. Galbraith. Inspector of Dead Letters, Richard Snow. Sub-Inspector of Postal Service, G. D. Pitman. General Post Office, Bourke street. For closing of mails, &c., see Post Office table.

Electric Telegraph.—Superintendent—S W. M'Gowan.

*** Office hours in Government Departments, from nine till four (Saturdays, nine till half-past twelve). Holidays—Christmas Day, New Year's Day, Good Friday and three following days, Whit-Monday, Queen's Birthday, Separation Day, and Proclamation of New Constitution.

GOLD OFFICE—TREASURY.

Escorts.—To Beechworth, Yackandandah, Chiltern, Morse's Creek, and Benalla, every alternate Monday.

To Jamieson and Wood's Point, every fourth Monday.

Gold received by the Beechworth Escort will be ready for delivery every alternate Wednesday, at 2 p.m.

Cash Parcels are conveyed to and from Beechworth, Benalla, Wood's Point, and Jamieson, under the following regulations:—

1. Parcels for escort will be received at the Gold Office, Melbourne, every alternate Monday, from 12 noon to 2 p.m.; and at the other Gold Offices during the hours hitherto observed.
2. Gold Coin to be packed in bags, not exceeding One Thousand pounds value in each.
3. Silver Coin in bags, not exceeding Fifty pounds value in each
4. Bank Notes in packages, the dimensions of which are not to exceed in length and breadth, the size of a bank note, containing not more than Five Hundred notes in one package, and to be wrapped in calico or canvas—the declared value and consignee's name and address to be marked on each parcel.

Escort Fees.—On Cash Parcels, one-half per Cent. On Gold from the Beechworth District, One Shilling per Ounce; and on Gold from other Gold Fields, Sixpence per Ounce.

No Escort Fee is charged on Gold upon which the duty has been paid.

Miners' Rights and Business Licenses may be obtained at the Receipt and Pay Office, Treasury, and at all the Country Gold Offices.

GOLD OFFICES ON THE GOLD FIELDS.

Ararat, A. H. Constable
Avoca, A. Mayrick
Ballarat, W. H. Barnard
Beaufort, R. McNeice
Beechworth, G. R. Berry
Benalla, H. Crofton
Blackwood, D. G. Stobie
Castlemaine, Canova Megson
Clunes, J. Fisher

Creswick, J. Fisher
Daylesford, H. Fowler
Dunolly, J. W. S. Butt
Heathcote, J. J. O'Meara
Chiltern, J. A. Mulligan
Jamieson, Thos. Smallman
Majorca, A. Reynall
Maldon, C. Megson
Maryborough, A. Reynell

Morse's Creek, A. L. E. Martin
Sandhurst, A. Langston
Smythesdale, H. Williamson
Stawell, G. W. Fitzsimons
Talbot, H. E. Jenkins
Tarnagulla, C. Maplestone
Wood's Point, G. J. Rumley
Yackandandah, G. Maynard

REGISTRATION OF BIRTHS AND DEATHS.

The parents of a child born or deceased, or the occupier of a house in which the event takes place, must give notice thereof to Deputy Registrar of the district. Births should be registered within 60 days after birth; and deaths before the funeral takes place. The Deputy Registrar should give certificate of registration to the undertaker, and attest place and date of interment.

VACCINATION.

The Deputy Registrar of Births and Deaths must, within 20 days after registration of any birth, give notice to the parents or guardian to have the child vaccinated, specifying the days and hours when the Government Vaccinator attends for the purpose. Parents or guardians refusing to attend to such notice are liable to a penalty of 40s. to £5.

CORPORATION OF THE CITY OF MELBOURNE.

WILLIAM BAYLES, MAYOR.

ALDERMEN.

Ward.		Retires.	Ward.		Retires.
Lonsdale	Edward Cohen	9th Nov., 1861	La Trobe	George Wragge	9th Nov., 1866
Bourke	John Thos. Smith	" 1867	Smith	John Harbison	" 1868
Gipps	Geo. Hayes	" 1866			

COUNCILLORS.

Ward.		Retires.	Ward.		Retires.
Lonsdale	Thomas Mobray	1st Nov., 1866	Gipps	Robert Flockhart, 1st Nov., 1862
	Jas. Stewart Butters	" 1867	La Trobe	Wm. Williams	" 1865
	William Bayles	" 1868		A. K. Smith	" 1866
Bourke	Orlando Fenwick	" 1864		Thomas Kenny	" 1863
	Samuel Amess	" 1867	Smith	Alexander McBean	" 1864
	Thomas Molburson	" 1868		Abraham Linacre	" 1867
Gipps	Joshua Cowell	" 1866		Joseph Stury	" 1868
	John Walker	" 1867			

AUDITORS.—Henri John Hart, and William Richard Virgo.

Town Clerk—E. G. FitzGibbon
Treasurer—John Cosgrave
City Surveyor—J. Kelly
St. Counsel—Hon. A. Michie, Hon. T. H. Fellows
City Solicitor—F. J. S. Stephen
Officer of Health—Dr. Eades
Chief Clerk—Samuel Masters
Building Surveyor—T. J. Everist
Inspector of Nuisances—James Andrews
City Insp., Insp. of Hackney Carriages—C. Dabbs
Revenue Inspector—W. J. Sugden

Inspector of Weights and Measures—G. Donald
Inspector of Lodging Houses, and Inspector of Lamps—A. Hartwell
Inspector of General Markets—G. Robinson
Inspector of the Cattle Market—Gen. Robertson
Poundkeeper—John Felstead
Messenger—Richard Gough
Hall-keeper—Thomas Byrne
Official Referees for carrying out provisions of Building Act—Nominated by Government: T. A. Eaton; by Corporation: J. Blackburn.

CHURCHES, &c.

Church of England.—Bishop of Melbourne—The Right Rev. Charles Perry, D.D. Dean and Archdeacon of Melbourne—The Very Rev. Hussey Burgh Macartney, D.D. Archdeacon of Geelong—The Venerable Theodore Carlos Benoni Stretch, A.M.

GENERAL INFORMATION.

Archdeacon of Portland—The Venerable Thomas Henry Braim, D.D. Archdeacon of Castlemaine—The Venerable A. Crawford, A.M. Chaplains of the Bishop—Rev. S. L. Chase, A.M., and Rev. G. Goodman, A.M. Chancellor of the Diocese—J. W. Stephen, A.M. Advocate—J. B. Bennett, Registrar—Hon. T. T. a'Beckett, M.L.C. Deputy Registrar—W. E. Morris.

Roman Catholic Church.—Melbourne—The Right Rev. the Bishop, J. A. Goold, D.D.; the Very Rev. the Vicar-General, J. Fitzpatrick, D.D.; Rev. J. J. Bleasdale, D.D., Rev. S. Riordan, St. Patrick's College, Very Rev. J. Lentaigne and Rev. W. Kelly. Gaol, Rev. D. Lordon. Benevolent Asylum, Rev. G. Barry. Stockades and Hulks, Rev. H. England.

Wesleyan Methodist Church.—Melbourne District.—J. S. Waugh, Chairman, Wesley College, near Prahran.

Geelong and Ballarat District.—W. L. Binks, Chairman of the District.
Castlemaine and Sandhurst District.—W. Hill, first Chairman of the District.

Presbyterian Church of Victoria.—Moderator, Rev. T. Hastie. Clark, Rev. L Hetherington.

Free Presbyterian Church of Victoria.—No. 1.—Melbourne—John Knox's—vacant. Brunswick—Rev. A. McVean. Connewarre—Rev. J. Gardner. Kilmore—Rev. E Meiklejohn, moderator. No. 2.—St. Kilda—Rev. A. Paul. Meredith and Lethbridge—Rev. A. MacThomson, M.A. Rev. A. McIntyre, no charge.

United Presbyterian Church of Victoria.—The Synod meets at Melbourne on the 1st Tuesday of each quarter. Rev. J. Henderson, Moderator.

Congregational Churches.—Melbourne District.—Melbourne, Collins street east—Rev. A. Henderson. Lonsdale st. west—Rev. T. Odell. Collingwood, Oxford st.—Rev. J. C. McMichael. Fitzroy, Victoria parade—Rev. W. S. H. Fielden. East Melbourne, Victoria parade—Rev. J. Bear. Carlton, Grattan street—vacant. Richmond, Lennox st.—Rev. W. R. Fletcher, M.A. Prahran, Commercial road—Rev. W. Moss. Brighton—Rev. W. R. Lewis. Emerald Hill—Rev. C. S. Y. Price. St. Kilda—Rev. A. Gosman. Kew—Vacant. Hawthorne—Rev. T. Laver. Jamesfield—Mr. G. Bell, junior. Williamstown—T. H. Jackson. Snappers Point—Rev. H. Grosbe. Brunswick—Rev. W. W. Pentland. Churches also at Geelong, Little River, Castlemaine, Kyneton, Dunolly, Daylesford, Forest Creek, Maryborough, Sandhurst, Inglewood, Ballarat, Beechworth, Rutherglen, Warrnambool, &c., &c.

Baptist Churches.—Melbourne, Collins street east—Rev. Jas. Taylor. Albert street—Rev. Isaac New. Lonsdale street east—Rev. J. Turner. Bourke street east—Rev. D. Allen. And at Ballarat, Beaufort, Castlemaine, Collingwood, Brunswick, Daylesford, Emerald Hill, Geelong, Kew, Kyneton, Maldon, Portland, Prahran, Sandhurst, St. Kilda, Tarnagulla, Warrnambool, Wangaratta, White Hills, &c. &c.

Union Churches.—Caulfield—Rev. W. Poole. Hawthorne—Rev. J. G. Perrin.

United Methodist Free Churches.—Fitzroy—Rev. T. A. Bayley. East Collingwood—Rev. E. Hughes. Richmond—Rev. J. Walker. And at St. Kilda, Brunswick, Geelong, Ballarat, Heathcote, &c.

Primitive Methodist.—Melbourne—Rev. M. Clarke. Collingwood—Rev. W. Gould. And at Geelong, Castlemaine, Bendigo, Campbellfield, Kilmore, Ballarat, Smythesdale, Beaufort, Talbot, Benalla, Heidelberg, Tarnagulla, &c.

Methodist New Connexion.—Melbourne, St. George's Hall—Rev. C. Linley.

Bible Christians.—Melbourne Circuit, Rev. J. Rowe. And at Geelong, Castlemaine, Ballarat, Camperdown, Sandhurst, &c.

German Lutheran Church.—Eastern Hill, Melbourne—Rev. Matthias Goethe. And at Ballarat, Smythesdale, Bendigo, Castlemaine, Maldon, Hamilton, &c.

Unitarian Christian Church, Grey street, Eastern Hill—Rev. Henry Higginson.

Welsh Calvinistic Methodist Church.—Latrobe street west, Rev. W. Hughes. And at Sebastopol Hill, Daylesford, Forest Creek, &c.

Plymouth Brethren—Protestant Hall, Stephen street.

Christians, or Disciples of Christ.—Carlton, Lygon street. And at Prahran, Brighton, Ballarat, Beechworth, Beaumaris, Chiltern, &c.

Christian Brethren.—Temperance Hall, Russell street.

Society of Friends' Meeting House.—6, Russell street south.

Hebrew Congregations.—"Shierith Yisrael," Bourke street west—Rev. E. Myers. "Mickva Yisrael," Little Lonsdale street east—Rev. Moses Rintel. Geelong—Mr. J. Goldstein. Ballarat—Rev. D. Isaacs. Sandhurst—Rev. Isaac Friedman.

COACHES.

Beechworth Line, from 35 Bourke street east.

Leave	Arrive	Leave	Arrive	Leave	Arrive
Melbourne, 11.45 a.m.		Beechworth, 4 p.m.		Wangaratta 10.45 a.m.	
Campbellfield	1.13 p.m.	Tarrawingee	7 a.m.	Chiltern	3.30 p.m.
Somerton	1.45 „	Wangaratta	8 „	Rutherglen	3.30 „
Donnybrook	2.30 „	Benalla	11.30 „	Barnawartha	4.30 „
Wallan Wallan	3.15 „	Violet Town	1.30 p.m.	Belvoir	6.30 „
Kilmore	4.30 „	Euroa	3.30 „	Albury	7 „
Broadford	5.45 „	Longwood	6.30 „	Leave	Arrive.
Tallarook	6.45 „	Avenel	7.30 „	Albury 11 p.m.	
Seymour	8 „	Seymour	9 „	Belvoir	11.30 p.m.
Avenel	9.45 „	Tallarook	10.45 „	Barnawartha	1.30 „
Longwood	12.15 „	Broadford	midnight	Chiltern	3 „
Euroa	1.45 a.m.	Kilmore	3 a.m.	4 a.m.	
Violet Town	4 „	Wallan Wallan	3.15 „	Wangaratta	8 a.m.
Benalla	8.15 „	Donnybrook	4 „	Leave Rutherglen 4 a.m. to reach Springs in time for onward despatch by Chiltern coach to Wangaratta.	
Wangaratta	10.15 „	Somerton	4.30 „		
Tarrawingee	11.30 „	Campbellfield	5 „		
Beechworth	3 p.m.	Melbourne	6.30 „		

To **Dandenong**, daily, at 4 p.m., from Star Hotel, Prahran. *Return.*—Dandenong, at 8 a.m.

To **Dromana**, Tuesday, Thursday, at 1 p.m., from 35 Bourke street east.

To **Jamieson**, via Longwood and Mansfield, Tuesday, Thursday, Saturday, at 11.30 a.m., from 35 Bourke street. Returning from Jamieson same days, at 4 a.m.

To **Kilmore**, daily, at 4.30 p.m., from 35 Bourke street, arriving at Kilmore, at 9.30 p.m. Returning from Kilmore, 9 a.m.

To **King's Creek**, Tuesday, Friday, at 1 p.m., from 35 Bourke street east.

To **McIvor**, Monday, Wednesday, Friday, at 7 a.m., from 35 Bourke street east, arriving at 5 p.m., same day. Returning from McIvor at 8.30 a.m., reaching Melbourne Tuesday, Thursday, Saturday, at 6 p.m.

To **McIvor**, via Kyneton, daily, by 7.15 p.m. train from Spencer street, arriving at McIvor at 4.30 a.m. Returning, leave McIvor daily, at 2.30 p.m., arriving by 11.15 p.m. train at Spencer street Station.

To **Merriang**, via Thomastown, Epping, and Woodstock, daily, at 3 p.m., from 35 Bourke street east. *Return.*—6.45 a.m.

To **Sale**, via Oakleigh, Dandenong, and intermediate places, daily, at 5 p.m., and Monday, Wednesday, Friday, at 7 a.m., from 35 Bourke street east.

To **Schnapper Point**, daily, at 1 p.m., from 35 Bourke street east. *Return.*—Schnapper Point, 7.30 a.m. An extra coach, Tuesday, Thursday, Saturday, at 12.30 *Return.*—Monday, Wednesday, Friday, from Dromana at 6 a.m. Also, Tuesday, Thursday, Saturday, at 12.45, from Bush Inn, Elizabeth street. *Return*, from Mornington Hotel, Monday, Wednesday, Friday, at 8 a.m.

To **St. Andrew's**, Tuesday, Thursday, Saturday, at 10.30 a.m., from the Star Hotel, Swanston street, via Eltham and Caledonia. *Return.*—St. Andrew's, Monday, Wednesday, Friday, 10 a.m.

To **Whittlesea**, via Janefield, Morang, and Yan Yean, daily, at 3 p.m. from 35 Bourke street east. *Return.*—Whittlesea, 6.45 a.m.

To **Wood's Point**, via Jamieson and Mansfield, Monday, Wednesday, Friday, at 7 a.m. from 35 Bourke street east. Returning from Jamieson, Monday, Wednesday, Friday, at 4 a.m.

To **Wood's Point**, via Healesville and Marysville, Yarra Track, Monday, Wednesday, Friday, at 7 a.m., and Tuesday, Thursday, Saturday, at 5 p.m, from 35 Bourke street. Returning from Marysville early, at 0 a.m.

To **Yea**, Monday, Wednesday, Friday, at 7 a.m., from 35 Bourke street east. Returning from Yea, Tuesday, Thursday, Saturday, at 6 a.m.

CARRIAGE AND CAB FARES.

By the Day.—For any 12 hours between 5 a.m. and 10 p.m., carriage £3; cab, £1 10s.

By the Hour.—First hour, Carriage, 6s.; cab, 3s. Subsequently, 5s.; and 2s. 6d. One-half extra between 10 p.m. and 5 a.m.

GENERAL INFORMATION.

By Distance.—Not exceeding a mile, carriage, for one or two persons, 2s.; cab, 1s. For three or more, carriage, 4s.; cab, 2s. For every half-mile beyond, one-half the rate per mile. Half-fare back allowed when over two miles from the stand.
For Calling off the Stand, and not further employing the same, carriage, 3s.; cab, 1s.
For Omnibuses and Omnibus Cabs.—Between 6 a.m. and 7 p.m., 3d. per mile; between 7 p.m. and 10 p.m., 4d. per mile; between 10 p.m. and 6 a.m., 6d. per mile.
For Detention.—Every 15 minutes (except for the purpose of returning), carriage, 1s. 6d., cab, 6d.

The driver of every Hackney Carriage is bound to produce, on demand, a copy of the Fares as fixed by the City Council, and also to have a copy fixed conspicuously inside his carriage.

THE TRAVELLERS' ROAD GUIDE.

The postal distance and bearing from Melbourne, route, and means of conveyance.

Alberton, 203 miles, S E—steamer to Port Albert
Albury (N.S.W.), 207 miles, N E—via Beechworth by coach.
Alma, 107 miles, N W—rail to Castlemaine, thence by coach.
Alphington, 5 miles, N E—Heidelberg bus.
Amherst, 111 miles, N W—Ballarat by rail, thence by coach.
Amphitheatre, 128 miles, N W—rail to Castlemaine or Ballarat, thence by coach.
Apsley, 258 miles, W N—Geelong by rail, thence by coach.
Ararat, 136 miles, N W—Ballarat by rail, thence by coach.
Armstrong's, 140 miles, N W—Ballarat by rail, thence by coach.
Ascot, 115 miles, N W—Ballarat by rail, thence by coach.
Avenel, 84 miles, N E—on Beechworth road, by coach.
Avoca, 130 miles, N W—Castlemaine or Ballarat by rail, thence by coach.
Avon Plains, 223 miles, N W—Ballarat by rail, thence by coach.
Axedale 101 miles, N—Sandhurst by rail, thence by coach.
Barcobie Marsh, 34 miles, N W—Keilor road by Sandhurst Railway, thence by coach.
Bairnsdale, 260 miles, E—Port Albert by steamer, and thence by coach.
Bald Hills, 144 miles, E—Port Albert by steam, thence by coach, via Sale, 60 miles, or via Rosedale, by horse 50 miles.
Ballan, 49 miles, N W—Keilor road by Sandhurst Railway, thence by coach.
Balmoral, 204 miles, W by N—Ballarat by rail, thence by coach.
Ballarat, 102 miles, W N W—by Geelong and Ballarat Railway.
Daringhurst, 91 miles, N N W—Castlemaine by rail, thence by coach.
Barkly, 148 miles, N W—Ballarat by rail, thence by coach.
Barnawatha, 187 miles, N E—Chiltern by coach.
Batesford, 43 miles, S W—on Geelong and Ballarat Railway.
Beaufort, 134 miles, W N W—Ballarat by rail, thence by coach.
Beechworth, 166 miles, N E—by coach.
Belfast, 188 miles, S W—steamer.
Benalla, 119 miles, N W—Castlemaine by rail, thence by coach.
Belvoir, 208 miles, N E—via Wangaratta by coach.

Benalla, 134 miles, N E—on the Beechworth road by coach.
Berwick, 30 miles, E S E—by coach via Dandenong, three times a week.
Bet Bet, 108 miles, N W—Castlemaine by rail, thence by coach.
Birregurra, 80 miles, S W—Geelong by rail, thence by coach, Winchelsea.
Blue Mountain Diggings, 62 miles, N W—Woodend by rail, thence 14 miles W by horse.
Branxholme, 214 miles, W—Ballarat by rail, thence by coach.
Bright, 225 miles, N E—by coach via Beechworth.
Bradford, 48 miles, N—via Kilmore, by coach.
Broadmeadows, 10 miles, N—on Sydney road by coach.
Brown's Diggings, 109 miles, N W—Ballarat by rail, thence by coach.
Buckland, 223 miles, N E—by coach via Beechworth.
Boninyong, 408 miles, W by N—by Geelong and Ballarat Railway, thence by car.
Burrumbeet, 109 miles, W by N—Ballarat by rail, thence by coach.
Campbellfield, 10 miles, N—by coach.
Camperdown, 130 miles, W S W—Geelong by rail, thence by coach, via Colac.
Carlsruhe, 57½ miles, N by W—Sandhurst Railway.
Cardigan, 103 miles, N W—Ballarat by rail, thence by coach.
Carisbrook, 101½ miles, N W—Castlemaine by rail, thence by coach.
Carngham, 119 miles, W by N—Ballarat by rail, thence by coach.
Casterton, 272 miles, W—Geelong by rail, or steamer to Portland, thence by coach.
Castlemaine, 77½ miles, N N W—Sandhurst Railway.
Cathcart, 136 miles, W N W—Ballarat by rail, thence by coach.
Cavendish, 192 miles, W by N—Geelong by rail, or Portland by steamer, thence by coach.
Chewton, 74½ miles, N by W—Castlemaine rail, thence by cab.
Chiltern, 192 miles, N E—on Beechworth road by coach.
Clunes, 120 miles, N W—Ballarat by rail, thence by coach.
Clydesdale, 84½ miles, N by W—Castlemaine by rail, thence by coach.
Coghill's Creek, 121 miles, W N W—Ballarat by rail, thence by coach.
Colac, 93 miles, S W—Geelong by rail, thence per coach.

GENERAL INFORMATION.

Coleraine, 205 miles. W—Ballarat by rail, thence by coach, or Portland by steamer, thence by coach.
Cowie's Creek, 4½ miles, S W—on Geelong Railway.
Cressy, 87 miles, S W—Geelong by rail, thence by Warrnambool coach.
Cranbourne, 29 miles, S S E—Dandenong by coach.
Creswick, 109 miles, N W—Ballarat by rail, thence by coach.
Crowlands, 144 miles, N W—Rail to Castlemaine, thence by coach.

Dandenong, 19½ miles, S E—coach daily.
Darlington, 138 miles, W by S—Geelong by rail, thence by Warrnambool coach.
Daylesford, 78 miles, N W—Malmsbury or Castlemaine by rail, thence by coach
Digby, 264 miles, W—steamer to Portland, thence by coach.
Donnelly's Creek 90 miles, E—by steamer to Port Albert, thence by coach to Sale 50 miles, thence by coach, to Bald Hills 20 miles, and thence by horse or waggon 23 miles.
Donnybrook, 18½ miles, N—on Beechworth road by coach.
Digger's Rest, 20½ miles, N by W—on Sandhurst Railway.
Duck Ponds, 39½ miles, S W—Geelong Railway.
Dunkeld, 170 miles, W—Ballarat by rail, thence by coach.
Dunolly, 107 miles, N W—Castlemaine by rail, by coach.

Echuca, 156 miles, N—by rail, on the Murray River, the boundary of Victoria and New South Wales.
Egerton, 62 miles, W N W—by rail to Keilor Road Station, thence by coach.
Elphinstone, 71 miles, N N W—by rail via Kyneton.
Elsternwick, 6 miles, S—Brighton Railway.
Eltham, 14 miles, N N E—coach via Heidelberg.
Essendon, 6 miles, N—Essendon Railway.
Euroa, 107 miles, N by E—on Beechworth road by coach.

Framlingham, 156 miles, W by S—steamer to Warrnambool, thence by coach or rail to Geelong, thence by Warrnambool coach.
Frankston, 27 miles, S—by coach.
Fryers Town, 84½ miles, N by W—Castlemaine by rail, thence by car.

Geelong, 46 miles, S W—railway.
Gisborne, 31 miles, N—on the Sandhurst Railway.
Glendaruel, 114 miles, N W—Ballarat by rail, thence by coach.
Glengower, 83½ miles, N N W—Castlemaine by rail, thence by coach.
Glenlyon, 70 miles, miles, N N W—Carlsruhe by Sandhurst Railway, thence by coach.
Glenorchy, 197 miles, N W—Ballarat by rail, thence by coach.
Gaffney's Creek, 145 miles, E N E—by coach to Big river, thence by horse.
Gordon's, 84 miles, W N W—Ballarat by rail, thence by coach.
Great Western, 159 miles, W by N—Ballarat by rail, via Beaufort.
Guildford, 88½ miles, N by W—Castlemaine by rail, thence by coach.

Hamilton, 219 miles, W—Ballarat by rail, thence by coach.
Harrow, 231 miles, W by N—Ballarat by rail, thence by coach.
Hawthorn, 75 miles, N—Sandhurst by rail, thence by coach.
Heidelberg, 5 miles, E N E—by coach, running morning and evening from Swanston street.
Hepburn, 84 miles, N W—by rail to Castlemaine, thence 22 miles by coach.

Hexham, 160 miles, W by S—Geelong by rail, thence by coach.
Heywood, 254 miles, W by S—Portland by steamer, thence by coach, or Ballarat by rail, thence by coach.
Horsham, 222 miles, W N W—Ballarat by rail, thence by coach.
Huntley, 113 miles, N—Sandhurst by rail, thence by coach.
Indigo, 187 miles, N E—on Beechworth road by coach.
Inglewood, 129 miles, N N W—Sandhurst by rail, thence by coach.
Inverleigh, 61 miles, W by S—Geelong by rail, thence by coach.
Italian Gully, 113 miles, N W—Ballarat by rail, thence by coach.

Jamieson, 170 miles, N N E—via Longwood, and Mansfield by coach.
Jericho (West), 138 miles, N N W—Sandhurst by rail, thence by coach.
Jericho, 119 miles, E—by Yarra Track to Matlock, by Longwood and Jamieson to Wood's Point, or by Steamer to Port Albert, thence by coach to Sale and Bald Hills.
Jordan, 122 miles, E—by same road as to Jericho.

Kerang, 162 miles, N N W—Sandhurst by rail, thence by coach.
Kilmore, 37 miles, N—on Beechworth road by coach.
Kingower, 129 miles, N N W—Sandhurst by rail, thence by coach.
Kingston 96 miles, N W—Ballarat or Castlemaine by rail, thence by coach.
Kyneton, 62 miles, N by W—Sandhurst Railway.
Lake Learmonth, 109 miles, N W—Ballarat by rail, thence by coach.
Lal Lal, 93½ miles, W—on Ballarat Railway.
Lancefield, 37 miles, N—Lancefield road Station, by rail.
Landsborough, 170 miles, N W—Ballarat by rail, thence by coach.
Larpent, 87 miles, S W—Geelong by rail, thence by coach.
Learmouth, 102 miles, N N W—Ballarat by rail, thence by coach.
Lethbridge, 61½ miles, W—on Geelong and Ballarat Railway.
Lexton, 125 miles, N W—Ballarat by rail, thence by coach via Learmouth.
Little River, 29½ miles, S W—on Geelong Railway.
Liston, 116 miles, N W—Ballarat by rail, thence by coach.
Lockwood, 103 miles, N N W—Sandhurst by rail, thence by coach.
Longwood, 95 miles, N N E—on Beechworth road by coach.

Majorca, 103 miles, N W—Rail to Castlemaine, thence by coach.
Maldon, 94½ miles, N N W—Castlemaine by rail, thence by coach.
Malmsbury, 57 miles, N by W—Sandhurst Railway.
Mansfield, 145 miles, N E—by coach via Avenel.
Marong, 111 miles, N by W—rail to Sandhurst, thence by coach.
Maryborough, 104 miles, N W—Castlemaine by rail, thence by coach.
Matlock, 110 miles, E—Healesville (New Chum) by coach, thence by horse.
Melton, 20 miles, N W—Keilor Road Station by rail, thence by coach.
Meredith, 104 miles, W—on Geelong and Ballarat Railway.
Merino, 261 miles, W—Geelong by rail, or steamer to Portland, thence by coach.
Merton, 170 miles, N E—via Avenel and Longwood by coach.
Miner's Rest, 104 miles, W N W—Ballarat by rail, thence by coach.

GENERAL INFORMATION.

Moonee Ponds, 4 miles, N—Essendon Railway.
Mollagul, 118 miles, N W—Sandhurst by rail, thence by coach.
Morang, 14 miles, N E—by coach on Plenty road.
Mortlake, 137 miles, N W—by Belfast coach from Geelong twice a week.
Mount Blackwood, 64 miles, N W—Keilor road by rail, thence by coach.
Mount Egerton, 60 miles, N W—Keilor road by rail, thence by coach.
Mount Rouse, 112 miles, N W—Ballarat by rail, thence by coach.
Moonambel, 134 miles, N W—Ballarat by rail, thence by coach.
Murchinson, 128 miles, N—Hunnymede by rail, thence via Rushworth by mail-coach.

Newbridge 121 miles, N W—Sandhurst by rail, thence by coach.
Newstead, 84½ miles, N N W—Castlemaine by rail thence by coach.
Navarre, 142 miles, N W—Ballarat by rail, thence by coach.

Omeo, 290 miles, E N E—Port Albert by steamer, thence by coach, 50 miles to Sale, thence 125 miles by horse.

Penshurst, 149 miles, W—Belfast by steamer or rail to Geelong, thence by coach.
Pentland Hills, 42 miles, N W—Keilor road by rail, thence by coach.
Pitfield, 100 miles, W S W—Leigh Road by rail, thence by coach.
Port Albert, 204 miles, S E—steamer.
Portland, 255 miles, S W—steamer.
Pyalong, 52½ miles, N—via Kilmore by coach, Beechworth road.

Quartz Reefs, (Pleasant Creek), 116 miles, N W—Ballarat by rail, thence by coach.
Queenscliff, 62 miles, N—by steamer, or to Geelong by railway, thence by coach.
Queenstown (Caledonia Diggings), 29 miles, N E—by coach via Eltham.

Raglan, 179 miles, W N W—Ballarat by rail thence by coach.
Haywood, 118 miles, N N W—Sandhurst by rail, thence by coach daily.
Redbank, 137 miles, N W—Ballarat by rail, thence by coach.
Riddell's Creek, 36½ miles, N—on the Sandhurst Railway.
Rokewood, 64 miles, W—Leigh road Station by railway, thence by coach.
Rosedale, 143 miles, E S S—Port Albert by steamer, thence by horse, or overland by horse.
Rushworth, 127 miles, N—Hunnymede by rail, thence 30 miles by coach.
Rutherglen, 186 miles, N E—Beechworth road by coach.

Sale, 140 miles, E S E—Port Albert by steamer, thence by coach.
Sandhurst 100½ miles, N N W—railway
Sandy Creek, 128 miles, N W—Castlemaine or Sandhurst by railway, thence by coach.
Scarsdale, 119 miles, W by N—Ballarat by rail, thence by coach.
Sebastopol, 99 miles, W—Ballarat by rail, thence by coach.
Seymour, 64 miles, N—on Beechworth road by coach.
Shelford, 60 miles, W S W—Leigh road Station, by rail, thence by coach.

Skipton, 116 miles, W by N—Ballarat by rail, thence 30 miles by coach.
Smeaton, 103 miles, N W—Ballarat by rail, thence by coach.
Smythesdale, 107 miles, W by N—Ballarat by rail, thence by coach.
Snapper Point, 39 miles, S—steamer or coach.
Snowy Creek, 263 miles, N E—Port Albert by steamer, thence by coach, 50 miles to Sale, thence by horse; or via Beechworth by coach and horse.
Somerton, 13 miles N—on Beechworth road by coach.
Springs, 118 miles, N W—Ballarat by rail, thence by coach.
Stawell (Pleasant Creek), 177 miles, N W—Ballarat by rail, thence by coach.
Steiglitz, 91 miles, W—Geelong by rail, thence by coach or Meredith station by rail, thence 7 miles by horse; railway to Meredith.
Stratford, 169 miles, E S E—Port Albert by by steamer, thence by coach via Sale, or overland by horse.
Streatham, 129 miles, W by N—Ballarat by rail, thence 44 miles by coach.
St. Arnaud, 160 miles—Castlemaine or Ballarat by rail, thence by coach.
Sunbury, 26 miles, N—on Sandhurst Railway.
Swan Hill, 231 miles, N N W—Sandhurst by rail, thence by coach.

Talbot (Back Creek), 100 miles, N W—Ballarat or Castlemaine by rail, thence by coach.
Tallarook, 55 miles, N—on Beechworth road by coach.
Tarnagulla, 128 miles, N W—Sandhurst or Castlemaine by rail, thence by coach.
Taradale, 82 miles, N N W—on Sandhurst Railway.
Tarrawingee, 168 miles, N E—on Beechworth road by coach.

Violet Town, 118 miles, N E—on Beechworth road by coach.

Wahgunyah, 183 miles, N E—on Beechworth road by coach.
Wangaratta, 149 miles N E—on Beechworth road by coach.
Warrandyte, 19 miles, E—by coach.
Warrnheip, 91 miles, W N N—by Geelong and Ballarat Railway.
Warrnambool, 170 miles, S W—steamers, also coach from Geelong.
Wedderburn, 147 miles, N N W—Sandhurst by rail, thence by coach.
Wickliffe, 159 miles, W S W—Ballarat by rail, thence by coach.
Werribee, 19 miles, S W—on Melbourne and Geelong Railway.
Winchelsea, 76 miles, S W—Geelong by rail, thence by coach.
Woodend, 48½ miles, N—Sandhurst Railway.
Wood's Point, 129 miles, E—by Yarra Track, or by coach to Longwood and Jamieson, or, by Yea, by coach to Big River.

Yackandandah, 177 miles, N E—via Wangaratta by coach.
Yandoit, 92½ miles, N W—Castlemaine by rail, thence by coach.
Yea, 76 miles, N N E—by coach via Broadford.

GENERAL INFORMATION. xv.

COUNTRY DISTRICTS.

ALBURY.
(In New South Wales, on the border of Victoria, 204 miles from Melbourne; 378 from Sydney).

LAW, &c.—Judge, South West Dist., H. R. Francis. Crown Prosecutor, D. G. Forbes. Clerk of the Peace and Reg. Dist. Court, Albury, H. S. Elliott. Police Mag., M. P. Brownrigg, R.N. Clerk of the Bench, Dis. Reg. Crown Lands Agent, F. Brown. Attorneys: S. F. Blackmore, W. M. Miller, G. C. Thorold, and O. T. Fleming. Com. of Crown Lands, C. G. N. Lockhart. Dist. Surveyor, T. Wood.
BANKS.—New South Wales: Manager, J. W. Jones. Commercial: T. B. Gaden.
MISCELLANEOUS—Surgeons: Drs. Keatinge, Barnett, and Wilkinson. Postmaster, — Stone. Electric Telegraph—Station Masters: N. R. W., C. Kraegan; Victoria, R. W. Deverill. Municipal Council: Mayor, S. F. Blackmore. Newspapers: *Border Post and Federal Standard*, and *Albury Banner*. National School, Mr. and Mrs. McCready, teachers.

AMHERST.
(114 miles from Melbourne, 8 from Maryborough, 12 from Avoca. Pop. mun., 4,600.)

LAW, &c.—P. C. Crespigny, P.M. Clerk of Petty Sess., T. Freeman. Postmaster, J. P. Smith, Hackett and Co.'s Office. Deputy-Registrar, W. Wood. Coroner and Public Vaccinator, Dr. Dow. Police, Sen. Constable Woods.
* MISCELLANEOUS.—Hospital: House Surgeon, Dr. Rose. Schools: Church of England, Mr. Finlay; Presbyterian, Mr. Nicholl; Wesleyan, Mr. Burchett.

ARARAT.
(134 miles from Melbourne—Ballarat line. Pop. Elec. Dis., 3,081; Municipality, 1570.)

LAW, &c.—Chairman of Gen. Ses., Judge of C. of Mines and County C., J. L. Clarke. Pol. Magis., Coroner, Vis. Jus., Chinese Protector, Com. of Crown Lands, Warden, &c., J. G. Taylor. Super. of Police, T. E. Langley. Clerk of the Peace, County C., Clerk of Pet. Sessions, Court of Mines, Warden's Clerk, F. P. Cope. Postmas. and Tel. Sta. Mas., K. L. Murray. Dep. Reg., J. Cannon. Pub. Vac., J. Galbraith. Local Jus.—J. L. Clarke, J. G. Taylor, J. Richardson, C. Campbell, J. M. Saunders, G. Thompson, F. Ganson, G. Logan. Mayor, T. Walker. Town Clerk, J. Campbell.
BANKS.—New South Wales, J. M. Saunders. London Chartered, J. B. Littlejohn. Bank of Victoria, W. Blackburn.
COACHES.—To Ballarat, Maryborough, and Pleasant Creek, daily.
MISCELLANEOUS.—Mining Board: Chairman, E. Salisbury; Clerk, J. Payne. Road Board: Chairman, G. Thomson; Clerk, J. Maclean. Barrister, J. Lamont. Solicitor, J. Y. Presswell. Hospital: President, K. L. Murray; Secretary, J. Cannon. Mechanics' Institute, J. Campbell, Secretary. News Agent, J. Cannon. Newspaper, *Ararat Advertiser*.

AVOCA.
(120 miles from Melbourne, and 16 from Maryborough. Population: Electoral District, 18,035; Municipality, 1,447.)

LAW, &c.—Police Magistrate and Warden, C. W. Carr. Local Justices: L. Ogilby, J. Quarterman, C. F. Cameron. Sup. Police, J. Mason. Gold Receiver, A. Meyrick. Clerk of Peace, C. of Mines, County C., and Petty Sess., &c., J. Coffin. Coroner, L. Worsley. Dep.-Reg, W. Goodshaw. Pub. Vaccinator, W. S. Morris. County C. Bailiff, J. Racon. Telegraph Station Master, J. Wondward. Poundkeeper, J. Batchelor. Min. Reg., R. English. Shire Council: E. Snell, President; H. Hall, Clerk.
BANK.—Victoria, Leslie Ogilby.
COACHES.—To Melbourne (via Maryborough) and Ararat daily; to Ballarat (direct) daily.

d

BACCHUS MARSH.

(34 miles from Melbourne—Ballarat Line.)

LAW, &c.—Police Magistrate, J. C. Thompson. Local Justices : J. Young, W. Rae. Clerk of County Court, Clerk of Petty Sessions, and Commissioner for taking Affidavits, Victoria and N. S. W., J. S. Cooper. District Road Board : Chairman, R. Lawson ; Secretary, W. E. Standfield. Public Vaccinator, W. Rae. Deputy-Registrar of Births and Deaths, Electoral Registrar, and Agent for Curator of Intestate Estates, J. S. Cooper. County C. Bailiff, W. E. Standfield. Postmaster, T. Tantuman. Police : Sen. Constable Kiernan in charge.

BANK.—National, T. N. Binney.

COACHES.—Daily to and from Keilor Road Station and Ballarat ; also to and from Bacchus Marsh and Keilor Road Station daily.

MISCELLANEOUS.—Mechanics' Institute, W. E. Standfield. Bacchus Marsh and Pentland Hills Farmers' Society, Sec., W. E. Standfield. Schools : Central School, A. Millie ; Roman Catholic, W. Marshall.

BALLARAT.

(96½ miles from Melbourne, 54 from Geelong, 35 from Raglan, Fiery Creek. Population, Electoral District, 34,580—Municipalities, East, 14,000 ; West, 11,000.

GOVERNMENT OFFICIALS.—Warden, Com. of C. Lands, and Guardian of Minors, J. Cogden. Clerks in Warden's Office ; S. D. S. Huyghue ; A. Livingstone. Chinese Interpreter, Ah Com. Receiver and Paymaster, W. H. Barnard. District Surveyor, Thomas Adair. Surveyor, W. O'Brien. Draughtsman, F. G. Miles. Postmaster, H. J. N. King. Police Superintendent, H. Hill ; Sub-Inspector, — Ryall. Electric Telegraph Station Master, W. P. Bechervaise. Sheriff, Major R. Wallace. Registrar of County Court and Clerk of the Peace, F. Greene ; Deputy-Registrar and Bailiff, W. Tweedie. Gaol: Keeper, W. McGee ; Matron, Mrs. S. McGee. Coroner, G. Clendinning, M.D. Deputy-Registrar, W. T. Pooley. Powder Magazine Keeper, A. Livingstone.

LAW.—Police Magistrates : S. T. Climold, W. H. Foster. Local Justices: A. Fiskin, J. Victor, D. Fitzpatrick, W. H. Bacchus, T. Learmonth, S. Learmonth, J. Oddie, W. R. Rodier, J. McPhillimy, J. McIntosh, C. J. Little, J. S. Strachan, W. C. Smith, J. Baker, J. B. Humffray, C. Neal, S. Wilson, T. Bath, R. M. Gibbs, G. Clendinning, C. Dyte, and H. Clarke. Clerks of Petty Sessions : District Court, — Hogarth ; Ballarat East, G. W. F. Patterson.

COURT OF MINES.—Judge of the Court, J. W. Rogers ; Clerk, Francis Green.

MINING BOARD.—F. C. Downes, Chairman ; Clerk, H. Wood ; meets at the Board Room, Camp.

MUNICIPAL COUNCILS.—Ballarat West—G. Duncan, Mayor ; Town Clerk, J. Comb. Ballarat East—G. Clendinning, Mayor ; Town Clerk, W. B. Rodier.

BANKS.—Australasia, Manager, Michael Elliott ; Victoria, W. Robertson ; N. S. Wales ; W. Ochiltree ; Union, J. Williamson ; London Chartered, G. G. Mackay ; Colonial, A. S. Park ; National, M. Morrison ; Savings' Bank, Actuary, W. T. Pooley ; Ballarat Banking Co., W. V. Duther. Discount, J. Wynne. Land Mortgage, J. Oddie and Co.

RAILWAY TERMINUS.—Lydiard street, R. Manby, Station-master. Ballarat East, C. Beckett, Station-master.

COACHES leave Craig's, the George, Buck's Head, Unicorn, and Provincial Hotels daily, or the principal townships.

MISCELLANEOUS.—St. Patrick's Society : Sec., J. O'Brien. Caledonian Society : Sec., J. Anderson. Hospital : Sec., E. C. Moore ; Resident Surgeon, W. P. Whitcombe. Chamber of Commerce: Sec., J. B. McQuie. Ballarat Gas Company : W. Cameron, Chairman. Shire Council : Sec., J. H. Mather. Places of Amusement : Theatre Royal, Charlie Napier Theatre, Temperance Hall, Mechanics' Institute, and Caledonia Hall. Newspapers : Star, Miner, and Evening Post.

BALLAN.

(Between Melbourne and Ballarat, and 49 miles from Melbourne.)

LAW, &c.—Police Magistrate and Com. of Crown Lands, J. M. Clow, visiting Ballan once a fortnight. Local Justices: C. H. Lyon, Peter Inglis, D. Macpherson, Walter

Duncan. Judge of County Court, &c., J. G. Forbes. Clerk of Petty Sessions and Com. of the Sup. Court for taking Affidavits, J. S. Cooper. Police: Sen. Constable Walsh. Postmaster and News Agent, G. Flack. Public Vaccinator, J. Joppling. Deputy-Registrar, W. Scott. Elect. Registrars, J. Tanner and S. Cooper. Poundkeeper, H. Cooper. Shire Council: Chairman, C. H. Lyon; Clerk, G. Cooper.
MISCELLANEOUS.—Mechanics' Institute: S. Leith, Sec. Common School: W. Scott. Roman Catholic: D. Ryan.
COACHES, Daily, between Keilor Road Station and Buninyong Road Station, passing through Ballan.

BEAUFORT, FIERY CREEK DIGGINGS.
(124 miles from Melbourne, 28 from Ballarat, 23 from Ararat.)

LAW, &c.—Judge of County Ct. and Ct. of Mines, J. L. Clark. Clerk of Ct. of Mines, County C., and Court of P. Sess., Com. of Supreme Court, Gold Receiver, and Elect. Reg., C. W. Minchin. Bailiff, W. E. Nickols. Elec. Tel. Station Master and Postmaster, G. Allan. Police Sergeant, R. Chamberlain. Shire of Ripon: Secretary, J. Wotherspoon. P.M. and Warden, F. R. Pohlman. Public Vaccinator, J. Johnston.
BANK.—Victoria, W. Moudell (acting).
COACH to and from Ararat, Beaufort, and Ballarat, daily.
MISCELLANEOUS.—Grammar School, W. Humpage; Common School, Mr. Grenville.

BEECHWORTH, OVENS.
(185 miles from Melbourne—Sydney line. Pop. Elec. Dis., 15,701; Municipality, 2,500.)

LAW, &c.—District Judge and Chairman of Gen. Sess., T. S. Cope. Com. of Crown Lands, Warden, Coroner, and P.M., W. H. Gaunt. Local Justices: G. E. Mackay, G. B. Kerferd, W. Telford, A. Rogers, J. J. Bowman, F. Brown, W. Witt. Judge of Court of Mines, T. C. Cope. Clerk of Peace and of County C., Court of Mines and Pet. Sess., and Elect. Registrar and Com. for Taking Affidavits, &c., A. Drury. Receiver and Paymaster, G. R. Berry. Sup. of Police, F. A. Winch. Sheriff, W. G. Brett. Bailiff, E. G. Nethercott. Governor of Gaol, J. B. Castieau. Postmaster, S. Byrchall. Telegraph Stationmaster, R. D. Hodgson. Pub. Vaccinator, Dr. Dempster. Mayor, W. Witt. Town Clerk, W. H. C. Darrall.
BANKS.—New South Wales, Manager, J. Bently; Victoria, A. K. Sheppard; Australasia, F. W. Morrah; Oriental, W. M. Hyndman.
COACHES.—Bevan and Co.'s Mail line to Melbourne. Crawford's line, daily, to Yachandandah, Crawford's line, three times a week, to Albury. Hooper's Mail line, daily, to Bright. Growler's Creek and Buckland. Daily coaches to Chiltern, Indigo, Wahgunyah, and Stanley.
MISCELLANEOUS.—Hospital: Resident Surgeon, A. L. Slater. Athenaeum: President, J. Castieau. Benevolent Asylum: President, W. G. Brett. Schools: Grammar, J. H. Cuzner; Common, T. Moldran; R. Cath., J. Austin. Mining Board: D. Fletcher, Chairman; — Alderdice, Clerk. Agricultural and Horticultural Society: His Honor Judge Cope, President. Bible Society: W. G. Brett, Sec. Young Men's Christian Association: Rev. J. K. Macmillan, Pres. Fire Brigade: H. A. Crawford, Capt. Newspapers: *Ovens and Murray Advertiser, Constitution.*

BELVOIR.
(205 miles from Melbourne.)

LAW, &c.—Police Magistrate: M. F. Brownrigg, R.N. Local Justices: W. Huon, J. T. Fallan, and J. J. Keating. Sergeant of Police, Acting Clerk of Pet. Sess., Elect. Registrar and Deputy-Registrar, J. Bambrick. Customs Officer, J. Chapman. Postmaster and Electric Tel. Station Master, J. Coverdale. Poundkeeper, H. McIlree. Common School, — Browne.

BENALLA.
(134 miles from Melbourne. Population, 700.)

LAW.—P.M. and Warden, W. Piper. Local Justices, Dr. Lumsden, and W. M'Kellar. Coroners, W. Piper and J. Spark. Clerk of Bench, H. Crofton. Surveyor, T. Nixon. Police Sup., F. M'Crae Cobham.

xviii   GENERAL INFORMATION.

MISCELLANEOUS.—Post Office: Postmaster, C. Croft; Mail closes daily for Melbourne at 11.30 a.m., and for Beechworth, daily, at 6 p.m. (Sundays excepted.) Common School, Court House, and Electric Telegraph Office.

BLACKWOOD GOLD FIELD.

(54 miles from Melbourne. Population, 1,000.)

LAW.—P.M. and Warden, J. M. Clow. Clerk of the Bench, D. G. Stobie. Clerk to the Court of Mines, D. G. Stobie. Guardian of Minors and Chinese Protector, J. M. Clow. Deputy Registrar, D. G. Stobie.

MISCELLANEOUS.—Gold Receiver, D. G. Stobie (clerk-in-charge.) The Gold Escort starts from Golden Point every alternate Wednesday. Mining Surveyor, E. G. Magness. Schools (two); Church of England.

BRIGHT (MORSE'S CREEK).

(42 miles from Beechworth. Head Quarters—Buckland Division. Population of Buckland District, 3,900, including Chinese.)

LAW, &c.—P.M., War., Cor., Com. Crown Lands, A. C. Wills. Clerk of County Court, Court of Mines and Pet. Ses., Agent for Curator of In. Estates, Agent Board Land and Works, and Dep.-Reg., A. L'E. Martin. Public Vaccinator, C. J. M. Dowd. Police, Constable Harkins. Mining Sur., R. H. Stone. Mining Reg., L. C. Kinchela. Postmaster, W. S. Hazelton. Road Board, H. W. De Mole, Pres.; L. C. Kinchela, Clerk.

BANKS.—Oriental, W. H. De Mole. Australasia, W. W. Duke.

BELFAST, PORT FAIRY.

(186 miles from Melbourne. Pop. Elec. Dis., 2,338; Municipality, 2,300.)

LAW.—Stipendiary Magistrate, G. Stewart. Superintendent of Police, S. S. Furnell. Collector of Customs, P. Nicholson. Receiver and Paymaster, P. Nicholson. Harbour Master and Pilot, J. B. Mills. Immigration Agent, P. Nicholson. Local Guardian of Minors, G. Stewart. Clerk of the Peace, County C., and Pet. Ses., and Registrar, W. E. Wheeler. Postmaster and Tel. Station Master, J. A. Lynar. Coroner, Dr. Jermyn. Mayor, R. H. Woodward. Town Clerk and Surveyor, W. Barrett.

BANKS.—Australasia, T. Ingram. Victoria, W. Young. Savings' Bank, Actuary, R. Allen.

STEAMERS.—Every week from Melbourne. Lord, Croaker, and Co., agents.

COACHES leave the Star of the West Hotel, for Warrnambool, Camperdown, Colac, and Geelong, Tuesday, Thursday, and Saturday, at 4 p.m., through from Warrnambool to Geelong and Melbourne in one day.

NEWSPAPERS.—Weekly; *Belfast Gazette* and *Banner of Belfast*.

SCHOOLS.—Church of England, W. Conroy and Mrs. M. A. Braim. Wesleyan, W. Bedford and A. Witton. Roman Catholic, Mr. O'Callaghan and Mr. Roe.

MISCELLANEOUS.—District Council: P. Duffus, Chairman. Engineer and Secretary, D. J. Howes. Benevolent Asylum: Secretary, D. J. Howes; Surgeon, W. Loftus, M.D. Mechanics' Institute; President, R. H. Woodward; Librarian, A. Youngman. Temperance Society: Secretary, W. Pawling. Cricket Club and Western Turf Club: President, R. H. Woodward; Hon. Sec., F. G. Yorke. Lloyd's Agent, H. Flower. News Agent, R. Allen.

BUNINYONG.

(86¾ miles from Melbourne, 7 from Ballarat. Pop. Municipality, 1,500.)

LAW, &c.—P.M. and Warden, C. W. Sherard. Local Justices, P. Hedrich, T. Sheppard, R. Gillespie, A. Fisken. Mayor,—Bishop. Elec. Tel. and Postmaster, P. R. Arkins. Police Sergeant, W. F. Smith. Clerk of Petty Ses. and Elec. Reg., D. Oliver. Dep. Reg., Dr. Casey. Mining Reg., R. M. Harvey. President Shire Council, Mr. Bacchus.

BANK.—National, Manager, R. Gillespie.

MISCELLANEOUS.—Schools: Common, Church of England, T. Bedford; R. Cath.,—Duggan; Presbyterian, J. McLellan. Newspaper, *Buninyong Telegraph*. News Agents, T. and L. Ashburner.

GENERAL INFORMATION. xix.

CALEDONIA DIGGINGS, QUEENSTOWN.

(28 miles from Melbourne.)

LAW, &c.—P.M., Warden, and Com. Crown Lands, J. A. Panton. Clerk of Petty Ses., J. B. Drummond. Min. Reg., C. Cole. Postmaster and Dep.-Reg., J. C. Knoll.
COACHES every Monday, Wednesday, and Friday, at 8 a.m.; returning from Star Inn, Swanston street, alternate days, at 10.30 a.m.

CARISBROOK.

(101¼ miles from Melbourne. 5 miles from Maryborough. Pop. Municipality, 2,000.)

LAW, &c.—Judge of Court of Mines and County Court, His Honor M. F. Macoboy; Stip. Mag. and Warden, Crawford A. D. Pasco, R.N. Local Justices: W. A. Smith, A. Heynell. Clerk of Courts and Com. for taking Affidavits, D. B. Daly. Bailiff, G. Richards. Police Inspector, Ximines. Postmaster and Elect. Tel. Master, J. A. B. Smith. Mayor, W. Crooks. Town Clerk, G. Read.
COACHES.—To Melbourne, viâ Newstead and Castlemaine, 8.30 a.m. To Melbourne, viâ Maldon and Castlemaine, 3 p.m. To Majorca and Talbot, 2 p.m. To Maryborough hence next day. To Avoca and Dunolly, 2 p.m. A parcel delivery, carrying passengers to Maryborough and Majorca, twice a week.
SCHOOLS.—Common, Mr. and Miss Clark; Girls' Day School, Mrs. Fraser.
MISCELLANEOUS.—Mechanics' Institute: D. Preshaw, Sec. Cricket Club, W. Long. Sec. Agricultural and Horticultural Society, George Read, Sec. Poundkeeper, F. G. Hull. Cemetery: G. Read, Sec. Total Abstinence Society: L. Burland, Sec. Newspapers: *Maryborough Advertiser, Carisbrook and Majorca Independent.*

CARNGHAM.

(119 miles from Melbourne, 17 from Ballarat. Population, 3,500.)

LAW, &c.—J. P. Hamilton, P.M. and Warden. Local Justices; P. Russell, T. Hepper. Clerk of Petty Sessions, R. M'Niece. Dep.-Reg., E. J. Jones. Public Vaccinator, T. R. Nason. Police: Constable, J. Menagh.
POST OFFICES.—Township, A. Henderson; Snake Valley, J. Greig; Preston's Hill, C. Franklin.

CASTERTON.

(272 miles from Melbourne, 40 from Hamilton, and 60 from Portland.)

LAW, &c.—P.M. and Com. of Crown Lands, C. Fotheringaugh. Clerk of Petty Sess. and Agent of Board of Land and Works, G. Cue. Local Justices, F. Henty, W. H. Tuckett, J. H. Jackson, J. S. Murray, and G. Carmichael. Coroner, Dep. Reg. and Pub. Vaccinator, C. Radford. Surgeons, T. M. Wyly, M.D., C. Radford, F.R.C.S.E. Postmaster, E. C. Courtis. Telegraph, E. L. Merchant. Police Serg. and Insp. of Slaughter-houses, W. B. Price. Poundkeeper, R. Havis. Shire Council: G. Carmichael, President.
COACHES.—For Hamilton, viâ Coleraine, Mon., Wed., Fri., 10 a.m. For Penola, Tues., Thurs., Sat., 12 noon. For Portland, Tues., Thurs., Sat., 5 a.m.
MISCELLANEOUS.—Common School, R. W. Bell.

CASTLEMAINE.

(78 miles from Melbourne, 23 from Sandhurst, per rail, 11 from Maldon, and 28 from Maryborough. Borough and Market Town, pop., 9,664; Electors for the Legislative Council, 230; Assembly, 2,340.)

GOVERNMENT OFFICIALS.— Warden, Commissioner of Crown Lands, Guardian of Minors, and P.M., J. E. N. Bull. Sup. of Police, F. A. S. Reid. Sub-Treasurer and Gold Receiver, C. Megson. District Surveyor, T. Couchman. Postmaster, E. H. Stalart. Tel. Station Master, T. Green. Coroner, D. Mackay. Pub. Vac., T. McGrath. Dep. Reg., J. Rogers. Elec. Reg., R. Curle.
LAW, &c.—Judge of County C., Court of Mines, and Chairman of Gen. Sess., J. G. Forbes. Clerk of the Peace and Registrar, H. N. L. S. Kentish. Sheriff, R. Colles.

GENERAL INFORMATION.

Local Justices, A. J. Smith, J. Mesars, W. Froomes, F. W. Tracey, G. Isaacs, J. Ball, D. Mackay, N. Fitzgerald, B. Butterworth, J. W. Burnett, J. Roche. Clerks of Petty Sess., H. N. L. S. Kentish, H. L. Warde, J. W. Pearce, C. Anderson.
MINING BOARD.—Chairman, J. C. Atkinson. Clerk, A. Poole.
BOROUGH COUNCIL.—Mayor, G. Cunnack. Town Clerk, J. Davis.
BANKS.—Australasia: Manager, D. Trail. Victoria: T. Young. N. S. Wales: J. Farran. Colonial: J. Ball. Oriental: Agent, A. Kerr. English and Scottish: H. Isaacs. Savings' Bank, Actuary.
COACHES.—Cobb's, daily to Muckleford, Newstead, Maldon, Maryborough, Avoca, Amherst, Ararat, Dunolly, Tarnagulla, Daylesford, Yandoit, Creswick, and Ballarat, and all the Western and North Western districts. Conveyances hourly to Chewton, Campbell's Creek, Guildford, &c.
MISCELLANEOUS.—Hospital, Sec., T. W. Courtney. Benevolent Asylum, Sec., J. Hartley, Mechanics' Institute, Sec., E. Finlayson. Fire Brigades, Sec. H. Christophers. Philharmonic Society, Sec., A. T. Hodgson. Agricultural and Horticultural Society, Sec., C. W. Nicholson. Schools—National, Church of England, Roman Catholic, Wesleyans, Primitive Methodists, &c. Theatre Royal. Newspapers—*Mount Alexander Mail, Daily News.*

CHILTERN.

(131 miles from Melbourne.)

LAW, &c.—Judge of County C. and Court of Mines, T. S. Cope, P.M., Warden, Com. of Crown Lands, Chinese Protector, Coroner, and Guardian of Minors, J. Le M. Carey. J. P. for New South Wales, Captain Carey. Clerk of C. of Mines and Petty Sess., Clerk of County Court, J. A. Mulligan. Police, Sen. Const. Duffy. Territorial Magistrates, D. Reid and J. L. Brown. Public Vaccinator, C. W. Rohner, M.D. Mayor, J. Wertheim. Dep. Registrar, T. R. S. Carwithen.
BANKS.—New South Wales: A. Cameron.
POST OFFICES.—Chiltern, Telegraph Officer. Christmas Town, W. Witt. Wahgunyah, Main and Baldock.
COACHES.—Daily to Melbourne, Beechworth, and Albury. To various leads, every half hour.
MISCELLANEOUS.—Schools: Common, Roman Catholic. Petty Sessions at Indigo: Mon., Wed., and Fri. At Chiltern: Tues., Thurs., and Sat. Newspaper, *Federal Standard.* News Agents, Geo. Lyon and W. C. Hunter.

COLAC.

(92 miles from Melbourne, 30 miles from Camperdown.)

LAW, &c.—Judge of County Ct., His Honor C. B. Brewer. Clerk of Pet. Sess., Elect. and Dep. Reg., G. Dunderdale. Local Justices: H. Murray, A. Dennis, R. Calvert, J. D. Bromfield. Coroner, Dr. T. Rae. County Ct. Bailiff, B. J. Miller. Poundkeeper, W. Bradley. Postmaster and Electric Teleg., E. Smith. Elect. Ret. Officer, J. D. Bromfield. Police Serg., W. Child. Shire Council: Chairman, H. Murray; Clerk, P. C. Wilson. Public Vaccinator, Dr. Rae. Coms. for taking Affidavits, J. R. Lane and G. Dunderdale. J.P. empowered to consent to the Marriage of Minors, H. Murray.
BANK.—National, J. Hinckley.
MISCELLANEOUS.—Schools: Roman Catholic, J. McCormack; Common, G. Archer. Agri. and Horti. Society, J. Chapman, Sec. Cricket Club, E. Smith, Sec. Temperance Hall, W. Smith, Librarian.

COLERAINE.

(205 miles from Melbourne, 60 from Portland, 21 from Hamilton.)

LAW, &c.—Police Mag., C. Featherstonaugh. Clerk of Petty Sessions, Com. of Supreme Ct. for taking Affidavits, and Elect. Reg., G. Cue. Local Justices, A. Turnbull, W. Learmouth, G. Trangmar. Constable in charge, J. G. Gray. Inspector of Slaughter House, J. G. Gray. Poundkeeper, D. Barry. Public Vaccinator, J. Baird. Postmaster and Deputy Registrar, G. Trangmar.

GENERAL INFORMATION.

COACHES.—A mail car to carry six passengers passes through Coleraine each alternate day from Hamilton to Penola, S. A., by Casterton.
MISCELLANEOUS.—Book Club, A. Turnbull, Sec. Cricket Club, G. Trangman, Sec. Schools: Church of England, Mr. and Mrs. J. McDonald; Roman Catholic, Miss Buckley.

COY'S DIGGINGS.

(126 miles from Melbourne, 33 miles from Bunnymede. Pop., 500.)

LAW, &c.—Postmaster, A. Corbett. Police cons. in charge, T. Flint.
MISCELLANEOUS.—Common School, F. Scott.

CRANBOURNE.

(29 miles from Melbourne.)

LAW, &c.—Chairman of Court of Petty Sess., J. S. Adams. Clerk of the Bench and Com. for taking Affidavits, J. Dobson. Road Board: Chairman, A. Patterson; Sec., E. J. Tucker. Elect. Reg., W. Tucker. Postmaster, A. Thompson. Police, Constable Watson.
MISCELLANEOUS.—Common School, A. Thompson.

CRESWICK.

(107½ miles from Melbourne, 65 from Geelong, 11 from Ballaarat. Pop. Elec. Dis. 32,938. Borough, 3,700.)

LAW, &c.—P.M. and Warden, C. C. Dowling. Local Justices: A. Lewers, T. Cooper, W. B. Lees, G. Russell, E. Royce, R. Richardson. Clerk of Petty Sessions, G. L. Hutchinson. Judge of Court of Mines and County Court, J. L. Clarke. Clerk, George L. Hutchinson. Warden, C. C. Dowling. Police: Sergeant Archibald in charge. Sub-Treasurer, J. Fisher. Coroner, W. B. Lees. Mayor, S. Lewers. Town Clerk, J. Reed. Mining Registrar, J. Stovenson. Public Vaccinator, R. C. Lindsay.
SCHOOLS.—National, Church of England, and Wesleyan.
BANKS.—Australasia, H. B. Chomley. New South Wales, A. Lewers.
COACHES leave for Ballarat at 9, 10 a.m., 12 noon, 4 and 4.30 p.m. For Clunes, &c., 2 a.m. (mail) and 2 p.m. Arrive from Ballarat, 11 a.m., 12 noon, 3, 5, 6 p.m. From Clunes, &c., 10 a.m. and 4 p.m.
MISCELLANEOUS.—Postmaster and Teleg. Station Master, J. Thwaites. Mechanics' Institute, J. Thomas, Sec. Hospital, H. Starke, M.D., Resident Surg. Newspapers: *Creswick Advertiser* (tri-weekly paper). News Agent, J. Roycraft.

DAYLESFORD.

(78 miles from Melbourne, 2½ from Spring Creek; 23 from Castlemaine. Pop. municipality, 3,500.)

LAW, &c.—Warden and P.M., W. H. Drummond. Receiver and Paymaster, H. Fowler, Clerk of Petty Sess., County C., and C. of Mines, C. C. Robertson. Coroner, J. M'Nicholl. Police, Sub. Insp. Culkin. Bailiff, F. A. Newton. Mayor, G. Patterson. Town Clerk, W. G. Hart.
BANKS.—Union, Z. W. Carlisle. National, W. M. Alexander. Victoria, J. Jamieson. Colonial, J. Resnick.
COACHES.—Leave the Booking Office, Jamieson's Hotel, daily (Sundays excepted) for the undermentioned places, as follows:—At 4 a.m. for Glenlyon, Malmsbury, and Melbourne. At 7.30 a.m., Shepherd's Flat, Franklinford, Guildford, Castlemaine, Sandhurst, Melbourne. At 8.30 a.m., Blanket Flat, Deep Creek, Ararat, Mount Prospect, Creswick, Clunes, Ballarat, Geelong, Talbot. At 9 a.m., Coomoora, Dyer's, Glenlyon, Red Hill, German's, Kyneton Road, Malmsbury, Melbourne. At 4 p.m., Glenlyon, Malmsbury, Melbourne. Melbourne passengers leaving Daylesford at 9 a.m. reach Malmsbury in time for the 1.27 p.m. train, arriving at Melbourne at 4 p.m. Leaving Daylesford again at 4 p.m., will reach Malmsbury in time for the 8.42 p.m. mail train to Melbourne. Daylesford passengers returning from Melbourne can leave by the 12.15 noon train, arriving at Malmsbury at 2.48 p.m., in time for the 3 p.m.

coach, arriving at Daylesford at 5 p.m. Daylesford passengers leaving again by the 7.15 p.m. mail train, reaching Malmsbury at 9.48 p.m., in time for the 10 p.m. mail coach to Daylesford, arriving there at 1 a.m.

MISCELLANEOUS.—Deputy Reg., W. G. Hart. Mining Surveyor, Ambrose Johnson. Postmaster and Telegraph Station Master, J. O'Connell. Newspapers, *Daylesford Mercury* and *Daylesford Express* (tri-weekly). News Agent, A. Draper.

DIGBY.

(254 miles from Melbourne, 41 from Portland.)

LAW, &c.—P.M. and Com. of Crown Lands, C. Fetherstonhaugh. Clerk of Petty Sess., Agent to Board of Land and Works, and Com. for taking Affidavits, J. H. Quinn. Local Justices: J. Coldham, F. Henty, and S. P. Winter. Dep. Reg. and Pub. Vaccinator, C. Eastwood. Postmaster, R. I. Mercer. Insp. of Slaughter Houses, F. Keon. Poundkeeper, A. J. Farley. Police, Sen. Cons. Keon.

COACHES.—For Melbourne and Portland, via Heywood, Tuesday, Thursday, and Saturday, 8 a.m.; returning Monday, Wednesday, and Friday, 1 p.m.

MISCELLANEOUS.—Common Schools, Mr. and Mrs. Eastwood.

DONNYBROOK KALKALLO.

(19¼ miles from Melbourne, Sydney road.)

LAW, &c.—Local Justices: J. Sherwin, Dr. T. Wilson, F. R. Godfrey. Clerk of Pet. Sessions, Com. for taking Affidavits, T. Somerville. Dep. Reg., Postmaster, and Elect. Reg., P. Crichton. Poundkeeper, Kalkallo, W. B. Gadd. Public Vaccinator, C. J. M. Dowd. Police: Sen. Cons., G. Skinner. Inspector of Slaughter-houses, G. Skinner. Surveyor, D. R. McGregor.

COACHES.—To Melbourne, Kilmore, and Beechworth, daily.

MISCELLANEOUS.—Common School, E. Chew.

DANDENONG.

(20 miles from Melbourne.)

LAW, &c.—Judge of County Court, His Honor J. G. Forbes; Clerk, J. Dobson; Petty Sess. Court, R. C. Walker, J.P., Chairman; Clerk of the Bench, J. Dobson. Police Sen. Cons., Murphy. Returning Officer: Mornington, R. C. Walker, J.P. Electoral Registrar: Mornington, J. Dobson. Public Vaccinator, Charles Phillips. Dep. Reg., Com. for taking Affidavits, and Postmaster, J. Dobson. Poundkeeper, William Davies. Inspector of Slaughter-houses, Senior Constable Murphy. Market Commissioners: R. C. Walker, Chairman.

SCHOOLS.—Denominational, A. Hemmings.

COACHES.—Daily (Sundays excepted), from 35 Bourke street, at 2 p.m., returning at 8.30 a.m.

DUNOLLY AND BURNT CREEK.

(107 miles from Melbourne, 32 from Castlemaine, 22 from Maldon, and 14 from Maryborough. Pop. municipality, 2000.)

LAW, &c.—P.M, and Warden, F. K. Orme. Clerk of Petty Sess., J. Miskelly. Coroner, G. Cook. Receiver and Paymaster, J. W. S. Butt. District Surveyor, P. Chauncy. Police: Sen. Con., R. J. Webb. Mining Registrar and Surveyor, R. J. McMillan. Deputy Registrar, Dr. Pierce. Postmaster and Telegraph Station-master, E. Smith. Mayor, — Daly. Town Clerk, C. Dicker. Shire of Bet Bet: P. McBride, Pres.; G. Cook, Sec.

BANKS.—London Chartered, J. A. Eddie. Victoria, W. Fairclough.

COACHES.—To Castlemaine, via Maldon, Daily at 6.30 a.m. and 2 p.m. To Maryborough, Tallot, Clunes, Creswick, and Ballarat, at 6.30 a.m and 2.15 p.m. To Tarnagulla, Inglewood, and Sandhurst, daily, at 6.30 a.m. To St. Arnaud, Peters, and Cochrane's, at 6.30 a.m. Agent, G. Simpson.

MISCELLANEOUS.—Hospital: Dr. McGregor, Res. Surgeon. Church of England School, J. Thomas. Public Library, W. H. Carwardine, Sec. Newspaper, *Dunolly and Bet Betshire Express*. Bookseller and General News Agent, W. Vesey.

ECHUCA.

(Hopwood's Ferry, River Murray, 166 miles from Melbourne.   Pop. Borough, 1,200.)

LAW, &c.—P. M. and Deputy Sheriff, C. E. Strutt. Local Justices : R. Glass, Dr. Crossem, Dr. Barker, and J. Shackell. Judge of County Court, C. B. G. Skinner. Clerk of Petty Sessions, County Court, Reg. of Imports, T. Bannett. Public Vaccinator, Dr. Crossen. Deputy Reg., D. W. Forbes. Police Serg., J. Cleary. Poundkeeper, G. Jamieson. Postmaster and Tel. Sta. Master, D. W. Forbes. Customs; T. Wardman, for N. S. W. Road Board; Chairman, R. J. Glass; Clerk, J. Shackell. Mayor, F. Payne. Town Clerk, C. E. Pascoe.

BANKS.—Victoria, — Gillies. New South Wales, — Lewers.

COACHES.—To Deniliquin, daily, Sunday excepted. A coach runs from Runnymede to Rushworth and Murchison.

BOATS ply between Echuca and Wahgunyah, and Echuca and Goolwa, S.A. Melbourne Agent, J. Halfey, 104 Bourke street west.

MISCELLANEOUS.—Northern General Association; President, J. P. Row; Treasurer, J. Crisp. Common School. Echuca Bridge across the River Campaspe; Hopwood's Pontoon Bridge across the River Murray. A Punt plies on the Murray at the Pontoon Bridge, and at Moama across the Murray two miles higher up. Murray Fishing Company. Railway Terminus. Newspaper, *Riverine Herald*, bi-weekly. News Agent, A. Carpenter.

ELTHAM.

(14 miles from Melbourne, via Heidelberg, direct route to Caledonian Diggings.)

LAW, &c.—Police Magistrate and Warden, J. A. Panton. Local Justices, H. Stooke, H. Dendy. Clerk of Petty Sessions, J. B. Drummond. Deputy Registrar, Mr. Clark. Inspector of Slaughter-yards, and Police Constable, P. Lawlor (in charge).

COACHES.—From Star Inn, Swanston street, for the Caledonia Diggings, via Eltham, Tuesday, Thursday, and Saturday; returning Monday, Wednesday, and Friday. Booking Office, Fountain Hotel, Eltham.

MISCELLANEOUS.—Common and Church of England Common Schools. Cricket Club, W. B. Andrew, Sec. Postmaster, T. Hanniford. Poundkeeper, T. Batt. Road Board: H. Stooke, Chairman; C. S. Wingrove, Secretary.

EPPING.

(13 miles from Melbourne.)

LAW, &c.—Res. Ter. Magistrate, T. H. Rawlings. Deputy Registrar, T. Dignan. Postmaster, W. Mitchell. Public Vaccinator, Dr. R. Bowie, Northcote. Police; Constable Johnston.

COACH.—Melbourne to Morriang. Leaves Melbourne, 3 p.m.; Morriang, 7 a.m. Delivery at Northcote, Preston, Thomastown, Epping, and Woodstock.

MISCELLANEOUS.—Common Schools, S. P. Moore and T. Dignan. Road Board, E. Hastings, Chairman. Trustees of Cemetery, T. H. Rawlings, Chairman. Cricket Club S. P. Moore, Sec.

GISBORNE.

(31 miles from Melbourne and 46½ from Castlemaine. Pop. Municipality, 423.)

LAW, &c.—Police Magistrate, J. C. Thompson. Clerk of the Bench and Elect. Reg., H. Carroll. Bailiff, H. R. Dixon. Police Sergeant, — Hall. Public Vaccinator, G. O. Rigby, M.D. Town Clerk, J. Thompson. Railway Stationmaster, Mr. Wills. Dep. Registrar, A. M'Gregor. Poundkeeper, H. R. Dixon. Postmaster and Elec. Tel. Stationmaster, D. Shiels. Gisborne Farmers' Soc. ; Secretary, S. B. Lee.

MISCELLANEOUS.—Bible Society: Secretary, J. Whitelaw. Common School: W. M. Pye. Mechanics' Institute: T. P. Smith, Sec.

c

GENERAL INFORMATION.

GEELONG.
(Pop., 23,037; Municipality, 14,784.)

THE CORPORATION OF GEELONG.
R. DE B. JOHNSTON, MAYOR.

ALDERMEN.

Ward.			Retires.	Ward.			Retires.
Bellerine	..	R. Upston	.. 9 Nov., 1867	Barwon	..	T. N. Couves	.. 9 Nov., 1865
Kardinia	..	J. Hedrick	,, 1867	Thomson	..	I. Boynton	,, 1865
Villamanata		R. de B. Johnstone	,, 1866				

COUNCILLORS.

Ward.			Retires.	Ward.			Retires.
Bellerine	..	W. P. Noonan	.. 31 Oct., 1865	Villamanata	..	J. Brearley	.. 31 Oct., 1867
		W. Matthews	,, 1866	Barwon	..	J. Whitchell	,, 1865
		W. Carpenter	,, 1867			W. Ashmore	,, 1866
Kardinia	..	W. Morris	,, 1865			W. Veitch	,, 1867
		A. C. McDonald	,, 1866	Thomson	..	J. Holdsworth	,, 1865
		R. Reeves	,, 1867			Jas. Oddy	,, 1866
Villamanata		M. S. Levy	,, 1865			J. M. Garrall	,, 1867
		J. M. Anderson	,, 1866				

Town Clerk, W. Weire. Treasurer, H. Roebuck. Surveyor, R. Balding. Rate Collectors, &c, C. Power, S. Trotman. Town and Lodging House Inspector, &c., J. Tweedale. Inspector of General Market, T. Inglis. Inspector of Haymarket, L. Ryan. Town Herdsman, W. Luxmoor.

BOROUGH OF SOUTH BARWON.—Mayor, S. Brearley. Town Clerk, J. Richardson.
BOROUGH OF NEWTON AND CHILWELL.—Mayor, P. Huddart. Town Clerk, J.

Prince of Wales Hotel, Wednesday and Saturday, at 6 a.m., and for Warrnambool, Tuesday and Friday, at 5 a.m.

AGRICULTURAL AND HORTICULTURAL SOCIETY.—Office: 48 Moorabool street. President, H. C. Hope. Treasurer, A. Douglass. Secretary, James Campbell.

HORTICULTURAL IMPROVEMENT ASSOCIATION.—President, A. S. Robertson. Secretary, Wm. Batson. Treasurer, W. Clarkson.

LADIES' BENEVOLENT ASSOCIATION.—Pres., Mrs. Hewlett. Sec., Mrs. Burn.

AUXILIARY TO THE BRITISH AND FOREIGN BIBLE SOCIETY.—Secretaries, Rev. G. Goodman and B. W. Wheatland. Treasurer, J. S. Turner.

MECHANICS' INSTITUTE.—Great Ryrie street. B. W. Wheatland, Secretary.

VOLUNTEER FIRE BRIGADE.—T. Thompson, Foreman.

INFIRMARY AND BENEVOLENT SOCIETY.—Secretary, John Middlemiss. Resident Surgeon, D. B. Reid.

ORPHAN ASYLUMS.—Secretary, J. Campbell. Saint Augustine's Orphanage, Newton Hill, Patron, Very Rev. Dean Hayes.

GORDON GOLD FIELD.

(On the Melbourne and Ballarat main line of road, 15 miles from Ballarat. Pop., 500.)

LAW, &c.—Police Magistrate, and Warden (non-resident), J. M. Clow; Resident Territorial Magistrates, W. H. Bacchus, of Poerewur, and A. Fiskin, of Lal Lal. Clerk of Petty Sessions (non-resident), D. Stolie. District Mining Surveyor, — Davilson, of Buninyong.

MISCELLANEOUS.—Postmast, C. Marx. Surgeon, J. Wilcocks. News Agents, Irwin and Major.

HAMILTON.

(219 miles from Melbourne, 53 from Portland, and 60 from Port Fairy. Population of the Municipality, 1500.)

LAW, &c.—Chairman of General Sessions, and Judge of County Court, J. L. Clarke. Crown Prosecutor, J. F. Nolan. Clerk of the Peace, County C. and Pet. Ses., Elec. Reg., Dep. Reg., H. Garton. Paymaster, Receiver, and Land Officer, E. Wrixon. Police Magistrate, Dep. Sheriff, and Vis. Justice, Crown Lands Com., and Guardian of Minors, C. Fetherstonaugh. Local Justices, A. Learmonth (Terri.), P. Henty, E. Henty, J. Coldham, J. G. Jackson, R. Officer, C. Officer, S. P. Winter, C. P. Cooke, A. Turnbull, T. McKillar, J. Mackersey, P. Learmonth. Coroners, C. Fetherstonaugh and A. Learmonth. Returning Officer, W. Skene. Election Auditor, H. Cox. Public Vaccinator, E. Govett. Police Sub-Inspector, — Kabat. Inspector of Slaughter Houses, R. Kennedy. Poundkeeper, R. Hounfield. Postmaster, C. Rogers. Electric Telegraph Station Master, W. Weston. Mayor, A. Learmonth. Town Clerk, J. S. Jenkins.

BANKS.—Bank of Victoria, Manager, D. Williamson. National Manager, D. McPherson. Savings' Bank, Actuary, Alexander Learmonth.

COACHES.—For Dunkeld, Wickliffe, Fiery Creek, Emu Creek, Skipton, and Ballarat daily, at 1 a.m.; returning at 8.30 p.m. For Branxholme, Greenhills, Haywood, and Portland, Tuesday, Thursday, and Saturday, at 6 a.m.; returning on Monday, Wednesday, and Friday, at 3 p.m. For Redruth, Colerane, Casterton, and Penola, Wednesday and Saturday, at 5 a.m.; returning on Tuesday and Friday, at 7.30 p.m. For Cavendish, Balmoral, Harrow, Apsley, and Lake Wallace, on Tuesday and Saturday, at 5 a.m.; returning on Monday and Friday, at 3 p.m. For Penshurst, Caramut, Hexham, and Mortlake, Thursday, at 6 a.m.; returning on Monday, at 9 a.m.

SCHOOLS.—Common, Mr. and Mrs. Phillips; Corresponding Patron, R. Garton. Roman Catholic, — Nicholas and Mrs. Flinn. Presbyterian, — Fraser. German Lutheran, O. Mueller.

MISCELLANEOUS.—Pastoral and Agricultural Association. Secretary, Alex. Learmonth. Mechanics' Institute, Secretary, J. Doig. Cricket Club, Secretary, W. Vale. Turf Club, Secretary, N. J. Uren. Ancient Order of Foresters, Secretary, W. Mott. Hospital and Benevolent Asylum, Secretary, J. H. Game. Shire of Dundas, Secretary, J. Walpole. Newspapers, Hamilton Spectator, and Free Press.

HAPPY VALLEY.

(93 miles from Melbourne; 24 from Ballarat; 120 viâ Ballarat from Melbourne. Pop., 3,500.)

LAW, &c.—Postmaster, R. Wreford. Deputy Registrar, T. Lea. Sen. Constable, P. Royan. Vaccinator, T. Hoskins.
BANKS.—Australasia, W. H. Comyns.
COACHES.—For Smythesdale and Ballarat, twice a day.
MISCELLANEOUS.—Common School, T. Lea. Catholic, Mrs. Howe. News Agents, Wreford and Co.

HEATHCOTE.

(70 miles from Melbourne and 31 from Sandhurst. Pop. Municipality, 1,200.)

LAW, &c.—Judge of County Court and Court of Mines, C. R. G. Skinner. P.M., Warden, Dep. Sheriff, Chinese Protector, and Guardian of Minors, W. Willoby. Clerk of County C., Court of Mines, Petty Sess., Com. for taking Affidavits, Gold Receiver, and Elect. Reg., J. J. O'Meara. Bailiff of the County Court and Court of Mines, Richard Carkeet. Local Justices: C. Robinson, R. Cocks, W. H. Robertson and E. Field. Police: Head Quarters, McIvor District; Sup. of Police, B. T. Wilson. Shire Council: Mr. Matthewson, Chairman. Postmaster and Elec. Teleg. Stationmaster, A. F. Sutton. Dep. Registrar and Returning Officer, Dr. Robinson. Poundkeeper, J. Hamilton. Mayor, Dr. Robinson. Town Clerk, T. Lea.
POST OFFICE.—Post to Melbourne, viâ Sandhurst, daily, at 2 p.m.; Kyneton, Mon., Wed., Fri, at 2.30 p.m.; viâ Kilmore, Tues., Thurs., Sat., at 8 a.m.; to Redcastle, and Costerfield, Tues., Thurs., Sat., at 8 a.m.
BANKS.—Oriental, James Campbell, Manager.
COACHES.—To Kilmore and Melbourne, Tues., Thurs., Sat., at 8 a.m. To Sandhurst, daily, at 2 p.m. To Kyneton, to meet trains, Mon., Wed., Fri.
MISCELLANEOUS.—Solicitors, J. Millett, W. G. Adamson. Newspapers: McIvor News and McIvor Times. Mechanics' Institute, Mr. Adams, Secretary. Hospital, Dr. C. Robinson.

HEIDELBERG.

(8 miles from Melbourne.)

LAW, &c.—Police Mag., J. A. Panton. Clerk, J. B. Drummond. Public Vaccinator, Dr. G. S. Butler. Postmaster and Registrar of Births and Death, R. Fuge. Road Board: Chairman, T. Harmson; Clerk and Treasurer, R. G. Durham. Electoral Registrar, R. G. Durham.
COACHES.—From Britannia Hotel, Swanston street, daily, at half-past 9 a.m., half-past 4 and 6 p.m. Leaves Heidelberg, daily, at 8 and half-past 9 a.m., and half-past 2 p.m. The Wood's Point coaches, viâ Yarra Track, go and return daily through Heidelberg.
MISCELLANEOUS.—Common School, C. Mattingley. Catholic, P. O'Brien. Police Inspector of Slaughterhouses, Sen. Constable Harty.

INGLEWOOD.

(For Kingower, Jericho, and Korong.—132 miles from Melbourne, 14½ from Tarnagulla, 49 from Castlemaine, 39 from Maldon, 28 from Sandhurst. Pop. Municipality, 1,700.)

LAW, &c.—General Sessions, Court of Mines, and County C. Judge, F. M. Macc boy. Clerk, W. Hanly. Police Magistrate, G. M. Lowther. Territorial Magistrates S. Rinder, J. Wilson, J. S. Robertson, H. Hunter, P. McVean. Warden, G. M Lowther. Receiver of Revenue, &c., S. Wyman. Mining Reg. and Surveyor, W. G Couchman. Commissioner of Crown Lands, G. M. Lowther. Coroner, H. H. Radcliffe. Dep. Reg. and Public Vaccinator, G. Crosland. Postmaster in charge of Telegraph, L. O. Peyton. Police, Serg. W. Acton. Road Board: Chairman, H. Hunter Clerk, S. Rinder. Mayor, M. Ward. Town Clerk, A. McNaughton.
BANKS.—New South Wales, T. K. Johnston. London Chartered, J. R. Gardine Victoria, J. D. Mills.

GENERAL INFORMATION.

COACHES.—For Tarnagulla, Dunolly, Maryborough, Talbot, Cariabrook, Creswick, Ballarat, daily, at 10.30 a.m. To Newbridge, Bullock Creek, and Sandhurst, meeting 7.15 train to Melbourne, daily, 2.30 p.m.
MISCELLANEOUS.—Hospital: Sec., H. J. Congreve; Surgeon, H. H. Radcliffe. Newspapers: *Inglewood Advertiser.*

JAMIESON.

LAW, &c.—P.M. and Warden, G. Harrison, Capt. R.N. Coroner, and Dep. Sheriff, J. H. Alley. Receiver of Revenue, Acting Clerk of Petty Sessions, T. Smallman. Public Vaccinator, J. Nicholson, M.D. Postmaster and Electric Telegraph, W. Andrews. Mayor, W. G. Power. Police: Serg. Baber.

KEILOR.

(10 miles from Melbourne.)

LAW, &c.—Police Court sits, alt. Tuesday, at 10 a.m. J. C. Thompson, P.M., visits from Gisborne. Local Justice, P. Phelan. Clerk of the Bench and Com. of the Supreme Court for taking Affidavits, T. Somerville. Poundkeeper, E. Bonfield. Road Board; Chairman, W. Taylor, M.L.C. Clerk, Elect. Reg., Dep. Reg., and Postmaster, R. G. Ely. Public Vaccinator, J. Gibson. Senior Constable, G. Bird.

KILMORE.

(37 miles from Melbourne, Sydney Road. Pop. Elec. Dis., 2,694; Municipality, 1,725.)

LAW, &c.—Chairman of Quarter Sess., Judge of County Court and Court of Mines, C. B. G. Skinner. P. Magistrate, Dep. Sheriff, and Warden, A. Murchison McCrae. Clerk of the Bench, Elect. Reg., Clerk of the Peace, and Gold Receiver, E. Barry. Land Officer, Col. of Imports, Agent of the Bd. of Land and Works, Gold Fields and Warden's Clerk, E. M. Cairnes. Inspector of Police, and Inspector of Distilleries, M. Page. Postmaster and Tel. Master, H. B. Bristow. Coroner, D. N. Nicolson. Dep. Reg., J. W. Osborne. Mayor, Town Clerk, J. Flynn.
BANKS.—Oriental, C. R. W. Fraser. Colonial, M. Hayes.
COACHES to and from Melbourne to Beechworth, Albury, and Deniliquin, daily (Sundays excepted). To Yea, on Mon., Wed, Fri.
SCHOOLS—Common, Roman Catholic, and Free Presbyterian.
MISCELLANEOUS.—Notary Public, Mr. Twigg. Public Vaccinator and Coroner, Dr. Nicholson. Newspapers, *The Examiner, Kilmore Free Press.*

KYNETON.

(52 miles from Melbourne, and 25½ from Castlemaine. Pop. Elec. Dis., 7,304; Municipality, 2,004.)

LAW, &c.—Stipendiary Magistrate and Com. of Crown Lands, J. C. Thomson. Clerk of Petty Sessions, &c., H. Weigall. Judge of County Court and Court of Mines, J. G. Forbes. Deputy Registrar, J. Conway. Police, Superintendent, R. Green. Postmaster and Elec. Tel. Manager, G. Groves. Returning-Officer, C. Young. Shire Council, W. Thomson, President. Town Clerk, J. Apperly.
BANKS.—New South Wales, H. B. Stiles. Colonial, W. G. Blair. Savings' Bank; Actuary, Frank Robertson.
MISCELLANEOUS.—Hospital, A. Purdue, Sec. Mechanics' Institute and National School. Farmers' and Cricket Clubs. Kyneton Agricultural Association, R. Harper. Newspapers, *Kyneton Observer,* and *Kyneton Guardian.*

LANCEFIELD.

(37 miles from Melbourne.)

LAW, &c.—Pol. Mag. and Com. of Crown Lands, A. M. McCrae. Local Justices, C. S. Haley, J. B. Phipps. Clerk of Petty Sessions, Agent of the Board of Land and Works, and Serjeant in Charge, J. Rennie. Elect. Reg. and Deputy Reg., Dr. Phipps.

Public Vaccinator, Dr. Birnie. Guardians of Minors, C. S. Haley and Dr. Phipps. Road Board: Chairman, C. S. Haley, J.P. Engineer and Clerk, T. Gannon.
Coach leaves Lancefield daily (Sundays excepted), at 6 a.m., for Lancefield Road Station, in time for the train arriving in Melbourne at 10.30 a.m.; and leaves Lancefield Road Station for Lancefield on arrival of the 12.15 p.m. train from Melbourne.
Miscellaneous.—Postmaster, R. Onians. Poundkeeper, A. Madigan.

LANDSBOROUGH.

(170 miles from Melbourne, 32 miles from Avoca.)

Law, &c.—Police Mag., Warden, Com. of Crown Lands, and Coroner, J. Daly. Receiver and Paymaster, A. H. Aston. Clerk of Petty Sessions, R. E. Johns. Local Justice, F. Lowe. Post-Office, J. Johnston. Dep. Reg. of Births and Deaths, W. H. Puddicombe. Pub. Vac., M. Brisbane. News Agent, Godfrey Morgan. Police, Sen. Cons. Blanc.
Banks.—London Chartered, J. S. Trew.

LINTON.

(110 miles from Melbourne, via Ballarat, 21 miles from Ballarat.)

Law, &c.—Police Magistrate, Warden, and Com. of Crown Lands, J. P. Hamilton. Local Justices: S. Lewers and M. H. Baird, Coroner, T. Hopper. Poundkeeper, N. Matthews. Gold Receiver, Elect. Registrar, Clerk of Petty Sessions, and Com. for taking Affidavits, R. McNiece. Mining Registrar and Surveyor, J. Montgomery. Postmaster, W. J. Hugill. Police, Constable Kennedy. Public Vaccinator, F. L. Hooper. Deputy Registrar, T. Taylor. Shire Council: S. Lewers, J.P., Chairman.
Banks.—New South Wales: S. Lewers, agent.
Coaches.—Daily, for Ballarat and Smythesdale, at 2.45 p.m.; Shipton and the Western District, at 7 a.m. For Pitfield, Shelford, Rokewood, and Leigh road Station, at 8.15 a.m. Monday, Wednesday, and Friday.
Schools.—Common School, vacant. Wesleyan, M. Wilson.

MALDON.

(84 miles from Melbourne. Tarrangower the district, Maldon the township. Pop. Municip., 3,300)

Law, &c.—Magistrate and Warden, vacant. Clerk of the Bench, J. Nott. Mining Surveyor, R. Nankiville. Telegraph Station and Postmaster, F. A. G. Farrar. Returning Officer, T. C. Cooper. President of Shire, J. Warnock. Town Clerk, J. B. Jones. Police, Senior Constable Greer.
Banks.—New South Wales: C. T. Cowle. Victoria, W. P. Smith.
Coaches.—Cousin's Coach leaves for Castlemaine at 9 a.m., Returning from Cumberland Hotel, Castlemaine, at 3.15 p.m., waiting arrival of Melbourne train. Cobb & Co.'s leave for Castlemaine at 5.30 p.m., returning from Castlemaine, 10.30 p.m. For Dunolly and Maryborough, 12.15 a.m.
Miscellaneous.—Newspaper: Tarrangower Times.

MALMSBURY.

(63½ miles from Melbourne. Pop. Municipality, 1,600.)

Law, &c.—Police Magistrate, J. C. Thomson. Local Jus., Dr. E. Davy, R. B. Tucker, and J. Tyson. Clerk of Petty Sessions, J. L. Willis. Police, Sen. Constable Holmes. Dep. Regis. and Pub. Vac., Dr. E. Davy. Elec. Regis., F. E. Adamson. Postmaster, J. Tyson. Mayor, — Evans. Town Clerk, F. E. Adamson. Borough Treasurer, R. B. Tucker.
Miscellaneous.—Mechanics' Institute: President, R. B. Tucker; Secretary, F. E. Adamson. Common School, Mr. and Mrs. Adamson.

GENERAL INFORMATION. xxix

MARYBOROUGH.

(104 miles from Melbourne, on the Castlemaine Road. Pop. Elec. Dis., 7,000; municipality, 2,477.)

LAW, &c.—Judge of County Court and Court of Mines, M. F. Macoboy; Police Magistrate, C. A. D. Pascoe. Sub-Treasurer, Alfred Reynell. Coroner, F. M. Laidman, J.P. Officer in charge of Escort, Inspector Leech. Clerk of County Court, Court of Mines, Petty Sessions, and Clerk of the Peace, R. A. Montgomery. Gov. Surveyor, F. B. Raymond. Chairman of Mining Board, — O'Farrell. County Court and Sheriff's Bailiff, G. Richards. Mayor, D. Christian. Town Clerk, T. Gardner.
BANKS.—Victoria, M. McLeod, Manager. London Chartered, J. Anderson. Union, G. Smith. Savings', J. Gardiner, Actuary.
MISCELLANEOUS.—Postmaster, G. Collett. Hospital: Secretary, T. Bregazzi. District Coroner, F. M. Laidman.

MEREDITH.

(70½ miles from Melbourne, on the Geelong and Ballarat line of railway.)

LAW.—P.M., Warden, and Com. of Crown Lands, J. M. Clow. Clerk of Petty Sessions, R. Singleton. Territorial Magistrate, J. Munro, of Native Creek. Solicitor, G. King. Police, Sen. Const. R. Hadfield in charge. Road Board, W. J. Reid, chairman; D. Hamilton, clerk and treasurer. Postmaster, C. L. Nugent. Common School, J. Vickers.
COACH, carrying the mail, leaves Steiglitz for Meredith (Sundays excepted), at 10.45 a.m., returning at 2.45 p.m. from Meredith.

MOONAMBELL, LATE MOUNTAIN CREEK.

(134 miles from Melbourne, 12 from Avoca, 35 from Ararat. Pop., 500.)

LAW, &c.—Warden, C. W. Carr. Local Justice, H. Fletcher. Clerk of the Court, R. E. Johns. Telegraph and Post-office, J. F. Hayes. Police, Constable Larkan. News Agent, F. Data.
COACHES.—Daily to Melbourne, Inglewood, Ararat, Ballarat, Back Creek, and Geelong. Also to Ballarat, via Laxton, and to Landsborough and St. Arnaud.

MORNINGTON.

(35 miles from Melbourne, eastern coast of Port Phillip Bay.)

LAW, &c.—W. Templeton, P.M. Courts of Petty Sessions and Revision : A. B. Balcombe, J.P., Chairman. Local Justices : J. Barker, E. Lintott, J. Butchart. Clerk of Petty Sessions and Elec. Reg., Dep. Reg. and Com. for taking Affidavits, W. Armstrong. Surgeon and Public Vaccinator, J. P. Lane. Registrar of Marriages, J. E. Worrell. Police : Senior Constable McAdam. Road Board: Secretary, W. H. Hobson. Electric Telegraph Manager and Postmaster, T. Gay.
MISCELLANEOUS.—Common School, J. E. Worrell. Sec. to Public Cemetery, Athenæum, and Cricket Club, W. Armstrong. News Agent.

MOUNT EGERTON GOLD FIELD.

(74 miles from Melbourne, 13 from Ballarat. Pop., 500.)

LAW.—Magistrate and Warden, J. M. Clow (see Gordon): Deputy Registrar, — Scott.
MISCELLANEOUS.—School (Church of England), Master, — Scott. Postmaster and Elect. Reg., E. O. Withenlen. Mail to and from Melbourne and Ballarat, via Bunninyong Station, daily (Sundays excepted).

MURCHISON.

(On the Goulburn, 134 miles from Melbourne, 34 from Runnymede Railway Station. Pop., 300.)

LAW, &c.—Postmaster, C. M. Stewart. Police Cons. in charge, M. Timothy. Poundkeeper, R. Wilson.

GENERAL INFORMATION.

COACHES.—Thrice a week to and from Coy's Diggings, Rushworth, Moora, Colbinabin, and Runnymede Railway Station.
MISCELLANEOUS.—Common School, T. Meagher. Murchison Punt, P. Fryer.

OMEO.

(From Melbourne, 290 miles; Port Albert, 175; Sale, 12; Bairnsdale, 75.)

LAW, &c.—Police Magistrate, Warden, Coroner, and Guardian of Minors, A. W. Howitt. Local Justices: J. C. McLeod and T. Lewis. Acting Clerk of Petty Sessions, Clerk to the Warden, Mining, Electoral, and Deputy Registrar, Registrar of Marriages, Licensing Officer for the Board of Land and Works, and Com. for taking Affidavits, W. Phipps. District Surveyor, T. W. Cooper. Member of Mining Board, N. P. Newman. Postmaster, A. Alibert. Police, Senior Constable Reid.

PENTLAND HILLS.

(42 miles from Melbourne, via Bacchus Marsh.)

LAW.—Pol. Mag., C. Shuter. Local Justice, R. Lawson. Police: Mounted Con-Quinn. Postmaster, H. W. Simmons. Dep. Reg., N. P. Webbe. Pub. Vaccinator, W. Rae.
COACHES.—To and from Keilor road and Buninyong Station, Blackwood, and Ballan, daily. Ballarat, three times a week.
MISCELLANEOUS.—Common School, Mr. Heaps.

PITFIELD.

(Wardy Yallock District, 53 miles from Geelong, on the Portland road.)

LAW, &c.—Coroner, T. Hopper. Deputy Registrar, A. W. Crowe. Police, Constable Mayes.
POST-OFFICE.—Mails to Melbourne and Geelong, Mon., Wed., Fri.; and to Lintons, Tues., Thurs., Sat. Postmaster, W. Ramble.
SCHOOL.—Church of England Common School, A. W. Crowe.

PORT ALBERT, PALMERSTON, ALBERTON, AND TARRAVILLE.

(Population, 6,428.)

LAW, &c.—Local Justices: D. Turnbull, J. Hool, W. R. Belcher, G. Hogg, and the President of the Alberton Shire Council. Clerk of Petty Sessions, County Court, and Clerk of the Peace, Captain Kelaill. Petty Sessions held at Tarraville, Monday; at Palmerston, Tuesday and Friday; at Alberton, Wednesday. Crown Lands Office, Palmerston, open on Thursday and Friday. Com. of Crown Lands, Res. Magis., Dep. Sheriff, Visiting Justice, and Warden, C. J. Tyers.
BANKER.—Victoria: W. H. Parr.
NEWSPAPER.—Gippps Land Guardian, published every Friday, at Port Albert.
MISCELLANEOUS.—Coroner, Dr. Goldie. Col. of Cus. and Immi. Agent, W. R. Belcher. Harbour Master, D. Fermater. Pilots: G. A. Phillips and — Harrison. Shire Council: Sec., A. H. Carruthers. Paymaster and Receiver, W. R. Belcher. Postmasters: Port Albert, J. Ferris; Tarraville, J. F. Liston; Alberton, Neils Christensen. Police: Alberton, Cons. McElgunn; Palmerston, Sen. Cons. Carden; Tarraville, Cons. Smallman. Common Schools: Alberton, Mr. and Mrs. Peppers; Tarraville, Mr. and Miss Broadfoot; Palmerston, Mr. and Mrs. Frost.

PORTLAND.

(235 miles from Melbourne.—Pop. Municipality, 2500.)

LAW, &c.—Police Magistrate, J. Blair. Local Justices, E. Henty, T. Must, T. Finn, H. E. Brewer, M.D., J. Trangmar, and C. Croaker. Clerk of the Bench, Registrar of County Court, and Clerk of the Peace, E. Manning. Sheriff, visited from Ararat. Sheriff's Bailiff, — Fricker. County C. Bailiff, H. Beauvais. Governor of

GENERAL INFORMATION. xxxi.

Gaol, T. F. Hyland. Com. of Sup. Court for Taking Affidavits, J. Blair, P.M., P. Scott, E. Manning. Com. Sup. Court, S. Australia, E. Manning. Notary Public, P. Scott. Dep. Reg., E. Atkinson. Sup. of Police, H. R. Barclay. Com. for taking Acknowledgments of Married Women, Registrar of Imported Live Stock, E. Manning Poundkeeper, S. Hazeldine. Inspector of Distilleries, H. R. Barclay. Tel. Station and Postmaster, F. Braim. Collector of Customs, W. A. Moore. Landing Waiter, E. Wardell. Lighthouse-keeper, L. Barton. Harbour Master, J. Fawthrop. Immigration Agent, W. A. Moore. Receiver and Paymaster, W. A. Moore. Coroner, H. E. Brewer, M.D. Thos. Must, Mayor. E. Atkinson, Town Clerk and Borough Treasurer Shire Council, J. Trangmar, President.

BANKS.—Union, W. A. Stokes. Australasia, D. W. Gallie. Victoria, F. C. Oswald Savings Bank, J. Smith, Actuary.

COACHES.—Cobb and Co.'s Royal Mail Coaches leave Mac's Hotel, Portland, daily, at 6 a.m., for Geelong, Casterton, Hamilton, Melbourne, &c. Return Coaches arrive at Portland at 3 p.m.

NEWSPAPERS.—*Portland Guardian*, twice a week. *Western Times*, twice a week.

SCHOOLS.—Common, C. S. Dunbar. Ch. of England, J. Dempster. R. Catholic, vacant.

STEAMERS.—The *Western*, from Melbourne, every Tuesday, Capt. Lucas. Leaves Portland for Belfast, Warrnambool, and Melbourne, every Friday. Agents, Messrs. Henty and Co.

MISCELLANEOUS.—Benevolent Asylum : J. Blair, P.M., Pres. ; T. E. White, Surgeon; R. Clay, Secretary. Building Society, H. Clay, Sec. Cricket Club, J. R. Y. Goldstein, Sec. Mechanics' Institute, W. Flannigan, Sec. Botanical Gardens, W. Alllitt, Curator. Land Officer, W. A. Moore.

QUEENSCLIFF.

(Distant, by sea, from Melbourne, 32 miles; distant, by land, from Geelong, 20 miles.)

LAW, &c.—Local Justices, J. D. Owens, M.D., G. White, J. Elder. Clerk of Petty Sessions, and Com. for taking Affidavits, E. Singleton. Tide Surveyor, H. E. Brown. Assistant Immigration Officer, H. E. Brown. Health Officer, A. P. L. Robertson, M.D. Light Houses: Superintendent, W. Foy. Pilots, Resident: Messrs. Dwyer, Caught, Neil, W. N. Reid, J. Nicholson, C. Kennedy, W. Rochet. Pilot Boats: Schooners "Proserpine," "Hip," and cutter "Corsair." Inspector of Nuisances, Senior Constable Goudenough. Postmaster and Deputy Registrar, C. Dod. Telegraph Station Master, J. Payton. Telegraph, Point Lonsdale, Miss F. Green. Signal Master, W. Peacock; Signal Master, Point Lonsdale, Capt. Preston. Electoral Registrar, C. Dod. Acting Pub. Vac., G. R. Ridley. Lloyd's Agent (acting), E. Singleton. Mayor, C. Kennedy. Town Clerk, R. Jordan.

COACHES.—The Mail leaves for Geelong daily.

MISCELLANEOUS.—Common School, Mr. Jordan. Mechanics' Institute, R. Jordan, Sec. Crick Club, C. C. Simpson, Sec. Bible Society, R. Jordan, Sec. Telegraph and shipping agent, and agent for Greville and Co. (Reuter's agents), H. Small.

ROKEWOOD.

(86 miles from Melbourne, 42 miles from Geelong, 27 miles from Ballarat.)

LAW, &c.—P. M., J. P. Hamilton. Local Justices: T. Russell, J. Elder. Clerk of Pet. Sess., Senior Constable Harding. Deputy Registrar, T. J. Landers. Public Vaccinator, W. Scott. Coroner, Dr. Hoppor. Poundkeeper, D. McAndrew.

MISCELLANEOUS.—Common School, T. J. Landers. Coach three times a week from Leigh road Station and Lintons.

RUSHWORTH.

(122 miles from Melbourne, 22 miles from Runnymede Railway Station. Population, 600.)

Surveyor and Registrar, and Collector of Imports, H. R. Nicholas. Road Board: W. Wigg, Chairman; H. R. Way, Clerk. Deputy Reg., H. Hicks. Public Vaccinator, J. P. Hiely. Police, Serg. Donally.

BANK.—Victoria, T. W. Renbow.

COACHES.—To Runnymede, to meet the 6 p.m. Train to Sandhurst, Mon., Wed., Fri., at noon. To Whroo, Coy's Diggings, and Murchison, Tues., Thurs., Sat., at 5.30 p.m.

MISCELLANEOUS.—Mechanics' Institute, W. C. Walbran, Sec. Mutual Improvement Society, J. A. Adamson, Sec. Common School, E. Smith; Presbyterian, — Robinson.

SALE.

(Sale, distant from Melbourne, overland, 140 miles: to Port Albert, 60 miles: to Bairnsdale, 50.)

LAW, &c.—Com. of Crown Lands, Warden, Land Officer, &c., W. H. Foster. Judge of County Court, C. B. Brewer. Clerk of Peace and Registrar, R. Quinan. Local Justices: W. Pearson, A. McArthur, W. Gardner, W. Montgomery, A. Arbuckle, J. Inglis, E. Slade. Superintendent of Police, E. Slade. District Surveyor, W. T. Dawson. Road Engineer, — Crawley, C.E. Coroner, A. Arbuckle. Mayor, N. Guthridge. Town Clerk, C. R. Geoghegan. County Ct. Officer and Poundkeeper, H. M. Pearson. Postmaster and Telegraph Master, W. Collier.

BANKS.—Victoria, Chas. B. Sibbald. National, C. F. T. Farran. Australasia, — Cromley.

MISCELLANEOUS.—Mechanics' Institute, T. Topping, Sec. Cricket Club, F. Webb, Sec. Turf Club, W. Pearson, Sec. Leeson's Museum, open daily, admission free. Common School, W. Bryant. Hospital, C. F. T. Farran, Sec. Newspapers, *Gippsland Times* and *Gippslander*.

COACHES.—For Melbourne, daily. For Bald Hills, Mon., Thurs., Sat., 6 a.m.; returning Tues., Fri., Sun. For Bairnsdale, Mon., Thurs. at 9.30 a.m.; returning Wed., Sat. For Port Albert, Tues., Fri., at 5 a.m., arriving at Port Albert at 2 p.m., immediately after which the steamers start for Melbourne, where they arrive on Wednesday and Saturday.

STEAMERS to Bairnsdale, Mon., Thurs., 8 a.m.; Tues., Fri. 7 a.m.

SANDHURST.

(100½ miles from Melbourne. Pop. Elec. Dis., 16,824; municipality, 15,000.)

LAW, &c.—Police Magistrates, L. M'Lachlan, C. Mollison, and G. Webster; Territorial, C. Mollison, C. Williams. J. F. Sollivan, J. J. Casey, J. F. Williams, J. W. Williams, W. Bannerman, J. McIntyre, Dr. Ponnds, R. F. Howard, L. Macpherson, Wardens, C. Mollison and G. Webster. Sub-Treasurer, A. Langton. Chinese Interpreter, Wat-a-chee, Chairman Gen. Sess., C. R. G. Skinner. Clerk of Petty Sessions, J. T. Sanders. Clerk of Peace and Reg. of County Court, G. Bartrop. Sup. of Police, H. M. Chomley. Inspector of Roads, T. W. McCulloch. Mayor, J. McIntyre. Town Clerk, G. A. Fletcher. Dep. Reg., D. Buchan.

BANKS.—Australasia, J. Lawford. Victoria, G. Vallentine. New South Wales, W. Bannerman. Colonial, M. Tolmie. Union, J. Orr. Savings' Bank, Actuary, J. White. Oriental, J. Anderson.

COACHES to Inglewood, daily. Mail conveyance to Heathcote, daily. Conveyances to the various out-districts throughout the day.

FIRE BRIGADES.—Captain, Peel. Municipal, J. Trant, Foreman.

NEWSPAPERS.—News Agent, J. N. Macartney, Pall Mall. *Bendigo Advertiser*, *Bendigo Independent*, *Bendigo Evening News*.

MINING BOARD.—Chairman, R. O. Smith. Clerk, J. Burnside.

SURVEY OFFICE, View Point.—District Surveyor, J. H. Taylor. Contract Surveyor, H. Walker.

MISCELLANEOUS.—Mechanics' Institute, Sec., D. Marshall. Agricultural and Horticultural Society, M. Mill, Sec. Place of Amusement: Lyceum Theatre, Pall Mall. Benevolent Asylum, J. Boyd, M.D., Sec. Telegraph Station, Mitchell street, R. Deverell. Bendigo Waterworks, Stand Pipe and Office, Pall Mall. Temperance Hall, View Point. District Hospital, Dr. P. McGillivray, Resident Surgeon. Rifle Corps, J. H. Taylor, Commanding Officer.

SHELFORD (UPPER LEIGH).

(24 miles from Geelong, and 11½ from Leigh Road Station, Ballarat Line.)

LAW, &c.—Territorial Magistrates, G. Russell, Chairman, R. L. Bell, J. Kinnimouth. Poundkeeper, H. M. Wilson. Deputy Registrar, Mr. Philp. Postmaster, H. M. Wilson. Shire Council, R. L. Bell, President. Police, Sen. Cons. Wilson.

MISCELLANEOUS.—Mechanics' Institute, Secretary pro tem., J. A. McCrae. School.—Presbyterian, G. Y. Hunt and Miss Pittbladdo.

SKIPTON.

(Emu Creek, 30 miles from Ballarat, on the main road to Hamilton.)

LAW, &c.—Police Magistrate, F. R. Pohlman. Local Justice, J. Aitken. Clerk of Pet. Sess. and Sen. Constable, A. Gray. Poundkeeper, J. Daly. Dep. Reg., Elect. Reg, and Postmaster, A. M. Elder.

MISCELLANEOUS.—Western District Pastoral and Agricultural Association, Sec., T. Shaw.

SMYTHESDALE.

(107 miles from Melbourne, 12 miles west of Ballarat. Pop. Municipality, 1,800.)

LAW, &c.—Police Magis., J. P. Hamilton. Local Justices: R. H. Lock, T. C. Burke. Judge of County C., and Court of Mines, Judge Rogers. Clerk of Petty Sessions, W. B. Nicholson. Resident Warden, J. P. Hamilton. Mining Surveyor, John Lynch. Inspector of Police, J. H. H. Stoney. Registrar of Births and Deaths, Richard Kelland. Coroner, Dr. Hopper. Public Vaccinator, H. Barnett. Postmaster and Tel. Station Master, J. Nicol. Mayor, — Papenhagen. Town Clerk, R. Kelland.

MINING BOARD.—Members, Bickett and McDonald.

BANKS.—Australasia, T. U. Burke. Union, J. Clapperton.

MISCELLANEOUS.—Argus Agent, R. T. Vale. Cricket Club, Secretary, W. Young. Turf Club, Secretary, R. Kelland. Fire Brigade, W. McGowan, Sec. Mechanics' Institute, C. Tembrink, Sec.

SNOWY CREEK.

(287 miles from Melbourne.)

LAW, &c.—Warden in Charge, A. W. Howitt, P.M. at Omeo. Police Station at Junction of Mitta Mitta, Sen. Constable Pepper. Postmaster, W. Thompson. Mining Registrar, Elec. and Dep. Reg., H. Trench. Mail from Melbourne, via Yackandandah, weekly.

ST. ARNAUD'S.

(150 miles from Melbourne.)

LAW, &c.—Judge of County Court and Court of Mines, F. M. Macoboy. P.M., Warden, and Com. Crown Lands, J. Dale. Clerk of County C., C. of Mines and Petty Sessions, Elect. Reg., and Commissioner of Supreme Court for taking Affidavits, O. W. Collins. Bailiff, Alfred Shaw. Collector of Imposts, A. F. Bradshaw. Agent of Board of Land and Works, W. Sewell. Coroner, Health Officer, and Public Vac., E. J. Lock. Local Justices, J. W. Walker, R. McLachlan, A. G. Anderson, W. H. Agnew, W. R. C. Baker, W. Williamson. Mining Reg. and Surveyor, J. Phillips. Postmaster, B. J. Mullin. Mayor, J. W. Walker. Town Clerk and Deputy Reg., T. B. Golden. Police, Sergeant Moran. Shire Council—W. Williamson, Chairman ; C. H. Raven, Secretary. Revenue Officer, &c., T. Seaver.

BANKS.—Victoria, M. F. Sharkey, Manager.

COACHES leave the St. Arnaud Hotel, daily, for Melbourne, via Dunolly and Castlemaine, at 6 a.m., and via Avoca and Ballarat, at 3 a.m. To Mt. Jeffcott, Wednesday and Saturday.

MISCELLANEOUS.—Common Schools; J. B. Richards and J. J. Mullins.

STAWELL (PLEASANT CREEK).
(177 miles from Melbourne ; Ballarat line.)

LAW, &c.—Warden and P.M., B. Smith. Local Jus., B. Smyth (Dep. Sheriff), E. J. Bennett, D. Scallan, J. Childs, J. Holt. Chairman of Gen. Sess., J. L. Clarke. Clerk of Courts and Electoral Registrar, H. H. Roberts. Postmaster and Telegraph master, E. Johnson. Coroner and Deputy Registrar, E. J. Bennett. Police, Sup. M'Culloch.
BANK.—Oriental, H. P. Wilson, manager.
MISCELLANEOUS.—Hospital : President, D. Scallan, J.P.; Secretary, C. Playford. Shire Council : President, D. Scallan, J.P.; Treasurer and Secretary, H. Keiley. Mechanics' Institute : President, J. Dalton; Secretary, J. H. Dane. Mining Surveyor, J. D'Alton. Newspaper, *Ararat Advertiser*.

STEIGLITZ.
(Distance from Meredith Railway Station, 7 miles. Population, 1000.)

LAW.—Judge of Court of Mines, J. W. Rogers. Clerk, R. Singleton. Resident Police Magistrate, Warden, Commissioner of Crown Lands, Chinese Protector, and Guardian of Minors, J. M. Clow. Deputy Registrar, R. Singleton. Electoral Registrar, B. Goulden. Clerk of Petty Sessions, Warden's Clerk, Agent for Board of Land and Works, Commissioner for Taking Affidavits, R. Singleton. District Mining Surveyor, T. Woolgrove. Postmaster, W. R. Cowper.
COACHES.—A coach, carrying the mails, leaves the Post-office, Steiglitz, daily, at 10.45 a.m., arriving at Meredith Railway Station at 12 noon, returning at 2.45 p.m.
MISCELLANEOUS.—Cricket Club, R. Robinson, Sec. Mechanics' Institute, R. Robinson, Sec.

SWAN HILL.
(231 miles from Melbourne, on the Murray River.)

LAW, &c.—Magistrates : Chairman, B. W. Gammow, S. H. Officer, P. Beveridge, S. Lintott, T. Macredie. Coroner, R. W. Gammow. Superintendent of Police, D. D. Chambers. Agent of Board of Land and Works, Sen. Constable J. Hickey. Tel. Sta. Master, A. Krom. Road Board : Chairman, Thos. Fenton.
COACHES leave every Wed. and Sat. at 8 a.m., arriving in Sandhurst on Thursday and Sunday. "Haines' Lower Murray Line" leaves every Saturday at 4 a.m., and arrives in Wentworth, River Darling, N.S.W, on Monday evening.

TALBOT (BACK CREEK).
(109 miles from Melbourne via Castlemaine, 127 via Ballarat ; 10 from Maryborough. Pop., 8,000.)

LAW, &c.—Judge of Court of Mines, Gen. Sess., and County C., M. F. Macohoy. Warden and P.M., P. C. Creydigny. Local Justices : Dr. Dow, J. Quarterman, J. P. Smith, J. S. Stewart. Clerk of the County Court, Court of Mines and Petty Sess., T. Freeman. Deputy Reg. of Births and Deaths, W. Wood. Coroner and Public Vaccinator, Dr. Dow. Police, Serj. Boyle. Postmaster and Telegraph Master, J. Colles. Elect. Reg., W. Wood. Mayor, M. Cohn. Town Clerk, I. Andrews.
BANKS.—Bank of Australasia, John Wighton. Bank of Victoria, — Long. London Chartered Bank, — Fowler.
COACH OFFICES, Commercial and United States Hotel.
MISCELLANEOUS.—Schools : Church of England, — Vance ; Common, J. Harris ; R. Catholic, J. Clarke. Fire Brigade, I. Andrews, Captain. Mechanics' Institute, J. Fletcher, Sec. Hospital : Dr. Dow, Surgeon ; F. B. Salmon, Sec. Newspaper, *Talbot Leader*.

TARADALE.
(67¾ miles from Melbourne, 10 from Castlemaine. Pop. Municipality, 1,600.)
LAW, &c.—P.M. and Warden, T. D. S. Heron. Local Justices : R. Strickland, J. Johnson, W. Reynolds. Clerk of County Court and Petty Sessions, N. J. B. Rigbye.

GENERAL INFORMATION.

Deputy Registrar, D. Wilson. Postmaster and Elec. Tel. Station Master, J. B. Matthews. Mayor, D. Wilson. Town Clerk, C. Mackinson. Police, Serj. Brown.
BANKS.—National : W. Richardson, Manager.
SCHOOLS.—National, J. Wilson. Denominational (R.C.), J. Analy.
MISCELLANEOUS.—Solicitors, J. L. & Austen, and C. Makinson. Cricket Club: Sec., C. Makinson. Amateur Dramatic Society : J. B. N. Rigbye. Concert at Albion on Saturday. Newspaper : *The Express*, weekly.

TARNAGULLA.

(117 miles from Melbourne, 9 from Dunolly, 15 from Inglewood, and 30 from Sandhurst.)

LAW, &c.—Police Magistrate, F. K. Orme (via. from Dunolly.) Judge of County Court and Court of Mines, M. P. Macoboy. Clerk of Petty Sessions, J. Miskelly (via. from Dunolly.) Postmaster and Tel. Office Manager, C. M. Maplestone. Mayor, J. Ray. Town Clerk, E. N. Francis. Gold Receiver, C. M. Maplestone. Police, Sen. Cons. Fahey.
BANKS.—Union, H. S. Hooke. Colonial, A. H. Willis.
COACHES.—To Inglewood, daily, at 8 a.m.; Kangaroo Flat, 7 a.m.; Dunolly, 12 noon daily.
MISCELLANEOUS.—Newspaper, *Courier*.

VAUGHAN.

(3 miles from Fryerstown, 8 miles from Castlemaine, 75 miles from Melbourne.)
LAW, &c.—Chairman of Bench, T. D. S. Heron, P.M., J. B. Malcolm, J.P. Clerk of Pet. Sess., E. Townsend. Postmaster and Elect. Reg., J. Chapman. Dep. Reg., J. S. Mackenzie. Common School, 642. Police, Sen. Cons. Bailey.
BANK.—Victoria, E. Gilliland.

WANGARATTA.

(150 miles from Melbourne, on the Sydney road. Population, 900.)

LAW, &c.—P.M. and Land Officer, R. W. Shadforth. Local Jus.: J. D. Reid, W. A. Dobbyn, G. Mackay, D. H. Evans. Clerk of Courts, and Dep. Reg. and Elect. Reg. for Trawinger division of Murray and Eastern Provinces, A. L. Ely ; Elect. Reg. for Wangaratta division of Murray Boroughs and Eastern Provinces, W. Shields. Guardian of Minors, R. W. Shadforth. Coroner, W. A. Dobbyn. Coms. for taking Affidavits, &c., W. A. Dobbyn, A. L. Ely. Engineer of Roads and Bridges and Town Surveyor, F. Ilyloy. Teleg. Station Master, and Postmaster, W. Shields. Poundkeeper, A. Tone. Agent for Curator and Intestate Estates and Land Officer, A. L. Ely. Police: W. B. Montfort. Mayor, W. A. Dobbyn. Town Clerk, Z. Porter.
BANKS.—New South Wales, J. Aitken, manager.
SHIRE COUNCIL.—T. Finn, J. P., President. W. Clapham, Secretary.
COACHES.—Mail coaches pass through, daily, to and from Melbourne, Beechworth, Chiltern, Rutherglen, and Albury.
MISCELLANEOUS.—Schools: Common, R. Catholic, four private.

WARRANDYTE.

(18 miles from Melbourne, on the south bank of the Yarra Yarra.)

LAW, &c.—Court of Mines, His Honor Judge Forbes. Court of Petty Sessions: Chairman, Warden, District Commissioner Crown Lands, and Guardian of Minors, J. A. Panton. Clerk of Court of Mines, Clerk of Petty Sessions, Com. for taking Affidavits, and Elec. Reg., J. B. Drummond. Police Station: Senior Constable in charge, and one mounted.
MISCELLANEOUS.—Church of England School: Mistress, Miss Blair

WARRNAMBOOL.

(About 170 miles from Melbourne. Steamers twice a week. Pop. municipality, 2700.)

LAW, &c.—P. M. and Com. of Crown Lands, L. W. Gillen. Clerk of the Bench, J. M. Ardlie. Coroners, L. W. Gillen and R. H. Harrington. Col. of Cus., Imm. Agent, and Sub-Treasurer, A. W. Musgrove. Harbour Master and Pilot, Capt. Helpman. Landing Waiter, A. C. Farquharson, Reg. of County and Clerk of Peace, J. M. Ardlie. Government Engineer, S. Parker. District Surveyor, R. D. Scott. Postmaster and Elec. Tel. Station Master, T. Rackham. Mayor, J. W. M. Aitkin. Town Clerk, T. Raingill. Shire Council: Chairman, E. Bostock; Secretary, A. Davies. Police, Serj. Johnston.

BANKS.—Australasia, W. H. Palmer; Victoria, R. B. Paterson; Savings' Bank, T. Raingill, actuary.

COACHES.—From Commercial hotel, for Geelong, Tuesday, Thursday, and Saturday, at 11 p.m., via Terang, Camperdown, and Colac. From Evans and Gleeson's booking office, Sunday, Tuesday, and Thursday. at 10 p.m., via Camperdown and Colac; Monday and Friday, at 12 noon, via Mortlake. For Belfast, Tuesday, Thursday, and Saturday, at 4 p.m., and Tuesday and Saturday, 11 a.m.

MISCELLANEOUS.—Hospital and Benevolent Asylum; President and Treasurer, F. P. Stevens; Secretary, A. Davies. Argus and Bradshaw's Guide, W. Davies. Steamers to and from Melbourne, Western and Edina, twice a week. Government moorings laid down fit for the largest vessels. Schools: Common, W. M'Leish; Church of England, W. Robb; Wesleyan, W. B. Stocks. Mechanics' Institute: Secretary, H. T. Read. Cricket Club: Secretary, J. L. Wall. Temperance Society: Secretary, W. Robb. Bible Society: Secretary, W. H. Palmer. Christian Association: Secretary, J. M. Ardlie. Newspapers: Warrnambool Examiner and Sentinel. Fire Brigade: Secretary, J. D. Burnie. Caledonian Society; Secretary, A. B. Mackay.

WHROO.

(116 miles from Melbourne, and 5 miles from Rushworth. Pop., 350.)

LAW, &c.—Postmaster, and Deputy Registrar, J. H. Collier. Public Vaccinator, J. Hembrough. Constable in charge, T. Flint.

COACHES.—Three times a week to and from Murchison (Goulburn River), Rushworth, Coy's Diggings, Moora, Colbinabbin, and Runnymede Railway Station.

MISCELLANEOUS.—Mechanics' Institute, A. Henry, Sec. Common School, H. Carter.

WOODEND.

(48 miles from Melbourne, per Railway.)

LAW, &c.—P.M., J. C. Thompson. Local Justices; H. Muntz, J. Davies, and J. Harper. Clerk and Com. for taking Affidavits, J. L. Willis. Assist. Clerk of Petty Sessions, A. S. Dought. Dep. Registrar, W. H. Greeves. Postmaster, R. Nicholson. Mayor, T. Patterson. Town Clerk, C. Lilley. Rail Station Master, R. H. Francis. Tel. Operator, J. Fraser. Road Board; Chairman, J. Savage; Secretary, J. J. Stammers. Police: Serg. Drought, in charge. The Police Court is held on Tuesday and Friday.

MISCELLANEOUS.—Mechanics' Institute: Secretary, J. Spalding.

WOOD'S POINT.

(110 miles from Melbourne, via Yarra Track—230 via Longwood and Jamieson. Estimated Population, 2,500.)

LAW, &c.—Chairman of Gen. Sess., Judge of County C. and C. of Mines, T. L. Cope. P.M. and Warden, A. P. Akehurst. Ter. Magis., J, Drysdale, A. Nash, S. Iffla, and G. Pendlebury. Rec. of Revenue, G. J. Rumley. Clerk C. of Mines, County C. Pvt Sess., and Clerk of the Peace, A. R. Hornbuckle. Bailiff and Dep. Elect. Reg., C. Blythman. Sub-Insp. of Police, A. R. Smith. Mining Surveyor and Registrar, A. B. Ainsworth. Coroner, Public Vaccinator, and Dep. Reg., S. Iffla. Postmaster and Telegraph Master, W. P. Hamilton. Official Assignees' Agent, C. Harker. Dep Official Liquidator for the winding-up of Mining Companies, W. Downing. Mayor, P. Perkins.

GENERAL INFORMATION.

xxxvii.

BANKS.—Colonial, J. McCoy. Union, J. Embling. Victoria, O. Pendlebury.
MISCELLANEOUS.—Newspapers, *Mountaineer* and *Leader*. Upper Goulburn Hospital: Hon. Surgeons, S. Iffla, A. Nash. Common School, Mr. and Mrs. Wilton. Fire Brigade: Captain, — Collier; Secretary, R. Morgan.

STEAMERS FROM MELBOURNE.

TO
Adelaide.—Coorong or Aldinga, about every fourth day. A.S.N. Co.'s Steamer, monthly. Fares: Saloon, £6 6s.; Second Cabin, £3 3s.
Belfast.—Western or Edina, Tuesday and Saturday. Fares: Saloon, £3 10s.; Return, £5 5s.; Fore Cabin, £1 15s.; Return, £2 12s. 6d.
Dromana.—Reliance, Wednesday, at 10 a.m., from Queen's Wharf.
Geelong.—For Cargo: Express, from Queen's Wharf, daily 4 p.m. Saturday, 3 p.m.
Hobart Town.—Southern Cross, three times a month, from Queen's Wharf. Saloon, £4 10s.; Return, £7 10s.; Fore Cabin, £3.
Launceston.—Derwent, about twice a week; from the Queen's Wharf. Fares: Saloon, £2 2s.; Return, £3 10s.; Fore Cabin, £1.
King George's Sound.—P. and O. Co.'s and Branch Mail Steamer, once a month.
New Zealand.—OTAGO, CANTERBURY, AND WELLINGTON.—Claud Hamilton, Aldinga, Alhambra, Omeo, Gothenburg, Albion, Rangitoto, &c., weekly.
Port Albert.—Charles Edward or Samson, Tuesday and Friday, at 11 a.m., from Queen's Wharf. Fares, Cabin, £2 5s.; Return, £3 15s.; Steerage, 17s. 6d.
Portland.—Western, Tuesday. Fares: Saloon, £4; Return, £6; Fore Cabin, £2; Return, £1.
Queensland.—For Brisbane, via Sydney, per A.S.N. Co.'s Steamers, about twice a week.
Queenscliffe.—Reliance, Tuesday and Friday, at 9 a.m., from Railway Pier.
Schnapper Point.—Reliance, Wednesday, at 12 noon, and Saturday, 2 p.m., from Railway Pier.
Sydney.—Rangatira, Wonga Wonga, Alexandra, City of Melbourne, &c., about twice a week, from Railway Pier, at 2 p.m. Steerage, £2. Return tickets, First Class, £9.
Warrnambool.—Western or Edina, Tuesday and Saturday. Saloon, £3; Return tickets, £4 10s.; Fore Cabin, £1 10s.; Return, £2 5s.

POSTAL.

GENERAL POST OFFICE, CORNER OF BOURKE STREET EAST AND ELIZABETH STREET.

TOWN AND SUBURBAN DELIVERY.

There are four deliveries daily by letter carriers in Melbourne within the following boundaries:—On the north, by the south side of Victoria street; on the east, by Spring street (including the Parliament Houses); on the south, by the River Yarra; on the west, by Spencer and Adderley streets. The letter carriers will leave the General Post Office at 8 a.m., 11 a.m., 2 p.m., and 5 p.m.

Letters intended for any of the above deliveries are required to be posted at the General Post Office not less than fifteen minutes before the times stated.

The delivery of letters, &c., by letter carriers, in Hotham, Fitzroy, and Collingwood, will take place three times daily, commencing at 8 a.m., 1 p.m., and 4 p.m.; and in Carlton and East Melbourne at 8 a.m., 12 noon, and 4 p.m.

Closing of Mails.—Notices of time of closing Mails to all parts of the world are posted up in front of the Post Office, on receipt of notice from Agents.

Registered Letters are received daily from 9 a.m. to 4 p.m., but must be posted one hour prior to the closing of the Mails, at Melbourne, except where Mails are closed at 9 a.m. and 9.30 a.m., in which case they must be posted before 4 p.m. on the previous days.

Newspapers must be posted one hour before the closing of the Mails by which they are intended to be forwarded.

GENERAL INFORMATION.

RATES OF POSTAGE CHARGEABLE ON LETTERS, NEWSPAPERS, BOOKS, PACKETS, Etc.

Letters.

Not exceeding half (½) an ounce ... 2d.
Exceeding half an ounce, but not ing one (1) ounce ... ... 4d.
And for every half-ounce or fraction of half an ounce, two-pence additional.

Ship Letters,

Or Letters transmitted out of the Colony by Sea to destination, or to nearest port, as opportunity occurs.
Not exceeding half (½) an ounce ... 6d.
Exceeding half (½) an ounce, but not exceeding one (1) ounce ... ... 1s.
And for every half ounce or fraction of half an ounce, sixpence additional.

Letters and Newspapers for the United Kingdom.

Letters for any part of the United Kingdom.

Viâ SOUTHAMPTON.

Not exceeding half (½) an ounce ... 6d.
Exceeding half (½) an ounce, but not exceeding one (1) ounce ... ... 1s.
And for every ounce or fraction of an ounce, one shilling additional.

Viâ MARSEILLES.

Not exceeding half (½) an ounce... 10d.
Exceeding half (½) an ounce, and not exceeding one (1) ounce ... ... 1s. 8d.
And for every ounce or fraction of an ounce, one and eight-pence additional.

NEWSPAPERS.

Not exceeding five (5) ounces in weight.
Viâ Southampton ... ... 1d. each
Viâ Marseilles ... ... 3d. each

Registered Letters.

For the Registration of Letters, stamps to the value of sixpence must be affixed, in addition to the postage.

Letters Containing Gold or Silver

Are charged only the ordinary rates; but it is necessary to pay the Registration Fee, 6d., and also the gold duty, if the letter is to be sent out of the colony.

Letters for Officers on Board Her Majesty's Ships.

Letters forwarded viâ the United Kingdom for Officers on Board Her Majesty's ships on any foreign or colonial

Under half (½) an ounce ... ... 1s.
Exceeding half (½) an ounce, but not exceeding one (1) ounce ... ... 2s.
And for every ounce or fraction of an ounce, two shillings additional.

Soldiers and Sailors' Letters.

From or to any non-commissioned officer, privately soldier, seaman, or marine, employed on actual service in the army, navy, or marines.
Under half (½) an ounce ... 1d.
If forwarded to any place viâ the United Kingdom ... ... 2d.

Provided that the postage be prepaid by stamps (unless sent from parts beyond seas), the corps, regiment, detachment, or ship being given in the handwriting and with the signature of the commanding officer, and otherwise posted in accordance with the requirements of the 10th clause of the Act 17 Victoria, No. 30.

Letters of the above class exceeding half (½) an ounce in weight are to be charged the ordinary rates of postage.

Exemption from Postage Rates.

Letters on the Government Service, contained in official envelopes or covers, described on the outside thereof as being "On Her Majesty's Service," and attested with the signature of the Governor, or impressed with "a frank stamp" with the title of a Responsible Minister of the Crown thereon, or the title of the officers in command of any portion of Her Majesty's land and sea forces, and the officers of Her Majesty's Ordinance or Commissariat respectively, are exempt from postage.

The *Government Gazette* in Printed covers, with the words "On Her Majesty's Service," open at both ends, and bearing the imprint of the Government Printer (if received at the General Post Office from the Office of the Government Printer, but not otherwise) to be exempt from postage.

Letters, newspapers and packets, sent by post from any place beyond the limits of the colony are to be transmitted and delivered free of charge, except in cases where it is necessary to collect postage under an arrangement with the country or colony from which such letters, packets, and newspapers, have been received.

Books, &c.

GENERAL INFORMATION.

following countries and British colonies the Book-Post System has been extended to:—

the United Kingdom	Gibraltar
India	New South Wales
Ceylon	South Australia
Mauritius	Tasmania
Hong Kong	New Zealand
Malta	Western Australia

and Queensland,

to which Countries or Colonies book-packets posted in conformity with the regulations may be sent at the following rates:—

Not exceeding four (4) ounces ...	6d.
Above four (4) ounces and not exceeding eight (8) ounces ...	1s.
Above eight (8) ounces and not exceeding one (1) pound ...	2s.
Above one (1) pound and not exceeding one-and-a-half (1½) pounds ...	3s.
Above one-and-a-half (1½) pounds and not exceeding two (2) pounds	4s.

and so on, adding one shilling for every additional half-pound or fraction of half-pound up to three pounds.

Book Packets may be forwarded to the United Kingdom via Marseilles, upon payment of twopence for every four ounces or portion of four ounces, in addition to the above rates.

REGULATIONS.

Every book-packet must be sent either without a cover, or in a cover open at the ends or sides.

No book-packet must exceed two (2) feet in length, and one (1) foot in breadth or depth, or three (3) pounds in weight.

A book-packet may contain any number of separate books, almanacs, maps, or prints, and any quantity of paper, vellum, or parchment (to the exclusion of letters, whether sealed or open) and the books, maps, papers, &c., may be either printed, written or plain, or any mixture of the three.

On the cover or outside of the packet, in addition to the name and address of the person to whom the same is to be delivered, the sender thereof shall be at liberty to subscribe a statement of the contents thereof, together with his name and address.

The books, &c., may be in any binding, mounting, or covering, whether such binding be loose or attached. In the case of prints or maps,

If a packet addressed to the United Kingdom, India, Ceylon, Mauritius, Hong Kong, Malta, Gibraltar, Tasmania, Western Australia, South Australia, or New Zealand, be not sufficiently prepaid, according to its weight, but nevertheless a single book-rate be prepaid, it will be forwarded, charged with the deficient book-postage, and with an additional book-rate. This does not apply to book-packets addressed to New South Wales or Queensland, which must be fully prepaid.

In the event of a book-packet addressed to any place being posted altogether unpaid, or prepaid less than a single rate, it will be detained and sent to the Dead Letter Office.

Book-packets correctly posted will be delivered according to their addresses without further charge.

PACKETS.

Rates of Postage and Conditions of Transmission.

1. Bankers' Packets.

Bankers' Packets containing only notes, orders, cheques, or passbooks, sent by or to any bank or banker.

2. Packets containing Law Papers, &c.

Packets containing process of, or proceedings or pleadings in, any court; briefs, cases, and instructions for counsel and their opinions thereon respectively; deeds, affidavits, policies of assurance, letters of attorney, depositions, or recognizances.

The endorsement "Law Papers" is not sufficient.

3. Packets open to Inspection containing Patterns or Samples of Merchandise.

Packets containing patterns or samples of merchandise.

The patterns or samples must not be of intrinsic value. This rule excludes all articles of a saleable nature, and indeed whatever may have a value of its own apart from its mere use as a pattern or sample; and the quantity of any material sent ostensibly as a pattern or sample must not be so great that it can fairly be considered as having on this ground an intrinsic value.

These packets must bear the following endorsement:— "Pattern (or sample) of Merchandise only," together with the name and address of the sender; but

GENERAL INFORMATION.

4. Packets open to inspection containing Prices Current, &c.

Packets containing prices current and catalogues.

These packets must be sent either without covers or in covers open at the ends or sides, and must be endorsed "Prices Current only," or "Catalogues only," as the case may be, together with the name and address of the sender.

5. Packets open to inspection containing Acts of Parliament, &c.

Packets containing Acts of the Victorian or Imperial Parliaments, or printed Votes and Proceedings of either House thereof respectively, or Returns or Copies of Returns made by or to any officer in the Public Service.

These packets must be sent either without covers or in covers open at the ends or sides, and must bear one of the following endorsements, according to the facts of the case:—

"Acts of Victorian Parliament only,"
"Acts of Imperial Parliament only,"
"Printed Votes and Proceedings of Legislative Council only,"
"Printed Votes and Proceedings of Legislative Assembly only,"
"Printed Votes and Proceedings of House of Lords only,"
"Printed Votes and Proceedings of House of Commons only,"
"Copies of Returns on Public Service only," together with the name and address of the sender.

6. Packets open to inspection containing Pamphlets, Maps, &c.

Packets containing pamphlets, maps, plans, music, photographs, if not on glass or in cases closed against inspection, magazines, reviews, placards, almanacs, prospectuses, paintings, engravings, printers' proofs, or periodical publications.

These packets must be sent either without covers or in covers open at the ends or sides, and must bear one of the following endorsements, according to the facts of the case:—

"Pamphlets only," "Maps only," "Plans only," "Music only," "Photographs only," "Magazines only," "Reviews only," "Placards only," "Almanacs only," "Prospectuses only," "Engravings only," "Printers' Proofs only," "Paintings only," "Periodical Publications only," together with the name and address of the sender.

7. Packets open to inspection containing a single Printed Book.

Packets containing a single printed book.

These packets must be sent either without covers or in covers open at the ends or sides, and must bear the following endorsement:—

"A Single Printed Book only."

together with the name and address of the sender.

Not exceeding four oz. ... ... 2d.
For every additional two oz. or fraction of two oz. ... .. 1d.

On each packet sent direct by ship to any place beyond the colony to which the Book Post has not been extended, One Shilling must be paid in addition to the above rates; and in cases where these packets are forwarded through the United Kingdom, the British letter rate of postage thence to destination must also be paid.

Packets, unless posted in accordance with the above directions, will not be transmitted or delivered.

MONEY ORDERS.

Lists of the Money Order Offices in South Australia, Western Australia, New Zealand, Queensland, and the United Kingdom, may be seen, and further information obtained at any Money Order Office in Victoria.

Money Orders may be obtained and made payable at the Post Offices in Victoria, marked in the table of Inland Mails.

GENERAL INFORMATION.

Rate of Commission:

For any sum not exceeding £5—*Sixpence*
Exceeding £5, but not exceeding £10—*One Shilling.*

Money Orders will be issued at all Money Order Offices in Victoria, payable in New South Wales, South Australia, Western Australia, New Zealand, and Queensland. Money Orders will also be issued at all Money Order Offices in the before mentioned colonies, payable in Victoria.

Rate of Commission:

For any sum not exceeding £5—*One Shilling.*
Exceeding £5, but not exceeding £10—*Two Shillings.*

Money Orders will be issued at all Money Order Offices in Victoria, payable in Great Britain and Ireland. Money Orders will also be issued at all Money Order Offices in the United Kingdom, payable in Victoria.

Rate of Commission:

For any sum not exceeding £2—*One Shilling.*
Exceeding £2, but not exceeding £5—*Two Shillings and Sixpence.*
Exceeding £5, but not exceeding £7—*Three Shillings and Sixpence.*
Exceeding £7, but not exceeding £10—*Five Shillings.*

No Money Order will be issued for a larger sum than Ten Pounds.
Money Orders must be obtained between the hours of Ten a.m. and Three p.m.

EXCHANGE OF POSTAGE STAMPS FOR MONEY.

Victorian postage stamps will be received in exchange for money, a charge of 5 per cent. being made upon the value of stamps purchased or according to the following scale, viz. :—

For stamps not exceeding in value, 1s. 8d., the charge to be One Penny.
For stamps exceeding in value 1s. 8d., but not exceeding 3s. 4d., the charge to be Twopence.

CONSULS AND CONSULAR AGENTS.

*** The date indicates the day on which the appointment was gazetted in Victoria.

Argentine Confederation—Vacant. April 10, 1862.
Brazil—J. B. Were, 22 Collins street west.
Bremen—Adolph Schlöstein, 38 Flinders lane west. Oct. 16, 1860. Acting Consul, Nali Cleve.
Belgium—Gustave Rechx, 89 Queen street.
Chili—J. B. Were, 22 Collins st west, May 5, 1852.
Denmark—J. B. Were, 22 Collins street west. December 8, 1852. Vice-Consul at Geelong, H. J. Henty. September 15, 1859.
France—Le Comte de Castelnau, Apsley place, West Melbourne. June 23, 1863. Vice-Consul, Henry Follet, Apsley place.
Hamburgh—Adolph Schlöstein, 38 Flinders lane west. August 20, 1858. Acting Consul, Nali Cleve.
Hanover—A. Kauffmann, 122 Collins street west. August 3, 1855. Acting Consul, Nali Cleve.
Italy—Chevalier Giuseppe Biagi, Consul. July 22, 1864. Signor Carlo Cossu, Vice-Consul, 30 William street.
Lubec—J. B. Were, 22 Collins st west. July 6, 1853.
Netherlands—Consul-General, John William Pless Van Amstel. January 3, 1862.

xlii.   GENERAL INFORMATION.

Vice-Consul, Daniel Ploos Van Amstel, 49 Collins street west.   Acting Vice-Consul, Edward Ploos Van Amstel.
Portugal—Consul-General, J. B. Wero, 22 Collins street west.   June 11, 1851.   Consul, R. Cooper, 26 Queen street.
Prussia—M. Adalbert Kruge, 60 Queen street.
Russia—Vice-Consul, James Damyon, Custom House, Market street.   July 13, 1857.
Spain—Vice-Consul, J. J. Marshall, 60 Flinders lane east.   Jan. 30, 1863.   Acting Vice-Consul, G. F. Agnew.
Sweden and Norway—J. B. Were, 22 Collins street west.   Nov. 26, 1851, Oct. 5, 1858.   Vice-Consul, at Geelong, Herbert James Henty.   January 29, 1859.
United States, North America—William Blanchard, 91 Chancery lane.

ELECTRIC TELEGRAPH.

Gen. Superintendent—S. W. McGOWAN.   Head Office, corner of William street and Flinders lane.

MELBOURNE, from or to	Ten Words s. d.	Each ad. word. s. d.	MELBOURNE, from or to	Ten Words s. d.	Each ad. word. s. d.	
Ararat, Avoca	3 0	0 2	Sale	3 0	0 2	Murrurundi, Muswellbrook, Newcastle, Orange, Parramatta, Penrith, Picton, Queanbeyan, Scone, Singleton, Sofala, South Head, Tambaroora, Tamworth, Tenterfield, Tumut, Urana, Wagga Wagga, Wellington, Windsor, Wollombi, Wollongong, Yass, Young, at slightly varying rates.
Ballarat	3 0	0 2	Sandhurst	3 0	0 2	
Beaufort	3 0	0 2	Sandridge	1 0	0 1	
Beechworth	3 0	0 2	Seymour	3 0	0 2	
Belfast	3 0	0 2	Smythesdale	2 0	0 2	
Belvoir	3 0	0 2	Snapper Point	1 0	0 1	
Benalla	3 0	0 2	St. Arnaud	3 0	0 2	
Bunlayong	3 0	0 2	Stawell	3 0	0 2	
Camperdown	3 0	0 2	Streatham	3 0	0 2	
Cape Schanck	3 0	0 2	Swan Hill	3 0	0 2	SOUTH AUSTRALIA.
Casterton	3 0	0 2	Talbot	3 0	0 2	ADELAIDE 5 0 0 3
Castlemaine	3 0	0 2	Tarnadale	3 0	0 2	Alberton, Auburn, Blanchetown, Burdon, Burra Burra, (Kooringa), Clare, Dry Creek, Freeling, Gawler Town, Glenelg, Goolwa, Gumeracha, Hahndorf, Kadina, Kapunda, Kincraig, Lobethal, Lyndoch, McDonnell Bay, McGrath's Flat, Milang, Moonta, Mt. Barker, Mt. Gambler, Nairne, Peninsular, Penola, Port Adelaide, Port Elliot, Riverton, Robe Town, (Guichen Bay), Roseworthy, Salisbury, Smithfield, Strathalbyn, Tanunda, Victor Harbor, Wallaroo, Waterval, Wellington, Willunga, Woodside, Yankalilla, at slightly varying rates.
Carisbrook	3 0	0 2	Tarnagulla	3 0	0 2	
Chiltern	3 0	0 2	Wahgonyah	3 0	0 2	
Clunes, Colac	3 0	0 2	Wanurattu	3 0	0 2	
Collingwood	0 6	0 1	Warrnambool	3 0	0 2	
Creswick	3 0	0 2	Williamstown	1 0	0 1	
Daylesford	3 0	0 2	Wood's Point	3 0	0 2	
Dunolly	3 0	0 2	Yackandandah	3 0	0 2	
Echuca	3 0	0 2	Geelong	1 6	0 2	
Geelong	1 6	0 1	Little Rivet	1 6	0 2	
Gisborne	1 0	0 1	Werribee	1 0	0 1	
Hamilton	3 0	0 2	Geelg. Jnr.	1 0	0 1	
Heathcote	3 0	0 2	Spencer st.	1 0	0 1	
Hexham	3 0	0 2	Ballarat W.	2 6	0 2	
Inglewood	3 0	0 2	Woodend	1 4	0 1	
Jamieson	3 0	0 2	Castlemaine	2 0	0 2	
Kerang	3 0	0 2	Sandhurst	2 4	0 2	
Kilmore	1 6	0 1	Runnymede	3 0	0 3	
Kyneton	2 0	0 2	Echuca	3 0	0 3	
Longwood	3 0	0 2				
Mahlon	3 0	0 2	NEW SOUTH WALES.			QUEENSLAND.
Malmsbury	2 0	0 2	SYDNEY 5 0 0 4			BRISBANE 5 0 0 4
Maryborough	3 0	0 2	Albury, Armidale, Bathurst, Braidwood, Berrima, Braidwood, Campbelltown, Cassilis, Cooma, Deniliquin, Dubbo, Forbes, Glen Innes, Goulburn, Grafton, Gundagai, Hartley, Hay, Kiama, Kiandra, Kyamba, Liverpool, Maitland East, Maitland West, Merriwa, Moama, Morpeth, Mudgee.			Banana, Rigge's Camp, Cape Moreton, Cleveland, Dalby, Dunwich, Durah, Gatton, Gayndah, Gladstone, Golden Fleece, Hawkwood, Ipswich, Lytton, Marlborough, Maryborough, Pilot Station, Rockhampton, St. Lawrence, Toowoomba, Warwick, Wangaroo, same price.
Mooramiel	3 0	0 2				
Mortlake	3 0	0 2				
Otway	3 0	0 2				
Newstead	3 0	0 2				
Point Lonsdale	3 0	0 2				
Port Albert	3 0	0 2				
Portland	3 0	0 2				
Queenscliffe	3 0	0 2				
Red Bank	3 0	0 2				
Rutherglen	3 0	0 2				

W. H. WILLIAMS, Printer, 23 Post-office place, Melbourne.

THE AUSTRALASIAN INSURANCE COMPANY.

ESTABLISHED 1857.

Head Offices:
COLLINS STREET WEST, MELBOURNE.

Subscribed Capital: £500,000.
Paid-up Capital: £125,000.   Reserve Fund: £70,000.

Board of Directors:
Hon. ALEXANDER FRASER, Esq., M.L.C., *Chairman.*
JAMES GRAHAM, Esq., *Vice-Chairman.*
EDWARD COHEN, Esq., M.L.A. | Hon. W. J. T. CLARKE, Esq., M.L.C.
E. P. S. STURT, P.M. | JOSEPH GRIFFITHS, Esq.

Auditors:
JAMES FOWLER, Esq. | THOMAS THORP, Esq.

Bankers:
BANK OF NEW SOUTH WALES.
COLONIAL BANK OF AUSTRALASIA.

Solicitors: | **Standing Counsel:**
Messrs. MALLESON & ENGLAND. | ARCHIBALD MICHIE, Esq., Q.C.

Medical Officers:
W. H. CAMPBELL, Esq., F.R.C.S.E. | J. B. MOTHERWELL, Esq., M.D.

Marine Surveyor: | **Actuary:** | **Architect:**
Capt. W. G. GRAVE. | G. E. COWLEY, Esq. | J. E. AUSTIN, Esq.

Secretary:
E. L. MONTEFIORE, Esq., J.P.

GEELONG BRANCH:
Directors.—ROBERT B. RONALD, Esq., ALEX. BUCHANAN, Esq.
Secretary.—GEORGE FRASER, Esq.

Fire Risks taken at lowest current rates.

Marine Risks accepted at current rates, and losses made payable either at the Head Office, Melbourne, or at any of the Agencies of the Company in Great Britain, India, or the Colonies, at the option of the assured.

Life Policies issued on very favourable conditions. No extra charge to members of Volunteer Brigades. Very extended geographical limits allowed. Claims paid within one calendar month after proof of death.

Particular attention is directed to the fact that the funds belonging to the Life Branch are protected by special Act of Parliament against any claim arising out of the Fire and Marine Branch; a substantial guarantee is thus afforded to policy-holders.

Agricultural Agent:
Mr. HENRY STEVENSON, 90 Queen street, Melbourne.

J. HALLENSTEIN & CO.,
TANNERS, CURRIERS, & LEATHER MERCHANTS,
Importers of French and English Calf,
GRAFTS, CLOSED LEGS, ELASTIC-SIDE UPPERS, GRINDERY, &c., &c.,
118 SWANSTON STREET, MELBOURNE.

Hides and Bark Purchased.

Prize Medallist at the Victorian Exhibition, 1862.

H. SCHREIBER,
Mathematical Instrument Maker,
MATHEMATICAL INSTRUMENT MAKER TO MAGNETIC OBSERVATORY,
110½ Queen Street, Melbourne.
THEODOLITES, LEVELS, MICROSCOPES, &C.,
Made according to Drawings, Repaired and Adjusted.
SMALL MACHINERY DONE.

GEORGE WRIGHT,
LATE
HAGERTY & WRIGHT,
WHOLESALE AND RETAIL
TIN, SHEET-IRON, AND ZINC WORKER.
THE TRADE SUPPLIED WITH
BLOCK AND SHEET TIN, GALVANIZED IRON, ZINC SPOUTING AND RIDGING, &c..
39 & 41 LITTLE BOURKE STREET EAST,
Two doors from Swanston street.

A. G. CROSS,
3 AND 13 LONSDALE STREET,
Upholsterer, Palliasse and Mattrass Manufacturer.
THE TRADE SUPPLIED WITH PALLIASSES AND MATTRASSES,
And all descriptions of Hair, Wool, Fibre, and other Materials, at the lowest possible price.
MATTRASSES RE-MADE.

JAMES K. KENNEDY,
PLUMBER, GASFITTER, AND IMPORTER,
168 ELIZABETH STREET.
Sheet Lead and Zinc, Pumps, Lead and Iron Pipes, Plain and Ornamental Gutters, Plumbers' Brass Work, &c.
FIRST-CLASS CERTIFICATE. VICTORIAN EXHIBITION, 1862.

ESTABLISHED 1843.

BLUNDELL & FORD,

Mercantile Stationers,

PRINTERS,
LITHOGRAPHERS, ENGRAVERS,
And Account-book Manufacturers.

STEAM PRINTING DEPARTMENT.

This Department, being replete with the most extensive selection of Type and Machinery of the latest improved construction, offers unusual facilities for the expeditious and satisfactory execution of every class of Printing entrusted to them, comprising—

Book Work	Forms of Public Companies	Tables & Statements
Pamphlets	Prospectuses	Ship Cards
Periodicals	Circulars	Show Cards
Parliamentary Bills	Hand Bills	Charter Parties
Appeals	Mercantile Reports	Policies
Newspapers		Bills of Lading

Brokers' Catalogues, Custom House Forms, &c.

MANUFACTURERS' ILLUSTRATED CATALOGUES.

Prices Current, Market Reports and Freight Lists,
IN ALL LANGUAGES,
With the most scrupulous regard to punctuality and expedition.

POSTING BILLS OR PLACARDS,
In all colors and of any dimensions.

Contract Notes, Share Certificates, Cheques, Coupons, Bonds, Receipts, &c., numbered consecutively and perforated.

STEREOTYPING & ELECTROTYPING.

ACCOUNT BOOKS.

The manufacture of Account Books commands the especial attention of BLUNDELL AND FORD, whose selection of only first-class materials, aided by the most experienced workmen in the various branches, ensures the judicious application of the various patents, and all the new improvements which have of late years been introduced, to ensure durability, elasticity, and that most desirable feature to the Book-keeper, a perfectly free and even opening. For all first-class Books a scrupulous regard is paid to the quality of the paper, procuring a smooth surface and such an amount of tenacity as to leave nothing to be desired.

MANUFACTURING STATIONERS

STATIONERY ESTABLISHMENT, 44 COLLINS STREET WEST, MELBOURNE.

STEAM PRINTING WORKS AND ACCOUNT BOOK MANUFACTORY, 51 & 53 FLINDERS LANE WEST.

Melbourne Commercial Stationery Warehouse,
67 COLLINS STREET EAST, MELBOURNE.

J. W. PEARSON & CO.,
STATIONERS,
Engravers, Lithographers, Embossers,
AND GENERAL PRINTERS;
ACCOUNT-BOOK MANUFACTURERS, PAPER RULERS, AND BINDERS.

Mining Share Scrip Plates engraved, lithographed, and printed; also, Plans and Prospectuses. Companies' Dies and Presses; **Shareholders' Register, Call, and Transfer Books, ruled to pattern.** J. W. P. & Co.'s New and complete patterns of
Mining Companies' Books kept on hand in every style of Binding.
Also Wages, Cash, and Contingency Sheets, Call Notices, and Receipts.

A SUPERIOR ASSORTMENT OF STATIONERY
ON HAND: INCLUDING
Superior hand-made Letter and Note Papers; Foolscap, ruled and plain; thick water-lined Linear Papers; Envelopes, all sizes; Mitchell's, Dawson's, and Gillott's first-class Pens; Pocket Books; Wallets; Metallic Books. Hobbs' Japanned Deed Boxes, with patent locks and two keys, all sizes. Cabinets and Cases. Cash and Day Books, all sizes; Ledgers and Account Books, good paper; Memorandum Books; Inkstands, large assortment, Embossing Presses, &c., &c.

Arms, Crests, Initials, Monograms, &c., neatly engraved; Note Paper and Envelopes, embossed, plain, and in colours; Sketches made, and Crests found. See specimens.

Just Published, fine Steel Engraving portraits of the
LATE HON. RICHARD HEALES,
the and **HON. J. M. GRANT.**
Carte de visite size, 1s. each; by post, 1s. 2d. To be had of all Booksellers.

Portraits of the late Governor, Sir Chas. Darling, from a steel plate, size 18 x 10; a few copies on hand. Proof Copies, 2s. 6d. each; sent post-free on receipt of stamps.

PEARSON & CO.'S NEW MAP OF VICTORIA.
Second edition; corrected to 1866.

This Map is, without doubt, the best Map ever published; great pains having been taken to make it really useful for the offices and convenient for the pocket.
The Map being divided into squares, with an alphabetical Key, any place can be found at once.
The Publishers have determined to make it the cheapest Map ever published in the colonies.

PRICE.—Plain sheet, 1s.; coloured, 1s. 6d.; in stiff cover, coloured, with key, 2s. 6d.; mounted on cloth, in case, coloured, with key, 3s. 6d. Mounted on rollers varnished, 7s. 6d. Post free on Victoria, on receipt of stamps.

THE MASONIC DIRECTORY for 1866. Price 6d.; per post, 8d.
SOLD BY ALL BOOKSELLERS.

CARPET
AND
FLOOR-CLOTH
WAREHOUSE,
27 COLLINS STREET EAST,
MELBOURNE.

W. HICKINBOTHAM

Desires to inform his customers in the country districts that their orders by letter will receive every attention.

CARPETS AND MATTINGS
MADE TO ANY SIZE.

Floor Cloths, all widths, suitable for Rooms and Passages.

ALSO,

- Brussels
- Tapestry
- Velvet Pile
- Kidderminster, and
- Felt Carpets
- Hearth Rugs
- Door Mats
- Coir Matting
- Damask
- Rep
- Muslin Curtains
- Lace Curtains
- Cornices

- Cornice Poles
- Bullion Fringe
- Looping Tassels
- Utrecht Velvet
- Table Covers
- Chints Furniture
- Blankets
- Counterpanes
- Sheetings
- Towellings
- Mattrasses
- Palliasses

LAW, SOMNER, & CO.,

WHOLESALE AND RETAIL

SEEDSMEN,

87 SWANSTON STREET, MELBOURNE;  260 PITT ST., SYDNEY; AND OCTAGON, DUNEDIN, N. ZEALAND

CALENDAR OF GARDENING OPERATIONS,

Giving Instructions for each Month of the Year,

To be purchased of all Seedsmen throughout the Colonies.

CARRON IRON FORGE AND MILL,
DUDLEY STREET;
WAREHOUSE AND OFFICE, 139 COLLINS STREET WEST.

ROBERT AMOS
HAS FOR SALE—

Iron—Rod, Bar, Sheet, Plate, Angle, T and Hoop; Shafting, Round and Square, 3 to 11-inch; Pig Iron; White and Grey Heramabibes; Kentledge; English Coke, Coal-Dust and Charcoal Powder; Tile Copper, Block Tin, Spelter, Sheet Copper, Quick-silver, Retorts, Blasting Powder; Oils—Colza, Castor, Olive, Kerosene and Chinese; Anti-friction Grease; Cotton-Waste Engine-Packing; Galvanized Sheet-Iron; Screws and Nails; Bolts and Nuts; Cornish Boilers; Boiler Plates and Boiler Rivets; Punching and Shearing Machine; Plate-bending Rollers; Horizontal, High-pressure, and Portable Engines; Crab Winches and Derrick Cranes.

Having added one of Condie's 40-cwt. Steam Hammers to the Plant at the Iron Mill, I am now prepared to receive and execute

ORDERS FOR FORGING OF ANY WEIGHT OR DESCRIPTION,
As well as to produce
IRON OF SUPERIOR QUALITY, OF THE FOLLOWING SIZES:
Round and Square, from ⅜ to 2 inches; Flat Iron, ½ x ¼ up to 4 x 1 inch; Half-Round, Converse, Bevelled, and Sash Bar Iron; Fire-bar, Angle, and T Iron; Mining Rails, 20 to 30-lbs. per yard.

Scrap Iron (Maleable and Cast) bought for Cash.

MALDEN ISLAND GUANO,

£7 5s. per Ton
(BAGS INCLUDED), DELIVERED IN MELBOURNE.

Each Bag is branded
PHOSPHATIC GUANO,
FROM
MALDEN ISLAND.
B. B. NICHOLSON & CO.,
59 Bourke st. west,
MELBOURNE.

The undersigned are the only Importers of this valuable Guano, which contains nearly 80 per cent. Phosphate, with small quantities of Sulphate and Carbonate of Lime, but quite free from Sand or Earthy Matter.

The above Guano will be found a most useful manure when applied to all soils, but especially so when put on those that are poor or exhausted from overcropping.

It is well known that the soils of the Colony are deficient in all sorts of Lime; the Malden Island Guano is rich in those constituents; therefore more suitable, as a manure, than the hot and stimulating Peruvian, which can only be used successfully in forcing crops on rich lands. For all general agricultural purposes the Malden Island Guano will be found better than the Peruvian, and costs only half the price.

£7 5s. per Ton, Bags included, delivered in Melbourne.

B. B. NICHOLSON & CO.

59 *Bourke street west, Melbourne.*

J. COCKBILL'S
BONE MILLS,
YARRA BANK,
Near Melbourne Gas Works.

TOWN OFFICE:—23 LITTLE BOURKE STREET WEST.

J. C. respectfully returns thanks to the farmers, gardeners, and others for the liberal support accorded to him. He begs to assure his customers that the utmost attention will be given to supply them with a first-rate article. He collects bones from all the principal butchers in Melbourne and vicinity; none but fresh bones are ground.

Bone Dust, any Grist, £6 10s. per ton, bags included. Bones prepared for Fruit Trees.

Orders delivered free at railway station, or on board ship. Five shillings per ton allowed for bags, and five shillings per ton by taking from the mill.

TOWN AGENTS:—
Mr. HOME, Engineer, corner of Elizabeth and Latrobe streets.
Messrs. REYNOLDS, Victoria Seed Stores, 35 and 37 Swanston street.
Mr. LINCOLNE, Agricultural Agent, 48 Bourke street west.
Mr. DAVID MACLEAN, Storekeeper, PRAHRAN.

PRIZE MEDALLIST, LONDON EXHIBITION, 1862.

C. NETTLETON,
PHOTOGRAPHIC ARTIST,
19 MADELINE STREET
(Near Public Baths).

Carte de Visite Portraits, 15s. per dozen. A choice collection of Views of Victoria always on sale. All descriptions of Photographic Portraits taken.

MR. E. POULTON,
ARCHITECT AND SURVEYOR,
190 MORAY STREET,
EMERALD HILL.

OFFICE: 58 ELIZABETH ST., MELBOURNE.

WILKINSON & CO.,
VICTORIA GRINDING AND BLACKING MILLS,
59 DUDLEY ST., WEST MELBOURNE.

Manufacturers of Coke and Charcoal Blacking and Coal Dust. Wood (cut), Coke, Coals, Redgum Charcoal, always on hand.

W. DAVIS,
Importer of Jewelry, Perfumery, Cutlery, Fancy Goods, Brushware, &c.,
111 RUSSELL STREET, MELBOURNE.

MISCELLANEOUS DEPOT.

CLELAND'S ORIGINAL STORE,
The oldest establishment and principal place of the kind in Victoria.

The highest Price given for Ladies' and Gentlemen's Left-off Clothing.

The largest, cheapest, and best stock of Ladies' and Gentlemen's Second-hand Clothing of every description, with a variety of Miscellaneous Articles too numerous to mention. Letters promptly attended to. A respectable Suit for either Lady or Gentleman, from 10s.

Cleland's, 87, 89, and 91 Stephen street, Melbourne.

HENRY GENDERS,

56 Elizabeth street, Melbourne,

GENERAL NEWSPAPER AND

ADVERTISING AGENT,

PRINTER, PUBLISHER,

BOOKSELLER AND STATIONER.

ADVERTISEMENTS AND SUBSCRIPTIONS FOR EVERY NEWSPAPER AND MAGAZINE PUBLISHED.

COUNTRY ORDERS PUNCTUALLY ATTENDED TO.

ENGLISH NEWSPAPER AND PERIODICAL DEPOT.

ADVANCES ON WOOL, STATIONS, STOCK, &c.

R. GOLDSBROUGH & CO.,
WOOL BROKERS,
STOCK AND STATION AGENTS,

BOURKE AND WILLIAM STREETS, MELBOURNE,

ARE PREPARED TO MAKE LIBERAL

CASH ADVANCES, on most favourable terms, on the
ENSUING CLIP OF WOOL,
Whether for Sale or Shipment; also

ON STOCK, STATIONS, AND ALL DESCRIPTIONS OF SQUATTING SECURITIES.

Station Accounts, and all Departments of Financial Business in connection with the Pastoral Interest, promptly attended to.

Auction Sales of Wool and Pastoral Produce held **Weekly**, during the Season.

STANDARD HOTEL.

JOHN CHURCHMAN, Proprietor.

EASTERN MARKET,
Corner of Stephen and Little Collins streets,

MELBOURNE.

J. W. HOME,
MANUFACTURER AND IMPORTER,
a'BECKETT ST. and corner of ELIZABETH and LATROBE STREETS,
MELBOURNE.

Stationary and Portable Engines, Force and Lift Pumps, Agricultural Implements, Wine Presses and Grape Mills, Wool Presses (patent), 2, 4, and 6-horse Bone Mills, AND ALL DESCRIPTIONS OF GENERAL MACHINERY.
Illustrated Catalogue sent free by post.

T. FLINTOFF & CO.,
British Wines, Liqueur, Cordial, Malt Vinegar,
AND BLACKING MANUFACTURERS.
Manufactory, 97 Webb st., Fitzroy; Warehouse, 18 Queen st., Melbourne.
ESTABLISHED 1853.

T. FLINTOFF and Co.'s celebrated Orange, Stomach, Stoughton and Brandy Bitters.
T. FLINTOFF and Co.'s celebrated Malt Vinegar, in hhds., qr.-casks, and 2, 3, and 4 dozen cases.
T. FLINTOFF and Co.'s celebrated Japan Blacking, in large, middle, and small size bottles.
T. FLINTOFF and Co.'s celebrated Paste Blacking, in small and large tins ; packets in gross and half-gross boxes.

J. NEEDHAM, SENR., & SON
(After 38 years' experience)
Having made further improvements in their well-known and hitherto highly successful method of

INSTRUCTION IN WRITING,
Invite all bad writers to give them a call at their establishments,
145 & 84 ELIZABETH ST.

The system established by them is calculated to enable any one to acquire a good Commercial Hand in a very few lessons, and on the most reasonable terms. *Bona fide* specimens of original writing, and improvements in each case, can be seen at the Head Offices, 83 and 84 Elizabeth street.

BOOK-KEEPING, by single and double entry, taught practically in one week. The FRENCH and GERMAN LANGUAGES taught.—EVENING CLASSES.

PETER SKIRVING

RESPECTFULLY announces to his friends throughout the Western District that he has always in stock a choice and very excellent assortment of **New Seasonable Goods**, comprising Imported Clothing, Hosiery, Shirts, Hats, &c., and all the various articles included in the Outfitting Trade. Visitors, therefore, can at once be furnished with every requisite for a complete and fashionable outfit.

But he would more particularly call attention to those goods of his **own Manufacture**, viz., **Colonial Clothing**; being made on the premises, thoroughly shrunk, and of excellent material, they are unrivalled for town or country wear, and the fast-increasing demand shows how high they already stand in public estimation.

In garments made to measure, it has been his constant aim to produce durable and moderately-priced articles, and, having always on hand a large variety of the season's Tweeds, he is enabled now to make to order, for cash, fashionable and superior

TWEED TROUSERS

at the extremely moderate price of

Twenty-Two Shillings per Pair,

An amount not more than is generally charged for imported goods.

Trusting, therefore, that his endeavours to produce a good article, at a moderate price, may meet with continued support and approval, all orders, either personally or by post, shall be promptly executed.

PETER SKIRVING,

EDINBURGH HOUSE,
58 MOORABOOL STREET,
GEELONG.

GEELONG SAVINGS' BANK.

TRUSTEES.

Hon. Robert C. Hope, M.D.
John Guthrie, Esq., J.P.
George Thomas, Esq.
James Balfour, Esq., J.P., M.L.A.
James O. Carstairs, Esq., M.D.

Alfred Douglass, Esq., J.P.
John R. Morris, Esq., J.P.
Vincent W. Giblin, Esq., J.P.
Thomas M. Harrington, Esq.

Open for RECEIVING DEPOSITS, DAILY, from 10 till 2 o'clock, and on SATURDAY EVENING, from 6 till 8 o'clock;
And for MAKING PAYMENTS TO DEPOSITORS on WEDNESDAY, from 10 till 2 o'clock.

ALFRED B. REED, Actuary.

GEORGE WISE,
Bookseller, Stationer, and Librarian.

English Papers and Periodicals supplied by every mail.
A good assortment of De la Rue's PLAIN AND FANCY STATIONERY always on hand.

81 MOORABOOL STREET, GEELONG.

W. F. DUCKER & Co.,
AUCTIONEERS,
Accountants, Arbitrators, Valuators, Auditors, Loan and Share Brokers,

House, Land, Estate, and General Commission Agents.

LITTLE MALOP STREET WEST, GEELONG.

PRESTON'S HOTEL,
GREAT RYRIE STREET, GEELONG.

J. F. GRIGGS
(Late of the Frenchman's Hotel, Creswy),

Has opened the above central hotel, and solicits the patronage of the public, assuring them that every article retailed by him will be of the best quality, and that the general arrangements of the hotel will be such as to ensure the further support of all who may favour him with one visit.

GOOD STABLING FREE.

STONEHAM'S
TEMPERANCE HOTEL,
PROVIDENCE RISE,
YARRA STREET, GEELONG,
NEAR THE WHARF.
STABLING FREE.

STEAM PACKET HOTEL,
YARRA STREET, GEELONG.

Excellent Accommodation as a Family and Commercial Hotel. Wines, Spirits, and Ales, of the best quality.

FIRST-CLASS BEDROOMS FOR SINGLE GENTLEMEN.

TIMOTHY RIEDY, Proprietor.

Persons visiting Geelong will find this Hotel very conveniently situated near the Pier.

Yarra street, Geelong, 1866.

VULCAN FOUNDRY.

HUMBLE & Co.,
ENGINEERS, SMITHS,
Iron and Brass Founders,
LITTLE MALOP STREET, GEELONG.

Wool Presses,   Thrashing Machines,
    Agricultural Implements,   Crab Winches,
    Wood's Patent Wool-Washers,

AND EVERY DESCRIPTION OF

MINING PLANT, MADE TO ORDER,
ON THE SHORTEST NOTICE.

JOHN TREMAIN,
PASTRYCOOK AND CONFECTIONER,
MALOP STREET, GEELONG.

Superior Dining Rooms and Restaurant,
MOORABOOL STREET, GEELONG.
G. HAASY, Proprietor.

TERMINUS HOTEL,
MERCER STREET, GEELONG.
MARY BEDFORD, Proprietor.

The above is a First-class Family and Commercial Hotel. The Wines, Spirits, and Liquors are of the very best quality, and charges moderate.

Geelong Homœopathic Pharmacy, 39 Ryrie st., Geelong,
(Nearly opposite the Mechanics' Institute)

CONDUCTED by JOHN OWEN (successor to EDWARD G. GOULD), Dispenser to the Geelong Homœopathic Dispensary, Homœopathic Chemist. Medicine Chests and Books, for family use. Cases re-filled. All the Standard Books and Periodicals. Veterinary Medicines.

R. ROCHE, Moorabool street, Geelong,
(Opposite the Grammar School)
WHEELWRIGHT, BLACKSMITH, AND SHOEING SMITH;
Waggon, Dray, and Spring Cart Maker.
ALL NEW WORK WARRANTED.

J. STOCK, Whitesmith and Machinist,
MERCER STREET, near Railway Station, GEELONG.

ESTABLISHED 1857.—Maker and Patentee of Green's TABACI SECTOR. Wool and Wine Press Screws to order, and all kinds of Machinery made and repaired. Country orders punctually attended to.

JOHN CURNOW,
Hay, Corn, and General Produce Store,
GREAT RYRIE STREET, GEELONG.

E. STONE, 6 Ryrie street west,
(Two doors from Moorabool street)

WHOLESALE and Retail Dealer in Haberdashery, Jewelry, Watches, Cutlery, Toys, Stationery, Perfumery, Brushware, Fancy Goods, Berlin Wools, &c. Storekeepers, Hawkers, &c., supplied at Melbourne Prices.

NORTH GRANT

Family and Commercial Hotel,

BRIDGE STREET, BALLARAT.

THOS. WIGGINS, Proprietor.

The above is a First-class Family and Commercial Hotel, affording every comfort and convenience to travellers of every description.

The Wines, Spirits, and Liquors are of the first quality, and charges strictly moderate.

BIGNELL'S UNION HOTEL.

WILLIAM BIGNELL, Proprietor.

STURT STREET, BALLARAT.

The above is a First-class Family and Commercial Hotel, affording every comfort and convenience which expense and attention can procure.

The Wines, Spirits, and Liquors are of the best brands, and the tariff moderate.

JOHN WALKER & Co.,

ENGINEERS & FOUNDERS,

UNION FOUNDRY,

DRUMMOND STREET,

BALLARAT.

C. HUMPHRIS,

ENGINEER & MACHINIST,

(Opposite the Railway Station)

ARMSTRONG AND LYDIARD STREETS,

BALLARAT.

Steam Engines, Mining and Agricultural Machinery, repaired at lowest charges. Smiths' Work and Brass Castings, at the shortest notice.

SOLOMON & BARDWELL,

PHOTOGRAPHERS,

STURT STREET,

BALLARAT.

VISITORS TO BALLARAT ARE INVITED TO CALL AND EXAMINE SPECIMENS.

PANORAMAS OF BALLARAT ON SALE.

TYNAN BROS.,

Agricultural Implement Manufacturers,

STURT STREET,

BALLARAT.

MINING MACHINERY.

Mining Companies and others requiring STEAM ENGINES or any other description of Machinery for Mining purposes, are invited to inspect the stock on Sale by the undersigned, comprising—Steam Engines, Boilers, Pumps, Winding Gear, Puddling Machines, Quartz-crushing Batteries, &c., at half the usual prices.

THOMAS DAVEY & CO.,
IRON MERCHANTS & IMPORTERS OF MACHINERY,
BALLARAT.

QUEEN'S ARCADE FURNISHING BAZAAR,

LONSDALE STREET EAST, MELBOURNE.

LONSDALE STREET EAST, MELBOURNE.

COHEN BROTHERS,
UPHOLSTERERS
AND
MANUFACTURERS
OF EVERY DESCRIPTION OF
DINING AND DRAWING ROOM, LIBRARY, OFFICE, AND BEDROOM FURNITURE, BEDDING, &c.,

Invite Parties about to Furnish to inspect their spacious Premises, at the above address, which are replete with a large and varied Stock of

CABINET FURNITURE, IRON AND BRASS BEDSTEADS, CARPETS and all kinds of UPHOLSTERY.

Messrs. COHEN BROTHERS beg to call the especial attention of the Public to their long experience in the Manufacturing Department, and beg to inform them that they can and will supply Goods at Twenty per cent. less than any other firm in Victoria.

The House where you can get the best value for your Money:

QUEEN'S ARCADE FURNISHING BAZAAR,
LONSDALE STREET EAST, MELBOURNE.

BRANCH ESTABLISHMENTS:
Maclaggan Street, Dunedin,
Weld Street, Hokitika, and } New Zealand.
Revill Street, „

SOLE PROPRIETORS,

ADVERTISEMENTS.

Go where you get the best Value for your Money,

QUEEN'S ARCADE
FURNISHING BAZAAR,

Where you can inspect the Manufacturing of every article of Furniture, suitable for the Cottage or the Mansion.

A LARGE ASSORTMENT ALWAYS ON HAND OF

ENGLISH AND AMERICAN FURNITURE,

DIRECT FROM THE MANUFACTURERS.

CHESTS OF DRAWERS,
TOILET, CHIMNEY, AND OTHER GLASSES,
ESPECIALLY MADE FOR THE CLIMATE.

A CHEAP STOCK OF
SOFAS, COUCHES, AND EASY CHAIRS,
IN HAIRCLOTH AND LEATHER, ARE ALSO OPEN FOR INSPECTION.

TABLES AND WASHSTANDS,
IN ENDLESS NUMBERS, AND OF ALL WOODS AND MAKES,
AND EVERY REQUISITE FOR

HOUSE FURNISHING

MANUFACTURED ON THE PREMISES.

AN IMMENSE STOCK OF
BRASS AND IRON BEDSTEADS AND BEDDING,
IN GREAT VARIETY.

SOLE PROPRIETORS,

COHEN BROTHERS,
QUEEN'S ARCADE FURNISHING BAZAAR,
LONSDALE STREET EAST, MELBOURNE.

BRANCH ESTABLISHMENTS:

MRS. FRANCIS,
VICTORIA REGISTRY OFFICE,
ARMSTRONG STREET,
Six doors from Mair st., Ballarat.

Servants of all classes carefully selected for private families, hotels, stations, farms, town or country, personally, or by order.
ALL ORDERS PROMPTLY EXECUTED.

CAESAR KIESER, M.D.,
CONSULTATION ROOMS,
118 MAIR STREET,
BALLARAT.

RICHARD KING,
Veterinary and Shoeing Forge,
VICTORIA STREET, BALLARAT EAST.

SIX PRIZES OBTAINED IN BALLARAT FOR SHOEING.

THOMAS TRENGROVE,
VETERINARY SURGEON.
Shoeing Forge:
BATH'S STREET.
Private Residence:
STURT AND URQUHART STREETS.

BALLARAT COLLEGE,
STURT STREET, BALLARAT.
Established July, 1864.

PRINCIPAL, ROBT. OLIVER McCOY, M.A., Glasgow and Melbourne.

COLLEGE COMMITTEE.

The Rev. William Henderson (Convener); the Rev. Duncan Fraser; Michael Elliot, Esq., Bank of Australasia; George Gordon Mackay, Esq., London Chartered Bank; John Winter, Esq., Lauderdale; Gilbert Duncan, Esq., Mayor of Ballarat; James Johnston, Esq., Mount Lodge; William Strachan, Esq., Melbourne.

LECTURERS.
Rev. WILLIAM HENDERSON, *English Language and Literature*.
ROBERT FAWELL HUDSON, M.D., *Natural Science*.

MASTERS.

English and Classics	ANDREW CHAMBERS, B.A., Honorman in French, English, Classics, and Mathematics, Queen's University.
Mathematics and Commercial Subjects	JOHN STRUDWICKR.
Vocal Music	AUSTIN T. TURNER.
Instrumental Music	AUSTIN T. TURNER.
Reading and Elocution	THOMAS PADMORE HILL.
Drawing	CANUTE ANDERSEN (of the Royal Society of Fine Arts, Copenhagen).
French	CANUTE ANDERSEN.
German	CANUTE ANDERSEN.
Dancing and Deportment	HENRY S. NUGENT.
Gymnastics	WILLIAM TIMMERMAN.

Terms, including Vocal Music and admission to Lectures:—
(PAYABLE QUARTERLY IN ADVANCE.)

SENIOR DEPARTMENT (per quarter).—Day Pupils, 3 Guineas; Day Boarders 7 Guineas; Resident Boarders, 18 Guineas.
JUNIOR DEPARTMENT (per quarter).—Day Pupils, 2 Guineas; Day Boarders, 6 Guineas; Resident Boarders, 16 Guineas.
EXTRA BRANCHES (per quarter).—Instrumental Music, 3 Guineas; Drawing, 1 Guinea; French, 1 Guinea; German, 1 Guinea; Dancing and Deportment, 1 Guinea; Gymnastics, ½ Guinea.

The CURRICULUM OF STUDY embraces a complete course of instruction in all the branches of a thorough English, Commercial, Mathematical, and Classical Education. For Junior Boys the course is elementary, and comprises Spelling, Reading, Writing, Arithmetic, Grammar, Geography, History, the elements of Latin, Music, and Natural Science. The utmost care is taken that every boy is well grounded in the subjects taught, before being advanced to a higher stage.

There are two definite courses of study, each connected with the termination of the Elementary Course—the one affording a complete preparation for the University and Learned Professions; the other for Mercantile life and the ordinary avocations of business. In the former, special attention is given to Latin, Greek, and Mathematics; in the latter, Modern Languages and the usual Commercial Branches occupy the chief place. In both Courses alike, English in all its branches forms a principal part, and, from its vast importance, receives marked attention.

VOCAL MUSIC is included in the regular course of study. There are also open to all the Students of the College, without extra charge, Special Courses of Lectures on the English Language and Literature, Natural Science, and other interesting and important subjects, by gentlemen of acknowledged ability.

CLASSIFICATION.—All the boys are classified according to their progress in English, Classics, Mathematics, Modern Languages, and Commercial subjects, respectively, without reference to their proficiency in any of the others.

The Religious Instruction is Scriptural, without regard to Denominational distinctions. In this branch the attendance or non-attendance of the pupils is altogether optional, and in accordance with the wishes of parents and guardians. Particular attention is directed to the moral conduct and demeanour of the Pupils.

PHYSICAL EDUCATION.—The Physical comfort of the pupils, while at work, is secured by large and well-ventilated class-rooms; each class has a separate room. The situation of the College in the highest and healthiest part of the town, in a very spacious reserve, offers seasonal facilities for cricket, foot-ball, and every variety of healthful exercise. All the pupils of the College have the opportunity of being instructed in the Art of Swimming, at the splendid Baths recently constructed at Ballarat.

In the BOARDING DEPARTMENT, the advantages of instruction in the public classes are combined with the careful supervision and training of the boarders by the Principal and Resident Masters, in the preparation of their work.

A. McINTOSH,
BOILER MAKER
AND
GENERAL BLACKSMITH,
YUILLE STREET, BALLARAT.

Tanks, Trucks, and Cages made to order on the shortest notice, and moderate terms.

HICKMAN & SON,
Boiler Makers, Blacksmiths, &c.,
68 MAIR STREET, BALLARAT.

Boilers, Tanks, Girders, &c., made on the shortest notice, and at moderate prices.

G. JACKSON,
CARRIAGE BUILDER,
AND
GENERAL SMITH,
BRIDGE ST., BALLARAT.

JOHN GIBB & Co.,
ENGINEERS, MILLWRIGHTS,
AND
AGRICULTURAL MACHINE MAKERS,
Mair street, above Market Square, Ballarat.

PRIZE MACHINE—REAPING, MOWING.
All kinds of Machinery made and repaired without delay. Iron and Brass Castings.

J. WARREN WHITE,
Stock & Share Broker, General Commission Agent,
LYDIARD STREET, BALLARAT.

Cash advances made on Freehold, Mining Scrip, and other Securities.

Agent for LONDON AND AUSTRALIAN AGENCY COMPANY, "Limited," (late J. H. Clough & Co.,) where Wool can be received, cartage paid, and forwarded to the Company's stores, Melbourne.

Proposals received for advances on coming Clip and Station properties.

STATION AND STORE SHEEP ALWAYS ON HAND.

W. GLENNIE,
BOOT AND SHOE WAREHOUSE,
Opposite *Star* Office,
STURT STREET, BALLARAT.

R. DIXON,
BOOKSELLER AND STATIONER.
Combs, Brushes, and Perfumery. All kinds of Fancy Goods.
TOBACCO, CIGARS, MATCHES, PIPES, &c.

Hotels, Storekeepers, and Hawkers, supplied with all kinds of China, Glass, and Earthenware, at Melbourne Prices.

ALMANACS, WHOLESALE AND RETAIL.

235 MAIR STREET, Ballarat.

J. R. GRUNDY,
WHOLESALE
Tobacco and Cigar Merchant,
114 MAIN ROAD, BALLARAT EAST.

ADVANCE BALLARAT!
J. WALKER
(LATE MORRISON & WALKER),

PRACTICAL HATTER,
78 BRIDGE STREET, BALLARAT.

The best selection of Hats and Caps in the District. Every style of Hat made to order and a perfect fit guaranteed.

WILLIAM HERD,
FAMILY GROCER,
WINE AND SPIRIT MERCHANT,
COMMERCIAL ROAD, TARNAGULLA.

JOHN PIERCE,
WHOLESALE
GROCER, IRONMONGER,
WINE AND SPIRIT MERCHANT,
COMMERCIAL ROAD, TARNAGULLA.

C. WALLER & COMPANY'S
Royal Mail Line of Coaches
LEAVES
LEWIN'S GOLDEN AGE HOTEL, Tarnagulla; and
GUNN'S GLASGOW ARMS, Kangaroo Flat, Bendigo;
DAILY.
C. WALLER & Co., Proprietors.

London Chartered Bank of Australia.

INCORPORATED BY ROYAL CHARTER, 1852.

PAID-UP CAPITAL, ONE MILLION STERLING.

LONDON OFFICE, 17 CANNON ST., CITY, E.C.

MARYBOROUGH BRANCH.

AGENCIES AT

TALBOT, MAJORCA, REDBANK, LANDSBOROUGH.

**INTEREST ALLOWED ON DEPOSITS.
DRAFTS ISSUED.
GOLD PURCHASED OR RECEIVED FOR ASSAY.
JAMES ANDERSON, Manager.**

THE PORTLAND GUARDIAN

(ESTABLISHED 1843)

PUBLISHED EVERY MONDAY AND THURSDAY,

HAS A

WIDE CIRCULATION IN THE WESTERN DISTRICT,

AND WILL BE FOUND

A SUITABLE MEDIUM FOR TRADE ADVERTISEMENTS
Meant to meet the eye of settlers in Normanby and the colony generally.

The *Guardian* is filed in most of the public institutes of the colony; by Gordon & Gotch, Melbourne; F. Algar Holloway, and G. Street, London; and by Willert & Berger, Paris; by whom orders for the paper, and advertisements, will be received.

WILLIAM COOPER.

PROPRIETOR AND PUBLISHER,

GAWLER STREET, PORTLAND.

BUSH INN,
PURNAM.

JOHN KAVANAGH, Proprietor.

A well selected stock of Wines, Spirits, and Liquors always on hand. Good Accommodation and moderate charges.

SUPERIOR STABLING.

CRESSY HOTEL,
CRESSY.

A. JONES, Proprietor.

The above Hotel affords excellent accommodation to travellers of every description.

The Wines, Spirits, and Liquors are of the best quality.
Stabling, superior.

MOUNT ELEPHANT HOTEL AND STORE

D. WATSON, Proprietor.

Wines, Spirits, and Liquors of the best brands and choicest description always on hand.

JOHN CAMERON,
Saddler and Harness Maker,
MORTLAKE.

ELTHAM FAMILY HOTEL,
ELTHAM.

Wines and Spirits of the best quality. Good Stabling.
B. O. WALLIS, Proprietor.

POST-OFFICE STORE,
DARLINGTON
(ELEPHANT BRIDGE).

SHOLTO DOUGLAS HODGSON,
DRUGGIST, &c., and
GENERAL STOREKEEPER.

Drugs, Groceries, Drapery, Ironmongery, &c., of the best quality, and at reasonable prices.

ROBERT MILLS,
Wholesale and Retail
GROCER AND PROVISION MERCHANT,
VINCENT STREET,
DAYLESFORD.

CRAMOND & DICKSON,
DRAPERS, GROCERS, IRONMONGERS,
AND
WINE AND SPIRIT MERCHANTS,
PENSHURST.

MELBOURNE, SANDHURST, and ECHUCA RAILWAY.
RUNNYMEDE STATION.

GRIFFIN & LAWRENCE,
FORWARDING & COMMISSION AGENTS,
LICENSED CARRIERS, &c.

Goods forwarded to all parts of the surrounding district.
Waggons dispatched daily for Rushworth and the Goulburn River District.
Wool or Goods stored.

JAMES SHACKELL & CO.
GENERAL AUCTIONEERS,
FOR VICTORIA AND NEW SOUTH WALES;
LAND, STOCK, STATION, AND WOOL AGENTS;
ARBITRATORS AND VALUERS;
RIVER STEAM BOAT AND CUSTOM HOUSE AGENTS.
BUSINESS PREMISES:
HALL OF COMMERCE AND COMMERCIAL CHAMBERS,
HIGH STREET, ECHUCA.

GOULBURN RIVER
STEAM SAW MILLS,
AND
CARRON TIMBER YARD,
ECHUCA.
ALEXANDER AMOS & Co., Proprietors.

W. W. MOORE,
COMMERCIAL TIMBER YARD,
Contractor, Undertaker, &c.,
HIGH STREET, ECHUCA.

N.B.—*Building Materials of every description always in Stock. Joiners' Work made on the premises, workmanship guaranteed.*

A TRIAL RESPECTFULLY SOLICITED.

Royal Hotel and Livery Stables,
VIEW POINT, SANDHURST.

The Proprietor begs to call the attention of Travellers and others visiting Sandhurst to the above, which is replete with every convenience. The table will be found liberally supplied. Charges strictly moderate. In the Billiard Room is one of Thurston's best tables. A civil marker always in attendance.

WINES, SPIRITS, AND ALES OF THE CHOICEST BRAND.
Livery and Bait Stables.   Saddle and Harness Horses on Hire.

A. TURNER, Proprietor.

JAMES INGLIS,
GROCER,
WINE, SPIRIT, AND PROVISION MERCHANT,
AND
General Storekeeper,
WHITE HILLS, SANDHURST.

HUNTLY
STEAM SAW MILLS
HOSKINS & COMPANY, Proprietors,
HUNTLY.

Orders promptly attended to.

HENRY SULOSHIN,
AUCTIONEER, VALUATOR,
Land and Estate and General Commission Agent,
DENILIQUIN, NEW SOUTH WALES.

N.B.—Parties in Victoria desiring information about Persons or Districts situate in or near the Murray, Murrumbidgee, Darling, and Back countries in New South Wales, apply above address.

BURTON'S RED BANK HOTEL
MATHOURA,
Half-way between Echuca and Deniliquin.

First-class Accommodation for Families and Gentlemen. Beautiful garden and vineyard. Fishing and shooting. The choicest Wines, Spirits, Beers, &c. Good Stabling and attentive Grooms. Cobb & Co.'s Coaches daily. Hay, Oats, Chaff, and Stores for Overlanders. Good Yards for Cattle.

HENRY BURTON, Proprietor.

BURTON'S NATIONAL CIRCUS travels annually from Adelaide to Rockhampton, performing at all the Townships and Gold-fields.

TAYLOR'S
ROYAL FAMILY HOTEL,
END STREET, DENILIQUIN,
NEW SOUTH WALES.

HOT AND COLD BATHS.
J. TAYLOR, Proprietor.

SANDERS & SON,
Nurserymen, Seedsmen, & Florists,
DENILIQUIN.

Gardens Laid Out and attended to by the Day, Week, or Year.

Contracts for Gardens, Orchards, &c., on the lowest possible terms. Seeds of all descriptions always on hand.

CAFE DE PARIS.
EDWIN & ST. TEUS,
PASTRY COOKS, CONFECTIONERS, & FRUITERERS
(Opposite the Telegraph Office),
DENILIQUIN.
FAMILIES AND THE TRADE SUPPLIED.

TATCHELL'S ROYAL HOTEL,
INGLEWOOD.

PRIVATE SITTING ROOMS.   LOFTY BEDROOMS.
FIRST-CLASS STABLING.   SADDLE HORSES AND BUGGIES.

TABLE D'HOTE, SIX O'CLOCK.

JAMES WILSON & CO.,
Wholesale General Merchants.

Wines, Spirits, Groceries, Timber, Iron, Furniture, Paints, Oils, Paperhangings, &c.

BROOKE STREET, INGLEWOOD; AND BROADWAY, DUNOLLY.

E. HILLILES,
Soda-water, Ginger Beer, & Cordial Manufacturer,
HIGH STREET, AVOCA.

Agent for COHN BROTHERS, Talbot Brewery.

THOMAS COOPER,
GENERAL AGENT,
AND
Share Broker,
ALBERT STREET, CRESWICK.

MOUNT BLOWHARD HOTEL,
AND
POST-OFFICE STORE.

The above hotel is situated

HALF-WAY BETWEEN BALLARAT & CLUNES,

Where every attention will be paid to travellers and the general public.

Best quality of Wines, Spirits, and Oilmen's Stores, always on hand.

DAVID WILSON, Proprietor.

MOUNT IDA HOTEL,
HIGH STREET, HEATHCOTE.

PRIVATE APARTMENTS FOR FAMILIES AND TRAVELLERS.

BILLIARD ROOMS.

Saddle and Harness Horses on hire.

A. H. R. MORRIS, Proprietor.

T. WALDER & Co.,
GENERAL STOREKEEPERS,
NUGGETY HILL AND CHAPEL HILL,

FRYER'S CREEK.

GOLD BOUGHT IN ANY QUANTITY. THE HIGHEST PRICE GIVEN.

WALTER JOHN GILLARD,
Saddler and Harness Manufacturer,
MAIN STREET, KINGSTON.

Farmers and Squatters supplied with a first-class article, of colonial manufacture, at moderate prices.

N.B.—Repairs executed neatly.   Orders punctually attended to.   A trial most respectfully solicited.

MOORE BROTHERS,
WHOLESALE AND RETAIL
STOREKEEPERS, IRONMONGERS, &c.,
WHOLESALE
Wine, Spirit, Timber, and Iron Merchants.

FLOUR, OATS, BRAN, CHAFF, &C.
BOOT, SHOE,
AND
GENERAL OUTFITTING ESTABLISHMENT.
CHINA, GLASS, AND EARTHENWARE.

FRYER'S TOWN;
AND AT
Latrobe street east, Melbourne.

PATRICK FOGARTY,
GENERAL STOREKEEPER,
(POST-MASTER FOR THE DISTRICT)
MAIN ROAD, LAMPLOUGH.

RAILWAY HOTEL AND STORE,
OPPOSITE THE RAILWAY STATION,
RUNNYMEDE.

The above hotel is replete with every convenience for travellers and others. Choice selection of Wines, Spirits, Ale, &c.

FIRST-CLASS STABLING.   MODERATE CHARGES.

GEORGE SCOTT, Proprietor.

Advertisements.   31

JAMES GORIE,
TAILOR AND CLOTHIER,
LIEBEG STREET,
WARRNAMBOOL.

JOHN PERRY,
COACHBUILDERS', IRONMONGERS',
AND
WHEELWRIGHTS' TIMBER MERCHANT.

STEAM-BENT and SAWN TIMBER

ON HAND and BENT TO ORDER.

Laterwood	Redgum	Circular Fronts	Elm
Hickory	Bluegum	Roof Sticks	Blackwood and
Ash	Ash	Seat Arms	Box Naves
Ironbark	Beech and	Foot Rails	Hickory, Ash
Blackwood	Oak	Lazy Backs	Oak, Ironbark
Gincgum	Felloes	Top Rails	Beech, Blackwood
Shafts and	Felloe Rims	Loo Table and	Blue and Red Gum
Spokes	Fender Ends	Sieve Rims	Plank

AMERICAN AND ENGLISH AXLES AND SPRINGS.

JOHN PERRY, 165 and 167 Russell street, and 83 Lonsdale street.
Country Orders Promptly attended to.

WM. McDONALD,
Agricultural, General Seedsman, & Florist,

128
Bourke st. east,
MELBOURNE.

128
Bourke st. east,
MELBOURNE.

(Opposite the Wax Works.)
EXPERIENCED GARDENERS RECOMMENDED.

T. ROBINSON & Co.,
MILLWRIGHTS, ENGINEERS, AND AGRICULTURAL IMPLEMENT MANUFACTURERS AND IMPORTERS,
247 ELIZABETH STREET, MELBOURNE.

T. ROBINSON & CO.'S Patent Post-Hole Borer for Wire Fencing.

This Machine is specially adapted for Boring Holes in Fencing that is already fixed, so as to insert Wire between the Rails. One Man will bore a Mile of upright fixed Fencing per day ready to receive the Wire.

Wind Mills (self-regulating); Grass Mowing Machines for Station Use; Improved Water-Lift for Sheep Washing, Irrigating, &c.; extra strong Wool Presses; Earth Scoops and strong Wood Ploughs; Iron Whim Work; Wood, Iron, and Canvass Water Buckets; Water Carts, with Teak Hose and Pump complete; Mowing and Reaping Machines, Horse Hay Rakes; Thrashing Machines, Horse and Steam Power.

Agricultural Implements and Machines of every description.
247 ELIZABETH STREET, MELBOURNE.

STANDARD HOTEL.
JAMES CHURCHMAN, Proprietor.
EASTERN MARKET,
Corner of Stephen and Little Collins streets,
MELBOURNE.

LANG & CO.,
LIME AND CEMENT MERCHANTS,
38 QUEEN STREET,

Have always on Sale—Bendo and Geelong Roche Lime, landing daily. Best brands Portland Cement and Plaster of Paris, Laths, Nails, Plasterers' Hair. Glazed Earthenware Drain Pipes, Bends and Junctions. English, Colonial, and Chinese Paving Tiles, Fire Bricks, Fire Lumps, and Fire Clay.
Chimney Tops, Hearthstones, Chimney Pieces, &c., &c.

GIPPS LAND STEAM NAVIGATION COMPANY
(LIMITED).

THE COMPANY'S FAST AND FAVOURITE STEAMSHIPS,

SAMSON, Captain LAPTHORNE;
AND
CHARLES EDWARD, Captain Darby;

LEAVE THE QUEEN'S WHARF,

EVERY TUESDAY AND FRIDAY.

AT ELEVEN A.M.

Passengers are conveyed to Sale by Coach, leaving immediately on the Steamer's arrival.

PASSAGES AT REDUCED RATES.

For information apply to the Company's Offices,

97 Collins street west, Melbourne.

The Land Mortgage Bank of Victoria
(LIMITED),
FOR DEPOSITS AND LOANS ON FREEHOLDS.

Incorporated under the Companies' Statute, 1864.

CAPITAL—Authorised, £500,000; Subscribed, £50,000; Paid-up, £10,000.
OFFICES: COLLINS STREET WEST.

Directors.
HON. C. J. JENNER, M.L.C., CHAIRMAN.
HON. JOHN M'CRAE, M.L.C., VICE-CHAIRMAN.

HON. D. E. WILKIE, M.D., M.L.C. | WILLIAM DETMOLD, Esq., COLLINS STREET.
ROBERT BYRNE, Esq., J.P., M.L.A. | JOHN SPENCE OGILVY, Esq., QUEEN ST.
JOSEPH CLARKE, Esq., WAREHOUSEMAN. | GEORGE WHARTON, Esq., J.P., ARCHITECT.

Solicitor—JOHN HUGHES CLAYTON, Esq.
Accountant—WILLIAM SINCOCK, Esq.
Manager—WILLIAM PATERSON MUIR, Esq.
Bankers—THE NATIONAL BANK OF AUSTRALASIA.

Deposit Receipts are issued, and Interest is allowed at the following rates:—

On Deposits for 12 Months (fixed) .. .. 7 per cent. per annum.
Do. 6 Months do. .. .. 5 do. do.
Do. 3 Months do. .. .. 4 do. do.
Do. at Call .. .. 2½ do. do.

The Deposits of the Bank are secured by the whole of its Invested Funds, and by the additional guarantee of the uncalled Capital.

The investment of the funds of the Bank is restricted by the Articles of Association to Real Estate in Victoria, and the amount of Deposits can never exceed the subscribed capital, thus affording to Depositors the most undoubted security.

The Bank also acts as General Financial Agent, and undertakes the Investment of the Capital of Absentees, Trustees, and others, in first-class Mortgages in Victoria, to pay Investors 8 per cent. per annum, the interest on such investments being guaranteed and paid half-yearly, at the Offices of the Bank.

W. PATERSON MUIR, Manager.

Agencies:
Geelong—A. C. Macdonald, Esq. Sandhurst—John McIntyre, Esq. Ballarat—Messrs. J. Oddie & Co.

JUST ISSUED, THE
NEW ZEALAND DIRECTORY,
For 1866-67,
WITH
CORRECT AND COMPLETE MAP,

Including Wellington, Auckland, Dunedin, Christchurch, Nelson, Hokitika, Greymouth, Napier, Wanganui, Picton, Blenheim, Lyttleton, Invercargill, Bluff, &c.

Price, ONE GUINEA. Sold by all Booksellers, and by

STEVENS & BARTHOLOMEW, Proprietors and Publishers,

48 FLINDERS LANE EAST.

OFFICE FOR PATENTS.
ESTABLISHED 1857.

PATENTS OBTAINED FOR GREAT BRITAIN, AMERICA,
AND ANY OF THE COLONIES, BY

E. WATERS, LATE HART & WATERS,
Little Collins street east, Melbourne.

WILLIAM DETMOLD,
Account-Book Manufacturer,
BOOKBINDER AND PAPER RULER.

Country Orders attended to with punctuality and dispatch.

35 Collins street east, Melbourne.

SNOW BROS. & Co.,
Licensed Railway Carriers,
Forwarding and General Commission Agents,

3 LITTLE COLLINS STREET WEST, MELBOURNE;

AND

KENEDY STREET, CASTLEMAINE.

Merchandise, Passengers, and Luggage Forwarded daily to all parts of the Colony. Goods Collected. Bills of Lading promptly attended to.

Advertisements.

NOTICE OF REMOVAL.

S. WALLWORTH,
HAT AND CAP MANUFACTURER AND IMPORTER,

Begs to announce that he has REMOVED from No. 4 Bourke st. to

9 BOURKE STREET EAST,

Nearly opposite his former premises, and adjoining the establishments of Messrs. Charlwood & Sons and Robertson & Moffat.

9 BOURKE STREET EAST, MELBOURNE.

Melbourne Stone and Marble Works,
CORNER OF
LONSDALE AND STEPHEN STREETS.

CHAMBERS & CLUTTEN,
STONE MERCHANTS,
Statuary, Monumental, and General Masons.

MINTON'S PATENT PAVING PLASTER AND CEMENT.

MARBLE AND SLATE CHIMNEYPIECES.

SLABS AND PAVING.

J. NICHOLSON,
Agricultural Implement Maker,
21 & 23 BOUVERIE ST., NORTH MELBOURNE.

Nicholson's Patent Self-acting Side Delivery Reaper. Nicholson's Patent Back Delivery Reaper.

For Prices and further particulars apply to the Patentee and Sole Manufactuer.

Advertisements.

G. E. A. KENNEY,

SADDLER,

67 STEPHEN STREET

(Near Eastern Market).

Colonial Riding Saddles made to order.

Trade, Storekeepers and Squatters supplied.

T. P. CLEMES,

Hat Manufacturer and Importer,

158 BOURKE STREET EAST,

(Near the Haymarket Theatre,)

MELBOURNE.

GOYDER'S HUNT CLUB HOTEL
LIVERY AND LETTING STABLES,
LITTLE COLLINS STREET EAST,
NEAR POLICE COURT.

S. HARDING begs to inform his friends and the public he has taken the above stables, and hopes by strict attention and moderate charges to obtain a share of their patronage.

BUGGIES, CARRIAGES, SADDLE HORSES,
HUNTERS, &c., FOR SALE AND HIRE,
HORSES BROKEN IN TO DOUBLE AND SINGLE HARNESS, OR SADDLE.

An Entrance in Royal Lane (opposite Theatre Royal) and Little Collins street. Gates always open and Grooms in attendance.

CHARGES STRICTLY MODERATE.

THE COMMERCIAL BANK OF AUSTRALIA LIMITED.

Duly Registered and Incorporated on the 3rd May, 1866, under "The Companies Statute, 1864;" Limiting the Liability of Shareholders to the extent of their shares.

HEAD OFFICE:
30 COLLINS STREET WEST, MELBOURNE.

CAPITAL, £500,000
(WITH POWER TO INCREASE TO £1,000,000)
IN 50,000 SHARES OF £10 EACH.

DIRECTORS:
GIDEON SCOTT LANG, ESQ., ST. KILDA (CHAIRMAN).
JOHN MACKENZIE, ESQ., J.P.
THOMAS MITCHELL, ESQ.
LESLIE JAMES SHERRARD, ESQ.

GENERAL MANAGER:
GEORGE VALLENTINE, ESQ.

SECRETARY AND INSPECTOR OF BRANCHES:
JAMES NAPIER, ESQ.

BANKERS:
THE COLONIAL BANK OF AUSTRALASIA.

SOLICITOR:
JOHN HUGHES CLAYTON, ESQ.

It is confidently expected that the Bank will be in a position to commence business on the 1st September. The terms on which business is to be conducted will be announced by separate advertisement.

THE
NATIONAL BANK OF AUSTRALASIA,

Incorporated by Acts of the Victorian and South Australian Parliaments.

CAPITAL - - £1,000,000.

IN 200,000 SHARES OF £5 EACH.

Directors.
THE HON. SIR FRANCIS MURPHY
(Speaker of the Legislative Assembly), CHAIRMAN.
ANDREW SUTHERLAND, Esq. | GEORGE MARTIN, Esq
THE HON. SIR JAMES FREDK. PALMER
(President of the Legislative Council).

Auditors.
THE HON. H. M. MURPHY, M.L.C. | HENRY HENTY, Esq., M.L.A.

Solicitors.
MESSRS. MALLESON AND ENGLAND.

FREDERICK WRIGHT, GENERAL MANAGER.
ALFRED PRIESTLEY, ACCOUNTANT

BRANCHES IN VICTORIA.

Bacchus Marsh	MANAGER: THOMAS N. BINNEY.
Ballaarat	ACTING-MANAGER: JOHN SALMON.
Buninyong	ACTING-MANAGER: THOMAS WALTERS.
Carngham	MANAGER: W. L. A. ELSTON.
Clunes	MANAGER: ALEXANDER G. DAVIDSON.
Colac	MANAGER: FREDK. J. HICKLING.
Coleraine	MANAGER: W. W. OSWALD.
Collingwood	MANAGER: F. W. THOMAS.
Daylesford	MANAGER: WILLIAM M. ALEXANDER.
Emerald Hill	MANAGER: JAMES M. CAMPBELL.
Geelong	LOCAL DIRECTORS: JAMES SIMSON, Esq. JOHN L. CURRIE, Esq. MANAGER: ROBERT GILLESPIE.
Hamilton	MANAGER: D. MACPHERSON.
Prahran	MANAGER: GEO. E. TOLHURST.
Richmond	MANAGER: CHAS. BAEYERTZ
Sale	MANAGER: CHARLES F. T. FARRAN.
Sandridge	MANAGER: W. LE CREN.
Scarsdale	MANAGER: M. W. RICHARDSON
Taradale	MANAGER: W. J. BUDD.
Bairnsdale Agency	ALEX. W. CUNNINGHAM, AGENT.

BRANCHES IN SOUTH AUSTRALIA.

ADELAIDE:

LOCAL DIRECTORS.

HON. A. BLYTH, Esq., M.P. | J. PEACOCK, Esq., M.P.
THOMAS GRAVES, Esq. | HON. A. SCOTT, M.L.C.

EDMUND MACKENZIE YOUNG, Manager.
RICHARD G. PROLE, Accountant.

Angaston	Acting-Manager: G. THOMSON.
Auburn	Manager: T. J. PLEYDELL.
Clare	Acting-Manager: W. GOOCH.
Gawler	Manager: J. T. WILLIAMS.
Kadina	Manager: C. FURNISS.
Kapunda	Manager: ROBERT NAIRNE.
Kooringa	Acting-Manager: W. H. ROSMAN, Jun.
Moonta	Acting-Manager: V. HANSEN.
Mount Barker	Manager: WILLIAM GRAY.
Mount Gambier	Manager: A. W. McGREGOR.
Nuriootpa	Manager: F. KARUTH.
Penola	Manager: W. F. REMINGTON.
Port Adelaide	Manager: H. D. O'HALLORAN.
Port Augusta	Acting-Manager: C. PAXTON.
Robe	Manager: HENRY LAW.
Strathalbyn	Manager: T. EVANS.
Wallaroo	Acting-Manager: H. C. HODGE.
Willunga	Acting-Manager: DANIEL BARKER.
Port MacDonnell Agency	T. MUST & CO., Agents.

WESTERN AUSTRALIA.

Perth Branch ... Manager: JOHN F. LAW.

FOREIGN AGENCIES.

New South Wales The Commercial Banking Company of Sydney.
Tasmania The Commercial Bank of Van Diemen's Land.
New Zealand—The Bank of New Zealand.
Queensland—The Commercial Banking Company of Sydney.
India and China—The Chartered Mercantile Bank of India, London and China.
Cape of Good Hope—The London and South African Bank.
Scotland—The National Bank of Scotland.
Ireland—The National Bank, The Provincial Bank of Ireland, The Ulster Banking Company.

LONDON OFFICE: 10 CORNHILL, E.C.

Directors.

J. W. MUTTLEBURY, Esq., Managing Director.
F. J. SARGOOD, Esq. | G. S. WALTERS, Esq.

Solicitors.

MESSRS. MAYNARD & SON.

THOMAS M. HARRINGTON, Manager.

The Melbourne Banking Corporation Limited.

INCORPORATED UNDER "THE COMPANIES STATUTE 1864."

Capital, fully subscribed, One Million (£1,000,000) Sterling.

WITH POWER TO INCREASE TO TWO MILLION.

Paid-up Capital, One Hundred Thousand Pounds (£100,000) Sterling.

DIRECTORS:

The Hon. J. P. BEAR	The Hon. Capt. MacMAHON
The Hon. WILLIAM HIGHETT	G. P. DESAILLY, Esq., J.P.

MANAGER: F. COOK, Esq.
SOLICITORS: Messrs. NUTT AND MURPHY.

Rates of Interest allowed at this Bank for Deposits.

On Fixed Deposits, without option of earlier withdrawal:—	On Deposits, with option of withdrawal on DEMAND, at call rate of interest:—
For 12 months, 7¼ per cent. per annum.	For 12 months, 6 per cent. per annum.
" 9 " 7 " "	" 6 " 6 " "
" 3 " 6 " "	" 3 " 6 " "
" 1 " 5 " "	" 1 " 6 " "

On Deposits at call, 5 per cent. per annum.

Interest is payable half-yearly on 12 months Fixed Deposits.

Special arrangements will be made as to rates of interest and period of lodgement for sums of £5,000 and upwards.

This Bank, in addition to a General Discount Business, advances on Wool, Stock, and Stations, and staple articles of Merchandise, and is also open to receive proposals for legitimate financial operations of every kind.

HOURS OF BUSINESS, 10 to 4.
SATURDAYS, 10 to 12.

FREDK. COOK, *Manager*.

MELBOURNE, 4th April, 1866.

THE
Australian Alliance Assurance Company.

ESTABLISHED FOR THE

ASSURANCE OF LIVES,

Fire Insurance, Guarantee, and Marine Insurance.

CAPITAL, £250,000.

Directors:

Hon. R. S. ANDERSON, M.L.C., CHAIRMAN.
JOHN HALFEY, Esq., M.L.A.
Hon. JAMES STEWART JOHNSTON.
Hon. CAPTAIN MACMAHON, M.L.A.
MICHAEL O'GRADY, Esq., M.L.A.
Hon. D. E. WILKIE, M.L.C.

Principal Offices:
COLLINS AND ELIZABETH STREETS WEST, MELBOURNE.

MICHAEL O'GRADY,
MANAGING DIRECTOR.

ESTABLISHED, 1840.

FULTON & SHAW,
ENGINEERS & IRONFOUNDERS, MILLWRIGHTS,
BLACKSMITHS,
SHIPSMITHS, AND BOILERMAKERS,
FULTON'S FOUNDRY,
137 FLINDERS STREET WEST, MELBOURNE.

McCALL, BLACK, & Co.,
Boiler Makers, Engineers, Shipsmiths,
IRON SHIPBUILDERS, &C.,
131 FLINDERS ST. & 138 FLINDERS LANE WEST
(FORMERLY FULTON'S PREMISES),
MELBOURNE.

Repairs of every description on Boilers and Iron Vessels, executed with despatch.

BANK OF AUSTRALASIA.
INCORPORATED BY ROYAL CHARTER, 1835.

PAID-UP CAPITAL, £1,200,000.
GUARANTEE FUND, £200,000.

HEAD OFFICE: 4 THREADNEEDLE STREET, LONDON, E.C.

ESTABLISHMENTS IN THE COLONIES.
SUPERINTENDENT, J. J. FALCONER, Esq.
GENERAL INSPECTOR OF BRANCHES, DAVID CHARTERIS McARTHUR, Esq.

BRANCHES AND AGENCIES:

VICTORIA.—Melbourne, Williamstown, Geelong, Belfast, Portland, Warrnambool, Ballarat, Creswick, Smythesdale, Happy Valley, Castlemaine, Blackwood, Talbot, Majorca, Sandhurst, Beechworth, Bright, Yackandandah, Sale, Grant, Walhalla.
NEW SOUTH WALES.—Sydney, Maitland, Newcastle.
QUEENSLAND.—Brisbane, Ipswich.
TASMANIA.—Hobart Town, Launceston.
SOUTH AUSTRALIA.—Adelaide, Kooringa, Port Lincoln.
NEW ZEALAND.—Wellington, Auckland, Christchurch, Dunedin.

FOREIGN AGENCIES:

MANCHESTER.—Union Bank of Manchester.
PENZANCE.—Messrs. Batten, Carne, and Carne.
SCOTLAND.—Bank of Scotland.
IRELAND.—Provincial Bank of Ireland.
FRANCE.—The Comptoir d'Escompte de Paris.
BERLIN.—Messrs. Platho and Woolff.
CAPE COLONY AND NATAL.—London and South African Bank.
CALIFORNIA.—British and Californian Banking Company.
INDIA, CHINA, JAPAN, MAURITIUS, AND BOURBON.—The Chartered Mercantile Bank of India, London, and China; and the Comptoir d'Escompte de Paris

BANK OF VICTORIA.

Incorporated by Act of Council.

Capital, £1,000,000; in 20,000 Shares of £50 each.
RESERVE FUND, £100,000.

ESTABLISHED, OCTOBER, 1852.

Directors:
The Hon. HENRY MILLER, M.L.C., Chairman.
The Hon. WM. HIGHETT, M.L.C., Deputy Chairman.
GERMAIN NICHOLSON, Esq., J.P.   K. B. WIGHT, Esq.
JOSEPH SUTHERLAND, Esq.   E. P. S. STURT, Esq., J.P.

Auditors:
J. D. PINNOCK, Esq.   H. N. HULL, Esq.

General Manager:
JOHN MATHESON, Esq.

Solicitors:
Messrs. VAUGHAN, MOULE & SEDDON.

Head Office, Melbourne:
John Matheson, General Manager.   Richard Shaun, Accountant.   E. G. Harrison, Branch Inspector.

London Office:
Directors—Edmund Westby, Esq.; Richard Gibbs, Esq.; Robert Sutherland, Esq.
H. L. Taylor, Manager.

BRANCHES:

GEELONG.—Local Directors—The Hon. J. F. Strachan, M.L.C.; A. B. White, Esq. Vincent W. Oftlis, Manager.
ECHUCA.—E. F. Gillen, Manager.
SANDHURST.—*With Agencies at Epsom, Raywood, and Eaglehawk.* George Vallentine, Manager.
BUCKWORTH.—T. W. Heubow, Acting Manager.
CASTLEMAINE.—*With Agencies at Vaughan and Malmsbury.* Thomas Young, Manager.
MALDON.—J. B. Griffiths, Acting Manager.
MARYBOROUGH.—*With Agencies at Inglewood, Talbot, and Dunolly.* Murdoch McLeod, Manager.
RAGLAN.—*With Agency at Ararat.* James Mason, Manager.
AVOCA.—*With Agency at St. Arnaud.* Leslie Ogilby, Manager.
BALLAARAT.—*With Agency at Sebastopol.* W. P. Smith, Acting Manager.
HAMILTON.—T. H. R. Andrews, Acting Manager.
PORTLAND.—Local Director—James Blair, Esq., P.M. F. C. Oswald, Manager.
BELFAST.—Local Director—George Stewart, Esq., P.M. William Young, Manager.
WARRNAMBOOL.—Robert R. Paterson, Manager.
MORTLAKE.—H. G. Kollerm, Manager.
PORT ALBERT.—W. H. Parr, Manager.
SALE.—*With Agencies at Rosedale and Wolhalla.* C. R. Sibbald, Manager.
BEECHWORTH.—A. K. Sheppard, Manager.
DAYLESFORD.—John Jamieson, Manager.
WAHGUNYAH.—A. Williamson, Acting Manager.
TACKANDANDAH.—W. K. Longshaye, Acting Manager.
GRANT.—A. R. Mackenzie, Acting Manager.
WOOD'S POINT.—*With Agencies at Donnelly's Creek and Jericho.* Gerard Pondlebury, Acting Manager.
HEATHCOTE.—W. Mendell, Manager.
KILMORE.—C. R. W. Fraser, Acting Manager.
STAWELL.—
HORSHAM.—

AGENCIES:

NEW SOUTH WALES   The Australian Joint-Stock Bank and Commercial Banking Company.
QUEENSLAND..   ..   The Australian Joint-Stock Bank and Commercial Banking Company.
SOUTH AUSTRALIA   The South Australian Banking Company.
TASMANIA   ..   ..   The Bank of Van Diemen's Land and Bank of Tasmania.
INDIA   ..   ..   Chartered Mercantile Bank of India, London, and China.
MAURITIUS   ..   ..   Chartered Mercantile Bank of India, London, and China.
NEW ZEALAND   ..   The Bank of New Zealand.

SAVINGS BANKS IN VICTORIA.

Commissioners of Savings Banks in the Colony of Victoria.

THE HON. JAMES HENTY, J.P., M.L.C., Chairman.
THE HON. THOMAS H. POWER, J.P.
THE HON. S. G. HENTY, J.P., M.L.C.
DAVID OGILVY, Esq.
JOHN BENN, Esq.

Comptroller of Savings Banks and Secretary to the Commissioners of Savings Banks.

CHARLES FLAXMAN, Esq., J.P.

OFFICES: MARKET STREET, COLLINS STREET WEST.

The Savings Banks in Victoria are under the immediate management of local trustees, appointed by the Commissioners of Savings Banks, who are appointed by His Excellency the Governor in Council, and who have the general control of the administration of the Savings Banks, and the sole investment of the funds, in accordance with the provisions of "The Savings Banks Statute, 1865."

Savings Banks are now established in the following places, viz.,—Melbourne, Geelong, Castlemaine, Sandhurst, Ballarat, Portland, Maryborough, Belfast, Warrnambool, Kyneton, and Hamilton.

By Order of the Commissioners of Savings Banks,

CHARLES FLAXMAN, Comptroller and Secretary.

Office of the Commissioners of Savings Banks,
Melbourne, July, 1866.

MELBOURNE SAVINGS BANK.

ESTABLISHED 1841.

TRUSTEES.

JOHN GOODMAN, Esq., J.P.
JOHN MACKENZIE, Esq., J.P.
GERMAIN NICHOLSON, Esq., J.P.
J. T. SMITH, Esq., J.P.
SAMUEL THORP, Esq.
T. J. SUMNER, Esq., J.P.

E. D. WIGHT, Esq., J.P.
CRAWFORD MAINE, Esq.
GEORGE STEVENSON, Esq.
F. J. BLIGH, Esq.
CHARLES HEAPE, Esq.
WILLIAM HENRY CUTTS, Esq., M.D.

ACTUARY,
JAMES BUOCK, Esq.

OPEN FOR DEPOSITS AND PAYMENTS:
DAILY.

From Ten till Three o'clock, except SATURDAY, when the Bank is open from Six till Eight o'clock in the Evening, for receipt of Deposits only.

OFFICE: CORNER OF MARKET STREET, FLINDERS LANE WEST.

DERWENT & TAMAR
FIRE AND MARINE
ASSURANCE COMPANY.

BOARD OF DIRECTORS.
CRAWFORD M. MAXWELL, Esq.
GEORGE SALIER, Esq.   JOHN BRENT, Esq.
ISAAC WRIGHT, Esq.   R. CLEBURNE, Esq.

MANAGER
HENRY B. TONKIN, Esq.

MARINE DEPARTMENT.

RISKS on Hulls, Freight or Merchandize, accepted at current Rates.

POLICIES granted in triplicate and made payable in London if required.

LOSSES promptly settled.

FIRE DEPARTMENT.

INSURANCES on first-class Buildings, on Merchandize or Furniture, effected at lowest Rates.

Jas. Henty & Co.,
AGENTS.

THE
DERWENT & TAMAR
FIRE & MARINE ASSURANCE
COMPANY.

ESTABLISHED 1838.

HEAD OFFICE:
MACQUARIE STREET, HOBART TOWN.

HENRY B. TONKIN, Manager.

LONDON OFFICE:
12, ST. HELEN'S PLACE.

RICHARDSON BROS. & CO., Agents.

Melbourne Branch:
11, LITTLE COLLINS STREET WEST.

Jas. Henty & Co.
Agents.

www.ingramcontent.com/pod-product-compliance
Lightning Source LLC
Chambersburg PA
CBHW020858020526
44116CB00029B/356